W9-CQM-312

PSYCHOLOGY

PSYCHOLOGY

SECOND EDITION

DIANE E. PAPALIA
University of Pennsylvania

SALLY WENDKOS OLDS

McGRAW-HILL BOOK COMPANY

NEW YORK
ST. LOUIS
SAN FRANCISCO
AUCKLAND
BOGOTÁ
CARACAS
COLORADO SPRINGS
HAMBURG

LISBON
LONDON
MADRID
MEXICO
MILAN
MONTREAL
NEW DELHI
OKLAHOMA CITY

PANAMA
PARIS
SAN JUAN
SÃO PAULO
SINGAPORE
SYDNEY
TOKYO
TORONTO

This book was set in Optima
by York Graphic Services, Inc.
The editors were Rhona Robbin,
James D. Anker, and Susan Gamer;
the designer was Joan E. O'Conner;
the production supervisor was Diane Renda.
The photo editor was Inge King;
the bibliographer was Marthe Grice;
the permissions editor was Elsa Peterson.
R. R. Donnelley & Sons Company was
printer and binder.
Cover: Pablo Picasso, *Bather with Book*;
oil, pastel, and charcoal on canvas, 1937;
Collection Musée Picasso, Paris
(Art Resource).

Acknowledgments appear on pages A 1 to
A 4, and on this page by reference.

PSYCHOLOGY

1234567890 DOCDOC 89321098

Library of Congress Cataloging-in-Publication
Data

Papalia, Diane E.
 Psychology.

 1. Psychology. I. Olds, Sally
Wendkos. II. Title.
BF121.P34 1988   150   87–16998
ISBN 0-07-048534–8

ISBN 0-07-048534-8

ABOUT

THE AUTHORS

 **DIANE E. PAPALIA** is a professor who has taught thousands of undergraduates at the University of Wisconsin. She received her bachelor's degree, majoring in psychology, from Vassar College, and both her master's degree in child development and family relations and her Ph.D. in life-span developmental psychology from West Virginia University. She has published numerous articles in professional journals, mostly on her major research focus, cognitive development from childhood through old age. She is especially interested in intelligence in old age and factors that contribute to the maintenance of intellectual functioning in late adulthood. She is a Fellow in the Gerontological Society of America. She is also affiliated with the University of Pennsylvania.

 **SALLY WENDKOS OLDS** is an award-winning professional writer who has written more than 200 articles in leading magazines and is the author or coauthor of six books addressed to general readers, in addition to the three textbooks she has coauthored with Dr. Papalia. She received her bachelor's degree from the University of Pennsylvania, where she majored in English literature and minored in psychology. She was elected to Phi Beta Kappa in her junior year and was graduated summa cum laude. Her book *The Complete Book of Breastfeeding*, a classic since its publication in 1972, has just been issued in a completely updated and expanded edition. Among the topics of her other books are concerns of working parents, sexual development throughout life, and development of values by children.

DIANE E. PAPALIA and SALLY WENDKOS OLDS are coauthors of the extremely successful textbooks *A Child's World* (now in its fourth edition) and *Human Development* (fourth edition scheduled for publication in 1989).

TO

OUR FAMILIES

Jonathan L. Finlay
Anna Victoria Finlay
Madeline and Edward
Papalia
Edward, Jr., Daphne, Marie,
and Edward Papalia, III

David Mark Olds
Nancy and Dorri Olds
Jennifer, Manfred,
and Stefan Moebus

whose interest, inspiration,
confidence, and love
make it all possible

CONTENTS

IN BRIEF

CONTENTS

LIST

OF BOXES

PREFACE

Aside from fulfilling a requirement for a social science course, what is the point of taking a course in introductory psychology? We, the authors of this book, believe that psychology underlies the most important learning we are capable of—finding out more about ourselves and about the people whose lives intersect with ours. Not until people have some basic knowledge of themselves and others can they put any of their other learning to work in an effective way. We believe that every literate person should take at least one course in psychology. In this firm conviction, we have tried to think about the most effective ways to present psychological concepts, both to students for whom this will be the only course they will take in the subject and to those who will go on to make psychology the basis of their life's work. With this in mind, let's look at what we consider the most important elements of this book.

OUR AIMS FOR THIS EDITION

It is hard to imagine that anyone could be bored by the study of how people think and behave. Yet basic facts and theories *can* be presented so drily that they seem remote from the excitement of new discoveries about how people live, how they learn, and how they love. It is also hard to imagine anyone's not stretching his or her horizons through the study of psychology. On the other hand, the temptation is great to present these topics in a "pop psychology" way that sugarcoats information and fails to give it a meaningful context. In this book we have sought to avoid both these traps, and to make it easier for the student to learn and for the instructor to teach.

First and foremost, we recognize psychology as a science, and throughout this book we treat it as such. We scrutinize research reports to evaluate their findings, and respect theories that meet the rigorous requirements established by scientific seekers after truth.

Our aims for this edition remain the same as for the first edition of this book: to present the basic matter of psychology— its areas of study, its methods, its findings, and their implications—as clearly as possible, with as much attention as possible to practical value, and with a constant focus on encouraging students to think for themselves as they read. We do not want our readers to accept our words blindly; rather, we want them to learn how to evaluate our biases, as well as those they will encounter elsewhere in life.

What are our biases? First, we're unquestionably prejudiced toward people. While we present information about animal studies when appropriate, we do so primarily to emphasize what they teach us about our own species. (In Chapter 6, for example, we show how the study of animal biology helps us learn about human memory.) Second, we're oriented toward the here and now. While we report the findings of basic research, we always keep our eyes closely focused on the practical applications of the research we cite. (In Chapter 1, we show how students can apply research findings about memory to help them do better in school.) Finally, in recognition of the enormous amount of research going on today, we're closely tuned into the present moment. Again, while we report the classic research and theories that have built the foundations of psychology, we have made special efforts to be up to date, and we have included "cutting edge" studies that were going on even as the book was being set in type. (In Chapter 2, for example, we report evidence about a new drug that shows strong promise of helping patients who are mentally and physically disabled by Alzheimer's disease and who until now have not been able to lead anything like a normal life.)

In our respect for the individual and in our humble awareness of human fallibility (including our own), we don't pretend to know all the answers. While we highlight our own views on ethics and on numerous controversial issues, we leave room for students to search their own consciences to determine the morality of various research projects, to weigh opposing arguments about controversial issues, and to reach their own conclusions. In fact, we encourage this kind of critical thinking in the belief that it will serve students well when they see or hear stories in the media about "breakthrough" discoveries in psychology or talk with people who announce their own pet theories as "scientific facts."

THE SECOND EDITION

Organization

This book has seven principal parts. In Part I, "Psychology as a Science," we introduce the student to the goals, history, and methods of psychology. Part II, "Biological Foundations of Behavior," comprises three chapters: Chapter 2, on the biological structures and functions of the brain and nervous system; Chapter 3, on the mechanisms of sensation and perception; and Chapter 4, on states of consciousness. In Part III, "Learning, Memory, and Cognitive Processes," we include four chapters: Chapter 5 deals with learning, Chapter 6 with memory, Chapter 7 with intelligence, and Chapter 8 with language and thought. The two chapters in Part IV, "Life-Span Developmental Psychology," cover development throughout life, from conception through old age. Chapter 9 discusses the influences of heredity and environment, conception, prenatal development, and physical, intellectual, and social-emotional development in childhood; Chapter 10 deals with these aspects of development from adolescence through old age. Part V, "Motivation, Emotion, and Sexuality" consists of Chapter 11, on motivation and emotion; and Chapter 12, on gender roles and sexuality—relating both these topics to motivation, emotion, and behavior. Part VI, "Personality, Abnormality, and Health," consists of four chapters. Chapter 13 examines theories of personality and ways to measure it, Chapter 14 looks at abnormal psychology, and Chapter 15 describes many ways to treat persons with psychological problems. Then, Chapter 16 examines the new field of health psychology and discusses the links between personality, lifestyle, and both physical and mental health. In the final two chapters of the book—in Part VII, "Social Psychology"—we look at the ways by which people influence and are influenced by others, both in group situations and in intimate relationships. Chapter 17 takes up social influence; Chapter 18 examines attraction and relationships.

The structure of the book offers various options for teaching introductory psychology. As the preceding description shows, all the chapters that are "standard" in most psychology texts have been included: biology and behavior, sensation and perception, learning, memory, motivation and emotion, child development, personality, abnormal psychology, therapy, social influences, and so on. We have also given full-chapter treatment to other high-interest and important topics that are often treated very briefly, if at all, such as health psychology, sexuality and gender roles, intelligence, language and thought, adolescent and adult development, and intimate relationships.

While we have covered these topics in a way that seems logical to us, we recognize that some instructors may want to organize their courses differently because of personal preference or scheduling requirements. All the chapters are self-contained and can, therefore, be presented in a variety of different sequences. An instructor who chooses to emphasize the developmental-social-personality approach might, then, teach Chapters 1, 5, 6, 7 (optional), and 8 through 18. An instructor who takes more of an experimental-physiological approach could teach Chapters 1 through 7, 9 and 10 (optional), and 11 through 15. Either of these arrangements would provide a course of 13 or 14 chapters, rather than all 18.

Content

The preceding description of chapter organization provides a brief overview of the subject matter in this edition. It cannot, however, convey the full sweep of its content. Psychology is a dynamic, rapidly growing discipline. Therefore, while retaining the scope, emphasis, and level of the first edition, we have made many significant changes, even though it has been only 3 years since the publication of the first edition. We have updated material whenever new findings or interpretations have been available, reorganized material to make it more effective, and added completely new sections, including two new chapters. Among the important changes are the following:

■ *New chapters:* Chapter 12, "Sexuality and Gender Roles," presents some material that originally appeared in various chapters throughout the first edition, plus some completely new discussions, such as gender differences in communication, psychosexual dysfunctions and their treatment, and a life-span perspective on human sexuality. By focusing on these issues in a single chapter, we are able to highlight the differences between biological sex and socially determined gender roles. We are also better able to trace the relationship between these topics and those treated in the other chapter in Part V, centering on motivation and emotion.

Chapter 16, "Health Psychology," reflects a major emerging area of interest and research in psychology. It updates material on stress and coping that appeared in the first edition. It also contains completely new material on the relationship between psychology and mental and physical health, including the influences of various lifestyles and habits and the impact of the health care system.

■ *New sections:* Among the most important additions to this edition are new sections on ethics in animal research; sex, handedness, and the brain; additional aspects of perception, including perception of biological motion; "flow states"; the use of operant conditioning to encourage use of seat belts; Sternberg's triarchic theory of intelligence; Gardner's theory of multiple intelligences; artificial intelligence; stress and resilience in children; the relationship between adolescent thought processes and behavior; cognitive explanations of achievement motivation; Plutchik's eight primary emotions; controversies relating to emotion; helping the elderly improve intellectual per-

formance; suicide; the borderline personality; seasonal affective disorder (SAD); couples therapy; excerpts from the proposed revision of DSM III; loneliness; power in marriage; and the development of intimate relationships. Throughout the book, descriptions of studies (many new to this edition) help students understand the design and operation of psychological research.

■ *New organization:* Several presentations have been reorganized for greater clarity and easier comprehension. Chapter 2, "Biology and Behavior," is one example of an improved account of challenging material. Material on life-span development is now presented in two chapters instead of the three in the first edition. While some material was deleted—in deference to the limited coverage that can be devoted to developmental issues in an introductory psychology course—the most important classic and new material remains. Attribution theory is now discussed in one chapter rather than two. Practical study tips are now in Chapter 1, so that they can be of maximum help to students (rather than in Chapter 6, "Memory," as in the first edition).

■ *Important revisions:* Throughout the book, numerous sections have been significantly revised and often updated as well. Besides the ones already mentioned, these include creativity (which now includes the work of Amabile); whether apes can learn language; theories of motivation (which has been completely rewritten for ease of understanding); the person-situation controversy; causes of psychological disorders; drug therapies; and why people become committed blood donors.

■ *New visual aids:* Many new tables, charts, graphs, and other visual ways of presenting data have been added to supplement presentations in the text.

Special Features

Several features are new to this edition of *Psychology.*

■ Every chapter presents one or more boxes with one of two major thrusts. The "In the Forefront" boxes highlight issues that are important in contemporary psychology because of new interest, new theoretical formulations, or new research findings. They are often controversial and are as current as today's newspaper, covering such topics as Alzheimer's disease, legal implications of memory research, developing children's abilities, family violence, and the mind and the immune system. The "Psychology in Your Life" boxes draw out practical ways to apply research findings in daily life. They cover such topics as preparing for a career in psychology, practical application of hypnosis, teaching tricks to an animal, improving memory, becoming more creative, the effect of child-rearing styles on children's behavior, the value of lie detectors, helping to prevent suicide, losing weight, and the possibility of legislating helping behavior.

■ Vignettes describing personal experiences in the lives of both authors open every chapter. These introductions—sometimes dramatic, sometimes humorous—capture the reader's interest, lead into the subject matter of the chapter, and present personal glimpses into the authors' lives that are rarely afforded to students.

REVIEWERS' AND USERS' COMMENTS ON THE BOOK'S SPECIAL FEATURES

One of this book's major strengths, as indicated by academic reviewers who either reviewed the first edition or saw the manuscript of this second edition before publication, is its effective integration of theory, research, and application—as described earlier in the section "Our Aims for This Edition." The consensus of reviewers was that these aspects are integrated here more *consistently* than they are in many other books. Other elements especially noted by reviewers include the book's attention to high-interest and timely topics, its references to "cutting edge" studies as well as to classic ones, and its approach to ethical issues. The writing style has been commended for its clarity, its ability to hold the reader's interest, and its engaging qualities—all elements designed to make both the teaching and the learning of psychology easier and more rewarding.

LEARNING AIDS

You'll find in this book a number of basic teaching aids whose value has been demonstrated through experience and research. These include:

■ *Part overviews:* At the beginning of each part, an overview provides the rationale for the chapters that follow.

■ *Chapter overviews:* At the beginning of each chapter, an outline clearly previews the major topics included in the chapter.

■ *Preview questions:* At the beginning of each chapter, a few key questions highlight the most important issues to be addressed.

■ *Chapter summaries:* At the end of each chapter, a numbered summary clearly restates the most important points.

■ *Highlighting of key terms:* Whenever an important new term is introduced in the text, it is highlighted in

boldface italic and defined. These terms are listed at the end of the chapter and appear in both marginal and end-of-book glossaries.

■ *"Running" glossary:* All key terms are defined in the margin where they first appear in each part of the book, and some of these definitions are repeated, where appropriate, in subsequent chapters. This gives instructors more latitude in teaching the chapters; instructors can use the order dictated by their own preference.

■ *Extensive illustrations:* Since one picture is often worth a thousand words, many of the points in the text are underscored pictorially through carefully selected drawings, graphs, and photographs (many in full color to illustrate important points better and to enhance the reader's enjoyment).

■ *Pedagogically sound legends:* The legends for these illustrations also serve a teaching purpose by emphasizing important points made in the text, posing questions calling for students' thought, or bringing in interesting new information.

■ *End-of-book glossary:* The extensive glossary at the back of the book repeats the marginal definitions of key terms.

■ *Bibliography:* A complete listing of references enables students to evaluate the sources of major statements of fact or theory.

■ *Suggested readings:* Annotated lists of recommended readings (classic works or lively contemporary treatments) are provided for students who want to explore issues in greater depth than is possible within these covers.

■ *Index:* Separate indexes, by subject and by author, appear at the end of the book.

SUPPLEMENTARY MATERIALS

An extensive package of newly revised supplementary materials add to the value of this edition as a teaching and learning tool.

■ *Study Guide with Readings,* by Virginia Nichols Quinn of Northern Virginia Community College and Jolyne S. Daughtry of California State University, Fresno, includes readings from both professional journals and popular magazines on topics covered in the text. It also includes such standard elements as outlines, objectives, key terms, and concepts; and 800 questions with answers. Questions from the study guide are also available on a computer disk, interactive microcomputer software designed for use by students.

- Two *Test Banks* are available. One, developed by Virginia Quinn to ensure consistency with the Study Guide in level and types of questions, contains 2000 questions keyed to the learning objectives in the Study Guide and the Instructor's Manual. This Test Bank can be used with several computer-generated testing systems. Correct answers and text page references are included for all questions. An alternative Test Bank by James J. Johnson of Illinois State University is also available.

- *Instructor's Manual,* also by James Johnson, includes chapter outlines, learning objectives, key terms and concepts, mini-lectures, demonstrations, short-answer and essay questions, and a media guide. It also has a distinctive "Teaching the Chapter" section for each chapter, which integrates all these elements to assist the instructor.

- *Psychworld,* by John C. Hay of the University of Wisconsin in Milwaukee, is an elaborate, colorful, and intriguing generic software package that contains 14 simulations of classic psychology experiments. Professors can use it in the classroom, and students can use it in a lab. It enables the user to perform such activities as identifying different sections of the brain and varying reinforcement patterns for a pigeon pecking at food.

- *Slides and Transparencies,* three packages from McGraw-Hill, include 100 generic slides (in *The McGraw-Hill Introductory Psychology Slide Set*), 100 generic transparencies (in *The McGraw-Hill Introductory Psychology Overhead Transparency Set*), and 50 transparencies keyed specifically to this book (in *Overhead Transparencies to Accompany Papalia-Olds: Psychology, Second Edition*). Booklets for instructors describe each slide and transparency.

- *McGraw-Hill/CRM Films and videotapes* are also available to adopters.

We hope that we have been able to communicate the excitement we feel about the study of psychology. We want to share this with you, our readers, as much as we want to share any of the concepts, principles, and philosophies contained within these pages. For if we succeed in this, we know we will have enriched your lives as the study of psychology has enriched ours.

ACKNOWLEDGMENTS

We are indebted to many colleagues and friends whose help was invaluable in the gestation and birth of this book, and in its appearance in this second edition. For contributing their deeply informed expertise in specific subfields, we're grateful to Jason Brandt and Howard Egeth, both at Johns Hopkins University; Robert Franken, at the University of Calgary; and Howard Hughes, at Dartmouth College (all of whom worked on the original edition). We're also grateful to Paul Wellman, Texas A & M University; Margaret Matlin, State University College of Arts and Science at Geneseo; and Herbert Petri, Towson State University (who helped us with the second edition). We also appreciate the contribution of Virginia Nichols Quinn, Northern Virginia Community College, who wrote the Appendix on statistics for both editions.

This edition of *Psychology* continues to reflect many insightful suggestions which were offered by reviewers of the first edition. Nearly 50 psychologists have provided constructive and thorough evaluations of the current edition. These reviewers, who are affiliated with both two- and four-year institutions, are listed on page xxii.

We deeply appreciate the strong support we have received from our publisher. Rhona Robbin, our editor for both editions, has become a friend not only to both the authors, but also to the readers of this book, who will benefit from her careful attention to detail, her dedication to clarity, and her perceptive questions that continually forced us to re-evaluate our presentation. Susan Gamer gave this project painstakingly careful attention through the production process. Joan O'Connor and the other creative people in the art department produced a striking cover and book design. Inge King found compelling and pedagogically perfect photographs. Elsa Peterson pursued and obtained needed permissions. Joanne Heiser and others at McGraw-Hill helped in ways large and small.

We would also like to express special thanks to two special research assistants—Julie Jensen, a doctoral candidate at the University of Wisconsin; and Martha Seidel, of Port Washington, New York. In addition to their efforts in tracking down innumerable elusive reports, articles, and papers, Julie helped to compile and prepare the bibliography and the glossary, and Martha drew up charts and tables and prepared the manuscript for transmission to our publisher. Both of them cheerfully and enthusiastically assisted in other ways too numerous to list.

This list would not be complete if we didn't acknowledge the continuing encouragement of our husbands, Jonathan Finlay and David Mark Olds. In deference to our deadlines on both editions, they postponed things they wanted to do and did things that needed to be done. In support of our aims, they asked the right questions and made us come up with answers. They knew when to hold our hands and when to make us laugh. Throughout, they were there for us when we needed them, and this book is better for that.

Thank you, one and all. We could not have done it without you!

Diane E. Papalia   *Sally Wendkos Olds*

ACADEMIC

REVIEWERS

For their reading of all or part of the manuscript in various stages of development, and for the helpful comments they offered, we thank the people listed below.

Diane E. Papalia
Sally Wendkos Olds

Andrew Baum
  Uniformed Services University
  of the Health Sciences
Ray Baumeister
  Case Western Reserve University
Amy D. Bertelson
  Washington University-St. Louis
John G. Carlson
  University of Hawaii
John J. Colby
  Providence College
Verne C. Cox
  University of Texas-Arlington
Jeff Cross
  Allegheny College
Nancy Dixon
  Tennessee Technical University
Robert Emery
  University of Virginia
C. Davis Gallacher
  American River College
Grace Galliano
  Kennesaw College
Marian Gibney
  Phoenix College
Richard Griggs
  University of Florida

Joseph Grosslight
  Florida State University
Sandra Harrison
  Mercer University
Glen R. Hawkes
  Virginia Commonwealth University
Robert W. Hayes
  Boston University
Vernon F. Haynes
  Youngstown State University
G. William Hill IV
  Kennesaw College
Morton Hoffman
  Metropolitan State College
Robert Hogan
  University of Tulsa
Jean Hollenshead
  Louisiana State University–Shreveport
John Hovancik
  Seton Hall University
Janet Hyde
  University of Wisconsin
James J. Johnson
  Illinois State University
John R. Lakey
  University of Evansville
Jane Ellen Maddy
  University of Minnesota–Duluth
Margaret Matlin
  State University College
  of Arts and Science, Geneseo
Ralph R. Miller
  State University of New York
  at Binghamton
Marilyn Milligan
  Santa Rosa Junior College

Letitia Anne Peplau
  University of California at Los Angeles
Richard S. Perrotto
  Queensborough Community College
Herbert L. Petri
  Towson State University
Harvey Pines
  Canisius College
Clare Porac
  University of Victoria
Derrick L. Proctor
  Andrews University
Virginia Nichols Quinn
  Northern Virginia Community College
John S. Rosenkoetter
  Southwest Missouri State University
Fredric Shaffer
  Northeast Missouri State University
Gene F. Smith
  Western Illinois University
Robert Solso
  University of Nevada–Reno
Shelley E. Taylor
  U.C.L.A.
Jeanne L. Thomas
  University of Wisconsin
James Turcott
  Kalamazoo Valley Community College
John Uhlarik
  Kansas State University
Gail Walker
  Alfred University
Paul J. Wellman
  Texas A & M University
Janet P. Wollersheim
  University of Montana

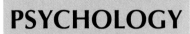

PSYCHOLOGY

PART

I

PSYCHOLOGY AS A SCIENCE

The study of why people do what they do has long been a favorite topic of philosophers and poets, historians and novelists, and everyone else, including neighborhood gossips. Psychology focuses on these same issues, within a scientific framework.

Psychology is the scientific study of behavior and of mental processes. Although a large body of psychological research uses animals (like rats, dogs, and monkeys) as subjects, in this book we emphasize what psychology reveals about what most of us consider the highest order of animals, human beings.

■ *Chapter 1,* "Introduction to Psychology," presents some of the issues and findings to be discussed in the rest of the book. We look at the roots of this relatively young science— the offspring, in a sense, of two more ancient disciplines, philosophy and physiology. We look at different schools of thought within psychology and at how different viewpoints influence the nature of research projects. We examine the various techniques employed by research psychologists. And we give a contemporary overview of the field, showing the many settings in which psychologists work and the many facets of the work they do.

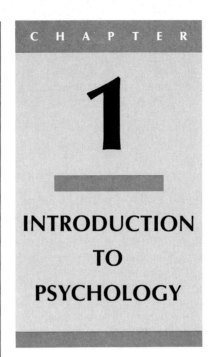

CHAPTER

1

INTRODUCTION TO PSYCHOLOGY

- How did psychology grow from its roots in philosophy and physiology to become an independent science?

- How did the controversies surrounding the early schools of psychological thought shape today's science of psychology?

- What do contemporary psychologists do?

- What are some possible careers in psychology?

- How do psychologists study behavior?

- What are the ethical principles that guide psychological research?

My husband and I were shopping for a stroller for our daughter in a baby furnishings store in Madison, Wisconsin. We found one that we liked, but neither my husband nor I could figure out how to open it from its folded position—nor, as it happened, could the salesman. Finally the salesman turned to us and said, "Let me show you one you don't have to have a Ph.D. to open." My husband then pointed to me and said, "But she has a Ph.D." So there we were—he with his M.D. in pediatrics and I with my doctorate in life-span development—neither of us able to master the intricacies of a baby stroller!

But then, that wasn't why I had become a psychologist or had chosen my specialty in the first place. Why had I? As I look back, I realize that my interest in the way people behave began very early in life. One of my favorite early books was my parents' copy of Gesell and Ilg's book on child development. I used to pore over it, read what children my age were supposed to be doing, and try to figure out whether I was normal.

I carried my interest in child development with me through the years, and I went on to major in psychology at Vassar College. Then, when I was pursuing a master's degree in child development and family relations at West Virginia University, I took a course in the work of the influential developmental theorist Jean Piaget. As I learned about Piaget's theories on how children think, memories of my grandmother kept coming back to me.

I had been very close to my grandmother throughout my growing-up years. I spent many hours listening to her tell vivid stories of her childhood in Italy. As she grew older I was impressed with how much she could still remember about her childhood and how much time she spent reviewing the details of her early life. I wondered how much of this was normal. And I wondered if Piaget's way of thinking and of analyzing development could be applied to studying intellectual functioning in later life. I became so interested in intelligence in old age and in the factors that contribute to the maintenance of intellectual functioning during this time of life that I decided to take my doctorate in life-span developmental psychology. I still find this subject intriguing as I see the many different ways in which people develop throughout life.

—From the notebooks of Diane Papalia

The study of development over the life span is just one branch of the science known as *psychology*. Psychologists study many aspects of behavior and mental processes that have practical implications for the lives of all of us. They study topics like these underlying the opening to this chapter—why some people learn to read at an early age but seem to have little mechanical facility, while others have a keenly developed sense of spatial relations but may have trouble following words on a page; what personality factors influence career choices; how we remember and forget and what the biological basis for memory is; what kinds of psychological changes occur during old age; how we choose our spouses and become attached to our parents and children—and many other issues that affect our day-to-day lives.

In this book you'll read about psychological study of all these topics and about the practical implications of both research and theories. You'll read about much more that is relevant to your own life. For the essence of this field is the study of you.

When psychologists study the human brain, they learn about *your* brain. When they study the way people learn, they find out how *you* learn. When they study influences on human intelligence, they discover what has affected the development of *your* intelligence. No field of study has more relevance for your own life than psychology does.

In this chapter we review the way the field of psychology developed and how it functions today. We talk about the various specialties in psychology and the kind of work that you yourself might do if you decide upon psychology as a vocation. We look at the methods of study that psychologists use as well as the criteria you can use to determine for yourself how scientific these methods are and how valid are the reports you read in newspapers, magazines, and professional journals. Finally, we consider the very important ethical questions pertaining to psychological research— and the standards you might use to judge the ethicality of any particular study.

WHAT IS PSYCHOLOGY?

Psychology is the scientific study of behavior and mental processes. Let's look at this definition word by word. The term *psychology* comes from the Greek *psyche* (*soul*) and *logos* (*word* or *discourse*) and reveals the original definition as discourse about the soul (later, about the mind). *Scientific study* implies using **scientific method,** a systematic, objective, and organized way to get information. Scientific method makes use of such tools as observation, description, and experimental investigation. *Behavior* is defined broadly as actions that can be readily observed, such as physical activity and speaking. We are also concerned with *mental processes* that occur even though they cannot be observed directly, such as perceiving, thinking, remembering, and feeling.

Psychology Scientific study of behavior and mental processes.

Scientific method Systematic, objective, and organized way to get information, involving observation, description, and experimental investigation.

WHAT ARE THE GOALS OF PSYCHOLOGY?

Psychology is a multifaceted science. Psychologists are not content with merely describing behavior. They go beyond this to try to explain, predict, and sometimes modify behavior to enhance the lives of individuals and to improve society in general. Let's take a brief look at the various goals of psychology.

■ *Description* is telling about what actually occurs. It is a major source of information about both ordinary and extraordinary mechanisms and events and the relationships between them. For example, through description we might find that a relationship exists between education and longevity, that is, that better-educated people tend to live longer. We would not know why the relationship existed—just that it did. Determining the *why* is another step in psychological research.

Description Information about what is actually occurring.

■ *Explanation* is telling why events occur. There are often a number of possible reasons for a given phenomenon. In the example just cited, it is possible that better-educated people live longer because they know more about staying well and what to do when they get sick. It is also possible that higher education and longevity are both associated with a third factor, like having enough money to pay for education and good health care. The purpose of explanation is to eliminate all the possible explanations except the correct one.

Explanation Information about why events occur.

■ *Prediction* is the forecasting of future events on the basis of past events. For example, IQ tests are known to be good at predicting success in school. There are also areas in which prediction is not so firmly established but would nevertheless be very useful; for example, it would be important to know whether programs discouraging smoking would lead to longer life for people in general, or for specific

Prediction Forecast of future events on the basis of past events.

One immediate use to which you can put findings from psychological research is in your study habits for your college courses. If you apply the following principles, all based on research in memory, to your own situation, you're likely to see results in better retention of the material you learn. (Furthermore, the better grades you're apt to earn may be so effective in rewarding you for your efforts that they'll motivate you to do still better, according to principles established by research in learning.)

Some of these principles have been summed up in a method known as SQ3R. SQ3R stands for the five systematic steps in the method: survey, question, and three R's—read, recite, and review. Let's see how you can use these steps with this textbook.

1   *Survey:* The first time you read a new chapter, give it an overall look to get what business executives often call the "big picture." Read the chapter title, the overview at the beginning, the outline, the main headings, and the end-of-chapter summary. Look briefly at the key terms listed at the end of the chapter. Read the picture captions.

TIPS ON MORE EFFECTIVE STUDYING

2   *Question:* Ask yourself questions about the material before you read it and while you're actually reading it. Some helpful questions appear at the beginning of each chapter; others are given in the study guide that accompanies this book; and you can come up with your own by rephrasing section headings or key sentences as questions. Such questions help to identify important points.

3   *Read:* Read each chapter, one section at a time. Underline or highlight headings, key terms (shown in **boldface italic** and defined in the margins), and major points. If you don't understand something, mark the passage so that you can get help with it. Take notes on the *most*

important points as you go along, putting what you learn in your own words.

4   *Recite:* Recite key points silently or aloud. This procedure, known by memory experts as *rehearsal,* helps fix information in your mind. It may be helpful to speak into a tape recorder, and then play back the tape while you're getting dressed, driving, or doing some other activity, increasing your exposure to the material. Taking notes is also a form of recitation, especially when you give yourself cues for retrieval. You can do this by using headings in your notes and making up personally meaningful catchphrases, visual images, or both that you associate with various blocks of material. Some doctor with a sense of humor, for example, taught medical students the sentence "Never lower Tilly's pants—mother might come home," to help them remember the bones of the wrist, whose names start with the first letters of the words of this sentence: navicular, lunate, triquetrum, pisiform, (greater) multangular, (lesser) multangular, capitate, and hamate.

categories of people (such as those at high risk or those of a particular sex, income level, or ethnic group).

Modification Change in, or control of, aspects of the environment in order to change behavior.

■ **Modification** involves changing or controlling aspects of the environment to change behavior in a way that would benefit both the individual and society. (The box above, "Tips on More Effective Studying," is an example.)

Before we try to change a behavior, we need an accurate *description* of it, an *explanation* of the behavior and its consequences, and some basis for *predicting* the results of the change. Determining why people eat well or poorly, why they do or do not use seat belts, or why they do or do not smoke enables psychologists to think of ways to encourage health-promoting behaviors. The explanations we propound influence our proposals for changing behavior. For example, a psychologist who explains depression as the result of irrational thought patterns and a psychologist who explains it as the result of a biochemical imbalance in the brain will propose very different therapies.

We can see, then, that these goals are not mutually exclusive; each one contributes something to our knowledge of human beings.

5 *Review:* After you have read a chapter, review it. You can do this by repeating steps 1 and 2. You can also go over your notes and think about the material. You'll get the best results if you do this kind of reviewing two or three times, once right after reading the chapter, then once again—before a quiz or midterm if one is scheduled—and then again before the final exam.

Other useful principles are embedded in the following guidelines.

6 In general, the best way to remember material is to make it yours by making it personally meaningful. It is especially easy to make associations with your own life and your own experience in a course like psychology. For example, try to remember some of the times you personally have experienced some of the phenomena we talk about in this book (like the tip-of-the-tongue phenomenon discussed in Chapter 6, in which you're sure you know something, but it eludes you). Do

exercises presented in the text and study guide. Answer quizzes. In other course material you may have to stretch to make connections with your own life, but you can do it using your imagination. For example, in studying a foreign language, you can fantasize yourself making a new friend using that language. Or to make history come alive, you might imagine yourself living in the time and place you're learning about.

7 Combine verbal and visual images of your material whenever possible.

8 Concentrate on paying attention. Much apparent "forgetting" is caused by not really taking in the material in the first place.

9 Study the topics that are most difficult for you or the topics that you consider most important either first or last, since research has shown that you are most likely to forget what you learn in the middle.

10 Allot extra time for studying difficult subjects. The more time you devote to material, the better you're likely to remember it.

11 Focus on the most important points. Don't try to remember every little detail.

12 Eliminate as much interference from other information as possible. Instead of studying two similar subjects close together (like two science courses), plan your schedule so you study something very dissimilar between them. Instead of studying for two tests on the same day, plan to study one subject, go to sleep, and wake up early to study the other. The material from the first will have been integrated sufficiently so that you'll be less likely to confuse the two topics in your mind.

13 Spread out your study periods before an exam, since relearning over several days works better than doing it all in one day.

These principles will, of course, apply to any subject that you study and any information that you want to remember, in or out of school. Once you get into the habits of applying them, you'll be in a better position to appreciate some of the ways in which psychology has made a contribution to your life.

HOW THIS BOOK PRESENTS THE STUDY OF PSYCHOLOGY

In this book we discuss many attributes that are universal among human beings, many that are widespread, and some that are unique. The elements of this text itself also fall into these categories. Most of the topics we discuss are to be found in any good book in introductory psychology, and in the way it is organized it is similar to other books in the field. It is unique, however, in some aspects of coverage, organization, and special features that enhance interest and aid learning—and, most important, in the way it reflects the points of view of its authors. Let's look, then, at some of the distinctive features of this book.

We Celebrate the Human Being

While many of the most important experiments in psychology have been performed on nonhuman animals—such as rats, pigeons, and monkeys—our emphasis in these pages will be what psychological research and theory tell us about human beings. When we do discuss important animal studies, we do so in order to shed light on human behavior.

We Are Practical

Throughout this book we emphasize the way research findings can be applied (used) to solve practical problems. We do report on basic research, which is performed in the spirit of intellectual curiosity, and on the kinds of questions psychologists ask as they explore the universe of the mind; but whenever possible we translate the results of such studies into knowledge that can be applied to better the human condition. (For example, the box "Tips on More Effective Studying" offers suggestions based on research findings on learning and memory that may help you do better in this course, as well as in your other studies.)

We View Psychology as a Dynamic Science

Because we recognize that new facts about human beings are constantly being learned and new concepts are continually being formed, we include in our discussions of psychological phenomena both the important classic work in the field and the most recent reports of research and thinking on the cutting edge.

We Present a Picture of Psychology on a Wide Canvas

For convenience, we have divided the study of psychology into seven major parts. In Part I we look at the scientific and historical aspects of the field. In Part II we consider how human beings are "wired" biologically and how this influences behavior. In Part III we look at intellectual processes—how people learn, remember, think, and use language—and at what intelligence is. In Part IV we look at physical, cognitive, and personality development throughout life. In Part V we see how humans are motivated and what role our emotions, gender, and sexuality play in our lives. In Part VI we explore issues of personality and of psychological disorders and their treatment; we also examine how psychological factors affect health, including how people cope with stress. Finally, in Part VII we examine the way people get along with one another, both in close relationships and in groups.

If this description sounds as if we were cutting human beings into arbitrary pieces, like a jigsaw puzzle, it is for the sake of simplicity. When we study the human being, we learn that the various aspects of our natures interact and add up to a cohesive whole. By the time you have finished reading this book, you will have a better understanding of the way all these parts fit together.

HOW PSYCHOLOGY HAS EVOLVED

A Brief History of Psychology

In a sense the history of psychology reaches back to ancient times when people began to ask questions about human nature and tried to explain human behavior. The early Greek and Roman philosophers wondered what the mind was and where it was located. Aristotle (384–322 B.C.) introduced the concept of the mind as a *tabula rasa* (*blank slate*) that was empty until it was "written upon" by experience. Nineteen centuries later the British philosopher John Locke (1632–1704) adopted this term to express his agreement with this view of the human mind. An opposing view was held by the French philosopher René Descartes (1596–1650), who believed that we are born with certain ideas and abilities. Descartes also maintained that the mind and the body are separate but have a great deal of influence over each other. These theoretical forays into the nature of human beings were not true psychology, however, because they expressed opinions rather than the results of scientific investigations. Psychology as a science is little more than 100 years old, as can be seen in Table 1-1, which lists some of its milestones.

RAPHAEL
SANTIVS
PINX

IN ÆDIBVS
VATICA
NIS.

RAPHAEL PINXIT.

THE SCHOOL OF ATHENS.

Psychology has come a long way since the time of Plato and Aristotle, shown surrounded by other philosophers in this print. The ancients pondered many of the same issues that preoccupy us today, but contemporary psychologists use more scientific methods to arrive at their conclusions.

TABLE 1-1 FAMOUS FIRSTS IN PSYCHOLOGY

1875	First course in experimental psychology offered at Harvard University by William James. The first psychology lecture James attended was his own.
1878	First Ph.D. in psychology in the United States awarded to G. Stanley Hall.
1879	First laboratory for psychological research founded in Leipzig, Germany, by Wilhelm Wundt.
1879	First American student works with Wundt in Leipzig (G. Stanley Hall).
1881	World's first professional journal of psychology established in Germany by Wilhelm Wundt.
1883	First psychology laboratory in the United States established at Johns Hopkins University by G. Stanley Hall.
1886	Publication of first American textbook in psychology—*Psychology* by John Dewey.
1887	First professional journal of psychology in the United States established by G. Stanley Hall (*American Journal of Psychology*).
1888	First professorship of psychology in the world established at the University of Pennsylvania (James McKeen Cattell named).
1890	Publication of William James's classic textbook, *The Principles of Psychology* (which took him 12 years to write, instead of the 2 years he had originally estimated).
1892	American Psychological Association founded, largely through the efforts of G. Stanley Hall, who served as its first president. (It grew to 400 members by 1920 and now has more than 50,000 members.)
1900	Publication of Sigmund Freud's landmark book, *The Interpretation of Dreams*.

(Culver Pictures)

What turned psychology from a philosophical search into a science? It was principally the application of the tools and techniques that had been used successfully in the natural sciences. When people who were looking for answers to certain puzzles and problems turned from relying on their own intuition and experience to carefully collecting information through systematic observation and controlled experiments, they transformed themselves from philosophers into scientists.

Psychology is, then, the child of two parents: philosophy (the pursuit of wisdom through logical reasoning) and physiology (the study of the life processes of an organism, such as respiration, digestion, and reproduction). During the eighteenth and nineteenth centuries, physiological researchers used the newly invented microscope to examine animal and human cadavers (dead bodies), making important discoveries about the functions of the spinal cord, the electrical nature of nerve impulses, and other biological mechanisms. These advances in science explained a great deal about the functions of the human body and led to questions about how sensation and perception operate. Such questions were taken up by experimental psychologists in Germany, most of whom had been educated in medicine or physiology. The interest of the German physicist Gustav Fechner (1801–1887) in the psychological experience of physical phenomena led to scientific exploration of such processes, setting the scene for the birth of the new science of psychology. Psychology's efforts to understand how people think, feel, and act continue to rest on a knowledge of human biology. Let's see how this science has evolved to its present state.

Schools of Thought in Psychology

Controversy swirls around many psychological issues, mostly because of basic differences in the way different psychologists see the nature of human beings. Within the field, bitter disputes have erupted—as happens in any enterprise filled with creative, strong-minded innovators. Some of these controversies are eventually resolved when one viewpoint comes to be generally accepted, but others have continued for years and show no signs of leading to any universal agreement. Many of these controversies were born in the very early days of psychology, with the emergence in the late nineteenth and early twentieth centuries of a number of different schools—groups of psychologists who shared a theoretical outlook. As these schools flourished, and then often declined, the history of psychology was written. Seven schools of thought are summarized in Table 1-2 and discussed in the following sections.

Structuralism   Wilhelm Wundt, M.D. (1832–1920), is usually called the "father of psychology." He called himself a psychologist, he formally established psychology as an independent and organized discipline, he set up the first laboratory for psychological experimentation in Leipzig, Germany, and many of the early leaders in the field were his students there.

Analytic introspection Technique developed by Wundt that uses self-observation to analyze the mind or break it down into its component elements.

Wundt merged both physiological and philosophical traditions into the field of psychology. His book *Principles of Physiological Psychology* (published in two parts in 1873 and 1874) established psychology as a laboratory science that used methods derived from physiology. Wundt wanted to study the basic structure of the human mind (what it *is*) rather than its functions or purposes (what it *does*). To do this, he developed the method of **analytic introspection.** He made new the centuries-old technique of introspection, or self-observation, by adding precise experimental controls. He then proceeded to analyze or break down the mind into its component elements (such as the basic experience of seeing a color). Wundt emphasized physiological experiments, much of them involving fairly simple means, for example, measuring reaction time (the time it takes to react to a new stimulus, like the fraction of a second between the flashing of a bright light and the blinking of a subject's eye). His work ran into considerable resistance, however, partly because some of his

TABLE 1-2 SEVEN SCHOOLS OF THOUGHT IN PSYCHOLOGY

School of Psychology	Time Period	Basic Belief	Techniques Used
Structuralism	Late nineteenth century to early twentieth century	The structure of mind is of prime importance.	Analytic introspection, reaction-time experiments
Functionalism	Late nineteenth century to early twentieth century	The uses and functions of the mind are more important than its structure.	Mental tests, questionnaires, objective observations
Gestalt psychology	Early twentieth century to present	The whole is greater than the sum of its parts.	Studies in perception
Psychoanalysis	Late nineteenth century to present	Behavior is controlled by powerful unconscious urges.	Clinical observation
Behaviorism	Early twentieth century to present	Psychology should focus only on observable events and behaviors.	Scientific method, conditioning
Humanistic psychology	Mid-twentieth century to present	Psychology should focus on uniquely human experiences.	Discusssion of feelings
Cognitive psychology	Present	Psychology should focus on how the mind acquires, stores, and processes information.	Experiments in memory, thinking, information processing

colleagues thought that too much examination of the mind could cause insanity, while others felt that such experiments would "insult religion by putting the human soul on a pair of scales" (Hearst, 1979, p. 7).

One of Wundt's students, Edward Bradford Titchener (1867–1927), named Wundt's approach **structuralism** and brought it to America. Titchener believed the new science of psychology should analyze consciousness by reducing it to its elemental units: the structure of the human mind was made up of more than 30,000 separate sensations, feelings, and images, and nothing else.

It's not hard to see why structuralism died with Titchener in 1927. First, it left out such important topics as motivation, individual differences, and psychological disorders. Furthermore, isolating the individual elements of the human mind seemed unnatural and silly to many people. For example, a structuralist could not say, "I see a penny," because such a statement fails to break the penny down into its various characteristics—that it is small, round, flat, copper-colored, and made of metal—and referring to the object as a penny, rather than in terms of the elements that an observer would see, would be interpreting the object, not describing it. Similarly, a structuralist could not say that two people standing at different distances were the same size, because the visual image of the more distant person is smaller than that of the closer person. Finally, the method was not truly scientific, because each introspectionist (who had to be rigorously trained in the method) described his own sensations uniquely and there was little consistency from one observer to another.

Structuralism School of psychology, developed by Wundt and Titchener, that emphasized the study of elements of the mind.

(Library of Congress)

(Archives of History of American Psychology)

Above: William James, an early functionalist.

Right: Wilhelm Wundt (at center), the "father of psychology" and founder of the structuralist school.

Functionalism *School of psychology, represented by James and Dewey, concerned with what the mind does rather than its elements or structure.*

Functionalism   *Functionalism* is considered the first truly American system of psychology. It was both more scientific and more practical than structuralism, a school that the early functionalists William James (1842–1910) and John Dewey (1859–1952) objected to as irrelevant. They and the other functionalist thinkers wanted to amass knowledge that they could apply in everyday life. In their concern with the way an organism adapts to its environment, they wanted to know how the mind functions—what it *does.* The functionalists broadened the scope of psychology. They developed many research methods beyond introspection, including questionnaires, mental tests, and objective descriptions of behavior. They also broadened their subject base beyond trained introspectionists, using children, animals, and the mentally retarded.

John Dewey (whose 1896 paper attacking the structuralists' idea of breaking down behavior into its elements is widely credited with launching functionalism) turned this pragmatic philosophy toward education. He felt that the emphasis of education should be not on the subject matter but on the needs of students, a radical view at the time. Dewey founded school psychology and left a lasting impression on the American system of public education.

American psychology is still functionalist in its outlook, with its emphasis on scientific methods of data collection and on the practical application of the knowledge gained from these methods.

Gestalt *School of psychology that emphasized the pattern formed by the elements in the mind rather than the individual elements themselves.*

Gestalt Psychology   Early in the twentieth century the German psychologists Max Wertheimer (1880–1943), Kurt Koffka (1887–1941), and Wolfgang Kohler (1887–1967) founded the **gestalt** school. These theorists advanced the idea that it is not the individual elements in the mind that are important (as the structuralists had maintained), but the *gestalt,* the pattern that these elements form in constructing a unified whole. (*Gestalt* is a German word that means *form* or *pattern.*) For example, they emphasized the importance of a new entity formed by its different elements, such as a melody formed by the combination of individual notes, or the perception of a leafy tree, its form much more than a mere combination of patches of light, shade, and

(Bettmann Archive)

Max Wertheimer, a gestalt psychologist.

(National Library of Medicine)

Sigmund Freud, the founder of psychoanalysis.

separate shapes. The gestaltists acknowledged consciousness; they just refused to look at it in little pieces. They held that the whole is greater than the sum of its parts, a viewpoint that had particular impact on the study of perception.

The **phi phenomenon,** the basis for what we experience as movies, was the cornerstone of a classic demonstration in perception that gave rise to the gestalt movement. In this experiment subjects sat in a dark room in which two spots of light alternately flashed on and off. When the time period between flashes was more than 0.2 seconds, the subjects saw two flashing lights, but when the interval was less than this they saw a single moving light. In other words, they saw apparent motion where there was actually none, just as we do at the movies when we see a series of individual frames in quick succession. The individual impressions on our retinas are not perceived as such but are perceived in a way that gives rise to an experience of a different order—apparent motion, which is a distinctive perceptual experience. This demonstration, showing that it is practically impossible to reduce conscious experience to its separate parts, supported the gestaltists' thesis.

Phi phenomenon Perceptual phenomenon used in a classic demonstration in perception that gave rise to the gestalt movement, in which stationary lights alternately flashed on and off are perceived as being apparent motion.

Psychoanalysis When Sigmund Freud (1856–1939) developed the psychotherapeutic technique called **psychoanalysis,** he complemented Wundt's "psychology of consciousness" with his "psychology of the unconscious." Unlike the laboratory-centered approaches described above, psychoanalysis did not try to be a pure science. Its emphasis was not the amassing of knowledge about the normal mind but the immediate application of a new way to treat people who showed abnormal behavior. It drew much of its data from clinical observation rather than controlled laboratory experimentation. Freud believed that powerful biological urges, most often sexual in nature, influenced human behavior. He felt that these drives were unconscious and that they created conflict within the individual and between the individual and the standards of society.

The Freudian approach generated storms of controversy, some of which are still raging today, as will be discussed in a number of places in this book. Some of Freud's disciples (like Erik Erikson) modified his basic approach, while others (like Carl Jung, Alfred Adler, and Karen Horney) broke away from him. The psychoanalytic school sees people in constant conflict between their biological urges and the need to tame them. While it has had an enormous influence on psychological thought, it has never become part of mainstream experimental psychology.

Psychoanalysis Therapeutic approach, developed by Freud, that aims to eliminate anxiety by giving the patient insight into unconscious conflicts which affect behavior and emotions.

Behaviorism *School of psychology that emphasizes the study of observable behaviors and events and the role of the environment in causing behavior.*

Behaviorism With the publication of an article by John B. Watson (1878–1958) in 1913, "Psychology as the Behaviorist Views It," a new school, **behaviorism,** was born. This school grew out of studies of animal behavior. The behaviorists saw no point in trying to figure out what people were seeing or feeling (as the structuralists did) or how they were thinking and why (as the functionalists did). They believed that these issues could not be addressed objectively and scientifically. Instead, they focused on what they could actually see people doing. In other words, they studied *observable* behaviors and events. They replaced introspection as a research method with laboratory studies of a basic type of learning called *conditioning*. They believed that if they could determine how a person or animal would respond to a particular kind of stimulus they could learn what was most important about behavior. With this orientation, the nature of the research shifted to experiments with animals and work on learning. The behaviorists emphasized the role of the environment in shaping human nature and played down hereditary characteristics.

B. F. Skinner (b. 1904) is not only the leading behaviorist today; he is one of the most important influences in all of psychology. The major thrust of his work has been in the area of operant conditioning, a type of learning in which an animal or person learns to make certain responses to get a reward or to avoid punishment. While Skinner used rats and pigeons to determine the effects of different patterns of reinforcement (rewards), he also did a great deal of work directly applicable to people. One of his inventions was the "aircrib," a roomy, temperature-controlled box in which he raised his own daughter for the first two years of her life. (It never became commercially successful, although it was much talked about.) Far more influential were the teaching machines that he popularized and the behavior modification programs that he developed using the same principles of reinforcement that he used with rats and pigeons.

The major contribution of behaviorism was its emphasis on the study of observable behaviors and events, as opposed to earlier introspective measures. Behaviorism also expanded the scope of psychology to include the study of animals as a way to learn more about people. This school helped psychology become a truly scientific discipline and shaped the field for years to come, despite a deliberate simplicity that prevented it from dealing satisfactorily with any psychological factors that could not be seen, which included almost all emotion and thought. A major objection to behaviorism has been its denial of cognitive processes. This concern has given rise to the cognitive approach, which we will discuss shortly. Still, behaviorism had a major impact and is still an important presence on the American psychological landscape.

(Bettmann Archive)

John B. Watson, the founder of behaviorism.

(J.R. Holland/Stock, Boston)

B. F. Skinner, the most prominent contemporary behaviorist.

(Doug Land)

Carl Rogers, a humanist and the founder of client-centered psychotherapy.

Humanistic Psychology *Humanistic psychology,* often called the "third force" (since it came after behaviorism and psychoanalysis), began in the early 1950s and has become increasingly influential since then. Humanistic psychologists, like Abraham Maslow (1908–1970) and Carl Rogers (1902–1987) protest against what they consider the narrowness of the first two forces. They maintain that behaviorism tells us about behavior but little about people, while psychoanalysis tells us about the emotionally disturbed but not about the healthy. Humanistic psychology has sought to expand the content of psychology to include such uniquely human experiences as love, hope, happiness, humor, affection, responsibility, and a desire for meaning in life, all aspects of our lives that are usually not studied or written about in scientific ways because they resist being defined, manipulated, and measured (Schultz, 1981). Humanistic psychology emphasizes a person's need to *self-actualize,* that is, to find self-fulfillment through the development of his or her unique potential. We'll see the current impact of this orientation when we discuss Maslow's theory of motivation and Rogers's theory of personality and the psychotherapeutic approach that grew out of it.

Humanistic psychology School of psychology, considered the "third force" in psychology, that emphasizes healthy human behavior.

Cognitive Psychology The most recent psychological school is an outgrowth of mainstream experimental psychology that seeks to find out what kinds of thought processes go on in the mind. *Cognitive psychology* represents a resurgence of interest in the earliest area of emphasis in psychology, the study of consciousness. Today's cognitive psychologists, however, study consciousness in a much more carefully controlled, objective, scientific way. These psychologists are not content with analyzing behavior in terms of simple stimulus-response connections but seek instead to understand the ways by which the mind processes information—that is, how it perceives, organizes, remembers, and uses data. They see people as actively engaged in information processing. This rapidly growing field is influencing the study of psychology in many ways, as you'll see throughout this book. For example, one interesting perception phenomenon studied by cognitive psychologists is the Stroop effect, shown in Figure 1-1. This effect demonstrates that in some situations the mind processes information virtually automatically.

Cognitive psychology Psychological school concerned with the way the mind processes information.

Name the colors	Read the words	Read the words	Name the colors
🌸	PINK	PURPLE	YELLOW
🌸	GREEN	RED	BLACK
🌸	GREY	GREY	GREEN
🌸	BLUE	BLUE	RED
🌸	YELLOW	BROWN	BLUE
🌸	RED	YELLOW	ORANGE
🌸	PURPLE	ORANGE	GREY
🌸	ORANGE	GREEN	BROWN
🌸	BROWN	PINK	PINK
🌸	BLACK	BLACK	PURPLE
A	B	C	D

FIGURE 1-1 *The Stroop effect shows how hard it is to ignore certain stimuli. You can demonstrate this to yourself. First, name the colors of the flowers in column A; you should be able to do this quickly. Then read the color names in columns B and C; this should be easy, too. Finally, name the colors in column D; now you may find yourself responding more slowly. When laboratory subjects are asked to name the colors of words like those in column D, written in colors different from the ones the words describe, they respond much more slowly, showing that it is difficult to ignore the meanings of the words. (Source: Stroop, 1935.)*

CONTEMPORARY PSYCHOLOGY

Areas of Specialization in Psychology

FIGURE 1-2 *Below: Current major fields for American psychologists. (Because of rounding, and because some respondents to the survey did not specify a major field, numbers do not add up to 100 percent.) (Source: Stapp, Tucker, & VandenBos, 1985, p. 1324.)*

FIGURE 1-3 *Bottom of page: Primary employment settings for American psychologists. (Source: Stapp, Tucker, & VandenBos, 1985, pp. 1326–1327.)*

Psychology is a complex science encompassing many different ways of looking at the human mind and human behavior and of applying the knowledge it has acquired. Being so varied, the field offers a rich selection of professional opportunities for people of widely differing interests, personalities, and abilities. The American Psychological Association lists more than 40 divisions to which its members may belong, depending on their interests and abilities. See the box "Preparing for a Career in Psychology" (opposite) and Figures 1-2 and 1-3 (below) for graphic presentations of the subfields and settings in which psychologists with doctoral and master's degrees work.

On the following pages, you'll find thumbnail sketches of several specialties in the field. These descriptions can give you an idea of the kinds of work that psychologists are doing today.

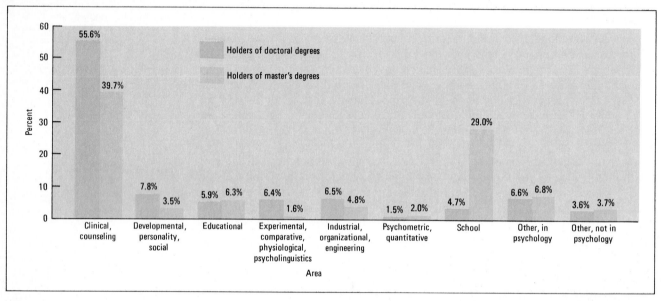

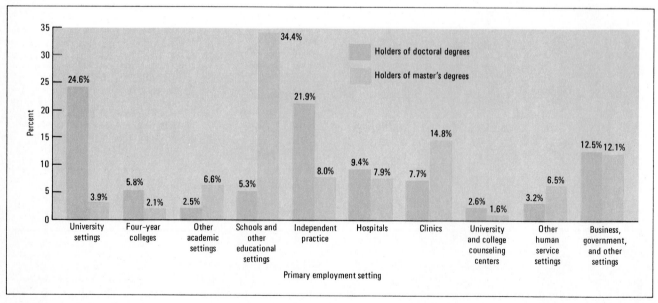

By taking this course you will fulfill your first requirement for a major in psychology. If you decide that this field is for you, you'll be taking more courses offered by the psychology department. Some junior and community colleges grant associate's degrees that prepare you to work in various psychological settings—for example, as an aide in an institution or school. If you're enrolled in a four-year college, you'll be getting your bachelor's degree with a major in psychology, which may prepare you for employment as a welfare caseworker or as a worker in a rehabilitation program, a community health center, or some other psychological facility. Or you may find that your psychology background is especially helpful for a career in any of a number of fields, such as advertising or labor-management relations.

If you decide to pursue further education in the field, you can go on for a master's degree (usually one to two years of graduate school), which may help you find employment as a school psychologist, in a clinic (particularly a community health center),

PREPARING FOR A CAREER IN PSYCHOLOGY

or with a business or government agency. Clinical or counseling work attracts the largest number of master's-level psychologists (39.7 percent), followed by school psychologists (29 percent) (Stapp, Tucker, & VandenBos, 1985). (See Figures 1-2 and 1-3.)

The next higher step is a doctorate. Most psychologists in the traditional areas of research and clinical work prepare for their careers by earning a Ph.D. (doctor of philosophy) degree, which entails three to six years of postgraduate study. A Ph.D. candidate must design and carry out an independent research

project, and describe it in a detailed report called a *doctoral dissertation*. In addition, the candidates will take courses that give a broad background in the different subfields and provide intensive training in a specialty. Clinical psychologists with doctoral degrees have received training and supervision in their specialty; to practice they need to be licensed. Doctoral-level psychologists work in a variety of settings, including colleges and universities, hospitals and clinics, businesses, government agencies, and private practice. More than half do clinical or counseling work (Stapp, Tucker, & VandenBos, 1985).

If you want a doctorate with a more practical focus, you might instead pursue the Psy.D. (doctor of psychology) degree. Instead of a research dissertation, Psy.D. candidates usually conduct a project related to their future goal, which might be in psychotherapy, school psychology, or one of the other subfields. Preparation generally takes about the same time as for the Ph.D.

Clinical Psychology   Upon hearing that you're studying psychology, your friends and family may ask you for advice or accuse you of "analyzing" everything that they say. They are reflecting the common belief that the clinical psychologist represents the entire field—which is understandable, since this is the largest specialty in psychology. *Clinical psychologists* diagnose and treat emotional and behavioral disorders that range from mild to very severe. *Abnormal psychology*, a related specialty, is devoted to the study of such disorders. Clinicians work much like psychiatrists, who also treat disturbed people but who have a medical degree and can prescribe medications.

Counseling Psychology   Your college probably operates a counseling service where you could go for help with problems revolving around your academic work, your career goals, the way you get along with your fellow students, or other aspects of your adjustment to life. *Counseling psychologists* give and interpret psychological tests, interview and observe clients, and offer suggestions for resolving problems.

Personality psychology   What makes one person trusting and another suspicious? What makes him honest and her devious? What makes you optimistic and me pessimistic? Are our personalities formed by our early experiences, or are we born the way we are? Are we likely to show the same personality characteristics in most situations, or do most of us show different faces in different settings? All these questions are investigated by *personality psychologists,* who measure and describe personality through interviews and specially designed tests and who formulate theories about its development.

Clinical psychologists Psychologists who diagnose and treat emotional and behavioral disorders.

Abnormal psychology Scientific study of the causes of emotional and behavioral disorders.

Counseling psychologists Psychologists who administer and interpret psychological tests, interview and observe clients, and help resolve clients' problems.

Personality psychologists Psychologists who study and assess individual differences in personality.

(©Vladimir Lange/Image Bank)

Counseling psychologists offer support and practical advice for resolving problems of everyday living. Many of them work at college counseling centers to help students cope with problems concerning their academic work, career plans, and social lives.

Educational psychologists
Psychologists who do research on the learning process.

School psychologists Psychologists who work directly with schoolchildren and their parents and teachers to deal with school-related problems.

Experimental psychologists
Psychologists who study basic psychological processes in animals and humans.

Physiological psychologists
Psychologists who study the relationship between physiological processes and behavior.

Educational and School Psychology Do children learn better with classmates of about the same level of ability? How can we help both gifted and mentally retarded children to develop to their fullest potential? What can schools do to overcome social, physical, and cultural handicaps? ***Educational psychologists*** look to psychological principles and techniques for help in answering questions like these. ***School psychologists*** work directly with schoolchildren and their parents and teachers to help the children get the most from their school years. They focus on helping youngsters who are having difficulty in school, often by diagnosing academic and emotional problems and recommending appropriate remedial programs. Educational psychologists most often work as professors and researchers in college-level departments of education, while school psychologists work in elementary schools.

Experimental Psychology Are you interested in the phenomenon of color blindness? Do you wonder how we are motivated by our sex drives? Would you like to know why somebody's name may be "on the tip of your tongue" but you can't quite say it? All these topics are investigated in experimental psychology. ***Experimental psychologists*** study such basic psychological processes as sensation and perception, learning, memory, cognition, motivation, and emotion. They work mostly in the laboratory and may use animals as well as human beings in their research. The name of this specialty is somewhat misleading, however, since psychologists in *all* the subfields conduct experiments and experimental psychologists use other research techniques as well.

Physiological Psychology Why is it that people with a spinal-cord injury can show the familiar knee-jerk reflex even though they can't move their legs voluntarily? Why do injuries to certain regions of the brain cause memory loss, while others cause speech disorders? How does a baby's cry activate the mother's mammary glands to produce milk? These questions are among those studied by ***physiological psychologists,*** who study the biological bases of behavior, especially the nervous system and the endocrine system. While they sometimes study human beings who have suffered injury to some part of the brain or spinal cord, they more often conduct research with animals such as rats, cats, and monkeys.

Developmental Psychology   When do babies learn that an object which they can't see still exists—so that they can understand that a parent who walks out of the room will very probably return? How do the hormonal changes of adolescence affect young people's emotional development? Do old people really suffer a decline in their intellectual abilities? *Developmental psychologists* study change over the life span, with some concentrating on particular times of life (such as infancy or old age) and others concentrating on relatively specific issues that persist throughout life (like the development of moral reasoning from childhood through adulthood). They describe, explain, predict, and sometimes try to modify behavior from birth through old age.

Developmental psychologists Psychologists who describe, explain, predict, and modify changes in behavior throughout the life span.

Health Psychology   Health psychology, a fairly new field, is concerned with psychological influences on staying healthy and getting well. *Health psychologists* look at the many ways in which the mind affects the body. They focus on the role of psychology in helping people to adopt health-promoting lifestyles, to prevent and recover from illness, to deal with stress, and to use and expand health care systems.

Health psychologists Psychologists who focus on the role of psychology in helping people to adopt health-promoting lifestyles, to prevent and recover from illness, to deal with stress, and to use and expand health care systems.

Social Psychology   What makes people go along with a group even when they disagree with what the group is saying or doing? Why do people sometimes rush to the aid of accident victims and at other times ignore their plight? What attracts people to one another? These are some of the questions studied by *social psychology,* the branch that studies the way we affect and are influenced by other people, both in groups and in intimate relationships. *Applied social psychologists* use such knowledge to solve practical problems that arise in public relations and advertising, in communities composed of members of different ethnic backgrounds, in the workplace, and in just about every kind of situation in which people are together.

Social psychology Scientific study of how we feel, think, are affected by, and act toward other people.

Applied social psychologists Social psychologists particularly concerned with solving practical problems related to people in groups.

Psychometrics   You've undoubtedly taken various kinds of ''intelligence'' tests throughout your school years, some of which may have yielded an IQ (intelligence quotient). In applying for certain jobs or seeking vocational or emotional counseling you may have taken personality tests that aimed to assess your social and emotional characteristics. *Psychometric psychologists* design such tests by identifying the characteristics they want to measure, developing the tests, and then developing statistical methods to interpret the scores.

Psychometric psychologists Psychologists who develop psychological tests and methods to score and interpret them.

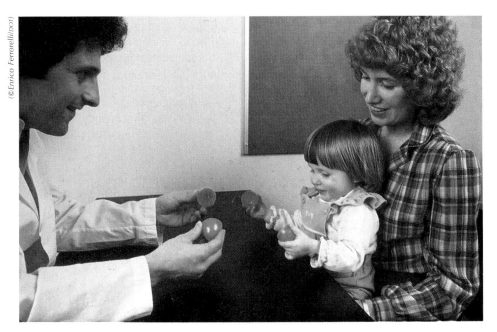

(©Enrico Ferrorelli/Iton)

The developmental psychologist Andrew N. Meltzoff is interested in the appearance of imitative behaviors—how soon children begin to imitate others and what kinds of actions they copy.

Industrial and organizational psychologists *Psychologists concerned with working people, work, and the workplace.*

Engineering psychologists *Psychologists concerned with designing, evaluating, and adapting machines to meet human needs.*

Theory *Explanation of the cause of behavior; theories organize data and provide directions for research.*

Hypothesis *Prediction about the results of research.*

Research *Systematic and objective collection of data.*

Data *Information collected through research.*

Industrial and Organizational Psychology   People and their work are the province of *industrial and organizational psychologists,* who focus on making the workplace more fulfilling and more productive, for both workers and their employers. These personnel specialists develop procedures for matching the job to the worker, for training workers, for evaluating internal organization, and for examining issues related to supervision, communication, and morale.

Engineering Psychology   This book was written on a word processor. People using this system can modify it for their own comfort by adjusting the brightness of the letters on the screen, tilting the screen to the most comfortable angle, and moving the keyboard to the best height and location. The kind of thought that goes into designing machines to meet human needs is the work of *engineering psychologists.* These applied experimental psychologists design, evaluate, and adapt equipment so that it can be used efficiently and effectively.

Some Other Specialties   Among the other psychological subfields are *comparative psychology,* which focuses on comparing behaviors across species; *psycholinguistics,* which is concerned with the study of language; and *quantitative psychology,* which undertakes statistical analysis of research findings.

How Psychologists Study Behavior

Since you've already seen how differently various psychologists conceptualize human behavior and how differently they apply psychological knowledge, it shouldn't come as a surprise that the methods by which psychologists gather their information are just as varied. The one thing they all have in common, however, is that scientific method guides all their approaches. This method is characterized by the systematic and objective collection of data. We'll now look at the most important research techniques used by contemporary psychologists, examine their strengths and weaknesses, and see how they contribute to our understanding of human beings. We'll look at the participants in such research and at the ethical issues that arise.

Theories, Hypotheses, and Research   Before researchers launch a particular project, they may develop a tentative *theory* to explain a particular behavior. A theory is a systematic attempt to explain behavior. Theories organize information, suggest explanations for phenomena, and provide direction for research. Theories generate *hypotheses,* tentative predictions (what could be called "educated guesses") about the results of the study. The researcher tests hypotheses by conducting *research,* the systematic and objective collection of data. *Data* (a plural noun; the singular form is *datum*) represent the information collected, a body of facts (such as scores on tests). We then make sense of the data by analyzing them using various statistical techniques, the most important of which are described in the Appendix. Often researchers modify their original theories considerably as their research fails to prove their original hypotheses. Theorizing is an important part of this process, since theories provide a framework for organizing the findings from research studies and for fitting them into our general state of knowledge.

As you become familiar with the ways these techniques are used, you'll be able to develop the kind of healthy skepticism that careful scientists develop in analyzing the results of their own and others' studies. You'll be able, for example, to read a newspaper report about an "exciting discovery" and ask yourself, "Was this experiment carefully set up? Were there enough subjects to warrant drawing a general conclusion? Are the findings clear-cut or ambiguous? Are there other possible explanations for the results besides those given by the researchers?"

Who Takes Part in Psychological Research?   SUBJECTS   A major element in any research project is the makeup of the people or animals being studied. Those whose

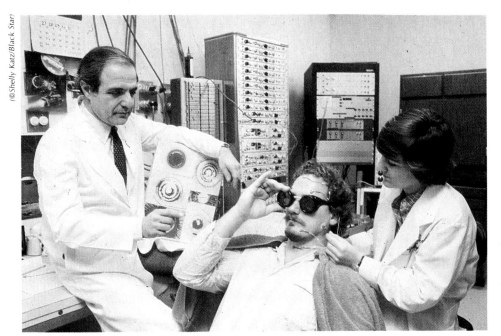

Much of what we know about sleep comes from laboratory experiments with college students, who are the most popular subjects for psychological research because they're convenient, inexpensive, and well motivated. Overreliance on this subject pool may lead to misleading conclusions.

reactions or responses are studied in psychological research are called **subjects.** For psychological researchers, two particularly important sources of subjects are college students and animals.

Subjects *Participants in research.*

College students Modern psychology has sometimes been referred to as the "science of the behavior of the college sophomore" (Rubenstein, 1982). Some 80 percent of contemporary psychological research uses college students (who make up only 26 percent of 18- to 24-year-olds) as subjects (Rubenstein, 1982; Schultz, 1969). Why are students so popular with researchers? Like Mount Everest, they are *there.* They are on the campuses where so much research is done, and they require little outlay of scarce research funds: they can be motivated by modest rewards—course credits for participating in research studies or relatively small cash payments.

But there are a number of problems with heavy reliance on a subject pool consisting of college students. For one thing, they tend to be from a fairly narrow social range, being predominantly white and middle-class. Further, they are even more limited as to age. Thus, we cannot generalize research findings from this group to other segments of the population that differ in age or social class. For example, most of what we "know" about normal sleep is based on the sleep of college students; other research has shown that patterns of sleep vary greatly over the life span. The data we have about young adults do not necessarily apply either to children or to older adults. It is probably dangerous to apply to the general public research findings based only on studies of this one group, whether the research is on forming friendships, falling in love, and conforming to group standards or even on basic psychological processes like sensory abilities and memory.

Animals Psychology has also been called the "science of the white rat," in recognition of the role this animal has played in so many research studies. Why do so many psychologists—whose field is, after all, the study of human behavior—do research on subjects like mice, pigeons, monkeys, chimpanzees, and even such primitive organisms as snails? This is partly a matter of convenience: since animals are less complex than people, we can often isolate a particular kind of behavior and get clearer, faster results. Because animals have shorter life spans than people, we can often follow the results of an experimental treatment into old age or into future

Animal research often has important implications for human beings. This rat is a subject in experiments that make use of its keen sense of smell to detect genetic traits affecting the immune systems of mice. Findings may help to improve procedures for transplanting tissue in humans.

An 11-year-old boy who was never able to accept an invitation to sleep over at a friend's house because he had been wetting his bed every night can now look forward to this pleasure because of a device that cured his bed-wetting. The device was developed out of an understanding of learning principles derived from research with pigeons and rats. A 3-year-old girl with a visual defect, astigmatism, is less likely to develop an irreversible defect in adult vision now than she would have been in the past. This is the result of studies that show the effects of uncorrected visual deprivation in kittens. A woman who was paralyzed on one side because of a brain injury can now hold and carry her grandchild in her arms as the result of physical therapy techniques developed through research with monkeys (Miller, 1985c).

These are just some examples of how people have benefited from psychological research conducted with animals. Such research has also been valuable in controlling pain; in the development of drugs to treat anxiety, psychoses, failing memory, and such neurological disorders as Parkinson's disease; and in developing treatments for many other human problems. It has also benefited ani-

ETHICS IN ANIMAL RESEARCH

mals, as authorities increasingly turn from killing troublesome animals to discouraging them from undesirable behavior by using chemicals that produce unpleasant tastes and nausea. The impetus for developing these chemicals arose from lab experiments that found that rats avoided certain flavors that they had tasted just before they felt sick.

Many advocates of animals' rights say, however, that such advances could have been accomplished without subjecting defenseless animals to uncomfortable or even cruel experimental procedures. What are these alternatives? They include observing animals living under natural conditions, using case studies, using embryos rather than

mature animals, turning to plants or tissue cultures of animals, or simulating animal models with computers. The general feeling among researchers is that while all these methods are valid in complementing other research, none of them takes the place of working with animals to study behavior (Gallup & Suarez, 1985).

Actually, investigations using animals make up a very small proportion of the total psychological research being conducted today. They account for only about 7 to 8 percent of all research and are conducted by only about 5 percent of psychologists (APA, undated). Of these animals, more than 90 percent are rodents and birds, about 5 percent are monkeys and other primates, and hardly any are dogs or cats. Few of the studies involve pain, stress, or deprivation. To safeguard the rights of those animals that are used, the American Psychological Association (undated) has formulated guidelines to be followed by researchers. These include compliance with any relevant laws; supervision that ensures comfort, health, and humane treatment; efforts to minimize discomfort, illness, and pain; and humane ways of terminating the animals' lives when that is required.

generations. There are other practical considerations. There are also ethical reasons for using animals in some research. We do many things with animals that we would not dream of doing with human beings, such as performing surgery that removes sections of an animal's brain and seeing how the animal is affected, and separating baby monkeys from their mothers and observing their development. Are such techniques ethical when applied to animals? This is a controversial and often highly emotional question, as we see in the box "Ethics in Animal Research."

We have learned a great deal from animal studies about learning, memory, attachment, the biology of the brain, and so forth, since animals and people are similar with regard to some processes and functions. But again, we have to be careful when we generalize findings from animals to human beings. Pigeons are not people, and we need to allow for differences between animals and humans.

Population All the members of a group being studied.

Samples Subgroups of a target population.

SAMPLING   Its is usually impossible to test all the members of a group (called a **population**) that a psychologist wants to study, for example all children from disadvantaged homes or all 1989 college graduates. Researchers therefore select subgroups, or **samples,** of these populations. They aim for a sample large enough to be representative of the population but small enough to be manageable in a study. Careful thought should go into selecting a sample. For example, if you wanted a sample of all the people over 70 years old in the United States, you wouldn't draw all your subjects from Florida but would choose people from various places around the country. You would probably try for a balance of urban and rural residents of various racial and ethnic origins, and of both sexes and married and single persons.

The most representative sampling procedure is random sampling. In a **random sample,** each member of the population has an equal chance of being selected. Depending on whom you want to study, this is sometimes done by choosing, say, every tenth name in a telephone directory (in which case you're narrowing your population to those people who have telephones listed in their names), or in a list of couples who have just applied for marriage licenses, or in a list of first-year students enrolled in a particular college. Another way to get a random sample would be to put all the names of people in the population you want on separate pieces of paper, put all the papers in a drum, shake it up, and withdraw, say, one-fifth of the slips.

Random sample Sample in which each member of the population has an equal chance to be chosen for study.

Samples are most reliable when they are **stratified,** that is, when they show a proportional representation of various important characteristics found in the larger population. For example, in a survey of the sexual attitudes and behaviors of the elderly, you would probably want your sample to reflect the proportions of males and females, urban and rural dwellers, and married and single persons that exist in the entire population. (Stratification is discussed in more detail in the Appendix.)

Stratified sample Sample that shows a proportional representation of various important characteristics found in a larger population.

Basic and Applied Research   One psychologist may ask, "How do people learn?" Another may ask, "How can we help retarded children learn how to care for themselves?" One may wonder, "What causes aggression?" Another wonders, "How can we reduce gang wars in our cities?" In both these examples, the first kind of question inspires **basic research** (or *pure* research), while the second kind is related to **applied research** (or *practical* research). The two orientations complement each other. Psychologists doing basic research look for answers that increase the total fund of human knowledge; although they are not addressing an immediate practical problem, the results of their work are often used in very down-to-earth ways. For example, a basic researcher may tell us what infants seem to like to look at, and then an applied researcher will use those findings to develop colorful mobiles to be hung over babies' beds.

Basic research "Pure" research that focuses on looking for answers which increase the total fund of human knowledge.

Applied research Research that addresses immediate practical problems.

Research Methods   The various systematic and objective techniques that psychologists use all have their own strengths and weaknesses. Each of the following methods has made a major contribution to our understanding of human behavior. As we survey them briefly, we will note the place each has earned in psychology.

CORRELATIONAL RESEARCH   Many of the techniques described here seek to discover **correlations,** or associations, between two or more variables. **Variables** are properties that vary, or can be varied for the purpose of an experiment, among members of a group. They include such factors as sex, race, age, IQ scores, reaction time, and exposure to different environmental influences. Suppose, for example, you wanted to find out whether men who view violent pornography are more likely to inflict harm upon women. The variables in this case would be the amount and kind of pornography viewed and the frequency and nature of violent acts.

Correlation Measure of the relationship (association) between variables.

Variables Properties that vary, or can be varied for the purpose of an experiment, among members of a group.

Researchers are interested in two properties of correlations: (1) their direction, that is, whether they are positive or negative; and (2) their strength. The direction is *positive* when an increase in one variable is related to an increase in another variable; it is *negative* when an increase in one is related to a decrease in the other. For example, if a high proportion of convicted rapists (relative to men in the general population) read magazines containing violent pornography, there is a positive correlation between these two variables. If rapists are *less* likely to read this material than are men who do not harm women, there is a negative correlation. If rapists are just as likely as nonabusers to read it, there is no correlation. The words *positive* and *negative*, then, do not imply value judgments; they simply refer to the direction of a relationship between variables.

The strength of a correlation between variables is expressed by a figure known as a **correlation coefficient** (symbolized as *r*). This value can vary between +1.0 (a perfect positive correlation) and −1.0 (a perfect negative correlation). The closer the correlation coefficient (*r*) is to 1, the stronger the relationship is in either direction. The closer *r* is to 0, the weaker the relationship is. A correlation of 0 signifies that no relationship exists. Most relationships between psychological variables have a value of less than 1, since perfect correlations rarely occur.

Correlations are important because they allow us to make predictions, to estimate one variable from the value of another variable. If, for example, there is a positive correlation between seeing violent pornography and committing aggressive acts, we would predict that people who do the former are more likely to do the latter. Obviously, the higher the correlation coefficient between two variables, the greater our ability is to predict one from the other.

One shortcoming of correlational research is that correlations do not allow us to draw conclusions about cause and effect. Even when two variables are strongly related, we cannot conclude that one of them caused the other or which one is the cause and which the effect. It is possible that the two variables are related because both stem from a third factor. In fact, this appears to be the case with a considerable body of recent findings about violent pornography. While there is a positive correlation between seeing violent pornography and inflicting harm upon women, there is no clear evidence that the pornography causes the aggression. It is possible that a cause-and-effect relationship operates in the opposite way, that is, that aggressive men want to justify their inclinations and are thus more apt to look at materials that depict a combination of sex and violence. It is also possible that some third factor— perhaps a history of having been abused themselves as children—causes such men both to look at violent pornography and to commit acts of violence.

We'll say more about cause-and-effect relationships when we talk about experiments. The uses of correlation as a statistical technique are described in greater detail in the Appendix.

CASE HISTORIES The story of "Dora," an appealing, bright 18-year-old who was brought by her father to the famous Dr. Sigmund Freud after her parents had found a suicide note she had written, is as dramatic and complex as any plot we're likely to see on daytime television. Freud analyzed Dora through her dreams, her nervous mannerisms, and her reports, uncovering a tangle of relationships between Dora and her parents, her brother, her governess, her friends, a friend of her father's who tried to seduce her, and the friend's wife, who turned out to be her father's mistress.

Freud (1905/1963) then used his considerable literary ability to illustrate his interpretation of her problems. In *Dora: An Analysis of a Case of Hysteria,* he wrote what amounted to an in-depth psychological study, a detective story, and a description of the way psychoanalysis works. Freud was one of the most skillful practitioners of the **case history** or **case study** method, in which intensive information is collected about one or just a few people.

The psychoanalytic case history is only one type. Those used by other practitioners often include other information such as test scores and medical histories. The case history method is especially useful in a clinical setting, where we need information to decide what kind of therapy to offer a particular person. Case studies are one of the earliest methods used by psychologists. They provide rich descriptions of behavior and can be the source of hypotheses that will form the basis of more carefully controlled research. They do have limitations, however. For one thing, since they are subjective, we have to rely on the accuracy and objectivity of the reporter. No two people would be likely to interpret and treat a case in exactly the same way; we are all governed by our own biases. Another drawback is the danger

Correlation coefficient Decimal value that indicates the strength and direction of a relationship, ranging from +1.0 (perfect positive correlation) to −1.0 (perfect negative correlation).

Case history; case study Research method in which intensive information is collected about one or very few individuals.

in drawing' a general conclusion about human nature on the basis of one or two people.

SURVEYS   When psychologists need information about a large group of people, they cannot use the case study method, because it is not valid to generalize from the experiences of one person. Therefore, they turn to survey methods such as questionnaires and interviews.

Questionnaires   Researchers may design a written questionnaire which they send to a random sample of the population they want to reach. Sending a questionnaire to a sample of female college seniors at a large urban university could give us information about the students' religious preferences, political leanings, premarital sexual experiences, and so forth, which we could then generalize to the population as a whole.

We might also find important relationships between two or more questions. We might, for example, find a correlation between political attitudes and sexual experience if students with liberal attitudes were more active sexually. We would say, then, that there was a relationship between liberal politics and sexual permissiveness.

While questionnaires can provide a lot of information about a lot of people in a short time, they have drawbacks. Answers are sometimes suspect because subjects' memories may be faulty, or they may give answers they think they ''should'' give; there is no way to follow up a response to explore its meaning or to delve deeper. Furthermore, we cannot draw any conclusions about cause and effect from answers to questionnaires.

Interviews   Psychologists or trained interviewers often ask questions in person. Often the interviews are **standardized,** so that everyone is asked the same questions, but sometimes respondents are asked to clarify or elaborate upon their answers. In Jean Piaget's interviews with children, he was more interested in the reasoning underlying the subjects' answers than in the answers themselves, and so he adapted each interview to the individual child. In this way he opened a window into children's minds and attained many insights into their thought processes. During the

Standardized   *Using the same measurement instruments and testing procedures for all participants.*

(Steve Skloot/Photo Researchers)

Researchers who draw on interview data, like this psychologist interviewing a prisoner, need to remember that interviewees' faulty memories, as well as their desire to please the interviewer and put themselves in a good light, may distort the truth.

1940s Alfred Kinsey and his associates interviewed thousands of people about their sexual behavior in a study that still remains as the most comprehensive ever done on male and female sexual practices.

Interviews (like questionnaires) are subject to respondents' faulty memory and conscious or unconscious distortion of answers. People being interviewed may feel constrained to give the answers that they think the interviewers want, or the answers that they think will give the most favorable impression of themselves. Those answering questions on a sensitive topic like sex may, for example, exaggerate either their naiveté or their experience. Furthermore, interviews can be expensive and time-consuming.

Sometimes questionnaires and interviews are used in the same study. In these cases, researchers will collect a large number of questionnaires and will then interview a subsample of the subjects who filled out questionnaires. The interview subjects may be selected at random, or they may be chosen because their answers on the questionnaires interested the researchers. Combining these two approaches provides depth as well as breadth.

NATURALISTIC OBSERVATIONS   Just like biologists who observe the feeding habits of raccoons in their natural habitats, psychologists often observe human behavior in nursery schools, subway trains, singles' bars, or whatever natural environment is appropriate for the population and the behavior under study. Researchers often keep careful records of their observations, such as tape-recording the interactions between husbands and wives, recording the number of instances of aggression by preschoolers, or carefully describing the responses of passengers in an elevator to some staged incident. Such records can provide valuable information about what people do in real-life situations.

Like every other study method, however, this one has drawbacks. Sometimes the presence of an observer can affect the subjects' behavior: if they know they are being watched, they will behave differently. Researchers address this problem in several ways—by staying in a situation long enough so that the subjects get used to them, by blending into a crowd, or by remaining behind a one-way mirror through which they can observe others but cannot be seen themselves. Observation can be time-consuming and tedious, especially if the observer has to wait for a given behavior to occur. And it is hard for an independent investigator to verify observations, since events are unlikely to recur in exactly the same way.

Probably the biggest disadvantage of naturalistic observation—and of all the methods discussed so far—is that the observer cannot manipulate the variables and therefore cannot make statements about cause and effect. If, for example, we note that children who often watch violent television shows act aggressively, we cannot say that the television shows make them more aggressive; maybe aggressive children are more likely to view that kind of show. What naturalistic observation does help us do is generate a hypothesis that we can then test in an experiment.

EXPERIMENTS   Experiments—a particularly important research method for modern psychologists—test hypotheses about causes and effects. In an experiment, researchers manipulate, or change, one aspect of a situation, called the **independent variable,** and observe its effect upon one aspect of behavior, called the **dependent variable.** The dependent variable thus *depends* upon the independent variable. For example, if you wanted to find out whether a special computer instruction program helped students learn the material in introductory psychology, you could design an experiment along the lines of the one described in Table 1-3.

A well-designed experiment needs two groups of subjects, an **experimental group** and a **control group.** Subjects are randomly assigned to one group or the other. Random assignment ensures that the two groups are similar in every way except for their exposure to the independent variable. The experimental group is

Independent variable   Factor which is manipulated by the experimenter.

Dependent variable   Factor which may or may not change as a result of experimental manipulation of an independent variable.

Experimental group   Group of subjects exposed to an independent variable.

Control group   Subjects who are not exposed to the independent variable; their performance is compared with that of the experimental group.

TABLE 1-3   DESIGN FOR AN EXPERIMENT

Procedures	Rationale
1 Frame your research question: "Does computer-assisted instruction improve students' learning of the information and concepts in introductory psychology?"	You have chosen a problem that interests you and is relevant for either basic or applied research.
2 Review the literature on the topic.	You want to know what other work has been done, and you want a basis for formulating your hypothesis.
3 State your hypothesis: "The use of these computerized materials improves learning."	This is the statement you will seek to support or not support.
4 Specify your operational definition of learning: the score on the final examination in the course.	You need an objective way to measure your findings.
5 Specify your independent and dependent variables: The independent variable is the computer learning program; the dependent variable is the score on the final examination.	You have developed a systematic framework for arriving at your data.
6 Identify the population you're concerned with: all students taking introductory psychology at your college. (Let's say there are 1000.)	This is the group that might ultimately be affected by your findings, but it is probably so large that you could not include everyone in your experiment.
7 Choose a sample, a subgroup of the population. You could do this by picking every tenth name of students enrolled for this course, coming up with a sample of 100.	If the sample is chosen randomly so that each member of the population has an equal chance of being selected, you can generalize your results from the sample to the population.
8 Assign the subjects randomly to either the experimental or the control group. You could do this by picking names out of a hat, or choosing every other name.	Random assignment controls for subject differences such as IQ, sex, age, geographic background, learning ability, study habits.
9 Manipulate the independent variable by exposing only the experimental group to the treatment (computer-assisted learning, in addition to traditional instruction), while the control group does not receive the treatment (receiving only traditional instruction).	All other conditions, such as class size, time of instruction, and student-teacher ratio, are the same for the two groups.
10 Measure the dependent variable: give members of both the experimental and control groups the final exam in introductory psychology.	All subjects receive the same final exam.
11 Determine your results: calculate the average final exam score for both groups.	Statistical techniques are used to determine whether the two groups differ significantly in average scores on the final exam.
12 Analyze your findings: "Students in the experimental group scored significantly better on the final exam on average than those in the control group."	Because of the various objective, systematic controls, we can conclude that exposure to the treatment caused the statistical difference (improved scores on the final exam), which probably represents improved learning.
13 Draw your conclusion: "The findings support the hypothesis that the use of this computerized instruction program enhances learning."	Because of this evidence, you may decide to apply your findings by offering computerized materials to all students of introductory psychology.

(Albert Bandura)

Through a series of laboratory studies, Albert Bandura and his colleagues concluded that children learn to be aggressive by seeing other people acting aggressively. Here we see an adult punching a "Bobo" doll, and then we see children who saw this adult. They're behaving more aggressively than children who saw a quiet adult.

Treatment *Experimental manipulation.*

exposed to the independent variable; the control group is not. The researcher then compares the two groups. (Statistical methods for determining the significance of the difference between the experimental and the control group are explained in the Appendix.)

If the experimental group, which has been exposed to a **treatment** (administration of the independent variable), behaves differently from the control group, which has not been exposed, we can assume that the treatment is responsible for the difference. If we did not have a control group, we would not know whether some other factor was responsible for the change in behavior. (In an experiment like the one described in Table 1-3, for example, another factor might be the superiority of a textbook that was being used.) Some more complex experiments use more than one experimental group and more than one control group.

Let's see how these principles work in both a laboratory and a field experiment.

A laboratory experiment In a laboratory experiment (as the term implies) researchers bring subjects into a psychological laboratory. One classic experiment was an investigation of the power of a bad example (Bandura, Ross, Ross, 1961). The researchers hypothesized that children who saw adults acting aggressively would copy their behavior while children who did not see these models would not behave aggressively. To test this hypothesis, 72 preschool boys and girls were divided into three groups. One experimental group of 24 children saw an adult hitting and punching a rubber doll; the second experimental group of 24 saw an adult playing quietly with tinker toys; and the third group, the controls, did not see any adults. (Seeing an aggressive or nonaggressive adult, then, was the *independent* variable; the children's aggressive or nonaggressive behavior was the *dependent* variable.)

The results supported the hypothesis. When children were observed in a free play situation, those who saw the aggressive adults behaved aggressively. The children who saw the nonaggressive adults and those in the control group showed very little aggressive behavior. This experiment seems to bear out the researchers' theory that children learn to be aggressive by seeing aggressive models, whom they then imitate. The question remains, however, whether the cause-and-effect relationships discovered in this carefully set-up laboratory situation could be generalizable to settings outside the psychological laboratory.

A field experiment In a field experiment, researchers introduce a change into a real-life setting. One example is a study we can refer to as "plant power" (Langer & Rodin, 1976). The researchers wanted to see whether it would be possible to slow down or reverse the decline in health, alertness, and activity that usually occurs among old people in nursing homes by giving these people the chance to make decisions and exert some control over their lives.

The researchers tested and rated a total of 91 persons on various measures of happiness and activity and then divided them into two groups that scored about the same on these measures. The 47 people in the experimental group were told that they were responsible for seeing that they got good care, for making decisions about how they spent their time, and for changing things they did not like. They were also asked to choose and care for a plant. The 44 people in the control group were told that the staff was responsible for caring for them and making them happy. They were handed a plant and were told that the nurses would water and care for it.

Three weeks after the experiment began, 93 percent of the experimental subjects were more active, more alert, and happier, and were involved in many different kinds of activities. In the control group, however, 71 percent were weaker and more disabled. A follow-up evaluation 18 months later showed that the benefits persisted. Only 15 percent of the experimental subjects had died in this period, compared with 30 percent of the control subjects (Rodin & Langer, 1977). The results of this study can be more logically generalized to the "real world," since it took place outside of the lab. The researchers did, however, acknowledge one difficulty common among field experiments. Because of ethical and practical considerations, they were not able to control all the important factors (in this case, random assignment of subjects and certain aspects of the nurses' involvement).

Strengths and weaknesses of the experimental method Because experimental procedures can be tightly controlled, they can be used to demonstrate cause-and-effect relationships as no other method can. Furthermore, because these procedures can be standardized, other investigators can **replicate,** or repeat them to see whether they get the same results.

We've already pointed out two difficulties: that of generalizing from laboratory findings to the real world (a problem with lab experiments) and that of maintaining sufficient control over a field situation (a problem with field experiments). Another problem may stem from **experimenter bias.** An experimenter who expects (or wants) a certain result to occur may unwittingly communicate these expectations to the subjects and thus influence the results. Such bias may be prevented by the **double-blind technique,** in which neither the subjects nor the experimenter knows which subjects are in the experimental group and which are in the control group. (In the **single-blind technique** the subjects do not know which group they are in, but the experimenter knows.)

In testing a drug that is supposed to alleviate depression, for example, the control group may be given a **placebo** (a treatment that seems to be the same as the experimental treatment but in fact has no physiological effect), but neither the subjects nor the experimenters know which subjects have received a pill or injection containing an active chemical and which have received an inert substance. Under such circumstances experimenters would not be tempted to evaluate the subjects according to what they *think* should happen.

Ethics in Psychological Research

When Steve Kaufman, an 18-year-old college student, agreed to take part in an experiment on the effect of hypnotism on problem-solving ability, he didn't realize that during the course of the experiment he would become partially deaf through hypnosis, that he would be placed in a room with two other students who he thought

Replicate *Repeat an experiment using the same methods and procedures to see whether the same results are obtained.*

Experimenter bias *Influence on experimental results caused by the experimenter's expectations.*

Double-blind technique *Procedure in which neither subject nor experimenter knows who is in the experimental group and who is in the control group.*

Single-blind technique *Technique in which subjects do not know if they are in the experimental group or the control group.*

Placebo *Treatment that seems the same as the experimental treatment but has no physiological effects.*

were fellow subjects but were actually confederates of the experimenter, or that he would become convinced that these two were deliberately excluding him from their conversation and laughing at him (Hunt, 1982). By the time he learned what was going on, his experience had confirmed the experimenter's hypothesis—that deafness makes people paranoid, a highly significant conclusion for middle-aged and old people who are losing their hearing (Zimbardo, Andersen, & Kabat, 1981). During the course of the experiment, Steve had some anxious, upsetting moments, but afterwards, when he was *debriefed* (told the actual purpose of the procedures), he expressed a feeling of pride that he had played an important role in this research.

This experiment demonstrates a major ethical issue in psychological research today—the use of deception. This study and a number of others have been denounced by some critics for deceiving subjects into taking part in an experiment for which they were not prepared (Baumrind, 1985). But defenders point to the obvious fact that this and other experiments in social psychology would be impossible to perform without deception, and that, in fact, a great deal of psychological knowledge has come to us precisely through such techniques. Recently, there has been less emphasis on deception, and this has resulted in a change in the nature of many psychology experiments, a change that some psychologists feel has seriously restricted the pursuit of psychological knowledge. This issue—along with certain other ethical issues—is still not completely resolved.

During the 1970s, the U.S. Department of Health, Education, and Welfare mandated the establishment of institutional review boards to review psychological research from an ethical standpoint. As a result, colleges and other research facilities usually have committees that review proposed research plans of investigators before they are allowed to proceed. In 1982, the American Psychological Association (APA) developed a set of guidelines on ethical issues to protect human subjects while permitting important research to continue.

Essentially, these are the most important principles:

■ *Subjects should be protected* from both physical and mental harm. Experimenters are obliged to consider the best interest of the subjects in the design and execution of their research studies. They must treat participants with respect and with concern for their dignity. They need to evaluate their designs to determine whether the subjects in them will be at significant or minimal risk of harm.

■ All subjects should give their *informed consent* to participate in research studies. In order to do this, they need to know what their participation will involve, what the study is about, what any risks might be, and anything else that might influence their decision about participating. The only time this obligation can be relaxed, according to the APA, is in a case when a study is considered to hold minimal risk for the subject.

■ Before experimenters design a study involving *deception,* they should try to come up with alternative procedures that would be equally effective. If this is impossible, the investigators must then ask themselves whether this study is really necessary—whether its results will be sufficiently important to justify its use. If so, the investigators must then be sure that whatever deception is used will not harm the subject, and they must debrief the subject as soon as possible afterwards.

■ *Subjects must be able to decline to participate in a study or to withdraw* from it at any time, even if they are students, clients, or employees of the investigator.

■ *The chief investigator in a research project is responsible* not only for his or her own ethical conduct, but also for that of collaborators, assistants, students, and employees working on the project. All these people are also responsible for their own behavior.

■ If a subject does suffer any harm from participation, *the investigator is obliged to detect and to correct any undesirable consequences,* including any long-term effects.

■ Investigators are obliged to guarantee the *right of privacy* to participants. All information obtained from participants must be kept confidential unless subjects agree in advance that it may be divulged.

These principles were developed to safeguard the rights of human participants in research. As we have pointed out, however, many psychological studies are performed with animal subjects. What rights do these subjects have? For a discussion of this issue, the cause of storms of emotional controversy, refer to the box "Ethics in Animal Research."

At various points throughout this book, we'll be turning our attention to ethical issues when discussing specific research projects. Meanwhile you might want to keep ethical considerations in mind when evaluating the studies you read about here and elsewhere.

You'll want to read this text with a critical eye, looking not only at ethical issues but also at the value of the information presented, for the field in general and for your own life in particular. We have presented data that we feel are important and that have met the tests of scientific validity. We've found the collection and presentation of these findings to be an exciting and challenging task, especially since the field of psychology continues to grow and to enrich our lives with what it can tell us about ourselves. We wish you a good journey along the most exciting route of all, the one that leads into the very nature of your own being.

SUMMARY

1 Psychology is the scientific study of behavior and mental processes. Psychologists describe, explain, predict, and modify behavior.

2 Psychology as a science is just over 100 years old. Its two main historical roots are philosophy and physiology.

3 During the late nineteenth century and the twentieth century, a number of different schools of thought in psychology emerged. These schools represented different theoretical outlooks concerning psychological issues.

4 Wilhelm Wundt, the "father of psychology," set up the first laboratory for psychological experimentation in Leipzig, Germany, in 1879. He developed the technique of analytic introspection in an attempt to study the basic structure of the mind.

5 E. B. Titchener named Wundt's work structuralism and brought it to America. Titchener attempted to analyze consciousness by reducing it to its elemental units.

6 The first truly American psychological school was functionalism. Functionalists were concerned with applying knowledge in practical situations, particularly educational settings. Early functionalists include William James and John Dewey.

7 Gestalt psychologists believed that the whole is greater than the sum of its parts. They believed experiences could not be broken down into elements. The German psychologists Max Wertheimer, Kurt Koffka, and Wolfgang Kohler founded this approach.

8 With the development of psychoanalysis, Sigmund Freud started a "revolution of the unconscious." His approach focused on the unconscious drives that motivate behavior.

9 Behaviorists focus on observable behaviors and events. They emphasize the role of the environment in shaping behavior. Behaviorism was launched in 1913 with John B. Watson's article "Psychology as the Behaviorist Views It." Today, the most prominent behaviorist is B. F. Skinner, who developed the basic principles of operant conditioning and applied these principles to the solution of practical problems.

10 Humanistic psychologists such as Abraham Maslow and Carl Rogers have been concerned primarily with healthy human behavior. They believe that the psychoanalytic and behaviorist approaches are too narrow.

11 The most recent psychological school is cognitive psychology, which is concerned with how the mind processes information.

12 There are a number of different subfields in psychology. These include clinical and abnormal, counseling, personality, educational and school, experimental, physiological, developmental, health, social, industrial and organizational, and engineering psychology, and psychometrics. There are career opportunities in psychology for people with different interests, abilities, and academic credentials.

13 Psychologists use a variety of research techniques in collecting psychological data. The scientific method, characterized by systematic data collection and objectivity, is

matter which research technique is used. In _____ng research, an experimenter often begins with a _____ory, or explanation, about the cause of behavior. On _____ e basis of this theory, the researcher generates hypotheses, or predictions, about the results of the study. A research project is then designed to test the hypotheses. The data collected are analyzed using appropriate statistical techniques, and the original theory is supported or modified on the basis of these findings.

14 College students and white rats have been somewhat overrepresented as subjects in psychological research.

15 Since psychologists usually cannot test all members of target populations, they select subgroups, or samples, of these populations. In a random sample, each member of the population has an equal chance of being selected. Stratified samples show various characteristics in the same proportions as they are found in the population.

16 Research is generally classified as either basic (aimed at increasing knowledge for its own sake) or applied (aimed at solving a problem).

17 Data-collection techniques include correlational research, case histories, surveys (including questionnaires and interviews), naturalistic observation, and experiments. Each technique has particular strengths and weaknesses, and all have their value in psychological research.

18 In correlational research, associations between variables are assessed. Two important properties of correlations are their direction (positive or negative) and their magnitude (strength). A correlation is expressed as a number ranging from −1.0 to +1.0.

19 In a case study, intensive information is gathered about one or a few subjects.

20 Using survey methods, psychologists can gather information about large groups of subjects. They may use questionnaires, or they may conduct interviews. Sometimes questionnaires and interviews are used in the same study.

21 In naturalistic observation, subjects are observed in some natural setting rather than in the experimental laboratory.

22 When psychologists want to make statements about cause-and-effect relationships, they design experiments. These are highly controlled procedures that can be readily replicated by the same or other experimenters. In an experiment, the psychologist manipulates the independent variable and observes the effect of this manipulation on the dependent variable.

23 Subjects in an experiment should be randomly assigned to one of two groups of subjects. The two groups of subjects in an experiment are the experimental group—the group that receives the experimental condition or treatment (the independent variable) and the control group—the group that does not receive the experimental treatment. By comparing the experimental and control groups, researchers can determine the effects of the treatment.

24 Psychological experiments are usually done in the laboratory, although they may also be carried out in the field.

25 In designing research, psychologists must consider ethical guidelines developed to protect subjects.

KEY TERMS

Abnormal psychology (page 17)
Analytic introspection (10)
Applied research (23)
Applied social psychologists (19)
Basic research (23)
Behaviorism (14)
Case history (24)
Case study (24)
Clinical psychologists (17)
Cognitive psychology (15)
Control group (26)
Correlation (23)
Correlation coefficient (24)
Counseling psychologists (17)

Data (20)
Dependent variable (26)
Description (5)
Developmental psychologists (19)
Double-blind technique (29)
Educational psychologists (18)
Engineering psychologists (20)
Experimental group (26)
Experimental psychologists (18)
Experimenter bias (29)
Explanation (5)
Functionalism (12)
Gestalt (12)

Health psychologists (19)
Humanistic psychology (15)
Hypothesis (20)
Independent variable (26)
Industrial and organizational psychologists (20)
Modification (6)
Personality psychologists (18)
Phi phenomenon (13)
Physiological psychologists (18)
Placebo (29)
Population (22)
Prediction (5)
Psychoanalysis (13)
Psychology (5)

Psychometric psychologists (19)
Random sample (23)
Replicate (29)
Research (20)
Samples (22)
School psychologists (18)
Scientific method (5)
Single-blind technique (29)
Social psychology (19)
Standardized (25)
Stratified sample (23)
Structuralism (11)
Subjects (21)
Theory (20)
Treatment (28)
Variables (23)

SUGGESTED READINGS

AMERICAN PSYCHOLOGICAL ASSOCIATION. (1982). *Ethical principles in the conduct of research with human participants*. Washington, DC: Author. A guidebook by the APA to the ethics of psychological experimentation.

DIENER, E., & CRANDALL, R. (1978). *Ethics in social and behavioral research*. Chicago: University of Chicago Press. Contains an interesting discussion of the ethical issues faced by psychologists in designing and carrying out research.

HEARST, E. (Ed.). (1979). *The first century of experimental psychology*. Hillsdale, NJ: Erlbaum. A collection of articles tracing the development of the subfields of experimental psychology during its first 100 years.

KOCH, S., & LEARY, D.E. (Eds.).(1985). *A century of psychology as science*. New York: McGraw-Hill. This monumental volume contains the analyses of over 40 authorities concerning the successes and failures of scientific psychology during its first 100 years.

NORDBY, V.J., & HALL, C.S. (1974). *A guide to psychologists and their concepts*. San Francisco: Freeman. A highly readable presentation of the lives and major concepts of 28 important psychologists from the past and present.

SCHULTZ, D. (1975). *A history of modern psychology*. New York: Academic. A fascinating account of the most important schools of psychology and the people associated with them.

SUPER, C., & SUPER, D. (1982). *Career opportunities in psychology*. Skokie, IL: VGM Career Horizons. A report on the many opportunities for careers in psychology.

WOODS, P.J. (1976). *Career opportunities for psychologists*. Washington, DC: American Psychological Association. A collection of articles on careers in psychology, emphasizing emerging and expanding areas.

P A R T

II

BIOLOGICAL FOUNDATIONS OF BEHAVIOR

U nderlying everything human beings feel and do is the complex mechanism of the physical self. To understand human behavior, then, we need to understand the basic biological structures and processes that provide information about the world and enable people to respond to it.

■ In *Chapter 2,* "Biology and Behavior," we explore the intricate workings of the brain and the nervous system, to see how they control every mental and physical process that human beings are capable of. Some of our knowledge about biological influences on behavior is as fresh as today's newspaper, since researchers continue to find ever more sophisticated tools for studying the nervous system and treating neurological disorders.

■ In *Chapter 3,* "Sensation and Perception," we describe how information is received through the various senses, including the five "special" senses—vision, hearing, touch, taste, and smell. We also investigate how the brain interprets and organizes such information to create meaningful patterns of perception.

■ Then, in *Chapter 4,* "States of Consciousness," we consider how the ability to sense, to perceive, and to act depends on states of consciousness. People experience the world differently, and behave differently, depending on whether they are awake and alert, asleep, or in an altered state induced by meditation, drugs, or hypnosis.

C H A P T E R

2

BIOLOGY AND BEHAVIOR

■ What methods are used by psychologists to study the brain?

■ How do the cells of the nervous system communicate with other nerve cells?

■ What is the spinal cord, and how does it participate in sensation, movement, and reflexes?

■ What are the somatic and autonomic nervous systems, and how do they influence behavior?

■ What are the components of the central nervous system?

■ What are the regions that make up the brain, and what is known of their functions?

■ How are the left and right hemispheres of the brain different in structure and function?

■ What is the endocrine system?

When I answered the telephone in New York early one July morning in 1979, I heard an unfamiliar voice announcing every parent's nightmare: "I'm a nurse at Good Samaritan Hospital in Phoenix, Arizona. Your daughter, Dorri, is here. She was in an automobile accident, and she has a concussion and multiple bruises, but it looks as if she's going to be all right." My husband and I got a flight out that afternoon, and after rushing to the hospital's Neuro-Intensive Care Unit, we walked past a patient with a swollen and discolored face before we realized that she was our 17-year-old daughter.

The neurosurgeon in charge told us that there had been injury to the brain, and there was some swelling, but there was no blood clot, no pressure, nothing that required surgery. He explained, "When there's a blow to the skull, the brain is shaken around inside like a mass of Jell-O. The brain is bruised and may be injured most severely directly opposite the place where the skull was hit. In your daughter's case, this is the area that controls the intellect. I think she'll recover totally, but it might take weeks or even months. Till then she'll be forgetful and not as quick as she was." He also told us that she might not be able to go away to college in the fall; we'd have to wait and see.

The fact that Dorri could move her fingers and toes was a good sign. So was her ability to understand what was said to her and to answer the questions she was asked every couple of hours for three days ("Where are you?" "What year is this?" "How many fingers am I holding up?"). She was still somewhat disoriented, though. She didn't know she was in a hospital, she said the year was 1964 (when she had been 2 years old!), and she didn't know she had been in a crash (she thought she had fallen down a flight of stairs). This was to be expected. If she continued to make progress throughout the crucial first 72 hours, the doctor would consider her out of danger. He would be ordering a CAT scan, a test (described later in this chapter) that would tell him the extent of her injury; he expected it to confirm his optimistic outlook. (It did.)

Five days after the accident Dorri could not remember anything about the two days just before it and the two days just after it. We were reassured that her intellect would be okay, however, when her father wanted to know whether she knew how to use the call button on her bed and asked, "Do you know how to call for the nurse?" In a hoarse voice she croaked, "Nurse! Nurse!"—and then grinned at us. Maybe her sense of humor wouldn't be impaired after all.

Dorri was lucky. She didn't suffer one possible effect of severe head injury—epilepsy. Nor did her accident have other serious permanent effects. She made a full recovery, both physical and mental, although the bruises we could see healed more quickly than the ones we couldn't. Two weeks after her injury she said, "I feel as if my brain is filled with air," as she was playing Scrabble and having trouble keeping score. Her memory for recent events was spotty for a few months, and to this day she has gaps in her memory for some events during the year after the accident. She did go to college in the fall, *though, and made a respectable showing. She eventually remembered most of what happened just before and just after the accident (although some of the details got lost forever), and today the only evidence that she ever suffered such a major trauma is a faint thin scar on her upper lip.*

—From the notebooks of Sally Olds

While any injury is unwelcome, of course, trauma to the brain seems most frightening because of the vital role the brain plays in organizing our lives. It is, for example, this one collection of nerve cells that told your body to wake up this morning, that allowed you to recognize where you were, that directed you to get up out of bed, to move your arms and legs. It allowed you to remember that you had a class to attend and how to get there, to understand the words you hear and read, and to formulate your own thoughts and to express them in speech. This same organ tells you when you're happy, sad, fearful, enraged, or in the grip of some other emotion.

Virtually all the subject matter included in the study of psychology is traceable to processes within our brains or to interactions between our brains and other organ systems in our bodies. Physical shortcomings or defects can interfere with the brain's work, and no other part of the body can replace it. (This is why an injury to the brain can have such drastic and irreversible consequences.) Programmed in our biology—in the brain and other parts of the nervous system—are the crucial elements that separate human beings from all other animals of earth, sea, and sky. These crucial elements are the nerve cells, which permit us to think in abstract terms, to speak, to write, to study ourselves. All these activities are thought to be beyond the reach of other animals.

For as long as people have studied the brain, they have been awed by its complexity. For centuries theorists have tried to explain the mysteries of how the brain works in terms of the most advanced technology of the day. During the seventeenth century, the French mathematician and philosopher René Descartes compared it to the science of hydraulics (the study of fluids), suggesting that information might be transmitted in the form of fluids through a system of pipes and tubes. Later, others compared brain activity to the gears and wheels of clockworks, to electrical cables, and to a telephone switchboard. Today's favorite analogy is the computer, since the brain, like the computer, is a processor of information. None of these comparisons is totally accurate, because the brain is still vastly more complicated than anything people have been able to invent. Still, the electrical analogy is apt, since minute electrical currents in brain cells direct our every activity.

In this chapter we look at the biological basis of human behavior, at the way the brain receives and transmits information and communicates with other parts of the body. We look closely at the basic building blocks of the nervous system—the neurons (nerve cells) and the glial cells—and the basic means of communication among these cells. We describe the various components of the nervous system. We discuss ways of studying the brain, how advances in technology help us understand its functions, and some of the controversies in interpreting our present knowledge. Finally, we'll discuss another system, the endocrine system, which is closely related to the nervous system.

Unless you have a strong interest in science in general or biology in particular, you may find the material in this chapter more challenging than anything else in this book. It isn't always easy to relate the structures of the nervous system to your everyday life or to become as involved in neurology as in the experiences of some of the real people you'll meet later on. Furthermore, you'll encounter many terms that are probably new to you. We urge you, however, to explore with us the complexities of the human brain and nervous system. As you learn about the physiological underpinnings for the way you think and act, you'll be in a better position to understand learning, memory, stress, motivation, physiologically based emotional problems, and other topics that are dealt with later in this book.

THE NERVOUS SYSTEM

How the Nervous System Is Studied

As we've said, the human brain and nervous system are of enormous interest to the human species. What brings about the countless activities we are engaged in all the time, asleep or awake, sick or well? To find out, physiological psychologists—now usually called *neuroscientists*—have developed a variety of ways to study the **nervous system.** The nervous system is a network of cells whose functions are to detect stimuli, guide motor responses, and provide the framework for mental processes.

The Pseudoscience of Phrenology   One popular practice in the nineteenth century involved feeling the bumps on people's heads. According to **phrenology,** your psychological attributes correspond to the swellings and hollows in your skull, which reflect the development of particular areas of your brain (see Figure 2-1). In other words, areas of the brain exist for such traits as secretiveness, calculation, and self-esteem, and if those areas are well developed, you have the trait in question. How were these areas decided upon? One amorous widow was noted to have a hot neck; thus, the phrenologist Franz Gall associated a region just above the neck with ''amativeness'' (from the Latin term for love). Several bankers had bumps in the region that came to be identified with ''acquisitiveness'' (which meant a tendency toward acquiring without permission, or in other words, stealing) (Fancher, 1979).

Nervous system   Network of cells whose function is to detect stimuli, guide motor responses, and provide the framework for mental processes; it consists of the brain, the brain stem, the spinal cord, the cranial and peripheral nerves, and the ganglia.

Phrenology   Pseudoscientific approach which contends that psychological attributes correspond to swellings and hollows in the skull, reflecting the development of particular areas of the brain.

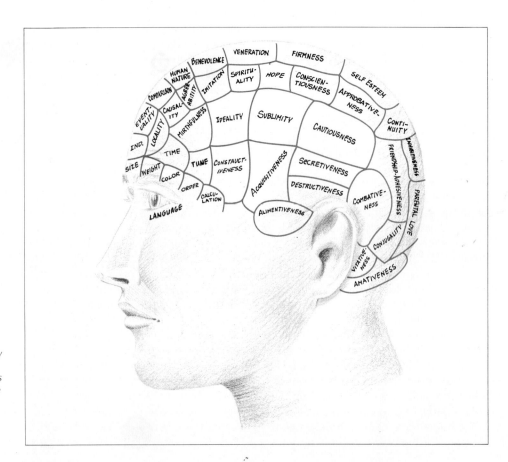

FIGURE 2-1   *This nineteenth-century phrenology chart shows different regions of the brain that were supposedly linked to the development of different personality characteristics. Its anatomical inaccuracies are most obvious in its placement of ''language'' under the eye, an area where no brain tissue exists. (Source: Kolb & Whishaw, 1980.)*

Most of the tenets underlying phrenology are clearly unscientific and have been completely discredited. For one thing, the theory was based on faulty anatomy. Some of the areas of the skull shown in Figure 2-1 do not even lie over the brain. Furthermore, the way these areas are charted does not correspond in any way to functionally significant divisions of the brain.

This theory is historically important, however, since it introduced the concept of *localization of function*—that is, the idea that certain regions of the brain control distinct functions of body and mind. This concept, a major focus of contemporary brain research, remains controversial. The heart of the controversy is whether a specific function is localized in a small region of the brain or controlled by widely distributed brain regions.

Surgery: Destroying a Part of the Brain   The oldest study technique is still in use—operations in which researchers create lesions (areas of brain damage) in the brains of experimental animals. They then observe the impact of such damage on the animals' behavior. For example, damage to one particular small region in the brain of a rat produces such extreme overeating that the animal soon becomes obese. For obvious reasons, this technique is not used on human beings, but researchers have obtained similar kinds of knowledge from studying persons who have suffered brain damage because of strokes or head injury, or who have had **psychosurgery,** the deliberate destruction of brain tissue to improve a psychiatric disorder. (This treatment is discussed in Chapter 15, along with other therapies for emotional problems.) Such people often show severe deficits that have taught us a great deal about the relationship between specific areas of the brain and particular psychological functions.

Psychosurgery *Brain surgery performed to overcome psychiatric disorders.*

Electrical and Chemical Stimulation of the Living Brain   Neuroscientists sometimes stimulate various brain regions electrically or chemically. Electrical stimulation is performed on patients who are about to receive therapeutic brain surgery (for example, to remove a tumor). To stimulate the brain electrically, scientists implant electrodes into the brains of anesthetized, but conscious, persons. (Electrodes are very thin wires, insulated everywhere except at their tips, that carry low-intensity electric currents.) The electrodes activate the electrical portion of the neurons (nerve cells) at the electrode tip. Subjects can report what they are feeling or can show the effects of the stimulation through their behavior. Electrical stimulation of the brain is painless in most areas, since there are no pain receptors in the brain itself. Subjects feel pain only when the pain pathways of the brain are stimulated (Penfield & Roberts, 1959).

To stimulate the brain of an animal chemically, researchers introduce specific chemicals into specific brain regions through a cannula (a thin metal tube). Introducing chemicals into the brain has produced behavioral changes in eating, drinking, aggression, docility, mood, sexual activity, and memory.

Modern Techniques   Modern technology has made possible a variety of new study techniques that are *noninvasive,* that is, they do not require physical entry into the brain. The following methods yield information that can be valuable in diagnosing injuries and disorders and in expanding our knowledge of the way the brain works.

ELECTROENCEPHALOGRAPHY   Electroencephalography is the recording of the electrical signals of the brain, which take the form of waves. The very small electrical potentials of the brain cells are amplified thousands of times and are recorded on paper. This record is called an *electroencephalogram* (EEG). Abnormal wave patterns on the EEG are very helpful in the diagnosis of epilepsy, brain tumors, and other neurological disorders. A new EEG technique called *evoked potentials* uses high-speed computers to construct brain-wave patterns that appear in response to a specific stimulus such as a word, a tone, or an electric shock.

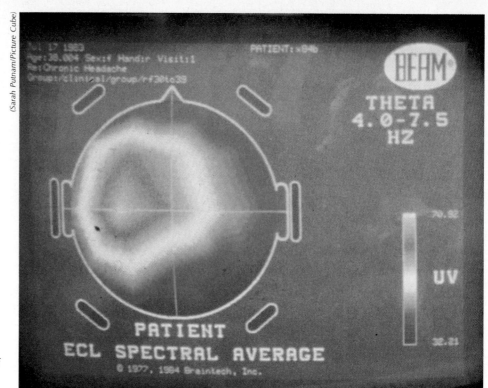

(Sarah Putnam/Picture Cube)

The wave patterns generated by electrical signals in the brain, as shown here on an electroencephalogram (EEG), yield information about brain function during sleep, during various states of consciousness, and in the presence of certain neurological disorders.

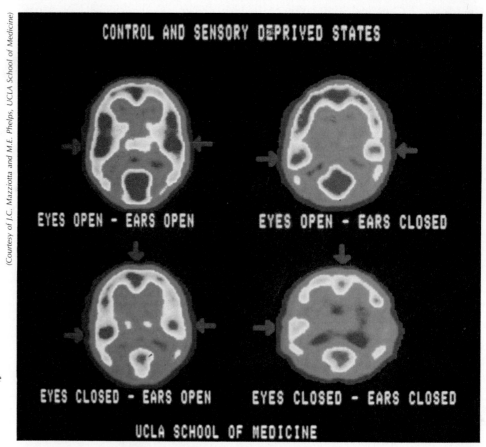

(Courtesy of J.C. Mazziotta and M.E. Phelps, UCLA School of Medicine)

This computerized image produced by a PET scanner shows activity in a normal brain. High metabolic activity is shown by red shades and low activity by blue shades. Note the changes that occur in the visual cortex (bottom of image) and auditory cortex (left and right sides) when the eyes and ears are either open or closed.

COMPUTERIZED AXIAL TOMOGRAPHY   Computerized axial tomography (CAT) uses x-ray images taken from many points around the head. A computer analyzes these multiple images and arranges them into an image that represents a "slice" of the brain. The newest CAT scanners produce very clear pictures of brain anatomy and can be used to diagnose the extent of brain damage from an injury as well as a variety of neurological disorders, including strokes and tumors.

POSITRON EMISSION TOMOGRAPHY   A positron emission tomography (PET) scan is like a "movie" version of the CAT scan. Thirty minutes before the scan is performed a harmless radioactive sugar is injected into the subject. The sugar travels quickly to the brain cells, which absorb it as glucose (which very literally becomes "food for thought"). Since blood flow and sugar utilization are related to neuronal activity, tracking the path of the radioactive sugar lets scientists see which brain areas are active during various tasks and mental operations.

The PET scan uses radiation-sensitive detectors to record the location in the brain of molecules that have been labeled with the radioactive sugar. A computer then constructs intricate and detailed color pictures of the brain. The newest version of the PET scan can examine seven "slices" of the brain in 1 minute, putting these images together in a way that tells us what parts of the brain are most active at any one time.

MAGNETIC RESONANCE IMAGING   Magnetic resonance imaging (MRI) uses radio waves and magnetic fields to produce three-dimensional images of the ridges, folds, and crevices of the brain. Like the CAT scan, MRI also produces a static picture, but one that is much sharper and more detailed. In addition to revealing anatomical detail, it may also give physiological and biochemical information about organs and tissues. It is particularly helpful in diagnosing problems involving soft tissue, such as tumors and other abnormalities of the brain. (This technology was originally called *nuclear magnetic resonance.*)

We can better appreciate the capabilities of these new study techniques when we recognize the enormous complexity of the human nervous system, as described in the following section.

How the Nervous System Works

Scientists have been able to look at the purely physical workings of the brain and nervous system and to describe the actions involved. In this section we examine the cells in this system and the electrical and chemical processes that provide the forces for their important work.

Cells: The Basis of All Behavior   Everything that we do depends on the action of the billions of cells of the nervous system. These building blocks of behavior are of two basic kinds: neurons and glial cells.

The **neurons,** or nerve cells, do the vital job of receiving and sending information to other parts of the body. There are three types of neurons—sensory neurons, motor neurons, and interneurons:

■ **Sensory (afferent) neurons** transmit information from the body organs (such as skin or muscles) to the brain.

■ **Motor (efferent) neurons** transmit information from the brain to the muscles and glands of the body.

■ **Interneurons** connect the sensory and motor cells, carrying messages from neurons in one part of the brain or the spinal cord to those in another.

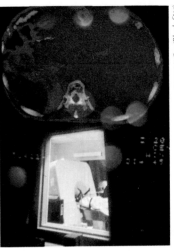

Magnetic resonance imaging (MRI) uses radio waves and magnetic fields to produce three-dimensional images of the brain. Patients remain inside the unit for 5 to 30 seconds. They do not feel anything, but some become claustrophobic or bothered by the loud noise of magnetic fields grating on metal. Some hospitals supply patients with a little bell to signal technicians that they want something.

Neurons *Nerve cells that receive and send information to other parts of the body.*

Sensory (afferent) neurons *Nerves that transmit information from the body to the brain.*

Motor (efferent) neurons *Nerves that transmit information from the brain to the muscles and glands of the body.*

Interneurons *Intermediary neurons that send messages from one kind of neuron to another.*

Glial cells *Cells that support and protect neurons.*

Myelin *Fatty tissue that covers some axons, allowing impulses to travel faster.*

Dendrites *Narrow, branching extensions of a neuron's cell body that receive incoming signals from other neurons.*

Axon *Tail-like fiber extension of a neuron that carries nerve impulses to other neurons.*

Resting membrane potential (RMP) *Difference in ions across the neuron membrane.*

FIGURE 2-2 *Each neuron, or nerve cell, is specialized for function. These drawings show the different shapes and sizes of neurons in various parts of the nervous system.*

The neurons are supported and protected in various ways by the **glial cells** (or glia). One type of glial cell covers parts of the neuron with a sheath, or covering, composed of a fatty tissue called **myelin.** Other types of glia help remove dead nerve cells, while some form a lining to prevent toxins from entering the brain, and others support the neurons in other ways.

An estimated 100 billion neurons (Hubel, 1979) and at least the same number of glia are present in the human nervous system. Neurons vary widely in size and in shape, depending largely on the different functions they perform. Some examples of different kinds of neurons are shown in Figure 2-2.

Despite their differences, all neurons have certain characteristics in common. They all have a cell body with a cell nucleus (a center). The nucleus contains the cell's genetic information (the programming that determines what each cell does) in deoxyribonucleic acid (DNA). Most have **dendrites,** narrow, branching extensions of the cell body, which receive incoming signals from other neurons. The longer and more complex a neuron's dendrites, the more connections can be made. Most neurons have a tail-like extension called an **axon,** which may be as short as a tiny fraction of an inch, as for a brain neuron, or as long as 2 or 3 feet, as in the case of some neurons in the spinal cord. A neuron receives information from other neurons through its dendrites and cell body. It transmits information through its axon (see Figure 2-3a).

Electrical and Chemical Activity: Keys to Communication Our brains are incredibly busy centers of electrical and chemical activity for as long as we live—even during sleep. The neuron, the basic unit of the nervous system, is responsible for the electrical and chemical activity of the nervous system. The neuron membrane, a thin porous layer of tissue, is responsible for the electrical characteristics of the nerve cell. If we were to insert into the neuron a microelectrode, a tiny wire connected to a voltmeter (see Figure 2-3b), we could measure the difference in electrical potential between the inside and the outside. The inside of the neuron would have a more negative electrical charge than the outside, the difference being about −70 millivolts (a *millivolt* is 1/1000 volt). Charged particles called *ions* are found inside and outside of the membrane (see Figure 2-3c). There are many sodium ions (NA+) outside the cell and many potassium ions (K+) inside the cell. This difference in ion concentration across the membrane is called the **resting membrane potential (RMP).** It exists because there are more positive ions outside the cell than in it. Thus, each neuron is like a battery in that the difference in ions across the membrane represents potential energy.

The nerve cell, however, does not remain at rest. Small pores in the membrane allow one of the two kinds of ions to enter or leave the cell. For example, if a pore

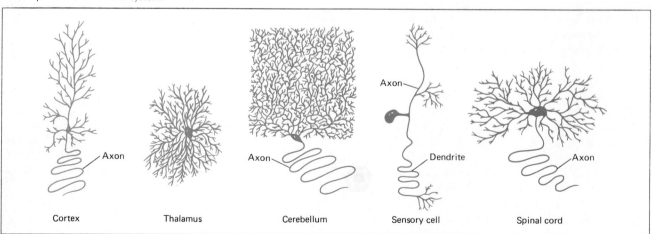

Cortex   Thalamus   Cerebellum   Sensory cell   Spinal cord

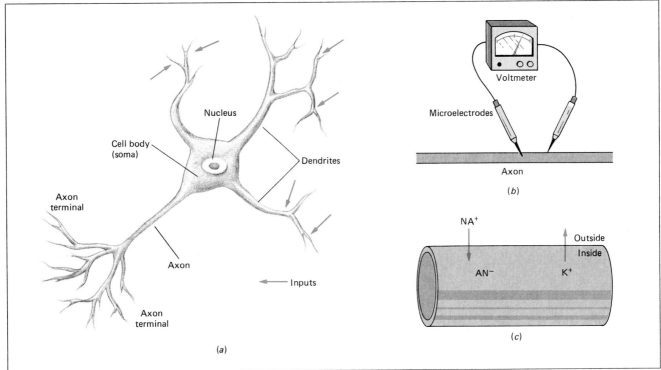

that allows sodium ions to enter opens, the inside of the cell will become more positively charged (see Figure 2-4a, page 46). Or, if a different set of pores open, potassium ions from inside the cell will exit, making the inside even more negatively charged (see Figure 2-4b). These ion movements are important: they form the basis for the electrical activity of nerve cells. (Indeed some poisons act by preventing the membrane pores from opening. For example, a chemical found in the Japanese puffer fish blocks the sodium pores and eliminates electrical activity in nerve cells, thus causing paralysis of body systems and ending in death. Little wonder that the Japanese have a saying, "Only a fool eats the puffer fish.")

The "firing" of a neuron, or the sending of a nerve impulse down its axon, is known as the **action potential (AP)** (see Figure 2-4c). The AP occurs when pores that allow NA+ ions to enter the cell open, thus causing the inside of the cell to become more positive and moving the membrane potential past its threshold (about −60 millivolts). The **threshold** is the value of membrane potential when the NA+ pores are completely open. (As with the "threshold" of a light switch it is the point at which it is either on or off.) If the membrane potential does not reach threshold there is no AP—that is, the neuron does not fire at all, since the AP operates on an all-or-none principle (like an on-off light switch, rather than a dimmer switch, which can provide gradients of light). The action potential is a change in membrane potential in which the membrane potential quickly reverses itself (as NA+ ions enter the cell) and then returns to resting level (as K+ ions leave the cell). Normally, the AP is generated at the axon hillock (refer to Figure 2-3) and then quickly moves down the axon toward the axon terminal. The **axon hillock** is a swelling near the connection between an axon and the cell body. The **axon terminal** is the far end of the axon.

Impulses travel faster along axons that are covered with the fatty substance myelin. Since myelin acts as an electrical insulator, the AP cannot occur beneath the myelin sheath, but instead jumps rapidly between the nodes (gaps) in the myelin (see Figure 2-5, page 46). The process of **myelinization** (the formation of myelin on axons) extends through at least the first 70 years of life in human beings, and dendrites continue to grow and become more elaborate. In old age, however, there is a

FIGURE 2-3 *(a) Schematic diagram of a typical neuron, showing the cell body, nucleus, dendrites, and axon. (b) Electrical potential across the neuron membrane is measured using a microelectrode connected to a voltmeter. (c) Neuron axon, showing the ions found inside and outside the cell membrane; these contribute to the electrical activity of the neuron. Arrows indicate the direction in which an ion will flow if a membrane channel opens for it.*

Action potential (AP) *"Firing" of a neuron, or the sending of a nerve impulse down its axon, from one end of the neuron to the other.*

Threshold *In an action potential, the value of membrane potential when the NA+ pores are completely open.*

Axon hillock *Swelling near the connection between an axon and the cell body.*

Axon terminal *Far end of the axon.*

Myelinization *Process that forms myelin on axons.*

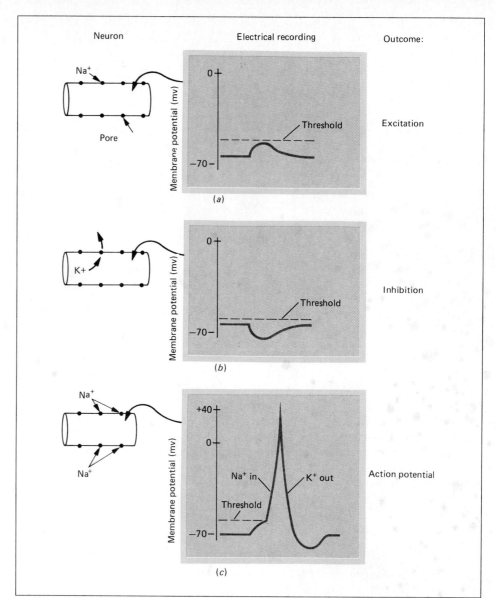

FIGURE 2-4 *(a)* Excitatory change in potential caused by a small movement of NA⁺ ions into the neuron. The change does not pass the threshold. *(b)* Inhibitory change in potential caused by a small movement of K⁺ ions out of the neuron. *(c)* Action potential consists of a slow rise in membrane potential from resting level until a threshold value is reached. At this time the membrane potential rapidly rises to near +40 millivolts (mv) and then returns to resting level. The rising phase is caused by the inward flow of NA⁺ ions, whereas the downward phase is caused by K⁺ ions leaving the cell.

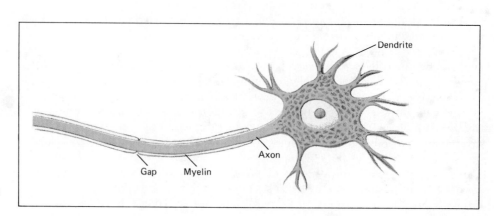

FIGURE 2-5 *A myelin sheath is formed around a neuron axon by layers of fatty material. Myelin serves to speed up nerve cell conduction.*

shriveling of dendrites and, thus, less communication among cells. The enormous growth in human abilities that takes place during the first ten years of life parallels the process of myelinization and the growth of dendrites during this period. Also, neurons die as we age, and massive neuron death is correlated with a decline in mental function. Massive neuron death occurs in some disorders, such as ***Alzheimer's disease*** (see the box "Alzheimer's Disease").

Neurotransmitters: Chemical Messengers   When you touch a hot stove and instantly pull your hand away, you are acting on information received by sensory neurons (that an intense stimulus is present) and sent by motor neurons (ordering your muscles to move your hand). Since these are different neurons, they must communicate with each other in some way. How do the neurons receive and pass along such information?

ACTION AT THE SYNAPSE: NEUROTRANSMITTERS AT WORK   Neurons communicate with each other at specialized junctions called ***synapses.*** A synapse is a junction between the membrane of one neuron and another. The ***synaptic cleft*** is a tiny physical gap between these membranes. When the action potential reaches the end of an axon, it causes release of a chemical called a ***neurotransmitter*** into the synapse. Neurotransmitters are stored within ***synaptic vesicles,*** packets of protein located at the axon terminal of the sending neuron. A neurotransmitter released into the synaptic cleft attaches to a ***receptor site,*** a protein complex on the membrane of the dendrite (the receiving portion of the neuron.) Neurotransmitters control electrical activity by causing the receptors to which they bind to open and close the ion pores. (See Figure 2-6 for a diagram of a typical synapse.)

   Not only are there many different transmitter substances, but individual neurons can send more than one neurotransmitter. Further, every receiving cell has many different receptor sites, which are specialized for different types of neurotransmitters. The effects of neurotransmitters depend on the amount of the chemical sent: small

Alzheimer's disease   *Irreversible dementia characterized by memory loss, confusion, and other intellectual and personality deterioration.*

Synapse   *Junction between the axon of one neuron and the dendrites or cell body of a second, where neurons communicate with each other.*

Synaptic cleft   *Tiny physical gap between the membrane of one neuron and another.*

Neurotransmitter   *Chemical involved in transmitting messages between neurons.*

Synaptic vesicles   *Specialized organs on the axon terminal of the sending neuron which squirt neurotransmitters into synapses.*

Receptor sites   *Specialized molecules on receiving neurons that bind with a neurotransmitter.*

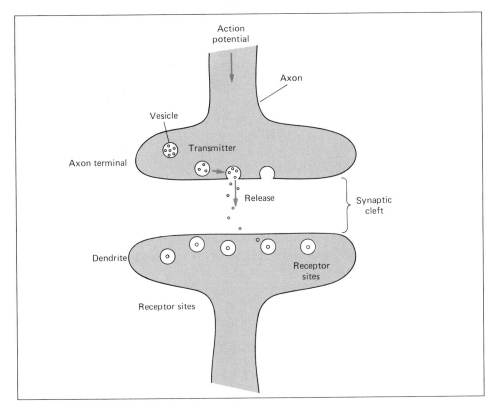

FIGURE 2-6   *Typical synapse. (For more detail, see Figure 2-7, page 50.)*

A once brilliant scientist now lies diapered in a bed with side rails. A once active business executive now cannot even cook a simple meal because she forgets to turn off the stove and has twice started kitchen fires. These people are victims of Alzheimer's disease. This degenerative disorder of the brain is a type of **dementia,** a term that describes a variety of conditions characterized by loss of memory, confusion, and personality changes.

Dementia is not, of course, an inevitable part of aging; it affects only 5 percent of people over 65. Most old people are in good mental health, and most of those who do suffer some memory loss are not suffering from dementia. (The word *senility* was long used to describe various kinds of dementia, but it is no longer used, since it is not a medical diagnosis but a ''wastebasket term'' for a range of symptoms.)

Alzheimer's disease wreaks havoc on established personality patterns and robs a person of intelligence, awareness, and even the ability to control bodily functions. It affects all aspects of functioning and has become one of the most dreaded conditions of old age. While it sometimes strikes in middle age, most victims are over 65.

The first signs of this affliction

IN THE FOREFRONT

ALZHEIMER'S DISEASE

are often not picked up immediately. They might include a tendency to garble phone messages, an inability to play a game of cards or tennis, or sudden outbreaks of extravagance. The most prominent early symptom is memory loss, especially for recent events. More symptoms follow, such as confusion, irritability, restlessness, agitation, delusions, hallucinations, and impairment of judgment, concentration, orientation, and speech. As the disease progresses, symptoms become more pronounced and disabling. By the end, the victim cannot understand or use language, does not know family members, and cannot eat without help.

Alzheimer's disease is estimated to affect from 500,000 to 1.5 million Americans, some 20 to 30 percent of those who live to their mid-eighties. Afflicted people survive for varying lengths of time, and by and large, the

earlier the condition appears, the shorter survival time is. When it occurs in people aged 55 to 70, survival time averages 8.5 years, but some people live for 20 years with the disorder (Alzheimer's Disease and Related Disorders Association, Inc.; Heston & White, 1983). In living patients the diagnosis of Alzheimer's disease has until recently been made only by ruling out other conditions, since the only definitive diagnosis has been by examination of the brain at autopsy (Heston & White, 1983). The development of magnetic resonance imaging (MRI), however, has improved diagnostic accuracy where this technique is available (Summers et al., 1986).

The brain of a person with Alzheimer's disease shows a number of specific changes, including loss of neurons in the cortex and in other brain structures, enlarged ventricles (caused by the death of neurons, which are consumed by glial cells, and reduced activity of the chemical acetylcholine in several areas of the brain. Symptoms resulting from acetylcholine deficiency include memory loss, visual hallucinations, and changes in cognition and emotional reactions. While some of these changes are also found to a limited extent in normal aging, they are more

amounts cause small changes in membrane potential; larger amounts cause greater ones. This entire process is electrochemical—electrical within the neuron and chemical between axon and dendrite. It is also a circular process, since an AP causes the release of a transmitter, which brings about electrical changes that cause another AP.

Neurotransmitters in the synapse can either *excite* the receiving neuron, making it fire its own impulses, or *inhibit* it from firing. In the ''hot stove'' example, sensory neurons in your fingers that are specially designed to feel pain send impulses that excite the motor neurons that control the biceps muscle of your arm, making it contract so that you flex your arm and pull away from the heat. At the same time, a ''copy'' of the message goes to the motor neurons that control your triceps muscle (which is used to extend your arm straight), inhibiting those neurons from firing, so that the triceps will be relaxed enough to allow your biceps to work. Inhibition is caused by chemicals that open K+ pores, thereby allowing K+ ions to leave the cell and making the inside of the cell more negative (see Figure 2-4*b*). The cell is thus harder to fire, since a stimulus must push the resting membrane potential past the threshold (a fixed point, perhaps −70 millivolts), and a larger change in membrane potential is required to reach the threshold.

Neurons can receive many synaptic inputs at about the same time from different pronounced in Alzheimer's disease, and they are more likely to occur in the area of the brain associated with memory, the hippocampus (Hyman, Van Hoesen, Damasio, & Barnes, 1984).

We don't know what produces this disorder. There does appear to be a genetic association: about 1 in 3 cases seems to be hereditary, especially when it occurs early in life (Kokmen, 1984; Kolata, 1981). A specific brain disorder may be responsible, such as a defect in the manufacture of acetylcholine or some other biochemical abnormality (Coyle, Price, & DeLong, 1983; Heston & White, 1983; Kokman, 1984; Sajdel-Sulkowska & Marotta, 1984). Very recent research has revealed a chromosomal defect in at least one type of Alzheimer's disease, which runs in families (Goldgaber, Lerman, McBride, Saffiotti, and Gajdusek, 1987). Other theories include the possibility that Alzheimer's disease is the result of a viral infection, a defect of the immune system, or even due to aluminum poisoning. Scientists have recently found a protein in the brains of sufferers of Alzheimer's disease that does not seem to be present in normal brains (Wolozin, Pruchnicki, Dickson, & Davies, 1986). While it is not yet known whether the protein causes the disease, is caused by the disease, or has no relevance to the disease, its discovery may prove to be an aid in diagnosis or in finding the cause of this devastating ailment.

Much current research focuses on the role of acetylcholine, since a sizeable body of data indicates that changes in the activity of this neurotransmitter may cause changes in memory. For example, drugs that block acetylcholine receptors impair the memory of healthy volunteers, whereas drugs that activate acetylcholine transmission improve memory (Sitaram, Weingartner, & Gillin, 1978). Such findings may lead to improved therapy for the disorder, including such treatments as giving patients drugs that will improve acetylcholine activity.

In one recent study, THA—tetrahydroaminoacridine, a chemical that increases the release of acetylcholine—was given to 17 patients for periods ranging from 3 to 26 months (average, 12.6 months), alternating with a placebo so that during the placebo periods the patients could serve as their own controls (Summers et al., 1986). The subjects were given a number of cognitive tests before and after treatment. These demonstrated significant improvement. More dramatic than the increased test scores were the differences in the subjects' daily lives. One subject who previously had to be fed could now eat normally at the family table, one was able to go back to work part time, one woman was able to resume most of her homemaking tasks, and one retired man was able to go back to his daily golf game. While THA is not a cure for Alzheimer's disease and is less effective at the more severe end stages, its use shows promise in greatly improving the lives of patients and their families.

Patients are sometimes helped by other drugs that relieve agitation, lighten depression, or help them sleep. Proper nourishment and fluid intake are important, and exercise and physical therapy may be beneficial. Memory aids can help everyday functioning. Probably the biggest help to both patient and family is the social and emotional support that can come through professional counseling and support groups (Heston & White, 1983; LaBage, 1981; Lazarus et al., 1981).[*]

[*]For more information: Alzheimer's Disease and Related Disorders Association, Inc., 360 No. Michigan Ave., Chicago, IL 60601.

sources, and it is the sum total of the excitatory and inhibitory synaptic currents that decide whether a given cell will fire. Each neuron then acts like a tiny calculator, adding up information (in the form of excitatory and inhibitory synaptic currents) from many sources and making "decisions" about whether to pass that information on to other cells.

Since each nerve cell can receive messages from about 1000 other nerve cells, the number of synaptic connections in the human brain probably exceeds 1 trillion (1000 billion). This very high number of communicative possibilities underlies everything we think, feel, and do. No wonder the human brain is still the most complicated mechanism in the known universe.

WHAT ARE NEUROTRANSMITTERS? It is difficult to prove that any specific chemical acts as a neurotransmitter, although researchers have identified a number of substances that are likely candidates. They meet these criteria: they are released by neurons; they can generate excitatory or inhibitory electrical currents; and the enzymes that break them down occur naturally in the brain. Among the brain chemicals considered to be neurotransmitters are dopamine, which is found in many different neuron systems in the brain and may play a role in motor and intellectual functions; serotonin, which can influence sleep; norepinephrine, which can influence memory; and the endorphins, which are natural pain relievers (Carlson, 1986).

We often learn what these substances are supposed to do when something goes wrong. For example, there is strong evidence that faulty transmission of dopamine can lead to at least two disorders. Too much dopamine in certain brain regions may cause the psychological disorder schizophrenia (discussed in detail in Chapter 14), and too little in another brain area may lead to the nervous disorder Parkinson's disease, an ailment characterized by involuntary shaking. Researchers have come to these conclusions by observing the effects of certain chemicals on persons affected with these disorders. Schizophrenics are often helped by a class of drugs known as *phenothiazines,* which are known to block transmission in synapses that use dopamine, suggesting that overactive dopamine synapses are a factor in schizophrenia. People who suffer from Parkinson's disease are helped by a drug called *L-dopa,* a substance that the brain can convert into dopamine (Kolb & Whishaw, 1980).

Some neurons that provide pleasurable sensations in the body also seem to use dopamine, and it is believed that addictive drugs like cocaine and opiates may act by raising dopamine activity in a specific area of the brain (Rolls et al., 1974). Another neurotransmitter, **acetylcholine,** may be implicated in Alzheimer's disease, a serious degenerative disorder of the central nervous system.

Psychoactive drugs can act on neurons in many ways that affect our sensations, our perceptions, our thinking processes, or our motor behavior. They can cause the release of a neurotransmitter from the axon, block the release of a transmitter from the neuron, and activate or inactivate the receptors located on the dendrite. For example, nicotine acts on the receptors for acetylcholine to speed up nervous activity, sometimes making people jittery (see Figure 2-7). Botulinum toxin (which is sometimes found in improperly canned or stored food and is responsible for a severe form of food poisoning) blocks the release of acetylcholine. This causes the diaphragm to stop working and prevents breathing.

Acetylcholine *Neurotransmitter that has been implicated in Alzheimer's disease.*

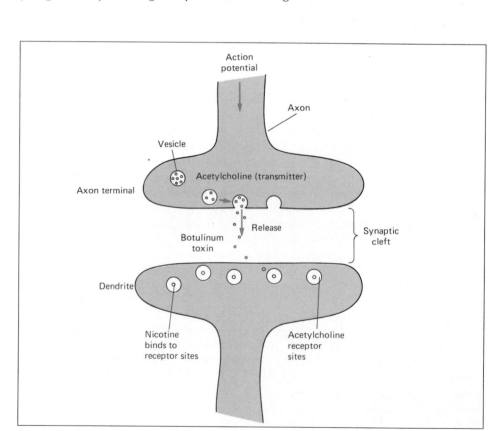

FIGURE 2-7 *Synapse that mediates the transmission of acetylcholine, with some drugs that can affect its activity.*

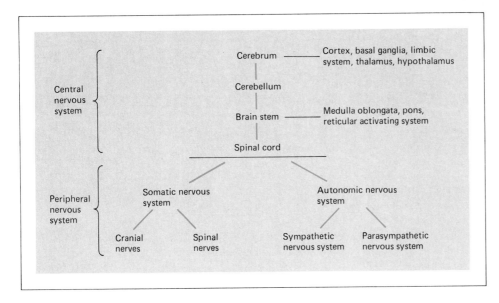

FIGURE 2-8 *Overview of the mammalian nervous system, showing its major divisions (central and peripheral) and its subsystems.*

Components of the Nervous System

An Overview   The brain may be the most obvious component of the highly complex human nervous system, but it is not the only one. The nervous system consists of two main divisions—the central nervous system (CNS) and the peripheral nervous system (PNS), both shown in Figure 2-8. But this division into two systems is actually an artificial one, developed only for convenience in studying the overall nervous system, which functions as a single unit.

The **central nervous system** consists of the spinal cord and the brain. The spinal cord is a long bundle of nerve cells that runs through the hollow spaces of the vertebrae, the bones that make up the backbone. The human brain is a spongy organ that accounts for only a tiny fraction of total body weight. The brain of an adult weighs only about 3 pounds. As small as it is, it contains a number of specialized structures, which we will discuss later in this chapter.

The **peripheral nervous system** is made up of two kinds of **nerves,** or bundles of axons. These connect the spinal cord with the muscles, glands, and sensory receptors. Sensory neurons form sensory nerves that transmit information from your body organs (such as skin or muscles) to your brain. Motor neurons form motor nerves that transmit information from your brain to the muscles and glands of your body. Motor nerves can be part of either of the two subsystems of the PNS, the somatic or the autonomic nervous systems.

We'll describe the various elements of the nervous system, going from the simplest structures to the most complex. Thus we'll look first at the spinal cord, then at the peripheral nervous system, and then at the most complex organ in the human body, the brain.

The Spinal Cord   STRUCTURE AND FUNCTIONS OF THE SPINAL CORD   The function of the spinal cord is crucial to the operation of the peripheral nervous system. The **spinal cord** is a long, stemlike structure that consists of nerve cell bodies and axons. (If we were to take a cross section of the spinal cord, we would see a gray *H* in the center, surrounded by white matter. The gray part is a mass of the cell bodies of neurons; the white matter is composed of myelinated axons that look white because of the fatty myelin covering. See Figure 2-9, on page 52.) The spinal cord operates as a pathway, taking sensory information to the brain and carrying motor signals from the brain to the body. It controls all the body's activities from the neck down, from

Central nervous system   Brain and spinal cord.

Peripheral nervous system   Network of sensory and motor nerves that control muscles and glands.

Nerves   Bundles of axons.

Spinal cord   Long, stem-like structure that consists of nerve cell bodies and axons.

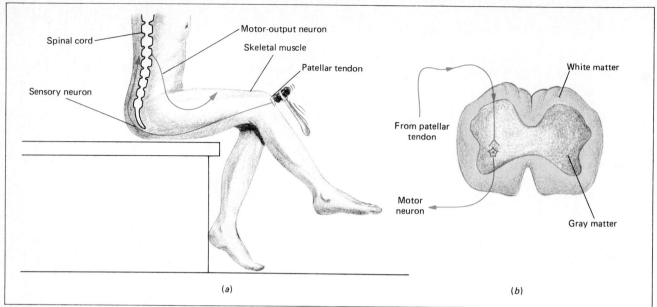

Spinal cord

Motor-output neuron

Skeletal muscle

Sensory neuron

Patellar tendon

White matter

From patellar tendon

Motor neuron

Gray matter

(a)

(b)

FIGURE 2-9 *(a) The patellar, or knee-jerk, reflex is a simple reflex that has only one synapse between sensory input (what you feel) and motor output (what you do).* *(b) Cross section of the spinal cord, showing the sensorimotor connection.*

Reflex *Inborn, unlearned, involuntary reaction to stimulation.*

the simplest sensorimotor reflexes to the most carefully planned and executed maneuvers.

An injury to the spinal cord, which most often occurs through a gunshot wound, a diving or gymnastics accident, or an automobile crash, can be devastating. It can result in the loss of all sensation and movement abilities of the body parts that would ordinarily send or receive signals through the neurons of the spinal cord. Thus, while the legs and arms of someone whose spinal cord was injured at the neck may still be intact, they can be paralyzed as the result of the injury.

REFLEXES AND THE SPINAL CORD   When you blink at a loud noise or pull your hand away from a hot stove, you are demonstrating a reflex. A **reflex** is an involuntary response to a stimulus. It is one of the simplest forms of behavior, a connection between sensory input and motor output that we share with the lower animals. Human beings have many reflexes, all of which are supported by connections between sensory and motor neurons that appear to be built into our systems through our genetic structure.

In the familiar patellar (knee-jerk) reflex, the brain itself does not participate directly, since both kinds of neurons involved in this reflex—sensory and motor—are located in the spinal cord (see Figure 2-9). This is a dramatic demonstration of the fact that you can make some responses to sensory stimulation without being consciously aware of the stimulus.

Some reflexes persist in people whose lower limbs are paralyzed because injury to the spinal cord has cut off communication between the brain and the spinal cord. They do not receive sensory information from the spinal cord and thus do not feel pain, even if something ordinarily painful occurs to a paralyzed part of the body. Since information cannot travel along a pathway from the brain to the rest of the body, they have no *voluntary* control over affected muscles. However, persons with spinal cord injuries do exercise some *involuntary* control because of synaptic connections that are completely within the spinal cord. Thus, people with this kind of injury will still move a leg away after a pinprick, even though they are not conscious of the sensation of pain.

Other more complex reflexes (blinking at a puff of air, withdrawing your hand from a source of pain, or contracting the pupils of your eyes in bright light) involve many synapses and an unknown number of interneurons. All our reflexes follow the same basic patterns of coupling between the sensory and motor systems.

The Peripheral Nervous System   Your ability both to see this book and to pick it up relies on the bundles of nerve fibers known as peripheral nerves. The sensory nerves, which transmit information from your sensory organs (your skin, for example) to your brain, are one kind of peripheral nerve. The motor nerves, which transmit information from your brain to your muscles (telling your arms to reach out and your hands to close around the book), are another kind of peripheral nerve. Motor nerves can be part of either the somatic or the autonomic nervous system, the two subdivisions of the peripheral motor system.

SOMATIC NERVOUS SYSTEM   The nerves that directed your arms and hands to pick up this book are part of the ***somatic nervous system,*** which controls involuntary reflex actions as well as those actions you voluntarily choose to perform. (*Somatic* comes from the Greek word meaning *body*. In this case it refers to the framework of the body, as opposed to the internal organs.) These nerves control the striated muscles of the body, so-called because they appear striped (striated) when seen under a microscope. Let's look at the way this system works.

The movements you make are accomplished through your muscles and the way they are attached to your bones, skin, and other muscles. This applies to all movements—large ones like running and jumping, and small ones like subtle changes in facial expression. As we noted earlier, muscles work together, sometimes in antagonistic (opposing) pairs. When you raise your forearm, for example, you contract your biceps muscle. The muscle antagonistic to the biceps—the triceps—relaxes. In certain movements other muscles work together in synergistic (cooperative) ways. When you lift a barbell, the biceps work together with forearm and finger muscles that allow you to hold onto the bar, with back muscles that maintain posture, and with leg muscles that either straighten or bend your knees. Some muscles that work as synergists in one movement will act as antagonists in another. Different patterns of muscular contractions produce different movements. And all these patterns are coordinated in the nervous system.

The strength of a muscle contraction depends on two factors: the number of active motor neurons and the frequency of the impulses they send. These impulses are sent by synaptic transmission as described earlier; the neurotransmitter involved in such muscle movements is acetylcholine. The motor neurons synapse onto muscle fibers and release acetylcholine, which crosses the synaptic gap between the nerve terminal and the muscle fiber. This causes the muscle fiber to contract. Meanwhile, circuits within the spinal cord and brain stem simultaneously inhibit antagonistic muscles.

By modifying the number of neurons involved and the frequency of their impulses, the brain can produce an amazing variety of complex movement patterns. Thus a pianist produces an arpeggio or a chord, a tennis player slams a ball or lobs it lightly, a driver maneuvers along a winding mountain road or drives straight ahead on an open highway.

AUTONOMIC NERVOUS SYSTEM   While you are lifting that heavy barbell, your body is functioning in other ways, too. Your heart is beating, your breathing goes on, and your digestive system is active. All these activities are being conducted by two other kinds of muscles—cardiac (heart) muscles and smooth muscles. Smooth muscles control the throat, the viscera (internal organs such as stomach and intestines), the diaphragm (which controls breathing), and other organs. Both cardiac and smooth muscles are controlled by the endocrine system (which we'll discuss later in this chapter) and the autonomic nervous system. Let's see how the ***autonomic nervous system*** controls these life-support functions that are usually considered involuntary,

This clown couldn't be playing with fire this way if his muscles were not working together under control of the somatic nervous system.

Somatic nervous system   *Part of the peripheral nervous system that controls reflex and voluntary actions.*

Autonomic nervous system   *Part of the peripheral nervous system that controls involuntary functions; consists of parasympathetic and sympathetic divisions.*

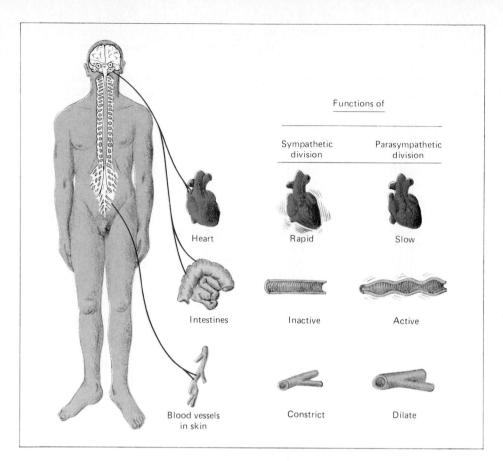

Functions of

Sympathetic division	Parasympathetic division
Rapid	Slow
Inactive	Active
Constrict	Dilate

Heart

Intestines

Blood vessels in skin

FIGURE 2-10 *The sympathetic and parasympathetic divisions of the autonomic nervous system often have opposing effects in many body parts. (Source: Adapted from Rosenzweig & Leiman, 1982.)*

or beyond conscious control. In some cases, as will be explained in the discussion of biofeedback in Chapter 5, we may be able to exert control over these functions, but usually they work more or less automatically.

The autonomic nervous system consists of two divisions—the sympathetic and the parasympathetic. These operate quite differently and often have opposing effects in many body parts, as shown in Figure 2-10. While the striated muscles associated with the somatic nervous system contract only when they receive neuronal messages, the autonomic system's smooth muscles of viscera (body organs) and heart never relax totally but always generate some contractions. This is why heart muscle can continue to pulsate even after it has been removed from the body. To relax heart and visceral muscles, then, the muscles themselves (not just the motor neurons) must be inhibited. The sympathetic and parasympathetic divisions work in concert in the autonomic system: one division may stimulate a muscle and the other may inhibit it. The roles of the two systems change, depending on the target organ, so that each division is capable of triggering contraction or relaxation.

Sympathetic functions The sympathetic division works as a unit ("in sympathy") to mobilize the body's resources so that it can *expend energy*. It creates the fight-or-flight response to stress and the physiological signs of such emotional states as fear and anger. Sympathetic activation makes your heart beat faster, makes you breathe more rapidly, and makes you sweat. To provide the oxygen and glucose (an energy-providing sugar) you need for vigorous activity, it directs blood from your skin and your stomach to your skeletal muscles, and makes your adrenal gland release the hormone epinephrine (adrenalin).

Parasympathetic functions The parasympathetic system restores the body by *increasing its supply of stored energy*. How many times in your life have you been told not to go swimming right after eating? The reason for this warning lies in a dual action by the parasympathetic system, which directs blood to the stomach to help digestion and slows the heart. When so much blood has been diverted to the stomach that not enough reaches the muscles to enable them to engage in strenuous exercise, cramping may take place.

How the sympathetic and parasympathetic systems work together Most of the time, both sympathetic and parasympathetic divisions are active, and in balance. After you eat lunch on a hot day, for example, you both perspire (sympathetic activity) and digest your food (parasympathetic). For any given organ, however, the two systems are usually antagonistic. This antagonism is especially evident in the way the pupil of the eye dilates and constricts. In dim light the sympathetic system operates to make the muscles of the iris widen the pupil, thus letting in more light and improving vision. In very bright light, the parasympathetic division takes over, narrowing the pupil to let in less light, thus protecting the eye and enhancing vision. The drug belladonna, which eye doctors sometimes administer to widen the pupil for easier examination, mimics sympathetic activity. (The name *belladonna* is from the Italian for *beautiful woman*; the Italians, like many other people, associate large pupils with beauty.)

How the brain activates the autonomic nervous system The autonomic nervous system can be activated in different ways. What happens, for example, when you receive information through your senses—when you receive a painful injury, see a menacing figure, or hear a baby's cry? All these stimuli can produce an emotional reaction in your brain. It sends messages to the hypothalamus, which in turn activates such autonomic responses as a racing heart or quickened breathing. The hypothalamus is a small organ in the brain that plays a vital role in mediating between the brain and the endocrine system (as we'll see in the next section).

Effects of learning can also bring about autonomic responses, as many war veterans find out when their hearts begin to pound at the sound of a car backfiring, which may arouse the same kinds of reactions they would have had in combat. Reflex pathways in the spinal cord and the brain stem also activate autonomic responses. For example, filling the stomach with food (and thus stretching it) activates *stretch receptors* in the stomach, which send impulses to the brain. The brain in turn activates interneurons, which then activate neurons that increase the secretion of gastric juices.

A fundamental principle of the control of these and many other body systems is **homeostasis,** the maintenance of vital functions within their optimum range through coordinated automatic adjustments. Thus, when blood pressure rises, certain neurons in the brain that reduce the heart rate are activated, leading to lower blood pressure. Temperature regulation is another example of homeostasis. We have temperature receptors both inside and outside our bodies. When they report that our body temperature is too low, the blood vessels in the skin constrict (preventing heat loss), and we may shiver (producing heat). When body temperature is too high, we sweat, and our skin blood vessels dilate, allowing heat to escape. Moreover, we can produce homeostasis through voluntary behavior, for example, by putting on a sweater and drinking hot soup, or by taking off a shirt and drinking a glass of ice water.

Homeostasis Equilibrium (balance) of vital functions maintained by coordinated adjustments of the autonomic nervous system.

The Brain STRUCTURES OF THE BRAIN As we move up the spinal cord into the brain, the first major structures that we encounter are the medulla oblongata and the pons, which make up a portion of the brain stem. The medulla controls such basic life functions as breathing and heart rate; the pons regulates arousal, sleep, waking, and the perception of pain.

The structures of the central integrating systems, all located in the brain, link the sensory and motor systems, enabling them to interact. They consist of the brain stem (containing the medulla, pons, reticular formation, and the midbrain), the cerebellum, the cerebrum, the hypothalamus, the thalamus, the basal ganglia, the limbic system, and the cerebral cortex (see Figure 2-11 below). When we realize how finely these structures work together, we gain even more respect for the brain.

Brain stem *Part of the brain that contains the medulla, pons, reticular formation, and midbrain; it is responsible for many basic functions.*

Brain stem The **brain stem** is similar to brain structures in many lower animals and is responsible for many basic functions. It takes in information from several senses through sensory regions for vision, hearing, taste, balance, and touch in the facial area. It controls involuntary activity of the tongue, larynx, eyes, and facial muscles through specific motor neurons for these areas. It controls levels of sleep and arousal through the reticular formation, nestled within its central core. And it coordinates the motor neurons in the spinal cord that control such activities as walking and breathing and the beating of our hearts.

Reticular formation *Network of nerves located in the brain stem; it controls waking up and going to sleep.*

Ascending reticular activation system *Part of the reticular formation responsible for the waking process.*

Reticular formation The **reticular formation** is a network of interconnected nerve fibers and neuronal nuclei (collections of cell bodies of neurons) inside the central core of the brain stem. (*Reticular* means *netlike* or *tangled*.) A principal function of this structure is to wake us up and put us to sleep. The part of this nerve network that wakes us up is called the **ascending reticular activation system.** Damage to its arousal areas can result in coma, while damage to other areas can cause long-lasting insomnia. Electrically stimulating the reticular formation arousal areas of an anesthetized animal will wake it up.

The reticular formation also exerts control over motor activity, such as the balance and coordination involved in walking. In addition, it directs the more complicated reflexive movements. For example, the auditory startle reflex—the involuntary jump we give when we hear an unexpected loud sound—occurs at the end of a chain that begins with input to the auditory sensory nerve and ends with motor orders from the reticular formation to the spinal cord.

Cerebellum *Part of the brain connected to the back of the brain stem, involved primarily in the coordination of motor activity.*

Cerebellum The **cerebellum** is connected to the back of the brain stem by a thick set of fibers. This structure is involved primarily in the coordination of motor activity, especially the fine tuning of voluntary movements. It is the functioning of the cerebellum that enables a pianist to play a difficult and rapid arpeggio. This organ also

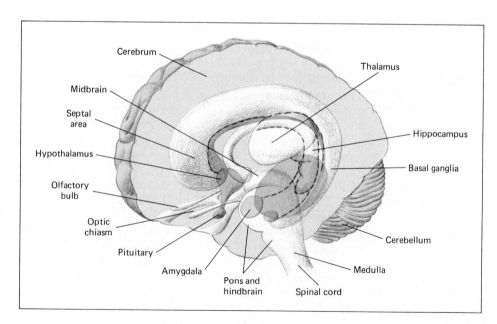

FIGURE 2-11 *The major structures of the brain include the brain stem, hypothalamus, thalamus, basal ganglia, hippocampus, septal region, and the cortex. (Source: Adapted from Kalat, 1984.)*

(M. Durrance/Photo Researchers)

This skier's dramatic and graceful movements are made possible by the normal functioning of the cerebellum, which helps to coordinate motor activity and maintain posture and balance.

helps to maintain posture and balance. Damage to the cerebellum will not affect a person's movements at rest, but will result in tremors when an affected person attempts any kind of intricate activity. The "punch-drunk" unsteady gait seen in many men who have boxed professionally is caused by damage to the cerebellum sustained by repeated blows to the head. Recent research suggests that the cerebellum also plays a role in motor learning and memory (McCormick & Thompson, 1984).

Cerebrum The **cerebrum,** the most highly developed section of the human brain, is also multifunctional. It contains the hypothalamus, which keeps many body systems in balance, largely through its close connection with the endocrine system; the thalamus, which acts as a relay center for the senses to the cortex; the basal ganglia, a large collection of cell bodies that are involved in bodily movements; the limbic system, which mediates emotional responses and is also involved in memory; and the cerebral cortex, the gray outer covering of the brain, which is involved in most higher-level functions such as thinking, remembering, and solving problems.

Cerebrum *Most highly developed part of the brain; it is multifunctional and contains the hypothalamus, thalamus, basal ganglia, limbic system, and cortex; the forebrain.*

Hypothalamus The **hypothalamus** is an important walnut-size organ. It lies just above the brain stem, in the cerebrum, as shown in Figure 2-11. It regulates hormone release and mediates between the brain and the endocrine system. The hypothalamus is often referred to as the "seat of emotion" because it is a source of a person's feelings. It sends its orders to the glands in the endocrine system, displaying emotions through physiological reactions. (You feel frightened or angry, for example, and your heart speeds up.) Its control of the pituitary gland allows the brain to control the endocrine system, and its receptors for hormones allow the endocrine system to exert control over the brain.

Hypothalamus *Small organ in the brain that plays a vital role in mediating between the brain and the endocrine system.*

In its sensitive position, the hypothalamus is the principal controller and organizer of the body's vital functions. It maintains homeostasis of many body systems. Behaviors connected with eating, drinking, temperature regulation, sexuality, anger, and fear are intimately involved with the endocrine system. Since all these are also involved with motivation, the role of the hypothalamus in regulating motivation is very important. This has been shown experimentally by inducing such motivated states as fear, anger, hunger, and sexual interest through electrical stimulation of specific hypothalamic sites. (We'll discuss the way the hypothalamus regulates hunger in Chapter 11.)

Thalamus *Part of the cerebrum that acts as a relay center for the senses to the cortex; it receives sensory information, which it sends to sensory areas of the cortex, and it sends motor information to the cortex.*

Thalamus   The thalamus lies deep inside the cerebrum, just above and to the rear of the hypothalamus (see Figure 2-11). At one time the **thalamus** was thought to be primarily a relay station for various kinds of sensory and motor messages. It does, in fact, send and receive signals related to vision, hearing, and pain. It also performs a number of other functions, however. It plays a role in voluntary movement. For this reason, surgical lesions were at one time often made in it to relieve symptoms of Parkinson's disease. People who had such surgery, however, often had problems afterward with language and memory. Depending on the placement of the lesion, some had trouble naming pictures, some had trouble thinking of words, some slurred their speech, and others had different problems. These and other findings have led to the conclusion that the thalamus may play an important role in these abilities (Crosson, 1984).

Basal ganglia *Collection of cell bodies near the thalamus; the structures it comprises seem to be important in controlling movement.*

Basal ganglia   The structures that make up the **basal ganglia** lie near the thalamus (see Figure 2-11). They seem to be important in controlling movement, since electrical stimulation of certain parts of the basal ganglia can inhibit movement and since damage often produces problems in initiating or completing a motor movement (as in victims of Parkinson's disease).

Limbic system *Part of cerebrum that mediates emotional responses and is involved in memory; it includes the septal area, the hippocampus, the amygdala, and parts of the thalamus.*

Limbic system   When you're furiously angry or curiously calm, you're showing effects mediated through your **limbic system.** This set of structures forms a border that encircles the upper brain stem (*limbus* is Latin for *border*). The limbic system consists of a number of nuclei (collections of neuronal cell bodies) and fibers that connect them to each other. The structures include the *septal area,* the *hippocampus,* the *amygdala,* and parts of the *thalamus* (see Figure 2-11). The system is arbitrarily defined and may have many functions. People or animals that have suffered injury to specific areas of the limbic system (like the amygdala) do not show some basic emotions (like rage); at the same time, these emotions may appear when these limbic structures are electrically stimulated. Amygdalectomy, the surgical destruction of the amygdala, has been performed—although never very widely—to alleviate uncontrollable rage in some psychiatric patients.

The different limbic structures seem to maintain a balance between opposite emotional states. Thus, while stimulation of the amygdala causes rage and damage to the amygdala causes tameness, the opposite holds true for the septum. Memory is also an important function of the limbic system, as evidenced by the degeneration of a section of the thalamus in persons with the memory disorder Korsakoff's syndrome (a neuropsychiatric disorder caused by prolonged and excessive use of alcohol). In Chapter 6 you'll meet a man whose hippocampus was surgically removed from both sides of his brain, resulting in an inability to create new memories. Psychosurgery, the intentional destruction of brain structures to modify behavior, has often damaged portions of the limbic system that lie buried under the cerebral cortex.

Cerebral cortex *Gray matter that surrounds most of the brain, involved in most higher-level functions, such as thinking, remembering, and problem solving.*

Cerebral cortex   If we compare the brains of a variety of mammals at different levels of evolutionary development, we see that the major differences in those brains is that the **cerebral cortex,** the gray matter surrounding most of the brain, is proportionately larger in more highly developed animals (see Figure 2-12). In human beings, this wrinkled covering makes up most of the brain. The greater number of nerve cells in the human cortex makes possible the many complicated mental operations we are able to perform.

The human cortex is also more convoluted, with deeper grooves. The many functions carried out by cells in the cortex require a large area; the wrinkling allows more surface area to fit into the small area bounded by the skull. Furthermore, the human cortex is not only relatively larger overall; it also has more area that does not have specific sensory or motor functions, and is therefore free for higher intellectual

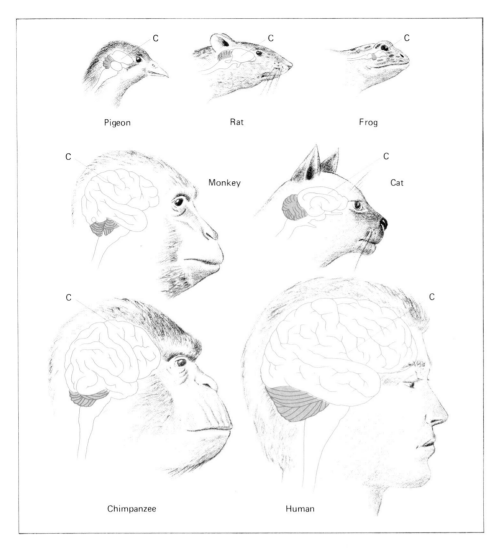

Pigeon

Rat

Frog

Monkey

Cat

Chimpanzee

Human

FIGURE 2-12 *Going up the evolutionary scale, the brain becomes proportionately larger, as we can see in this comparison of the sizes and shapes of the brains in different vertebrate animals, all shown about 4/10 life-size. The cortex (C) becomes progressively larger and more convoluted. (Source: Adapted from Rosenzweig & Leiman, 1982.)*

activities. This area is called the **association cortex** (see Figure 2-13, page 60). In the case of human beings, these intellectual activities allow the high levels of thought that we—and only we, in all the animal kingdom—are capable of. The cortex is the part of the brain that makes us human, the place where we take in and then sift and make sense of what we see, hear, and perceive in other ways. It is the site where we think, plan, speak, write, remember, and evaluate.

For convenience in studying and talking about the brain, neuroanatomists have divided each of the *hemispheres* (left and right halves) of the brain into four separate areas, called *lobes*. They are the *frontal*, the *temporal*, the *parietal*, and the *occipital* lobes (see Figure 2-14, page 60). The frontal lobe, is the most forward part of the cerebral cortex. The portion just behind the eyes and forehead is involved in planning, judgment, and emotion. Immediately behind this is a region that programs complex movement, and just behind this region is the area that controls movements of the various body parts. The *temporal* lobes play a major role in auditory perception and in some learning and memory functions. The *parietal* lobes play a major role in spatial and tactile perception. At the very back of the brain are the *occipital* lobes, an area primarily concerned with vision. While recent research points to some specialization within these lobes, each one is involved with a variety of different functions.

Association cortex *Area of the brain that receives input from many sensory and motor systems but does not have specific sensory or motor functions; it is free for such activities as language, thought, and memory.*

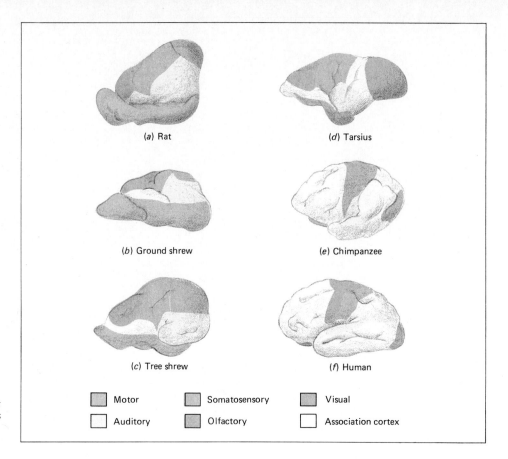

(a) Rat

(d) Tarsius

(b) Ground shrew

(e) Chimpanzee

(c) Tree shrew

(f) Human

- ▢ Motor
- ▢ Auditory
- ▢ Somatosensory
- ▢ Olfactory
- ▢ Visual
- ▢ Association cortex

FIGURE 2-13 *The human cerebral cortex is not only larger than that in most other animals but also has more areas that do not have specific sensory or motor functions; thus it is free for higher intellectual activities. (Source: Adapted from Hunt, 1982.)*

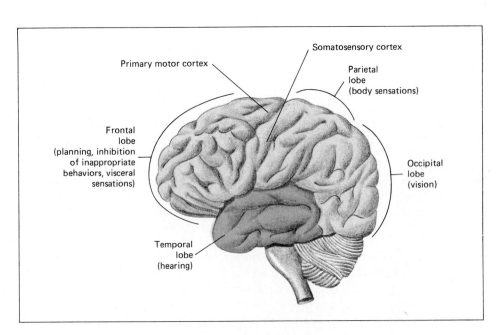

Primary motor cortex

Somatosensory cortex

Parietal lobe (body sensations)

Frontal lobe (planning, inhibition of inappropriate behaviors, visceral sensations)

Occipital lobe (vision)

Temporal lobe (hearing)

FIGURE 2-14 *Important subdivisions of the human cerebral cortex, with some of their primary functions. (Source: Adapted from Kalat, 1984.)*

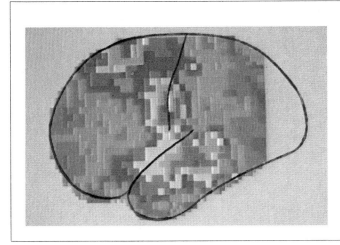
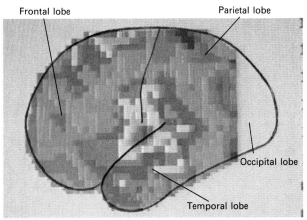

Frontal lobe   Parietal lobe

Occipital lobe

Temporal lobe

A dramatic—and colorful—demonstration of the localization of various brain functions can be seen in Figure 2-15. By monitoring the flow of blood to the brain, we can infer the importance of different areas in different operations. This illustration shows images averaged from the brain activity of nine different subjects, who engaged in a variety of activities, including speaking, following a moving object with the eyes, and listening to spoken words. Measurements of blood flow showed increased activity in different areas of the brain depending on what the subjects were doing at the time.

We have seen that different lobes of the cortex serve different functions. Moreover, each functional division within a lobe is organized *topically.* That is, parts of the body that are next to each other (like toes, feet, and ankles) send and receive signals to and from areas that are next to each other throughout the nervous system (as in the axons and within each functional area of the cortex). The primary cortex receives this direct input from the various senses or sends direct output to the motor system. The association cortex, which does not have specific sensory or motor functions assigned to it, is thus free for such functions as language, thought, and memory. It receives input from many sensory and motor systems.

The drawings in Figure 2-16 (page 62) show (in a somewhat grotesque way!) a schematic representation of two areas of the **primary cortex.** The primary motor cortex (2-16*b*) is located in the frontal lobe. This drawing shows the parts of the cortex that are responsible for the motor movements of different parts of the body. The primary somatosensory cortex (2-16*a*), just behind it (in the parietal lobe), receives direct information from the skin senses on different parts of the body. Figure 2-16*c* shows the areas in the cortex that receive signals from our senses for hearing and sight. The size of each area in drawings *a* and *b* that is devoted to a specific body part is a measure of how sensitive that part is to sensory stimulation (thus, the palm of the hand is drawn larger than the sole of the foot) and the degree of fine-motor control the part has (thus, the fingers are larger than the toes).

The sensory pathways lead to the primary sensory cortex, which includes the somatosensory, the auditory, and the visual. The motor pathways go from the primary motor cortex down the spinal cord and out to the muscles of the body. As we've seen, many structures in the nervous system, such as the basal ganglia and the cerebellum, participate in motor function.

The sensorimotor pathways between the hemispheres and the body parts they control are crossed, so that the right hemisphere controls the left side of the body and vice versa. Thus, when you stub a toe on your left foot, the "ouch!" signal goes to your right hemisphere. Motor signals cross sides, too, so that when you move your right arm, it is the result of a direction sent by your left hemisphere. Each eye projects

FIGURE 2-15 *Inferring localization of function from patterns of blood flow. In these CAT-scan images averaged from the brain activity of nine subjects, the colors indicate the average level of blood flow during speech: green areas show average flow; yellow and red areas show higher-than-average flow; blue areas lower-than-average flow. (The squared shapes are due to the recording and averaging procedure and don't accurately reflect the shapes of areas in the brain.) The areas in the cortex that control the activities of the mouth, tongue, and larynx are active, as is the area that directs auditory areas. (We hear ourselves speaking.) The mouth and auditory areas are more active in the left hemisphere than in the right. (Source: Lassen, Ingvar, & Skinhoj, 1978.)*

Primary cortex *Part of the cortex that receives direct input from various senses of the body and sends direct output to the motor systems.*

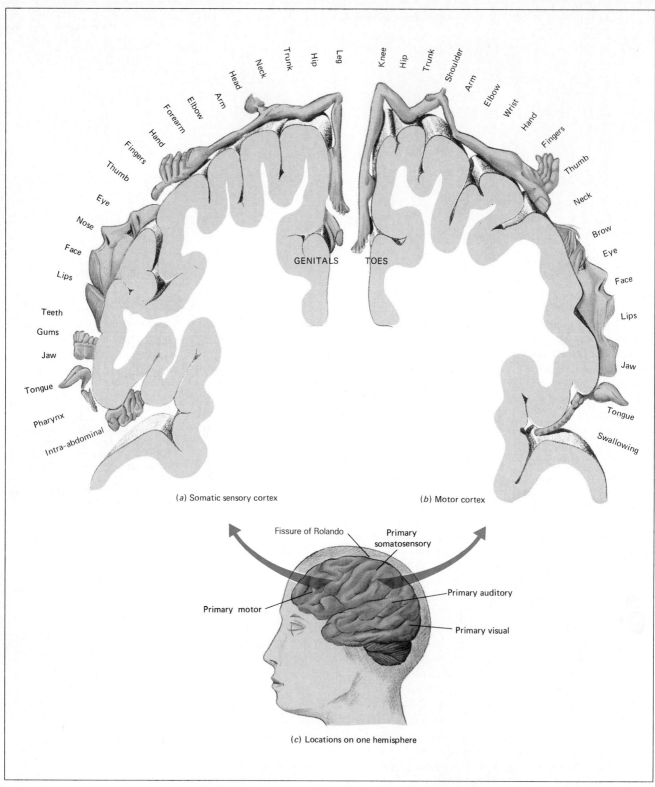

Thumb
Fingers
Hand
Forearm
Elbow
Arm
Head
Neck
Trunk
Hip
Leg

Knee
Hip
Trunk
Shoulder
Arm
Elbow
Wrist
Hand
Fingers

Eye
Nose
Face
Lips
Teeth
Gums
Jaw
Tongue
Pharynx
Intra-abdominal

Thumb
Neck
Brow
Eye
Face
Lips
Jaw
Tongue
Swallowing

GENITALS   TOES

(a) Somatic sensory cortex   (b) Motor cortex

Fissure of Rolando   Primary
                            somatosensory
Primary motor   Primary auditory
                                           Primary visual

(c) Locations on one hemisphere

FIGURE 2-16 *(a) The "sensory homunculus" is a diagram of the surface of the cortex that receives sensory information (like touch and temperature) from the skin. Note that adjacent body parts are arranged next to each other on the cortex and that some sensitive body parts (such as the face) have larger cortical areas, so that the shape of the homunculus is distorted. (b) The "motor homunculus" represents the area of the cortex that controls the muscles of the body parts. (c) Locations of the primary sensory cortex and motor cortex on one hemisphere.*

to both hemispheres, with the left visual field of each eye going to the right side of the brain and the right visual field of each eye going to the left side of the brain (see Figure 2-17).

"LEFT" AND "RIGHT" BRAINS: HEMISPHERIC LATERALIZATION   Each era has its own popular mythology—often resulting from misinterpretation or misapplication of sound scientific research. One of the myths of our time is the belief that the two hemispheres of the brain function separately as two different brains, and that some people (logical, analytical types) use the left brain most of the time, while others (creative artists) draw almost entirely on the right brain. The truth is that while some functions seem to be concentrated more on one side than the other, we do, in fact, use both sides in an integrated way; the two sides are more alike than they are different. The exercise of both logic and creativity requires the use of both hemispheres together, and there is no evidence that any of us are purely "left-brained" or "right-brained" (Levy, 1985).

Research and its implications   Let's look at the scientific research that gave rise to this intriguing myth—and at the more scientific but equally intriguing conclusions we can draw from it. The somatosensory cortex and the motor cortex have parallel functions in each hemisphere. With few exceptions most structures are found on both sides of the brain. The question is whether the same subcortical structure or cortical area on each side serves the same function. In some cases the two structures which look alike seem to perform separate functions. This is known as **hemispheric lateralization.** A different term, **asymmetry of the brain,** is used to express the concept of differences in size, organization, and function between the left and right hemispheres.

The region that seems to control language in the left hemisphere is larger than the comparable region in the right hemisphere, for example (showing asymmetry). Furthermore, the two sides of the brain do perform some different functions (showing hemispheric lateralization). For most people, the left hemisphere controls the ability to use language, handle numbers, and think analytically; it processes information sequentially, one bit at a time. The right side generally directs complicated spatial abilities, like pattern perception and aspects of artistic and musical performance; it tends to look at information globally, taking in an overall impression. The language centers in the brains of left-handed and ambidextrous people, however, are more likely to be evenly divided between both hemispheres, which is just one illustration of the way sex and handedness are related to the organization of our brains, as discussed in the box "Sex, Handedness, and Your Brain."

While we do have data to suggest that parallel structures on the two sides of the brain have their own functions to perform and are not just back-ups for each other, we also have reason to believe that our nervous system is "plastic," or adaptable. That is, if one structure is damaged, another area—sometimes in the other hemisphere, sometimes in the same hemisphere—may take over its function, especially when damage occurs early in life. In children who suffer an injury to the left hemisphere before the age of five, the right hemisphere apparently takes over the speech functions. If the injury occurs later in childhood, recovery is better than it would be for an adult, but the recovery apparently takes place within the left hemisphere, not by a shift to the right hemisphere. If such an injury occurs later in life, recovery is much more limited (Kolb & Whishaw, 1980.)

The two hemispheres are able to operate in concert with each other by communicating through a massive bundle of axons called the **corpus callosum** (refer back to Figure 2-17). If this body has been severed, as it sometimes is during operations performed to restrict epileptic seizures to one hemisphere, the two sides of the brain cannot communicate. (In such operations only the corpus callosum is cut; the brain itself is not touched.)

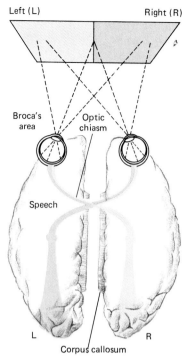

FIGURE 2-17   *Pathways of visual information in a bisected brain. Visual information from the left visual field is carried to the occipital cortex in the right hemisphere, whereas information from the right visual field is carried to the occipital cortex of the left hemisphere. In a normal person, the corpus callosum (a bundle of axon fibers) intermixes the sensory signals from both visual fields in both hemispheres.*

Hemispheric lateralization
Condition in which two structures of the brain, one in the left hemisphere and one in the right, look alike yet perform separate functions.

Asymmetry of the brain   *Concept that there are differences in size, organization, and function between the left and right hemispheres of the brain.*

Corpus callosum   *Massive bundle of axons that enables the two hemispheres of the brain to communicate with each other.*

If you're right-handed, like about 90 percent of the population, the part of your brain that controls your language abilities is concentrated on the left side, and one specific area of your brain (the planum temporale, a region of the temporal lobe that is involved in speech) is larger than it is among your left-handed friends (Geschwind & Galaburda, 1985). In contrast, if you're left-handed or ambidextrous (able to use both hands more or less interchangeably), the language centers in your brain are more likely to be evenly divided in both hemispheres, and while your planum temporale is smaller than that of your right-handed friends, your corpus callosum is likely to be larger than theirs (Witelson, 1985).

Other differences have also been observed between right- and left-handed people. The left-handed, for example, are more likely to suffer from allergies, migraine headaches, and disorders of the immune system, like arthritis and ulcerative colitis (a severe inflammation of the colon); they're also more prone to dyslexia (a reading disability), hyperactivity (a behavior disorder), stuttering, and alcoholism (Geschwind & Galaburda, 1985). And they tend to have more extreme brain responses to various drugs, including an anticonvulsant, an antidepressant, and ordinary aspirin (Irwin, 1985). But the deck isn't stacked totally against left-handers: they're likely to be better at spatial tasks than right-handers (there is a disproportionately high number of left-handed architects and mathematically gifted children); and a left-

SEX, HANDEDNESS, AND YOUR BRAIN

handed person who suffers a stroke is (other things being equal) likely to make a more complete recovery from it than a right-handed person.

What does all of this have to do with sex? The first connection is that men are more likely to be left-handed than women are, and right-handed women are more likely to be purely right-handed (that is, they use the right hand for virtually everything.) Second, males are more likely to fit most of the "left-handed" conditions listed in the previous paragraph than females are. Third, females seem to have an edge in verbal abilities: they start speaking earlier and remain more fluent with words throughout life.

Research on fetal development in people and in animals has given rise to some intriguing theorizing that ties these observations together. These theories relate to the concept of asymmetry of the brain—that there are differences in size, organization, and function between the left and right hemispheres.

One such theory, proposed by

Geschwind and Galaburda (1985), suggests that the levels of the male hormone testosterone affect the way a fetal brain develops by directing cells to migrate to different places in the brain. Levels of testosterone are higher for male fetuses, and also, it is believed, for the fetuses of mothers undergoing stress. Furthermore, prenatal conditions may be more critical for males, whose brains develop later, and for the left hemisphere of the brain, which matures later than the right. If the left hemisphere becomes less developed, the right hemisphere may become more highly developed, causing left dominance in the body and causing a language center to develop in the right hemisphere rather than the left.

Another psychologist who has studied men's and women's brains has also concluded that there are some differences between them (mainly, different sites in the brain for producing speech, defining words, and fine-motor hand movements). But while a basis for these differences may begin in utero, patterns of brain organization may continue to change throughout life, often in response to changing levels of various hormones (Kimura, 1985).

Still, abilities overlap so much on most tests of cognitive ability between males and females and between the right- and left-handed that there is more variability within each of these categories than between them. So knowing whether you're male or female, or which hand you hold your spoon with, tells us little about your intellectual potential.

Roger Sperry, a Nobel prize winner, and his colleagues (especially Michael Gazzaniga) at the California Institute of Technology have done a great deal of research with such split-brain patients, learning much in the process about the way the brain works (Gazzaniga & LeDoux, 1978; Sperry, 1982). On the surface, split-brain subjects seem normal, and they seem to get through daily life fairly well. Special laboratory experiments, however, show how they are affected by the lack of communication between the two sides of their brains.

If such patients touch a pencil that is hidden from sight, they can report what it is if they feel it with the *right* hand, because the sensory signal will travel laterally to the left side of the brain, where the language center allows the word "pencil" to be found. However, if they feel it with the *left* hand, they know that it is a pencil and can point to it if it is shown along with other objects; but they cannot name it, because the right hemisphere cannot communicate this knowledge to the speech center. Such patients are suffering from disconnection syndromes. Their behavior demonstrates that the seat of language abilities is in the left hemisphere while that of spatial abilities is in the right.

Damage to different parts of the cortex results in many different kinds of disturbances. For example, damage to the association areas of the parietal lobes impairs the way people see spatial relations, as well as the way they perceive their own bodies. In severe cases, affected persons deny the existence of body parts opposite the side where the brain lesion is. They will not shave half their face, will not dress half their body, and, when questioned, will deny that an arm or leg is their own. Figure 2-18 illustrates the way one artist, after suffering a right-hemisphere stroke, ignored the left half of his face in a self-portrait. A **stroke** occurs when a blood vessel in the brain suddenly bursts or is blocked, thus preventing oxygen from reaching parts of the brain and causing damage to a specific area. A variety of symptoms can result, including paralysis of one entire side of the body, personality changes, and difficulties in speaking and writing. One current line of research in this area is described in the box "Brain-Tissue Grafts in People and Animals."

Stroke   Severe accident in the brain, occurring when a blood vessel in the brain suddenly bursts or is blocked, thus preventing oxygen from reaching parts of the brain and causing damage to a specific area.

How Damage to the Left Hemisphere Affects Language   The most dramatic examples of hemispheric asymmetries are in the domain of language. In the late 1800s, the French neurologist Paul Broca and others discovered that language disturbances, called **aphasias,** often occurred following damage to the left hemisphere due to a stroke or injury. When the right hemisphere was injured, however, language was rarely affected. Such findings have demonstrated that in most people the left hemisphere controls language abilities.

Aphasia   Language disturbance that often occurs following damage to the left hemisphere due to stroke or injury.

The kind of language deficit depends on where in the left hemisphere the damage has occurred. If the damage is in the left frontal lobe, in the region called *Broca's area* (see Figure 2-19 on page 66), it produces motor aphasia, which affects production of speech and writing. People have trouble finding the right words and often cannot name everyday objects, but what they do say has meaning. They write or speak very simple noun-verb sentences and rarely use adjectives, adverbs and other parts of speech. They usually understand what they hear and read, know what they want to say, and are painfully aware that they are not saying it.

Sensory aphasia occurs when damage is in the left posterior temporal area, in the area known as *Wernicke's area* after the researcher who discovered its function (see Figure 2-19). People with damage to this area have trouble understanding the speech of others, and while they themselves speak fluently, the sentences they utter make no sense. Typical responses of people with such disabilities can be seen in the following description (Geschwind, 1979):

> When shown a fork, a person with motor aphasia may say, "I know, it's a . . . Wait . . . ; you eat with it." Another patient, asked about a dental appointment, said: "Yes . . . Monday . . . Dad and Dick . . . Wednesday nine o'clock . . . 10 o'clock . . . doctors . . . and . . . teeth." (p. 186)

Damage to other parts of the left hemisphere produces other disorders: one in which patients can understand speech and speak fluently, but cannot repeat words spoken to them, and another in which people cannot read despite normal vision. Damage to the left visual cortex and the corpus callosum may leave a person unable to read, but able to write. Affected persons (usually stroke victims) can write a long passage from dictation, or even generate their own writing, but then cannot read what they have just written.

FIGURE 2-18   *Self-portrait of a stroke victim, Anton Raderscheidt, after damage to the right association cortex of the parietal lobe. The artist has failed to depict the left side of his face; he also ignores the left side of the canvas. (Source: P. H. Furst.)*

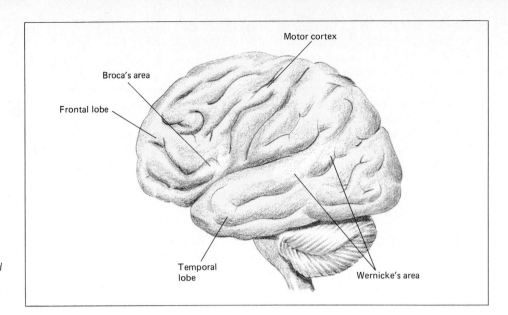

FIGURE 2-19 *Wernicke's area and Broca's area are two of the specialized language regions in the left hemisphere.*

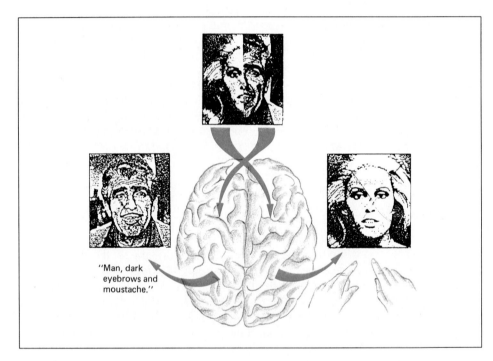

FIGURE 2-20 *When split-brain patients were shown pictures of faces that had been split down the center and recombined, like the one at the top here, they didn't notice the gross discrepancy between the two sides of the pictures. When asked to describe the face they saw, they reported the half-face on the right side, which registers in the left hemisphere (the man). But when asked to choose the face they saw from a set of similar faces, they picked the one that had been shown on the left side, which registered in the right hemisphere (the woman). It seems, therefore, that the right hemisphere is the one which recognizes faces. (Source: Levy, Trevarthan, & Sperry, 1972.)*

Brain injury or deterioration is one of the most devastating things that can happen to a person. It can transform personality, diminish capabilities, and result in complete incompetence. Once scientists thought that brain injury was irreversible, that injured cells in the brain could not recover, and that neural tissue could not survive transplantation. Some recent experiments with brain tissue grafts, however, have cast doubt on these beliefs and have offered new hope for persons with such brain-related disorders as Parkinson's and Alzheimer's diseases and spinal-cord injury.

Most of the research that has been conducted so far has taken place with mice, rats, and, recently, monkeys. Experimental brain-tissue grafts have, however, also been applied to human beings, with mixed results. Since 1982 Swedish scientists at the Karolinska Institute, which specializes in studying the neurochemistry of emotional disorders, have implanted fetal tissue into the brains of middle-aged and elderly victims of Parkinson's disease. These transplants have not produced lasting improvements, and much work remains to be done.

This disabling disease is among the better-understood neurological disorders. Its symptoms include increasing rigidity of the arms and legs, shaking, and loss of facial expression.

BRAIN-TISSUE GRAFTS IN PEOPLE AND ANIMALS

Its cause seems clearly related to a deficiency in the neurotransmitter dopamine. While the drug L-dopa can be used to increase the body's supplies of dopamine, patients develop a tolerance to the drug, need increasingly larger doses, and may suffer worse symptoms from an overdose. How else, then, could dopamine be provided to the brains of Parkinson's patients? Brain-tissue transplants offer one possible way.

Researchers discovered that they could induce symptoms like those of Parkinson's disease in rats and then cure them by transplanting neurons from fetal brain tissue, which contained the necessary dopamine. Fetal tissue seems to "take" (that is, to become attached to the brain of the host animal) better than adult tissue, possibly because it is fast-growing. However, while this method worked in

animals, it raised obv[ious is]sues for human being[s. A] source of dopamine was ne[eded,] and it was found in the adr[enal] glands in the Parkinson's patients' own bodies. These glands, located just above the kidneys in the lower back, produce dopamine, and losing part of one adrenal gland is not harmful, since the other adrenal gland will then increase its production of hormones.

After finding out that transplanting adrenal tissue into rats' brains eliminated Parkinsonian symptoms, neurosurgeons in Sweden performed the transplant in one woman and three men. They managed to stop the deterioration of one patient and to make temporary improvements in the condition of the others. Even temporary restoration of brain cell function may one day have far-reaching effects.

Meanwhile, this exciting work continues, as researchers seek new sources of transplant material and new applications of it. As one of these pioneering researchers says, "Today grafting is by no means the recommended treatment for any form of brain damage. But with our own work on humans and our American colleagues' work on other primates, we are clearly moving toward the day when reversing brain damage could become routine" (Olson, quoted in Kiester, 1986, p. 38).

Functions of the right hemisphere The right hemisphere is the part of the brain where spatial ability is located; it is more involved than the left hemisphere in artistic and musical experience and performance. In keeping with its pattern-perception ability, the right side lets us recognize faces and read people's facial expressions. This last ability has been established by a line of experimentation involving **chimeric stimuli**—stimuli that are not encountered in ordinary life (a chimera is an imaginary monster). One of these is a composite face, made up of the left side of a woman's face and the right side of a man's (see Figure 2-20, page 66). A person briefly shown this picture and asked to *describe* the face will answer, "A man with dark eyebrows and a mustache," showing that the left hemisphere (which controls language) "saw" the half-face on the right. But if shown the two original (plus other) faces and asked to *point* to the face seen, the participant will point to the woman's face. This demonstrates that the right hemisphere (which recognizes faces) "saw" the half-face on the left (Levy, Trevarthan, & Sperry, 1972). Our awareness of such specialized functions leads to a special amazement when we contemplate how the two sides of the brain work together to blend their many discrete abilities into one powerful instrument.

Chimeric stimuli *Stimuli that are not encountered in everyday life.*

THE ENDOCRINE SYSTEM

The nervous system is not the only biological system governing behavior. Both the central and the peripheral nervous systems work closely with the **endocrine system,** a series of ductless glands that secrete hormones directly into the bloodstream. **Hormones** are chemicals that can influence the rate or the direction of activity in distant target organs by speeding up or inhibiting the growth of cells in those organs. Table 2-1 lists the major endocrine glands, the hormones they secrete, and the principal functions of those hormones; Figure 2-21 shows the location of these glands in the body.

Hormones are active in the maintenance of homeostasis, the proper balance in the body's internal state. Thus, both the autonomic nervous system and the endocrine system work together to achieve equilibrium. The crucial coordinator of both systems is the hypothalamus, which provides the mechanism by which the brain exerts control over the endocrine system and by which the endocrine system exerts control over the brain. For example, the brain causes the release of hormones that affect body tissues (as in the effect of testosterone on the shape of the larynx, resulting in the deeper voices of males). Conversely, hormones may permanently alter the way brain cells are organized (as in the ability of estrogen to alter cells in the hypothalamus that govern adult sexual behavior).

TABLE 2-1 MAJOR ENDOCRINE GLANDS, HORMONES THEY SECRETE, AND THEIR PRINCIPAL FUNCTIONS

Gland	Hormone	Function
Adrenal gland		
Cortex	Aldosterone	Excretion of sodium and potassium
	Androstenedione	Growth of pubic and underarm hair; sex drive (women)
	Cortisone	Metabolism; response to stress
Medulla	Epinephrine, norepinephrine	Metabolism; response to stress
Hypothalamus*	Releasing hormones	Control of anterior pituitary hormone secretion
Kidneys	Renin	Control of aldosterone secretion; blood pressure
Ovaries	Estradiol (Estrogen)	Maturation of female reproductive system; secondary sex characteristics
	Progesterone	Maintenance of lining of uterus; promotion of pregnancy
Pancreas	Insulin, glucagon	Regulation of metabolism
Pituitary gland		
Anterior	Adrenocorticotropic hormone	Control of adrenal cortex
	Gonadotropic hormones	Control of testes and ovaries
	Growth hormone	Growth; control of metabolism
	Prolactin	Milk production
	Thyroid-stimulating hormone	Control of thyroid gland
Posterior	Antidiuretic hormone†	Excretion of water
	Oxytocin†	Release of milk, contraction of uterus
Testes	Testosterone	Maturation of male reproductive system; sperm production; secondary sex characteristics; sex drive (men)
Thyroid gland	Thyroxine	Energy metabolism; growth and development

*The hypothalamus, although it is part of the brain, secretes hormones; thus it can be considered to be an endocrine gland.
†These hormones are produced by the hypothalamus but are transported to and released from the posterior pituitary gland.
Source: Adapted from Carlson, 1986.

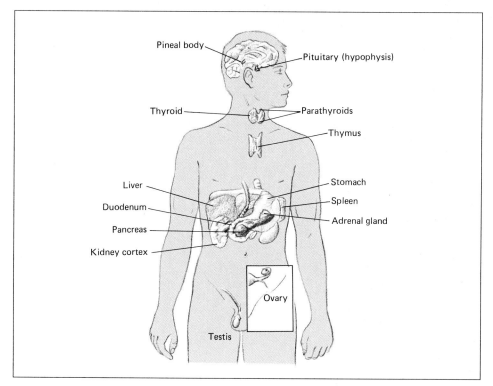

FIGURE 2-21 *The major endocrine (hormone-secreting) glands of the body are located in the brain and the periphery of the body. (Source: Adapted from Leshner, 1978.)*

Endocrine Glands

If we think of endocrine glands as members of an orchestra, the conductor would be the ***pituitary,*** the "master gland." This gland has two subdivisions: the anterior pituitary, which is made of the same embryological tissue as the throat and is a true endocrine organ, and the posterior pituitary, which is made up of nerve tissue and is, therefore, part of the nervous system. The pituitary gland controls the activity of all the other glands from its position at the base of the brain, directly below the hypothalamus.

The *anterior pituitary* secretes a large number of hormones. The hypothalamus controls the release of these hormones by means of hormone-releasing factors. For example, one of these factors, LHRH (luteinizing-hormone-releasing hormone), travels from the hypothalamus to the anterior pituitary to cause the release of LH (luteinizing hormone). Each of the anterior pituitary hormones affects the secretions of a different gland, which then affect other tissues of the body in various ways. For example, the adrenal gland releases a surge of adrenalin to let us respond to an emergency; the thyroid gland regulates growth and metabolism; the ovaries send out the female sex hormone estrogen, which regulates the menstrual cycle and allows a woman to become pregnant; and the testes secrete the male sex hormone testosterone, which maintains the sex drive and may also stimulate aggression. All of these are controlled by the anterior pituitary.

The *posterior pituitary* releases only two hormones, vasopressin, which controls the volume of urine (to conserve bodily fluids and therefore blood volume and pressure), and oxytocin, which stimulates contraction of the uterus during childbirth and then stimulates milk production in the mammary glands in the mother's breasts. Both these hormones are actually manufactured by neurons in the hypothalamus, transported down their axons, and released into the bloodstream. The hypothalamus directs all these functions: it either manufactures hormones itself or secretes releasing factors that cause other glands (like the pituitary) to release their hormones.

Pituitary Endocrine gland called the body's "master gland" because it controls the activity of all the other glands.

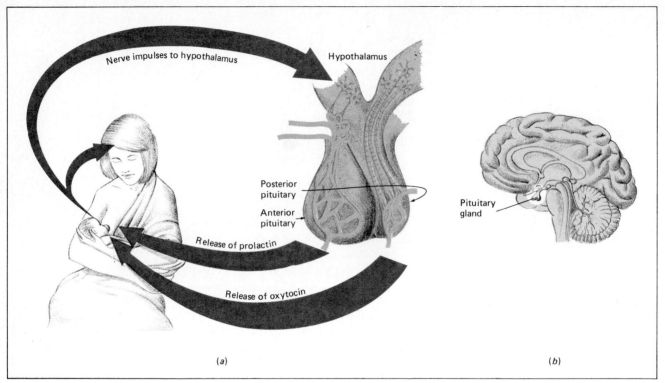

Nerve impulses to hypothalamus

Hypothalamus

Posterior pituitary

Anterior pituitary

Release of prolactin

Release of oxytocin

Pituitary gland

(a)

(b)

FIGURE 2-22 *(a) The let-down response in breast-feeding shows how brain and endocrine system work together to make milk and get it to the baby. The baby's suckling produces nerve impulses that direct the endocrine system to produce the hormone prolactin, which makes the milk, and another hormone, oxytocin, which causes contractions that send the milk into the area just behind the nipples where the baby can get to it. (Adapted from Rosenzweig & Leiman, 1982.)* **(b)** *Location of the pituitary in the brain.*

Neural-Endocrine Interactions

The let-down response experienced by breast-feeding mothers (which enables the mother to let down her milk to the baby) provides a classic example of neural-endocrine interactions (see Figure 2-22). The baby's suckling at the breast activates skin receptors in the mother's nipple, which transmit messages to the brain stem. Interneurons carry the message along to the hypothalamus, which signals the anterior pituitary to produce the hormone prolactin and the posterior pituitary to produce oxytocin. The prolactin stimulates the production of milk in the mammary glands, and the oxytocin causes the contractions that squeeze the milk through the ducts and into the milk pools behind the nipples where the baby can get to it.

Emotions play a powerful role in this reflex. Simply hearing her baby cry or just thinking about the baby at feeding time will often send a tingling rush of milk into the mother's breasts. On the other hand, anxiety or discomfort can inhibit the let-down reflex, and is the source of many breast-feeding failures (Eiger & Olds, 1987). This is just one example of the intricate interconnections between mind and body, between neurons and hormones.

The let-down reflex demonstrates the powerful control the nervous system has over the endocrine system. But the reverse also holds true. Endocrine hormones get into the brain and bind with neurons there, influencing the brain cells and the activities they direct.

Hormones can have two basic kinds of effects—activational and organizational. In activation, the effect is temporary. Thus, the brain's release of androgens might increase a person's sexual arousal at any specific time. An organizational effect, on the other hand, is permanent. Exposure to a hormone can permanently change some aspect of the way the brain is organized. The following finding, for example, suggests the possibility that even atypical sexual orientation may have a biological basis, perhaps reflecting the organizing influences of hormones during development of the embryo while the sexual organs are being set as either male or female.

In one experiment researchers administered estrogen to heterosexual men and women and also to a sample of exclusively homosexual men. In the normal ovulatory cycle of women, the secretion of estrogen stimulates luteinizing hormone (LH). In fact, when estrogen was injected into the women who participated in this study, more LH was released into their bloodstreams. This effect did not occur in the heterosexual men. The effect on the homosexual men was midway between the effects on the women and on the heterosexual men, suggesting that the brains of these men may be organized differently from those of heterosexual men (Gladue, Green, & Hellman, 1984). If further research confirms this finding, it will strongly suggest that there may be a biological basis for some types of homosexuality. Some scientists do believe this to be so, but up until now studies that have sought to prove it (usually on the basis of the amount of testosterone in the systems of heterosexual and homosexual men) have not resulted in positive results or firm conclusions.

While this chapter has peered through some windows into the brain, it seems that every time we answer one question about its workings, we raise dozens of other questions, which spur new research. It seems fairly safe to predict that psychobiology will never completely unravel the mysteries of how our brains function. Current brain research is exploring such topics as the factors that make one nerve cell different from another, the reasons why cell bodies do not always die even after their axons have been damaged, and the means by which some cells can take over the functions of other cells in some circumstances. When we can answer questions like these, we'll not only have more knowledge about this most mysterious realm—what one writer (Hunt, 1982) has called the "universe within"—but we'll also have clues that will assist us in helping those people whose brains are not functioning normally because of injury or illness.

SUMMARY

1 The study of the brain is much more sophisticated today than it was in the heyday of phrenology, an approach in which personality traits and mental abilities were thought to be related to bumps on the skull. Although phrenology was eventually discredited, it led to studies in which scientists used a variety of techniques to gain information about the relationship between mental function and the various areas of the brain. Invasive research techniques include surgery, electrical stimulation, and chemical stimulation; noninvasive techniques include the electroencephalogram (EEG), the computerized axial tomography (CAT) scan, the positron emission tomography (PET) scan, and magnetic resonance imaging (MRI).

2 There are two basic kinds of cells in the nervous system. Neurons (nerve cells) receive and send information to and from other neurons. The three types of neurons are sensory, motor, and interneurons. Glia (glial cells) support and protect the neurons. One type of glial cell covers parts of the neuron with myelin, a fatty tissue.

3 All neurons have a cell body with a nucleus that contains DNA, the cell's genetic information. Most neurons have dendrites (branching extensions of the cell body) and tail-like extensions called axons. Information from other neurons is received by a dendrite and then passed down the axon.

4 Communication between neurons involves both electrical and chemical actions. All neurons have a resting electrical charge across the neuron membrane that is produced by ions. The action potential—the "firing" of a neuron—begins at the axon hillock and sweeps down the axon to the axon terminal.

5 Neurons communicate with each other at synapses, physical gaps between the axon terminals and neighboring dendrites. When an action potential reaches the axon terminal, vesicles containing chemicals called neurotransmitters are released into the synapse. The chemical then diffuses to receptor sites on a neighboring dendrite. A neurotransmitter can either produce an action potential in the next neuron or inhibit that neuron so that no action potentials are produced. Some well-studied neurotransmitters are dopamine, acetylcholine, serotonin, norepinephrine, and the endorphins.

6 Psychoactive drugs influence our behavior by altering neuron transmission. Some drugs cause the release of neurotransmitters in certain parts of the brain, whereas other drugs either mimic a natural neurotransmitter or attach to dendrite receptor sites, blocking neural transmission.

7 Alzheimer's disease is characterized the disturbances in memory, language, and personality. Massive neuron death and reduced levels of the neurotransmitter acetylcholine have been observed in the brains of deceased victims of Alzheimer's disease. Chemical treatment of Alzheimer's disease with drugs such as THA may improve the cognitive activity of persons with mild cases.

8 The nervous system is composed of two major divisions: the central nervous system (CNS) and the peripheral nervous system (PNS). The brain and spinal cord make up the CNS. The two types of nerves that make up the PNS are the sensory nerves, which transmit information from the body to the brain, and motor nerves, which transmit information from the brain to the muscles and glands of the body.

9 The spinal cord is a long, stemlike structure that serves as a pathway between the body and the brain. Sensory and motor nerves enter and exit the spinal cord and make interconnections within the spinal cord. These interconnections allow reflexes, or involuntary motor responses to stimuli. The simplest type of reflex (the knee-jerk reflex, for example) occurs at a single synapse, whereas more complex reflexes (such as blinking at a loud noise) involve many synaptic connections within the brain and spinal cord.

10 The peripheral nervous system can be divided into the somatic nervous system and the autonomic nervous system. Motor nerves can be part of either division of the peripheral nervous system.

11 The somatic nervous system controls both reflex and voluntary actions. Motor neurons in the brain control the muscles of the face, neck, and head; motor neurons in the spinal cord control muscles in the rest of the body. Motor neurons release the neurotransmitter acetylcholine, which causes the appropriate muscle to contract.

12 The autonomic nervous system consists of the sympathetic and parasympathetic divisions, which often have opposing actions on the smooth muscles and glands of the body. The sympathetic division mobilizes resources to expend energy, for example, when you prepare to fight; the parasympathetic division restores the energy supply of the body, for example, during digestion.

13 The body has many systems that can only function within certain ranges (temperature, for instance). *Homeostasis* refers to the balance of vital functions maintained by coordinated adjustments of the central nervous system.

14 The brain contains a number of specialized structures: the brain stem (pons, medulla oblongata, and midbrain), the cerebellum, and the cerebrum (thalamus, hypothalamus, basal ganglia, limbic system, and cerebral cortex). Although we treat each as a specific structure, each is a part of an integrated system that records sensory inputs, integrates information, and then guides motor responses. In addition, these structures mediate thoughts, language, memory, etc.

15 The brain stem consists of the pons, medulla oblongata, and midbrain. The brain stem receives sensory information, controls muscle contractions, and is involved in the regulation of sleep and arousal, as well as more automatic functions (respiration, heart rate).

16 The cerebellum is connected by a thick set of fibers to the brain stem. The cerebellum is important for motor control (for example, coordinating and fine-tuning motor activity) and certain types of learning and memory.

17 The hypothalamus is an organ in the cerebrum involved in the regulation of hormone release as well as the maintenance of homeostasis in the body. Changes in eating, drinking, temperature regulation, emotion, and sexual behavior have been noted after stimulation of the hypothalamus.

18 The thalamus is a part of the cerebrum that lies just above the hypothalamus. It receives and integrates sensory information and participates in the control of voluntary movement, language, and memory.

19 The basal ganglia are a collection of nuclei located near the thalamus that modulate movement of the body. Stimulation of one part of the basal ganglia can arrest movement. Disorders of other parts of the basal ganglia can greatly interfere with normal movement.

20 The limbic system is a system of cell bodies and connecting fibers involved in emotional balance and memory. The nuclei of the limbic system include the septal area, the hippocampus, the amygdala, and parts of the thalamus.

21 The cerebral cortex is a layer of gray matter that surrounds most of the brain. The cortex is proportionately larger in more highly developed animals; in human beings it makes up a large portion of the brain. It is involved in the higher mental processes.

22 The cortex on each side (hemisphere) of the brain is divided into four lobes. Each lobe is somewhat specialized for various mental functions. The frontal lobe contains areas that are involved in motor control (on the opposite side of the body), planning, judgment, and emotion; the temporal lobe is involved in hearing, learning, and memory; the parietal lobe deals with spatial and tactile perception and with body image; the occipital lobe is primarily concerned with vision. The primary cortex is devoted to specific motor or sensory functions, whereas the association cortex participates in many higher mental functions, such as thought, speech, and memory.

23 Asymmetry of the brain is the concept that there are differences in size, organization, and function in the two sides of the brain, the left and the right hemispheres. The left hemisphere is involved in language and numeric and analytic thought; the right usually directs artistic, musical, and complex spatial abilities.

24 The two hemispheres communicate through the corpus callosum, a large bundle of axons. If this system of fibers is severed, as during a surgical procedure to control epilepsy, the two hemispheres of the brain cannot communicate. By studying how ''split-brain'' patients are different from normal persons, scientists have learned much about the functions of the two hemispheres.

25 Damage to the parietal lobe of one hemisphere can produce a disorder of spatial perception in which the person neglects the side of the body opposite to the side damaged. Damage to the left hemisphere can affect language abilities. When Broca's area of the left frontal lobe is injured, motor aphasia results, in which a person has difficulty in expressing thought in speech and writing. Damage to Wernicke's area in the left posterior temporal lobe produces sensory aphasia, in which a person speaks fluent nonsense and has difficulty in understanding other people's speech.

26 Important differences in health and function have been noted between left- and right-handed persons. More disorders of health (allergies, for example), dyslexia, and hyperactivity are noted in left-handers, but left-handers tend to be better at spatial activities. Males are more likely to be left-handed than are females.

27 Brain tissue grafts are used by researchers to explore the possibility that damaged neurons in the brain can be replaced. Parkinson's disease is a disorder in which damage to cells in the basal ganglia containing the neurotransmitter dopamine causes a loss in motor control. Grafts of fetal cells containing dopamine into the brain have par-tially reversed some of the symptoms of Parkinson's disease.

28 The endocrine system is a collection of glands that secrete hormones into the bloodstream. The hypothalamus coordinates the endocrine system and is largely responsible for homeostasis. The pituitary gland releases hormones that control the activity of other glands, including the adrenal glands, thyroid glands, testes, and ovaries. Each of these glands secretes one or more hormones which can have activational or organizational actions on the body systems. The mechanisms involved in breast-feeding demonstrate neural-endocrine interactions.

KEY TERMS

Acetylcholine (page 50)
Action potential (AP) (45)
Alzheimer's disease (47)
Aphasias (65)
Ascending reticular activation system (56)
Association cortex (59)
Asymmetry of the brain (63)
Autonomic nervous system (53)
Axon (44)
Axon hillock (45)
Axon terminal (45)
Basal ganglia (58)
Brain stem (56)

Central nervous system (51)
Cerebellum (56)
Cerebral cortex (58)
Cerebrum (57)
Chimeric stimuli (67)
Corpus callosum (63)
Dendrites (44)
Endocrine system (68)
Glial cells (44)
Hemispheric lateralization (63)
Homeostasis (55)
Hormones (68)
Hypothalamus (57)
Interneurons (43)

Limbic system (58)
Motor (efferent) neurons (43)
Myelin (44)
Myelinization (45)
Nerves (51)
Nervous system (40)
Neurons (43)
Neurotransmitter (47)
Peripheral nervous system (51)
Phrenology (40)
Pituitary (69)
Primary cortex (61)
Psychosurgery (41)
Receptor site (47)

Reflex (52)
Resting membrane potential (RMP) (44)
Reticular formation (56)
Sensory (afferent) neurons (43)
Somatic nervous system (53)
Spinal cord (51)
Stroke (65)
Synapses (47)
Synaptic cleft (47)
Synaptic vesicles (47)
Thalamus (58)
Threshold (45)

SUGGESTED READINGS

CALVIN, W. H. (1983). *The throwing madonna.* New York: McGraw-Hill. A series of clear, well-written essays on the brain by a neurobiologist who draws on his own research, on psychology journals, and on poetry, biography, and art. The title essay asks whether the reason most of us throw with our right arm is related to the fact that mothers often hold their babies with the left arm.

HUNT, M. (1982). *The universe within: A new science explores the human mind.* New York: Simon & Schuster. A fascinating book for the layperson that presents a wide range of information on every aspect of the mind, including the evolution and physiology of the brain; the way we think, remember, and solve problems; and the difference between human and artificial intelligence.

KLEINFIELD, S. (1985). *A machine called indomitable.* New York: Times Books. A gripping account of the development of magnetic resonance imaging (MRI) and its use in the detection of cancer, multiple sclerosis, and mental illness.

RESTAK, R. (1984). *The brain.* Toronto: Bantam. A readable, lavishly illustrated book based on the PBS television series *The Brain.* Contains chapters on the structure of the brain and on areas of brain research, including vision and movement, mental disorders, learning and memory, stress and emotion, and states of mind.

SACKS, O. (1985). *The man who mistook his wife for a hat and other clinical tales.* New York: Summit. An eloquent best-selling collection of case histories of people suffering from a variety of neurological disabilities. It explains the specific brain-mind relationships involved and shows the resourceful ways people can adapt to almost unbelievably strange disorders.

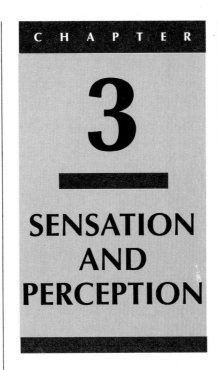

C H A P T E R

3

SENSATION
AND
PERCEPTION

■ How can what is seen and heard be described?

■ How does the sensory system work?

■ How are pressure and pain felt, and what are some effective ways to relieve pain?

■ How does the brain organize stimuli into meaningful patterns?

■ What roles do attention, expectation, and experience play in perception?

■ How do people know how far away objects are, and why do objects seem to stay the same size even when they cast images of different sizes on the retina?

If Miss Myers could see me now, in middle age, she wouldn't believe that the student who barely squeaked through her physical education classes at the Philadelphia High School for Girls now runs 2 miles every day, occasionally gears up for a 10-kilometer (6-mile) race, and has even, in some obscure events, won trophies in her age group.

Aside from the triumph of knowing that determination can win out over minimal athletic ability, I revel in the bouquet of sensory experiences that my morning run gives me. Before I began to run, I had never seen the sun blaze up through the trees over the little pond below the place where I live and work. I had not viewed the different moods of the early morning sky over the bay across the road, now pale pink with promise, now a jubilant azure. I had not heard the joyful singing of the birds as we greeted the day together. I had not drunk in the lush scent of the honeysuckle that grows in such profusion around the corner from my house.

Before I ran, I viewed the rain and the cold from inside as often as possible. I went out in "bad" weather only when I had to. Now each day, from the calendar's beginning to its end, signals a new adventure, a new experience, a new sensation. No day is a bad day for running.

I wake up, look at the temperature, and listen to the weather forecast as I never did before: Is this a day to keep as cool as possible in halter and shorts? Or is it one suited to T-shirt, or perhaps a long-sleeved shirt? Or would more layers be appropriate—cotton undershirt, silk turtleneck, wool sweater, hat, gloves, mittens, windbreaker, rain suit? Finding the right combination becomes a challenge. By dressing for the weather, I make each day mine. I embrace the caress of snow or the sting of rain on my face, the mist on my hair, the sweat on my skin, the wind against my chest. All these sensations are mine in the ever-changing world that now belongs to me every day.

Before I ran, I took my body for granted, paying attention to it only when I worried about my weight (like most Americans) or felt a twinge reminding me of my mortality (like most human beings). Running brought a new life to this compound of blood, flesh, muscle, and bone through the changes I felt—the new stamina that sends me flying up and down stairs from morning till night, ease in movement, comfort in breathing—or those signs of vulnerability like a shooting pain through a leg, an ache in the back, a bruise from a fall. This heightened consciousness of the physical brings in turn exhilaration or despair. Either way makes me more tuned into my senses than I have ever been before.

From the notebooks of Sally Olds

Your morning sensory experiences may be very different. You may be aware of the feel of plush carpet or icy tile under your bare feet, the sounds of activity outside your bedroom door, the time displayed on your digital clock, the aroma of freshly brewed coffee, the taste of your toothpaste. In these ordinary, unremarkable activities, you have used all your major senses—sight, hearing, smell, taste, and touch. Neither your mornings nor mine begin to scratch the richly textured surface of the vital role our senses play in our lives. From birth to death our senses are constantly bombarded by one stimulus after another, bringing us information and presenting us with decisions, first on how we are to perceive these stimuli and then on how we are to behave in response. In this chapter we'll look at the way we take in sensory information, from the basic operation of the sensory organs to the complex ways in which experience shapes our perceptions.

Before we go on, let's define some terms. A **stimulus** is any form of energy to which we can respond (such as light waves, sound waves, pressure on the skin, etc.). **Sensation** is the stimulation of our sensory organs and the transmission of information about this stimulation through the nervous system. For example, when a violinist plays a note, such qualities of that note as its loudness and its pitch represent sensation. **Perception** is the way our brain interprets these sensations to make them meaningful. For example, if you listen to several notes played on a violin and realize that they form a familiar tune, you have experienced a perception. Perception, then, results from a combination of sensation and previous sensory experiences. In real life it is often difficult to distinguish sensation from perception.

Stimulus *Form of energy which can elicit a response.*

Sensation *Stimulation of the sensory organs and the transmission of information about this stimulation through the nervous system.*

Perception *The way the brain interprets sensations to make them meaningful.*

PSYCHOPHYSICS: HOW OUR SENSES WORK ███████████████

Psychophysics is the study of the relationship between the physical aspects of stimuli and our psychological perceptions of them. In other words, psychophysics forms a bridge between the physical world and the psychological world. It examines our sensitivity to stimuli and the ways in which variations in stimuli affect the way we perceive them. Let's look at some of the findings from this branch of study.

Psychophysics *Study of the relationship between physical aspects of stimuli and psychological perceptions of them.*

Sensory Thresholds

At some time you have undoubtedly looked up at the night sky, seen no stars at all, looked away, and then looked back to see one faint glimmer. How bright did that first star have to be before you could see it? When a second star appeared, how much brighter would it have to be before you could say that it was brighter than the first star? These are both questions about "thresholds". The first question asks about an absolute threshold; the second asks about a difference threshold. In either case, the concepts of *threshold* and *sensitivity* have an inverse relationship. Thus, when you have a high threshold (as you have when you first look up at the dark night sky), you have low sensitivity (it's hard for you to see the stars). When you have a low threshold (after you've looked at the sky for a while), your sensitivity is higher (it's easier to see the stars).

Absolute Threshold   The **absolute threshold** is the lowest intensity at which a stimulus can be perceived. As you can see in Figure 3-1, our senses are incredibly sensitive. Laboratory tests have demonstrated that under ideal conditions the human senses are capable of perceiving stimuli as subtle as the estimated real-life equivalents shown in this illustration (Cornsweet, 1970; Hecht, Shlaer, & Pirenne, 1941). Of course, the phrase "under ideal conditions" is significant, since the sensitivity of our senses depends on the background level of stimulation. For example, you can see the stars best on a dark, moonless night. They are there in the daytime, but you can't see them at all because of the relative brightness of the sun. Similarly, you could hear a coin drop on a quiet street but not during a fireworks display.

Absolute threshold *Lowest intensity at which a stimulus can be perceived.*

In recent years, psychologists have come to appreciate that thresholds may not be as absolute as was once thought. According to **signal-detection theory,** an approach to psychophysics that considers both the sensitivity of the senses and the motivations of observers, our thresholds depend not only upon the sensitivity of the human senses, but also on our motivations (Gescheider, 1985; Matlin, 1983). For example, you've probably noticed that you're much more likely to think you heard the telephone ring if you've been anxiously awaiting an important call.

Signal-detection theory *Approach to psychophysics that emphasizes both the sensitivity of the senses and the motivations of observers.*

SIGHT
Candle flame seen from a
distance of 27 km (17 miles)
on a clear, dark night

HEARING
Ticking of a watch in a room
6 meters (20 feet) away

TASTE
One teaspoon sugar dissolved
in 2 gallons of distilled
water (1 part in 2000)

SMELL
One drop of perfume in
a three-room house (1 part
in 500,000,000)

TOUCH
The wing of a bee falling on
your cheek from a distance of
1 centimeter (0.39 inch)

FIGURE 3-1 *Absolute sensory thresholds established by laboratory experiments, as shown by equivalent real-life approximations of stimuli presented in the laboratory. (Source: Hecht, Shlaer, & Pirenne, 1941.)*

Difference threshold *Smallest difference in intensity between two stimuli that can be detected (also known as jnd: just noticeable difference).*
jnd *Difference threshold (just noticeable difference).*

Weber's law *Law of psychophysics which states that more intense stimuli require larger changes before those changes can be perceived, whereas less intense stimuli require smaller changes.*

Adaptation *Decrease in the response of the sensory system to continued stimulations.*

Difference Threshold   The ***difference threshold,*** also known as the ***jnd*** (just noticeable difference), is the smallest difference in intensity that you are able to detect. The size of this threshold is variable, depending not only on the background level, but also on the intensity of the original stimulus. If you have a 53-pound pack on your back and someone adds a 1-ounce letter to it, you won't feel the difference, but you will feel the addition of a 1-pound package. If the pack weighs 106 pounds, you won't feel the addition of 1 pound, but you will feel a 2-pound difference. This ratio between the size of the original stimulus and the size of the addition or subtraction that can just be detected is called ***Weber's law*** after the nineteenth-century German psychologist who first noticed that the larger the stimulus, the larger a change has to be before we can tell the difference. Weber worked out a set of ratios for different kinds of stimuli. These ratios hold true in the middle ranges of stimulation, but not for very weak or very strong levels of intensity. The ratios are shown in Table 3-1, on the opposite page.

Adaptation

Can you feel your watchband encircling your wrist? Are you conscious of the temperature in the room or the intensity of the light you're reading by? If none of these stimuli are so intense as to interfere with the primary focus of your attention (this book), chances are that you are not aware of any of them. In psychological terms, you have adapted to them. You have adjusted to a certain level of stimulation and are not consciously responding to it. ***Adaptation*** is the decrease in the response of the sensory system that accompanies continued stimulations.

This mechanism protects you from being distracted by the many stimuli that impinge upon your senses at any given moment. You aren't likely to notice such constant levels of stimulation unless they change—unless, for example, the watchband is so tight that it begins to hurt, the heat goes off and you feel your feet getting cold, or the lights flicker or dim—or unless someone brings your attention to one of these sensations. Our receptors for smell are the quickest to adapt, as you know from the many times that you've noticed a strong aroma (like the perfume on someone sitting near you), which you cease to be aware of within a few minutes. We can get used to many extremes of temperature, noise, brightness, odor, and other stimuli so that they fade from conscious awareness. The phenomenon of adaptation explains why a 40-degree day in early spring after a cold winter seems warm, but a 55-degree day in early fall after a hot summer seems chilly.

The degree to which we've adapted affects our sensitivity to stimulation. You can see this for yourself in another simple test. Get three bowls; fill one with ice-cold water, one with water as hot as you can stand it, and one with warm water. Put your left hand in the cold water and your right hand in the hot water. After a minute or so, put both hands in warm water. This water will feel hot to your left hand and cold to your right, showing the effect of adaptation.

What accounts for our lowered sensitivity as we adapt to various stimuli? We don't really know. The simplest theory is that the receptors become fatigued after being stimulated. A more complex theory suggests that specific mechanisms for adaptation may be located at higher levels of processing closer to the brain—but no one has yet discovered them (Matlin, 1983). The phenomenon has both benefits and drawbacks in daily life. It lets us focus our attention on what we're doing without being distracted by a variety of stimuli. It also, however, may dull our senses to stimuli that we need to be aware of (like the smell of leaking gas), keeping us from recognizing a dangerous situation.

The preceding phenomena—thresholds and adaptation—affect the way we perceive information that comes through our senses. We'll talk more about perception throughout this chapter, but first let's look at the actual physiological mechanisms that permit basic sensations to take place.

PHYSIOLOGY: THE SENSES

Vision

For most people, vision assumes more importance than any of the other sensory systems. More of the brain is devoted to mechanisms for vision than for any other sense, and it is what we see that gives us most of our information about the world.

Vision dominates information from the other senses. If you've ever seen a skillful ventriloquist in action, you probably wondered how he could make sounds come from the dummy. If you close your eyes while the ventriloquist is talking, you'll be aware that both voices come from the same place, but when your eyes are open and you see the dummy's mouth moving, what you see becomes more important than what you hear. This phenomenon, by which visual information assumes more importance in our minds than information from the other senses, is called **visual capture**. It is one of the many reasons we can't always trust the "evidence of our own senses."

What We See The human eye detects electromagnetic energy in the form of light waves. There are, however, many types and frequencies of electromagnetic waves, such as x-rays, ultraviolet rays, and infrared rays, that we cannot detect (see Figure 3-2 on page 80). An astonishingly small amount of light can be detected. As Figure 3-1 shows, you may not be able to see forever on a clear night, but the human eye can see a source of light that is as faint as a candle from a distance of about 17 miles (Hecht, Shlaer, & Pirenne, 1941). A powerful searchlight on the earth could be seen without a telescope by someone standing on the moon (Pirenne, 1948).

TABLE 3-1	WEBER'S RATIOS
Weight	1:53
Sound	1:11
Skin Pressure	1:7
Saltiness	1:5
Smell	1:10
Brightness	1:62

Note: This table can be used to calculate how much you have to increase a particular kind of stimulus in order to detect a change. To notice a difference in weight, for example, there must be an additional load equal to ⅟₅₃ of the original weight. For example, you could notice a difference between a weight of 53 pounds and a weight of 54 pounds, because the jnd for weight is ⅟₅₃: in this case, 1 pound. To detect a difference in sound, there must be a proportionately larger change, equivalent to ⅟₁₁ of the original stimulus.
Source: Adapted from Woodworth & Schlosberg, 1954.

Visual capture *Phenomenon by which visual information is more influential than information from the other senses.*

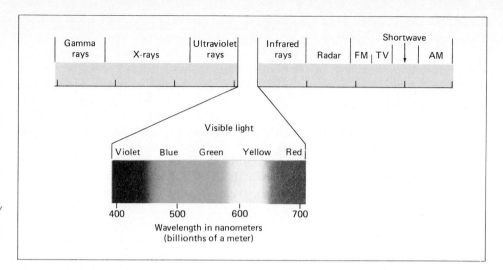

FIGURE 3-2 *Electromagnetic energy spectrum. The portion of the spectrum perceived as visible light is enlarged in the lower part of the figure.*

How We See: The Anatomy of the Eye   As you can see in Figure 3-3, the miraculous organ that is the human eye is a sphere containing a variety of structures. We can look at these structures in turn as we trace the path that light takes when it enters our eyes.

Light passes first through the ***cornea,*** the transparent tissue at the front of the eye. The cornea is made of the same materials as the ***sclera,*** the white outer part of the eyeball, but is transparent. The sclera, the "skin" of the eye, contains receptors for pressure, temperature, and pain.

The light then passes through a small hole called the ***pupil,*** which looks like a little black circle. The size of the pupil is controlled by the ***iris,*** the colored part of the eye, a pigmented set of muscles surrounding the pupil. Eyes with a great deal of pigment appear brown. Those with little or none are blue, and other colors are caused by varying amounts of pigmentation. The iris dilates the pupil (opens it wider) to let more light in under conditions of darkness, and constricts the pupil (makes it smaller) in bright lights.

Cornea *Transparent protective tissue at the front of the eye.*
Sclera *White outer part of the eyeball that contains receptors for pressure, temperature, and pain.*
Pupil *Small hole in the center of the iris which allows light to enter the eye.*
Iris *Pigmented set of muscles surrounding the pupil.*

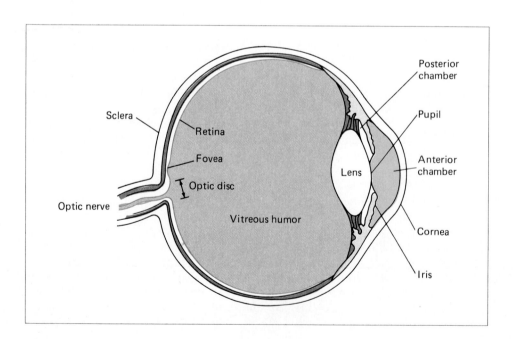

FIGURE 3-3 *Cross section of the human eye.*

FIGURE 3-4 (*a*) *Nearsightedness and farsightedness are caused by abnormalities in eye shape. In the normal eye (top), light is focused on the retina. When the eye is elongated (bottom left), nearsightedness results because the light focuses in front of the retina. When the eye is too short (bottom right), light focuses behind the retina, causing farsightedness.* (*b*) *A person with normal vision will see a "clockface" figure (A), while someone with astigmatism will have difficulty seeing some or all of the vertical lines (B) or the horizontal lines (C). (Source: Mitchell, Freeman, Millodot, & Haegerstrom, 1973.)*

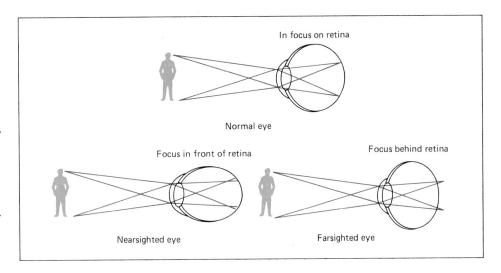

In focus on retina

Normal eye

Focus in front of retina

Focus behind retina

Nearsighted eye

Farsighted eye

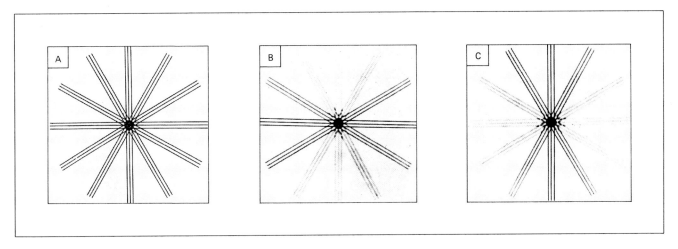

A

B

C

Lens *Disk-shaped elastic structure in the eye that focuses light into a clear image.*

Retina *Tissue lining the back of the eye and containing the light-sensitive rods and cones; it is the most important part of the eye.*

Accommodation *Process by which the lens changes shape to focus images at different distances onto the retina.*

Rods *Receptors on the retina that are sensitive to black and white but not to color.*

Cones *Receptors on the retina responsible for seeing color and small details.*

Ganglion cells *Cells in the eyes that carry all visual information to the brain.*

Optic disk *Part of the eye with no photoreceptors; when an image is projected on this disk, it hits a blind spot.*

Light then passes through the ***lens,*** an elastic structure in the shape of a round disk. The lens focuses the light into a clear image that is projected through a clear fluid to the photosensitive part of the eye, the ***retina.*** The lens changes its shape, becoming thicker in order to focus nearby images onto the retina, or thinner for images farther away, in a process known as ***accommodation.*** Problems with accommodation, together with problems of eye shape, cause either nearsightedness or farsightedness as shown in Figure 3-4a. These and other vision problems are described in the box "Common Vision Problems."

The most important and most complicated part of the eye is the retina, which contains photoreceptor cells called ***rods*** and ***cones.*** Each retina contains approximately 120 million rods and 6 million cones. As shown in the diagram in Figure 3-5, light passes through all the neurons before it reaches the photoreceptors (the rods and cones), where the visual responses originate. These responses are then transmitted through a complicated network of neurons to the ***ganglion cells.*** Each eye has about 1 million ganglion cells, which carry all visual information to the brain. The axons of these cells converge on one spot on the retina known as the ***optic disk*** (the "blind spot"). They send impulses to the brain, where the messages brought by the ganglion cells are decoded, so that we know what we see. (We will say more about this later in the chapter, when we discuss the way the brain organizes sensory information.)

FOCUSING DISORDERS

■ *Nearsightedness:* If the eyeball is too long, the lens cannot focus distant images on the retina, causing nearsightedness (*myopia*), a difficulty in seeing objects that are far away. Since the shape of the eye can change over time, periodic check-ups by an eye doctor can keep a lens prescription up to date.

■ *Farsightedness:* If the eyeball is too short, the lens cannot focus near images on the retina, causing farsightedness (*hypermetropia*), a difficulty in seeing objects that are close up. (See Figure 3-4a for a graphic comparison of normal vision, nearsightedness, and farsightedness).

■ *Astigmatism:* If the eyeball is not perfectly round, a condition called *astigmatism* results. People who are astigmatic cannot see equally well along horizontal and vertical axes; they have trouble seeing either sideways or up and down, as shown in Figure 3-4b. If severe astigmatism in children is not corrected with eyeglasses at an early age, there may be a permanent loss in the ability to see clearly either vertical or horizontal lines,

apparently because the appropriate neural connections do not develop in the visual cortex (Mitchell et al., 1973). Astigmatism in adults can usually be aided by corrective lenses.

DISORDERS OF EYE IMBALANCE

■ *Strabismus* ("crossed eyes," "wall-eyes," or "wandering eye"): This defect of the eye muscles affects 3 percent of the population (Sanders, 1986). The two eyes cannot focus together, so that an image that falls on one region in one eye will fall somewhere else in the other eye and will only be seen by one eye. People with this condition use their eyes one at a time, quickly alternating between them,

but if one eye has poorer vision than the other, they stop using that eye altogether. As a result, the vision in that eye worsens until good vision remains in only one eye. The condition is treated by covering the good eye with a patch to force the weaker eye to work harder, by exercises, or with surgery. If not corrected early (before age 5), permanent visual impairment will occur (Banks, Aslin, & Letson, 1975; von Noorden, 1981). Two such impairments are amblyopia and stereoblindness.

■ *Amblyopia* ("lazy eye" or "weak eye"): This condition seems to involve a problem in the processing of visual messages to the brain. Both eyes are normal, as are the optic nerve fibers, but for some reason the brain does not receive the visual information from one eye. As a result, the affected person has a fuzzy, distorted view of the world. Amblyopia, which occurs in 2 percent of the population, is the most common visual defect in children and the most common cause of legal blindness in children and young adults.

■ *Stereoblindness:* People who are

As you can see in Figure 3-5, the retina contains two different kinds of photoreceptors—the long, narrow rods and the thicker cones. The rods and cones both contain light-sensitive chemicals, but the two kinds of receptors have specialized functions and appear in different concentrations in different regions of the retina. The cones function best in bright light, where they are responsible for color vision and for

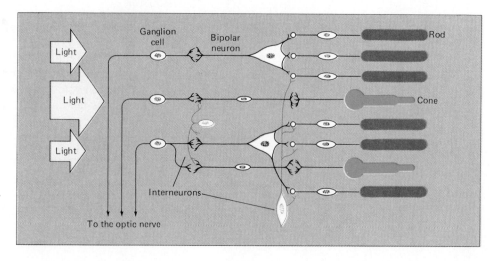

FIGURE 3-5 *Layers of the retina. Light passes through the ganglion cells and the bipolar neurons to the photoreceptors (the rods and cones). Sensory messages go back from these receptor cells through the bipolar neurons to the ganglion cells. The axons of the ganglion cells form the optic nerve, which sends visual messages to the brain. (Source: Hubel, 1963.)*

stereoblind cannot perceive depth, because of retinal disparity (discussed later in the chapter). About 5 to 10 percent of the population have stereoblindness (Richards, 1970).

DISORDERS OF AGING

■ *Presbyopia:* The farsightedness that affects most people past middle age takes its name from the Greek words for *old age* and *eyes.* A loss of elasticity in the lens makes accommodation difficult. That is, the eye cannot easily focus on near objects. People with normal distance vision can wear half-glasses that allow them to look through the glasses at nearby objects and to look over the tops of the glasses at distant objects. People who are both nearsighted and presbyopic wear bifocals, which have an upper lens that improves distance vision and a lower lens that helps in reading and doing close work.

■ *Cataract:.* Sometimes the lens loses its transparency, causing a condition known as a *cataract,* which results in a progressive, painless loss of vision. It can be caused by trauma, x-ray treatment, a disease such as diabetes, dietary deficiencies, or (most commonly) the degeneration of aging. Recent advances make the surgical removal of the lens a very quick and usually effective treatment. With new glasses, the patient often achieves excellent vision.

OTHER DISORDERS

■ *Night blindness:* This reduction of the ability to see in dim light often results from retinal disease or from a deficiency of Vitamin A. (Fortunately, Vitamin A deficiency is rare in the United States. Taking extra Vitamin A beyond the minimum daily requirement does *not* produce extrasensitive night vision, so enjoy your carrots for their taste and nutritional value, but don't expect them to help you see in the dark.) When a vitamin deficiency is at fault, the administration of vitamins will sometimes reverse the difficulty.

■ *Cornea damage:* If injured, the cornea can lose its transparency and become opaque like the sclera, thus preventing light from coming through. This kind of vision loss can be corrected through the transplant of a cornea from the healthy eye of a person who has just died. Corneal damage can be serious; if the cornea is scratched, it is important to see an opthalmologist (a physician who specializes in treating the eyes).

■ *Glaucoma:* If the canal between the sclera and the iris becomes blocked, too much liquid inside the eye can create an increase in pressure inside the eye. Persons with glaucoma have a smaller field of vision, see a colored halo around artificial lights, and can eventually become completely blind through damage to the optic nerve in the back of the eye. A person usually cannot feel the increase of pressure, but an opthalmologist can generally detect it at a fairly early stage and can control it with drops of medicine. Glaucoma affects some 2 percent of people over age 40, and about 50,000 Americans are blind because of it (Vaughan & Asbury, 1977).

---

small details. They are located mostly in and near the **fovea,** the central region of the retina, which contains no rods at all. Farther from the fovea there are fewer cones.

Rods appear in the peripheral retina, the region responsible for peripheral vision, that is, what we see from the corners of our eyes. Since the rods are more sensitive to light, they allow us to see in dim light. With the rods we see mostly outlines and shapes, all in black and white. This explains why we see little or no color or sharp detail in dim light or out of the corner of the eye. Rod-controlled peripheral vision does have an important role, however, which you can test by trying to see something in dim light, like a faint star. If you look slightly away from your target, you'll see it better than if you gaze right at it. The phenomenon becomes especially dramatic when you move your head back and forth and find that the star becomes clear when it is not at the center of your visual field, but it may disappear when you look straight at it.

The optic disk has no photoreceptors at all; an image projected on the disk therefore hits a blind spot in either eye. We usually don't notice this blind spot, for several reasons. (1) Because an image that hits the blind spot in one eye is hitting another place in the other eye, the other eye compensates. (In the exercise in Figure 3-6, only one eye is open, preventing the closed eye from compensating.) (2) Because we move our eyes very rapidly, we quickly pick up the image. (3) The visual system has a tendency to complete unfinished patterns, as we will discuss later in the chapter. For example, if an image of a straight line is registered on your retina, and part of that image falls on the blind spot, your visual system can "fill in the blank." To find your own blind spots, see Figure 3-6 (page 84).

Fovea *Region of the retina specialized for detail vision.*

FIGURE 3-6 *Finding the blind spot. Close your right eye and line up the lamp with your left eye; then move the book slowly back and forth. You'll see the genie disappear when it is about 1 foot from your eye. Why? Its image falls on your optic disk, which has no photoreceptors.*

Receptive field *Specific areas of the retina to which given ganglion cells respond.*

Visual cortex *Part of the cerebral cortex that is concerned with vision.*

How We See: Beyond the Retina RETINAL GANGLION CELLS AND THEIR RECEPTIVE FIELDS What kinds of messages do our brains receive from 2 million ganglion cell axons? Recordings of the activity of individual ganglion cells show that each cell receives input from a number of receptor cells and therefore "looks at" a particular part of the visual field. The message it sends to the brain apparently lets the brain know which ganglion cells have been stimulated, since there is a relationship between an object's location in space and its location on the retina. The area of the retina to which a given ganglion cell responds is called the cell's **receptive field.** Thus, the ganglion cells encode retinal images. That is, they put information about what we see into sequences of action potentials (explained in Chapter 2). This information gathered by the ganglion cells then travels toward the brain.

VISUAL CORTEX Information from the ganglion cells is transferred to other neurons, which carry it to the **visual cortex,** the part of the cerebral cortex that is concerned with vision.

There appear to be three kinds of neurons in the visual cortex that differ from the ganglion cell in terms of the stimuli to which they respond, according to research conducted primarily by David H. Hubel and Torsten W. Wiesel, who won the Nobel prize for medicine in 1981 for their work in this area (Hubel & Wiesel, 1959, 1979). The three kinds of neurons are called *simple cells, complex cells,* and *hypercomplex cells.* Simple cells respond most vigorously to lines. However, they are quite picky about the kinds of lines they choose to respond to. Even a slight rotation in a line's orientation may produce a drastic decline in the response rate of a particular simple cell. By contrast, complex cells respond most vigorously to moving stimuli, like a vertical line that is moving back and forth (Lennie, 1980). Finally, hypercomplex cells respond most vigorously to moving lines and to angles of a specific size (Hubel, 1982). A typical hypercomplex cell is so selective that it responds vigorously only if a right angle consisting of lines of a certain size moves diagonally downward and toward the left!

The cells in the visual system become increasingly specific as we move from the retina to the brain. The rods are relatively easy to please; they need only a modest amount of light. The cones are slightly more demanding, as we'll see, because they need light waves of a certain wavelength. Neither rods nor cones require a particular pattern of stimulation. Within the brain, the cells become more and more demanding until we reach those very particular hypercomplex cells, which respond only to stimuli forming specific angles, sizes, and movement patterns.

Through the action of these cells, the visual cortex seems to change images into "line drawings" in the brain, which lets the visual system analyze parts of a pattern. This mechanism may be the way we detect the differences between the letters printed on this page. (Later in the chapter we'll see what happens when young animals see lines in only one orientation, either vertical or horizontal.)

Adaptation to Light and Dark When you go to the movies on a sunny afternoon, you first have to adapt to the dark; then, when you come out of the theater, you have

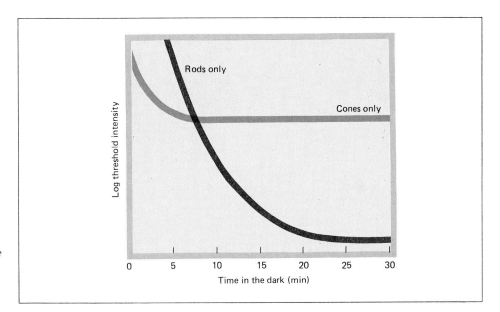

FIGURE 3-7 *Dark adaptation. After a test flash, there is a decrease in visual threshold as a function of time in the dark. The upper curve in this graph shows cone sensitivity; the lower curve shows rod sensitivity. (Source: Cornsweet, 1970.)*

to adapt to the light. When you first walk into the dark auditorium, it takes a while before you can see clearly enough to walk down the aisle without bumping into things or people. Gradually, your eyes adapt and you can see more clearly. Your detection threshold, the level at which you begin to see, drops as a function of the time you spend in a dim light. As the detection threshold drops, sensitivity increases.

Both rods and cones begin to become more sensitive to light as soon as you step into a dark place. For the cones, the adaptation process is over within the first 10 minutes, whereas the rods continue adapting for another 20 minutes. As we said before, rods are much more sensitive than cones in dim light. After 30 minutes, you are seeing as well as you are going to see in the dim light. Figure 3-7 shows the time course of dark adaptation and the different effects on rods and cones. Light adaptation is much faster than dark adaptation, and it takes you only about a minute to readapt to the daylight after you come out of the theater (Matlin, 1983).

Color Vision   The human sense of color is not, of course, limited to the primary colors. If you have normal color vision, you can discriminate hundreds of thousands of colors. Exactly how do our eyes see colors produced by the mixing of lights? Two major theories explain how we see colors, the trichromatic theory and the opponent process theory. We'll look at both of them (in color, of course), and we'll see that they are actually compatible with one another.

First, let's define *color vision*. When we see light waves, our sensations depend on three different qualities—their *wavelength* (see Figure 3-8), their *intensity*, and their *purity*. Color vision is the ability to discriminate by wavelength. If your color vision is normal, you'll be able to tell colors apart regardless of the intensity of each wavelength. Let's see what these terms mean.

The wavelength—the distance between the tops of the waves—is what chiefly determines what we think of as color and what scientists call hue. As you can see by looking again at Figure 3-2, the shortest wavelengths in the rainbow are seen as the color violet, the longest as red.

The *intensity* of light is the amount of energy in the waves. The greater the intensity of the light wave, the brighter it appears—in most cases. There are some exceptions, one of which can be seen in Figure 3-9 (page 86). The center square in each larger square reflects the same amount of light to the eyes. However, the one on the left looks brighter in contrast with its dark background than does the one on the right against its white background.

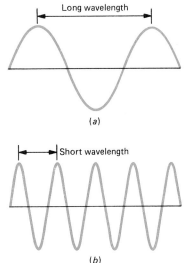

FIGURE 3-8 *Examples of light waves: (a) long wavelength; (b) short wavelength.*

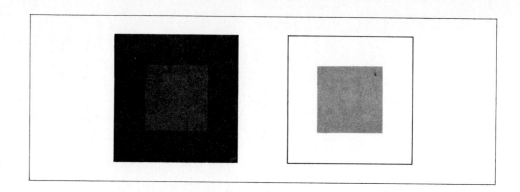

FIGURE 3-9 *Simultaneous brightness contrast. Gray on black looks brighter than gray on white.*

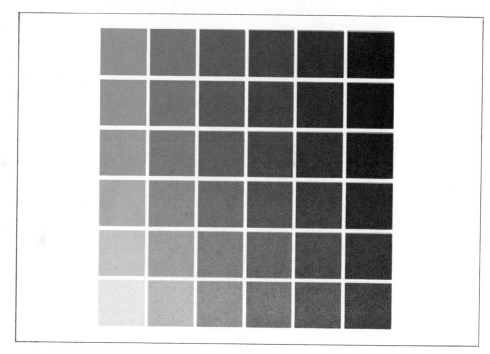

FIGURE 3-10 *Variations of intensity and saturation make these squares of the same color look different. In the far left column the squares are saturated (pure) blue. Moving to the right, the pure blue is increasingly diluted with gray of equal intensity (brightness), so that the squares on the far right are the least saturated blues that can be told apart from pure gray. The intensity of the squares decreases from top to bottom, so that the bottom ones appear less bright.*

The *purity* of a light wave depends on whether what we see is composed primarily of waves of the same length (in which case we'll see a bright, "pure" color) or of mixtures of different wavelengths (in which case a color will be duller). The purest hues are said to be *highly saturated*. You can see the effects of intensity and saturation in Figure 3-10.

White light contains all wavelengths. You don't need all the colors of the spectrum to make white light, however—only one pair of complementary colors, as shown in Figure 3-11*a*. Complementary colors are pairs of hues that, combined with each other, produce gray or white. They're opposite each other on a standard color wheel (see Figure 3-11*b*).

Trichromatic theory Theory that the visual system contains three color mechanisms (for red, green, and blue), and that combinations of the responses of these three mechanisms produce all sensations of color.

TRICHROMATIC THEORY OF COLOR VISION Combinations of the three colors red, green, and blue can produce every other color. The **trichromatic theory** maintains that the visual system contains three color mechanisms (for red, green, and blue light), and that combined responses of these three mechanisms produce all perceived colors. Although this theory was developed in the 1800s, it was not supported experimentally until the 1960s (Brown & Wald, 1964; Marks, Dobelle, & Mac-Nichol, 1964). Experiments showed the existence of three types of cones, each of which has its own kind of visual pigment made up of molecules that absorb the light

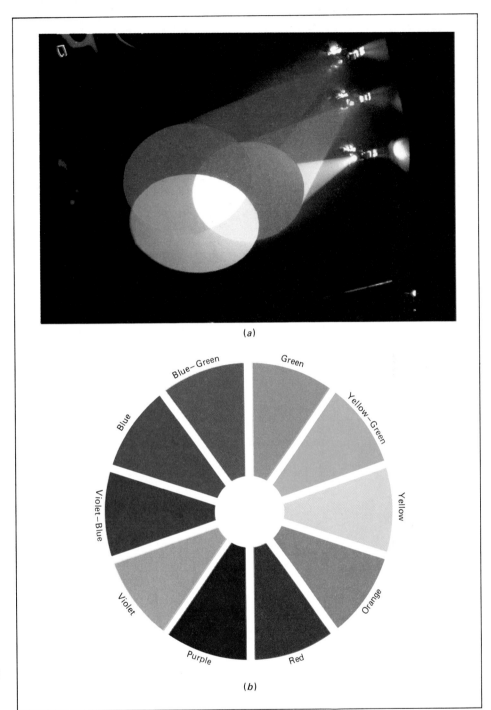

(a)

(b)

FIGURE 3-11 *(a) Additive color mixture. Different mixtures of lights produce different colors. Here we see what happens when green and red lights are combined, and when green, red, and violet lights are combined. (Source: Fritz Goro, Life Magazine, © Time, Inc., 1944.) (b) Color wheel. Any two colors that are opposite each other are complementary colors; that is, combining them produces gray.*

and activate the visual process. Each kind of cone absorbs light at its own wavelength very effectively (peaking at either red, green, or blue), but is less effective at other wavelengths. The combined outputs of each of the three cone systems can signal the presence of any wavelength within the human range of perception.

OPPONENT-PROCESS THEORY OF COLOR VISION   While the trichromatic theory explains the effects of mixing colors of different wavelengths, it cannot explain some other phenomena of color vision. One phenomenon is the afterimage, which *can* be

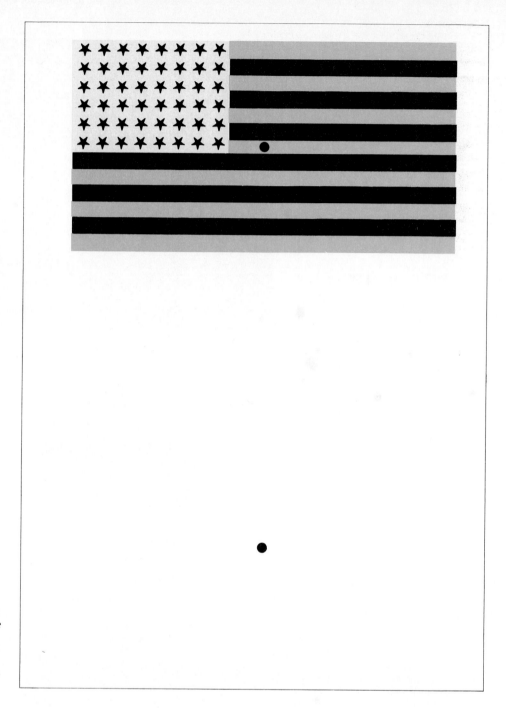

FIGURE 3-12 *Afterimage. To see a "normal" American flag, stare at the dot in the middle of the flag for 30 to 45 seconds. Then look at the dot in the white space below to see an afterimage in the familiar red, white, and blue.*

Opponent-process theory *Theory proposing the existence of opposite processes that occur in the cells of three systems—a blue-yellow system, a red-green system, and an achromatic black-white system.*

explained by the **opponent-process theory,** first proposed by Hering (1920) and then developed by Hurvich and Jameson (1957) and DeValois and DeValois (1975). After you see a very brief flash of a very intense light (like the flashbulb of a camera or the high beams of an oncoming car at night), you see a series of both positive and negative afterimages. In a positive afterimage, the image is the same color as the original light; in a negative afterimage, the complements of the original colors are seen. Negative afterimages also occur after you've been staring at colored objects for a long time. You can see how this works by following the instructions for Figure 3-12.

The opponent-process theory proposes the existence of opposite processes that occur in the cells of three systems—a blue-yellow system and a red-green system (each of which is sensitive to a pair of complementary colors), along with an achromatic (no hue) system of black and white, which codes intensity. We see reds, for example, because red wavelengths excite some of the cells in the red-green system while inhibiting ''opposite'' cells (those excited by green wavelengths). The blue-yellow system works similarly. The black-white system essentially responds to different levels of brightness (Hurvich, 1981). Let's see how this system explains colored afterimages.

When you stare at the yellow field of the flag, you are fatiguing the yellow system, while the blue system is inhibited, since the cells in that system do not respond to yellow wavelengths. The same thing happens with the green stripes and the black stripes and stars. As a result, after you look away from this image at plain white paper, the complementary systems will take over for the various fatigued systems, and you'll see the colors that are opposite those you originally stared at.

FIGURE 3-13 *Test of color deficiency. What numbers, if any, do you see in these circles? People with normal color vision see the number 32. If you don't see the number, you have a red-green color deficiency. (Source: Dvorine Color Vision Test.)*

The trichromatic and opponent-process theories are compatible, because they may operate at different levels in the visual system. The trichromatic system explains functioning at the receptor level: since we have three kinds of color receptors, we can see three different colors and their variations. The opponent-process theory applies to higher levels of the visual system, such as the ganglion cells and beyond. Combining the two theories suggests that the three cone mechanisms of trichromatic theory are the basis for the action of the opponent processes. The combination of both theories helps to explain the fairly common defect known by laypeople as *color blindness* and by scientists as *color deficiency*.

COLOR DEFICIENCY Some people cannot see all the differences in color. Most of those who have a problem in distinguishing colors don't see reds and greens, some don't see blues and yellows, and a very few see things only in shades of gray, black, and white (see Figure 3-13). More males than females are color-deficient; the defect is more common among some racial groups than others (see Table 3-2); and it is hereditary, usually passed on by a recessive gene carried by the mother (Pokorny & Smith, 1986).

It is possible that color-deficient people are missing one or more cone systems. The missing cone system leaves the opponent-process system without input, and the person is therefore unable to distinguish between the two opposing colors. Thus, someone missing the red cones cannot tell the difference between red or green and sees them in shades of gray. People who see no colors at all may be missing all the visual pigments in the cones, or possibly all the cones, so that they see only with their rods.

TABLE 3-2 INCIDENCE OF COLOR DEFICIENCY (PERCENTAGE OF POPULATION)

Racial Groups	Males	Females
Caucasians (Northern Europeans, Americans, and Australians)	8.08	0.74
Asians (Japanese, Chinese, and others)	4.90	0.64
American blacks, Native Americans, Mexicans, and Inuit (Eskimos)	3.12	0.69

Source: Adapted from Hurvich, 1981, p. 267.

Hearing

A great deal of what we know about the world comes to us through our ears. Probably the commonest use to which we put our sense of hearing is in communicating with other people (Evans, 1982). In today's world, most of our contact with those we are close to, either personally or professionally, is either face-to-face or over the telephone. It could hardly be an accident that our keenest hearing is in the frequency range of the human voice.

What We Hear   Do you remember the western movies that showed Indians putting an ear to the ground to listen for the wagon train, or to the railroad track to listen for the "iron horse"? The Indians were showing awareness of the fact that sound can travel in any medium—through air, water, metal, or the ground. Like light, the sound that we hear comes to us in the form of waves.

How do sound waves travel? Sound waves are actually movements of the molecules in the medium. The motion of the sound source alternately pushes molecules together (compressing the air, making it denser) and pulls them apart (rarefying the air, making it thinner), causing vibrations in the form of sound waves. When sound is generated by a loudspeaker, the air pressure goes up during compression and drops during rarefaction. Thus sound waves are actually changes in air pressure that move at about 1100 feet (340 meters) per second. As you can see in Figure 3-14, the pattern of sound waves resembles the pattern of the ripples that spread out after you've tossed a pebble into a pond. A similar process is taking place in both situations—waves of energy are passing through a medium, temporarily displacing molecules. Sound needs a medium: in a vacuum, a ringing bell would be as silent as a scream in a nightmare.

We differentiate among sounds according to three basic measures—loudness (a function of the amplitude, or intensity, of sound waves), pitch (a function of frequency), and timbre (a function of the complexity of the waveform).

LOUDNESS   The loudness, or intensity, of sound is measured in **_decibels (dB),_** which are a measure of the amplitude (height) of sound waves: the higher the decibel level, the louder the sound. Figure 3-15 shows the decibel levels of a number of common sounds. Regular exposure to 80 decibels or more, and even a single exposure to much higher levels, can cause permanent hearing loss.

PITCH   Sound waves are repetitive changes in air pressure. The number of cycles (complete waves) that occur per second are measured in hertz (Hz). Human beings normally hear sounds in the range between 20 and 20,000 Hz. The higher the frequency, the higher the pitch of a sound and the shriller it will seem. Most human speech occurs in the range between 100 to 3500 Hz.

Human ears are most sensitive to the high end of this range (from about 3000), the range of high-pitched human screams. (It's tempting to speculate that the scream then evolved accordingly, as a survival mechanism that would be sure to be heard and attended to.) Dogs can hear up to about 80,000 Hz, which explains why you can buy a special dog whistle to call your pet without disturbing your neighbors. Bats and dolphins have even more impressive hearing ranges—beyond 100,000 Hz.

TIMBRE   The quality that makes your voice sound different from someone else's, even though both of you may have the same pitch and loudness, is timbre. This is related to the complexity of the waveform. Figure 3-16 shows several waveforms, of differing complexity, produced by different musical instruments. These variations are one of the reasons the same notes sound different depending on whether they are played on a violin or a flute.

Now let's look at the way the human ear hears and discriminates so many different sounds.

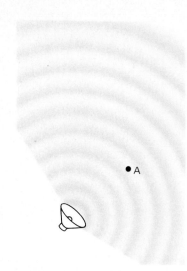

FIGURE 3-14 *Sound from a loudspeaker creates cyclic movement of molecules in the air, as they are pushed together (compressed) and then pulled apart (rarefied).*

Decibels (dB)   Measurement of the loudness or intensity (amplitude) of sound waves.

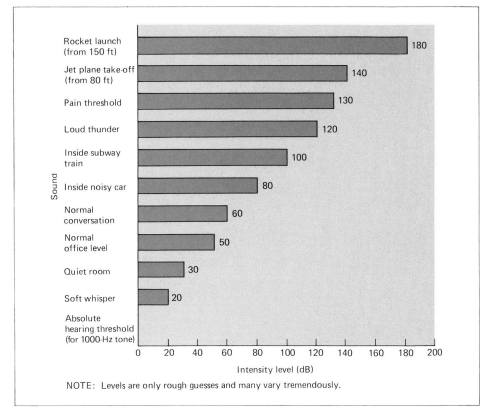

FIGURE 3-15 *Sound levels in decibels (dB) for some common sounds. (Source: Levine & Shefner, 1981.)*

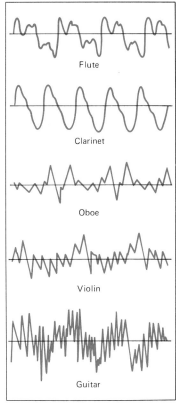

FIGURE 3-16 *Sound waves of several kinds of complex tones produced by musical instruments. (Source: Matlin, 1983.)*

How We Hear: The Anatomy of the Ear What we generally think of as the ear—that flap on the side of the head that serves variously as a hat rack or a jewelry stand—is only one small part of a complex structure, as you can see in Figure 3-17 (page 92).

Let's follow a sound wave through the center of that skin-covered cartilage known as the outer ear (the **pinna**) and see where it takes us. The outer ear funnels sound waves into the middle ear through the tubelike ear canal (**auditory meatus**). This is lubricated by wax glands and protected by its lining of tiny hairs that keep out dirt and bugs. At the end of the ear canal is the eardrum (**tympanic membrane**), which vibrates in response to sound waves entering the ear. As the eardrum vibrates, it nudges a tiny bone, the "hammer" (**malleus**), which moves the "anvil" (**incus**), which moves the "stirrup" (**stapes**). (These three bones in the ear, named for their shapes, are the three smallest bones in the body.) The stirrup presses against a small membrane-covered region called the *oval window*, which leads to the inner ear.

The inner ear, a coiled, snail-shaped structure filled with fluid, is called the **cochlea.** When the stirrup presses against the oval window, it transmits sound energy to this fluid, creating pressure waves in it that cause the **basilar membrane** inside the cochlea to move at the same rate as the vibrations of the sound wave itself. Lying on the basilar membrane are rows of hair cells, with tiny hairs (cilia) protruding from them. When the basilar membrane moves up and down, the cilia are bent, causing currents in the hair cells. These currents cause the dendrites of auditory nerve fibers to fire, sending impulses to the brain (Scharf & Buus, 1986). These impulses represent the sound, and the brain processes this information to let us know what we are hearing.

Thus, the hair cells are the receptors for hearing (corresponding to the rods and cones for vision), and the auditory nerve fibers transmit sensory information to the brain (corresponding to the ganglion cells in vision).

Pinna *Outer ear.*

Auditory meatus *Ear canal.*

Tympanic membrane *Eardrum; a tissue that vibrates as sound waves enter the ear.*

Malleus *Tiny bone in the ear; the "hammer."*

Incus *Tiny bone in the ear; the "anvil."*

Stapes *Tiny bone in the ear; the "stirrup."*

Cochlea *Coiled, fluid-filled structure; the inner ear.*

Basilar membrane *Tissue inside the cochlea that moves at the same rate as the vibrations of the sound wave.*

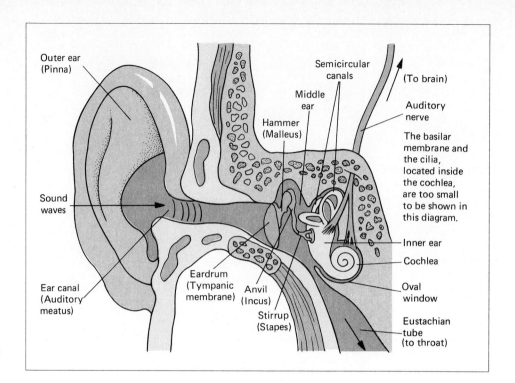

Labels in figure:
Outer ear (Pinna)
Semicircular canals
Middle ear
(To brain)
Auditory nerve
Hammer (Malleus)
The basilar membrane and the cilia, located inside the cochlea, are too small to be shown in this diagram.
Sound waves
Inner ear
Cochlea
Oval window
Eardrum (Tympanic membrane)
Anvil (Incus)
Ear canal (Auditory meatus)
Stirrup (Stapes)
Eustachian tube (to throat)

FIGURE 3-17   *Cross section of the ear.*

Place theory   *Theory that the ability to hear a sound of a certain pitch depends on the particular spot on the basilar membrane which is stimulated.*

Frequency theory   *Theory that the frequency by which the basilar membrane is stimulated determines what pitch is heard.*

HOW WE HEAR SOUNDS OF DIFFERENT FREQUENCIES: PLACE VERSUS FREQUENCY THEORY   How do we hear the different notes in a bar of music? How do our ears tell the difference between the high-pitched piping of a flute and the deeper tones of a bassoon? Two explanations for this ability are the place theory and the frequency theory.

According to **place theory,** we hear a certain pitch depending on the particular spot on the basilar membrane that it stimulates. According to **frequency theory,** it is the frequency with which the basilar membrane is stimulated that determines what pitch we hear. A variation of frequency theory is the *volley principle,* which suggests that groups of nerve fibers form "squads," and that individual neurons take turns firing in volleys.

A number of locations on the basilar membrane have been identified as being sensitive to high and middle-range frequencies, but none has been found to be sensitive to very low frequencies (von Békésy, in Wever, 1960). Thus, the place theory cannot explain our hearing of very low pitches. Frequency theory, on the other hand, cannot explain our hearing of sounds above 4000 Hz, since neurons cannot fire fast enough to handle more than 1000 impulses per second, even in volleys (Matlin, 1983). Place theory, then, seems to explain how we hear high-pitched sounds (above 3000 Hz, as in the warning tone of a civil-defense alert), and frequency theory explains our hearing of very low-pitched sounds (below about 100 Hz, like the hum in a bad stereo system). It's likely that both principles may operate in the middle range of sounds—between 500 and 4,000 Hz—which may explain why we hear sounds in this range particularly well. Understanding how we hear in this range may help us to help the hearing-impaired hear what most of us consider the most important sounds in the world, other people's voices.

HOW WE CAN TELL WHERE SOUND COMES FROM   From birth infants will turn their heads to a sound coming from one side, showing that they can locate sounds in space (Castillo & Butterworth, 1981). This ability obviously has important survival value. How can we tell where a sound is coming from? The two major ways both rest on the fact that our ears are on different sides of our head.

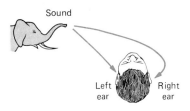

If an elephant trumpets right in front of you, the sound waves will travel the same distance to reach each ear, and you will perceive the sound as coming from straight ahead. But if the elephant is off to your left, the sound will travel a shorter distance to your left ear than to your right. It will therefore be heard in that ear a fraction of a second sooner, and you will perceive the sound as coming from your left. Another clue to sound is the difference in intensity between the sounds reaching the two ears. If this elephant trumpets off to your left, your right ear is in a "sound shadow" created by your head, so the sound is louder in your left ear (see Figure 3-18). Time of arrival is more important in locating low-frequency sounds, while intensity differences are more important for high-frequency sounds.

FIGURE 3-18 *Sound traveling toward the left and right ears.*

Suppose you have no hearing in one ear. This does not mean you can't locate sounds in space at all, because there are also monaural cues. Since experiments have shown that covering the nooks and crannies of the outer ear with putty impairs localization, we know that these parts of the ear help us locate sounds. These cues, however, work well only for complex acoustic signals like human speech, again showing how well adapted we are for getting along with others of our species.

Hearing Loss   When the Swedish navy wanted to track a suspected submarine in local waters, it had trouble finding sailors whose hearing was keen enough to use the sensitive listening devices. One navy captain ascribed the problem to permanent damage to the ears of young people caused by years of listening to loud rock music. Similar hearing loss has been seen among high school and college students who listen to a lot of loud music, among students who are "addicted" to headphones, and among people who work in noisy environments (Brody, 1982). People with this kind of hearing loss are often afflicted with **tinnitus,** a continuous ringing or hissing sound. In this kind of loss, called **sensorineural hearing loss,** either the hair cells of the cochlea or the auditory nerve has been damaged. This is similar to the hearing loss which commonly comes with advancing age, caused by the normal tendency of hair cells to die off in later life. This kind of loss, called **presbycusis** (from the Greek words for *old age* and *hearing*), is particularly marked for high-frequency sound and in situations with a lot of background noise (see Figure 3-19). It is difficult for hearing aids to handle these hearing disorders.

Tinnitus   *Continuous ringing or hissing sound in the ears.*

Sensorineural hearing loss   *Hearing loss due to damage to the hair cells of the cochlea or to damage to the auditory nerve.*

Presbycusis   *Hearing loss for high-frequency sounds.*

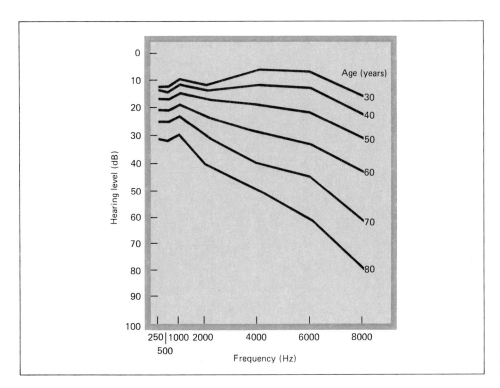

FIGURE 3-19 *Hearing loss as a function of frequency and normal aging. Hearing losses increase with age, especially for high-frequency sounds. (Source: Witbourne, 1985.)*

Sensorineural hearing loss can be prevented by avoiding excessive noise. Under federal law, employers whose workers are regularly exposed to noise levels of 85 decibels or more are required to provide some kind of hearing conservation program (Brody, 1982). You can help yourself by keeping the volume in your head-sets low and by not sitting too close to the speakers when you attend rock concerts.

The other major type of hearing loss is **conductive deafness,** caused by a ruptured eardrum or a defect in the bones of the middle ear, in which sound waves are prevented from reaching the cochlea. This kind of impairment is easier to treat, either by surgery or a hearing aid that picks up sound from a bone behind the ear and transmits it directly to the cochlea, bypassing the middle ear.

Conductive deafness *Hearing loss, caused by a ruptured eardrum or a defect in the bones of the middle ear, which prevents sound waves from reaching the cochlea.*

The Skin Senses

What is generally known as the "sense of touch" really involves several different senses, since the skin contains receptors for pressure, pain, heat, and cold. As long ago as the early 1800s, scientists knew that the skin has a variety of receptors to feel different sensations, and that the different kinds of receptors respond to different kinds of stimuli. These receptors are made up of nerve fibers. They are so specific that when the individual fibers are stimulated, they will produce the sensation for which they are programmed, no matter what the stimulus. The experiments of von Frey, for example, suggested that when a "cold spot" is stimulated, you will feel a sensation of cold even if the stimulus itself is hot. Similarly, a cold stimulus applied to a "warm spot" will produce a sensation of warmth. However, researchers have not been able to find a consistent relationship between such "spots" on the skin and the types of receptors directly below them.

Pressure We are much more sensitive to touch (pressure) in some parts of our bodies than in others, as shown in Figure 3-20. According to laboratory tests, in

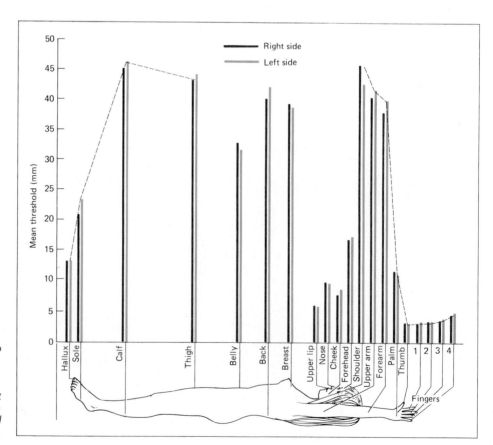

FIGURE 3-20 *Two-point discrimination thresholds. Mean threshold values represent the minimum distance between two points that is required for a person to sense two probes rather than one. The closer this distance is, the more sensitive the body is. The shortest lines in the figure show that the most sensitive parts of the body are thumb and fingers, lips, cheeks, big toe, and forehead. (Source: Weinstein, 1968.)*

which a hair-like fiber is touched to the skin, our most sensitive parts are our face (especially our lips) and our hands (especially our fingers). The relative sensitivity of most body regions has been demonstrated scientifically by the two-point-discrimination threshold—the ability of a person to tell whether a single probe or two probes very close together are being applied to the skin. There is a close relationship between the ability to tell whether one or two probes are being applied to a particular part of the body and the size of the area in the cortex that represents this part of the body. There is also a close relationship between this threshold and the number of nerve fibers for each body region. The most sensitive areas have a more skin receptors than the less sensitive area.

Pain   The sense of pain serves a valuable function by signaling danger—letting us know, for example, when tissue is being destroyed by fire, injury, or illness—so that we can avoid harm. Once we are injured, however, pain can be physically and emotionally draining, and so a great deal of research has explored the mechanisms that give rise to physical pain with the aim of finding ways to reduce or eliminate it.

So far, we're not sure whether a specific pathway for pain exists in the brain, but it does seem likely. Certain sensory nerve fibers respond only to pain, while others seem to signal pain along with other sensations. If pain pathways do exist, how does the brain control them? Dramatic light has been shed on this question by research over the past 10 years, which has demonstrated that the brain itself produces opiatelike substances that reduce or eliminate pain (Elton, Stanley, & Burrows, 1983; Rivlin & Gravelle, 1984; Wall, 1978). These substances, called **endorphins,** are not neurotransmitters but neuromodulators which adapt synaptic connections in certain ways. The endorphins seem to fill in the body's pain receptors in such a way that pain signals cannot get from the spinal cord to the brain (Fields & Basbaum, 1978). An endorphin called **enkephalin** is a very powerful pain killer when injected into animals or human beings.

Various situations seem to activate the brain's own mechanism against pain. One is physical exertion: marathon runners, for example, often do not feel the excruciating pain caused by pounding the pavement for more than 26 miles until after they have completed the race (Carr et al., 1981; Zaslow, 1987). Fear and stress are also common inhibitors of pain. A common phenomenon of war is the injured soldier who does not feel the pain from a bullet wound until after the battle is over. This

Endorphins   *Opiatelike substances released by the brain which prevent pain signals from reaching the brain.*

Enkephalin   *Endorphin that is a powerful painkiller.*

(Lewis Portnoy/Stock Market)

These marathon runners probably won't feel the punishment they're giving their bodies until after they have completed the race, because of the way the brain inhibits pain in certain situations.

phenomenon is seen in other stressful situations, like the often reported instances of parents' exposing themselves to what would ordinarily be painful ordeals to save their children from danger (Bolles & Fanselow, 1982).

Acupuncture, placebos, hypnosis, and prepared childbirth methods are all commonly known to block pain. The big question is how they do it. *Acupuncture* is an ancient Chinese technique in which thin needles are inserted into the body at a number of carefully charted locations. The technique is widely used in China today, allowing some 90 percent of patients undergoing surgery to forgo any other pain relief. *Placebos* are substances that contain no active ingredients but that are presented as if they did. *Hypnosis* is a state of heightened suggestibility in which a person is susceptible to the influence of the practitioner who induced the state. Finally, prepared childbirth methods, such as the Lamaze method, relieve pain during childbirth by teaching women about the process of childbirth and by teaching them how to substitute useful responses to labor contractions (like special kinds of breathing) for counterproductive ones (like fear and tension) (Matlin, 1983).

These methods probably work for a variety of reasons. Acupuncture may work for the same reason some doctors pinch a patient's right arm before giving a shot in the left arm—when one area is stimulated, the pain in another is sometimes lessened. Placebos may alter our perception of pain; we may still feel something, but we may be less likely to consider the sensation painful. Hypnosis may work similarly, enabling the subject to prevent a sensation from reaching the level of awareness at which it is perceived as painful. And the success of prepared childbirth methods may rest partly on a kind of conditioning brought about by prenatal training and practice (conditioning as a type of learning is explained in Chapter 5), and partly on their ability to turn the woman's attention toward breathing and other body functions and away from the pain of the contractions.

The drug naloxone reverses the action of the natural pain reliever enkephalin, apparently by blocking the receptors in the brain for opiates. Researchers sometimes administer naloxone to see whether the brain's own opiate system is inhibiting pain. If the subject feels pain after receiving the naloxone, the conclusion is that the opiate system in the brain is probably what is relieving pain in a given situation. Using this approach, researchers have determined that acupuncture and placebos seem to activate the brain's own opiates, but that hypnosis does not (Mayer, Price, & Rafii, 1977; Pomeranz & Chiu, 1976). Obviously, research along these lines has valuable implications for the well-being of the human race.

The Chemical Senses

While people often think of taste and smell as minor senses, they play a major role in our lives. One researcher calls them the "gateways or monitors of all the nutrients—all the air and all the life-sustaining chemicals—that come into the body" (Doty, quoted in P. Morgan, 1984, p. 37). They can save our lives by enabling us to detect dangerous gases or poisons, and they certainly enhance our lives by allowing us to enjoy aromas and flavors. Let's take a look at these valuable *chemical senses,* so called because they respond to the chemical substances in various stimuli, to see what they do for us and how they do it.

Smell (Olfaction)   Most of us take our sense of smell for granted, and it has been historically undervalued because it holds a "lowly" place on the evolutionary ladder, being most highly developed among lesser species. But it plays an extremely important role in human lives right from birth. As infants we recognize our mothers' scents, and throughout life we continue to respond to the smells of the important people in our lives; we associate events in our lives with the odors that were present at the time; we choose our foods, our environments, and some say even our romantic partners on the basis of smell.

Smell is a powerful means of communications among human beings (Filsinger & Fabes, 1985). Babies turn their heads more often to breast pads that their mothers

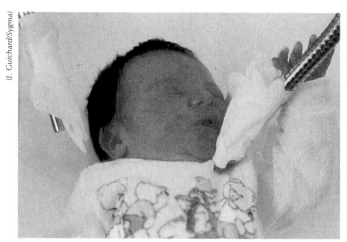
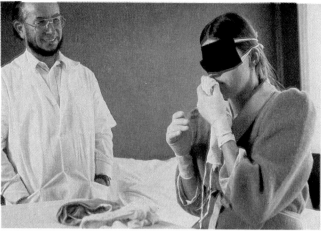

Three-day-old infants, like this one, show more peaceful behavior when they smell pieces of gauze that were worn by their mothers than when they smell cloth worn by other women. And blindfolded mothers can tell the smell of T-shirts worn by their own babies from shirts worn by other babies.

had worn than toward those worn by other nursing mothers at a very early age—6 days according to one study (Macfarlane, 1975), 6 weeks according to another (M. Russell, 1976). Sisters and brothers can identify T-shirts worn by their siblings versus those worn by strangers (Porter & Moore, 1981). Another odor you're apt to recognize is your own. If presented with a T-shirt you wore along with T-shirts worn by a man and a woman you don't know, you're likely not only to sniff out your own scent, but you will also probably be able to tell which of the other shirts was worn by a man and which by a woman (M. Russell, 1976).

Furthermore, your sense of smell is important in your day-to-day life. You sniff milk in the carton; if it's sour, you throw it out. If your nose is accosted by something that makes it wrinkle—and you realize that your new puppy isn't housebroken yet—you know you have some cleaning up to do. The fragrance of newly mown grass wafts into your nostrils—and after you rejoice in the coming of spring, you remind yourself it's time to cut your own lawn.

How does this vital sense function? Odors come into the body as molecules in the air, either through the nostrils or from the back of the mouth, into the smell receptors in the nasal cavity. The nasal cavity is lined with the **olfactory mucosa,** a mucous membrane that contains the smell receptors, which have hairlike projections (cilia) that catch the molecules and send an electrical signal through nerve fibers to the olfactory bulb. It is here that the signals sent by the receptors are processed and then sent to the brain.

Do you remember the last time you had a cold and couldn't smell anything? Even though the taste buds in your tongue were not affected, you couldn't really taste what you were eating. Your taste sensations themselves were not really impaired, but what most of us call "taste" is actually flavor, a global sensation that also includes the sense of smell. Figure 3-21 (page 98) graphically depicts the close relationship between the senses of taste and smell. It shows the olfactory pathways, through which some molecules of whatever we eat or drink make their way from the mouth up into the nasal passages to the olfactory receptors. It was actually your impaired sense of smell, then, that resulted in your food's "tasting" dull.

It is hard to study the sense of smell for several reasons. For one thing, it is difficult to control odors and to determine when and in what degree of concentration an odor reaches a receptor cell. Most of the molecules that enter the nose are absorbed by the lining of the nose before reaching the receptors. Further, it is hard to classify odors. They are so complex that we don't know how to identify the fundamental physical variables that produce a given smell, as we can do for visual and auditory wavelengths that produce a given sight or sound. Researchers have come up with several theories, but so far none of them satisfactorily explains our olfactory mechanisms.

One branch of this research has sought to determine how many different odors

Olfactory mucosa *Mucous membrane that contains the smell receptors.*

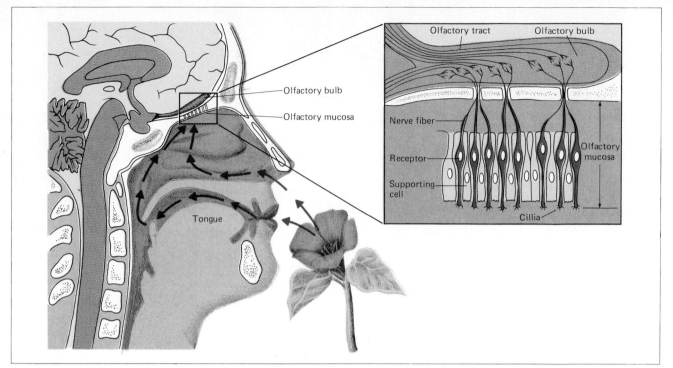

FIGURE 3-21 *Molecules of substances that we smell, eat, or drink travel from the mouth to the nasal passages to the olfactory receptors in the brain. (Source: Adapted from Amoore, Johnston, & Rubin, 1964.)*

people can identify. Although the average person can name only a few, some scientists believe that an untrained person can distinguish at least 200 and that an expert can distinguish as many as 10,000 (Engen, 1982). Recent research shows that it is harder for people to think of names of smells than to tell the difference among them. When people are given the right names, they can name correctly most of 80 different odors (Cain, 1981).

This shows the importance of cognition in sensation. In fact, some researchers have suggested that older people have trouble identifying the flavors of foods not only because they cannot identify the smells connected to the tastes, but, even more important, because they have difficulty remembering the names of tastes and smells (Schiffman & Murphy, cited in Cain, 1981, p. 55).

Taste (Gustation)   No matter what makes your mouth water—a hot fudge sundae, a double cheeseburger, the finest imported caviar, or a juicy red slice of watermelon— it's obvious that your sense of taste adds a great deal to your enjoyment of life. Your sense of taste also has survival value—at least in the wild, since most poisonous substances in nature have a bitter or otherwise unpleasant taste. In any case, with the vast smorgasbord of different flavors that we can tell apart, it's surprising that our receptors for taste distinguish among only four different sensations: sweet, salty, sour, and bitter. Human beings describe virtually all tastes in terms of combinations of these four qualities (McBurney & Gent, 1979).

Often when we talk about taste, we really mean flavor. This sense of the food we eat is heavily dependent on odor. The delicate fragrance of cinnamon or the assertive aroma of steak not only makes our mouths water ahead of time; it influences our experience of the food as we eat it. Flavor is also influenced by other aspects of the food that we experience through other senses, such as texture (is it chewy or creamy?) and temperature (foods taste different depending on whether they're steaming hot, ice-cold, or lukewarm).

Papillae   Taste buds on the tongue.

Our receptors for taste are located on the tongue, along the edges of the taste buds, the little bumps called *papillae*. These taste buds are distributed in different places on the tongue, as shown in Figure 3-22. The tip of the tongue is most sensitive

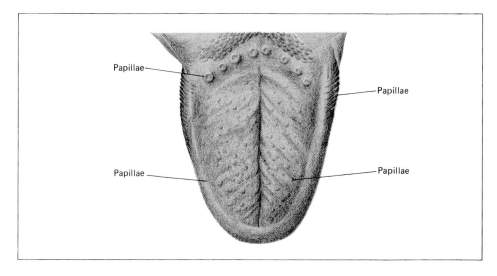

FIGURE 3-22 *The tongue, showing different types of papillae.*

to sweet, salty, and bitter tastes, the sides to sour (McBurney & Collings, 1984). These regional differences only describe the zones of greatest sensitivity. All areas of the tongue that have papillae (that is, all areas except the middle of the tongue) can sense all taste qualities.

As you can see from Figure 3-23, nerve fibers convey information from the cells within the taste bud to the brain. These individual nerve fibers are also differentially sensitive to the four basic tastes. While they respond to all four taste stimuli, they respond best to only one (M. Frank, 1973).

Have you ever wondered why some people have a "sweet tooth" while others never eat dessert, or why some people love hot, spicy foods while others prefer bland foods, or why some people salt their food even before they taste it while others want little or no salt? Some of these food preferences are undoubtedly the result of

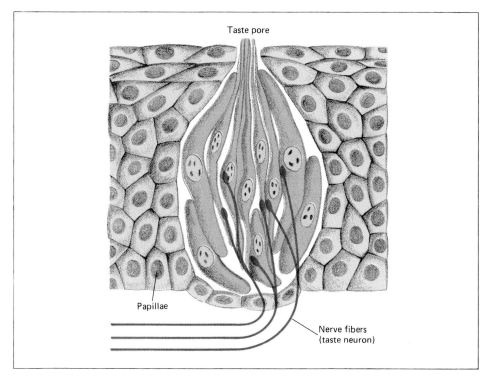

FIGURE 3-23 *A taste bud is made up of taste cells and supporting cells.*

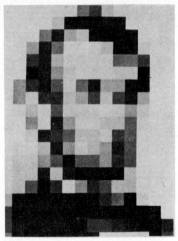

FIGURE 3-24 *If you look at this computer-processed portrait, your sense of vision will tell you that you're looking at an arrangement of geometric forms of varying shapes, sizes, and intensities. If you squint or move away from the picture, you'll see something else: the face of the sixteenth president of the United States will emerge from this pattern. Squinting, moving away, or defocusing lets us perceive an overall pattern that is not visible when we concentrate too closely on the geometric forms. Comic-book illustrations, made up of many tiny dots, illustrate the same concept.*

Gestalt psychology *School of psychology that emphasizes the pattern formed by the elements in the mind rather than the individual elements themselves.*

Gestalt laws *Principles, described by gestalt psychologists, that govern the ways by which the perceptual system organizes sensory information.*

learning, but others may well be due to hereditary differences in our taste buds. This is the conclusion of some interesting studies done with a bitter-tasting substance, phenylthiocarbamide (PTC). Laboratory experiments have shown that about one person in three cannot taste this chemical, apparently because of the absence of a particular "bitter" taste bud. The same people who cannot taste PTC usually do not object to the bitter taste of caffeine and are likely to use less sugar in their coffee (Bartoshuk, 1974).

Taste cells die and are replaced by new cells about every ten days, but as we age fewer new cells are generated. Thus, the older we are, the fewer taste buds we have. This may be one reason that many old people find that food doesn't taste as good as it once did.

PERCEPTION: HOW THE BRAIN ORGANIZES SENSORY INFORMATION

There's an old story about two people out for a walk in a little town that boasts a church known the world over for its tower bells. One turns to the other to say, "Aren't those bells magnificent?" and the other answers, "I can't hear you because of all that noise." The same sort of exchange goes on in any household that contains a lover of symphonies and a devotee of rock music. The same sounds may be perceived very differently by different people.

Perception is more than what we see, hear, feel, taste, or smell. It is also the meaning that we ascribe to these sensations. We arrive at this meaning by the way our brain organizes all of the information we take in through our senses. Reading this book, for example, you see more than an assortment of little black marks on a white page. You see letters that make up words. Because you have learned how to read, your brain organizes these little marks as symbols that represent meaning. The same process takes place in many other areas of life as we interpret sensory information.

Gestalt Laws of Perceptual Organization

While psychologists have established the individual elements, or basic units of visual and auditory patterns, what we see and hear is much more than the sum of those units. You can see this in Figure 3-24, where apparently meaningless shapes produce an instantly recognizable picture. We routinely organize lines and shadings into scenes and individual sounds into speech and music. Thus, these bits of information become meaningful patterns.

As we noted in Chapter 1, **gestalt psychology** emphasizes the significance of overall patterns. (The German word *Gestalt* means *form* or *pattern*.*) This approach is particularly applicable in perception. Look at the picture in Figure 3-25, for example. We see more than a random selection of lines. We even see more than the front half of a lion, a tree, and the back half of a lion. We immediately know that the front and back of the lion are parts of the same animal, even though the picture itself does not show this continuity. We know because we impose a structure on what we see. Gestalt psychologists proposed that certain laws of perceptual organization encourage an overall pattern to emerge from what would otherwise be a random assortment of isolated lines.

This picture illustrates one of the **gestalt laws** that govern the ways in which the perceptual system organizes sensory information. The lion image demonstrates the law of continuity, by which our minds continue in the direction suggested by the stimulus. Other basic rules described by gestalt psychologists include the law of proximity (we group elements that are near each other), the law of similarity (we group elements that are like each other), and the law of closure (we complete unfinished patterns). These are illustrated in Figure 3-26.

*In German, all nouns are capitalized, but *gestalt* is usually not capitalized in English.

FIGURE 3-25 *We see more than a random selection of lines—more than a front half of a lion, a tree, and the back half of a lion. By the rule of continuity we impose our own structure on this drawing so that we see a lion behind a tree.*

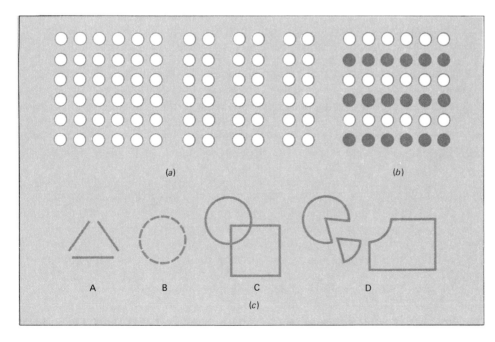

(a)

(b)

A   B   C   D

(c)

FIGURE 3-26 (*a*) *Rule of proximity. The pattern on the left can be seen as either rows (across) or columns (down) because the circles are spaced equally in both directions. The pattern on the right appears as pairs of columns because the horizontal spacing has been altered. (*b*) Rule of similarity. We now see the circles in rows because we group together elements that look alike (the colored circles and plain ones). (*c*) Law of closure. We fill in the gaps. Thus we see A and B as a triangle and a circle, respectively; and we see C as a circle and a square, not as the assortment of incomplete figures shown in D.*

FIGURE 3-27 *Pattern in which figure and ground may exchange roles. It may be seen either as two silhouetted faces or as a white vase.*

The gestaltists have pointed out another common way of organizing sensation—dividing it into a *figure* (the object we focus our attention on) and a *ground* (the background for the focal object). When figure-ground relations are ambiguous, our perceptions of figure and ground shift back and forth. You can see this in Figure 3-27. When you look at it one way you see a white vase on a dark background; viewed another way, it becomes two dark profiles facing each other over a white background. This figure dramatically demonstrates the active nature of our perceptual system, since you can choose between two different perceptions from the same stimulus. You can't, however, see them both at the same time.

The figure-ground effect applies to other sensations, too, involving touch, taste, smell, and hearing. In a bar of music we may hear the melody as the figure, with the chords as the ground, until a change in volume or rhythm brings a chord to the center of our consciousness. Or, sitting in a classroom, we can attend either to the lecture or a conversation behind us. While extremely quick reversals of figure and ground can occur, we cannot simultaneously attend to both. So when we're studying, listening to music, and watching television, we may think we're paying attention to all three at once, but what is actually happening is that we're rapidly bringing each stimulus into consciousness in turn.

Bottom-Up and Top-Down Processing in Perception

Bottom-up processing *Explanation of pattern recognition that emphasizes the contribution of the stimulus.*

Top-down processing *Explanation of pattern recognition that emphasizes the observer's expectations and knowledge.*

You're on your way to psychology class when you hear strains of music issuing from an open window and recognize one of your favorite melodies. As you stand listening, you spot your psychology professor heading toward class. Since you don't want to be late again, you move on your way. Now—how did you recognize the music and how did you recognize your professor?

There are two ways of looking at the way we recognize patterns: bottom-up and top-down processing. **Bottom-up processing** (also known as *data-driven processing*) emphasizes the importance of the stimulus. In this explanation, information (data) comes in from our sensory receptors, and we recognize simple, low-level features (such as individual musical notes of the sounds of particular instruments, or individual facial features—a nose with a bump in the middle, a wide mouth, a jutting chin). We then combine these features in a way that lets us recognize more complex patterns (a melody, a familiar face). Before you read further, look at the line fragments in Figure 3-28 and see whether you can identify them as part of a larger pattern. We'll come back to them in a little while.

FIGURE 3-28 *Do these line fragments represent anything to you?*

Top-down processing (also called *conceptually-driven processing*) emphasizes the importance of the observer's expectations and knowledge. This explanation rests on the idea that we have concepts about the way the world is organized and that our expectations are based on those concepts. Thus, we begin by recognizing a whole, complex pattern, and we then break it down into its simpler elements. First we hear the melody, and then we identify the notes; first we recognize the face, and then we look at the nose, mouth, and chin.

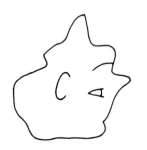

FIGURE 3-29 *Hold the page upside down: Can you identify the line fragments you saw in Figure 3-28? They're now easily recognized in context. (Source: Palmer, 1975.)*

In recognizing your professor, for example, the expectations you had formed from knowledge and memory (that is, experience) helped you. You saw a person near the psychology building at a time when you expected him to be there, dressed in his favorite green tweed jacket. If you had seen him on a tennis court in another town at another time, you might have had trouble recognizing him at first because you had no expectation of seeing him in that context ("The face is familiar, but . . . ").

When we try to explain perception by either of these processes, we come up with a paradox. We can't recognize a face until we recognize that one nose, mouth, or chin is different from another and until we learn to tell different ones apart. On the other hand, we can't recognize features until we know they're part of a face. (Looking at Figure 3-29, you can now see that the meaningless squiggles in Figure 3-28 suddenly assume shape as a nose, eye, ear, and mouth.) How, then, do we manage to recognize anything? The answer lies in the conclusion that perception proceeds in both directions at once. We need bottom-up processing to allow stimuli to come in from the outside. However, without top-down processing our perception would be extremely slow and inefficient; top-down processing provides the way in which our experience influences our perception.

Word-Superiority Effect   We see how this operates in the ***word-superiority effect***. (Before going on, look at Figure 3-30.) This term denotes the principle that a letter can be identified faster when it is part of a word than when it is not, a fact first demonstrated about a century ago (J. M. Cattell, 1885–1886). Cattell showed people letter displays for 10 milliseconds and then asked them to report as many letters as they could. When people saw strings of single letters, they reported only four of five letters. When they saw words, they reported three or four entire words, which, of course, contained many more letters. This principle has been demonstrated several times since (Reicher, 1969; Solman, May, & Schwartz, 1981).

You can see how this principle affects the speed of reading. If you had to look closely at every single letter in every word, you would read at a snail's pace. Furthermore, in most of your reading, you don't even have to read every word closely, since the other words in a sentence give clues to each other. Thus, in reading the sentence, "John pounded the nail with a ———," you tend to know the missing word without even reading it, since the cues provided by the words already read limit the number of possibilities for the last word (Just & Carpenter, 1980). This principle is illustrated by the ambiguous figure presented in Figure 3-30. As shown in Figure 3-31, you'll read it as a *B* or a *13*, depending on how it's presented.

Phonemic Restoration Effect   The same principle of using context to provide clues can be seen in an explanation for the way we perceive what we hear. The ***phonemic restoration effect*** occurs when a speech sound is replaced by a loud noise. Even though people cannot hear the speech sound, they report hearing it, claiming that they can hear that sound as clearly as any that they actually did hear (Warren, 1984).

In one experiment, subjects heard one of the four following sentences, which differ only in the final word (the * represents a loud cough that replaced a speech sound).

1   It was found that the *eel was on the axle.
2   It was found that the *eel was on the shoe.
3   It was found that the *eel was on the orange.
4   It was found that the *eel was on the table.

The subjects' reports on what they had heard depended upon which sentence had been presented to them. *Wheel* was the word reported by those who heard the first sentence; *heel*, *peel*, and *meal* were reported by those who heard sentences 2, 3, and 4 (Warren & Warren, 1970).

Clearly, the illusion that we have heard the sound we *expect* to hear is very strong. This illusion is the basis for the advice that is given to people with hearing problems—to search the context for cues when they are unsure of a specific speech sound.

Attention

While your psychology professor may not make a formal assignment asking you to attend a party for course credit, you can, in fact, study one psychological phenomenon—attention—in this kind of situation. (This experience can illustrate the relevance of this field to your everyday life—and also show you that sometimes you *can* combine work with play.) ***Attention*** is a state of focused mental activity. ***Selective attention*** involves concentrating on some stimuli while ignoring others. ***Divided attention*** occurs when you try to focus on more than one activity at the same time, often with a reduction in performance.

FIGURE 3-30   *What does this look like to you?*

FIGURE 3-31   *Hold the page upside down: Here we see that the context in which a stimulus appears influences how we perceive it. The B and the 13 are identical.*

Word-superiority effect   *Principle in pattern recognition based on the observation that a letter can be identified faster if it is part of a word than if it stands alone.*

Phonemic restoration effect   *Phenomenon in which a listener reports hearing a speech sound that has been omitted from a passage.*

Attention   *State of focused mental activity.*
Selective attention   *Concentration on some stimuli while others are ignored.*
Divided attention   *Concentration on more than one activity at the same time, often with a reduction in performance.*

To see how these phenomena operate, observe yourself when you arrive at the party. There will be a place where food and drinks are served, there will be a number of physical features in the room, and there will be a number of people (some known to you, some not) engaged in several different conversations. Of all these separate kinds of messages, what will you notice? If you're a connoisseur of art, you may first notice the paintings on the walls. If you're very hungry, you may focus on the food. If you see a group of people that includes someone you know and like—or would like to get to know—the people may take center stage for you.

As you're talking to these people, you won't have any trouble dividing your attention between the conversation and the canapés (remembering your parents' admonition not talk with your mouth full). It is difficult, though to divide your attention between two different conversations. When engaged in conversation, you generally don't pay attention to the other talk going on around you. It will just be a buzz in the background—unless you happen to hear something of special interest to you, perhaps your own name. In that case, your selective attention will shift, and you'll pay so much attention to the conversation behind you that you may be embarrassed to find that someone in the group you're with has just asked you a question—and you didn't even hear it.

Psychologists have studied selective and divided attention in a number of ways. One technique is called **shadowing technique,** or **dichotic listening,** in which one message is presented to one ear and another to the other ear. Usually people focus on one of the messages and hear very little of the other, sometimes not even noticing that the second message is spoken in a different language or doesn't make any sense. People do, however, tend to notice the gender of the other speaker and pick up their own names, and they sometimes absorb some of the meaning in the second message (Matlin, 1983).

The value of both selective and divided attention is obvious. Since our senses are often bombarded with many messages at the same time, we can't pay attention to all of them. Often, however, we have to be able to handle more than one at a time, or as one popular saying has it, to be able to "walk and chew gum at the same time." And the ability to switch our attention to more important stimuli as they arise allows us the flexibility that is vital not only for survival but for accomplishing our own personal aims.

Perceptual Constancy

When you say good-bye to your friend Mary and watch her walk down the street, her image on your retina gets smaller and smaller. You don't see her as the "incredible shrinking woman," however. You know that she's staying the same size and that the reason she looks smaller is the growing distance between you. This awareness that objects in our environment remain the same even though they may look different because of varying conditions in the environment is known as **perceptual constancy.** We maintain a stable view of the world and the people and objects in it by a number of means.

One explanation of perceptual constancies, the **unconscious-inference theory,** rests on the principle that we temper our sensory input with what we know from experience. If we know certain basic information—like the true size or shape of an object—we make unconscious inferences when that object *seems* different. According to this theory, we unconsciously know that nearby objects look bigger because they cast a larger image on the retina, so that if we know the distance between our eyes and an object, we can derive the size of the object (Rock, 1983).

According to another explanation, the **ecological theory,** the relationships between different objects in a scene give us information about their sizes (Gibson, 1979). Thus, when your friend is farther away from you, the relationship between her size and the size of the surrounding trees and cars remains the same, so you see all the sizes as remaining constant, despite the change in retinal image. Similarly,

Shadowing technique *Technique in which one message is presented to one ear and another to the other ear.*

Dichotic listening *Another term for "shadowing technique."*

Perceptual constancy *Awareness that objects and events in the environment remain the same even though they may appear different because of varying environmental conditions.*

Unconscious-inference theory *Theory that perceptual constancies are a result of what is known from experience.*

Ecological theory *Theory that the relationships between different objects in a scene give us information about their sizes.*

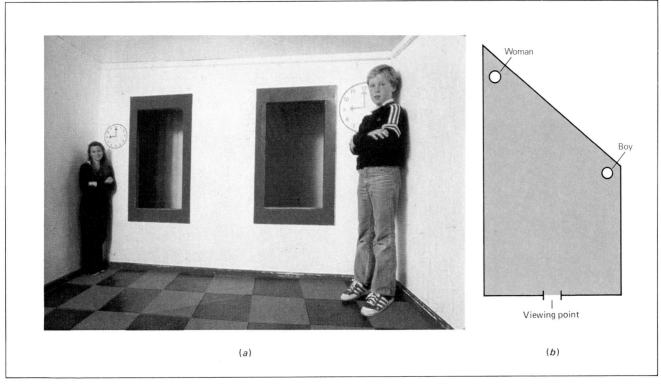

(a) (b)

FIGURE 3-32 (a) The woman in this photo taken in the Ames room is actually taller than the boy, although he looks like a giant next to her. (Source: Baron Wolman/Woodfin Camp.) (b) View of the Ames room. This diagram explains the illusion: the woman is almost twice as far from the viewer as the boy is, but from the viewing point the difference in distance is not apparent. (Source: Gregory, 1973.)

when you look at this book in dim light, the ratio between the white of the page and the black of the letters appears to remain constant even though the actual amount of light reflected differs.

The Ames room (shown in Figure 3-32) draws on the ecological theory to mislead the viewer into a distortion of the sizes of the people in the room. In the photograph of an observer's view of the room (Figure 3-32a), the woman on the left looks much smaller than the boy on the right, even though he is in fact smaller. This is because the room was designed to look like a normal rectangular room when viewed from one particular observation point. As you can see from the drawing in Figure 3-32b, the room is shaped so that the woman is almost twice as far away from the viewer as the boy. Furthermore, the floor and the ceiling both have abnormal slopes. The relationships between the sizes of the windows and walls have been altered, changing the relationships between the people and their environment and thus fooling the viewer. Perceptual constancy, then, needs a context.

Perceptual constancies are important, because they free us from depending entirely on the characteristics of the retinal image when we try to perceive the nature of an object. They make our perceptions object-oriented rather than retina-oriented. They help us maintain a realistic sense of the world we live in.

Constancy affects almost every area of perception, and it holds true with regard to the other senses. For example, if we hear the very faint sound of a fire engine, we recognize the siren and, knowing that it's ordinarily loud, assume that it's far away. We are able to relax, free from worry that our own house is on fire. Most of the research, however, has been conducted on four kinds of constancies: size, shape, brightness, and color.

Size Constancy We maintain a sense of size by our knowledge of how big an object is, by our knowledge that things that are far away look smaller than they really are, and by our knowledge of the size of an object relative to other objects whose size we know. (See Figure 3-33, page 106.)

Depth perception *Ability to judge how far away an object is.*

Shape Constancy An object seems to stay the same shape even though it may be viewed from a different distance or angle. Thus, the end of an oil drum remains circular, even though the shape that it produces on the retina may be an oval. (See Figure 3-34.)

Brightness Constancy We see the brightness of an object as constant even under different lighting conditions, so whether you read this page in bright sunlight or semidarkness, you still know that the paper is white and the printing is black.

Color Constancy We tend to see the color of an object as remaining constant and assume that when it appears to be lighter, darker, or of a different hue, it's the lighting that makes it look different. Color constancy cannot, however, compensate for all of the wide ranges of appearance that colors take on in different lights. When we are choosing a specific color for a reason, we need to see it in the kind of light we'll use it in. Thus, in choosing wallpaper, a decorator examines it in daylight; a woman selecting make-up to wear in the evening should look at it in a softer glow.

Depth Perception

Wesley Walker, a professional football player with the New York Jets, has to make fine judgments of speed and motion every time he makes a play. As a wide receiver, he has to estimate where the ball will land while both he and it are still in motion, and he has to keep modifying his estimate as he runs after the ball. Obviously, he needs a keen sense of depth perception, and judging from his success in the stadium, he has it—despite the fact that he is nearly blind in his left eye ("Visual cues," 1983).

Depth perception—the ability to judge how far away objects are—is not, of course, important only to football players. It is vital for anyone who drives a car, walks in the street, or performs the most elementary motor activities. How, then, do we judge the distance of objects? In two major ways: those that depend on the vision of both eyes working together (binocular cues) and those that depend on only one eye (monocular cues).

FIGURE 3-35 *Stereoscopic photos of the football player "Mean" Joe Greene, former defensive lineman for the Pittsburgh Steelers. The left eye sees the view on the left, and the right eye sees the view on the right. In the photo on the right, player 23 seems closer to Greene, showing that our two eyes perceive the world just a little differently. (Source: Stereograph by Michael Chikiris.)*

Binocular cues are cues of distance that depend on the fact that we have two eyes. The major binocular cue is called **binocular disparity,** which means that each eye has a slightly different view of the world. The way the brain combines these two images creates the impression of depth. When you "see double," you are seeing the separate views of both your eyes; for some reason (possibly fatigue, intoxication, or a weakness of the eye muscles) the two views are not being fused.

You can easily demonstrate this difference in what your eyes see. Close your right eye and hold one finger upright about 8 inches in front of your left eye. Then position a finger from your other hand behind the first finger so that the second finger is completely hidden. If you now close your left eye and open your right eye, you'll be able to see the previously hidden finger. This slightly different view of your fingers seen by each eye demonstrates the principle of **stereopsis**—the basis for 3D movies and slide viewers, which project a slightly different image to each eye and thus create the illusion of depth. The stereoscopic photographs of two football players in Figure 3-35 show a scene the way it would be seen by each eye. The brain determines the speed of an object (say, a ball being thrown to you) through stereomotion, that is, processing the change in the disparity between the two images of the object as it moves closer or farther away.

Wesley Walker and other people with sight in only one eye can still play tennis or football, drive a car, or fly an airplane by depending on **monocular cues,** which are cues about distance that require only one eye.

The monocular cues include size, motion parallax, partial overlap, texture gradients, linear and atmospheric perspective, and shading.

■ Size is a prime cue: Nearby objects look bigger because they cast a larger image on the retina. As a thrown ball comes closer it gets bigger, and, based on the rapidly changing retinal image, the brain can quickly calculate speed and direction. When the body is moving, too, the brain also takes this into account, and the monocular cue of motion parallax becomes important.

■ Motion parallax means a change in position due to movement (*parallax* means a change in position). In this phenomenon, objects seem to move at different speeds and, sometimes, in different directions as you move in relation to them. You may notice this particularly when you're riding in a car or train, where nearby objects move past your field of vision faster than distant ones do. Bushes seen outside a bus window seem to fly by, compared with distant mountains, which "move" much more slowly. The speed of the apparent movement is directly related to

Binocular cues *Cues in depth perception that depend on both eyes.*
Binocular disparity *Cue in depth perception that is based on each eye's having a different view of the world.*

Stereopsis *Basis for 3-D movies and slide viewers, which project a sightly different image to each eye and thus create an illusion of depth.*

Monocular cues *Cues about the distance of an object that can be seen with just one eye.*

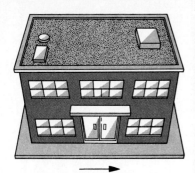

(To be fixated on)

Your movement

FIGURE 3-36 *Motion parallax. If you fixate on a tree about 50 feet away and then move your head from left to right, the bench in front of the tree will seem to move to the left, while the building behind the tree will seem to move to the right.*

FIGURE 3-37 *Texture gradient. This magnificent photograph of the Dumont dunes in California demonstrates an important monocular cue to depth. The fact that the sand grooves closer to us seem more widely spaced than those in the distance allows us to draw inferences about the distances involved. (Source: © C. Max Dunham/Photo Researchers.)*

distance. You can also see how the phenomenon works in this way: Stand up, look out a window at something about 50 feet away, and fixate on it. Then move from right to left at the window and notice how objects in front of your target seem to move in the opposite direction (from left to right) and objects farther away than the target seem to move in the same direction as your own movement (see Figure 3-36).

Other important monocular cues include these:

- Partial overlap (interposition): When one object is in front of and partially blocks our view of another object, it is clear that the one in front is closer.

- Texture gradient: When we look at a textured surface—whether a natural texture, like a grooved sand dune, or one composed of many objects close together, like a roomful of barrels—the elements closer to us seem to be more widely spaced than those that are farther away (see Figure 3-37).

- Linear perspective (convergence of parallel lines): When two lines that we know are parallel appear to be converging, we infer that the point where they appear to be closer together is more distant from us than the point where they appear far apart (see Figure 3-38).

- Atmospheric perspective: We see objects that are far away from us less clearly than nearby objects. The farther ones look fuzzier because of haze, smog, and dust in the air, and they also look bluer than closer objects. (Remember the "purple mountains' majesty"?)

- Shading is another cue to depth. By noting where the shadows fall, we often get a sense of the size and distance of an object. Artists who specialize in *trompe l'oeil* painting, which "fools the eye," use shading skillfully to make the viewer think that a flat painting actually has three-dimensional elements in it (see Figure 3-39).

FIGURE 3-38 *Linear perspective. When we see the parallel lines of the squares in the street and the fronts of the buildings converging to a vanishing point in the distance, we get an illusion of depth. (Source: Museum of Art, Pittsburgh.)*

FIGURE 3-39 *Shading is an important cue to depth perception. In the original of this painting the artist's use of shading almost makes you feel as if you could pick up the violin and play it. (Source: Jefferson Chalfant, "Violin and Bow," 1899; collection of Metropolitan Museum of Art, New York, George A. Hearn Fund, 1966.)*

Depth perception appears to be either an innate ability or something learned extremely early. When babies as young as six months are placed on a "visual cliff" consisting of a flat, glass-covered board that creates an illusion of a chasm, they will not crawl on the side that looks deep, even to reach their mothers (Walk & Gibson, 1961). Two- to three-month-olds show slower heart rates on the "deep" side than on the "shallow" side, suggesting that they are responding to their perception of depth (Campos, Langer, & Krowitz, 1970); see Figure 3-40.

Visual Illusions

While perceptual constancies help us perceive the world accurately, our perceptual systems are not infallible. We're subject to many false perceptions, called ***illusions.*** Some illusions are caused by misleading context, as in the size illusion produced by the Ames room, seen earlier in Figure 3-31, and in the Mueller-Lyer and Ponzo illusions.

Look at the lines in Figure 3-41*a* (page 110). Ignoring the angled lines on the end of each vertical line, decide which vertical line is longer. If you measure them, you'll see that they are both the same, but it's hard to believe, because the one on the right looks longer to virtually everyone. The Mueller-Lyer illusion, as this is called, is caused by those angled lines. Perhaps the effect is caused by the tendency of our eyes to be drawn back into the center of the line on the figure at left and for them to move out into space on the figure to right. Or the effect may be related to a false impression of depth, as indicated in Figure 3-41*b*.

The Ponzo illusion, shown in Figure 3-42 (page 110), confuses us because of the illusion of depth caused by the converging railway tracks, which makes us expect the rectangle in the distance to appear smaller. When it does not, we assume it's larger than the one in the foreground of the photo.

FIGURE 3-40 *Babies perceive depth, and the illusion of depth, from a very early age. Even the mother cannot induce this baby to crawl across what looks like a cliff. (Source: © Enrico Ferorelli/DOT.)*

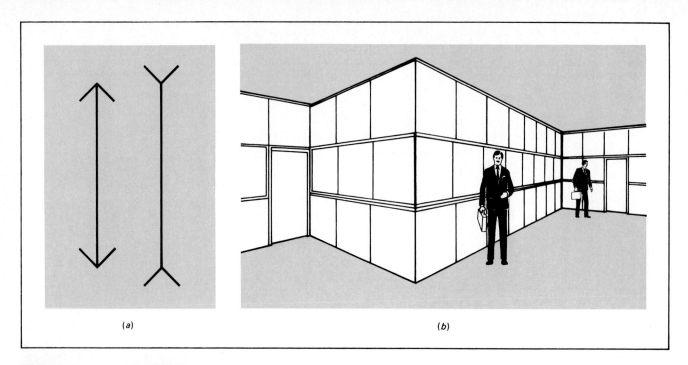

(a)   (b)

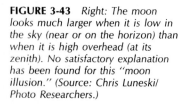

FIGURE 3-42 *Above: Ponzo illusion. Although these bars are of equal length, the one on top looks longer, because our experience with converging lines makes us think that it is farther away. The less experience people have with perspective, the less susceptible they are to this illusion. (Source: © J. Barry O'Rourke/Stock Market.)*

FIGURE 3-43 *Right: The moon looks much larger when it is low in the sky (near or on the horizon) than when it is high overhead (at its zenith). No satisfactory explanation has been found for this "moon illusion." (Source: Chris Luneski/ Photo Researchers.)*

Another startling illusion is the "moon illusion," which makes the moon look much larger when it's low in the sky than when it's high overhead (see Figure 3-43). Since the second century after Christ, scientists have been trying to explain this illusion; and despite extensive research in the 1980s, the explanation is still unclear (Baird, 1982; Reed, 1984).

Illusions *False perceptions.*

The Role of Experience

While some of the concepts we've been talking about seem obvious, they're far from universal. The use of perspective to show depth in painting (as in Figure 3-38), for example, is a fairly recent artistic convention. Roman paintings of the first century B.C. showed only an elementary perspective. Not until the time of the Renaissance did artists discover that by using the principles of perspective, they could add a convincing feeling of depth to their paintings. Even now, there are some cultures that apparently do not recognize linear perspective as showing depth.

Experience is crucial in perception. This was shown in research comparing American college students with English-speaking students at the University of Guam (Leibowitz, 1971). On the western Pacific island of Guam, there are no railroads and relatively few perspective cues. Thus, it came as no great surprise when the Guamanian students did not respond as strongly to the Ponzo illusion (Figure 3-42) as the American students did. Both groups of students saw line drawings of the illusion, as well as photographs with texture depth cues and perspective depth cues. For the Guamanian students, adding texture and perspective cues did not increase the force of the illusion; for the Americans, these cues increased it by about 200 percent.

This is explained by the ***theory of misapplied constancy.*** Apparently, the American students, who were used to judging distance by such cues as texture and perspective, interpreted cues in the illusion as cues for maintaining size constancy. The Guamanian students, who were less used to considering these cues, were not so influenced by them and were able to see the pictures more accurately. As one psychologist has written, "Ironically, the more knowledge and experience we acquire, the less accurately we perform on some illusions!" (Matlin, 1988).

Theory of misapplied constancy *Theory that inappropriate interpretation of cues in an illusion is the result of having learned cues for maintaining size constancy.*

Similar findings emerged from an experiment comparing two groups of Native Americans (Pedersen & Wheeler, 1983). The members of one group had lived all their lives in rectangular houses, where they would have seen corners like those in Figure 3-41. The other group had lived at least the first 6 years of their lives in hogans, traditional Navajo round houses. Those who were more familiar with corners were more susceptible to the Mueller-Lyer illusion. In effect, they were misapplying the cues for constancy that they had learned from their environments.

Cultural differences are also obvious in other ways. While you would look at the drawing in Figure 3-44 and know immediately that the hunter was trying to spear the

FIGURE 3-44 *Members of remote tribes who are unfamiliar with pictorial cues for depth think that this picture shows the hunter trying to spear the elephant in the distance, not the antelope up close. (Source: Deregowski, 1972.)*

If you run, walk, or bike after dark, you probably use reflector patches so that you won't be struck by a car. (If you don't, you should.) These patches, attached to the heels of your shoes, the back of your shirt or jacket, or the spokes of your bicycle, signal that you are a moving object. How do drivers who see your safety patches reflected from their headlights realize not only that you're moving, but that you are a human being? A major part of the answer to this question comes from a series of experiments that have proven that we can get a tremendous amount of information about objects by seeing their patterns of movement, even if we can't see the objects themselves.

First, we can tell whether something is alive or is an inanimate object. Then, we can usually tell whether it's a human being, whether it's male or female, and what a person is doing (walking, dancing, running, painting, or lifting a box). We can often tell from a walker's gait whether it's someone we know. We begin picking up these clues in our infancy, as early as 4 to 6 months (Fox & McDaniel, 1982), and we continue to acquire and use such information throughout life.

How do we know that it's the movement itself that gives us this information and not clues such as hairstyle, clothing, and body contours? Researchers of the phenomenon of **biological motion,** the patterns of movement of living organisms, follow a technique pioneered by the Swedish psychologist Johansson (1973). In such experiments an "actor" wears black clothes, and the

PERCEPTION OF BIOLOGICAL MOTION

experiment takes place in a pitch-dark room. Small light bulbs are then attached to certain spots on the person's body, and the person engages in a variety of activities. When a person wearing 12 such lights (attached to shoulders, elbows, wrists, hips, knees, and ankles) is sitting still, observers say the lights look like a Christmas tree or a constellation. As soon as the person starts to move, however, it becomes clear immediately that this is indeed a person.

It takes only $\frac{1}{10}$ (0.1) second (the equivalent of two frames in a motion picture) to recognize, entirely from the movement of these 12 little lights, that the person is performing some familiar activity, like walking (Johansson, 1975). Furthermore, viewers can almost instantly tell the difference between walking and jogging, they can detect a limp, and they can recognize when such lights are on a dancing couple. It takes an average of only 4.4 seconds to recognize whether a walking set of lights is a male or female (Cutting & Proffitt, 1981).

We can see how this works by analyzing differences in movement between men and women. From

Some Like It Hot to *Tootsie,* moviegoers have burst into laughter at seeing a man trying to walk like a woman. It's hard to do, largely because much of the difference in male and female gaits stems from anatomical differences. Men, for example, typically have broader shoulders than women, and women usually have wider hips than men. When you walk, as your left leg steps out, your right arm swings forward. As your limbs alternate, your body shifts from side to side. As you can see from Figure 3-46, the center of movement for this shift is lower for men than for women. This is probably the major clue that lets observers tell the difference between the sexes, even when they view not the people themselves, but a computer-created display based on typical male and female body measurements (Runeson & Frykholm, 1983).

It's fascinating to note that when actors are conscious of trying to walk in gender-specific ways, either according to their actual gender or the other one, it is harder for observers to attribute gender correctly. This is probably because the actors' self-conscious attempts result in awkward movements that obscure natural patterns (Runeson & Frykholm, 1983).

Like many other human abilities, the perception of biological motion probably has strong survival value (even if you're not a late-night jogger), and it's possible that our quick recognition of such movements even before we are conscious of them may be due to a fixed pathway in the visual system from the retina to the cortex (Johansson, 1975).

antelope, some people from other cultures would ignore the size cues and assume that the hunter was aiming for the elephant (Deregowski, 1980).

We also see differences in the way people from different cultures react to various tastes, smells, and physical sensations, on the basis of their earlier experiences. Much of the way we organize our sensations is based on what we've learned.

Research has shown an actual physical change that occurs in response to early experience. Young cats that have been fitted with goggles (like those shown in Figure 3-45) which allow them to see only vertical lines, will in maturity be unable to see horizontal lines and will bump into horizontal boards right in front of them (Hirsch & Spinelli, 1970). If the goggles let them see only horizontal lines, they will be effectively blind to vertical columns. This seems to be due to modifications in the cortex. Apparently, most of the neurons in the visual cortex are programmed to respond to the lines only in the direction (vertical or horizontal) that the cats have been permitted to see. This does not happen when the same procedure is carried out with adult cats, suggesting that crucial cells in the visual cortex develop early in life. Thus the possibility arises that there is a critical period in the development of vision. A *critical period* is a specific time during development when an animal or person needs to have appropriate experiences to bring about normal adult functioning.

The relevance of these findings for human beings lies in some recent findings about astigmatism, a visual defect in which a person has difficulty seeing lines in a particular orientation, either vertical or horizontal. (Refer back to the box "Common Vision Problems" and Figure 3-4b.) If astigmatism is not corrected with eyeglasses at an early age, children are likely to have a permanent loss of visual acuity for either vertical or horizontal lines (Mitchell et al., 1973). Similarly, children with strabismus who use only one eye at a time will have poor depth perception all their lives unless they receive treatment before age 5 (Banks, Aslin, & Letson, 1975).

As you'll see elsewhere in this book, there is a basis for the belief that there may be critical periods for various other kinds of development, such as learning language skills or sexual behaviors. Apparently brain development is preprogrammed to conform to certain sequential patterns. One kind of perception that appears very early in life is the response to *biological motion,* described in the box "Perception of Biological Motion." Analyzing gender-related differences in movement helps explain perception of biological motion, and these differences are in turn related to the "center of movement" in males and females—as shown in Figure 3-46.

FIGURE 3-45 *This kitten is wearing training goggles. One lens contains horizontal stripes and the other vertical stripes. The eye that sees only horizontal stripes will be blind to vertical lines when the animal matures, and the eye that sees only vertical stripes will be blind to horizontal lines.*

Critical period *Specific time during development when an animal or person needs to have appropriate experiences to bring about normal adult functioning.*
Biological motion *Patterns of movement of living organisms.*

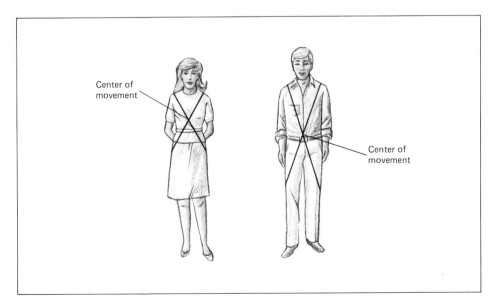

FIGURE 3-46 *Men and women walk differently because of gender-related anatomical differences that result in a lower center of movement for males than for females.*

In this chapter we've seen how the brain helps us organize and give meaning to the information that comes to us through our sensory organs. In Chapter 4, we'll see how the state of consciousness we are in at any particular moment influences the way we sense and perceive the world around us.

SUMMARY

1 Sensation is stimulation of the sensory organs and the transmission of information about this stimulation through the nervous system. Perception is the way the brain interprets these sensations to make them meaningful. Psychophysics is the study of the relationship between the physical aspects of stimuli and psychological perceptions of them.

2 The absolute threshold is the smallest intensity of a stimulus that can be perceived. The difference threshold is the smallest detectable difference in intensity. Signal-detection theory is a recent approach in psychophysics that emphasizes both the sensitivity of the senses and the motivations of observers.

3 Adaptation is the decrease in the response of the sensory system with continued stimulations. Adaptation may involve mechanisms in the higher levels of perceptual processing as well as fatigue of the receptors.

4 In vision, the human sees electromagnetic energy in the form of light waves. The most important part of the eye is the retina, which contains photoreceptors, the rods and cones. Information from the photoreceptors is passed on to the retinal ganglion cells. The information eventually reaches the visual cortex, where three kinds of neurons analyze the stimulation into patterns.

5 Common vision problems include nearsightedness, farsightedness, astigmatism, strabismus, amblyopia, stereoblindness, presbyopia, cataracts, night blindness, cornea damage, and glaucoma.

6 Two theories of color vision apply to different levels in visual processing. Trichromatic theory, which operates at the receptor level, proposes that the visual system contains three color mechanisms (one for red, one for green, and one for blue), and that all colors of the spectrum can be produced by these three mechanisms. Opponent-process theory, which operates at higher levels in visual processing, proposes that there are three systems at work in visual processing—two in which pairs of complementary colors are opposed (a yellow-blue system and a red-green system) and one system for black and white.

7 In hearing, sounds are distinguished according to three basic attributes: loudness, pitch, and timbre. Sound makes the eardrum move, and this movement is eventually transmitted to the hair cells in the inner ear, which are the receptors for hearing. Auditory nerve fibers transmit auditory information to the brain.

8 According to place theory, a certain pitch is heard depending upon the particular spot on the basilar membrane that is stimulated. Frequency theory maintains that a certain pitch is heard depending upon the frequency with which the entire membrane vibrates. High-pitched sounds can be best explained by place theory; low-pitched sounds can be best explained by frequency theory. Pitches in the middle range can be explained by both theories.

9 The direction from which a sound is coming is known because sound waves reach one ear before the other, because the sound shadow decreases the intensity for one ear, and because the shape of the outer ear provides additional information.

10 The two major kinds of hearing loss are sensorineural deafness, in which the hair cells have been damaged (sometimes by loud noises, including loud music), and conductive deafness, caused by a ruptured eardrum or bone defect.

11 The sense of touch is really several different senses, including the senses of heat, cold, pressure, and pain. Some parts of the body are much more sensitive to touch than others, as evidenced by their lower two-point-discrimination thresholds. Pain serves an important function by signalling danger. The brain produces endorphins, substances that reduce or eliminate pain. Acupuncture, placebos, hypnosis, and prepared childbirth also have the potential to block or alter the perception of pain.

12 Smell plays an important role in human life. Molecules reach the olfactory mucosa, and information about smell is then conveyed to the olfactory bulb and on to the brain. The average person can name only a few smells but can discriminate among at least 200 smells.

13 Tastes can be described in terms of sweetness, saltiness, sourness, and bitterness. Flavor typically depends heavily upon odor; texture and temperature are also important determinants of flavor. The receptors for taste are contained in the taste buds; nerve fibers from the taste buds convey information to the brain.

14 In perception, the brain organizes lines and shadings into scenes and individual sounds into speech and music. The gestalt laws such as continuity, proximity, and closure take part in the organization process.

15 Pattern recognition can be approached from two viewpoints. The concept of bottom-up processing focuses on the way the sensory receptors register information. The concept of top-down processing emphasizes the observer's expectations and knowledge. Both approaches are necessary for accurate and efficient pattern recognition. Two examples of the importance of top-down processing are the word-superiority effect and the phonemic restoration effect.

16 Attention is a state of focused mental activity. Two important kinds of attention are selective attention, in which

people concentrate on some stimuli and ignore others; and divided attention, in which people try to focus on more than one activity at the same time, often with a reduction in performance.

17 Perceptual constancy is the effect on perception of an awareness that objects in the environment remain the same even though they may look different because of varying conditions in the environment. Perceptual constancies free people from depending too heavily on the characteristics of the retinal image when they try to perceive the nature of an object. Examples include size constancy, shape constancy, brightness constancy, and color constancy.

18 Humans judge distance using binocular and monocular cues. Binocular cues, which require the use of two eyes, include binocular disparity, which means that each eye has a slightly different view. Monocular cues, which re-

quire only one eye, include size, motion parallax, partial overlap, texture gradient, linear perspective, atmospheric perspective, and shading.

20 Experience is crucial in perception. People raised in cultures with little experience with perspective or rectangular objects do not respond to illusions in the same way as American students. Other research, with animals, has indicated that there may be a critical period in the development of vision; if certain kinds of visual experiences are not provided at specific stages of development, normal perception will not occur in adulthood.

21 Humans can quickly identify specific kinds of biological motion, the patterns of movement in living organisms. For example, even when a person is represented only by several spots of light, viewers can easily determine whether the person is walking or jogging and whether the person is female or male.

KEY TERMS

Absolute threshold (page 77)
Accommodation (81)
Adaptation (96)
Attention (103)
Auditory meatus (91)
Basilar membrane (91)
Binocular cues (107)
Binocular disparity (107)
Bottom-up processing (102)
Cochlea (91)
Conductive deafness (94)
Cones (81)
Cornea (80)
Critical period (112)
Decibels (dB) (90)
Depth perception (106)
Dichotic listening (104)
Difference threshold (78)

Divided attention (103)
Ecological theory (104)
Endorphins (95)
Enkephalin (95)
Fovea (83)
Frequency theory (92)
Ganglion cells (81)
Gestalt laws (100)
Gestalt psychology (100)
Illusions (111)
Incus (91)
Iris (80)
Just noticeable difference (jnd) (78)
Lens (81)
Malleus (91)
Monocular cues (107)
Olfactory mucosa (97)

Opponent-process theory (88)
Optic disk (81)
Papillae (98)
Perception (77)
Perceptual constancy (104)
Phonemic restoration effect (103)
Pinna (91)
Place theory (92)
Presbycusis (93)
Psychophysics (77)
Pupil (80)
Receptive field (84)
Retina (81)
Rods (81)
Sclera (80)
Selective attention (103)
Sensation (77)

Sensorineural hearing loss (93)
Shadowing technique (104)
Signal-detection theory (77)
Stapes (91)
Stereopsis (107)
Stimulus (77)
Theory of misapplied constancy (111)
Tinnitus (93)
Top-down processing (102)
Trichromatic theory (86)
Tympanic membrane (91)
Unconscious inference theory (104)
Visual capture (79)
Visual cortex (84)
Weber's law (78)
Word-superiority effect (103)

SUGGESTED READINGS

COREN, S., & GIRGUS, J. S. (1978). *Seeing is deceiving: The psychology of visual illusions.* Hillsdale, NJ: Erlbaum. An extended and readable treatment of visual illusions.

COREN, S., PORAC, C., & WARD, L. M. (1984). *Sensation and perception* (2d ed.). New York: Academic. A middle-level textbook with clear explanations of details on psychophysics and the sensory systems.

ENGEN, T. (1982). *The perception of odors.* New York: Academic. This interesting book includes information on topics such as memory for odors, odor mixtures, and measuring the pleasantness of odors.

MATLIN, M. W. (1983). *Perception.* Boston: Allyn & Bacon. This student-oriented textbook emphasizes applications of perception to everyday life.

WARREN, R. M. (1982). *Auditory perception: A new synthesis.* New York: Pergamon. This summary of research on hearing includes coverage of sensory aspects of audition as well as topics such as speech perception and the interaction of vision and hearing.

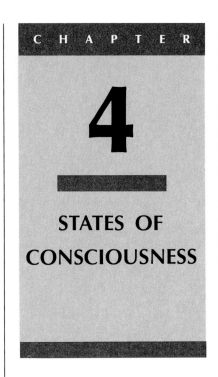

C H A P T E R

4

STATES OF CONSCIOUSNESS

PREVIEW QUESTIONS

■ Can consciousness be studied?

■ What is the difference between normal and altered states of consciousness?

■ What are the stages and characteristics of sleep?

■ Why do people sleep, and why do they dream?

■ What is meditation? Is it an effective therapy?

■ Is hypnosis a unique state of consciousness? How is it used in law and in therapy?

■ What are the effects of psychoactive drugs?

A few nights before I was to take a trip from my home in Madison, Wisconsin, to New York City to meet with my coauthor and our editors about the preparation of this second edition of Psychology, *I had a dream. I dreamed that I was 75 years old and that Sally Olds was 85 years old. We looked exactly the way we now do, we were both wearing bright red suits, and we were in the New York offices of our publisher, in a conference room with a panoramic view of the Manhattan skyline. Our editors were urging us to revise this book "just one more time," for its ninety-seventh edition.*

This dream exemplifies some of the characteristics of altered states of consciousness, which we'll be talking about in this chapter. For one thing, I was asleep, which in itself is a different state from the usual conscious, waking state. For another thing, I fully accepted inconsistencies in the dream that seemed jarring once I was awake—for example, our ages. First, no matter how much research is put into slowing down the aging process, it's unlikely that we'll look the same in our seventies and eighties as we do now. Second, since the difference between our birth dates is greater than 10 years, one of us would have to be a different age from that in the dream. Furthermore, since even the most ambitious revision schedules for textbooks usually don't exceed one every 2 or 3 years, it would be impossible to prepare 97 editions in one lifetime!

The meaning this dream had for me is another question altogether, one you may want to think about as you read in this chapter about the significance of the content of our dreams and why we remember some and forget others.

—From the notebooks of Diane Papalia

Sleep and dreaming are among the altered states of consciousness that we discuss in this chapter in contrast to the normal state of consciousness. Consciousness is one of those concepts that seem straightforward but are surprisingly hard to define. Its very familiarity makes laypersons take it for granted and challenges psychologists to come up with precise descriptions. We need such descriptions to pin down the state well enough so that when you and I say "consciousness," we know we are both talking about the same state.

WHAT IS CONSCIOUSNESS?

The word *consciousness* itself (from the Latin, *knowing things together*) was first used in the seventeenth century by Francis Bacon. Later in the century, John Locke defined it as the "perception of what passes in a man's own mind" (1690, p. 138). In the early nineteenth century, the new science of psychology was often referred to as the "science of consciousness." Wilhelm Wundt, working in the middle to the late nineteenth century, used introspective methods to study consciousness, and Edward B. Titchener, his student, analyzed consciousness by reducing it to elemental units. (See Chapter 1 for a brief discussion of Wundt's and Titchener's work.)

The study of consciousness received a major setback in psychological circles when the behaviorists exerted their influence. In 1913, the year before he was elected president of the American Psychological Association, John B. Watson issued his behaviorist manifesto, in which he proclaimed, "The time has come when psychology must discard all reference to consciousness." Agreeing with Watson's proposition that psychology could be scientific only if it studied observable, measurable behaviors, most psychologists dropped the study of what goes on inside the human brain. Those who persisted in delving into thoughts and feelings tended to study them within a neurological and physiological framework rather than a psychological one. Not until the middle of the twentieth century did the study of consciousness again become respectable in psychological circles.

Today the emphasis in the study of this commonplace yet elusive phenomenon is on defining it and describing its various levels, called *altered states*. While there is no universally agreed-upon definition of **consciousness,** we can adopt as a working definition "our awareness of ourselves and of the world around us."

Consciousness Our awareness of ourselves and the world around us.

THE NORMAL STATE OF CONSCIOUSNESS VERSUS ALTERED STATES

Just as news reports do not point out the circumstances in daily life that proceed more or less normally, but rather those that disrupt the usual course of events, the study of consciousness has concentrated on altered states rather than the usual state. Before we go on to discuss these other levels, let's see how they differ from the normal condition.

Your normal state of consciousness is generally considered to be the one in which you spend most of your waking hours. Any qualitative change from your usual state is considered an **altered state of consciousness (ASC).** *Qualitative* is the key word, since the difference has to be one of *kind,* not just of *degree.* It's not a question, for example, of your being more or less alert. You have to feel as if your mental processes are working in a different way from the way they usually function. You may be aware of mental functions that don't operate at all in your usual state, you may see or hear or feel things that normally you don't perceive, you may be more preoccupied than usual with your internal sensations or the way you think, you may actually think differently, and you may be out of touch with reality (Ludwig, 1966; Tart, 1969). Often you may be in a borderline state, as when you are dozing, lying out in the hot sun, and you realize that you don't know whether you have been awake or asleep.

Altered state of consciousness (ASC) Any qualitative change in consciousness from the normal waking state.

The concept of normality varies from one person to another. One person may be only dimly aware of time, another conscious of it almost to the minute. Awareness of bodily sensations, visual images, and surroundings vary considerably among people. Your normal state of consciousness is likely to differ from another's in countless ways.

Normality also differs depending on physical settings, cultures, and time. A normal state of consciousness for a cowboy in the American west during the nineteenth century was undoubtedly quite different from the normal state for a priest in Asia during the fourteenth century. As Tart (1969) points out, "Many 'primitive' people believe that almost every normal adult has the ability to go into a trance state and be possessed by a god; the adult who cannot do this is a psychological cripple. How deficient Americans would seem to a person from such a culture" (p. 3).

Characteristics of Altered States of Consciousness

We have all experienced changed states of consciousness when we have been asleep, dreaming, or sick with high fever, and many of us have experienced the kind of total absorption in a task that makes us lose track of time and place. Some of us

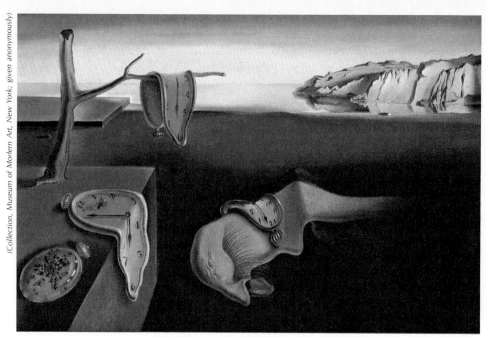

(Collection, Museum of Modern Art, New York; given anonymously)

In this famous surrealist painting, "The Persistence of Memory," Salvador Dali projects the mood of an altered state of consciousness. He blends the actual (these are recognizable objects) with the imaginary (we have never seen watches like these), creating dreamlike images. The watches imply a sense of distorted time, commonly felt by people in an altered state.

have also experienced the ASCs that come from meditation, hypnosis, and drugs. While all of these experiences differ from each other, they have some characteristics in common, such as the following (Ludwig, 1966).

Alterations in Thinking   You experience varying degrees of change in concentration, attention, memory, and judgment. You're not sure what is real and what isn't, and you get mixed up between cause and effect. Things that ordinarily seem inconsistent suddenly go unquestioned, as in a dream when one minute you are on a beach under a summer sun, and the next minute are faced by mountainous snowdrifts.

Disturbed Time Sense   You may feel that time is either standing still or moving very fast. Totally immersed in a creative activity, you may not realize that you have worked all day until the darkening shadows let you know how many hours have elapsed.

Loss of Control   You may resist loss of control as you fight the onset of sleep. Or you may eagerly give up self-control as you try to go into a mystical state or a trip induced by a hallucinogenic drug. Sex therapists have found that one factor preventing some people from experiencing orgasm is their fear of losing control.

Change in Emotional Expression   You may show your emotions much more freely, like the man who weeps copiously, laughs uproariously, or violently beats his wife only when he is drunk. Or you may become withdrawn, not showing any emotion at all, in a meditative state.

Change in Body Image   You may have a sense of being out of your body, feeling very heavy or very light, or feeling that certain body parts have shrunk or grown, or become rubbery or rigid.

Perceptual Distortions   You may see visions, hear voices or strange music, or feel you are perceiving things in a heightened way. Paintings done by people under the influence of drugs or in schizophrenic episodes generally show distortions.

Change in Meaning or Significance You may have an "a-ha!" experience, in which you feel you have attained some exciting new insight. The dreamer, the meditator, the drunkard—all may feel as if they have finally hit upon the meaning of life. In all too many cases, however, once the state is passed, the insight has either withered away or become humdrum. Some creative people, however, transform such insights into works of art or breakthrough theories.

Sense of the Indescribable "I can't explain it," you may say. While part of your problem may be a deficient vocabulary to describe experiences so far outside your ordinary realm, another may be an element of amnesia, and another may be that your thinking processes were so dulled or different during the experience that you were not sufficiently aware of what was happening to you to be able to describe it.

Feelings of Rejuvenation You may experience a sense of rebirth after emerging from certain kinds of ASCs, such as very deep sleep. People also have this sense after certain primitive puberty rites and religious conversions.

Hypersuggestibility The hypnotic trance is, of course, the prime example of the tendency of a person in an altered state to express beliefs and perform actions suggested by another person. However, this might occur in other circumstances as well. Ludwig explains this suggestibility in terms of various attributes of the altered state, including the loss of contact with reality, the diminished critical faculties, and the acceptance of contradictions.

Bringing On Altered States

The way you induce a particular altered state has a lot to do with the kind of state you want to induce, the kind of person you are yourself, and the circumstances around you. Methods of induction vary from overstimulation to the withdrawal of stimulation, as in the following examples (adapted from Ludwig, 1966):

■ *Repetition, monotony, restricted movement:* Solitary confinement, trudging across unmarked Arctic slopes, driving along miles of high-speed highway, immobilization after surgery.

The monotony of traversing mile after mile of a high-speed highway unbroken by interesting scenery can put drivers in a less alert state of consciousness.

The description of writers and artists so caught up in creative work that they lose track of time, forget appointments, are oblivious to activity around them, and go without food or sleep is familiar. The description of such a state as an *altered state,* however, is new. Also new is the concept that such a state can apply to many different tasks, including such apparently humdrum ones as tightening screws on an assembly line—*if the* workers are able to lose themselves in the task at hand. Such states of intense concentration are known as *flow states.*

After 10 years of studying peak performers in a number of different fields (such as athletes, composers, dancers, chess masters, surgeons), researchers at the University of Chicago found that when such people described times they had "outdone themselves," the descriptions had the

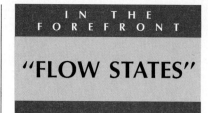
flavor of an altered state. They lost track of time and perceived events as going either very quickly or very slowly; their sensory perceptions and bodily sensations were different; they focused almost effortlessly on the task at hand without being conscious of irrelevant thoughts and sensations (like a ringing doorbell); and they experienced a sense of *euphoria,* or extreme happiness. They also showed decreased cortical activity (Goleman, 1986).

People seem to get into these states when they are faced with

greater demands than usual, but not so great that they feel overwhelmed. The investigators found that people often create their own conditions for flow. They increase the challenge in boring jobs. For example, an assembly-line worker may become immersed in the job of tightening screws by continuing to experiment with ways to do the job faster. Or they divide a complex problem into manageable parts and then fling themselves into one part at a time.

One psychologist, Ellen Langer, has compared a similar state of active attention, which she calls *mindfulness,* to meditation. "We're trying to achieve the same goal as meditation, but in a western way," she says. "We try to get people to see the moment more creatively by paying more active attention" (Langer, Beck, Janoff-Bulman, & Timko, 1984; Langer, Chanowitz, & Blank, 1985).

- *Barrage of stimulation, extensive activity:* "Third degree" grilling, brainwashing, crowd influence (as in a revivalist meeting or tribal ceremony), frenzied dancing, prolonged masturbation, long-distance running, emotional conflict.

- *Mental concentration:* Praying, sentry duty, reading, writing, problem solving, turning one's full attention to an absorbing task, listening to a charismatic speaker. Creative, productive activity can lead to the condition described in the box "Flow States."

- *Passivity:* Daydreaming, drowsiness, meditation, autohypnotism, soothing music, free association during psychoanalysis, muscular relaxation (as in sunbathing).

- *Physiological factors:* Changes in body chemistry brought about by drugs, dehydration, sleep deprivation, fasting, hyperventilation, fever, illness, withdrawal from addicting drugs.

Now let's take a look at some of these altered states, beginning with one that we all experience practically every day of our lives—sleep.

SLEEP

We can see the impact of technology on psychology when we look at what has happened in the growing field of sleep research. Until about 60 years ago, scientists had focused almost entirely on the waking state. This changed with the invention in 1929 of the **electroencephalograph,** an instrument that measures brain-wave activity. In 1937, Loomis and his associates discovered that stages of sleep were related to EEG states. Research in the 1950s and 1960s resulted in the publication of a standardized sleep stage scoring manual, which made it possible for researchers working in different sleep labs to analyze their data according to one standard (Rechtschaffen & Kales, 1968).

Electroencephalograph Instrument that measures brain-wave activity.

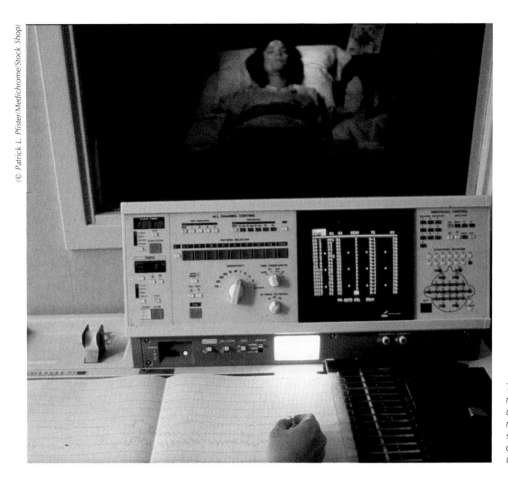

Thanks to volunteers who have spent nights in sleep laboratories hooked up to various measuring devices, we now have a large body of data on stages of sleep, frequency of dreaming, and other aspects of this universal experience.

For most of what we have learned about sleep, we are indebted to volunteers, many of them college students, who agree to spend varying numbers of nights in sleep laboratories, hooked up to such measuring devices as the electroencephalograph; the **electromyograph,** which measures muscle movements; and the **electrooculograph,** which measures eye movements. The electrodes that provide the data for these devices are placed on subjects in virtually all sleep laboratories in the same standardized way known as the *international 10-20 system* (Jasper, 1958).

It was in the 1950s, with a series of studies conducted at the University of Chicago, that sleep research really came into its own. Eugene Aserinsky, a graduate student working with Nathaniel Kleitman, was studying the eye movements of sleeping infants. He noted times when the eyes moved very quickly, in patterns very similar to waking eye movements, and that these times were followed by periods of little or no eye movement. This discovery led to the distinction between *REM (rapid-eye-movement) sleep* and *NREM (non-rapid-eye-movement)* sleep, which show different brain-wave patterns, breathing and heart rates, and dream patterns (Aserinsky & Kleitman, 1953). It also led to differentiation among four stages of NREM sleep.

Electromyograph *Instrument that measures muscle movement.*

Electrooculograph *Instrument that measures eye movements.*

REM (rapid-eye-movement) sleep *Sleep associated with dreaming; also called active or paradoxical sleep.*

NREM (non-rapid-eye-movement) sleep *Four sleep stages, each with distinct EEG patterns, not typically associated with dreaming.*

Aspects of Sleep

Stages and Kinds of Sleep   The two types of sleep (REM and NREM) and the stages within them show unique kinds of activity in many body processes, not just a simple reduction of activity in all systems (Williams, Holloway, & Griffiths, 1973). As we progress through the four stages of non-REM sleep (stages 1 through 4 in Figure 4-1, page 124), our sleep gets progressively deeper. From the deepest stage we move back up through the stages and into REM sleep, which is associated with dreaming.

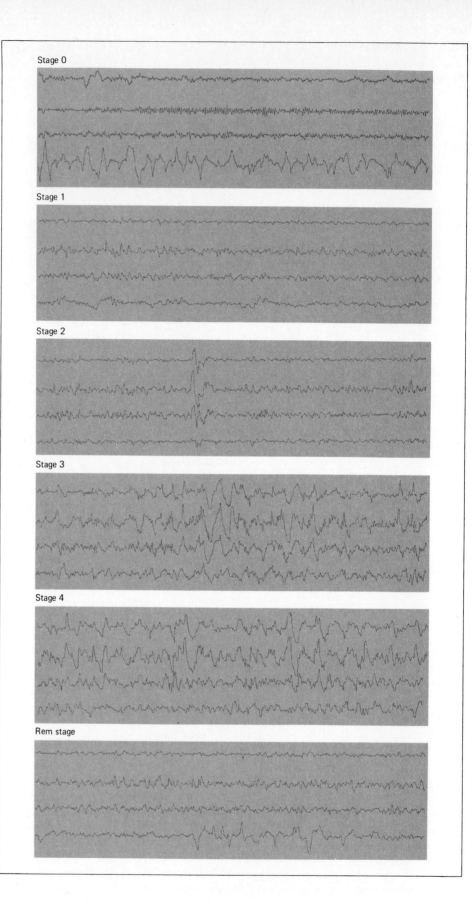

FIGURE 4-1 *EEG tracings of stages of wakefulness and sleep. Stage 0 is the stage of wakefulness. In stages 1 through 4, sleep becomes progressively deeper. REM sleep, which is represented in the final tracing, is associated with dreaming. (Source: Webb, 1984.)*

Adults typically have four to six sleep cycles per night, later cycles showing longer periods of REM sleep.

Researchers identify the stages of sleep by EEG patterns. An EEG tracing shows the *amplitude*, or voltage level, of brain waves (represented as the height of each wave in the pen movements on the paper) and brain-wave *frequency* (the rate of up-and-down pen movements). When you are fully awake, an EEG of your brain waves will show small, fast *beta* waves. Just before you fall asleep, when you are relaxed but still awake, your brain waves would show an *alpha* rhythm of larger, slower waves (8 to 12 cycles per second). Your eyes begin to close, your breathing and heart rates slow, and your body temperature drops. (See Figure 4-1 for graphic depictions of these processes.)

NON-REM SLEEP *Stage 1* For just a few minutes after you fall asleep, you are in the stage of light sleep, during which you can be awakened fairly easily. Your eyes move more slowly, beginning to roll from side to side. Your brain waves are 3 to 7 cycles per second, a little slower than they were just before you fell asleep. Your breathing becomes irregular and your muscles relax.

Stage 2 As you drift into a deeper sleep, one of two brain wave patterns that occur only in this stage will show up on your EEG. One, demonstrating short bursts of brain activity, is the *sleep spindle* (12 to 14 cycles per second, so called because on an EEG they look like thread wrapped around an old-fashioned sewing spindle, or spool). The other is a *K complex*, a low-frequency, high-amplitude wave.

Stage 3 As you sleep more deeply, your brain slows down even more, and a *delta* rhythm (0.5 to 2 cycles per second) appears.

Stage 4 When delta waves become more prominent, they signal your descent into the deepest sleep of all, during which you are very hard to arouse. If suddenly awakened, you may sit bolt upright, disoriented and confused. It usually takes about 30 minutes to reach this point, and you will remain in this deep sleep for 30 to 40 minutes. You will then rise through levels 3, 2, and 1, completing a 90-minute cycle that occurs throughout the night. At some point you will emerge into a very different stage—REM sleep.

REM SLEEP You have been asleep for about 90 minutes. Your eyes, which had been quite still, suddenly dart around as if you are watching something. The breathing and heart rates that had been slow and regular speed up irregularly, and your blood pressure rises. Your brain-wave tracings move back into a pattern very similar to those of the stage 1 EEG. In this stage, known as *emergent stage 1*, it is very hard to wake you up, as opposed to the initial stage 1, when it is very easy.

Rapid-eye-movement sleep is also known as *active* or *paradoxical* sleep, because all the brain-wave signs are so similar to the waking state, even though you are clearly asleep. Another paradox is that even though there are many signs of brain activity, the muscles are so relaxed that movement is impossible. This is why sleepwalking never occurs during REM sleep. Your first episode of REM sleep may last for about 10 minutes, while later episodes may last for as long as 1 hour. This is the time when you are most likely to dream.

If you are a woman, the blood flow into your vagina is altered during REM sleep. If you are a man, your penis is likely to become erect. This is because REM is a time of physiological arousal, not because of any sexual dream content. The discovery of nocturnal penile tumescence (NPT) has made it possible for sex therapists to determine whether a particular man's impotence has a physiological or emotional cause. If a man does not have erections during sleep, doctors look for a physical reason, but if his sleeping erections are normal, they look for psychological causes.

Characteristics of Sleep Sleep is universal in mammals and common in much of the rest of the animal kingdom. There are, however, wide differences in the amount of sleep various species need. Some animals sleep a lot (the bat, for example, sleeps about 20 hours a day), and others sleep very little (like the elephant, which sleeps only 2 to 4 hours a day). Many lower animals seem to go through periods of REM and NREM sleep, just as human beings do.

During sleep your brain is still functioning at a high, if different, level. You will wake up even from a fairly deep sleep in response to a stimulus with a special meaning (Williams et al., 1973). This explains why a new mother can sleep through the wailing of fire sirens outside her window but wake up at a whimper from her baby in the next room. During sleep your brain apparently categorizes incoming signals as "important" or "unimportant" and wakes you up or lets you sleep on accordingly.

The awareness of the brain's functioning during sleep has tantalized researchers and busy students with the possibility of learning during sleep. Wouldn't it be wonderful if you could turn on a cassette by your bed at night and wake up in the morning with a brain full of new knowledge! Unfortunately, however, "no study has been able to convincingly show an ability to learn complex verbal material during sleep" (Webb & Cartwright, 1978, p. 227). It looks as if we'll have to keep studying the old-fashioned way—awake.

Circadian Rhythms When Thomas Edison invented the light bulb, he probably didn't realize the extent to which he would change people's lives. This invention freed us from the sleep-wake pattern most of humanity had always observed. Jet planes that rush us from one time zone to another, 24-hour businesses and services that require personnel to work at odd hours, and television that seduces us into late-night viewing habits have also changed our lives. Still, none of these inventions changed the human body, and today our inner mechanisms are often in conflict with our external technology.

Circadian rhythms Biological patterns in body functions that occur about every 25 hours.

Plants, animals, and human beings still operate by inner daily time clocks. These **circadian** (from the Latin for *about a day*) **rhythms** govern the amount of sleep we need during a typical day. What if people didn't have to eat or sleep or be awake at any special time? An experiment in the early 1960s placed subjects in a windowless basement apartment with no clocks, no radio or television, or anything else to indicate the time of day or night (Aschoff & Wever, 1962/1982). The participants ate and slept whenever they wanted to. Through this study and others, we have learned that most human beings drift into a 25-hour day.

Our body temperature also follows a 25-hour pattern, fluctuating in a rhythm that correlates with our sleeping patterns. Most of us go to bed when our body temperature is falling and sleep for 7 or 8 hours. If our schedule changed so we went to bed when body temperature was at its peak, we would sleep much longer—15 or 16 hours. So the *time* we go to sleep, not how long we have been awake, generally seems to be more important in determining how long we will stay asleep.

This information has many practical applications. One relates to shift workers. Since it takes several days for a person to adjust his or her circadian rhythms to a new schedule, it makes sense (for optimal physiological functioning) for people who work the night shift to continue on that shift for a long enough period to allow adaptation. Having to switch from day (8 A.M. to 4 P.M.) to swing (4 P.M. to midnight) to night (midnight to 8 A.M.) shifts every week or more often can take a heavy toll.

The consequences of tampering with circadian rhythms can be severe. Insects and mice whose day-night cycle is changed weekly show 5 to 20 percent decreases in their life spans. People working on frequently changing schedules are often prone to sleep and digestive ailments (Moore-Ede, Sulzman, & Fuller, 1982). Furthermore, these effects can create hazards for others. Airline pilots' erratic schedules and travels across time zones contribute to fatigue, which is being blamed increasingly for accidents. The fact that the accident at the Three Mile Island nuclear power plant occurred at 4:00 A.M. with a new night crew suggests that a loss of efficiency may have contributed to the disaster (Moore-Ede et al., 1982).

Why We Sleep   If we rest quietly in bed, eyes closed and muscles relaxed, will such rest do the same for our bodies that sleep does? According to research, the answer is no. Rest alone cannot replace sleep (Webb & Cartwright, 1978). No one knows for sure why we sleep, even though sleep students have pondered and researched this puzzle. Most of the experiments have involved depriving people of sleep and then looking at the consequences. It has been found that people are surprisingly adaptable with regard to amount of sleep, but they cannot do without it totally for a prolonged period.

WHAT CAUSES SLEEP?   Researchers have not yet learned exactly what tells our body that sleep is necessary, but one recent discovery may provide some clues. When a "sleep-promoting substance" isolated from human urine was injected into the brains of rabbits, the rabbits showed a 50 percent increase in slow-wave sleep, a sleep that appeared normal under testing. This sleep was similar to the deep, nondreaming state that occurs in animals that have been deprived of sleep and are then allowed to sleep when they want (Krueger, Pappenheimer, & Karnovsky, 1982). It is possible that this substance affected the reticular formation in the brain, which, as we saw in Chapter 2, is the structure that controls sleep and arousal. Identification of a sleep-promoting factor might help researchers to develop a safe, natural sleeping pill.

FUNCTIONS OF SLEEP   What does sleep do for us? The traditional wisdom has long been that it had an ability to restore bodies and brains from the fatigue of daily activity. A recent study, which found an increase in slow-wave sleep and in total sleep time in subjects who had run a 92-kilometer (57-mile) road race, seems to support this theory (Shapiro, Bortz, Mitchell, Bartel, & Jooste, 1981). Since research has shown that there is continuous activity of one kind or another during sleep, however, this is probably not the whole story. Another possibility is that we sleep not to *restore* our bodies after we get exhausted, but to *prevent* exhaustion. If we're sleeping, we can't be doing all the other things that would tire us out.

   Still another explanation is the evolutionary theory advanced by Webb (1971), which proposes that we sleep because of ancient adaptive patterns that once ensured survival. By curling up at night inside caves, early humans remained safe from predatory animals and other perils of the dark; those who slept at night survived and passed down their nocturnal sleeping patterns to their descendants. This theory explains the different sleep schedules of different animals—those whose predators are up and about during the day sleep at night. But it doesn't, or course, answer the big question: Why do animals sleep at all? So far, there is no answer.

FUNCTIONS OF REM SLEEP   To find out whether REM sleep has special value, the psychiatrist William Dement (1960) conducted experiments in which he awakened subjects each time they entered REM sleep and then let them go back to sleep. Over a period of three to seven nights, this procedure reduced REM sleep by about 75 percent. After this time, the same procedure was followed for NREM sleep. Those subjects who had been awakened during REM sleep became more anxious and irritable and had trouble concentrating. They caught up on their lost REM periods by showing more REM sleep on the "recovery night," the first night when they could sleep without being interrupted.

   The body's making up for lost REM sleep—whether this loss is the result of deliberate interruption (as in a sleep lab) or of using drugs or alcohol—is known as **REM rebound**. After reviewing some 80 studies of human beings and animals, Webb (1975) concluded that while REM is hard to suppress and insists on making up for its absence, it cannot be linked to any particular psychological function.

When the editors of the magazine "Fine Woodworking" asked readers to report injuries, they found that, of 952 shop accidents, the greatest number—more than one-third—had occurred between noon and 3 P.M. Since part of this time is taken for lunch, when no work is done, and since most hobbyists (70 percent of the magazine's readers) aren't in their shops at all during those hours on weekdays, the injury rate for this time period is disproportionately high. It seems likely that a decrease in efficiency after lunch is to blame.

REM rebound   *The body's making up for lost REM sleep.*

SLEEP DEPRIVATION   What happens when animals and people are not allowed to sleep at all for various periods of time? Relatively little of a physiological nature occurs—if the loss of sleep is not *too* great. Human beings often develop hand tremors, double vision, droopy eyelids, and a lower pain threshold after 5 to 10 sleepless days. Animals often lose a lot of weight, possibly because of the stress the animal is under to stay awake and because of the total disruption of the body's biorhythms (Webb, 1975).

What about the ability to function? Here, too, there are symptoms, but they are not so severe as we might have supposed. People who have gone without sleep for as long as three nights can still carry out most tasks fairly well. They have the most trouble with tasks that take a long time; tasks that are difficult or complex, requiring several different operations; tasks that must be finished in a short period of time; tasks that use recently acquired skills; tasks that require new short-term learning; and tasks for which they receive no feedback as to how well they are doing (Webb & Bonnet, 1979).

One study *has* shown brain tissue damage and death in rats who suffered *prolonged* sleep deprivation (Rechtschaffen, Gilliland, Bergmann, & Winter, 1983). This study compared a severely sleep-deprived group of rats with a moderately sleep-deprived control group. The control rats were active, had healthy-looking fur, responded to stimuli, and showed no outward signs of pathology. The experimental rats, however, developed yellowed, ungroomed fur, skin lesions, and swelling of the paws, and they became very weak and unable to maintain their balance. Electroencephalograms showed declines in brain function, and some of the rats died. This study underscores the fact that organisms can adapt to moderate loss of sleep, but that severe sleep deprivation can be catastrophic. It also supports the notion that sleep serves a vital physiological function.

Another study showed that the quality of sleep may be as important as its length. One group of young adults volunteered for an experiment in which they were awakened after each minute of sleep all night long for two consecutive nights (Bonnet, 1985). They then had two undisturbed recovery nights. Their total sleep time was only 1 hour less than usual during the experimental nights, since they usually went back to sleep quickly, but the repeated awakenings took a heavy toll on their functioning. They did poorly on addition problems and tests of reaction time, and they felt sleepy. By the middle of the second disruption night, they became confused on awakening, could not make sense of what the experimenter was saying, could not perform simple tasks (like saying "A" when asked to give the letter that precedes B). They were experiencing "sleep drunkenness," the confusion that results from arousal during sleep (Bonnet, 1985, p. 18). The disruption affected their sleep patterns considerably. Wakefulness and stage 1 sleep increased dramatically, stage 2 was reduced, and stages 3 and 4 and REM sleep virtually disappeared.

Persons totally deprived of sleep get confused and disoriented and become irritable, but their personalities are likely to remain intact. They do show an overwhelming need to sleep and have to struggle hard to stay awake. Few human beings, however, can match the ingenuity of one experimental rat reported by Webb (1975) that had been kept from sleeping by a cage floor made up of a slowly rotating wheel surrounded by water:

> He managed to climb to the top of his chamber, up smooth steel walls, and hook his teeth into a meshed wire covering the chamber. There he was found sleeping while suspended by his teeth! (p. 121)

Research seems to contradict the common feelings most of us have when we have slept too little the night before. The reason we don't feel well after not sleeping well or enough may have more to do with factors other than the actual loss of sleep itself—the stress we are under that prevented our sleeping in the first place, or the energy we are expanding in whatever we are doing when we are not sleeping, whether it's working, playing, or worrying (Webb, 1975).

These findings may seem to indicate that sleep isn't that important, after all. But this is certainly not the case. Even though little or no physical or psychological damage seems to result from occasional loss of sleep, such deprivation does, of course, have other effects. Real damage can occur when the driver of a car or the operator of heavy machinery succumbs to a need for sleep and goes off the road or gets a limb caught in a machine.

CAN WE LEARN TO SLEEP LESS? With all that we have to do and want to do, most of us could use a few extra hours in the day. One intriguing possibility is the notion of plucking those hours from the time we ordinarily spend sleeping. Is this feasible? According to some research, it is (Friedmann et al., 1977; Mullaney et al., 1977).

Investigators selected four couples in long-term, stable relationships—eight men and women in their twenties who had no sleep disturbances, no evidence of drug abuse, and no chronic physical complaints or serious personality disturbances, and who wanted to reduce their sleep time. Three couples ordinarily slept about 8 hours per night, the fourth about 6.5 hours. For the first 3 weeks of the study (the baseline period), the subjects slept their normal amounts. Then at 2-week intervals they went to bed 30 minutes later, keeping their morning wake-up time constant. When the 8-hour sleepers were down to 6.5 hours, they continued to reduce their sleep time by 30 minutes, this time at 3-week intervals. Those who got below 5.5 hours stayed at this sleep time for 1 month before trying to reduce it further. The subjects stayed in the study for 4 to 6 months, by which time the former 8-hour sleepers were sleeping from 4.5 to 5.5 hours per night; the other couple reduced sleep time to 5 hours per night.

The percentage of REM sleep remained constant, which meant that there was less of it altogether. REM sleep did tend to occur earlier in some subjects. There was less stage 2 sleep, no reduction in stage 3, and an increase in stage 4 sleep. This increase in both the amount and percentage of the deepest sleep stage indicates that the sleep of these subjects became more efficient as there was less of it.

During the study, the subjects were not significantly more tense, angry, depressed, or confused. As sleep levels dropped, however, they did report being more tired, and when they were sleeping less than 6 hours per night they found it hard to get up in the morning. They felt less efficient, but they did just as well on tests of performance, and in school or on the job. At the lowest levels of sleep several complained of eye problems—blurred vision, itching, and dryness. It often took 7 to 10 days to adapt to new reduced sleep levels. They did adapt, though, so that one year after the end of the study, six of the subjects were sleeping an average of just over 6 hours per night—less than they had before the program began. The only subjects who reverted to the baseline were the two who had slept 6.5 hours in the first place.

So it seems that by reducing sleep gradually, it is sometimes possible to shave an hour or two off of total sleep time. There are limits, however: none of the subjects in this study lowered their sleep time to less than 4.5 hours. It is apparently a very rare person who can get along with less sleep than this. Sleep patterns change across the life span, and age seems to be related to the amount of sleep that people need, as indicated in the box "Sleep throughout the Life Span" (page 130).

What Is Your Sleep Personality Profile? Sleep patterns vary among people along a number of dimensions. While little of the research is conclusive, it raises interesting questions.

HOW LONG DO YOU SLEEP? If you regularly sleep less than 6 hours a night, not because you have insomnia but because this is all the sleep you need, you're consid-

The next time you say, "I slept like a baby," remember that new babies usually wake up every 2 to 3 hours around the clock. Fortunately for all concerned (especially their parents), this pattern soon changes. Sleep patterns keep changing throughout the life span.

INFANCY
Newborn babies sleep an average of about 16 hours every day. One healthy baby may sleep as little as 11 hours, another as much as 21.5 (Parmalee, Wenner, & Schulz, 1964). They start to sleep through the night at varying ages, generally in the first 3 to 6 months, and by 6 months, more than half their sleep takes place at night. Newborns generally have six to eight sleep periods, which alternate between quiet and active sleep. Active sleep, probably the equivalent of the REM sleep of maturity, appears rhythmically in cycles of about 1 hour and accounts for 50 to 80 percent of the newborn's total sleep. Over the first 6 months, REM sleep diminishes in both total time and percentage of sleep time (to about 30 percent), and cycle lengths become more consistent (Coons & Guilleminault, 1982).

CHILDHOOD
In early childhood the average amount of sleep declines, with wide individual differences. Preschoolers tend to sleep through the night with

SLEEP THROUGHOUT THE LIFE SPAN

one daytime nap, and between the ages of 6 to 16 sleep drops from 11 to 8 hours. By age 5, REM sleep accounts for only a little over 2 hours (Webb & Bonnet, 1979). Stage 4 sleep is at its highest proportion in early childhood, with 100 minutes or more seen in 2-year-olds.

ADOLESCENCE
Teenagers are less likely to wake up spontaneously in the morning and are apt to sleep later and take afternoon naps, possibly due to a chronic lack of sleep associated with contemporary life styles (Anders, Caraskadon, & Dement, 1980).

YOUNG ADULTHOOD
We know the most about the sleep habits of 18- to 22-year-old college students, the group that provides the largest pool of research volunteers. On average, they take 5 to 15 minutes to fall asleep, awaken only once every other night, and stay awake for less than 5 minutes. No sex differ-

ences show up, and both sexes average between 7 and 8 hours at night (ranging from about 6 to 10 hours), with great variability from day to day. While they go to bed at varying times, they tend to have more regular times for awakening. They spend the most time—about half the night—in stage 2 sleep and spend about one-fourth the night in REM sleep. The first REM period (about 10 minutes) is the shortest, with later periods getting progressively longer, up to 1 hour in length. Almost all stage 4 sleep occurs in the first 4 hours after falling asleep.

LATER ADULTHOOD
At age 25 or 30, the amount of stage 4 sleep drops dramatically so that by age 35 it accounts for less than 40 minutes a night. By age 50, some people have none of this very deep sleep (Webb & Bonnet, 1979). Sleep patterns undergo major changes for most people between early adulthood and late middle age. People over 60 often become "night prowlers" in the home because they wake up more often, have more trouble falling asleep again, sleep more lightly, and have fewer periods of deep sleep.

Women's sleep patterns do not change as dramatically as those of men, and in general women's patterns tend to resemble the sleep of men ten years younger (Webb, 1975).

ered a "short sleeper." If you usually sleep more than nine hours, you're a "long sleeper." Is there a relationship between length of sleep and personality? It depends on which study you read.

When Webb and Friel (1971) compared 54 17- and 18-year-old first-year college students, they found no significant differences between short and long sleepers in scores on personality or aptitude tests, or in physical examinations. However, when Hartmann, Baekeland, and Zwilling (1972) conducted the same kind of study with 29 men over age 20, two different personality types emerged. Short sleepers tended to be energetic, efficient, outgoing people who were satisfied with themselves and their lives, rarely complained, and were somewhat conforming, socially and politically. They handled stress by keeping busy and denying it. Long sleepers were depressed, anxious, nonconforming, critical, and unsure of themselves. They dreamed more than short sleepers and were more likely to be artistic and creative.

Although clinical observations suggest that short sleepers are "high drive" people and long sleepers are "down" and "depressed," Webb (1979) maintains that the research to date has not demonstrated this difference. It is possible that more sophisticated kinds of tests would identify differences more consistently, but at the moment we just don't know.

DO YOU NEED MORE SLEEP AT CERTAIN TIMES IN YOUR LIFE? About one out of three people is a *variable sleeper* whose sleep needs change for weeks at a time at different periods of life (Hartmann & Brewer, 1976). If you need less sleep when things in your life are going well and more when you change jobs or schools, when depressed or under stress (especially after the death of a family member or the end of a love affair), or when you have to expend more mental activity, you are a variable sleeper. Physical factors also play a part, since both pregnancy and illness require extra sleep. Since these findings mirror the differences between long and short sleepers and since it's the need for REM sleep that seems to change, these findings seem to suggest that REM sleep may help to restore psychic equilibrium at times of stress and upheaval.

HOW SOUNDLY DO YOU SLEEP? Are you the kind of heavy sleeper who sleeps through thunderstorms, slammed doors, and the sudden flooding of a room with light? Or a light sleeper who is awakened by a whisper or a light seeping into the room through a closed door? Most people stay in the same classification from one night to another (Zimmerman, 1970). Light and heavy sleepers awakened during REM sleep report about the same number of dreams, but when awakened from NREM sleep, light sleepers are much more likely to report dreaming, and heavy sleepers are more likely to report drifting kinds of thoughts such as those in daydreams.

Even if you are ordinarily a heavy sleeper, a stimulus with special meaning for you—your name whispered in your ear or the sound of an expected friend's tapping lightly on your door—may rouse you, confirming the continuing activity of your brain even during the deepest stages of sleep.

Dreaming

Dreams assumed an important, if mysterious, place in people's lives long before the Bible reported Joseph's prophetic interpretation of the Pharaoh's dreams of lean and fat cattle. Some 4000 years later, Sigmund Freud, recognizing that dreams came not from divine forces but from the dreamer's own mind, drew from them clues to the workings of the unconscious. But not until the middle of this century have dreams become accessible to scientific research. This is, again, a result of technology: until outside observers could tell when someone was dreaming, the only people who could identify dreams were the dreamers themselves. Once scientists had made the connection between REM sleep and dreaming and had the tools that would enable them to tell when a dream was occurring, they could begin to solve some of the puzzles locked in our dreams.

What *is* a dream? A dream is a mental experience that occurs during sleep, consisting of a series of vivid, usually visual, and often hallucinatory images. In dreams we jump bizarrely from one time and place to another, among people who may be dead, fictional, or unknown. When we are dreaming we accept such strange happenings without question (as Diane Papalia accepted the inconsistencies in the dream described at the beginning of this chapter).

Criteria of Dreaming How do researchers know when someone is dreaming? Four criteria have evolved:

1 *Increase in pulse and breathing rates.*
2 *Typical brain-wave EEG of an emergent stage 1 pattern.* This sign during REM sleep is reliably associated with dreaming. Although some sleepers awakened during NREM sleep report having been dreaming, their dreams are usually much

shorter, less distinct, and more like waking thoughts than like typical dream images.

3 *Lack of body movement.* That terrifying sensation of being frozen to the spot while someone is chasing you or of opening your mouth to scream but being unable to utter a sound may have a basis in the fact that we are unable to move our muscles while we are dreaming. This "dreamer's paralysis" may be due to a brain chemical that inhibits the motor neurons that ordinarily cause our muscles to contract (Chase, 1981). If such inhibition did not occur, we might act out our dreams and wouldn't get the rest that sleep provides. Furthermore, since our sense of judgment is suspended when we dream, we might get ourselves into dangerous situations.

4 *Appearance of rapid eye movements.* Earlier dream researchers thought that the movements that can be seen under the closed eyelids of a sleeper were related to the action in the dream. The typical side-to-side movements indicated that you were looking at the scene in your dream; vertical movements were thought to occur in those dreams where the action was up and down. Newer evidence, however, indicates that eye movements are probably unrelated to dream content. Cats raised in the dark, which have never seen anything, still show eye movement during sleep, as do adults who have been blind for as long as 55 years and who "hear" their dreams rather than "see" them (Webb & Bonnet, 1979).

Patterns of Dreaming   After monitoring the sleep of thousands of volunteers, dream researchers have come up with answers to some of the most common questions about dreaming.

WHAT IS A TYPICAL NIGHT OF DREAMING LIKE?   Your first dream, occuring after about 90 minutes of sleep, lasts about 10 minutes. You have a total of four to six periods of dreaming throughout the night, for a total of 1 to 2 hours of dream time.

IS IT POSSIBLE THAT I NEVER DREAM?   All subjects in dream laboratories have "reported dreaming upon being awakened at appropriate times" (Kleitman, 1960, p. 241). Everyone seems to dream every night, but some people remember dreams more clearly.

WHY DON'T I REMEMBER MY DREAMS?   Most people don't remember most of their dreams, for a variety of reasons. Freud (1900) attributed this forgetting to the repression of anxiety-laden thoughts, but recent research has found that people are *more* likely to remember very emotional dreams, and that a more important reason for forgetting seems to be distraction upon awakening. We're more likely to remember our dreams if we wake up soon after having them, are not distracted by other thoughts or activities, and deliberately try to remember them, for example, by keeping a dream diary (D. B. Cohen, 1974; Cohen & Wolfe, 1973). Individual differences in visual memory also affect dream recall; people who are better at remembering what they see during the waking state remember more about their dreams (Cory, Ormiston, Simmel & Dainoff, 1975).

There is also a theory of "state-dependent amnesia." When we're awake and alert we don't remember experiences that occurred in another state, like sleep, unless we're barely out of the state, as when we're awakened immediately after dreaming. When this happens, we do remember our dreams, including the very emotional ones, indicating that forgetting may have a physiological, state-related basis (Hobson and McCarley, 1977).

Another explanation for the forgetting of dreams is that they are *meant* to be forgotten. The very purpose of REM dreaming, say Crick and Mitchison (1983), is to clear our brains of unnecessary information so we won't be troubled by obsessions and hallucinations during our waking hours. They maintain that the brain has a "reverse learning mechanism," triggered by the intense electrical activity in the cortex that occurs during REM sleep, which erases various random memory associations that have formed during the day. This helps the cortex to work better and helps prevent the recurrence of dreams. (Those dreams that do recur are, they say, the ones that have tended to awaken us, possibly because they produce anxiety.)

A full explanation of the remembering and forgetting of dreams would probably involve a combination of psychology and physiology. Some people seem to forget emotional dreams for the same reasons that they repress anxious thoughts in waking life, and others forget unemotional dreams because they're not memorable (Koulack & Goodenough, 1976). It's harder to remember a dream if you were under stress before falling asleep (Goodenough, 1967; Koulack, 1970). The dream we remember tends to be the one dreamed most recently, just before awakening. This dream also tends to be the longest, most vivid, and most emotional of the night. When we remember an earlier dream, it may be because we awakened at that point (either because of the dream itself or for some other reason) or it may be because we've had this same dream before. The dreams we remember are probably not typical of most of our dreams (Cartwright, 1978).

HOW MUCH TIME DO MY DREAMS REALLY TAKE?   The notion that a long and complicated dream actually takes place in the space of a moment may owe its origin to the report given in 1861 by André Maury, who ascribed a long and complicated dream about being guillotined during the French Revolution to the fact that the top of his bed had fallen upon the back of his neck, just where the guillotine blade would have struck. Laboratory research, however, has determined that dreams take varying amounts of time, and that sleepers awakened either 5 or 15 minutes after REM onset correctly estimate the length of their dreams as either 5 or 15 minutes long. People seem to tell dream time fairly accurately (Webb & Bonnet, 1979).

DO OBJECTIVE ASPECTS OF MY ENVIRONMENT DURING SLEEP AFFECT THE CONTENT OF MY DREAMS?   As André Maury's experience would suggest, the external environment can affect the content of dreams. However, this effect is not always strong. When a bell rang in the sleep lab, a ringing bell showed up in only 20 out of 204 dreams, and only 5 out of 15 dreams told by sleepers who had gone without fluids for 24 hours contained any content related to thirst (Kleitman, 1960). There is, however, some carry-over from the waking environment into dreams. Studies of subjects who during their waking hours wore goggles that gave everything a reddish tint had more dreams with the color red or with colors near red in the spectrum than they did when they didn't wear the red goggles (Roffwarg, Herman, Bowe-Anders, & Tauber, 1976).

Content of Dreams   Where do the "stories" of our dreams come from? Most of them appear as a montage of the day's events in somewhat altered form. On the basis of some 10,000 dreams reported by normal people, Calvin Hall (1966) concluded that most dreams are commonplace. They are most often played out in familiar settings, such as a house, although the house is usually not the dreamer's own home. The most popular room is the living room, followed by—in order—bedroom, kitchen, stairway, basement, bathroom, dining room, and hall. The room is often a composite of several rooms the dreamer has known. Women's dreams more commonly take place indoors, men's out-of-doors.

In only 15 out of 100 dreams is the dreamer alone. We dream most often about the people we're emotionally involved with—our parents, spouses, and children. Men dream more often about male friends and acquaintances, while women dream of both sexes equally. About 4 out of 10 dream characters are strangers. What do we do in our dreams? Mostly, we engage in ordinary everyday activities, more often related to leisure than to work. (In this respect, Diane Papalia's dream is unusual.) We tend to walk, run, or ride rather than float or fly. Most dreams have negative tones, with apprehension the most common emotion, and hostile acts more than twice as common as friendly ones.

A comparison of the dreams of college students in 1950 and in 1980 shows that, despite many changes in society, students are still dreaming about the same things that students dreamed about 30 years ago, and the sex differences that showed up then still exist. This conclusion came from analyzing the dreams of these two groups of students according to content categories that included aggressive, friendly, and sexual interactions; misfortunes; outdoor and indoor settings; and clothing and weapons. According to the "continuity hypothesis," dreaming is "continuous" with waking life, and people dream about their concerns and preoccupations (in Diane Papalia's case, the major task of revising this book). So, either human nature does not change or 30 years is too short a time for social changes to affect dream content (Hall, Domhoff, Blick, & Weesner, 1982).

Why We Dream An activity all of us engage in every night must serve an important function. Let's look at some of the possible explanations for the purpose of dreaming.

FULFILLING WISHES AND GUARDING SLEEP Freud placed great importance on the function of dreams, calling them the "royal road to the unconscious." He believed that their *psychological* purpose was to let us express the wishes we repress during our waking lives. At the same time, he believed that they served the *biological* function of acting as the "guardians" of sleep. It does appear that when we move into REM sleep, we seem to be trying to wake up, perhaps because our emotional conflicts are insisting on surfacing. If we can deal with these conflicts in dreams, we can remain asleep—confirming this view of dreams as guardians of sleep.

Freud called the part of a dream that we remember its *manifest content*. According to Freudian theory, the events in a dream express through symbolism what is really behind the dream, the *latent content,* or *dream-thoughts*. These are the desires and conflicts we have repressed, most of which are sexual. The individual dreamer transforms latent content into manifest content by *dream-work*, which uses symbols and other kinds of psychological short-hand to make the dreamer's deepest desires more acceptable. Freudians might interpret a young man's dream of walking up the steps to his mother's house, carrying his open umbrella, as a dream of making love to his mother, because of such symbols as a long object for the penis (with the opening of the umbrella a symbol for an erection), an enclosed place (the house) for the vagina; and the activity of walking up stairs for the act of sexual intercourse.

Modern-day interpreters of dreams recognize their symbolism but are more likely to interpret symbols in a variety of ways, depending on a person's unique situation, rather than limiting them to sexual meaning. "For different persons, boarding a train may either represent a flight from a problem, engaging in a new adventure, worry about car repairs, or, simply, a concern about making a plane reservation for an upcoming trip" (Webb, 1975, p. 149). The manifest content may not stand for something else in the dreamer's past but may, in fact, show a straightforward picture of present concerns (Foulkes, 1964).

RESOLVING PERSONAL ISSUES AND SOLVING EVERYDAY PROBLEMS Alfred Adler (1936) called dreams the "factory of the emotions." Their job in this "factory" is to awaken the emotions so that the dreamer will be pushed into solving real-life problems in a realistic way. The dreamer's problems are not repressed in the Freudian sense, but are issues the dreamer is well aware of and wants to resolve. Thus, there is a continuity of thought during waking and sleep.

C. G. Jung (1933) held that dreams help us learn about ignored or suppressed aspects of ourselves. The unconscious is an instrument of self-discovery, not a repository of uncomfortable forces. Dreams provide the images that compensate for any psychic imbalance in our waking lives and help us plan our future. Jung believed that it was not necessary to look for a hidden meaning in a dream—that the manifest content would give us its personal significance. (Freud's, Adler's, and Jung's theories about personality development are discussed in Chapter 13.)

We seem to use dreams to dispel the anxiety around experiences, often by "rehearsing" things we will have to do. People commonly dream about going away to college, taking a trip, working at a new job, getting married, and having a baby just before such events. (Some people even dream about revising a textbook.) "Dreams are often safe experiments to prepare the way for coping with a future which may be anxiety provoking" (Cartwright, 1978, p. 28).

MAINTAINING SLEEP DURING PHYSIOLOGICAL ACTIVATION OF THE BRAIN   Hobson and McCarley (1977) explain the purpose of dreaming by describing its origins in basic physiological processes. The bizarre shifts and symbols of dreams may be, not the product of disguised unconscious thoughts, but the logical results of the way the brain functions during sleep. The brain creates electrical energy, and the forebrain becomes especially active during REM sleep. Rapid bursts of electrical activity in different parts of the brain determine what we dream about and how we put dream images together. The largely random or reflex process by which the various parts of the brain are stimulated accounts for illogical shifts in time, place, and other dream elements. Since such stimulation brings forth incomplete information, the brain tries to fill in with other material culled from memory, becoming like "a computer searching its addresses for key words" (p.1347). This explanation looks at dreaming as a cognitive process that may give us clues to the learning process. At the same time, it virtually ignores the psychological ramifications of dreams, lending no particular significance to the events and people we dream about or to our emotions about them.

Finally, then, we don't have conclusive research evidence to explain why we dream. The quest for this evidence continues.

Sleep Disorders

Whether it's sleeping too little, sleeping too much, or doing things during sleep that we'd rather not do (like walking and talking), a variety of sleep disorders affect people throughout the life span.

Narcolepsy   *Narcolepsy,* an uncontrollable need to sleep for brief periods, usually during the day, is accompanied by loss of muscle tone (cataplexy). It is sometimes accompanied by hallucinations as well. These occur as people are falling asleep or waking up and can be frightening, since they are so vivid that the sleeper often thinks they are really happening. Some 3 to 4 hours after waking up, the narcoleptic feels overpoweringly sleepy and often falls asleep while talking, standing, or even moving about. The person may go into many very short episodes of sleep, lasting 5 to 15 seconds, and eventually has to take a nap.

Narcolepsy is not associated with any kind of emotional disorder, yields normal EEGs, runs in families, and may be a genetic disturbance of the mechanism that regulates REM sleep. Treatment includes amphetamines for the sleepiness and antidepressants for the loss of muscle tone. Narcolepsy generally shows up for the first time between ages 10 and 25, affects between 2 and 10 people in 10,000 (some 250,000 people in the United States), and may last throughout life (Dement & Baird, 1977; Fenton, 1975).

Insomnia   About 1 in 3 Americans suffers from *insomnia.* Insomniacs spend anxious hours tossing and turning in bed, trying to go to sleep at bedtime (the biggest problem for 8 out of 10) or after awakening during the night (NIH, 1984). Half of these insomniacs consider their problem serious, and of these, half report high levels of emotional distress. Virtually anything can cause an inability to sleep, including poor

As this narcoleptic dog shows, nonhuman animals, too, sometimes experience an uncontrollable need to sleep.

(Courtesy of Dr. William Dement, Sleep Disorders Center, Stanford University)

Narcolepsy   *Disorder characterized by an uncontrollable urge to sleep.*

Insomnia   *Difficulty getting to sleep, staying asleep, or both.*

The following dos and don'ts offered by sleep experts may help you get to sleep and stay asleep.

- Follow a regular schedule: go to sleep and get up at about the same time every day, even on weekends.
- Do some exercise every day, fairly early in the day.
- Do not eat or drink anything containing caffeine after midday. This includes coffee, tea, cola drinks, and chocolate.
- Develop a relaxing before-bed routine. Avoid stimulating work or play, family arguments, and stressful activities. Do whatever relaxes you—take a hot bath, read, watch television, listen to music.
- Eat or drink something before bedtime. Grandma's old remedy of hot milk has now achieved scientific validity. An ingredient found in certain foods—including milk and such carbohydrates as sweets, bread, pasta, and rice—has been

SUGGESTIONS FOR POOR SLEEPERS

found to induce sleep. (This substance, *tryptophan*, is an amino acid that turns into the neurotransmitter *serotonin*.)
- Do not drink a large quantity of beer, wine, or liquor before you go to bed. These drinks may help you *fall* asleep, but they interfere with your *staying* asleep. When the sedative effects of alcohol wear off, you're likely to wake up. Furthermore, alcohol may trigger or dangerously worsen the disorder *sleep apnea*.

- Get into bed only when you plan to go to sleep. Using your bed as a center for working, studying, paying bills, talking on the telephone, and watching television detracts from the association between getting into bed and falling asleep.
- Sleep in the dark. Get room-darkening windowshades or blinds or wear sleep goggles.
- Sleep in quiet. If you can't (or don't want to) kick out your snoring roommate, get earplugs. You might also get an electrical "white noise" machine to block out outside noises.
- Don't worry about *not* sleeping. The more you worry about how tired you'll be the next day, the harder it will be for you to go to sleep. Remember that human beings are flexible and can function quite well on little sleep; then get up and do something relaxing or boring (like reading a dull book—unlike this one) until you start to feel sleepy.

health, high stress, an irregular life style, inadequate nutrition, drug use, and emotional problems. Most people go through occasional periods of insomnia, but for the majority normal sleeping patterns soon return.

Treatment should begin with a search for a specific psychiatric or medical condition. If such a condition is found, treatment of the condition often clears up the insomnia. Caution should be exercised in prescribing sleeping pills, since they carry risks of lowered daytime performance, potential negative effects from interactions with other drugs (especially alcohol), the possibility of overdose and drug dependence, and the danger of suppressing breathing. When drugs are given, the smallest possible dose should be taken for the shortest period possible (NIH, 1984a). Treatments which do not involve drugs include exercise; reduction or elimination of caffeine, drugs, and alcohol; and use of biofeedback and other stress-reduction and relaxation techniques.

There is no simple cure for a complicated complaint with so many possible causes, but sleep researchers have come up with commonsense measures that have helped many. See the box "Suggestions for Poor Sleepers."

Sleep apnea *Sleep disorder characterized by periods of interrupted breathing.*

Sleep Apnea *Sleep apnea* was once called the "Pickwickian syndrome" after a fat messenger boy, Joe, in Charles Dickens's *Pickwick Papers,* who fell asleep while knocking on a door. It is characterized by loud snoring, poor sleep at night, extreme daytime sleepiness, and brief periods when breathing stops during sleep (Anders et al., 1980; Brouillette, Fernbach, & Hunt, 1982). The syndrome may affect intellectual functioning, possibly because the flow of oxygen to the brain is continually interrupted. This accounts for a report that some 35 percent of affected children were diagnosed as borderline mentally retarded (Guilleminault, Eldridge, & Simmons, 1976). Many patients are obese men over age 40 whose airway may be obstructed by a thick neck, previous surgery, or a jaw deformity. Treatment may include a

Cures for insomnia are just as numerous as its causes. When sleep will not come, the important thing to remember is that human beings are flexible and can often function quite well on very little sleep.

tracheostomy (a surgical opening of the windpipe) that functions during the night and is closed off during the day, significant weight reduction, and drugs (Anders et al., 1980; Cherniak, 1981; NIH, 1984a; Orr, Martin, & Patterson, 1979; Parkes, 1977).

Night Terrors (Pavor Nocturnus) Night terrors are a very different phenomenon from nightmares; but, like nightmares, they begin to appear in early childhood, and about 1 in 4 children between ages 3 and 8 will suffer from one or the other (Hartmann, 1981). In a ***night terror*** the sleeper awakens abruptly in a state of panic, during stage 4 sleep. He or she may scream and sit up in bed, breathing quickly and staring unseeingly ahead; is not aware of any frightening dreams or thoughts; goes back to sleep quickly; and in the morning will not remember awakening. These episodes usually go away by themselves as the child matures neurologically. Night terrors do not signal underlying emotional problems and probably are an effect of sudden awakening from very deep sleep. Generally, medication is not required. The psychiatrist and sleep researcher Ernest Hartman suggests that night terrors may be a mild neurological disorder in which an electrical discharge is set off, as in a minor epileptic seizure. They may be a symptom of delayed maturation of the central nervous system.

Night terrors Sleep disorder consisting of panic attacks which typically occur within an hour of falling asleep.

Nightmares Night terrors usually occur within an hour of falling asleep; ***nightmares***, by contrast, come toward morning, during REM sleep (Hartmann, 1981). Unlike night terrors, nightmares are often vividly recalled. *Persistent* nightmares, especially those that make a child fearful and anxious during waking hours, may be a signal that a child is under too much stress and may benefit from individual or family counseling. Repetitive themes in nightmares often indicate a specific problem that a person cannot solve when awake and that, consequently, comes to the fore during sleep.

Nightmares Frightening dreams most likely to appear in childhood; they occur during REM sleep.

MEDITATION

In our battery of survival mechanisms, the fight-or-flight reaction is one of the most powerful. This arsenal of responses, which equips us to react to perceived danger, includes increases in heart and breathing rates, blood pressure, blood flow to the muscles, and oxygen consumption. When humans were threatened by wild animals

Meditation has its origins in Buddhism, a religion practiced widely in Asia. Many people who meditate, however, do so not for religious reasons but because they believe that it will reduce tension. While some psychologists share this view, others maintain that meditation is no more effective than ordinary rest in reducing arousal.

Meditation *Altered state of consciousness induced by a refocusing of attention.*

and hostile tribes on all sides, they needed the heightened alertness such responses brought. In most situations in contemporary life, however, our health and survival might be better served by a state in which we take in less oxygen, release less carbon dioxide, breathe more slowly, and have a slower pulse rate.

While some physicians and therapists claim that **meditation** can bring about this latter state (Benson, 1983), controversy surrounds this position. One school of thought maintains that meditation is no more effective than ordinary rest in reducing arousal. In reviewing the research comparing meditating and resting subjects, Holmes (1984) found no difference in heart or breathing rates, electrical activity of the skin, skin temperature, blood pressure, oxygen consumption, or other physiological measures.

Part of the problem in assessing meditation rests on the fact that there is no single easily described meditative state. Despite considerable research over the past 20 years, this phenomenon retains an aura of mysticism. Some researchers describe it as a state of relaxed wakefulness in which bodily processes are slowed down (Wallace & Benson, 1972). Others note that the body processes of *experienced* meditators show a great deal of activity, possibly reflecting the intensity of their concentration (Corby, Roth, Zarcone, & Kopell, 1978). Still others have found that the EEGs of meditators show much time spent in stages 2, 3, and 4 of actual sleep (Pagano, Rose, Stivers, & Warrenburg, 1976). At present, then, the meditative state defies precise definition.

People get into the meditative state in a variety of ways. They may whirl or dance, sit still and concentrate on a nonsensical question, look at or imagine looking at an object, or repeat a prayer, a word, or a chant. The technique best known in the west is the easily learned **transcendental meditation (TM)** developed by Maharishi Mahesh Yogi. Transcendental meditation is practiced by some 500,000 to 2 million people worldwide (Benson, 1975). In two daily sessions of 15 to 30 minutes, meditators sit in any comfortable position, closes their eyes, and concentrate on their **mantra**, a specific word or thought that has been given especially to each meditator and is not publicly revealed. The purpose of repeating the mantra is to prevent distracting thoughts.

In this state, people seem to be able to do things they are ordinarily not capable of—for example, controlling such autonomic systems as skin resistance to electricity, heart and breathing rates, and reflex reactions to heat, cold, and pain. It's not

Transcendental meditation (TM) *Best-known meditative technique in the west, developed by Maharishi Mahesh Yogi.*

Mantra *Specific word or thought used repetitiously by someone practicing transcendental meditation.*

surprising, then, that proponents claim that regular periods of meditation can help people deal with stress.

Meditation has been used in various therapeutic programs to reduce insomnia; to cut back the use of alcohol, tobacco, and other drugs; to reduce blood pressure in hypertensive patients (Benson, 1975; 1983); and to reduce the pain of angina pectoris, a frequent sign of heart disease (Kanellakos, 1978). Critics dispute the effectiveness of such programs. Some find no evidence that meditation reduces stress (Holmes, 1984), and others point out the ironic tendency for some meditators to become even *more* tense when they try to relax (Heide & Borkovec, 1983; 1984). Such "relaxation-induced anxiety" may result from the unusual feelings and thoughts that arise in the meditative state or from a fear of losing control.

Some meditators seek to create a new positive condition, rather than to overcome a negative one. After taking a "vacation" from ordinary awareness, such meditators feel that they return to full, conscious awareness even more alive to the sights and sounds around them that had faded into the backgrounds of awareness simply from being taken for granted. This freshness of perception gives them the sense of being reborn.

HYPNOSIS ▰▰▰▰▰▰▰▰▰▰▰▰▰▰▰▰▰▰

A woman bites into a lemon and raves about the sweetness of a "peach." An old man talks in the babyish lilt of a 3-year-old as he expresses his feelings upon his father's death. A woman who was a witness to a fire describes a suspicious-looking man on the scene whose features, dim in her conscious memory, seem clear to her now. All these people are demonstrating the power of a little-understood phenomenon, hypnosis. Let's explore its mysteries.

Most people believe that if you are hypnotized you will fall asleep, lose touch with your surroundings, be able to remember details hidden from conscious memory, do whatever the hypnotist tells you to do, and forget whatever you did under the hypnotic spell when you wake up. But this is not the case.

What Is Hypnosis?

The hypnotic state is very different from the sleeping state, and there is much disagreement as to whether the hypnotic state can accurately be called a trance. It has been difficult to identify physiological differences between hypnotized and unhypnotized people in terms of brain-wave patterns, eye movements, pulse and breathing rates, or galvanic (electrical) skin response. But recent research does show that highly hypnotizable subjects change from left-hemisphere to right-hemisphere dominance as they go into hypnosis (MacLeod-Morgan, 1982).

The definition of hypnosis is controversial and often depends on such elusive reports as what the hypnotist or the subject does or on subjects' reports of how they feel—criteria that are unsatisfactory by scientific standards. Hypnotized people see this state as different from their normal state. They feel more susceptible to outside influence and less able to tell what is real and what is not; they fantasize more and experience changes in body image (Crawford, 1982). Such self-reports are, of course, highly subjective and cannot be confirmed. The problem of definition is so thorny that some scientists say the hypnotic state doesn't exist at all.

We believe that there is such a thing as the hypnotic state, that it is different from the normal state of consciousness, and that some day we may have the tools to define or identify it—as we now have rapid eye movements as a criterion to identify, more or less, the state of dreaming. We define **hypnosis** as a procedure, practiced by a person with special skills, which induces a condition of heightened suggestibility in which the subject's perceptions change along lines suggested by the practitioner.

Hypnosis *Procedure which produces a state of heightened suggestibility or susceptibility to outside influence.*

This woodcut based on a drawing by Honoré Daumier satirizes the once popular belief, originally put forth by the Austrian physician Franz Mesmer, that electrical magnetism in people's bodies controlled their health. Here, a "mesmerizer" puts a patient into a trance and issues suggestions. Although such patients often seemed cured of their ailments, a royal commission discredited Mesmer and his methods.

Neodissociation theory of hypnosis
View that a hypnotized person is functioning on more than one level of awareness.

Some common behaviors observed among hypnotized people are rigidity of the arm, loss of voluntary control, hallucinations, failure to feel pain, amnesia, and responsiveness to posthypnotic suggestion (performing an action *after* coming out of the hypnotic state in response to a suggestion made *during* hypnosis) (Hilgard, 1977).

Who Can Be Hypnotized?

As much as you might like to become hypnotized, you may never be able to. You may be among that 5 or 10 percent of the population who cannot "go under" no matter how hard you try. On the other hand, you may be among that 15 percent who are hypnotized so easily that they seem to be hypnotizing themselves. Or you may be like the great majority—responsive to some degree between these two extremes (Orne, 1977). Whatever your tendency, it is likely to remain with you throughout life. College students who had been tested for hypnotizability and then retested 8 to 12 years later showed remarkably stable scores (Hilgard, 1977). Susceptibility to hypnosis does change somewhat over the life span. Susceptibility is lowest among young children and highest among preadolescents; it declines slowly from that point on (Hilgard, 1977).

Some people seem to have more hypnotizable personalities, as suggested by a relationship between psychological characteristics and the ability to be hypnotized. Easily hypnotized adults are usually able to set aside ordinary reality and become deeply immersed in reading, music, or art. They tend to have been very imaginative children who often lost themselves in flights of fantasy (J. Hilgard, 1979). Furthermore, they are less likely to suffer from the more serious psychiatric disturbances, such as depression, anxiety, or schizophrenia (Spiegel, 1984). Susceptibility to hypnosis may be at least partly hereditary, since identical twins (who have the same genetic makeup) are more alike in this respect than fraternal twins (who are no more alike, genetically, than nontwin siblings) (A. H. Morgan, 1973).

How Can We Explain Hypnosis?

Is hypnosis a unique state—a trance? A number of different viewpoints on this issue range from the notion that hypnotized people are indeed in a trance to the view that they are role-playing. Let's take a look at the two most prominent theories representing these two divergent positions.

Split-Consciousness (Neodissociation) Theory   A young woman was told that she would awaken from hypnosis to find she had no hands but that this would not trouble her (E. R. Hilgard, 1970). When she was given a strong electric shock to the hands, she didn't feel anything—even though she hadn't been told she would feel no pain.

Her experience supports Ernest R. Hilgard's **neodissociation theory of hypnosis,** which holds that hypnosis represents a true altered state and that the hypnotized person is functioning on more than one level of awareness. This is similar to the common sensation of knowing, while you are asleep and dreaming, that what seems real is only a dream and that there is another, real, world beyond your present perceptions.

E. R. Hilgard (1977) coined the term "hidden observer" to explain a phenomenon he discovered during experiments in which subjects kept their hands in ice water for 45 seconds. Holding the hands in ice water usually produces intense pain; in Hilgard's experiment hypnotized subjects reported little or no pain, but when they were asked to give reports as if from a "hidden observer" (either by a kind of automatic writing or by pressing a key with one hand while the other was in the ice water), about half of the particularly "good" subjects showed that they did feel pain at some level of awareness. Apparently, through hypnosis, they were blocking this pain from full consciousness.

Cognitive-Behavioral Theory According to the *cognitive-behavioral theory of hypnosis,* the hypnotic state does not depend on any trance-induction techniques and can occur even in their absence (Barber, 1970). It depends on the subject's readiness to think along with and imagine the themes suggested by the hypnotist; in other words, the "hypnotized" subject is playing a role. If the hypnotist says the subject will not feel pain, will not be able to lift an arm, or will become a 4-year-old again, the subject in the right frame of mind will go along with these themes and behave accordingly. Subjects with passive, negative, or cynical attitudes will not think along with these themes.

Cognitive-behavioral theory of hypnosis View that the hypnotic state depends on the subject's readiness to "think with" the hypnotist.

In an interesting study conducted by Barber and Wilson (1977), 66 student nurses were divided into three groups of 22. Those in the first group were hypnotized in traditional ways; those in the second were given "think with" instructions designed to encourage them to focus their imaginative powers and to discourage negative and passive attitudes. The third group served as a control. The "think with" group was told: "Let me give you an example of the kind of tests I might give you. I might ask you . . . to feel as if you're looking at a television program." The experimenter then gave the subjects three ways they could respond: (1) They could say negative things to themselves, such as "This is ridiculous; there is no television there," and nothing would happen. (2) They could wait for a television screen to appear, and again nothing would happen. Or, (3) they could recall a program they liked and let themselves "see" it again in their mind's eye.

All three groups were then tested on a scale of creative imagination, which measured subjects' reports of arm heaviness, hand levitation, finger numbness, drinking imaginary water, smelling and tasting an imaginary orange, hearing nonexistent music, feeling imagined sunshine, sensing a slowdown of time, regressing to childhood, and feeling relaxed. The students in the "think-with" group achieved higher scores than those in either of the other groups, lending support to the view that hypnosis comes about because of the subject's ability to think along the lines suggested by the hypnotist.

At this point we cannot say whether either of these theories is correct. If we ever do arrive at a definitive explanation of hypnosis, that will affect its practical uses. Right now it is being used in a number of ways in everyday life, including aiding therapy and solving crimes; see the box "Practical Applications of Hypnosis."

Is Hypnosis Safe?

The Department of Health, Education and Welfare (1971) listed hypnosis among several procedures that it considered potentially stressful. However, one study that looked into the aftereffects of five different kinds of activities participated in by 209 introductory psychology students found being hypnotized to be no more troubling than taking part in a verbal learning experiment, attending a class, taking an examination, or college life in general (Coe & Ryken, 1979). In fact, examinations, college classes, and college life in general seemed to make students more anxious, fearful, depressed, or unhappy than hypnosis did, and the 70 students who had been hypnotized often found hypnosis a pleasant experience that left them refreshed and rested.

Can hypnosis make you do something you ordinarily wouldn't do, such as killing a person or taking off your clothes in front of strangers? One school maintains that you would resist such suggestions, while the other claims that a hypnotist could get you to do such things by couching his suggestions along lines you could accept, such as telling you that someone was threatening your life and killing him would be a matter of self-defense or that you're in a doctor's office where getting undressed would be appropriate.

TREATING AILMENTS

The list of ailments that have been treated with hypnosis is a varied one. Hypnosis has been used in the treatment of pain from childbirth, angina pectoris, burns, back problems, dental work, headaches, cancer, arthritis, and major surgery. In addition, it has been applied to a wide range of other conditions, including nausea due to the chemical treatment of cancer; obesity; insomnia; abuse of alcohol, nicotine, and other drugs; warts; asthma; nail biting; phobias; incontinence; apprehension before surgery; and various psychosomatic illnesses.

The effectiveness of hypnosis varies enormously depending on the patient, the practitioner, and the ailment. It is particularly effective in alleviating physical pain. Nonaddictive, inexpensive, and safe, it can be used alone or along with medical treatments (Long, 1986; Spiegel, 1984). Athletes or soldiers who fail to notice an injury are in effect hypnotizing themselves by focusing so completely on the competition or the battle that they are not conscious of the pain until later. Hypnosis subjects can often be taught to restructure their experience similarly, using techniques that help them shift their focus from the pain to something else.

Since hypnosis is physically relaxing, it is also effective in relieving anxiety, "the emotional equivalent of physical pain" (Spiegel, 1984, p. 5). People can learn how to use self-hypnosis to deal with phobias and to control physical conditions that are worsened by anxiety, such as asthma. Hypnosis also helps people receiving chemotherapy control their nausea. It can also be used to help people who have suffered traumas like rape, military combat, and accidents to remember the details of their experiences so that they can "work them through."

While hypnosis is commonly used to help correct bad habits like smoking, drinking, abusing drugs,

PRACTICAL APPLICATIONS OF HYPNOSIS

and overeating, it has been of value in such cases only insofar as it has helped people to cope with the stress connected with making the change (Spiegel, 1984; Wadden & Anderton, 1982). By and large, the conditions best treated by hypnosis are those over which a person *seems* to have no control (such as pain and asthmatic reactions). The addictive disorders present a complex problem of ingrained habits combined with the requirement the the subject give up some immediate gratification, like the pleasure of eating, smoking, or drinking. In contrast, those experiencing pain or difficulty in breathing are not dealing with habits or sacrifice and are highly motivated to change their experiences.

SOLVING CRIMES

An executive who had escaped from a hotel fire that killed 26 people testified at the trial of the man who was accused of being the arsonist (Feron, 1982). Earlier, the witness had undergone hypnosis to try to bring to consciousness details he might have forgotten. During his conscious testimony he described having seen a man "dressed in the uniform of those who serve coffee"; under hypnosis, he saw this man wearing a short-sleeved shirt and described him as "chunky, with perhaps a mustache," a description that might have helped the suspect, who was slightly built and clean-shaven. The jury, however, did not hear the testimony given under hypnosis, and it did convict the

defendant (Press, 1982). Would the hypnosis testimony have changed the verdict? Should it have?

The use of hypnosis in criminal trials is highly controversial. While police departments are using it more often these days, a panel of prominent researchers recently issued a statement warning that hypnotized witnesses and victims seem to offer *less* reliable "memories" than do people using ordinary recall (AMA, 1985). In one case, for example, a hypnotized child described the murder of his mother by his father, only to have the mother turn up alive after the father's conviction (Orne, in Colen, 1982). Problems arise because hypnotized subjects may transform their thoughts or fantasies into what they think are memories, and also because their suggestibility leads them to incorporate cues picked up during hypnosis into their recollections. The Council on Scientific Affairs of the American Medical Association recommends that hypnosis should be used *only* in the investigative stage to produce leads for follow-up and not in the courts, that informed consent should be obtained, and that hypnosis should be induced only by a skilled and legally knowledgeable psychologist or psychiatrist (AMA, 1985).

If you have a problem that you think hypnosis might help, you can consult an experienced, reputable practitioner to see whether you'd be a good candidate. To find one or to check credentials, you could contact the American Psychological Association, 1200 17th Street NW, Washington, D.C. 20036; the psychiatry department of the closest university-affiliated hospital; your local medical society; the American Society of Clinical Hypnosis, 2250 East Devon Avenue, Suite 336, Des Plaines, Ill. 60018; or the Society for Clinical and Experimental Hypnosis, 129-A Kings Park Drive, Liverpool, N.Y. 13088.

DRUGS

If you're a typical adult, you regularly take some kind of chemical that alters your state of consciousness. Maybe it's the cup of coffee that helps you wake up in the morning, the after-dinner cigarette that helps you relax, the glass of wine, beer, or liquor that puts you into a lighter mood, the marijuana that heightens your enjoyment of music, the tranquilizer that calms you during a crisis, or one of many other commonly used substances. From the beginnings of recorded history, people in every culture around the world have taken various substances that changed their states of consciousness. Sometimes these elements have helped people cope better, and sometimes they have created problems far worse than any that might have led to their use in the first place.

The Department of Health and Human Services (1980b) defines a **drug** as "any chemical substance that produces physical, mental, emotional, or behavioral change in the user" (p. 3). Those we are talking about here are the **psychoactive**, or mind-altering, drugs. They range from those common substances just described, through the coca leaves chewed by natives of the Peruvian Andes, the cocaine sniffed by people looking for a fast "high," the heroin injected by the junkie who steals to maintain an expensive habit, and the amphetamines swallowed by the fashion model trying to lose weight. A major concern is that many of these drugs are taken by young people (see Figure 4-2).

Why do people take these foreign substances? Sometimes just to enhance their enjoyment of everyday life, sometimes to deal with or escape from problems, sometimes to reach a state of mind that promises new experiences of a spiritual or aesthetic nature, sometimes just because it's the "thing to do." Often the reason a person *continues* to use drugs has little to do with the original purpose.

Drug abuse is the nonmedicinal use of a drug, resulting in physical, mental, emotional, or social impairment. It usually involves either physiological or psychological dependence. **Physiological dependence** is the body's need for the drug in order to function. This results from changes in the body caused by use of a drug. When the user stops taking the drug, withdrawal symptoms occur, such as vomiting,

Drug *Chemical substance that produces physical, emotional, or behavioral change in the user.*
Psychoactive *Able to change perception, mood, or thought processes; mind-altering.*

Drug abuse *Nonmedicinal use of a drug that results in physical, mental, emotional, or social impairment.*
Physiological dependence *The body's need for a drug in order to function, caused by use of the drug.*

FIGURE 4-2 *Prevalence and recency of use of eleven types of drugs among high school seniors, class of 1985. (Source: Johnston, O'Malley, & Bachman, 1986.)*

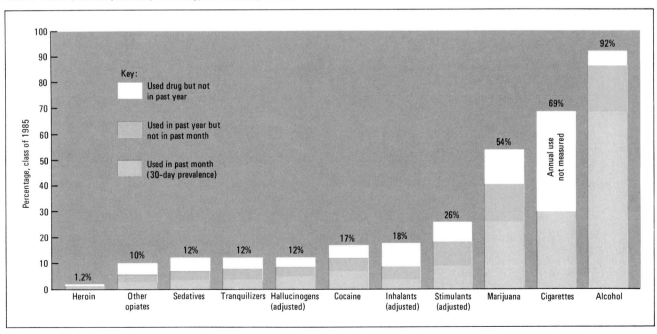

tremors, sweating, insomnia, or convulsion. To avoid such symptoms, the user continues to take the drug. **Psychological dependence** is the user's belief that he or she must have a given drug to feel good or normal, or just to survive, even in the absence of physical changes.

We'll take a look at some of the most common psychoactive drugs, how they change states of consciousness, and what they do to overall functioning in both the short term and the long term. (When pregnant women take these drugs, the fetus is often seriously affected. Some of these effects will be discussed in Chapter 9.)

Stimulants

Stimulants increase energy and wakefulness, elevate mood, and have other effects. Caffeine, nicotine, amphetamines, and cocaine are all stimulants.

Caffeine   The cup of coffee or tea, can of cola, or bar of chocolate that you sometimes take for a "pick-me-up" all contain the stimulant **caffeine,** which raises your heart and breathing rates and your blood pressure. It can stimulate you mentally and physically for brief periods of time, giving you short bursts of energy. In large doses (the amount in seven to ten cups of coffee) caffeine can make you restless, jittery, and irritable, give you headaches, or diarrhea, keep you from falling asleep or remaining asleep, interfere with your ability to concentrate, produce ringing in your ears, and at times, even produce mild delirium. Coffee can irritate the stomach lining, especially when taken on an empty stomach.

Americans ingest a lot of caffeine, mostly through coffee, with 1 out of 4 people over age 17 drinking six or more cups a day (Dusek & Girdano, 1980). Most adults seem to suffer no extreme side effects, but children who take in the amount of caffeine present in just 6 to 8 ounces of coffee (or the equivalent in cola or chocolate) often become anxious and have difficulty learning (Dusek & Girdano, 1980). Users develop high physiological and psychological dependence on caffeine (Bratter & Forrest, 1985).

Nicotine   *Nicotine,* the second most widely used stimulant, is present in the tobacco in cigarettes, cigars, and pipes. Smoking may help you feel more relaxed, but

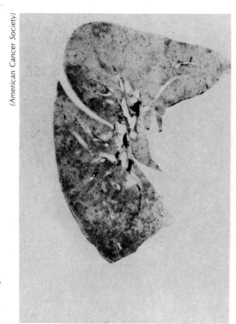
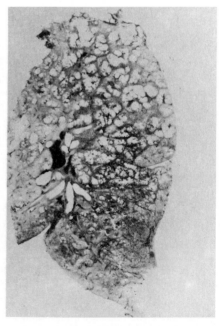

(American Cancer Society)

In normal lung tissue (left), air sacs are too fine to be visible. In damaged tissue from the lung of a heavy smoker (right), there are many greatly enlarged air sacs. Cigarette smoking is the major cause of death from cancer of the lung.

it is actually stimulating your heart and nervous system, raising your blood pressure and making your heart beat faster. If you have ever stopped smoking or tried to, you are familiar with the addictive properties of nicotine. Giving it up causes withdrawal symptoms such as irritability, cramps, headache, anxiety, nervousness, and depression.

Continuing to smoke has even worse effects. Cigarette smoking is the major cause of death from cancer of the lung, esophagus, larynx, and mouth, and it contributes to death from cancer of the pancreas, kidney, and bladder; it also contributes to heart disease and makes stomach ulcers worse (U.S. Public Health Service, 1982; Fielding, 1985a). Differences in the rates of cigarette smoking between men and women over age 30 may well account for much of the 7-year difference in life expectancy between the sexes (Miller & Gerstein, 1983). Smokers develop high levels of both physiological and psychological dependence on nicotine (Bratter & Forrest, 1985).

Fortunately, cigarette smoking is on the decline in this country. Only 19.5 percent of American high school seniors smoke daily now, compared with 29 percent in 1977; and 32 percent of adults smoke, compared with 42 percent in 1965 (U.S. Public Health Service, 1982; Johnston, O'Malley, & Bachman, 1986). People who want to stop smoking often look for help from counseling, behavior modification, hypnosis, or certain medications, but none of the official programs report impressive success rates. The great majority of people who have given up cigarettes have quit on their own (Fielding, 1985b). (For information on programs for quitting smoking, see Chapter 16.)

Amphetamines   People who take **amphetamines,** known collectively as "uppers" or "speed," do so for various reasons. Some find amphetamines helpful in focusing concentration on a demanding task like writing a paper. Others take them to stay awake to study, do a boring job, or drive long distances. Some athletes take them to marshal energy for a big game. Some dieters take them to suppress the appetite (which they do, but only for a short while.) Doctors often prescribe them for hyperactive children to lengthen attention span and control restlessness, to narcoleptics to keep them awake, and to sufferers of short-term depression. People who buy them on the street take them just to feel good—to gain self-confidence and feel they can meet any challenge life has to offer.

Amphetamines were once readily available without a prescription; later, they were still freely obtainable from easygoing physicians. However, they have led to so much abuse that they are now much harder to obtain legally. Doctors are now required by law to justify any prescriptions for them.

Amphetamines make the heart beat faster, harder, and sometimes irregularly; constrict blood vessels; raise blood pressure and blood sugar level; stimulate the adrenal glands; and increase muscle tension. The person taking them is apt to be very talkative, energetic, alert, in a good mood, and uninterested in sleep but very interested in sexual activity. These effects seem to occur because of the action of amphetamines on the brain chemicals dopamine and norepinephrine.

Abuse of amphetamines can lead to weight loss and malnutrition, pain in muscles and joints, a feeling of paralysis, and unconsciousness. It can also lead to *amphetamine psychosis,* which is characterized by paranoia, hallucinations, or inability to recognize familiar faces. Violence and aggression are common among heavy users, especially during the period of depression that often follows a high. Amphetamine users sometimes develop physiological dependence and often develop psychological dependence (Bratter & Forrest, 1985).

Cocaine   *Cocaine* ("coke"), a stimulant made from the leaves of the South American shrub *Erythroxylon coca,* has become alarmingly popular in recent years, and a growing number of medical emergencies and deaths have been related to its use. People are drawn to it because of the mild euphoria, increased heartbeat, and subtle

Amphetamines *Specific class of drugs that stimulate the central nervous system.*

Cocaine *Stimulant made from the leaves of the South American shrub Erythroxylon coca.*

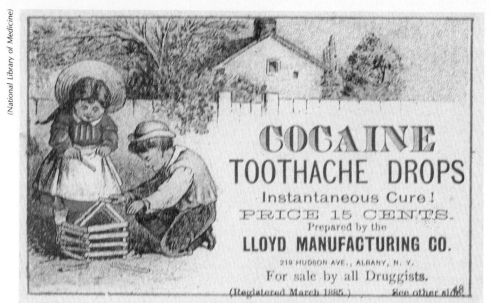

At one time cocaine was considered a benign treatment for a wide range of physical and psychological ailments; it was hailed by such authorities as Sigmund Freud.

sense of excitement that most users feel; but sudden death is possible even if only a small quantity (two or three "lines" or 60 milligrams) is taken. Death usually comes from paralysis of the respiratory system, heart rhythm disturbances, or repeated convulsions. "Crack," a very potent form of cocaine, is especially dangerous. Crack is purified cocaine in pellet form which takes effect in seconds and is more addictive than regular cocaine.

How does cocaine alter consciousness? Whether sniffed, smoked, or injected, it acts on the central nervous system to produce feelings of euphoria and excitement. Temperature and blood pressure rise, the pupils dilate, blood vessels constrict, and appetite diminishes. The user generally feels strong, energetic, and optimistic. Judgment is impaired, inhibitions are unblocked, and perception may be altered. Large doses often create hallucinations and may lead to paranoia, panic attacks, anxiety, depression, impotence, or insomnia. Cocaine may make a person dangerous to others. Users do not necessarily become physically addicted, but they may become psychologically hooked, since "coke" users often feel depressed and tired after its effects have worn off (Bratter & Forrest, 1985).

The number of people who had tried cocaine almost quadrupled between 1974 to 1982, from 5.4 million to more than 20 million; and the number of current users soared from 1.6 million in 1977 to between 4 and 6 million in 1982, the latest year for which we have official figures (Adams & Durell, 1984; Johnston et al., 1986). Use of cocaine by high school seniors increased in 1985; about 17 percent had tried it. Among 27-year-olds who were followed up after having been interviewed several years before as high school seniors, 40 percent had tried cocaine. Cocaine is thus the only illicit drug for which there is a substantial increase in active use with age (Johnston et al., 1986). Cocaine users do not fit the usual profile of drug abusers: many are successful, well educated, upwardly mobile professionals. But a large number have seen their professional and personal lives collapsing around them.

More than a million calls came in to the national 800-COCAINE hot line from May 1983 to June 1985, demonstrating the need for treatment of cocaine abuse (Johnston et al., 1986). Such treatment can consist of medications, psychotherapy, participation in group programs similar to those of Alcoholics Anonymous, exercise, and the promotion of good health and nutrition habits (Johnston et al., 1986; Wilbur, 1986).

(Wesley Bocxe/Photo Researchers)

Today, the dangers of cocaine are well known; it accounts for an increasing number of hospital emergencies and deaths. It is most dangerous in a highly concentrated form known as crack, which this man is smoking.

Hallucinogens

Hallucinogens, or psychedelic drugs, affect consciousness in many ways. They influence perceptions, thoughts, and emotions, making them all different from those of the normal waking state. Time and space expand and contract, delusions appear, logical judgment is suspended, and the imaginary visual, auditory, and tactile sensations that characterize hallucinations are experienced. Users may feel chills, nausea, tremors, and palpitations of the heart. Memory plays strange tricks, bringing long-buried images to vivid consciousness in unexpected ways. The combination of unfamiliar feelings may lead to euphoria or panic.

Marijuana, LSD, and PCP are hallucinogens. Let's consider them briefly.

Marijuana **Marijuana,** a derivative of the common plant *Cannabis sativa,* contains more than 400 chemicals, of which the mind-altering component is delta-9-tetrahydrocannabinol (THC). Marijuana increases heart rate and sometimes blood pressure, reddens the eyes, produces a dry mouth and throat. It alters the sense of time, making minutes seem like hours or vice versa. It impairs the ability to perform tasks requiring concentration, coordination, and quick reaction time. Mood often changes, possibly into euphoria, melancholy, or almost emotionless detachment. Powers of perception may seem heightened, so that colors are seen more vividly, music heard more acutely, physical sensations felt more intensely. Short-term memory is affected. Depending on the amount and strength of the marijuana and the underlying psychological condition of the smoker, confusion, anxiety, or delirium can result (Petersen, 1984; Relman, 1982). The use of marijuana interferes with the ability to drive an automobile or pilot a plane (Petersen, 1984).

Marijuana has several therapeutic uses. It is sometimes used in treating the eye disorder glaucoma, alleviating nausea caused by chemotherapy in the treatment of cancer, and treating such ailments as asthma, seizures, and spastic conditions (Relman, 1982).

The long-term effects of smoking marijuana are still unknown. There is no evidence of any permanent change in the nervous system or in brain function. Physical dependence does not seem to occur, although mild withdrawal symptoms do appear and psychological dependence sometimes occurs (Bratter & Forrest, 1985). Some research suggests that marijuana may affect both male and female reproductive sys-

Hallucinogens *Psychedelic drugs, such as LSD and PCP, that alter perception, thoughts, and emotions and produce hallucinations.*

Marijuana *Derivative of the plant Cannabis sativa, which contains the mind-altering component delta-9-tetrahydrocannabinol (THC).*

tems, but there is no proof that it affects either sex's fertility (Relman, 1982). It may have the same kinds of effects on the lungs that tobacco does, but this has not been firmly established (Petersen, 1984).

In recent years young people have been smoking less marijuana. High school seniors in 1985 smoked considerably less than those in the late 1970s; and although the decline in marijuana smoking among high school seniors did not continue between 1984 and 1985 (Johnston et al., 1986), the percentage of seniors smoking marijuana regularly (20 or more times a month) had dropped from 11 percent in 1978 to 4.9 percent in 1985. In 1985, only 26 percent of the survey group had used marijuana occasionally in the month before the survey, compared with the 37 percent who had done so in 1978. Furthermore, in 1985, 70 percent of seniors said that regular use of marijuana entailed "great risk," compared with only 35 percent in 1978, showing increasing concern about the dangers of marijuana. Similar declines were also noted since the late 1970s in the use of stimulants, sedatives, tranquilizers, LSD, and PCP. The use of heroin and other opiates and of inhalants remained relatively stable (Johnston et al., 1986).

LSD (d-lysergic acid diethylamide) Synthesized drug with psychoactive properties.

LSD *LSD (d-lysergic acid diethylamide)* was synthesized in the laboratory in 1938, and its psychoactive properties were discovered in 1943. During the 1950s it was used in psychotherapy, in treating drug and alcohol addiction and mental disorders, and to relieve pain in patients with terminal cancer. By the 1960s it had attracted a following among people seeking creative and spiritual visions, and Congress restricted its use as an experimental drug. It soon became easily available on the street.

LSD seems to work by affecting the production of the chemical brain transmitter *serotonin*. It is rapidly absorbed into the blood stream and disseminated throughout the body. Experiments on monkeys have shown that only 1 percent concentrates in the brain, mostly in the pituitary and pineal glands, but also in the hypothalamus, the limbic system, and the auditory and visual reflex regions (Snyder & Reivich, 1966). A frightening aftermath of use of LSD is the flashback. This is a spontaneous recurrence of the drug experience some time after taking the drug, without any more of it having been taken. A "bad trip" may recur after as long as 18 months, resulting in troubling and dangerous emotions. LSD can impair memory, attention span, and the ability to think abstractly and may bring about organic brain damage in some heavy users. Does it damage chromosomes? Research on this is inconclusive, with findings indicating that pure LSD does not seem to do so, but that street LSD, mixed with other substances, may.

Will LSD make you more creative? Many people claim that if you take LSD, you'll see and hear all sorts of things that may never have appeared in your normal waking life, and that you'll have new insights and answers to all sorts of questions. However, a drug cannot provide "the checks and balances between intuition and analytic reason required for genuine creation" (Grinspoon and Bakalar, 1979, p. 267). During the drug experience you can't transmit your new insights, partly because of the drug's effects on motor abilities. After taking LSD, users do not show any more creativity than they did before (Dusek & Girdano, 1980).

PCP (Phencyclidine hydrochloride) Stimulant, depressant, and pain killer.

PCP *PCP (phencyclidine hydrochloride)* is a frequently abused street drug that is a stimulant, a depressant, and a pain-killer, as well as a hallucinogen. Originally developed as an anesthetic, it is no longer used legally on human beings because of the agitation and thought disturbance it produces. Users take it for its few favorable effects—mood elevation, relaxation, stimulation, and heightened sensitivity—even though these seem greatly outweighed by the negative effects. These include memory and speech problems, depression, anxiety, paranoia, violence, hallucinations, convulsions, depersonalization, poor coordination, numbness, possibly psychosis, and sometimes even death from convulsions or interference with breathing. The most dangerous aspect of PCP is its utter unpredictability.

Other common hallucinogens are mescaline, peyote, psilocybin, STP, DMT, and nitrous oxide.

Depressants

Depressants operate by suppressing central nervous system activity. We'll look now at some of those most commonly used—and abused: alcohol, sedatives, tranquilizers, and narcotics.

Alcohol Seeing the exuberance of friends at a beer party or the violence of a drunken wife-beater, you might think that **alcohol** is a stimulant. It is not. It is a depressant of the central nervous system that causes blood pressure to drop while heart rate increases. The effects of alcohol vary. While small amounts tranquilize most people, others become stimulated, probably because the alcohol suppresses mechanisms that ordinarily control active behaviors, so that they lose their inhibitions and act exuberant, sociable, silly, or aggressive. Large amounts of alcohol tranquilize most people, dulling sensation, impairing judgment, memory, and muscular coordination, and eventually causing unconsciousness. Shakespeare recognized the effect of alcohol on sexuality: "Drink . . . provokes the desire, but it takes away the performance" (*Macbeth*, Act II, Scene iii).

Alcohol Central-nervous-system depressant that causes blood pressure to drop and heart rate to increase.

Alcohol is this country's number one drug problem. Ten million Americans are either "problem drinkers" or full-fledged alcoholics. Alcohol becomes a problem when it interferes with a person's ability to function on the job or in personal relationships and when the drinker cannot control the desire for or use of alcohol. People dependent on alcohol experience a variety of withdrawal symptoms. Drinking a large amount of alcohol in a single session can result in sudden death, and liver or heart disease can be brought on by excessive drinking over a period of years. Problems with alcohol can occur at any age and are significant among the elderly. Alcohol produces high levels of dependency, both physiological and psychological (Bratter & Forrest, 1985).

The mixture of alcohol and other drugs, especially tranquilizers, anticoagulants, barbiturates, and other sedatives, can cause depression, coma, or even death. Because alcohol impairs judgment, reaction time, and motor ability, one of its most lethal effects is the high number of traffic accidents caused by drivers who have been drinking, many of whom fall asleep at the wheel.

Considering all these dangers, why would anyone ever drink? In part, the answer is that most people can handle alcohol in moderation, and that for many people it enhances the enjoyment of life. Wine is a part of the rituals of many religions, a small amount of brandy is often recommended by doctors as a painkiller, and the relaxing qualities of alcohol contribute to social celebrations. With alcohol such a pervasive presence in modern society, people need to monitor themselves to determine whether they are among those who either should not drink at all or need to exercise special care. At the same time, societal institutions need to continue to develop ways to help those people who already have drinking problems regain their ability to become fully functioning. The most effective approaches so far have been group-oriented programs like Alcoholics Anonymous, which focus on drinkers' recognition of their problems, total abstinence, and the emotional support of other alcoholics (Zimberg, 1982).

Sedatives and Tranquilizers *Sedatives and tranquilizers,* which have a calming effect and bring on sleep, are of two kinds: barbiturates and nonbarbiturates. These "downers" are often used by people who have gone too far "up" on amphetamines. Unable to sleep or calm down, the "speed freak" turns to the drugs in this class to counteract the stimulants, thus boarding a chemical roller coaster. Sedatives are also taken by anxious people, people dealing with a life crisis such as the death of a

Sedatives and tranquilizers Central-nervous-system depressants that are calming and sleep-inducing.

family member, and insomniacs. Physicians often prescribe sedatives to relieve the anxiety of patients with heart, respiratory, gastrointestinal, or other physical illnesses.

Barbiturates are easily abused. They have profound effects, impairing memory and judgment, and sometimes leading to coma or even death. They are particularly dangerous when taken with alcohol, since the combination magnifies the effects of both these central-nervous-system depressants. Nearly one-third of accidental drug-related deaths are related to an overdose of barbiturates (U.S. Department of Health and Human Services, 1980b). Barbiturate users develop a tolerance, need greater and greater amounts, and eventually become addicted. Levels of physiological and psychological dependence vary for different drugs, however (Bratter & Forrest, 1985). Withdrawal can be a grueling experience, with tremors, nausea, abdominal cramps, vomiting, hallucinations, and a distorted sense of time and space; it can even lead to death.

Narcotics In today's climate it is hard to believe that **narcotics,** a class of depressant drugs which relieve pain and induce sleep, were used openly and widely in this country during the nineteenth and early twentieth centuries. **Opium** was used in China and India to heal, relieve pain, and give warriors courage. It appeared in this country in patent medicines for coughs, diarrhea, and just about every other human ailment. **Morphine,** an opium derivative, was freely given to injured soldiers during the Civil War and World War I. Then a promising new drug that seemed to have the advantages of opium and morphine, without their addicting properties, burst on the scene. Unfortunately, **heroin** did not live up to the expectations held for it, but instead became more of a problem than the other narcotics. Today it accounts for 90 percent of narcotics abuse in the United States (Shorter & McDarby, 1979).

Heroin users, who typically shoot a solution of the drug directly into the bloodstream with a hypodermic syringe, feel its effects quickly. They soon become euphoric, peaceful, content, and safe, detached from any dangers or challenges. Their breathing becomes slower and shallower, their pupils constrict, their sex drive diminishes, and they may experience intense itching, nausea, and vomiting. Despite these effects, they can hold a job and lead a relatively normal life—as long as they take the drug. Physical addiction occurs, with severe withdrawal symptoms when the drug wears off; and tolerance develops with prolonged use, so that heroin addicts need progressively greater amounts.

Within 4 to 6 hours after addicts stop taking the drug, they begin to experience discomfort, which becomes agony 12 to 16 hours after the last dose. Sweating, shaking, vomiting, running nose and eyes, chills, aching muscles, abdominal pain, and diarrhea are common (U.S. Department of Health and Human Services, 1980b). Withdrawal does not cause death, but an overdose can. Heroin users may contract serum hepatitis or AIDS (acquired immune deficiency syndrome) from using dirty needles. They also develop vein inflammations, skin abscesses, and lung congestion. A new form of heroin, called "black tar" because of its color and consistency, is causing an increase of drug deaths, because it is cheaper and more potent (Brinkley, 1986).

One controversial but sometimes effective way of countering addiction is to give the addict a daily dose of **methadone.** Methadone is also an addictive narcotic, but its effect lasts longer than that of heroin, and it is less likely to cause harmful side effects. However, people on methadone maintenance do report symptoms of physical withdrawal, as well as psychological problems. There is a need, therefore, for some kind of counseling support for people undergoing methadone treatment (NIDA, 1985).

Another approach tries to free addicts from physical or psychological dependence on *any* drug through group therapy and peer support, often at a residential treatment center. As users break their physical addiction, they progress to a halfway house and then to life in the community, perhaps with regular supportive help.

Narcotics *Central-nervous-system depressants used to relieve pain and induce sleep.*

Opium *Narcotic used to relieve pain and induce sleep.*

Morphine *Opium derivative used to relieve pain and induce sleep.*

Heroin *Addictive narcotic.*

Methadone *Addictive narcotic, sometimes used to treat heroin addiction.*

The major problem in curing heroin addicts is not releasing them from the physiological hold of the drug but meeting the underlying psychological needs that drove them to take it in the first place. Typical addicts have low self-esteem and self-confidence, are afraid of life, have a generally negative and pessimistic outlook, feel that whatever they do is futile, and look to heroin as a means of escaping reality (Dusek & Girdano, 1980). Such deep-seated psychological problems often defy resolution and send the "cured" addict back into the arms of the comforting drug. All the narcotics—opium, morphine, heroin, and methadone—are both physiologically and psychologically addictive (Bratter & Forrest, 1985).

Many people who originally sought altered states of consciousness through drugs have since discovered they can obtain some of the same benefits, without the same risks, from meditation, hypnosis, and other mind-altering techniques. Part of the appeal of long-distance running seems to lie in the "high" that many runners experience. Since the desire to enter other states of consciousness seems to be a basic human tendency, it is likely that people will continue to develop still more ways to expand or limit consciousness.

SUMMARY

1 Consciousness is awareness of oneself and the world around one. The normal state of consciousness is the normal waking state. Any qualitative change from the normal state is an altered state of consciousness. Such states include sleep and states induced by meditation, hypnosis, and drugs.

2 Characteristics of altered states of consciousness (ASCs) include the following: alterations in thinking, disturbed time sense, loss of control, change in emotional expression, change in body image, perceptual distortion, change in perceived meaning or significance, sense of experiencing the indescribable, feelings of rejuvenation, and hypersuggestibility.

3 Altered states may be induced in a number of different ways ranging from overstimulation to complete withdrawal of stimulation.

4 Flow states are states of intense concentration during which peak performance occurs.

5 While sleeping, human beings pass through four sleep stages that exhibit different brain-wave patterns. Sleep gets progressively deeper during the progression from stage 1 through stage 4. These four stages are called *non-REM (non-rapid-eye-movement) sleep.*

6 After progressing through the four non-REM stages, sleep gets progressively lighter. REM (rapid-eye-movement) sleep is entered about 90 minutes after falling asleep. This is the time when dreaming is most likely.

7 Sleep is universal in mammals and common in much of the rest of the animal kingdom, although there are wide differences in the amounts of sleep different species need. Circadian rhythms are daily rhythms that govern the sleep-wake pattern. Recently, a "sleep-promoting substance" isolated from human urine has been found to bring on a 50 percent increase in deep, nondreaming sleep in rabbits after injection.

8 There are a number of different theories about the function of sleep, including its role in restoring the body or preventing exhaustion. People deprived of sleep, especially when the extent of the deprivation is not prolonged, show minor physiological symptoms, including hand tremors, double vision, and lowered pain threshold. Sleep loss especially affects the ability to do complex or difficult tasks. People totally deprived of sleep are apt to become confused and irritable, although their personalities are likely to remain intact. People awakened repeatedly during REM sleep become anxious and irritable and have trouble concentrating. They "catch up" on REM sleep when they are allowed to sleep uninterrupted.

9 The average amount of sleep varies depending on age. Infants sleep the most, elderly people the least. Some research suggests that adults can learn to sleep less.

10 Research on personality differences between long and short sleepers is contradictory. People may need different amounts of sleep depending on their life circumstances.

11 A dream is a mental experience that occurs during sleep; it consists of a series of vivid, usually visual, and often hallucinatory images. The presence of dreaming is associated with the typical brain wave of an emergent stage 1 sleep pattern, an increase in pulse and breathing rate, lack of body movement, and rapid eye movements. People have four to six periods of dreaming each night, for a total of about 1 to 2 hours of dream time.

12 A number of theories exist as to why people forget their dreams. Freud maintained that forgetting is due to the repression of anxiety-laden thoughts; Hobson and McCarley point to state-dependent amnesia; Crick and Mitchison believe that dreams clear the brain of unnecessary material.

13 The contents of dreams are generally commonplace.

There appears to be a continuity between waking concerns and preoccupations and the content of dreams.

14 There are a number of very different theories about the reasons for dreaming. Freud believed that dreams guard sleep and that people dream to fulfill the wishes that they repress while awake. He believed that dreams have both manifest content (the actual description of dreams) and latent content (their underlying meaning). According to Freud, much of what people dream is symbolic of repressed desires and conflicts, most of which are sexual.

15 Adler believed that dreams assist people in solving problems. Jung thought that dreams help people learn about ignored or suppressed aspects of themselves.

16 Hobson and McCarley proposed an activation-synthesis model of dreaming. They believe that the bizarre shifts and symbols of dreams are not disguised unconscious thoughts but are the result of how the brain functions during sleep. During dreaming, parts of the brain are stimulated; which parts are stimulated determines what a person will dream about and how dream images will be put together.

17 Sleep disorders include narcolepsy (an uncontrollable urge to sleep), insomnia (an inability to sleep), sleep apnea (periods of sleep when breathing stops briefly), night terrors (panic attacks), and nightmares (frightening dreams).

18 There does not seem to be a single, unique meditative state. While Wallace and Benson describe meditation as a state of relaxed wakefulness, others have noted that experienced meditators show a great deal of activity in their body processes. The meditative technique best known in the west is transcendental meditation (TM), developed by Maharishi Mahesh Yogi. The therapeutic benefits of meditation are controversial.

19 Hypnosis is a state of increased suggestibility or susceptibility to outside influence. Some common behaviors among hypnotized people include rigidity of the arm, loss of voluntary control, hallucinations, failure to feel pain, amnesia, and responsiveness to posthypnotic suggestion. Not all people can be hypnotized.

20 Opinions differ on what hypnosis is. E. R. Hilgard believes that hypnotized people feel little or no pain because they block pain from full consciousness. He maintains that during hypnosis there is a dissociation or split in consciousness, that is, that the hypnotized person is operating on more than one level of awareness.

21 Cognitive-behavioral theory maintains that the hypnotic state does not depend on a trance-induction technique but, rather, depends on the subject's readiness to think along with and imagine the themes suggested by the hypnotist.

22 Hypnosis is being used in a number of practical settings. It has been used to treat a variety of medical conditions and has been particularly effective in alleviating pain. The use of hypnosis in criminal trials is highly controversial.

23 A drug is any chemical substance that produces physical, mental, emotional, or behavioral changes in the user. Psychoactive drugs are mind-altering. Drug abuse is the nonmedicinal use of a drug, resulting in physical, mental, emotional, or social impairment. Physiological dependence is the body's need of a drug in order to function. Psychological dependence is the drug user's belief that he or she must have the drug to feel good or normal, or just to survive.

24 Stimulants increase energy levels and wakefulness and elevate mood but potentially have a number of negative side effects. Stimulants include caffeine (in coffee, tea, cola, and chocolate), nicotine (in tobacco), amphetamines ("uppers"), and cocaine. Large amounts of caffeine can make the user jittery and irritable. Cigarette smoking is a major cause of several different types of cancer, as well as heart disease and a number of other conditions. Amphetamine abuse can lead to weight loss, malnutrition, dependency problems, pain, unconsciousness, and feeling of paralysis as well as amphetamine psychosis. Cocaine initially produces feelings of euphoria but impairs judgment, unblocks inhibitions, and alters perception. Even small doses occasionally result in death.

25 Hallucinogens are psychedelic drugs that alter perceptions, thoughts, and emotions. Hallucinogens include marijuana, LSD, and PCP. Depending on the amount and strength of marijuana taken, it can convey a sense of well-being or bring on anxiety, confusion, or delirium. Its long-term effects are unknown. LSD produces hallucinations and can impair memory, attention span, and the ability to think abstractly. It may be followed some months later by "flashbacks." PCP produces a number of largely unpredictable negative effects.

26 Depressants include alcohol, sedatives, tranquilizers, and narcotics. These drugs all depress central-nervous-system activity. Alcohol abuse is the country's leading drug problem. Sedatives and tranquilizers have a calming effect and bring on sleep. They are easily abused and are particularly dangerous when taken with alcohol, since both depress CNS activity. Narcotics such as opium, morphine, and heroin relieve pain and induce sleep. Today heroin accounts for 90 percent of narcotics abuse in the United States.

KEY TERMS

Alcohol (page 149)
Altered state of consciousness (ASC) (119)
Amphetamines (145)
Caffeine (144)
Circadian rhythms (126)
Cocaine (145)
Cognitive-behavioral theory of hypnosis (141)
Consciousness (119)
Drug (143)
Drug abuse (143)

Electroencephalograph (122)
Electromyograph (123)
Electrooculograph (123)
Hallucinogens (147)
Heroin (150)
Hypnosis (139)
Insomnia (135)
LSD (148)
Mantra (138)
Marijuana (147)
Meditation (138)
Methadone (150)

Morphine (150)
Narcolepsy (135)
Narcotics (150)
Neodissociation theory of hypnosis (140)
Nicotine (144)
Nightmares (137)
Night terrors (137)
NREM (non-rapid-eye-movement) sleep (123)
Opium (150)
PCP (148)

Physiological dependence (143)
Psychoactive (143)
Psychological dependence (144)
REM rebound (127)
REM (rapid-eye-movement) sleep (123)
Sedatives and tranquilizers (149)
Sleep apnea (136)
Stimulant (144)
Transcendental meditation (138)

SUGGESTED READINGS

BRATTER, T. E., & FORREST, G. G. (Eds.). (1985). *Alcoholism and substance abuse: Strategies for clinical intervention.* New York: Free Press. A thorough discussion of the causes, assessment, and treatment of alcoholism and substance abuse. The book emphasizes practical aspects of treatment.

KELLY, S. F., & KELLY, R. J. (1985). *Hypnosis: Understanding how it can work for you.* Reading, MA: Addison-Wesley. A straightforward account of hypnosis, with many fascinating case histories to show what hypnosis is and what it can and cannot do.

LEVY, S. J. (1983). *Managing the drugs in your life: A personal and family guide to the responsible use of drugs, alcohol, and medicine.* New York: McGraw-Hill. A practical guide to common drugs and how to deal constructively with them. Contains much useful information to help people make informed decision about the risks and benefits of drug use.

NARANJO, C. & ORNSTEIN, R. E. (1976). *On the psychology of meditation.* New York: Penguin. In the first part of this book, Naranjo discusses the spirit and techniques of meditation. In the second part, Ornstein describes the implications of meditation techniques for modern psychology.

WEBB, W. (1975). *Sleep: The gentle tyrant.* Englewood Cliffs, NJ: Prentice-Hall. A brief and easy-to-read discussion of experimental findings about sleep by a prominent researcher. This book has a practical orientation.

ZILBERGELD, B., EDELSTIEN, M. G., & ARAOZ, D. L. (Eds.). (1986). *Hypnosis: Questions and answers.* New York: Norton. Experienced clinicians answer 84 commonly asked questions about hypnosis, focusing on induction techniques and clinical applications.

PART

III

LEARNING, MEMORY, AND COGNITIVE PROCESSES

You could not be taking this course or reading this book if you did not have the abilities described in Part III—learning, remembering, and thinking. These abilities are not exclusively reserved for human beings; in fact, considerable controversy rages in psychological circles over the extent to which nonhuman animals can think and can learn a language. There is no controversy, however, about the fact that all normal human beings can perform all these mental processes.

■ In *Chapter 5,* "Learning," we look at some of the principles of learning and at the practical implications of psychological findings, which have been applied to such everyday concerns as using seat belts and teaching tricks to pets.

■ How do we remember? Why do we forget? These questions are posed and answered (to the best of current knowledge) in *Chapter 6,* "Memory." Much of the research on memory that has taken place so far aims to sort out the basic processes of remembering and forgetting; but here, too, we can turn to research for practical ideas about improving our memories.

■ *Chapter 7,* "Intelligence," takes up the controversial topic of intelligence, asking what it is, how we measure it, and what factors affect it. All these issues have been—and continue to be—hotly debated by educators, politicians, laypersons, and, of course, psychologists. We'll look at some exciting new directions in intelligence testing and talk about what's right and what's wrong with the tests in common use today. The chapter ends

with discussions of people at the two extremes of intelligence—the intellectually gifted and the mentally retarded.

■ *Chapter 8,* "Language and Thought," focuses on the cognitive abilities examined in the preceding three chapters, as we consider how both people and animals apply their intelligence to learn and remember, and in the service of thought and language. We examine the various theories that try to explain how we learn to speak and understand language, describe some apes who are said to know a language, and consider the important role of "motherese" in children's linguistic development. The kind of thinking that solves problems is discussed, along with suggestions for more creative problem solving.

CHAPTER

5

LEARNING

- What are the differences between the two basic types of associative learning, classical conditioning and operant conditioning?

- How did Pavlov's experiments with dogs, Thorndike's experiments with cats, and Skinner's experiments with rats and pigeons lead to basic laws of learning?

- How do psychologists use learning principles to deal with such practical problems as whether, how, and when to punish children; how to promote the use of safety belts in cars; how to teach tricks to animals; and how to control various bodily responses?

- What are the cognitive aspects of learning?

- How important is a sense of control in people's lives? How does lack of control undermine the ability to learn?

Learning to use a computer for writing reminds me of the days when my children were in the "terrible twos." When they were babies, I had felt that I was more or less in charge, that I could figure out when they were hungry or cold, do what needed to be done for them, and keep them reasonably happy. But when they got to the point where they balked at what I wanted them to do—and often absolutely refused—I realized that the center of power in the family had shifted. Changing from a typewriter to a word processor has given me the same feeling. When I worked with a typewriter, I felt as if I controlled my machine as well as my material. Now, however, it's a different story.

I try to perform some operation that I know my system is capable of (the manual tells me so), I think I'm following the instructions exactly—and I get a maddening error message on my screen. These phrases—"unknown command," "invalid drive," and "disk error"—are even more obnoxious than toddlers' back talk: "No!" "I don't want to!" "You can't make me!"

I remember, though, that when I needed to, I figured out ways to diminish my children's resistance—parents have to, if they are to survive. I assume, then, that I can do as well with the word processor; I persist; and as I become more familiar with the computer, I do (fortunately) get fewer and fewer of those frustrating little green messages in the lower right-hand corner of the black screen.

—From the notebooks of Sally Olds

Experience with a computer shows the importance of learning, since all organisms need to adapt to a changing world. (We don't see many people writing with quill pens these days!) It also demonstrates several aspects of learning that we discuss in this chapter. The way we learn to write, the way we learn to type, the way we learn to handle new technology—all follow basic principles that govern the way we learn most things in life. Most of us don't stop to think how many of our thoughts, feelings, and experiences are the product of learning. Youcangetsome ideaoftheimpactoflearningbyseeinghowharditistoreadthissentence,whichmakesallthe learnedpatternsandexperiencesyouhavehadwithreadingfailtowork. Learningiscrucial not only for improving our lives but for survival itself. It's important, therefore, to know how and under what conditions learning takes place.

In this chapter we explore the history of the study of learning, including the animal experiments from which important principles emerged. We examine the major types of learning, and we look at some practical implications to be drawn from psychological research on learning.

These red-crested cranes doing a mating dance are exhibiting a biologically patterned instinct: any pair will do the same dance as every other pair in the species. Human beings don't show instincts like this. We may have the same basic drive to mate, but we design a wide variety of ways to let a prospective partner know of our interest.

WHAT IS LEARNING?

As you watch a spider spin a graceful gossamer web, or see a bird drop worms into the wide-open mouths of nestlings, or peer at a column of ants carrying crumbs to the anthill, you are not watching any learned activity. All these behaviors are carried out by a sort of species-specific program that each of these creatures is born with, known as *instinct*. **Instincts** are relatively complex patterns of behavior that are biologically determined and usually important for the survival of a species. All members of a species show the same kinds of instinctive behavior. One swallow, for example, does not stay "home" while all the others migrate to Capistrano every year at some genetically programmed signal.

Instincts *Inborn, species-specific, relatively complex patterns of behavior that are biologically determined and usually important for species survival.*

Today, many psychologists and other observers of human behavior agree that human beings probably have no abilities which could properly be considered instincts. The prevailing professional opinion is that we come into this world with a functioning body, a few reflexes, a maturational timetable, and an infinite capacity for learning.

Reflexes, the closest thing human beings have to instincts, are inborn, unlearned, involuntary reactions to stimulation. These simple behaviors arise not from our planning or even from our will, but involuntarily in response to certain aspects of our environment. We blink at a bright light or a puff of air, kick out when we are tapped at a certain spot just below the kneecap, and, as infants, respond to a stroke on the cheek by turning the head, opening the mouth, and beginning to suck. Why don't we consider these reflexes learned behavior? To answer this question we need to define learning.

Reflexes *Inborn, unlearned involuntary reactions to stimulation.*

Learning is a relatively permanent change in behavior. It reflects a gain of knowledge, understanding, or skill, achieved through experience, which may include study, instruction, observation, or practice. Changes in behavior are reasonably objective and, therefore, can be measured.

This definition specifically excludes any ability or skill that is attained by **maturation,** the process by which biologically predetermined patterns of behavior unfold, more or less on schedule (walking, for example). The definition also excludes re-

Learning *Relatively permanent change in behavior, which reflects knowledge, understanding, or skill achieved through experience (which may include study, instruction, observation, or practice).*
Maturation *Unfolding of biologically determined patterns of behavior.*

FIGURE 5-1 *Continuum of learning. The various types of learning can be thought of as part of a continuum of adapting to the environment, in which each kind is related to and builds upon the ones before it.*

Habituation *Simple type of learning in which an organism stops responding to something that it has grown used to.*

Associative learning *Kind of learning in which an association is formed between two events. Two types of associative learning are classical conditioning and operant conditioning.*

Classical (Pavlovian) conditioning *Kind of learning in which a previously neutral stimulus (conditioned stimulus) acquires the power to elicit a response (conditioned response) after repeated pairing with an unconditioned stimulus that ordinarily elicits a particular response (unconditioned response).*

Operant (instrumental) conditioning *Type of learning in which the consequences of a behavior (that is, whether it is reinforced or punished) determine whether or not the behavior will be repeated.*

Cognitive learning *Learning involving mental activity (thought) as a step between stimulus and response.*

flexes, because they are innate, involuntary responses to stimulation rather than relatively permanent changes of behavior brought about by experience. Nor does learning include temporarily induced states brought about by physiological factors like illness, medication, or fatigue. If, for example, you perform much better on a test this week than you did last week, it may not be because you have actually learned in the meantime. Your first performance may not have been as good as it could have been because you were tired or not feeling well. Similarly, if your second performance is much worse, the explanation may again be fatigue or poor health rather than that you have forgotten something you had already learned.

The presence of learning can often be deduced by a change in behavior—but not always. There is a difference between learning and performance. Even though you have learned something, you may not demonstrate that learning by your behavior if you are not motivated and paying attention. College students' scores on a psychology exam, for example, may not adequately reflect what they have learned if, say, one of them had an argument with a roommate just before the test, another was suffering from a bout of hay fever, another slept poorly or not at all the night before, and another always becomes extremely anxious in a testing situation.

Despite the fact that performance is not necessarily a perfect indicator of learning, however, psychologists generally assess what people or animals have learned on the basis of what they do, because behavior is the only criterion they can observe and measure.

Because so much of what human beings do, both in and out of society, depends on learning, psychologists have devoted considerable attention to finding out how people learn. They have found that we learn in a number of different ways.

The various types of learning can be thought of as part of a continuum of adapting to the environment, in which each type is related to and builds upon the ones before it (Figure 5-1).

Habituation, the simplest kind of learning, is the phenomenon by which we "get used to" something, thus showing that we know what it is. In habituation, a person or an animal decreases the strength of response after repeated presentation of a stimulus. When habituation occurs, it shows that a stimulus has become familiar; a novel stimulus will cause the organism to respond again. In other words, habituation lets us stop paying attention to irrelevant stimuli, so that other learning can occur. (For example, if forest dwellers didn't get used to, and ignore, the usual birdcalls and chirping of insects, they couldn't attend to unusual noises that might signal the presence of predators.)

Associative learning is the next level. At this level (as the term implies), we form new associations between two events. There are two basic types of associative learning—classical conditioning and operant conditioning. In both, new responses seem to be "stamped" into a person or an animal automatically.

Classical (Pavlovian) conditioning allows us to predict the arrival of important stimuli, and that increases our ability to survive. (A wild dog that begins to salivate when it smells a familiar food is ready to swallow and digest quickly—an advantage in case a competitor for food arrives.)

Operant (instrumental) conditioning allows us to *do* something to get what we want or need, and this is another step up in adaptability. (A hunter who discovers that going to a certain place at a certain time of day and remaining very quiet will result in a catch will have a reliable source of food.)

Cognitive learning is a less automatic kind of acquisition of knowledge about the environment. Over the years, classical and operant conditioning have received a great deal of attention; but today, many psychologists are focusing more on cognitive learning and thus on the thought processes that go on in people and animals. Behaviorists say that the stimulus-response sequence is automatic; cognitive psychologists maintain that there is a step between stimulus and response. This step is mental activity, or thought. Thus cognitive learning allows us to be aware of experiences as they occur, anticipate future experiences, form expectations about outcomes, and adjust our behavior to bring about outcomes that we want. (Cognitive psychologists also believe that there are other types of learning besides associative learning, or conditioning; we will discuss these later in the chapter.)

ASSOCIATIVE LEARNING

Classical Conditioning

You meet your friend Jack at noon, in front of the science building, and head toward the student union. As you walk together, he tells you about the restaurant where he had dinner the night before. As he describes, in delicious detail, the pungent aromas and the subtle flavors of the food he ate, you realize that your mouth is watering. "Hey!" you say. "I'm like those dogs I just learned about."

Pavlov and His Dogs   "Those dogs" were the subjects in what is probably the most famous scientific experiment in the field of learning. Ivan Pavlov, a Russian physiologist who won the Nobel Prize in 1904 for his work on the digestive system, also had a great interest in studying the brain and the nervous system. His research into the workings of these two systems demonstrated the presence of the learning phenomenon that has come to be known as *classical conditioning*. Classical, or Pavlovian, conditioning involves some kind of reflex behavior. As we noted earlier, reflexes are involuntary responses to stimulation. We see in classical conditioning that the organism learns to make a reflex response (that is, becomes classically conditioned) to some stimulus which was previously neutral (that is, it did not bring forth this response). Let's see how this worked with Pavlov's dogs.

Pavlov knew that when he placed meat powder in a dog's mouth, saliva would flow, as the first step in the process of digestion. Salivation is an unlearned, or reflex, response to food. After noting that his dogs would salivate not only when they tasted the meat powder but when they first *saw* it, he designed an experiment that has become a landmark. First, a minor operation was performed on the laboratory dogs so that their saliva could be collected and measured. As a dog stood quietly on a table, loosely harnessed, an experimenter sounded a tone on a tuning fork, and then, 7 to 8 seconds later, moved a plate of meat powder within reach of the dog.

At first, the dog oriented, or paid attention to, the tone, but did not salivate upon hearing it—although the animals did salivate copiously while eating (see Figure 5-2).

FIGURE 5-2 *Apparatus used by Pavlov in classical conditioning studies. Saliva was collected through a tube in the dog's cheek and measured on the revolving drum to the left. At the beginning of a typical procedure, the dog would salivate only when meat powder, an unconditioned stimulus, was presented. Salivation to a conditioned stimulus, such as a tone, would occur after repeated presentations of tone and meat together.*

The experimenter then presented different combinations of the tone and food, varying the intervals between them. Eventually the dog salivated when it heard the tone, even before the meat appeared. Apparently, it had learned that the tone would soon be followed by food, and its salivary reflexes had been conditioned to respond to the tone as they did to the food itself.

How do we describe this phenomenon in psychological terms? In classical conditioning, an organism learns a new association between two events. In this experiment, an association was learned between the tone and the food. The food is called the **unconditioned stimulus (UCS).** An unconditioned stimulus is one that automatically elicits a response. Such a response is known as the **unconditioned response,** or **unconditioned reflex, (UCR).** It does not have to be learned. In this situation food automatically elicits salivation. Salivation is the UCR.

At the beginning of the experiment, the tone is a **neutral stimulus**—a stimulus that does not automatically elicit the response we are interested in, in this case salivation. During conditioning, the neutral stimulus (the tone) is *reinforced* by being repeatedly paired with the UCS (the food). Through this reinforcement, the neutral stimulus acquires the power to produce a learned response, salivation. Once the organism has learned to associate the food and the tone, and to respond essentially the same way to both, conditioning has occurred. At this point the tone is called the **conditioned stimulus (CS),** and salivation is the **conditioned response (CR).** A conditioned stimulus, then, is an initially neutral stimulus that, after repeated pairings with a UCS, comes to elicit a conditioned (or learned) response. The conditioned response occurs with the conditioned stimulus; but the unconditioned response occurs only with the unconditioned stimulus (Figure 5-3).

Pavlov (1927) and those who came after him believed that conditioning is strongly influenced by the timing of the **interstimulus interval,** the time between the presentation of the neutral stimulus and the UCS. Generally, it's most effective to present the neutral stimulus (in this case the tone) just before and overlapping with the UCS (the meat powder). This is called a *delayed relationship.* A *trace relationship* occurs when the CS (the tone—after conditioning has taken place) is presented and then withdrawn before the UCS (the meat powder) appears. If the tone sounds too far before the meat appears, the dog will have trouble learning the association between the two. If the tone sounds at the same time that the dog sees the meat (*simultaneous conditioning*), or afterward (*backward conditioning*), it might not notice the tone and might not learn to associate the tone with the meat. (See Figure 5-4.)

What happens when the experimenter changes the rules and begins to sound the tone without following it with the meat? The dog eventually learns that food is not forthcoming after all, and no longer salivates. This is the process of **extinction,** the gradual weakening of and failure to perform a conditioned response that occurs when the CS is presented repeatedly without the UCS.

After a conditioned response has been extinguished, **spontaneous recovery** may take place. Spontaneous recovery is the partial reappearance of a conditioned response that has been extinguished—with no additional learning trials. That is, there have been no further pairings of the UCS and the CS. How would this work? Several days after a dog has stopped salivating in response to the tone, taking it back to the lab where the original conditioning took place and again sounding the tone will make it start salivating again. This response shows that it has not forgotten the original learning but has inhibited the learned response. The spontaneously recovered response is usually weaker, however, than the original conditioned response (see Figure 5-5 on page 164).

Another Pavlovian concept is **stimulus generalization,** the tendency to transfer the conditioned response to a stimulus that is similar but not identical to the one originally paired with the unconditioned stimulus. For example, a dog that has learned to salivate to one tone may also salivate to a tone slightly higher or lower in pitch, to a bell, or to some other sound. **Discrimination** is the opposite of generalization; the organism learns to respond differentially to two similar stimuli. For exam-

Unconditioned stimulus (UCS) Stimulus that automatically elicits an unconditioned response, without the organism's having to learn (be conditioned) to respond.

Unconditioned response (unconditioned reflex) (UCR) Automatic response to an unconditioned stimulus.

Neutral stimulus Stimulus that does not automatically elicit a reflex response.

Conditioned stimulus (CS) Initially neutral stimulus which, after repeated pairings with an unconditioned stimulus, comes to elicit a conditioned response.

Conditioned response (CR) Response that comes to be elicited by a conditioned stimulus which has been repeatedly paired with an unconditioned stimulus.

Interstimulus interval Time interval between presentation of the neutral stimulus and the unconditioned stimulus.

Extinction Gradual weakening of and failure to perform a learned (conditioned) response.

Spontaneous recovery Reappearance of an extinguished response with no additional conditioning trials.

Stimulus generalization Tendency to respond in the same way to a stimulus that is similar (but not identical) to the one used in the conditioning trials.

Discrimination Learning to respond differently to two similar (but not identical) stimuli.

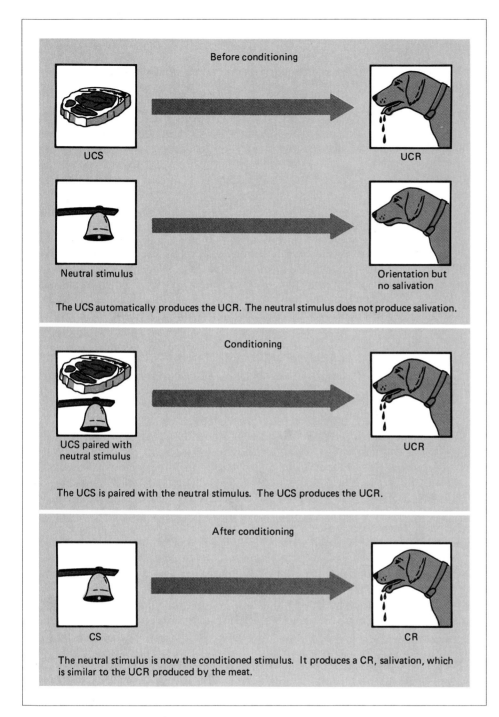

Before conditioning

UCS

UCR

Neutral stimulus

Orientation but no salivation

The UCS automatically produces the UCR. The neutral stimulus does not produce salivation.

Conditioning

UCS paired with neutral stimulus

UCR

The UCS is paired with the neutral stimulus. The UCS produces the UCR.

After conditioning

CS

CR

The neutral stimulus is now the conditioned stimulus. It produces a CR, salivation, which is similar to the UCR produced by the meat.

FIGURE 5-3 *Left: Classical conditioning. Classical conditioning occurs in three stages. The neutral stimulus eventually produces a conditioned response.*

FIGURE 5-4 *Below: Pairing of CS with UCS in four temporal relations. Acquisition of conditioning is quickest with the "delayed" sequence. (Source: Hulse, Egeth, & Deese, 1980.)*

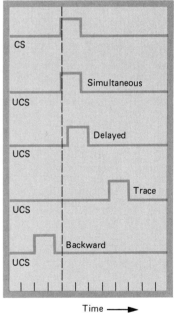

CS

UCS

Simultaneous

UCS

Delayed

UCS

Trace

UCS

Backward

UCS

Time ⟶

ple, a dog would salivate only to one specific tone—and not to one of a different pitch or to a bell.

Both these concepts have practical implications. If we were not able to generalize learning from one stimulus to another, getting along in the world would be very difficult. We would have to learn how to respond separately to every single situation we confronted. We would, for example, have to learn how to drive all over again every time we rented a different car, followed a new road, or were in a new driving situation. (Because of generalization, Sally Olds was able to transfer the motions she had learned at the typewriter to the keyboard of her computer.) It is equally impor-

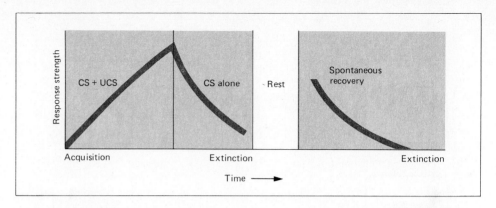

FIGURE 5-5 *Acquisition, extinction, and spontaneous recovery of a conditioned response. During acquisition, CS and UCS are paired, and learning increases. During extinction, CS is presented without UCS; responding weakens and eventually stops. After a rest period, spontaneous recovery occurs. In other words, the learned response reappears without further conditioning trials.*

tant to learn how to discriminate among different although somewhat similar stimuli. If we could not learn that when we see a green light at a traffic crossing we are supposed to keep on going, and that when we see a red light we are supposed to stop, chaos would reign on modern thoroughfares and traffic accidents would be the rule rather than the exception. (Because of discrimination, it's possible to learn—and sometimes to remember—that the shift lock on the computer works differently from the one on the typewriter.)

Pavlov used the concept of discrimination to create an *experimental neurosis* in some dogs (1927). First the dogs learned how to discriminate between a circle, which was a signal for food, and an ellipse (an oval, or elongated circle) which meant that no food would be forthcoming. When the circle and the ellipse were quite different from each other, the dogs quickly learned to salivate to the circle, but not to the ellipse. But when the experimenter gradually changed the shapes so that the two figures came to look more and more alike, the dogs could no longer tell the difference between the shape that signaled food and the one that did not. Once the dogs could no longer discriminate between the two shapes, they began to act strangely. They barked, acted fearful, and tried to destroy the conditioning apparatus.

Since all these behaviors are similar to those that we often see among anxious people, this last experiment may help us understand human anxieties. For one thing, it suggests that anxieties are *learned*. For another, the situation that the dogs were put in, in which they essentially lost control of their environment, resembles situations that many people often feel they are in—situations where they are unable to pick up cues from their environment. In such situations, people feel that they have no control over their lives. Later in this chapter we will talk about this emotionally debilitating condition, known as *learned helplessness*, which resembles the plight of the dogs.

Can People Be Conditioned?   A sales representative takes prospective clients out to dinner. If the prospects associate the salesperson's proposal with the favorable feelings engendered by a good dinner in a pleasant restaurant, they will be more likely to become clients than if the salesperson had approached them in less appealing surroundings. At least, this is the basis for much of the expense-account wining and dining that supports many expensive restaurants across the country.

A soldier sees a person in the uniform of an enemy nation. Having seen that uniform only in conjunction with stories of atrocities committed by people wearing it, the soldier immediately becomes enraged.

We are all conditioned to many aspects of the world about us. But we can often deal better with the world if we are aware of the mechanism that prepares us to feel spiritual as soon as we step into a church, patriotic when the flag passes by, emotional upon reading or hearing certain phrases of a poem or a bar of music. As the psychologist B. F. Skinner has pointed out, society uses the process of classical

Can people be conditioned? These flag-wavers at a political convention may be responding to associations laid down by society over the years: certain good feelings are allied with the display of our national symbols.

conditioning to "arrange for the control of behavior" (1953, p. 56). In addition, classical-conditioning procedures are used to help people overcome phobias (irrational fears), as well as undesirable habits like excessive drinking or smoking. One practical application of classical conditioning is described in the box "The Medical Potential of Classical Conditioning."

These are only two examples of the many ways in which we are conditioned, throughout our lives, to associate pairs of stimuli and to react accordingly. One of the most famous examples in the annals of psychology of a person who was conditioned is a child known in the literature as "little Albert."

LITTLE ALBERT John B. Watson, the "father of behaviorism," and Rosalie Rayner, the student who became his wife (1920), maintained that infants are born with three basic emotions: fear, rage, and love. They felt that children's early home lives are the laboratories in which they are conditioned to show these emotions and the more complex feelings that grow out of them. To test these beliefs, they brought Albert, a healthy, good-natured, emotionally stable 9-month-old boy, into the lab. The baby showed no fear with any stimulus—until they made a loud sound by striking a steel bar with a hammer just behind his head. Then Albert trembled and wept.

Two months later, they brought Albert back. Just as he was starting to touch a white rat (which he had shown no fear of at first), an experimenter sounded a loud noise. Albert jumped, fell forward, and cried. A week later, Albert again saw the rat at the same time that he heard the loud noise, was frightened, and cried. This happened again and again. Eventually, as soon as the baby saw the rat, he whimpered in fear. Albert's fear generalized to a rabbit, a dog, a seal coat, cotton wool, a Santa Claus mask, and Watson's hair. One month later, Albert was found to be still afraid of the Santa Claus mask, the fur coat, and in various degrees, the rat, the rabbit, and the dog. Watson and Rayner concluded that "directly conditioned emotional responses as well as those conditioned by transfer persist for a longer period than one month. Our view is that they persist and modify personality throughout life" (p. 12).

Since these psychologists believed so strongly in the power of early experience to bring about lifelong fears, their willingness to subject a healthy baby to these

Gloria, a 28-year-old former dancer, suffers periodically from rashes, pain, fever, and debilitating weakness. Her dancing career, like her general health, has fallen victim to systemic lupus erythematosis, or lupus. Lupus is a disorder of the immune system in which the body turns against itself. Gloria regularly takes cyclophosphamide, a drug which suppresses the immune response and keeps many of her symptoms under control. However, she often doubles over from the painful stomach cramps that are one of its side effects. If the dosage could be lowered to a level that would still be effective in controlling the symptoms of lupus but that would not produce the undesirable side effects, Gloria—and, of course, many others—would benefit greatly.

Recent research indicates that this may be possible. A psychologist and an immunologist have been able to classically condition rats and mice to suppress their bodies' immune response as a result of drinking sac-

IN THE FOREFRONT

THE MEDICAL POTENTIAL OF CLASSICAL CONDITIONING

charin-flavored water, after saccharin had been paired repeatedly with cyclophosphamide (Ader & Cohen, 1982). The researchers injected cyclophosphamide into the animals immediately after they received water sweetened with saccharin. The immune systems of the rodents that had received sweetened water along with the drug then reacted to the sweetened water alone as if it had the immunosuppressive qualities of the drug. When the classically conditioned mice received only half the

usual dosage of cyclophosphamide, bolstered with the sweetened water the animals had been conditioned to, their bodies' immune systems were suppressed as completely as if they had been given full dosages of the drug. These mice lived as long as other mice that received full dosages.

The implications of these findings for the human condition are exciting, since the usefulness of many drugs is limited by the severity of their side effects. If classical conditioning could fool human bodies into responding to greatly lowered dosages of powerful drugs, many people would have access to treatments that are now out of the question because of their side effects. This kind of research demonstrates the powerful influence of the mind over such autonomic body systems as the immune response, which we don't ordinarily think of as under our control. It also demonstrates the promise that psychology holds for advancing medical progress.

procedures seems especially irresponsible. They did acknowledge that the project was questionable and talked about the counterconditioning that they "would have done" if Albert had not been removed from the hospital before they could carry it out. They admitted, however, that they had known from the start that they would have access to Albert for only a short time. Experiments like this have given rise to the Code of Ethics of the American Psychological Association, which today would not allow such an intrusion into a child's psyche.

While psychologists have long faulted Watson and Rayner's *ethics*, serious criticism of their *conclusions* arose only recently. Let's look at some of the reservations voiced by Harris (1979). First, the results did not prove stimulus generalization, since separate conditioning trials were held for the rabbit and the dog. Second, Albert did not have as strong a fear reaction as indicated. In fact, he was ambivalent toward the animals after the experiment, sometimes letting them approach, sometimes reaching out to them, sometimes avoiding them but not crying. Furthermore, a number of researchers tried to replicate the work, but were unable to induce fears in infants by conditioning them to a loud noise (H. E. Jones, 1930; Valentine, 1930). Finally, while this study is usually considered a pure example of *classical* conditioning, the punishing aspect of the frighteningly loud noise interposes elements of *operant* conditioning, which will be discussed later. We have discussed this experiment in detail more because of its status as a classic study than because of its findings.

OVERCOMING FEARS   Suppose that Watson and Rayner had gone ahead with their expressed intention to free Albert of the fears they had instilled in him. How might they have gone about it? They spoke of pairing the feared objects with stroking of the child's erogenous zones (sensitive body areas that produce pleasurable sexual sensations when stroked, like the genitals and breasts) or feeding him candy or other food, or encouraging him to imitate a model (Watson & Rayner, 1920, p. 12). It's probably just as well that they never went through with the first approach, since they might have produced sexual pathology on top of Albert's other problems. Their other two suggestions, however, were used successfully by another student of Watson's, Mary Cover Jones (1924).

Peter was almost 3 years old—a healthy, normal child except for his exaggerated fears, which resembled Albert's laboratory-induced fears so closely that Jones said he "seemed almost to be Albert grown a bit older" (p. 153). No one knew what had made Peter so afraid of such objects as a white rat, a rabbit, a fur coat, a feather, and cotton wool. Jones wanted to "uncondition" Peter's fear to an animal and then see whether this "unconditioning" would generalize, without further training, to the other feared items.

First, she set up a modeling procedure, bringing Peter to the lab together with three other children who were not afraid of the rabbit. (Modeling, which we'll discuss in detail later, is the process by which people observe and imitate the behavior of others, who are called *models*.) Peter watched the other children playing near or with the rabbit, and gradually lost his own fear. He had begun by being afraid if the rabbit was even caged up anywhere in the room; eventually, he would let the rabbit nibble his fingers and would exult, "I touched him on the end."

After this advance, however Peter was hospitalized for 2 months with scarlet fever. When he came back to the lab, he was showing his old fears again, partly, no doubt, because both he and his nurse had been frightened by a large dog who jumped at them as they were leaving the hospital. At this point, Jones started a new phase of treatment, in which Peter got food he liked when the rabbit was present so that he would associate the rabbit with a pleasant experience. This method, called *counterconditioning*, was also effective in helping Peter overcome his fear, not only of the rabbit, but of the other objects and of strange animals, including a mouse and a tangled mass of angleworms. Therapeutic approaches based on these principles will be discussed in Chapter 15.

Operant Conditioning

In a large gambling casino on the boardwalk in Atlantic City, a middle-aged woman stands for hours in front of a metal box with pictures. Over and over again, she puts a coin into a slot and pulls down a lever to make the pictures come up in a certain pattern. Why does she engage in this monotonous, tiring behavior? She does so because from time to time a pattern she is trying for appears and coins cascade out of the machine, for her to scoop up and reinsert, in hopes of bigger and bigger returns. Here we see a prime example of operant conditioning.

How does operant conditioning differ from classical conditioning? Classical conditioning applies to reflex behaviors that follow a stimulus, like a dog's salivation in the presence of food. The food automatically elicits salivation, and through classical conditioning, a new stimulus like a tone eventually comes to elicit salivation. An association between two stimuli (the tone and the food) has occurred; the dog eventually learns that the tone means that food is on the way, and salivates to the tone. Nothing that the dog does has any effect: the dog's actions do not make food arrive or cause salivation. Rather, salivation is an automatic response.

In operant conditioning an association is also formed between two events. But in this kind of conditioning, organisms learn that by doing something, they can produce a particular outcome. In operant conditioning, also known as *instrumental conditioning*, organisms learn that by behaving in a certain way (in other words, by operating on the environment in some way), they become instrumental in either producing a reward or avoiding or escaping punishment. The outcome, then, is contingent on a particular behavior. The behaviors are strengthened (that is, they are more likely to occur again) if they are followed by reinforcement, and are weakened (less likely to occur again) if followed by punishment.

The starring role that Pavlov's dogs played in demonstrating the principles of classical conditioning was assumed for operant conditioning by Thorndike's cats and Skinner's rats and pigeons.

Thorndike: His Cats and His Law of Effect   While Pavlov was discovering the basic laws of classical conditioning in Russia, an American psychologist, Edward L. Thorndike, was discovering the "law of effect," which was an important foundation for the principles of operant conditioning. Thorndike put hungry cats inside locked "puzzle boxes." The cats could see and smell food that was placed outside the boxes but couldn't get at it unless they could learn some way to escape from the box. Gradually, the cats learned to pull on a piece of rope that would open the box so that they could get out and reach the food. Their learning achievement was the basis of Thorndike's doctoral dissertation (a research project required for a Ph.D. degree), which he received in 1898.

Trial-and-error learning *Learning by trying out a number of responses until the correct response is made.*

The cats learned by trial and error. ***Trial-and-error learning*** consists of trying out a number of responses until the correct response is made. The cats engaged in a number of different behaviors while they were in the box, and happened upon the right one only by accident. Once they learned the trick of opening the box, however, they were able to escape rapidly; and in subsequent sessions in the box, they did not engage in any of the unproductive behaviors they had initially tried but concentrated only on pulling the rope.

Law of effect *Thorndike's principle that when an animal's actions are accompanied or closely followed by a satisfying experience, the animal will connect the two and will be likely to perform the same actions in a similar situation.*

Thorndike explained the cats' learning by referring to the reward they got (the food) and the association they made between pulling the rope and eating. He called his explanation the ***law of effect*** (1911). This law states, basically, that when an animal's actions in any given situation are accompanied or closely followed by a satisfying experience, the animal will connect the actions with the satisfaction and will be likely to perform the same actions if a similar situation comes up again. When the animal's actions become linked with discomfort, the animal won't repeat those actions. In other words, behaviors that are reinforced will be repeated, and those that are punished will stop. The association, says Thorndike, is automatic. A related principle developed by Thorndike is the ***law of exercise,*** which states that the connection between stimulus and response becomes stronger through repetition. In other words, the more often a response is repeated in one situation, the more likely it is to be repeated in the future.

Law of exercise *Thorndike's principle that the connection between a stimulus and a response is strengthened by repetition.*

Skinner: Principles Derived from the "Skinner Box"   For many years, B. F. Skinner has been the foremost proponent of operant conditioning. He is concerned chiefly with the way behavior affects the environment to produce consequences and with the way a favorable consequence, or ***reinforcement,*** works to increase the probability that a behavior will recur. Skinner maintains that reinforcement is the basic means of controlling behavior. The kind of behavior that is influenced by reinforcement is called an ***operant.*** In Skinner's work with animals the operants were often pressing a bar or pecking.

Reinforcement *Event (or consequence) following a behavior which increases the probability that the behavior will occur again.*

Operant *Response that an organism makes to bring about an effect.*

In his laboratory work with rats and pigeons, Skinner designed an apparatus that has since become one of the most common tools of psychological research. This was a cage, or box, equipped with a simple mechanism that the animal itself could activate to get its reward. The mechanism was usually a bar or lever that the animal could press. Skinner also designed a moving paper tape that would automatically record the animal's behavior.

Skinner developed a standard procedure for studying operant conditioning, which can be applied to people as well as to animals. Briefly, this is how the procedure works:

1   Identify the response to be studied (that is, the *operant*). The easiest kind to study is a simple response like pressing a bar.

2 Determine the *baseline rate* of that response. That is, how often—if at all—does the animal normally emit the response before conditioning?

3 Choose something that you think will *reinforce* the behavior you want the animal to perform. Food is most often chosen, but other reinforcers are also used from time to time, such as the opportunity for a mother to reach her offspring or for an adult to reach a sexual partner.

4 Apply the reinforcer according to some set schedule until the animal has increased the response you want.

5 Stop awarding the reinforcer to see whether the animal's rate of response will drop back to the baseline rate. If so, *extinction* has occurred, and you can safely assume that the reinforcer was responsible for the animal's changed behavior.

A Note on Animal Studies Pavlov's dogs, Thorndike's cats, and Skinner's rats and pigeons demonstrate the important kinds of findings that can result from studying animals. Pavlov, Thorndike, and Skinner were interested in the principles behind the animals' actions, rather than in the animals or the actions themselves. They used animals instead of people for some of the reasons cited in Chapter 1—largely because animals are simpler organisms and therefore it is easier, faster, and cheaper to set up experiments using animals rather than people as subjects. With the knowledge of basic principles that we gain from animal studies, we can then generalize many of these findings and build on them to design research with people. In this way we expand our knowledge about living organisms in general and about people in particular.

Aspects of Operant Conditioning REINFORCEMENT There are two basic kinds of reinforcers: *positive* and *negative*. **Positive reinforcers** are stimuli that increase the probability of a response when they are *added* to a situation. Common experimental examples are such desirable things as food, water, and sexual contact. In real life, reinforcers can consist of smiles from people we love, good grades, gold stars, and athletic letters. **Negative reinforcers** are unpleasant stimuli whose *removal* from a situation increases the probability of a response. Common experimental examples are loud noises, very bright lights, and electric shocks. (By pressing a bar in the Skinner box, a rat can turn off an electric shock to its foot.) In real life a common negative reinforcement is stopping the nagging of a parent, partner, or roommate when we clean up a room, fill up the gas tank in the car, or wash a sinkful of dirty dishes.

In either case, the effect of the reinforcer is the same: it increases the response. Negative reinforcement is *not* the same as *punishment*. Both kinds of reinforcement—positive and negative—result in the probability that a given behavior will occur more often; but punishment is administered to make a behavior occur less often. We'll see how this works when we discuss punishment in more detail later in this chapter.

Reinforcers can be *primary* or *secondary*. **Primary reinforcers** are biologically important: they include food, water, sex, and escape from harmful conditions. **Secondary reinforcers** are *learned*; they become reinforcing only because of their association with primary reinforcers. In this category we would put such reinforcers as money, school grades, gold stars on a chart, and praise. Tokens, which can be exchanged for desired merchandise or for other kinds of rewards, can be effective secondary reinforcers to change the behavior of people in a variety of situations. How do you know what will serve as a reinforcement? According to Skinner (1953), the only way to know is to make a direct test. An event is reinforcing if it brings about an increase in the frequency of a specific response. No matter how good something might seem to you, it is not a reinforcer if it doesn't change an animal's or person's rate of response, or if it lowers the rate of response. Conversely, something that on the face of it does not seem like a reinforcer may actually be one.

An animal in a "Skinner box," like this rat, can trip a mechanism to get food. Skinner also designed a moving paper tape that would automatically record the animal's behavior. Here, an investigator using a computer records the data.

Positive reinforcer *Stimulus which when added to a situation increases the probability of the occurrence of a response.*

Negative reinforcer *Stimulus which when removed from a situation increases the probability of the occurrence of a response.*

Primary reinforcers *Objects or events that are biologically important, such as food and sex, and whose appearance increases the probability of the occurrence of a response.*

Secondary reinforcers *Stimuli that become reinforcing after becoming associated with primary reinforcers.*

The idea of reinforcement, along with other learning principles, has important implications for bringing up children. In many homes, for example, parents tend to ignore small children when they are quietly behaving themselves. But when Melissa starts to tease the cat, poke a finger in the baby's eye, or get into the cookie jar, her parents don't ignore her any longer. They may scold her, scream at her, or spank her. These behaviors do not seem like reinforcers, but if what Melissa wants is attention, that is what she is getting. The attention itself is the reinforcer for the child's obstreperous behavior.

In an experiment that has since become a classic, two psychologists decided to test the reinforcing power of attention to eliminate aggressive behavior among nursery school children (Brown & Elliott, 1965). Over an 8-week period, nursery school teachers focused on eliminating aggressive behavior among 3- and 4-year-old boys. They paid special attention to the children when they were being cooperative, saying things like, "That's good, Mike," and, "Look what Eric made." They tried to ignore aggression unless it seemed dangerous.

The average number of physically aggressive acts dropped from 41 during the week before treatment to 21 by the end of the treatment period, and the number of instances of verbal aggression fell from 23 to 5. Why did verbal aggression drop so much more? The answer is probably that it is harder to ignore fighting than threats and insults. In any case, both kinds of aggression were reduced, and the two most troublesome boys in the class became friendly and cooperative to a degree none of the teachers had thought possible.

Timing of reinforcement For reinforcement to be effective, it must be prompt. If it follows too long after an action, no learning will take place. The other events that take place during the period of delay will make the person or animal miss the connection between what was done and the feeling of pleasure that comes from the reinforcement. The major exception to this general rule is in regard to food preferences and aversions, which we'll discuss in the section on punishment.

Schedules of reinforcement *Patterns by which reinforcement is administered.*

Continuous reinforcement *Pattern of reinforcement by which the organism is reinforced every time that it emits the desired response.*

Partial reinforcement *Pattern of reinforcement in which the desired response is rewarded only part of the time; also called intermittent reinforcement.*

Schedules of reinforcement **Schedules of reinforcement** are patterns by which reinforcement is given. There are two broad categories of patterns—*continuous* and *partial*. If a pigeon gets food every time it pecks a particular spot, it is receiving **continuous reinforcement. Partial reinforcement** it also known as *intermittent reinforcement*. If the pigeon receives food only every tenth time it pecks the spot, it is receiving intermittent, or partial, reinforcement. Partial reinforcement is more common than continuous reinforcement.

Animals learn more quickly when they receive continuous reinforcement, but they will perform a behavior longer under intermittent reinforcement. Why is partial reinforcement more resistant to extinction? The answer is that an animal receiving continuous reinforcement quickly learns when no further reinforcement is forthcoming and quickly stops making the response; but an animal being reinforced only part of the time takes longer to recognize that reinforcement has stopped and, as a result, keeps making the response for a longer time.

The power of intermittent reinforcement also has important implications for child rearing. Here is a typical scenario: Three-year-old Michael, sitting in a supermarket cart, asks his mother for a box of cookies. The mother says, "No, we have some at home." Michael asks again. Again, his mother refuses. Michael starts to scream and flail about, trying to get out of the seat. His mother refuses one more time. Other shoppers look at the child, who is getting noisier and more out of control by the minute. Finally, the embarrassed mother grabs a box of cookies from the shelf and hurls them into Michael's lap. The child has learned something that he will use to his advantage in the future. He has learned that he has a tool for getting what he wants, that sometimes it will work and sometimes it won't, and that he might as well keep trying it. This is why it's important for parents to be consistent in deciding what they will and what they will not reinforce.

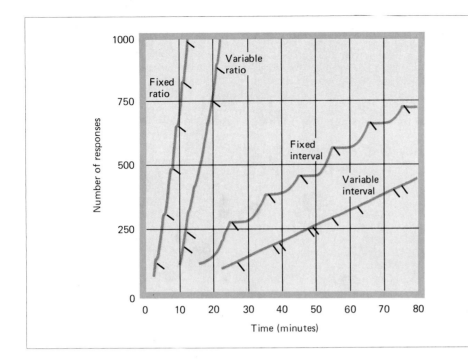

FIGURE 5-6 *Typical response curves for different reinforcement schedules. Note that both ratio schedules are associated with high levels of responding, as demonstrated by the steepness of the curve. The interval schedules are associated with intermediate rates of responding. Note the drop in responding immediately after reinforcement in the fixed-interval schedule; this produces the typical "scalloped" curve. The presentation of reinforcement is indicated by the small lines perpendicular to each curve. (Source: Adapted from Skinner, 1961.)*

Partial reinforcement can be given according to a number of different schedules. The most basic of these are **interval schedules of reinforcement** and **ratio schedules of reinforcement**. (See Figure 5-6.)

In *interval schedules,* a certain amount of time must pass before presentation of reinforcement. Thus a pigeon might get food every 5 minutes, regardless of the number of pecks it makes during that period, as long as it pecks after each 5 minute waiting period. Animals on a **fixed-interval schedule** will respond less immediately after reinforcement, since they have learned that they will not be reinforced again for some time.

On a **variable-interval schedule,** the time that must pass before a response will be reinforced is varied. The animal might get food every 5 minutes *on the average;* but sometimes it will be reinforced after only, say, 30 seconds, and at other times it might have to wait 10 minutes or more. Skinner (1953) points out that pigeons reinforced under this type of schedule give a "remarkably stable and uniform" performance (p. 102) that is very resistant to extinction. Skinner (1953) observed that pigeons will peck for as long as 15 hours straight, pecking two to three times per second, without pausing longer than 15 or 20 seconds during the entire time span.

In *ratio reinforcement,* the time interval does not matter. What does matter is number of responses. A pigeon will be reinforced, say, every tenth time it presses a bar; a writer will receive a check for every three completed chapters of a book. In a **fixed-ratio schedule,** like these, reinforcement is contingent upon making a fixed number of responses. Ratio reinforcement is the basis for sales commissions, the pay that most professionals receive, and certain kinds of industrial work.

An animal being reinforced by a high fixed ratio will respond less immediately after reinforcement, just as it will with fixed-interval reinforcement. Skinner (1953) notes that the same principle applies to people: "Wherever a piecework schedule is used—in industry, education, salesmanship, or the professions—low morale or low interest is most often observed just after a unit of work has been completed" (p. 103). (*Piecework* is the term used in industry to denote payment to workers on the basis of the number of units of work they complete. A tailor who gets paid for every finished garment is an example of ratio reinforcement.)

In a **variable-ratio schedule,** the organism is reinforced for variable numbers of

Interval schedule of reinforcement Partial reinforcement schedule that requires a certain amount of time to pass between the presentations of reinforcement.

Ratio schedule of reinforcement Partial reinforcement schedule that requires a certain number of responses to be emitted for reinforcement to be given.

Fixed-interval schedule Pattern of reinforcement under which the organism is regularly rewarded according to a fixed time period.

Variable-interval schedule Pattern of reinforcement by which the time period that must pass before a response is reinforced varies around some average.

Fixed-ratio schedule Pattern of reinforcement in which the organism is reinforced after making a specified number of responses.

Variable-ratio schedule Pattern of reinforcement in which the organism is reinforced after making a variable number of responses around some average number.

The allure of slot machines is gamblers' knowledge that they have a chance to win a lot of money. This woman may not be familiar with intermittent reinforcement and variable-ratio schedules, but these principles govern the slot machine's payoff—and its popularity.

responses, around some average number. Since the probability of reinforcement at any moment remains essentially the same, the animal continues responding on a constant basis. This kind of schedule is much more powerful than a fixed-ratio schedule with the same average number of responses, producing much more resistance to extinction. Gamblers using slot machines are being reinforced on a variable-ratio schedule. They know that the casino management has set these "one-armed bandits" to pay off according to some kind of average that will, in the long run, make money for the house. They also know, however, that occasionally there will be big payoffs, and they keep playing in the hope that they will be lucky enough to be around for one of those payoffs.

It is possible to combine interval and ratio schedules, to reward a certain number of responses made during a certain time period. A psychology student, for example, might get an A in a 16-week course if he or she gets a grade of 90 percent in each of four exams taken during that time span. A delayed reward system is described in the box "Using Operant Conditioning to Encourage Use of Seat Belts."

SUPERSTITIOUS BEHAVIOR Things looked bad to Tony LaRussa, manager of the Chicago White Sox. His team had lost 12 games out of 15, his job was in danger, and he had just received a death threat over the telephone. Maybe that's why he pulled his warm-up jacket around him, even though it was a hot, muggy night. That night his team won. From that time on, Tony put on his jacket every time the team played, no matter how blistering the weather. The White Sox won the next 9 games out of 11, and LaRussa said, "I don't put much faith in it but you never know" ("Sports people," 1982, p. B8).

Many athletes, actors, and gamblers wear "lucky" clothes, carry "lucky" charms, and perform "lucky" behaviors. They do it because on one or more occasions they associated success with one of these other events. According to Skinner, **superstitious behavior** is behavior that has been strengthened or weakened because it was accidentally reinforced or punished.

Pigeons can "learn" to be superstitious, too. In one series of experiments, Skinner (1953) gave pigeons a small amount of food every 15 seconds, no matter what they were doing. The first time a pigeon got food, obviously, it was doing something— if only standing still. The pigeon apparently made some connection between the

Superstitious behavior *Behavior that has been strengthened or weakened because it was accidentally reinforced or punished.*

One of the most challenging paradoxes of modern life is the fact that although people have a basic motivation for survival (according to which they will do whatever they can to save their lives and avoid injury), most people resist using lap and shoulder belts in cars, despite statistics proving that more than half of all traffic deaths and injuries could be avoided by the use of safety belts.

Psychologists have analyzed this contradiction and concluded that the major reason for it is that people are rewarded for *not* using safety belts. That is, most people travel unbelted because they consider the belts an uncomfortable nuisance, and most people who travel unbelted reach their destination without an accident. Arriving safely is in effect a reinforcement for not using a belt. Other reasons for not using safety belts also derive from learning principles. One is a lack of models. (See the section "Observational Learning" later in this chapter.) A recent survey by a group of graduate students found that fewer than 5 percent of television stars in prime-time "action" shows are shown wearing lap or shoulder belts (Geller, 1985).

To counter these disincentives, the psychologist E. Scott Geller and his colleagues have developed a number of programs based on learning principles to encourage drivers and passengers to wear safety belts. These programs, which have relied on various ways of reinforcing people for wearing belts, have been fairly successful and hold promise for being even more so. Let's take a look at one.

As we pointed out earlier, direct and immediate reinforcement has the best chance of changing behavior. However, a disadvantage of a program involving such direct reinforcement is that it would require stopping cars, checking for use of seat belts, and giving immediate rewards, all of which would cause unacceptable traffic jams. Geller (1984), therefore, developed a delayed-reward program at one large industrial complex.

USING OPERANT CONDITIONING TO ENCOURAGE USE OF SEAT BELTS

Every day for 4 weeks, observers noted *baseline* rates of use of shoulder belts at two gates where workers left for the day, to see how many people were using belts already. (Determination of the baseline rate tells us the extent of use before the program.) Ten days before the experiment went into effect, the employees' newspaper announced the kick-off day for a special safety-belt promotion program, and during the 3-week incentive program posters and signs told workers that wearing safety belts made them eligible for a daily lottery. Each day's winner would get a dinner for two at a local restaurant or a pair of basketball tickets.

Every day during the following 3 weeks, observers noted use of belts, recorded license plate numbers, randomly selected winners, and awarded prizes. The employees' newspaper printed the winners' names. The researchers assessed use during the program and then did follow-up assessments 1, 3, and 10 months later. As Table 5-1 shows, use of belts went up sharply during the incentive period and then dropped gradually over the year. Still, almost 1 year after the program ended, use was higher than it had been at the baseline, showing that some benefits were maintained. Geller recommends periodic incentive programs (intermittent reinforcement) to keep use high.

Other programs have coupled incentives with brief educational sessions consisting of a film and discussion; have involved handing fliers to drivers on campus parking lots, promising to users of seat belts the chance to win a prize; or have used flashing signs saying, "PLEASE BUCKLE UP—I CARE" (Geller, Bruff, & Nimmer, 1985; Geller & Hahn, 1984; Geller, Paterson, & Talbott, 1982). All were effective in varying degrees, showing some of the very practical results that research in learning principles can have.

TABLE 5-1   MOTIVATING USE OF SAFETY BELTS

Mean Use of Shoulder Belts at Exit Gate during Baseline, Incentive, and Follow-Up Conditions

Experimental Condition	Period of Study	Number of Observation Days	Percent Wearing Shoulder Belt
Baseline (before program began)	4 weeks	21	6.7
Incentive period (prizes awarded daily)	3 weeks	15	23.1
Follow-up 1	1 month after end of incentives	37	16.3
Follow-up 2	3 months after end of incentives	38	15.8
Follow-up 3	10 months after end of incentives	10	11.0

Source: Adapted from Geller, 1984.

Teaching an animal a trick involves operant-conditioning techniques like shaping, in which the trainer rewards any effort in the right direction, no matter how small. With a little effort, this dog may be as fit as its master.

activity and the food; and the second time it got the food, it was more likely to be doing what it had been doing previously than some other activity. The more it did this, the more the act was reinforced, since the food kept coming. Pigeons that have been conditioned in this way have started hopping from one foot to the other, turning sharply to one side, bowing and scraping, turning around, strutting, and raising their heads.

Such accidental connections have been the basis for the success of innumerable nonscientific medical "cures." Many medical conditions run their course over a certain time, and any measure that is taken to cure them will meet with success if it is adopted at the right time. Thus are "true believers" created.

SHAPING   A favorite saying among behavior modifiers is that the trick to encouraging children to do what you want is to "catch them being good" and then reward them. Suppose, though, that you never do catch a child doing exactly what you want him or her to do. What, then, can you reward? You reward any effort, no matter how small, that is going in the right direction. This is called **shaping,** and it can be very effective in bringing about all sorts of new behavior. To understand how shaping can be used with animals, see the box "How to Teach an Animal."

Shaping   *Reinforcement of responses that come progressively closer to the desired behavior until the desired behavior is reached.*

In shaping, you begin by reinforcing any response that is part of the desired behavior. Shaping proceeds by reinforcing responses that are closer and closer to the desired behavior. By reinforcing these "successive approximations" to the target behavior, you will eventually lead the subject to perform the desired behavior.

We'll talk more about the use of operant-conditioning principles in Chapter 15, when we discuss their applications in therapy.

BIOLOGICAL INFLUENCES ON LEARNING   Can any animal learn to do any trick? Long before Miss Piggy pranced into public consciousness, a real porker named "Priscilla the fastidious pig" was performing on television, as well as at fairs and conventions, turning on the radio, eating breakfast at a table, picking up dirty clothes and putting them into a hamper, running a vacuum cleaner, and answering *yes* or *no* (by lighting up signs) to questions posed by the audience.

Priscilla was the apt pupil of Keller Breland and Marian Breland (1951), a hus-

This is how you can use shaping to train a pet:

1   Choose your subject. You could pick any household pet, such as a mouse, a parrot, or a gerbil. (Skinner suggests saving any available children until you have had practice with less valuable material.) Let's say you want to teach your Samoyed dog, Sam, a new trick.
2   Choose a reinforcer. Food is usually the easiest to use. For food to be reinforcing, Sam has to be hungry. So don't try to teach him right after he has eaten.
3   Since reinforcement is most effective when given almost simultaneously with the desired behavior, and since it's hard to hand out food as quickly as you would like to, develop a conditioned reinforcer by pairing the food with something else. That something might be one of those little metal toys that make a "cricket" sound when you click them.
    Condition the cricket by getting together 30 or 40 small scraps of food or tiny dog biscuits.

HOW TO TEACH AN ANIMAL

Toss a few to Sam, one at a time, no oftener than once or twice a minute. As soon as Sam is eating all the scraps eagerly, sound the cricket—and then toss a piece of food. Wait about 30 seconds and repeat. When you sound the cricket, make no other movement. Sound the cricket and give food only when Sam is not facing you and is at spot where he receives food.
4   When Sam goes to the food place whenever you sound the cricket, you are ready to begin teaching.
5   Choose the behavior you want to teach. One relatively simple trick, good as a starter, is getting Sam to touch the handle on a low cupboard door with his nose.

6   Shape Sam's behavior by reinforcing anything that remotely resembles the behavior you want. First, reinforce any turn toward the cupboard. Then reinforce any move toward the cupboard. When Sam is standing close to the cupboard, reinforce any movement of his head that brings his nose close to the cupboard handle. Every time you reinforce one of these successive approximations to the target behavior, sound the cricket as nearly simultaneously with Sam's movement as possible, and then give him a piece of food. During the teaching do not touch Sam, talk to him, coax him, or in any other way divert his attention from the task at hand. As a normal dog, Sam should, according to Skinner, learn the desired behavior within 5 minutes.
7   Before you teach Sam another trick, extinguish this one by no longer reinforcing it. Eventually Sam will stop touching his nose to the cupboard handle and will be ready to learn something new.

Source: Based on Skinner, 1951.

band-and-wife team of psychologists who applied the principles of operant conditioning to teach chickens, a calf, a turkey, rats, hamsters, guinea pigs, ducks, pigeons, rabbits, cats, dogs, and crows. While their work was almost exclusively in entertainment, they believed that their techniques could be used to make farm animals more useful and to train dogs to work with the blind, hunt, do detective work, and guard children and property.

In 1961, ten years after publishing a first, enthusiastic paper about the promise of this new field, which they called *applied animal psychology,* the Brelands published a report about what they considered their "failures." These failures teach us a vital lesson about the biological parameters of learning.

In one experiment, the Brelands wanted to teach chickens to stand on a platform for 12 to 15 seconds. More than half the chickens would not stand still, but instead began to scratch vigorously, round and round, at the rate of about two scratches per second. The trainers changed the act and billed it as "dancing chickens."

In another experiment, they wanted to teach a raccoon to pick up coins and put them into a piggy bank. The raccoon quickly learned to pick up a coin but was very reluctant to let go, rubbing it against the inside of the container, pulling it back out, and holding it firmly for several seconds before finally dropping it in the "bank." Even though this behavior was not reinforced, the raccoon did so much of it that the act never worked out.

These failures of conditioning theory can be seen as triumphs of biology. The animals were persisting in carrying out behaviors that came to them instinctively and were resisting the most sophisticated use of operant-conditioning techniques. The limits to learning that the animals displayed are important because they show situations in which the laws of conditioning do not apply. Originally, researchers like the Brelands thought that they could teach an animal to make any response it was physically capable of. Experiments like the ones described here show us, however, that animals seem to have different capacities for learning. The responses that are easiest for animals to learn are the ones closest to behaviors they would ordinarily perform in their natural environment. In other words, different animals are prepared to learn different specific responses (such as scratching in chickens and rubbing in raccoons).

The Brelands used the term *instinctive drift* for the animals' tendency to perform their own instinctive behaviors, even when these behaviors delayed or eliminated reinforcement. The idea that "learned behavior drifts toward instinctive behavior" seems to have been confirmed by another study, in which pigeons learned to peck at a light even though the pecking actually *prevented* them from getting food (Williams & Williams, 1969). Reinforcement, then, is not all-powerful. It works best when animals are being taught to perform behaviors that are compatible with their natural responses (Wickelgren, 1977).

We can see this when we look at the way animals learn to avoid certain foods. A rat that eats a food which makes it ill as much as 12 hours later quickly learns to avoid that food. This is obviously a survival mechanism. Apparently, the kind of learning that helps an animal to survive in its basic environment will persist (Garcia & Koelling, 1966). Since rats depend on whatever food they can scavenge, they need to learn quickly which foods to stay away from. Such learning is relatively easy for rats, partly because they are conservative gourmets, tending to eat only one new food at a time. If they become nauseated soon after eating a new substance, they will be able to identify it and will thereafter avoid it. Interestingly, rats learn to avoid tastes associated with nausea but not tastes associated with pain. This may be because their biological systems are programmed to recognize nausea as associated with eating, whereas they do not recognize the same connection between pain and eating.

GENERALIZATION AND DISCRIMINATION   As in classical conditioning, *stimulus generalization* is the phenomenon whereby an animal or person learns a response to one stimulus and then applies it to other, similar stimuli. Thus a pigeon who learns to peck at a red card will also peck at a green card. If you want to teach the pigeon to discriminate between the two cards, you continue to reinforce pecks at the red card and stop reinforcing pecks at the green card. The red card is then said to be the *discriminative stimulus*—the stimulus that rewards, and thus controls, behavior. We say that the red card has acquired *stimulus control* over the pigeon's behavior. Since the red card signals potential reinforcement, the pigeon is likely to respond in a certain way when it is present (in this case, to peck).

EXTINCTION   How do you get an animal or person to stop responding in a certain way? You might do this by no longer reinforcing the response. As we have pointed out, how rapidly you can extinguish a response depends on the kind of reinforcement schedule you have been using. You can extinguish continuously reinforced behaviors faster than intermittently reinforced behaviors. Of the intermittently reinforced responses, you can extinguish the ones that were reinforced on a fixed schedule faster than those on a variable schedule. You can also get an organism to stop responding by using punishment, which we'll discuss below.

SPONTANEOUS RECOVERY   Just as in classical conditioning, animals and people whose operant behaviors have been extinguished may recover them. If you take a pigeon whose pecking behavior has been extinguished and put it back in the Skinner box at a later date, the pigeon may well start to peck again. And "cured" habitual gamblers may start to play blackjack again when they go back into a casino.

PUNISHMENT Rats receive a shock when they run up the wrong alley in a maze. Children get a spanking when they run into the street. Pigeons have their food taken away when they peck at a bar that the experimenter wants them to avoid. Motorists have to pay a fine when they run a red light. All these situations are examples of punishment. **Punishment** is a consequence that decreases (or aims to decrease) the probability that a behavior will recur. The first two types of punishment described here represent the presentation of an **aversive stimulus** (one that the subject does not like, such as a shock or a spanking), and the second two represent the *withdrawal* of a stimulus that the subject does like (food or money).

Clearly, punishment can and does take many forms. Its popularity seems to show that for most people the idea of punishing undesirable behavior seems more natural than rewarding desirable behavior—in child rearing, in family relations, at work, and in the community. Is this belief justified?

As we pointed out earlier, punishment is different from negative reinforcement. Punishment is administered for the express purpose of reducing the tendency to behave in a certain way, and it often succeeds. Administering an electric shock to an animal every time it presses a bar will make it stop pressing the bar. A child who is bitten by a dog he or she tries to pet will probably stop approaching strange animals.

In other cases, however, punishment seems to be ineffective. Thieves who have been imprisoned routinely steal again as soon as they are released. A dog that has been hit for eating food off the table will often continue to gobble up any meat it can find, as long as its owner is not around. A teenage girl who is "grounded" because she sneaked out to meet a boyfriend will devise more ingenious ways of getting out of the house without being caught.

Why does punishment work some of the time but not all the time? And when it does work, why does it still have so many drawbacks that most behavioral scientists, animal trainers, and authorities on child rearing recommend reinforcement instead?

How punishment works—or doesn't work Punishment often works dramatically right away, in an immediate situation. Its long-term effects are much more questionable. We can see this with rats that had been trained to press the bar in a Skinner box and were then slapped on the paw every time they pressed it. On the first day of the punishment trial, these rats pressed the bar less often than a control group of rats that were not punished for pressing but were not reinforced for it either. By the second day, however, there was no difference between the two groups of rats. The response was extinguished just as quickly in the rats that were not punished as in those that were (Skinner, 1938).

What factors determine the effectiveness or ineffectiveness of punishment? Ross D. Parke (1977) has identified timing and consistency as among the most important. Other research has shown that severity and the availability of an alternative, reinforced response are also significant elements.

Timing: Earlier is better than later. The shorter the time interval between a behavior and its punishment, the more effective the punishment will be. For example, if children are punished as they *begin* to do something that is forbidden (such as approaching an object they have been told to stay away from), they will do it less often than if they are not punished until *after* they have actually done it. The same principle applies to animals. It is of limited value to tell a child, "Wait until your father gets home," or to come home, find a table leg chewed up, and then hit the dog (by then happily napping). In practical terms, of course, it is not always possible to punish children, pets, or criminals as they are misbehaving or immediately afterward. Timing, therefore, is a factor that often works against the effectiveness of punishment.

Consistency: The more consistently a person or animal is punished, the more effective the punishment will be. Erratic punishment prolongs undesirable behavior more than no punishment at all. The father who punishes four-year-old Kimberly on one occasion for using four-letter words, rewards her with an amused smile on

Punishment *Event that when administered following a response decreases the probability of the recurrence of that response.*
Aversive stimulus *Stimulus that the subject does not like; a type of punishment.*

another, and ignores her on a third is helping to engrave these words in his daughter's vocabulary. Again, looking at the situation practically, parents, pet owners, and police officers are not always on the scene. Thus people and animals often get away with behavior on one occasion that they will be punished for on another. Inconsistency sabotages punishment, and in the real world inconsistency is unavoidable.

Availability of alternative, reinforced responses: A rat will quickly learn to take an alternative route in a maze if it is not only shocked for taking the wrong route but rewarded with food for taking the right one. A 3-year-old boy will learn not to poke his finger in his baby sister's eye if he is not only scolded for poking her eye but also shown how to touch her gently and then commended for being "a big boy who knows how to treat a baby." Skinner (1953) stresses the importance of specifying the kind of behavior that will avoid punishment—whether it is a different act or simply doing nothing (p. 189). Very often punishment doesn't work because the animals or people being punished realize what they should *not* be doing but keep on doing it because they do not know what they *should* be doing. (This is only one of the problems with punishment. In the following paragraphs we'll see what some of the others are.)

Problems with punishment Even if all the conditions that maximize the effectiveness of punishment could be met, we would still have to say that punishment is less desirable than reinforcement.

First, neither people nor animals learn new acceptable responses from punishment. Reinforcement helps people and animals make new associations in order to perform some new action, but punishment doesn't teach them what *to* do—it tells them only what *not* to do. Punishment leads them to suppress a behavior that they already know and are already doing. Furthermore, the behavior tends to be suppressed only in the presence of the punisher; when the person who administers the punishment isn't around, people and animals will go back to doing the very thing the punisher is trying to prevent.

If the impulse to carry out a suppressed behavior is strong enough and if the rewards for doing it are great enough, the behavior will emerge again. The teenage girl wants so desperately to be with her boyfriend that she is willing to risk whatever punishments her parents can dream up. The dog just cannot resist the tempting smell of meat left to defrost on a reachable kitchen counter, no matter how many times it is hit for snatching food. The rewards of the behavior more than make up for the punishment that might follow.

This principle is seen throughout society. Many people regularly break the law, knowing that they will eventually be punished: they get more from committing the transgression than they suffer from punishment. The president of a company that releases poisonous chemicals into the environment, for example, may decide that it is cheaper for the company to continue to do business as usual and pay fines from time to time than it is to overhaul the operations of the plant.

Another problem with the use of punishment is that what is a punishment for one person may be a reinforcement for another. As we pointed out earlier, the spanking that Melissa gets when she acts up may be a reinforcer, since it represents more attention than she gets when she is being good. If punishment is in some sense a reward, it encourages the very behavior it seeks to extinguish.

Even when punishment is effective in eliminating behavior that parents, teachers, or other agents of society consider undesirable, it may have unwanted side effects. People who are punished for sexual behavior in childhood or adolescence may encounter difficulties in forming healthy sexual relationships in adulthood. Children who are punished for being curious and exploring may withdraw into themselves and not ask questions that could stretch their mind and abilities. The feelings of guilt, rage, or fear that come from the suppression of natural impulses in childhood often cause emotional problems later in life. Children who are punished with physical abuse often grow up to abuse their own children.

"In the long run," says Skinner (1953, p. 190), "punishment does not actually eliminate behavior from a repertoire, and its temporary achievement is obtained at tremendous cost in reducing the overall efficiency and happiness of the group."

COGNITIVE PERSPECTIVES ON LEARNING

So far we have been talking about learning as a simple formation of associations. A dog learns to associate a tone with the taste and smell of food. A child becomes afraid of objects associated with a loud noise. A pigeon learns that if it pecks, it will get fed. A teenage boy learns that if he does his schoolwork, he'll get to shoot pool. We have interpreted these events in an environmental way. That is, it doesn't matter who or what the subject is. Whether it's a person or a pigeon, behaviorists feel that by knowing the reinforcement contingencies, we can explain and predict the behaviors.

Cognitive psychologists believe that there is more to the story. While they agree that classical and operant conditioning are important ways of learning, they maintain that they are not the only ways. Futhermore, they maintain that even in associative learning, more than a simple mechanistic explanation is needed to account for the important thought processes that intervene between the stimulus and the response.

At the core of cognitive interpretations of learning is the conviction that human beings—and even lower-order animals—are not just creatures of the environment but bring to it certain capacities for understanding the nature of the world and for demonstrating their understanding when motivated to do so. Although the environment certainly affects behavior, people and animals also have an important impact on their own learning. Learning is not only the result of external forces, like conditioning. It is also internal. A process that we cannot see is taking place.

Higher-level animals are capable of extremely complex learning. They learn concepts like *same* and *different, large* and *small, up* and *down, and left* and *right.* They learn by imitating other animals, not only animals like themselves but also those that are different. They learn how to use tools. They learn to cooperate with others like themselves. Furthermore, they put this learning to work in totally new ways to solve new problems. We cannot explain much of the elaborate learning shown by primates and by human beings simply by referring to principles of classical and operant conditioning.

How, then, do cognitive psychologists explain learning? In the following discussion, we look at their concepts of thought in associative learning, of latent learning, of cognitive maps, and of observational learning. Later, in Chapter 8, we describe some of the ways animals solve problems, apparently through flashes of insight.

Thought Processes in Associative Learning

As we noted earlier, cognitive psychologists maintain that in associative learning there is a step between stimulus and response—thought, or mental activity. Thus people and animals can be aware of conditioning experiences, can anticipate future ones, can form expectations about what will happen, and can therefore adjust their behavior to produce desired results.

Expectations are a particularly important aspect of this idea. For example, your poodle Samantha, who comes running to the kitchen as soon as she hears the rustle of dry dog food being shaken from the bag or the soft thump of the feeding dish being placed on the floor, has learned more than a simple mechanical response. Like Pavlov's laboratory animals, Samantha has developed an *expectation* that these previously neutral sounds will be followed by an unconditioned stimulus, like dinner. Cognitive psychologists maintain that such learned expectations are at the root of all learning, including classical and operant conditioning.

(Ira Wyman/Sygma)

Higher animals are capable of extremely complex learning. Crystal, a capuchin monkey taught by a professional animal trainer, has changed the lives of people who cannot perform simple, basic tasks. Here, Crystal feeds a woman whose arms and legs are paralyzed. The monkey also picks up books, turns the television on and off, opens the door, and helps shop for groceries.

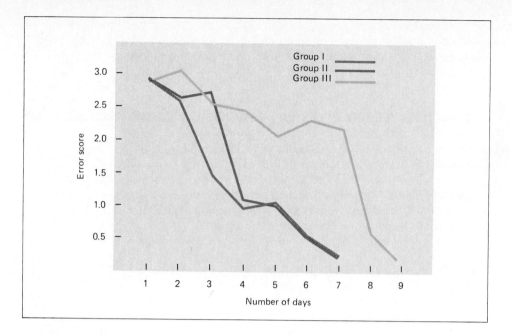

FIGURE 5-7 *Error scores for three groups of rats in Blodgett's study. (Source: Adapted from Blodgett, 1929.)*

Latent Learning

Latent learning is a type of learning that occurs but is not displayed until an organism is motivated to display it. Blodgett (1929) ran three groups of rats through a maze over a 9-day period. The rats in the first group were reinforced with food after every successful run, from the first day forward. Those in the second group found no food in the maze for the first 2 days (they were fed in their home cages during this time), but were reinforced for successful runs from the third day on. Those in the third group were treated similarly except that they did not find any food in the maze until the seventh day. Figure 5-7 shows the error scores for these three groups of rats, that is, the number of wrong turns they continued to make on each day.

It is clear from looking at the sharp drops in the error curves of the two groups of rats who received food later that they had been learning the maze even when they were not being reinforced for doing so. In the absence of reinforcement they had apparently meandered through it, not showing what they knew; but when they had a *purpose* for using their learning, they showed how much they had learned.

Edward C. Tolman conducted a number of experiments that confirmed these findings and that also confirmed his strong belief in the importance of purpose in learning, a belief which he expressed in his book *Purposive Behavior in Animals and Men* (1932). He also maintained that understanding, rather than conditioning, is the essence of learning, and that animals and people learn innumerable things throughout life for which they are reinforced by no other reward than the satisfaction of learning itself. Often, of course, they do not show this learning until they have some reason, or *purpose*, for doing so—as the rats did when they knew that they could get food by traversing the maze.

Latent learning sometimes appears in emergency situations—when, for example, a woman who has never driven a car has to get someone to the hospital and finds out that, just by being a passenger, she has learned enough to get the car where she has to go; or when a man who has seen the Heimlich maneuver demonstrated on television but has never practiced or consciously learned it puts it into action to save himself or someone else from choking on a piece of food.

Cognitive Maps

Tolman (1948), a behaviorist who took issue with the stimulus-response analysis of learning, likened that view of learning to a telephone switchboard, in which there is a very simple, straightforward connection between stimuli and responses, "incoming calls from sense-organs" and "outgoing messages to muscles" (p. 190). He agreed that stimulus leads to response, but felt that complicated, patterned brain processes were taking place between the two, and that an animal even as lowly as the rat is "surprisingly selective as to which of these stimuli it will let in at any given time" (p. 192). Tolman compared the concept of learning as a "telephone exchange" with his own concept, according to which learning takes place in something more closely resembling a map control room:

> The stimuli, which are allowed in, are not connected by just simple one-to-one switches to the outgoing responses. Rather, the incoming impulses are usually worked over and elaborated in the central control room into a tentative, cognitive-like map of the environment. And it is this tentative map, indicating routes and paths and environmental relationships, which finally determines what responses, if any, the animal will finally release. (p. 192)

Tolman developed his concept of **cognitive maps,** or mental maps of the environment, through a series of experiments in which rats learned how to negotiate a maze to get food and then found their initial routes blocked. The fact that they were still able to reach their goal quickly indicated that they had not simply learned to make responses like "turn left" and "turn right"; they had constructed a mental map of their environment. To construct this map they had undoubtedly used information gained from their senses (like the smell of the food), as well as kinetic clues about direction and distance. They processed this information in their brains and ended up knowing something they had not known before. The rats showed that they were *goal*-oriented rather than *response*-oriented; they could use any of "many paths to Rome."

Cognitive maps   *Mental maps of the environment.*

This map making ability is crucial to the way we manage our everyday lives. We see it when our favorite route to school is blocked by construction and we take for granted the need to figure out another route. We also see it when we break an arm and learn to do things with the left hand that we have always done with the right. It is the goal that counts, and cognitive creatures are not kept from reaching a goal by a limited repertoire of responses.

Observational Learning

Can you imagine learning how to knit, dance, play tennis, or drive a car without having seen someone else go through the motions? We learn specific skills like these, which we deliberately set out to learn, by watching other people carry them out. We also learn a great deal more simply by seeing and listening to other people. Learning based on observation and imitation of models is called **observational learning.**

Observational learning   *Learning based on the imitation of models.*

Parents who try to raise their children according to the principle, "Do as I say, not as I do," soon find that this won't work. Children *will* do what their parents do. If their parents hit them in anger, the children learn that this is an acceptable way to express their own anger. An experience familiar to virtually every parent of small children is the sudden awareness that the youngsters are copying in their play not only the parent's actions, but also his or her exact vocabulary and tone of voice. (Sometimes this recognition brings the parent up short. "Do I really act like that?" a mother may wonder, using her own learning to change her behavior!) As adults, many of the things we do and say and the way we relate to other people stem from the kinds of behaviors we observed our parents doing when we were younger.

The power of observational learning has been confirmed in experiments in which children who see an adult model punching, throwing, and kicking an inflated doll are more likely to act aggressively themselves when they have the chance to do the same thing than children who see a quiet model (Bandura, Ross, & Ross, 1961).

The cognitive psychologists who emphasize the role of learning by observation are adherents of **social-learning theory,** which will be analyzed in more detail in our discussions of developmental psychology (Part IV) and personality theory and psy-

Social-learning theory   *Theory, proposed by Bandura, that behaviors are learned by observing and imitating models and are maintained through reinforcement.*

(© Marc and Evelyne Bernheim/Woodfin Camp)

This boy from the Ivory Coast is learning how to weave baskets by watching an expert at work. Such observational learning is a popular and effective way to acquire a variety of skills.

Modeling *Type of learning that involves observing and imitating other persons' behaviors.*

chotherapy (Part VI). Albert Bandura, the most prominent social-learning theorist in the United States, has conducted many experiments that confirm the importance of observational learning, also called *vicarious learning* or ***modeling.*** The persons whose behavior we observe, and often imitate, are called *models.*

If all learning resulted from the rewards and punishments actually received by a given person, our capacity for learning would be severely restricted. We would have to go through every experience ourselves and would not be able to learn from the examples of others. Mistakes made through trial and error would be costly and often tragic. Society as we know it could not exist.

How Observational Learning Occurs   Bandura (1977) has identified the following four steps in the process of learning by observation:

1   Paying attention to and perceiving the relevant aspects of a behavior
2   Remembering the behavior, through either words or mental images
3   Converting the remembered observation into action
4   Being motivated to adopt the behavior

Let's see how this process might work. Suppose that you arrive in New York City from the small town where you have lived all your life. The friend you're visiting has told you to take a taxicab to her apartment. You have never taken a taxi in your life. You stand in the crowd outside the bus terminal, and you can't seem to attract a cab driver's attention. You look at the people who are successfully hailing cabs—and you note that they step into the street in front of the crowd, raise an arm in a characteristic gesture, and usually wave it around vigorously. Sometimes this works; sometimes it doesn't. You try it, with no luck. Then you see that the most successful people approach taxis that are letting passengers out and stand by the passenger door in such a way that they can step right in. You do the same, and you get your taxi. You have just learned—by observation—a valuable urban strategy.

Modeling can in certain instances be more effective than shaping in encouraging socially withdrawn children to become more sociable (R. D. O'Connor, 1972). Teachers from four different nursery schools in Illinois identified 80 children as "social isolates" who avoided playing with other children. The researchers put these youngsters in one of four categories: (1) those in the "modeling" group saw a film showing sociable children; (2) those in the "shaping" group received a total of 5 hours of praise and attention, during a 2-week period, as they showed signs of going toward other children, and also saw a film about fish; (3) those in the "modeling and shaping" group saw the film about children and also received praise and attention; (4) those in the control group saw the film about fish.

In this study, modeling was a faster agent of change than shaping, and the changes held up better: all 16 of the children who saw the film about children played more with other children afterward. Although the youngsters in the two "shaping" groups also played more with others right after the program ended, after 3 more weeks all the children in these two groups were as isolated as they had been before the program began.

Modeling has been demonstrated to be such a powerful influence on the behavior of both children and adults that it has become the basis for a popular psychotherapeutic approach in the treatment of phobias. With the help of specially planned programs, people who are afraid of dogs, snakes, the dark, or other things manage to overcome these fears, partly by seeing other people behave fearlessly. This approach will be described in detail in Chapter 15.

Self-Reinforcement The concept of *self-reinforcement* is important in the cognitive view of observational learning: people are seen to have a major impact on their own environment. They not only are dependent on the rewards and punishments that come to them from outside forces, but are also capable of rewarding and punishing themselves in a way that helps them develop new ways of behaving. Bandura (1977) uses the term *self-regulation* to encompass both reinforcing and punishing influences that people impose upon themselves.

How do people regulate their behavior? Mostly, they do this by developing standards and making efforts to live up to them. Very often they develop these standards in relation to what they have observed in other people. For example, a middle-aged woman who takes up running as a sport may assess her performance by comparing herself with other women of her own age and general level of physical fitness. If she runs faster than other 40- to 50-year-old casual athletes, she may feel highly reinforced even if she knows that she will never outdistance younger, more athletic women—or men. People who set unrealistically high standards for themselves are unlikely to obtain reinforcement for their efforts, a phenomenon we'll look at in Chapter 11, when we talk about motivation.

If we can understand how people learn, we can help them learn in more self-fulfilling, socially productive ways. Having such knowledge about learning imposes a special responsibility, of course, on social leaders and child rearers who are in a position to decide what they want others to learn.

PRACTICAL INSIGHTS INTO LEARNING

Psychological researchers are constantly exploring topics that have great relevance for people's day-to-day lives. We will talk about two issues: *biofeedback* and *learned helplessness*. Biofeedback is a way of learning to control body systems that were once thought beyond our reach. *Learned helplessness* is a mechanism through which some people have learned to feel helpless about controlling aspects of their lives that most of us take for granted.

Biofeedback

There have undoubtedly been times in your life when you have been conscious that your heart was beating faster. Generally, such an increase has to be enormous before

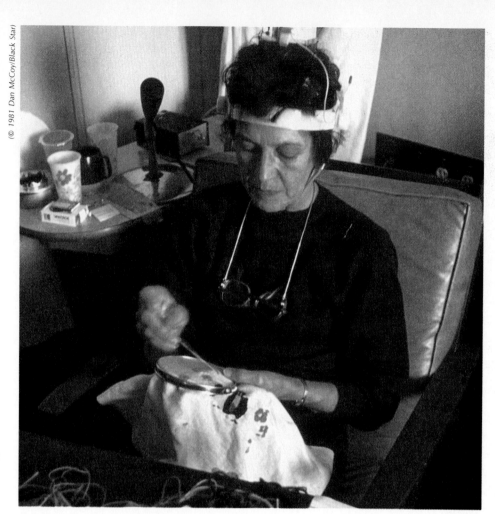

Through biofeedback, people learn to detect irregularities in their internal physiological processes and can often control such mechanisms as heart and breathing rates, blood pressure, and skin temperature. Such control enables people to treat their own tension headaches and holds promise for treating many other medical conditions.

Biofeedback *Technique that gives people information about their internal processes (like blood pressure and heart rate) so that they can learn to exert control over those processes.*

you notice it. But if you were suffering from a cardiac disorder in which it was dangerous for your heart to beat too quickly, it would be important for you to know when your heart was *starting* to speed up. Biofeedback can give you this information.

Biofeedback is a treatment technique through which people learn to monitor signals from their bodies (as in Figure 5-8), with the aim of improving their health by controlling various bodily processes. Why are we talking about this kind of psychophysiological therapy in a chapter on learning? Biofeedback is of interest here because it involves a very interesting question: Can people learn, through instrumental conditioning, to control responses of the autonomic nervous system? The answer to this depends on which expert you listen to. Advocates of biofeedback maintain that it is effective in treating a wide variety of conditions, including high blood pressure, irregular heartbeat, curvature of the spine, speech disorders, spastic muscles, epileptic seizures, motion and space sickness, migraine headaches, and pain from various causes (Lubar, 1985; N. E. Miller, 1985a, 1985b). Critics charge that there is no convincing evidence that biofeedback specifically treats *any* condition (Roberts, 1985). Let's look at this treatment.

What do people using biofeedback actually learn? They learn to detect such bodily processes as heart and breathing rates, blood pressure, skin temperature, salivation, muscle movements, and the galvanic skin response (the electric reactions of the skin to a stimulus). Usually they do this by using one or more of a variety of electronic machines specially designed for this purpose. The electromyograph measures muscle contractions, the electroencephalograph measures brain activity, and other machines monitor changes in blood flow, skin temperature, heart rate, breathing, and some kinds of gastrointestinal activity. Such machines monitor, amplify, record, and feed information to the client. "For patients, the biofeedback machine acts as a kind of sixth sense which allows them to 'see' or 'hear' activity inside their body" (USDHHS, 1983, p. 1).

What Biofeedback Does   It's not enough, of course, just to know what's happening. The ultimate aim of biofeedback is to enable you to *do* something about the condition you're getting data about. Physicians and psychologists alike used to believe that people had no control over the *autonomic* systems of the body—heart and breathing rates, blood pressure, skin temperature, salivation, and the galvanic skin response. During the 1960s, however, researchers in the United States became impressed by the reports of practitioners of various eastern disciplines who demonstrated that they could stop the heart rate, remain buried for long periods of time without suffocating, and seemingly experience no pain from such actions as piercing the skin with a sharp instrument, walking on red-hot coals, and swallowing broken glass. At about the same time, some psychologists were proposing that people and animals did not learn in two different ways—one way for autonomic responses and one for voluntary responses—but rather that one kind of learning controlled both kinds of functions (N. E. Miller, 1969).

Thus biofeedback was born. It is used primarily in clinical settings to treat some troubling condition, and is almost always used in combination with other therapeutic techniques, such as relaxation training, exercise, counseling, psychotherapy, medications, and stress management.

FIGURE 5-8   *Have you ever wanted to wiggle your ears and not been able to? Many years ago, several young men acquired this somewhat dubious skill in the course of studies on developing voluntary control over muscle movement. They gave themselves a mild electric shock through electrodes wired to their ears. The shock made their ears contract and wiggle. Then the men tried to move their ears on their own by clenching their jaws and knitting their brows. Because they remembered what a wiggling ear felt like, they could detect an extremely faint movement as a result of these strenuous efforts, which spurred them to enthusiastic practice, and eventually they perfected the ability. This principle—that to control a response, you must first be able to feel it—is the basis of biofeedback. (Source: Bair, 1901, cited in Runck, 1980.)*

Evaluating Biofeedback   The strength of biofeedback is the way that it helps people take charge of their own bodies. First, they learn how to listen to bodily signals and to recognize when something might lead to trouble. For example, a man who suffers from tension headaches can learn to sense tension in his neck before a headache comes on. Then, using special relaxation techniques, he can dispel the tension and prevent the headache. No one else is doing this for him. He is responsible for himself.

The key component of biofeedback may well be its ability to help people relax. Reducing tension often results in the alleviation of pain, and in changes in various kinds of bodily responses. Another major contribution that biofeedback makes is raising a person's consciousness about the kinds of situations that produce stress. Recognizing those situations, people often change the way they live so that they avoid or reduce the situations.

We do have to be cautious, however, in assessing the value of biofeedback. First, since biofeedback is usually used in combination with other kinds of treatment, it is difficult to determine which treatment is responsible for any apparent improvements. In many cases, success that seems to be due to biofeedback may reflect natural, possibly temporary, improvements in the condition itself, or be due to placebo effects, or be due to some other aspect of the treatment.

It seems, then, that while exploring the possibility of biofeedback as a treatment is useful, especially when other treatments have proved to be of little or no value, biofeedback cannot be looked upon uncritically as a cure-all. Time and continuing studies are still needed.

Learned Helplessness

What is Learned Helplessness?   Learned helplessness is an outcome of learning that occurs when a person or animal cannot control important events in the environment. It has motivational, cognitive, and emotional aspects. This phenomenon has important implications for the care of children, the ill, and the elderly.

During the 1960s a team of psychologists studying the relationship between fear and learning noticed that the dogs they were working with were behaving in bizarre ways. As part of one experiment, they gave moderately painful but not physically harmful electric shocks to the dogs. No matter how much the dogs struggled to get out of hammocks they had been placed in, barked, or wagged their tails, they could not escape the shocks. There was nothing the dogs could do to avoid being shocked. The next part of the experiment involved putting the dogs in a chamber divided into two parts by a barrier. By jumping over the barrier after a shock began, the dogs could turn off the shock; by jumping over it beforehand, they could avoid the shock completely.

Most dogs that are put into an apparatus like this, without ever having experienced shock before, will run about the chamber until they accidentally scale the barrier; once this happens, they then learn very quickly how to avoid the shock. This was what the experimenters expected their dogs to do once they had a chance. What happened was eerily different. At first, the dogs in this experiment ran around frantically for about 30 seconds. But then they stopped moving, lay down, and whined. After 1 minute, the shock was turned off. On all trials after that, the dogs gave up. They never did learn how to escape the shock (Seligman, 1975, p. 22).

This, then, is what Seligman termed **learned helplessness,** the conviction of animals or people that they are not in control—that nothing they can do will make any difference in changing some important feature of their lives. This demoralizing condition has been seen in dogs, cats, rats, fish, and nonhuman primates, as well as in human beings. What does learned helplessness do to people and animals? Since they believe that they can't do anything to change a situation, they don't have any motivation even to try. They are rendered incapable of learning a response that would in fact control the outcome. If the outcome is likely to be traumatic, they will be afraid and will then lapse into depression.

Fortunately, the experimenters who had caused learned helplessness in their laboratory dogs were able to figure out a way to reverse it. They *forced* the dogs to learn what would turn off the shock by leashing and dragging them from one side of the box to the other, with the barrier removed. As the dog's body scudded over the center of the chamber, the shock stopped, and eventually the dog learned to initiate the move itself. Complete and lasting recovery from helplessness has been effected in this way for both dogs and rats.

Preventing Learned Helplessness Seligman and his colleagues asked themselves the following questions, which they answered through lab experiments:

- ■ "What would happen if dogs learned how to escape shock *first,* before being presented with the unescapable shock?" They found that dogs which had 10 escape trials before being shocked did not thereafter lapse into the helpless state.

- ■ "What effects does a dog's early history have on its later tendency to become helpless?" The experimenters found that dogs raised in cages where they controlled practically nothing in their lives turned out to be much more susceptible to helplessness than other dogs.

These results confirmed earlier reports that wild rats which had been squeezed in the hands of an experimenter drowned within 30 minutes of being put in a water tank, compared with rats that had not been squeezed, which swam for 60 hours before drowning (Richter, 1957). Apparently, the squeezing took away from these rats the sense that they could save themselves.

These findings seem to hold great significance for the lives of human beings. Early experiences of mastery over the environment seem to immunize animals against the paralysis of helplessness, and early experiences of lack of control seem to predispose them to give up under adversity. Apparently, then, if we want to raise human beings who will exert the maximum effort toward improving their situation in life, we must imbue them early on with the sense that they have the power to do so.

Learned helplessness *Conviction that one's actions make no difference, which occurs when an organism learns that it cannot control important events in the environment.*

(© Elizabeth Hathon/Stock Market)

Babies whose signals bring responses learn that they have the power to affect their environment and therefore to exert a measure of control over their own lives. This helps to prevent the development of learned helplessness.

This implies that parents and others who work with small children should be sensitive to their needs and respond to cues that the children themselves give. What are some ways this can be done?

A baby's first signal showing that he or she needs something is the cry. Parents who take babies' crying seriously, and respond by feeding, changing, or just holding them, show these infants that they can make the world a more comfortable place. Parents don't have to worry about "spoiling" infants; a more serious error is ignoring the calls of these dependent little creatures for help in doing the things they cannot do for themselves.

Learned helplessness is a danger not only in childhood, but throughout life. Adults who feel powerless to escape from traumatic situations may give up and simply die. "Hex death"—death following a voodoo-type curse or pronouncement—is common in many societies around the world and is clearly related to the victim's sense of being helpless to prevent the death that has been prophesied. People who feel helpless because they have lost a loved one on whom they depended sometimes respond by dying themselves. The ill and the elderly who are institutionalized and deprived of control over the everyday details of their lives often respond by becoming weak or ill, or even dying. Learned helplessness is also discussed in Chapter 15 as it relates to depression and in Chapter 16 as it relates to stress.

People learn through every experience in life. When this learning shows them that they have little control over their lives, the result may be as devastating as death or as wasteful as the failure to try to achieve. When they learn that what they do does make a difference, they are inspired to make the most of their time here on earth. The vital importance of learning for the way we live our lives justifies the great interest and involvement that the topic of learning has received and continues to get from psychological researchers.

SUMMARY

1 Learning is a relatively permanent change in behavior that reflects knowledge, understanding, or skill, achieved through experience, which may include study, instruction, observation, or practice. Learning does not include changes brought about by factors such as maturation, fatigue, illness, or medication. Psychologists infer that learning has taken place through changes in performance.

2 There are several different types of learning. The simplest type is habituation, in which an organism eventually stops responding to a stimulus because it has grown used to the stimulus. The next level of learning is associative learning, in which an organism forms an association between two events. Two types of associative learning are classical conditioning and operant conditioning. Another type of learning is cognitive learning, in which the thought processes involved in learning are important.

3 Classical conditioning involves reflex (or involuntary) behavior. In classical conditioning, an animal or person learns to make a response to some previously neutral stimulus (that is, a stimulus which originally did not bring forth a particular response) paired repeatedly with an unconditioned stimulus. An unconditioned stimulus is one that automatically brings forth an unconditioned (unlearned) response. During conditioning, the neutral stimulus is reinforced by the pairings with the unconditioned stimulus. At the point when the neutral stimulus alone brings forth the response, the neutral stimulus becomes a conditioned stimulus and the response becomes a conditioned response. The principles of classical conditioning were demonstrated by Pavlov in his experiments with dogs.

4 Conditioning is influenced by the period of time between presentation of the conditioned stimulus and presentation of the unconditioned stimulus. Generally it is most effective to present the conditioned stimulus just before, and overlapping, the unconditioned stimulus. When the conditioned stimulus is presented repeatedly without the unconditioned stimulus, the conditioned response will be extinguished. Extinction is the gradual weakening of and failure to perform the conditioned response. When the conditioned response appears spontaneously, without additional pairings of the conditioned stimulus and the unconditioned stimulus, the organism is exhibiting spontaneous recovery.

5 Stimulus generalization is the tendency to make the conditioned response to stimuli similar to, but not identical with, the conditioned stimulus. Discrimination is learning to respond differently to two similar stimuli.

6 Principles of classical conditioning form the basis for a number of psychotherapeutic techniques and are useful in certain medical situations.

7 In operant conditioning, the organism emits a response known as an *operant*. The organism learns that by re-

sponding in a certain way, a particular outcome is likely to occur. When a response is reinforced, it is likely to be repeated. When it is punished, it is likely to be suppressed (not repeated). The basic principles of operant conditioning were developed by Thorndike and Skinner.

8   There are two kinds of reinforcers: positive and negative. Both increase the probability that a behavior will occur in the future. Positive reinforcers do this when they are added to a situation, and negative reinforcers when they are removed from a situation. Reinforcers are also classified as primary or secondary. Primary reinforcers are biologically important—that is, they satisfy needs such as those for food, water, and sex. Secondary reinforcers are learned; they become reinforcing because of their association with primary reinforcers.

9   Reinforcements are administered according to patterns or schedules. The type of reinforcement schedule chosen influences the rate of response and the rate of extinction. The two broad categories are continuous and partial (also known as intermittent) reinforcement. In continuous reinforcement, reinforcement is given after every response. In partial reinforcement, reinforcement is given after a certain number of responses have been emitted (this is a ratio schedule of reinforcement) or after a certain time period has passed (this is an interval schedule). Ratio and interval schedules may also be either fixed or variable.

10   Superstitious behavior is behavior that has been strengthened or weakened because it was accidentally reinforced or punished. In shaping, reinforcements are given for behaviors that come progressively closer to the desired behavior until the target behavior has been reached.

11   There are certain biological limits to what an organism can learn.

12   Generalization is responding similarly to similar stimuli; discrimination is responding differentially to different stimuli. As in classical conditioning, operantly conditioned responses are subject to extinction and spontaneous recovery.

13   In punishment, a behavior is followed by an unpleasant event. In one type of punishment, an aversive stimulus—one that the subject does not like—is presented; in another type, something that the subject does like is withdrawn. The purpose of punishment is to decrease the probability that a behavior will recur.

14   The effectiveness of punishment is associated with a number of factors such as its timing, its consistency, and the availability of alternative responses. Problems with punishment include the failure to provide new, acceptable responses to replace punished responses, the fact that what may be punishment for one may be reinforcement for another, and the undesirable side effects that sometimes result from punishment.

15   Recently, psychologists have been concerned with cognitive aspects of learning. These include thought in associative learning; latent learning and cognitive maps (as described by Tolman); and observational learning (as described by Bandura). In latent learning, people (or animals) do not demonstrate that learning has taken place until motivated to do so. In observational learning, people learn by observing and imitating the behavior of models. Self-reinforcement is people's self-regulation of their own behaviors by developing standards of behavior, often through observing others.

16   Through biofeedback, people learn to monitor signals from their bodies and to control various bodily functions. The therapeutic effectiveness of biofeedback is controversial.

17   Learned helplessness is an outcome of learning that occurs when a person or animal cannot control important events in the environment. This lack of control undermines the ability of animals and people to learn.

KEY TERMS

Associative learning (page 160)
Aversive stimulus (177)
Biofeedback (183)
Classical (Pavlovian) conditioning (160)
Cognitive learning (160)
Cognitive maps (181)
Conditioned response (162)
Conditioned stimulus (162)
Continuous reinforcement (170)
Discrimination (162)
Extinction (162)
Fixed-interval schedule (171)

Fixed-ratio schedule (171)
Habituation (160)
Instincts (159)
Interstimulus interval (162)
Interval schedule of reinforcement (171)
Latent learning (180)
Law of effect (168)
Law of exercise (168)
Learned helplessness (186)
Learning (159)
Maturation (159)
Modeling (182)
Negative reinforcer (169)
Neutral stimulus (162)
Observational learning (181)

Operant (168)
Operant (instrumental) conditioning (160)
Partial reinforcement (170)
Positive reinforcer (169)
Primary reinforcers (169)
Punishment (177)
Ratio schedule of reinforcement (171)
Reflexes (159)
Reinforcement (168)
Schedules of reinforcement (170)
Secondary reinforcers (169)
Shaping (174)
Social-learning theory (181)

Spontaneous recovery (162)
Stimulus generalization (162)
Superstitious behavior (172)
Trial-and-error learning (168)
Unconditioned response (unconditioned reflex) (162)
Unconditioned stimulus (162)
Variable-interval schedule (171)
Variable-ratio schedule (171)

SUGGESTED READINGS

BANDURA, A. (1977). *Social learning theory*. Englewood Cliffs, NJ: Prentice-Hall. A brief overview of social learning theory, written by the leading spokesperson for this approach.

LANGER, E. (1983). *The psychology of control*. Beverly Hills, CA: Sage. A thorough discussion of the importance of perceived control for a sense of mastery and the potentially devastating effects of lack of control.

PAVLOV, I. P. (1927). *Conditioned reflexes*. London: Oxford University Press. Pavlov's own discussion of the experiments that revealed the laws of classical conditioning.

SELIGMAN, M. E. P. (1975). *Helplessness: On depression, development, and death*. San Francisco, CA: Freeman. Drawing on experimental evidence, the author discusses the importance of a sense of control at all stages of the life span.

SKINNER, B. F. (1974). *About behaviorism*. New York: Knopf. An interesting and clearly written discussion of the way that the environment controls human behavior, as described by the most influential behaviorist in the United States.

STERN, R. M., & RAY, W. J. (1977). *Biofeedback*. Lincoln: University of Nebraska Press. The authors of this award-winning, very readable book provide information about the potential and limitations of biofeedback.

WATSON, J. B. (1924;1970). *Behaviorism*. New York: Norton. The classic statement of the principles of behaviorism by the founder of this school of psychological thought.

C H A P T E R

6

MEMORY

- ■ In the storage-and-transfer model of memory, how do the three types of memory—sensory, short-term, and long-term—function, and how do they differ from each other?

- ■ Is the storage-and-transfer model of memory compatible with the levels-of-processing model, which proposes that how well people remember depends on how deeply they process information?

- ■ Which factors influence what people remember?

- ■ Why do people forget?

- ■ What is the biological basis of memory?

- ■ What can be learned about memory by studying exceptional memory ability and memory disorders?

- ■ How can mnemonics help people to remember better?

For three long hours I was the only person in the jury room who was not convinced that the defendant (whom I'll call "Eddie Smith") was guilty. My fellow jurors could not go home because I knew how faulty eyewitness testimony can be (as you'll see in this chapter).

This case involved two men who apparently had run into each other at a local bar, had drunk the early part of the night away, and had then driven around in a liquory stupor, till they ended up at about midnight at a small gas station in a nearby town. They parked behind a building next to the closed station and, with a tire iron, broke a window through which they could glimpse some tools that looked worth stealing.

Before they could translate their boozy intentions into action, a pair of state troopers who had been driving around looking for a public telephone happened to spot one of them standing in front of the station holding the tire iron. The troopers drove into the station, overhead lights whirling and spotlights shining, and then saw the man I'll call "José Juarez" in a side alley with his arm through the window. The troopers ran after both men and caught Juarez. The local police later picked up Eddie Smith, who, they said, was the second would-be burglar.

How had they found Smith? When the local police officers were called by the state troopers, they were told to look for a young black man wearing a red sweatshirt. Eddie Smith not only fit that description but seemed to be the only black person on the streets of the mostly white suburb during those early-morning hours. When he was brought in, he was identified by the troopers, who had seen the second burglar twice—first for a fraction of a second as they drove into the gas station, and then a few minutes later (again for only a moment) in the dark alley where they caught Juarez.

My biggest problem was with this identification. Both the judge and the defense attorney had said that if we were not convinced "beyond a reasonable doubt" that Eddie Smith was guilty, it was our duty to set him free. Even the prosecutor had said that if we believed that the police picked him up and identified him simply because he was black and not because he was the offender, then we should "let him walk."

I had read too many accounts of scientific experiments showing the limitations of what people think they have seen. (As you'll read in this chapter, although eyewitness testimony is often relied upon in courts of law and often strongly believed, it is highly inaccurate in many instances. One experimenter has shown that information provided after an event can erase an accurate memory, substituting an inaccurate one.) I thought it very likely that a police officer looking for a black man in a red hooded jacket picked up the first such person he spotted and that the troopers, wanting to believe that they had their man, confirmed the identification.

Since I also had questions about some of the other testimony, I wrestled with the conflict between protecting the public from crime and sending a possibly innocent man to jail. My fellow jurors did not pressure me to change my opinion but shared their own reasoning with me, the court reconvened to let me rehear some crucial testimony, and I was finally convinced by the weight of testimony that did not rely on eyewitness identification. After our "guilty" verdict, the judge invited us into his chambers to talk about the case—and showed us the thick computer printout of Smith's previous convictions. While his past record did not, of course, prove his guilt in this case, I felt lighter. Not knowing this man's background, we had looked at the evidence and come up with a verdict that seemed just. This was one time when the system seemed to work.

—From the notebooks of Sally Olds

What cognitive and biological processes helped Christopher Walken learn his lines as Hamlet? Memory researchers have helped provide some answers. Their findings about the way memory operates have many practical implications for all of us.

Unfortunately, there have been times when faulty eyewitness identification has resulted in the imprisonment—or even execution—of the wrong person. Thus, we see the importance of recent research on eyewitness memory. These studies represent a new focus in the study of memory—directing our attention to the way memory actually operates in everyday life, rather than to the way we can make it function in a psychological laboratory. Research on memory has been going on for about 100 years, and much of it has been based in the laboratory, with a subject population made up mostly of students. Such work has provided a great deal of basic information about how memory works, even though this limited subject population is not representative of memory functioning throughout the life span. While the study of memory continues in the lab, there is a growing interest these days in the way memory operates in "real life." In this chapter, we discuss memory as a basic psychological process. In addition, we take up some of the practical implications of memory research—including what it tells us about the reliability of eyewitness testimony and how it suggests we might improve our memories.

MEMORY AS A COGNITIVE PROCESS

How Do We Remember?

Before you can begin to remember anything, you have to perceive it—to see it, hear it, or become aware of it through some other sense. Your memory works through three basic steps: first, you have to get material into your memory; second, you have to put it away; and, third, you have to find it so that you can take it out.

1 The first step in remembering requires you to encode whatever you want to remember. **Encoding** is the process of getting information into the memory system. You get information ready for storage by organizing it in some meaningful way. One way is by combining letters of the alphabet into words, combining words into sentences, and combining sentences into ideas. We also encode material by sound and meaning. Encoding is most effective when it involves making meaningful associations between new material and material already in memory. Only encoded information can be remembered.

2 Second, you put the material in **storage** so that it stays in memory.

3 The third, crucial step in this sequence is **retrieval,** or getting the remembered information out of storage. The thoroughness with which we prepare information for memory and store it determines the efficiency with which we retrieve it.

Encoding *Process of getting information ready for storage in the memory system by classifying it in some way.*

Storage *Process of keeping material in memory.*

Retrieval *Process of getting at information in memory.*

Forgetting can occur because of a problem in any of these three areas.

We regard memory as a topic in cognitive psychology because we see human beings as active processors of information. We act on information, rather than passively responding to it. The two most popular explanations of the way human memory works are the storage-and-transfer model proposed by Richard Atkinson and Richard Shiffrin (1968, 1971) and the levels-of-processing model of Fergus I. M. Craik and Robert S. Lockhart (1972).

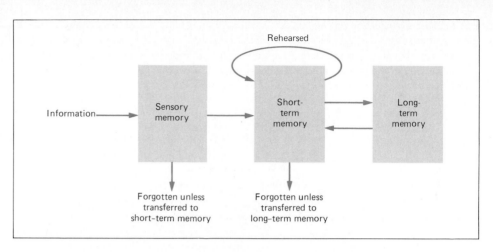

FIGURE 6-1 *Atkinson and Shiffrin's storage-and-transfer model of memory. Information comes through the senses and enters sensory memory. It may then enter short-term memory, where it remains for no more than a few seconds unless held longer by rehearsal. If it is not forgotten, it enters long-term memory, where it is organized and stored. When information is recalled, it is retrieved from long-term memory and transferred back to short-term memory. The capacity of short-term memory is limited, but the capacity of long-term memory is virtually limitless.*

Storage-and-transfer model of memory *Multistore model of memory proposed by Atkinson and Shiffrin which holds that there are three types of memory: sensory, short-term, and long-term.*

Sensory memory (SM) *Type of memory that involves material which comes through the senses. This material disappears very rapidly unless it is transferred into short-term memory.*

Short-term memory (STM) *Working memory, with a limited capacity; items remain in short-term memory for up to 20 seconds unless held there by rehearsal.*

Long-term memory (LTM) *Type of memory that seems to have unlimited capacity and may store information permanently.*

FIGURE 6-2 *Sperling's partial-report technique of assessing sensory memory. Subjects were shown a letter grid for less than 1 second. They then heard one of three tones and were instructed to report the letters from the first, second, or third row of the grid depending on whether they heard a high, medium, or low tone. For an array of letters of the size shown here, subjects typically were able to report 3 out of 4 letters in a row. (Source: Sperling, 1960.)*

A Storage-and-Transfer Model of Memory   According to Atkinson and Shiffrin's *storage-and-transfer model of memory,* all of us have three different types of memory. First, material comes through our senses—eyes, ears, nose, and so forth—into *sensory memory (SM)* (sometimes called *sensory register*). Depending on the particular sense involved, material lasts for from 1 second to a few seconds in sensory memory. Then this information either disappears or is transferred from sensory memory into *short-term memory (STM),* where it may last for approximately 20 seconds. If it does not disappear at this stage, it moves into *long-term memory (LTM),* where it may remain for the rest of our lives. Since this model proposes several storage systems, it is sometimes called the *multistore model of memory* (see Figure 6-1).

SENSORY MEMORY   With regard to sensory memory, you are a camera. You take an instantaneous "photo" of whatever you see, hear, smell, taste, or touch. For a fraction of a second, your brain absorbs the overall appearance of a room you step into, with its colors, shapes, and arrangements; or a buzz and rumble of sounds around you on a busy street; or a bouquet of fragrances in a summer garden. This information is the raw data of life. You can either act upon it by taking it into your memory or ignore and forget it. The way this kind of memory works has been demonstrated by a series of experiments performed by George Sperling.

The nature of sensory memory   Sperling's experiments demonstrated the short-lived but broad-based capacity of sensory memory. Before Sperling (1960) did his experiments, psychologists had performed many studies in which they showed people visual arrays of letters like the grid in Figure 6-2. No matter how many items were shown—from as few as eight to as many as twenty—most people could remember only four or five. The natural assumption was that this was the maximum number of items people could take in at a single glimpse.

Many people insisted, however, that they had seen more items but had forgotten the others during the time it took them to report the first four or five. Knowing this, Sperling devised his "partial report" experiment as part of his doctoral dissertation.

If you were a subject in this study, you would be shown a grid like the one in Figure 6-2 (or a similar grid with three rows of three letters each) for less than 1 second. After the grid was removed, you would hear a tone telling you to report all the letters you remembered from one of the rows. A high-pitched tone would mean the top row, a medium tone the middle row, and a low tone the bottom row.

No matter which tone you heard, you would probably report three letters in any row. Since you didn't know in advance which row you'd be asked about, you must have remembered about three letters from each row, or nine letters—about twice the earlier estimate of what people can absorb into sensory memory. The *percentage of*

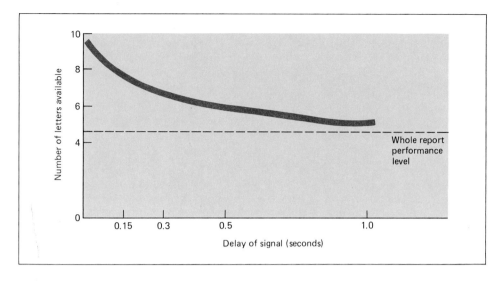

FIGURE 6-3 The fleeting nature of sensory memory. The longer the time between seeing the letter grid and being asked to report, the fewer letters subjects remember. (Source: Sperling, 1960.)

information you remembered would vary depending on whether you were shown a 3-by-3 grid (you would probably remember virtually everything) or a 3-by-4 grid (you would probably remember 75 percent). In either case, you would be reporting about nine items.

Sperling also established the fleeting nature of sensory memory. He found that if he sounded the tone after a delay of only 1 second, his subjects would remember very little (see Figure 6-3).

Kinds of sensory memory The kind of memory we have just been talking about, which involves vision, is known as **iconic memory.** (An *icon* is an image.) Apparently, iconic images fade more quickly than images in **echoic memory,** which involves hearing. (An *echo,* of course, is the repetition of a sound.) Echoic images last a bit longer, as you might have noticed if you have ever "heard" a radio continue to play *after* you turned it off. Although sensory information can enter through each of the five senses, most research has been done on the iconic and echoic systems.

Iconic memory *Visual sensory memory.*

Echoic memory *Auditory sensory memory.*

Pattern recognition in sensory memory When you receive information through the sensory register, you have to make it meaningful to get it into your short-term memory. You do this through a complex process in which you match incoming sensory information with information you already have in long-term memory. If you have a name for a stimulus, you will mentally use that name. For example, suppose you see the number 7. You will immediately recognize this pattern, as you will if you see it written as vii, VII, or *seven.* If you're used to the European style of writing numbers, you will also recognize 7. You'll recognize any of these patterns in a variety of sizes, colors, type faces, or handwriting. If, however, you have never heard of the numerical concept *seven,* you will not have anything in LTM to match the 7 you see, and so you will find it more difficult to learn and remember this new information.

The intricacy of the human mind is emphasized by our ability to recognize patterns. For example, no computer has yet been made that can "read" all the different versions of 7 as if they were the same. This kind of recognition is such a uniquely human ability that, as mechanized as our society gets, we may still need human beings to read handwriting and to make other similar distinctions.

SHORT-TERM MEMORY Sensory memory, then, is the information that comes to us through our senses. However, not all material in SM makes it into STM. The stimuli that we pay attention to in SM determine what gets into STM. We obviously do not pay attention to all the competing stimuli in SM. Rather, we selectively pay attention to some, and we forget the rest.

Short-term memory is our working memory—the active memory that contains information we are currently using. What happened the last time you had to look up a telephone number to make a call at a public booth, when you didn't have anything on which to write the number down? You probably repeated the number in your head two or three times before dialing. If a friend came up to speak to you before you reached the phone, you most likely forgot the number and had to look it up again. What does this common situation tell us about STM?

Short-term memory fades rapidly If you had not repeated the telephone number to yourself (that is, rehearsed the material), you would have forgotten the number within seconds. In a classic study by Peterson and Peterson (1959), subjects heard a *trigram* of three letters followed by a three-digit number (such as *ABC* 309). The subjects were then given a distractor task that asked them to count backward by 3s or 4s, beginning with the number just heard (309, 306, 303, etc.). This task prevented them from rehearsing the trigram. When a light flashed, the subject was asked to recall the letters *(ABC)*.

The subjects were tested eight times each, at recall intervals of from 3 to 18 seconds. After only 3 seconds, they were able to recall the trigram only 50 percent of the time, and recall got progressively worse, until by 18 seconds there was virtually none. These researchers concluded that when rehearsal cannot occur, short-term memory fades rapidly.

Rote rehearsal *Deliberate repetition of information to keep it in memory.*

Rehearsal helps to retain material in STM With **rote rehearsal** (simple repetition), you will be able to hold onto material in short-term memory for longer than 20 seconds. We saw this in the example of looking up a telephone number. Generally, however, rote rehearsal is not the best way to get information into long-term memory, the next step in the storage-and-transfer model. For that, more meaningful rehearsal, in which the material to be remembered is associated with material we already have in LTM, is best. We'll discuss this issue later in the chapter.

Short-term memory is like your attention span If you're distracted, you'll forget whatever is in short-term memory. This can be a nuisance sometimes, but it helps to preserve sanity. Suppose that you remembered every trivial transaction you were involved in all day long. Such information would interfere with your ability to go on with other activities and to take in new material. For example, if you were waiting on tables and could not put out of your mind the orders of the previous 10 customers after they had left the restaurant, you would have a hard time remembering the orders of your current customers.

The experience of a famous memory prodigy, known as S., bears this out (Luria, 1968). S. remembered *everything* and forgot nothing. As a result, he could not read, for the image from one passage would intrude upon his reading of the next one, and he would be ensnared in a thicket of overlapping images. He could not dismiss an image when it was no longer needed.

Capacity of short-term memory is small "The magical number . . . plus or minus two" usually defines the limits of STM (G. A. Miller, 1956). The magic number is 7, and as an average seven is the largest number of items we can keep in short-term memory. An item is a meaningful unit, such as a letter, digit, word, or phrase. Some people at some times, however, can remember no more than five items, and others can often remember up to nine. (Is it just a coincidence that American telephone numbers—without area codes—have exactly seven numbers?)

Chunking *Technique for expanding the capacity of short-term memory by grouping items together in the mind.*

We can expand the capacity of short-term memory One way to expand short-term memory is through **chunking,** or grouping items into meaningful units. You can remember telephone numbers more easily, for example, if you break them into three chunks—the exchange plus two groups of two-digit numbers, instead of seven numbers in a row. Chunking does not expand short-term memory indefinitely, however. Once you reach the limit of the amount of information you can store there, adding new information will cause the old information to be displaced, unless it has been stored in long-term memory.

How we find information in short-term memory   If we have stored information in STM, we can get at it very quickly. This has been demonstrated in experiments performed by Saul Sternberg (1966, 1967, 1969). If you were a subject in these studies, you would see a memory set consisting of letters or numbers, say the digits 5 8 4 2. (In the experiment, the memory set varied from one to six items—less than the seven-item capacity of STM.) Next, you would press a button that would flash a single digit, known as a *test item* or a *probe*, and you would say whether or not this had been in the memory set. If the probe was 4, you would say *yes*, but if it was 6, you would say *no*. You would be asked to answer as quickly as possible, but to avoid errors.

Through these experiments, Sternberg explored two issues—first, whether people examine items in STM one at a time (serial processing) or globally, all at once (parallel processing); and second, whether the search of material in STM is *self-terminating* (ends when we have found the test item in STM) or *exhaustive* (we scan all digits in the memory set). He concluded that retrieval from STM is serial (rather than parallel) and exhaustive (rather than self-terminating), and that retrieval is extremely rapid.

Sternberg examined the first question by varying the size of the memory set. If people examine everything in STM at one time, the size of the set should not affect response time. But if people examine items one at a time, the more items they have to look through, the longer the search will take. Sternberg found that searches for longer memory sets take longer, and concluded that people probably look for things one at a time.

For the second question, Sternberg hypothesized that if subjects used self-terminating searches, they would be able to answer *yes* faster than *no*. In other words, as soon as they found the test item in their memory, they would stop; but they would have to go through *all* the items to be able to say that an item was *not* there. Since subjects took equal amounts of time to give either a *yes* or a *no* answer, he concluded that scanning was exhaustive. Reaction time was measured in milliseconds, showing that the entire process of scanning STM, even though it is "exhaustive," is very fast.

How short-term memory and long-term memory work together   Imagine yourself as a carpenter in a workroom, with all your materials neatly organized on shelves. As you prepare to build a cabinet, you take wood, a saw, and a hammer from the shelves and put them on your workbench, saving some room to work on. Soon you realize that you need some nails and clamps, and so you lay them down on the bench, too. Before long your bench is such a jumble of tools and materials that there's no room to work. You stack some boards in a neat pile, but still things keep falling off onto the floor. So you put some of the materials and tools you're finished with back onto the shelves to leave some room to work on, and you go ahead to finish the job.

In this analogy, created by Klatzky (1980)—and expanded by us—the workbench represents short-term memory, known as *working memory*; the shelves represent long-term memory, the repository of much information we don't need at the moment but have stored. Short-term memory contains a limited amount of activated material in current use, while long-term memory contains a great deal of encoded, currently inactive material.

If we stretch this analogy and assume that the shelves have a magical ability to refill themselves when we take materials to the workbench, we can appreciate the way short-term and long-term memory overlap. Something can be in both STM and

LTM at the same time. You may have known the road over the river and through the wood to grandfather's house ever since you were a child, and so it is in your long-term memory. The next time you go there, though, you will be activating that knowledge into your short-term memory so that you can put your memory of the route to work for you.

Another way to look at the difference between these two types of memory, and at the way they are related, is to realize that, according to the model we have presented, everything we learn has to go through STM before it reaches LTM. Once it does, it is (at least theoretically) capable of being activated so that we can work with it. Whatever we want to retrieve from LTM has to go through STM before we can use it. Not all information, though, gets into LTM. Some of it falls off the workbench onto the floor, where it gets swept up and thrown out, rather than put on the shelves.

It is easy and more or less automatic to pick up materials from the workbench (and memories from STM), whereas you have to search for what you want on the shelves (or in LTM). However, once you have stored something on a shelf (in LTM), it is not as likely to fall off and disappear—even if you are distracted. What does happen is that material stored on the shelves for a long time sometimes gets warped or distorted. So do memories, as we'll see when we discuss forgetting.

The importance of transfer from STM to LTM Suppose that you never transferred anything from short-term to long-term memory. If you met someone today, you would have to learn his or her name again tomorrow, and the next day, and the day after that. If you went out, you would not be able to remember your way home from one day to the next. You would have to keep relearning the same information over and over again, because of the limited capacity of short-term memory.

"*The matters about which I'm being questioned, Your Honor, are all things I should have included in my long-term memory but which I mistakenly inserted in my short-term memory.*"

LONG-TERM MEMORY Let's get back to our analogy of the carpenter's workroom. Those shelves that represent long-term memory seem to have another magical quality: unlimited capacity. However, the way you place your tools on the shelves is crucial for later retrieval. If you throw everything on haphazardly, you may never be able to find the tool you want when you need it. If you organize the tools according to a system, they will be easier to find. Long-term memory is often described as similar to a card catalog in a library, a complicated filing system, or a book index.

Kinds of long-term memory Psychologists are now studying the different types of information in LTM, distinguishing between **procedural memory** (information about how to do various things, like riding a bicycle, solving puzzles, and playing golf) and **declarative memory** (knowledge about facts, like names, dates, faces, and golf scores). There are two types of declarative memory: episodic and semantic. **Episodic memory** (sometimes called *autobiographical memory*) is about our own experiences, and **semantic memory** is about meaning that is independent of our own experiences (Tulving, 1972).

The case of M. T. dramatically illustrates the presence of these different types of memory (D. L. Schacter, 1983). M. T., age 58, had developed, 8 years previously, a memory impairment diagnosed as Alzheimer's disease. (Alzheimer's disease is a progressive degenerative disorder of the brain that affects some 5 to 6 percent of the elderly; it is described in Chapters 2 and 10.) He had been playing golf for about 20 years—long before this disorder began. A psychologist who examined M. T. in the laboratory and found gross deficits in memory tests went out on the golf course with him, and during two rounds found certain aspects of M. T.'s performance markedly impaired while others seemed intact.

M. T. played golf well—in some ways. He knew a lot about the game and used some 30 different golf terms correctly (showing good semantic memory); and he

Procedural memory *Memory for information about how to do various activities.*

Declarative memory *Knowledge about facts.*

Episodic memory *Type of declarative memory that involves memory about our own experiences; also called autobiographical memory.*

Semantic memory *Type of declarative memory that involves meaning independent of our own experiences.*

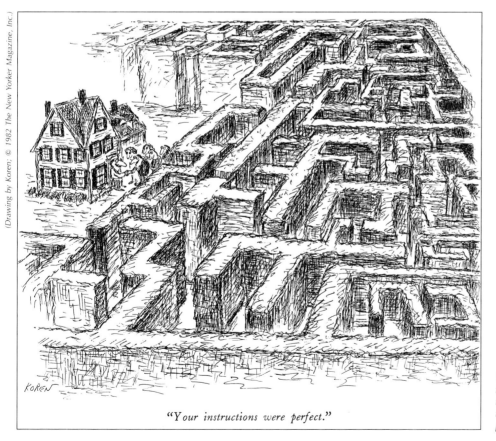

(Drawing by Koren; © 1982 The New Yorker Magazine, Inc.)

"*Your instructions were perfect.*"

The next time these visitors arrive, they'll have an easier time finding their way through the maze, since they'll have encoded the route in procedural memory.

could size up a situation, select the right golf club, and hit the ball exactly where it should go (showing good procedural memory). His game fell apart, though, because he kept forgetting where the ball was, and he kept forgetting the score (showing impaired episodic memory). A week afterwards, he denied that he had played the first of the two rounds.

We see, then, that some aspects of memory may decay while others continue to function. As we shall see when we discuss the biological basis of memory, it seems that declarative and procedural memory may be controlled by different mechanisms and different parts of the brain.

Encoding in long-term memory How would you get to your memory of your birthday in 1977? Suppose you had celebrated it with a picnic in Fairmount Park in Philadelphia. You might get to it by thinking of picnics or parks in general, of Fairmount Park, of Philadelphia, of the people you were with that day, of the foods you ate, of the mosquitoes that ate you, of birthday celebrations, of the aroma of new-mown grass, of the feel of the wind or the color of the sky on the day of the picnic, or of any of a number of other "indexes." You will have organized these memories (encoded them) in some way that makes sense to you.

The more associations you have with a piece of information, the easier it will be for you to remember it. You won't, however, store every single detail of an experience. You won't remember every word spoken during the 3 hours you were at the park, or every person seen, or every mouthful eaten. As one researcher writes, you will just remember the highlights:

> The brain condenses experiences for us. It seems to edit the boring parts in order to highlight the interesting parts and cross-reference them for storage. While there are many similarities in the ways in which different people's memories are organized, each memory is also unique. This is because memory is a result of a collection of life experiences, and everybody's life experiences are different. (Loftus, 1980, pp. 27–28)

Encoding by association: We can think of rehearsal as a continuum. We can memorize information by rote rehearsal (simple repetition) to get it into long-term memory. In general, though, the more elaborate the rehearsal (that is, the more associations you can make between the new material and information you already know), the more effective the encoding and storage of the material. This type of rehearsal, known as **associational rehearsal,** in which connections are made between new and old material, helps us remember information better in the long run.

We can see the differences between these two types of rehearsal in an example involving stalagmites and stalactites—mineral deposits that form in caverns (Figure 6-4). While we could memorize by rote the fact that stalagmites form from the bottom of the cave and stalactites from the top, we have a better chance of

Associational rehearsal *Process of encoding information in memory by making connections between new material and material already there.*

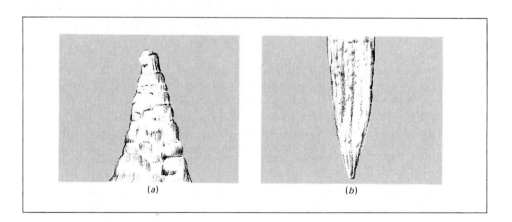
(a)   (b)

FIGURE 6-4 *(a) Stalagmite. (b) Stalactite.*

(Bill Gallery/Stock, Boston)

If this shopper clustered items in her memory before she went to the store (by categories like fruit, cleaning items, and beverages), she'd be more likely to remember to buy oranges after she had picked a perfect bunch of bananas.

remembering which is which if we associate the words with their meaning. The g in *stalagmite* is the initial letter of the word *ground,* reminding you that stalagmites form from the ground of a cave. The c in *stalactite* begins the word *ceiling;* it is easy, then, to remember that stalactites form from the ceiling, or top, of a cave. As we point out later, in the box "How Can You Improve Your Memory?" (page 222), associational rehearsal can help you remember many kinds of information.

Encoding by organization: Associational rehearsal is one kind of organization. Think back to the shelves in the workroom. The better you can organize material to stack on those shelves, the easier it will be to find it. When material is presented in an organized way—by categories of related items, for instance—it is easier to remember than when it is presented at random (Bousfield, 1953). When material is presented randomly, most people tend to organize it themselves by a technique known as **clustering,** that is, grouping items into categories, rearranging in the mind the order in which the items were presented. We impose our own subjective organization on unrelated items. This common way to convert material from short-term to long-term memory was used by the subjects in the following experiment.

Endel Tulving (1962) presented 16 unrelated words in 16 different sequences to 16 college women for 16 different trials. The words are listed in Figure 6-5. When the students were asked to give the words in any order that came to mind, they tended to remember the words in the same order on different trials, no matter how they had been presented. This suggests that the women had organized the words in their own minds. They organized the words in many different ways—meaning, sound, familiarity, and so forth. There were a number of common patterns, indicating either that the subjects discovered sources of organization in the material itself rather than imposing it arbitrarily or that the women's similar life experiences may have led them to similar styles of clustering.

The "tip of the tongue": You run into someone whose name you're sure you know, but no matter how hard you try, you can't come up with it. Is it Nadine, or Natalie, or Nadia? You know none of those are right—but you have the feeling you're on the right track. You try to remember where you met her. You keep probing

Clustering Technique for organizing material to be remembered into categories.

ACCENT	LAGOON
BARRACK	MAXIM
DRUMLIN	OFFICE
FINDING	POMADE
GARDEN	QUILLET
HOYDEN	TREASON
ISSUE	VALLEY
JUNGLE	WALKER

FIGURE 6-5 *Sixteen unrelated words used in Tulving's study of memory.*

until you visualize a party in a loft, and you see a woman wearing a red dress. Suddenly you remember. Her name is Natasha!

Sequences like this go on in our heads all the time; they are called **tip-of-the-tongue (TOT)** states. There are situations in which a person cannot recall a word, image, or other memory immediately but does have some knowledge of it. Sometimes we find such a memory quickly; sometimes we find it after several hours; and sometimes we never find it at all. After 56 college students heard definitions of 49 fairly uncommon words (such as *apse, nepotism, cloaca, ambergris,* and *sampan*) and were asked to supply the word, they came up with a total of 360 TOT states. One definition they were given was, "A navigational instrument used in measuring angular distances, especially the altitude of sun, moon, and stars at sea." Before you read the next paragraph, write down a word or words to fit this definition.

If you don't know the word, you're likely to search your memory and come up with words like *astrolabe, compass, dividers,* and *protractor,* all of which are similar in *meaning* to the target word. Or you might go off in a different direction, coming up with words like *secant, sextet,* and *sexton,* all of which resemble the *sound* of the word you're looking for. Most people encode material into memory according to two basic signals—how a word sounds and what it means (Brown & McNeill, 1966).

In all cases of positive TOTs (in which the target word was eventually recalled or recognized), 48 percent of subjects came up with a word that had the same number of syllables as the target word, 57 percent guessed the initial letter, and many came up with the correct prefix or suffix.

While 95 words similar in meaning were called forth, 224 words similar in sound were given. The researchers called this second kind of recall *generic* recall, or recall of the general type of the word, if not the actual word itself. Such generic recall can be *partial,* when only a letter or two, or a prefix or suffix, is remembered; or it can be *abstract,* such as "a two-syllable word with the stress on the first syllable."

These experiments show that we encode items in LTM in ways other than meaning alone, and that we retrieve a word or name by the way it looks or sounds, in addition to or instead of whatever it means. (By the way, did you ever come up with *sextant?*)

Dual-coding hypothesis: Other research has shown that we store, organize, and retrieve material in memory through two basic systems—one using words and one using images—and that these two systems seem to involve different kinds of processing. According to this *dual-coding hypothesis* (Paivio, 1975), we use imagery for information about concrete objects and events, and we use words for ideas and language. The two systems are independent but interconnected: either one can be approached individually, but they transfer information back and forth to each other. Some material seems to be stored in each of these systems, although controversy exists about the amount and type stored in each.

A Levels-of-Processing Model of Memory   There is another way of looking at how memory works. Some researchers (Craik & Lockhart, 1972; Craik & Tulving, 1975) disagree with the concept of memory as a division into three separate structures. Instead, they identify only one kind of memory and propose a **levels-of-processing model of memory**. This model is based on the idea that the ability to remember is dependent on how deeply we process information. We process material along a continuum of ever-increasing depth, running it through on levels that range from quite shallow to very deep. The deeper we process material, the longer it lasts.

How does this concept work? The shallowest level of processing, according to this model, involves your awareness of a sensory feature—what a word or number looks like or sounds like, what a food smells or tastes like, and so forth. As you recognize some kind of pattern in your sensory impression, you will process it more deeply. And when you make an association, that is, give a meaning to your impression, you will be at the deepest level of processing, the level at which you form the strongest and most enduring memory trace.

TABLE 6-1 TYPICAL QUESTIONS AND ANSWERS IN A LEVELS-OF-PROCESSING EXPERIMENT

Level of Processing	Depth of Processing	Question	Answer Yes	Answer No
Structural	Shallow	Is the word in capital letters?	TABLE	table
Phonemic (sound)	Intermediate	Does the word rhyme with *weight?*	Crate	Market
Category	Deep	Is the word a type of fish?	Shark	Heaven
Sentence	Deep	Would the word fit this sentence: "He met a ——— in the street"?	Friend	Cloud

Source: Based on Craik & Tulving, 1975.

If you had been a subject in a study that Craik and Tulving (1975) ran to test this thesis, you would have been asked to look at a number of different words. You would have been asked whether each word was in capital letters, whether it rhymed with a specific sound, whether it would fit into a given category, or whether it would fit into a particular sentence with a blank spot. To get a picture of the levels of processing for these words, see Table 6-1.

After these questions, you would have received a surprise quiz on the words, in which you would have been asked to recall or recognize them. Recall and recognition are two different measures of memory. **Recall** is a measure of retention in which the subject has to reproduce from memory material that has been learned previously. **Recognition** is a measure in which the subject is confronted with material that has been previously learned and is asked to identify it (see the box "Testing Memory: Recognition, Recall, and Relearning").

In these experiments, Craik and Tulving found that deeper levels of processing generally took longer to accomplish than the shallower levels and produced stronger memories of the words. Follow-up tests suggested that it was not the time itself but the depth of processing which was important. When a complex but shallow task was assigned (such as classifying vowel-and-consonant patterns according to a complicated formula), it took longer to carry out than an easy but deeper task (for example, deciding whether a word would fit into a sentence).

The levels-of-processing explanation has some gaps in it. For one thing, the type of test used to measure memory may well influence the conclusions drawn. In other experiments, questions like "Was there something in the words you saw that rhymed with *pain?*" gave better results than the sentence task (Morris, Bransford, & Franks, 1977). Apparently, then, there are cases where a shallower level of processing (the phonemic level in this case, as described in Table 6-1) gives better retention than a deeper level. In addition, another contradictory finding has appeared. When subjects are presented with the same item and the same encoding question more than once ("Does the word *train* have an *n* sound?"), they remember the item better (T. D. Nelson, 1977). The second presentation does not call for any deeper processing—it requires only more of the same—and so the explanation for better recall after two trials has to be sought outside the levels-of-processing model.

Furthermore, we don't yet have an objective way to measure depth of processing. We can't go by the time required, as we have seen. All we're left with is the intuitive assumption that processing by meaning is "deeper" than processing by physical characteristics. It may well be, but where is the proof?

What we can do is use the best parts of both explanations—the storage-and-transfer model and the levels-of-processing model. It is useful to think about memory in terms of short-term and long-term memory. At the same time, we recognize that they are related, not divided into two separate structures. Furthermore, we note that both models have some elements in common, like the emphasis in each one on the importance of meaningful associations.

Recall Measure of retention in which the subject has to reproduce from memory previously learned material.

Recognition Measure in which the subject is confronted with material that has been previously learned, and is asked to identify it.

Of the three basic ways used to test and study learning and memory, recognition and recall are most often used today. The most sensitive measure, relearning, is not commonly used today because it is so time-consuming, but it is historically important.

RECOGNITION

In tests of recognition you're given an array of possible answers, from which you're asked to choose the right one. These answers are cues that help you search your memory. Multiple-choice and true-false tests are tests of recognition. Recognition is usually easier than recall, since you're given the answer (even if it is one among several), and you have to perform only *one* memory task—deciding whether what you see (or hear, etc.) is a copy of the information you have in your memory.

RECALL

In tests of recall you may be given clues, but you have to pull the information out of memory yourself. Essay tests are tests of recall. The reason why recall is usually harder than recognition is that you have to go through *two* steps—generating possible answers from your memory and then identifying them.

There are two kinds of recall tests. In *free recall* you can reproduce the material in any order. In *serial recall* you have to reproduce the material in a particular sequence, usually the order in which it was originally presented. You might be shown

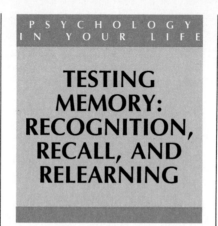

TESTING MEMORY: RECOGNITION, RECALL, AND RELEARNING

12 nonsense syllables and be asked to recall them by either free or serial recall. Or you might learn pairs of nonsense syllables and then be shown the first member of each pair and asked to recall the second.

RELEARNING

Relearning is a technique that tries to measure the amount of time you save in learning material if you had already learned it at some earlier time. It is easier, for example, to prepare for a comprehensive final exam in a subject if you have already learned the material earlier in the semester than if you are learning it for the first time during your "cram" session.

As a research method, testing for relearning takes a great deal of time because it involves teaching information, allowing enough time to go by for the information to be forgotten, and then presenting the same information again. The saving is calculated in one of two ways. One way is

judging the ease with which a person learns brand-new material compared with how that person relearns material he or she had learned earlier. The other is comparing two groups of subjects, one of which has been exposed to material earlier while the other has not.

In the first systematic study of memory, in 1885, Hermann Ebbinghaus demonstrated this concept. Ebbinghaus decided to use the most convenient, economical research subject around—himself. (This, of course, raises a problem—the possibility of experimenter bias.) Ebbinghaus invented the concept of the nonsense syllable—a set of three letters, arranged in consonant-vowel-consonant order—as the basis for his experiments. Why were nonsense syllables (such as SUJ, FUB, and HIW) used? Ebbinghaus felt that people would make various associations to meaningful items and would differ in their ability to learn and remember them. (Another problem with this work is that nonsense syllables are not all equally meaningless, and thus some are easier to learn than others.)

Ebbinghaus learned lists of nonsense syllables and determined how long it took him to learn them perfectly. He let enough time go by for him to forget the syllables and then relearned them, calculating the time it took him to recite them perfectly once again. The difference between how long it took him to learn the nonsense syllables the first time and how long it took him to relearn them gave him a measure of savings.

What Do We Remember?

We've already learned that we tend to remember meaningful, well-organized information. Material that is remembered well also has some other characteristics. Here are a few of them.

We Tend to Remember What Is Presented First and Last: Serial-Position Curve
If you have ever gone through a receiving line at a wedding or some other social affair, you may remember being introduced to eight or ten or so new people, one right after the other. By the time you had shaken the last hand, it's probable that you remembered the names of the two people you met first and the two you met last—and forgot the names of those in the middle.

Remembering the names of the first and the last people you meet in a receiving line—and forgetting those of the people in the middle— illustrates the primacy and recency effects. If you want to be remembered, try to stand at the beginning or end of a line.

This kind of experience incorporates the ***primacy effect*** (the tendency to remember items presented early in a list) and the ***recency effect*** (the tendency to remember items presented most recently, that is, last in a list). You can get a graphic picture of this phenomenon by looking at the ***serial-position curve*** shown in Figure 6-6. The curve shows that in a free-recall situation we tend to remember items presented first and last in a series and to forget those in the middle. One possible explanation for this is that the names presented first were the ones which entered your long-term memory, while the others made it only into your short-term memory. Because material in short-term memory is displaced by new information, the only names you could remember at the end of the line were those that had not yet been replaced, the last ones (Glanzer & Cunitz, 1966).

Primacy effect Tendency to remember the items presented first in a series.

Recency effect Tendency to remember the items presented last in a series.

Serial-position curve Curve of remembering which demonstrates that in free recall there is a tendency to remember items learned first and last in a series and to forget those in the middle.

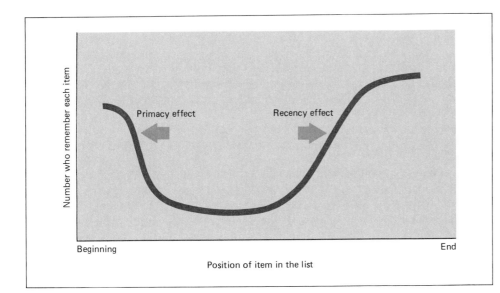

FIGURE 6-6 *Serial-position curve. This curve indicates that subjects are most likely to remember items at the end of a list (recency effect) and at the beginning (primacy effect) and are least likely to remember items in the middle. (Source: Loftus, 1980.)*

The serial-position curve is taken as evidence for the distinction between short-term and long-term memory. That is, we remember the final items (recency effect) because they are still in STM, and we remember the initial items (primacy effect) because they have entered LTM.

We Tend to Remember the Unusual: Von Restorff Effect If someone in the middle of the line had had a name that was famous or distinctive, you probably would have remembered it—provided it was not so difficult for you to pronounce or spell that you were unable to get it into your memory in the first place. This tendency to remember an unusual item, regardless of its position in a list, is named after von Restorff, the psychologist who first presented it.

We Tend to Remember Links to Emotionally Significant Events: Flashbulb Memories
Late in the nineteenth century, a researcher asked 179 middle-aged and old people whether they remembered where they had been when they heard that Abraham Lincoln had been shot (Colegrove, 1899/1982). Thirty-three years after the assassination, 127 of those questioned were able to give a full description, including the time of day, the exact location, and the identity of the person who had brought the news.

Flashbulb memory Vivid recollections of what one was doing when one heard about a significant event.

This kind of autobiographical memory has been called a **flashbulb memory,** a vivid recollection of what one was doing when one heard about a significant event (Brown & Kulik, 1977). It is "simply *there,* ready to appear in stunning detail at the merest hint. It's as if our nervous system took a multimedia snapshot of the sounds, sights, smells, weather, emotional climate, even the body postures we experience at certain moments" (Benderly, 1981, p. 71).

The snapshot is not complete, however. It usually includes certain basic elements, such as where you were, what you were doing before the shock, who gave you the news, what you did next, and how you and others felt about the event. But it generally captures some trivial details and leaves out others. You may remember who telephoned to tell you about the explosion of the shuttle *Challenger,* and at what time of day; but you may not remember what papers were on your desk or what you were wearing. You may remember a smell of formaldehyde mingling with the scent of cut flowers, as you sat in a hospital room listening to a red-bearded doctor tell you than an illness was even more serious than you had feared; but you may not remember the color of the walls.

(NASA photo)

The events that capture such memories can be moments out of history or out of your personal life. A flashbulb memory occurs at a moment of surprise, of shock, and of great personal, biological significance, according to Brown and Kulik. In 1977, they asked 80 people aged 20 to 60 to recall the circumstances in which they had first heard the news of nine public events (including seven killings or assassination attempts), as well as a personal, unexpected shock, such as the death of a friend or relative, a serious accident, or the diagnosis of a deadly disease. These subjects had flashbulb memories of a number of events—all but 1 had them for the murder of John F. Kennedy, and 73 out of the 80 had them for a personal shock. Some racial differences showed up: for example, 75 percent of the black subjects reported a flashbulb memory for the murder of Martin Luther King, Jr., but only 33 percent of whites did.

Most flashbulb memories, however, are of events that are significant personally rather than nationally (Brown & Kulik, 1977; D. C. Rubin, 1986). When a group of college students were asked to report the three most vivid autobiographical memories of their lives, almost all were of personally important events, for example, events involving injuries or accidents, sports, members of the other sex, and animals (Rubin & Kozin, 1984).

Brown and Kulik believe that the printing of such records in our memories held survival value in the days before communications media existed. It would have been important to remember significant events. Suppose that you saw a dangerous animal attack someone in front of you? Your life could be saved by remembering exactly

Millions of Americans will always remember what they were doing on January 28, 1986, when they heard the horrifying news that the space shuttle Challenger had exploded and that all seven crew members had been killed. Such a remembered moment is known as a "flashbulb memory."

what time of day it was, where you were, and what you were doing at the time of the attack, so that you could avoid such an encounter in the future.

We Reconstruct Memory by Filling in the Gaps   We can see how our retrieval mechanism works when we search our minds for a memory, using certain clues to lead us to our goal. Suppose that someone asks you what you were doing at 12 noon exactly 1 year ago today. First you'll establish the date; then you'll probably place yourself geographically; then you may think of your usual weekly schedule; then you'll narrow your possibilities until you come up with what you want. In the following example you can see that recalling this kind of memory is like solving a logical problem:

> January 7, 1977. Let's see, that was during Christmas break so I suppose I was at home. No, wait a minute, that year Christmas break ended January 6, that was before we switched schedules. So let's see, I must have been back at school. In fact that was review week so I assume I was in class. Let's see, we came back on a Monday, so the 7th would have been a Tuesday. What classes was I taking that term—Renaissance poetry, physics—wait, I must have been in statistics because it met over the noon hour on Tuesdays and Thursdays. Now I remember the review session. Dr. Shaw was having trouble with all the nervous students demanding to know if they were responsible for this or that particular piece of information. (Glass, Holyoak, & Santa, 1979, p. 119)

This process does help us come up with many elusive memories. However, it also leads us to "false" memories. Several lines of research—with childhood memories, with the reconstruction of stories read or heard, with parents' memories of their children's development, with eyewitness testimony—all lead to the same conclusion. In their zeal to be logical and to fill in the gaps, people often *invent* material and then are sure that they are *remembering* it. An example of this is presented in Figure 6-7.

FIGURE 6-7 *In a classic study of memory, subjects were briefly shown this picture and asked to describe it to someone who had not seen it, who was in turn asked to describe it to someone else, and so forth. In successive retellings, the razor, which in the picture is held by the white man, eventually came to be described as being held by the black man. This illustrates how people often reconstruct memory to fit in with their emotions and beliefs. (Source: Allport & Postman, 1958.)*

Here is another example: The parents of 47 three-year-olds were asked about various aspects of their children's development and their own child-rearing practices over the previous 3 years (Robbins, 1963). Researchers had a way to evaluate their answers, since all the parents had been participating in a longitudinal study since their children's birth.

The parents turned out to be poor reporters. They made mistakes about such "marker events" as the age when a child was weaned from breast or bottle, the age of bowel and bladder training, and the end of the 2 A.M. feeding. The mothers' memories tended to be distorted in the direction of currently popular professional recommendations. For example, they were more likely to report that they had fed on demand when they had not. The fathers' errors varied more randomly, possibly showing unawareness of current trends in child rearing (the study covered a period of time when fathers were less involved in their children's day-to-day care than many men are today).

Apparently, in the absence of memory for the events in question, these mothers filled in the gaps and created "memories" for dates and experiences they had forgotten. This report is especially significant when we realize how many research projects have been based on retrospective reports, that is, reports relying on subjects' memories. As this study shows, we cannot count on the accuracy of human memory. It seems that we fill in the gaps with material that reflects our own biases, knowledge, and expectations, and that we do this in a largely unconscious way (Loftus, 1980).

Filling in the gaps can have life-or-death implications when it takes place in eyewitness testimony—the kind of testimony that is believed most strongly by jurors and a kind that has been shown, both experimentally and in real life, to be distressingly prone to error. See the box "Legal Implications of Memory Research" (pages 210–211).

Why Do We Forget?

How much do you remember of what you learned over the past academic year? How many of your high school classmates could you name right now? How many times a week do you forget appointments, chores, and other details of everyday life? Before you groan in self-disgust, take heart: you are entirely normal. We all forget all kinds of things all the time. Psychologists have even shown that people forget in an orderly fashion and according to a number of well-established principles.

The pioneer memory researcher Hermann Ebbinghaus (1885/1913) gave us a picture of the *curve of forgetting* (see Figure 6-8), which shows that forgetting is very

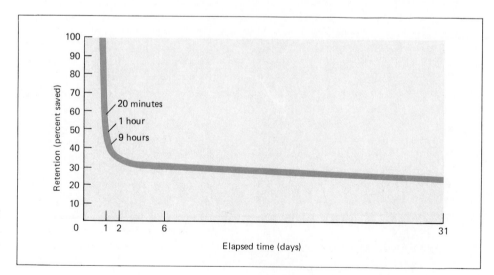

FIGURE 6-8 *Ebbinghaus's forgetting curve. Forgetting is initially very rapid and then slows down markedly. (Source: Ebbinghaus, 1885/1913.)*

rapid at first and then slows down markedly. After Ebbinghaus had learned a list of nonsense syllables, he forgot them in an orderly way—and quite rapidly. Just 20 minutes after having learned 13 syllables well enough to recite them twice in order without a mistake, he forgot about 40 percent of what he had learned, and by the end of the first hour he remembered only about 33⅓ percent. Over the next few days additional forgetting took place at a much slower pace, so that 6 days later he remembered 25 percent, and 1 month later, he still remembered about 20 percent. Ebbinghaus felt that the slowness of this forgetting strongly suggested that it would have taken a very long time to forget the series entirely (Sahakian, 1976).

When Ebbinghaus rehearsed the list 30 additional times immediately after learning it, he remembered the syllables much better, showing that extra time spent overlearning, or studying, material that you want to remember can often pay off. Eventually, however, the effects of overlearning decrease; and so overlearning needs to be done within reason.

Apparently, we forget for a number of different reasons. Each of the following theories probably gives us at least a partial answer to the question: Why do we forget? The complete answer, however, is still unknown.

How well eyewitnesses remember an event like an accident depends partly on how accurate their initial perception was. If they weren't paying close attention, or if it was dark outside, the scene will not have made enough of an impression on their memory for them to recall the details.

Motivated Forgetting: Repression Sometimes we forget material in long-term memory because *not* remembering seems to provide some personal benefit. Thus, you forget the name of someone you don't like or the dentist's appointment you don't want to keep. You repress (block from consciousness) memories that are sad, embarrassing, or painful. (Freud felt that repression is a defense mechanism to combat anxiety.) Or you glorify your past, bringing your memories into line with an ideal picture you would like to have of yourself—as in the case of the mothers in the study referred to earlier, who "remembered" themselves as having followed currently recommended practices (Robbins, 1963).

Repression is an unconscious process. It is triggered by our need to protect ourselves against the anxiety that we would feel if particular memories were retrieved. For example, Freud says that we do not remember the feelings of sexual attraction we once had for our parent of the other sex, because memories of those early sexual feelings would produce anxiety. We unconsciously repress those anxiety-producing experiences.

Decay of the Memory Trace The basic question about most other forgetting—unmotivated forgetting—is whether we forget simply because a memory deteriorates, or because even though a memory is there, possibly for as long as we live, we can't get at it to retrieve it. Some influential theorists, such as Shiffrin and Atkinson (1969) and Tulving (1974/1977), maintain that we lose material from short-term memory because of decay of an **engram,** a memory trace "engraved" upon the nervous system after learning has taken place. However, anything stored in long-term memory stays there forever and any forgetting of that material is due to difficulty in retrieval. Other researchers (Loftus, 1979, 1980) take strong issue with this point of view, claiming that there is little basis for the widespread belief in the permanence of long-term memories. Theorists who maintain that there is a memory trace and that it is subject to decay believe that it will persist when used but will eventually disappear if it is not used. We'll examine these possibilities below and then again later in this chapter, when we discuss the physiological basis for memory.

Engram Memory trace.

POOR PERCEPTION Sometimes your perception may have been too weak for something to make much of an impression in the first place. This may come about because of external conditions: noise, darkness, or some other circumstance that interferes with observation. If, for example, you saw a man in a moving car at least 60 feet away from you, who was visible only for the time it took the car to travel 50 or 60 feet, it would be hard to remember what the man looked like, because you never

EYEWITNESS TESTIMONY

Although testimony from witnesses who have seen a person or event is strongly believed in and often relied upon in courts of law, it is often highly inaccurate. Untold numbers of innocent people have been convicted of crimes they did not commit, usually because of mistaken identification (Houts, 1981; Loftus, 1983). In Elizabeth Loftus's many experiments in this area, she has shown that information provided after an event can erase an accurate memory, and people are prepared to swear that the second (inaccurate) impression is the true memory.

In one experiment (Loftus, Miller, & Burns, 1978), subjects saw a series of 30 color slides showing successive stages in an accident involving an automobile and a pedestrian. Half the subjects saw the car going toward an intersection with a STOP sign; the others saw a YIELD sign. The subjects were then asked, "Did another car pass the red Datsun while it was stopped at the STOP sign?" or, "Did another car pass the red Datsun while it was stopped at the YIELD sign?" Some subjects were asked a question consistent with what they had seen, and others were asked a misleading question.

Over 80 percent of subjects who heard the misleading question answered as if they had seen the slide

LEGAL IMPLICATIONS OF MEMORY RESEARCH

that corresponded to the question rather than the one they had actually seen. However, when no misleading question was asked, over 90 percent of subjects correctly identified the sign they had seen. Apparently, what people learn after an event can replace information they learned during it. When this happens, "in the process, the original information is forever banished from the subject's memory" (Loftus & Loftus, 1980, p. 416).

In another study, 150 subjects were shown a film of a traffic accident and asked questions about it. Those who were asked, "About how fast were the cars going when they smashed into one another?" gave higher estimates of speed than subjects who were asked how fast the cars were going when they "hit" one another. Furthermore, the subjects who heard the verb *smashed* were

more likely to say they had seen broken glass than were the ones who had heard the word *hit*. In fact, there was no broken glass in the accident. Obviously, hearing the word *smashed* gave these "witnesses" new information. Associating the word with higher speeds and more severe accidents, they filled in the gaps and drew their own conclusions (Loftus & Palmer, 1974/1982).

This study suggests that our memories respond to two kinds of information—data received during an event and data received afterward—and that the material which comes later may act like additional paint on a wet watercolor picture, seeping into the earlier impression and changing it forever.

These and other similar findings have enormous practical implications in a society in which a person can be imprisoned for life or even executed on the basis of testimony from witnesses who are convinced that they are telling the truth. What people *think* is the truth is often a hodge-podge of remembered events, statements by other people, and logical "filling in the gaps."

HYPNOSIS

A woman who witnessed her boyfriend's murder could not remember the incident because of two factors—the shock and the state of intoxica-

got a good look at him. Yet it was just this kind of eyewitness identification that helped to convict Nicola Sacco, a shoemaker, an anarchist, and the codefendant in the famous Sacco and Vanzetti trial, of murder and send him to his death in 1927 (Loftus, 1979).

Poor perception may also be due to some quality of the observer. You might be distracted; you might be under stress; or you might not be paying attention, because you don't think a particular item is terribly significant. This becomes a problem when bystanders who were not paying close attention are suddenly called upon to testify about a crime, an accident, or some other event that caught them by surprise. In ordinary life, it is possible that most people cannot remember names and faces because they have never learned them in the first place—they don't listen closely enough when they are first introduced to people. As is shown in the box "We Don't Learn What We Don't Need to Remember" (pages 212–213), we often forget infortion she had been in. Under hypnosis she gave previously unreported information that helped police find the killer (Stump, 1975). Hypnosis has successfully unblocked suppressed memories in a number of similar cases. But in other cases, it has apparently unleashed "memories" of events that never took place. An article in the *American Bar Association Journal* reported:

> People can flat-out lie under hypnosis, and the examiner is no better equipped to detect the hypnotic lie than any other kind. Even more serious, a willing hypnotic subject is more pliable than he normally would be, more anxious to please his questioner. Knowing even a few details of an event, often supplied in early contacts with police, may provide the subject with enough basis to create a highly detailed "memory" of what transpired, whether he was there or not. ("Hypnotized Man," 1978, p. 187)

Recent experiments testing the role of hypnosis in aiding memory have failed to demonstrate any value in the procedure (Dywan & Bowers, 1983; M. C. Smith, 1983). As we reported in Chapter 4, the American Medical Association recommends that hypnosis should be used *only* to jog witnesses' memories to produce leads for follow-up; it should not be used in testimony (AMA, 1985).

One technique that may account for some of the successes of hypnosis can be used successfully without inducing the hypnotic state and the high level of suggestibility that goes with it and is the source of many errors (M. C. Smith, 1983). This involves giving witnesses information about the context in which an event occurred—the sounds, sights, and smells. This technique is currently being used in a television program, *Crimestoppers,* which re-enacts unsolved local crimes in the hope that the dramatization might trigger recall in witnesses to the real crimes.

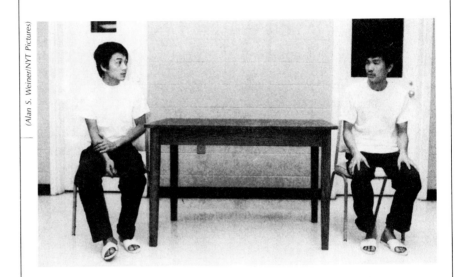

Because of a mistake, the wrong defendant was put on trial for murder in Georgia in 1985 and identified by witnesses. Both the man on the left—who had been charged with theft—and the actual murder defendant (right) were Vietnamese, and their height and weight were about the same. None of the white participants in the trial, including the lawyer of the man charged with theft, noticed the error. Had it not been caught, an innocent man might have been convicted.

(Alan S. Weiner/NYT Pictures)

mation that we are constantly exposed to. (Often we are right; this may be a way of keeping our minds uncluttered with unnecessary data.)

INABILITY TO REHEARSE   Sometimes a memory decays because we don't have the opportunity to rehearse what we want to remember. If you look up a phone number and are prevented from going over it in your head, you may not be able to remember it long enough to make your call and will almost certainly lose it right afterward. But this applies only to short-term memory. Once something has been stored in long-term memory, you don't have to keep rehearsing it.

Interference   A different theory of forgetting is that the reason we forget is not decay but interference. Other information, learned earlier or later, *interferes* with our memory. Let's consider the two kinds of interference.

Before you go on reading this, take out pencil and paper and draw a picture of an American penny—both sides—putting in as many details about pictures, numbers, and letters as you can think of. After you've done your best, look at the drawings in Figure 6-9. Which of these seems most accurate to you? Now take a penny out of your pocket and see how well you did in *recalling* what is on a penny, as shown by your own drawing, and in *recognizing* an accurate depiction of a penny. (This little exercise is fun to do with friends.)

If you're like most people, your performance was abysmal. When 20 adults (all citizens of the United States) were asked to draw both sides of a penny from memory, only one (an avid penny collector) put in all eight features listed in Figure 6-10. Only four people got as many as half

WE DON'T LEARN WHAT WE DON'T NEED TO REMEMBER

the features (Nickerson & Adams, 1979). Some examples of drawings are shown in Figure 6-11. In another experiment, the same researchers showed 127 adult citizens one of the drawings like the ones in Figure 6-9 and asked them to decide whether it

was accurate and if not, why not. Again, performance was generally poor, both in recognizing the accurate drawing and in spotting errors on the inaccurate ones.

A series of experiments showed that most people have very incomplete and imprecise memories of the details of an object that they have been handling constantly since childhood. Apparently, we don't store the details of a penny in our memory because we don't need to. We remember only what we need to remember. We can identify a penny by size and color, without looking at its features. We don't have to know which way Lincoln's head faces in order to recognize a penny as a penny. This study seems to show that recognition makes much smaller demands on memory than most of us believe.

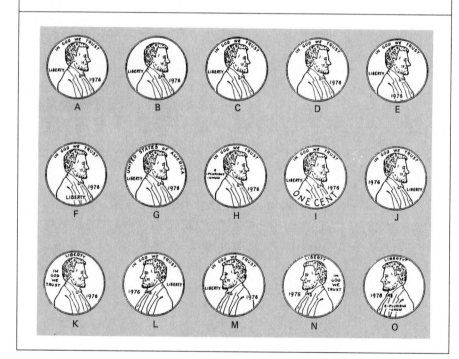

FIGURE 6-9 *Which is the "real" penny?*

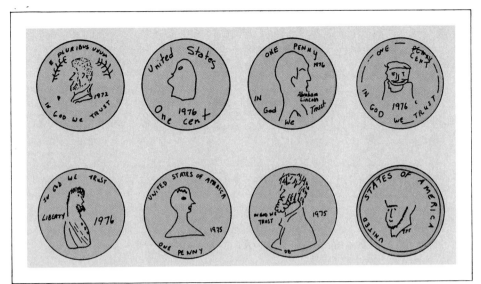

FIGURE 6-10 *Left: Examples of drawings of "pennies."*

FIGURE 6-11 *Below: Types of errors made in trying to draw a penny.*

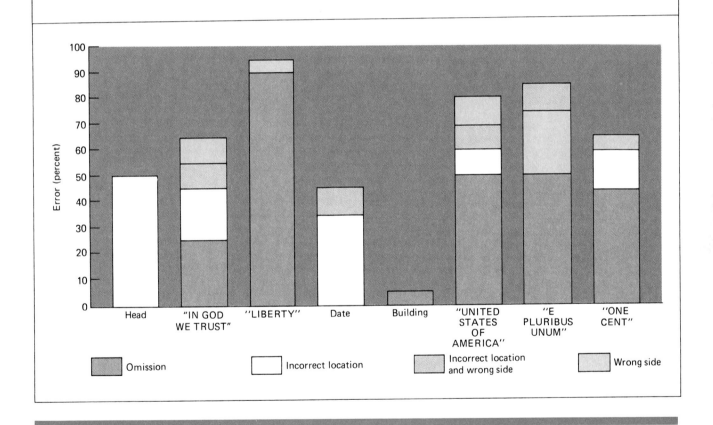

TABLE 6-2 EXPERIMENTAL DESIGNS FOR THE STUDY OF RETROACTIVE AND PROACTIVE INTERFERENCE

Group	Step 1	Step 2	Step 3
Proactive Interference			
Experimental	Learns A	Learns B	Retention test on B
Control	Rest	Learns B	Retention test on B
Retroactive Interference			
Experimental	Learns A	Learns B	Retention test on A
Control	Learns A	Rest	Retention test on A

Source: Adapted from Hulse, Egeth, & Deese, 1980, p. 308.

Proactive interference (PI) Situation in which information learned earlier inhibits the ability to remember new information.

Proactive interference (PI) describes a situation in which information that you have already learned interferes with your ability to remember new material. (The prefix *pro* means *before;* the interfering task is learned *before* you learn the task on which you are tested.)

In studies of proactive interference, an experimental group learns one list of words (material A) and then a second list (material B), and then is asked to recall the second list. A control group is asked only to learn and then recall the words in list B. The control group usually remembers the words better, indicating that the words learned earlier are interfering with the ability of the experimental group to remember the later ones. (See Table 6-2.)

In real life, this effect often shows up when you run into a woman you knew when she was single, who then took her husband's last name after marriage. Even though you have learned her married surname, you are apt to think of her by the name you first learned rather than the one you had to learn later—if you remember her name at all. The principle of proactive interference suggests that you would remember a person's name more easily if you had to learn only one name. (This may be one reason for a growing trend for married women to retain their birth names.)

Retroactive interference (RI) Situation in which information learned later inhibits the ability to remember previously learned information.

In **retroactive interference (RI),** information that we learn *later* causes a kind of barrier that interferes with our ability to remember material learned previously. (The prefix *retro* means *backward;* the interfering task, learned after you learned the task on which you are tested, exerts a backward influence.) The new material takes over, obliterating the old, even if we learned it well.

In studies of retroactive interference, the experimental group learns material A and then B, and then recalls A. The control group is not exposed to B at all. In these experiments, too, the control group remembers the material better, indicating that the experimental group's attention to new material is blocking the memory of the old material. (Again, see Table 6-2.)

Failure of Retrieval Have you ever seen someone you usually see at the beach or the tennis court in a situation where you are both wearing more formal clothes, and had a terrible time figuring out who that familiar-looking person could be? When one of you finally makes the connection, either is sure to say, "Oh, I didn't recognize you with your clothes on." That kind of forgetting is **cue-dependent forgetting,** the inability to remember information because appropriate retrieval cues are not present.

Cue-dependent forgetting Inability to remember information because appropriate retrieval cues are lacking.

In cue-dependent forgetting, the memory trace is there, but we cannot get at it—which shows that normal people often have difficulty retrieving memories, just as amnesiacs do. Our environment is different, the cues we depend on for retrieval are no longer present, and the memory is therefore inaccessible. In the example above, you are away from the environment where you usually see this person, and the person is dressed differently; in other words, the cues for recognition are not there. Many contemporary psychologists feel that we often can't get at our long-term memories because we don't have appropriate cues to call them up, rather than because there is decay or interference.

Tulving (1974/1977) has shown that if retrieval cues are given to subjects when they first learn something, the cues will help them remember it later on. Such cues may be words that rhyme with or are associated with a list of words a subject has learned, or the first letter or letters of the word. This suggests that material will be easier to retrieve if we encode it with a cue when we first commit it to memory.

Are Memories Permanent?   Which of the following two statements best reflects your own opinion?

1   Everything we learn is permanently stored in the mind, although sometimes particular details are not accessible. With hypnosis, or other special techniques, these inaccessible details could eventually be recovered.
2   Some details that we learn may be permanently lost from memory. Such details could never be recovered by hypnosis, or any other special technique, because the details are simply no longer there.

When Elizabeth F. Loftus and Geoffrey R. Loftus (1980, p. 410) asked 169 people (75 psychologists and 94 people in other occupations) to answer this question, they found that 84 percent of the psychologists and 69 percent of the others believed in the permanence of memories. Loftus and Loftus, however, maintain that many memories cannot be recovered because the memories no longer exist. As we pointed out in our discussion of eyewitness testimony, evidence from studies such as the one by Loftus, Miller, and Burns (1978) suggests that at least some memories are not permanent but can be "replaced" by information that is received after an initial event. If one memory can disappear because it is completely displaced by another, the notion that memory is permanent would seem to be disproved.

THE BIOLOGICAL BASIS OF MEMORY

For decades, psychologists have tried to pinpoint the physiological mechanisms that underlie memory—principally, how and where memories are stored in the brain. Research has given us some important clues about these mechanisms; but many of the findings have not been definitive, and the studies continue. Let's look at some of the most compelling theories and at the evidence for them.

How We Study Biological Aspects of Memory

Researchers study the way experience (and thus memory) affects both the structure and the chemistry of the nervous system, and how the nervous system enables us to learn and then to store what we learn in memory. Our data on memory come from two types of subjects, animals and people.

Laboratory Experiments   The most common laboratory approach is *somatic intervention (soma* means *body),* in which the experimenter changes some aspect of the nervous system (for example, by stimulating a part of the brain electrically or chemically) and then looks at the effects of the change on some behavior (such as speed of learning or retention of memory). In *behavioral intervention,* the investigator does something to affect a subject's behavior (such as providing formal training or an enriched environment) and then looks for structural or chemical changes in the subject's brain (such as changes in synaptic contacts or in transmitter levels in specific regions of the brain) (Rosenzweig, 1984). Experimenters usually use animals as subjects.

Studies of People with Memory Disorders   Researchers have also learned a great deal from studying people with defective memories. *Amnesia* is the general term for a variety of memory disorders that arise from different causes and that affect memory

Amnesia   General term for a variety of memory disorders that arise from different causes and affect memory in different ways.

in different ways. These disorders rarely come as they do in the movies, from a single blow to the head; nor do they disappear as they do in movieland, with another sudden shock. They are, however, the most frequent complaint of patients who have suffered strokes, infectious diseases of the brain, and traumatic injuries (as in Dorri's case, described in Chapter 2). Memory disorders are often the earliest signs of a number of neurologic illnesses, including Alzheimer's disease. Later in the chapter, we look at different kinds of amnesia.

How Memories Are Stored in the Brain

An influential model of the way the brain stores memories was proposed by one of the founders of physiological psychology, D. O. Hebb (1949). Hebb assumed that the neural bases in short-term memory and long-term memory were different stages of the same memory-storage process. In short-term memory a circuit of neurons, which Hebb called the *cell assembly,* fires in repeated patterns, creating a memory trace. This trace is unstable; but if it is maintained long enough, it causes a permanent change in the physical structure of the brain. For material to go from short-term to long-term memory, an actual physical change of the brain is required. This change may involve better synaptic transmission, the formation of new synapses, or the elimination of unused synapses—or any combination of these. The shift from a fragile memory trace to a permanent change in physical structure is called **consolidation.** It represents the two phases of memory, short-term and long-term.

Consolidation Shift of a fragile memory trace to a permanent change in physical structure; this shift represents the two phases of memory, short-term and long-term.

The findings from several lines of research support the basic thrust of Hebb's theory. Evidence for the existence of an unstable short-term memory that has not been consolidated into long-term memory can be seen in the effects of electroconvulsive shock on animals (usually rats) and human beings. The experimenter places electrodes on an animal's head and passes an electric current—strong enough to produce a seizure—through the animal's brain. If the animal is shocked immediately after having learned a task, such as running a pathway in a maze, it will lose all memory of the experience. But if the shock is delayed for some time after the learning experience, perhaps 1 hour or so after a rat has learned a maze, the animal does not forget what it has learned.

Why should this difference exist? We presume that when the shock to the brain comes immediately after learning, it disrupts the specific neural firing patterns that provide the code (the system of symbols) for short-term memory. Once the code has been established, it is not so vulnerable to disruption. Thus when the shock comes sometime afterward, it has no effect on material that has already been coded and consolidated into long-term memory (Duncan, 1949).

Another form of support for Hebb's theory is the fact that electroconvulsive therapy, which is sometimes used to treat severe depression, often produces amnesia (Scovern & Killman, 1980). Further support can be found in cases of traumatic amnesia. People who have suffered head injuries are more likely to lose memories for events that occurred just before their injury than they are for events in the more distant past, say, 3 months earlier. Presumably, that older information is now permanent; but the events that occurred just before the trauma were not firmly fixed and were easily dislodged from memory.

Still other evidence supports the notion that long-term memory is based on changes in brain structure having to do with dendritic spines. These are thornlike projections on dendrites, the parts of neurons that carry nerve impulses toward cell bodies (as described in Chapter 2). The number of dendritic spines in the brain correlates roughly with experience, a finding that has emerged from postmortem examinations of the brains of mentally retarded persons. (Mental retardation is characterized by an inability to learn and to store experiences.) Specifically, the number of these spines increases as a result of *learning* experiences (Crick, 1982). When electric stimulation is given to the **hippocampus,** a brain structure thought to be important in memory, the dendritic spines swell (Van Harreveld & Fifkova, 1975). Rats put in cages enriched by the presence of such stimulating objects as wheels to

Hippocampus Brain structure important in memory.

balance on, rocks to stand on, and objects to explore show more dendrites in the cortex than rats in standard cages (Rosenzweig, 1984).

Researchers have devoted considerable effort to trying to learn precisely how these structural changes come about. Since protein molecules serve as the building blocks for all cells, including neurons, much research has tried to determine whether learning experiences produce changes in **protein synthesis,** the body's building of protein molecules from amino acids. In a typical lab study of this process, a rat is injected with a drug thought to inhibit protein synthesis. The rat is then trained to do a particular task (like avoiding an electric shock) and is tested after training to see how well it remembers how to do the task. Twenty-four hours later, a normal rat will continue to avoid the place where it was shocked, showing that it remembers what it learned. A rat injected with a protein-synthesis inhibitor, however, will behave like one that received no training at all. This seems to show that protein synthesis is essential for memory (Davis & Squire, 1984; Rosenzweig, 1984).

The biochemical changes that seem to be most consistently correlated with memory are an increased number of synaptic contacts along specific pathways in the brain. Some researchers have studied a very primitive animal—the invertebrate sea snail *Aplysia* (see Figure 6-12), which has a simple, easily studied nervous system (Carew, Hawkins, & Kandel, 1983; Kandel, 1976).

Aplysia normally retracts its gill in response to tactile stimuli, such as would occur in turbulent waters, probably as a protective mechanism. When researchers squirt water at a certain spot on the snail (mimicking a stormy ocean), a nerve impulse in sensory neurons releases a neurotransmitter onto motor neurons, which in turn activates the muscles that retract the gill. But if the researchers squirt 10 times or more, say once every minute, less transmitter is released from the sensory neuron, apparently because repeated squirts cause chemical changes at the synapses. The snail has become habituated to the turbulence and has stopped releasing the transmitter; therefore the gill does not retract.

If the snail receives an electric shock and then a squirt of water, it becomes sensitized, and the gill-withdrawal reflex is more vigorous than ever. This seems to occur because other synapses become active and release the neurotransmitter *serotonin,* which facilitates transmission in the reflex pathway. Now more transmitter is released from the sensory neurons, which make direct contact onto the motor neurons. This simple animal can even respond to differential conditioning; that is, it can acquire two different conditioned responses to stimulation of different sites on its body. The mechanism of the conditioning appears to be an extension of the same mechanism that underlies the simpler form of learning known as *sensitization.*

Kandel and his colleagues are trying to explain more complex learning and memory phenomena in terms of changes in transmitter release for neurons. Working

Protein synthesis *The body's building of protein molecules from amino acids.*

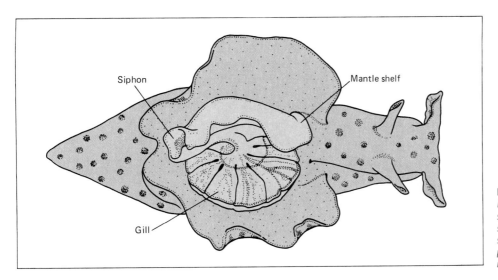

FIGURE 6-12 *Aplysia. This invertebrate, a sea snail, has a simple nervous system that is easy to study. Scientists have recently studied aplysia to establish the physiological bases for learning and memory. (Source: Kandel, 1979.)*

with a simple organism like aplysia may yield partial answers to such questions as why we adapt to constant stimuli (like a pervasive smell or loud noise level at a worksite) and why our behavioral responses become more vigorous under certain conditions. (If you were leaving a frightening movie, for example, you would be likely to experience a massive startle response at hearing a car backfire, whereas the same noise would probably have a much milder effect on you if you heard it as you were leaving church.) Basic research like this may help us find answers to some of the questions we ask about human learning and memory, including the relationship between classical and operant conditioning, the relationships between habituation and extinction, and the nature of the differences between short-term and long-term memory.

Where Memories Are Stored in the Brain

During most of his professional life, the physiological psychologist Karl Lashley was occupied by one consuming activity—a search for the *engram,* or memory trace. He tried for decades to find specific locations in the brain where memory traces existed.

In his research, Lashley taught rats various tasks, including running mazes and discriminating between stimuli; then he surgically produced lesions (injuries) in various parts of the rats' cortices; and finally, he tested the rats' memories for the tasks they had learned. But after all his research, he was unable to find a specific region of the cortex which when lesioned would invariably produce impairments in memory. He finally joked, "I sometimes feel, in reviewing the evidence on the localization of the memory trace, that . . . learning is just not possible" (1950, p. 477).

While it is probably true that memories do not settle into isolated chunks of brain tissue, more recent studies indicate that certain brain structures play a more important role in memory than others do. In particular, parts of the limbic system that lie under the temporal lobes seem essential for establishing new permanent memories. Data on the limbic system and memory follow in the next section. (See Chapter 2 for a review of these sections of the brain.)

Researchers now believe that different types of memory (such as procedural and declarative memory, defined earlier) involve different areas of the brain. One line of research, for example, has located one type of procedural memory in a particular region of the cerebellum. Investigators have classically conditioned rabbits to blink their eyes to a tone that has been sounded just before a puff of air. The rabbits will stop blinking in response to the tone if brain cells in a specific region of the cerebellum are destroyed, by either surgery or chemicals. But they will still blink to the puff of air, showing that the reflex itself is not affected—only the conditioned response is changed (McCormick & Thompson, 1984). The cerebellum is not the only seat of memory. Other research has shown that destroying parts of the hippocampus of an animal makes it impossible for the animal to learn more difficult tasks.

The importance of specific brain structures in the various types of memory has become dramatically apparent in studies of people suffering from memory disorders that seem to be linked to physical injury or illness. From such studies, researchers have concluded that different parts of the brain control short-term and long-term memory, as well as procedural and declarative memory. We'll see the basis for these conclusions in the following section.

MEMORY DISORDERS

We don't realize how much we depend upon memory for every aspect of day-to-day life until we see how devastating its loss can be. Simple lapses of memory are annoying; more severe losses can be life-threatening; major losses force people out of the world at large and into lonely pockets of isolation.

(Andy Schwartz/© Orion Pictures Corp.)

When the heroine in the movie Desperately Seeking Susan lost her memory, she was suffering from retrograde amnesia.

Organic Amnesia

H. M., age 58, does not know where he lives (in a nursing home) or what he ate at his last meal. Asked what year it is, his guess may be off by as much as 43 years. Although he is able to hold a conversation and can keep information as long as it stays in consciousness, even a moment's distraction will wipe out the memory. He understands puns and can do difficult crossword puzzles. He can draw an accurate floor plan of the house where he lived for 14 years, but thinks he still lives there even though he moved away over 12 years ago. H. M. has an ***organic amnesia*** that can be ascribed to a physiological injury or illness. He is famous in the psychological literature, for reasons that will soon be clear.

There are two basic kinds of memory loss. In ***anterograde amnesia,*** a disorder characterized by inability to create new permanent memories, patients typically cannot learn the names of their doctors or of the hospitals they are in, or any other new information they are exposed to *after* the traumatic event or illness that caused the amnesia. In ***retrograde amnesia,*** a disorder characterized by inability to recall information that had been learned *before* the onset of the amnesia patients may not remember experiences in their earlier life or the name of the president of the United States.

H. M. suffers from severe anterograde amnesia in declarative but not procedural memory. At age 10 he began to suffer such severe epileptic seizures that his life became a constant misery. No remedy helped. When he was 27 years old, in a desperate attempt to control his seizures, surgeons removed parts of both temporal lobes of his brain, as well as deeper structures, including almost all of the hippocampus. The seizures were greatly reduced in number and intensity, but this improvement in H. M.'s condition brought about a tragic side effect—loss of the ability to remember new information.

H. M. had no apparent memory problems before his operation (which took place in 1953). After it, while he remembered much that he had learned before the operation, he could not learn and remember the most basic facts. He has, however, been able to learn a variety of perceptual tasks (like mirror reading) and motor skills (like playing tennis), a fact which suggests that memory for such abilities may be different from other memories. (Once we have learned how to swim or ride a bicy-

Organic amnesia *Memory disorder that can be attributed to physiological illness or injury.*

Anterograde amnesia *Memory loss that is characterized by the inability to create new permanent memories.*

Retrograde amnesia *Memory loss that is characterized by the inability to recall information learned before the onset of the amnesia.*

cle, we do not forget how to do it.) H. M. has also learned how to solve puzzles and perform maze tasks, and he can improve with practice. He has no recollection, however, of ever having done these tasks.

H. M.'s brain surgery affected different types of memory differently. The fact that he could learn new skills indicates that his procedural memory was not affected; the fact that he could not remember events in his life after his operation shows impaired episodic memory. H. M.'s short-term memory seems relatively intact; his essential disorder seems to be in the transfer of information from fragile short-term storage to more permanent long-term storage. These differences imply that the different types of memory depend on different physiological structures.

H. M. has shown a few "islands of remembering," possibly because he still retains a small piece of hippocampus. He knows what an astronaut is (although his damage occurred long before the term was coined), that his parents are dead, and that someone named Kennedy was assassinated. For the most part, however, he is unable to form new memories.

The study of H. M.'s complex memory problems has given us many clues that different parts of the brain are involved in short-term and long-term memory and also in procedural and declarative memory (Corkin, 1984; Milner, 1966). For obvious reasons, bilateral temporal lobectomy (the technical term for the operation that caused H. M.'s amnesia) is no longer used as a treatment for epilepsy, but similar symptoms sometimes arise from diseases that attack the temporal lobes (Drachman & Arbit, 1966).

The hippocampus and the amygdala, both parts of the limbic system, have been shown to be crucial brain structures responsible for memory. (See Figure 2-13 in Chapter 2.) Patients who have had the cerebral cortex of their temporal lobes removed, without the destruction of the hippocampus and the amygdala, do not show the profound amnesia suffered by H. M. (Milner, 1970). Animal research supports this conclusion. Surgical lesions of both of these structures affect the ability to learn new information (Horel, 1978; Mishkin, 1982). Rats with lesions of the hippocampus have problems with spatial memory tasks (Olton, 1979), and monkeys with bilateral lesions of the hippocampus and amygdala develop memory deficits similar to H. M.'s (Mishkin, 1982).

Damage to regions of the brain other than temporal and limbic structures can also produce severe memory disorders. An instance of memory loss arising from injury to the thalamus can be seen in the case of a young man, N. A., who suffered a lesion in this part of the brain (Teuber, Milner, & Vaughan, 1968). A friend who had been fooling around with a miniature fencing foil accidently stabbed N. A. The foil entered a nostril and went to the base of his brain, causing a severe anterograde amnesia. N. A.'s memory loss is much milder than H. M.'s and is largely restricted to verbal activities (probably because his lesion occurred in a portion of the left thalamus). His retrograde amnesia is limited to only 1 year before his accident (Squire & Slater, 1978).

Another severe memory disorder, *Korsakoff's syndrome,* is a neuropsychiatric disorder caused by prolonged, excessive alcohol abuse, coupled with a deficiency in the vitamin thiamine. Affected persons suffer both anterograde and retrograde amnesia and fill in gaps in their memory with incorrect details. They can use language normally, but they have trouble carrying on a conversation because they can't think of anything to say (Talland, 1969). Postmortem examinations have shown that the lesions most typical of this syndrome are not in the hippocampus but in the thalamus and the hypothalamus (Butters & Cermak, 1980; Victor, Adams, & Collins, 1971).

Memory is not located in one single brain region. On the contrary, many brain structures are involved in memory. Damage to different locations produces slightly different memory disorders, causing a problem, for example, in declarative memory but none in procedural memory. Some of the new techniques for studying the brain, described in Chapter 2, may provide additional clues to the biological bases of memory.

Psychogenic Amnesia

The kind of amnesia most people are aware of is actually much rarer than the kind caused by organic brain damage. This is **psychogenic amnesia,** a memory disorder caused by emotionally disturbing events. It differs from organic amnesia in several ways. Patients with psychogenic amnesia usually display much worse retrograde than anterograde amnesia—the opposite of the usual situation in an organic amnesia. Furthermore, psychogenic amnesiacs often lose their personal identity; organic amnesiacs almost never do. The characteristics of psychogenic memory loss are poorly understood and have only recently begun to be explored through research (Kihlstrom & Evans, 1979).

Psychogenic amnesia Dissociative disorder in which a person may forget events that occurred during a certain time period; it usually follows a traumatic event and may end suddenly.

Theories of Amnesia

Precisely where memory breaks down is a controversial issue. Some of the cognitive processes that have been implicated are described below, but the most likely conclusion is that there is no one single cause; in any individual patient, one or more information-processing mechanisms may be faulty (Brandt, 1983).

Encoding   Research in recent years has supported the possibility that amnesiacs, especially those with Korsakoff's syndrome, analyze incoming information too superficially, failing to engage in the deep-level encoding that, according to depth-of-processing theory, makes for stable memory traces (Butters & Cermak, 1980).

Consolidation   Since experiments with electroconvulsive shocks have shown that information is most likely to be forgotten during a definite period of time after learning, it is possible that amnesia is caused by the failure to consolidate information into more permanent memory traces.

Retrieval   The tendency of some amnesiacs to make an unusual number of "intrusion errors" (that is, to report previously acquired information when they are trying to retrieve task-relevant material) suggests that faulty retrieval may be based on proactive interference, or excessive interference from previously learned information (Warrington & Weiskrantz, 1970). A clue that H. M.'s problem might involve retrieval can be seen in the fact that he could not name the president of the United States (even though he watched the news every night) until he was told that the name began with *N*. He then said "Nixon" (Corkin, 1984).

EXCEPTIONAL MEMORIES

The Russian psychologist Alexander Luria (1968) was stymied by a man he called *S.* Luria wanted to measure the limits of human memory, as exemplified by this famous memorist (a person with an exceptional memory), but he was thwarted because he could never establish a point at which S. forgot anything. No matter what task Luria posed or how long a time passed afterward, S. never forgot.

S. produced a veritable explosion of visual images with virtually everything he learned, an ability that fixed information in his mind, but that also produced difficulties for him, as we pointed out earlier. He had trouble reading or being read to, because images would form so quickly they would collide with one another in his mind, become contorted, and create mental chaos. Much of the time he was, however, able to distribute these images along a road or street he "saw" in his mind.

There have been other people whose feats of memory dazzle us. There is, for example, V. P. (Hunt & Love, 1972/1982), who, blindfolded, could play seven games of chess at the same time, and who constantly carried on correspondence chess games for which he kept no written record. There is "Nancy" (Gummerman & Gray, 1971), who could provide a 9-minute, 25-second, greatly detailed description

A substantial body of research has yielded many clues to ways you can improve your memory to help you in many aspects of your life.

You can improve both short-term and long-term memory. Even before either of these memory stages begins, you can give yourself a head start by paying close attention to what you will want to remember. You cannot remember something you have never seen or heard, and so if you want to remember it, you have to get it into your consciousness first.

REHEARSAL

You can improve your short-term memory by *rote rehearsal*, just going over and over something in your head, for the short time you need to hold onto it. You can also hold things better in short-term memory by *chunking*—organizing long lists or numbers so that you can remember them in seven or fewer chunks.

ORGANIZATION

The major improvement you can make, however, is in your long-term memory. The way you encode and store material will help you when you go to retrieve it. The all-embracing concept that will help you remember what you want to remember is *organization for meaningful association*. The more meaning you can give to something and the more associations you can make between the new information you are now learning and other information you already know, the better you'll remember.

MNEMONICS

If you ever took piano lessons, you must have learned both the sentence "Every good boy does fine," because the first letter of every word represents the lines in the treble clef, and the acronym, FACE, whose letters represent the spaces in the treble clef. In grammar school you probably learned the spelling rhyme, "*I* before *E* except after *C*, or when sounded like *A* as in *neighbor* or *weigh*." A device like these, to help you remember information, is known as a *mnemonic*, and an entire system to im-

HOW CAN YOU IMPROVE YOUR MEMORY?

prove or develop your memory is called *mnemonics*.

These systems really do work. When Gordon H. Bower (1973) gave 5 different lists of 20 words to 2 different groups of college students, those who had used mnemonics remembered an average of 72 out of the 100 items, while those using either simple or rote learning remembered only an average of 28. Some of the most popular of these systems are given on the next page. They all require time and attention until you get used to using them. People who have learned them, however, often swear by them, and some professional memorists base their performances on them.

Most of us rely less on the kind of internal memory aids represented by these mnemonic systems than we do on a variety of external aids, such as the ones listed at the end of this box. Writing something down usually requires less thought, but tying it to a mnemonic system frees you from reliance on paper and pencil. You might want to try one or two of the mnemonic systems described in the following pages and see how they work, compared with whatever system you have been using up until now.

The following memory systems all use visual imagery to help you make the associations that can help you to remember. Such systems seem to come naturally to some people with exceptional memories, like the memory whiz S. Other people, however, can also learn them and can often achieve remarkable results.

Method of Loci The method of loci is a mnemonic system that has a long

history, having originated in ancient Greece and been described by the Roman writer Cicero (the word *loci* means *locations* or *places* in Latin). It works through imagery, based on keying what you want to remember to the stops along a route that you take in your mind:

■ *Develop your route:* Think of an orderly progression of places that you are already familiar with—possibly your street, the sidewalk in front of your building, the outer door, the vestibule, the inner lobby, the stairway, the first landing, the landing in front of your door, the door into your apartment, your livingroom, your kitchen, your bathroom, and your bedroom. The same kind of progression could be set up for a private house, a rural setting, a walk along campus, or any other familiar route. Whichever one you choose, it's important to stick to the same route, so that you don't have to keep learning a new one.

■ *Make up an image associating each item you want to remember with each stop on your route:* Suppose that you want to remember to buy the following items—milk, eggs, tomatoes, bananas, sunflower seeds, tea, toilet paper, peanut butter, soap, and window cleaner. You might imagine puddles of milk covering your street, eggs splattered all over your outer door, tomatoes piled up so high in the vestibule that you can't get in, a big banana tree standing where the Christmas tree usually stands in the inner lobby, sunflower seeds sprinkled on the stairway, a giant teapot on the first landing, rolls of toilet paper piled high on the landing in front of your door, peanut butter smeared on the door into your apartment, soap bubbles awash in your livingroom, and a little gremlin busily cleaning your kitchen window. The more vivid your images, the better you'll remember them.

■ *When you want to remember your list, take a mental walk:* Ask yourself, "What did I put in the street? On the outer door? In the vestibule?" Remembering the scene at each stop will give you a cue to help you remember what's in it. You can also use this system for remembering people, errands, chores, and so forth.

Peg-Word Method Following are the steps to take in the method that uses peg words.

■ *Learn a series of words that correspond to the numbers 1 to 20:* The ones most often used for 1 to 10 are these—One is a bun. Two is a shoe. Three is a tree. Four is a door. Five is a hive. Six is sticks. Seven is heaven. Eight is a gate. Nine is wine. Ten is a hen.
■ *Make up a series of images that let you "hang" the items you want to remember on the pegs:* Each item interacts with one peg word. For the shopping list given before, you might imagine milk sloshing over a bun (or a quart of milk inside it—a milk sandwich), a broken egg in your shoe, a tree laden down with tomatoes, a bunch of bananas hanging on a door, bees carrying sunflower seeds into their hives, tea bags attached like flags to sticks, rolls of toilet paper decorating the gates of heaven, jars of peanut butter impaled on a gate, a wine bottle whose label declares the brand of soap you want, and a hen cleaning your window.
■ *When you want to remember the list, go through your peg words in numerical order:* The peg words serve as your cues, and the numbers will help you keep track of how many items you want to remember.

Narrative-Chaining Method If you have to remember only a single list of items, either of the above methods is good. But if you need to remember more than one list or a variety of different kinds of items, narrative chaining is more effective. This is how it works.

■ *Make up a story built around what-*

ever you want to remember: Let's go back to our shopping list. Imagine that you're a tourist visiting a farm, and the farmer asks you whether you want to milk the cow. You sit down on the milking stool to do it, but you didn't realize that there were a bunch of eggs on the stool, and when you sit down you smash them and come up covered with egg yolk. The farmer says, "I know what will remove the egg stains!" and rubs at your pants with a slice of tomato, making the stain worse, of course. You get so mad you throw a banana at her. She ducks, and the banana flies past her into a bag of sunflower seeds, puncturing the bag and sending seeds all over the barn floor. The farmer's husband runs in and says, "You two look pretty upset. Why don't you calm down with a nice cup of tea?" The three of you mop up the mess with gobs of toilet paper, and. . . . Well, you see how this works.
■ *To remember the list, remember the story.*

HOW TO REMEMBER NAMES AND FACES BETTER

■ Pay attention when you first hear someone's name. Many cases of "forgetting" a name are caused by never having absorbed it in the first place.
■ Use the name immediately. Say something like "Hello, Mary. Smith is an unusual name, isn't it?" Speaking the name out loud provides a valuable form of rehearsal. Use it once or twice more during your conversation or focus on it silently.
■ Make an emotional association with the person's face. Would you buy a used car from this person? Would you trust this person with money or a confidence? Does the person remind you of anyone you know?
■ Notice an outstanding physical feature and conjure up some kind of mental image that will hook the feature to the person's name. For example, if Mr. Bell has large ears,

imagine them as ringing bells (Lorayne, 1975).

POPULAR EXTERNAL MEMORY AIDS THAT HELP IN EVERYDAY LIFE

■ Write a note to yourself and put it where you are sure to see it (tape it to the bathroom mirror before you go to sleep at night or to the inside of the door you'll use to leave home in the morning).
■ Put an object you have to do something with (book to library or shoes to shoemaker) in a place where you can't miss it (such as in front of a door).
■ Write appointments, obligations, and activities in a daily diary or calendar, which you check automatically every morning.
■ Ask someone reliable to remind you of something.
■ Make lists of items you have to buy, activities you have to do, people you have to phone, assignments you have fulfill, etc.
■ Set an alarm or a kitchen timer to remind you to turn off the stove, leave your room for an appointment, make a phone call, or end one activity and begin another.
■ Change a ring you ordinarily wear on one finger to a different finger; transfer your watch to your other wrist or turn it to the underside of the customary wrist; or make some other change you'll be conscious of.
■ Write a note to yourself on your hand.
■ Integrate an activity into your everyday routine; for example, take a daily pill with your morning juice, instead of at haphazard times during the day. Keep your pillbox in a prominent spot.

Most of the preceding suggestions were used by 30 college students surveyed by John E. Harris (1978, in Gruneberg, Morris, & Sykes, 1978); they have also been used by the authors of this book. Such aids are especially recommended for older people, who often find that they are more forgetful than they used to be.

of a picture she had seen for only 30 seconds. Ulric Neisser (1982) feels that such abilities may be more common than we realize and that studying such people may shed light on the potential of human memory. While most of us cannot rival the memory abilities of people like this, we *can* improve our capacity for remembering material that is important to us. Some suggestions for doing this, based on research on memory and **mnemonics,** are given in the box "How Can You Improve Your Memory?"

Mnemonic   *Device to aid memory.*

We have seen how complex memory is and how it is inextricably tied to the entire learning process. Both learning and memory have major implications for the development and the measurement of intelligence, as we'll see in Chapter 7.

SUMMARY

1   Memory is the ability to encode, store, and retrieve material. Encoding is the process of getting something into the memory system. This is done by organizing material using a code. Encoding is most effective when it involves making meaningful associations between the new material and material already in memory. Storage is the retention of the material in memory; retrieval is getting material out of memory.

2   One important model of the way memory works is the storage-and-transfer model of Atkinson and Shiffrin. It proposes that there are three different types of memory: sensory memory, short-term memory, and long-term memory.

3   Sensory memory involves stimuli that come through the senses. Depending on the particular sense involved, material lasts from 1 second to a few seconds and then is either forgotten or transferred into short-term memory through a process of pattern recognition. Sperling demonstrated the fleeting nature of sensory memory.

4   Short-term memory is working memory. It has a limited capacity of about seven meaningful units. Information in short-term memory disappears in about 20 seconds unless it is held there through rehearsal. The amount of information can be expanded by chunking or grouping items into meaningful units. Sternberg found that retrieval from short-term memory is serial, exhaustive, and extremely rapid.

5   Long-term memory is a storehouse. It appears to have unlimited capacity and may store information permanently. There are different types of materials in long-term memory. Procedural memory is information about how to do things. Declarative memory is knowledge of facts. There are two types of declarative memory: episodic memory (sometimes called *autobiographical memory,* since it refers to personal experiences) and semantic memory (meaning).

6   Retrieval from long-term memory depends on how efficiently material was stored there. The more associations people make between an item they want to remember and what they already know, the more likely they will be to remember the item in the long run. In other words, people are more likely to remember material that is meaningful. Clustering is an organizational technique in which items to be remembered are rearranged into meaningful categories.

7   The tip-of-the-tongue phenomenon is a retrieval situation in which a person cannot recall information exactly although he or she has some knowledge of it. Research on this phenomenon indicates that information is coded in ways other than meaning alone, such as by sound.

8   Not all psychologists see memory as consisting of separate storage systems, as Shiffrin and Atkinson propose. Craik and Lockhart, for example, believe that the ability to remember depends on how deeply information is processed. The deeper the processing, the longer the material lasts. This is the levels-of-processing model.

9   Recognition, recall, and relearning are three ways to measure retention. In recognition, one must identify previously learned material. In recall, one has to reproduce previously learned material. In free recall, the material may be reproduced in any order; in serial recall, it must be reproduced in the order in which it was originally presented. The relearning technique measures amount of time saved learning material which had been learned originally at some earlier time.

10   The serial-position curve is a curve of remembering which demonstrates that in a free-recall situation there is a tendency to remember items presented first (primacy effect) and last (recency effect) in a series and to forget those in the middle. However, if there is an unusual item in the middle of the material to be remembered, there is also a tendency to remember it (von Restorff effect).

11   Flashbulb memories are vivid recollections of what one was doing when one heard about a significant event. They are a type of autobiographical memory. Flashbulb memories may once have had survival value.

12   Research has shown that at least some of what people "remember" is the result of mental reconstruction. People have a tendency to fill in gaps in their memories, and this may result in "creating memories." One area where this can occur is eyewitness testimony.

13   Hermann Ebbinghaus's curve of forgetting indicates that forgetting is initially quite rapid but then slows down markedly.

14   A number of theories have been proposed to explain why people forget. According to the theory of motivated forgetting, people forget material they need to forget. In other words, they unconsciously repress certain uncomfortable memories. Decay theory holds that certain memories fade with the passage of time if the information is not

used. Interference theory holds that some information is forgotten because other information interferes with or confounds memory. Proactive interference is a situation in which material learned first interferes with ability to remember new information. Retroactive interference is a situation in which information learned later interferes with remembering information learned previously.

15 Psychologists disagree about the permanence of memory. Some hold that forgetting is failure to retrieve. That is, sometimes information cannot be retrieved because the appropriate cues to retrieve it are lacking. Other psychologists maintain that at least some memories are permanently lost or altered in some way.

16 Some researchers have examined how memories are stored in the brain. They have relied upon both laboratory experiments (largely with animals) and studies of people with memory disorders.

17 Different processes are believed to occur for short-term and long-term memory. According to D. O. Hebb, in short-term memory a circuit of neurons, the cell assembly, fires in repeated patterns, creating an unstable memory trace that does not change the physical structure of the brain. For material to go from short-term memory to long-term memory, an actual physical change is required, taking the form of new connections between neurons. A number of lines of research support this distinction.

18 Recent research indicates that certain brain structures play an important role in memory. The parts of the limbic system that lie under the temporal lobes seem essential for the establishment of new permanent memories. It appears that different types of memory (such as procedural and declarative memory) involve different parts of the brain.

19 Amnesia is a general term for a variety of memory disorders. Organic amnesias are disorders arising from physiological injury or illness. A person with anterograde amnesia cannot create new permanent memories. Retrograde amnesia is a condition in which a person cannot recall information learned before the onset of the amnesia. Electroconvulsive therapy produces both types of amnesia. Persons suffering from Korsakoff's syndrome, a neuropsychiatric disorder caused by prolonged, excessive alcohol abuse, experience both anterograde and retrograde amnesia and fill in the gaps in their memories with incorrect details.

20 Psychogenic amnesia is a memory disorder caused by emotionally disturbing events. Theories of amnesia have considered difficulties in encoding, consolidation, and retrieval. Most probably there is no single cause for all amnesias. In any patient, one or more information-processing mechanisms may be faulty.

21 A memorist is a person with an exceptional memory.

22 A mnemonic is a device to aid memory. Useful mnemonics include the method of loci (in which items to be remembered are imagined as placed along a familiar route); the peg-word method (in which words to be remembered are associated with certain peg words or cues); and the narrative-chaining method (in which a story is made up containing the information to be remembered). External aids such as writing notes, making lists, and keeping an appointment calendar are also useful.

KEY TERMS

Amnesia (page 215)
Anterograde amnesia (219)
Associational rehearsal (200)
Chunking (196)
Clustering (201)
Consolidation (216)
Cue-dependent forgetting (214)
Declarative memory (199)
Echoic memory (195)
Encoding (193)
Engram (209)
Episodic memory (199)

Flashbulb memory (206)
Hippocampus (216)
Iconic memory (195)
Levels-of-processing model of memory (202)
Long-term memory (LTM) (194)
Mnemonic (224)
Organic amnesia (219)
Primacy effect (205)
Proactive interference (PI) (214)

Procedural memory (199)
Protein synthesis (217)
Psychogenic amnesia (221)
Recall (203)
Recency effect (205)
Recognition (203)
Retrieval (193)
Retroactive interference (RI) (214)
Retrograde amnesia (219)
Rote rehearsal (196)
Semantic memory (199)

Sensory memory (SM) (194)
Serial-position curve (205)
Short-term memory (STM) (194)
Storage (193)
Storage-and-transfer model of memory (194)
Tip-of-the-tongue (TOT) problem (202)

SUGGESTED READINGS

BADDELEY, A. (1982). Memory: A user's guide. New York: Macmillan. A beautifully illustrated, fascinating compendium of up-to-date information about memory, complete with tests and exercises to improve memory.

LOFTUS, E. (1979). Eyewitness testimony. Cambridge, MA: Harvard University Press. An absorbing book presenting evidence on the unreliability of eyewitness testimony.

LOFTUS, E. (1980). Memory. Reading, MA: Addison-Wesley. A comprehensive account, by a memory expert, of recent research findings on such topics as memory in old age, the use of computers as memory substitutes, and the effects of drugs on memory, with suggestions for improving memory.

NEISSER, U. (1982). Memory observed: Remembering in natural contexts. San Francisco: Freeman. A fascinating look at a generally neglected area of psychological research on memory and forgetting—their manifestations in everyday life.

CHAPTER

7

INTELLIGENCE

- How have different psychologists defined intelligence over the years? What are some of the ways they have devised for measuring it? Why has this been so controversial?

- What are the most important contemporary theories of intelligence?

- Why are standardization, reliability, and validity important in intelligence tests?

- What are the strengths and weaknesses of intelligence tests in use today?

- What are some promising new directions in intelligence testing?

- What role do heredity and environment play in influencing intelligence?

- What can be learned from studying extremes of intelligence—the intellectually gifted and the mentally retarded?

When I was in the fourth grade at the Academy of the Holy Angels in Fort Lee, New Jersey, I took a group intelligence test, along with the rest of my classmates. I don't remember taking the test itself, but I do have a clear memory of my teacher, Sister Mary Clovis, going around the room and telling each of us what his or her IQ was. To me, it was just a meaningless number; but since it seemed to mean something to my teacher, I repeated it to my parents at the dinner table that evening. When they both seemed overjoyed and made a big fuss over me, I realized that it meant something good.

The number meant that I was "smart," and therefore that I was expected to do well in school and in life. In many ways I have done well, but I'm not sure whether it was because of the intelligence which that number supposedly represented, or whether it was because I was lucky enough to be born to parents who wanted and loved me, who valued education, who encouraged me in my interests from an early age, who filled our house with books, who gave me music and dancing lessons, who made me feel good about myself, and who could afford to provide an environment that made it possible for me to accomplish many of my goals.

Furthermore, that number told only a little bit about me, in a narrow context. It said nothing about a wide range of abilities that, as we'll see in this chapter, are more and more being considered part of intelligence. It said nothing about whether or not I was good at solving problems, skilled in sizing up situations and people in real life, or able to function well on a day-to-day basis. The main things it said were that I could take tests well, that I was fluent with words (and to some degree with numbers), that I was good at certain kinds of logical reasoning, and that I would probably do well in school.

Still, the number was not infallible even for its most valid aim—predicting academic performance. Yes, I did well through high school, and I was accepted by a select college, Vassar. But because I was distracted by events in my personal life during my first 2 years at college, I did poorly there. Only by pulling myself together and working very hard in my last 2 years was I able to make up for my early college record and be admitted to graduate school.

—From the notebooks of Diane Papalia

In this chapter we look at a number of issues related to intelligence, several of which have had a major political and social impact. First, we look at the ways that psychologists have defined intelligence over the years, and at the resulting controversies. We then examine the whole area of intelligence testing and what intelligence tests can and cannot tell us. We look at the ways psychologists have measured—or tried to measure—intelligence, some of the uses and abuses of testing, and some promising new directions for assessing intelligence. We explore relationships—or their absence—between intelligence and other factors: heredity, environment, birth order, and sex. Finally, we consider extremes of intelligence: the intellectually gifted and the mentally retarded. In Chapter 8, on language and thought, we will deal with issues closely related to intelligence.

WHAT IS INTELLIGENCE?

Defining Intelligence

Debate over what intelligence is—and how to measure it—has gone on for decades and is still as heated as ever. Lewis Terman (1921), an early researcher who developed the Stanford-Binet Intelligence Scale, one of the most influential tests in this country, and who launched a major longitudinal study of gifted children that is still going on today more than 60 years later, defined intelligence as the *ability to think abstractly*. Jean Piaget (1952), the Swiss psychologist who applied his broad knowledge of biology, philosophy, and logic to meticulous observations of children and constructed complex theories about how children acquire knowledge, defined intelligence as the *ability to adapt to one's surroundings*. And David Wechsler (1944), the developer of widely used intelligence tests for different ages, came up with a practical definition—the ability to "act purposefully, to think rationally, and to deal effectively with the environment" (p. 3). Other psychologists define it as "whatever intelligence tests measure." The box "How Laypersons Judge Intelligence" reports on the way a number of ordinary nonprofessionals describe intelligence.

Recent conceptions of intelligent behavior stress that it is both goal-oriented (conscious and deliberate rather than accidental) and adaptive (leading to solving problems). When we use the term **intelligence** in this book, we are referring to a *constant interaction between inherited ability and environmental experience, which results in a person's being able to acquire, remember, and use knowledge; to understand both concrete and (eventually) abstract concepts; to understand relationships among objects, events, and ideas; and to apply and use all these abilities in a purposeful way to solve problems in everyday life.*

Intelligence *Ability to adapt or appropriately alter a behavior in pursuit of a goal.*

This definition is—deliberately—extremely broad. While intelligence results from the interplay between heredity (our inherited capabilities) and environment (our experiences), it is difficult to estimate the weight of each influence. This issue—whether intelligence is inherited or acquired—represents a long-standing controversy in the intelligence literature. Today most psychologists agree that heredity and environment interact to influence intelligence, but there is considerable disagreement on the relative importance of each factor.

Our definition blends the practical and adaptive with the abstract. We recognize, for example, that the verbal abilities you need to get along in mainstream American society are different from the abilities you would need if you lived in a culture where you had to hunt and fish to survive.

Theories of Intelligence

While there are almost as many theories of intelligence as there are definitions, we will focus our discussion on a few important approaches. The first approach we'll examine is exemplified in the theories of Spearman, Thurstone, Guilford, and Cattell and Horn. It uses a statistical technique known as *factor analysis** to discover the nature of intelligence. This orientation, known as the *psychometric approach*, emphasizes measurement of intelligence and individual differences in intelligence.

---

*Factor analysis is a statistical technique employed to determine the "factors" underlying a group of test scores. A factor is composed of a group of tests or measures that correlate highly: that is, the scores on these tests cluster together. For example, people who score highly on reading tests also tend to score highly on vocabulary tests and other verbal measures. This pattern suggests that there is an underlying factor, or element, common to those tests—verbal ability. Through factor analysis, then, we are able to determine the underlying element common to a group of measures that correlate highly

TABLE 7-1 FACTORS UNDERLYING PEOPLE'S CONCEPTIONS OF INTELLIGENCE, ACCORDING TO LAYPERSONS' RATINGS

1 Practical problem-solving ability

Reasons logically and well.
Identifies connections among ideas.
Sees all aspects of a problem.
Keeps an open mind.
Responds thoughtfully to others' ideas.
Sizes up situations well.
Gets to the heart of problems.
Interprets information accurately.

Makes good decisions.
Goes to original sources for information.
Poses problems in an optimal way.
Is a good source of ideas.
Perceives implied assumptions and conclusions.
Listens to all sides of an argument.
Deals with problems resourcefully.

2 Verbal ability

Speaks clearly and articulately.
Is verbally fluent.
Converses well.
Is knowledgeable about a particular field of knowledge.
Studies hard.
Reads with high comprehension.

Reads widely.
Deals effectively with people.
Writes without difficulty.
Sets aside time for reading.
Displays a good vocabulary.

3 Social competence

Accepts others for what they are.
Admits mistakes.
Displays interest in the world at large.
Is on time for appointments.
Has social conscience.
Thinks before speaking and doing.
Displays curiosity.
Does not make snap judgments.
Makes fair judgments.

Assesses well the relevance of information to a problem at hand.
Is sensitive to other people's needs and desires.
Is frank and honest with self and others.
Displays interest in the immediate environment.
Accepts social norms.
Tries new things.

Source: Adapted from Sternberg, Conway, Ketron, & Bernstein, 1981, p. 45

TABLE 7-2 FACTORS UNDERLYING PEOPLE'S CONCEPTIONS OF INTELLIGENCE, ACCORDING TO EXPERTS' RATINGS

1 Verbal intelligence

Displays a good vocabulary.
Reads with high comprehension.
Displays curiosity.
Is intellectually curious.
Sees all aspects of a problem.
Learns rapidly.
Appreciates knowledge for its own sake.
Is verbally fluent.

Listens to all sides of an argument.
Displays alertness.
Thinks deeply.
Shows creativity.
Converses easily on a variety of subjects.
Reads widely.
Likes to read.
Identifies connections among ideas.

2 Problem-solving ability

Able to apply knowledge to problems at hand.
Makes good decisions.
Poses problems in an optimal way.
Displays common sense.
Displays objectivity.
Solves problems well.

Plans ahead.
Has good intuitions.
Gets to the heart of problems.
Appreciates truth.
Considers the end result of actions.
Approaches problems thoughtfully.

3 Practical intelligence

Sizes up situations well.
Determines how to achieve goals.

Displays awareness of world.
Displays interest in the world at large.

Source: Adapted from Sternberg, Conway, Ketron, & Bernstein, 1981, p. 46.

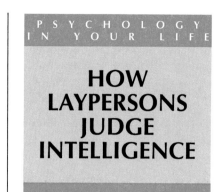

You probably have strong opinions about the intelligence of your friends, people you know at school or work, members of your family, and yourself. How, though, do you decide whether or not a person is "smart"? If you're like most of the people canvassed in one study (Sternberg, Conway, Ketron, & Bernstein, 1981), you base your opinions on the way other people act, and your ability to judge intelligence in others is similar to that of contemporary psychologists.

The psychologist Robert J. Sternberg and his colleagues interviewed or mailed questionnaires to 476 men and women—students, working people, supermarket shoppers, and people located by newspaper ads or the phone book. They also questioned 140 research psychologists who specialize in studying intelligence. Both experts and laypersons listed kinds of behavior that they thought characterized "intelligence," "academic intelligence," "everyday intelligence," and "unintelligence." Some 250 different behaviors emerged: 170 indicators of different aspects of intelligence and 80 signs of lack of intelligence.

Most of the intelligent behaviors can be grouped in three categories: (1) *practical problem-solving ability* ("identifies connections among ideas"), (2) *verbal ability* ("reads with high comprehension"), and (3) *social competence* ("thinks before speaking and doing"). Some of the most commonly cited illustrations of these abilities are given in Tables 7-1 and 7-2 (opposite page). Academic intelligence was composed of the same three basic categories, with a greater emphasis on academic skills, such as studying hard; and everyday intelligence consisted of practical problem-solving ability, social competence, character, and interest in learning and culture.

The ideas advanced by laypersons turn out to be very close to the newest ways of looking at intelligence. Ordinary people add social and cultural dimensions (such as sensitivity to other people's needs and desires, honesty, and the ability to get along well with others) to the cognitive dimensions (such as logical reasoning, display of curiosity, and rapid learning).

While people aren't very good at judging their own intelligence, they are good at describing the way they act, so that an outside observer can get a pretty accurate idea of their intelligence. When the subjects in this study rated themselves on the 250 behaviors, the researchers were able to predict quite well their overall scores on standard intelligence tests, as well as their scores on the parts of the tests that measure verbal ability, social competence, and ability to solve problems.

This finding points to a possibility in intelligence testing—a checklist that could supplement, or in some cases replace, the elaborate intelligence tests that follow most of us throughout our school and work years. A checklist has several advantages. It is simple; it focuses on typical performance rather than on the best performance a person is capable of; it is not stressful; it emphasizes behaviors that matter in the real world; and it can be tailored to different cultural groups and to behaviors important within a specific culture or subculture.

While there were some differences between the experts interviewed in this study (who emphasized motivation more) and the laypersons (who concentrated more on competence in getting along with other people), one of the most interesting conclusions from the study is the close connection between what the average person means by intelligence and what contemporary psychologists say it is (Sternberg et al., 1981).

Second, we'll consider two *new approaches* to the study of intelligence, Gardner's *theory of multiple intelligences* and Sternberg's *triarchic theory*.

Third, we'll examine an approach conceptualized by Piaget and known, accordingly, as the *Piagetian approach*. People who take this approach look at universal patterns of qualitative changes in the development of intelligence.

Psychometric Approach SPEARMAN: TWO-FACTOR THEORY An important debate among those taking the **psychometric approach** concerns the question whether intelligence is an overall general ability or a number of specific abilities. One of the earliest theorists, Charles Spearman (1904), proposed a **two-factor theory** of intelligence that explained intelligence as consisting of general intelligence and specific abilities. Spearman considered the g factor (general intelligence) much more important than specific abilities and characterized it as an inherited intellectual capacity

Psychometric approach *Orientation to the study of individual differences in the quantity of intelligence that emphasizes measurement using tests derived from factor-analytical statistical techniques.*

Two-factor theory *Spearman's theory that intelligence consists of two kinds of factors: the g factor (general intelligence), an inherited intellectual capacity which influences all-around performance; and several s factors (specific abilities), which account for the differences between scores on different tasks.*

that influences all-around performance. He maintained that several *s* factors (specific abilities) account for the differences between scores on different tasks—say, verbal and mathematical. Spearman developed the technique of factor analysis to isolate and compare these different factors. He justified the division into *g* and *s* factors by pointing to a common phenomenon: people who score high on one kind of test usually do well on others, but their scores on various abilities do differ somewhat.

THURSTONE: PRIMARY MENTAL ABILITIES   Using factor analysis on intelligence test scores of a large number of children, L. L. Thurstone (1938) identified seven **primary mental abilities.** These relatively distinct factors are, (1) *word fluency* (ability to think of words rapidly); (2) *verbal comprehension* (ability to define words); (3) *space* (ability to recognize a figure whose position in space has been changed); (4) *perceptual speed* (ability to detect similarities and differences between designs); (5) *reasoning* (logical thought); (6) *numbers;* and (7) *memory.* Thurstone maintained that these seven abilities were largely independent and that there was, therefore, no need to think in terms of an overall general (*g*) factor.

GUILFORD: STRUCTURE-OF-INTELLECT THEORY   J. P. Guilford (1959, 1982) believes that intelligence is much too complex to be discussed in terms of either a single *g* factor or even a few primary mental abilities, as Spearman and Thurstone did. He took factor analysis several steps further and developed a three-dimensional, cube-shaped model of intelligence made up of some 120 separate factors and called **structure of intellect.** Guilford recently expanded this model to include 150 factors. These separate factors result from the interaction of *operations* (the ways we think), *contents* (what we think about), and *products* (results of applying a certain operation to a certain content, or thinking a certain way about a certain subject). (See Figure 7-1.)

Primary mental abilities *Thurstone's theory of intelligence, which identified seven relatively distinct factors.*

Structure of intellect *Model of intelligence proposed by Guilford, according to which intelligence is the result of the interaction of operations, contents, and products.*

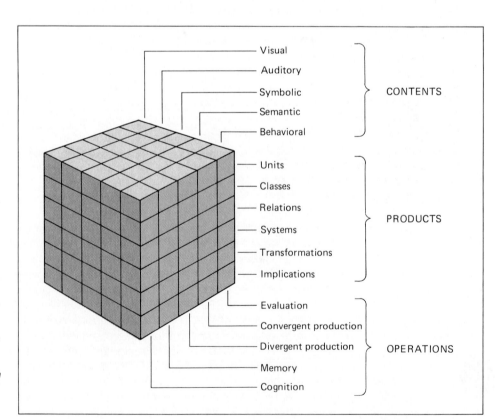

FIGURE 7-1 *Guilford's structure-of-intellect model. Guilford has proposed that there are 150 intelligence factors, resulting from an interaction of operations, contents, and products. (Source: Guilford, 1977.)*

CATTELL AND HORN: "FLUID" AND "CRYSTALLIZED" INTELLIGENCE   R. B. Cattell (1965) and J. L. Horn (1978) account for the large number of mental abilities described by Thurstone and Guilford by classifying them into two broad categories of intelligence, which they call *fluid* and *crystallized*. Suppose you are asked to group letters and numbers according to some criterion, to pair related words, to remember a series of digits, or to insert the next item in a logical sequence. The kind of intelligence you use for these tasks—to figure out relations between two different items or concepts, to form concepts in the first place, to reason, or to abstract—is **fluid intelligence**. These problems are novel for everyone taking a test, but their content (using letters, numbers, or shapes, for example) is familiar to everyone in a particular culture. These items, then, are supposed to be "culture-fair." (See Figure 7-2 for an example of a measure of fluid intelligence.)

Fluid intelligence is considered to be dependent on neurological development and relatively free from the influences of education and culture. It reaches its peak in the late teens and begins a slow, steady decline in the twenties. This decline, however, usually does not have much practical significance until late in life, because most people learn to compensate, often simply by allowing a little more time to solve these kinds of problems.

The other kind of intelligence in this theory—**crystallized intelligence**—involves the ability to use an accumulated body of general information to make judgments and solve problems. This kind of information has to be specially learned and is, therefore, dependent on education, experience, and culture. It includes knowing such things as the meanings of words, the customs of Peruvian Indians, and the proper fork to use at a formal dinner. Crystallized intelligence generally increases throughout the life span, until nearly the end of life. In fact, recent research on age differences in "world knowledge" (names of world leaders, signs of danger in the street, and so forth) found that people in their seventies remembered such information better than young and middle-aged adults (Lachman & Lachman, cited in Goleman, 1984a). (See Figure 7-3.)

Students of intelligence who emphasize the processes that go on in human thought criticize the factor-analytical models on a number of grounds (Sternberg, 1985b). For one thing, those models don't tell us *how* people arrive at their solutions to problems. Two people could attack a problem in totally different ways, or could get different answers right on the same intelligence test, and yet both might receive identical scores. Second, methodological difficulties with the factor-analytical techniques make it very hard to test one theory against another. Furthermore, factor

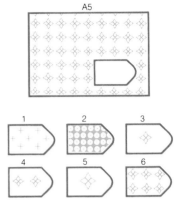

FIGURE 7-2   *This test item is a measure of fluid intelligence, since it represents a novel task that does not ostensibly depend on knowledge. Even without instructions, you can understand what you're supposed to do. However, if you come from a culture in which fill-in or matching exercises are common, you may do better on tests like this than people from other cultures. (Source: J. C. Raven, 1983.)*

Fluid intelligence   *Ability to solve novel problems; this kind of intelligence is influenced by neurological development.*

Crystallized intelligence   *Ability to use information that has been learned; this kind of intelligence is influenced by culture and education.*

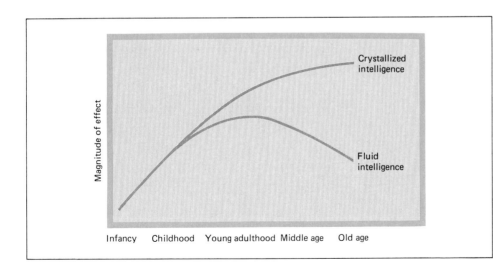

FIGURE 7-3   *Changes occur in two types of intelligence over a life span. While there is a decline in "fluid intelligence," there is a gradual increase through old age in "crystallized intelligence." (Source: Horn & Donaldson, 1980.)*

analysis depends not on defining intelligence as an entity of itself, but on looking for individual differences among test takers. One critic has asked whether identical twins, growing up together on a desert island, would ever give rise to the notion of intelligence if their mental abilities were exactly the same (McNemar, 1964, cited in Sternberg, 1985b). Two new approaches to intelligence, approaches that are not based on factor analysis, are Gardner's theory of multiple intelligences and Sternberg's triarchic model.

Two New Approaches GARDNER'S THEORY OF MULTIPLE INTELLIGENCES A new way to look at intelligence is provided by the ***multiple-intelligences theory*** of Howard Gardner (1985). While Gardner sharply disagrees with the previous theorists, does not use factor analysis, and deemphasizes measurement, his approach does have one major point in common with these other theories: the idea that intelligence is composed of a number of different specific abilities. Gardner also believes that until now intelligence has been defined too narrowly. He defines it as the "ability to solve problems, or to create products, that are valued within one or more cultural settings."

> **Multiple-intelligences theory**
> *Gardner's theory that intelligence consists of seven independent "intelligences" which involve the ability to solve problems or create products valued within one or more cultural settings.*

Gardner maintains that human beings have at least seven separate intelligences, each relatively independent of the others. They are: (1) linguistic (reading, writing); (2) logical-mathematical (using numbers, solving logical problems); (3) spatial (finding one's way around an environment); (4) musical (perceiving and creating patterns of pitch and rhythm); (5) bodily-kinesthetic (making precise movements, as in surgery or dance); (6) interpersonal (understanding others); and (7) intrapersonal (knowing oneself). In discussing musical intelligence, for example, he points to the emphasis in some cultures, such as the Japanese, on teaching large numbers of people, including very young children, to play musical instruments very well, and he explains the high rate of "musical illiteracy" in our society as the result of our schools' lack of interest in teaching musical competence. Gardner also emphasizes neurological underpinnings for these less traditional intelligences, along with those for the ones we are used to thinking of as aspects of intelligence.

Other theorists (Sternberg, 1985b) have questioned whether some of these abilities (specifically, musical, bodily-kinesthetic, interpersonal, and intrapersonal abilities) can properly be called *intelligences;* and Sternberg (1985b) charges that factor analysis has shown that at least some of the seven intelligences are not distinct from

(Alain Keler/Sygma)

Playing the violin at a very early age is not considered remarkable among the Japanese. They believe that everyone can learn to play an instrument, and they teach young children how to do it, using instruments specially sized for their little hands. The high rate of "musical illiteracy" in the United States may result from the fact that we do not consider musical competence a kind of intelligence.

one another (for example, that logical-mathematical and spatial abilities are so strongly related that it is hard to test for them separately). However, Gardner's theory does broaden the concept of intelligence beyond the traditional areas of linguistic, logical-mathematical, and spatial abilities.

STERNBERG'S TRIARCHIC MODEL Sternberg's very different way of looking at intelligence is currently challenging traditional views. Sternberg (1985a) conceptualizes intelligence as a triangle with three separate but interrelated "sides." His **triarchic theory of intelligence** is, accordingly, composed of three parts: an ability to analyze information to solve problems (componential), a creative ability that incorporates insight and new ideas (experiential), and a practical side that lets us size up a situation and succeed in the real world (contextual). While we are all influenced by all three parts, some of us are stronger in one aspect than another. Let's see what is involved in these three faces of intelligence.

Componential element The componential aspect of intelligence is its analytical, information-processing "side." This is what we use in approaching a problem, in deciding how to go about solving it, in monitoring ourselves as we're solving it, and then in evaluating our approach. If you're especially strong in this element, you're likely to be good at taking intelligence tests (especially doing problems like analogies). You're also a critical thinker who can spot strengths and the weaknesses in other people's arguments.

Experiential element The experiential element is the creative "side" of the intelligence triangle. It is the "aha!" ability—the ability to use insight and come up with new ideas. It incorporates the ability to separate relevant from irrelevant information, to put important facts together, and to blend new information with what you already know, allowing you to look at things in a new way. If you're strong in this element, you can look at a body of scientific data that other people have noted—but you're the one who comes up with an original theory. Or you might be a computer expert who comes up with a new way to program a machine, a therapist who hits upon an innovative strategy for helping a troubled client.

Contextual element Suppose that you're not "smart" in the first sense or creative in the second. You can still go far in the real world—maybe further than people who excel in the first two elements—if you're strong in the contextual element. This is the practical side of intelligence, the ability to learn from experience. You can size up a situation, figure out what you have to do to succeed, and go ahead and do it. You have "tacit knowledge": you know the kinds of things that are rarely taught, such as what kind of work is "hot" in your field, which people can help you, and how to get them to help. You know how to deal with everyday problems—like selecting an apartment and a roommate, or getting to work during a transit strike—and you apply this kind of commonsense approach to getting things done on higher levels, too.

The force behind the triarchic theory of intelligence is the expansive view it takes of different important abilities that, in varying combinations, help people achieve their goals. Sternberg has found that people can actually be taught to strengthen their abilities in all three areas, and he has begun to develop tests based on this theory to identify areas that individual test takers need to concentrate on. Some of these tests are discussed later in the chapter.

Piagetian Approach While the psychometric approach tries to quantify intelligence and measure individual differences, the **Piagetian approach** is concerned with universal patterns of intellectual functioning. Jean Piaget, whom you will be reading more about in Chapter 9, devised an elaborate theory of the way children acquire knowledge about the world and learn to solve logical problems. Piaget was inter-

Triarchic theory of intelligence Sternberg's theory describing three types of intelligence: componential (analytical ability), experiential (insight and creativity), and contextual (practical knowledge).

Piagetian approach Theory of intellectual development that describes qualitative changes in thinking which are typical of children of particular ages.

ested in discovering how intelligence is displayed by people in different stages of life, from infancy through adolescence. He described four stages of cognitive development which he regarded as universal (occurring in all normal people) and invariant (occurring in the same sequence in everyone).

Object permanence *Realization that an object or person continues to exist even if it can no longer be seen.*

Piaget stressed the adaptive nature of intelligence, the way it enables people to master their environment. He noted the way children who have not yet learned how to understand language show by their adaptive behavior that they are intelligent. One adaptive concept developed between 12 and 18 months of age is ***object permanence***, the realization that an object (or person) continues to exist even when out of sight. A number of standardized scales have been developed to measure the acquisition of such concepts, and one of these, Uzgiris and Hunt's Infant Psychological Development Scale, seems to predict intelligence later in childhood fairly well. Such scales represent a merger of the psychometric and Piagetian approaches.

Probably all these different approaches contribute something to our understanding of intelligence. At this point, however, it is hard to know which of these ways of looking at intelligence tells us most about its nature. The issue is significant, since the way this elusive quality is defined dictates the kinds of techniques that will be developed to test it. These techniques have changed over the years, and at present some exciting new ones are appearing that are consistent with some of the new ways of describing intelligence.

INTELLIGENCE TESTING

A Historical Overview

Most intelligence testing as we know it today is based on the psychometric approach. In recent years intelligence testing has become such a controversial political issue that it is hard to remember that such testing was born in the mid-nineteenth century out of an interest in the humane treatment of institutionalized retarded and disturbed persons in the United States and Europe.

Early Contributors The first intelligence tests were devised by two French physicians, of whom one emphasized verbal ability and the other stressed such performance tasks as inserting different-shaped blocks into holes in a board (Esquirol, 1838; Séquin, 1866/1907). Later in the century, Sir Francis Galton (1883), an English biologist who believed strongly that intelligence was inherited and that keen sensory discrimination held the key to intelligence, developed various measures such as the Galton bar (to estimate length visually) and the Galton whistle (to judge highest audible pitch).

Another important early contributor was the American psychologist James McKeen Cattell, who in 1890 coined the term *mental test.* He developed easily administered tests that focused on such simple tasks as reaction time, word association, keenness of vision, and weight discrimination. Since scores on his tests did not predict college grades, as Cattell had hoped, the tests were forgotten. Their failure apparently lay in the fact that the tasks were not complex enough to measure intelligence.

(National Library of Medicine)

Alfred Binet, pioneer in the study of intelligence.

Alfred Binet Not until 1905 did intelligence testing as we know it become part of the educational scene. At that time, school administrators in Paris wanted to relieve overcrowding by removing from class those children who didn't have the mental capacity to benefit from an academic education. Because of a new law, however, all children, including retarded children, were required to have several years of public education (Fancher, 1985). The psychologist Alfred Binet was asked to devise a test to identify children who could benefit from special help, outside the regular schools.

A variation of this test, devised by Binet and his colleague Theophile Simon, is still widely used.

Binet invented the term *mental level* to express a child's test score. This level, later widely called **mental age,** corresponded to the age of the normal children who had received a similar score on these items during the preparation of the test. Binet and Simon had given the tests they had devised to large numbers of normal children between the ages of 3 and 13. A child who passed all the test items that had been passed by 80 to 90 percent of the normal 3-year-olds in the standardization groups would be considered to have a mental age of 3. (*Standardization* is explained later in this chapter.) Binet did not regard intelligence as fixed and urged that students who did poorly on his test be given "mental orthopedics" (compensatory training) to increase their intelligence.

The term *IQ* (for **intelligence quotient**) was devised later to translate mental age into a number that could be used for all age groups. IQ is the ratio of a person's mental age (MA) to chronological age (CA) multiplied by 100. The equation looks like this:

$$IQ = \frac{MA}{CA} \times 100$$

When mental age is the same as chronological age, the IQ of the test taker is 100, which is average; when mental age is greater than chronological age, the IQ is over 100; and when mental age is less than chronological age, the IQ is under 100. Thus:

■ A 10-year-old child (CA = 10) whose test score yields a mental age of 10 years (MA = 10) has an IQ of 100.

■ A 10-year-old (CA = 10) who scores a mental age of 8 (MA = 8) has an IQ of 80.

■ A 10-year-old (CA = 10) who scores a mental age of 12 (MA = 12) has an IQ of 120.

The distribution of IQ scores in general population takes the form of a bell-shaped curve. That is, the great majority of scores will cluster around the middle, with fewer and fewer at either end. (See Figure 7-4.)

Mental age *Assessment of intellectual ability, determined by administering an intelligence test and matching the test taker's score with the average age of those who have scored similarly during the standardization of the test.*

Intelligence quotient (IQ) *Mathematical score computed by dividing an individual's mental age (MA) by his or her chronological age (CA) and then multiplying by 100: IQ = (MA/CA) × 100.*

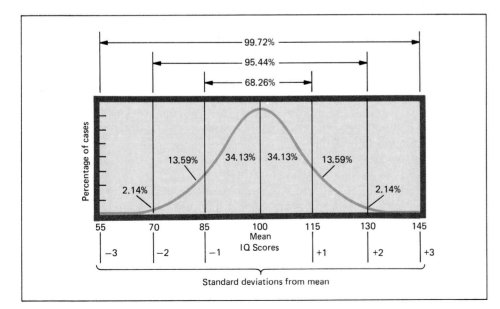

FIGURE 7-4 *Percentage distribution of cases in a normal curve. In a normal distribution of IQ scores, most of the population falls in the middle range of scores; extremely high and extremely low scores are rare. This curve indicates that on an IQ test with a mean (average score) of 100 and a standard deviation of 15, 68.26 percent of the population have IQs between 85 and 115; 95.44 percent of the population have IQs between 70 and 130, and 99.72 percent of the population have IQ scores between 55 and 145.*

Deviation IQ   One problem with this traditional calculation of IQ was that the same IQ did not mean the same thing at different ages, because the variability in scores is not the same at all age levels. For example, an IQ of 110 might have meant that the test taker in one age group (say 7-year-olds) was superior to 84 percent of his or her peers, but in another age group (say, 10-year-olds), an IQ of 115 might be required for that degree of superiority.

To deal with this problem, David Wechsler, who developed a number of important IQ tests that we discuss later in this chapter, developed the "deviation IQ." To understand what this means, we must first understand the concept of standard deviation. **Standard deviation** is a measure of variability of scores. It is defined as the square root of the average squared deviation around the mean. In the preceding example, let's say that the standard deviation for 7-year-olds is 10 and that the standard deviation for 10-year-olds is 15. As we pointed out, it might take a higher IQ score (115) for a 10-year-old to maintain the same position in relation to peers (1 standard deviation above the mean—superior to 84 percent), then it would for a 7-year-old (who requires an IQ of only 110).

Wechsler converted scores attained at any age so that they always had a mean of 100 and a standard deviation of 15. Thus, at any age, a subject had to attain a score of 115 to be superior to 84 percent of his or her peers. Now, both 7- and 10-year-olds need IQs of 115 to be 1 standard deviation above average, that is, to be superior to 84 percent of their peers. Where does the "84 percent" come from? If you look at Figure 7-4, you will see that an IQ score of 115 is superior to the scores at lower levels. Adding up the percentages in these four lower-level blocks (2.14+13.59+34.13+34.13) yields a total of 83.99, rounded off to 84.

Subsequent Tests   The Binet-Simon tests set the stage for all the intelligence tests that were to follow, even though subsequent tests differ in a number of ways. For one thing, all the Binet-Simon tests were administered only to individuals, but significant growth in IQ testing came with the development of group tests at the time of World War I. The term *mental age* and *IQ* captured the fancy of the public, as well as the psychological profession, and the heavily verbal content of these tests influenced the nature of most other tests, even though nonverbal tasks have been used increasingly in recent years.

Binet's tests leaped the English Channel and the Atlantic Ocean and became widely used in Great Britain and the United States. Lewis Terman, a psychologist at Stanford University, revised them; the result became known as the *Stanford-Binet Intelligence Scale* and was standardized on American children. Since 1916, the Stanford-Binet has been revised and updated several times, most recently in 1985, but after three-quarters of the century some of the original items are still included.

Intelligence Testing Today

Before we take up some of the hotly debated political and philosophical issues regarding intelligence testing, we'll focus on its more technical aspects—kinds of tests in most common use, strengths and weaknesses of each kind, and (to begin with) criteria for developing both intelligence and personality tests. (We'll talk specifically about personality tests in Chapter 13.)

Developing Tests   TEST CONSTRUCTION AND STANDARDIZATION   Constructors of a test must first decide what they want it to evaluate and predict. They then develop a large pool of items that seem to fit their purpose, inventing new items, or adapting items that have been used in other tests, or both. Construction and **standardization** go hand in hand in these early stages. Constructors standardize a test by developing uniform procedures for both giving and scoring it. To make the testing situation as identical as possible for all subjects, testers give the same directions, the same materials, and the same demonstrations; impose the same time limits; and so forth.

Standard deviation   Measure of variability of scores; the square root of the average squared deviation around the mean.

Standardization   In test construction, development of procedures for giving and scoring a test; test items are administered to a large group of subjects representative of the population for whom the test is intended in order to determine the distribution of test scores.

Test constructors try out their prospective items on a group of subjects like the ones for whom they are devising the test. (If the test is supposed to predict the ability of ghetto children to benefit from an educational program, for example, it would be given to a sample of children from an inner city, not to a group from a wealthy suburb.) They analyze the answers from the sample group, keeping the items that differentiate among people of different abilities and discarding the ones that do not. The final step involves giving the refined test to a different group—a large, representative group known as the *standardization sample.*

At this point the test designers establish **norms,** so that they can standardize scoring. A norm is a normal or average performance. The average performance in the standardization sample is determined to get a basic norm, and then the frequency of deviations around this average is calculated to assess the superiority or inferiority of other scores. Norms, then, are standards of performance.

Norms *Standards of test performance.*

RELIABILITY   A test is *reliable* when it is consistent in measuring the performance of an individual or a group. How do we calculate **reliability?**

The most common way of calculating reliability is to give the same person or group the same test more than once **(test-retest reliability)**. However, consistency between scores can be undermined by a number of different factors, including differences in testing conditions or in the physical circumstances of the test taker. If you're in a quiet room one time and a noisy one the next, or if you're tired on one occasion and alert on another, your scores are likely to be fairly different from time to time. Another factor that creates problems with calculating reliability by retesting is practice. People are likely to do better on the test the second time they take it, because they have become familiar with the general aims of the test, the principles underlying the items, or the actual items themselves, or simply because they feel more comfortable in the testing situation.

Reliability *Consistency of a test in measuring the performance of an individual or a group.*
Test-retest reliability *Degree of similarity in scores when a test is given to the same person or group more than once.*

Therefore, testers often use other ways to establish reliability. One way is to develop **parallel forms** of a test, alternative forms which are very similar, but not identical, in format, content, and level of difficulty. Instructions must also be comparable. This eliminates the possibility that a subject will become familiar with specific items, but it does not get around the effects of practice in taking this *kind* of test. Another method is **split-half reliability.** Split-half reliability can be calculated after a single administration of the test, by seeing how a test taker did on half the test items compared with the other half. Usually the test is split according to odd- and even-numbered items. This procedure gives a measure of the test's internal consistency.

Parallel forms *Alternative versions of a test which are so similar that they should yield similar scores; a way to measure reliability.*

Split-half reliability *Degree of similarity in scores on half of the items in a test compared with the other half.*

VALIDITY   A test is *valid* if it measures what it is supposed to measure, as judged by how well scores on the test correlate with other measures.

One kind of **validity** is **content validity**—a test's ability to show a broad picture of whatever you want to measure. For example, a final exam in psychology has content validity if it covers everything the course covered, rather than only one or two topics. It is much easier to determine content validity for achievement tests, like final exams, than for intelligence tests, which cannot draw on a particular course of instruction or on basic content.

Validity *Degree to which a test measures what it is supposed to measure.*
Content validity *Degree to which a test covers a representative sample of the material under consideration.*

Criterion-related validity measures the relationship between test performance and some outcome that is completely independent of the test; that is, one does not affect the other. Criteria vary, depending on individual tests and what they measure. The two types of criterion validity are *concurrent* and *predictive*. Concurrent validity is related to test performance and a situation in the present (for example, a child's IQ and his or her present classroom grades). Predictive validity looks at the relationship between test performance and some future situation (like scores on the Scholastic Aptitude Tests taken in high school and grades during the first year of college).

Criterion-related validity *Measure of the relationship between test performance and some independent outcome (criterion).*

DO INTELLIGENCE TESTS MEASURE APTITUDE OR ACHIEVEMENT?   If you were to encounter an analogy in an intelligence test ("Hat is to head as shoe is to _____"), what would it measure? Would it measure reasoning ability? Yes, it would. Would it measure your ability to determine relevant information? Yes, it would. Would it measure your ability to see relationships among different items? Yes, it would. All these are elements of aptitude, or general intelligence. Would it also measure what you had learned? Yes, again, it would. In this very simple analogy, you would need to know what a hat and a shoe are and how they are ordinarily used. This kind of question requires a certain base of learning, even though the learning may be so universal in your culture that you can't imagine anyone not having it. It seems, then, that as far as analogies are concerned, intelligence tests measure *both* aptitude and achievement—and we could draw the same conclusion about other types of items in intelligence test.

Developers of intelligence tests have usually aimed at measuring unlearned ability. However, R. J. Sternberg (1979) refers—somewhat ironically—to "a bit of conventional wisdom among those in the field" that achievement tests measure what you have learned recently, while IQ tests measure what you learned in the more distant past (p. 47).

Once it is recognized that the items on most traditional intelligence tests reflect to a great extent what we have learned, a question arises: Who are "we"? Here, *we* is generally taken to mean members of the dominant culture in the United States—middle- and upper-middle-class whites. Because these tests may be biased in favor of members of the dominant culture (among other reasons), many efforts have been made to assess "pure" unlearned intelligence, but so far it has not been possible to separate what people might be capable of learning from what they have already learned. Later in this chapter, we'll talk about some of the new ways psychologists are tackling this challenge.

Tests in Use Today   You might have had your intelligence measured on a test designed specifically for infants, for children, or for adults. You might be tested as an individual or in a group. (Individual tests are used primarily in clinical settings, in conjunction with counseling or therapy; group tests are used for mass screening, primarily in educational, military, and business settings.) You might have your motor ability or your verbal ability tested—or both. We'll take a look at some of the traditional measures of intelligence, and then at several new kinds of tests whose designers are responding to some of the criticisms of current testing practices.

STANFORD-BINET INTELLIGENCE SCALE   Still given as an individual test to one person at a time, the Stanford-Binet is used primarily for children, although it may also be given to adults. It takes about 30 to 45 minutes to test a child and up to 1½ hours to test an adult. Test takers at different age levels have to answer six items at each level (except for the "average adult," who is given eight items), but no one is expected to answer all the items. Many test items tap verbal abilities at all age levels beyond infancy, with items involving vocabulary, analogies, interpretation of proverbs, and so forth.

The examiner begins by presenting items on a level slightly below the expected mental ability of the person taking the test. If the examiner has misjudged, and the subject has trouble with any of these initial items, the examiner drops back and gives the subject easier items. Eventually a "floor," or basal age, is established—a level at which the person passes all items. The examiner then goes through higher levels until a level is reached at which the person fails all items; once this ceiling age is reached, testing stops. The IQ is the subject's basal age plus "credit," in months, for items passed above this.

Generally, a person's IQ is considered roughly equal to those in a range of 10 points higher or lower, since one person's score may vary that much from test to test. While some guidelines have been developed to interpret IQ scores, there are no hard and fast rules. Many people with average IQs have made outstanding achievements, while some at the extreme upper levels do not distinguish themselves at all. On the low end of the scale, retardation is defined by the way a person acts, as well as by IQ.

It is important to remember that IQ can be modified. Changes in environment often produce changes in IQ scores, as we'll see when we discuss the influence of environment on intelligence.

The Stanford-Binet test is very reliable, especially for older test takers (school-children, adolescents, and young adults, as compared with very young children) and for people at the lower end of the IQ scale. It is impressively valid in predicting achievement in school: IQ scores correlate significantly with high school and college grades: they correlate highly with grades in verbal courses like English and history, and moderately with grades in courses like biology and geometry. These correlations (ranging from .40 to .60) are not surprising, since this test was originally developed to predict success in school.

A correlation does not, of course, need to be a perfect (1.0) in order to have meaning. But when correlations are less than perfect, as these are, it appears that performance in school is also influenced by other factors, such as nutrition, child-rearing practices, motivation, teachers' expectations, and educational opportunities.

Compelling evidence that even this well-standardized, popular test does not measure "pure" intelligence can be seen in changes in test takers' scores over the many years it has been administered. Test takers of all ages have been doing better on the test in recent years, with improvements especially notable among preschoolers and those age 15 and older (Anastasi, 1976). A person who scores 100 now has passed more items than one who scored 100 in 1937. The higher scores of adolescent and adult test takers probably reflect increased years of education for this age group. The higher scores of young children may be related to increasing literacy and higher educational levels of parents, as well as the impact of radio and educational television on the children themselves.

WECHSLER SCALES   David Wechsler originally developed his own test because he considered the Stanford-Binet too oriented toward children, even with the addition of more difficult items geared to adults. As he put it, "Asking . . . an ex-army sergeant to give you a sentence with the words, 'boy,' 'river,' 'ball,' is not particularly apt to evoke either interest or respect" (1939, p. 17). He first developed a test for adults (1939, 1955, 1981), then one for schoolchildren (1958, 1974), and finally one for preschoolers. All three contain two separate scales—verbal and performance—which yield separate scores as well as a full-scale IQ. This approach allows us to analyze test scores to see precisely where someone may excel or be behind most other people. It also overcomes some of the objections to the heavily verbal content of tests like the early versions of the Stanford-Binet.

Wechsler Adult Intelligence Scale (WAIS-R)   WAIS-R (the *R* stands for *revised*, and the most recent revision was in 1981) contains six verbal subtests (Information, Comprehension, Arithmetic, Similarities, Digit Span, and Vocabulary) and five performances subtests (Digit Symbol, Picture Completion, Block Design, Picture Arrangement, and Object Assembly); see Table 7-3 (page 242).

WAIS-R includes specially developed norms for adults and the elderly and is very reliable. It is valid on several measures, including relationship to job category (white-collar workers do better in verbal IQ, while skilled workers do better in performance IQ) and prediction of work adjustment for mental retardates released from institutions (Anastasi, 1976). Table 7-4 (page 243) shows the distribution of overall IQ scores on this test in a standardization sample of adults. You can see that the great majority of people attain scores in the middle ranges. Only about 26 percent of the people in this sample have scores of 110 or over, the range usually considered to reflect that of the college population. This distribution of IQ scores is valid only for WAIS-R; it does not necessarily apply to other IQ tests.

(© Sepp Seitz/Woodfin Camp)

A psychologist administers the Block Design Test, a subtest of the Wechsler Adult Intelligence Scale (WAIS). This is one of five performance and six verbal subtests, which yield separate verbal performance scores, as well as a full-scale IQ.

TABLE 7-3 VERBAL AND PERFORMANCE SUBTESTS OF THE WAIS-R

Verbal Scale

Subtest	Ability Tested	Sample Questions
1 Information	Factual knowledge	How many senators are there in the United States Senate? What was Marie Curie famous for?
2 Digit span	Memory for a series of numbers	*Digit forward:* Subject repeats numbers in the order presented ("2–7–5–8–6–2–5–8–4"). *Digit backward:* Subject repeats numbers in reverse order of presentation.
3 Vocabulary	Knowledge of word meanings	What do the following words mean? "Enormous . . . obstruct . . . tirade."
4 Arithmetic	Ability to solve math problems in one's head	How many hours will it take a person to walk 24 miles at the rate of 3 miles per hour?
5 Comprehension	Understanding social rules and conventions; understanding familiar sayings	Why do people pay taxes? What does this saying mean? "One swallow doesn't make a summer."
6 Similarities	Detecting relationships	In what way are a poem and a statue alike?

Performance Scale

Subtest	Ability Tested	Sample Questions
1 Picture completion	Identifying important details; recognizing familiar objects	Determine missing parts in pictures such as a door without a doorknob and a female profile with no eyebrow.
2 Picture arrangement	Understanding a social or cultural situation	Put a set of pictures in a logical sequence to tell a story. In one, subject must arrange pictures to show work on a house, from beginning to end.
3 Block design	Perceiving forms; eye-hand coordination	Using actual blocks, reproduce a series of block designs pictured on cards.
4 Object assembly	Analysis by sight; assembly skill; grasp of relationship between whole and parts	Arrange pieces of jigsaw puzzles correctly (including manikin, profile, hand, and elephant).
5 Digit symbol	Learning new task; visual and motor dexterity; speed and accuracy	Use a coding system in which symbols represent numbers.

Note: By examining the individual scores on these eleven subtests, psychologists can determine a test taker's strengths and weaknesses, can prescribe special remediation in particular areas, and can make predictions about aptitudes for particular activities.
Source: Wechsler, 1981.

TABLE 7-4 INTELLIGENCE CLASSIFICATIONS ON WAIS-R

IQ	Classification	Percent Included in Standardization Sample
130 and above	Very superior	2.6
120–129	Superior	6.9
110–119	High average	16.6
90–109	Average	49.1
80–89	Low average	16.1
70–79	Borderline	6.4
69 and below	Mentally retarded	2.3

Note: This table shows distribution of IQ scores on WAIS-R (full-scale IQ) and classifications at each level. Percentages in the last column indicate proportion of people in the standardization sample of 1880 adults that scored in each category. Source: Adapted from Wechsler, 1981.

Wechsler Intelligence Scale for Children (WISC-R) WISC-R (revised in 1974) is tailored for children age 6 to 16. It has separate verbal and performance scales that let us identify problems with language development (when the verbal score is much lower than the performance score) or with perceptual and motor development (when the performance score is much lower). Its reliability is good. The verbal items are very similar to those on the Stanford-Binet, and so WISC IQ correlates highly with Stanford-Binet IQ and gives rise to the same charges of cultural bias against test takers from low socioeconomic groups.

Wechsler Preschool and Primary Scale of Intelligence (WPPSI) WPPSI is used with children from 4 to 6½ years old, takes about 1 hour, and is sometimes given in two separate sessions, since young children are distracted easily and tire out soon. Reliability is good on this test, too, although it has not been revised since 1967. There is some relationship with socioeconomic status, since children of professionals score higher than children of unskilled workers (Anastasi, 1976).

GROUP TESTS As the United States entered World War I, the American Psychological Association (APA) pressured the government to administer group intelligence tests to all recruits. The immediate rationale was to help place soldiers in appropriate jobs. But for the APA, which not only administered but also developed the tests, the major incentive was to generate data on large numbers of people and to advance the "science" of intelligence testing. The written Alpha test was given to recruits who could read and write, and the performance-type Beta test was administered to recruits who were illiterate or did not speak English. The tests did not help in job placement (except for screening recruits out of officer training), but they did generate a mass of data on some 3 million people. Although the use of scores achieved on these tests led to many abuses, the tests themselves became models for the group tests that most of us have encountered in school and in applying for jobs, and that many people have encountered in the armed services.

They have several drawbacks, though. For one thing, that clinical interpretation, which takes time on an individual test, gives the examiner an opportunity to establish rapport and to use clinical insight in assessing test takers' ability. This opportunity is not available with group testing. Thus preschoolers, who need rapport with the examiner, cannot be tested in a group.

The best thing about group tests is that they can be administered quickly and easily. Also, good norms are generally provided for their scores, and they do not require the kind of clinical interpretation that individual tests call for.

Furthermore, the multiple-choice nature of most group tests penalizes creative thinkers who offer a different slant on questions and provide unusual answers. One high school student in Cocoa Beach, Florida, who correctly solved a geometry prob-

Question:

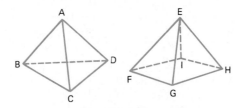

44. In pyramids ABCD and EFGHI shown above, all faces except base FGHI are equilateral triangles of equal size. If face ABC were placed on face EFG so that the vertices of the triangles coincide, how many exposed faces would the resulting solid have?

(A) Five   (B) Six   (C) Seven
(D) Eight   (E) Nine

Discussion of solution:

Depending on whether the faces considered are those of the original two solids or those of the combined solid, both choices (A) Five and (C) Seven have merit as correct answers. When the question was originally scored, only choice C was considered correct. Although seven of the original faces remain exposed, the solid that results if face ABC is placed on face EFG contains but five distinguishable faces. Some of the faces of the original figures (for example, faces ABD and EGH in the diagram below) lie in the same plane and form a parallelogram when the solids are placed together. The diagram provides an illustration.

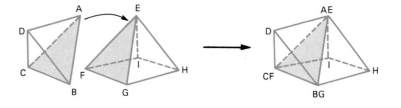

FIGURE 7-5 *Problem on the Preliminary Scholastic Aptitude Test and Daniel Lowen's solution. (Source: Educational Testing Service.)*

lem on the Preliminary Scholastic Aptitude Test (PSAT) had his answer marked "wrong." He appealed the decision and won—and the Educational Testing Service was forced to raise the scores of 240,000 other students as well (Fiske, 1981); see Figure 7-5. This story had a happy ending, but there are undoubtedly many more cases when a question is ambiguous, a student is not given credit for an unusual answer, and no one questions the decision.

What's Right—or Wrong—with Intelligence Testing?   The controversies over intelligence testing are as stormy as those between advocates of gun control and the National Rifle Association. Are the tests themselves all right for certain specified purposes but dangerous when used in the wrong way by the wrong people? Or is the whole concept of intelligence testing as we know it a mistake that is bound to have unfavorable consequences for society? Let's take a look at the basis for some of the arguments for and against testing.

THE VALUE OF TESTING INTELLIGENCE   There are many situations in which it is useful to have some method of predicting academic performance. Intelligence tests do this quite well. Test scores can alert parents and teachers to the fact that a child will need special help, can suggest the extent of that help, and sometimes can indicate what kind of help will be most useful. High school students' performance on intelligence tests can help them decide which colleges to apply to—and can help a college decide whether a student will be able to keep up with the level of work it requires. IQ tests provide one way to establish whether a special educational program—like Head Start, which was designed for children from economically disadvantaged families—improves children's performance enough to justify the necessary expenditures of effort and money. Sometimes such tests are used to provide opportunities by identifying and offering scholarships to gifted youngsters whose families cannot afford to send them to college or are not educationally oriented and might not even consider the possibility.

IQ tests have a number of strengths that help them accomplish these aims. They are well-standardized instruments whose norms, validity, and reliability are well established. They are readily available and often easy to give. Since many researchers have used them, results in any given situation can be compared with those in other studies. At the moment, they are the best available predictor of school performance and the best available measure of mental retardation.

Testing does have many valid and socially beneficial uses, then. But we need to be aware of a number of problems in the tests themselves and in the ways they are sometimes misused or misinterpreted.

SOME PROBLEMS WITH INTELLIGENCE TESTS   There *is* life after school. One would not, however, know this from most intelligence tests. These tests most often measure the kinds of abilities that we use in doing schoolwork, ask questions related to the kinds of information and skills we have learned in the classroom, and bear little or no relevance to the world beyond school and the situations we are likely to encounter in daily life. Furthermore, the score on a test does not tell us about how the mind actually works to solve a problem, or where in the process a person may excel or falter. Finally, individual test scores do not tell us about a person's potential for growth (Gardner, 1985). Two people may attain the same score at one time in their lives, and yet go on to two entirely different levels of accomplishment and intellectual fulfillment, as we'll see later in this chapter when we discuss the careers of a number of bright children who were followed through adulthood.

MISUSE OF INTELLIGENCE TESTS   Intelligence tests can be, and have been, misused in several ways. It is sometimes held, for example, that they are used to justify certain forms of racial discrimination; educators and others have frequently overrelied on them; and they tend to underestimate the intelligence of the elderly and of handicapped children. These problems are discussed in the following paragraphs.

"Rationalization" of racial discrimination   Ever since the 1920s, when Terman found that Spanish-Indian, Mexican, and black test takers tended to score in the 70-to-80 IQ range, one expert after another has used this information to maintain that intelligence levels are inborn and unchangeable, and that test scores demonstrate the superiority of whites over everyone else. Such convictions have been used to justify providing a poorer education to minority-group children and keeping adults out of jobs. There *are* differences in IQ scores between racial and ethnic groups, but they don't always favor whites or Anglo-Saxons: for example, today the average citizen of Japan has a higher IQ than the average American.

On the average, black children tend to score some 15 points lower than whites on IQ tests, attaining an average IQ of about 85. There is, of course, some overlap: some blacks score higher than almost all whites, and many blacks score higher than most whites. Furthermore, urban northern blacks as a group score higher than rural southern blacks. The range of scores within any ethnic or racial group goes from very low to very high, indicating that the differences in scores among individuals of the same group are much greater than the differences in average scores between groups (Brody & Brody, 1976).

In 1969 Arthur Jensen, a California professor of education, outraged many readers (and excited others) with an article in the *Harvard Educational Review*, "How

Much Can We Boost IQ and Scholastic Achievement?" Jensen pointed to a large body of evidence suggesting that genetic factors seem to determine much of the differences in measured intelligence among members of the same ethnic groups—white Europeans and Americans, for example. (The impact of heredity is discussed later in this chapter, along with other influences on intelligence.) He believed that if there is a large genetic factor *within* a group, it stands to reason that the differences in IQ scores *between* different groups (such as blacks and whites in the United States) can also be ascribed to heredity.

While the vast majority of psychologists do not agree with this position, and consider the argument dubious, it has been used to suggest that compensatory education is a waste of teachers' time and efforts and of taxpayers' money. If intelligence is determined almost entirely by our genes, an enriched environment can do nothing.

There are a number of flaws, however, in this point of view. First and foremost, the only way to determine that heredity was in fact the major influence on intelligence, and the major source of differences between groups, would be to study people who grow up in nearly identical environments. In the United States today, this is impossible. Black children, for example, are more likely to be poor, to come from large families, and to attend overcrowded schools. Furthermore, even when blacks and whites have similar levels of education and income, there are still vast social pressures that affect the two racial groups differently, so that their motivation and confidence in testing situations are different.

Later in this chapter we discuss the relative influences of heredity and environment in some detail. The research findings lead us to believe that environmental factors are largely responsible for group differences. We also believe that the erroneous assumption that blacks are genetically and unalterably less intelligent than whites may create many self-fulfilling prophecies. Parents, teachers, and others who think a child is dull may lower their expectations, may not devote to the child the kind of attention that would encourage him or her to do better, and may undermine the child's self-confidence. They may discourage ambitious educational and career goals, and end up producing an adult who lives down to everyone's expectations. Furthermore, when intelligence tests that discriminate against a major portion of the population are used to screen applicants for schools and jobs, people who do not do well on the test will be deprived of future opportunities to do well in life.

Overreliance on testing   After a 4-year study, a panel named by the National Academy of Sciences (1982) concluded that standardized tests *are* reliable predictors in narrowly defined areas of performance (such as grades during the first year of college), but that they also reflect inequities in the educational and home backgrounds of many minority-group youngsters. Is there a way to get around this problem? The authors of the report warn against rigid overreliance on such tests for placing children in special classes, for admitting students to college, and for hiring job applicants. They recommend the use of flexible criteria that take into account motivation and other factors. They also suggest that the Scholastic Aptitude Test (SAT) (which you have probably taken), or any college entrance examination, is usually an unnecessary expense and inconvenience, since most applicants (other than those applying to a very few highly selective schools) are accepted at the college of their choice.

Underestimation of IQ in the elderly   Older people may not do as well on intelligence tests as younger adults, particularly when a test asks them to solve problems they have never seen before. Even when elderly test takers do know an answer, they may not be able to give it. Impairments in vision, hearing, coordination, and agility often make it hard for them to absorb instructions or carry them out. Speed of response is another factor: when elderly test takers are allowed as much time as they need to finish a task, they do better than when they are timed (Bromley, 1974). Physical conditions such as fatigue, high blood pressure, and various other ailments

Because older people often don't do as well on tests as younger adults, their intelligence tends to be underestimated. This woman's age, 80, did not keep her from earning a college diploma.

also seem to interfere with performance (Schaie & Gribbin, 1975). Anxiety may also affect an old person, especially one who has never seen a machine-scored answer sheet and may be too embarrassed to ask questions. Finally, the test items may have so little relevance to the life of an older test taker that he or she is not motivated to make much effort to answer them.

Such tests, then, may limit the ability of older people to get a job or to go back to college. To avoid closing off opportunities to the elderly, the psychological community is beginning to devise new kinds of tests that will more realistically assess intellectual ability in late life. Such tests would include measures of wisdom and practical problem solving. (For a continuation of this discussion of intellectual activity in old age, see Chapter 10.)

Underestimation of the intellectual abilities of handicapped children Traditional intelligence tests often underestimate the intelligence of children with various motor and speech handicaps. Considered mentally deficient, these children are then consigned to classes for the retarded and prevented from realizing their intellectual potential. Tests like those discussed in the next section can be administered to handicapped children for a truer picture of their ability.

NEW DIRECTIONS IN INTELLIGENCE TESTING Ever since the concept of intelligence testing was born, one psychologist after another has tried to improve the tests already in use, to overcome the shortcomings every one has had. Wechsler's addition of performance tasks to lessen the verbal emphasis of earlier IQ tests was one such innovation. In recent years, a number of other approaches have been tried.

Zelazo and Kearsley's information-processing approach It is virtually impossible to predict intelligence scores in adulthood, or even in childhood, on the basis of scores of normal children tested before the age of 2. One reason for this is the heavy emphasis on motor skills in intelligence tests for infants. This emphasis also causes the tests to underestimate the intelligence of physically handicapped children. To overcome such limitations, Zelazo and Kearsley (1981) developed a completely new testing approach. Drawing on research which shows that even infants only a few days old can become habituated to sounds, sights, and smells, and thus demon-

(© Richard Howard 1982)

This 2-year-old boy is taking part in a new kind of intelligence test. Electrodes attached to his chest record his heart rate, which speeds up when events taking place before him violate his expectations. (In this case, light bulbs are turned on and off in response to movements of a wand.) Researchers will see how quickly he learns what to expect, and thus estimate his intelligence level. The child shown here was at one time considered slow; but this test indicated that he was of normal intelligence.

Habituation *Simple type of learning in which an organism stops responding to a stimulus it has grown used to.*

strates the presence of memory in infants, Zelazo and Kearsley test children from the ages of 3 months to 3 years in a special way. (**Habituation** is a form of learning evidenced by subjects' no longer responding to stimuli that they have grown used to.)

The baby or toddler sits, usually on the mother's lap, in a room set up like a puppet theater. Through wires attached to the chest, the child is hooked up to an instrument that records changes in heartbeat, while hidden observers watch and record facial and physical changes. Over a 45-minute period the child sees or hears five episodes that are designed to set up expectations and then to create a surprise by changing the expected pattern. In one of the little dramas, a toy car rolls down a ramp and knocks over a doll. A hand stands the doll back up and rolls the car back up the ramp. The same action occurs six times. The seventh time, the doll does not fall down when it is hit by the car. This happens twice more, and then there are a few more trials of the original sequence.

The child reacts to these events in a number of ways: by staring at the stage, pointing, or clapping, waving, twisting, or turning to the mother. At two points—the first time the doll does not fall down and the first time it falls down again—the child's heart is likely to speed up; and the child may frown the first time the doll does not fall and smile the next time it does. The researchers have charted the ways children typically react and have developed standards for different age levels, paying special attention to the speed with which a child reacts to the episodes. In this way, they have been able to assess intellectual development quite apart from motor development. Thus they can test children with major physical handicaps whose intelligence would be vastly underestimated by traditional tests.

This approach has advantages for testing normal children as well, since we don't have to worry about whether the child understands, likes, or is willing to cooperate with the examiner. The test itself is so interesting that the child usually pays attention to what is going on.

Considering the environment One recent attempt to take into account environmental factors and the way a child functions in daily life is embodied in the System of Multicultural Pluralistic Assessment (SOMPA), developed by the sociologist Jane Mercer and now being used in some states to place students in special-education programs. This battery of measures for 5- to 11-year-olds includes a medical exam, a Wechsler IQ test, and an interview with the parents. The interview yields information about the environment (how many people live in the home, their levels of education, etc.) and the child's level of social competence (how many classmates the child knows by name, whether the child prepares his or her own lunch, etc.).

Thus, a 9-year-old girl, say, who scored only 68 on the Wechsler IQ test might be eligible for placement in a class for the mentally retarded. But when we take into account her impoverished cultural background (a family living on welfare in an urban ghetto) and compare her with other children from similar backgrounds, we realize that her IQ score of 68 is only 9 points below the mean for that group. Moreover, her adaptive-behavior scores might show that she is unusually capable of taking care of herself and getting along in her community. Then her estimated learning potential, or "adjusted IQ," would be 89, and this would mean that she belongs in a regular class which takes her background into account (Rice, 1979).

Culture-free and culture-fair intelligence tests   When a group of immigrant children in Israel were asked to provide the missing detail in a picture of a face with no mouth, they said that the body was missing. They were not used to considering a drawing of a head as a complete picture and "regarded the absence of the body as more important than the omission of a mere detail like the mouth" (Anastasi, 1976, p. 347). This experience illustrates the difficulties in designing a test that can measure innate intelligence without introducing cultural bias.

It is possible to design a test that does not require language. Examiners use gestures, pantomime, and demonstrations for tasks such as tracing mazes, finding absurdities in pictures, putting the right shapes in the right holes, and completing pictures. But even with tasks like these, our way of thinking and behaving is affected much more broadly by our culture than most of us realize. Like the Israeli children, we need to be familiar with commonly accepted artistic conventions. We also need to be familiar with objects pictured, as the biology professor Stephen Jay Gould (1981) confirmed when he gave the army Beta test to his present-day Harvard university students. He found that many of them were stumped by an item in which they had to supply the missing part of a Victrola, although the test assumed that their

Cultural differences affect intelligence scores in a number of ways. These Zimbabwean boys making toys out of wire and the American boy constructing a model car may be showing the same kind of spatial abilities. The challenge for testers is to devise tasks to measure such abilities in people from both cultures.

"innate intelligence" would tell them it was the horn. (Unfamiliarity with many items in the army tests helps to explain why so many recruits in World War I did poorly on it.)

Furthermore, our standards of behavior exert a powerful influence. A person living in a culture which emphasizes the importance of doing something thoroughly, even it that means doing it slowly, will do poorly in tests that value speed and the number of items answered. On the other hand, children from poor families tend to rush through a test, marking their answers almost at random and finishing ahead of time (Anastasi, 1976). Whether this is because they are not interested in the test, do not care about the results, do not expect to do well at it, or just want to get it over with quickly, the end result is that their scores underestimate their ability.

Recognizing the impossibility of designing a "culture-free" test, test makers have tried to produce "culture-fair" tests—tests that deal with experiences common to various cultures. But they have found that it is almost impossible to screen for culturally determined values and attitudes and that the tests almost always favor people from the same culture as the test constructor. Some conditions also differ among cultures: "intrinsic interest of the test content, rapport with the examiner, drive to do well on a test, desire to excel others, and past habits of solving problems individually or cooperatively" (Anastasi, 1976, p. 345). Ironically, some of these supposedly culture-fair tests have yielded larger discrepancies between the scores of black and white children than verbal tests do (Anastasi, 1976). These nonlanguage tests seem to be heavily loaded with cultural baggage that we cannot allow for because it is largely invisible.

Even as test makers continue their efforts to devise tests that minimize cultural influences, the ultimate question remains: If we could devise a test that had no relevance to culture, what would we be measuring? We have to ask: Doesn't intelligence have something to do with how well people perceive and adapt to their culture? Isn't culture so pervasive that it is bound to affect every aspect of our intelligent functioning?

Recognizing cultural differences It may be impossible to eliminate cultural bias from intelligence tests that try to compare one regional, ethnic, or social group with another. One way to get around this might be to test each group in its own cultural idiom, choosing test elements, vocabulary, conventions of time, and so forth separately from the background of each group (Garcia, 1981). If testers paid less attention to identifying people who will do well in the future and focused more on opening up opportunities for minority groups and economically disadvantaged people—as Gordon and Terrell (1981) suggest—we would have come full circle. Alfred Binet, who devised the earliest intelligence tests, felt that the tests could provide a valuable service by identifying children who needed special help—and then giving them help to improve their functioning in school. The early translators of Binet's tests, including Terman and Goddard, took the opposite view, setting the stage for years of using intelligence tests to screen out people who were less qualified rather than to make them more qualified.

Testing for competence David C. McClelland (1973) did not believe research findings showing that success in careers is virtually unrelated to college grades—or, by extension, to intelligence tests (whose only reliable correlations are with grades in school). He therefore conducted his own survey of some of his former students at Wesleyan College, 15 to 18 years after college graduation. His results confirmed the earlier research. There was no difference between a group of straight-A students and a group of students whose averages were C− or below. There were lawyers, doctors, research scientists, and teachers in both groups. Recognizing that standards for admission to graduate and professional schools are stricter today, so that the C− students probably could not enter even second-rate law schools or medical schools if they were applying now, McClelland points out how our society might be depriving itself of some excellent practitioners, simply by screening out people who do not do well on traditional tests.

McClelland proposes some nontraditional methods of testing. One is *criterion sampling,* in which tests are developed to sample what the test taker is actually expected to do in real life. The best example of such a test is the road test you take to get a driver's license. You are thrust into the situation you'll be in when you're driving on public roads.

This principle can be applied in many other areas. Instead of giving applicants for a police academy paper-and-pencil tests that ask them to define words like *quell* and *lexicon,* which they don't need to know to do their job, testers should find out what a good police officer does and what he or she needs to know. McClelland suggests following good officers on their rounds, making a list of the things they do, and then sampling from that list in screening applicants. For example, it is probably more important for an officer to know street language than "dictionary" words.

Developing such tests will not be easy, McClelland concedes. "It will require new psychological skills not ordinarily in the repertoire of the traditional tester. What is called for is nothing less than a revision of the role itself—moving it away from word games and statistics toward behavioral analysis" (p. 8). His other suggestions include these:

- *Giving follow-up tests:* Such tests should assess what someone has learned through experience, instead of trying to measure intelligence as an inborn, unchangeable trait.

- *Testing realistic behavior:* Most tests ask the subject to choose among several clearly defined choices, but life does not usually work in this tightly structured way. McClelland recommends the development of test items to which there are many correct answers, with one that is best. Test takers could be faced with a checkbook-balancing problem or an airline-scheduling problem, in which basic information would be given to enable them to come up with the best solution.

Testing for practical intelligence   Getting along in life depends on much more than the ability to answer questions about analogies, solve number problems, and deal with the other items commonly found on intelligence tests. To measure some of the abilities that are important for succeeding at work, in personal relationships, and in everyday life, Sternberg has devised a number of experimental questionnaires and tests, in line with his triarchic theory of intelligence. One valuable kind of practical intelligence, for example, is the ability to look at a situation and figure out what is happening, what important relationships exist, and where power lies. How do you test for this? One way is to show test takers photos of two people and ask them to determine which is the employer and which the employee, or whether a couple is romantically involved or not. (See whether you can answer these questions for the photos shown on page 252.)

Assessing multiple intelligences   Gardner (1985) believes that it is possible to assess a person's "profile" of the seven intelligences that he says we all have to a greater or lesser degree. Such assessments can begin very early in life, with experiences designed specifically for different ages. In monitoring spatial abilities, for example, we might hide an object from a 1-year-old, ask a 6-year-old to do a jigsaw puzzle, and give a Rubik's cube to a preadolescent. Similar progressions can be developed for each of Gardner's seven intelligences.

Early and continuing assessment (from infancy through adolescence) can tell us which of a child's strengths can be developed for special achievement, which more modest endowments can be enhanced, and which genuine obstacles (like tone deafness, which would affect "musical intelligence") need to be recognized. To develop such profiles, Gardner believes in observing children for about 5 to 10 hours over a

Above: One form of intelligence, according to Sternberg, is the ability to "read" nonverbal cues like body language. Can you tell which of these couples is romantically involved and which just posing together? (Turn the page upside down for the answer.)

Below: Can you read nonverbal cues well enough to determine which person in each pair is the employer and which the employee? (Turn page upside down.)

In the photos of the couples, the "real couple" is shown on the right. People who are actually romantically involved tend to be more relaxed, to stand closer together, to touch more, and to be more alike in dress, age, and socioeconomic status. In the photos of employers and employees, the employer is on the right in the photo at the right, and on the left in the photo at the left. The boss tends to be older, better dressed, and more relaxed, and to look directly at the employee (while the employee tends to look away from the boss).

month or so in regular classroom activities—a more time-consuming process than the present short-answer IQ tests usually given, but perhaps a more rewarding way to help people realize their potential.

Should we get rid of all the tests now in use until better instruments can be developed? Despite their drawbacks, probably we should not. While they are not perfect, they are all we have, and if used properly, they are better than nothing at all. As long as we are aware of the dangers in overreliance on tests, we can use what we have and carefully weigh the results. The bottom line in evaluating intelligence tests is that the kinds of decisions for which test scores are sometimes misused (like placing children in certain classes or hiring job applicants) are decisions that would be made with or without the information that test scores provide. Without the scores, the decisions might well be made on a basis that is even less justifiable, such as the evaluation of a biased teacher or personnel director. While current tests are far from perfect, then, if they are well designed, administered, and interpreted, they can benefit both the individual and society. In any case, IQ (or any other) test scores should never be used in isolation. A responsible test administrator will report scores in the context of interpretation and will make recommendations based on other relevant information as well (such as background information about the test taker and scores from other tests). Meanwhile, of course, the psychological community is constantly engaged in the effort to improve testing methods.

INFLUENCES ON INTELLIGENCE

If I had any desire to lead a life of indolent ease, I would wish to be an identical twin, separated at birth from my brother and raised in a different social class. We could hire ourselves out to a host of social scientists and practically name our fee. (Gould, 1981, p. 234)

Why do Professor Gould's fantasies run along these lines? The answer is that the situation he describes would make him and his brother extremely rare specimens—people with identical genes but different environments. Psychologists have been tracking down people like these for over half a century, and are still looking for more, to try to answer the old nature-versus-nurture question: How much of our intelligence is determined by our genes, and how much by our means?

It is difficult to establish with any certainty the relative roles of heredity and environment in determining intelligence. The only way we could do this would be to compare children who have different heredity but who grow up in identical environments or to compare children who have identical genes but who grow up in different environments.

The first alternative is impossible, since no two children—not even identical twins—grow up in identical environments; each person's experience is unique. This is especially significant when we talk about differences in IQ between groups, since if this is true for two children in the same family, it is much truer for children from different racial groups, different socioeconomic levels, and different neighborhoods. In the United States, black children are more likely to come from poor families, and so any comparison of whites and blacks must take into account the effects of poverty, cultural differences, and race. Even controlling for financial circumstances does not eliminate the problem, since the cultural heritage of black and white children differs in innumerable subtle ways.

The second alternative—comparing the IQs of identical twins who grew up in different environments—has been attempted but has met with difficulty because such twins are hard to find. Other ways of trying to measure the relative input of heredity and environment include studies of adopted children and their biological and adoptive families, comparisons among relatives of various degrees of closeness and unrelated persons, and measures of intelligence before and after a known change in environment.

Heredity

The belief that intelligence is hereditary is an old one. Sir Francis Galton (1869/ 1979) based his studies of eminent men largely on his belief that heredity, race, and class (this last attribute attained by virtue of the first two) were the basic determinants of achievement; he estimated the chances for relatives of the most eminent men to achieve eminence themselves. (This tack may have been influenced by the fact that Galton himself was Charles Darwin's cousin.) Given the point of view Galton started out with, his conclusion is not surprising: The closer the blood tie, the better the chance for fame.

Heritability *Proportion of variance in a trait that is due to genes.*

Binet, who developed the first intelligence test, believed that intelligence scores were often the result of past experience and education and that they could be improved with special help. But the translators of his tests in this country—such as Terman and Goddard—took a strong hereditarian point of view. This point of view has influenced psychological thought throughout the twentieth century, culminating in Jensen's (1969) adamant argument that heredity accounts for about 80 percent of the differences in IQ and environment for only about 20 percent. What evidence has been cited to bolster this belief in the heritability of IQ? (**Heritability** is the proportion of variance in a trait that is due to genes; it applies to differences among individuals in a group rather than between groups.) Let's consider some sources of evidence.

Twin Studies   Professor Gould's dream of fame and fortune is based on the efforts of numerous social scientists who, since the beginning of this century, have tried to fix the proportions of heredity and environment by comparing identical twins raised together and apart and fraternal twins raised together and apart. Separated twins have been hard to find; and even when they are located, they are often found to have been reared in very similar environments, by relatives, friends, or like-minded adoptive parents (Eysenck & Kamin, 1981).

For years hereditarians pointed to the research of the British psychologist Cyril Burt, which appeared to be the most complete study of separated identical twins. Burt reported that 53 pairs of separated twins were remarkably similar in IQ, despite differences in their upbringing. The amazingly high correlations, over time and under different research conditions, turned out to be the "fatal flaw" in Burt's work, however. They made critics suspicious of the findings and eventually led to the exposure of the study as a hoax. Compelling evidence surfaced, showing that Burt had invented many of his data. The twins themselves, two "colleagues," and the statistics that were supposed to prove his theory never really existed (Hearnshaw, 1979; Kamin, 1974).

The disclosure of Burt's fakery has eliminated the most persuasive evidence for the heritability of intelligence. It has not eliminated *all* the evidence, of course. There is still a body of classical research which compared 40 pairs of separated identical twins and found high correlations in intelligence (Shields, 1962). These twins, however, were reared similarly and often had been in touch with each other over the years. Furthermore, the more the twins' family environments differed, the less alike their IQ scores were. The IQs of twins raised by relatives (one by the mother, for instance, and the other by an aunt or grandmother) had a correlation of .83; the IQs of those raised by unrelated families had a correlation of only .51. (Correlation is discussed in Chapter 1, and the meaning of correlations like these is expanded on in the Appendix.) Since the twins' genes were, of course, identical, such differences offer clear evidence that there is a strong environmental component in intelligence (Kamin, 1974).

Efforts to locate and study separated twins continue. An ongoing study has reported findings on a number of pairs of identical twins and fraternal twins who have been reared apart. High degrees of similarity have been found in the identical twins in mental abilities, emotional disturbances, temperament, and such disorders as phobias and speech impediments (Bouchard, 1981; Bouchard, Heston, Eckert, Keyes, & Resnick, 1981; Ecker, Heston, & Bouchard, 1981). This study still supports the importance of environment, however. When twins grew up in vastly different environments, as did two brothers, one of whom was raised by a poorly educated fisherman and the other by a much more cosmopolitan family, differences in IQ were greater—in this case, the twin with the more sophisticated background had an IQ 20 points higher.

Adoption Studies   Researchers compare children's IQs with those of their biological mothers and their adoptive parents (although they often use the biological mother's educational level as a measure, since IQ data for her may be unavailable). For children who were adopted as infants, similarities with the biological mother point to the influence of heredity; similarities between these children and their adoptive parents point to the influence of environment.

Two major adoption studies found a strong influence of heredity in IQ scores, an influence that seems to become stronger as children grow older. In Texas, Horn (1983) compared the IQs of adopted children in several age groups, from 3 to over 10, with those of their adoptive parents and their biological mothers. The resemblance between children and the mothers they had been separated from since they were less than 1 week old was twice that found between the children and the adoptive parents who had raised them from infancy.

In Minnesota, researchers compared IQs of adopted children with those of their adoptive siblings and parents and with the educational levels of their biological mothers. Young siblings scored similarly, whether related by blood or adoption, but adolescents' scores had no correlation with those of their adoptive siblings. Furthermore, the adolescents' IQs correlated more highly with their biological mothers' levels of schooling than with their adoptive parents' IQs. Scarr and Weinberg (1983) concluded that the family environment is more important for a young child, but that by adolescence we find our own niche in life based on our innate abilities and interests.

The evidence from research shows, then, that both heredity and environment play a significant part in determining intelligence. Although there are some differences of opinion, most behavior geneticists conclude that the heritability of intelligence is about 30 to 50 percent. In other words, 30 to 50 percent of the difference in IQ among American and European whites may be the result of genetic differences (Gardner, 1985). The corollary of this, of course, is that 50 to 70 percent of the difference may be attributable to the environment. As we pointed out earlier, it is difficult to pinpoint the proportion of responsibility borne by these two influences, since the way they interact makes it impossible to look at them as distinct, separate ingredients.

One way to explain the contributions of nature and nurture may be found in Scarr and Weinberg's concept of finding one's "niche." Finding our place in the world is not automatic; the richer an environment is, the more niches it presents. An impoverished environment will offer few niches, and although some people will fit into them, others may find none—no avenues leading to a position where they might do well. Similarly endowed people in a rich environment, on the other hand, would find their places and flourish. We seem to see here a demonstration of the way heredity often provides a foundation on which environment can build. Thus our inheritance may determine our intellectual potential, but environmental factors are important in shaping how well or poorly that potential is reached.

It is easy to see the way this principle works with a simple example: height. A boy born with genes for tallness will, in an optimum environment, grow up tall. But if he does not get enough to eat, his growth will be stunted and he will be prevented from expressing his genetic endowment. It appears that the same principle may operate with regard to intelligence.

Environment

Social Environment What has happened to Japan since World War II? It has not only achieved a high position in the world's marketplace as a manufacturer of all sorts of goods, from transistors to automobiles, but has also undergone vast changes in the way its people live. Psychologists are particularly interested in these societal shifts, because the average IQ among Japanese children age 6 to 16 is now the highest in the world, having risen by some 7 points over the past generation. Young Japanese now have a mean IQ of 111, compared with 100 for Americans; their superiority shows up particularly on block design, mazes, picture arrangement, and object assembly (R. Lynn, 1982). More than three-quarters of Japanese children have higher IQs than the average American or European; and while only about 2 percent of Americans and Europeans score over 130, about 10 percent of Japanese now reach this level.

"It seems doubtful whether a rise of this magnitude could be accounted for by a change in the genetic structure of the population. Instead, the explanation probably lies largely in environmental improvements" (R. Lynn, 1982, p. 223). Among the changes in Japanese society that have probably contributed to the rise in scores are the assimilation of previously isolated peasant communities, as almost 40 percent of the population moved from the country to the cities and married people from other areas; rapid economic growth that brought improvements in welfare, health, and education; and the growing exposure to the western culture that developed intelligence tests (A. M. Anderson, 1982).

The impact of environment on intelligence scores has also been seen in the United States. Between 1932 and 1978, representative samples of Americans who took the Stanford-Binet and Wechsler IQ tests scored higher every year than the sample in the year before. Over the 46-year period the total gain in average IQ was 13.8 points (Flynn, 1984). While there are a number of possible explanations, the two that seem most plausible are rising educational levels and rising socioeconomic levels. In any case, the change seems due to environmental factors rather than hereditary ones, since genetic endowment does not change so quickly.

Family Environment   Additional evidence of the importance of environment comes from a study of 130 black and interracial children who had been adopted by 101 white families in Minnesota (Scarr & Weinberg, 1976). These families were well above the average in education, occupation, income, and IQ—in short, they were the kinds of families that usually rear children who do well on IQ tests and in school. The children's biological mothers were at a slightly lower social level, averaging 4 to 5 years less schooling than the adoptive mothers. When these adopted children were tested, they averaged 106—higher than the average IQ of 90 usually achieved by black children reared in their own homes in the area. Furthermore, the adopted children were performing above the national norms on the standard scholastic achievement tests.

These researchers conclude that if all black children had environments like the ones provided by the adoptive families in this study, their IQ scores might well be 10 to 20 points higher. It is not the interracial aspect of the adoption that seems important, but the presence of elements that encourage intellectual skills. Here again, it seems obvious that IQ is not a fixed trait, present from birth, but a changeable one that is responsive to changes in the environment. Even when a trait has a high degree of heritability, it can still be modified by the environment.

An elegant intertwining of genetic and environmental issues becomes clear in this study. The power of *heredity* shows in the fact that the IQs of the adopted children were not quite as high as the IQs of the adoptive parents' biological children, and in the similarity in the correlations between children and their biological mothers *and* fathers, since both parents contribute equally to a child's genetic endowment. The impact of *environment* comes through in the importance of the caretaking parent. While the correlation in IQ between father and biological child was the same as that of mother and biological child (.34), the father's correlation with an adopted child (.07) was considerably lower than the mother's correlation (.29) with an adopted child. The closer resemblance in IQ between children and their adoptive mothers, compared with children and their adoptive fathers, shows the importance of the caretaking environment, which is most typically provided by the mother. We see, then, the influence of both nature and nurture.

What goes on in homes that produce children who do well on intelligence tests, in school, and in life in general? A number of studies (Clarke-Stewart, 1977; White, 1971) have shown that certain parental characteristics are associated with intellec-

Care givers of achieving children provide a special climate for the development of intelligence; they encourage the children's independence, creativity, and growth in warm and caring ways.

tual growth. Parents of achieving children tend to be sensitive, warm, and loving. The accept their children's behavior, letting them explore and express themselves. When they want to change aspects of children's behavior, they appeal to reason or to feelings rather than setting rigid rules. They use fairly sophisticated language and teaching strategies, and they encourage their children's independence, creativity, and growth by reading, teaching, and playing. They give their children a sense of control over the environment: the children know that what they do counts. The children respond by expressing curiosity, being creative, exploring new situations, and doing well in school. Such a "climate for excellence" need not be created exclusively by children's biological parents, however. Other relatives and care givers outside the family (such as providers of day care) can all contribute to a child's intellectual growth.

Nutrition   Another factor that influences intellectual development is nutrition. Severe early malnutrition seems to retard intellectual development by affecting brain development, the "orienting response" (which shows that a baby is paying attention to some sight or sound), and the ability to pay attention (Lester, 1975; Winick, Brasel, & Rosso, 1969). Giving a pregnant mother, a new baby, or a preschooler extra food, more nutritious food, or both often has positive effects on the child's intelligence (Harrell, Woodyard, & Gates, 1955; Lloyd-Still, Hurwitz, Wolff, & Schwachman, 1974).

It seems clear, again, that *both* heredity and environment exert some influence on the intellectual heights any of us can reach. Since we cannot do anything about heredity but can do a great deal about environment, it makes sense for us to continue to ask which environmental factors seem most important in encouraging intellectual development and, as individuals and members of society, to do as much as we can to introduce those factors into the lives of all children.

Birth Order

A number of studies have found that firstborn and only children are particularly likely to be high achievers. They are more likely to be listed in *Who's Who,* to earn Ph.D.s, and to become national merit scholars (Helmreich, 1968; Sutton-Smith, 1982). This pattern of achievement may occur because they are more apt to go to college, and to be admitted to elite colleges; these accomplishments in turn are probably related to the fact that they do better in school at earlier ages and aim higher than other children (Sutton-Smith, 1982).

Recent research on intelligence has confirmed this trend. Among 400,000 19-year-old Dutch men tested for intelligence, firstborns scored better on average than second-borns, who in turn scored better than third-borns, and so forth (Belmont & Marolla, 1973). Family size seemed to have an effect, too, since, in general, the men who grew up in smaller families had higher scores. Other research has found that middle-born children tend to be underachievers (Bayer, 1967). Some of these differences may be closely related to social class, however, since it is only the firstborn children of middle- and upper-middle-class families who actually do better in school and have the higher goals noted above (Glass, Neulinger, & Brim, 1974).

Why should birth order affect intellectual functioning? Robert Zajonc (1976) has come up with a mathematical model, emphasizing not only birth order itself but also the family configuration. According to this model, a person's intelligence is affected by the average intellectual level in the family, uncorrected for age. The more children there are, the more they bring the average down. When the children are widely separated by age, however, they are better able to develop their intellect, thus raising the average. This model has been used to predict intelligence among large groups of children in the United States and several European countries, but it is limited in its applicability to individual families (Zajonc & Bargh, 1980).

The most obvious explanation for the impact of birth order is that when parents spend more time with children and expect more from them, the children will achieve more. This is consistent with Zajonc's model and also with observations of mothers, who do tend to behave this way with their first children (Sutton-Smith, 1982). There are other possibilities, too. Firstborn children may be motivated to outperform those interlopers, their younger siblings, who have, in the words of Alfred Adler (1928), "dethroned" them from their original position in the family. They may also be more inspired by their adult models, their parents, than their younger brothers and sisters are.

Sex

Your sex is not likely to affect your overall IQ. This is not surprising, since both the Wechsler and the Stanford-Binet tests were designed to eliminate any sex bias. Even using other tests, investigators have found very few differences between the sexes. A persistent thread running through the research literature, however, has been sex differences in some specific abilities. If you are a woman, you are more likely to excel in verbal ability; if you are a man, you are more likely to excel in spatial ability. Of course, you may not fit this general pattern. While group differences between the sexes do exist in these abilities, there is considerable overlap between male and female scores and there is great variability among persons of the same sex. The highly controversial issue of cognitive differences between the sexes is discussed in detail in Chapter 12.

EXTREMES OF INTELLIGENCE ▬▬▬▬▬▬▬▬▬▬▬▬▬▬▬▬

The Intellectually Gifted

When Robert R. Sears was a little boy in California, his teacher gave his name to Lewis Terman, who was looking for exceptionally bright children, with a view to following them through life to see which ones would achieve success. Robert was tested for intelligence (scoring over 140, the requirement for inclusion in the study), school achievement, character, personality, and interests. He was examined medically, his physical measurements were taken, and his parents and teachers were interviewed for case-history material and a rating of his personality.

The data that emerged for the 1500 children studied demolished the popular stereotype of the bright child as a puny, pasty-faced bookworm. On the contrary, these children were superior all-around: healthier, taller, better coordinated, better adjusted, and more popular than the average child.

Over the years the Stanford University researchers kept in touch with as many of the original subjects as possible. Their intellectual, scholastic, and vocational superiority continued. They were ten times more likely than an average group to have graduated from college and three times more likely than other students to have been elected to honorary societies like Phi Beta Kappa. By midlife, they were highly represented in listings such as *American Men of Science* (which includes women) and *Who's Who*. Almost 90 percent of the men* were in the two highest occupational categories: the professions and semiprofessions and the higher echelons of business (Terman & Oden, 1959).

These unusually bright people turned out not to be especially creative, producing neither any great musicians nor any exceptional painters (Goleman, 1980). It is possible that the tests and other methods of selection tended to screen out the highly creative in favor of the highly competent. Or "perhaps it is unfair to expect that among this particular pool of intelligence there would happen to be a Beethoven or an Einstein" (Goleman, 1980, p. 34). Another possibility is that only some of these youngsters' abilities were encouraged while others were neglected. The box "Developing Children's Abilities" describes the kinds of special encouragement that seem to help gifted youngsters fulfill their potential.

Robert Sears did his fair share to advance the reputation of "Terman's children," becoming a prominent psychologist who directed a major study of child-rearing practices (R. Sears, Maccoby, & Levin, 1957), head of the psychology department at Stanford University (a post held earlier by Terman), and then dean of the university. Now, more than 60 years after the study began, Dr. Sears and his wife, Pauline, also a psychologist, are examining the trends that have emerged over the years from this longitudinal study of the intellectually gifted (Sears, 1977; Sears & Barbee, 1978).

While most of these adults were more successful than the average person in our society, there was a range of achievement within the group itself. When the life histories and personalities of the 100 most successful ("A") men and the 100 least successful ("C") men were compared, a number of differences emerged. The A's made more money, had higher-level occupations, came from more advantaged families and more stable homes, were better adjusted as children, were encouraged to be independent, felt more parental pressure to excel in school and go to college, were healthier, were better-educated, were more active physically, and were happier in family life. Even as children, they were more ambitious—more goal-oriented, self-confident, persevering, and eager for acknowledgment for their achievements. Obviously, factors other than intelligence affect success, since the average intelligence level in both groups was about the same.

In 1972, at an average age of 62, the original subjects reported on their sources of life satisfaction (P. Sears, 1977; R. Sears, 1977). Overall, the men and the employed women rated work highly, and the women at home rated family life highly; but both men and women gave the highest rating to family life. Both men and women needed to feel competent. Sixty-nine percent of the women said that they would choose their work and lifestyle again. The happiest women had been working outside the home for years, had been single for a long time, and had no children.

What does this study tell us? Does it suggest that people who score high on intelligence tests do well in life? Does it imply that labeling children "bright" early in life creates a self-fulfilling prophecy which helps them do better later on? Does it

---

*Because of different societal attitudes toward careers for men and women, the sexes were evaluated separately. Both sexes made a good showing.

IN THE FOREFRONT

DEVELOPING CHILDREN'S ABILITIES

Most of us are awed by outstanding ability, especially when it shows up early in life. In an effort to explore the origins of unusual talent, the Development of Talent Research Project studied more than 120 high achievers who, before the age of 35, had become internationally known in various fields: as concert pianists, sculptors, Olympic swimmers, tennis players, research mathematicians, and neurologists (Bloom, 1985). (The specific artistic, psychomotor, or cognitive fields can also be described in terms of the seven intelligences proposed by Gardner, 1985).

The researchers wanted to find out why people of such outstanding accomplishments are so rare, what their patterns of development are, and what role their families, teachers, and schools play in their eventual success. The findings emphasize the importance of early encouragement of talent.

All these achievers had received encouragement, nurturance, education, and training from an early age. Their parents played a major role by generating pride in the youngsters' achievements, inspiring them to work hard, comforting them when they failed, and removing obstacles when possible. Most of these accomplished people became intensely involved in their field before the age of 12, and often before the age of 10, when other activities (like school) became secondary in their lives. In most cases one or both parents, a sibling, or some other relative showed a personal interest in the child's talent because this person had special ability in the same area. These relatives often encouraged the children to take part in activities in these areas as early as age 3 to 7, and they rewarded any signs of interest and capability.

Next in importance to parents and other relatives was the child's first teacher. The first teacher often imparted a sense of joy and playfulness before the pupil needed a teacher who would make more rigorous demands. This, too, was vital in inducing the young people to put forth their best efforts.

The third vital factor was the youngsters' own commitments of time and energy. As the children grew up, their talent continued to assume the most important role in their lives. Adolescents often devoted 15 to 25 hours a week to the activity, and they chose their friends from fellow participants.

A number of differences showed up between the specific kind of training these youngsters received and the teaching available to the typical schoolchild. First, these young people received special training for their unique talents, with much of their instruction coming from parents, tutors, and coaches on a one-to-one basis. Their training, unlike the typical school curriculum, emphasized not what a teacher wanted to teach, but what this particular child needed to learn. Instead of a standard course of study, learning goals and tasks were set for this one child.

Second, their teachers had a "longitudinal" approach. They knew the children well, expected to remain with them for several years, and emphasized long-term goals and individual progress over a period of time. The typical classroom teacher, on the other hand, has a "cross-sectional" approach, being responsible for children for only 1 year and judging them by comparing them with their classmates.

Third, these talented young people experienced emotional "highs" from regular participation in public events, such as recitals and contests. These events provided a series of short-term goals to work toward and gave them benchmarks of progress. When they performed well, the praise and rewards inspired them to continued effort; and when they did poorly, they were motivated to try to do better next time. In contrast, typical schoolchildren today have few experiences like these. At one time, school life was full of events like spelling bees, debates, writing competitions, and scientific and mathematical projects; but today's schools seldom emphasize such events (Bloom, 1985).

Three basic patterns showed up in the relationship between development of talent and overall schooling. For some of the children, their special abilities and their school life were separate spheres, and school was essentially a neutral factor. Aside from occasional minor scheduling adjustments made by the schools, these youngsters were expected to meet the demands of both their talents and their schools. For example, they would get up early in the morning to swim or play the piano and then continue to practice in the evening. For others, school was a negative factor, because their teachers and schoolmates did not value their talents, and they were torn in allocating their time and energy. For still others, school was a positive factor. These youngsters' schools did encourage them: often a particular teacher showed special interest, their peers were appreciative, or school events provided opportunities for recognition.

This study confirms the findings of Harvard University's Project Zero—named to reflect what its founders considered the state of knowledge about creativity. In Project Zero, children are observed as they take part in a range of artistic activities. Here, too, the three elements essential for artistic success have been found to be inborn talent, encouragement of that talent, and a person's own drive to excel (Gardner, 1979).

indicate the "rich and powerful have more opportunities, and therefore do better in life" (McClelland, 1973, p.5)? To some extent the answers to all these questions may be *yes*.

But it must be noted that the study sample was not representative of the population of the United States. All the subjects were Californians, most came from relatively advantaged homes, Jewish children were overrepresented, and black and Asian children were underrepresented. The most interesting findings to emerge from the study may well be those *within* the sample, such as the differences between the very successful A's and the less successful C's. Among people with so much in common, what differences mattered? The answer to a question like this might help us to improve the lives of people at all levels of intelligence—and society.

The Mentally Retarded

At the other extreme of the IQ spectrum are people whose intelligence is *below* average. The most widely accepted definition of mental retardation includes below-average general intellectual functioning, deficiency in the level of adaptive behavior appropriate to current age, and the appearance of such retardation before age 18 (DSM III, 1980). It is important to note that while low-level intellectual functioning (as detected by IQ tests) is one component, behavioral performance is also important.

There are several levels of retardation, as shown in Table 7-5. Persons in the "borderline" and "mild" categories account for about 80 percent of all retarded people and may constitute about 15 percent of the American population (DSM III, 1980; Zigler & Seitz, 1982). These people can hold jobs and function fairly well in society. Those at the very lowest levels, by contrast, have to be cared for constantly, usually in institutions.

We also categorize retardation another way—in terms of whether it is organic, with a known physical cause; or familial, in which case we cannot identify a specific organic cause.

TABLE 7-5   LEVELS OF MENTAL RETARDATION

Type of Retardation	IQ Range*	Level of Functioning
Borderline	70–85	May be able to function adequately in society.
Mild	50–70	"Educable": Can learn academic skills up to sixth-grade level, and can support self minimally, with special help at times of unusual stress.
Moderate	35–49	"Trainable": Can learn up to second-grade level, care for self, and do skilled work in sheltered workshop, with supervision and guidance.
Severe	20–34	Will not learn to talk or practice basic hygiene till school years; cannot learn vocational skills; may be able to perform simple work tasks under close supervision.
Profound	Below 20	Requires constant care and supervision.

*Scores are not rigid, since level of adaptive behavior is also important.
Source: Adapted from DSM III, 1980; Grossman, 1983.

Children with Down's syndrome are limited in intellectual potential but not in personality; they are often cheerful and sociable. Recent programs have enabled many of them to achieve much more than was thought possible in the past, as seen in this lively little girl's enjoyment of a picture book.

Organic retardation *Generally severe mental retardation with a physical cause.*

Down's syndrome *Chromosomal disorder caused by an extra chromosome 21 (or sometimes by the attachment of chromosome 21 to another chromosome), resulting in mental retardation and often heart defects and other physical abnormalities; the most common chromosomal disorder.*

Organic retardation may have a number of different physical causes. It may stem from a chromosomal disorder like Down's syndrome, which also produces certain distinct physical characteristics. It may result from a disorder of metabolism, like phenylketonuria (PKU). Or it may be caused by problems during the prenatal period such as maternal illness, infection, or drug ingestion. Sometimes it accompanies a major physical birth defect like hydrocephaly, in which a baby is born with an abnormally large head. In this and other instances, the cause is unknown, although it is clearly physical in origin. This type of defect can usually be detected before or shortly after birth. About 1 in 4 mentally retarded persons—some 2 million people—are in this category. Their IQs are usually below 50, and they are equally likely to come from the highest social classes as from the lowest (Zigler & Seitz, 1982).

Down's syndrome is a disorder of the chromosomes, the tiny rod-shaped particles that carry the genes—the transmitters of heredity. Characteristic features of Down's syndrome include a downward-sloping skin fold at the inner corners of the eyes; small head; flat nose; protruding tongue; defective heart, eyes, and ears; short height; reduced fertility; and mental retardation, generally to a moderate degree. The syndrome is caused by an extra twenty-first chromosome (giving the child a total of 47 chromosomes instead of the normal 46) or the attachment of part of the twenty-first chromosome onto another chromosome. It is the most common chromosomal disorder and occurs once in every 700 live births. Older women are at greater risk for bearing children with Down's syndrome; women over age 40 run a risk of more than 1 percent of bearing a baby with Down's syndrome.

It is hereditary only about 3 percent of the time, usually among younger parents. The risk is above average, then, in families that already have one afflicted child. Among older parents, chromosomal accidents are almost always to blame (Smith & Wilson, 1973), possibly because the mother's ova deteriorate over time or because of some problem with the father's sperm, which seems to be implicated in about 1 in 4 cases (Abroms & Bennett, 1981). Babies with Down's syndrome are equally likely to be male or female and of any socioeconomic level.

Since children with Down's syndrome tend to be cheerful and sociable, a growing number are being cared for by their biological parents or in foster or adoptive homes, rather than in institutions (Oelsner, 1979). Programs that offer supportive exercises and activities have been able to improve the limited intellectual abilities of these children (Hayden & Haring, 1976). As a result, many learn simple skills and can, in time, help to support themselves.

In **familial retardation** the cause is more elusive, probably involving a complex interaction between genetic factors and such environmental influences as poor nutrition, mild lead poisoning, and lack of social or intellectual stimulation. It is usually less severe than organic retardation, is most common among the lower socioeconomic classes, and often appears in several members of the same family. Often it is not diagnosed until a child goes to school, and even then the diagnosis may be controversial.

Familial retardation   Retardation for which no physical cause can be found; it is generally less severe than organic retardation and probably involves an interaction between genetic and environmental factors.

The way a mentally retarded person gets along in the world depends on society's attitudes toward retardation and its willingness to take action to prevent retardation in the first place, provide supports for the retarded and their families to make it easier for people to live in the community, and offer humane institutional care for the most severely affected. Prevention seems most feasible for organic retardation. In fact, Zigler and Seitz (1982) maintain that if techniques like genetic counseling, amniocentesis, routine screening and health care for newborns, prenatal health care, and nutritional services for pregnant women and infants had been in full use for the past generation, the number of persons with organic retardation could have been reduced from about 2 million to 1 million.

A number of intervention programs have been successful in improving levels of functioning of many people who are mildly to moderately retarded. As a result, many are able to be more independent and to live in the community. Such additional supports as day care centers, hostels for retarded adults, and homemaking services for families caring for retarded children are enormously valuable. From a societal point of view, they are also financially sound when compared with the high cost of institutional care. The schools can also play an important role in providing special educational services for people in the upper ranges of retardation, to enable them to become contributing members of society to the best of their ability.

SUMMARY

1   There has been considerable debate over the nature and meaning of intelligence. Most recent conceptions stress that it is both goal-oriented and adaptive. In this book intelligence is defined as a constant interaction between inherited ability and environmental experience, which results in a person's being able to acquire, remember, and use knowledge; understand both concrete and (eventually) abstract concepts; understand relationships among objects, events, and ideas; and apply and use all those abilities in a purposeful way to solve problems in everyday life.

2   There are almost as many theories of intelligence as there are definitions. One group of theories, the psychometric approach, has focused on whether intelligence is best described as a general ability or a number of specific abilities.

3   Spearman's two-factor theory proposes that there are two types of intelligence. The more important g factor (general intelligence) influences overall performance, and s factors (specific abilities) account for different scores on different types of intellectual tasks.

4   According to Thurstone, intelligence is composed of seven primary mental abilities: word fluency, verbal

comprehension, space, perceptual speed, reasoning, number, and memory.

5   Guilford's structure-of-intellect model includes 150 factors that result from the interaction of operations, content, and products.

6   Cattell and Horn propose that there are two broad types of intelligence: fluid intelligence and crystallized intelligence. Fluid intelligence is required to solve novel problems; crystallized intelligence involves the ability to use knowledge acquired over time.

7   Gardner's theory of multiple intelligences proposes that there are at least seven separate types of intelligence: linguistic, logical-mathematical, spatial, musical, bodily-kinesthetic, interpersonal, and intrapersonal.

8   Sternberg's triarchic theory describes three types of intelligence: componential (analytical ability), experiential (insight and creativity), and contextual (practical knowledge).

9   The Piagetian approach considers universal qualitative changes in thought that occur in an invariant sequence of stages.

10   It was not until 1905 that the kind of intelligence testing used today was developed in the laboratory of Alfred

Binet in Paris. The intelligence test he developed there was a forerunner of the modern-day Stanford-Binet Intelligence Scale.

11 In developing a good intelligence test, a number of factors having to do with test construction must be considered. First, a test must be standardized; that is, uniform procedures must be developed for giving and scoring it, and it must be given to a large, representative standardization sample in order to develop norms or standards of performance. A good test must also be reliable (consistent in measuring performance) and valid (accurate in measuring what it is supposed to measure).

12 A wide range of intelligence tests are in use today. Some, such as the Stanford-Binet and the Wechsler scales (WAIS-R, WISC-R, and WPPSI), are administered individually. The Stanford-Binet test is an excellent predictor of academic success, but it has been criticized for its heavy verbal emphasis. The Wechsler tests include two major types of subtests: verbal and performance. Group tests, such as the Scholastic Aptitude Test, have well-established procedures for administration and scoring and can be given to many persons at one time.

13 Although intelligence tests are particularly useful in predicting academic performance, they have been used in ways that have underestimated the abilities of people from racial minorities, the elderly, and people with various motor and speech handicaps.

14 In recent years, psychologists have developed an array of novel measures of intelligence. These include measures that are based on information processing, measures that consider a child's everyday environment (SOMPA), culture-free and culture-fair tests, tests that assess job-related competence, and tests that assess practical intelligence (these are based on the work of Sternberg) and multiple intelligences (these are based on the work of Gardner).

15 Psychologists today believe that heredity and environment interact in influencing intelligence. However, there is considerable disagreement about the relative contribution of each factor. Twin studies and adoption studies indicate that intelligence is partly determined by heredity. However, environment plays a critical part in determining the expression of intellectual potential.

16 A number of studies have indicated that firstborns and only children are particularly likely to be high achievers. When birth-order effects exist, they are most likely to be the result of different experiences (particularly within the family) undergone by firstborns and later-borns.

17 There are no sex differences in overall IQ. However, females tend to excel in verbal abilities and males in spatial abilities. There is considerable overlap between scores of males and females, and there is great variability among persons of the same sex.

18 Terman's longitudinal study of gifted children (the subjects had measured IQs over 140) indicated that these children were healthier, taller, better coordinated, better adjusted, and more popular than the average child. Studies following this sample in adulthood indicate that the subjects maintained their intellectual, scholastic, and vocational superiority, although a range of levels of success were achieved.

19 Mental retardation includes below-average general intellectual functioning, deficiency in the level of adaptive behavior appropriate to current age, and the appearance of such retardation before the age of 18. Organic retardation has a physical basis and affects about 25 percent of retarded people. Familial retardation, affecting the remaining 75 percent, probably involves an interaction of environmental and genetic factors.

20 Intervention programs have been successful in helping people with mild to moderate retardation to be more independent and better able to live in the community.

KEY TERMS

Content validity (page 239)
Criterion-related validity (239)
Crystallized intelligence (233)
Down's syndrome (262)
Familial retardation (263)
Fluid intelligence (233)
Habituation (248)

Heritability (254)
Intelligence (229)
Intelligence quotient (IQ) (237)
Mental age (237)
Multiple intelligences (234)
Norms (239)
Object permanence (236)
Organic retardation (262)

Parallel forms (239)
Piagetian approach (235)
Primary mental abilities (232)
Psychometric approach (231)
Reliability (239)
Split-half reliability (239)
Standard deviation (238)

Standardization (238)
Structure of intellect (232)
Test-retest reliability (239)
Triarchic theory of intelligence (235)
Two-factor theory (231)
Validity (239)

SUGGESTED READINGS

BLOOM, B. S. (Ed.). (1985). *Developing talent in young people*. New York: Ballantine. An absorbing report of a project in which researchers interviewed 120 accomplished young pianists, sculptors, swimmers, tennis champions, mathematicians, and research neurologists, and their parents, teachers, and coaches. The book emphasizes the importance of parents' and teachers' active development of the young people's abilities.

EYSENCK, H. J., & KAMIN, L. (1981). *The intelligence controversy*. New York: Wiley. A lively debate about whether intelligence is the result of heredity or environment, by two prominent advocates of each point of view, complete with attacks, counterattacks, and rebuttals.

FANCHER, R. E. (1985). *The intelligence men: Makers of the IQ controversy*. New York: Norton. A fascinating account of the key players in the nature-nurture IQ controversy from the nineteenth century to the present.

GARDNER, H. (1983). *Frames of mind: The theory of multiple intelligence*. New York: Basic Books. A view of intelligence which draws upon research in cognitive psychology and neurophysiology to argue that people are born with the potential to develop several different types of intelligence. The author suggests ways to mobilize these intelligences for maximum benefit to society and individuals.

HEARNSHAW, L. S. (1979). *Cyril Burt, psychologist*. Ithaca, NY: Cornell University Press. An authoritative biography of a major figure in British psychology, written by a fellow psychologist who came to the project with vast admiration for Burt. Faced with clear evidence that Burt had made up his studies on identical twins reared separately to support his own convictions that intelligence is inherited, Hearnshaw became a historian, revealing Burt's scientific fraud.

KERR, B. A. (1985). *Smart girls, gifted women*. Columbus, OH: Ohio Psychology. A thought-provoking book that considers the question: Why don't gifted women achieve more in their careers? Drawing on information revealed in a variety of studies, the author points out principles for guiding gifted girls and provides specific suggestions for parents.

STERNBERG, R. (1985). *Beyond IQ*. Cambridge: Cambridge University Press. Sternberg's statement of the triarchic theory of intelligence.

CHAPTER

8

LANGUAGE AND THOUGHT

■ How does language develop?

■ What is the role of "motherese" in children's language development?

■ Are the years before puberty a critical period for acquiring language?

■ What is the relationship between language and thought?

■ Can apes learn language?

■ How does the ability to categorize objects and events impose a sense of order?

■ What is the difference between routine and creative problem solving?

■ How can people be more creative?

A few years ago I took a trip to the Netherlands. I went into a grocery store to buy some cheese, and the cheerful, friendly shopkeeper spoke to me in flawless English. As I was finishing my purchase, a German tourist came in, and the shopkeeper immediately switched to fluent German. Before I left the store, a similar scene was enacted with a French shopper. I was impressed, not only by the fact that this merchant was able to conduct his business transactions in all these different languages, but by the expansive nature of these brief exchanges. With every encounter, he would insert some expression of interest in the purchaser—a comment, a question, or a joke—that put the conversations on a slightly more personal level than the mere exchange of guilders for goods.

Having just come from a visit to France, where I had used what I remembered of my high school French, I realized what a difference it makes to be able to speak to people in their own language. Part of my vacation in France was spent in little towns where (unlike the big cities) people's command of English was no better than my knowledge of French. I was able to make my wants known in a rudimentary way. I could get a hotel room; I could get a meal; I could buy a train ticket. But I couldn't do many of the things I ordinarily take for granted.

I couldn't exchange the kind of small pleasantries that color so many casual encounters throughout a typical day, as the Dutch merchant did. I couldn't speak with my counterparts in the French university system. I couldn't get a feeling for the way people thought about politics, about family life, or about any of the other issues I like to talk about. I couldn't explore any aspects of my academic research, intellectual functioning at different ages in life.

On a very personal level I realized how vital language is for the most basic interchanges we have with other people. I also realized how closely language is tied in with many of the psychological processes that affect my life—what I learned and how I learned about it, how I use my intelligence, what I remember. And I realized how much of a barrier the inability to speak the same language erects between people who would like to understand each other.

—From the notebooks of Diane Papalia

You would expect the science of psychology, defined in Chapter 1 as the scientific study of behavior and mental processes, to include the study of the way people think and speak. But for many years, American psychologists paid little attention to either thought or language.

For much of the first half of the twentieth century, experimental psychology was behaviorist in its orientation. Trying to get away from the ponderings of philosophers and be more scientific, it focused only on behavior, on what could be seen and measured. The behaviorists believed that psychologists could not properly study "thinking," because they could not observe it directly and therefore could not measure it objectively. They coined the term *mentalism* and generally used it somewhat contemptuously to describe interpretation of behavior in terms of mental processes as opposed to observable acts.

Today, although the rapid twists and turns that our brains take when we think are still not readily available to scientific measure, we are making enormous strides in this area. Most psychologists now seem to feel that the study of mental activities is not only possible but very important. With the rise of **cognitive psychology,** the branch of the science that strives to understand human thought, a "cognitive revolution" has done much to foster our understanding of mental processes.

In thinking we're able to use symbols to stand for things, events, and ideas. This allows us to manipulate concepts and images, so that we can acquire knowledge, remember it, and use it to solve problems. The subjects we'll talk about in this chapter—language, formation of concepts, problem solving, and creativity—are all considered by psychologists to be aspects of thinking. The impact of cognitive psychology goes beyond these topics, however, as you'll note throughout this book. The influence of the "cognitive revolution" can now be seen in the study of virtually every issue discussed in these chapters.

Human thought is complex, and resistant in many ways to the kind of study that yields definite answers about its nature. But thanks to the ways various researchers have solved some of the problems of studying it, we now have access to some of its secrets. One of the most absorbing topics studied by cognitive psychologists is the development of language, a basic tool for most human thought.

Cognitive psychology *Psychological school concerned with the way the mind processes information.*

LANGUAGE ▬▬▬▬▬▬▬

"Does the bus stop here?" "I've come up with some possible solutions—here's my report." "I love you." "What time will you be back?" "Ladies and gentlemen of the jury. . . ." "Please stop at the store and pick up milk, bread, and apples." "To be or not to be, that is the question." "If you agree to limit your nuclear weapons, we'll limit ours."

Language is indispensable for normal human interaction. Think about its role in your day-by-day functioning, in your relationships with other people, in your ability to do your work, in your enjoyment of leisure activities, and in the governance of the nations of the world. A human world without language is unimaginable. If you've ever been in a country where you didn't speak the language, you know how much of a handicap you suffered. The occasional stories that surface of rare people without any language, like the young Helen Keller or the abused and neglected "Genie" (whom we'll meet in this chapter), are among the saddest we hear. Without language, we wouldn't be able to build a society, establish and enforce laws, pass on knowledge, or do most of the things that we take for granted as part of human life.

The study of language is important for other reasons, too. Human language represents a special form of abstract and symbolic thinking. While some other animals communicate with each other, no other species—including the great apes, our closest relatives—come remotely close to our language abilities. Furthermore, we store information in our minds through language, we solve problems using language, and the language we use influences how we perceive the world around us. No wonder cognitive psychology devotes so much emphasis to the study of language!

The frustration experienced by someone in an unfamiliar country, like this tourist asking directions of a Parisian policeman, underscores the importance of language, which is usually taken for granted in such everyday transactions.

Studying Language

Some Basic Definitions   Before we talk about the study of language, we need to learn a few terms and their meanings, such as those presented in the following paragraphs.

Linguistics *Study of language.*

LINGUISTICS **Linguistics** is the study of language, including speech sounds, meaning, and grammar.

Language *Way of communicating through spoken sounds that express specific meanings and are arranged according to rules.*

LANGUAGE **Language** is a means of communicating through spoken sounds (or through gestures, as in the case of American Sign Language, used by the deaf), which express specific meanings and are arranged according to rules.

Grammar *Rules of sound, meaning, and syntax in a language.*

GRAMMAR **Grammar** is a set of rules that specify the three basic components of every language—*sound, meaning,* and *structure*. It is a general term that includes rules of sound, rules of meaning, and rules of syntax. Let's look more closely at these basic types of rules, focusing on a simple sentence, "The astronaut skates on the moon."

Sound Even our short "sample" sentence illustrates the wealth of sounds that make up a language. To analyze those sounds, linguists break them down into small units. The term **phoneme** refers to the minimal unit of sound. In the word *skates,* such sounds as the long *a* and the *t* (sounding like a blade hitting the ice) are phonemes. *Skates* also has a phoneme made of two letters, the hiss of the *s* linked to the explosion of air in the *k*. English has 46 basic speech sounds; some other languages have as many as 85 or as few as 15.

Phoneme *Minimal sound unit of spoken language.*

Semantics *Study of meaning in a language.*
Morpheme *Smallest meaningful element of speech.*

Meaning **Semantics** is the study of meaning in a language. The **morpheme** is the smallest element of speech that has meaning. Made up of phonemes, it consists of a word stem, and possibly a prefix or a suffix or both. The word *skate* is composed of three phonemes (*sk, a,* and *t* sounds). It consists of one morpheme. The meaning is different, depending on whether we're talking about a skate on someone's foot (the noun) or the act of gliding around the rink (the verb). Words like *skates* and *skating,* which consist of the word stem plus a prefix or suffix, have two morphemes each (as in *skate* and *s*). *Ice-skating* (prefix, word stem, and suffix) has three morphemes. We can see how the addition of a prefix changes the meaning of the word: we now know that we are talking about someone on blades rather than wheels.

Syntax *Body of rules for structuring a language.*

Structure **Syntax** is a set of rules for structuring a language—that is, for ordering words into sentences. Thus, English syntax for this sentence dictates that the article *the* comes first, followed by the noun, and then the verb, as in "The astronaut skates." We wouldn't say, "Skates astronaut the," or "Astronaut the skates," or "The skates astronaut." Placement of the phrase *on the moon* also follows English syntax. In some other languages the order of words would be different.

The structure of a language can become very complex. In English, for example, the 46 smallest units of sound (phonemes) can be put together in different ways to form more than 100,000 units of meaning (morphemes). These can add up to more than 500,000 words. And the number of original sentences that can be made up of these words is limited only by the imagination and linguistic abilities of all the English-speaking people in the world.

How Psychologists Study Language Abilities Psychologists investigate language abilities in many different ways. To learn about the production of speech, they observe how people speak and then analyze their speech. To learn about understanding speech, they observe how people respond to the speech of others. An important way to learn about human linguistic abilities is to study how they first appear among young children.

In recent years, researchers have devised ingenious methods of studying the language abilities of infants and young children. One method involves observation of sucking. Infants who are sucking on a pacifier while listening to a sound decrease their rate of sucking when they habituate to (get used to) the sound. They increase their rate when a new sound is presented, thus showing the experimenter that they can tell the difference between one sound and another. A second measure of habituation is heart rate, which increases in response to a new sound but decreases when habituation takes place. The rate at which babies turn their heads toward a new sound is a third behavioral measure. A fourth way to measure discrimination of sounds is through an *auditory-evoked response (AER)*. In this procedure, electrodes fastened to a baby's scalp measure the brain responses elicited by sounds, and differences in these responses are interpreted as evidence that the baby is discriminating between sounds (Molfese, Molfese, & Carrell, 1982).

It is easier, of course, to study the language abilities of older children than to study sound differentiation in infants. Researchers tape-record samples of the children's speech, perhaps for 1 or 2 hours a week, and then analyze what they say. Since it is often important to know what children are doing as they are speaking, videotaping has become popular. To test children's ability to hear or reproduce speech sounds, the children are asked to imitate a word or a sentence. To find out what they know about linguistic rules, they may be asked to say something. For example, a child may be shown a drawing of a funny-looking creature and told, "This is a wug. There's another one. There are two . . . ?" Children who say "wugs" have shown that they know how to make plurals in English, since they could not have heard this made-up word anywhere else. To measure comprehension, researchers ask children to choose among pictures or objects, or to act something out: "Make the (toy) horse kick the (toy) cow."

Learning a Language

How Children Learn a Language   Long before a child says his or her first word, generally sometime between 12 and 18 months of age, an enormous amount of language learning has taken place. Some of this learning occurs so early that it seems as if the basic form and structure of a language system are programmed into our genes, so that we are born with built-in mechanisms for the acquisition of language. One-day-old babies will move their bodies, for example, in the same rhythm as the adult speech sounds they hear around them (Condon & Sander, 1974). Three-day-old babies can tell their mother's voice from a stranger's (DeCasper & Fifer, 1980). And 1-month-old babies can tell the difference between sounds as alike as *pah* and *bah* (Eimas, Siqueland, Jusczyk, & Vigorito, 1971).

PRELINGUISTIC SPEECH   Before babies say that first real word—an event that ushers in the beginning of linguistic speech—they utter a variety of sounds in a sequence tied fairly closely to chronological age. These sounds constitute prelinguistic speech. First babies *cry*, and their crying takes on different patterns, intensities, and pitches to indicate hunger, sleepiness, anger, or pain. At about 6 weeks they *coo* when they are happy, and at about 6 months they *babble*, repeating a variety of simple consonant and vowel sounds (*ma-ma-ma-ma*). During the second half of their first year, they listen to sounds around them, *accidentally imitate* these sounds, and then imitate themselves. At about 9 or 10 months they *consciously imitate* other people's sounds even though they do not understand them. During these last three stages babies acquire their basic repertoire of sounds, and during their second year they string these sounds together in ways that mimic the patterns and rhythms of sentences, even though they make no sense—at least to anyone besides the baby (Eisenson, Auer, & Irwin, 1963; Lenneberg, 1967). Some milestones in early speech development are shown in Table 8-1 (page 272).

LINGUISTIC SPEECH   Linguistic speech is characterized by the use of words, that is, spoken sounds which stand for specific meanings.

First words   It's a major family event when a baby says his or her first word. This

TABLE 8-1   LANGUAGE MILESTONES

Age, Months	Language Development
6	Changes from cooing to babbling with introduction of consonants
12	Imitates sounds Understands some words Applies some sounds regularly to signify person or object (that is, uses the first words)
18	Uses repertoire of 3 to 50 words Makes patterns of sound and intonation that resemble discourse Makes good progress in understanding
24	Uses more than 50 words Uses two-word phrases Is more interested in verbal communication No longer babbles
30	Uses new words almost every day Makes utterances of three or more words Has excellent comprehension Makes many mistakes in grammar
36	Has vocabulary of some 1000 words; about 80% intelligible Uses grammar close to colloquial speech of adults Makes fewer syntactic mistakes

Source: Adapted from Lenneberg, 1969.

usually happens at about 1 year. This word can be any simple syllable and can have a variety of meanings; the meaning at any given time has to be interpreted by those close to the infant, in terms of the context in which it is said. The baby may point to a cracker or toy and say "Da" (meaning: "I want that"); or may crawl to the door and say "Da" (meaning: "I want to go out"); or may smile at the father and say "Da" (meaning: "I'm glad you're home, Daddy"). These first words are called **holophrases** because they express a complete thought in a single word.

Holophrases *First spoken words; they express a complete thought in a single word.*

Children differ considerably in the kinds of words they use first (K. Nelson, 1973, 1981). Among the first 50 words spoken by one group of eighteen 1- and 2-year-olds, the most common were *names* of things, either in the general sense (*da* for *dog*) or in the specific sense (the name of one particular dog). Others were *action* words (*bye-bye*), *modifiers* (*hot*), words that express *feelings or relationships* (*no*), and a very few words that fulfill a solely *grammatical function* (*for*) (K. Nelson, 1973).

After children acquire a few words at about 1 year, there seems to be a plateau of several months when they add very few additional words (K. Nelson, 1979). This may be a period during which their understanding of language grows, when they use words more to structure their own thinking than to communicate.

First sentences At 26 months, Nancy said her first four-word sentence. She looked up from the stroller in which she was riding and told her father, "I dropped my shoe"—clearly a practical thing to be able to say. Some children speak in sentences earlier than this, some later. While prelinguistic speech is fairly closely tied to chronological age, linguistic speech is not.

Brown's stages of language: Roger Brown (1973a, 1973b), who has done a great deal of work on this phase of language acquisition, maintains that knowing a child's age tells us very little about his or her language development. Brown prefers to discuss syntactic skill in terms of stages that correspond to the **mean length of utterance (MLU),** the average length of utterances in morphemes (units of meaning). In stage 1 the child first begins to combine morphemes and words; in this stage the MLU is over 1.0. In stage 2, when the MLU is 2.0, the child can actually utter as

Mean length of utterance (MLU) *Average length of utterances, in morphemes.*

This little girl seems to be remembering what it felt like to touch the cactus. She's probably using a single word to describe it—perhaps a modifier like "sharp" or "hurt." Such modifiers are often among children's first spoken words, along with names of things ("flower"), words that express feelings ("ouch") and action words ("touch").

many as seven morphemes, even though the mean, or average, is only two. The child advances with each increase of 0.5 MLU, up to stage 5.

Stage 1 is primitive speech, when tense and case endings, articles, and prepositions are missing (as in "That ball," "More ball," "All gone ball," "Hit ball," "Big ball," "Book table," "Go store," "Mommy sock"). When the MLU is 1.5, the child may string two basic relations together ("Adam hit" + "Hit ball") to get a more complicated relation ("Adam hit ball").

In *stage 2,* children acquire morphemes, such as articles (*a, the*), prepositions (*in, on*), plurals, verb endings, and forms of the verb *to be* (*am, are, is*). Children start to use these forms gradually, sometimes over several years. In his intensive study of three children (Adam, Eve, and Sarah) Brown (1973a) noted that the rate of development even among such a small sample is great, but that the order in which the children acquired the different constructions was almost constant.

Children leave stage 2 at a variety of ages, and their speech becomes longer and more complex. Speech in *stage 3* has been called **telegraphic speech** because it contains many utterances, like "Mama put dolly table," which sound like telegrams. This term is misleading, however, because it implies that children edit their sentences as adults edit telegrams.

Characteristics of stages 1, 2, and 3: Just as children are not miniature adults, neither is their speech a simplified version of adult language. It has a character all its own, with its own rules—even though these rules change over time. Children speaking German, Russian, Finnish, Samoan, and English show similar patterns (Slobin, 1971). How, then, do young children form their speech in stages 1, 2, and 3?

Telegraphic speech *Speech that is characterized by many utterances and that sounds like words in a telegram.*

■ *They simplify:* Children utter just enough to get their meaning across, omitting many parts of speech that adults consider essential (as in "Nancy go store" for "I want to go to the store" or "No drink milk" for "I don't want to drink any more milk").

■ *They overregularize rules:* At the beginning of stage 3, many children who had earlier used the correct words for *mice, went,* and other exceptions to grammatical rules start to say things like *mouses* and *goed.* Why? They have not regressed to a lower stage. Instead, they have learned rules of grammar for forming past tense and plural nouns and are now using these rules consistently. They still need to learn the exceptions to the rules.

■ *They overextend concepts:* Sometimes children apply concepts too broadly. The tendency of young children to call all men *Daddy* and all furry creatures *kitty* is exemplified by one child who called not only her mother but both her older sisters *Mom*—an overextension of the caretaking role (Nelson, 1973).

■ *They understand certain grammatical relations that they cannot yet express:* Children early in stage 1 may understand that a dog is chasing a cat, but they cannot explain the complete action. They may say, "Puppy chase," "Chase kitty," or "Puppy kitty," but not until the end of this stage will they be able to string together "Puppy chase kitty."

Characteristics of stages 4 and 5: In *stage 4,* children's grammar is close to that of adults, even though children are still learning some syntactic niceties. They can string together two sentences, but they still make a lot of grammatical mistakes. They often cannot use the subjunctive ("I wish we were going swimming today") or make up tag questions ("You are coming, aren't you?"). And they cannot deal with the meaning in such sentences as "John promised Mary to shovel the driveway"; they think that Mary is going to do the shoveling (C. Chomsky, 1969).

Stage 5, embodying full competence, occurs by late childhood. No change in handling syntax occurs beyond puberty, but vocabulary and style continue to improve into adulthood. Relatively little research has been done on these last two stages.

Theories about Language Aquisition   The major theories about why and how children learn language range along a continuum with regard to the relative influence of environment and heredity. The **learning theorists** believe most strongly in the power of the environment while the **nativists** are most convinced that people have an inborn capacity for learning language. We'll look at views at either extreme and then examine one based on interaction between heredity and environment.

Learning theorists   *Theorists who believe that the environment is most influential in learning language.*

Nativists   *Theorists who believe that there is an inborn capacity for learning language.*

LEARNING THEORIES   According to the behaviorist B. F. Skinner (1957), we learn language the way we learn everything else—through reinforcement, discrimination, and generalization. In this view, parents shape their children's production of speech by reinforcing sounds that are like adult speech. Children learn to generalize and abstract from the sounds they are reinforced for, and eventually they produce effective language. Evidence favoring this viewpoint is the greater amount of babbling by babies reared at home in comparison with babies reared in an institution. Presumably, the babies at home are noticed and reinforced more often than those in institutions, who vocalize less (Brodbeck & Irwin, 1946). Evidence against this behaviorist viewpoint is the fact that parents generally do not correct the grammar of their young children (Brown, Cazden, & Bellugi, 1969); this suggests that something other than direct learning (through reinforcement or partly through reinforcement) is taking place.

Social-learning theory   *Theory, proposed by Bandura, that behaviors are learned by observing and imitating models and are maintained through reinforcement.*

Social-learning theory stresses the importance of observation and imitation (Bandura, 1977; Mowrer, 1960). Children hear their parents speak, copy them, are reinforced for this behavior, and thus learn the language. Certainly this theory explains some aspects of language acquisition, since children in English-speaking nations speak English rather than French or Swahili. But imitation does not explain many aspects of language development. For one thing, many of the things children say are novel. The little girl who did not know the word for *knee* and called it an *elbow of the leg* had not heard this description before and so could not have imitated a model. For another, it is highly unlikely that children come up with words like *mouses* and *goed* through observation and imitation. Furthermore, children often fail to imitate what they hear, as in this interchange:

"She said, 'My teacher holded the baby rabbits and we patted them.'
I asked, 'Did you say the teacher held the baby rabbits?'
She answered: 'Yes.'
I then asked: 'What did you say she did?'
She answered again: 'She holded the baby rabbits and we patted them.'
'Did you say she held them tightly?' I asked.
'No,' she answered. 'She holded them loosely.'" (Gleason, 1967)

NATIVISM According to the view held by nativists, human beings have an inborn capacity for acquiring language and learn to talk as naturally as they learn to walk. Noam Chomsky (1965, 1968) of the Massachusetts Institute of Technology proposes that the human brain is specifically constructed to give us this innate ability. This inborn ability to acquire language is known as the **language acquisition device (LAD).** LAD enables children to analyze the language they hear and to extract grammatical rules, with which they are able to create new sentences that they have never heard before. Our brains are programmed to extract these rules; all we need is the basic experience that will activate our innate language capacity.

Language acquisition device (LAD) Inborn ability to analyze language to extract grammatical rules.

What is the evidence for this viewpoint? First, all normal children learn their native language. They master not only the basics but also highly complex aspects of grammar, in the same age-related sequence. Second, human beings have certain biological characteristics which seem to suggest that they are programmed for language. We are, for example, the only species with a brain larger on one side (the left) than the other. This size difference suggests that there may be an innate mechanism for language in the left hemisphere. Third, certain brain injuries may impair our language abilities without affecting other mental and motor skills; this may indicate that we have a localized structure specifically designed to provide language capacity (Lenneberg, 1969). Finally, the "ongoing dance of the neonate with human speech"—the tendency of newborns to move at the same tempo as the speech sounds they hear—suggests that even before birth something in the brain may lay down the form and structure of language (Condon & Sander, 1974).

In explaining the development of speech, however, the extreme nativist approach has its shortcomings. Some learning has to take place, of course, if children are to learn the rules of English rather than the rules of German or Japanese. Also, this theory does not take into account the considerable individual differences which do exist among children. And, finally, Chomsky has not addressed issues related to the meaning of the words children use or to the social context in which they use these words.

MOTHERESE: HOW CARETAKERS STRUCTURE THE CHILD'S LANGUAGE ENVIRONMENT Today, many psychologists believe that language develops through interaction between children and those who care for them. Infants enter the world with some inborn language capacity, as seen in their ability to discriminate fine variations in sounds, to distinguish and respond to their mothers' voices as compared with the voices of other women, and to move in rhythm with adult speech. This basic capacity lets them benefit from the specialized environmental input called *motherese.*

When you're with a baby or toddler, do you find yourself talking simply and pitching your voice higher than usual? If so, you're speaking **motherese,** something most adults do almost automatically. Motherese is useful in helping children learn a language. The term itself reflects the fact that most research in this area has focused on language between children and their mothers; but it is actually more general. It refers to language addressed to children by mothers, fathers, other adults, and even older children, who generally talk to small children differently from the way they speak to their age-mates. Studies of the social context of language learning have led to explorations of the way adults talk to children, and to the conclusion that such modifications in speech are helpful in teaching children their native language.

Motherese Specialized kind of conversation that is addressed to young children and is important for language acquisition.

What is the function of motherese? Emotionally, it provides a framework for

Fathers, too, speak "motherese," a simplified form of speech in which word endings are omitted, pronouns are avoided, sentences are short, and a great deal of repetition occurs. These modifications of usual adult speech seem to help children learn their language.

social interaction between adult and child, helping to develop their relationship. Socially, it teaches a child how to carry on a conversation—how to introduce a topic, comment and expand on an idea, and take turns talking. Linguistically, it teaches a child how to use new words, how to structure phrases, and how to put ideas into language. It seems to be vital to the learning of speech.

How do adults change their speech in talking to small children? Catherine E. Snow (1972) examined the speech of middle-class mothers and of women who had no children themselves and were rarely with children. Mothers and nonmothers alike made similar adjustments, speaking quite differently to 2-year-olds and to 10-year-olds. For the 2-year-olds, they simplified what they said, repeated it either exactly or by rephrasing the same idea, and used fewer pronouns and verbs.

These findings need some qualification, however. For one thing, the actual presence of the child seems to be significant. In some experiments, the adults were asked to make tapes addressed to children of these ages. When the children were not present, the adults did not modify their speech as much. Also, some studies have found that motherese does not begin to function fully early in infancy—it functions only when babies respond with a glimmer of understanding to what adults are saying (Molfese, Molfese, & Carrell, 1982). And third, mothers tend to overestimate the conversational abilities of infants; but as they attribute skills to infants and talk to them accordingly, the children develop the skills. Children, then, are active partners in conversations, showing by their expressions, their actions, and their own speech how closely they are following adults' speech.

It has also been shown, in other studies, that adults speaking to small children modify *what* they talk about as well as *how* they talk. They tend to talk about down-to-earth, everyday topics—what children can see or hear, have just seen or done (or are about to see or do), or might want to know. As Snow (1977, p. 41) points out, "Mothers make very predictable comments about very predictable topics," a tendency that helps children learn language because they can add their own knowledge to what they hear to help them work out meaning.

The importance of motherese in learning speech is reflected in the language retardation of children with normal hearing who grow up in homes with deaf parents who communicate with them through sign language. No matter how fluent the children are in signing (showing their ability to learn a language) and no matter how much television they watch, they do not develop fluency in spoken language unless adults speak to them, which may not happen until they go to school.

Case study: A home without motherese. In one family, both parents of two little boys were deaf (Sachs, Bard, & Johnson, 1981). The mother was warm and loving, but she was able to speak very few words and said hardly anything to her children except an occasional *no*. She did not sign to them, because she wanted to motivate them to use normal speech. The children's speech did not develop normally, because they had little contact with hearing adults. They did watch television, and at 2½, Jim, the older child, began to use a few words he had heard on television, mostly from commercials. At age 3 years, 9 months, Jim spoke considerably below age level, in a very soft monotone. He had trouble understanding words spoken to him, and what he did say was peculiar in structure ("Where is it plane?" "Where the wheels plane?" "That enough two wing"). However, he was a persistent little boy who tried hard to communicate, often rephrasing his words to get his ideas across.

After Jim attended six sessions of speech therapy, many of his unusual speech patterns disappeared and he was talking like a typical 4-year-old ("He's stopping crying," "I say 'bye' to my mommy"). He continued to receive therapy, and his first-grade teacher reported that he was a well-adjusted, popular child. Her only complaint may have had something to do with Jim's making up for lost time. She protested that he chatted too much with other children!

Jim's brother, Glenn, was almost 2 years younger. His speech developed more normally, because he had Jim. Glenn started speaking late (by 1 year, 8 months, he still was not talking), but he never used the kind of deviant language structures that

Jim had used. At 4 years, 9 months, Glenn was speaking normally. This was proba- bly because Jim spoke to him a great deal. Jim taught Glenn the names of items and interpreted his little brother's speech for outsiders.

These children illustrate some important facts about language development. Jim's experience shows that an important part of learning a language involves learn- ing linguistic forms. This seems to depend a great deal on feedback, which Jim did not have. Being spoken to (for example, through television) is not enough; one-to- one conversation is essential. Glenn's experience shows that feedback does not have to be given by an adult with full command of the language. He apparently got enough from his brother to enable him to develop normal patterns of speech. He may have learned simpler ideas than he would have gotten from an adult speaking motherese, but he learned enough to use the patterns of his native language.

It seems, then, that language development is based on an innate mechanism which depends both on maturation and on certain kinds of language experience for its full flowering.

Three Controversies in Linguistics

Controversy 1: Is There A Critical Period for Acquiring Language?   You may know an older person who came to the United States 20, 30, or more years ago and yet still speaks with a pronounced foreign accent. On the other hand, if you know someone who came to this country as a small child, he or she probably speaks unaccented English, like a native. This common phenomenon is one reason for thinking that there is a critical period in learning a language.

A **critical period** is a specific "sensitive time" during development, a time when certain events have their greatest impact. With regard to language, the idea of a critical period would imply that the brain of a child who has not yet reached puberty is organized to encourage the acquisition of language, but that something happens in the brain during the early teens which changes this linguistic capacity.

Eric Lenneberg (1969), one of the strongest proponents of the critical-period theory, offers other evidence for it. He points to the fact that language correlates better with motor development, an important index of maturation, than it does with chronological age. Furthermore, he notes that children who suffer injury to the left hemisphere of the brain before their early teens may lose some speech ability but will quickly regain it if the right hemisphere is intact. However, if such lesions occur during adolescence or adulthood, loss of language skills is likely to be irreversible. Left-right specialization does not take place until puberty, according to Lenneberg. Until then, the right hemisphere can take over if injury occurs to the left. He maintains that the critical period "coincides with the time at which the human brain attains its final state of maturity in terms of structure, function, and biochemistry" (p. 639).

A poignant test of this hypothesis was in the case of "Genie," a girl discovered in 1970 (Curtiss, 1977; Fromkin, Krashen, Curtiss, Rigler, & Rigler, 1974; Pines, 1981). From the age of 20 months until her discovery at age 13½, Genie (that was not her real name) had been kept confined in a small room where no one spoke to her. When Genie was brought to a hospital in California, she weighed only 59 pounds, could not straighten her arms or legs, could not chew, had no control over bladder and bowel functions, and did not speak. She recognized only her own name and the word *sorry*.

Genie's linguistic progress during the following 9 years (until her mother re- gained custody and cut her off from the professionals who had been caring for her and teaching her) both disconfirms and supports the critical-period hypothesis. The fact that Genie learned any language at all after the age of 13 may refute the notion of a critical period, but then again, it may not. Genie did acquire quite a bit of language ability, learning many words and stringing them together in primitive though rule- governed sentences. Yet even after 9 years of progress and intensive work with

Critical period *Specific sensitive time during development when certain events have their greatest impact.*

psycholinguists, she never used language normally. She never asked questions, and 4 years after she had begun putting words together, "her speech remained, for the most part, like a somewhat garbled telegram" (Pines, 1981, p. 29).

The fact that she was just beginning to show signs of puberty at age 13½ may indicate that she was still in the critical period, although near its end. The fact that she had apparently said a few words before being locked up at the age of 20 months may mean that her language-learning mechanisms had been triggered early in the critical period, thus allowing later learning to occur. And the fact that she was so abused and neglected may have retarded her so much—emotionally, socially, and intellectually—that she cannot be considered a true test of the critical period. A number of examinations suggested that Genie was using her right hemisphere to learn language, possibly because development of the left hemisphere is limited to a critical period following the acquisition of language at the proper time (Curtiss, 1977).

Controversy 2: Does Thought Structure Language, or Does Language Structure Thought?   While we have only one word for *snow*, the Inuit (Eskimos) have several. They have different words for *snow packed hard like ice, falling snow,* and *snow on the ground.* The question is: Do they think differently about snow because they have the vocabulary to do so? Or have they made up those words because they think differently? Can the Inuit make discriminations among types of snow that we, with our meager vocabulary of "snow words," cannot?

Linguistic-relativity hypothesis
Whorf's view that language affects perception and thought; also known as the Whorfian hypothesis.

LINGUISTIC-RELATIVITY HYPOTHESIS   The idea that the language we use affects the way we perceive and think is known as the **linguistic-relativity hypothesis,** or the *Whorfian hypothesis,* after its most vigorous modern proponent, Benjamin Lee Whorf (1956). Whorf maintains that language does not simply provide a neutral means for giving voice to ideas, but instead plays an active part in shaping those ideas. Thus people who speak different languages perceive the world differently and think differently.

As fascinating as Whorf's observations are, they are not decisive. People from Florida can distinguish different types of snow and can describe them with phrases. Furthermore, if these Floridians go to Colorado to ski, they are likely to add new "snow words" to their vocabulary—like *powder, corn,* and *ice.* They can learn to make distinctions among different kinds of snow. The question, then, is: Are the new words helping the Florida skiers to make finer discriminations? Or are the new words merely tools to help them express something they have already noticed?

The Whorfian hypothesis raises a "chicken or egg" problem: Which comes first—the thought or the word? An opposing point of view is that you have a thought first and then talk about it; and that when you talk about something frequently, you are likely to develop a word for it (Brown & Lenneberg, 1954).

Recent efforts to make the English language less sexist (gender-biased) have built on the view that language structure shapes a person's view of reality and, therefore, carries serious psychological implications. Thus, a language that uses masculine words to apply to both sexes (*mankind*) and defines occupational titles by sex (*policeman, stewardess*) puts forth a stereotyped view of people and sets limitations for both males and females. The use of gender-biased words sets in motion thought processes that have implications far beyond the particular words. Masculine words conjure up masculine images and feminine words inspire feminine images. Shifting to more inclusive words (*police officer, flight attendant*) frees both speaker and listener (or writer and reader) from gender-role stereotyping. (For more on such stereotyping, see Chapter 12.)

TESTS OF THE LINGUISTIC-RELATIVITY HYPOTHESIS   To test the Whorfian hypothesis, Brown and Lenneberg (1954) developed the concept of *codability* of words. Highly codable words are those to which speakers of the same language respond quickly,

and on whose meaning they agree. (Here, *agreement* implies that the meaning of a word will be consistent not only between different people but also for one person on different occasions.) If codability is applied to colors, *red* is highly codable and *mauve* is not. Brown and Lenneberg found that the most codable colors are remembered the best. For many years, this finding was believed to demonstrate the effect of language on perception and memory.

More recently, however, the concept of codability was applied in color-naming and memory tests given to English-speaking Americans and to some members of the Dani—a stone age tribe in New Guinea which has just two names for color, emphasizing brightness rather than hue (Heider & Olivier, 1972). The Americans, with their large color vocabulary, named many more colors. However, when subjects were shown a single color chip for 5 seconds and then 30 seconds later were asked to pick it out from an array of 40 chips, the two groups performed similarly. Not having names for colors did not prevent the Dani from perceiving and remembering them. Colors that were highly codable in English were remembered best by both groups, suggesting that certain colors are remembered best by everyone, despite differences in language. These findings have led many psychologists to discard the Whorfian hypothesis, although others think that color naming is the wrong place to look for an effect of language on thought.

Whether or not the Whorfian hypothesis is tenable, we can say that the development of language gives us a symbol system which lets us label people, places, events, and objects in our lives. Through these labels we can communicate with others in our culture who attach similar meanings to these labels. In our discussion of concept formation later in this chapter, we'll see how people learn to apply similar labels to stimuli that they categorize into concepts.

Controversy 3: Can Animals Learn Language? During the 1970s, Washoe, Sarah, Lana, and Nim Chimpsky created a stir in linguistic circles (Gardner & Gardner, 1969; Premack & Premack, 1972; Rumbaugh & Gill, 1973; Terrace, 1979). These celebrities were chimpanzees who had been taught to communicate through such mediums as American Sign Language (ASL), the set of hand gestures used by deaf persons (Washoe and Nim); Yerkish, an artificial visual language (Lana); and another artificial language which uses plastic chips of different colors and shapes (Sarah). Earlier studies had recognized the impossibility of actually teaching apes to speak

It's not surprising that natives of lands like the one shown here have a much richer vocabulary for different kinds of ice and snow than people who live in more temperate climates. A question debated by linguists is whether the Inuit (Eskimos) think differently about snow because they have the vocabulary to do so, or whether they make up words because they think differently. That is: Which comes first, thought or language?

because of their inadequate vocal apparatus (Hayes, 1951; Kellogg & Kellogg, 1933), but these new researchers seemed to be getting around the problem by using nonvocal languages. (ASL is considered a language even though it does not include one definitive feature of language, spoken sounds, since it does embody the other crucial elements, especially rules that allow signers to create new sentences.)

Enthusiasm greeted news of Washoe's definition of a duck as a "water bird"; Sarah's ability to follow such directions as "Sarah insert apple pail banana dish"; Lana's ability to "say," "Please machine give juice"; and Nim's 16-sign utterance, "Give orange me give eat orange me eat orange give me eat orange give me you." The trainer of Koko, a gorilla, even said, "Language is no longer the exclusive domain of man" (Patterson, quoted in Terrace, 1979).

However, critics of these and other projects that have tried to teach apes various kinds of language state that the apes' performances do not demonstrate ability to learn language as we define it (Limber, 1977; Terrace, 1985, 1979; Terrace, Petitto, Sanders, & Bever, 1979). It all seems to come down to the fact that while apes can learn to use meaningful symbols, can generalize them correctly to new situations, and can communicate after a fashion with human beings, they do not learn the creative aspect of language. Particularly, they do not know how to use rules to create an infinite number of new expressions and complex sentences.

One psychologist (Terrace, 1979) initially felt that "his chimp," Nim Chimpsky, was using a grammar—until he analyzed videotapes of Nim's "conversations" with a teacher. At that point, he discovered that word sequences, although they seemed like sentences, were in fact subtle imitations of the teacher's sequences. Furthermore, even though Nim learned more and more words, he did not show the kind of increase in mean length of utterance that accompanies normal human speech development. Nim was not as grammatically competent as he had first seemed, and, according to Terrace, neither were any of the other "talking" apes.

Apes differ from humans in another way. The first vocabulary of human babies usually includes various nouns, which the children say with obvious delight—not necessarily because they want the items in question, but just to show that they have noticed something in their world and want to share this awareness with other human beings. This spontaneous naming does not occur in chimps. They can learn to communicate names of objects, but only after intensive drilling, and they do so only to get something. In fact, Terrace (1985) believes that apes do not understand the fact that it is possible to refer to an object by its name, or the fact that the names they express could be any symbol to be used to demand something.

One possible exception was a 4-year-old pygmy chimp, Kanzi, who showed the most advanced linguistic abilities ever documented in an animal (Savage-Rumbaugh, Sevcik, Rumbaugh, & Rubert, 1985). Kanzi was the only primate that seemed able to use a symbol to identify a concept and to ask for a particular food or drink that was not in plain sight. Kanzi expressed himself by punching geometric symbols on a keyboard. Kanzi also commented on his actions, described what he planned to do, and apparently understood spoken words. Furthermore, he came up with creative responses to novel situations. For example, when a companion chimp, Austin, was moved out of the compound, Kanzi seemed to miss him. After several nights without his friend, Kanzi typed the symbols *Austin* and *TV*. When he saw a videotape of Austin, Kanzi made loud sounds of pleasure and then went happily to sleep. Of course, in this exchange, Kanzi was still using nouns to get something he wanted. Still, Kanzi went so far beyond other chimps in understanding complex sentences, in learning many symbols without intensive drilling, and in other linguistic abilities that researchers hope to use the pygmy chimpanzee to understand how human language first developed.

At this point none of the apes have shown the kind of creative, complex production of meaningful phrases that are part of a full-fledged language. However, none of them have had the many years of language training, or the intensity of training, that children receive automatically before they are able to understand and speak a language. So far it has not been possible to provide such training, because chimpanzees

(Elizabeth Rubert)

Kanzi, the pygmy chimp who has shown the most advanced linguistic abilities ever documented in a nonhuman animal, examines the computer language board from which he selects symbols to identify concepts and ask for items.

become unmanageable and dangerous as they grow older. Meanwhile, the research with Kanzi seems to hold the most promise for discovering language abilities in animals other than human beings.

One of the limitations in apes' use of language is their literalness. They do not talk about any concepts that cannot be seen and touched. So far, the ability to express thoughts about such abstract concepts, and, in fact, the ability to form concepts at all, seems to be an exclusively human capacity.

FORMATION OF CONCEPTS

If you were asked what you have in your closet, you might answer, "Clothing." Or you might say, "Jackets, jeans, shirts, and shoes." In either case, you would not feel that you had to describe every individual object in the closet. Both these answers demonstrate a vital aspect of human thought, the ability to organize a variety of different objects, events, and people into concepts, or *categories*. In forming categories we group together items that have defining features in common. These concepts range from fairly narrow ones like *pullover sweaters,* to broader ones like *tops* (including sweaters, blouses, and T-shirts), *sportswear, outerwear,* and so forth, to the general category of *clothing.*

The world would be a much more chaotic place for us if we could not use language and form concepts. Concepts allow us to generalize, and thus to give order to a world full of unique objects and happenings. With this order, we know how to act when we meet new members of a category, and so we don't have to relearn how to behave at each encounter. We can generalize from previous experience and formulate general rules for thought and action.

By having a concept of *car,* we know that this is a four-wheeled vehicle with the potential for taking us someplace—and also the potential for damage. Since we have this concept, we can apply it to new cars (such as foreign ones or racers) that we have never seen before. Early in life, then, we learn to stay out of the way of fast-moving cars, trucks, and buses, because we have formed the concept that speed and a large vehicle can be a dangerous combination. On the more abstract level, systems of morality, justice, and government rest on a foundation of concepts.

Well-Defined Concepts

Well-defined concept *Concept specified by a set of unambiguous features, connected by a rule.*

A **well-defined concept** is a concept that can be specified by a set of clear, unambiguous *features* (such as color, size, composition, shape, and function), connected by a *rule,* or a relationship among them. Thus a baseball is a spherical object of a certain composition, size, weight, *and* texture, used for the purpose of playing a particular game. An eligible candidate for the presidency of the United States is someone who was born in this country *and* is over 35 years old. A promising applicant for college is a high school student who has achieved good grades, *or* has scored high on aptitude or achievement tests, *or* has an interesting extracurricular background. The rules or relations in these examples are indicated by the words *and* and *or*. In the first two examples, *all* the features have to be present for membership in the category *(and)*; in the last example, *only one* of the three features has to be present *(or)*.

In studying the way people form concepts, researchers often use a series of symbolic forms that differ in such features as size, shape, and color, and then ask subjects to tell which items are examples of an *undefined* concept. The experimenter does not define the concept in question for the subject, but requires him or her to determine what the concept is ("all green circles") by figuring out which stimuli are and are not positive examples of the concept in question. In this way it is possible to see the kind of reasoning used in forming concepts.

People usually use systematic strategies rather than trial and error (guessing). This shows that concept formation is a thinking process. As such, it goes far beyond the automatic strengthening or weakening of associations between stimulus and response that the behaviorists envisioned. In fact, people do better in solving concept-formation problems if they have had training in formal logic (Dodd, Kinsman, Klipp, & Bourne, 1971) or a great deal of practice in learning concepts in the laboratory (Bourne, 1967, 1970).

Also, people usually focus on one feature at a time. If the first positive example was "3 red circles in 2 borders," subjects may choose "3 *green* circles in 2 borders." If they are told that the second item is *not* an instance of the concept, what do they know? They know that color is crucial because it is the only feature which has changed between the two examples. If they are told that the second item *is* an instance, they know that color is not relevant, but that number of circles or borders or shapes might be.

If subjects feel like gambling, after they have been told that the first positive instance is "3 red circles in 2 borders," they might choose "2 *green* circles in 2 borders." If this *is* an instance, they have learned two facts—that both number and color are irrelevant. If this is *not* an instance, they don't know which was crucial—changing the color or changing the number. This "focus gambling" is like the kind sometimes used in the game Botticelli, in which players try to guess which famous person another player is thinking of, by asking questions that can be answered only *yes* or *no*. If I ask, "Is this a living American male?" and you say, "Yes," I have three pieces of information, but if you say, "No," I don't know whether any of these attributes apply. If I had asked, "Is this person living?" I would have one definite, specific piece of information, no matter what your answer was.

Ill-defined Concepts

What Are Ill-Defined Concepts? The concepts we have just described are considered well-defined, because there is no likelihood of confusion between red and green, between circles and squares, or between one border and two. All these distinctions are very clear. But in real life, where we cannot control conditions the way we can in a laboratory, we most often deal with **ill-defined concepts.** In these, the features of one category often overlap those in another, making it difficult to distinguish between them.

Ill-defined concept *Concept for which the features and rules that connect members of a category are not obvious.*

What, for example, is the difference between a magazine and a book? Is it the fact that a book is bound and a magazine is stapled? Is it the fact that a book is issued once and a magazine periodically? Is it the fact that a book is sold in bookstores and a magazine at newsstands? Suppose a publisher issues a yearly publication in a binding like that used for books. Is it a magazine, even though most magazines are published weekly or monthly? Is it a book? If the publisher calls it a book, does that make it a book? If bookstores refuse to sell it, does that make it a magazine? Who decides?

In ill-defined concepts, then, the features and the rules that connect members of a category are not obvious. Thus it is difficult to learn ill-defined concepts simply by learning a specific definition. Instead, they tend to be learned by experience with members of the category. The concept *clothing*, for instance, is usually taught by example, not by definition. Young children learn to distinguish coats from hats not by being given lists of the features of each, but by being told, "This is a coat. That is a hat." In other words, we learn what constitutes a concept by being given a series of examples and abstracting the rules for concept "membership" from these examples.

For example, you know what a game is. Come up with a definition for *game* before reading on.

Game = ———————————————

Now check your definition. Does it include checkers but exclude dancing? Does it distinguish between amateur and professional sports? Should it? What are its features? What rules connect them?

Aspects of Ill-Defined Concepts TYPICALITY Even though many different items may fit into a particular concept category, some things have a firmer place in it than others. Some items seem to be more typical (that is, better examples) of a concept than others. To see how this works, let's suppose that you are asked to answer *yes* or *no* as quickly as possible to such questions as "Is a robin a bird?" and "Is a penguin a bird?" Most people correctly answer both questions *yes* but reply more quickly to the question about robins than the one about penguins (Rips, Shoben, & Smith, 1973). A robin is more typical of *bird* than a penguin is, probably because it has more of the defining features of the category *bird*: a robin not only lays eggs and has feathers and wings, but also flies (which a penguin does not). When asked to rate the **typicality** of different kinds of fruits (pictured in Figure 8-1 on page 284), subjects rated orange and apple as "good" examples, apricot and tangerine as "intermediate," and grapefruit and berry as "poorest." These ratings correlated with reaction times—answers affirming the more typical examples were given faster (Rosch, 1975).

Typicality *Degree to which a particular item is a good example of a concept.*

FAMILY RESEMBLANCE One way of explaining typicality is the theory of **family resemblance.** You may, for example, look like your father, especially around the eyes. Your sister's nose may look like his. But you and your sister may not look much like each other. In a family, members resemble each other in various ways, and the essence of this family resemblance is an overlap of similarities. Members of a natural language category may be linked by the same type of "family resemblance" in which all the members have at least one feature in common with another member and some members share many features (Wittgenstein, 1953).

Family resemblance *Degree to which members of a category have features in common.*

To test the theory that typicality is related to degree of "feature overlap," college students were asked to rate the typicality of 20 objects from each of 6 categories (furniture, vehicle, fruit, etc.) (Rosch & Mervis, 1975). Another group of students was asked to list the attributes possessed by each item (for *bicycle*, the features might include "two wheels," "pedals," and "you ride on it"). When the scores of the two groups were compared, typicality and family resemblance ratings correlated very highly. The more features an item has in common with other members of a category, the more it will be considered a "good"—that is, a representative—member.

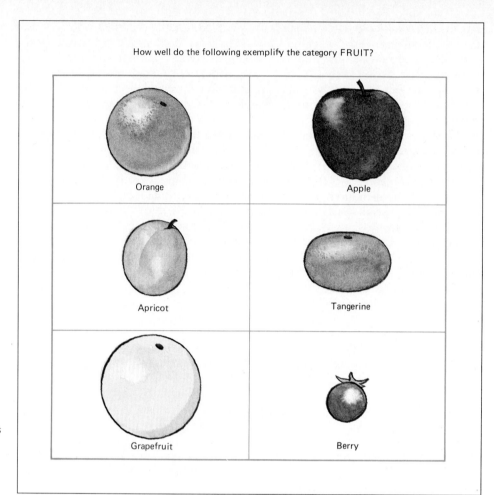

How well do the following exemplify the category FRUIT?

Orange

Apple

Apricot

Tangerine

Grapefruit

Berry

FIGURE 8-1 *Right: Typicality in concept formation. Regardless of personal preferences, we can say that apples and oranges are "better" (more typical) examples of the category "fruit" than are the other fruits shown here. Our basis for saying this is the finding that subjects in research studies, asked whether these various foods were fruits, needed less time to affirm the top two as fruits than they did for the other four. (Source: Rosch, 1975.)*

FIGURE 8-2 *Basic-level category: chair. The object pictured here can be categorized in a number of different ways. The basic level is the one that takes most subjects the least time to classify. In this case, the basic level is "chair," a higher-order category is "furniture," and a lower-order category is "kitchen chair."*

BASIC-LEVEL CATEGORIES   In the real world, concepts are not arbitrary combinations of features and rules. Nor do they necessarily look, sound, or feel alike. Yet there is a basic level of abstraction at which we naturally divide things into categories (Rosch & Mervis, 1975).

For example, what would you call the object shown in Figure 8-2? You would probably say, "A chair," the answer most likely to be given by both children and adults. Yet this object also belongs to a higher-order category (*furniture*) and a lower-order category (*kitchen chair*). People *can* classify an object (like a chair) in any of several ways. They could correctly indicate that it is a *chair*, a *kitchen chair*, a *piece of furniture*, or a *manufactured object*.

Reaction-time tasks show that people classify fastest at the basic level (such as *chair*). This suggests that basic-level categories are the ones we use in our daily dealings with objects. These basic-level categories are probably the ones that children learn to use earliest in naming and classifying objects (Rosch, Mervis, Gray, Johnson, & Boyes-Braem, 1976).

With the ability to form concepts, we can make generalizations about the world that let us impose our own order on its complexity; we can communicate with other people; and we can solve at least some of the many problems we encounter as we go through life.

PROBLEM SOLVING

Consider this: It's Saturday night. Sara is getting married tomorrow afternoon. The shoes that go with her wedding dress are in the store where she bought them, being repaired. She has forgotten to pick them up, and now the store is closed, not to reopen till Monday. Sara has a problem. Finally, Sara's mother remembers that a friend of hers is a friend of the sister of the man who owns the shoe store. She calls her friend, who calls her friend, who calls her brother, who takes pity on the distraught bride and arranges to meet her at the store early the next morning to give her the shoes. Sara gets married in full wedding garb, and everyone is happy. The problem has been solved.

Finding an answer to a question or a way out of a predicament—that is, solving a problem—is a cognitive activity aimed at a goal. In this case, the goal is obtaining something (a pair of shoes) before a certain time (Sunday afternoon). Problem solving can be either *routine* (using existing procedures) or *creative* (developing new procedures). In the case of Sara's mother, the use of a familiar tool (the telephone) and a familiar activity (contacting people) puts the solution in the category *routine*. What creative procedures might Sara (or her mother) have devised for this problem?

Unlike language, problem solving seems to be common among animals of lower orders. To explain how both people and animals solve problems, psychologists turn to one of several theories.

Theories about Problem Solving

Learning Theory   The learning-theory approach to problem solving is exemplified in the work of Ivan Pavlov, John B. Watson, and Edward Lee Thorndike, whose philosophies and research were all introduced in Chapter 5. According to Thorndike, cats placed in "puzzle boxes" learned to pull a string to get out by a trial-and-error process, rather than by a sudden flash of insight. He believed that the cats were learning a new habit only because of a reward, or reinforcement—getting out of the box—and did not understand why tugging on the string led to escape.

Gestalt Theory   Sultan, a chimpanzee, was the star of the most famous experiments exemplifying the gestalt approach (explained in Chapter 1), which were conducted by Wolfgang Kohler (1927). If bananas were placed outside Sultan's cage, out of reach, and he was given a stick, he would use the stick to pull the bananas to him. Sultan's problem occurred when neither of two sticks he had was long enough to reach the bananas. He tried both to no avail and then walked away. Suddenly, however, he went back and figured out a way to put one stick inside the other, making the combination long enough to reach the bananas. According to Kohler, Sultan used **insight,** or what is often known as an *"aha!"* experience. He came up with a completely new, creative solution to his problem, which he continued to use in similar situations. (Repeat uses fall into the category of routine problem solving.)

Insight   *Sudden, creative solution to a problem.*

A recent experiment found that pigeons which had been trained to climb, peck, and push a box aimlessly for long periods of time managed to use these activities to solve a new problem, for which they had *not* been trained (getting a banana). In the suddenness, directness, and continuousness they displayed in solving the problem, these pigeons showed insight. The birds that had acquired relevant skills "solved the problem in a remarkably chimpanzee-like (and . . . human-like) fashion" (Epstein, Kirshnit, Lanza, & Rubin, 1984, p. 61).

Similar flashes of insight may have occurred to black bears in the Great Smoky Mountains National Park. These bears have become expert at stealing food from human beings. One creative bear, nicknamed the "Deep Creek leaper," climbed a tree from which a camper had suspended a pack containing food; when the bear was

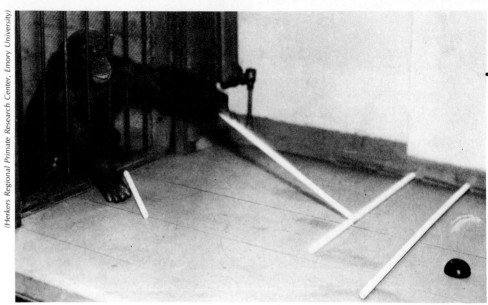

(Herkers Regional Primate Research Center, Emory University)

The chimpanzee Sultan is shown here using one stick to move another stick toward him. Sultan was the first primate (aside from human beings) observed to use insight to come up with a completely new, creative solution to a problem.

above the pack, it leaped from the tree, grabbing the pack on its way down. A female was spotted stretching full length up a pole so that a cub clinging to her shoulders could reach a pack at the top ("Frequent bear forages," 1983).

Information-Processing Theory   According to the information-processing approach (discussed in Chapters 5, 6, and 7), problem solving is a complex activity comprising several processes: registering information, retrieving from memory material that is related to this information, and using both registration and retrieval in a purposeful way.

Let's now take a look at the processes involved in problem solving.

Stages of Problem Solving

Generally, psychologists believe, we go through several stages in solving problems. According to one approach (Bourne, Dominowski, & Loftus, 1979), we *prepare*, we *produce*, and we *evaluate*.

Stage 1: Preparation   First, we need to understand what a problem is. Our interpretation of a problem, and thus our ability to solve it, can be affected by the way it is presented, as seen in Figure 8-3. Duncker (1945) gave one group of subjects three cardboard boxes, one holding matches, one holding thumbtacks, and one holding candles. He then asked them to mount a candle upright on a nearby screen. These subjects had a great deal of trouble solving the problem, although a second group of subjects, given the same materials, solved it much more easily. The difference lay in the way the materials were presented. The second group had received the boxes empty; thus they could visualize one of the boxes as a base on which to mount a candle. The first group suffered from what the gestalt psychologist Karl Duncker considers a major barrier to effective problem solving, **functional fixedness.** This is an overreliance on old ways of seeing and doing things that keeps a person from thinking of novel possibilities. In this instance, people had trouble overcoming the notion that the boxes were containers and thus could not see them as candle holders.

Functional fixedness *Overreliance on traditional ways of solving problems, which inhibits novel solutions.*

Stage 2: Production   Once we understand the problem, we need to generate possible solutions. Simple problems may require nothing more than getting correct infor-

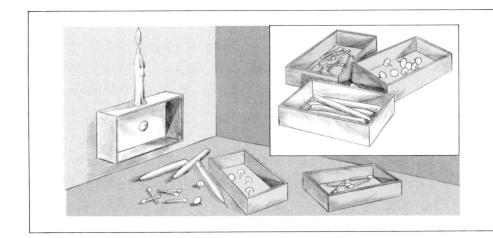

FIGURE 8-3 *Candle problem: an example of functional fixedness. Subjects in one group were given three cardboard boxes (one holding matches, one holding thumb tacks, and one holding candles) and were asked to mount a candle upright on a nearby screen. Their difficulty in solving the problem contrasted with the relative ease of another group of subjects who received the same materials, with the boxes empty. The first group had trouble seeing the boxes as candle holders rather than containers; it was easier for the second group to visualize one of the boxes as a base.*

mation from long-term memory. More complicated problems require more complex strategies. The two basic kinds of solution strategies are algorithms and heuristics.

An **algorithm** is a strategy that exhausts every possible answer until a correct solution is reached. Used diligently, it guarantees a correct solution (if one exists). For example, given the anagram UHB, an algorithm would put the three letters in every possible combination (BUH, BHU, HBU, UBH) until the correct order (HUB) is found. Algorithms are rarely used, partly because they don't exist for many problems and partly because when they do they can be too time-consuming.

A **heuristic** is a rule of thumb for finding a solution. It *may* lead to a solution more quickly than an algorithm can, but it is not guaranteed to lead to a solution at all. Heuristics may involve *planning* that ignores some information while focusing on other information (for example, solving a three-letter anagram quickly by realizing that the vowel probably goes between the two consonants and not even trying out words that don't fit this pattern). Or it may involve a *means-end analysis* that tests for a difference between the state that currently exists (your king in check in a chess game, meaning that you'll lose if you don't get it out of check) and one that is desired (winning the game)—and then doing something to reduce the difference (planning moves that will first get the king out of check and will then, one move at a time, put you in a stronger position). Heuristics may also involve *working backward*, figuring out what the ideal situation would be (Sara's possession of the shoes), determining what step will lead to the ideal, and determining what has to be done before that step can be taken (contacting the owner of the store, who can be reached by his sister, who can be called by her friend, etc.).

Stage 3: Evaluation Once we have arrived at a solution, we have to decide how good it is. For some problems, this is easy. If we unscramble an anagram and come up with a word, we know we're right. If we get the shoes in time for the wedding, we've solved the problem. Many problems, however, have less precise goals, and so the adequacy of their solutions is harder to judge. There may be more than one possible solution, and we then have to determine which one is best. (This is often the case in a multiple-choice exam, in which two answers may be correct but one is better.)

When a problem is solved in a moment of insight, evaluation is so quick that the people or animals are not aware of it. They know only that they have come up with a solution.

Before we say more about insight, we want to emphasize that the three stages we've just presented are not necessarily gone through 1–2–3. Often there's a great deal of moving back and forth as we produce a possible solution (stage 2), evaluate it (stage 3), and then go back to reinterpret the problem (stage 1).

Algorithm Problem-solving strategy in which every possible answer is exhausted until a correct solution is arrived at.

Heuristic Problem-solving strategy consisting of a rule of thumb for finding a solution; it may lead to a solution more quickly than an algorithm can, but it will not necessarily lead to a solution at all.

Insight and Problem Solving

How can two men play five games of checkers and each win the same number of games without any ties? How can you plant a total of ten trees in five rows of four trees each? If you have black and brown socks in your drawer in a ratio of 4 to 5, how many socks will you have to take out to make sure of having a pair the same color? How did the museum director know that an "old Roman coin" stamped with the date 350 B.C. was a fake?

How Insight Works   Problems like those just mentioned are generally solved through insight rather than from laborious computation. From study of the way people reach their conclusions, Sternberg and Davidson (1982) identified three necessary intellectual processes. *Selective encoding* is the ability to *encode* information (to see what is relevant, even if that is not obvious, and to sort it out from what is irrelevant). *Selective combination* is the ability to *combine* different and seemingly unrelated bits of information. And *selective comparison* is the ability to discover a nonobvious relationship between new and old information. The role of selection is important in all three types of information processing.

Let's see how the three types are related to our questions:

■ If you assumed that the checkers players were playing against each other, faulty *encoding* got in the way of your solution. Since there were no ties and each player won the same number of games, they could not have been playing against each other.

■ If you did not think of planting the trees in a nonparallel pattern (see Figure 8-4), you were not *combining* the facts productively.

■ If you did not realize that you need to draw out three socks to be sure of a pair, you were misled by the irrelevant 4 to 5 ratio and neglected to use existing knowledge (of any three items of two different kinds, two are bound to be the same). You failed to use selective *comparison*.

■ The final problem also demonstrates that selective *comparison* (which depends on knowledge) can be important. (The meaning of "B.C." and the fact that coins are stamped with the date when they are first made are a combination that leads to the conclusion: the coin could not have been stamped "B.C." 350 years before the birth of Christ.)

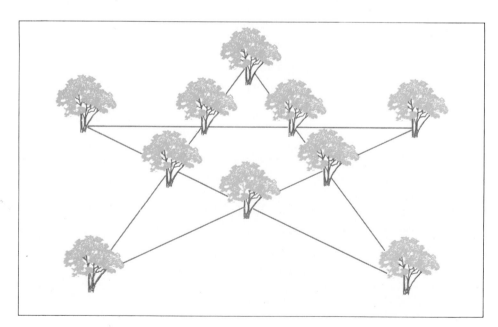

FIGURE 8-4   *Ten trees can be planted in five rows of four each if they are arranged in this nonparallel pattern.*

Other elements which are important for solving problems with insight are the basic processes of planning, production, and evaluation; motivation (leading the solver to exert necessary effort); and style (being impulsive at some times, reflective at others).

Insight and Intelligence   The insight required to solve problems like these correlates with IQ but is not the same, as Sternberg and Davidson (1982) found when they gave a battery of tests to 30 urban residents. They included tests of intelligence, insight, deductive reasoning, and inductive reasoning. In ***deductive reasoning,*** we draw a conclusion that is *certain* if the information given is true, as in "If all robins are birds and all birds lay eggs, then all robins lay eggs." In ***inductive reasoning,*** we draw a *probable* conclusion, as in "Mary and John live in the same house and have the same name, and Mary has a picture of John on her desk; therefore Mary and John are married." While Mary and John could be siblings or lovers with the same name, the conclusion is probably correct (J. R. Anderson, 1980, p. 329).

High correlations showed up between insight and IQ, and between insight and inductive reasoning: but the correlation between insight and deductive reasoning was much more modest. The best indicators of IQ were insight problems that required the subject to sort out relevant from irrelevant information. The poorest indicators were "trick" questions that the subjects misread (see Figures 8-5, below, and 8-6, on page 290). Performance on insight problems does, then, provide a good measure of intelligence. It would be interesting to see a similar test of the relationship between insight and creativity.

The study of information processing has grown along with the use of computers, starting in the 1950s. Scientists have tried to figure out how people solve problems so that they could program computers to use similar processes, producing ***artificial intelligence.*** Meanwhile, as they have made efforts to break down the processes of human thought in order to program computers, they have learned more about thinking; see the box "Artificial Intelligence" (page 292).

Deductive reasoning   *Logical process in which conclusion is certain if the information given is true.*

Inductive reasoning   *Logical process in which the conclusion drawn is probably correct.*

Artificial intelligence (AI)   *Branch of research that programs computers to solve problems by simulating human thought processes.*

Water lilies double in area every 24 hours. At the beginning of the summer there is one water lily on a lake. It takes 60 days for the lake to become covered with water lilies. On what day is the lake half covered?

FIGURE 8-5   *Sternberg and Davidson found this problem a good predictor of IQ. To solve it, people have to recognize the key fact: that the number of lilies doubles every 24 hours. The answer is day 59. (Source: Sternberg & Davidson, 1982.)*

A farmer has 17 cows. All but nine break through a hole in the fence and wander away. How many are left?

FIGURE 8-6 *Sternberg and Davidson found this problem a poor predictor of IQ, since solving it depends only on a careful reading of the second sentence. The answer is 9. (Source: Sternberg & Davidson, 1982.)*

CREATIVITY

Creativity Ability to see things in a new and unusual light and to come up with unusual solutions to problems.

Einstein's development of the theory of relativity; Newton's discovery of the law of gravity; Shakespeare's plays; Picasso's paintings; Henry Ford's development of assembly-line production; the government's creation of the social security system—all these are examples of creativity. **Creativity** is the ability to see things in a new and unusual light, to see problems that no one else may even recognize the existence of, and then to come up with new, unusual, and effective solutions. Creativity can thus be thought of in terms of solutions to problems. The poet writing a sonnet is solving a problem, as is the scientist seeking a new alloy, the musician composing a symphony, the sculptor chiseling a form from a block of marble, or the social planner trying to bail out the financially troubled social security system.

Measuring Creativity

Standard intelligence tests measure *convergent* thinking (Guilford, 1967), the ability to come up with a single correct or best answer. It is hard to measure *divergent* thinking, the ability to come up with new and unusual answers to a problem, but researchers have used their own creativity to devise several tests. They ask questions like these: "List all the uses you can think of for a brick." "Name all the words you can think of that start with *a* and end with *d.*" "Suppose that all humans had eyes in back of their heads as well as in front. List all the consequences and implications you can think of." Then these items are scored for *quantity* (how many different answers you came up with), *originality* (how different your answers are from those given by others), and *usefulness* (how practical your answers are).

So far these tests have been more significant in research than in educational or vocational counseling. One problem is that scores depend heavily on speed, and creative people do not always give quick responses. Another is that while the tests are reliable (consistent), there is little or no firm evidence of their validity—their ability to predict creativity in real life. Results are mixed with regard to whether they really measure creativity in nontest situations (Anastasi, 1976). In one study, advertising copywriters judged high on creativity did better on several tests of divergent thinking than subjects judged low (J. M. Elliott, 1964). But in another study, there was little correlation between creativity and divergent thinking in a group of research scientists (Taylor, Smith, & Ghiselin, 1963). This kind of discrepancy is not surprising. There may be many specific kinds of divergent thinking. Guilford (1967) claims at least 24. It is difficult to know just which ones are required for any given real-life problem. In addition, creativity seems to involve more than just divergent thinking. Motivation, knowledge, training, independence of spirit, and purposefulness all seem to play a part in creative work (D. N. Perkins, 1981). Some of these qualities may be encouraged by certain social practices.

Another way of assessing creativity is to ask people with experience in a field in question (who do not need to be creative people themselves) to judge creative work (Amabile, 1983). The judges should make their evaluations independently of each other, according to their own criteria rather than criteria imposed on them, and they should assess both technical and aesthetic aspects. They should rate work relative to other work rather than to some absolute standard. Each judge should view the products under consideration in a different random order. This is, of course, a subjective approach to measuring creativity. It seems promising precisely because the very nature of creative output cries out against attempts to measure it objectively.

If Sir Isaac Newton had not been creative enough to see things in a new and unusual light, he could have watched a million apples fall and never discovered the law of gravity.

Creativity and Intelligence

We all know bright people who do well in school or on the job but who exhibit "little evidence of the quality that advances rather than enhances the status quo" (Goertzel & Goertzel, 1962, p. 280). These people are intelligent but not creative. We also know people who test poorly and muddle their way through school but who constantly come up with original ideas. These people score high in creativity but low in intelligence. It seems, then, that creativity and intelligence often do not go hand in hand.

In fact, investigators have found only modest correlations between creativity and intelligence in schoolchildren (Anastasi & Schaefer, 1971; Getzels & Jackson, 1963). And findings for adults are similar—as least beyond a certain level of intelligence. In one study, architects, mathematicians, and research scientists (all well above average in intelligence, with IQs ranging from 120 to 140) were divided into two groups. One was composed of people who *had* made distinguished contributions to their fields; the other consisted of people who were competent practitioners but had *not* made distinguished contributions. No differences in IQ showed up between the two groups. Nor were grades in school related to creativity later in life, a fact which suggests that beyond a certain level, higher IQs do not predict creativity (McKinnon, 1968). Of course, the range of IQs in this study was quite narrow. It seems likely that a greater relationship between IQ and creativity would appear in subjects with a wider range of intelligence.

Influences on Creativity

A Swiss school that the great physicist Albert Einstein attended when he was 15 may well have been crucial in his development of the innovative theory of relativity. Having to go to this school to do remedial work turned out to be a blessing, since the school's humanistic orientation gave him the kind of freedom he thrived on. It emphasized the search for knowledge through work that the students initiated themselves and pursued individually (Holton, 1972). This school was in strong contrast to a regimented, militaristic school Einstein had previously attended, which he later said had robbed him of scientific interest for an entire year (Einstein, 1949).

A physician is confronted by a sick patient. The doctor powers up a computer, feeds information into it about the patient's symptoms and test results, and then asks the machine a series of questions, such as: "Was the patient seriously burned?" and "Were bacteria seen in the stain of the culture?" From the answers to these and other questions, the computer tells the doctor which specific organisms are causing the patient's infection (Waldrop, 1985). MYCIN, a computer program specially designed to diagnose infectious diseases, is one of a number of "expert systems" designed since the late 1960s by specialists in the rapidly growing field of artificial intelligence.

Artificial intelligence (AI) is the overall term given to a branch of research that programs computers to solve problems by making them "think" the way human beings do. An *expert system*, one kind of artificial intelligence, is a computer program that follows a set of rules and reaches conclusions much as a human expert would.

MYCIN, like other expert systems, operates according to a series of *if-then* rules. In other words, if statement A is true, then conclusion B is warranted. This is one way in which human beings reason. AI researchers try to analyze the way people solve a problem; then they write a computer program accordingly. If the program solves the problems they set, their analysis may be correct.

The major difficulty for AI researchers is isolating the various steps in solving problems. Ironically, it seems easier to do this for sophisticated problems requiring specialized information. It is much harder to break down the steps in human thought for the kinds of things that we do every day, such as talking to each other, using common sense (knowing about a lot of things and using what we know in a variety of situations), or recognizing a friend (Schank & Hunter, 1985).

ARTIFICIAL INTELLIGENCE

For example, try to list everything that a child has to do to make a tower out of three blocks—how to find the next block, how to move a hand to pick it up, how to hold it, what direction to move it in, how to put it on the stack, and so forth. How does the child know what to do next? At one time dozens of people worked with the "block problem." Graduate students wrote theses about it, and several computer programs were developed (which, among other things, told the computer not to pick up the block on the bottom of the stack). At the end the machine was about as good as a normal 3-year-old (Waldrop, 1985).

If a computer is no better than a person, what are the practical applications of AI? In a test of MYCIN's ability to diagnose meningitis, MYCIN was right 69 percent of the time, and human experts were right 68 percent of the time (R. M. Mason, 1985). The fact that it is as good as a human expert means that the computer could become a valued assistant to a busy doctor. In other fields (like geology, insurance, military tactics, and nuclear engineering), expert systems have solved problems much more quickly than human beings could.

There are also other potential benefits. If this research can help us learn more about how people think, we may be able to help people think better. As AI researchers have tried to write programs that can read, for example, they have been forced to learn how people read. This knowledge can help educators improve ways to teach reading. We already

know, for example, that expectations are important in reading (and in computer problem solving): people can figure out unfamiliar words if they are familiar with a subject. This implies that beginning readers will learn faster if they are asked to read passages on subjects they know something about.

At the moment, the field of artificial intelligence is full of unanswered questions, such as the following:

- Can computers be programmed to use several different thought operations at the same time, the way people seem to do (taking in new information about a number of different subjects at the same time that we're retrieving other information from memory)?
- Can computers be taught to learn—to take in new information that will change their store of knowledge?
- Can computers make the kinds of distinctions that come so easily to us—for example, recognizing words in a language whether the person speaking them has a southern drawl, a western twang, or a foreign accent?
- Will computers ever learn to deal with the ambiguities we do not even think about as we determine meanings of words depending on context? (For example, one story that goes the rounds in AI circles is about a computer that translated the English phrase "The spirit is willing, but the flesh is weak" into Russian as "The vodka is strong, but the meat is rotten"—Rose, 1986).
- For that matter, can a computer ever be programmed to have a sense of humor?

If the answers to these questions are all *no*, we can be confident that no computer programmed by people will ever be mentally superior to people.

Some of the following suggestions, which are based on research and thinking on creativity, may help you be more creative in your work, your hobbies, and your daily life.

WHAT DO YOU WANT TO DO?
- Take time to understand a problem before you begin trying to solve it.
- Get all the facts clearly in mind.
- Identify the facts that seem to be the most important before you try to work out a detailed solution.

HOW CAN YOU DO IT?
- Set aside a sizable block of time to focus on a particular problem, rather than attending to it in scattered sessions.
- Work out a plan for attacking the problem.
- Establish subgoals: solve part of the problem and go on from there. You don't have to do everything at once.
- Write out your thoughts. This allows you to capture important points and to come back to them later. It also allows you to look for patterns.
- Imagine yourself acting out the problem. (With the sock problem mentioned on page 288, for instance, you might imagine yourself going to the drawer and beginning to fish out socks.)
- *Actually* act out the problem. (Go to the sock drawer.)

- Think of a similar problem you've solved in the past and build on the strategy you used then.
- Use analogies whenever possible: see whether you can generalize from a similar situation to your current problem.
- Use several different problem-solving strategies—verbal, visual, mathematical, acting. Draw a diagram to help you visualize the problem, or talk to yourself out loud, or "walk through" a situation.
- Look for relationships among various facts.
- Trust your intuition. Take a guess and see whether you can back it up.
- Play with ideas and possible approaches. Try looking at the same situation in a number of different ways.

HOW CAN YOU DO IT BETTER?
- Try consciously to be original, to come up with new ideas.
- Don't worry about looking foolish if you say or suggest something unusual or if you come up with the wrong answer.
- Eliminate cultural taboos in your thinking (such as gender stereotyping) that might interfere with your ability to come up with a novel solution.
- Try to be right the first time, but if you're not, explore as many alternatives as you need to.
- Keep an open mind. If your initial approach doesn't work, ask whether you made assumptions that might not be true.
- If you get stuck on one approach, try to get to the solution by another route.
- Be alert to odd or puzzling facts. If you can explain them, your solution may be at hand.
- Think of unconventional ways to use objects and the environment. Look at familiar things as if you've never seen them before.
- Consider taking a detour that delays your goal but eventually leads to it.
- Discard habitual ways of doing things and force yourself to figure out new ways.
- Do some brainstorming with one or more other people. This involves trying to produce as many new and original ideas as possible, without evaluating any of them until the end of the session.
- Strive for objectivity. Evaluate your own ideas as you would those of a stranger.

Would Wolfgang Amadeus Mozart have composed some of the most beautiful music the world has ever known if his genius had not been recognized and nurtured at an early age? His father, a fine musician and composer himself, taught Wolfgang, shown here with his sister, and furthered his musical education in many other ways.

For many years, research on creativity emphasized the personality characteristics of people who produced original work. In recent years, more researchers have investigated the "social psychology of creativity" by looking into the various social forces that tend either to encourage creativity or to squelch it.

What Makes People Creative?   Teresa Amabile's review and analysis of research on creativity (1983) has identified a number of factors that seem to help people get their creative juices flowing. From factors like the following, she has drawn important implications for encouraging both children and adults to be more creative.

- *Intrinsic motivation*—pursuing an activity for its own sake, not to please others or to reap rewards (like fame and money).

- *Choice*—having the opportunity to choose which task to perform and then to select a way of doing it.

- *Stimulation*—being in a physical environment that is cognitively and perceptually stimulating.

- *Inspirational models*—coming into contact with creative people who serve as examples or mentors.

- *Freedom from evaluation*—performing a task without fear of being judged foolish or inadequate.

- *Independence*—performing a task without a sense of being observed by others in a critical way.

Implications for Education and Child Rearing   Research findings suggest that the following practices will help young people develop the kinds of attitudes and activities that will result in more creative outputs (Amabile, 1983).

- *Provide a stimulating environment.* School and home should be tailored as much as possible to a child's special interests and aptitudes. Children who show a flair for drawing, for example, would benefit from access to a variety of art materials and from special classes where they could learn how to use these materials. Children who show no single special interest should be provided with a variety of experiences and materials.

- *Emphasize the positive.* Teaching methods should focus on fostering a child's strengths rather than criticizing weaknesses. Children should also be encouraged to focus on their strengths, so that they will not be too harsh on themselves. For instance, a child who has a good sense of rhythm but a poor memory for melody should be encouraged to play the drums instead of being berated for not being able to play the violin.

- *Allow children to be themselves.* Tolerating—and even encouraging—nonconforming, unpredictable behavior gives children more room to grow and expand than forcing them into conventional molds. Questions or comments that might seem impertinent to a parent or teacher are often a clue that a child is looking at life in an original way. Discouraging such expressions can discourage the thinking as well. This does not mean that no limits should be set on unacceptable behavior; it means setting reasonable limits.

- *Help children to avoid peer pressure.* Many gifted children do best when taught in special settings; all youngsters benefit from knowing that they do not have to be "just like everybody else."

- *Develop the right balance between giving children warm support and smothering them with affection.* Children need respect and confidence from adults, which often seem to occur in a secure, somewhat distant affection that gives them breathing space.

- *De-emphasize traditional sex roles.* Traditional sex roles and other rigid social conventions constrain children from developing and expressing their own interests and abilities.

- *Expose children to cultural diversity.* When children see how people in other social circumstances, from other racial and ethnic groups, and in other countries do things, they become aware that there are usually many ways to do practically anything.

- *Expose children to creative models early in life.* Children who see creative people, without being encouraged to imitate the particular forms other people's creativity takes, are apt to be inspired to express originality themselves.

Implications for Creativity in Adults   Adults, too, are more creative in certain conditions. The following elements seem to foster creative work in the arts, the sciences, and industry (Amabile, 1983). Furthermore, a number of specific approaches seem to encourage creative problem solving (see the box "How to Be More Creative," on page 293).

- *Minimum of stress.* People who are secure in their jobs, are not worried about paying their bills, and are in good health are more likely to do creative work. Society in general, and employers in particular, can play a role in supporting creative people. People should not have to worry that they will be fired if they make a mistake, for example; and financial grants to creative people often result in increased output.

- *Choice.* Deciding what job to work on and how to go about it promotes a more creative approach. Complete choice is not always possible; but the more autonomy workers and artists have, the more creative their output is likely to be. Autonomy implies giving people high levels of responsibility and little interference from supervisors.

- *Rewards.* The rewards that seem to lead to creative work are very high and come as unexpected bonuses. These provide recognition of outstanding performance but are not used to control behavior.

- *Opportunities to play.* People who are encouraged to use their time and resources without having to produce work that is immediately useful can often produce important ideas. This is the concept behind basic research, as opposed to applied research.

- *Encouragement of new ideas.* Employers and supervisors who encourage innovation and are open to new ideas will get them. Those who make fun of unusual notions will not.

It's clear, then, that much more than talent is involved in creativity. As you can see from the preceding discussion, different issues arise in encouraging creativity in children and in adults.

Chapters 9 and 10 explore a number of ways in which our development changes throughout life, from conception through old age.

SUMMARY

1 In thinking, people use symbols to stand for things, events, and ideas. This enables them to manipulate concepts and ideas. A major concern of cognitive psychology is the study of human thought processes that include language, concept formation, problem solving, and creativity.

2 Language is a means of communicating, generally through spoken sounds that express specific meaning and are arranged according to rules.

3 Every language has a grammar, a set of rules that govern sound, meaning, and structure. The phoneme is the minimal unit of sound. Semantics is the study of meaning in a language. The morpheme is the smallest element of meaningful speech. Syntax is the set of rules for structuring words into sentences.

4 Prelinguistic speech occurs in a sequence that is tied fairly closely to chronological age. Prelinguistic speech includes crying, cooing, babbling, and imitating sounds.

5 Linguistic speech is characterized by the use of words. Holophrases are single words that express a complete thought. They are the earliest form of linguistic speech, generally occurring around age 1. The second year of life is important for the development of language comprehension.

6 Mean length of utterance is the average length of utterances in morphemes. A child in stage 1 has an MLU over 1.0 and in stage 2 has an MLU of 2.0. The child advances with each increase of 0.5 MLU, up to stage 5.

7 Speech in early childhood is different from adult speech. Young children simplify, overregularize rules, overextend concepts, and cannot yet express certain grammatical relationships (even though they understand these relationships).

8 Learning theorists emphasize the role of the environment in language acquisition. According to Skinner, language is learned through reinforcement, discrimination, and generalization. Social-learning theorists emphasize the roles of observation, imitation, and reinforcement. Although these theories can account for why children learn to speak a particular language, they fail to account for novel speech.

9 Nativists, such as Noam Chomsky, believe that human beings have an inborn capacity for language acquisition. This inborn ability is the language acquisition device (LAD). It enables children to extract grammatical rules from the language they hear and to use these rules to create new sentences. While this approach accounts for novel speech and the rapidity with which children acquire language, it fails to consider individual differences and the learned aspects of language.

10 Today psychologists believe that language develops through interaction between care giver and child. The infant has some innate capacity to learn language, as demonstrated in his or her ability to discriminate fine variations in sound, respond differentially to the mother's voice, and move in synchrony with adult speech.

11 The innate capacity to acquire language probably allows the child to benefit from a specialized kind of speech known as *motherese*. Motherese is language addressed to small children by people who interact with them. Its characteristics include high pitch, simplification, and repetition. These modifications appear to be important in language learning.

12 Lenneberg proposed that the years before puberty are a critical period for language acquisition. Although there is some evidence to support this assertion, no clear-cut conclusions can as yet be drawn.

13 According to the linguistic-relativity hypothesis (the Whorfian hypothesis), language affects perception and thinking. Research has not conclusively supported this viewpoint.

14 Psychologists disagree about whether animals can learn language. Although apes can learn to use meaningful symbols, can generalize them to new situations, and can communicate with humans to some extent, they seem unable to learn the creative aspects of language.

15 An important aspect of human thought is the ability to organize different stimuli into concepts, which are categories of objects, events, or people. This ability enables humans to impose order on a world full of unique objects and events.

16 A well-defined concept is one that can be specified by a set of clear, unambiguous features (such as color, size, shape, and function), connected by a rule or relationship among them.

17 Most concepts are ill-defined. That is, the features of one category often overlap with those of another, making it difficult to distinguish between them. In ill-defined concepts, the features and the rules that connect members of a category are not obvious.

18 Some examples of categories are more typical (that is, better examples) than others. The theory of family resemblance can be used to explain typicality. Basic-level categories are those used in daily dealings with objects.

19 Problem solving is a cognitive activity aimed at a goal. It can be either routine (using existing procedures) or creative (developing new procedures).

20 There are several theories of problem solving. Learning theory is concerned with the trial-and-error process of solving problems. Gestalt theorists consider the role of insight in solving problems. Information-processing approaches consider problem solving to be a complex activity consisting of several processes.

21 Stages of problem solving include preparation, production, and evaluation. In the preparation stage, the problem is clearly defined. At this stage, functional fixedness (overreliance on old methods) can hinder problem solving. In the production stage, possible solutions are generated. Two basic kinds of solution strategies are algorithms (which exhaust every possible solution until the correct one is discovered) and heuristics (which are rules of thumb that can lead to a solution more quickly than an

algorithm will, but do not necessarily lead to any solution at all). In the evaluation stage, the adequacy of the solution is considered.

22 There appear to be three intellectual processes involved in solving problems by insight: selective encoding, selective combination, and selective comparison. The ability to use insight to solve problems is related to IQ but is not the same.

23 Creativity is the ability to see things in a new and unusual light, to see problems that others may not recognize, and then to come up with new, unusual, and effective solutions. Creativity is, then, a type of problem solving. While standard intelligence tests measure convergent thinking (the ability to produce the one best answer), creativity is a matter of divergent thinking (the ability to produce new and unusual answers). Various social forces tend to either encourage or restrict creativity.

KEY TERMS

Algorithm (page 287)
Artificial intelligence (AI) (289)
Cognitive psychology (269)
Creativity (290)
Critical period (277)
Deductive reasoning (289)
Family resemblance (283)
Functional fixedness (286)

Grammar (270)
Heuristic (287)
Holophrases (272)
Ill-defined concept (282)
Inductive reasoning (289)
Insight (285)
Language (270)
Language acquisition device (LAD) (275)

Learning theorists (274)
Linguistic-relativity hypothesis (278)
Linguistics (270)
Mean length of utterance (MLU) (272)
Morpheme (270)
Motherese (275)
Nativists (274)

Phoneme (270)
Semantics (270)
Social-learning theory (274)
Syntax (270)
Telegraphic speech (273)
Typicality (283)
Well-defined concept (282)

SUGGESTED READINGS

AMABILE, T. M. (1983). *The social psychology of creativity.* New York: Springer-Verlag. A discussion of creativity that includes material about factors which undermine and enhance creativity. The book contains many suggestions for enhancing creativity at home, school, and work.

BROWN, R. (1973). *A first language: The early stage.* Cambridge, MA: Harvard University Press. A classic book that describes the language development of three children—Adam, Eve, and Sarah.

CURTISS, S. (1977). *Genie: A psycholinguistic study of a modern-day "wild child."* New York: Academic. The absorbing story of the discovery and treatment of Genie, a girl who never developed normal language abilities because of the extreme neglect she suffered during most of her childhood.

JOHN-STEINER, V. (1985). *Notebooks of the mind: Explorations of thinking.* Albuquerque: University of New Mexico Press. Drawing on information from interviews, diaries, biographies, letters, and laboratory studies, the author provides an account of creativity that focuses especially on its development.

KOHLER, W. (1927). *The mentality of apes.* New York: Harcourt, Brace, & World. Kohler's own discussions of his classic studies on insight in apes.

LINDEN, E. (1986). *Silent partners: The legacy of the ape language experiments.* New York: Times Books. A disturbing look at human responsibility for the "talking" apes after the apes grew old and the funding ran out. The author follows the lives of the best known of these apes, and in this moving book documents their present situation, displaced from both the human and the animal world.

PART

IV

LIFE-SPAN DEVELOPMENTAL PSYCHOLOGY

From that fateful moment of creation when each of us was conceived, to that fatal final moment when we expel our last breath, our lives are governed by one overriding principle: change. As long as we live, we are in the process of becoming something other than what we were. Throughout life, we have the potential to change, to grow, to develop. This process of development is what Chapters 9 and 10 are about.

■ Part IV presents the life span in two segments. *Chapter 9*, "Early Development," discusses the first 12 years or so of life, from conception until adolescence. After we examine prenatal development, we turn our attention to the amazingly competent newborn, whose wide-ranging abilities have only begun to reveal themselves to us through innovative psychological measures. We look at the physical, the intellectual, and the socioemotional aspects of development during childhood as we see the enormous strides that youngsters make in controlling their bodies, in understanding and using intellectual concepts, and in expressing their unique personalities.

■ In *Chapter 10*, "Development from Adolescence On," we trace development as young people assume adult status, and then we see the persistence of development as people grow physically, intellectually, and emotionally. The struggles still being waged with issues of identity foster growth, even through the final step in this struggle, dealing with death.

Our development is a continuous thread that marks conception; weaves through childhood, adolescence, and adulthood; and is snipped off only at the grave. The pattern made by this thread is formed by many influences: the biological influences that provide our genetic heritage and dictate the unfolding of new abilities as we mature—and the kaleidoscope of experiences that we have through life. We explore the impact of such influences as we discuss human development.

■ How do heredity and environment work together to influence development?

■ How much development occurs before birth?

■ What are some of the hazards that can affect the developing fetus?

■ What are the most important physical, cognitive, and personality changes between birth and adolescence?

■ How does stress affect children? Why are some children more resilient than others?

■ How do children form bonds with their mothers, their fathers, and other important people?

■ How do parents and children influence each other?

One of my earliest memories revolves around the birth of my only sibling. When Eddie arrived, I was 4 years old. I probably had mixed feelings about the event—both excitement at the idea of having someone right in my own house to play with and anxiety about being "dethroned" as the "little princess" that I was in my family. The only feelings that I can remember now, however, were disappointment and frustration at not being able to go to the hospital to see either my mother or my baby brother.

I don't remember this as an unhappy time, since I spent those few days with my grandmother, whom I adored. To this day, when I sometimes come across a soap with a strong floral scent like the kind my grandmother used, I remember the happy time I spent with her in her apartment. Another joyful memory of my brother's birth is of my mother tossing chocolates down to me as I stood with my father outside the hospital, looking up at the window of her room. Now I know that it was my mother's hand that threw the chocolates, but at the time I was told—and believed without question—that they were from the baby. Naturally, this helped sweeten the atmosphere and helped me to accept the changes he would bring to my life. It also shows my parents' sensitivity to my feelings, which helped smooth this transition in my life, as it did at many other crucial times.

—From the notebooks of Diane Papalia

Developmental psychologists
Psychologists who study stability and growth in human characteristics and behavior throughout the life span.

Many of the aspects of this early memory reflect the kinds of issues dealt with by ***developmental psychologists,*** who study stability and change in human development throughout the life cycle. They believe that growth and change are possible at every stage of life. They are concerned, for example, with the way memory develops—and they have found that most people's earliest memories are for events that occurred between the ages of 3 and 7, and often revolve around the birth of a sibling (Kihlstrom & Harackiewicz, 1982). They also study the way we are affected by various events and people, and by the experience of birth itself.

In this chapter, we'll begin with a look at the study of human development: how researchers examine it, and what influences affect it. Then we'll consider prenatal development: how it takes place, and some hazards of the prenatal environment. Next, we'll discuss development in infancy and childhood in terms of three closely interrelated aspects: ***physical development*** (changes in the body, such as height, weight, brain development, and the acquisition and refinement of motor skills); ***cognitive development*** (changes in thought processes, which affect learning, language, and memory); and ***psychosocial development,*** or *emotional and social development*—changes in the emotional and social aspects of the personality (and

Physical development *Changes in the body such as changes in height, weight, brain development, and motor skills.*

Cognitive development *Changes in thought processes, which affect learning, language abilities, and memory.*

Psychosocial development *Changes in the emotional and social aspects of personality.*

therefore sometimes referred to as *personality development*). In Chapter 10, we'll continue the story of development by examining physical, cognitive, and psychosocial development in adolescence and adulthood.

We define *development* as the ways by which people's physical, cognitive, and psychosocial characteristics change throughout life. Such development is complex, systematic, and age-related. Change can be *quantitative* and thus fairly easy to measure, such as growth in height and weight and the expansion of vocabulary. Or it can be *qualitative*—changes in kind that are more complex and involve "leaps" in functioning. Qualitative changes distinguish a talking child from a nonverbal baby, a mature adult from a self-absorbed adolescent. These changes trace the growth of intelligence, creativity, sociability, and morality. But even these leaps result from a series of small steps that we continue to take as long as we live.

HOW WE STUDY DEVELOPMENT

Research Methods

Two major approaches are used to collect information about development: the *cross-sectional* method and the *longitudinal* method. Each of these has its strengths. Each also has weaknesses, however, and to make up for these, the *cross-sequential* method was designed. Let's look at the three approaches.

Cross-Sectional Method   In the **cross-sectional method,** psychologists compare people of different ages at the same point in time, giving us information about *age differences* in behaviors, abilities, or growth patterns. A major problem with this method is the danger of confusing age differences with the effects of <u>cohort</u>. Suppose, for example, that a school has changed its methods of teaching first-grade vocabulary during the past year (say, by introducing computer-assisted techniques). Since the older children will have had different experiences, we can't attribute differences between them and the younger ones solely to the effect of age. The change in teaching method experienced by the younger children might account for some of the difference between the two age groups. Furthermore, cross-sectional data are usually presented as group averages (that is, how the average 4-year-old or 12-year-old performed), and so it is difficult to pinpoint individual differences.

Cross-sectional method   Data-collection technique in which subjects of different ages are measured on one occasion, providing information about age differences in behavior.

Longitudinal Method   In the **longitudinal method,** psychologists trace the development of one or more people at more than one point in time, giving us information about *age changes*. This design gives us information about individual developmental patterns rather than group differences, but it is costlier and more time-consuming than the cross-sectional method (see Figure 9-1, page 304, for a comparison of the two methods). Furthermore, we have to take human factors into account. When subjects take the same or similar tests more than once, they will probably do better on the later tests because they have had practice; and by using people who volunteer for and stay with research projects, we are getting a self-selected sample that differs in a number of ways from those who did not participate in the first place or who drop out before the study is finished (for example, the subjects are probably brighter and of higher socioeconomic status).

Longitudinal method   Data-collection technique in which the same people are measured more than once to see behavioral changes over time.

Cross-Sequential Method   To make up for drawbacks in both the cross-sectional and the longitudinal methods, a number of sequential strategies were designed. One such strategy, the **cross-sequential method,** combines the cross-sectional and longitudinal approaches. People in a cross-sectional sample are tested more than once, and the results are analyzed to find differences that show up over time for different groups of subjects. Although this is a more complex and time-consuming approach, use of this method has helped us arrive at a more realistic assessment of intellectual functioning in adulthood, as we'll see in Chapter 10.

Cross-sequential method   Data-collection technique which combines longitudinal and cross-sectional strategies.

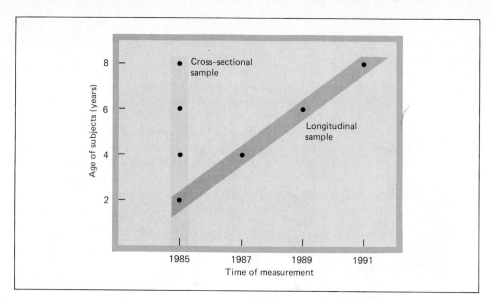

FIGURE 9-1 *The two most important ways to obtain data about development. In a **cross-sectional** study, people of different ages are measured at one time. Here, groups of 2-, 4-, 6-, and 8-year-olds were tested in 1985, to obtain data about age differences in performance. In a **longitudinal** study, the same people are measured more than once. Here, a sample of children were first measured in 1985 when they were 2 years old. Follow-up testing was scheduled for 1987, 1989, and 1991, when the children would be 4, 6, and 8, respectively. This technique shows age changes in performance.*

Influences on Development

Normative and Nonnormative Influences   Developmental psychologists consider three major types of influence on development—normative age-graded, normative history-graded, and nonnormative life events (Baltes, Reese, & Lipsitt, 1980). Normative events occur in a similar way for all people in a given group. Thus **normative age-graded influences** include biological markers like puberty and cultural markers like entry into formal education. **Normative history-graded influences** are common to people of a particular generation, or *cohort* (people growing up at the same time in the same place). The history that takes place during a person's lifetime—such as a major economic depression or a war—leaves indelible impressions. Furthermore, people who grow up in a time when medical advances in treating common illnesses keep both young and old alive, who can pick up a telephone and call someone on the other side of the world, and who can board an airplane and arrive on a distant continent in a single day are bound to be different in some ways from their ancestors, whose historical context was very different. **Nonnormative life events** (like suffering a serious injury or winning a lottery) do not happen to most people; but when they do occur, they are likely to have a major impact.

Heredity and Environment   The study of development begins at the very beginning, with the origin of life, as we learn about the earliest influences we are likely to encounter and ask what we are born with and what we acquire.

Throughout this book, we talk about many different human abilities—how we perceive the world, for instance, and how we act toward people and situations in it. One question that has preoccupied students of humanity for centuries is how we develop these abilities. Do we inherit them, or do we learn them? Throughout history, opinions about this have varied, ranging between two extremes: that we are entirely the product of nature (our inherited traits), or that we are entirely the product of nurture (our experiences).

Most contemporary thinkers recognize that it is difficult or impossible to separate nature and nurture completely: the two interact in various ways to make each of us a unique person. But the **nature-nurture debate** still goes on. Its results are important, since they determine the way we construct both our society and our personal lives.

Normative age-graded influences Biological and environmental influences on development that are highly similar for all people in a given age group.

Normative history-graded influences Biological and environmental influences on development common to people of a particular generation.

Nonnormative life events Biological and environmental influences on development that, while not happening to most people, may have a major impact on those who do experience them.

Nature-nurture debate Controversy over the relative influence of inherited traits (nature) and experience (nurture) on development.

RELATIVE EFFECTS OF HEREDITY AND ENVIRONMENT In any particular m
influenced by heredity, there is a range of possible responses, depend
environment. Body size, for example, is dependent on biological process
genetically regulated. Even so, a range of sizes is possible, depending on
tion of the growing child. Such potential variability is known as a *reacti*

In general, it seems that our heredity predisposes us toward, and sets
certain behaviors, but our environment determines their expression. Yo
gence, for example, may be determined in large part by genes you inher
your parents, but the kind of home you grew up in, the degree to which y
encouraged to pursue intellectual interests, the kind of education you recei
your own decisions in life have all had—and will continue to have—an effe
way your intelligence will flower. Similarly, if you inherited shortness as
trait, you may never reach a height of 6 feet, but if you are well cared for,
grow taller than you would if you were kept in cramped quarters and given t
food, too little exercise, and too little love.

Researchers have developed a number of methods to determine the
contributions of heredity and environment to various traits. These methods i
the following:

- *Studies of twins*: When identical twins (who have exactly the same genetic legacy) are more alike than fraternal twins (who are no more alike than any siblings), a hereditary basis for a trait seems indicated. Identical twins who have been raised in different homes are especially sought after because they have identical heredity but different environments; but they are hard to find. Even when we can locate them, their cultural environments usually turn out to be quite similar, and so it may be unwarranted to conclude that similarities between such twins reflect only heredity.

- *Adoption studies*: When adopted children are more like their biological parents and siblings, we see the influence of heredity; when they resemble their adoptive families more, we see the influence of environment.

Above: Computers are one kind of normative history-graded influence. We don't know yet how they will change people's lives—whether they will affect boys and girls differently, increase the gap between affluent and poor students, or affect children's social activities. But we suspect that children who grow up in the "computer age" will be different in some ways from the generations before them.

(© George Ancona 1984/International Stock Photo)

Below: Twins are often subjects of research that seeks to determine which traits show a large hereditary influence and which ones seem to be determined more by environmental factors.

(© Erika Stone/Peter Arnold)

■ *Consanguinity studies*: By examining as many blood relatives as possible in a particular family, we can discover the degree to which they share characteristics and whether the closeness of a relationship affects the degree of similarity.

■ *Selective breeding in animals*: If animals can be bred for a certain characteristic (like the ability to run mazes or the tendency to become obese), we conclude that the trait is at least partly hereditary, and we generalize these findings to human beings, validly in some cases, less so in others.

Other lines of research concentrate on determining possible environmental causes for particular characteristics. These include:

■ *Prenatal studies*: By investigating the relationship between various conditions in people and the experiences of these people's mothers during pregnancy, we can often identify a specific cause for a specific condition. In the 1960s, researchers did this sort of detective work to identify an innocent-seeming tranquilizer called *thalidomide* as the agent that had caused thousands of children to be born without arms or legs.

■ *Manipulation of the environment*: Making changes in diet, exercise opportunities, intellectual enrichment, and sensory stimulation in one group of animals or people, and then comparing this group with a control group, enables us to draw conclusions about the effects of such environmental differences. A dramatic example of this kind of manipulation showed up in a classic study of enrichment, when 13 apparently retarded 2-year-olds were moved from their orphanage to an institution for mentally retarded young adults, who doted on the children and lavished care on them. As adults, all 13 were functioning in the community, married, and raising their own normal children; by comparison, 12 who had remained in the orphanage for a much longer time had a much lower average IQ, and 4 were still institutionalized (Skeels, 1966; Skeels & Dye, 1939).

■ *Comparisons of actual histories*: By interviewing parents about their child-rearing practices (remembering to discount the effects of faulty and distorted memories!) and by comparing other life-history factors, researchers can sometimes isolate specific environmental influences on specific characteristics.

Our ability to manipulate either the heredity or the environment of human beings is, of course, limited by both ethical and practical considerations. We cannot, for example, mate human beings for selective characteristics, and we would not separate identical twins, make adoption placements, institutionalize children, or prescribe questionable drugs to pregnant women for experimental purposes. We therefore have to rely on animal studies or after-the-fact observations of events that have occurred naturally.

HEREDITARY CHARACTERISTICS   On the basis of studies using the techniques described above, researchers have concluded that heredity exerts an important influence on human development. Physical traits seem to be the ones most strongly determined by heredity, but there is evidence for substantial hereditary influence on intellectual and personality characteristics, too. The results of many studies point to a strong hereditary basis for the characteristics listed in Table 9-1. Most of these traits are also influenced by the environment.

HOW GENETIC TRAITS ARE TRANSMITTED   *Creating a new life*   The moment of conception is a split-second event when a sperm from the father unites with an ovum (sometimes referred to as an egg) from the mother to form a one-cell **zygote,** containing the new person's complete hereditary endowment. Which sperm joins which ovum has tremendous implications for the kind of person the new being will become (see Figure 9-2).

Zygote *One-cell organism resulting from the union of sperm and ovum.*

TABLE 9-1 SOME CHARACTERISTICS WITH HEREDITARY COMPONENTS

Physical traits

Height, and, to a lesser extent, *weight* (Newman, Freeman, & Holzinger, 1937)
Pulse and *breathing rates, blood pressure,* and *perspiration* (Jost & Sontag, 1944)
Patterns of tooth decay, voice tone and pitch, and *posture* (Farber, 1981)
Obesity (Stunkard, Foch, & Hrubec, 1986)
Age of first menstruation (E. Petri, 1934)
Age of death (Jarvik, Kallmann, & Klaber, 1957)

Intellectual traits*

Word fluency, memory, timing of language, and *Piagetian stages of intellectual development*
   (Wilson, 1980)
Maze-running abilities in rats (Tryon, 1940)
Scores on various intelligence tests (Bouchard & McGue, 1981; DeFries & Plomin, 1978; Horn,
   1983; Scarr & Weinberg, 1983; Wilson, 1983)

Personality and emotional disorders

Shyness (Daniels & Plomin, 1985)
Extroversion, emotionality, and *activity* (Vandenberg, 1967)
Anxiety and *obsession* (Gottesman, 1962; Inouye, 1965)
Autism (Ritvo, Freeman, Mason-Brothers, Mo, & Ritvo, 1985)
Schizophrenia (Gottesman, 1979)
Special aptitudes and interests (especially in the arts and athletics), and *mannerisms* (such as a
   firm handshake) (Farber, 1981)

* For a discussion of environmental contributions to intelligence, see Chapter 7.

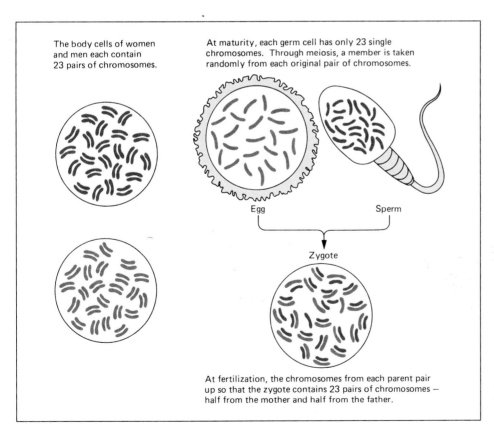

The body cells of women and men each contain 23 pairs of chromosomes.

At maturity, each germ cell has only 23 single chromosomes. Through meiosis, a member is taken randomly from each original pair of chromosomes.

Egg   Sperm

Zygote

At fertilization, the chromosomes from each parent pair up so that the zygote contains 23 pairs of chromosomes — half from the mother and half from the father.

(b)

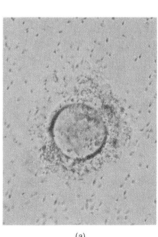

(a)

FIGURE 9-2 *Genetic transmission. Conception is a split-second event when a sperm unites with an ovum. Which sperm joins which ovum has tremendous implications for the kind of person the new being will become. (Sources: **a**, Alexander Tsiaras, Science Source/Photo Researchers; **b**, Papalia & Olds, 1982.)*

Chromosomes *Tiny rod-shaped particles that carry genes, the transmitters of inheritance.*

Genes *Tiny segments, carried on the chromosomes, that transmit hereditary characteristics.*

Genotype *Genetic composition of a person; the genotype may differ from the phenotype because of the possession of recessive genes.*

Phenotype *Observable characteristics of a person.*

Alleles *Alternative forms of a gene. When alleles are identical, a person is homozygous for a trait; when alleles are dissimilar, the person is heterozygous.*

Homozygous *Possessing two identical alleles for a trait.*

Heterozygous *Possessing two dissimilar alleles for a trait.*

Autosomal dominant inheritance *Pattern of inheritance in which a specific gene is dominant; if it is inherited, it manifests itself in the person.*

Autosomal recessive inheritance *Pattern of inheritance in which a trait appears only if a person inherits two genes for it, one from each parent. If the person inherits only one gene for the trait, it will not appear in the person but may be passed on to his or her children.*

Sex-linked inheritance *Pattern of inheritance in which genes for certain characteristics (often undesirable) are carried on an X chromosome. The genes are transmitted by the female and are generally expressed in the male.*

Multifactorial inheritance *Pattern of inheritance in which a trait is expressed either by a combination of several genes or through the interaction of genes with environmental factors.*

Sperm and ovum each contain 23 rod-shaped particles called **chromosomes,** of which 22 are *autosomes* (chromosomes that do not have to do with sex) and 1 is a sex chromosome. The autosomes are the same for both sexes. The mother's sex chromosome is always an X, but the father's may be either an X or a Y. If the father's sperm contains an X chromosome, the sex of the new being will be female; if the father's sperm contains a Y chromosome, the sex will be male.

Each of the zygote's 46 chromosomes contains about 30,000 segments strung along it like beads. These segments are the **genes,** which are made up of deoxyribonucleic acid (DNA) and which determine all our hereditary characteristics. The assortment of genes we inherit constitutes our **genotype;** the characteristics that can be seen make up our **phenotype.** These are not always the same. For example, people may have brown eyes (their phenotype) but carry genes for both brown and blue eyes (their genotype). This difference is due to the fact that genes come in alternative forms called **alleles.**

Patterns of genetic transmission   When you inherit identical alleles from both parents, you are **homozygous** for a trait; when you inherit different alleles, you are **heterozygous.** If you are homozygous for brown eyes, you will have brown eyes and will transmit only genes for brown eyes to your children. If you inherit one allele for brown eyes and one for blue eyes, you will have brown eyes yourself, since genes for brown eyes are dominant over genes for blue eyes, which are recessive. However, you could pass on either allele to your children. If you and your spouse both pass on genes for blue eyes, your child will have blue eyes. While your pattern is that of **autosomal dominant inheritance,** your child's pattern will be **autosomal recessive inheritance.**

Another major pattern is **sex-linked inheritance,** in which recessive genes for a specific (generally undesirable) trait are carried on the X chromosome passed on by mothers. Females with these traits rarely express them, since the recessive gene is usually countered by a dominant gene on the X chromosome received from the father. Males—who have only the one X chromosome—do not have that protection: if they receive the X-linked gene, they express the trait.

The final form of inheriting characteristics is known as **multifactorial inheritance.** It is a more complicated combination of genes or an interaction between genetic predispositions and environmental factors that bring them out.

Some characteristics follow one of these patterns; others, another. For example, hair type (curly or straight) is either autosomal dominant or autosomal recessive, baldness is sex-linked, and height and weight are probably multifactorial. Some diseases and birth defects are inherited according to these patterns. For example, *achondroplasia* (a kind of dwarfism) is inherited by autosomal dominance (see Figure 9-3a). Autosomal recessive conditions (like *Tay-Sachs disease*, a central-nervous-system disorder) are often killers in childhood (see Figure 9-3b). The blood-clotting disorder *hemophilia* is a sex-linked condition (see Figure 9-4, page 310), and *spina bifida* (a defect in the closure of the vertebral canal) is one of the conditions believed to be transmitted multifactorially.

As we examine influences on development—normative and nonnormative factors, heredity, environment—it is important to remember that the relationships among us and the people, places, and events in our lives are almost never one-sided. This is also important when we come to consider aspects of development—physical, cognitive, and psychosocial—and stages of development over the life span. *Individuality* and *interaction* are the keys to understanding development. We all bring a unique genetic legacy into the world and then have a unique set of experiences. Our individual strengths, abilities, and predispositions are affected by influences from the environment. These influences make us act in ways that elicit new experiences. The

Right: Parents often enjoy seeing similarities between themselves and their children—the shape of a face, the color of hair, a fleeting expression. Such resemblances result from the legacy of genes that parents pass on to their children, according to several different patterns.

characteristics inside us constantly intermesh with factors outside us, and we find ourselves in a never-ending cycle of acting and reacting. As our bodies, for example, set boundaries on what we can do, the things we do affect our bodies. As our parents influence us, we influence them. We are not passive recipients of various influences; instead, we actively contribute to our own development and often show resilience in overcoming negative influences.

FIGURE 9-3 *Below: (**a**) How autosomal dominant inheritance works. (**b**) How autosomal recessive inheritance works. (Source: March of Dimes, 1983.)*

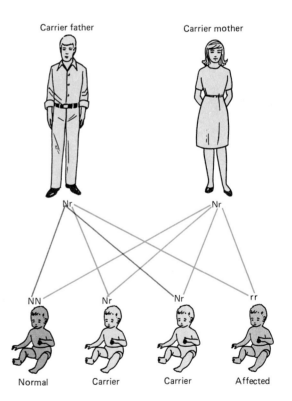

One affected parent has a single faulty gene (D) which *dominates* its normal counterpart (n).

Both parents, usually unaffected, carry a normal gene (N) which takes precedence over its faulty recessive counterpart (*r*).

Affected father   Normal mother

Carrier father   Carrier mother

Dn   nn

Nr   Nr

Dn   nn   Dn   nn

NN   Nr   Nr   rr

Affected   Normal   Affected   Normal

Normal   Carrier   Carrier   Affected

Each child's chances of inheriting either the D or the n from the affected parent are 50 percent.

The odds for each child are
1. A 25% risk of inheriting a "double dose" of r genes which may cause a serious birth defect
2. A 25% chance of inheriting two Ns, thus being unaffected
3. A 50% chance of being a carrier as both parents are

(a)

(b)

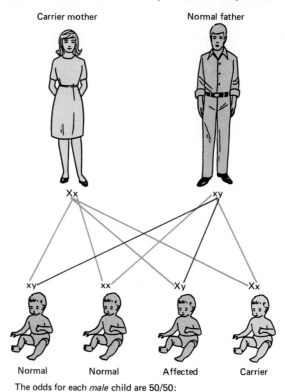

In the most common form, the female sex chromosome of an unaffected mother carries one faulty gene (X) and one normal one (x). The father has normal x and y chromosome complement.

Carrier mother   Normal father

Xx   xy

xy   xx   Xy   Xx

Normal   Normal   Affected   Carrier

The odds for each *male* child are 50/50:
1. 50 percent risk of inheriting the faulty X and the disorder
2. 50 percent chance of inheriting normal x and y chromosomes
For each *female* child, the odds are
1. 50 percent risk of inheriting one faulty X, to be a carrier like mother
2. 50 percent chance of inheriting no faulty gene

FIGURE 9-4 *How sex-linked inheritance works. (Source: March of Dimes, 1983.)*

ORIGINS: PRENATAL DEVELOPMENT

Recognizing that what happens before birth is crucial to what happens afterward, scientists have devoted increasing attention to the prenatal period, when the fetus develops inside the mother's body. In this section, we'll look at the three stages of prenatal development, and at some prenatal hazards.

Stages of Prenatal Development

There are three stages of prenatal development: the germinal stage, the embryonic stage, and the fetal stage. Each has its own characteristics.

During the **germinal stage** (fertilization to 2 weeks), the zygote enters a period of rapid cell division resulting in an increasingly complex organism that possesses rudimentary body organs. In this stage protective and nurturing organs develop, such as the umbilical cord (the long structure that connects the embryo to the placenta, and that brings oxygen and nourishment to the baby and absorbs its body wastes) and the amniotic sac (the membrane that encases the fetus).

In the **embryonic stage** (2 to 8–12 weeks), the embryo grows quickly, and the major body systems (respiratory, alimentary, and nervous) and organs develop. Be-

Germinal stage *First stage of pregnancy (fertilization to 2 weeks), characterized by rapid cell division and increasing complexity of the organism.*

Embryonic stage *Second stage of pregnancy (2 to 8–12 weeks), characterized by rapid growth and development of major body systems and organs.*

cause of this rapid growth and development, this stage is the time of greatest vulnerability to prenatal environmental influences. Almost all developmental birth defects (such as cleft palate, incomplete limbs, and blindness) occur during the critical first trimester (3-month period) of pregnancy. Three out of four spontaneous abortions (miscarriages) also occur during this stage, affecting an estimated 30 to 50 percent of all pregnancies. Chromosomal abnormalities are found in half of all spontaneous abortions (Ash, Vennart, & Carter, 1977), and some 30 percent of them may be caused by a symptomless herpes virus in the uterus (Goldsmith, 1985).

The *fetal stage* (8–12 weeks to birth) begins with the appearance of the first bone cells at about 8 weeks; by 12 weeks the organism is fully in the fetal stage. During this period, the body grows about 20 times in length, so that at birth, the average newborn measures about 20 inches. The form of the body changes, and the various body parts receive "finishing touches." A full-term birth occurs approximately 266 days after conception.

Fetal stage Final stage of pregnancy (8–12 weeks to birth), characterized by rapid growth and continued development.

Hazards of Prenatal Development

If a pregnant woman is under stress, will her baby be affected? Will the baby be affected if she has x-rays taken while she is pregnant, if she gets sick, or if she smokes marijuana? How does her nutrition affect her unborn child? Questions like these have been—and continue to be—the subject of research in the relatively new field of prenatal psychology. Most of our knowledge about prenatal hazards has been gleaned from animal research or from studies in which mothers reported on such factors as what they had eaten while pregnant, what drugs they had taken, how much radiation they had been exposed to, and what illnesses they had had.

Influences in the prenatal environment affect different fetuses differently. Some environmental factors produce birth defects in some cases but have little or no effect in others. We still do not have all the answers to questions about prenatal influences, but research suggests that the timing of an environmental "insult," its intensity, and its interaction with other factors are all important. For example, we have known for more than 50 years that radiation can cause gene mutations and that x-rays are most dangerous before the sixth week of pregnancy, at the time of major organ development (Murphy, 1929). What, then, do we know about other prenatal influences?

Maternal Nutrition A woman's diet during pregnancy can have important effects on the future health of her child. Women who have been malnourished for long periods—before or during pregnancy—are more likely to have complications during pregnancy and childbirth, and to bear low-birthweight babies or babies who are born dead or die soon after birth (Burke, Beal, Kirkwood, & Stuart, 1943; Read, Habicht, Lechtig, & Klein, 1973). Although supplementing the diets of pregnant women reduces these problems (Jacobson, 1977; Prentice, Whitehead, Watkinson, Lamb, & Cole, 1983), good long-term nutrition for both mother and child is best.

The National Center for Health Statistics (1986) recommends a weight gain of about 26 to 35 pounds. A woman who gains significantly less weight than this is more likely to have a baby under 5 pounds, to miscarry, or to bear a stillborn baby. Weight gains above 35 pounds are associated with slightly higher risks to the fetus. Other research has established the importance of eating breakfast during pregnancy, since pregnant women who skip breakfast show changes in the levels of various bloodstream substances that are not shown by nonpregnant women (Metzger, Ravnikar, Vileisis, & Freinkel, 1982). (For a diagrammatic representation of where the weight goes, see Figure 9-5, page 312.)

Maternal Illness A number of illnesses contracted during pregnancy can have serious effects on the developing fetus, depending partly on *when* the mother gets sick. Rubella (German measles) before the eleventh week of pregnancy is almost certain to cause deafness and heart defects in the baby (Miller, Cradock-Watson, & Pollock,

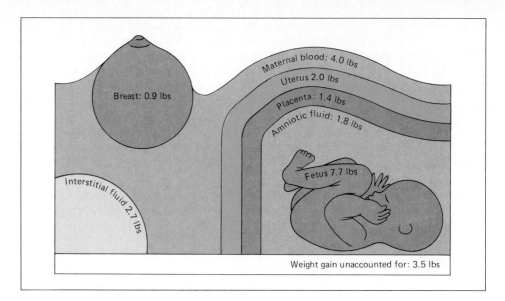

FIGURE 9-5 *Distribution of weight gain in an average pregnancy. (Source: Newton & Modahl, 1978.)*

Labels within figure:
Breast: 0.9 lbs
Maternal blood: 4.0 lbs
Uterus 2.0 lbs
Placenta: 1.4 lbs
Amniotic fluid: 1.8 lbs
Fetus 7.7 lbs
Interstitial fluid 2.7 lbs
Weight gain unaccounted for: 3.5 lbs

1982). Diabetes, tuberculosis, and syphilis have been implicated in problems of fetal development, and both gonorrhea and genital herpes can have harmful effects on the baby at the time of delivery. Herpes can cause blindness, other abnormalities, and even death in the newborn (Sullivan-Bolyai, Hull, Wilson, & Corey, 1983). A new danger for infants is acquired immune deficiency syndrome (AIDS), which can be contracted by a fetus if the mother has the virus in her bloodstream (M.F. Rogers, 1985). Recently, head and facial abnormalities have appeared in children infected with the AIDS virus in utero (Marion, Wiznia, Hutcheon, & Rubinstein, 1986).

Maternal Drug Intake A woman who is, or thinks she might be, pregnant should be very careful about taking any drug, whether prescribed or over the counter. She needs to weigh long-term potential effects on her unborn child against any discomfort she is feeling, and should consult her doctor about the safety of any medication. The hormone *diethylstilbestrol (DES),* which for many years was prescribed (ineffectually) to prevent miscarriage, has had serious effects on some of the children whose mothers took it and has been linked to abnormalities of the cervix and vagina and childbirth problems among female children (Barnes et al., 1980; Herbst, Ulfelder, & Poskanzer, 1971) and infertility and reproductive abnormalities among male children (Stenchever et al., 1981).

A pregnant woman enjoying an after-dinner cigarette may not think that she is taking a potent drug. Research shows that she is. Pregnant women who smoke are more likely to bear low-birthweight and premature babies and to have spontaneous abortions, stillbirths, and babies who die soon after birth (Lincoln, 1986). Their children are at higher risk for behavior problems like hyperactivity and short attention span, for school problems (Naeye & Peters, 1984), and for childhood cancer (Stjernfeldt, Berglund, Lindsten, & Ludvigsson, 1986). A "fetal tobacco syndrome" characterized by retarded fetal growth may be caused by smoking during pregnancy (Nieberg, Marks, McLaren, & Remington, 1985). In addition, passive smoking (smoking by the father during the pregnancy) has been related to reduced birthweight (Rubin, Krasilnikoff, Leventhal, Weile, & Berget, 1986). Even having tobacco smoke in the air seems to affect the fetus.

Some alcoholic women have given birth to babies who suffer from a rare ailment termed **fetal alcohol syndrome,** characterized by mental, motor, and growth retardation (Golden, Sokol, Kuhnert, & Bottoms, 1982; Jones, Smith, Ulleland, & Streissguth, 1973; Wright et al., 1983). Even when their intelligence is normal, these children are apt to have problems with schoolwork (Shaywitz, Cohen, & Shaywitz, 1980). Since many alcoholic women have alcoholic husbands, it is significant that sperm samples from alcoholic men are often highly abnormal (Lester & Van Thiel,

Fetal alcohol syndrome *Group of symptoms including mental, motor, and growth retardation affecting the offspring of some women who drank heavily during pregnancy.*

1977). And taking one or two alcoholic drinks per day has been associated with growth retardation in the offspring (Mills, Graubard, Harley, Rhoads, & Berendes, 1984).

Heavy use of marijuana may also contribute to earlier delivery and other difficulties (Fried, Watkinson, & Willan, 1984; Hingson et al., 1982). The mother's overall lifestyle is significant. A general lifestyle combining smoking, drinking, marijuana, poor nutrition, and so forth has a serious impact on fetal and child development, even though the impact of each of these is relatively minor by itself. More powerful drugs are even more dangerous: women who use cocaine during pregnancy are more likely to miscarry and more likely to have children with neurological impairments (Chasnoff, Burns, Schnoll, & Burns, 1985).

Risks Associated with the Father We need more research on the father's role in causing birth defects. Advanced paternal age has been implicated in Down's syndrome and some rare genetic effects, and the father's drinking of alcoholic beverages is suspected to be a contaminant of sperm. More research is needed with regard to men's exposure to chemicals at work, the drugs they take, their health, and other factors in their lives.

Fortunately, most of the time fetal development is normal, and pregnancy ends with the delivery of a healthy baby. Let's see how we develop after we make our appearance in the outside world.

THE BODY: EARLY PHYSICAL DEVELOPMENT

At the Beginning

The way babies grow in height and weight is obvious and enormous, as is their surge in motor abilities. But some other abilities are less apparent, a fact that has led people to underestimate the capacity of infants to perceive and respond to a great variety of events in their everyday world. Research in recent years, which has used a variety of ingenious study techniques, has shown that human infants are very sophisticated little beings. Even though they are dependent in many ways, they are extremely competent.

New arrivals do not look like the babies in magazine ads. They are usually wrinkled, with a misshapen head and a squashed nose resulting from the trip through the birth canal, and may be covered all over their bodies by a downy fuzz (*lanugo*). Their appearance changes during the **neonatal period,** the first 28 days of life. During this time of transition from life in the uterus to an independent existence, all the newborn's body systems—circulatory, respiratory, gastrointestinal, and temperature regulation—adjust to functioning on their own, with no help from the mother's systems.

Neonatal period *First 28 days of life.*

Even at this threshold of life, newborn babies can do much more than most people realize. From birth they blink at a bright light, follow a moving target, and turn toward light at a window. Although their visual acuity is relatively poor, it will improve with age (Vaughan, McKay, & Behrman, 1979).

Newborns also turn their heads toward a sound, move in time to human speech, and respond to pain (for example, they try to withdraw from a needle and are wakeful after being circumcised or being pricked for blood). Before 1 week of age, they prefer to look at a human face rather than at other patterns, recognize their mother's voice and smell, and are more alert when held at an angle or upright rather than lying down. By 2 weeks, they recognize their mother's face (MacFarlane, 1978).

How do we know all this? Techniques devised by ingenious researchers have let us discover that the infant's world is not as William James described it in 1890: "one great blooming, buzzing confusion."

Some of the most interesting research on infants' vision—which measures aspects of infants' thought as well—is in the area of visual preference. If we see that a baby spends a longer time looking at one item rather than another, we conclude that the baby can tell the difference between the two and for some reason likes one of them better. Robert L. Fantz (1956) designed a special apparatus in which infants can lie and look at visual stimuli that differ in color, complexity of pattern, dimensionality, and familiarity. By measuring the length of time an item is reflected in the baby's cornea, an observer can tell what the baby likes to look at. Babies prefer curved lines to straight, color to black-and-white, complex patterns to simple ones, three-dimensional to flat patterns, pictures of faces to pictures of other things, and new sights to familiar ones (Fantz, 1963, 1964, 1965; Fantz, Fagan, & Miranda, 1975; Fantz & Nevis, 1967).

Habituation *Simple type of learning in which an organism becomes used to a stimulus and stops responding to it.*

Another way to determine infants' capabilities is through the phenomenon of **habituation,** in which babies stop responding to a stimulus they've gotten used to (see the section "Learning in Infancy," later in this chapter). In this way we've learned that newborns can distinguish among at least four distinct smells and prefer sweet tastes (MacFarlane, 1978). By 3 days after birth, infants can already distinguish between new speech sounds and those they have already heard (Brody, Zelazo, & Chaika, 1984). The babies in one experiment steadily stopped responding to familiar words; but when they heard new words, they became more attentive. By 1 month, babies can tell the difference between sounds as close as *pah* and *bah* (Eimas et al., 1971).

In another study, infants less than 3 days old showed that they could tell their mothers' voices from those of strangers and that the mother's voice seemed to have special importance (DeCasper & Fifer, 1980). By sucking on a nipple, the babies were able to turn on a recording. Sometimes the infants would hear their mother reading a story; at other times, they would hear another woman reading a story. They sucked about 24 percent more to produce the mother's voice. This early preference may be important in developing attachment between mother and child.

Early sensitivity to sounds may provide a way to estimate infants' intelligence. Most attempts to measure infants' intelligence using traditional psychometric tests (see Chapter 7) have been disappointing, but a recent study found a highly significant correlation between the ability of 4-month-old infants to discriminate between sounds and their IQ scores at age 5. This suggests that auditory sensitivity may be one of the earliest indicators of cognitive functioning (O'Connor, Cohen, & Parmelee, 1984).

From research like this, we know that we enter this world as creatures who are ready to interact with the people and objects around us. And we see how competence in one domain, the physical, affects our development in the cognitive and psychosocial domains.

Growth

During their first 3 years, children grow more quickly than they will at any other time throughout life. By the first birthday, they usually triple their birthweight, from an average birthweight of 7½ pounds for a normal full-term baby to about 22 pounds. At the same time, they increase their height by about one-half, from an average length at birth of 20 inches to about 30 inches. Between the first and third birthdays, they grow about another 8 inches and gain another 10 pounds. While the average boy is larger and heavier than the average girl, the difference is not significant.

Physical growth slows down somewhat after this, but it is more rapid during the next 3 years than it will be between about ages 6 and 12, after which time the pubertal growth spurt occurs. For the next few years, girls tend to be larger than boys of the same age. Normal children show such a wide range in height that "if a child who was of exactly average height at his seventh birthday grew not at all for two years, he would still be just within the normal limits of height attained at age nine" (Tanner, 1973, p. 35).

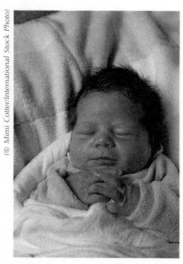

(© Mimi Cotter/International Stock Photo)

Because of some ingenious research, we now realize that newborn babies like this one are amazingly competent.

Skill	Age when shown (percent of babies tested)		
	25%	50%	90%
Rolling over	2 months	3 months	5 months
Sitting without support	5 months	6 months	8 months
Standing holding on	5 months	6 months	10 months
Standing alone well	10 months	12 months	14 months
Walking well	11 months	12 months	14½ months
Walking up steps	14 months	17 months	22 months
Jumping in place	21 months	22 months	36 months

FIGURE 9-6 *Ages when babies acquire motor skills can vary widely and still be regarded as "normal." (Source: Adapted from Denver Developmental Screening Test.)*

Motor Development

The next time you're near a baby who is not yet walking, notice all the things that he or she can do with the hands. This exemplifies the **cephalocaudal principle**—that development proceeds from head to toe, with the upper body parts developing before the bottom ones. You'll also note that babies learn to use their arms and legs before they have fine control over their fingers and toes, in line with the **proximodistal principle**—that development proceeds from near to far, with the parts of the body near the center developing before the extremities.

Figure 9-6 shows the leaps in motor development that take place in all normal children. Notice, however, that although these changes are universal, there is a wide "normal range" of ages when particular skills develop. Many normal children achieve these abilities before or after the age noted. One child may walk well at 11 months; another may not walk alone until 17 months; both are perfectly normal. We have to remember that the study of development is not only a study of the usual but also a study of individual differences: in every aspect of development, at every stage of life, there is a wide range of normality.

Another important aspect of motor development is reflex behaviors. When we blink at a bright light or kick out a foot after being tapped lightly on the knee, we are not acting in a deliberate, planned, voluntary way. We are reacting through a **reflex**,

Cephalocaudal principle Principle that development proceeds in a head-to-toe direction; upper parts of the body develop before lower parts.

Proximodistal principle Principle that development proceeds in a near-to-far direction; parts of the body near the center develop before the extremities.

Reflex Involuntary reaction to stimulation.

TABLE 9-2 SOME PRIMITIVE REFLEXES IN HUMANS

Name of Reflex	Stimulation	Behavior	Approximate Age of Dropping Out
Rooting	Cheek stroked with finger or nipple	Head turns; mouth opens, sucking movements begin	9 months
Moro (startle)	Sudden stimulus such as a loud noise or being dropped	Extends legs, arms, and fingers; arches back, draws back head	3 months
Darwinian (grasping)	Palm of hand stroked	Makes such a strong fist that baby can be raised to standing position if both fists are closed around a stick	2 months
Swimming	Put in water face down	Well-coordinated swimming movements	6 months
Tonic neck	Laid down on back	Head turns to one side; assumes "fencer" position; extends arms and legs on preferred side, flexes opposite limbs	2 months
Babinski	Sole of foot stroked	Toes fan out, foot twists in	6-9 months
Walking	Held under arm, with bare feet touching flat surface	Makes steplike motions that look like well-coordinated walking	2 months
Placing	Backs of feet drawn against edge of flat surface	Withdraws foot	1 month

an involuntary response to stimulation. Human beings have an arsenal of reflexes, some of which are clearly instrumental for survival and stay with us throughout life. The primitive reflexes are present at birth, drop out at various times throughout the first year, and provide an index for a baby's neurological development. Table 9-2 gives a list of primitive reflexes.

How Maturation and Deprivation Affect Physical Development

Maturation *Unfolding of biologically determined patterns of behavior, programmed by the genes.*

Both physical growth and the development of motor skills like walking and running are strongly influenced by **maturation,** the unfolding of biologically determined patterns of behavior that are programmed by the genes. Such behaviors tend to unfold in a predetermined pattern within certain ranges. These behaviors can rarely be hurried, even through the most vigorous attempts to train a child in, say, walking stairs, before he or she is ready (Gesell, 1929). Furthermore, they persist despite deprivation. Even children who suffer from abuse and neglect learn to sit up, to crawl, to walk. Only when deprivation is unusually severe is development substantially affected.

One classic example of such severe deprivation and its effect on motor development was seen among institutionalized children in Iran, who were hardly ever handled by their overworked attendants. As babies, they were in their cribs almost all the time, lying on their backs—never on their stomachs—and never put into a sitting position. They drank from propped bottles, had no toys, and were not taken out of bed until they could sit unsupported. They often did not sit alone till 2 years of age, as compared with about 6 months for the average American child—and for children in another Iranian institution, who had a more normal upbringing. When the children in the understaffed institutions did start to get about, they did not crawl on their hands and knees but scooted on their behinds. Apparently, lack of practice in using upper-body muscles had retarded their development. Even among these children, however, the retardation seemed only temporary. School-age children at one of the understaffed institutions, who presumably had also been retarded as toddlers, now worked and played normally (Dennis, 1960).

THE MIND: EARLY COGNITIVE DEVELOPMENT

Even though infants do have some adaptive capacities at birth, their enormous leaps in intellectual functioning are still to come—learning about the world and the people in it, figuring out how to make their wants known, learning to speak and understand language, remembering what they have learned and how to use it. How do these vast developments come about?

In this section, we'll consider cognitive development—the development of thought processes. We'll begin by discussing the most influential theoretical approach to cognitive development, that of Jean Piaget. We'll go on to examine two significant aspects of cognitive development—learning and memory.

Piaget: A Theory of Cognitive Development

The most influential explanation of intellectual development in modern times was put forward by the Swiss biologist and philosopher Jean Piaget (1896–1980), who formulated a theory to explain the various levels of cognitive development. He presumed an increasing ability to acquire knowledge that proceeds in an orderly sequence, closely related to age. He was specifically interested in how children acquire knowledge and understanding of their world.

Piaget considered children active constructors of their own cognitive world, rather than passive reactors to influences in the environment. His background in biology led him to give maturation an important place in his theory, but he went beyond this to emphasize the interaction between maturation and experience. In other words, children have to be ready for new development to occur, but if they do not have certain types of experiences at crucial times, they will not achieve the level they are capable of. These experiences include direct contact with physical objects, as well as education.

How did Piaget formulate this theory? He developed it not through standardized experimental procedures, but through his observations of his own children and through a flexible way of questioning children and basing additional questions on the children's initial responses. He devised this technique early in his career, when he was working in Binet's laboratory in Paris, trying to standardize an intelligence test (as described in Chapter 7). Piaget became interested in the wrong answers that children gave him. In exploring the reasons behind wrong answers he found that children of similar ages tended to make the same mistakes. One of his most important and enduring contributions to our knowledge of children's thought processes is the recognition that children think in ways which are qualitatively different from the ways adults think. Children's thought evolves through a series of four stages, culminating in adult logic. As children progress through these stages, they view their world in increasingly complex ways.

Piaget's stages of cognitive development are shown in Table 9-3 (page 318). Let's now take a look at three of them. We'll discuss the fourth stage in greater detail in Chapter 10, since, typically, it does not appear until adolescence.

Sensorimotor Stage (Birth to 2 Years)   Infants learn about their world through their senses and motor behaviors, rather than by thinking about it in the way that older children and adults can. The sensorimotor stage is a time of learning through action, as babies go from responding primarily through reflexes to organizing their activities in relation to the environment. They learn how to coordinate information from the

TABLE 9-3 PIAGET'S STAGES IN COGNITIVE DEVELOPMENT

Ages	Cognitive Stages
Birth to 2 years	*Sensorimotor:* Infant changes from a being who responds primarily through reflexes to one who can organize activities in relation to the environment.
2 to 7 years	*Preoperational:* Child develops a representational system and uses symbols such as words to represent people, places, and events.
7 to 12 years	*Concrete operations:* Child can solve problems logically if the problems are focused on the here and now.
12 years to adulthood	*Formal operations:* Person can think in abstract terms and deal with hypothetical situations.

different senses and to produce goal-directed behavior. They also learn the concept of object permanence.

Object permanence *Awareness that an object or person does not cease to exist when out of sight.*

Object permanence, the most important achievement of the sensorimotor period, is the realization that an object (or person) continues to exist even if it can no longer be seen. Up to about 4 months of age, babies do not look for an object they no longer see, but between 4 and 8 months, they will search if they see it being hidden. If it is moved several times, however—even right in front of their eyes—they will look for it only in the first place they saw it being hidden. Between 12 and 18 months, they can follow moves that they see, but they will not search for an object if they did not see it being hidden. Generally, not until after 18 months of age do children have a mature sense of object permanence. Only then can they follow the movements of an object, look for an object in the last place they saw it, and look for something they have not seen being hidden.

The concept of object permanence has many practical implications. For one thing, children who have achieved it are better able to handle separation from their parents because they know that these important people still exist and will return. They can also go to a closet to look for a favorite toy or item of clothing and take other actions that involve remembering where someone or something might be.

The age-old game of peekaboo provides hours of excitement for children who are just developing the notion of object permanence. Is Mommy still there, although she can't be seen? Toddlers usually stay interested in asking and answering that question far longer than their adult playmates.

(© Jean-Claude Lejeune/Stock, Boston)

Preoperational Stage (2 to 7 Years)   At about age 2, children make a qualitative leap forward, thanks to their new ability to use symbols such as words to represent people, places, and objects. The kind of "pretend" play that 2-year-olds engage in, making one thing stand for something else, is a sign that they are in the preoperational stage.

Preoperational children can think about objects that are not right in front of them, imitate actions they do not see at the moment, learn how to use numbers, and learn to use language—the most remarkable of symbol systems—in a sophisticated way. They are beginning to understand that an object continues to be the same thing even if its form changes. If, for example, they see water being poured from a pitcher into a glass, they realize that it is the same water. (Later they will realize that if the pitcher is *emptied* into the glass, it is also the same *amount* of water.) And they can understand relationships between two events (like flipping a switch and seeing a light go on).

There are, however, major limitations in thought. Children at this stage generally fail to take all aspects of a situation into account; they focus on only one aspect, ignoring others that may be just as important. Also, they do not understand that actions can be reversed to restore an original state. And they are still governed by **egocentrism;** they cannot consider another person's point of view. Instead, they assume that everyone sees the world just as they do, and that they are the cause of all significant events. For example, a little boy may hide or close his eyes and think that because he can't see you, you can't see him. Or a little girl may feel that she caused her parents' divorce ("If I hadn't been bad, Mommy and Daddy wouldn't have fought so much").

Egocentrism   *Inability to consider another's point of view; a characteristic of preoperational thought.*

Some recent critics maintain that Piaget overstated children's egocentrism by posing problems that were too difficult for them. They point to recent studies showing that children in this stage *can* take another person's point of view and can communicate information effectively if they understand the task at hand (Dickson, 1979) and that even 4-year-olds change their way of speaking when they talk to 2-year-olds (Shatz & Gelman, 1973).

Concrete Operations Stage (7 to 12 Years)   In the stage of concrete operations, children again make a qualitative leap as they shed their egocentrism and begin to understand and use new concepts. They can classify things into categories, deal with numbers, take all aspects of a situation into account, and understand reversibility. They are much better at putting themselves into another's place—a capacity which has implications for understanding other people and making moral judgments.

The concept of conservation, which has probably intrigued more researchers than any other aspect of Piagetian theory, brings out the difference between the preoperational stage and the concrete operations stage. **Conservation** is the ability to recognize that two equal quantities of matter remain equal (in substance, weight, length, number, volume, or space) even if the matter is rearranged, as long as nothing is added or taken away.

Conservation   *Piagetian term for the awareness that two stimuli that are equal (in length, weight, amount, etc.) remain equal despite perceptual alteration, so long as nothing has been added to or taken away from either stimulus.*

Conservation of substance is tested as follows: a child is shown two balls of clay and agrees that they are equal; the child is said to "conserve substance" if he or she recognizes that even after one of the balls is rolled into the shape of a worm or a pancake (or is divided into several smaller balls), both lumps still contain the same amount of clay. Weight conservation is tested by asking whether the ball and the worm weigh the same. For conservation of volume, the question is whether the ball and the worm displace an equal amount of liquid when placed in glasses of water.

Children develop the ability to conserve the different dimensions at different times. At age 6 or 7, they can conserve mass, or substance; at 9 or 10, weight; and by 11 or 12, volume. This age difference is intriguing, since each problem is based on exactly the same principle, but it does seem to hold true for most children. Even though the age of acquisition may vary, children master mass first, then weight, and then volume. This shows how concrete children's thinking is at this stage, since they are unable to generalize the same principle to all content areas at the same time.

The reasons children give for their answers give us clues to their thinking. Children in the concrete operations stage show that they understand reversibility ("You can always turn the sausage back into a ball"), identity ("It's the same clay; you haven't added any or taken any away"), and compensation ("The ball is shorter and thicker, but the sausage is longer and narrower"). Preoperational children who say that the sausage has more clay or weighs more because it is longer show that they are fooled by what the clay looks like and that they are thus focusing on only one aspect of the situation. They also may have trouble understanding the precise meaning of the words *more, less,* and so forth. And since their memory is not so well developed, they may not remember that the two lumps were equal to begin with.

Formal Operations Stage (12 Years and Older)   The stage of formal operations heralds the ability to think abstractly. People in this stage can approach a problem that is not physically present, work out a hypothesis, and go about testing it systematically. Piaget originally felt that this qualitative leap was made by all normal youngsters at about age 12; but he later changed his stance, maintaining that different kinds of experiences might delay the arrival of this stage until later in the teens. Other researchers have discovered that some people may never attain formal operations (Papalia & Bielby, 1974; Tomlinson-Keasey, 1972). (As was noted earlier, formal operations are discussed further in Chapter 10.)

Piaget's theory has been criticized on a number of grounds. For one thing, he concentrated on the average child and was not especially concerned with individual differences in development. For another, he did not place much emphasis on the impact of education and culture on cognitive development. Furthermore, he drew many conclusions about infants' development from his observations of his own children, a very small sample (three). Finally, he did not use standardized experimental procedures. Still, his analysis of intellectual growth has opened the door to a novel way of evaluating the development of logical thinking, has inspired more research than that of any other developmental theorist in the last few decades, and has stimulated many practical changes in the way children are taught and cared for.

Learning

Learning in Infancy   Learning is one aspect of early cognitive ability. In recent years, researchers have tried to determine at what age babies can learn and what types of learning they are capable of. We've found out that children learn as early as the first day of life. They learn to make sucking movements with the mouth as soon as they see their mothers, and they learn to recognize sounds, patterns, and smells. Such early learning is possible because it builds upon powers that human beings are born with, such as reflexes and basic sensory capabilities. These inborn survival-promoting abilities can be thought of as a "gift of the species" (Lipsitt, 1982, p. 63).

There is no controversy about this enormous capacity for learning, which opens up a world of possibilities for the human infant, especially as the baby's brain matures and the cerebral cortex takes over many activities, allowing new learning to take place. Major questions still exist, however, about the *ways* by which babies learn.

As we saw in Chapter 5, human beings can be *conditioned* to associate pairs of stimuli—in other words, to learn. In classical conditioning the learner forms a new association between a previously neutral stimulus and an unconditioned stimulus, and in operant conditioning the organism learns that making a particular response will bring about either reward or punishment. Researchers have set up experiments in both classical and operant conditioning and have tried to determine how early human beings can be conditioned.

According to the most recent research, it seems possible to classically condition newborn infants. Newborns have learned to suck when they hear a buzzer or tone;

to exhibit the Babkin reflex (turning the head and opening the mouth) when their arms are moved (instead of in response to the usual stimulus, pressure on the palm of the hand); to dilate and constrict the pupils of the eyes; to blink; and to change the heart rate (Rovee-Collier & Lipsitt, 1982).

However, operant conditioning, or learning by a reinforcement system, seems easier to establish in early infancy, especially when it is based on existing behavior patterns, such as reflexes, rather than on behaviors the infant would not ordinarily perform. For example, infants as young as 2 days old have learned to apply the sucking reflex to suck on a nipple that did not produce any milk. Their reward was music, produced by their sucking. Infants whose sucking turned the music off (which was *not* a reward) did not learn to suck on the nipple (Butterfield & Siperstein, 1972).

Later Learning   It is clear, as the discussion of learning in infancy shows, that learning occurs in several ways. (Yet another type of learning, social learning, is discussed later in this chapter.) Children—like adults—continue to learn along the lines described in Chapter 5.

Memory

Memory in Infancy   What do babies know? What can they remember? When we see a baby beginning to make sucking motions with the mouth when the mother comes into sight, we deduce that the baby remembers that she is the one who brings food. This does not happen at birth: research has shown that a delay interval of only 1 second will interfere with the memory of a 1-month-old (Watson, 1967). As infants mature neurologically, their memories get better.

Because researchers have come up with creative methods of studying memory, we now know that some aspects of early memory are much better than we could have imagined. We are aware that some degree of memory exists at 1 week of age. How do we know this? A major source has been research establishing the existence of visual-recognition memory, a baby's ability to remember something previously seen.

There are several ways to test infants' memory, one of which makes use of habituation. Babies may be shown a particular design several times, while sucking on a nipple. When they first see the design, they will probably stop sucking so that

(© James Kilkelly/DOT)

This baby boy is taking part in a test of infants' memory. When he first sees the doll's face, he stops sucking on the nipple so that he can pay attention. As he becomes used to seeing the face, he'll go back to sucking. He'll stop again, though, when he is shown something new on the screen. This indicates that he remembers what he has seen.

they can pay attention to it. After they have seen the same design several times, they tend to continue sucking, showing that they have become used to it. When a new design is shown, however, they will again stop sucking. This shows that they have stored some information about the design they saw originally: they must remember enough about it to recognize that the new design is different.

During the first week of life, babies can discriminate patterns that are considerably different from each other. If patterns differ in several ways (such as size, number, hue, and brightness), neonates can tell them apart. Not until the third or fourth month can they tell things apart that differ in only one way, such as orientation, form, or patterning. By 5 months of age, they can make even more subtle distinctions—for example, between black-and-white photos of two unfamiliar faces (Fagan, 1982).

One practical application of these findings about infants' memory is the development of tests that may be able to predict later intelligence. A baby's visual-recognition memory may be able to tell us about later intellectual development. This is implied by the fact that tests of infants' visual-recognition memory are good predictors of verbal intelligence in 4- and 7-year-olds (Fagan, 1982; Fagan & McGrath, 1981).

Memory in Childhood Between the ages of 2 and 5, memory improves considerably. Researchers have tested children through "memory games," asking them to *recognize* (point out familiar items) or *recall* (summon items from memory when they cannot see them) a series of toys or pictures that they saw a short time before. As in adulthood, recognition is easier than recall. Four-year-olds recognize about 90 percent of items they have seen, but they can recall only about 35 percent (Myers & Perlmutter, 1978).

As children develop intellectually, their memory improves, partly because they develop strategies that help them to remember. By the second grade, children spontaneously use *rehearsal* (that is, silent or spoken repetition of something we want to remember, like a phone number), and they can be taught to rehearse even earlier, in first grade (Flavell, Beach, & Chinsky, 1966).

Later in childhood, at about the fifth-grade level, youngsters begin to use strategies like *clustering* (organizing materials in categories, such as birds, foods, and items of clothing) and *chunking* (organizing material in sections—for example, learning a phone number by remembering the area code, then the telephone exchange, and then the last four digits) (Appel et al., 1972; Forman & Sigel, 1979). Such strategies will help them remember the billions of items of information they will need to keep in their minds throughout their lives.

Learning and memory are not, of course, the only aspects of cognitive development. Other aspects of intellectual development—such as language and intelligence and its measurement—are covered elsewhere in this book.

THE PSYCHE: EARLY EMOTIONAL AND SOCIAL DEVELOPMENT

In the first days of life, babies are already manifesting their unique temperaments; they are gaining a sense of the world—whether it is friendly and caring or cold and hostile—and they are responding to and evoking responses from the people around them. The way we develop emotionally depends on what we bring into the world and what we find in it. In turn, we affect others and contribute to our own future emotional development. And so it goes, throughout life.

In this section we'll consider an important theory of social and emotional, or psychosocial, development—Erik Erikson's. Then we'll discuss five significant aspects of social and emotional development in early life: emotional expression, temperament, attachment, identification, and getting along with peers.

TABLE 9-4 ERIKSON'S STAGES OF PSYCHOSOCIAL DEVELOPMENT

Ages	Psychosocial Stages
Birth to 12–18 months	**1** *Basic trust versus basic mistrust:* Baby develops sense of when and whom to trust, when to protect self by being cautious.
12–18 months to 3 years	**2** *Autonomy versus shame and doubt:* Child develops a balance of independence and recognition of limitations.
3 to 6 years	**3** *Initiative versus guilt:* Child develops ability to try out new activities in the pursuit of goals, is not overwhelmed by failure, and begins to question propriety of activities.
6 years to puberty	**4** *Industry versus inferiority:* Child learns skills of the culture, gains self-esteem through competence, and keeps the role of work in proper perspective.
Puberty to young adulthood	**5** *Identity versus role confusion:* Adolescent must determine own sense of self, especially in terms of work goals. Problems may result in either impulsive behavior or extended immaturity.
Young adulthood	**6** *Intimacy versus isolation:* Person seeks to find a balance between making commitments to others and maintaining own individuality.
Middle adulthood	**7** *Generativity versus stagnation:* Mature adult is concerned with establishing and guiding the next generation and also with developing own creativity, which may require a period of attention to self.
Late adulthood	**8** *Basic Integrity versus Basic despair:* Elderly person achieves an acceptance of own life, coming to terms with approaching death; some despair is inevitable.

Erikson: A Theory of Psychosocial Development

The psychoanalyst Erik Erikson (b. 1902) developed the only major theory of normal human development that covers the entire life span. Erikson (1950) built on the Freudian concept of ego to consider society's influence on the developing personality. He outlined eight stages of development throughout life, each of which depends upon the successful resolution of a *crisis,* or turning point. Each crisis is an issue that needs to be resolved at a particular point in development; "resolution" of a crisis implies achieving a balance between two alternatives (see Table 9-4). Whether and how such resolutions occur will have an impact on personality development.

We'll look at Erikson's first four crises of psychosocial development here, and at the last four in Chapter 10.

Crisis 1: Basic Trust versus Basic Mistrust (Birth to 12–18 Months)   Constant, reliable care is the basic determinant of the successful resolution of the first crisis, **basic trust versus basic mistrust.** Babies pick up cues about such care primarily from the satisfaction of their feeding needs, but also from the way they are handled, protected, and kept safe and comfortable. Children who have trust in their mother (whom Erikson views as the primary caretaker) are able to let her out of their sight, because they know she is certain to return. At the same time, their trust in the mother becomes a standard against which they can measure others and determine whom to trust and whom to mistrust.

Crisis 2: Autonomy versus Shame and Doubt (12–18 Months to 3 Years)   Building upon the sense of trust already established, children at the second crisis, **autonomy versus shame and doubt,** are now exploring their environments with newly developed skills in moving around and in dealing with language. They are learning how

Basic trust versus basic mistrust
According to Erikson, the first crisis of psychosocial development. From birth to 12–18 months, an infant develops a sense of whether or not the world can be trusted; the feeding situation and the quality of the mother-infant interaction are important determinants of the outcome of this stage.

Autonomy versus shame and doubt
According to Erikson, the second crisis of psychosocial development. Between 12–18 months and 3 years, the child develops a balance of autonomy (independence, self-determination) and shame.

independent (autonomous) they can be and what their limitations are. A healthy sense of doubt helps them set their own limits, and the development of shame marks the beginning of a sense of right and wrong. The parents' role at this stage is to provide the right amount of control. Too much control may inhibit the child's autonomy; but if there is too little control, the child may become compulsive about controlling himself or herself.

Crisis 3: Initiative versus Guilt (3 to 6 Years) The basic conflict of the third crisis, *initiative versus guilt,* is between initiative in planning and carrying out activities and guilt over what the child wants to do. Children have to learn how to regulate these aspects of personality so that they can develop a sense of responsibility and still be able to enjoy life. If too much guilt develops, children overcontrol themselves, stifling their initiative and preventing the free expression of their personality.

Crisis 4: Industry versus Inferiority (6 Years to Puberty) Children must learn the skills of their culture, either in school or from adults or older children. Productivity and a sense of competence are important, tempered by the child's awareness of how much still has to be learned. The stage of *industry versus inferiority* coincides with the timing of the Piagetian *concrete operations stage,* which makes possible many productive achievements. Children who feel inferior to their peers may retreat to the safety of the family, stifling cognitive and productive development; children consumed with the importance of industriousness may neglect the emotional sides of their personality.

Erikson's theory has been criticized on several counts—most especially, it is said that an antifemale bias emerges from his acceptance of prevailing cultural standards (Gilligan, 1982) and that the imprecise definition of his concepts makes it difficult to confirm them through research. The great strength of his theory is its broad-based viewpoint, which takes in the entire life span. (As we noted earlier, we'll examine Erikson's crises 5 through 8 in Chapter 10, since they occur in adolescence and adulthood.)

Emotional Expression in Early Life

Expressing Emotions How can we tell what is happening in a baby's mind? We try to figure this out on the basis of what we can see—crying, smiling, laughing, and the way babies, and then older children, respond to those around them. Recent research suggests that babies show a wide range of different feelings, even in the early months of life; that specific feelings appear in a typical sequence; and that even adults who are observing babies they do not know can distinguish a variety of emotional expressions.

In one study, the facial expressions of 30 infants (10 each at the ages of 5, 7, and 9 months) in such circumstances as playing games with their mothers, being surprised by a jack-in-the-box, getting shots from a doctor, and being approached by a stranger were recorded on videotape. A panel of judges were trained with Izard's *Facial Expression Scoring Manual* (FESM), which gives verbal descriptions and photographs of brow, eye, and mouth regions of nine facial patterns that express fundamental emotions (Izard, 1971, 1977). These judges then classified the expressions. Then untrained subjects—college students and female health service professionals (mostly public health and school nurses)— were asked to identify the babies' expressions. These volunteers were able to identify such expressions as joy, sadness, interest, and fear accurately, and anger, surprise, and disgust to a lesser degree (Izard, Huebner, Resser, McGinnes, & Dougherty, 1980). When the subjects were trained with FESM, they became even more accurate.

Initiative versus guilt According to Erikson, the third crisis of psychosocial development, which characterizes children from about 3 to 6 years. Children develop initiative when they try out new things and are not overwhelmed by failure.

Industry versus inferiority According to Erikson, the fourth crisis of psychosocial development, which occurs during middle childhood. Children must learn the skills of their culture or feel inferior.

While we can't be positive that these babies did have the emotions they were credited with, the fact that the judges and the untrained subjects agreed so closely in identifying the various expressions does seem to indicate that the babies were showing a variety of different feelings. Also, the fact that the babies' expressions resembled adults' expressions in similar situations seem to provide some basis for attributing similar emotions to young infants and adults.

(Rhona Robbin)

The extent to which babies influence their own environment shows up in individual differences in the amount of smiling they do. A happy, cheerful baby like Andrew, who freely bestows smiles and gurgles on the people in his life, is likely to form a more positive relationship with them than he would if he smiled less readily.

SMILING A baby's smile is an irresistible means of communication. The probability is high that an infant's smile will elicit a smile from any adult within range (Gewirtz & Gewirtz, 1968), and these reciprocal smiles go far to cement the bonds between babies and the important people in their lives. Babies smile fleetingly at the age of 1 week and more frequently at 1 month; at 3½ months, they smile more at familiar faces than at unfamiliar ones (Kreutzer & Charlesworth, 1973).

Infants vary considerably in their smiling (Tautermannova, 1973), and the differences can be significant. A happy, cheerful baby who rewards parents' caretaking efforts with smiles and gurgles is quite likely to form a more positive relationship with them than a baby who smiles less readily.

LAUGHING At about the fourth month, babies start to laugh out loud—when they are kissed on the stomach, when they hear certain sounds, and when they see their parents do unusual things. As babies grow older (7 to 9 months), they laugh more often and at more different things. They are more likely to laugh at complex situations like a game of peekaboo, or in potentially upsetting situations where laughter helps them discharge tension (as it does with adults, too).

We see, then, a relationship between emotional and cognitive development. By laughing at the unexpected, children show that they know what to expect (Sroufe & Wunsch, 1972); by using laughter at difficult times, children demonstrate competence.

CRYING Crying is the most powerful way—and sometimes the only way—that babies can make their needs known. It is, therefore, a vital means of communication. Babies cry for many reasons, and experienced parents and laboratory researchers are often able to tell whether the babies are hungry, angry, in pain, or frustrated (Oswald & Peltzman, 1974; Wolff, 1969).

Parents often wonder how to respond to their babies' crying. If they come whenever the child cries, do they risk creating a spoiled child who whines and fusses at every frustration? The evidence says *no*. Babies whose cries of distress bring relief are apparently able to gain a measure of self-confidence from the knowledge that they can affect their own lives. By the end of the first year, babies whose care givers respond promptly and caringly to their crying cry less than those whose cries are not answered so well (Ainsworth & Bell, 1977; Bell & Ainsworth, 1972). In fact, the more a care giver ignores, scolds, hits, commands, and restricts a baby, the more the baby cries, frets, and acts aggressively (Clarke-Stewart, 1977).

Babies who are carried more cry less (Hunziker & Barr, 1986). One 12-week experiment divided pairs of 4- to 12-week-old babies and their mothers into two groups. The parents in the experimental group were asked to carry their babies for 3 hours or more every day in baby carriers or in their arms (carrying time averaged 4.4 hours per day). The babies in the control group were carried at their usual rate, which averaged 2.7 hours per day (see Figure 9-7, page 326). The babies in the experimental group cried less than the babies in the control group, especially in the evening.

The Timing of Emotional Expression As children mature, they certainly express a wider variety of emotions (see Table 9-5, page 326). It is possible that the time when they first express various emotions is closely tied to maturation of the brain. Research

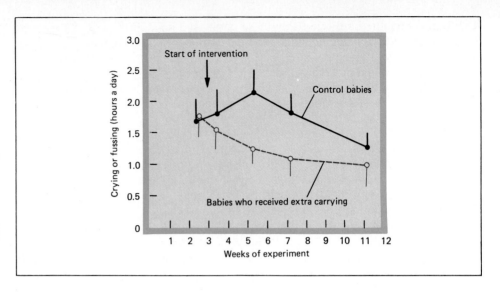

FIGURE 9-7 *Babies cry less when they are carried more. The dotted line represents babies who received extra carrying (an average of 4.4 hours total each day) in a 12-week experiment. The solid line represents a control group of babies who were carried at their usual level (an average of 2.7 hours per day). During the first 3 weeks of the study, the amount of crying was about the same for both groups. From then on, the difference was striking. The control babies showed the typical pattern of increased crying and fussing, peaking at 6 weeks and then decreasing. The babies who received extra carrying showed a steady decrease. (Source: Adapted from Hunziker & Barr, 1986, p. 644.)*

shows that the right frontal regions of the brains of 10-month-olds are more active during positive emotions, and the left frontal regions are more active during negative emotions. The basis for this brain organization may exist at birth (Fox & Davidson, 1984), and the chronology may have survival value. An expression of pain from a helpless 2-month-old may bring needed help; at 9 months, in the same situation babies may express anger, which may mobilize them to do something to help themselves—to push away another child, for example (Trotter, 1983).

However, experience also plays a role. Abused infants show fear several months earlier than other babies, a fact which suggests that they have learned fear through unhappy experiences (Gaensbauer & Hiatt, cited in Trotter, 1983).

Furthermore, the same emotional response can have different meanings at different ages. In early infancy, crying usually signals physical discomfort; later on it is more likely to mean emotional distress. Early smiles often come spontaneously as an expression of internal well-being; after a few months of age, smiles are more often social signals through which the baby shows pleasure in other people.

TABLE 9-5   TIMES OF EMERGENCE OF INFANTS' EMOTIONAL EXPRESSIONS

Expression of Fundamental Emotions	Approximate Time of Emergence
Interest	Present at birth
Neonatal smile (a sort of half smile that appears spontaneously for no apparent reason)	Present at birth
Startle response	Present at birth
Distress (in response to pain)	Present at birth
Disgust (in response to unpleasant taste or smell)	Present at birth
Social smile	4–6 weeks
Anger	3–4 months
Surprise	3–4 months
Sadness	3–4 months
Fear	5–7 months
Shame, shyness, self-awareness	6–8 months
Contempt	Second year of life
Guilt	Second year of life

Source: Adapted from Trotter, 1983, pp. 14–20.

Temperament

One baby seems to smile and laugh almost all the time, hardly ever crying, while another reverses the pattern. Such differences often show up right from birth, demonstrating distinct differences in *temperament*—a person's characteristic style of approaching people and situations. After following 133 babies from birth, researchers identified 9 different aspects of temperament that appear inborn (Thomas, Chess, & Birch, 1968): (1) activity level; (2) regularity in biological functioning (sleeping, eating, eliminating); (3) readiness to accept new people and situations; (4) adaptability to change; (5) sensitivity to noise, light, and other sensory stimuli; (6) mood (cheerfulness or unhappiness); (7) intensity of responses; (8) distractibility; and (9) persistence. Biological differences may be at the root of such temperamental diversity. Newborns with lower levels of the enzyme monoamine oxidase (MAO) are more active, more excitable, and crankier than those with higher MAO levels (Sostek & Wyatt, 1981). Previous research has established a probable genetic basis for such variations.

Certain combinations of these nine temperamental traits produce three distinctive personalities. About 40 percent of the children studied can be described as *easy* children: they're happy most of the time; adjust easily to new situations; and sleep, eat, and eliminate on a fairly predictable schedule. About 10 percent are *difficult*: they cry easily, are irregular in body functions, and take a long time to adjust to a new routine. And about 15 percent are *slow to warm up*: mild in their responses, with a need to take time adjusting to new experiences and people (Thomas & Chess, 1977). Of course, many children do not fit neatly into any of these categories.

The significance of such characteristics lies in the degree to which children create their own worlds. One of the major trends in recent research has been the exploration of the degree to which children affect their parents, as well as the other way around. Some children are more likely, for example, to suffer abuse—premature and low-birthweight babies, temperamentally difficult children, hyperactive and retarded children, and youngsters who make other special demands on their parents (Reid, Patterson, & Loeber, 1982). Research has shown that when experimenters encourage children to ask their parents for help, the children act more dependently and their parents become bossier and more restrictive; when the children are encouraged to be independent, their parents are less likely to interfere (Segal & Yahraes, 1978).

A child's temperament, therefore, is an important element in the way other people will act toward him or her. It is easier to be warm and loving to a baby who is usually cheerful and whose wants you can anticipate and meet easily than it is with a baby who cries constantly, resists being cuddled, and often seems impossible to please. Parents who get along best with difficult or slow-to-warm-up children are the ones who have learned how to adapt their child-rearing patterns to their children's individual needs (Thomas & Chess, 1977). Some children, in fact, seem to change their behavioral styles over the years, apparently reacting to the kind of handling they get from their parents. Some of the ways in which parents and children affect each other are explored in the box "How Parents' Child-Rearing Styles Affect Their Children" (page 328).

Attachment

If you've ever seen a baby who watches a mother's every move, smiles at her when she comes near, gurgles to her, cries when she leaves the room, and then squeals with joy upon her return, you've seen a baby who has formed a first attachment to another person. **Attachment** is an active, affectionate, reciprocal relationship specifically between two people, as distinguished from all other persons. While babies do

Attachment *Active, affectionate, reciprocal relationship specifically between two people; their interaction reinforces and strengthens the attachment, or bond. Often refers to infant's relationship with parents.*

HOW PARENTS' CHILD-REARING STYLES AFFECT THEIR CHILDREN

What makes Mary burst into tears of frustration when she can't finish a jigsaw puzzle, while Gary will shrug and walk away from it, and Cary will sit with it for hours until he finishes? What makes Polly independent and Molly a clinger? What makes Tim ready to hit out at the slightest provocation and Jim loath to fight? One answer lies in the basic temperament children are born with. Another very important influence on behavioral styles is the early emotional environment—how children are treated by their parents.

The psychologist Diana Baumrind set out to discover relationships between different styles of child rearing and the social competence of children. She reviewed the research literature and conducted her own studies with 95 families of children in nursery school. Using a combination of long interviews, standardized testing, and observations at school and home, she identified three categories of parenting styles and linked them to children's behavior (Baumrind, 1967, 1970; Baumrind & Black, 1967).

Authoritative parents exert firm control when necessary, but they explain why they take a stand and encourage children to express their opinions. They feel confident in their ability to guide their children, while respecting the children's interests, opinions, and unique personalities. They combine firm control with encouragement and love. Their children know that they are expected to perform well, fulfill commitments, and carry out duties in the family. They know when they are meeting expectations and when it is worth risking their parents' displeasure to pursue some other goal. They seem to thrive on their parents' reasonable expectations and realistic standards, and they are most self-reliant, self-controlled, assertive, exploratory, and content.

Authoritarian parents value unquestioning obedience and punish their children forcibly for not conforming to set and quite absolute standards. They are somewhat detached, controlling, and distant. Their children tend to be discontented, withdrawn, and distrustful.

Permissive parents make few demands on their children, set few rules, and hardly ever punish. As preschoolers, their children are immature—the least self-reliant, self-controlled, or exploratory.

On the basis of her research, Baumrind (1970) has recommended that parents who want to raise competent, socially responsible, independent children should do the following things:

- Teach by example, that is, behave the way you want your children to behave.
- Reward behaviors you want to encourage and punish behaviors you want to discourage, giving explanations in both cases.
- Show interest in children.
- Bestow approval only when the child has earned it.
- Demand achievement and the meeting of standards, while being open to hearing the child's point of view.
- Encourage original thinking.

Baumrind's work raises important issues about child-rearing practices, but before we conclude that parenting is all, we have to remember what children bring to the family. Through their own inborn temperaments, children influence their parents. It is possible, for example, that "easy" children will elicit an authoritative attitude from their parents, while "difficult" children may make tyrants out of theirs.

form attachments to their fathers, their brothers and sisters, their grandparents, and other consistent care givers, most of the research on early attachment has focused on the bond between mother and child.

Mother-Child Attachment For attachment to take place between two people, each has to reach out and respond to the other. Mothers (and others) do this by being sensitive to babies' needs, picking up their signals, and holding the babies closely. Babies do their share by smiling, crying, clinging, and looking into their mothers' eyes. As early as the eighth week, babies initiate some of these behaviors more toward their mothers than toward anyone else and gain a sense of power and competence when their mothers respond warmly (Ainsworth, 1969).

PATTERNS OF MOTHER-CHILD ATTACHMENT Different levels of attachment exist; and they can be measured in terms of Mary D. Salter Ainsworth's *strange situation*. The strange situation is a sequence with eight parts: (1) Mother and baby enter an unfamiliar room. (2) Mother sits down, and baby is free to explore. (3) An unfamiliar adult enters. (4) Mother leaves baby alone with stranger. (5) Mother returns, and stranger leaves. (6) Mother leaves baby alone. (7) Stranger comes back. (8) Finally, stranger leaves, and mother returns (Ainsworth, Blehar, Waters, & Wall, 1978). One-year-olds observed in this sequence were characterized as securely attached, avoidant, or ambivalent:

■ *Securely attached* children use the mother as a safe base from which to explore, returning to her occasionally for comfort, acting distressed when she leaves, and going to her when she returns.

■ *Avoidant* children rarely cry when the mother leaves but stay away from her when she returns, seeming to be very angry.

■ *Ambivalent* children are anxious before separation, become very upset when the mother leaves, and on her return seek close contact but also resist it by kicking or squirming.

What causes these different patterns, which seem to persist at least until age 5 (Arend, Gove, & Sroufe, 1979; Matas, Arend, & Sroufe, 1978; Sroufe, Fox, & Pancake, 1983; Waters, Wippman, & Sroufe, 1979)? Probably, the cause is a combination of the infants' temperaments and the mothers' patterns of handling their children. The mothers of the securely attached babies, for example, were most sensitive to them, while the mothers of the avoidant babies were the angriest; furthermore, the ambivalent babies were temperamentally "difficult" (Ainsworth, 1979).

What was it about these women that made them act so differently toward their babies? Many different factors enter in, including a mother's personality, her attitude toward children, and her present circumstances. Outside events influence attachment, as shown by recent research which found that almost half of a group of 43 babies changed their attachment patterns between the ages of 1 year and 19 months (Thompson, Lamb, & Estes, 1982). Some of the babies became more securely attached; some became less so. Both kinds of changes were associated with changes in care-giving, such as the mothers' taking jobs outside the home and providing other kinds of care for their children. Changes that affected the babies' everyday lives "forced a renegotiation, so to speak, of the mother-infant relationship" (p. 148).

Early development of a strong bond between parent and child seems to have far-reaching effects. For one thing, securely attached babies are more sociable with strangers, probably because they trust their mothers and generalize this trust to other people (Thompson & Lamb, 1983). This supports Erikson's emphasis on the initial crisis in psychosocial development, "trust versus mistrust."

Several long-lasting effects of attachment have been found. When securely attached 18-month-olds were followed up at the age of 2, they turned out to be more enthusiastic, more persistent, more cooperative, and in general more effective than children who had been insecurely attached as babies (Mates, Arend, & Sroufe, 1978). At 3 years, securely attached children receive more positive responses from playmates than insecurely attached children do (Jacobson & Wille, 1986). At 3½, securely attached children are described as "peer leaders, socially involved, attracting the attention of others, curious, and actively engaged in their surroundings" (Waters, Wippman, & Sroufe, 1979). At 4 and 5 years, children who had been securely attached at 12 and 18 months were now likely to be independent, while those who had been anxiously attached earlier were likely to be dependent on their nursery school teachers and to have trouble getting along with other children and doing things appropriate for their age (Sroufe, Fox, & Pancake, 1983).

HOW MOTHER-CHILD ATTACHMENT OCCURS How do babies and mothers become attached to each other? Often it is not love at first sight. Only about half of one group

(Jonathan Finlay)

Both Anna and her mother contribute to the attachment between them by the way they act toward each other. The way the baby molds herself to her mother's body shows her trust and reinforces the mother's feelings for her child, which she then displays through her sensitivity to the baby's needs. Again we see how babies actively influence their own worlds.

of new mothers reported that they had positive feelings when they first saw their babies, but by 3 weeks love was taking hold and by 3 months most were strongly attached (Robson & Moss, 1970).

Attachment seems to depend on the mother's sensitivity, which lets the baby form expectations of her as generally accessible and responsive (Ainsworth, 1979). Mike wakes up and cries, for example; his mother comes into the room. He is hungry; she feeds him. He is wet; she changes his diaper. He smiles; she plays with him. Thus Mike develops what Erikson calls a *sense of trust*. What happens, though, when babies' signals are not picked up? The babies become anxious, not knowing what to expect, and fail to form a strong attachment.

Erikson felt that the feeding situation was paramount in developing a sense of trust, but Harry Harlow and Margaret Harlow's classic experiments with monkeys have shown that food is not the crucial path to a baby's heart. In one famous study, monkeys were separated from their mothers 6 to 12 hours after birth and raised in the laboratory. The infants were put in cages with one of two surrogate "mothers"—one a plain cylindrical wire mesh form; the other covered with terrycloth. Some monkeys were fed from bottles connected to the wire "mothers"; others were fed by the warm, cuddly cloth ones. When the monkeys were allowed to spend time with either mother, they all spent more time clinging to the "cloth mother," even if they were being fed by the "wire mother." Monkeys with cloth mothers also explored more than those with wire mothers (Harlow, 1958; Harlow & Zimmermann, 1959). Apparently body contact can be even more important than food.

Not surprisingly, though, having a warm, cuddly cloth mother to cling to does not provide adequate mothering. The monkeys with cloth mothers did not grow up normally, had difficulty mating, and were unable to mother their own infants (Harlow & Harlow, 1962; Suomi & Harlow, 1972). Obviously, mothers have to *do* something—not just stand there and allow themselves to be clung to—to let their children develop normally. There is, by the way, an encouraging sequel to the story of these motherless monkeys: slightly younger normal monkeys were able to rehabilitate them very successfully (Suomi & Harlow, 1972, 1978). These "therapist" monkeys made normal social overtures, eventually eliciting normal playfulness in the unmothered monkeys.

In a series of classic experiments, Harry Harlow and Margaret Harlow showed that food is not the most important way to a baby's heart. When infant rhesus monkeys could choose whether to go to a wire surrogate "mother" where they could feed from a bottle or to a terrycloth "mother" that offered warmth and softness but no food, the babies spent more time clinging to the cloth mother.

Is there a critical period in the development of mother-child attachment? Harlow's success in rehabilitating monkeys deprived of normal mothering argues against the theory that primate animals, like some of the lower species, must receive mothering at a critical, early period. Among sheep and goats, however, certain standardized rituals occur right after birth to cement the mother-child relationship. If these rituals are prevented or interrupted, neither mother nor baby will recognize the other, no attachment will take place, and the baby is likely to die or develop abnormally.

Klaus and Kennell (1976) proposed that the first hours after birth constitute a critical period for bonding between mother and child, and that if the two are separated then, the attachment needed for the baby's healthy development may be harmed. Their pioneering research, which promoted the beneficial effects of extended close contact right after birth between mother and baby, was widely accepted and has been quite influential in changing many restrictive hospital practices that kept mothers and babies apart. While these changes do seem more humane and natural, recent research indicates that they are not critical for the relationship between mother and child. As a result, Klaus and Kennell (1982) have modified their original position.

After analyzing more than 20 follow-up research projects, Michael E. Lamb (1982a, 1982b) concluded that early contact between a mother and her newborn has no lasting effect on either one, although it may have slight short-term effects on *some* mothers in *some* circumstances. Awareness that such early separation does not do permanent harm is particularly important for adoptive parents, for parents of sick and low-birthweight infants, and for parents in other circumstances which entail an unavoidable separation after birth.

Happily, human beings are remarkably **resilient**, and many babies overcome extremely damaging early experiences to grow up as well-adjusted adults. How this occurs is currently an issue of great interest to psychologists, as discussed in the box "Stress and Resilience in Childhood" (page 332).

Resilient children *Children who bounce back from unfortunate circumstances; invulnerable children.*

"STRANGER ANXIETY" If you've ever tried to pick up a baby over the age of 8 months whom you don't know very well, and have been greeted by howls of fear and desperate attempts to go back to the safety of familiar arms, you don't have to

STRESS AND RESILIENCE IN CHILDHOOD

While childhood is often romanticized as a carefree, blissful time of life, we all experience stress in our early years, some of us more than others. Normal childhood stress takes many forms—including illness, the birth of younger siblings, interaction with older siblings, frustration when we can't have or do what we want, the temporary departures of parents. Some children encounter more severe stress brought on by parents' divorce or death, hospitalization, physical or sexual abuse at the hands of adults, devastation by natural disasters like tornadoes or human disasters like war, or the day-in, day-out stress of poverty. Some observers feel that the pressures of modern life produce "hurried children" who are under stress in a way that children of earlier generations were not (Elkind, 1981).

EFFECTS OF STRESS

What are the effects of children's being separated from their parents in wartime, being kidnapped, or being interned in concentration camps? A number of researchers have studied effects of these and other stressors, including a variety of experiences that come under the umbrella of poor parenting. All such events have the potential for affecting the emotional development of children.

The way a child reacts to a particular stressful event depends on many different factors. First is the *event* itself; different stressors affect children differently. In many cases, events are stressful because of their impact on children's interactions with family members and other important people. When these interactions are disturbed, when children feel that their parents cannot take care of them or do not love them, stress is apt to be especially severe. *Age* is also a consideration, as researchers have learned from the different ways children of different ages react to their parents' divorce (Wallerstein, 1983; Wallerstein & Kelly, 1980). *Sex* is a factor, too: by and large, boys are more vulnerable. Children who do well in *school* seem to respond better to stress, but it is not clear why. Perhaps the high self-esteem of achieving children helps them cope better; perhaps these chil-dren are better at solving problems in everyday life as well as in their schoolwork; or perhaps there is some inherited factor that makes them achieve in school *and* handle stress (Rutter, 1984). Other areas which seem significant, but on which there has been little research, are *inherited differences* in ability to handle stress; the effect of *difference in temperament*, which seems at least partially genetically determined; and *intelligence* (Rutter, 1983). In addition, other factors have surfaced from the study of "resilient" children.

RESILIENT CHILDREN

Known variously as *invulnerables* and *superkids*, resilient children are youngsters who "bounce back," who rise above the most unfortunate circumstances—situations that blight the emotional development of other children. Resilient children include the children of schizophrenic parents who do not develop emotional illness themselves, children of the ghetto who go on to distinguish themselves in the professions, and neglected and abused children who go on to form close intimate relationships and to lead fulfilling lives. Life has dealt these children a bad hand, but nevertheless they are creative, resourceful, independent, achieving, and enjoyable to be with. How do they do it?

Stranger anxiety *Normal wariness of strangers that usually begins at about 8 to 12 months of age.*

worry that you did anything wrong. The baby is showing a perfectly normal (although not universal) wariness of strangers, known as **stranger anxiety**, which—although rare in the first 6 months of life—is common by 8 to 9 months of age and is likely to increase throughout the rest of the first year.

Why do infants all over the world begin to become afraid of strangers at about this age, reach a peak of distress at about 15 months, and accept strangers at about 3 years? This phenomenon occurs among blind babies, babies held almost constantly on their mothers' bodies, and babies raised in such disparate settings as nuclear families, communes, and day care centers; and it appears at about the same time as object permanence. The reason for it may have to do with development of learning and memory (Kagan, 1982). An infant's new ability to learn and to remember the good feelings experienced in the presence of a familiar caretaker, combined with anxiety at not being able to predict what it will be like to be with a stranger, may give rise to stranger anxiety.

Stranger anxiety also seems to be related to temperament. "Easy" children, for example, show little stranger anxiety; difficult and slow-to-warm-up children show more (Thomas & Chess, 1977).

Several research studies have identified a number of "protective factors" that operate to reduce the effects of stressors (Anthony & Koupernik, 1974; Garmezy, 1983; Rutter, 1984). They include:

■ *Personality*: Resilient children are adaptable enough to cope with changing circumstances; they think positively, and they are friendly, sensitive to other people, and independent. They have a high level of self-esteem. The mystery is whether they were born with the predisposition to such a personality or whether they developed it in response to factors such as those below.

■ *Family*: The child is likely to have a good relationship with parents who support each other, or, failing that, to have a close relationship with at least one parent. If he or she does not have such a relationship with a parent, there is likely to be at least one relative or other adult who is close to the child, who expresses interest and obviously cares for the child, and whom the child trusts.

■ *Learning experiences*: These children are likely to have had experience in solving social problems.

They have observed positive models—parents, older siblings, or others—dealing with frustration and making the best of a bad situation. They have faced challenges themselves, they have worked out solutions, and they have learned that they can affect outcomes and exert a measure of control over their lives.

■ *Limited risk factors*: Children who were exposed to only one of a number of factors strongly related to psychological disorder (such as marital discord, low social status, overcrowding at home, a disturbed mother, a criminal father, and experience in foster care or institutions) are often able to overcome stress. But when two or more of these factors exist together, the child's risk of disturbance increases four times or more (Rutter, quoted in Pines, 1979). When children are not besieged on all sides, they can often marshal their strength to cope with adverse circumstances.

■ *Miscellaneous positive experiences*: Successful experiences with sports, music, or other children can help to make up for a dismal home life, and a good marriage in adulthood can

compensate for poor relationships earlier in life. Early deprivation can often be overcome by a nurturing environment later on. Sometimes therapy helps. As one psychiatrist has written, "The emotionally traumatized child is not doomed, the parents' early mistakes are not irrevocable, and our preventive and therapeutic intervention can make a difference at all age-periods" (Chess, 1983, p. 976).

All this research does not, of course, mean that what happens in a child's life does not matter. In general, children with unfavorable backgrounds have more problems in adjustment than those with favorable backgrounds. More often than not, however, the human race seems to be governed by what Jerome Kagan (1979) has called "growth for health," the ability to make a good adaptation to life, once given a favorable, responsive environment. What happens in childhood does not necessarily determine the outcome of a person's life.

Many people do have the strength to rise above the most difficult circumstances. We are constantly rewriting the stories of our lives, as long as we live.

Father-Child Attachment Most of the psychological literature about attachment has, as we said, focused on the mother-child tie, while the father has hovered in the shadows. In recent years, however, a surge of research interest in father-child bonds has reflected changes in our society—many fathers (including research psychologists) are now assuming a much larger role in the care of their children.

The impression that this is a healthy trend is confirmed by recent research, which has shown that infants form attachments to their fathers in the first year of life; and that fathers often become attached to their babies within the first 3 days after birth; and that the father-child bond throughout childhood has important implications for children's healthy development (Greenberg & Morris, 1974; M. E. Lamb, 1981; D. Lynn, 1974).

How do mothers' and fathers' relationships with their children differ? First, mothers spend more time with their children. Second, mothers do different things. Mothers tend to hold their babies to *take care* of them—to feed, bathe, or change them—while fathers pick up their babies to *play* with them, usually more boisterously than mothers do (M. E. Lamb, 1979). On the other hand, fathers who take care of their babies seem to do just as good a job as mothers. They touch, look at, talk to,

(Nola H. Lynch)

Fathers are very important in their children's lives. The attachment between these two has already started to form, and the impact of the father-child bond will influence many aspects of this baby's life, for years to come.

rock, and kiss their children as much as mothers do; respond equally well to the babies' signals; and are just as effective in feeding them (Parke, 1978). Still, when both parents are present, the mother usually gives basic care and the father plays with the baby.

Fathers differentiate their children more by sex than mothers do, even during the babies' first year of life (Snow, Jacklin, & Maccoby, 1983). By the second year the difference intensifies; fathers talk more to and spend more time with their sons (M. E. Lamb, 1981). For these reasons fathers seem to affect the development of gender identity and gender roles (see "Identification" later in this chapter) more than mothers do.

Sibling Attachment   If you have brothers and sisters, your relationships with them are likely to be the longest-lasting you'll ever have with anyone. They began in infancy, long before you might meet a future spouse, and are apt to persist into old age, probably long after your parents will have died. The intensity of these relationships and their special character are rarely duplicated. Siblings are people who share your roots, who emerge from the same font of values, who deal with you more objectively than your parents do, and who are more candid with you than practically everyone else you'll ever know.

Sibling relationships are probably even more important today than they were in days gone by, because of changes in society (Cicirelli, 1980). With higher rates of divorce and remarriage, brothers and sisters tend to become closer to each other than to either their parents or their stepparents. Another change is the increased responsibility among middle-aged siblings for the care of aging parents, an issue that can either draw siblings closer together or inflame old rivalries. Not surprisingly, your siblings are a major influence in your life. What is surprising is the small amount of research on this unique relationship.

Until recently, the main interest in the influence of siblings revolved around birth order and its effects on development. Over the past few years, however, researchers have become more interested in interaction among siblings themselves rather than between parents and their different children, in the way siblings affect each other throughout life rather than just in childhood, and in process rather than effect (M. E. Lamb, 1982).

The relationship between these brothers is likely to be among the longest-lasting either one will ever have. Sibling relationships are probably even more important today than they were in earlier times, because of changes in society that bring siblings closer together. While rivalry usually exists to some degree, it's often overshadowed by positive aspects of the sibling tie.

When 3-year-old Melissa's baby sister was born, she reacted to the news with apparent joy—but she told her nursery school class that the baby was a boy, and she kept forgetting the baby's name. Melissa is a beautiful example of the ambivalence with which many children react to the birth of a sibling and of how they get along with their siblings throughout life. Most people grow up with at least one sibling, and the influence of one child on another begins even before the birth of a second child, as the anticipated birth affects both the parents and the firstborn. The potential for rivalry is present in the "dethroning" of the first child, which was first pointed out by Alfred Adler (1928), a disciple of Freud. Adler did not invent sibling rivalry, which has been around since Cain and Abel, but he emphasized the influence on personality development of competition, jealousy, and hostility among siblings.

Some rivalry exists in all sibling relationships; however, it need not be the dominant theme (Dunn, 1985). Often the positive aspects of the sibling tie are uppermost—the ability siblings have to learn from each other and enjoy each other's company; the support they give each other against pressures from outsiders and even from parents; and the security created by familiarity and shared experiences. Preadolescent siblings often become each other's primary confidants and sources of emotional support (M. E. Lamb, 1982), and many siblings tend to stay close throughout adulthood, often becoming closer in old age (Cicirelli, 1982).

Identification

How do children develop a sense of who they are? They do this partly by looking at the people around them and seeing whom they want to be like. Through **identification,** children adopt certain characteristics, beliefs, attitudes, values, and behaviors of another person or group. Identification is one of the most important personality developments of early childhood.

Identification *Process by which a person acquires certain characteristics, beliefs, attitudes, values, and behaviors of another person or group; one of the most important personality developments of early childhood.*

Psychoanalysts, who originated this concept, see it as an outgrowth of the Oedipus and Electra complexes (discussed in Chapter 13). Unable to compete with the same-sex parent for the love of the other-sex parent, children resolve their conflicts by identifying with the same-sex parent. This is sometimes termed *identification with the aggressor,* since the child sees the same-sex parent as a rival and potential aggressor.

Social-learning theorists consider identification a result of copying a model, who may be a parent, but who might also be a sister or brother, a neighbor, a teacher, a playmate, or a celebrity—particularly an athlete or an entertainer. Furthermore, children often model themselves on several people, picking up different characteristics from each. They choose their models largely on the basis of two main characteristics—power and nurturance (Bandura & Huston, 1961).

According to Jerome Kagan (1958, 1971), four interrelated processes establish and strengthen identification:

1 *Children want to be like the model.* A little boy, for example, feels that if he's like a sports idol, he'll be able to do what the athlete can do.
2 *Children believe they are like the model.* They think they look like the model, tell jokes like the model, walk like the model. This identification is often buttressed by other people's comments ("You have your father's eyes").
3 *Children experience emotions like those the model is feeling.* When a little girl sees her mother cry after the mother's brother has died, the child feels sad and cries too—not for an uncle she may barely have known, but because her mother's sadness makes her feel sad.
4 *Children act like the model.* In play and in everyday conversation, children often adopt a model's mannerisms, voice inflections, and phrasing. Many parents are startled to hear their own words and their own tone of voice come out of the mouths of tots.

Through identification, then, children come to believe that they have the same characteristics as a model. Thus, when they identify with a nurturant and competent model, they are pleased and proud; but when the model is inadequate, they may feel unhappy and insecure.

Getting Along with Peers

Beginning in infancy, we human beings are social creatures who are intensely interested in other people—and especially in other people about our own size. Even very young babies are fascinated by each other. From the age of 6 months, babies will smile, touch, and babble to another baby, and will tend to cry if another baby near them has been crying for a long time (Hay, Pedersen, & Nash, 1982; Vandell, Wilson, & Buchanan, 1980). These responses become increasingly common toward the end of the first year and are more likely to occur when the babies are not distracted by the presence of either adults or toys.

Toddlers become even more social, and their sociability has more purpose. A 10-month-old may hold out a toy to another baby—but is as likely as not to offer it when the other baby's back is turned. During the second year of life, children's social skills sharpen, and they learn when such offers have the best chance of being accepted and how to respond to other children's overtures (Eckerman & Stein, 1982).

Real friendships, though, usually do not emerge until sometime after 3 years of age. Even at this point, they are at a relatively primitive level compared with the form they will take in later years. The distinctive ways children of different ages think about friendship emerged dramatically in a study about how people's ideas about this important relationship develop over the life span. Robert Selman and Anne Selman (1979) interviewed more than 250 people between the ages of 3 and 45 to get a developmental perspective on friendship.

Up until about 9 years of age, children tend to define friendship in terms of themselves. Egocentric preschoolers think about their own convenience ("She's my friend—she lives on my street"). Slightly older children consider a good friend as someone who does what *they* want him or her to do ("He's not my friend anymore, because he wouldn't go with me when I wanted him to"). Not until the age of 9 or so, when children are well into the cognitive stage of concrete operations, with the flexibility of thought such development allows, do friendships become more mutual. Still, children of this age may become possessive of each other and jealous of their friends' other friends.

With the coming of adolescence, people respect their friends' needs for both dependency and autonomy. Friends are especially important during these years of transition from childhood to adulthood, as teens break their early dependency on their parents, try out different roles in the process of achieving identity, and experiment with different ways of being (Coleman, 1980; Selman & Selman, 1979).

In this very brief overview of infancy and childhood, we've seen how much progress is made during these stages in the three realms we've been discussing—the physical, the cognitive, and the psychosocial. We've also seen how many different factors influence this development. Now let's follow these youngsters as they move into adolescence and then into adulthood, where they'll grapple with the issues of defining their individual identity and giving purpose to their lives.

SUMMARY

1 Developmental psychologists are concerned with stability and change in physical, cognitive, and psychosocial characteristics throughout the life span. They see development as a lifelong process with the potential for growth and change at all stages of life.

2 The two traditional data-collection techniques used by developmental psychologists are the cross-sectional and the longitudinal methods. In the cross-sectional method groups of people of different ages are compared at the same point in time, yielding information about age differences. In the longitudinal method, psychologists trace the development of one or more people at more than one point in time, obtaining information about age changes. Each method has its strengths and weaknesses. Sequential strategies, such as the cross-sequential method, have been developed to overcome some of the problems with the traditional techniques.

3 Three important influences on development are normative age-graded influences (biological and cultural markers that occur in a similar way for all people in a given group), normative history-graded influences (influences common to people of a particular cohort), and nonnormative life events (events that do not happen to most people but that can have a major impact on those who do experience them).

4 The nature-nurture debate concerns the relative influence of heredity and environment (experience) on development. Twin studies, adoption studies, consanguinity studies, selective breeding in animals, prenatal studies, studies that manipulate environmental conditions, and studies that compare life-history factors all provide information about the relative influence of heredity and environment.

5 Conception occurs when a sperm from the father unites with an ovum from the mother to form the one-cell zygote. Sperm and ovum each contain 23 chromosomes, giving the normal zygote 46 chromosomes. About 30,000 genes are located on each of the chromosomes. The genes that are inherited constitute the genotype; the characteristics that can be seen make up the phenotype.

6 Genes come in alternative forms called alleles. A person who inherits identical alleles from each parent is homozygous for a trait; a person who inherits different alleles is heterozygous. A dominant gene for a particular trait is one that is always expressed; a recessive gene is expressed only when the dominant gene is not present. There are a number of patterns of genetic transmission, including autosomal dominant inheritance, autosomal recessive inheritance, sex-linked inheritance, and multifactorial inheritance.

7 There are three stages of prenatal development. During the germinal stage (fertilization to 2 weeks), the zygote is in a period of rapid cell division resulting in an increasingly complex organism. In the embryonic stage (2 to 8–12 weeks), the embryo grows quickly, and the major body systems and organs are formed. The fetal stage (8–12 weeks to birth) begins with the appearance of the first bone cells. This period is characterized by rapid growth and changes in body form.

8 The organism is particularly vulnerable during the first trimester (3-month period) of pregnancy. The developing child can be affected by such maternal factors as nutrition, illness, and drug intake.

9 The neonatal period covers the first 28 days of life, a time of transition from prenatal to postnatal existence. Neonates are extremely competent; they can use all their senses from birth and display a variety of specialized responses.

10 According to the cephalocaudal principle, development proceeds from head to toe: upper-body parts develop before lower-body parts. According to the proximodistal principle, development proceeds from near to far: parts near the center of the body develop before the extremities.

11 Reflexes are involuntary reactions to stimulation. In the

first few months of life infants show a variety of primitive reflexes that will drop out as neurological development progresses.

12 Both physical growth and motor development are strongly influenced by maturation, the unfolding of biologically determined patterns of behavior, programmed by the genes. During the first 3 years, the child grows more quickly than at any other time after birth. The growth rate slows down after this until the child reaches the prepubertal growth spurt, at about age 12.

13 Physical development may also be influenced by deprivation.

14 According to Jean Piaget, children actively construct their own cognitive worlds. Piaget saw cognitive development as occurring in an invariant sequence of four age-related stages: sensorimotor (birth to 2 years), preoperational (2 to 7 years), concrete operations (7 to 12 years), and formal operations (12 years and older, or perhaps never for some people). These stages represent qualitatively different ways children adapt to and think about the world. During the sensorimotor stage infants learn about the world through their senses and motor behavior. Their most important achievement is object permanence, the realization that people and objects continue to exist even if they can no longer be seen. During the preoperational stage children become more proficient in using symbols. Their thinking shows a high degree of egocentrism, or inability to consider the viewpoint of another. Children in the concrete operations stage begin to think logically although they cannot think abstractly. They understand number, classification, and conservation. During the formal operations stage, people are able to think abstractly, test hypotheses, and deal with problems that are not physically present.

15 Infants are capable of some types of learning from the first days of life.

16 Memory develops rapidly in infancy and childhood. At about the second grade, children spontaneously use rehearsal as a memory strategy; at about the fifth grade they use clustering and chunking.

17 Erik Erikson proposed a theory of psychosocial development that consists of eight stages throughout life. Each stage involves the resolution of a crisis or issue. How a person resolves each crisis affects his or her personality development. The four childhood stages are basic trust versus basic mistrust (birth to 12–18 months); autonomy versus shame and doubt (12–18 months to 3 years); initiative versus guilt (3 to 6 years); and industry versus inferiority (6 years to puberty).

18 Infants appear to experience a variety of emotions and display a range of emotional expressions.

19 There are individual differences in temperament, or characteristic styles of responding, which are present from birth. According to the findings of one major longitudinal study, most children can be classified into one of three types: easy, difficult, and slow to warm up. A child's temperament can influence how others respond to him or her.

20 Diana Baumrind has identified three child-rearing approaches: authoritative, authoritarian, and permissive. Each is associated with characteristics in the child.

21 Attachment is an active, affectionate reciprocal relationship between two people. Infants form attachments not only to their mothers but also to their fathers, siblings, and others. Infants show a variety of attachment patterns including securely attached, avoidant, and ambivalent. These attachment patterns are related to later development. Although attachment is affected by what both people do, there is no persuasive evidence that extended contact immediately after birth is critical for bonding.

22 Normal childhood stresses take many forms and can affect the healthy emotional development of children. Resilient children are particularly able to bounce back from unfortunate circumstances. Often, the presence of one or more protective factors reduces the effects of stress.

23 Stranger anxiety is a normal wariness of strangers that typically begins between 8 and 12 months of age. Not all children show stranger anxiety.

24 Relationships between siblings in childhood are typically characterized by positive feelings, not just jealousy.

25 Identification is the process whereby a child takes on the values and behaviors of another person or group. Psychoanalysts say that this is the result of identification with the aggressor (same-sex parent), which is an outcome of the Oedipus-Electra complex. Social-learning theorists see identification as the result of observing and imitating models.

26 Beginning in infancy, human beings express an interest in peers. The peer group becomes more important as children enter middle childhood.

KEY TERMS

Alleles (page 308)
Attachment (327)
Autonomy versus shame and doubt (323)
Autosomal dominant inheritance (308)
Autosomal recessive inheritance (308)
Basic trust versus basic mistrust (323)
Cephalocaudal principle (315)
Chromosomes (308)
Cognitive development (302)
Conservation (319)

Cross-sectional method (303)
Cross-sequential method (303)
Developmental psychologists (302)
Egocentrism (319)
Embryonic stage (310)
Fetal alcohol syndrome (312)
Fetal stage (311)
Genes (308)
Genotype (308)
Germinal stage (310)
Habituation (314)
Heterozygous (308)

Homozygous (308)
Identification (335)
Industry versus inferiority (324)
Initiative versus guilt (324)
Longitudinal method (303)
Maturation (316)
Multifactorial inheritance (308)
Nature-nurture debate (304)
Neonatal period (313)
Nonnormative life events (304)
Normative age-graded influences (304)

Normative history-graded influences (304)
Object permanence (318)
Phenotype (308)
Physical development (302)
Proximodistal principle (315)
Psychosocial development (302)
Reaction range (305)
Reflex (315)
Resilient children (331)
Sex-linked inheritance (308)
Stranger anxiety (332)
Zygote (306)

SUGGESTED READINGS

BELLINO, J. H., & WILSON, J. (1985). *You can have a baby*. New York: Crown. A full study of the way fertilization works, how it can go wrong, and what can be done to assist it. Written for the layperson, it is as complete as a textbook.

BRINGUIER, J. (1980). *Conversations with Jean Piaget*. Chicago: University of Chicago Press. Fourteen conversations with Piaget that give insight into the man as well as his theory of cognitive development.

DUNN, J. (1985). *Sisters and brothers*. Cambridge, MA: Harvard University Press. A beautiful little volume summarizing knowledge about sibling relationships by a researcher on this topic.

GREENBERG, M. (1985). *The birth of a father*. New York: Continuum. This first-person account of what it means to become a father is written by the psychiatrist who coined the term *engrossment* to describe the father's sense of absorption, preoccupation, and interest in his baby. It is written with sensitivity and humor, and the chapter "Who Changes the Diapers?" is a gem.

KAGAN, J. (1984). *The nature of the child*. New York: Basic Books. A beautifully written and compelling argument against the idea that early experiences have irreversible effects. Kagan believes that people have the ability to change throughout life and that later events transform childhood experiences.

KLAUS, M. H., & KLAUS, P. H. (1985). *The amazing newborn: Making the most of the first weeks of life*. Reading, MA: Addison-Wesley. Over 125 wonderful photos of newborns, some just minutes old, show some of their capabilities. The authors, a renowned researcher and a psychotherapist, report the latest scientific findings on newborns, and give practical suggestions for parents.

SINGER, S. (1985). *Human genetics* (2d ed.). New York: Freeman. A solid account of genetic principles and how they apply to people. Beginning with Mendel's principles, it considers genes, gene pools, genetic disorders, and genetic counseling.

WHITE, B. L., KABAN, B. T., & ATTANUCCI, J. S. (1979). *The origins of competence*. Lexington, MA: Heath. The final report of the Harvard Preschool Project focusing on the interrelationship between child-rearing practices and the development of competence in the first few years of life.

CHAPTER

10

DEVELOPMENT FROM ADOLESCENCE ON

■ How does the capacity for growth continue beyond childhood?

■ What roles do love and work play in the lives of adults?

■ Does adult development occur in fairly predictable stages or through small, unpredictable changes?

■ How does the search for identity evolve from adolescence through adulthood?

■ How does the aging process affect people physically, intellectually, and emotionally?

■ How do dying people and those close to them deal with death?

The summer before I was to enter my junior year at the University of Pennsylvania, I worked in Cleveland, Ohio, as a counselor at a residential center for emotionally disturbed children. I had been thrilled to get this job through the college placement office, because I was planning to become a clinical psychologist specializing in working with children. I thought that this summer job would be a wonderful apprenticeship. It did turn out to be a valuable learning experience—but not in the way I thought it would.

What I learned was that I was not cut out to do the kind of work I had been planning for years to do. As I was on my way home to Philadelphia at the end of the summer, I realized that I had not done my job nearly so well as I would have liked to and that I no longer felt that this kind of work was right for me.

I had probably overreacted to the difficulties of being plunged into a demanding situation with no experience and no special training in working with children who needed a great deal of support. Whether my self-assessment was accurate or not, however, it was intense, and I was determined to change my major from psychology. At the time, though, I had no idea what to choose as my new major. I did not know what kind of work I wanted to do or how to prepare myself for it, and I had to choose my major quickly. Later I realized that I could have gone into some other branch of psychology, but at that time I was so disappointed at the failure of my dream that I wanted to leave the field altogether.

Since English had always been a subject I liked and did well in, I decided to major in English literature, without having any clear sense of what I might do after college. Eventually I began to write professionally. My first articles were about children. I went on to write about children's psychological development, and then about a variety of mental health issues relating to children and adults. In writing about psychological topics I had come full circle, back to my original interest in psychology. I had finally found a career that suited my interests, my abilities, and my personality.

—From the notebooks of Sally Olds

The role of work in one's life is one of the most prominent issues for most people, from their adolescent years through most of all of their adulthood. It encompasses the search for identity and the marriage of interests and abilities, and it very often affects and is affected by basic personality issues and important personal relationships. All these concerns come to the fore in a new way in adolescence. Adolescence is the point at which we teeter between the childhood we are leaving behind and the adulthood we are embarking upon. Freud's definition of maturity—the capacity to love and to work—gives due weight to what for most people are the two most important elements of their adult lives.

In this chapter we explore some aspects of the physical, cognitive, and psychosocial development that occurs beyond childhood. In adolescence and adulthood, people become more deeply invested in the concerns that will absorb them throughout the rest of life—getting a firm grasp on the sense of self, finding and concentrating on a life's work, and forming and handling the intimate relationships that have so much to do with happiness and well-being. The specific issues vary over the life stages of adolescence and early, middle, and late adulthood, but there always *are* issues. We always have more questions than we have answers. As we keep looking for answers, we keep developing.

ADOLESCENCE

Adolescence with its physical changes and its foreshadowing of adulthood, can be considered a kind of rebirth. Postpubertal adolescents look almost as different from their childhood selves as a butterfly does from a caterpillar. There is nothing subtle or gradual about this transformation. After the bit-by-bit development of childhood, the changes of adolescence come like a sudden storm. The entire body form changes, so that adolescents now *look* like adults, even if their emotions and intellectual abilities are not yet mature. Boys sound different; girls are affected by a new life rhythm that will stay with them for the next several decades; both are becoming absorbed with adult concerns.

The process begins with **pubescence**. In this stage of rapid growth the primary sex characteristics (the organs directly involved in reproduction) mature and the secondary sex characteristics (all other body changes not directly tied to reproduction, such as breast development, growth of body and facial hair, and changes in the voice) appear (see Table 10-1). After about 2 years, this stage ends in **puberty,** when a person is sexually mature and able to reproduce. While the average age of puberty is 12 for girls and 14 for boys, there is a tremendously wide normal age range (see Table 10-2). The end of adolescence is even harder to mark, since it is defined by social, legal, and psychological measures, such as being self-supporting, choosing a career, being eligible to vote or join the military, marrying—or, as one parent defines it, "not calling home collect any more."

Pubescence *Time of the life span just before puberty, characterized by rapid physiological growth, maturation of reproductive functioning, and development of primary and secondary sex characteristics.*

Puberty *Physiological point at which an individual is sexually mature and able to reproduce.*

TABLE 10-1 PRIMARY AND SECONDARY SEX CHARACTERISTICS

Primary Sex Organs

Female	Male
Ovaries	Testes
Fallopian tubes	Penis
Uterus	Scrotum
Vagina	Seminal vesicles
	Prostate gland

Secondary Sex Characteristics

Girls	Boys
Breasts	Pubic hair
Pubic hair	Axillary hair
Axillary hair	Facial hair
Increased width and depth of pelvis	Voice chance
	Skin change
	Broadening of shoulders
Voice change	
Skin change	

TABLE 10-2 PHYSIOLOGICAL CHANGES OF ADOLESCENCE, IN USUAL SEQUENCE

Girls' Characteristics	Age of First Appearance
Growth of breasts	8-13
Growth of pubic hair	8-14
Body growth	9.5-14.5 (average peak, 12)
Menarche	10-16.5 (average, 12.5)
Underarm hair	About 2 years after pubic hair
Oil- and sweat-producing glands (acne)	About the same time as underarm hair

Boys' Characteristics	Age of First Appearance
Growth of testes, scrotal sac	10-13.5
Growth of pubic hair	10-15
Body growth	10.5-16 (average peak, 14)
Growth of penis, prostate gland, seminal vesicles	11-14.5 (average, 12.5)
Change in voice	About the same time as penis growth
First ejaculation of seminal fluid	About 1 year after beginning of penis growth
Facial and underarm hair	About 2 years after appearance of pubic hair
Oil- and sweat-producing glands (acne)	About the same time as underarm hair

Physical Development: Physiological Changes

Menarche *First menstruation.*

Menarche, the first menstrual period, occurs at an average age of 12.5 years in the United States. This event signals a girl's sexual maturity, even though she may not be fertile for the first few cycles. As a marker of maturity, menarche is psychologically important. Girls who have begun to menstruate are more conscious of their femaleness, more interested in boys, and more inclined to adorn their bodies than girls who have not (Grief & Ulman, 1982). Although some girls express joy and excitement at the arrival of menstrual periods, or accept it matter-of-factly, many react with shame, embarrassment, and fear. Often this is because they are poorly prepared; girls who are prepared have more positive attitudes (Koff, Rierdan, & Sheingold, 1980). Another problem seems to be an overemphasis by adults on cleanliness and hygiene at the expense of the girls' psychological needs (Whisnant & Zegans, 1975). Then, our society's cultural taboo against discussing menstruation openly (even within many families) serves to prevent the development of rituals to celebrate this entry into womanhood and reinforces negative attitudes (Grief & Ulman, 1982).

What can be done to make menstruation a more positive experience? First, it is important to prepare young girls by telling them about menstruation as soon as their breasts and pubic hair begin to develop. Celebrating the menarche with a family ritual might also be appropriate to emphasize its role as a signal of a girl's entry into womanhood. Other ways to encourage positive attitudes include maintaining an open, matter-of-fact attitude among all family members, including men and boys; letting girls know that they can continue with all their normal activities during the menses; reassuring them that they are normal; encouraging them to ask questions; and helping them cope with the practical aspects of menstruation.

For boys, the physiological "marker" that is the closest counterpart to menstruation is the presence of sperm in the urine. This is found in about one in four 15-year-olds (Richardson & Short, 1978), but it is not readily observed and so has never achieved the same emotional or symbolic significance that menstruation has.

Both sexes appear to reach full adult height and sexual maturity earlier today than they did in previous centuries, probably because of improved nutrition, but this trend has leveled off in recent years (Dreyer, 1982; Schmeck, 1976). We see in this historical change the effects of the interrelationship between heredity (which has a significant influence on the timing of maturation) and environment.

Adolescents are acutely aware of their physical appearance. Boys want to be tall and broad-shouldered; girls want to be slim but bosomy. The importance of good looks in adolescence looms large. Adults who considered themselves attractive as teenagers are more self-confident and happier than those who felt unattractive, and there is some evidence that these differences do not disappear until the mid-forties (Berscheid, Walster, & Bohrnstedt, 1973).

Furthermore, both sexes want to be in step with their peers and are uncomfortable when they mature much earlier or later. Late maturing has especially pronounced effects for boys, as has been shown in some classic studies (Mussen & Jones, 1957). Until their early thirties, late-maturing boys may continue to feel less self-assured, but then they turn out to be more flexible, assertive, and insightful (M. C. Jones, 1957). The effects of late or early maturation on girls is less clear; research has produced contradictory findings (Jones & Mussen, 1958).

Adolescents become acutely conscious of their appearance as they get used to the new form their bodies have taken. Teenagers tend to be more concerned about their appearance than about any other aspect of themselves.

Cognitive Development: Formal Operations and Moral Reasoning

In this section we'll look at two significant aspects of intellectual development in adolescence: abstract thought and thinking about morality. Two cognitive-developmental theorists are of greatest importance here: Piaget, whose final stage of cognitive development—called *formal operations*—may be reached at this point in the life span; and Kohlberg, who examined and theorized about the cognitive underpinnings of moral growth.

Piaget's Formal Operations Stage (11–12 Years to Adulthood) The stage of *formal operations* is the point at which a person is able to think abstractly and deal with hypothetical situations. The ability to think abstractly may be considered a "cognitive definition" of maturity.

Formal operations According to Piaget, the final stage of cognitive development, characterized by the ability to think abstractly.

According to Piaget (1972), formal operations are usually reached during adolescence—sometime between the ages of 11 or 12 and 20. Adolescents can now think in terms of what *might* be true, not just what they can see in a concrete situation. Since they can imagine a great variety of possibilities, they can think of hypothetical situations, consider all aspects of a situation, and approach an intellectual problem systematically.

We can see this development of thought by the different reactions to the following story:

> Only brave pilots are allowed to fly over high mountains. A fighter pilot flying over the Alps collided with an aerial cable-way, and cut a main cable causing some cars to fall to the glacier below. Several people were killed. (Peel, 1967)

A child still at the Piagetian level of concrete operations said, "I think that the pilot was not very good at flying. He would have been better off if he went on fighting." This child assumes that there is only one possible reason for an event—in this case, the ineptness of the pilot. By contrast, a young person who had attained the level of thought Piaget called formal operations said:

> "He was either not informed of the mountain railway on his route or he was flying too low; also his flying compass may have been affected by something before or after take-off, thus setting him off course causing collision with the cable." (Peel, 1967)

Elkind (1984) has looked at how cognitive development at the formal operations stage is reflected in adolescents' behavior; see the box "Cognition and Behavior in Adolescence" (page 346). It's interesting to try to trace links between formal operations and the behaviors and concepts (such as the *imaginary audience* and the *personal fable*) that are characteristic of adolescence.

However, formal operational thought—unlike the earlier Piagetian stages—does not always occur. It seems that a certain level of cultural support and education is essential if formal operations are to be achieved. In fact, many American adults—perhaps as many as half—apparently never reach this stage at all (Clayton & Overton, 1973; Kohlberg & Gilligan, 1971; Papalia, 1972).

Imaginary audience "Observer" who exists only in the mind of an adolescent who is as concerned with the adolescent's thoughts and behaviors as the adolescent is.

Personal fable Conviction, typical in adolescence, that a person is special, unique, and not subject to the rules that govern the rest of the world.

Moral Development According to the theories of Piaget (1932) and Lawrence Kohlberg (1964, 1968), the way people think about moral issues depends not only on their character and upbringing but also on their level of intellectual development. Let's now consider Kohlberg's "stages of moral reasoning" and the work of another theorist, Carol Gilligan, who has focused on moral development in women.

KOHLBERG: STAGES OF MORAL REASONING Kohlberg defined *moral development* as the development of a sense of justice and concentrated on how people think about morality rather than on what they actually do.

To test his subjects' moral reasoning, he devised a set of "moral dilemmas," such as the following:

> In Europe, a woman was near death from a special kind of cancer. There was one drug that the doctors thought might save her. It was a form of radium that a druggist in the same town had recently discovered. The drug was expensive to make, but the druggist was charging 10 times what the drug cost him to make. He paid $200 for the radium and charged $2,000 for a small dose of the drug. The sick woman's husband, Heinz, went to everyone he knew to borrow the money, but he could only get together about $1,000, which is half of what it cost. He told the druggist that his wife was dying, and asked him to sell it cheaper or let him

When you were an adolescent, you thought as an adolescent, and the way you thought colored the way you acted. It may be interesting for you to look back at your own actions and attitudes during those years and to see whether you get any insight into your own life history from the descriptions below of some typical adolescent behaviors and the underlying thinking processes that are associated with them (Elkind, 1984). It may also be interesting to think of adolescents you know now and see whether the descriptions apply to them. Understanding the root causes of behavior can be helpful to parents and to teachers and others who work with adolescents. What, then, are some of the hallmarks of adolescent thought and behavior?

■ *They find fault with authority figures.* Young people have a new ability to imagine an ideal world. As they do so, they realize that the people they had once worshipped as near-perfect fall far short of their ideal, and they feel compelled to try to bring reality closer to fantasy by pointing out all the shortcomings they notice. Adults who do not take this criticism personally, but look at it as a necessary stage in teenagers' cognitive and social development, will be able to answer such comments matter-of-factly. They may even take the opportunity to point out that nothing—and nobody (not even a teenager)—is perfect.
■ *They are argumentative.* Adolescents want to practice their new ability to see the many nuances in an issue. Sometimes they seem to be "picking fights"; when this happens, adults can sometimes steer the argument into one about principles rather than personalities. In this way young people can stretch their reasoning ability without getting sidetracked in personal feuding.
■ *They are self-conscious.* A boy who hears his parents whispering "knows" they are talking about him; a girl who passes a couple of

COGNITION AND BEHAVIOR IN ADOLESCENCE

boys laughing raucously "knows" they are ridiculing her. The extreme self-consciousness of young adolescents owes a great deal to the concept of the imaginary audience. Adolescents can now put themselves into the mind of someone else; that is, they can think about someone else's thinking. Since they have trouble distinguishing what is interesting to them from what is interesting to someone else, however, they assume that everyone else is thinking about the same thing they are thinking about—their favorite topic, themselves. Thus they create an *imaginary audience,* an observer as concerned with their thoughts and behavior as they are themselves.

The imaginary audience stays with us to a certain degree in adulthood. Who among us has never agonized over what to wear to an important event, thinking that the other people there would actually care what clothes we had on—and then realized that most people were so preoccupied with the impressions they themselves were making that they did not even notice our carefully chosen outfit? Since this self-consciousness is especially agonizing in adolescence, however, it is important that adults avoid any public criticism or ridicule of young teenagers.
■ *They are self-centered.* "The biggest thing is that they just don't think it's going to happen to them. As my mother would say, 'They don't believe fat meat is greasy.'

They feel . . . invincible, and they are risk takers" (Shipp, 1985, p. A16). The speaker, a coordinator of pregnancy prevention programs for a large school system, is describing the *personal fable.* This is the conviction, particularly strong among young teens, that they are special, and not subject to the natural rules that govern the rest of the world. The personal fable accounts for a great deal of self-destructive behavior: it occurs because teenagers think that they are magically protected from harm. A girl thinks *she* can't get pregnant; a boy thinks *he* can't get killed on the highway; youngsters who experiment with drugs think *they* can't get hooked. "These things only happen to other people, not to me" is the unconscious assumption that helps to explain much risk-taking. The task for young people is to maintain a sense of individuality while developing a realistic awareness of the ways in which they are not exempt from the natural order of things.
■ *They are indecisive.* Teenagers often have trouble making up their minds about even the simplest things because they are suddenly aware of the multiplicity of choices in virtually every aspect of life.
■ *They seem hypocritical.* Young adolescents often fail to recognize the difference between expressing an ideal and working toward it. Thus they can march against pollution while littering along the march route. They need to realize that thinking does *not* make it so, that they have to act upon their values to bring about change.

The more adolescents talk about their personal theories and listen to those of other people, the sooner they arrive at a mature level of thought (Looft, 1971). As the thought processes of adolescents mature, they are better able to think about their own identities, to form adult relationships, and to determine how and where they fit into society.

pay later. But the druggist said, "No. I discovered the drug and I'm going to make money from it." So Heinz got desperate and broke into the man's store to steal the drug for his wife. Should Heinz have done that? Why or why not? (Kohlberg, 1969)

Kohlberg developed a system for scoring people's reasoning about these dilemmas, and then identified six stages (organized on three levels) in the development of moral judgment, described in Table 10-3 (page 348). Although children begin to think about issues of right and wrong at a very early age, Kohlberg maintains that they cannot attain the highest stages of moral reasoning at least until adolescence, and that some people never reach these levels.

Why does moral development depend on cognitive development? This is so largely because children cannot judge the morality of another person's actions until they can put themselves in the place of all the people who would be affected by those actions—the actor, as well as everyone that his or her actions would affect. Until they have developed social role-taking skills, they cannot weigh the effects of their own behavior, let alone anyone else's.

Kohlberg's theory has generated many research projects, which have confirmed some aspects of it but left others in question. The stages he outlined do seem to apply to American boys and men, but they are limited in their applicability to women and to people in nonwestern cultures (Edwards, 1977; Gilligan, 1982; Nisan & Kohlberg, 1982). Also, the relationship between moral judgment and moral behavior is far from clear-cut (Kupfersmid & Wonderly, 1980). Still, Kohlberg's influential theory has enriched our thinking about the way moral development occurs, has strengthened the association between cognitive maturity and moral maturity, and has stimulated both research and theory elaboration.

GILLIGAN: MORAL DEVELOPMENT IN WOMEN Carol Gilligan (1982) has studied moral development in women, which seems to rest on an extension of role-taking. Since Kohlberg defined morality as justice rather than compassion and based his research on male subjects, and since tests of moral judgment are usually based on Kohlberg's theory, some research suggests that women score lower than men on these tests. Gilligan maintains that women define morality as the ability to take another person's point of view and as willingness to sacrifice oneself to ensure the well-being of another. Her research shows that women see morality not in terms of abstractions like *justice* or *fairness*, but as a responsibility to look out for a specific other person or persons. Her sequence of development can be seen in Table 10-4 (page 349).

Gilligan contrasts Kohlberg's "morality of rights" with her own "morality of responsibility" by recalling two stories from the Bible. The abstract morality exemplified by Kohlberg's stage 6 made Abraham ready to sacrifice his son when God demanded it as proof of faith. Gilligan's person-centered morality can be seen in the story of the woman who proved to King Solomon that she was a baby's real mother when she agreed to give up the infant to another woman rather than see it harmed. To attain the highest levels of morality, Gilligan argues, justice and compassion must exist side by side.

Personality and Social Development: The Search for Identity

Psychosocial development in adolescence is most strongly characterized as a search for personal identity. In this section, we'll look at Erik Erikson's fifth crisis of development, identity versus role confusion; we'll then discuss three important psychosocial aspects of adolescence: "adolescent rebellion," work, and sexuality.

Erikson's Crisis 5: Identity versus Role Confusion (Puberty to Young Adulthood) The most important task of adolescence is to find out "who I really am"—although this task, or quest, is not completed in adolescence but is a theme we return to for the rest of our lives. Erik Erikson described the search for identity in adolescence as the fifth crisis of development: ***identity versus role confusion*** (1968).

Identity versus role confusion
According to Erikson, the fifth crisis of psychosocial development, in which an adolescent must determine his or her own sense of self or suffer from idertity confusion.

TABLE 10-3   KOHLBERG'S SIX STAGES OF MORAL DEVELOPMENT

Levels	Reasoning	Typical Answers to Heinz's Dilemma

Level I: Preconventional (ages 4 to 10 years)

Emphasis in this level is on external control. The standards are those of others, and they are observed either to avoid punishment or to reap rewards.

Stage 1: Punishment and obedience orientation. "What will happen to me?" Children obey the rules of others to avoid punishment. They ignore the motives of an act and focus instead on its physical form (size of lie) or its consequence (amount of physical damage).

Stage 1:
Pro—He should steal the drug. It isn't really bad to take it. It isn't like he didn't ask to pay for it first. The drug he'd take is only worth $200; he's not really taking a $2,000 drug.
Con—He shouldn't steal the drug. It's a big crime. He didn't get permission; he used force and broke and entered. He did a lot of damage, stealing a very expensive drug and breaking up the store, too.

Stage 2: Instrumental purpose and exchange. "You scratch my back, I'll scratch yours." Children conform to rules out of self-interest and consideration for what others can do for them in return. They look at an act in terms of the human needs it meets and differentiate this value from the act's physical form and consequences.

Stage 2:
Pro—It's all right to steal the drug because she needs it and he wants her to live. It isn't that he wants to steal, but it's the way he has to use to get the drug to save her.
Con—He shouldn't steal it. The druggist isn't wrong or bad; he just wants to make a profit. That's what you're in business for, to make money.

Level II: Morality of conventional role conformity (ages 10 to 13)

Children now want to please other people. They still observe the standards of others, but they have internalized these standards to some extent. Now they want to be considered "good" by those persons whose opinions count. They are now able to take the roles of authority figures well enough to decide whether some action is "good" by their standards.

Stage 3: Maintaining mutual relations, approval of others, the golden rule. "Am I a good girl (boy)?" Children want to please and help others, can judge the intentions of others, and develop their own ideas of what a good person is. They evaluate an act according to the person doing it or the person's motive, and take circumstances into account.

Stage 3:
Pro—He should steal the drug. He was only doing something that was natural for a good husband to do. You can't blame him for doing something out of love for his wife; you'd blame him if he didn't love his wife enough to save her.
Con—He shouldn't steal. If his wife die, he can't be blamed. It isn't because he's heartless or that he doesn't love her enough to do everything that he legally can. The druggist is the selfish or heartless one.

Stage 4: Social system and conscience. "What if everybody did it? People are concerned with doing their duty, showing respect for higher authority, and maintaining the social order. They consider an act always wrong, regardless of motive or circumstances, if it violates a rule and harms others.

Stage 4:
Pro—You should steal it. If you did nothing, you'd be letting your wife die; it's your responsibility if she dies. You have to take it with the idea of paying the druggist.
Con—It is a natural thing for Heinz to want to save his wife, but it's still always wrong to steal. He still knows he's stealing and taking a valuable drug from the man who made it.

Continued

TABLE 10-3 CONTINUED

Levels	Reasoning	Typical Answers to Heinz's Dilemma

Level III: Morality of autonomous moral principles (age 13, or not until young adulthood, or never)

This level marks the attainment of true morality. For the first time, the individual acknowledges the possibility of conflict between two socially accepted standards, and tries to decide between them. The control of conduct is now internal, both in the standards observed and in the reasoning about right and wrong. Stages 5 and 6 may be alternative methods of the highest level of reasoning.

Stage 5: Morality of contract, of individual rights, and of democratically accepted law. People think in rational terms, valuing the will of the majority and the welfare of society. They generally see these values best supported by adherence to the law. While they recognize that there are times when there is a conflict between human need and the law, they believe that it is better for society in the long run if they obey the law.

Stage 6: Morality of contract, of universal ethical principles. People do what they as individuals think right, regardless of legal restrictions or the opinions of others. They act in accordance with internalized standards, knowing that they would condemn themselves if they did not.

Stage 5:
Pro—The law wasn't set up for these circumstances. Taking the drug in this situation isn't really right, but it's justified to do it.
Con—You can't completely blame someone for stealing, but extreme circumstances don't really justify taking the law in your own hands. You can't have people stealing whenever they get desperate. The end may be good, but the ends don't justify the means.

Stage 6:
Pro—This is a situation which forces him to choose between stealing and letting his wife die. In a situation where the choice must be made, it is morally right to steal. He has to act in terms of the principle of preserving and respecting life.
Con—Heinz is faced with the decision of whether to consider the other people who need the drug just as badly as his wife. Heinz ought not to act according to his particular feelings toward his wife, but should consider the value of all the lives involved.

Source: Adapted from Kohlberg, 1969; and Kohlberg, 1976, in Lickona, 1976.

TABLE 10-4 GILLIGAN'S LEVELS OF MORAL DEVELOPMENT IN WOMEN

Level	Description
Level 1: Orientation of individual survival	First, a woman concentrates on what is practical and best for her. The she makes the transition from selfishness to responsibility as she thinks about what would be best for other people.
Level 2: Goodness as self-sacrifice	This stage begins with her thinking that she has to sacrifice her own wishes to what other people want, being worried about what they will think of her, and feeling responsible for what they do. She tries to manipulate other people, sometimes through guilt. She then makes the transition from "goodness" to "truth," taking into account her own needs, *along with* those of others. Her own survival returns as a major concern.
Level 3: Morality of nonviolence	Finally, she has elevated the injunction against hurting anyone to include herself, thus establishing a "moral equality" between herself and others.

Source: Gilligan, 1982.

TABLE 10-5   ERIKSON'S STAGES OF PSYCHOSOCIAL DEVELOPMENT

Ages	Psychosocial Stages
Birth to 12–18 months	**1** *Basic trust versus basic mistrust:* Baby develops sense of when and whom to trust, when to protect self by being cautious.
12–18 months to 3 years	**2** *Autonomy versus shame and doubt:* Child develops a balance of independence and recognition of limitations.
3 to 6 years	**3** *Initiative versus guilt:* Child develops ability to try out new activities in the pursuit of goals, is not overwhelmed by failure, and begins to question propriety of activities.
6 years to puberty	**4** *Industry versus inferiority:* Child learns skills of the culture, gains self-esteem through competence, and keeps the role of work in proper perspective.
Puberty to young adulthood	**5** *Identity versus role confusion:* Adolescent must determine own sense of self, especially in terms of work goals. Problems may result in either impulsive behavior or extended immaturity.
Young adulthood	**6** *Intimacy versus isolation:* Person seeks to find a balance between making commitments to others and maintaining own individuality.
Middle adulthood	**7** *Generativity versus stagnation:* Mature adult is concerned with establishing and guiding the next generation and also with developing own creativity, which may require a period of attention to self.
Late adulthood	**8** *Integrity versus despair:* Elderly person achieves an acceptance of own life, coming to terms with approaching death; some despair is inevitable.

Note: This table also appears as Table 9-4; it is repeated here for the reader's convenience.

You'll remember from Chapter 9 that Erikson advanced a theory of psychosocial development according to which there are eight developmental stages, at each of which there is a crisis, or turning point. (See Table 10-5.) Negotiating a crisis successfully means achieving a favorable balance of the factors or elements involved in it. By the time we reach adolescence, with its fifth crisis, we have—it is hoped—successfully resolved the preceding four. What brings on this new crisis?

The sudden changes in their bodies bewilder young people and make them ask who they have been and who they are becoming. "Am I the same person I used to be?" they wonder; "What will I be like from now on?" As teenagers continue to question and puzzle over their greatest preoccupation, their life's work, they are in danger of becoming confused. This confusion may result in a person's taking an excessively long time to settle on a career. (Erikson himself wandered around Europe for 7 years after leaving school before he even considered the possibility of becoming a psychoanalyst.) Confusion may also show up in childish impulsivity, hero worship, or intolerance of others (Erikson, 1965).

Falling in love is seen by Erikson as an attempt to define identity. By sharing intimate thoughts and feelings, the adolescent offers up his or her own identity, sees it reflected in the loved one, and is better able to clarify the self.

Erikson's concept of identity has received more research attention—and support—than any other aspect of his theory. Research with college students has found four different categories of identity, which are related to several personality characteristics such as intimacy, commitment, and sense of self (Marcia, 1966). Other research with undergraduates has confirmed Erikson's point that people who have resolved their own identity crises, especially with regard to their occupational goals, are better able to develop intimate relationships with other people (Kacerguis & Adams, 1980).

Erikson sees falling in love during adolescence as an attempt to define identity. As an adolescent couple share intimate thoughts and feelings, each one sees the self reflected in the other, and each is better able to answer the question, "Who am I?"

"Adolescent Rebellion": Fact or Myth? The first psychologist to formulate a theory of adolescence, G. Stanley Hall (1916), contended that the physiological changes of adolescence would necessarily bring about psychological reactions and that the teenage years must be a time of storm and stress. The anthropologist Margaret Mead (1928) challenged this view after going to the South Pacific and observing that teenage girls in Samoa did not undergo stress at the onset of adolescence but accepted it easily.

Mead's conclusions about the Samoans' smooth transition from childhood to adulthood have been questioned recently because of findings that delinquency shows up more often in adolescence than at any other time of life in Samoa—just as it does in the United States, England, and Australia (D. Freeman, 1983). But a number of researchers have found that for most young people, adolescence is just one more of life's transitions, no stormier than any other (Bandura, 1964; Offer & Offer, 1974).

There is a certain amount of conflict between adolescents and their parents, much of which results from teenagers' search for identity. Young people feel a constant tug between wanting to break away from their parents and realizing how dependent they really are on them. Adolescents' ambivalent feelings are often matched by their parents' ambivalence. Torn between wanting their children to be independent and wanting to keep them dependent, parents often find it hard to let go. One study of 27 boys found that such conflict is particularly strong between a boy and his mother, who finds herself losing authority and power (Steinberg, 1981).

Family discord increases during early adolescence, stabilizes for a while, and then decreases after the young person reaches 18 years of age (Montemayor, 1983). This may be because the generations have worked out most of the issues between them—or because the young person is now living away from home. Most of the tension arises from arguments about mundane matters like schoolwork, friends, chores, siblings, and cleanliness, and it is generally not severe enough to be described as "storm and stress." Why, then, does this myth persist? According to Albert Bandura (1964), the answer is, at least partly, that the myth is self-perpetuating. Bandura believes that troubled adolescence is often a self-fulfilling prophecy: when society expects young people to be rebellious, some of them oblige. Also, researchers may pay more attention to certain troublesome segments of the adolescent population and surprisingly little to the bulk of typical teenagers (Adelson, 1979).

(©Alan Carey/Image Works)

The search for identity often leads to some conflict at home, as both adolescents and parents cope with ambivalence about young people's need to become independent. Most of the tension arises from arguments about mundane matters like schoolwork, friends, chores, siblings, and cleanliness, and it is generally not severe enough to be described as "storm and stress."

Erikson (1968) has offered another explanation for the tumult in some adolescents' coming of age. While young people who are gifted and well prepared for the future will eagerly embrace the responsibilities of adulthood, those who feel overwhelmed and ill-equipped to deal with new technology and new roles are, on the contrary, likely to "resist with the wild strength encountered in animals who are suddenly forced to defend their lives. For, indeed, in the social jungle of human existence there is no feeling of being alive without a sense of identity" (p. 130). This theory seems to shed some light on recent riots in English and American cities by young men who are chronically out of work and have lost all hope of being employable.

Work and Careers   Work looms large in Erikson's concept of development in adolescence. At about age 17, teenagers are supposed to be entering a phase in which they realistically plan for their future careers (Ginzberg et al., 1951), but recent research shows that many high school seniors are still not making realistic educational and career plans. In one study of more than 6000 high school seniors in Texas, many were found to have very limited knowledge about occupations, and even less knowledge about the kind of education that would be appropriate for them. Moreover, relatively few seemed to be making good matches between career choices and their own interests (Grotevant & Durrett, 1980).

A greater proportion of teenage students are working today than at any other time in the past 25 years—about half of all high school juniors and seniors and some 30 percent of freshmen and sophomores (Cole, 1980). Some work because their families need the income; others work because they want the independence that comes from earning their own money.

Yet work does not seem to benefit teenage students' educational, social, or occupational development as much as you might think (Greenberger & Steinberg, 1986). Teenagers who work are no more independent in making financial or other decisions affecting their lives than their classmates who do not hold jobs (Greenberger & Steinberg, 1986). Most students who work part-time do not learn the kinds of skills that will be useful later in life (Hamilton & Crouter, 1980). And those who work during high school are not likely to earn any more money afterward than they would have had they not held jobs (Greenberger & Steinberg, 1986).

Work does not, then, seem to aid development in adolescence. In fact, there appear to be a number of "hidden costs." Teenagers who work, especially those who put in more than 15 or 20 hours per week, show declines in school grades, involvement with school, and attendance in school. Furthermore, there is a correlation between working and certain antisocial behaviors. Some teenage workers spend the money they earn on alcohol or drugs, develop cynical attitudes toward working, and cheat or steal from their employers by the time they have been on a job 6 or 7 months. Working teenagers tend to spend less time with their families and feel less close to them. Furthermore, they have little contact with adults on the job, and they are usually exposed to sex-stereotyped occupational roles (Greenberger & Steinberg, 1986).

Some of these negative correlations may be caused not by working itself, but by the factors that motivate some teenagers to take jobs. That is, they may already be uninterested in school, alienated from their families, and prone to drink or take drugs whenever they can afford to. In any case, however, working does not seem to help such young people manage their lives any better. Part of the reason is probably the fact that the kinds of jobs teens can get are usually of a menial, dead-end nature and are completely unrelated to their life goals. While some adolescent workers do learn how to manage both money and time, how to find a job, and how to get along with a variety of people, in general work experience seems less important than a solid academic foundation. Adults who want to help adolescents prepare themselves for future careers would probably do better to offer young people incentives to stay in school and do their best rather than encourage them to take after-school jobs.

Sexuality Sexuality comes to the fore during adolescence, but it is still not most young people's primary interest. Generally, it ranks lower among teenagers than choosing future work, understanding other people, and even participating in sports (Kermis, Monge, & Dusek, 1975). When sex *is* of prime interest, it is usually in the context of a relationship, apparently engaged in more because of the young person's search for identity through intimacy than for impulsive physical gratification. Aside from their interest in sex, adolescents also have other compelling concerns—friendships, school, sports, the struggle to be independent from their parents while still needing some guidance from them, and, of course, issues of identity and intimacy. Sexual development in adolescence is discussed in Chapter 12.

EARLY AND MIDDLE ADULTHOOD

Hindu texts written in the second century described life as a "series of passages, in which former pleasures are outgrown and replaced by higher and more appropriate purposes" (Sheehy, 1976, p. 355). From that point, however, until the twentieth century, the concept of development throughout adult life was, for the most part, ignored by scientists, even though artists recognized the ways in which adults keep developing.

Now, developmental psychologists are looking closely at how we develop as grown-ups, dividing adult life into several stages. With fewer specific physical criteria to signal change from one period to another and with a bewildering array of social markers, the beginnings and endings of stages are even more arbitrary than the age divisions of childhood. For our discussion, we divide adulthood into three parts: young adulthood (20 to 40–45 years), middle adulthood (40–45 to about 65), and old age (from 65 or 70 on).

What does knowing a person's age really tell us in adulthood? It doesn't tell us very much, since individual lives diverge so drastically, with all of us doing different things at different times. Biology shapes much of what we do in childhood, but individual personality and life events play a much larger role in adult life. The older we get, the less our age tells about us. For example, two 40-year-old women may resemble each other physiologically, but the one who had three children in her twenties, stayed home with them, and is just starting to carve out a vocation has a very different outlook on life from that of her childless age-mate with a well-established career.

Traditionally, most adults have had strong feelings about the time in life when certain activities are considered acceptable (Neugarten, Moore, & Lowe, 1965). People are keenly aware of their own timing and describe themselves as "early," "late," or "on time" with regard to when they married, settled on a career, had children, or retired. This sense of timing seems to be shaped by environmental expectations, often affected by social class. The entire life span is speeded up for working-class people, who tend to finish school earlier than those in the middle class, take their first jobs sooner, marry younger, have children earlier, and become grandparents sooner (Neugarten, 1968).

In recent years, however, as affluence has filtered down, as medical advances have kept people vigorous, and as the life span has lengthened, age-based expectations have become more flexible. We are more accepting of 40-year-old first-time parents and 40-year-old grandparents, 50-year-old retirees and 75-year-old workers, 60-year-olds in blue jeans and 30-year-olds in college presidencies. As Neugarten and Hagestad (1976) point out, "We seem to be moving in the direction of what might be called an age-irrelevant society; and it can be argued that age, like race or sex, is diminishing in importance as a regulator of behavior" (p. 52).

We are much more flexible when it comes to dealing with the basic developmental tasks of adulthood. Most of us still choose a career in young adulthood, but many of us change careers in middle age, and sometimes again in old age. We may become independent of our parents in our twenties, our forties, or our sixties. We may form our first intimate love relationship in our teens—or not until midlife. We may conceive our first child at 20 or at 40. Yet some things seem more age-related than others. It is not until middle age, for example, that most people acknowledge the limitations of their bodies or accept the certainty of their own death. (Some ill or handicapped people do this early in life, of course; and some people never think about these issues, denying them altogether.)

Physical Development: Continuity and Change

Health These are years of good health and energy, especially in our twenties and thirties. Significant changes do not take place until about age 50, and even then they are slight and gradual. We are at the peak of our muscular strength and our manual dexterity at about 25 or 30 (Troll, 1985). In our twenties, we are also at the peak of our reproductive capacities, and we see and hear most sharply. Gradually, we become farsighted and less able to hear high tones. Taste, smell, and sensitivity to pain, touch, and temperature remain stable until at least 45 or 50.

Most changes in health from young adulthood to middle age are relatively minor. But the organ systems are not as efficient as before, tending to lose some of their reserve capacity; men's sexual capacity declines somewhat; and high blood pressure may become a problem. Metabolism also changes, and people of both sexes tend to put on weight.

How do people cope with physical changes, and, therefore, with the awareness that they are aging? Past health history, family attitudes, and individual personalities play a large part. So does sex. Women know more about health, think more and do more about preventing illness, think they are more susceptible to illness, and are more sensitive to symptoms. They are also more apt to express fears and worries about their health, and seek out doctors more often (in addition to obstetrical and gynecological care). Finally, they are also more likely to be hospitalized, most often for surgery associated with the reproductive system (Nathanson & Lorenz, 1982).

What accounts for these gender differences? Biological factors may make women more aware of the body and its functioning, and cultural standards may dictate medical management of physical processes. Employment may be a factor. Employed women report less illness than homemakers, possibly because workers want to protect their jobs, and the greater proportion of male employees may add to the sex differential (Nathanson & Lorenz, 1982).

Midlife Changes Menopause in women and the male climacteric are major events of midlife—menopause is, of course, universal among women, and the climacteric is becoming an increasingly recognized syndrome among men. Both events have a physical and a psychological element, although the ratio of the physical to the psychological varies.

MENOPAUSE Typically, at about age 50 a woman stops menstruating and can no longer bear children; but this can happen normally several years earlier or later (Lennon, 1982). The time (some 2 to 5 years) during which a woman's body undergoes the various physiological changes that bring on **menopause** is known technically as the **climacteric**.

Many myths have sprung up around the menopause, associating it with a number of physical and psychological conditions. However, it is now clear that many of these so-called symptoms have no direct relationship to menopause.

The only physical symptoms that seem directly related to the reduction of the body's production of the female hormone estrogen are hot flushes (sudden sensations of heat that flash through the body), thinning of the vaginal lining (which can make sexual intercourse very painful), and urinary dysfunction (caused by tissue shrinkage) (Ballinger, 1981). The administration of artificial estrogen often dramatically resolves these problems, but since women who receive estrogen replacement therapy (ERT) have a higher risk of cancer of the lining of the uterus (Hoover, Gray, & Fraumeni, 1977), the benefits of this treatment must be weighed against its risks. Fortunately, research has now demonstrated that when artificial progesterone is given along with estrogen, the risk of developing this kind of cancer falls *below* the risk for women who receive no estrogen at all (Bush et al., 1983; Hammond, Jelovsek, Lee, Creasman, & Parker, 1979).

At one time menopause was blamed for a number of psychological problems, especially depression, but recent research shows no reason to attribute psychiatric illness directly to physical changes in a woman's body. Emotional problems that appear among middle-aged women and seem to be linked to menopause are more probably an *indirect* result.

It appears, for example, that the timing of menopause may be important. If menopause occurs when women expect it to—during middle age—there is no special psychological distress associated with it. But if it occurs earlier or later, so that it violates expectations, a woman runs a higher risk of becoming distressed or depressed (Lennon, 1982). (Thus we see that the timing of events can influence how we deal with them and how normal we perceive ourselves to be.)

Also, some emotional problems of middle-aged women are probably caused by environmental pressures—by society's negative attitude toward aging, which reminds a woman that menopause marks the end of her youth. In cultures that value older women, few problems are associated with menopause (Ballinger, 1981). A society's view of aging seems to influence the well-being of menopausal women far more than hormonal levels in their own bodies do.

MALE CLIMACTERIC Despite the fact that men can continue to father children until quite late in life, there are some biological changes in middle-aged men. These include decreased fertility, a decrease in the frequency of orgasm, and an increase in impotence (Beard, 1975). Furthermore, men seem to have cyclic fluctuations in the production of hormones (Kimmel, 1974).

About 5 percent of middle-aged men are said to experience symptoms such as depression, fatigue, sexual inadequacy, and vaguely defined physical complaints

Menopause *Cessation of menstruation, which typically occurs at about age 50.*

Climacteric *Medical term for menopause and the changes that occur at this time in a woman's life.*

(Henker, 1981). Since researchers have found no relationships between hormone levels and mood changes (Doering, Kraemer, Brodie, & Hamburg, 1975), it is probable that most men's complaints are just as much the result of environmental pressures as women's are. Some of their problems may be related to disturbing life events, such as illness of a man or his wife, problems with work, children leaving home, or the death of parents.

PSYCHOLOGICAL ASPECTS OF PHYSICAL CHANGES   Although both sexes suffer to some extent from our society's worship of youth, there is a "double standard" of aging which makes midlife especially difficult for women. Gray hair, coarsened skin, wrinkles, and crow's feet may make a man look distinguished, masterful, and attractive; but for a woman, they are simply signs that she is "over the hill." The feminine look is "smooth, rounded, hairless, unlined, soft, unmuscled—the look of the very young; characteristics of the weak, of the vulnerable" (Sontag, 1972, p. 9). Once these signs of youth have faded, so has a woman's value as a sexual and romantic partner. Homosexual men also suffer greatly from the loss of their appeal as they age (Berger, 1982). And even heterosexual men, who historically have had the most leeway in growing old naturally, are often at a disadvantage in the job and promotion market as they reach middle age.

Society's false values, added to the real losses people are apt to suffer as they get older, create undue burdens, sometimes leading to what has been called the *midlife crisis,* which we talk about later in this chapter. Not until attaining maturity is seen as a positive phenomenon for both sexes, rather than as a consignment to the social waste heap, will human beings in our society be able to make the most of most of their lives.

Cognitive Development: Intellectual Growth or Stagnation?

For many years it was believed that general intellectual activity peaked at about age 20 and then declined. The good news is that this is not so: certain types of intelligence continue to develop throughout life. In Chapter 7, we talked about two kinds of intelligence, fluid and crystallized. **Fluid intelligence,** as demonstrated by the ability to solve new problems, such as spatial-relations tasks, does peak in the late teens and then begins a slow, steady decline. But **crystallized intelligence**—as demonstrated by verbal abilities, for example—appears to increase throughout adulthood, even into old age.

Furthermore, different types of intelligent behavior may gain strength during adulthood, and this development may offset any decline in fluid intelligence. One such characteristic is wisdom—"good or sound judgment regarding the conduct of life" (Dixon & Baltes, 1986, p. 224). In addition, intellectual growth may occur in professional areas; for example, knowledge and productivity may increase (Baltes & Kliegl, 1986).

Adults focus their intellectual energies on solving real problems. In this process, they accept contradiction, imperfection, and compromise as part of adult life. This difference in the nature of adult thought, as compared with less mature thought, shows up in the ways people of different ages respond to different kinds of problem-solving tasks.

Which do you think you would be better at—playing a game of "twenty questions" or figuring out what to do about a flooded basement? Nancy Wadsworth Denney and Ann M. Palmer (1981) asked 84 adults between the ages of 20 and 79 to solve two kinds of problems—a traditional one like those that regularly appear in intelligence tests, and a practical one reflecting the kind of real-life situation adults regularly face. The traditional task was like the game "twenty questions": the subject was shown 42 pictures of common objects and told to find out which one the examiner was thinking of by asking questions that could be answered *yes* or *no.* Subjects were scored by the number of questions it took to get the answer and the

Fluid intelligence *Ability to solve novel problems; this kind of intelligence is influenced by neurological development.*

Crystallized intelligence *Ability to use information that has been learned; this kind of intelligence is influenced by culture and education.*

percentage of questions that eliminated more than one item at a time ("Is it an animal?") compared with those that eliminated only one ("Is it the cow?").

The practical task described nine real-life situations. The subjects were asked what they would do in situations like these: a vacuum cleaner they had bought from a door-to-door salesperson stopped working after 2 or 3 weeks, their basement was flooded, the refrigerator was not cold, an 8-year-old was 1½ hours late coming home from school, or they were stranded in a car during a blizzard. They were scored according to whether they came up with any solution at all and, if so, to what degree the solution involved their own actions as opposed to reliance on other people.

The way people responded to these questions reveals something important about adult intelligence. The older the subjects were, the worse they did on "twenty questions," but people in their forties and fifties were best at solving the practical problems. The middle-aged, then, are good at using abilities they have had experience using in daily life. We need to look at findings like these and ask ourselves what the point of intelligence is, after all. Is it to solve abstract problems or to play games? Or is it to solve the many problems that face us every day of our lives as individuals and as members of society?

Personality and Social Development: Theories and Issues

If you've ever reread a diary entry or a letter you wrote some years ago, you may well have done so with a sense of amazement: "Is that the way I thought then? This could have been written by someone else." We often receive a similar shock at a reunion of our high school class, finding that the boy voted "most likely to succeed" never again achieved the success he knew in school and that the mousiest girl in the class is now an attractive, successful dynamo. Happily, people are unpredictable.

Few of us have the same outlook on life at 40 that we did at 20; we usually change our views, showing the growth and development that take place during adulthood. This growth comes from many sources—the people we meet, the reading we do, the experiences we undergo, the challenges we face. Recent longitudinal studies of adults have dramatically illustrated the kinds of developmental tasks we deal with over the years. These tasks, as we'll see, are remarkably similar for large groups of people, even though the details—the specific circumstances and actions—vary widely.

Yet despite the changes that occur in our lives and our thinking, we *are* still the same people. And we do tend to carry certain basic traits with us in all the twists and turns of life's pathways. If we had sunny dispositions in junior high school, we're likely to be cheerful as 40-year-olds; if we were complaining as adolescents, we're apt to be querulous as adults; if we were assertive at 20, we're likely to be outspoken 10 years later (Block, 1981; Haan & Day, 1974; Livson, 1976).

Does this mean that our personalities are set in stone early in life? Does it mean that change, growth, and development are not possible, after all? No, it does not, because while some aspects of personality remain stable, other aspects show evidence of considerable change. For example, we are apt to show great leaps in self-esteem and in a sense of control over our lives, as a result of our accomplishments (Brim & Kagan, 1980). Furthermore, the wisdom we accumulate over the years enhances our growth and changes us.

The two threads of stability and change are intertwined throughout our lives, with some of us showing more stability and others more change. We can see this duality in Corazon Aquino, who became president of the Philippines at the age of 53, after having lived for years as a self-effacing housewife. President Aquino surprised many people with the toughness, determination, and sense of authority she showed when she began governing her country. Had this woman changed? Of course she had. Still, some elements of her personality remained stable over the years. The absolute devotion she once showed to her family she later showed to her country. Even as she led a revolution, she maintained her calm manner. Her strong religious faith, her moral integrity, and her sense of humor were noted by people who had known her as a schoolgirl, as a wife and mother, and as the leader of her country (Komisar, 1987).

One personality change common in midlife is the tendency to express aspects of our personality that we have repressed during our younger years (Cytrynbaum et al., 1980). Sometimes these newly flowering traits are ones usually thought of as more appropriate for the other sex. With the recognition at this stage of life that some of our basic goals have already been achieved—children reared, career established, identity in large measure achieved—both men and women feel freer to veer from the stereotypical male or female they had originally modeled themselves after. They allow themselves to express long-buried aspects of their personalities. Many women become more assertive, competitive, and independent; many men become more nurturant, passive, and dependent. The significant aspect of such change is not that it is "contrasexual" but that any trait which has been repressed for the first half of life may now flower with increased self-confidence and relaxation.

One other common personality change, which may help uncover such buried characteristics, is the tendency for people to become more introspective as they grow older. Younger people invest more of their energies in action rather than thought, but people at midlife and beyond tend to think about themselves more, analyzing what they have done in their lives and why they have done it (Cytrynbaum et al., 1980).

On the following pages, we'll discuss some theories of psychosocial development in early and middle adulthood, and then go on to look at two psychosocial issues that are important at this stage of life: work and parenthood. (Other important issues—such as sexuality, marriage and divorce, and human relationships—are taken up elsewhere in this book.)

Theoretical Approaches   ERIKSON: CRISES DURING EARLY AND MIDDLE ADULT-HOOD   Erikson (1963) maintains that the search for identity begun in adolescence continues as adults focus on different issues at different stages of life. But he also envisions two new crises in early and middle adulthood: intimacy versus isolation and generativity versus stagnation. It is interesting to note that in a recent interview, Erikson has increased his emphasis on the necessity of achieving a balance between two extremes in each crisis (E. Hall, 1983).

Erikson's crisis 6: Intimacy versus isolation (young adulthood)   The young adult is now ready to make a commitment to a close relationship with another person, risking temporary ego loss in situations requiring self-abandon (like coitus and orgasm, marriage, and very close friendships). While a certain degree of isolation is crucial to maintain one's individuality, too much may prevent the ability to merge with another in an intimate bond and may lead to loneliness and self-absorption. Erikson's original view of the sixth crisis, **intimacy versus isolation,** was limited; he defined a "utopia of genitality" to include mutual orgasm in a loving heterosexual, child-producing relationship, thus eliminating from the realm of healthy development homosexuals, single people, and childless people. Also, he omitted any discussion of career development, a major issue in the identity formation of the young adult.

Recently, Erikson has expanded on the implications of the decision not to have children. While he recognizes the rationale behind such an option, he calls upon childless persons to recognize that they are defying an instinctive urge: they need to acknowledge the sense of frustration and loss that may accompany this decision and to channel their procreative tendencies in other directions (E. Hall, 1983).

Erikson's crisis 7: Generativity versus stagnation (middle adulthood)   At about age 40, people face the need to resolve the crisis of **generativity versus stagnation.** Generativity involves guiding the next generation; it can be expressed by having and

Intimacy versus isolation *According to Erikson, the sixth crisis of psychosocial development, in which the young adult seeks to find a balance between making commitments to others and maintaining his or her own individuality.*

Generativity versus stagnation *According to Erikson, the seventh crisis of psychosocial development, characterizing midlife. The mature adult is concerned with establishing and guiding the next generation or else experiences stagnation (personal impoverishment).*

Marriage represents a turning point in most people's lives, as they make a commitment to a close relationship with another person. According to Erikson, such a commitment is essential for resolving the sixth crisis, intimacy versus isolation. Maintaining a balance between merging with another and retaining one's separate identity is a challenge for young adults.

nurturing one's own children, by teaching, by taking on younger protégés, or by doing other productive and creative work that will live on. The major emphasis is still on wanting to have and guide one's own children, thus demonstrating "belief in the species." But Erikson stresses the potential for generativity in any kind of work and in a concern for the future shown in political and volunteer activities (E. Hall, 1983). Some degree of stagnation can serve to let creativity lie fallow for a while, but too much can result in self-indulgence or even physical or psychological invalidism. Here again, Erikson seems to overemphasize the universal value of parenthood and to give insufficient recognition to the need for self-nurturance that often emerges at this time of life, after people have been focusing on others, either through work or through the family.

LEVINSON: STAGES IN ADULT DEVELOPMENT   The study of how we develop as adults is relatively new—it is only quite recently that researchers have looked at normal adult development. Several of them have concluded that there is a predictable sequence of age-related stages throughout adult life, a concept that is intriguing but also somewhat questionable, as we shall point out later, in our evaluation of this research.

A major researcher who has identified "typical" profiles of adult development is Daniel Levinson of Yale University, who, with his colleagues, interviewed in depth 40 men aged 35 to 45 (10 each from 4 different vocations: biologists, business executives, novelists, and hourly workers in industry), asking them about work, religion, politics, education, leisure, and personal relationships. While the sample was small and predominantly white, this work was important because it gave rise to a comprehensive theory of adult development (Levinson, Darrow, Klein, Levinson, & McKee, 1978). Levinson then went on to interview 45 women, for whom he found similar stages of development (Levinson, 1986). He maintains that all people in all cultures, classes, and cohorts go through the same basic age-related sequence of stages. These stages, unlike those identified by theorists such as Piaget, do not progress to higher levels; later stages are no "better" than earlier ones (Levinson, 1986).

Levinson ties the findings from his work to his overall concept that the goal of adult development is the creation of a **life structure,** a pattern or design of life that

Life structure   *According to Levinson, the basic pattern of a person's life consisting of both internal and external aspects.*

TABLE 10-6 LEVINSON'S DEVELOPMENTAL PERIODS

Stage	Description	Ages
0	Preadulthood	Conception to age 22
1	Early adult transition	17–22
2	Entry life structure for early adulthood	22–28
3	Age 30 transition	28–33
4	Culminating life structure for early adulthood	33–40
5	Midlife transition	40–45
6	Age 50 transition	50–55
7	Culminating life structure for middle adulthood	55–60
8	Late adult transition	60–65

Note: Stages 6, 7, and 8 are proposed.

consists of internal aspects made up of dreams, values, and emotions, and external aspects such as participation in work, family, and religious life. This structure evolves throughout life. Its primary aspect is a person's relationship with people, groups, institutions, objects, places, cultures, and other aspects of the outside world. The central elements of a person's life structure are usually marriage, family, and occupation.

According to Levinson, the life cycle is a sequence in which we alternately build structures and change structures. As we build parts of a structure, we go through a period of stability; then, as we keep evaluating the structure, we change it.

Levinson's typical sequence of stages of development through the adult years is shown in Table 10-6 and described below:

0 *Preadulthood (conception to age 22):* During these early years, people become biologically and psychologically separate from their parents and develop as individuals. By the end of this period, they are at the threshold of a more independent, responsible adult life.

1 *Early adult transition (17 to 22 years):* People feel halfway out of the family and sense a great need to get all the way out. They have a tenuous sense of their own autonomy and feel that real adult life is still around the corner.

2 *Entry life structure for early adulthood (22 to 28 years):* People are building an adult life. They are established in a chosen lifestyle, independent of their parents, and pursuing immediate goals without asking themselves whether they are following the right course.

3 *Age 30 transition (28 to 33 years):* People ask themselves, "What is life all about, now that I am doing what I am supposed to?" and "Is what I am the only way for me to be?" They often reassess both work and family patterns. At this time, for example, career women may think about having a baby, and homemakers may begin to work outside the home.

4 *Culminating life structure for early adulthood (33 to 40 years):* People make deeper commitments to work, family, and other important aspects of their lives, setting specific goals and timetables. Toward the end of this period, they break away from the authorities in their lives and work at attaining senior status in their own right.

5 *Midlife transition (40 to 45 years):* In this period of transition between early and middle adulthood, people question virtually every aspect of their lives and values, with an increasing awareness that time is limited. They may lose their mooring for a time as they make the transition to the second half of life. They come to terms with the fact that the first part of adult life is over and they will not be able to do all that they had planned before they grow old and die. The transition may be smoothly managed, or it may assume crisis proportions, depending on their personalities and the specific situations they find themselves in.

For those who build a satisfying life structure, "middle adulthood is often the fullest and most creative season in the life cycle. They are less tyrannized by the ambitions, passions and illusions of youth. They can be more deeply attached to others and yet more separate, more centered in the self" (Levinson et al., 1978, p. 62).

The following three periods are tentatively proposed; the research to flesh out the tasks of these years has yet to be done:

6 *Age 50 transition (50 to 55 years):* People have an opportunity to modify and perhaps improve the entry life structure.
7 *Culminating life structure for middle adulthood (55 to 60 years):* This provides the framework for concluding middle adulthood.
8 *Late adult transition (60 to 65 years):* This boundary period separates and links middle and late adulthood.

CLAUSEN: CHOICES AND COMMITMENTS IN ADULT DEVELOPMENT   Another view of adult development—associated with Clausen—is that there is no necessary age-related sequence of periods of stability and transition (as Levinson proposes), but rather that people tend to change in small ways throughout life or to make major transitions when these are called for, with their age at the time having very little relevance (Clausen, 1986). Some people undergo more transitions than others, because of their personalities, their experiences in childhood and adolescence, and social and economic forces beyond their control.

Using as a basis the Berkeley longitudinal studies—which followed people born in the late 1920s up to the age of 53 to 62—researchers looked at various personality traits, such as dependability, self-confidence, and *cognitive commitment* (defined as interest in intellectual matters) (Clausen, 1986). Because of differing societal expectations for men and women, their personalities as adolescents seemed to have different long-term effects. Men who had shown "planfulness and competence" as adolescents (that is, the ability to plan ahead and meet responsibilities and to function productively, with self-confidence) had more stable and satisfying careers and marriages than the other men in the study. Women who had been self-confident in high school were more apt to have stable, satisfying marriages, but women's personalities as teenagers did not seem related to later success in careers. Findings like these contradict Levinson's view that the preadult era is only a prelude to adult living, and that all people go through the same basic sequence of personality changes in early and middle adulthood.

EVALUATION OF RESEARCH ON ADULT DEVELOPMENT   One problem with most of the research we have is that it is based on small samples of white, middle-class men; another is that none of the stage-related studies have focused on elderly people. Increasingly, however, populations studied are broadening, and it may now be possible to determine whether the approximate sequence, if not the specific ages, of developmental stages is appropriate for women, nonwhites, and people of lower socioeconomic status, as Levinson maintains.

The major question about the "age and stage" concept is that if it is taken literally, we would expect to find a common pattern of development in all people. This, of course, does not happen. An adult's chronological age tells us less than his or her personality and history. Furthermore, many of the same issues recur over and over again throughout adulthood, requiring both reflection and action. While we need to remember the limitations of this research, then, looking at its findings does help us identify developmental threads that run through the lives of many people. Its most important message is its challenge to the notion that people's life histories are written early and that nothing of significance happens in adulthood in terms of emotional and personality development. These studies emphasize how adults continue to change, develop, and grow during middle age, and probably beyond. Personality continues to evolve throughout life. The end of adolescence does not mean the end of growth, and each age period is significant.

The work we do and the way we do it are major determinants of self-esteem. This is true for both sexes, especially now that more American women are working outside the home than ever before. Women value the noneconomic benefits of their jobs (interest and contact with people) more than men do, and women more often say that they would continue to work even if they did not need the money.

Two Psychosocial Issues of Early and Middle Adulthood WORK AND ADULT DEVELOPMENT Only recently has work been getting the research attention it deserves, in view of its central place in the lives of most people. "What do you do?" is usually the first question strangers ask us. What we do for pay usually takes up at least half of our waking hours. And what we do and how we do it often play a major role in our self-esteem.

Perhaps the increased interest in work (as shown by some of the longitudinal research on adulthood, whose findings will be discussed later) parallels changes that have taken place in American society. One demonstration of these changes is a report that presents findings from two national studies, of more than 2000 adults each, one made in 1957 and the other almost 20 years later, in 1976 (Veroff, Douvan, & Kulka, 1981).

What has happened in the work world over this generation? Women have moved into it in ever-increasing numbers, so that by 1969 more mothers of school-age children were out working than were staying at home. Meanwhile, men were showing more concern about their family roles, more young people had entered the work force, workers were thinking more about leisure and retirement, and people in the "baby boom" generation (born between 1945 and 1965) were pursuing higher educational goals. Some of these broad changes undoubtedly affected differences in the attitudes people in the 1970s displayed toward their work, compared with those in the 1950s.

About 12 or 13 percent of both sexes at both times (1957 and 1976) mentioned their jobs as a source of happiness, but in 1976 more people saw their jobs as a source of worry and more women saw them as a source of unhappiness. The women's answers probably reflect the greater importance their jobs held for them; a woman's job is no longer just a source of pocket money or even needed income but is now an important part of "identity validation." When a job does not live up to this promise, disappointment is keener.

The importance people give their jobs often depends on their principal values and their stage in life. In the 1976 study, married workers who had children rated their occupations below their roles as spouse and parent, confirming Erikson's emphasis on the importance of generativity. Older men who greatly valued self-actualization considered work more of a source of self-actualization than marriage, but still rated work lower than parenthood. Women seemed to value the noneconomic benefits of their jobs (interest and contact with people) more than men did, and women more often said that they would continue to work even if they did not need the money (Veroff et al., 1981). This may reflect the contrast between work and the social isolation and low prestige of homemaking, which many women and few men have experienced.

Overall, while Americans today seem to value family roles over work roles, work is still a strong area of concern—and it is stronger than ever for some people, especially young single women. The most sweeping changes with regard to work over the past 20 or 30 years have affected women, a fact confirmed by other researchers. An intensive study of about three hundred 35- to 55-year-old women in the Boston area found a strong relationship between paid work and a sense of pride and power, especially for women in high-prestige occupations (Baruch, Barnett, & Rivers, 1983). Work has a major impact on a woman's feeling of well-being.

HOW PARENTHOOD AFFECTS DEVELOPMENT Parenthood can be a creative experience in self-growth as parents go through its several stages: anticipating what parenthood will be like, adjusting to new demands and learning how to meet them at every stage of children's growth, and then disengaging from the active parental role as children mature (Group for the Advancement of Psychiatry, 1973). Through their children, parents get a chance to relive their own childhood experiences and to work out issues they have not resolved with their own parents. In addition, they are influenced by their children, who bring their unique personalities and demands to this intimate, intensely emotional relationship.

Many women greet pregnancy with mixed emotions. They feel special, potent, and creative; but at the same time they may also feel a loss of individual identity, and they may worry about the future. No matter how much a woman may want a baby, she can find it depressing to see her familiar body looking and feeling so different. Furthermore, contemplating the unknown often arouses anxiety, and a woman can never imagine ahead of time all the changes a baby will bring to her life. All these feelings—positive, negative, and ambivalent—are normal.

While we know less about the father's reaction to an impending birth, he also experiences conflicting emotions. He is apt to feel virile and powerful, excited at the prospect of carrying on his genetic lineage, while at the same time feeling inadequate about his ability to be a good father, worried about the new responsibilities a baby will bring, and estranged by the physical and emotional changes in his wife.

Parenthood is more likely to be a freely chosen option today than at any earlier time in history. As parenthood has become more and more a matter of choice, so has acceptance of people who decide not to have children. Still, most people in their thirties have children, and most find parenthood a significant experience and a major source of satisfaction (Veroff et al., 1981).

Parenting does, of course, affect different people in different ways. By and large, the sexes hold different viewpoints. Women tend to think that the nicest thing about having children is the love and warmth in the relationship; men focus on their role in influencing and forming the character of a child. When asked to describe the changes children bring to a person's life, women reflect difficulties in meeting society's expectations for a "good mother" by focusing on restrictions on their freedom.

Different people also respond differently to the physical, psychological, and financial stresses of parenthood. Some cannot meet these challenges; they may abuse, neglect, or abandon their children or become physically or emotionally ill themselves. Most, however, cope to a greater or lesser degree. Parents often turn to support systems such as family, friends, and neighbors, or get help from professionals and from books and articles on child rearing. Adoptive parents develop, basically, much as biological parents, even though they face special experiences and have to deal with special challenges. Successful parents tend to define their situation positively, putting parental responsibilities first; they concentrate on one set of responsibilities at a time; and they are willing to compromise their standards (such as those for neatness or promptness) when necessary (Miller & Myers-Walls, 1983; Myers-Walls, 1984; Paloma, 1972).

By the time grown children leave the parental home, their mothers are usually ready to let them go. For years the **empty nest** was considered a problem for women—a crisis that occurred when the youngest child left home. More recently, it has been found to be a crisis that does not really exist. While some women experience problems at this time, they are far outnumbered by those who are ready to invest their energies in other pursuits (Barnett, 1985; Brecher & Editors of Consumer Reports Books, 1984; L. B. Rubin, 1979). There is some evidence that this stage is harder on fathers, who may regret that they have not spent more time with their children in earlier years (L. B. Rubin, 1979); on parents whose children do not become independent when their parents expect them to (Harkins, 1978); and on women who have not prepared for the empty nest by reorganizing their lives (Targ, 1979).

Empty nest *Transitional phase of parenting after children leave the parental home.*

LATE ADULTHOOD

There is, of course, no arbitrary dividing line when old age begins. A vigorous-looking woman of 55 complains, "I hope I never get as old as I feel"; a frail 84-year-old talks about putting aside money for his "twilight years." There are tremendous differences among people in their later years. Some remain intellectually and physically hale well into their nineties, while others look, feel, and act old in their fifties. Bernice Neugarten (1975) refers to the "young-old," people age 55 to 75 who have retired from full-time work and are still vigorous and active, as compared with the "old-old" of 75 and over.

Senescence, the period of the life span when one grows old, begins at different ages for different people. We don't always know much about someone just by knowing when he or she was born. The official definitions of *old age* used to be 65—the age when people could be forced to retire from a job and were eligible for social security payments. In recognition of the fact that people are staying vigorous longer, however, even the legal definition of old age is now changing; mandatory retirement can no longer be implemented for most jobs before age 70, and politicians are considering raising the age for social security benefits.

Such trends have far-reaching implications for social policies, politics, fiscal stability, and family patterns in our society, as the elderly become a larger segment of our population. Today about 11.7 percent of the United States population—some 28 million people—are 65 or older; by the year 2030, the percentage will almost double, to 21.2 (U.S. Senate Special Committee on Aging, 1986). The fastest-growing segment of this population is people age 85 and over. This increase in the number of older people, especially the very old, makes many demands on our society's ability to provide health care and other supportive services.

Physical Development: Health and Aging

In this section we'll take a brief look at two theories of aging: "programming" versus "wear and tear." Then we'll go on to consider several physical aspects of aging: sensory and psychomotor functioning and general health status.

Theories of Aging   Why do our bodies age? We still do not have a definitive answer to this question. We do know, however, that aging is a complex process influenced by heredity, nutrition, disease, and various environmental factors. If you have chosen your ancestors well and followed good health practices, you should stay vigorous longer and live longer. Still, less favorable ancestry and poor health habits do not explain the aging process. What happens to the cells in our bodies? How are old cells different from young cells? What happens to make them different? Theories that try to answer these questions fall into two main categories, as follows.

"PROGRAMMING" THEORY   Since each species has its own pattern of aging and its own life expectancy, some theorists propose that aging must be programmed, or built into every organism in some way. Leonard Hayflick (1974), who studied the cells of many different animals, found that normal cells will divide only a limited number of times; for human cells, that number is about 50. He maintains that this limitation controls the life span, which for humans seems to be about 110 years. We may be born with genes that become harmful later in life, causing deterioration. One form of deterioration may take place in the immune system, which seems to become "confused" in old age, so that it attacks the body itself.

"WEAR AND TEAR" THEORY   The wear-and-tear theory compares our bodies to machines whose parts eventually wear out through continuous use and proposes that internal and external stresses (which include the accumulation of harmful by-products in our systems, such as chemical by-products of metabolism) aggravate the wearing-down process. As cells grow older, they are less able to repair or replace damaged components, and so they die. We know, for example, that the cells of the heart and brain do not replace themselves, even early in life. When they are damaged, they die. The same thing seems to happen to other cells later in life.

Sensory Functioning in Old Age   With age the acuity of the senses tends to decline, but there are great individual differences.

People over 65 are apt to have problems seeing in the dark, which often prevent them from driving at night. Half of the legally blind people in the country are over 65, but, fortunately, with the development of improved eyeglasses and contact lenses and of new surgical techniques for the removal of cataracts, many vision losses are at least partly correctable.

Hearing problems are more common than visual problems. Older people often have difficulty following a conversation when there is competition from a radio or a television set, when outside noises intrude, or when other people are talking at the same time. Here again, we see a close relationship between physical and emotional development: a hearing loss can contribute to an old person's loneliness and sense of isolation. The link between physical limitations and personality problems has been underscored by experiments which found that college students suffering from hypnotically induced partial deafness began to feel paranoid (Zimbardo, Andersen, & Kabat, 1981). People who may not admit to themselves that they have a hearing problem may develop personality quirks and become difficult to be with if they get the idea that others are whispering about them or are deliberately excluding them from conversations.

The elderly often complain that their food doesn't taste very good any more. This seems to be caused by a loss of sensitivity in taste and smell.

The vestibular senses, which help to maintain posture and balance, often deteriorate in old age, causing dizziness and falls.

Psychomotor Abilities   Older people can do most of the things they could when they were younger, but they do them more slowly. Their general slowing down affects the quality of their responses, as well as response time, since it takes them longer to assess the environment and make decisions. This slowdown has a number of implications. It depresses scores on intelligence tests, for example, since many of these tests must be completed within a certain time. On a more practical level, it affects the ability to drive, and thus the ability to be independent.

Are you one of those people who lie down every time they feel the urge to exercise—until the urge passes? If so, you should reconsider. Physical exercise has benefits throughout life. Aside from making you feel virtuous, it helps tone your muscles, keep your weight down, and protect you from heart disease. In old age it proves its worth again. Older people who have exercised throughout adulthood show fewer losses in speed, stamina, and strength, and in various underlying functions such as circulation and breathing (Bromley, 1974). Many of the effects we associate with aging may result more from failure to use our bodies and from adaptation to nondemanding physical circumstances, than from chronological age.

Health   HEALTH STATUS IN OLD AGE   Despite a widespread belief to the contrary, being old does not mean being sick and disabled. Most elderly people are reasonably healthy; 90 percent of people over 65 describe their health as fair, good, or excellent. Older people in the work force average only four or five absences a year, a rate similar to that among younger workers. A majority of the elderly (54 percent) report no limitations on their activities for health reasons; but about 40 percent report that they have had to curtail a major activity (compared with about 20 percent of people aged 45 to 64). Those most likely to suffer from handicapping health conditions are elderly people in rural areas and people over 85; those most likely to be in good health are people with high incomes (U.S. Bureau of the Census, 1983).

Chronic conditions are the most prevalent health problem for people over 65, with more than 80 percent reporting one or more. The most common are arthritis, rheumatism, heart problems, hearing impairments, hypertension, and impairment of the lower extremities, the hips, the back, or the spine. On the other hand, acute conditions like colds and flu are less common in old age. Old people visit the doctor an average of six times a year, compared with five times for the population in general; but they are hospitalized twice as often as younger people. Only about 5 percent of the elderly live in nursing homes; institutionalization is most prevalent

Most elderly people are reasonably healthy, and scenes like this one—an older man keeping pace with much younger competitors—are quite common across the United States.

among the very old. About 75 percent of elderly people in the United States die from heart disease, cancer, and stroke, although there has been a decrease in heart disease since 1968, especially for women (U.S. Bureau of the Census, 1983; U.S. Senate Special Committee on Aging, 1986).

At the middle of the nineteenth century, Americans could expect to live to an average age of 40 years, and by 1900 life expectancy had risen only to 49. But today the average life expectancy for someone born in 1983 is 74.7 years (U.S. Senate Special Committee on Aging, 1986; see Table 10-7). This record high is due largely to lower mortality rates in infancy and childbirth and to medical progress in treating diseases that used to be fatal early in life.

Dementia *Mental deterioration caused by organic brain disease; characteristic of about 10 percent of people over 65 years of age.*

DEMENTIA   The combination of physical and mental deterioration that we know as *senility* and that is known medically as **dementia** is not inevitable in old age. Only about 1 in 10 people over 65 show significant mental impairment (National Institute on Aging, 1980). When a person *is* disabled by such symptoms as forgetfulness, problems in paying attention, decline in general intellectual ability, and difficulties in responding to other people, there is usually a physiological explanation (Butler, 1975).

Alzheimer's disease *Irreversible dementia characterized by memory loss, confusion, and other intellectual and personality deterioration.*

Alzheimer's disease   Most cases of dementia are caused by **Alzheimer's disease,** a progressive neurological disorder that results in intellectual loss and personality deterioration. Its early symptoms include forgetfulness (especially for recent events); later symptoms are confusion, irritability, incontinence, and sometimes complete inability to speak or care for oneself (U.S. Department of Health & Human Services, 1985b). Some patients continue to function on less demanding levels (playing tennis, gardening, maintaining personal relationships) but lose their ability to cope with more complex tasks. There is great variability in the rate at which the condition worsens, and some people live many years with it.

The disease hardly ever occurs under age 50, but its incidence increases with age; 6 percent of people over 65 and 20 percent of people over 85 suffer from it (Heckler, 1985). Alzheimer's disease seems to be partly hereditary, running in certain families. It is generally diagnosed by eliminating other possibilities, since a definitive diagnosis can be made only by brain autopsy (Crook & Miller, 1985). The brains of victims of Alzheimer's disease show such changes as tangles of nerve fibers, plaques (abnormal flat areas), and cell loss. Sometimes, they also show a protein not found in normal brains, which may eventually help diagnose the disorder (Wolozin, Pruchnicki, Dickson, & Davies, 1986). Most brain changes occur in the hippocampus, the area of the brain associated with memory (Hyman, Van Hoesen, Damasio, & Barnes, 1984). (See Chapter 2 for a discussion of some neurological aspects of Alzheimer's disease.)

We don't know the cause of Alzheimer's disease. Researchers are currently investigating imbalances or deficits of neurotransmitters (especially acetylcholine), selective death of brain cells caused by a slow virus, accumulation of toxins in the brain, autoimmune defects, and genetic factors (Crook & Miller, 1985; Heckler, 1985).

A promising new treatment (described in Chapter 2) involves the administration of a chemical that increases the release of acetylcholine, which has brought about dramatic cognitive and social changes in patients. Other types of therapy include medication for agitation and sleeplessness, techniques to improve memory, and professional counseling to help both patients and the families who care for them.

Other kinds of dementia   About 1 in 4 cases of senile dementia are caused by a series of small strokes. Since such strokes can often be prevented by treating the high blood pressure that leads to them, they may be rarer in the future. And some syndromes which seem to be dementia may actually be due to a number of causes and may be treatable and reversible.

All too often, dementia-like symptoms in old people are not accurately diagnosed and not treated because senility is *expected* in old age. However, confusion, memory loss, and similar symptoms often respond well to proper treatment. For example, when such states arise from *overmedication* (especially with a combination of drugs that interact poorly with each other), the treatment is obvious—a reduction in dosage or a change of medicine. Other conditions that produce similar symptoms and are potentially treatable include *depression* (possibly resulting from poor health, surgery, the death of a spouse, or some other life event), *underlying disease* (alcoholism, malnutrition, or poor thyroid function), and *difficulty in adjusting to a social change* (like moving to a new apartment).

For most people, generalized intellectual deterioration is not a necessary part of old age, as we'll see in the next section.

Cognitive Development: Is Decline Inevitable?

Two of psychology's intellectual giants recently made public statements about their own lessened intellectual abilities in old age. The behaviorist B. F. Skinner (1982) stated that at 78 he found it harder to "think big thoughts" without losing the thread connecting one topic to another, he sometimes forgot things that he had said or written many years ago, and he was not as creative as he had once been. And at 74, the learning researcher Donald O. Hebb (1978) wrote that during his sixties he had started to become forgetful, to lose some command of his vocabulary, and to be troubled by irrelevant thoughts he could not get out of his mind (like the words of an old nursery rhyme).

Both men devised strategies to deal with what they perceived as major losses. Skinner gave up intellectually demanding leisure activities like chess and made special efforts to continue meeting with other scholars, and Hebb began to be more discriminating in what he read and stopped working at night. Both began to rely more on external memory aids (like hanging an umbrella on the front doorknob so that they would remember to take it when they went out).

As we pointed out earlier, crystallized intelligence holds up very well in old age,

TABLE 10-7 LIFE EXPECTANCIES FOR PEOPLE BORN IN 1983	
White females	78.8 years
Black females	73.8 years
White males	71.6 years
Black males	65.2 years

Note: Females can expect to live longer than males for reasons that are not clear. The discrepancy between blacks and whites reflects many socioeconomic differences, including a higher rate of premature births among blacks, poorer prenatal care, and less access to medical care in general.
Source: U.S. Senate Special Committee on Aging, 1986.

although fluid intelligence typically shows some decline. In certain ways, the elderly tend to use intelligence better than younger people. While they do not perform as well as younger people when facing a new problem whose solution requires geometric or spatial-relations abilities, they tend to be superior at remembering, combining, and drawing conclusions from information learned over the years. As Horn (quoted in Goleman, 1984b, p. C5) says, "The ability to bring to mind and entertain many different facets of information improves in many people over their vital years. . . . Older people can say the same thing in five different ways. In our research, they're better in this sort of knowledge than the young people we see." Why are some abilities maintained while others seem to decline? Nancy Denney (1982) has proposed that people maintain *exercised* abilities (the ones they use) and tend to show a decline in *unexercised* abilities. In our society we often use many of the crystallized abilities—but we call upon the fluid ones less often.

In certain areas, older people's performance may not reflect their true intellectual capacity. For example, since they do things more slowly, anything that requires speed puts them at a disadvantage. And when they take a test, they may have trouble seeing or hearing instructions or questions, may be too anxious to perform well, or may just not be motivated highly enough to make an effort. What we are talking about here, then, is a distinction between competence and performance. Recent efforts to improve the cognitive performance of the elderly are described in the box "Helping the Elderly Improve Intellectual Performance."

Sometimes the decline in intellectual abilities that has been attributed to old age is, instead, a precursor of death. Shortly before death, people often experience a sudden decline in intellectual performance known as *terminal drop* (Botwinick, West, & Storandt, 1978; Riegel & Riegel, 1972). This phenomenon actually affects people of all ages, but the higher death rates among the elderly have caused it to be associated with old age.

Personality and Social Development: Successful Aging

The years beyond age 65 constitute a normal stage of development during which people can experience growth as well as crises. Yet our society seems to be bent on preventing the elderly from experiencing their last years positively. We dismiss their ideas as outdated and irrelevant, rather than valuing the wisdom gained through experience and the links with the past. We force them into retirement while many are still eager and able to work. We accept illness and depression as inevitable baggage of old age. And we stereotype the elderly in countless ways, treat them according to our mistaken ideas of what they are like, and thus create self-fulfilling prophecies. As a society we fail, for the most part, to meet their needs for companionship, income, transportation, housing, health care, and safety. In the face of all this, it is amazing that so many old people age so successfully. How do they do it?

Let's examine some theoretical approaches to psychosocial development in late adulthood: Erikson's final life crisis—"ego integrity versus despair"—and the controversy between "activity" and "disengagement" as the key to successful aging. Then we'll consider a major life event of old age: retirement.

Psychosocial Theories ERIKSON'S CRISIS 8: EGO INTEGRITY VERSUS DESPAIR (LATE ADULTHOOD) According to Erikson, the final crisis in life is **ego integrity versus despair,** and the achievement of ego integrity represents a culmination of the successful resolution of the seven previous crises. It implies a love of the human ego, which is dependent on an acceptance of the life one has lived, without major regrets over what could have been or for what one should have done differently. People who cannot accept the basic way they have lived may sink into despair at the knowledge that there is no time now to start another life, no possibility of going back and doing things better (Erikson, 1963). People who have not continually evaluated and modified their life structure (as recommended by Daniel Levinson and his col-

Ego integrity versus despair
According to Erikson, the eighth and last crisis of psychosocial development. The elderly person achieves a sense of acceptance of his or her life, allowing the acceptance of death; the developmental alternative is despair, characterized by failure to accept one's life and thus one's ultimate end.

We've all had the experience of doing better on a given task at one time than at another. The results of an exam may show the effects of too little sleep the night before, of going into the test without having studied, of a head cold, of a testing room that's stuffy or chilly, of anxiety about some other aspect of our lives, or of an "I don't care" attitude. Paul B. Baltes and his colleagues have focused on various factors that influence test performance of older people and have tried to see whether creating optimal testing conditions and providing special training can improve their performance on intelligence tests.

The good showings made by elderly subjects in such research have given rise to two conclusions. First, the typical world of the elderly is "cognitively deprived;" second, given favorable conditions, older people can activate an intellectual reserve that enables them to function on a higher level. These conclusions are based largely on the Adult Development and Enrichment Project (ADEPT) that originated at Pennsylvania State University (Willis, Bleiszner, & Baltes, 1981).

In one study based on ADEPT, healthy volunteers (whose average age was in the seventies) were assigned randomly to one of three groups. Two experimental groups, a "trained" group and a "self-taught practice" group, met for about 5 hours each. People in the "trained"

IN THE FOREFRONT

HELPING THE ELDERLY IMPROVE INTELLECTUAL PERFORMANCE

group were taught the rules underlying figural relations; that is, they learned rules such as those needed to determine the next figure in a series. Those in the "self-taught practice" group met in small groups in which they worked with the same problems and used the same training materials, but they received no formal instruction in solving the problems. The third group, a control group, had no contact with the experimenters except for pretesting and posttesting.

All participants (in both the experimental and the control groups) were given an extensive pretest of cognitive and personality measures. They were then given posttests 1 week, 1 month, 6 months, and 1 year after training. The posttests were also extensive, taking several hours to administer. The tasks included ranged from those that were very similar to the materials used in training

and practice to those that were markedly different. Both training and self-taught practice resulted in better performance on the posttest measures that were very similar to the training materials. Both experimental groups improved more than the control group (Blackburn, Papalia, & Foye, 1986; Papalia, Blackburn, Foye, & Serlin, 1986).

The posttest scores after 1 year show particularly marked positive effects for people in the practice group. It seems that—at least for a group of healthy "young-old" people—the opportunity to work out their own solutions to problems (as seemed to occur in the "self-taught practice" group) may provide more durable learning than being taught a set of rules (Blackburn & Papalia, 1986).

Findings like these are especially noteworthy, since they show that practice and training can improve performance even on problems involving fluid intelligence (which is known to decline in adulthood, presumably as a result of neurological losses). Just as older athletes, then, may have to train longer and harder to achieve what came more easily earlier in life, older scholars may have to put forth extra effort to maintain their level of mental achievement. The fact that this now looks possible means that old age need not be a time of intellectual decline for people who are motivated to put forth an extra ounce (or pound) of effort.

---

leagues) can become desperately afraid of death. On the other hand, those who have accepted their lives can more easily accept the inevitability of death, at the end of a life lived as well as they knew how.

Despair has its healthy side, too, however. As Erikson asks, "How could anybody have integrity and not also despair about certain things in his own life, in the human condition? Even if your own life was absolutely beautiful and wonderful, the fact that so many people were exploited or ignored must make you feel some despair" (E. Hall, 1983, p. 27). Again, it is the balance that is important.

Old people often engage in what Robert Butler (1961) has called a *life review*, in which they go over the past and think about what to do with the future. In Ingmar Bergman's classic film *Wild Strawberries*, an elderly doctor realizes how cold he has been for most of his life and becomes warmer and more open in his last days. This film dramatically shows the fact often noted in real life that we are in control of our personalities and can make changes at any time in the life span, including old age.

The self-searching undergone by the hero of this movie was inspired by his sense of impending death, the experience we must all come to terms with in one way or another.

ACTIVITY VERSUS DISENGAGEMENT   There is more than one way to age successfully, and the route we take depends on our personality, our past, and our present circumstances. Two major theories, which take extreme, diametrically opposite views, have generated vast amounts of research. So far, neither one seems to offer a complete explanation. With this in mind, let's look at the either-or theories.

Activity theory: The more active you remain, the more fulfilled you will be in old age. Ideally, according to **activity theory,** an old person should stay as much like a middle-aged person as possible. In old age, you should keep up as many activities as you can and replace roles you have lost (such as spouse or worker) with other roles (like grandparent or volunteer).

Activity theory *Theory of aging that holds that in order to age successfully an individual must remain as active as possible.*

Research, however, has found that the degree of satisfaction which older people feel has little relationship to how busy they are (Lemon, Bengston, & Peterson, 1972). Solitary activities (reading, watching television, and working on hobbies) have no relationship to satisfaction, and structured group activities actually seem to diminish it (Longino & Kart, 1982). Enjoyment of life does seem to be related to older people's involvement in doing things with friends and family—a fact that underlines the importance of significant relationships (Longino & Kart, 1982).

Disengagement theory: You will be happiest if you withdraw gracefully from life. According to **disengagement theory,** it is normal and healthy for old people to cut down their activity and involvement, retreating into themselves and weakening their emotional ties to others. But much research has failed to support the contention that disengagement is inevitable, universal, or sought by the elderly. Disengagement has been found to be more closely tied to impending death than to age itself (Lieberman & Coplan, 1970).

Disengagement theory *Theory of aging that holds that successful aging is characterized by mutual withdrawal between society and the elderly person.*

Other research has found that some people are happiest when they stay busy, and some enjoy the tranquility of the rocking chair. The approach people take usually reflects their personality and the degree of activity they engaged in before middle age. There is equal promise of a happy old age for the person who loves being frantically busy at work, as a volunteer, and in the social whirl, as well as for the retiree who enjoys indulging in the luxury of leisure, possibly for the first time in his or her life (Neugarten, Havighurst, & Tobin, 1968; Reichard, Livson, & Peterson, 1962).

Retirement   What impact does leaving the world of paid work have? As our comments above would indicate, it depends on whom you ask. The following statements by retirees who took part in a nationwide longitudinal study (Streib & Schneider, 1971) express two common points of view:

> I dislike retirement. Personally I think it is better to keep busy. When you are not occupied and not useful, you feel like a back number. The world gets along without you. Sometimes I think about suicide. There is nothing to do but read—it's hard keeping occupied. . . . Yesterday I answered an ad. Retirement is the bunk. (p. 139)
> Retirement means everything to me! I'm so happy about the whole set-up. I'm having a good time. I don't have any trouble keeping busy. On Monday I gardened. On Tuesday I played 18 holes of golf. Sometimes I bowl. On Wednesday I did yard work all morning. On Saturday I went fishing. I read a lot. In the winter I go to my lodge, and play cards. I've had several job offers but I don't want to work. (p. 142)

For this man and many others, retirement provides an opportunity to use their skills in satisfying ways on a schedule they can arrange for themselves. The dual benefits— maintaining control over their lives and demonstrating their competence— enhance their self-esteem and benefit society in general.

What makes the difference? By and large, a person's reaction to retirement often depends on money and health. Not surprisingly, retirees who do not have money worries are more satisfied with retirement than are those who miss their income. Similarly, people who feel well enough to enjoy their leisure time are more satisfied than those who do not. This conclusion emerged from Streib and Schneider's study, and also from other cross-sectional studies of retirees (Barfield & Morgan, 1974, 1978).

Streib and Schneider began their study when all their respondents were gainfully employed. The researchers followed the subjects as they continued working, when they retired, and when (as some did) they returned to work after retiring. Streib and Schneider began with questions derived from role theory: What does it mean when we drop, disrupt, or alter a basic role such as "worker"? How does this affect health, actual and perceived economic situation, self-image, and satisfaction with life? Their findings were generally quite positive. Health does not decline after retirement, nor does satisfaction with life. Self-image does not change drastically, either; retirees do not feel suddenly old and useless. Although income does decline sharply, most people in this study felt prepared for this aspect of retirement and did not worry about money. This finding underscores the wisdom of preparing for retirement well ahead of time.

In general, the better educated workers are, the more prestigious their jobs; and the more money they earn, the longer they are likely to work.

Most research about the effects of retirement has concentrated on men, but with the increased role of work in the lives of women, this focus is changing. Streib and Schneider found that married women and single women tended to retire earlier than widowed and divorced women. The earlier retirement of single women seems to belie the importance work has in their lives, but it may also reflect the fact that they have probably been working more continuously than women in the other groups and that retirement may give them their first chance for the kinds of domestic and leisure activities that women in the other groups may have taken for granted and gotten tired of.

DEATH AND MOURNING:
AN IMPORTANT ASPECT OF DEVELOPMENT

At one time, death was very much a part of most people's daily lives. Death in childhood and infancy was common, and people of all ages succumbed to a frightening array of fatal illnesses. Death was feared, but its hovering presence was accepted as natural and normal.

With advances in medicine, death receded farther away from the center of most people's daily existence and eventually became one of the few topics we hated to talk about. Recently, however, a healthier attitude toward death has arisen—an attitude that seeks to understand it; to explore the emotional, moral, and practical issues surrounding it; and to make this inevitable outcome of our lives as positive as possible for both the dying and their survivors. *Thanatology*, the study of death and dying, is arousing much interest, with the recognition that dealing with death can teach us about life.

Thanatology *Study of death and dying.*

Attitudes toward Death and Dying

Young children consider death temporary and reversible; they often think that a dead person will return. But their understanding gradually develops, and during childhood virtually all youngsters learn that death comes to everyone and that it should be seen not as a punishment but as a normal part of the life cycle (Nagy, 1948). This gradual understanding is affected partly by cognitive development and partly by experience. Chronically ill children and children who have lost a parent become precociously aware of the meaning of death (Bluebond-Langner, 1977).

Adolescents and young adults rarely think about death, because it is usually not an imminent threat, either to themselves or to those around them. Usually it is not until middle age that most people come to terms with the fact that they themselves are going to die. This realization is often an impetus for a major life change. Knowing that time is limited, people take stock of their careers, marriages, friendships, parenting, and values—and often make major changes. Old people generally accept death more easily than the middle-aged.

Dealing with Death

Accepting One's Own Death Elisabeth Kübler-Ross (1969), a pioneer in the study of dying, evolved a concept of the dying process based on her work with several hundred dying patients. She maintains that most people go through five stages in coming to accept imminent death: first, *denial* ("This can't be happening to *me*!"); second, *anger* ("Why me?"); third, *bargaining* ("God, if you let me live to see my daughter graduate, I won't ask for anything more"); fourth, *depression* ("I won't be able to do the things I had planned"); and fifth, *acceptance* ("My time is close now, and it's all right").

Dr. Kübler-Ross has made a major contribution to our understanding of the dying and our ability to help the terminally ill, but her stages are not invariant for all people and should not be held up as a criterion for a "good death." Some people, for example, deal best with death by denying it; others find release in raging against it; and others skip one or more stages on the way to acceptance. We need to respect individual "death styles" just as we do life styles.

Facing the Death of a Loved One In the United States, bereaved people have no universal mourning rites to help them express grief and provide a structure for a new life. Mourners are expected to be brave, suppress their tears, and get on with the business of living. Yet the bereaved need to express and deal with their feelings of loss before they can reorganize their lives.

Like any other life crisis, widowhood affects people differently, depending on personality, the quality of the marital relationship, and other elements in a widowed person's life. Adjustment is easier when there are friends to confide in, to be with, and to count on in time of trouble.

Normal grief often follows a fairly predictable pattern (Schulz, 1978). First, a few weeks after a death, survivors react with shock and disbelief. Second, as the fact of the loss sinks in, this initial numbness gives way to overwhelming sadness. Some people cry almost constantly; many suffer physical symptoms like insomnia, shortness of breath, and loss of appetite; some fear that they will have an emotional breakdown; some drink too much or sedate themselves with tranquilizers. Third, beginning about 3 weeks after the death, and continuing for about 1 year, survivors often relive the death in their minds, in an obsessive search for its meaning. They may hallucinate the presence of the dead person—seeing the face, hearing the voice. Fourth, at the start of the second year after the death, the survivors become more active socially, getting out more, seeing people, resuming their interests. At this point, survivors feel stronger, knowing that they have come through an ordeal.

When people react to loss with an initial sense of well-being and then show personality changes like generalized hostility or irritability, when they sink into a long-lasting depression, or when they develop major physical symptoms like asthma or colitis, they can often benefit from some kind of help in managing their grief. This help can come from nonprofessional organizations like Widow to Widow and (for parents whose children have died) Compassionate Friends, or from short-term psychotherapy.

Widowhood Three out of four women can expect to suffer one of life's severest traumas, the death of a spouse—an event that heads Holmes and Rahe's list of stressful life events (1976). About half of all women become widows before age 56, and about half afterward. Middle age is thus the time when women most often have to deal with this loss, and old age is the time when they integrate their widowed status into their day-to-day life (Balkwell, 1981).

In 1984, 67 percent of women 75 and older were widows; the same percentage of men of this age were married (U.S. Senate Special Committee on Aging, 1986). This huge disparity occurs because women live longer than men, usually marry older men, and are much less likely to remarry after a spouse's death than men are. Elderly widowers are seven times more likely to remarry than elderly widows, who find fewer men of their own age available and who rarely marry younger men.

What does widowhood mean for day-to-day life? Men are more likely than women to die from a "broken heart." In one study of 4486 widowers over age 55, the death rate during the 6 months following their wives' deaths was 40 percent above the expected rate, and most of the men had died of heart ailments (Parkes, Benjamin, & Fitzgerald, 1969). Women are more apt to suffer from disabling chronic conditions (Verbrugge, 1979). Both sexes have a higher rate of mental illness than their married counterparts (Balkwell, 1981).

Helena Lopata (1977, 1979) of Loyola University has done extensive research with more than 1000 widows and widowers. A major problem for both sexes is economic hardship. When the husband was the principal breadwinner, his widow is now deprived of his income. A widowed man, on the other hand, now has to buy many of the services his wife had provided. Even when both spouses were employed, the loss of one income is often major. The greatest problem, though, is still emotional. Even in a bad marriage, the survivor feels the loss. The role of spouse has been lost, social life has changed from couple-oriented friendships to associations with other single people, and the widowed no longer have the day-in, day-out companionship that had become a basic part of their lives.

People deal with these problems in various ways. Men usually remarry, and women usually become friendly with other widows. Few choose to live with their married children. Younger widows often feel more competent after they have made basic adjustments to their husbands' death and carved out a more independent life (Lopata, 1973).

Like any other life crisis, widowhood affects people in different ways, depending on their personalities, the quality of the marital relationship, and other elements in their lives (such as work, friendships, and financial assets). Married people can prepare themselves for the possibility of widowhood by gaining a strong sense of their own indentity and a sturdy measure of self-sufficiency. A woman is less likely to be devastated by the loss of her husband if, while he was alive, she pursued her own interests and assumed a large role in every aspect of family planning and management, including financial matters. A man will cope better if he is used to handling day-to-day household tasks like cooking simple meals, doing laundry, and making social arrangements. The resilience of the human spirit, even in old age, can be seen in the way so many people do cope with this major loss, and go on to reorganize their lives in the face of it.

As we have seen, all stages of the life span are important. Development winds continuously along the corridors of our lives as we take different directions to discover who we are and to give purpose to our quest. We never have all the answers to life's questions. Our days are illuminated by the search for them, and this search persists right up to the end of life.

SUMMARY

1 Adolescence begins with pubescence, when the sex organs mature and the secondary sex characteristics develop. Puberty is the point when the individual is sexually mature and able to reproduce. Menarche, the first menstrual period, signals sexual maturity for girls. The closest physiological counterpart for boys is the presence of sperm in the urine.

2 According to Jean Piaget, adolescents are in the stage of formal operations and display the ability to think abstractly. This cognitive ability is reflected in behaviors such as being critical of authority figures, argumentative, self-conscious, self-centered, indecisive, and hypocritical.

3 Lawrence Kohlberg sees moral development as related to cognitive development. Moral development progresses through three stages: preconventional morality, conventional role conformity, and autonomous moral principles.

4 Gilligan objects to Kohlberg's narrow definition of morality as the development of a sense of justice, believing that women tend to see morality in terms of responsibility to look out for others.

5 Erik Erikson describes the crisis of adolescence as identity versus role confusion, in which a person tries to find out "who I really am."

6 Although there is some conflict between adolescents and their parents, particularly about mundane matters, many adolescents have good relationships with their parents and do not feel alienated from them. "Adolescent rebellion" appears to be largely a myth.

7 Although many teenage students are working today, work does not seem to have any great benefit for their educational, social, or occupational development; and it appears to have a number of costs.

8 Although many adolescents are sexually active, their sexual behavior often occurs in the context of a relationship.

9 During young adulthood (20 to 40–45 years) and middle adulthood (40–45 to about 65 years), health and energy are generally quite good.

10 For women, menopause typically occurs at about age 50. Society's attitude toward aging women seems to have a more profound effect on women's reaction to menopause than actual hormone levels do. Males also experience some biological changes during midlife including decreased fertility, orgasm frequency, and potency.

11 Certain types of intelligence may continue to develop throughout life. While fluid intelligence begins a slow, steady decline during adulthood, crystallized intelligence stays the same or may improve. Practical intelligence appears to peak in midlife.

12 There is potential for personality growth in adulthood. While some aspects of personality appear to remain stable, other aspects change.

13 According to Erikson, intimacy versus isolation is the crisis of early adulthood, and generativity versus stagnation is the major crisis during midlife. The young adult must make a commitment to another or risk isolation, according to Erikson. The adult in midlife must deal with issues related to establishing and guiding the next generation.

14 Daniel Levinson has identified a number of age-related "stages" of adult development. According to Levinson, the goal of adult development is the evolution of a life structure, a pattern of life consisting of internal and external aspects. He sees adult development as consisting of alternating periods of stability and transition.

15 Clausen holds that adult development does not involve age-related periods of stability and transition. Rather, people change in small ways throughout life and make major transitions when necessary.

16 Psychologists are assessing the impact of work during adulthood. While Americans seem to value family roles over work roles, work is still a strong area of concern.

17 Most couples react to pregnancy with mixed emotions. Although effective means of birth control make parenthood more a matter of choice than it was in the past, most adults do have children and most parents find this a major source of satisfaction. However, when children are ready to leave home, parents typically do not find that the "empty nest" constitutes a crisis.

18 An adult's chronological age does not tell much about him or her. Biology shapes much of what happens during childhood, but culture and individual personality play a larger role in adult development. Individual differences are extensive in adulthood, particularly in old age. Senescence, the time when one grows old, begins at different ages for different people. Age 65 is typically designated as the beginning of old age, although there are wide individual differences among 65-year-olds.

19 A number of theories have been advanced for physical aging, including the theory that aging is programmed into every organism in some way and the theory that aging is a result of continual wear and tear on the body.

20 Sensory problems are quite common in old age, although many of them can be remedied.

21 The elderly can do many of the same things they did when they were younger, although they tend to do things more slowly.

22 Old age is not synonymous with sickness and disability, although chronic conditions do affect more than 80 percent of the elderly.

23 Dementia, the physical and mental deterioration experienced by about 1 in 10 people over 65, is not universal. Most cases of dementia are caused by Alzheimer's disease, a progressive, incurable condition whose cause is not yet known. Other causes of dementia—for example, a series of small strokes, overmedication, depression, underlying disease, and difficulty in adjusting to social change—can often be prevented or treated.

24 Generalized intellectual deterioration is not an inevitable part of old age. Although elderly people may not perform as well as younger adults, older people's performance may not reflect their true intellectual capacity. Poor performance may be due to impaired sight or hearing, anxi-

ety, or lack of motivation. A number of attempts to improve older people's intellectual performance through "training" have been successful.

25 Erikson sees the life crisis of old age as the establishment of ego integrity, which is dependent on accepting the life one has lived. A person who cannot do this faces overwhelming despair, since it is now too late to start over.

26 Two important theories of successful aging are activity theory and disengagement theory. Activity theory holds that the more active older persons remain, the more fulfilled they will be. Disengagement theory maintains that successful aging involves a normal "mutual withdrawal" of an old person and society. Research indicates that there is no one pattern of successful aging. Different people adapt in different ways.

27 Good health and an adequate income are two important factors in adjustment to retirement.

28 American society has hated to talk about death; but recently there has been an increased interest in death and a healthier attitude toward it.

29 People's attitudes toward, and understanding of, death change throughout life.

30 Elisabeth Kübler-Ross suggests that people go through five stages in dealing with their own death: denial, anger, bargaining, depression, and acceptance.

31 Immediately after the death of a loved one, survivors often react with shock, disbelief, numbness, and sadness. This initial reaction may be followed by an attempt to give the death meaning, and by a feeling that the dead person is still there. After about a year, the survivor may become more active, feeling a sense of strength.

32 Widowhood will be experienced by most American women: half become widows by age 56. Widowhood affects people differently, depending on such factors as personality, life circumstances, and the quality of the marital relationship.

KEY TERMS

Activity theory (page 370)
Alzheimer's disease (366)
Climacteric (355)
Crystallized intelligence (356)
Dementia (366)
Disengagement theory (370)

Ego integrity versus despair (368)
Empty nest (363)
Fluid intelligence (356)
Formal operations (345)
Generativity versus stagnation (358)

Identity versus role confusion (347)
Imaginary audience (345)
Intimacy versus isolation (358)
Life structure (359)
Menarche (344)

Menopause (355)
Personal fable (345)
Puberty (343)
Pubescence (343)
Senescence (364)
Thanatology (372)

SUGGESTED READINGS

BARUCH, G., BARNETT, R., & RIVERS, C. (1983). *Lifeprints*. New York: McGraw-Hill. On the basis of their research with 35- to 55-year-old women, the authors explore factors in women's happiness and self-esteem, emphasizing the dual elements of work and family.

COLES, R. (1986). *The moral life of children*. Boston: Atlantic Monthly. A prominent child psychiatrist offers his rebuttal to the Kohlbergian theory that moral development rests on cognitive development and that schoolchildren are too young to live moral lives. Contains many moving quotations from children discussing morality in their own experience.

CSIKSZENTMIHALYI, M., & LARSON, R. (1984). *Being adolescent: Conflict and growth in the teenage years*. New York: Basic Books. A detailed portrait of the day-to-day world of typical middle-class teenagers: what they do, how they feel, and what they think about. A readable account of what it's like to be an adolescent.

ELKIND, D. (1984). *All grown up and no place to go*. Reading, MA: Addison-Wesley. A thought-provoking book about the difficulties involved in being and raising teenagers today. Elkind argues that today's teens are unprepared to face adult challenges at an early age, resulting in many problem behaviors. The chapter relating formal operational thinking to behaviors such as self-centeredness, self-consciousness, and argumentativeness is outstanding.

GILLIGAN, C. (1982). *In a different voice*. Cambridge, MA: Harvard University Press. A discussion of the misrepresentation of women by the major theorists in developmental psychology, with an emphasis on women's moral development.

GREENBERGER, E., & STEINBERG, L. (1986). *When teenagers work*. New York: Basic Books. An absorbing and controversial analysis of research on the impact that working has on teenagers. The authors conclude that working during the teen years entails a number of hidden costs that affect development negatively.

HERR, J. J., & WEAKLAND, J. H. (1979). *Counseling elders and their families*. New York: Springer. A practical guide to the problems of the elderly. Written primarily for health professionals, but other readers will also find this a useful aid in problem solving.

KÜBLER-ROSS, E. (1969). *On death and dying*. New York: Macmillan. A moving book that inspired a new interest in death. The author draws upon case studies and actual dialogues with dying patients to back up her pioneering concept that there are five stages in dying.

LEVINSON, D. J., DARROW, C. N., KLEIN, E. B., LEVINSON, M. H., & McKEE, B. (1978). *The seasons of a man's life*. New York: Ballantine. A detailed report of this research team's findings about male development from early adulthood through middle age. Highly readable, with interesting case histories. The authors propose a number of theoretical concepts that guide adult development.

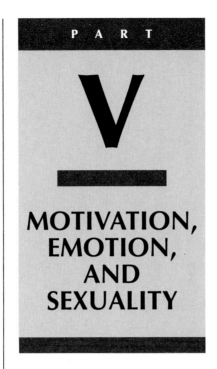

V

MOTIVATION, EMOTION, AND SEXUALITY

The links between body and mind become especially clear when we talk about the forces that motivate us toward certain behaviors. A major element of motivation lies in the way we feel emotionally in any given situation. Both motivation and the emotions affect and are affected by our maleness or femaleness.

■ In *Chapter 11,* "Motivation and Emotion," we delve into the complexities of motivation, and how it affects our day-to-day lives, especially with regard to eating, achievement, aggression, curiosity, and arousal. We look at some of the theories proposed to explain why some people behave one way and others another, or why the same person acts differently in different situations. We describe basic emotional states and some of the theories that explain why they occur and how they affect us.

■ We then bring together in one chapter many aspects of a subject that has been a major focus of study by motivational researchers—our sexual drive and our gender roles. In *Chapter 12,* "Sexuality and Gender Roles," we look at the many ways our biological sex and our culture's attitudes toward sex and gender affect our lives. We look at differences and similarities between the sexes, and we explore physical and social influences on them. These issues are especially relevant today, in light of recent societal changes that have blurred traditional gender roles and altered our thinking about sexuality.

C H A P T E R

11

MOTIVATION AND EMOTION

- ■ Do human beings have instincts?

- ■ How do physiological drives, learning, the need for stimulation, the desire for self-actualization, and cognitive factors motivate behaviors?

- ■ Why do people get hungry, and why do they eat (especially too much)?

- ■ How do biological and environmental factors influence aggressive behavior?

- ■ Is there a need to achieve?

- ■ How important is level of arousal in motivating behavior?

- ■ What is the experience of emotion?

- ■ Are emotions inborn?

- ■ What comes first, thinking or feeling?

Why was I gasping for breath, my teeth chattering, in freezing water? Why was I struggling to stay relatively horizontal with my feet in front of me, when they seemed to want to point downward to make me vertical? Why indeed? I was on a rafting trip on the Colorado River, where I had been enjoying riding the rapids on the snout of our polypropylene raft, getting that sudden splash of icy water, being carried up on the crest of a wave before being plunged down into its trough. Between the rapids I reveled in the magnificence of the Grand Canyon, whose ages-old majestic rock formations could be appreciated as they could not from the summit.

Now, though, I was swimming Fishtail Rapid even though I was neither a strong swimmer nor a lover of icy water. My life vest was keeping me afloat, and I was too busy concentrating on avoiding the rocks and breathing while being tossed about by the waves to think about the coldness of the water. I got a little nervous when our guide told me to swim to the right below the rapid, and I was having trouble battling the current. I finally made it and clung for dear life to a rock until our raft caught up with me and a couple of pairs of strong arms pulled me aboard. Then I was absolutely euphoric, having conquered my initial fear of jumping in, and I could hardly wait for the next swimmable rapid.

When my husband and I returned to New York, friends asked us why we had paid as much money to fly west, camp out by a riverbank, eat peanut butter sandwiches for lunch, and alternate between sweltering under the Arizona sun and shivering in the frigid water as they had paid to luxuriate in a resort where their every wish was catered to. Today, 9 years after that rafting trip, it still stands out as a high point in my life.

What explains why one person tries to keep life as comfortable and risk-free as possible, why another (like me) is exhilarated by small amounts of risk and discomfort, and why a third sets out to scale a Himalayan peak, even though there is a 1 in 10 risk of dying and an even greater risk of losing a finger or toe to frostbite? What accounts for people's decisions on leisure activities, career goals, personal habits, choices of friends and lovers—the whole range of behaviors we engage in?

—From the notebooks of Sally Olds

Almost as soon as we begin to put sentences together, we start to ask, "Why?" Aside from wondering why the world is as it is—an aspect of curiosity that spurs scientists, artists, explorers, and others to do their finest work—most of us spend a great deal of time wondering why we and those around us behave in certain ways. Why, for example, did you eat that second doughnut this morning after you had resolved to lose 10 pounds? Why did your roommate spend so many hours on a homework assignment for a one-credit course? Why are you sexually attracted to someone who doesn't seem to know you're alive, and why can't you work up any enthusiasm at all for someone who's obviously crazy about you? Why might a mugger not only steal your wallet, but cruelly beat you for no apparent purpose?

When we ask questions like these, we're asking about **motivation,** the force that energizes behavior, gives direction to behavior, and underlies the tendency to persist. This definition of motivation recognizes that in order to achieve goals, people must be sufficiently aroused and energetic, must have a clear focus, and must be able and willing to commit their energy for a long enough period of time to fulfill their aim.

A major element in motivation is the way we feel. Our **emotions** are subjective reactions to our environment that are accompanied by neural and hormonal responses; they are considered adaptive reactions that affect the way we think and are generally experienced as either pleasant or unpleasant. Often emotions do motivate us, but emotion and motivation don't always overlap. Emotions are often inner-directed, whereas motivation is goal-directed. Furthermore, there are many times when we may be motivated in particular directions without feeling emotional. Still, the two areas are linked. We act quite differently toward someone we trust than toward someone we're afraid of, and we respond to incidents differently when we're feeling cheerful than when we're feeling sad or angry. In other words, our emotional states often affect (motivate) our behavior.

It's often hard to distinguish between motivation and emotion, then, since the two are so closely linked. We often do things because they make us feel good and avoid doing things that make us feel bad. Sometimes, however, we do things even though we know they'll make us unhappy and we don't do things even though we think they'd make us happy. Researchers are beginning to be able to explain such paradoxes, especially when they focus on people's reactions to stress (see Chapter 16) and on the emotional disturbance of depression (see Chapter 14).

If you've ever wondered why people endanger their own lives to save strangers, eat themselves into obesity or starve themselves to death, fly into a jealous rage, torture people who've done them no harm, become addicted to drugs, become "workaholics," climb forbidding mountains, or set out for unexplored territory, then you've asked some of the same questions posed by motivation and emotion researchers. Some of the major issues that confront human beings have aroused so much interest that entire fields of study have grown up around them, many of which are treated in other sections of this book.

In this chapter we'll concentrate on only a few of these topics—hunger and eating, aggression, achievement, curiosity, and arousal. We'll look at the way researchers study the motivational and emotional factors associated with them, the way various components of motivation and emotion contribute to our behavior in these areas, theories that have been developed to explain motivation and emotion, and questions that still persist. Although there will be some overlap in our discussion of these two important phenomena in our lives, after a brief look at what determines them we'll be treating them separately: first we'll take up *why* we do what we do, and then *how* we feel.

DETERMINANTS OF MOTIVATION AND EMOTION ▮▮▮▮▮▮

Both motivation and emotions are influenced by three kinds of factors—biological, learned, and cognitive. The way we eat, for example, is determined by a combination of the bodily sensations of hunger caused by our need for food (a biological factor); our preference for, say, steak over fried ants (a learned factor); and our knowledge about the nutrients in various kinds of foods, which might lead us to choose milk over a soda (a cognitive factor). In asking why people behave as they do, we need to look at each of these components.

Emotional states like fear, anger, and excitement are characterized by such

Motivation *General term for the force responsible for arousal, direction, and persistence of behavior.*

Emotion *General term for a person's subjective reaction to the environment. Emotions involve neural and hormonal responses. When activated, emotions elicit an adaptive reaction that the individual experiences as pleasant or unpleasant.*

physiological signals as a rapid heartbeat and breathing rate, high blood pressure, and a flushing of the skin. Such changes are apparently caused by the activation of certain parts of the brain and the production of various hormones in the body. Emotions also have their learned and cognitive aspects, which contribute to the differences in the ways different people react to the same experiences. While one person may feel a thrill while diving off a high board, another is terrified by the very idea of going into deep water. Sometimes we respond to our feelings unthinkingly (screaming, crying, laughing, or running away), and sometimes we respond in ways that we've learned are appropriate (climbing a tree to get away from a bear or counting to 10 to prevent an angry outburst). Sometimes we label ambiguous feelings with the names of emotions that we think are pertinent to the situation. In the end, the combination of our biological, learned, and cognitive reactions affects both the way we think about the world around us and the way we act (Kleinginna & Kleinginna, 1981).

MOTIVATION ■■■■■■■■■■■■■■■■■■■■■

Theories of Motivation

Psychologists have developed a number of different theories about why we behave the way we do, and have followed different approaches to try to confirm or refute them. In this section we'll discuss some of the most important theories, ranging from early approaches focusing on instinct to contemporary cognitive models.

Instinct Theories   Birds don't stop to consider different possible ways to build a nest; those of any particular species all build their nests the same way. Ants don't think about how to get food; they carry out the same kind of food-gathering behavior that goes on in every other anthill populated by the same species. Behaviors like these are *instincts:* genetically programmed, inborn behaviors that occur in all members of a species and require no learning. Some of the oldest theories of motivation attributed human behavior to instincts.

Instinct Inborn, species-specific, relatively complex pattern of behavior that is biologically determined and usually important for the survival of a species.

Among lower-order animals, instincts are manifested in relatively complex patterns, like building nests, gathering food, and hibernating. The wide acceptance of Charles Darwin's theory that human beings evolved from lower animals provided a hospitable climate for talking about instincts in humans, especially toward the end of the nineteenth century and the beginning of the twentieth. William McDougall, an important early theorist who believed that *all* behaviors were instinctive, developed long lists of instincts, citing such traits as curiosity, gregariousness, and the care parents give their children.

Why didn't these early instinct approaches hold up? First, there was no general agreement about the basis for determining which behaviors should be considered instincts—that is, for distinguishing among reflexes, instincts, and learned behaviors. Thus, theorists disagreed about how many instincts existed and what they were. Second, if a behavior is instinctive, all members of a species should exhibit it. This is not the case with human behavior, and instinct theorists had no explanation for individual differences among cultures and people. Finally, labeling something an instinct only describes but does not explain it (Petri, 1986).

Ethologist Scientist who studies behavior in its natural environment.

Still, instinct theories have come into fashion again from time to time. Today, *ethologists* (biologists who study behavior in natural settings, primarily among animals) have revived interest in the possibility of human instincts. They point, for example, to facial expressions that are found among people in many different cultures, such as the "eyebrow flick" (see Figure 11-1). However, even though some behaviors may stem from genetic programming, the concept of instinct is still far too narrow to account for all human motivation.

FIGURE 11-1 *Eyebrow flick. A brief lifting of the eyebrows, usually accompanied by a smile, is a greeting signal which shows recognition and may also indicate that there is no intention to harm. Because it appears in many different cultures, ethologists suggest that it may be instinctive. Here it is shown by a Balinese (left) and a Papuan (right). The picture at the left in each pair is before recognition; the picture at the right, after recognition. (Source: Eibl-Eibesfeldt, 1971/1972.)*

Drive Theories SIGMUND FREUD: UNCONSCIOUS MOTIVATORS Freud's complex theories are discussed in detail in Chapter 13. Here we'll mention only his concept that unconscious forces motivate much human behavior (Freud, 1915/1949a). The two types of forces that he proposed—life *(eros)* and death *(thanatos)*—are often referred to as instincts but are more properly considered **drives,** forces within an organism that motivate behavior. Eros includes reproductive and sexual urges, and thanatos includes aggressive forces. There are problems with the Freudian view: it is hard to verify through research and hard to predict behavior from it. But the idea that much behavior is unconsciously motivated is important.

Drive *Force inside an organism that motivates behavior.*

CLARK HULL: DRIVE-REDUCTION MODEL Clark Hull's theory of "drive reduction" is the most important of the American drive theories (Hull, 1943). According to Hull, a physiological need, such as hunger or thirst, creates an undesirable state in the body of a person or animal. An individual with this need is in a state of tension and is motivated to reduce the tension by fulfilling the need.

Drive theory is related to the concept of balance within the body. According to the principle of homeostasis (explained in Chapter 2), the body is self-regulating; when changes move vital functions out of some optimal range, there are mechanisms that return it to a balanced state. When the body is not at an optimal level in some way (when it is hungry, thirsty, or tired, for example), the appropriate drive is activated and the animal or person tries to bring the body back into balance (by getting food, liquid, or rest). Whatever helps the organism achieve this is reinforced, is learned, and is then repeated when the need recurs. (Suppose a raccoon, driven by hunger, happens to find food in a garbage can. If this occurs on several occasions, the raccoon will learn to seek out garbage cans whenever it is hungry.) Drive theories hold that reducing the drive brings about learning.

Hull believed that some human behavior stemmed from inborn drives reflecting basic biological needs ("primary drives") and that other drives developed from experience ("secondary" or "acquired" drives). An example of a learned secondary drive is "little Albert's" acquired fear of furry animals (discussed in Chapter 5).

Why did drive theory fall out of favor? For one thing, it didn't take into account the thinking that underlies much human behavior. For another, it didn't account for activities that increase tension (like Sally Olds's rafting trip). Nor did it account for the kind of motivation that leads us to drink, not to reduce thirst, but because we're at a party where everyone is holding a glass; or to raid the refrigerator, not because we're hungry, but because we've just seen a mouth-watering commercial. Learning theories that emphasize rewards and punishment and learning by observation (described in Chapter 5) help to explain this kind of behavior.

Opponent-Process Theory: Sensory Stimulation Human beings (like some of our relatives in the animal kingdom) seem to need a certain amount of stimulation. We're curious, we need to explore our environments, we need to change our lives in

Opponent-process theory
Explanation, proposed by Solomon, that an initial state will be opposed by an opposite reaction in the central nervous system that reduces the intensity of the first state and produces its opposite. Thus, an initially negative state will be followed by a positive state, and vice versa.

some way on a fairly regular basis. As we'll see later in the chapter, we generally perform at our best when we are moderately aroused, although individuals vary, some needing more arousal and some less. We also need different amounts of arousal at different times and with regard to different tasks. A high enough level of stimulation seems critical for normal functioning.

The **opponent-process theory** aims to explain the process by which various stimuli affect the brain. Richard Solomon and his colleagues propose that an initial state will be opposed by an opposite reaction in the central nervous system that reduces the intensity of the first state (Hoffman & Solomon, 1974; Solomon, 1980; Solomon & Corbit, 1974). In other words, if something feels very good (like taking an addictive drug), then, after long enough use, an unpleasant state will occur when the user stops taking it. Now the person continues to use the substance not for the pleasure it brings, but to avoid an unpleasant state (such as the severe discomfort of withdrawal symptoms) (Siegel, Sherman, & Mitchell, 1980).

Contrariwise, some activities that arouse negative feelings at the beginning end up by making people feel good. For example, people who participate in a high-risk sport like parachuting, or people who donate blood, at first experience fear and anxiety (negative emotions). But the more often they jump from an airplane or give blood, the more positive are the feelings surrounding the activity. And the parachutist's exhilaration and sense of competence or the blood donor's sense of having helped someone in need is felt as even more positive because the initial feelings were so negative (Piliavin, Callero, & Evans, 1982).

Abraham Maslow's Theory: Hierarchy of Needs   If you are gasping for air or suffering from starvation, you have one overriding motivation—basic survival. Not until that is ensured can you turn your attention to other concerns, which may be those of safety—freedom, say, from fear and pain. Feeling relatively safe, you can then seek intimacy in your relationships with family, friends, and lover. Once comfortably nurtured by affectionate ties with other people, you can focus on meeting your need for self-respect. Then, when you feel healthy, safe, loved, and competent, you can seek the self-actualization that comes from pursuit of knowledge, appreciation of beauty, playfulness, self-sufficiency, insight into truth, and other growth-producing values.

Self-actualization   *Self-fulfillment.*

This is the theory of motivation proposed by the humanistic psychologist Abraham Maslow (1954/1970). Maslow envisions a *hierarchy of needs,* leading up to the satisfaction of the highest need, the need for **self-actualization,** or self-fulfillment. Before people can meet this need (called a "being" need), they need to meet other, lower-level "deprivation" needs, such as physiological requirements (like food or air), safety, "belongingness" (through love, work, or group participation), and self-esteem (see Figure 11-2). Maslow did not regard the hierarchy as totally rigid; he maintained that higher needs can become active even if lower needs are only partially satisfied.

This theory explains certain behaviors, but it is also open to criticism. For one thing, the progression does not necessarily go in order for all people all the time. History is full of accounts of self-sacrifice, in which people have given up what they need for survival so that another (a loved one or even a complete stranger) might live. For another, it is hard to test the theory, since the people Maslow studied as self-actualized persons were either people he knew personally who remained anonymous or historical figures who were dead. Finally, Maslow himself stated that most people do *not* become self-actualized. A theory that does not apply to most people has limited usefulness.

Cognitive Theories   If a strange woman steps on my toe, I can interpret the action in several different ways: she's doing it on purpose, she's drunk, she's clumsy, or she's disabled. The interpretation I choose affects the way I'll act—whether I'll snarl, move away, smile reassuringly, or try to help her. According to one cognitive ap-

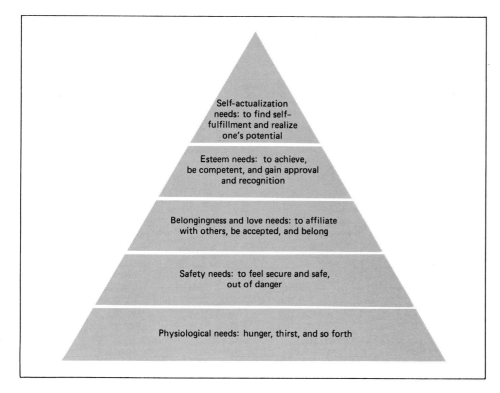

FIGURE 11-2 *Maslow's hierarchy of needs. According to Maslow, human needs have different priorities. First comes survival, represented by the needs at the base of the pyramid. Starving people will take great risks to obtain food; once they know that they will not die of starvation, they have the luxury of worrying about their personal safety. Then, needs for security must be met, at least in part, before people can even think about meeting their needs for love. As each succeeding layer of needs is addressed, says Maslow, a person is motivated to look to the needs at the next higher step, until he or she achieves the highest level of being, self-actualization.*

proach, the way we respond to events depends on how we *interpret* them (how we think about them).

A second cognitive approach stresses the way we think about *goals* as a major motivating factor. **Incentives,** for example, are external, learned goals that motivate behavior. Incentives differ from person to person and from time to time within the same person. Your desire to become a psychologist may be the incentive that has led you to take this course. Your wish to get a high grade-point average may be the incentive that leads you to take careful notes on your class lectures. If your career goal changes, however, and you decide you'd rather be a guitarist in a rock band, your behavior in psychology class may change because your incentive has changed. (But musicians can benefit, too, from knowing about psychology!) The important things to remember about incentives are that they are learned products of your thinking processes and that they can change.

Incentives *External, learned goals that motivate behavior.*

A third cognitive approach stresses the importance of *expectations* in motivating behavior. This is an essential element in the concept of **locus of control.** People who have an *internal* locus of control believe that they are responsible for what happens to them; people who have an *external* locus of control believe that outside factors (like luck) are responsible (Rotter, 1966, 1975). Thus, if you attribute doing well on a test to your own ability and to the time and effort you spent in preparation, you probably have a sense that you're in control of your life, a feeling that is associated with high self-esteem and achievement. If you attribute it to luck, you probably believe that your life is controlled by fate, other people, or some other force.

Locus of control *Concept that explains events according to whether they result from efforts under one's control (internal) or from outside factors over which one has no control (external).*

Each of the theories of motivation has something to offer, since motivation is multidimensional; but no one theory can account for the motivation of all behavior. In animals a number of behaviors seem to be determined by instincts that are programmed into the genes, but very few human behaviors can be explained this way. Physiology plays a role in human motivation, especially with regard to such basic need states as hunger and thirst, but learning, too, plays a role in when and how we'll satisfy these needs. Learning plays a critical role in the development of new

An apple a day can help keep the pounds away. Since fruits increase insulin levels for only a short time, they can satisfy hunger without making us want to eat again soon. Sweets, however, keep insulin levels higher for longer periods of time, often making us hungry again soon after eating.

motives (like acquired fear) and in determining the incentives (goals) that motivate behavior. As Freud pointed out, much of our behavior seems to be motivated by factors we are not consciously aware of. We may, for example, not be aware of the need for certain levels of sensory stimulation, which we maintain by exploring our world. After we meet our most basic goal, we can pursue higher-level incentives and goals, possibly culminating in self-actualization. Finally, such cognitive factors as our thoughts and expectations and our sense of control over our lives affect motivation.

Now let's turn to several specific areas of behavior that are often studied by motivation researchers—hunger and eating; aggression; achievement; and arousal, curiosity, and boredom. (We'll discuss ramifications of sexual motivation in Chapter 12.)

Hunger and Eating

Most of us tend to take for granted the daily, life-sustaining activity of eating; but food means more than fuel for the body. Virtually every society has developed rituals revolving around food. Food may symbolize love, social bonding, and affluence. The way we eat may reflect our attitudes toward ourselves, our families, and our society. Let's look at the various components driving us to the dinner table, the snack bar, or the four-star restaurant.

How the Body Regulates Hunger How does our body tell us that we want or need food? It seems to do so in two different ways. Short-term regulation controls food intake from meal to meal or from day to day. Long-term regulation, on the other hand, controls body weight, which for most people remains quite stable over time. Both types of regulation depend on homeostasis, with short-term regulation seeming to center on levels of glucose (sugar) in the blood and long-term regulation on body stores of fat.

SHORT-TERM REGULATION One cause of hunger (or more precisely, for most of us, appetite) seems to be a low level of glucose in the blood. Glucose is an important source of energy; when levels are too low, specialized body cells detect an imbalance and send signals that motivate us to eat. More than 50 years ago, researchers manipulated blood glucose levels in dogs by transfusing blood from a starved dog to one that had just eaten, and vice versa (Templeton & Quigley, 1930). When the blood from the hungry dog was given to the recently fed dog, it developed stomach contractions even though its stomach was full; and when blood from the dog that had just eaten was given to a hungry dog, the stomach contractions of the hungry dog stopped. The unfed dog did eat, however, as soon as food was available.

These findings have been complemented by research with people who have diabetes, a disorder caused by a disturbance of the body's mechanism for producing insulin, a necessary hormone that converts blood glucose and carbohydrates into energy. Since diabetics don't produce enough of their own insulin, they either inject it or take it orally. After taking insulin, they experience stomach contractions and feelings of hunger (Goodner & Russell, 1965). Since insulin tends to be secreted whenever glucose levels increase, it has been difficult to conclude whether hunger is caused by changes in levels of glucose or insulin. Recently, research that manipulated the two independently found that hunger follows changes in insulin rather than glucose (Rodin, 1983).

One implication of this finding is that eating can prime us to become hungry! When we begin to eat, our insulin levels rise, explaining why we may be more hungry *after* snacking on a candy bar than we were *before* we ate it. Sugar, which leads to increased glucose in the blood, raises our insulin levels more than many other foods; furthermore, it keeps insulin levels higher for longer periods of time. Therefore, eating sweets often makes us hungry again after a short period of time. On the other hand, fruits, which contain the "fruit sugar" fructose, increase insulin levels for only short periods of time. Thus, fruits can satisfy hunger without making us want to eat again soon (Rodin, 1983).

LONG-TERM REGULATION: SET-POINT THEORY   Most of us tend to reach a certain body weight, and to stay close to that weight for a long time, with minor fluctuations. This may be because we're equipped with a *set point,* a mechanism that maintains an individual's usual weight. The set point controls body fat the way a thermostat keeps room temperature at a certain level. It varies from person to person, so that two people of the same height may be "programmed" at different body weights.

Set point   *Mechanism that maintains an individual's usual weight.*

   Research with rats suggests that such a mechanism may be located in the hypothalamus. When surgical lesions are made in one site in the hypothalamus (the *ventromedial nuclei*), rats tend to become obese. They don't eat until they burst, but they do put on weight until they reach some new maximum level, and then they reduce their food intake and maintain their weight. When rats are lesioned at another site (the *lateral hypothalamus*), they tend to stop eating. If they are force-fed subsistence-level diets for 2 or 3 weeks, they begin to eat again and maintain the low weight they have dropped to. (If they were not force-fed, they would die.) These two hypothalamic sites—the ventromedial nucleus and the lateral hypothalamus—may work together to determine an individual's set point (Keesey & Powley, 1975). The way these sites affect appetite is shown in Figure 11-3.

   According to set-point theory, some people have higher set points than others. When people fall below their set points, as by dieting, they feel deprived and eat more. This explains why some people gain more after going off a diet that was temporarily successful (Bennett & Gurin, 1982).

   What accounts for individual differences in set points? Recent research in Denmark suggests that we may inherit our set points—that heredity, not environment, plays the main and perhaps the only role in determining whether we'll be fat or thin (Stunkard et al., 1986; see Chapter 16).

   Other research, however, suggests that environment does play a part and that set points can be raised or lowered. People who exercise daily often eat less than people who are less active, suggesting that physical activity may alter the *basal metabolism rate,* which controls the amount of energy the body expends while at

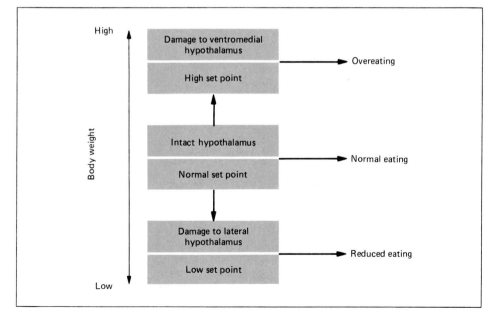

FIGURE 11-3   *Damage (or lesions) to the ventromedial hypothalamus will raise the set point; damage (or lesions) to the lateral hypothalamus will lower the set point.*

rest. The more energy we expend, the more calories we use up (Thompson, Jarvie, Lahey, & Cureton, 1982). Also, when people diet often but keep regaining the weight they have lost (the "yo-yo syndrome"), their metabolism seems to change so that they put on weight more easily with the same caloric intake (Kolata, 1986).

There is also research indicating that the fat cells of people who become overweight or obese are more numerous than those in people of normal weight—and larger, because they are filled with more fat. When a fat cell gets larger, it can store more fat and become larger still (Salans, Knittle, & Hirsch, 1968). This may have some effect on the set point.

Why We Eat the Way We Do   Let's look at some of the theories that seek to explain eating patterns, especially *overeating* patterns.

PREPARATION FOR FAMINE   Some theorists look to our early evolutionary history to explain the inability of many people to control their food intake, holding that the tendency to retain fat was originally adaptive. At one time, human beings didn't have a dependable food supply and would go for long periods of time on a subsistence level before having the chance to eat their fill. To deal with periodic food shortages, they developed the capacity to store energy in the form of fat. When a large animal was killed, they would gorge themselves on it and put on extra weight, which would sustain them over a time of scarcity.

Beta-endorphin, a chemical linked to the conservation and expenditure of energy, may be responsible for this kind of fat storage, according to a group of researchers who have shown that genetically obese mice have high beta-endorphin levels (Margules, Moisset, Lewis, Shibuya, & Pert, 1978). Since recent work with humans has failed to find a direct link between beta-endorphin levels and obesity, however (O'Brien, Stunkard, & Ternes, 1982), the evidence for this theory is far from conclusive.

ENJOYMENT OF SENSORY QUALITIES OF FOOD   One reason for eating is the sensuous pleasure it gives us. We like biting into and chewing a tender steak, we like the crispness of a fresh salad, we like the rich flavor of a chocolate mousse. Humans and most animals seem to be born with a preference for sweet foods. Rats will learn to press a bar to get the sweet taste of a nonnutritive food additive like saccharin, and human beings often select sweet foods over others that have more nutritive values (Nisbett, 1968).

We receive pleasant sensations of taste and texture via nerves that link receptors in the mouth to the lateral hypothalamus. When one of these nerves was cut in a group of rats, they stopped eating (Zeigler, 1973, 1975), probably because they got no more pleasure from their food than you would if your meals consisted of a tasteless semiliquid. One reason for the success of commercial liquid diet preparations is their uninteresting blandness. In one experiment, when obese people were told they could eat all they wanted of such a substance, their calorie intake dropped from about 3000 calories a day down to 500, while the intake of normal subjects on this kind of diet continued at about 2400 calories a day (Hashim & Van Itallie, 1965); see Figure 11-4. This isn't a practical solution for obesity, since we can't control the environment of most fat people, but it does demonstrate the seductive qualities of appealing food. It also raises the question of the different ways that people react to food, suggesting that taste and texture are more important factors for obese people than for people of normal weight.

LEARNED CUES FOR EATING   Do you ever look at your watch and, after finding out what time it is, decide that you're hungry? Do you eat more popcorn when the bowl is on your desk than when it's in the other room? Do you eat more when you're the guest of an unusually good cook than you do at home? If your answer to any of these

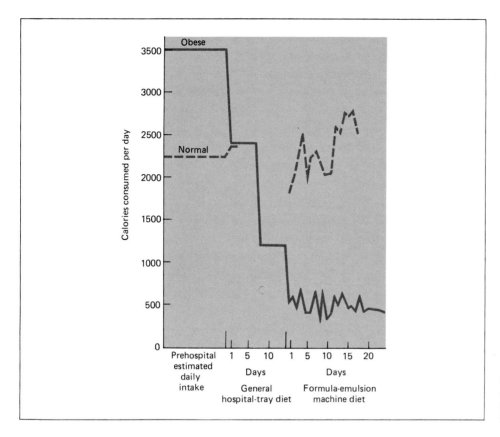

FIGURE 11-4 *Effect of a formula-emulsion diet on the eating behavior of a normal subject and an obese subject. (Source: Schachter, 1971.)*

questions is *yes,* you're responding to *external* rather than *internal* cues for eating. Internal cues are those that originate within our bodies—stomach contractions, low blood glucose or insulin levels, or any other indication that we require nourishment. External cues are those outside our bodies, such as time of day, ads and commercials, sensory qualities of food, or simply availability of food; they are factors in the environment that we have learned to associate with eating.

After conducting a series of experiments in which he found that overweight people ate more or less food than people of normal weight did in response to various external cues, Stanley Schachter concluded that obese people are more influenced by external cues and people of normal weight by internal ones (Goldman, Jaffa, & Schachter, 1968; Schachter, 1971; Schachter & Gross, 1968). He found, for example, that obese people ate more than people of normal weight when they were in a room with a clock set to show that it was close to dinnertime, and they ate less food when they had to expend effort (by shelling nuts, for example). Then Judith Rodin (1981) found that "externals" (people who eat more in response to external cues) show a large insulin reaction when presented with a sizzling steak, whereas "internals" do not.

There may be a physiological difference between "external" and "internal" eaters, but follow-up research has not been able to replicate Schachter's findings to differentiate between normal and overweight people (Rodin, 1981). Many people of normal weight are also affected by external cues, but they do not overeat. Still, the management of external cues is the basis for many behavior modification approaches to dieting. If you're an "external" eater but you can change your environment so that it presents you with fewer cues for eating, you'll be likely to eat less. Some basic guidelines for putting this into practice, along with other findings about eating and weight, are given in the box "Losing Weight by Applying Psychological Principles" in Chapter 16.

Aggression

The tiny town of Old Snake River, Texas, seems like an unlikely spot for an epidemic of violence. Yet within one year, one woman killed her husband, who had frequently beaten her; another woman killed her husband while he was talking on the phone to his girlfriend; a third woman killed her teenage son; and a fourth woman was raped and murdered. In response, almost the entire population of 200 in Old Snake River armed itself against "undesirable outsiders," creating, of course, the danger of more violent attacks among neighbors and relatives (Strasser, 1984).

Aggression—any behavior intended to hurt or destroy someone or something—is all around us. In most places around the world, not least in the United States, aggression often explodes into **violence,** destructive action against people or property. At times, however, the aggressive impulse is confined to competition, verbal attack, or some other expression of hostility short of physical injury. When we talk about aggression, we are talking about behavior that is meant to do harm. (There's also a definition of *aggressiveness,* which incorporates competitiveness and assertiveness and does not involve inflicting injury, but in this discussion we will focus on the definition of *aggression* above.)

Scientists have offered a variety of explanations for aggressive behavior—inherited tendencies, the results of experience and learning, and an interaction between these two major forces. By and large, it looks as if we are born with a predisposition toward aggressiveness, and then we learn when we should express this tendency and when we should inhibit it.

Do We Inherit a Tendency toward Aggression?

In view of the widespread appearance of aggression among nonhuman animals, some sociobiologists suggest that it's adaptive behavior that has developed over the course of evolution (Barash, 1977). Animals threaten or attack other animals whenever they compete for any commodity in short supply, such as food, space, or a mate; when they're in pain or discomfort; when they're frustrated in reaching some goal; when they're up against a competitor they have a chance of defeating; and when strangers appear. Human beings often become aggressive under similar circumstances.

The ethologist Konrad Lorenz (1966) has proposed that an aggressive *instinct* exists in all animals, including humans, as a genetically determined, inevitable trait. The anthropologist J. Robin Fox (1983) suggests that human beings are "wired" for aggression—that the drive is an essential and functional part of the organism and is always available. It can be easily turned on, and it can also be turned off when the expression of aggression might interfere with some other goal. However, the fact that some cultures and some individuals in every culture show practically no aggression while others show a great deal suggests that although we may inherit the tendency to act aggressively, other factors determine to what extent we will express aggressive behavior.

Is There a Biological Basis for Aggression?

A biological basis for aggression, or at least a predisposition toward it, is indicated by a considerable body of research. Certain brain structures are implicated in the regulation of aggression. Electrical stimulation of certain areas of cats' brains causes normally nonaggressive cats to attack rats, even if the cats are busy eating at the time (Roberts & Kiess, 1964). Different brain structures are involved in the expression of different types of aggression, such as rage, attack, predatory behavior, and defensive behavior (Moyer, 1976). In some instances lesions of the brain may be involved, as in the case of Charles Whitman, who went on a shooting spree in Texas in 1966—a tumor of the temporal lobes was probably the cause of his sudden violence (Johnson, 1972). In a study of several hundred excessively violent people, more than 90 percent showed evidence of brain dysfunction and neurological defects (F. A. Elliott, 1982). These defects may have altered their ability to inhibit aggressive behavior.

Aggression *Any behavior intended to hurt or destroy someone or something.*

Violence *Destructive action against people or property.*

(Wide World Photos)

On the night of July 31, 1966, Charles Whitman, an introspective 25-year-old, killed his wife and mother. The following morning he went to the administration building of the University of Texas, where he shot the receptionist and then barricaded himself in the tower. Using a high-powered rifle with a telescopic lens, he proceeded to shoot anyone in range. Over the next 90 minutes, he killed 14 people and wounded 24. His shooting spree ended only when he himself was shot and killed by the police. In a note he had written before any of the killings, he described agonizing headaches he had been suffering for several months and unusual and irrational thoughts, including violent impulses, that had been tormenting him. The autopsy that he had requested showed a brain tumor of the temporal lobes.

Various hormones and brain chemicals have also been linked to aggression. One is the male hormone testosterone. Among humans, as among most other animal species, males are generally more aggressive than females (Maccoby & Jacklin, 1974). In nearly all societies around the world, the men do the hunting and the fighting; in the United States, they commit more violent crime than women; and many lab experiments have found men to be more aggressive than women, whereas very few have found women more aggressive than men (Myers, 1983). In one study of young criminals, those with a history of violent and aggressive crimes had higher testosterone levels than those with a nonviolent history (Kreuz & Rose, 1972).

Some researchers have pointed to an increase in irritability and hostility just before the menses of some women and have suggested that this is caused by changes in female hormones—a marked drop in progesterone and a rise in estrogen (Dalton, 1977). In recent years, the name **premenstrual syndrome** (PMS) has been given to this condition, and medication is sometimes prescribed, even though the existence of the syndrome is still questioned.

One experiment measured blood pressure rates of persons taking part in a competitive, aggression-inducing task (Frodi, 1976). Blood pressure rates in this condition were found to be similar to rates that are present when high levels of the neurotransmitter norepinephrine are released in the brain. This similarity gives rise to the suspicion that norepinephrine may be associated with aggression. A low level of glucose in the blood, which marks the state of hypoglycemia, has also been implicated in aggression. In one group of people, under normal conditions only 7.7 percent were aggressive, but when they were moderately hypoglycemic, 84.6 percent were aggressive (Bolton, 1973). And the link between alcohol and aggression has been well established, in research as well as in everyday observation of people who become violent only when they're drunk (Pihl, Zeichner, Niaura, Hagy, & Zacchia, 1981). The effects of alcohol are probably largely due to the way it reduces inhibitions, but they may also come from its ability to produce a hypoglycemic state.

A promising line of research is now taking place on the role of various substances in the brain that cause fear, which reduces aggression and which is notably absent among violence-prone sociopathic people (Redmond, 1983).

It seems clear, then, that various hormones and chemicals can increase the likelihood of aggression.

What Triggers Aggression?   Hormones and chemicals do not actually produce aggressive behavior. What they do is lower our threshold for expressing aggression. In other words, if I encounter a situation that would call forth an aggressive response, I'm more likely to make that response if I have a higher level of these substances coursing through my body. Among the kinds of experiences that bring out aggressive responses are *frustration* (the thwarting of some goal-directed behavior), *insults, negative evaluations,* and *depression.*

WE ARE FRUSTRATED   How do you feel when someone cuts in front of you in traffic or in a checkout line when you're in a hurry? Chances are that you want to "get back" at the intruder.

Frustration doesn't *always* bring about aggression; it's likely to do so only when it's intense and unexpected or arbitrary (Baron, 1977). You're less likely to become angry when you're refused a job if you weren't counting on getting it and if you think the interview was fair. Furthermore, frustrated people aren't likely to become aggressive, no matter how angry they get, unless the stage is set for aggression. The "stage setting" may consist of cues for aggression, such as an atmosphere that promotes violence (seeing a violent movie would be an example); the presence of weapons that remind you how they can be used to hurt someone; or an already existing dislike for a person who has frustrated you (Berkowitz, 1979).

Social conditions can create a chronic state of frustration. A major study of about 10,000 men born in 1945 in Philadelphia, Pennsylvania, found that about

Premenstrual syndrome
Psychological and physical state experienced just before and during the early phases of a menstrual period, characterized by physical discomfort and psychological tension.

6 percent became chronic criminals. These men accounted for almost half of all the delinquent acts of the entire group. In a related study of men born in 1958, 7.5 percent of the men accounted for two-thirds of the murders, three-quarters of the rapes, and two-thirds of the aggravated assaults committed by the entire group. In both cohorts the clearest single predictor of a man's chronic criminal activity was his having been the victim of violence himself as a boy (Ledger, 1983). Other common factors were such elements of social deprivation as poverty, low IQ scores, and an unstable home life. Still, when we consider that many of the other men had encountered the same kinds of social conditions as boys and did not turn to criminal activities, we're left wondering what made the difference. So far, researchers have not been able to pinpoint specific differences between the chronic criminals and those who may have been arrested once but then got into no further trouble with the law.

WE ARE INSULTED OR RECEIVE A NEGATIVE EVALUATION   Children learn from an early age that calling people names is almost sure to make them angry, and laboratory researchers have confirmed the aggression-eliciting power of insults by acting rudely toward subjects, sometimes questioning their intelligence (Baron, 1977). Similarly, most of us have felt angry at teachers who gave us a lower grade than we felt we deserved or supervisors who rated our work below the level we thought fair. Here, too, intent is important. We're much less likely to become angry if an evaluation—no matter how negative—seems to be fair than if it seems to be arbitrary and undeserved.

WE ARE DEPRESSED   Although literature and religion often hold out examples of people who become ennobled through suffering, it often seems that in real life the more we suffer ourselves, the more we want to make other people suffer. Depressed people, for example, often become hostile and aggressive. Children may act out depression through fighting, biting, and destructive actions, and depressed adults often express hostile feelings (Berkowitz, 1983).

How Do We Learn to Be Aggressive?   How do we *learn* when to discharge frustration and anger through aggression? How do we learn that it's all right to hurt other people in certain circumstances? What in our environment teaches us? Social learning theorists consider aggression to be behavior that's learned as a result of rewards and punishments, as well as through imitating models.

WE LEARN FROM PEOPLE AROUND US   Parents usually teach their children not to hit other children first, not to hit smaller children, and not to hit their parents. But when parents tell their children not to hit but then hit them themselves, they're sending mixed messages and providing a double incentive toward violence. Aside from suffering pain and humiliation, which is likely to elicit an aggressive reaction, the children see an example of an adult with whom they identify acting aggressively. Such parents provide a "living example of the use of aggression at the very moment they are trying to teach the child not to be aggressive" (Sears, Maccoby, & Levin, 1957, p. 266).

Parents exert a great deal of influence over children's aggressiveness. One major study found that the parents of children who were aggressive in school were less nurturant and accepting, punished their children for aggression at home, and, in general, gave them little support (Eron, 1980).

WE LEARN FROM SOCIETAL ATTITUDES   When social scientists compare violent societies (like our own) with those in which very little violence occurs, they find a number of differences. In the valley of Oaxaca, Mexico, for example, there are several nonviolent communities, surrounded by others showing a more typical level of violence (Paddock, 1975). What are the differences? The nonviolent communities have very different attitudes toward sex differences, rearing boys and girls very similarly and showing practically no signs of *machismo,* or the necessity for male dominance in employment and income and within the family. They discipline their children quite differently, correcting them verbally most of the time and rarely spanking. Adults ignore children's misbehavior when possible and teach children to ignore mistreatment by other children. Children are also kept much closer to home in these nonviolent communities.

In our society, even today, after many changes in the roles of men and women, the prevailing attitudes are more like those of the more violent Mexican ones—the man is expected to be the head of the household, children and adults alike are expected to get even with anyone who does them an injury, and corporal punishment is taken so much for granted as a way of disciplining children that even nonfamily members like teachers are often expected to spank youngsters.

DO WE LEARN FROM TELEVISION?   What are children to conclude about aggression and violence when they sit before the television set and watch grisly killings, beatings, and mayhem day after day? Between the 6 violent acts per hour of prime-time network television and the 17 violent acts per hour of Saturday morning cartoons, the average child has witnessed the violent destruction of more than 13,400 persons during the 10 years between his or her fifth and fifteenth birthdays (Sabin, 1972; Prial, 1983).

Research on the effects on aggressive behavior of seeing televised violence has gone on since the 1950s, and the most common conclusion by social scientists has been that seeing violence on the screen makes children more aggressive in real life. A report issued in 1982 by the National Institute of Mental Health states that this effect is true across all geographic and socioeconomic levels, for both sexes, and for normal children as well as those with emotional problems. It concludes that television encourages aggressive behavior in two ways: children imitate what they see on television, and they also absorb the values transmitted and come to accept aggression as appropriate behavior.

A subsequent review of all the published research literature on the link between violence on television and aggression comes to a different conclusion, however, maintaining that although there is an association between the two, "there is little convincing evidence that viewing violence on television in natural settings causes an

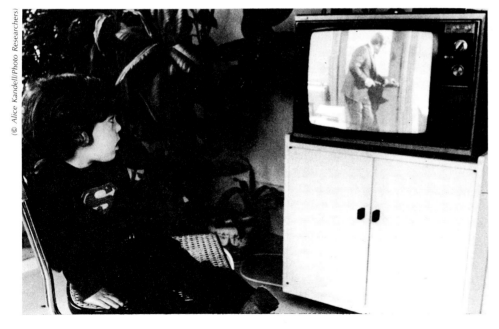

Between the ages of 5 and 15 the average child in the United States has seen the violent destruction of more than 13,400 people. Researchers conclude that seeing violence on the television screen encourages aggressive behavior, as children imitate what they see and come to accept aggression as appropriate.

increase in subsequent aggressiveness" (J. L. Freedman, 1984, p. 243). The author of this review cites mixed findings from field studies, some of which have found increased aggressiveness after watching violence on television, some no effect, and some even a reversed effect.

The issue, then, is not so clear-cut as common sense would have us think. For one thing, the context in which the violence is shown probably has an effect, one key issue being whether violent actions are rewarded or punished. Another question seems to be parental involvement in children's reactions to what they see on television. When parents let their children know that violence is not an acceptable means of settling disputes, watching television does *not* lead to more aggression (Dominick & Greenberg, 1971; Huesmann, Eron, Klein, Brice, & Fischer, 1983).

Still, there is a correlation between watching violence on television and acting aggressively. Aggressive children watch more television in general, identifying more strongly with aggressive characters, and are more likely to believe that on-screen aggression reflects real life (Eron, 1982). It's possible that people who are aggressive for other reasons like to watch scenes of aggression. In other words, the aggressiveness in their personalities causes them to watch the violent television and not the other way around. This explanation receives support from a study that shows that early patterns of television viewing do not help us to predict which children will turn out to act aggressively later in life (Milavsky et al., 1982).

Contradictory findings were noted by one researcher, who followed up 427 young adults whose viewing habits had been studied when they were in third grade. He found that the single best predictor of a young man's aggressiveness at the age of 19 is the violence of the television programs that he liked to watch at the age of 8 (Eron, 1980). He then found a similar relationship for girls and women and concluded that third-graders may be at a critical period of development in which they are unusually susceptible to the effects of television (Eron, 1982).

One explanation for the contradictory findings on this issue lies in the complexity of the influences upon children. It's difficult to attribute human behavior to any one environmental factor; rather, it's the combination of influences in people's lives that exerts a global effect. The conclusions from one in-depth longitudinal study show how television and parents interact to affect children. Jerome L. Singer and Dorothy G. Singer (1983) followed more than 100 children from the age of 4 through the age of 9, observing them directly, interviewing their parents (about their own values, child-rearing techniques, and family lifestyles), and examining logs of the television programs the children watched. They then looked at a number of cognitive and personality measures for the children. These authors concluded that children were more likely to have problems if as preschoolers they watched a great deal of television, especially if it was not monitored by parents; if they watched a lot of violent programs; if the parents themselves used physical force to punish the children; and if the parents did not hold values stressing imagination, curiosity, or creativity. Thus, television emerges as an important influence in children's lives, but as one that sits firmly in a context of family values.

It seems, then, that although we may well inherit a tendency to act aggressively, and although aggression seems to have a biological basis, the way we express or inhibit aggressive behavior is shaped by the world around us. A disturbing manifestation of aggression is its high level among family members, a topic explored in the box "Family Violence" (pages 398–399).

Achievement

You may be trying to earn the highest grade possible in this course, make the dean's list, graduate with honors, and go on to reach the top of your chosen profession. Or you may be content to pass the course, get through college somehow, and take a job that will give you a living but won't hold out the promise of high achievement. If the first sentence describes you, you probably have high achievement needs; if the second is more accurate, your achievement needs are lower. In 1938, Murray defined the need to achieve (expressed as *nAch*) as a desire or tendency "to overcome obstacles, to exercise power, to strive to do something difficult as well and as quickly as possible" (pp. 80–81). Achievement motivation is generally considered to exist in situations that embody competition against a recognized standard of excellence. In 1953, psychologists began to measure the strength of this need, using the ***Thematic Apperception Test (TAT)*** to do so (McClelland, Atkinson, Clark, & Lowell, 1953).

The TAT is made up of a set of purposefully ambiguous pictures showing people in different kinds of situations. If you were taking this test, you would be asked to write a story indicating what led up to the event shown in the picture, what's happening now, and what will happen in the future. The assumption underlying the test is that people are inclined to write stories about themes that are important to them. (For this reason the TAT is often used as a general personality test, as explained in Chapter 13.) McClelland and his associates devised a system for scoring "achievement imagery." They analyzed the content of stories about the TAT pictures to see whether the writers had used achievement imagery or had used words related to achievement. In other words, did people talk about setting difficult goals, persisting, overcoming obstacles, and so forth? Through answering these questions, they rated the test takers' needs for achievement.

A cognitive way to look at achievement motivation has been proposed by Weiner (1972, 1974, 1985). This theory emphasizes the achiever's (or nonachiever's) interpretation of the reasons for success or failure. You can attribute your score on a psychology test, for example, to either internal or external causes. Your locus of control, in other words, can be internal or external. *Internal* causes are the ones you bring to the exam—your ability and how much effort you put forth. *External* causes are those you have no control over—the difficulty of the task, and luck. Both internal and external causes can be either *stable* (relatively unchanging from one time to another) or *unstable* (showing wide fluctuations); see Figure 11-5.

The way people look at stability and instability factors also influences what they expect for the future. If you think you have not done well because you haven't put forth enough effort (an unstable factor) and not because you don't have the ability (a stable factor), you may resolve to try harder next time and expect to succeed. If you think you don't have the ability to succeed, you're likely to develop an attitude of helplessness—that no matter what you do, you can't change the outcome.

People who have a high *nAch*—a high need to achieve—tend to exhibit characteristic behavioral styles and personality traits. Given a choice of hard, easy, and in-between tasks, they usually pick the in-between tasks, which seem to present

nAch *"Need to achieve." According to Murray, this need is characterized by a desire or tendency "to overcome obstacles, to exercise power, and to strive to do something difficult as well and as quickly as possible."*

Thematic Apperception Test (TAT) *Projective personality test in which the test taker makes up stories about ambiguous pictures; these stories are scored for themes.*

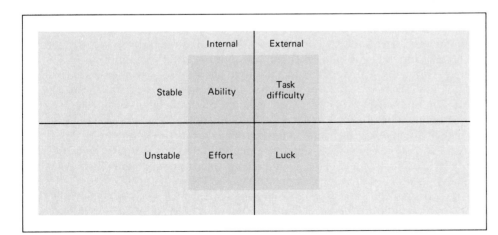

FIGURE 11-5 *One cognitive approach to achievement motivation stresses people's interpretations of the reasons for their success or failure. The characteristics in the boxes show the interaction of two major dimensions—internal or external locus of control and stability or instability—for different traits. Effort, for example, falls under internal locus of control, since people can control the amount of effort they put into a task; and it is unstable, since it can fluctuate widely from one time to another. Which of these boxed characteristics seem to be most predictable? (Source: Adapted from Weiner, 1974.)*

Whether aggression is the result of inherited tendencies, of learning, or of a combination of both, it is tragically present in countless families. A growing interest among psychologists in family issues has led to an increased amount of research into the causes, prevention, and treatment of family violence. The American home is the most violent place in this violent country. In this "haven from the outside world," parents beat, kick, and punch their children and even use weapons on them; husbands and wives assault, shoot, and stab each other; and adults batter, tie up, and neglect their elderly parents.

The actual numbers of such attacks are staggering; the evidence suggests that almost four million 3- to 17-year-olds are abused by their parents every year; almost 2 million people are abused by their spouses; and between 500,000 and 2½ million old people are abused by family members and other caretakers (Pedrick-Cornell & Gelles, 1982). The most common relationship between murderers and their victims is membership in the same family (FBI, 1983). Even college students who are dating often become violent toward each other; one study indicates that 1 out of 5 have experienced violence themselves and 6 out of 10 know of someone else who has experienced violence (Makepeace, 1981).

Note: Where no other reference is given, findings are reported in Belsky, 1980.

IN THE FOREFRONT

FAMILY VIOLENCE

WHY PEOPLE HURT THE ONES THEY LOVE

Researchers who have tried to explain and prevent abuse in the home have come up with various contributing causes. Jay Belsky (1980) has proposed a multilevel model that focuses first on the characteristics of the individual abuser and victim, and then broadens its focus to include the family, the community, and the larger culture.

ABUSER

Abusers often hate themselves for what they do and yet feel powerless to stop. "It's a fallacy that the abused child is unwanted or unloved. Abusive parents often haven't had good parental role models of their own, and many have been programmed for violence. When there is stress, they strike out at the kids" (Fontana, quoted in Francke, 1983).

Abusive parents are likely to have been mistreated in their own childhood and to have felt rejected by their parents. Deprived of good parenting themselves, they don't know how to be good parents to their

own children. They don't know how to make a baby stop crying, for example, and will sometimes lose all control when they can't get their children to do what they want them to. Furthermore, they often look to their children to take care of them and become furious when this does not happen. They are often grossly ignorant of normal child development, holding unrealistic expectations about when children can be toilet-trained, can stay clean and neat, and can mature in other ways. They have more confrontations with their children and are less effective in resolving problems (Reid, Patterson, & Loeber, 1982).

People who abuse their elderly parents often do so out of a sense of rage that the tables are turned and they cannot look to their parents for care but must instead care for their parents.

VICTIM

Abused children tend to need or demand more from their parents. They're more likely to have been premature or of low birthweight; to be hyperactive, mentally retarded, or physically handicapped; or to show other behavioral abnormalities (Reid et al., 1982). They show more difficult behavior than other children—almost 50 percent more, in one study. Abused old people tend to have special characteristics: they tend to be female, older than average, and in poor health (Pedrick-Cornell & Gelles, 1982).

---

enough of a challenge to be interesting but not enough to be discouraging (Atkinson, 1957; Raynor & Entin, 1982). This has been shown in studies involving such tasks as spelling, arithmetic, tossing a ring over a peg, and solving anagrams. This choice of moderate difficulty seems related to a desire to attribute success to one's own efforts and abilities (Weiner, 1985). In other words, if a task is so easy that almost anyone can do it or so hard that practically no one can, you can't tell how you stack up. It's in the middle range that you can get the kind of feedback that lets you test yourself. People with high *n*Ach are more restless, more interested in finding new ways to do things, and more likely to take personal responsibility for the way they perform. They also tend to exhibit some less attractive traits, such as a greater tendency to cheat and a relative lack of sensitivity to other people (McClelland, 1985).

It's possible that the need for achievement may be at least partly inherited. People with high *n*Ach show a higher level of physiological activation than people

FAMILY CLIMATE

Abusive parents are more likely to have marital problems than other couples and to fight physically with each other. They have more children and have them closer together, and their households are more disorganized. They experience more stressful events than other families (Reid et al., 1982). Stress is also a factor in abuse of the elderly; an abusing adult child often perceives the victim as a source of intolerable stress because the demands of caretaking have become overwhelming (Pedrick-Cornell & Gelles, 1982).

Social isolation of a family also plays a role. Families in which violence occurs tend to be those that cut themselves off from neighbors, other relatives, and friends and consequently have no one to turn to in times of stress and no one to see what's happening within the family.

COMMUNITY

The outside world can create a climate for family violence. Unemployment, job dissatisfaction, and chronic financial hardship are all closely correlated with child and spouse abuse. Men who are unemployed or unhappy in their jobs are more likely to maltreat their wives and children (Gil, 1971; McKinley, 1964). During a 6-month period of rising unemployment in Birmingham, Great Britain, the rate of wife beating rose, too (Steinmetz & Straus, 1974).

CULTURE

A culture sets the stage for violence in the attitudes it passes on to its citizens. Murders are 10 times more common in the United States than in Great Britain, and rates of assault and battery are 5 times more common than in Canada. More than 9 out of 10 American parents spank their children, almost 9 out of 10 Americans feel that children need strong discipline, and half of American adults approve of teachers hitting students for "good reasons"—like being noisy in class, destroying school property, or hitting someone else (Stark & McEvoy, 1970). In countries where parents rarely spank children, child abuse is rare.

An additional contributing factor to family violence is the belief that a child is the property of its parents, and a wife of her husband. In staged "assaults," bystanders are more reluctant to interfere when a man is believed to be hitting his wife or a parent his or her own child than when the victim of the attack is a stranger (Shotland & Straw, 1976).

HELPING FAMILIES IN TROUBLE OR AT RISK

All these factors interact in different ways for different families, sometimes causing abuse, sometimes not. The particular circumstances in any one case would dictate the means of preventing or overcoming abusive patterns.

To prevent abuse, the United States Attorney General's Task Force on Family Violence (1984) recommends the institution of a broad-based education and awareness program, sponsored both by the federal government and the private sector. This would include 24-hour toll-free hot lines, education for teachers and health care providers, and media campaigns.

Gerald R. Patterson and his colleagues at the Oregon Social Learning Center have achieved good results with abusing families by using a dual approach: teaching parents how to handle their children better and, at the same time, providing skilled therapeutic help related to whatever other stresses the parents are facing (Patterson, Chamberlain, & Reid, 1982).

One of the most effective ways of helping the victims of abuse is to treat their abusers as criminal offenders. People who are arrested for family violence are less likely to continue to mistreat their families (Sherman & Berk, 1984).

Steps to help families in which old people are abused or neglected include becoming aware of the problem, developing and using shelters for the victims of abuse, and providing support services (such as homemakers, visiting nurses, and home health visitors) to those taking care of the elderly (Pedrick-Cornell & Gelles, 1982).

---

with lower nAch (McClelland, 1985). When they concentrate, their muscles are tenser; this may be due to higher anxiety levels or to other causes, or there may be an inborn component to the drive to succeed. Whether or not this is so, there do seem to be ways to increase nAch.

Certain styles of child rearing seem to influence children to become high achievers (Feshbach & Weiner, 1982). In one classic study, Winterbottom (1958) found that mothers of children with strong achievement motivation tend to encourage independence and mastery before their children are 8 years old, expecting their youngsters to know their way around the city and to do well in competition. A recent 14-year longitudinal study of 544 young adults who had come from impoverished families in the rural south found that the most important factors influencing whether they got the jobs they wanted were achievement motivation, self-confidence, and family factors (including the parents' own levels of education, their expectations for their children, and their child-rearing values and practices). It's likely that the family factors helped to inspire both the self-confidence and the achievement motivation (Schiamberg & Chun, 1986).

Achievement performance can be improved later in life. Men who took part in a 3- to 6-week training course (in which they learned about the importance of taking risks, about the future-orientation of achievers, and about ways to set their own goals) achieved more afterwards than men who had not taken the course (McClelland & Winter, 1969). Other approaches try to change people's explanations for success or failure. Since low achievers tend to think they have little ability and won't succeed anyway, they don't try hard. This results, of course, in a self-fulfilling prophecy, since people who don't make the effort to achieve are more likely to fail. Some programs concentrate on simply instructing people about the role of effort in success (Ostrove, 1978).

Aside from anecdotal evidence in personal cases, we don't know whether nAch cuts across different areas of people's lives; researchers have not sought to find out whether someone with a high need for achievement will be just as competitive, for example, on the tennis court as in the law court, or whether people have different achievement needs in different areas of their lives. Our knowledge about whether people's needs for achievement remain fairly stable through life is fairly limited. There does seem to be some evidence that college men in their early twenties with high nAch tend to end up in entrepreneurial jobs (McClelland, 1965).

It's not surprising that a 1976 national study found that American men with high nAch were positively oriented toward work. They tended to be satisfied with their jobs, to consider their jobs interesting, not to see work as interfering with family, and to prefer work to leisure. They reported few symptoms of ill health, considered themselves happy, and did not take drugs to relax (Veroff, Douvan, & Kulka, 1981). This study did not find the same kind of work satisfaction among women with high nAch, possibly because the respondents had been brought up in a time when women's achievement motivation was expressed in marriage, motherhood, and leisure activities rather than at work. But the women, like the men, reported a high sense of well-being and satisfaction with life; and the differences found between men and women may cease to exist as a result of our society's growing emphasis on the value of work in women's lives and the value of family in men's lives.

Arousal, Curiosity, and Boredom

Anyone who has ever spent much time in the company of a 3-year-old knows that human beings are very curious creatures from a very early age. We want to know about everything—why people act as they do; why events occur; how things work; what's on the other side of a hill, a mountain, or an ocean. To satisfy our boundless curiosity, we begin as infants to touch, to put new objects in our mouths, to take our first faltering steps away from home. As we grow older, we continue to process the information that comes in through all our senses, we explore our surroundings, we ask questions, we study, we puzzle, we think. We seem to do many things for no reward other than satisfying our curiosity. Most psychologists believe that a basic motivational system underlies this behavior, and that curiosity and arousal are related in important ways. The other side of these phenomena is boredom, and researchers are just beginning to look at its impact on why we do what we do.

How We Become Aroused   Have you ever read the same paragraph six times before realizing that you were just too sleepy to know what the words meant? Can you think of times when you came home from an exciting evening, planning to study, but then found that you were too "hyper" to sit down and concentrate? We're in the best position to analyze what we see, hear, and feel when we are in an optimal state of arousal. *Arousal* is a physiological state which we experience as an ability to process information, to react to an emergency, and to experience a wide range of emotions.

Arousal Physiological state which we experience as an ability to process information, to react to an emergency, and to experience a wide range of emotions.

If we're drowsy or hyperstimulated, we don't process information well. To satisfy our curiosity, we need to be at a relatively high level of arousal.

What's happening in our bodies when we are at a high level of arousal? A number of things are taking place. Let's start in the cortex. As we learned earlier, brain-wave patterns can be measured by an electroencephalogram. When we are in a state of moderate arousal, in which we're alert and attentive, our EEG patterns show irregular, fast, short spikes (beta waves). In this state there's also an increase in other physiological responses: heart rate and blood pressure go up. At the same time, glucose is released into the blood, and other reactions take place to prepare the body for expending energy. These responses are referred to as **autonomic arousal,** since they are mediated by the autonomic nervous system.

What produces these signs of cortical and autonomic arousal? There seems to be some biological mechanism, probably located in the reticular formation in the brain stem. This system, as we saw in Chapter 2, controls our levels of alertness and also plays a primary role in putting us to sleep. Incoming sensory stimulation activates sensory neurons, which stimulate the reticular formation. This in turn activates the cortex and other brain centers (such as the hypothalamus) that control autonomic arousal. Because the reticular formation activates these various brain centers, it has come to be called the **reticular activation system (RAS).**

How We Feel about Arousal   Human beings tend to prefer a moderate level of arousal—not so high that we're excited and disorganized and not so low that we're drowsy (Berlyne, 1971; Eysenck, 1967). The relationship between arousal and feeling state is shown in Figure 11-6, which demonstrates people's differing reactions to a variety of stimuli, ranging from the very simple and very familiar to the very complex and strange. Most people apparently like a stimulus that's moderately complex or moderately new.

Most people try to maintain a moderate level of arousal. Usually we do this by controlling our level of external stimulation. When we feel overstimulated, we're likely to retreat to a quiet spot where we can be alone; and when we feel understimulated, we will probably seek out stimulation—maybe a noisy place full of people.

There are, however, large individual differences in the degree of arousal people feel comfortable with. You may be a very active person who likes or would like to engage in activities that carry risk and adventure, a very sociable type who likes meeting and being with unconventional people. If so, you're what one psychologist

Autonomic arousal   Heightened activity of a number of physiological responses such as heart rate and respiration. The increased action is controlled by the autonomic nervous system.

Reticular activation system (RAS)   System of nerve pathways and connections within the brain stem.

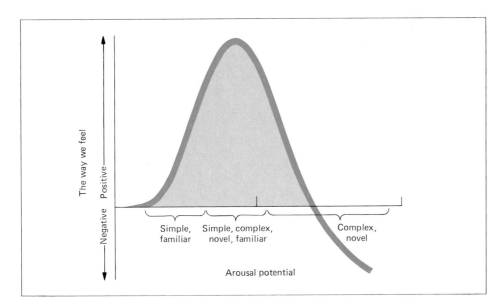

FIGURE 11-6   *Hypothetical relationship between the way we feel and the arousal potential of a stimulus. People are in the best frame of mind when faced with a stimulus that is moderately complex or moderately novel. A stimulus that is too simple and familiar or too complex and strange produces less pleasant feelings. (Source: Berlyne, 1970.)*

This man, scaling cliffs above Monte Carlo, in Monaco, is an excellent example of what the psychologist Frank Farley would call a type T personality, with the capital T standing for "thrill seeker."

Yerkes-Dodson law *According to Yerkes and Dodson, optimal level of arousal varies depending on what you are doing. If you are doing something very easy, you'll do best at a high arousal level; if you're doing something more complicated or more difficult, you'll do best if your arousal level is somewhat lower.*

has termed a "sensation-seeker" (Zuckerman, 1979) and what another has dubbed the *type T personality,* the capital *T* standing for "thrill seeker" (Farley, 1986a). If, on the other hand, you prefer familiarity, stability, and a sense of peace, you're low on the sensation-seeking scale—a *type t personality,* with a lowercase *t.*

Such differences in preferred arousal levels may be inherited, according to research findings that one of the chemicals that regulate this tendency is, at least in part, genetically determined (Zuckerman, Buchsbaum, & Murphy, 1980). Also, some preliminary evidence of differences in biological responsivity between "big T" and "little t" personalities has been found (Farley, 1986b). It's possible that some people are born with different levels of arousability. Those with unusually low levels are not very responsive to either mental or physical stimuli, and therefore they need very high levels of stimulation to arrive at optimal levels. These are the people who take physical, emotional, and intellectual risks in their search for stimulation—risks that may lead to fame or infamy. Those who become aroused very easily don't seek out highly stimulating experiences and environments, but instead look for certainty, familiarity, and predictability in their lives. Most people seek some middle level of stimulation.

Since diversity helps a species survive, it's possible that such differences in sensation seeking may contribute to the vigor of the human race. In any case, the existence of people with such widely differing tendencies certainly helps keep life interesting.

How Arousal Affects Performance   Not only do most people like to feel moderately aroused, but most of us are most efficient in this state. You've probably noticed yourself that you can't do your best work when you're excited and jumpy, or when you're extremely relaxed. You write your best papers, do your best studying, put forth your finest efforts at anything when you're in a state of moderate arousal. Figure 11-7 shows the relationship between arousal and your best efforts.

According to the **Yerkes-Dodson law,** stated in 1908 by two psychologists, the optimal level of arousal varies depending on what you're doing. If you're doing something very easy, you'll do best at a high arousal level; if you're doing something more complicated or more difficult, you'll do better if your arousal level is somewhat lower. Since the discovery in 1949 of the reticular activation system, D. O. Hebb (1955) provided a new way of looking at how stimulation affects performance. Hebb said that the crucial determinant was not the stimulus itself but the state of arousal that it produced. A very strong stimulus produces high arousal; a weaker stimulus produces low arousal.

Arousal narrows our attention. A narrowed focus, brought about by a strong stimulus and high arousal, helps us to concentrate on only one task. But when we need to solve problems in which we have to consider a number of factors and many possible solutions, we need to take a broader approach. This has survival value. Animals that see an enemy (a strong stimulus that causes high arousal) focus their attention on one task—getting away. At such a time, they will tend to use a familiar escape route. When there is no immediate threat, they need to be at a lower level of arousal, to process information about the environment effectively enough to learn new routes.

According to Hebb, performance increases as arousal increases—up to a point. After the optimal level is reached, further increases in arousal don't help performance but actually interfere with it. Hebb's model not only predicts performance, but predicts the kinds of tasks that human beings and animals are inclined to select. According to Hebb, we select tasks that provide us with optimal levels of arousal; and we often shift from one level of arousal to another, choosing to be quiet after being overstimulated or doing something new when we're bored. Individuals differ according to the level of arousal each finds comfortable. If you prefer to work in a state of high arousal—for example, in a room where people are constantly coming and going, where the walls are covered with vivid posters, and where loud music is

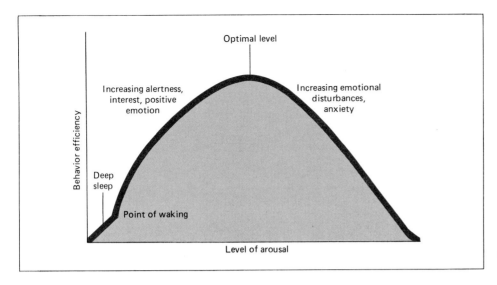

FIGURE 11-7 *Hypothetical relationship between behavioral efficiency and level of arousal. (Source: Hebb, 1955.)*

playing—but your roommate likes to work alone in a quiet, sparsely furnished room, you'll have to do some careful negotiating—or else switch roommates.

Our bodies have mechanisms for reacting to and dealing with new objects and events. In laboratory experiments, subjects faced with novel experiences have responded with autonomic arousal, increased galvanic skin response (the skin's reaction to a weak electrical current), dilation of the pupils, and other signs of arousal (R. Lynn, 1966). There seems to be a clear evolutionary reason for this kind of reaction: it can save your life. For example, if you were suddenly to encounter a bear on the path, you'd need good cortical arousal to analyze how best to deal with this novel event, and you'd need autonomic arousal to provide the necessary energy backup to do whatever you'd decided was the appropriate action—climbing a tree, shooting, or shouting for help.

Effects of Sensory Deprivation   Most of us today are beset on every side by a bewildering variety of sounds, sights, smells, movements, and other stimuli. Modern life—especially modern urban life—is a hubbub of stimulation, which some people (like type T sensation seekers) thrive on and others long to escape. Some do escape, not by leaving the city, but by regularly isolating themselves from stimulation. One way to do this is by immersion in a sensory deprivation chamber or tank, a facility that has become commercially available in some large cities, What does this do to people? Apparently, the effect depends partly on the individual and partly on the length of time one remains isolated from stimulation.

Some years ago a group of psychologists at McGill University built a sensory isolation chamber designed to keep stimulation to a minimum. They offered students who agreed to participate $20 a day and asked them to be prepared to stay as long as possible. It sounded like an easy way to earn money, since the students were to do nothing at all. They were simply to lie motionless in this chamber whenever they weren't eating or drinking the adequate amounts of food and water available to them. They couldn't see anything but constant light, because they wore translucent goggles; they couldn't touch things, because they wore cardboard cuffs over the hands and lower arm; and they couldn't hear anything, because the monotonous hum of an exhaust fan drowned out all other sounds. It turned out, however, that doing nothing was hard to do. Nearly all the subjects said the experience was unpleasant, and more than half asked to leave within 48 hours, since they found sensory deprivation for such an extended time intolerable (Heron, 1961).

Other researchers have found some benefits from sensory deprivation, including improvements in certain sensory abilities: faster response to a tone signal, a lower

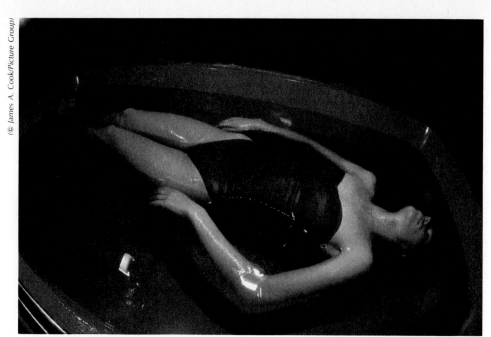

After floating in warm water in a dark sensory-deprivation tank, this woman may come out feeling refreshed by a brief respite from the hubbub of daily life. She may also experience a sharpening of cognitive processes. Most people, however, seem to find this kind of deprivation intolerable for any extended period of time.

two-point-discrimination threshold (described in Chapter 3), and increased sensitivity to sweet and bitter tastes. Certain cognitive processes seem to be sharpened, also, like rote learning of lists of words and recall or recognition of previously learned material. (While performance on such simple tasks is often improved after deprivation, however, performance on more complex tasks is impaired.) Among the therapeutic benefits of sensory deprivation has been its use in a program that helped people to stop smoking (Suedfeld, 1975).

Most people, though, seem to need a great deal of sensory stimulation and find the kind of deprivation we're talking about here intolerable for any extended period of time.

Boredom   Who would be your candidate for the most boring celebrity of the year? The Boring Institute has given this honor to movie stars, athletes, royalty, and the entire cast of the nighttime television soap opera *Dynasty*. The institute, which is the brainchild of a public relations counselor, pokes fun at all sorts of contemporary phenomena that evoke a yawn (Caruba, 1986). Boredom, though, has a much more serious side, one that is just now achieving the attention it deserves. It has been cited as a contributing factor in marital instability, juvenile delinquency, and overeating (Darden & Marks, 1985a). Recently, boredom has been blamed for the failure of airport guards to detect smuggled weapons, for automobile accidents caused by a lapse of attention to the demands of driving, and for failures of vital inspections at nuclear power plants, airport control towers, and nursing stations in hospitals (Warm & Dember, 1986).

Many of our society's important institutions rest on the vigilance of appointed monitors who check to be sure that systems are functioning as they should be. The problem is that monitoring tasks tend to be repetitive and monotonous, and the reticular activation system (RAS) in the brain of the monitor works best under varied, changing conditions. The RAS slows down, therefore; the person becomes drowsy and less efficient; and vital information does not get through. Scientists who have studied such drops in vigilance recommend several strategies to help people maintain their attentiveness, including mild physical exercise (getting up and walking around), sensory stimulation (music, bright lights, an uncomfortably warm or cool environment), and variation (switching from one kind [...] Dember, 1986).

Boredom seems to be the result of a kind of adaptatio[...] tolerance level for stimulation. Once we adjust to levels of [...] satisfying, they lose their ability to interest us and we become [...] den & Marks, 1985a). We then go on to seek a new level of stim[...] changing our activities or by escalating the stimulation level. Or we [...] enjoy our boredom, taking advantage of it to let the mind lie fallow lo[...] recharge (Darden & Marks, 1985b). Boredom thus has a positive side wh[...] vates us to try new activities and face new challenges.

Arousal is an important element in emotion, as well as in motivation, as we'll se[...] our discussion of theories explaining the psychological ramifications of our emo[...] tions. As we pointed out earlier, our feelings are an important element in motivating our behavior. And our own behavior and that of others are important elements in making us feel a wide range of emotions. Let's see what psychology has found significant about human emotions.

EMOTION

Imagine that you're driving along a highway, thinking about your plans for the evening, when suddenly you're jolted into full arousal by the sight of a truck looming toward you on your side of the highway. You swerve into the shoulder of the road, narrowly averting the careening truck. What are you likely to be feeling after you realize that you're safe?

Later in the evening you arrive on time, to meet the person you're in love with, the person you've just decided you want to marry (although you haven't communicated this desire yet). Your true love is not at the meeting place. As you wait you pace back and forth, looking at your watch. Fifteen minutes pass, then half an hour. Finally your lover arrives. What do you feel now? What do you feel later in the evening when you learn that the person you love returns your feelings and wants to marry you?

Classifying Emotions

Fear, anger, relief, anxiety, happiness—these are some of the labels you might have given to some of your feelings in situations like these. What do these words mean? You know how *you* felt in these situations, but would you know what other people meant if they used the same words? In an effort to understand human feelings, psychologists have categorized emotions in various ways. According to Izard (1977, 1979), 10 fundamental emotions are important for survival of either the individual or the species: (1) *interest-excitement*, (2) *joy*, (3) *surprise*, (4) *distress-anguish*, (5) *anger*, (6) *disgust*, (7) *contempt*, (8) *fear*, (9) *shame*, and (10) *guilt*. Each of these emotions has three essential components—a neurological activity, a subjective feeling, and an expression. Because the basic 10 interact with each other, they can create a very large pool of possible feelings. These emotions serve as the basis for personality and motivate behavior.

In a similar classification system, Plutchik (1962, 1980, 1983) named eight primary emotions: (1) *fear*, (2) *anger*, (3) *joy*, (4) *sadness*, (5) *acceptance*, (6) *disgust*, (7) *expectancy*, and (8) *surprise*. He also sees the emotions as adaptive for survival, and as interacting with each other to produce more complex feelings. In Figure 11-8, Plutchik's primary emotions are shown inside the wheel, and some of his simple two-emotion combinations are shown on the outside of the wheel. Many of the emotions we feel are more complex than this diagram can show, according to Plutchik, since they differ in intensity and persistence. For example, you may feel a

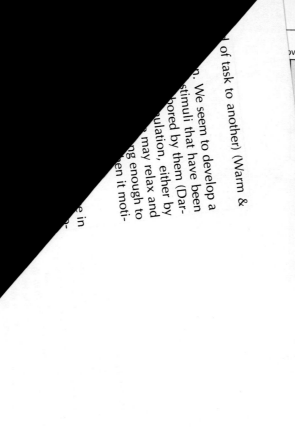

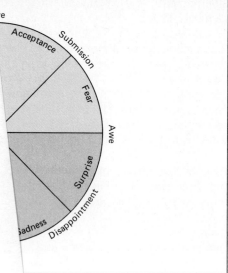

...n the street, but this feeling is of a ...ld feel at losing someone you love, ...lasting.

...otional state? Are you interpreting ...me chemical in your body or the ...your brain? Or is the strong feeling you're aware of a ...tive thing that owes its existence to the thought processes in your brain that created it and labeled it? Historically, emotion theorists have focused on answering these questions. The principal theories of emotion see this feeling state as physiological, as cognitive, or as a product of the interaction of physical and mental factors.

James-Lange Theory: Feelings Are Physical   How would you react if you were walking along a dark street and were suddenly accosted by a mugger? According to traditional theory, you would see the mugger, feel afraid, and then experience the physiological sensations connected with the emotion of fear—pounding heart, quickened breathing, sweaty palms, weakness in the knees. You would then act in a way that seemed appropriate—fight, shout, faint, or run away. Two scientists working at the same time—the psychologist William James (1884) and the physiologist Carl Lange (1885/1922)—both questioned this traditional assumption. James and Lange argued instead for a reversal of this sequence—that the basis for emotions arises from our perception of such physiological sensations as changes in heart rate and blood pressure and contractions of visceral and skeletal muscles (see Figure 11-9).

According to this theory, when you're insulted, you don't feel angry and then experience the physiological symptoms of rage. Your heart and breathing speed up and your muscles tense and you then interpret these body changes to yourself as "I'm angry." This theory assumes that our physiological responses are different for each emotion, which is not *always* the case. Although the theory has a certain measure of validity, it does not provide a complete explanation for the experience of emotion.

The feedback from physiological responses is not *necessary* to experience an emotion, but it can be important. As will be seen in what follows, Schachter and Singer (1962) showed how it can help to make an emotional response more intense.

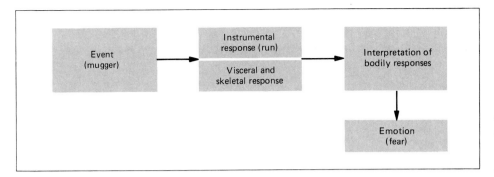

Cannon-Bard Theory: Feelings Are Cognitive In 1927, Walter Cannon argued against the James-Lange position; his argument was later extended by Philip Bard (1938). Both Cannon and Bard pointed to laboratory research suggesting that the physiological reactions which accompany different emotions are the same from emotion to emotion—in other words, that heart and breathing rates increase and muscles tense whether people are nervous, angry, afraid, or in love. If we depended only on our physiological responses, we wouldn't be able to distinguish one emotion from another. Furthermore, they claimed that people are not normally aware of most of the internal changes (like contractions of visceral organs, such as the kidney or the liver) and that even animals that were surgically prevented from experiencing such physiological sensations showed typical emotional reactions. They proposed instead that the emotional experience and the physiological arousal occur at the same time, rather than one after the other (see Figure 11-10). They further suggested that the important factor in feeling the emotion was not the physiological response, but our cognitive labeling of the event itself. If we thought we had something to fear, we would be afraid.

How does this happen? According to Cannon and Bard, when you encounter the mugger, nerve impulses carry this information to two important places in your brain. Your cortex, the site of the higher thought processes, tells you that the mugger is a threat to your personal safety, and this realization, this thought, is enough to produce fear. At the same time, said Cannon and Bard, your thalamus produces a variety of nonspecific physiological changes (that is, they are not specific to any particular emotion but arise in response to any emotion). These changes are referred to as the *stress* reaction, or the *fight-or-flight* reaction. This reaction prepares you to expend energy and deal with potential injury. If you were then to discover that the threatening-looking person was not a mugger but just someone coming up to ask you directions, both sites would shut down. According to Cannon and Bard, the cortex

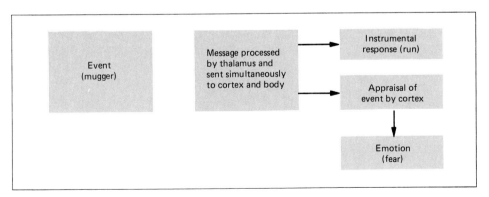

would turn off your feelings of fear and the thalamus would cancel the physiological reaction. (Today, it seems clear that it is the hypothalamus, rather than the thalamus, that is involved in this mechanism.)

The Cannon-Bard theory made use of the research that had been done to date on the role of the thalamus in emotion. Its major shortcoming was its failure to recognize the complexity of emotional experiences and the way they can be influenced by a person's interpretation of physiological feedback.

Schachter-Singer Theory: Emotions Depend on Double Cognitive Labeling   How we appraise an event and how we evaluate what's going on in our bodies are the two kinds of labeling that underlie the theory proposed by the psychologists Stanley Schachter and Jerome Singer (1962). They questioned the concept implicit in the Cannon-Bard theory that physiological responses play no role whatsoever, and maintained that both physiological arousal and a cognitive label are necessary for the full experience of emotion (see Figure 11-11). If either one is absent, the subjective emotional state will not be complete.

Schachter and Singer performed a number of interesting laboratory experiments. In some of them they told subjects that they were testing the effects on vision of a new vitamin supplement. They injected the subjects either with *epinephrine,* a hormone produced by the adrenal cortex that causes autonomic arousal (such as faster heart rate and breathing, flushing, and hand tremors), or with a placebo of an inactive salt solution. They then put the subjects in one of two situations. Half of them waited to take the eye test in a room with a person who pretended to be euphoric, sailing paper airplanes, shooting wads of paper, or using a hula hoop. The other half waited with a person who pretended to be angry at being injected or at filling out a questionnaire, and who finally stormed out of the room. Meanwhile, the experimenters had told half the ''epinephrine subjects'' in each situation (euphoria and anger) that the injection would cause certain physiological effects; the other half were not informed of the effects of the injection. The ''placebo subjects'' received no information.

By and large, the experiment confirmed the researchers' hypothesis. The ''epinephrine subjects'' who had *not* been told of the probable effects of the injection claimed to be especially happy or angry and acted accordingly, while the ones who *had* been informed did not have a particularly emotional reaction. Apparently, the uninformed subjects, not knowing about the effects of the drug, noticed their arousal, cast about for an explanation, and concluded that it must be due to an emotion. In looking for an emotion, they hit upon the most available explanation

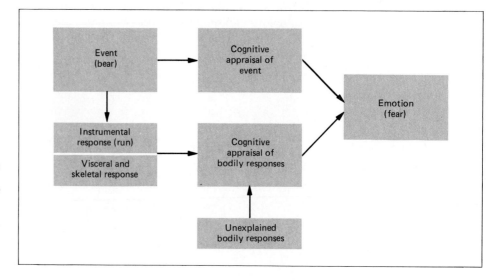

FIGURE 11-11 *Schachter-Singer theory of emotion. Emotion is due to two related but independent cognitive operations: appraisal of the event and appraisal of bodily reactions. The intensity of an emotion depends on how the person appraises bodily responses. Unexplained bodily reactions can increase perceived intensity.*

One reason why roller coasters are so popular with lovers may be a possible association in people's minds between the physiological sensations brought on by fear and those brought on by sexual arousal. In one study, men who met an attractive woman on a high, swaying bridge were more likely to phone her later than those who met her on a sturdier, lower, safer bridge.

and fitted their emotion to the situation at hand. The informed subjects, on the other hand, attributed their physiological arousal to the effects of the drug.

A similar effect seemed to occur in another intriguing experiment that took place on a suspension footbridge that swayed above a rocky canyon more than 200 feet deep. When young men standing on this bridge were approached by an attractive young woman who asked them to take part in a study that involved writing thoughts inspired by a picture she showed, they seemed (on the basis of their writing) to have been more sexually aroused than young men who were approached by the same woman on a sturdier, lower, safer bridge. Furthermore, the men on the "high fear" bridge were more likely to phone the woman afterwards (Dutton & Aron, 1974). Apparently the men in the "high fear" situation tended to attribute whatever signs of arousal they felt—swiftly beating heart, clammy hands, quickened breathing—to sexual arousal in the presence of a likely candidate. Could the implications of this study lead people in love to take the objects of their affection to someplace frightening to intensify their feelings? Maybe that's why roller coasters and Ferris wheels seem to be so popular with lovers.

Follow-up research has confirmed some elements of Schachter's theory. It seems as if increased arousal (which can come from the injection of a drug like epinephrine, from physical exercise, or from being in a frightening situation) can *intensify* an emotion we already feel (Reisenzein, 1983). Considerable support has been found for the suggestion that people show more intense emotional reactions when they experience increases in arousal that they can't attribute to some other source. Research has not, however, supported the suggestion that reducing arousal automatically leads to a reduction in emotional intensity (Reisenzein, 1983). In other words, arousal can enhance intensity but doesn't necessarily cause it.

On the whole, however, subsequent research has given only modest support to this theory. The original study (Schachter & Singer, 1962) has been criticized for its methodology, and attempts to replicate it have usually been unsuccessful (H. L. Petri, 1986). Psychologists are still debating about the conditions that give rise to emotion and about the relative contribution of cognitive and physiological elements.

Facial-Feedback Theory: Facial Expressions Lead to Emotions   Recent findings about the effects of our facial expressions show a definite connection with theories

A professional actor, Tom Harrison, is shown in these frames from a videotape as he responds to instructions such as, "Raise your brows and pull them together" (left), "Now raise your upper eyelids" (center), and "Now also stretch your lips horizontally, back toward your ears" (right). Researchers designed these instructions to portray the facial expressions that accompany fear, and in fact the actors who followed the instructions showed more bodily signs of fear than they did when they just thought of a frightening experience.

that William James enunciated a century ago. James wrote, "If we wish to conquer undesirable emotional tendencies in ourselves, we must assiduously go through the outward motions of those dispositions we prefer to cultivate" (1884). James is said to have followed his own advice to get over his grief after his parents' deaths.

To test the impact of "putting on a happy face" (or a facial expression of another emotion), researchers enlisted professional actors to take part in a two-phase experiment on emotion (Ekman, Levenson, & Friesen, 1983). In the first phase, the actors were asked (as in "method acting") to think of an emotional experience in their own lives that mirrored each of six emotions being studied—surprise, disgust, sadness, anger, fear, and happiness. In the second phase, the senior researcher coached each subject, with the help of a mirror, to assume certain expressions. He didn't ask the subjects to *feel* a certain way but simply had them contract specific facial muscles, thus creating smiles, frowns, and other expressions common in the six emotional states. In both phases, the subjects' autonomic nervous system responses were recorded—heart rate, temperature of left and right hands, resistance of the skin to the passage of a very weak electrical current, and muscle tension in the forearm.

Two significant findings emerged from this set of studies. First, this research found that physiological responses differed according to the emotion being studied. Hearts beat faster in anger and fear than in happiness, hands were colder in fear than in anger, and certain other physical differences showed up. Different emotions do seem to elicit different responses, at least to some degree. This indicates that the James-Lange theory seems to have some validity. We do get feedback from our bodies, and we often get different kinds of feedback for different emotions. Second, a major—and surprising—finding was that when subjects just moved their facial muscles, they produced more pronounced physiological signs of emotion than they did when they thought of emotional experiences. The advice in the popular song to "put on a happy face" when you're feeling low may be psychologically sound, after all. Acting happy may make you feel happy.

Questions about Emotion

Are Emotions Inborn? Suppose you were asked such questions as "How would you feel if . . ." " . . . a friend visited?" " . . . your child died?" " . . . you saw a dead pig that had been lying around a long time?" If you were like the subjects in a series of studies of people around the world from a wide variety of cultures, you would express happiness with a smile, sadness with lowered eyes and downturned mouth, and disgust with a wrinkled nose. Furthermore, if you saw pictures of strangers expressing these emotions, you would be able to recognize the feelings they were showing (Ekman & Friesen, 1971).

The finding that some facial expressions seem to be universal supports the idea that the emotions behind them are part of our legacy as human beings (Ekman, Friesen, & Ancoli, 1980; Ekman & Oster, 1982). This view is further confirmed by studies of infants which show that beginning at birth babies express several different emotions and that these expressions become more distinctive over the next few months (Izard et al., 1980). Studies like these support Izard's and Plutchik's view that we have a fundamental set of emotions, programmed into the brain.

But even if emotions are innate, the way we express them reflects the society we live in and our personal experiences in that society. If the expression of an emotion is an integral part of it, as Izard maintains, then our emotions can be said to be influenced by learning. For example, in some cultures it's considered appropriate to wail loudly, even scream, at the death of a close family member, and anyone who did not do so would be thought unfeeling. In others, however, a few quiet tears are considered the "right" way to express sorrow, and giving vent to more impassioned demonstrations of grief would be considered melodramatic. Another clue to the influence of learning and the environment can be seen through observing abused children, who express fear (a "universal" emotion) at an earlier age than other children do (Gaensbauer & Hiatt, 1984, in Trotter, 1983). These children's unfortunate early experiences may have taught them to be more sensitive to fear.

Which Comes First—Thinking or Feeling?   You see a mugger coming toward you in a dark alley, and you're afraid. Which comes first, the fear, quickly followed by your thoughts about what is about to happen—or your cognitive analysis of your situation, quickly followed by the emotion? This question is at the heart of a controversy currently being addressed by two prominent psychologists, Robert Zajonc (1980, 1984) and Richard S. Lazarus (1982, 1984).

"EMOTION IS PRIMARY"   Arguing that feeling is "the first link in the evolution of complex adaptive functions that eventually differentiated animals from plants," Zajonc (1980, p. 156) maintains that emotion is basic and independent from thought. His theory rests on a number of bases.

First, *emotion is universal among animals.* We don't know whether rabbits think, but we do know that they show fear of snakes. Even if they do process events cognitively (that is, think), a rabbit facing a snake has no time to think about how dangerous the situation is—how likely the snake is to attack, whether this is a poisonous snake, and so forth. If the rabbit is going to survive, it must run fast—possibly as soon as it sees a movement that *might* be a snake. Second, *emotions are inescapable.* We may be able to control the expression of a feeling, but we can't control the feeling itself. Third, *feelings are not easily changed.* When we take an instant dislike to a person, a food, or a piece of music, we're not likely to change our mind about it. If feelings were secondary to logical thought, they might not persist so stubbornly. And fourth, *we communicate our feelings nonverbally,* for the most part. It's hard to put feelings into words, which suggests that emotion is experienced outside of, and ahead of, the cognitive system.

"THOUGHT IS PRIMARY"   Countering Zajonc's view, Lazarus contends that thought is a necessary condition of emotion. He bases his argument on several kinds of evidence.

First, he maintains that an immediate emotional reaction to a stimulus doesn't mean that there's no cognitive appraisal of that stimulus. The rabbit *knows* that a slight rustle in the grass or a dimly perceived shape can signify danger. The appraisal is instantaneous, and *it is this appraisal that engenders the fear.* Second, *the fact that someone is thinking does not necessarily mean that the thought is rational and logical.* Cognitive therapy (described in Chapter 15) is based on just this premise, that faulty belief systems cause distressing emotional states. Third, *some emotions are based more on thought than others;* fear may be intuitive, but anxiety results from thinking about the negative aspects of a situation. And finally, people in different cultures experience different feelings about similar situations, feelings that are based on the values, commitments, and beliefs of their societies.

Which is primary, then? Both these schools of thought can marshal convincing arguments, based on research and other evidence, for their points of view. Neither argument appears, at this time, to be subject to proof, and intelligent thinkers are to be found on both sides of the controversy.

Cognitive-Chemical Interactions in Emotion

Most of us have accepted the idea that the chemicals in our body affect the way we feel, think, and act. This is, after all, the rationale for taking psychoactive drugs that simulate the action of natural neurotransmitters. More recently, moreover, we have been discovering that the way we feel, think, and act affects the chemicals our bodies secrete. Males in a position of dominance, for example, seem to secrete more of the neurotransmitter *serotonin*. When members of a college fraternity were measured for serotonin levels, the officers were found to have higher levels than other members. Evidence that the leadership led to the serotonin, and not vice versa, comes from research with monkeys (Raleigh, McGuire, Brammer, & Yuwiler, 1984).

Dominant males in colonies of vervet monkeys have been shown to have twice as much circulating serotonin in their blood as other males. When the leader is isolated from the group, his serotonin levels drop. When another male assumes the dominant role, his serotonin level rises to about twice its normal level. Then, when the original leader returns, his serotonin level rises again and the deposed monkey's drops again.

Other research with monkeys (Brady, 1967, 1975) has shown that monkeys that are in control of an event secrete more of the neurotransmitter norepinephrine. High levels of this chemical usually lead to feelings of optimism and enthusiasm; low levels are associated with depression (Schildkraut & Kety, 1967). Before taking part in studies involving avoidance of shock, the monkeys' levels of norepinephrine and epinephrine were fairly low, but after the monkeys had learned how to avoid a painful electric shock, their norepinephrine levels soared. This adaptive mechanism helps to explain why people who feel they have control over their lives have a much more positive outlook, as we saw when we discussed the phenomenon of learned helplessness in Chapter 5. Often, people who believe that they have control feel better even when they don't exercise it, which is a powerful argument for seeing life as a series of challenges rather than a series of blows dealt by fate.

Polygraph test *Lie-detector test.*

The well-established fact that a relationship exists between our emotions and our bodies is the basis for the development of the lie detector, or ***polygraph*** (see Figure 11-12). Since most people tend to feel anxious when they lie, and since there are a number of common physical signs of anxiety—such as faster heartbeat and breathing rate and increased perspiration—the notion that judging whether someone is telling the truth by measuring some of these physical signs is seductive. The ancient Hindus tried to do it by requiring people suspected of crimes to chew a mouthful of rice; those who couldn't spit it out onto a sacred leaf were judged guilty. Why? People who are afraid tend to salivate less, and this would cause the rice to stick in their dry mouths and be impossible to spit out. Our technically advanced modern polygraph is based on the same physiological relationship, but it isn't always reliable, as shown in the box "Lie Detectors: Foolproof or Fraudulent?"

In Chapter 12, we'll take a look at aspects of people's lives that are strong motivating forces and are also closely associated with the emotions: gender and sexuality.

FIGURE 11-12 *Measures in a typical polygraph test. This represents tracings in a polygraph recording. The top tracing shows breathing rate; the middle tracing shows electrodermal response (EDR); the bottom tracing shows blood pressure. The subject—who claimed not to have seen an envelope, containing money, which was stolen— was asked whether the envelope was brown (1), red (2), blue (3), yellow (4), or gray (5). You can see the sharp rise in EDR when question 3 was asked. The subject finally admitted to having taken the money and having returned it, in its blue envelope. Electrodermal response is the most accurate of the three measures.*

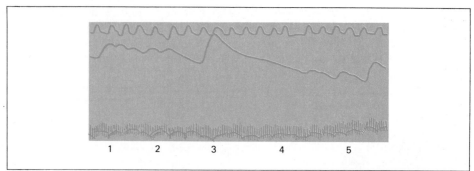

Your chances of being hooked up to a lie detector at some point are greater now than they were several years ago. Increasing numbers of government agencies and private employers have been requiring job applicants and current employees to take polygraph tests, and law enforcement agencies have turned to them more and more to help solve crimes. The consequences of "failing" a lie-detector test may include being fired from a job (with a consequent reputation for lying or theft); being refused government security clearance (with this fact going on one's record); or indictment on a criminal charge, a trial, and perhaps a prison term. What should you do if you're asked to take such a test? Are these tests useful and ethically justifiable? Let's look at the evidence.

Suppose that Ms. A., the owner of Scooper Dupers, an ice cream parlor, finds a persistent shortage in the cash register—a discrepancy between the amount of ice cream being sold and the cash taken in. She questions her 12 employees and is unable to figure out who is either stealing money or giving away ice cream. She administers lie-detector tests to all 12. Six "fail" the test and are fired. The question is: Have the real culprits been fired?

People selling such tests often tell prospective customers that psychologists have *proved* that they work. This is not true. What psychologists have found is that on a probability basis, they "detect" more people who are lying than people who are not. In any particular instance, however, the tests are not foolproof. (This is like the probability that when we toss a coin, we don't know on any given toss whether heads or tails will come up, but we do know that if we toss enough coins, we'll turn up half heads and half tails.)

Because results of lie detector tests have a high error rate, Ms. A. is likely to be firing one or more honest employees. To see how this could be, let's see how these tests, called *polygraph tests,* work.

The examiner reminds the subject of his or her right not to take the test and has the person sign a consent form testifying that the test is being

LIE DETECTORS: FOOLPROOF OR FRAUDULENT?

taken "voluntarily." (An important ethical issue here is how voluntary such a step can be when the subject feels that refusing to take the test will make him or her the object of suspicion.) The examiner then discusses the questions that will be asked. Some are irrelevant ("Are you in the United States?"), some are designed to elicit an emotional response ("Besides what you told me about, have you ever stolen anything?"), and some are related to the specific purpose of the test ("What color was the envelope containing the stolen money?").

Before the examiner actually asks the questions—usually no more than 12 questions over a time period of 3 to 4 minutes—devices are attached to the subject's body. These measure breathing rate, blood pressure, and *electrodermal response (EDR),* an index that detects changes in the resistance of the skin to the passage of a very weak electric current. This last measure, EDR, is the most accurate. (See Figure 11-12.) The subject cannot see either the examiner or the machine's record of his or her responses.

The tests do show that certain physiological responses reflect a high level of emotionality. But they don't necessarily prove that the emotions are linked to lying. The theory underlying these tests is that persons who are guilty of whatever wrongdoing the test is being given to uncover will respond emotionally to the key questions and that these measures can correctly identify emotional responses. Often this is so: people show greater changes from their *baseline* scores (the scores they show when they're answering irrelevant questions) when they're lying than when they're telling the truth.

There are, however, many fac-

tors that affect a person's score on a test. Some people react emotionally to certain words or phrases even when they're telling the truth. Those who believe that the lie detector is effective in detecting lies are more likely to receive accurate readings from it than people who don't (probably because they'll be more nervous about being found out when they lie than people who don't think that lie detectors work). It's also possible to reduce detectability in a number of ways. Laboratory studies have shown that it's harder to detect lying by subjects who have taken tranquilizers, people who are not paying close attention to the questions, habitual liars, those of the same ethnic group as the examiner, and those who were later-born children in large families (Waid & Orne, 1982).

The principle underlying polygraph testing is that people who show anxiety are lying. Yet, as the authors of a recent review of the psychological literature on these tests have pointed out, anxiety can stem from many causes other than lying (for example, the anxiety some people feel just from having to take the test). They conclude that the tests can sometimes detect deception at rates that are better than chance, especially when the test is conducted by an experienced examiner who asks narrowly focused questions of a subject who believes in the test. These psychologists point out, however, that the tests often indicate that a truthful person is lying or that a liar is telling the truth, thus giving rise to scientific skepticism about them (Saxe, Dougherty, & Cross, 1985). Such skepticism was voiced in a recent resolution adopted by the American Psychological Association maintaining that scientific evidence for the validity of polygraph tests to detect deception is unsatisfactory, and that if the test is to be given at all, it should be administered only in narrowly defined situations and by well-trained examiners (American Psychological Association, 1986). At present, civil liberties organizations are trying to ban the use of polygraph tests and are counseling people who have been asked to take them (American Civil Liberties Union, 1985).

1. Motivation is the force that energizes and gives direction to behavior, and that underlies the tendency to persist. Current research focuses mainly on the factors that arouse and energize behavior. Emotions are subjective reactions to our environment that are accompanied by neural and hormonal responses. They are generally experienced as pleasant or unpleasant and are considered adaptive reactions that affect the way we think.

2. Motivation is multidimensional and cannot be explained by any single theory. Different theories emphasize the importance of instincts (inborn patterns of behavior), drives (internal tension states, such as hunger, that propel people or animals to act and which may be unconscious), and needs (which may be physiological or psychological and which operate in a hierarchical way, so that we generally satisfy those most basic for survival first). One need is for sensory stimulation, and one explanation for some kinds of behavior is the opponent-process theory. Cognitive approaches stress the importance of our interpretation of events, of our incentives, and of our locus of control.

3. Some kinds of behavior often studied by motivational researchers are hunger and eating; aggression; achievement; and arousal, curiosity, and boredom.

4. Subjective feelings of hunger are linked to insulin levels (a biological factor). Insulin is released when we eat and is important in the conversion of blood glucose and carbohydrates into energy. When insulin levels are high, we get hungry.

5. Theories about why people become obese include these. First, there is a possibility that we are perpetuating an evolutionary mechanism by which we eat when we can and store energy in the form of fat against the possibility of famine. Second, in some people, the *set point,* the mechanism controlled by the hypothalamus that signals us to stop eating when an ideal weight has been reached, may be higher than average. Third, people who are addicted to the taste and texture of food may eat too much of it. Fourth, people who respond to *external* cues (like time of day, ads for food, or the availability of food) may eat more than people who respond to *internal* cues (like stomach contractions or low blood glucose or insulin levels). Most current diet programs try to get overweight people to eat less and exercise more.

6. A number of theories try to explain the cause of aggression, any behavior intended to harm someone or something. Biological theories point to the implication of several brain structures in the regulation of aggressive behavior and to hormones and other brain chemicals, such as testosterone, estrogen, and norepinephrine. Learning theories emphasize our observations of other people's actions and the messages we get from our culture. Violence depicted on television seems to teach an acceptance of aggressive behavior to both adults and children. Events that trigger aggressive behavior include frustration, negative evaluation, and insults.

7. Human beings have different needs to attain goals by putting forth their best efforts. This need to achieve (nAch) is often measured by the Thematic Apperception Test (TAT). nAch may be partly inherited, but it can also be spurred by certain child-rearing techniques or incentives. Locus of control also seems to influence achievement.

8. Arousal is a physiological state that we experience as an ability to process information, react to an emergency, or experience a wide range of emotions. Curiosity is a desire to learn about new events or objects. Human beings are curious animals who seem to become aroused as they process information in the absence of any reward other than the satisfaction of their curiosity. Although different people find different levels of arousal satisfying, most of us feel most comfortable and do our best work at a moderate level. Individual differences may be inherited. Boredom is a state of low arousal that seems to be associated with some behaviors.

9. There are several different ways of classifying emotions. Most theories concentrate on a few basic emotions that interact to produce more complex feelings. The major explanations for emotions are based on physiology, cognition, or the interaction of physical and mental factors. The James-Lange theory suggests that we base the way we feel on physical sensations like increased heart rate and muscle contractions. The Cannon-Bard theory suggests that feelings are purely cognitive, since physical reactions are the same for different emotions and people can't tell one emotion from another on the basis of physiological signs. The Schachter-Singer theory maintains that emotions are due to both our cognitive appraisal of an event and our bodily reactions: people notice physiological changes, note what is going on around them, and label their emotions according to both kinds of observations. The facial-feedback theory proposes that our facial expressions influence the way we feel.

10. Two major questions about emotions are whether they are inborn or learned, and which comes first, thinking or feeling.

11. When people experience an event as uncontrollable, they feel more negative about it than when they feel they can direct its outcome. Feelings of control are linked to the brain chemical norepinephrine.

12. Lie detectors (polygraph tests) are not very reliable in determining a subject's truthfulness by monitoring such physiological signs as breathing rate, blood pressure, and electrodermal response. This is because people sometimes react emotionally to questions that they answer truthfully and at other times are able to mask emotional responses when they are lying.

KEY TERMS

Aggression (page 392)
Arousal (400)
Autonomic arousal (401)
Drive (385)
Emotion (383)
Ethologist (384)
Incentives (387)

Instinct (384)
Locus of control (387)
Motivation (383)
nAch (397)
Opponent-process theory
  (386)
Polygraph test (412)

Premenstrual syndrome
  (393)
Reticular activation system
  (RAS) (401)
Self-actualization (386)
Set point (389)

Thematic Apperception Test
  (TAT) (397)
Violence (392)
Yerkes-Dodson law (402)

SUGGESTED READINGS

GEEN, R. G., & DONNERSTEIN, E. I. (Eds.). (1983). *Aggression: Theoretical and empirical reviews: Vol. 1. Theoretical and methodological issues,* and *Vol. 2. Issues and research.* New York: Academic. Provides comprehensive coverage of developments in the field of aggression since the 1970s. Includes both theoretical and applied research.

MASLOW, A. H. (1971). *The farther reaches of human nature.* New York: Viking. Discusses how people can become self-actualized. Maslow's humanistic view is presented clearly and forcefully.

SPENCE, J. T. (Ed.). (1983). *Achievement and achievement motives.* New York: Freeman. Brings together the current research and thinking about achievement motivation.

STUART, R. B. (1978). *Act thin, stay thin.* New York: Norton. The condensed version of a classic book on dieting. In this book Stuart explains why his behavioral approach to dieting works.

TIGER, L. (1979). *Optimism: The biology of hope.* New York: Simon & Schuster. Presents the case that humans are inclined to be optimistic. Tiger traces the origins of this tendency through our evolutionary history, showing how and why this tendency evolved.

ZUCKERMAN, M. (1979). *Sensation-seeking: Beyond the optimal level of arousal.* Hillsdale, NJ: Erlbaum. Packed with information about the sensation seeker. A must for anyone interested in this topic.

CHAPTER

12

SEXUALITY AND GENDER ROLES

■ Which differences between the sexes actually exist, and which are myths?

■ How do gender differences arise?

■ How do standards for male and female behavior affect adjustment?

■ What is known about the physiological basis for the human sexual response?

■ How does human sexuality develop and function across the life span?

■ What is known about what determines heterosexual and homosexual orientation?

■ How prevalent is sexual dysfunction, and what can be done about it?

■ What triggers sexual arousal?

■ Does pornography cause sexual violence against women?

Most of the players at the Port Washington Tennis Academy are more or less in my league: our enthusiasm far outweighs our ability. Some, however, are known around the world, mostly because of the academy's commitment to finding and training talented young players. Since the editor of one of the magazines I sometimes write for knew that I live 5 minutes away from the academy, she asked me to go to an exhibition match held a few years ago between Billie Jean King and Renee Richards. King's opinion about Richards's right to compete on the women's tennis circuit might provide an article.

Richards strode onto the court wearing gold hoop earrings and a very short lavender dress that now and then uncovered tiers of ruffles on her panties. The extreme "femininity" of her outfit contrasted sharply with her height (6 feet 2 inches), her broad shoulders, and her well-muscled arms and legs. She lost to King, and at the press conference afterwards, when I asked her how she felt about her game, she smiled, shook her head, and said, "Dick never would have served that poorly." Who was Dick? He was Renee Richards before her sex-change operation, when she was Richard Raskin, a New York opthalmologist, an amateur tennis player, and a man.

The question whether Richards was a man or a woman was a source of controversy in tennis circles. Did the sex-reassignment operation and the hormones she received in conjunction with it make Richards a woman and therefore eligible to compete against other women? Or did she retain the athletic advantages of male power and strength and of years of competing with men that gave her an unfair advantage over other women? I held the latter point of view, but the New York Supreme Court ruled that Renee Richards could play as a woman, without having to pass the chromosomal test that is often used to determine a person's biological sex when it's in question.

—From the notebooks of Sally Olds

Issues like these raise the questions: What constitutes sex and gender? What makes us male or female, and what are the differences and similarities between the sexes? How do differences show up, and which ones are inborn and which imposed by our upbringing? These are some of the questions which psychologists are interested in, and which we examine in this chapter. We talk about how gender is determined and how that in turn affects our feelings about our identity as males or females. We talk about the changes that have occurred in our society as traditional gender roles have become blurred. And we discuss the physiological and the psychological facets of sexuality and their ramifications for other aspects of our lives, from birth through old age. Finally, we talk about various sexual and gender-identity disorders (such as the one that makes people like Richard Raskin feel that they are trapped in the bodies of the wrong sex) and the kinds of therapies available to treat them. These subjects are of interest to psychologists in virtually all areas of specialization, since they revolve around issues that affect us profoundly. As we'll see, sexual drive and gender role are prime motivating forces for many aspects of our behavior, not just those that are clearly sexual in nature.

GENDER AND GENDER IDENTITY ▰▰▰▰▰▰▰▰▰▰▰

When long hair for boys and men came into fashion during the 1960s, many older people would say with irritation, "I can't tell these days whether people on the street are boys or girls." When you look at the situation dispassionately, why should the sex of a perfect stranger matter, anyway? It matters because a person's sex is a prime identifying trait. It's usually the first characteristic we notice about someone, and we're distinctly uncomfortable when we can't recognize it. Our sex to a large extent determines how we think of ourselves and how other people think of us. In recent years a great deal of research, discussion, and controversy have centered on the extent and cause of sex and gender differences.

To understand the arguments in this controversy, we need to be familiar with a few important terms and the way we use them in this book. The terms *sex* and *gender* are often used interchangeably, to designate the categories *male* and *female*. In this book we use the term **sex differences** to refer to actual physical differences between males and females. We use the term *gender* to refer to aspects of behavior that may or may not be tied to biology. Thus, **gender identity** is the awareness that develops in early childhood that one is male or female. **Gender roles** are the behaviors, attitudes, and interests that a culture says are appropriate for males and females. **Gender stereotypes** are exaggerated generalizations about masculine and feminine attitudes and behavior that sometimes reflect reality, but often do not. A wide variety of stereotypes exist, such as the belief that men are active and aggressive, while women are passive and dependent.

Sex differences *Physical differences between males and females.*

Gender identity *Awareness, developed in early childhood, that one is male or female.*

Gender roles *Behaviors, attitudes, and interests that a culture says are appropriate for males and females.*

Gender stereotypes *Generalizations about masculine and feminine attitudes and behavior.*

Sex and Gender Differences

In addition to the physical differences between the sexes, research shows that there are some psychological differences but that these tend to be quite small. We get a skewed view of the differences that do exist, because studies that yield similarities are less likely to be published than those that show differences. Furthermore, because the differences that do exist are usually small, there is generally a large overlap between men's and women's abilities (Matlin, 1987). That is, in any given area where there are differences, the differences usually show up in small groups of scores at the extremes of measurement, but most of the scores for both sexes cluster in the middle.

You won't see any references to the "opposite sex" in this book, then, because in most ways men and women, and boys and girls, are more alike than they are different. Let's take a look at some of the research on differences—and similarities—between the sexes.

How Do Males and Females Differ?   PHYSICAL DIFFERENCES   Aside from their distinctive anatomies, there are other biological differences between the sexes. Males and females are born with different patterns of **chromosomes,** the tiny particles that carry **genes,** the transmitters of inherited characteristics. Normal human beings have 46 chromosomes in each cell, two of which determine their biological sex. Females are born with two X sex chromosomes (XX), and males are born with one X chromosome and one Y (XY).

The difference in chromosomes seems to give the female a lifelong health advantage. Males are more vulnerable in many ways from conception on. Although 120 to 170 males are conceived for every 100 females, only 106 baby boys are actually born for every 100 girls. Boys have a higher likelihood of being spontaneously aborted, of being born dead, or of dying in the first year of life (Rugh & Shettles,

Chromosomes *Tiny rod-shaped particles that carry genes; in the normal person, there are 46 chromosomes in each cell.*

Genes *Transmitters of inheritance, carried on the chromosomes.*

1971). Shepherd-Look reports, "Until adulthood it is difficult to find a pathological condition in which the incidence among females is higher than among males" (1982, p. 408). At all ages, males die at higher rates than females (Lewis & Lewis, 1977).

Why are males more vulnerable? Explanations include the possibility of protective genes on the X chromosome, harmful genes on the Y chromosome, and a more efficient mechanism in females for forming antibodies to fight against infection (Purtilo & Sullivan, 1979). Whatever the basic cause of their vulnerability, poverty makes it worse—showing how biology and environment interact (Birns, 1976).

There are, then, distinct biological differences between the sexes, which influence development in certain important ways. Since gender roles vary so much from one culture to another, however, biological differences can provide only a partial explanation for them, and learning must account for much of what we consider masculine or feminine.

PSYCHOLOGICAL DIFFERENCES   A flood of recent research on cognitive and personality differences between males and females has shown that these differences are less clear-cut than physical differences. Are boys and men better at math than girls and women? The answer depends on what kind of mathematical problems we study. Do girls and women communicate better than boys and men? The answer to that question depends on how we define *communication*. Are males more aggressive and females more sensitive to other people's feelings? In both cases, the answer seems to be *yes*, but not by much.

Cognitive differences   A new level of discussion of gender-based differences seems to have resulted from the publication, in 1974, of a major analysis of more than 2000 studies on this topic, which found only a few clear-cut dissimilarities between boys and girls (Maccoby & Jacklin, 1974). In most cognitive areas studied, including general intelligence, learning, memory, formation of concepts, reasoning tasks, problem solving, and creativity, there were no differences between males and females.

Only three consistent cognitive differences were noted, all of which usually develop in middle childhood. After about the age of 10 or 11, girls do better on a wide range of tasks involving word skills and boys excel in mathematics and in spatial relations. Analysis of the data shows that these "well-established" differences are present but are very small (Hyde, 1981).

More recently, larger differences have shown up among mathematically gifted seventh- and eighth-graders who have taken the math portion of the Scholastic Aptitude Test (SAT); the male to female ratio is about 13:1 for scores above 700, scores that are attained by about 1 in 10,000 students (Benbow & Stanley, 1980, 1983).

When researchers have analyzed findings like these, however, they have found interesting differences in specific skills *within* cognitive areas (Deaux, 1985). For example, although boys do better on algebra problems, girls do just as well in arithmetic and geometry and better in computation (Becker, 1983; Marshall, 1984). Whereas boys do better on some measures of spatial skills (the ability, for example, to visualize what an object would look like if it were seen from a different angle), girls do just as well on other measures that require a more analytic strategy and that are more closely related to mathematical and scientific reasoning (Linn & Petersen, 1985). These fine points are relevant when we look at reasons for the superiority of one sex over the other in certain abilities, as we will see later in this chapter.

It is also noteworthy that these gender differences are changeable. Training in math skills can significantly improve performance by both males and females. As a possible reflection of different emphases in education over the past 20 years, the gap between males and females in verbal, mathematical, and spatial skills has narrowed significantly (Deaux, 1985). It is important, therefore, that parents and teachers be careful not to underestimate specific abilities in any of these cognitive areas by either sex. There is *no* basis for discouraging young people from pursuing career goals

(© Peter Miller/Photo Researchers)

This girl's absorption in an abacus illustrates the interest that math holds for many girls—despite research findings which suggest that, on the average, boys perform better in this subject. When considering an individual student, it's important to recognize that training can improve skills—and that many girls are better at math than many boys.

more commonly associated with the other sex. What matters is not any overall difference between males and females—it's how good a particular boy is in writing or how good a particular girl is in math that will affect the chances for success.

Personality differences It's harder to measure personality than cognitive abilities, and therefore even harder to determine when gender differences in personality appear. The expression of our personality traits is often affected by the situation we're in, as we'll see in Chapter 13. Thus, personality differences may show up on one occasion and not on another. In fact, such differences show up more in situations that encourage gender stereotypes. Women seem to act more "feminine" and men more "masculine" when they know that someone is watching them (Unger, 1985). For this reason, it is quite possible that laboratory experiments *overestimate* the degree of personality differences that actually exist in the real world (Matlin, 1987).

Two personality traits that are often associated more with one gender are aggressiveness (usually considered characteristic of males) and empathy (usually considered characteristic of females). Let's look briefly at each of these.

From an early age boys play more boisterously, roughhouse more, fight more, and try more often to establish dominance over other children; and in virtually every society around the world, adult men are more aggressive than women (Maccoby, 1980). In an analysis of the literature on gender and aggressive behavior, Eagly and Steffen (1986) found that, on the average, men are more aggressive than women and that this difference is greater when we talk about the kind of aggression that causes physical pain or injury, as opposed to psychological or social harm. The same investigators also found that women and men think differently about aggression, and that this probably affects the way they behave. Women feel more anxious and guilty about their aggressive behavior, are more conscious of the harm that aggression does to its victims, and are more concerned about the danger their aggression might bring to themselves. We see, then, how a trait that may be partly hormonally based is greatly accentuated by the gender roles created by culture.

Another body of research suggests that girls and women are more likely to be empathic, that is, to have such an intimate understanding of other people's feelings that when others are happy, they're happy, and when others are sad, they're sad (Hoffman, 1977).

Stereotypes about the way men and women communicate are drummed into our ears from the time we're babies. In television comedy series, in comic strips, in nightclub acts, and in everyday conversation, we see or hear about the strong, silent man and the gossipy, gabby woman. We expect men to use language they wouldn't use "in front of ladies," and we don't expect "ladies" to use such language at all. In recent years, a spate of studies have explored these beliefs to see which ones are true (some are) and which ones have no basis in fact (some are directly the reverse of reality).

Girls and women seem to be better at handling words in every stage of life. For example, they begin to talk earlier, do better on the verbal tasks of intelligence tests, and find it easier to learn new languages. Besides verbal ability, however, verbal communication includes the way words are used—speech patterns and content, for example, and voice quality (Matlin, 1987). It also has a nonverbal component, involving signals sent by our bodies and our facial expressions. Although there is considerable overlap in men's and women's communication patterns and individual differences within a sex are very great, a fair number of gender differences do show up in both kinds of communication, especially in nonverbal communication.

GENDER DIFFERENCES IN COMMUNICATION

VERBAL COMMUNICATION

When we look at the *amount* of talking that men and women do, we see that the stereotype is completely wrong. Yes, little girls seem to talk more than little boys, but among adults, the roles reverse and men talk more. In one study, men talked about 4 times longer than women when subjects of both sexes were asked to describe three artistic works (Swacker, 1975). Men speak for longer periods of time, and even when they're groping for the right words, they "hold the floor" by saying "um," "er," or "ah" 3 times more than women do (Frances, 1979). Furthermore, men interrupt much more (E. Hall, 1984).

Women, then, are not gabbier than men. Nor do they gossip much more, and their gossip is not at all different in kind from that of men. Gossip, defined in one study as conversation about any third person, was found to account for 71 percent of women's conversation and 64 per-

cent of men's; both males and females said positive things 27 percent of the time and negative ones 25 percent (Levin & Arluke, 1985).

Two typically female characteristics tend to make women seem unsure of themselves. One is a tendency to speak with a raised inflection at the end of a sentence. Thus, asked when she'll be ready to leave her office, a woman says, "In about an hour?" implying, "If that's all right with you." Another is the "tag" question. Rather than say simply, "This textbook is boring," a woman may add, "isn't it?" This pattern might indicate that the speaker isn't sure enough of her opinion to state it flatly without confirmation—or that she's trying to show openness and sensitivity to another person's views (Lakoff, 1973; Miller & Swift, 1976).

Women's voices are higher than men's partly because their vocal cords are shorter, lighter, and less muscular, but also because they seem to form words differently to produce words in "gender-appropriate" pitch (Matlin, 1987). Men swear more, and older women (in their seventies) use more words like *lovely, delightful,* and *dearest* (Hartman, 1976; Jay, 1980). Still, reading the transcribed testimony of courtroom witnesses, for example, does not allow us to determine the sex of the witness (O'Barr & Atkins, 1980). Apparently, the setting and the

But close analysis of the findings indicates that even though differences may exist, they're not large—certainly not large enough for us to predict aggressive or empathic behavior simply by knowing a person's sex. Gender accounts for a relatively small amount of the variability among people on these traits; there is a wider variation among members of the same sex than there is between one sex and the other (Hyde, 1981, 1984). Furthermore, the differences vary according to the way these traits are measured. When women report on their own levels of empathy, they come out far ahead of men; when girls' and women's nonverbal reactions to other people's emotional states are noted by an observer or by a physiological measure and compared with boys' and men's, no gender differences show up (Eisenberg & Lennon, 1983). Reported gender differences for aggression vary in the opposite direction, tending to be larger under direct observation, projective tests, or reports by peers, and smaller for self-reports or reports by parents or teachers (Hyde, 1984). Finally, differences in empathy and aggression vary according to the situation, sometimes showing up quite strongly, sometimes disappearing (Matlin, 1987). Thus, even these apparently "well-established" differences are questionable, and at best modest.

speaker influence the kind of language used.

Finally, men and women tend to talk about different things. In general, women are more likely to talk about feelings, while men talk about objects and events. Women discuss personal topics like family matters and relationships; men talk about cars, sports, current events, and music. Women listen to each other, showing understanding, whereas men like to give logical advice for solving everyday problems (Haas & Sherman, 1984).

NONVERBAL COMMUNICATION

Men and women send different signals without words, too. Men "own" more space: they take up more room with their bodies, tending to sit and stand with legs apart and hands on hips or reaching out. Women, on the other hand, look less relaxed and tend to keep their bodies more tightly contained, with legs together and hands folded in front or at their sides. Women use less personal space than men, and are likely to sit and stand closer to other people. Men and women don't show any differences, however, in the amount of touching they do. Women smile and laugh more and maintain more eye contact with the people they talk to. They

tend to be better at reading other people's facial expressions—that is, at figuring out how other people are feeling on the basis of how their faces look (E. Hall, 1984).

CAUSES OF GENDER DIFFERENCES IN COMMUNICATION

Although we don't have clear explanations for these differences, theories abound. One emphasizes women's subordinate social position. People who had less power would probably smile more to please those with more power, would take up less room with their bodies and less time with their words, and would work harder at understanding other people's feelings so that they could respond to them (Matlin, 1987). Some linguists reject this viewpoint on the ground that women behave like this with other women even more than with men (E. Hall, 1984). It is still possible, however, that the attitudes behind this kind of behavior are the basis for women's overall style of communicating, which might not vary much on the basis of other people's different levels of power.

Another theory, which is compatible with the first, emphasizes women's attention to and practice of various behaviors. For example, the way women hold their bodies proba-

bly results from years of socialization. Girls are instructed to look "ladylike" and to deal with the confining aspects of tight skirts or the potential immodesty of short ones. Girls and women may be urged to smile more than males are. When these lessons are delivered over and over again, they are taken seriously.

MAKING CHANGES

Because some of these differences in behavior work to the disadvantage of one sex or the other, it might be worth making efforts to change them. It's interesting to speculate on the changes that might occur in society if women brought their facial expressions into line with their feelings and didn't feel obliged to smile when they were angry or sad or were concentrating on an activity, and if men smiled more. What would happen if women claimed more space by loosening up their body posture and claimed more time by not permitting themselves to be interrupted? And what would happen if men paid more attention to other people's facial expressions to understand their feelings? If both men and women moved in the direction of each other's strengths, we might all improve our ability in this basic element of social life, communication.

Other psychological differences A number of other areas have been studied for gender differences. For example, some research suggests that men and women tend to think about moral issues in different ways, with men showing concern about justice and fairness, and women seeing morality as responsibility for a specific person or persons (Gilligan, 1982; Kohlberg, 1964, 1968). Gilligan (1982) cites biblical examples of this difference in morality: Abraham was ready to sacrifice the life of his son when God demanded it as proof of faith; but a woman proved to King Solomon that she was a baby's mother when she agreed to give up the infant to another woman rather than see it harmed. However, a subsequent analysis of the literature on moral development found little evidence of gender differences (Walker, 1984).

This situation, in which some studies contradict others, is typical. Girls and boys, and women and men, do behave differently in virtually every society around the world, but when we go beyond the culturally based differences to try to find underlying differences in male and female personalities, we find ourselves in very murky waters. (For a discussion of communication, which encompasses both cognitive and personality factors, see the box "Gender Differences in Communication.")

Why Do Males and Females Differ?   The nature-nurture debate—the controversy about the relative influence of heredity and environment—rages nowhere more fiercely than over the causes of differences between males and females. It is simplistic, however, to think of nature and nurture as either-or influences. Yes, there are definite biological differences between the sexes, including differences in maturation (in general, girls mature earlier) and in hormone levels. And yes, the fact that people with basically the same biological legacy act very differently, depending on when and where they live, shows that cultural and social factors play a major role. The weight of the evidence seems to suggest that biological tendencies exist, but that learning modifies these tendencies—either accentuating them or discouraging them—and that no inborn tendencies are unchangeable. Let's look at some of this evidence.

Androgens *Male sex hormones.*

HORMONES AND THEIR EFFECTS   One basic difference between the sexes is a different hormonal balance. All embryos begin life with undifferentiated body structures, and not until about the sixth week, when **androgens** (male sex hormones, including *testosterone*) flood the bodies of those babies destined to be male do masculine body structures begin to form (Hoyenga & Hoyenga, 1979; Money & Ehrdardt, 1972). If little or no testosterone is present, female body structures begin to form at about the eleventh or twelfth week. The presence or absence of testosterone, then, is critical for sexual differentiation.

In recent years a number of researchers have explored the effects of the sex hormones on the development of brain structures. It's possible that such structural differences might help to explain differences in behavior between the sexes. Evidence from research with animals indicates that hormones circulating before or at about the time of birth can cause differences in the behavior of males and females. It is often risky to make assumptions about human beings on the basis of findings about rats, guinea pigs, dogs, sheep, or even our closer relatives, monkeys; but some scientists believe that there may be similarities.

Although different species of animals develop differently, in general, low levels of androgens (male sex hormones) before or at about the time of birth result in female characteristics, whereas higher levels result in male characteristics. Researchers have come to these conclusions after conducting many animal experiments in which they have manipulated hormone levels. Since, for both ethical and practical reasons, this cannot be done with human beings, most human research has relied on two types of subjects—persons who have had unusual prenatal exposure to hormones, and persons born with certain disorders, such as abnormal production of or sensitivity to sex hormones.

One team of researchers who explain behavioral differences in terms of hormones cites the cases of nine girls whose mothers had received synthetic progestins during pregnancy and who were born with abnormal external sexual organs (Ehrhardt & Money, 1967). After surgery, the girls looked normal and were capable of normal female reproduction. Though raised as girls from birth, they were called "tomboys," liked to play with trucks and guns, and competed with boys in active sports. There may be something in fetal masculinization that affects that part of the central nervous system that controls energy-expending behavior. However, the parents of these girls may have been influenced by their daughters' genital masculinity at birth, or the girls' own awareness of their endocrine problems may have led to their tomboyish behavior. Furthermore, tomboyishness is common, and since there was no control group, we don't even know how different from the norm these girls were, if at all.

ENVIRONMENTAL INFLUENCES   In some cases, small differences that exist between the sexes are encouraged and accentuated by societal forces. In other cases, the culture actually creates differences, apparently as part of a universal phenomenon: in every society, some roles are considered appropriate for females and some for males (although the roles themselves differ from culture to culture). How are beliefs about roles handed down in any culture?

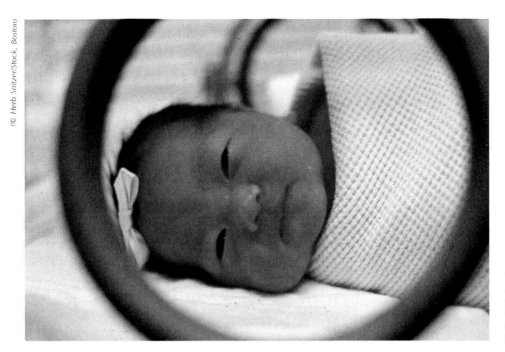

The pink bow in this baby's hair announces her biological sex to all who see her and sets the stage for her being treated in ways that her culture prescribes as suitable for girls.

Parents Even in these "liberated" times, parents treat their sons and daughters differently from infancy, often without realizing it. In one study, women who had small children of both sexes, and who said that they didn't see any differences between boys and girls in infancy, were given the chance to play with a 6-month-old baby, variously labeled as a boy or a girl. When these women thought the baby was a girl, they were more likely to offer "her" a doll; when they thought the baby was a boy, they were more likely to offer "him" a train (Will, Self, & Datan, 1976). Furthermore, parents seem to be more actively involved with their male infants (H. A. Moss, 1967; Shepherd-Look, 1982) and to treat them more roughly (Yarrow, Rubenstein, & Pederson, 1971). Middle-class and better-educated mothers talk to their daughters more than to their sons (Maccoby & Jacklin, 1974). Such differences in treatment may help to explain males' aggressiveness and females' fluency with words.

In many ways, however, parents treat their sons and daughters about the same. They have similar expectations for their children with regard to dressing and bathing themselves, they impose similar limits on how far from home children may go, and they impose similar limits on aggression; and mothers, at least, have similar expectations with regard to competence. Fathers consistently show more gender-stereotyping behavior, from their children's infancy on. They tend to pay more attention to sons; to emphasize competence for sons but relationships for daughters; and to encourage dependency in their daughters while stressing achievement, careers, and occupational success for their sons (Shepherd-Look, 1982).

Fathers, however, can also help both sons and daughters feel good about themselves in regard to gender identification without limiting their potential for success in a career or for becoming nurturant persons. Adults who function well at work and in their heterosexual relationships are most likely to have had warm relationships with fathers who were competent, strong, secure in their own masculinity, and nurturant toward their children. The son of such a father is apt to identify with him; and the daughter of such a father will be able to carry over her good feelings from her relationship with him to relationships with other males in her life. Conversely, the children of a punitive, rejecting father or a passive, ineffectual one are less likely to function well (Biller, 1981).

The media By the time the typical child has graduated from high school, he or she has watched more than 25,000 hours of television, including 360,000 commercials

(Action for Children's Television, undated). What messages are conveyed in this "megaviewing?"

Children will have seen about twice as many males as females on the television screen, and they will have observed that men and women on television act quite differently—more differently, in fact, than real-life men and women. Until very recently, television was one of the most effective media for spreading highly gender-stereotyped attitudes. Traditionally, males on television have been more aggressive, more active, and more competent than females, who have often been portrayed as submissive, inactive, and interested primarily in keeping house or becoming more beautiful (Mamay & Simpson, 1981; Sternglanz & Serbin, 1974). It isn't surprising, then, that children who watch a great deal of television develop more traditional attitudes about gender than those who watch little television (Frueh & McGhee, 1975). (However, it is also possible that parents with more traditional attitudes about gender are also more permissive about television.) Similar content-analysis studies have found highly gender-stereotyped behaviors and attitudes in children's books (Weitzman, Eifler, Hokada, & Ross, 1972).

With the growth of awareness of the damaging effects of such stereotyped messages, the publishers of children's books and the producers of television shows and commercials have become more sensitive to the need to portray healthier images of men and women. As a result, women on television are more likely to be working now, are smarter, and are less likely to be portrayed as family servants; men are more often shown taking care of children and doing the weekly marketing. Television portrayals still tend to lag behind real life, but they are moving away from the rigid gender-role stereotyping that has been characteristic for years.

Cultural attitudes   In the 1930s, the anthropologist Margaret Mead (1935) dramatically demonstrated the influence of culture on male and female behaviors when she reported on three tribes in New Guinea whose behavioral patterns did not conform to western stereotypes. Among the Arapesh, *both* men and women are "placid and contented, unaggressive and non-initiatory, non-competitive and responsive, warm, docile, and trusting" (p. 56), and men and women alike are nurturant toward children. Among the cannibalistic Mundugumor, "*both* men and women are expected to be violent, competitive, aggressively sexed, jealous and ready to see and avenge insult, delighting in display, in action, in fighting" (p. 213); the occasional mild or nurturant man or woman is a social misfit. The Tchambuli tribe does have separate expectations for males and females, but these are directly opposite to those in most societies. The woman is dominant, impersonal, and hardworking, while the man is less responsible, more concerned about personal appearance, and more emotionally dependent.

In most cultures around the world, men are more aggressive, have more authority than women, and usually do the dangerous, physically strenuous jobs, while the women do routine work closer to home. These patterns undoubtedly developed because the average man is taller, heavier, and more muscular than the average woman, and the woman is the one who bears and nurses babies. Today, however, when most work can be performed as well by a 90-pound woman as a 200-pound man and when women are bearing fewer children and breast-feeding them more briefly, cultural attitudes about gender roles are changing.

An important aspect of these cultural roles is the amount of power women and men have in society. People with less power may need to be more aware of the feelings of those with more power so that they can respond appropriately; in addition, leaders may be freer than followers about expressing their feelings. Thus, "woman's intuition" may more accurately be referred to as "subordinate's intuition" (Snodgrass, 1985). Similarly, if women are more likely to conform to other people's ideas in social situations (a tendency noted by some research), it may be due to their typically inferior social status compared with men, rather than anything having to do with sex or gender (Eagly, 1983; Eagly & Carli, 1981).

In recent years, of course, we've seen a great deal of change in our society with regard to gender-related attitudes and behaviors. Women have been achieving more power in the world of work, in politics, and within the family, and both men and women have shown interest in developing aspects of themselves that have not been part of traditional gender stereotypes. Research has found changed attitudes toward the roles of women and men, shifting toward more egalitarian attitudes and away from beliefs in traditional roles. Younger and better-educated people and those with higher incomes may have changed most, but a trend in this direction has shown up in most populations studied (Deaux, 1985).

As one sociologist has written:

> We can create any type of gender role society that we want—the most that biology can do is make some changes more difficult to accomplish, but there is no evidence of the inevitability of any aspect of gender role. The key question is better put as what type of gender role system do we desire and are we willing to receive the rewards and pay the cost of achieving that system? (Reiss, 1980, p. 61)

How Do Ideas about Gender Affect Our Lives? Despite the fact that boys and girls are more alike than different, myths persist about the differences between them. These myths take shape as gender stereotypes, beliefs that males and females have—and should have—certain distinctive characteristics. Our culture, like other societies around the globe, defines some behaviors, emotions, and attitudes as acceptable for males, others for females. Boys are expected to be dominant, aggressive, active, independent, and competitive; girls are expected to be nurturant, compliant, and dependent.

The wholesale acceptance of gender-typed societal restrictions has many far-reaching implications. People often deny their natural inclinations and abilities because they're ''unmasculine'' or ''unfeminine,'' often forcing themselves into ill-fitting academic vocational, and social molds. Sometimes not until adulthood do these stereotypes exert their fullest influence. (In middle age, however, it's common for each sex to take on behavior usually associated with the other—for women to become more assertive and men to become more sensitive to other people (Neugarten, 1968; Cytrynbaum et al., 1980).

Convinced that gender stereotyping constricts both men and women, preventing persons of either sex from achieving their potential, Sandra L. Bem (1974, 1976) developed a concept of psychological well-being, according to which the healthiest person is one whose personality includes a balanced combination of the most positive characteristics normally thought of as being appropriate for one sex or the other. Such a person, whom Bem describes as **androgynous,** might be assertive, dominant, self-reliant (''masculine'' traits), as well as compassionate, sympathetic, and understanding (''feminine'' traits).

Androgynous *Personality type integrating both typically ''masculine'' and typically ''feminine'' characteristics.*

Bem (1976) found that stereotyping restricts people in even the simplest, most everyday behaviors. Masculine men won't choose to prepare a baby bottle or wind yarn, and feminine women won't choose to nail boards together or attach artificial bait to a fishing hook, even if they could earn more money by doing these ''cross-gender'' activities than by doing gender-typed tasks. The major effect of femininity in women is not the inhibition of traditionally masculine behaviors, but often the inhibition of any behavior at all in a situation where the woman isn't sure about the right thing to do. On the contrary, androgynous men and women show the most freedom to judge a particular situation on its own merits and to take action on the basis of what seems most effective rather than what seems most ''appropriate'' for their gender.

Most contemporary psychologists subscribe to Bem's goal of freeing the human personality from the ''restricting prison'' of gender-role stereotyping (1976, p. 59) in the interest of healthy development throughout childhood and in adolescence and adulthood.

Theories of Gender Identity

Children are not born knowing what sex they are or knowing the implications of gender. How, then, do they learn that they are male or female; that this basic element of their identity will, in the normal course of events, never change; and that certain kinds of behavior are expected of them? To explain how biological and environmental factors interact to produce people who think of themselves as male or female and act accordingly, three major theories have evolved. The two theories most often invoked today are *social learning theory* and *cognitive developmental theory*. The third theory is Freud's psychoanalytic theory, which was in fact the first important attempt to explain gender identity. Freudian theory holds that gender typing is the indirect result of anatomy and of a child's identification with the parent of the same sex—in many ways, an outgrowth of the Oedipus and Electra complexes (discussed in Chapter 13). Very few contemporary thinkers consider this a valid explanation, and so we'll consider only social learning theory and cognitive-developmental theory here.

Social-Learning Theory   Social-learning theorists (whose point of view was introduced in Chapter 5) propose that children learn to act like boys or girls by imitating the parent of the same sex (especially when that parent is seen as nurturant, competent, and powerful), and that they are then rewarded for behavior their parents and other adults think is appropriate and punished for behavior deemed inappropriate.

Although this theory seems to make sense, it has been hard to prove. First, children do imitate adults, but research findings imply that they don't necessarily imitate the parent of the same sex, or even necessarily a parent at all. When children are tested on masculinity or femininity, they are no more like their own parents than like a random group of other children's parents, and those who test similarly to their own parents score no closer to the parent of the same sex than to the one of the other sex (Hetherington, 1965; Mussen & Rutherford, 1963).

Second, although there are differences in the way parents treat sons and daughters, there are more similarities than differences, especially on important issues (Maccoby & Jacklin, 1974); for example, parents discourage fighting and encourage helping behavior for both boys and girls. It's possible that parents do treat sons and daughters more differently than the literature shows, however. Most of the studies we have deal with mothers' treatment of their children, and most focus on children age 5 and younger. Since fathers gender-type more than mothers and since sex differentiation increases with age, any analysis that does not take these factors into account is likely to be skewed (Block, 1978). It's also possible that parents transmit gender-role standards in ways so subtle that they cannot be measured by present research methods.

Cognitive-Developmental Theory   According to Lawrence Kohlberg (1966), gender typing comes about as a natural corollary of cognitive development. Children don't depend on other people's serving as models to imitate or as dispensers of rewards and punishments; instead, they actively categorize themselves as "male" or "female" and then organize their lives around their gender. By the age of 2 or 3, a boy knows that he is a boy, decides he wants to do the things boys are supposed to do, does them, and is then rewarded by feeling secure in his gender identity. Sometime between the ages of 5 and 7, children achieve what Kohlberg calls "gender conservation," the realization that they will always be male or female. (At earlier ages, this awareness is not always present, as was clear in the case of Eric, who, at the age of 3, commented to his mother, "When I grow up I want to be a mommy just like you so I can play tennis and drive a car.")

Gender-role concepts, then, change as cognitive development advances. In fact, the brighter the children, the more quickly they adapt to the gender-role stereotypes of their cultures, since they notice the physical differences between the sexes, learn the societal prescriptions for the role of each gender, and try to live up to their role (Greenberg & Peck, 1974).

Gender Identity Disorders

Sometimes gender identification goes awry, so that a person feels uncomfortable with his or her biological sex and behaves in ways that are generally associated with the other sex. In this case, he or she is said to have a rare condition known as a *gender identity disorder.*

Gender Identity Disorder of Childhood   In a *gender identity disorder of childhood,* a young child, usually under 4 years old, develops a "profound disturbance of the normal sense of maleness or femaleness" (DSM III, 1980, p. 264). This is not just a rejection of stereotypical behavior— that is, it is not simply tomboyish or sissyish behavior, but something that goes far deeper. A little girl with this disorder might want to play house only if she can be the father, insist that she'll grow up to become a man, and want to play *only* with boys. A little boy might cross-dress (dress in girl's or women's clothes), want to play only with girls, always take the role of a woman in fantasy play, and use "girlish" gestures and actions.

A common pattern emerges in these cases: often the parents gave the child a name usually associated with the other sex, wanted a child of the other sex, or actively encouraged cross-dressing and other cross-gender behavior. Sometimes, for example, it is found that a mother taught her son how to put on makeup (Davison & Neale, 1986). Some researchers, however, have suggested that there is a hormonal basis for some cases (Ehrhardt & Money, 1967; R. Green, 1976). Most children, of course, engage in varying amounts of "cross-gender" play and dress-up with *no* gender identity conflicts, and parents do *not* have to worry that encouraging little girls to be assertive or little boys to be nurturant will cause gender confusion.

Transsexualism   Sometimes a child with a gender identity disorder grows up to be a *transsexual,* a person who (like Richard Raskin, described at the beginning of this chapter) feels that he or she is "trapped" in the body of the wrong sex, wants to live as a member of the other sex, and may want to be rid of his or her genitals. To be diagnosed as transsexual, the person must have felt this way for at least 2 years. Transsexuals usually suffer from anxiety and depression and often seek sex-change surgery to change their genitals so they can be sexually active as a member of the sex they feel themselves to be. Before the operation, they receive sex hormones to make them look like the other sex (in skin texture, hair growth, or breast formation, for example), and they begin to live as a member of that sex. An estimated 1000 transsexuals receive sex-change operations each year in the United States, even though it is highly controversial whether those who have had the surgery show better adjustment than those who have not (Davison & Neale, 1986). Some transsexuals respond well to behavior therapy (described in Chapter 15) that helps them bring their gender identity into conformity with their anatomy.

Gender identity disorder *Psychosexual disorder in which a person feels uncomfortable with his or her sex and behaves in ways that are generally associated with the other sex.*

Gender identity disorder of childhood *Disorder in which a young child develops a profound disturbance of the normal sense of maleness or femaleness.*

Transsexual *Person who has felt for at least 2 years that he or she is "trapped" in the body of the wrong sex, wants to live as a member of the other sex, and may want to be rid of his or her genitals.*

Right: Dr. Richard Raskin, a New York ophthalmologist, in 1974. Raskin, a transsexual, felt "trapped" in a man's body and decided to seek a sex-change operation. About 1000 transsexuals a year undergo such an operation.

Far right: After the sex-change operation, Raskin became Renee Richards, whose eligibility to play in a women's tennis tournament caused considerable controversy.

Our sexual behavior is one obvious manifestation of our gender, and one realm of development in which differences between the sexes are very obvious, even though there are many similarities here, too. Our physical endowment equips us for sexual behavior, provides a mechanism that makes it enjoyable, and readies us for a variety of reinforcing stimuli from the environment. Sexuality is a physical, a psychological, and a social phenomenon. It is a major motivating factor for our behavior and often has far-reaching effects on our lives. Our sexuality encompasses both our beliefs and our behaviors related to erotic stimulation; it is influenced by our biology, our emotions, and our culture.

Human sexuality was almost ignored by researchers until the 1940s, when Alfred Kinsey and his colleagues began to ask people what they did sexually and to make some observations of sexual activity (Kinsey, Pomeroy, & Martin, 1948; Kinsey, Pomeroy, Martin, & Gebhard, 1953). Then, in the 1950s, another pioneering team, William H. Masters, M.D., and Virginia E. Johnson began to discover what happens in the human body from the beginning of erotic stimulation up to and beyond the point of orgasm. (Masters & Johnson, 1966). Their study eventually included interviews with men and women of a wide range of ages, the use of sophisticated instruments to measure physiological responses, and direct observation and motion-picture recording.

To conduct their study program, it was necessary for Masters and Johnson to find volunteers who would be willing to engage in sexual activity under observation in the laboratory. Eventually, 694 men and women, including 276 married couples, agreed to participate in the research. All these volunteers possessed one crucial ability, the capacity to reach orgasm during both masturbation and sexual intercourse while being observed, and during the 12-year research program they experienced more than 10,000 orgasms in the lab. A particularly valuable group of observations were made through the use of newly developed instruments, such as an artificial penis made of clear plastic, powered by an electric motor and containing an optical system that enabled the observation and recording of internal bodily changes (Brecher, 1971). Masters and Johnson discovered basic facts about human sexuality that had never been known before. They opened the way to further study and to the application of these findings to therapy for a wide range of sexual dysfunctions.

Physiology of Human Sexual Response

Masters and Johnson identified four stages of sexual response, based on two basic physiological processes: *vasocongestion* (the flow of blood into a region's blood vessels as a result of the dilation of the vessels) and *myotonia* (the contraction of muscles in the genitals and throughout the body). The sexual response pattern is the same, regardless of the kind of stimulation—intercourse, manual or oral stimulation, masturbation, or even fantasy. Female orgasms derived from vaginal stimulation were once considered "more mature" than those resulting from clitoral stimulation, but we now know that the intensity and physiology of orgasm are the same, no matter how the orgasm is reached.

Erogenous zones Sexually sensitive areas of the body.

The pleasurable sensations associated with sexual contact go far beyond intercourse alone. We have many sexually sensitive areas in our bodies, known as **erogenous zones,** and people often experience arousal or orgasm from being touched in these spots. Besides the genital region (clitoris and vagina, penis and testes), the erogenous zones usually include the breasts, thighs, lips, anus, and buttocks—and may also include such other sites as the ears and armpits, depending on the individual. Different people are sensitive in different parts of their bodies; what one person may ignore, another may find highly erotic. (Figures 12-1, opposite, and 12-2, page 432, show the human sexual response.)

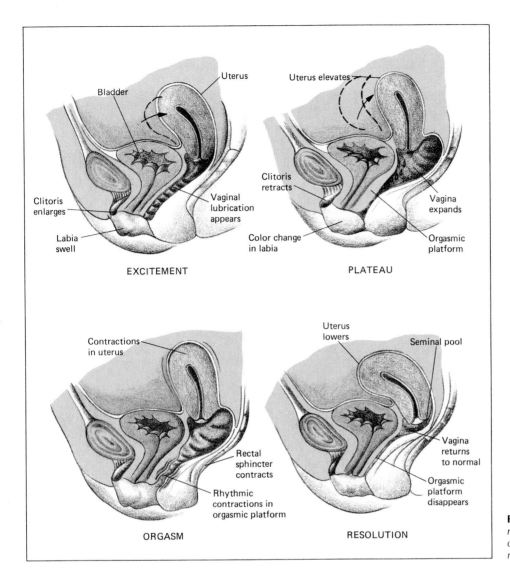

Uterus

Bladder

Clitoris
enlarges

Labia
swell

Vaginal
lubrication
appears

EXCITEMENT

Uterus elevates

Clitoris
retracts

Color change
in labia

Vagina
expands

Orgasmic
platform

PLATEAU

Contractions
in uterus

Rectal
sphincter
contracts

Rhythmic
contractions in
orgasmic platform

ORGASM

Uterus
lowers

Seminal pool

Vagina
returns
to normal

Orgasmic
platform
disappears

RESOLUTION

FIGURE 12-1 *Female sexual response. External and internal changes in the female sexual response cycle.*

Sexual Response Cycle EXCITEMENT In sexual excitement, the beginning stage of the response cycle, the female experiences lubrication of the vagina, enlargement of the breasts, erection of the nipples, swelling of the glans (tip) of the clitoris, and an expansion of the upper two-thirds of the vagina. In the male's excitement stage, the penis becomes erect, the skin of the scrotal sac smoothes out, and the testes are drawn closer to the body. Both sexes may experience an increase in pulse rate and blood pressure—and, late in this phase or early in the next one, a transitory rash called a *sex flush*.

PLATEAU In the plateau stage, vasocongestion is at its peak. The woman's vaginal walls thicken; the opening becomes smaller, enabling the vagina to grip the penis snugly; the clitoris draws up into the body; the uterus enlarges; and the color of the inner labia deepens. The man's penis is completely erect, the testes are enlarged, and a few drops of fluid (which may contain active sperm) appear at the tip of the penis. Breathing, pulse rate, and blood pressure continue to mount for both sexes.

ORGASM In both sexes, orgasm consists of a series of rhythmic muscular contractions of the pelvic organs at about 0.8-second intervals. The male orgasm has two

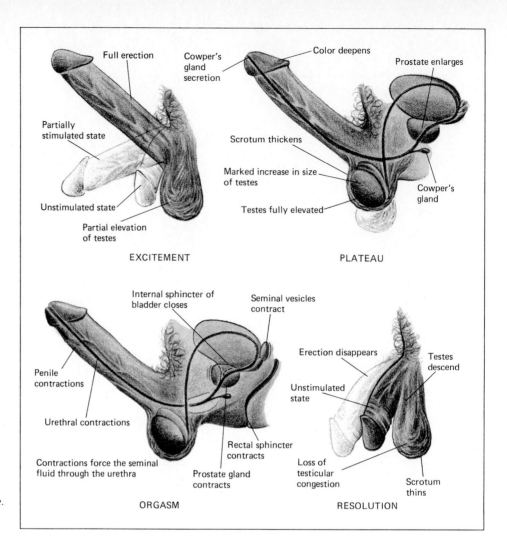

FIGURE 12-2 *Male sexual response. Internal changes in the male sexual response cycle.*

stages: first, "ejaculatory inevitability," that is, the sense the ejaculation is about to occur and cannot be stopped; and second, ejaculation itself, during which semen is forcefully expelled from the penis. In the female orgasm, the uterus also contracts.

RESOLUTION   In the final phase, resolution, the body returns to the unaroused state. For women, this reversal of the preceding processes usually takes 15 to 30 minutes but may take up to 1 hour for those who have been aroused but have not experienced orgasm. Men enter a *refractory period,* a time during which they are incapable of having an erection or an orgasm. This period may last only a few minutes for some men, or for as long as 24 hours in others. It is longer for older men. Women do not experience a refractory period, so that multiple orgasms are possible for them.

Problems can arise at any point in this response cycle, as we'll see when we discuss sexual dysfunctions later in this chapter.

Arousal of Sexual Desire   What makes a person want sex at all? Research points to the interaction of physiology and learning.

HORMONES   A number of studies have tied hormonal activity to sexual behavior in animals, although the connection between sex hormones and arousability or sexual activity in human beings has not been well established. Of the androgens (the male sex hormones), **testosterone** is the most studied. During the life cycle, when testosterone levels are high, the male is more inclined to engage in sexual behavior. During adolescence, testosterone levels rise; it is during these years that many boys begin to masturbate to orgasm. Women have testosterone in their bodies, too, and there is evidence that women with high levels of testosterone engage in sex more frequently and enjoy it more (Persky, Lief, Strauss, Miller, & O'Brien, 1978).

Testosterone Primary male hormone produced by the testes.

Of the two major female sex hormones, **estrogen** and **progesterone,** estrogen has been linked specifically to female sexual arousal in animals. In virtually all animals except humans, females permit sexual intercourse only during those times in the reproductive cycle when estrogen levels are high (the time when they are fertile). Although the human female *may* tend to be more interested in sex when estrogen levels are high (Adams, Gold, & Burt, 1978), she is just as likely to engage in it when estrogen levels are low (Morris, 1969).

Estrogen Female sex hormone.
Progesterone Female sex hormone.

The relationship between sex and physiology is dramatically underscored by the large number of commonly used drugs that can impair sexual functioning in both men and women. Heavy use of alcohol is a major impediment to normal sexual functioning. Among 188 men in a recent study who suffered from impotence, medications were the single largest cause of their dysfunction. Drugs may also interfere with sexual desire in both sexes, with the ability to ejaculate in men, and with the ability to reach orgasm in women. They may do this by altering the production or action of sex hormones; by interfering with the autonomic nervous system, blocking the stimuli needed for a normal sexual response; or by altering emotional mood or level of arousal (H. S. Kaplan, 1979; Slag et al., 1983). Fortunately, nearly all drug-related effects on sexuality disappear when a person stops taking the drug.

STIMULATION   What makes us start thinking about sex at a particular time? The ethologist Desmond Morris (1977) suggests that sexuality is triggered by "gender signals," clues that enable us to recognize another person as male or female and that, in fact, emphasize maleness or femaleness. Anything that differentiates the sexes attracts our attention: the genitals; the breasts and rounded buttocks of women; the broad shoulders and flatter buttocks of men; and culturally imposed gender signals like clothing and hairstyles.

We don't know exactly why certain physical characteristics of another person appeal to us. It may be because they remind us of someone else (like a parent), because they represent a societal ideal of beauty, or because we've learned in some other way to associate a certain mix of physical features with sexual arousal. When we do find we are sexually attracted to someone, our first response is to maintain visual contact; our next response is to get physically close; and if the other person is receptive, we'll move to touch him or her and then to escalate this touch into sexual contact.

Because human beings are capable of symbolic thinking, we can be aroused not only by the sight of a flesh-and-blood person in front of us, but also by pictures, films, and descriptions of nudity and sexual behavior. Both males and females show such arousal (Mosher & Abramson, 1977). Exposure to erotic materials has been shown to increase the output of sex hormones, which we know are important for sexual arousal (LaFerla, Anderson, & Schalch, 1978).

LEARNING   There is a great deal of evidence that learning plays an important role in the mature sexual response. Most of this evidence comes from research with animals, and the assumption is that if learning plays an important role in the sexual behavior of animals, if probably plays an even greater role in humans. Monkeys that do not have a chance to play with other monkeys their own age when they are young seem motivated to be sexually active when they mature, but they do not know what to do—how to engage in appropriate sexual behavior (Harlow, 1962; Harlow & Harlow, 1969). Apparently, the presence of peers somehow stimulates young monkeys to practice certain behaviors in play (such as components of the mature sexual response) that are important for mature sexual behavior.

The importance of learning also emerges from a report that mature male rats seem to be attracted to females that resemble those that suckled them early in life—a rodent's equivalent of wanting a girl just like the girl who married dear old dad. In one study, baby rats lived with and were suckled by dams (adult females) whose nipple and vaginal odors were altered with a lemon-scented chemical. After weaning, they were not exposed to this scent again. Baby rats in control group A were raised by dams whose scent was altered by a salt solution, and those in control group B, by dams who were painted with the lemon scent—but only on their backs. At maturity (about 100 days of age), the experimental rats were paired with normal female rats or with females whose vaginal odors were lemon-scented. The experimental rats, those suckled by lemon-scented mothers, ejaculated more quickly with lemon-scented mates and more slowly with normal females. Those in control group A showed the opposite pattern, and those in control group B mate as quickly with either type of female. These findings suggest that male rats are more aroused sexually by females whose scent is similar to one they experienced as sucklings (Fillion & Blass, 1986). This study makes an interesting case, then, for the effects of certain types of infantile experience on adult sexual behavior—at least for rats.

The importance of early sexual learning is undoubtedly crucial in human beings, also. We don't have the same kind of data (since, for obvious ethical and practical reasons, we cannot bring up children for the sake of a scientific experiment), but learning seems to play a considerable role in our choice of sexual partners and in the way we act with these partners. The importance of learning in people's choice of sexual partners is shown by the widely varying standards of attractiveness from one culture to another, or even at different times within the same culture. In addition, sex therapists often comment on the preponderance of repressive upbringing among people with sexual dysfunctions (D. O'Connor, 1982).

COGNITIVE FACTORS Since human beings are thinking creatures, it's not surprising that the way we think affects the way we act, sexually as well as otherwise. For example, two different personality types—*extroverts* and *introverts*—seem to think differently in many ways. Extroverts like change and variety, like to be with other people, and tend to act impulsively; introverts prefer the familiar, enjoy solitude, and are more reflective. In a study of British students, Eysenck (1976) found that extroverts petted more, engaged in intercourse more, and tried more different sexual positions than introverts; they were also more satisfied with their sexual experiences. Eysenck suggested that introverts may be more inhibited by feelings of guilt. Other research has shown that people often associate sexual arousal with feelings of guilt, and therefore are inclined to label sexually arousing situations as disgusting or nauseating (Mosher, 1965; Mosher & Abramson, 1977).

EMOTIONAL FACTORS Intimacy and sexuality are often closely intertwined. Although many people seek and enjoy sexual activity without emotional involvement, one of the most popular sexual standards in our culture stresses the tie between affectionate feelings and sexual feelings (Reiss, 1986). As people become more intimate, their relationship often becomes more sexual; conversely, sexual connection often promotes intimacy. In our society, sex with love is considered the ideal intimate relationship.

A Life-Span Perspective on Human Sexuality

Human beings are sexual even before birth, if we can judge from ultrasound photographs of male fetuses showing erections (Calderone, 1983). Our sexual development then proceeds, interacting with every other aspect of our development—physical, cognitive, social, and emotional—throughout life. Sexuality takes different forms, of course, as people face different developmental tasks (Olds, 1985). Some typical events are described in the box "Sexual Turning Points throughout Life" (pages 438–439).

Childhood   The early years are important for the development of sexual beliefs and values. During the first few years of life, children become aware of their bodies. The way they feel about these bodies—whether they feel comfortable and proud or ashamed and fearful—depends in large part on the attitudes displayed by their parents and other adults. How these adults respond to the perfectly normal masturbation that children naturally engage in and to their just as normal curiosity about other people's bodies has a great impact on the attitudes formed in childhood and carried throughout life.

Sigmund Freud, the first person to set sexuality into a theoretical framework that emphasized its importance in the development of personality, made much of sexual development early in childhood (discussed in Chapter 13) and minimized its presence in later childhood (1905/1949). He called the years from the age of 6 to puberty the "latency stage," maintaining that this was a time when children are relatively uninterested in sex. In fact, during these years children do engage in sex play, masturbate, and ask sexual questions, and today psychological researchers and theorists generally agree that the latency period does not exist (Hyde, 1986).

Adolescence   The most dramatic sexual turning point in the human life span comes sometime between the ages of 10 to 14 for most people, when our biological clock brings about **pubescence.** In this stage, a time of rapid growth, the reproductive functions and sex organs mature, representing the **primary sex characteristics** (the organs directly involved in reproduction—the ovaries and vagina; the penis and testes); and the **secondary sex characteristics** (the characteristics of adult male and female bodies that do not involve reproductive organs, including the breasts, body and facial hair, and the mature voice) appear. After about 2 years, this stage ends in **puberty**, when the person is sexually mature and able to reproduce. The average age of puberty is 12 for girls and 14 for boys, but there is a very wide range of ages considered normal.

Sexual activity (not necessarily intercourse) is a typical part of contemporary teenage experience, rather than an expression of frustration or personal dependency (Dreyer, 1982). By the age of 16, about 1 out of 4 white boys and girls, 1 in 2 black girls, and 9 out of 10 black boys have had sexual intercourse (Chilman, 1980; Zelnik, Kim, & Kantner, 1979). Most adolescents do not have more than one sexual relationship at a time, have strong moral feelings about sex, and disapprove of exploitation and of casual sex outside a caring relationship (Zelnik, Kantner, & Ford, 1981).

The biggest change in adolescent sexual behavior is among girls, who are now more sexually active than they used to be. Overall, boys and girls today are acting more like each other than like their parents of the same sex. They also hold similar standards for appropriate behavior for both sexes, perhaps heralding an eventual end to the double standard that has traditionally allowed boys more sexual freedom (Coles & Stokes, 1985). Still, differences remain between the sexes. Girls are more likely to have their first intercourse with a steady boyfriend, whereas boys are more likely to have theirs with a girl they know casually; and a girl's first partner is usually 3 years older than she is, whereas a boy's is 1 year older (Dreyer, 1982; Zelnik, Kantner, & Ford, 1981; Zelnik & Shah, 1983).

One major difference between the sexes, of course, is the fact that only girls can get pregnant. They are doing so, in this country, at an alarming rate. The teenage birth rate in the United States is among the highest in the western world, with 1 in 10 teenage girls becoming pregnant every year (Dryfoos, 1985). Of the 1 million pregnancies that occur every year among adolescents, 38 percent end in abortion, 13 percent in miscarriage, 22 percent in babies born out of wedlock, and 17 percent in

Pubescence   *Time of the life span just before puberty, characterized by rapid physiological growth, maturation of reproductive functioning, and the development of primary and secondary sex characteristics.*

Primary sex characteristics   *Characteristics directly related to the sex organs and involved in reproduction.*

Secondary sex characteristics   *Body changes occurring during adolescence that do not involve reproductive organs, such as breast development, growth of body and facial hair, and voice changes.*

Puberty   *Physiological point at which a person is sexually mature and able to reproduce.*

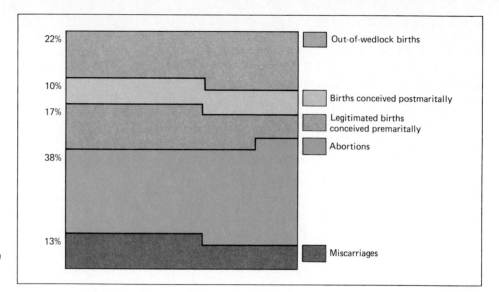

FIGURE 12-3 *Outcomes of teenage pregnancies. Percentage distribution of the outcomes of 1,142,000 pregnancies among women under 20 years old in 1978. (Source: Guttmacher, 1981.)*

Legend:
Out-of-wedlock births
Births conceived postmaritally
Legitimated births conceived premaritally
Abortions
Miscarriages

22%
10%
17%
38%
13%

babies born to parents who married after the pregnancy occurred; only 10 percent occur among married women (Alan Guttmacher Institute, 1981); see Figure 12–3. Nine out of ten teenage mothers choose to keep their babies, at least at first.

Why do so many young girls become pregnant? Many are reluctant to accept the fact that they are sexually active (Oskamp & Mindick, 1981; Oskamp, Mindick, Berger, & Motta, 1978). They prefer to think of themselves as having been swept away in a moment of passion (''forgivable'') rather than having expected to engage in intercourse (''immoral''). They are not ready to think of themselves as sexually mature and responsible, and do not, therefore, plan ahead to prevent conception. Others do not use birth control because they don't know about contraception, don't know where to get birth control devices, are afraid their parents will find out they're having sex, or believe they can't become pregnant (because they're too young, they're having intercourse for the first time, or they're doing it standing up, or for some other reason) (Dreyer, 1982; Alan Guttmacher Institute, 1981; Zelnik, Kantner, & Ford, 1981).

The problems of adolescent parenthood are rooted in the problems of society in general. A teenage mother is likely to drop out of school and get caught up in a cycle of welfare dependency, and her children are likely to have more problems with health, school, and behavior—an effect that may be due to the fact that there is only one parent in the home, and to the family's economic and social problems (Chilman, 1982). A growing number of communities are instituting programs aimed at preventing teenage pregnancy, with varying degrees of success. The programs vary in their emphasis on information, on encouraging the postponement of sexual relations, and on improving adolescents' self-esteem. So far, the last approach seems the most effective (Carrera, 1986).

Adolescents' attitudes are considerably more conservative than their behavior. Although most boys say they don't want to marry a virgin and only half the girls want to be virgins when they marry (only 20 percent of them will be; Tanfer & Horn, 1985), most teenagers disapprove of casual sex and also of sex between couples who are ''going together'' or ''in love.'' Most of the adolescents surveyed in one study approved of sexual intercourse only between couples planning to marry (Coles & Stokes, 1985).

Young Adulthood   As young people cross the threshold from adolescence into adulthood, they face a set of new sexual goals, revolving around achieving sexual independence (developing their own moral code, instead of passively accepting or

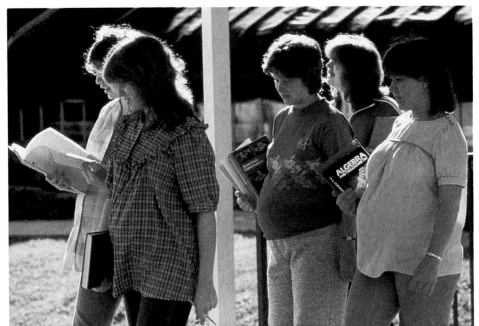

One of the worst consequences of teenage pregnancy is that many girls will drop out of school and drift into lifelong financial dependency. These girls go to a school in Fort Worth, Texas, especially oriented toward pregnant students aged 12 to 21. Some of the girls keep their babies; others place them for adoption. Either way, the mothers can continue their own education.

mindlessly rebelling against that of their parents), sexual responsibility (being ready to face the emotional and reproductive implications of sexual behavior and acting accordingly), and sexual competence (learning sexual skills). This is an age of experimentation and an age when sexuality often merges with an emotional commitment to another person.

More and more young people are having sexual experiences before marriage, and the later people marry, the less likely they are to be virgins on their wedding day. Premarital intercourse is now the usual course for most American women. Of unmarried women in their twenties who have never been married, 82 percent have had sexual intercourse, and more than 50 percent are currently sexually active (Tanfer & Horn, 1985).

Over the past 30 years, sexual attitudes and behaviors in our society have undergone marked changes, with more people engaging in premarital sex, with more of them having a succession of partners rather than only the one they will eventually marry, and with more egalitarian attitudes toward sexual standards for both men and women. Although some observers have referred to these changes as a "sexual revolution," they are more in the nature of a sexual *evolution*: they are an extension of trends begun earlier in this century.

In recent years, some observers have suggested that the revolution is over and that more conservative attitudes and behaviors are becoming prevalent (Hyde, 1986). This is questionable, however, and the conclusion one draws depends on which of many contradictory signs one considers valid. A series of studies at one Ohio campus, for example, found lower rates of premarital sexual activity in 1980 than had been found a decade earlier (Clatworthy, 1980). On the other hand, a 10-year study of undergraduates at a small southern university found that between 1970 and 1981 rates of premarital sex rose, age at first intercourse dropped, and average number of partners increased (Earle & Perricone, 1986). It seems, though, that the major change in sexual behavior among young American adults has been, not an avoidance of sexual activity, but an increasing discrimination in choice of partners (Ehrenreich, Hess, & Jacobs, 1986). The recent decrease in casual sexual activity among both heterosexuals and homosexuals has occurred principally in response to two incurable diseases spread by sexual contact.

Until fairly recently, most students of human nature thought of growth and development as phenomena that exist during childhood and that stop abruptly at the end of adolescence. According to this view, sexual development will have come to a stop at just about the time most people have barely begun to express themselves as sexual beings. The truth, as we pointed out in Chapters 9 and 10, is that almost every kind of human growth takes place throughout the entire life span. As long as we live, we are in the process of becoming something other than what we are. Thanks to a number of recent studies of development in adulthood, we now accept the notion that there are certain predictable patterns in our development throughout life. Such patterns, highlighted by specific experiences and decisions, are especially significant in charting our sexual development.

In our development, we often come to sexual turning points—events or experiences that have a pivotal impact on our sexuality (Olds, 1985). The way we behave at these times determines our attitudes, our feelings, and our actions from that time on. All of us have many such

SEXUAL TURNING POINTS THROUGHOUT LIFE

turning points, since our sexual development is so intertwined with every other aspect of our lives. Some of these turning points are universal; others are as individual as a fingerprint. Even those turning points that are based on biology and are, therefore, common to many lives all occur differently, depending on the individual context (Masters, 1983). There are definite relationships between our sexuality and our stages in life, in society, and in history. The following experiences represent some typical turning points for people living in the 1980s in the United States, although not all people experience all these

sexual passages, or experience them in the sequence given here.

1 *First childhood awareness of oneself as a sexual being, when one gets a good or bad feeling about the body.* Children's feelings about sexuality usually stem from the attitudes of the adults around them, shown often by the adults' reactions toward masturbation and normal childhood curiosity. Negative feelings also arise from such traumatic events as incest or molestation.

2 *Physical changes of puberty that force recognition of sexual maturation.* Physical maturation leads to the expression of sexual orientation (heterosexual or homosexual), the awareness of sexual responsiveness, and the development of sexual responsibility (as shown by taking responsibility for making decisions about reproduction).

3 *First sexual intercourse.* Significant factors in one's first sexual intercourse are one's age, who one's partner is and what the relationship is with that partner, and one's feelings about oneself.

First, genital herpes—an annoying condition—became a concern. But then a far more serious threat appeared: acquired immune deficiency syndrome (AIDS), a fatal disorder that destroys the body's immune system (Lyons, 1983). In the United States, the two groups most affected by AIDS have been homosexual men and intravenous drug abusers; but the AIDS virus has also been spread in some cases by heterosexual intercourse, and there is concern that this mode of transmission will increase. While medical researchers seek to find a cure for AIDS, sexually active people are urged to practice "safe sex," which avoids the exchange of bodily fluids between partners.

Another means of avoiding AIDS is to have monogamous relations with an uninfected partner, a situation that often occurs in marriage. Sex is usually more frequent in the first year of marriage than it will ever be again; and the more frequent it is then, the more frequent (compared with other marriages) it will be in the future (Greenblat, 1983). Husbands and wives are having sexual intercourse more often and engaging in more varied sexual activities than their same-age counterparts did in the past several decades (Hunt, 1974). This change seems due to many factors—a generally more liberated attitude toward sex in society in general and a resulting increase in information and advice on sexual matters; the greater reliability of contraceptive methods; the availability of legal and safe abortion; and the women's

4 *Becoming a sexual individual.* To become sexual individuals, people must develop their own sexual values, neither totally accepting nor mindlessly rebelling against the values of their parents.

5 *Falling in love.* The first romantic love affair, whether it includes sexual expression of that love or not, is a passage because it arouses sexual feelings and opens one up to sexual possibilities.

6 *Making a commitment to a partner.* Moving in, becoming engaged, and getting married all have important sexual ramifications: sexuality is a major factor leading to what is often the most important relationship of a lifetime.

7 *Conceiving a child.* This outcome of sexual activity affects people's feelings about their own sexuality, about their partner's sexuality, and about the relationship in general. An inability to conceive a child when one is wanted is also an important influence on all these feelings.

8 *Becoming a parent.* Parenthood

can affect one's sense of oneself as a sexual person, and its demands can affect a marriage. For many people, the early years of parenthood constitute the worst period in their entire lives, as far as their sexuality is concerned.

9 *Career change.* Any important change in a person's work situation—being promoted, being demoted, being fired, getting a new job, or retiring—can affect that person's sexuality and its expression.

10 *Divorce.* Divorce may bring on celibacy, promiscuity, or a new sexual health.

11 *Extramarital sex.* A person's first, or only, affair outside his or her marriage can provide a signal that there are problems in the marriage or with the person, or it may represent a sexual passage that can be dealt with in a way that strengthens both the marriage and each partner in it.

12 *Physical changes of middle age.* Age-related differences in sexual functioning can suggest new ways of being sexually active or can lead to a diminution of sexual interest.

13 *Empty nest.* Being alone can

offer a couple a sexuality as free as the kind they could engage in at the beginning of their life together, with the benefits of years of experience and familiarity, or it can show them that they have little in common now that the children who have kept them together are gone. Single parents may either welcome the new freedom or suffer from a sense of loneliness.

14 *Illness or surgery.* Heart attack, hysterectomy, mastectomy, and other common illnesses and operations can have far-reaching effects on sexual identity and sexual activity.

15 *Widowhood.* The death of a long-term sexual partner can be either a devastating loss or an opportunity to seek a new, perhaps even more compatible partner.

Although all these turning points are significant, their ultimate impact is often due not so much to the experience or event itself, but to the way people respond to them. What may overwhelm one person may provide an opportunity for growth and development for another.

liberation movement, which has helped many women to acknowledge their sexuality.

Sexual adjustment in marriage requires learning about oneself and one's partner, and then developing the communication skills to implement this learning. The time needed to make a good sexual adjustment varies from couple to couple and is often contingent on other aspects of the marriage. Problems with sex may be a symptom of other marital difficulties or may be due to a couple's sexual naiveté. In either case, professional marriage counseling or sex therapy can often help.

Extramarital sex also seems to have increased in recent years, especially among women. In Kinsey's surveys of more than 30 years ago, 51 percent of men and 26 percent of women reported extramarital intercourse (Kinsey et al., 1948, 1953). Now, according to estimates based on more recent studies, between one-half and three-fourths of married men and between 34 and 43 percent of married women have extramarital sex by age 40 or 50 (Nass, Libby, & Fisher, 1984; Thompson, 1983). This change, too, seems to result from changed societal attitudes.

Middle Adulthood Middle-aged people, too, are engaging in sexual activity more often and in more varied ways than ever before (Brecher & Editors of Consumers Reports Books, 1984; Starr & Weiner, 1981). Sexual activity is different during the

(Don Klumpp © 1978/Image Bank)

Sexuality can be a vital force throughout life. Many men and women enjoy fulfilling and satisfying sexual relationships throughout middle and late adulthood, including some form of active sexual expression.

Heterosexuals *People who are sexually attracted to persons of the other sex.*

Homosexuals *People who are sexually attracted to persons of the same sex.*

(© Costa Manos/Magnum)

While researchers have sought to discover why some people are sexually attracted to partners of the same sex, we still don't have definitive answers.

middle years, partly because of physiological changes in men. Middle-aged men usually want sex less frequently than in their earlier years; they now have fewer spontaneous erections and more often need direct stimulation; their orgasms come more slowly and sometimes not at all; and they experience a longer refractory period. Men who become anxious over these changes may experience difficulty getting or keeping erections and may, as a result, withdraw from sex. Women may not lubricate as quickly or as extensively as they once did; their breasts, clitoris, and labia may not become as engorged; and their nipples may not become as erect.

However, men who have been sexually active during their younger years are likely to continue to be sexually active through their older years (Masters & Johnson, 1966, 1981), and women often report improved sexuality, thanks to their having overcome the effects of inhibition and inexperience (L. B. Rubin, 1983).

Late Adulthood   One of our most prevalent stereotypes about the elderly has been that old people are and should be sexless, and that those who are not are perverted. In recent years, however, as researchers have gathered more information on sexual behavior late in life, they have found that sexuality can be a vital force throughout life (Adams & Turner, 1985; Brecher & Editors of Consumers Reports Books, 1984; Starr & Weiner, 1981; Weinberg, 1982). Both men and women can usually continue some form of sexual expression as long as they live (Masters, 1986).

The physical changes that begin in middle age become more intense in old age. Men usually find that it takes longer for them to have an erection and that when they do, it is not as firm as in earlier years; ejaculation usually takes longer, too, and in some men it may not occur at all. Older women, though, are still able to reach orgasm, especially if they have been sexually active over the years. Both men and women are still able to enjoy a fulfilling and satisfying sexuality. This is especially likely if they define sexuality not only as sexual intercourse, but also as caressing, fondling, and oral and manual erotic activity.

Sexual Orientation: Heterosexuality and Homosexuality

What makes people become sexually attracted to persons of the other sex or to persons of the same sex? A great deal of research has been carried out to answer this question, and we have many theories but no definitive answers. **Heterosexuals** (people who are sexually attracted to persons of the other sex) and **homosexuals** (those sexually attracted to persons of the same sex) show similar physiological responses during sexual arousal and are aroused by the same forms of tactile stimulation. Large-scale studies have indicated that homosexual men act in most ways like heterosexual men and that lesbians (homosexual women) are very similar to heterosexual women (Bell & Weinberg, 1978; Blumstein & Schwartz, 1983). The major difference is in the sex of the person preferred as a partner.

A number of hypotheses have been advanced to account for the existence of homosexuality. The oldest is that it represents a kind of *mental illness*. In a classic study, Hooker (1957) could find no evidence to support this contention. Her conclusions and those of other researchers (along with political lobbying and changes in public attitudes) eventually led the American Psychiatric Association to stop classifying homosexuality as a "mental disorder."

Other theories include the possibility of a *genetic factor*, a *hormonal imbalance*, a *family constellation* with a dominating mother and a weak father (thought by some to cause male homosexuality), and a *chance learning* situation, in which a young person who has been seduced by someone of the same sex will then develop a preference for that sex. So far, no scientific support has been found for the family-constellation and chance-learning theories; and only tentative evidence has been found for the genetic and hormonal theories. (One recent study was the first to find a biological difference between heterosexual and homosexual men, a different hormone-response pattern to estrogen stimulation. Since the homosexual men in this

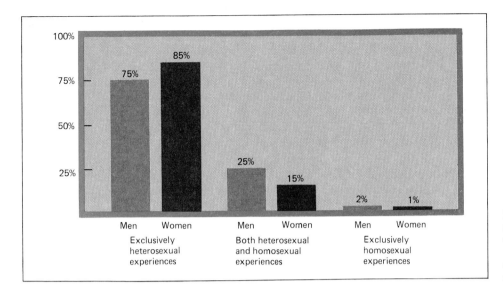

FIGURE 12-4 *Incidence of heterosexual and homosexual orientation. Figures do not add up to 100 percent for each set, because of rounding. (Source: Adapted from Hyde, 1986.)*

study were at the extreme end of homosexual orientation, the findings may not apply to all homosexuals; Gladue, Green, & Hellman, 1984.)

Another hypothesis is that there are probably several different reasons why a person becomes heterosexual or homosexual, and that interaction among various hormonal and environmental events is crucial. This broad hypothesis seems to have garnered the most support (Bell, Weinberg, & Hammersmith, 1981; Durden-Smith & DeSimone, 1982; Masters & Johnson, 1979). It's interesting to note that homosexual behavior is one kind of sexual behavior which has not increased in incidence over the years and the incidence of which appears to be similar in a number of cultures (Hyde, 1986); see Figure 12-4.

Psychosexual Problems and Their Treatment

Psychosexual Dysfunction Problems commonly arise at various points in the sexual response cycle, including the point before any physical changes occur, when someone first feels sexual desire. When a person only occasionally is not "in the mood" for sex, or does not become aroused, or does not experience orgasm, there is no reason to label this a dysfunction, or even to consider it a problem. It is only when a disturbance in the response cycle is not caused by a physical condition (as the result of physical abnormalities, illnesses, or medications) and is "recurrent and persistent" (DSM III, 1980, p. 276) that a diagnosis is made of **psychosexual dysfunction**. Even then, it is likely that the condition can be successfully treated. The following dysfunctions tend to begin early in adulthood, to have variable courses, and to be caused by or result in troubled marital and love relationships.

INHIBITED SEXUAL DESIRE (ISD) Lack of interest in sex, known as **inhibited sexual desire (ISD)**, is usually considered dysfunctional only if the affected person is almost never interested in sex and is concerned about it, or if he or she wants sex much less often than his or her partner and the disparity causes problems between them. ISD, which seems to be more common among women, is the problem most often brought to sex therapists today (H. S. Kaplan, 1979).

INHIBITED SEXUAL EXCITEMENT A man's partial or complete failure to attain or keep an erection is also known as *impotence,* and a woman's partial or complete failure to attain or keep vaginal lubrication and swelling is sometimes called *frigidity* (this term

Psychosexual dysfunction *Recurrent and persistent disturbance in the sexual response cycle that is not caused by a physical condition or by medications.*

Inhibited sexual desire (ISD) *Persistent lack of sexual interest that is of concern to a person.*

Inhibited sexual excitement *For a man, partial or complete failure to attain or keep an erection; for a woman, partial or complete failure to attain or keep vaginal lubrication and swelling.*

is rarely used any more). Both kinds of ***inhibited sexual excitement*** may have organic causes, but they're more often believed to be psychological in origin. A man's problem, for example, may begin when he experiences difficulty with erection after drinking too much, being worried about his job, or simply being tired. The next time he makes love, he worries that the same thing will happen again; and the more he worries, the likelier it is that he will have the same trouble, until he has a full-fledged problem.

Inhibited female orgasm *Situation in which a woman can become sexually aroused but is unable to reach orgasm.*

INHIBITED FEMALE ORGASM   A woman who becomes sexually aroused but is unable to reach orgasm is experiencing ***inhibited female orgasm.*** She may be ignorant about sex or have trouble communicating the kind of stimulation she needs; she may be afraid of losing control; or she may have to learn how to become orgasmic, possibly through masturbation.

Inhibited male orgasm *Inability to ejaculate.*

INHIBITED MALE ORGASM   Inability to ejaculate, ***inhibited male orgasm,*** is relatively rare, and may result from a biological problem in the ducts, or from such psychological causes as fear of impregnating a woman or of losing control, or from trying to delay ejaculation for too long.

Premature ejaculation *Situation in which a man's ejaculation regularly occurs before he wants it to.*

PREMATURE EJACULATION   When ejaculation regularly occurs before the man wants it to, he is experiencing ***premature ejaculation,*** probably the most common sexual dysfunction among men. Some men ejaculate prematurely with a new partner; some at times when they are anxious about their sexual performance; and some simply because they reach a climax at lower levels of sexual excitement than other men (Spiess, 1977). Sometimes a man or his partner simply has unrealistic expectations.

Vaginismus *Involuntary spasms of the vaginal muscles.*

VAGINISMUS   In ***vaginismus,*** involuntary spasms of the vaginal muscles prevent intercourse, or even the insertion of a finger. The condition may be caused by anxiety, fear of pregnancy, or negative attitudes about sex, but affected women often achieve sexual satisfaction through clitoral stimulation.

Dyspareunia *Painful intercourse, most common in women.*

DYSPAREUNIA   Painful intercourse, known as ***dyspareunia,*** is more common among women, but can also affect men. It's almost always caused by a physical problem such as an infection in the genital area, a structural disorder, scar tissue, or lack of lubrication.

Sexual burnout *Boredom with the same sexual routine, marked by a sense of physical depletion and emotional emptiness, and a negative sexual self-concept.*

SEXUAL BURNOUT   Possibly 20 percent of men and women at midlife experience ***sexual burnout*** (Masters, Johnson, & Kolodny, 1986). This condition, marked by a sense of physical depletion and emotional emptiness and a negative sexual self-concept, seems to stem from boredom with the same sexual routines. The affected person despairs of the possibility of rekindling erotic passion or pleasure. In almost all cases, people recover spontaneously, but about 10 percent of those affected become celibate, never to resume sexual activity.

CAUSES OF SEXUAL DYSFUNCTION   Because our sexuality is so closely intertwined with every other aspect of our lives, problems with sex may be traced to one or more of innumerable causes (Masters & Johnson, 1970; Masters, Johnson, & Kolodny, 1986). Medical conditions, such as diabetes and alcoholism (the two most common organic causes of impotence), infections, injuries, hormonal insufficiencies, and circulatory problems, are sometimes to blame. So are both prescription drugs and street drugs. An upbringing marked by severely antisexual attitudes, stressing the evil and dirtiness of sex and bodily pleasures, is often associated with various dysfunctions. Anxiety, guilt, depression, and poor self-esteem are also associated with them, although it's often hard to tell which comes first—the problem with sex or the emotional problem. Ignorance about one's own or one's partner's body and the acceptance of cultural myths (such as "the male must set the pace of sexual activity" or "old people can't have sex") are sometimes to blame.

One of the most common causes of sexual dysfunction is a problem in the relationship, either a simple problem of communication or a conflict between partners. There is no reason, in most cases, to assume that a sexual problem stems from a deep-seated personality problem. Many people with sexual problems "have completely normal personalities, no signs of emotional illness, and simple, straightforward explanations for their problem" (Masters, Johnson, & Kolodny, 1986, p. 480).

Paraphilias Another group of psychosexual disorders, known as ***paraphilias*** (formerly known as *sexual deviations*), are characterized by sexual arousal *only* in response to bizarre imagery, objects, or acts. People (more often men) with these disorders are aroused by nonhuman objects (such as shoes, animals, or specific articles of clothing), by sexual activity involving humiliation or suffering (inflicting harm on someone else or being beaten or bound oneself), or by engaging in sex with a nonconsenting partner (as in rape, including forced oral-genital activity) (DSM III, 1980).

Paraphilia Sexual arousal only in response to bizarre imagery, objects, or acts.

The cause of such tendencies is unknown. Psychoanalytic theories ascribe them to anxiety about normal sexual contact, and cognitive and social learning theories attribute them to incidents in a person's past. For example, according to this view, if a boy had his first orgasm while masturbating in his sister's room after rummaging through her underwear drawer, this might set up an association whereby he might from then on need to see, feel, or wear women's underpants to become sexually aroused.

The implications of the paraphilias can be significant; they can range from difficulty in maintaining a normal sexual relationship to becoming a public danger to women or children. (Some people believe that violent pornography encourages men to act out their fantasies of hurting women or of having forced sex with them, and attempt to forbid the publication of certain ***erotic, obscene,*** and ***pornographic*** materials. For a discussion of this issue, see the box "Is There a Link between Pornography and Sexual Violence against Women?" on pages 444–445.) Treatment usually involves some sort of behavior therapy (as described in Chapter 15), to break the association between sexual arousal and the specific factor, to teach the person new social skills, and to create a new association for more normal sexual interaction (Freeman-Longo & Wall, 1986).

Erotica Materials designed to arouse sexual desire.

Obscenity Legal term for materials that are offensive to community standards, appeal to prurient interests (lust), and lack serious scientific, educational, literary, political, or artistic value.

Pornography Sexually oriented materials that a given individual or group considers morally or aesthetically objectionable.

Sex Therapy Therapy for sexual dysfunction owes a great debt to the publication of Masters and Johnson's book *Human Sexual Inadequacy* (1970), in which the authors described the short-term behavior therapy approach they had been using to treat a wide variety of sexual problems. Some practitioners had used some of the same techniques for some time, others have since modified the Masters and Johnson approach considerably, and some subsequent researchers have questioned Masters and Johnson's reports of success (Zilbergeld & Evans, 1980). Still, this pioneering team added new elements and combined old ones in a way that virtually created sex therapy as we know it today. ***Sex therapy*** is treatment designed to remove specific obstacles to sexual functioning. As practiced today, it is usually behaviorally oriented, emphasizing the current situation and focusing on specific behavioral changes on the part of the person or persons coming for treatment.

Sex therapy Treatment designed to remove specific obstacles to sexual functioning.

MASTERS AND JOHNSON'S PROGRAM In the sex therapy practiced by Masters and Johnson, the couple is regarded as the patient; clients without partners sometimes bring a surrogate partner for the purpose of the therapy. The therapists work as a two-sex team. Some sessions take place among all four participants, and some only between each client and the therapist of the same sex. The couple leave their home and go for 2 weeks to a clinic in St. Louis. For 1 hour a day (after the first day) they participate in therapy, and then they do "homework" in their motel.

In recent years, there has been a disturbing upsurge in filmed and printed portrayals of men raping, mutilating, or otherwise hurting women. The more graphic depictions of sexually linked brutality have repelled many people; some have concluded that such imagery must contribute in some way to the high rates in our society of sexually violent crimes against women and children. Some feminist groups have joined forces with some politically conservative organizations to press for laws against sexually explicit materials that "subordinate, objectify, or degrade" women. The Attorney General's Commission against Pornography issued its official report in July 1986, calling for an all-out war against pornography, recommending more stringent federal and state laws and more vigorous prosecution of persons charged with breaking the law.

If violent pornography does cause sex crimes, there might be a compelling argument for exempting it from the provisions of the First Amendment to the Constitution, which protect freedom of speech. This would be an extremely grave step, however, since any such exemption could lead to further erosion of the First Amendment. Therefore, we have to ask the basic question: How valid is the belief that pornography causes violence? To answer this question, some researchers have devised laboratory experiments, others have explored the history of exposure to pornography of violent sex offend-

IS THERE A LINK BETWEEN PORNOGRAPHY AND SEXUAL VIOLENCE AGAINST WOMEN?

ers, and others have examined the links between the availability of sexually explicit materials in a culture and that culture's rate of violent sex crimes.

First, we need to define terms. *Erotica* are materials that are designed to arouse sexual desire. *Pornography* seems to be erotica that somebody, for some reason, doesn't like—that is, sexually oriented materials which a given person or group considers morally or aesthetically objectionable. *Obscenity* is the *legal* term for materials that are offensive to community standards, appeal to prurient interests (lust), and lack serious scientific, educational, literary, political, or artistic value. When we talk about pornography, then, you and I may be talking about very different things.

Although some people object to

any form of sexually explicit material, no evidence has appeared that has linked nonviolent erotica to any form of sexual aggression. On the other hand, most people agree that any material depicting children involved in sex acts with adults should be restricted, and, in fact, such activity is prohibited by child protection laws. Most of the current debate centers on films, videocassettes, and magazine portrayals of sex-linked violence against women, which is the subject of about 10 percent of X-rated films available today (Rimmer, 1984). Let's see what the facts are.

EXPERIMENTS
Researchers have put male college students in situations in which female confederates (working with the experimenters) anger them, have shown films to the men, and have then given the men the opportunity to administer electric shocks to the women. In one experiment, one group of men saw a violent erotic film, a second saw a violent nonerotic film, a third saw a nonviolent erotic film, and a fourth group saw a film that was neither violent nor erotic. The men who were most willing to administer shocks to the women were those who had seen the violent films, whether they were erotic or not (Donnerstein, 1984; Malamuth, 1984; Malamuth & Donnerstein, 1984).

Other experiments show attitude changes. Men who see films showing a woman becoming aroused by rape (a common theme in hard-core por-

Throughout the 2 weeks, the couple promise not to engage in any sexual activity not expressly recommended by the therapists. The first 2 days are taken up with physical examinations and detailed social and sexual histories. Then the therapists interpret the difficulty as they see it, emphasizing it as a problem in the relationship, not as a problem in either partner.

To alleviate anxiety and avoid the phenomenon of "spectatoring" (monitoring one's own performance), the couple are instructed in an exercise known as *sensate focus*. Back in their motel room they undress and take turns touching each other in various pleasurable ways. They are specifically instructed not to engage in intercourse. Over the next few days the touching escalates to concentrate more on the erogenous zones and specifically the genitals, and eventually leads to intercourse. During the sensate focusing period, they receive specific guidance depending on the nature of their sexual dysfunction (Masters & Johnson, 1970).

nography) see the victim as more responsible for her own rape than those who see films in which the woman seems to suffer. The men in the former group thus fall prey to a common myth—that rape is a sexually arousing act instead of the terrifying one that actual rape victims describe. Such depictions seem to teach that this kind of aggression is acceptable, a worrisome lesson. These opinions can be reversed by a simple debriefing in which the men are told that the feelings of the women they saw being aroused by rape are not typical (Malamuth & Check, 1984). Attitudes are not behaviors, however; although these viewpoints are disagreeable, they don't necessarily turn men into rapists.

The evidence from these studies is worrisome, however, in light of findings that about 35 percent of college men say they would rape if the situation were right and they were sure they would not be caught (Malamuth, 1981). Enough "normal" men do force themselves upon women or pressure them into having sex to make "date rape" distressingly prevalent (Hyde, 1986). Are these men's attitudes influenced by pornography—or by societal standards that hold out rape as one way men can prove their masculinity?

STUDIES OF CRIMINALS
Does seeing pornography make a man a sex offender? The evidence from studies of convicted offenders seems to say no. In one study, jailed sex offenders were found to have had less exposure to sexually explicit materials than were prisoners convicted of other offenses (Gebhard, Gagnon, Pomeroy, & Christenson, 1965). More recently, studies have found that jailed sex offenders and persons both in and out of prison with a record of nonsex offenses had had similar exposure to erotica, and that more violent rapists had had no more exposure than less violent rapists (Reiss, 1986). It is not clear, however, what kind of sexual material these prisoners had seen; if we separated violent from nonviolent material, we might see different results. We also have to remember that studies of men in prison tap only a small proportion of rapists: most rapes go unreported and most rapists are not apprehended (Hyde, 1986).

CROSS-CULTURAL STUDIES
In Japan, bondage and rape are often featured in sexually oriented novels, cartoons, and movies, but Japan has one of the lowest rates of reported rape of any industrialized country (Abramson & Hayashi, 1984). After Denmark relaxed its laws against written and visual erotica in the late 1960s, there was no increase in rape or other sex offenses (Kutchinsky, in press). Apparently, then, other cultural factors operate to encourage or discourage sexual crimes. One of these seems to be a society's level of machismo, the cultural attitude that defines masculinity in terms of physical aggression, sexual conquests, and risk-taking, and another is the degree to which a society considers men superior to women (Reiss, 1986). As one sociologist writes, "A cultural milieu in which women are always perceived as sex objects contributes to the devaluation of women" (McCormack, 1985, p. 199). Such settings provide a more fertile soil for sexual violence against women.

What are we to conclude from all this research? First, we need to recognize that the studies themselves are limited. The findings that we do have provide no strong evidence for linking violent pornography to violent action. Nevertheless, the issue arouses strong passions, and thoughtful people disagree on the right course society should take.

There are those who hold that any means are justifiable to suppress material that glorifies violence, brutality, and the subjugation of women and that may produce a social climate in which sexual aggression is more acceptable.

On the other side of the debate, free-speech advocates maintain that outlawing material which has not been found to be legally obscene is, in the final analysis, even more dangerous to our society than permitting its production. The difficulty comes in defining exactly what is to be outlawed, in allowing some authority to dictate what viewers and readers can have access to, and in opening the doors to the suppression of a wide range of unpopular materials.

Some of the principles underlying this approach include its behavioral emphasis (that is, its emphasis on changing the couple's behavior, without dwelling heavily on the past to uncover the reasons for it); its narrow focus, which results from the short term of the therapy; its restriction against sexual intercourse until the therapists feel a couple are ready for it; its sensate focus exercise; its emphasis on treating the couple, not the individuals; and its reliance on the two-therapist team.

SEX THERAPY TODAY   Most sex therapists today build on and modify Masters and Johnson's prototype, generally concentrating on the same basic aims. They seek to reduce anxiety about performance, to provide information about normal sexual functioning and about special techniques, to train clients in communication skills, and to change attitudes that might get in the way of satisfactory sexual functioning (Heiman, LoPiccolo, & LoPiccolo, 1980). Some therapists have discarded some of

Masters and Johnson's elements, considering them unnecessary: the two-therapist team, for instance, or daily therapy sessions for a short time as opposed to weekly sessions over a long time. Others add elements, such as vibrators to help women become orgasmic, or a greater emphasis on marital therapy when relationship problems seem to be causing the sexual difficulty.

The effectiveness of sex therapy varies, depending on the particular dysfunction and the particular client. Therapy for premature ejaculation and vaginismus has the highest success rates: 90 to 95 percent. Efforts to deal with the other dysfunctions have success rates ranging from about 30 to 80 percent (Heiman et al., 1980). The most resistant problem, for which no figures on success rate are available, is inhibited sexual desire.

In the early 1960s, there were many cases of sexual dysfunction that were fairly easy to treat. Many people needed nothing more than permission to be sexual, information, or specific suggestions. In those days there were few good books on sex, and the social climate was just beginning to accept sexuality as a natural function. Over the past 20 years, however, sex has achieved new prominence, and the people who come for therapy are those who have more complicated needs. They've read the books, seen the films, accepted their right to be sexual—but they're still anxious and having sexual difficulties. As Masters (1983) has said, "We don't see the easy cases anymore."

Sexuality and gender issues are, as we have pointed out, important aspects of development throughout life. Both of them exert a major impact on personality development, which will be discussed in Part VI.

SUMMARY

1 The term *sex differences* refers to actual physical differences between males and females. The term *gender* refers to aspects of behavior that may or may not be tied to biology. Gender identity is the awareness that one is male or female. Gender roles are those behaviors, attitudes, and interests that a culture says are appropriate for males and females. Gender stereotypes are exaggerated generalizations about masculine and feminine attitudes and behaviors.

2 Some physical differences are plain. Males are born with an X chromosome and a Y chromosome in each cell, while females have two X chromosomes. Males are more vulnerable to a variety of physical problems throughout life. Cognitive and personality differences are less clear-cut. Girls tend to do better on a range of verbal tasks and boys on mathematics and spatial relations, but these differences are quite small. There is some evidence that males are more aggressive and females more empathic, although there are methodological problems with the studies underlying these generalizations. There appears to be a wider variation among members of one sex than there is between one sex and the other. One area where gender differences appear is in communication, especially nonverbal communication, although there is still considerable overlap between males and females.

3 Explanations for sex and gender differences include hormonal effects and environmental influences such as parental child-rearing patterns, messages in the media, and cultural attitudes.

4 The uncritical acceptance of gender stereotypes (for example, that males should be dominant and aggressive while females should be nurturant and dependent) can have far-reaching implications. Sandra L. Bem maintains that the healthiest person is one whose personality includes a balanced combination of the most positive characteristics associated with each sex. Such a person is described as androgynous.

5 The two most influential theories of gender identification are social learning theory and cognitive developmental theory. Social learning theorists propose that children learn to act like boys and girls by observing and imitating models (most frequently, the parent of the same sex) and by being reinforced for appropriate behavior. Cognitive-developmental theorists believe that gender typing is related to a child's intellectual understanding that he or she is of a particular sex and is therefore expected to act in certain ways.

6 Gender identity disorder of childhood is a profound disturbance of the normal sense of maleness or femaleness. It has been related to both hormonal factors and parental child-rearing methods. Some children who experience gender identity disorder grow up to be transsexuals, people who feel "trapped" in the body of the wrong sex.

7 The pioneering work of Masters and Johnson has identified four stages of sexual response: excitement, plateau, orgasm, and resolution. Sexual desire is aroused by a combination of factors. Testosterone, one of the androgens (male sex hormones), is an important source of arousal for both males and females; and the female hormone estrogen is linked to female sexual arousal. Other

factors include "gender signals," physical characteristics, learning, and cognitive and emotional factors.

8 Human beings are sexual creatures even before birth. However, sexuality takes different forms throughout the life span, as people deal with different developmental tasks. The early years are important for the development of sexual beliefs and values. With the dramatic physical changes of pubescence and puberty, people become sexually mature and able to reproduce. Sexual activity is a typical part of the experience of contemporary teenagers, and adolescent pregnancy is an important concern. During young adulthood, individuals want to achieve sexual independence, sexual responsibility, and sexual competence. This is a stage when sexuality often merges with an emotional commitment to another person. Although the physiological changes of middle and old age, especially in men, result in differences in sexual activity compared with earlier ages, older adults can and often do engage in some form of active sexual expression as long as they live.

9 We do not know what causes heterosexuality (sexual attraction to someone of the other sex) or homosexuality (sexual attraction to someone of the same sex), although it is likely that an interaction between various hormonal and environmental events is crucial.

10 Sexual dysfunctions are recurrent and persistent disturbances in the sexual response cycle that are not caused by a physical condition or by medication. These include inhibited sexual desire (the psychosexual dysfunction for which sex therapy is most frequently sought), inhibited sexual excitement, inhibited female orgasm, inhibited male orgasm, premature ejaculation, vaginismus, dyspareunia, and sexual burnout. Causes of sexual dysfunctions include medical conditions, drugs, attitudes toward sex and sexual pleasure, emotional problems, ignorance, and problems in the relationship between partners.

11 Paraphilias are psychosexual disorders characterized by arousal only in response to unusually bizarre imagery, objects, or acts. Their causes are typically unknown and treatment usually involves behavior therapy.

12 There is no compelling evidence that links nonviolent erotica (materials that arouse sexual desire) to any form of sexual aggression. In addition, there is no strong evidence linking violent pornography to violence against women. Other cultural factors, such as a society's level of machismo (the extent to which males are viewed as superior to females), are more likely to provide a setting for sexual violence against women.

13 Sex therapy is treatment designed to remove specific obstacles to sexual functioning. It is often behaviorally oriented. Its success depends upon the particular dysfunction, with treatment for premature ejaculation and vaginismus having the highest success rates.

KEY TERMS

Androgens (page 424)
Androgynous (427)
Chromosomes (419)
Dyspareunia (442)
Erogenous zone (430)
Erotica (443)
Estrogen (433)
Gender identity (419)
Gender identity disorder (429)
Gender identity disorder of childhood (429)

Gender roles (419)
Gender stereotypes (419)
Genes (419)
Heterosexuals (440)
Homosexuals (440)
Inhibited female orgasm (442)
Inhibited male orgasm (442)
Inhibited sexual desire (ISD) (441)
Inhibited sexual excitement (442)

Obscenity (443)
Paraphilia (443)
Pornography (443)
Premature ejaculation (442)
Primary sex characteristics (435)
Progesterone (433)
Psychosexual dysfunction (441)
Pubescence (435)
Puberty (435)

Secondary sex characteristics (435)
Sex differences (419)
Sex therapy (443)
Sexual burnout (442)
Transsexual (429)
Testosterone (433)
Vaginismus (442)

SUGGESTED READINGS

HALL, J. A. (1984). *Nonverbal sex differences: Communication accuracy and expressive style.* Baltimore: Johns Hopkins University Press. A complete and up-to-date review of the literature that concludes that sex differences in nonverbal communication (that is, in body posture, personal space, touch, facial expression, and decoding ability) are greater than sex differences in other areas.

HYDE, J. (1986). *Understanding human sexuality* (3d ed.). New York: McGraw-Hill. An exceptionally readable textbook covering a wide range of topics in the area of sexuality: physical and hormonal factors; contraception; sex research; variations in sexual behavior; sexual dysfunction; and sex and religion, law, and education.

MASTERS, W. H., JOHNSON, V. E., & KOLODNY, R. C. (1986). *Sex and human loving.* Boston: Little, Brown. An overall look at sexuality, summarizing for general readers the information in the earlier books of Masters and Johnson and adding material on a broad range of sexual issues.

MATLIN, M. W. (1987). *Psychology of women.* New York: Holt. A comprehensive and readable review.

OLDS, S. W. (1985). *The eternal garden: Seasons of our sexuality.* New York: Times Books. A description of sexual development throughout life, through personal accounts. Several people ranging in age from 20 to 83 tell of significant turning points in their own lives; their stories are then interpreted in the light of both classic and contemporary research.

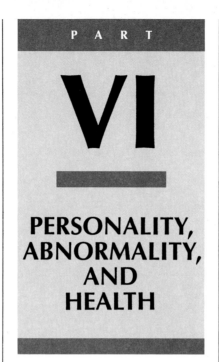

PART

VI

PERSONALITY, ABNORMALITY, AND HEALTH

ndividuality—for good and for ill—and the pursuit of both mental and physical health are the meat of Part VI of this book; for many people these subjects are the overwhelming reason for the existence of the science of psychology. We first take up the riddle of individual personality— what it is that makes us the way we are—and attempt to provide some answers. Then we look at the difficulties that arise when the way some people are undermines their ability to function normally. We examine various attempts through the years to treat those suffering from various kinds of psychological disturbances. We also explore the relationship between psychological issues and both mental and physical health.

■ In *Chapter 13*, "Theories and Assessment of Personality," we first ask what makes each person unique and examine some of the explanations offered by various students of personality. We look at the theories of Sigmund Freud, who focused on the conflict between

biological urges and the need to tame them; those of B. F. Skinner, the behaviorist, and Albert Bandura, the social-learning theorist, both of whom examined the role of the environment; and those of Abraham Maslow and other humanists, who considered the potential we have to fulfill ourselves. In the remainder of Chapter 13, we look at ways in which psychologists measure personality—through interviews; through projective techniques like the interpretation of inkblots; and through more objective tests, which are usually pencil-and-paper tests.

■ *Chapter 14*, "Abnormal Psychology," discusses the ways we define emotional disturbance and abnormal behavior and the difficulties we have in deciding what is "abnormal." It describes and tries to shed some light on the causes of a range of emotional disorders, from mild depression that affects almost all of us at times to the break with reality that characterizes schizophrenia.

■ In *Chapter 15*, "Therapy," we point out the three most widely used ways of treating psychological disorders: *psychotherapy*, which relies most heavily on talking to help individuals change their attitudes and behavior; *medical treatment*, which uses physical techniques like drugs, electric shock, and surgery; and *social* or *environmental intervention*, which focuses on changing the individual's environment in some way. We also look at some of the many differences within the three approaches.

■ *Chapter 16*, "Health Psychology," focuses on the relationships among the various biological, psychological, and social factors that promote wellness and cause illness. We discuss stress and show how one's interpretation of a potentially stressful event influences one's ability to cope with it. We examine both the psychological and the physical aspects of such health-related behaviors as eating, exercising, smoking, and drinking. We also look at the psychological ramifications of physical illness.

C H A P T E R

13

THEORIES AND ASSESSMENT OF PERSONALITY

- How does Freud's psychoanalytic view of personality portray people as being in a constant struggle to tame their biological urges?

- What points of view were taken by the personality theorists Jung, Adler, Horney, and Erikson, who broke away from Freud?

- How do Maslow's self-actualization theory and Rogers's person-centered theory emphasize each person's potential for self-fulfillment?

- How do Skinner's radical behaviorism and Bandura's social-learning theory focus on the role of the environment?

- How does Allport's psychology of the individual look to individual traits to explain personality?

- How does temperament affect the way people approach situations and other people?

- Which is more important in determining behavior—characteristics of the person or characteristics of the situation?

- How can personality be assessed?

- What ethical concerns are related to personality tests?

We were about to go to a party where the only person I would know was my husband, Jonathan. Just before we left the house, I turned to him and asked plaintively, "Are you going to stay close to me tonight? Or are you going to walk away and leave me alone with all those strangers?" In his obvious anticipation of the party (where he would know only one or two people himself) and his warm, reassuring smile, I could see a major difference between his personality and mine—and a big reason why I had been attracted to Jonathan in the first place.

I hate to go to new places full of new people, whether it's a social gathering or a professional meeting. My husband, on the other hand, is energized by anything or anybody unfamiliar. My initial reaction when faced with a new idea is usually, "No. I can't do it: I don't have the time. It doesn't fit in with my schedule, my life, my abilities, my personality." His initial reaction to a new proposition is, "Why not?" I like to be introduced to life gradually, putting my big toe in unfamiliar waters before I get my ankles wet. He dives right in.

—From the notebooks of Diane Papalia

The way people respond to new situations is just one kind of personality characteristic, one among many. After a few minutes of conversation with someone new, it's usually possible to glimpse many facets of that person's personality. At the same time, of course, you're usually revealing something about yourself. In our dealings with other people, and also in our solitary pursuits, we clearly show that each of us is unique, with a personality like that of no one else on earth. This is precisely the psychological definition of ***personality***—the constellation of relatively consistent ways of dealing with people and situations that puts the stamp of individuality on each of us. Our attitudes, our values, our opinions, and our emotions are the cornerstones of our individuality, but it is the way we act upon these states of mind that determines what others will see as our personalities.

No one, of course, is 100 percent consistent—always receptive to new ideas or always resistant to them; always generous; always friendly; always tolerant; always callous; always honest. But as you know from your own experience and your read-

Personality *Constellation of relatively consistent ways of dealing with people and situations that makes each person unique.*

ing of literature, certain characteristics do predominate in our psychological makeup, so that we can be described by the traits that seem to govern our behavior much of the time.

A great puzzle in psychology, and the one that has led to countless theories and research projects, is: What makes people develop these characteristics? Why is one man so generous that he would give away his last dollar to a stranger, while another finds it painful to spend even modest amounts? Why does one woman accept people essentially as they are, while another has room in her life only for those who think and act the way she does? Why is one person loud and another quiet? Why is one "all wired up" and another "laid-back"? Why is one ready to question authority at every turn, while another finds comfort in established structures?

For answers to these questions, observers of human nature have formulated complex theories. We will look at the most important of these theories, which fall into four broad categories: *psychoanalytic* theory, *humanist* theory, *environmental* (or *learning*) theory, and *trait* theory. According to learning theory, one's personality is determined by experiences outside oneself, in the environment; according to the other three schools of thought, our personalities are formed within ourselves, arising from basic inborn needs, drives, and characteristics.

We will also explore other questions related to personality, such as whether a person reacts similarly over a broad range of circumstances, or whether the situation a person is in dictates how he or she will act. And we'll examine the field of personality testing—how much tests can tell us and whether their use is ethical.

THEORIES OF PERSONALITY DEVELOPMENT

As you read about the theories we discuss in this chapter, ask yourself how each one might account for the personality characteristics you've noticed in your friends. Consider also how each theory differs from the others along the dimensions indicated by the following questions. How do you think the answers to these questions (the answers are summarized in Table 13-1) affect the degree to which each theory has become accepted by professionals and by broad segments of society?

1 Does the theory consider behavior to be motivated largely by conscious factors or unconscious factors?
2 How did the theory originate—from looking at normal people, from observing troubled persons who have sought out psychotherapy, or from observing animals in the laboratory and then generalizing to human beings?

TABLE 13-1 CHARACTERISTICS OF MAJOR PERSONALITY THEORIES

Theory	Principal Motivation for Behavior		How Theory Originated			Can Theory be Measured Precisely?		Principal Causes of Behavior		Basic View of People			Focus of Theory		Principal Interest	
	Conscious	Unconscious	Normal People	Troubled People	Animals	Yes	No	Biological	Environmental	Good	Bad	Neutral	Observed Behaviors	Internal Traits	General Laws of Behavior	Individual Uniqueness
Psycho-analytic		X		X			X	X			X			X	X	
Humanistic	X	X	X	X			X	X		X				X		X
Environ-mental	X				X	X			X		X		X		X	
Trait	X		X			X		X			X			X		X

(Bettmann Archive)

Sigmund Freud, originator of the psychoanalytic view of personality, and the most influential personality theorist in history

Psychoanalysis *Therapeutic approach, originally developed by Freud, that aims to eliminate anxiety by giving the patient insight into unconscious conflicts which affect behavior and emotions.*

Id *According to Freudian theory, the aspect of personality that is present at birth; the id operates on the pleasure principle and is characterized by the desire for immediate gratification.*

Libido *In Freudian theory, sexual energy.*

Eros *In Freudian theory, life instincts.*

Thanatos *In Freudian theory, death instincts.*

Pleasure principle *In Freudian theory, the operating principle for the id, which attempts to gratify needs immediately.*

3 How easily can researchers design programs to test the theory? Are terms defined precisely? How much research actually has been generated?
4 Does the theory emphasize biological or environmental causes of behavior?
5 Does the theory see people as basically good, basically bad, or neutral?
6 Does the theory focus on behavior that can be seen or on internal traits?
7 Is the principal interest of the theory in universal laws of behavior or in individual uniqueness?

Psychoanalytic Approaches

Classical Psychoanalytic Theory: Sigmund Freud   Sigmund Freud (1856–1939), the most famous personality theorist the world has ever known, revolutionized people's thinking about the development of personality. Much of the terminology he used has entered the common vocabulary, so that most of us have heard the terms *id, ego, superego, oral* and *anal personalities, libido, penis envy, Oedipus complex*, the *unconscious,* and many others. We'll take a look at what these and other terms mean in the context of Freudian theory.

A BRIEF HISTORY OF FREUDIAN THEORY   Freud's life spanned the second half of the nineteenth century and most of the first half of the twentieth; his work left the world forever changed in the way people saw certain aspects of human personality. In some ways, he presented a totally new vision of the human mind; in other ways, he was a product of his own upbringing and of the Victorian era in which he lived. Freud began his career in Vienna, where he lived for almost 80 years. As a physician in private practice, he became interested in the treatment of nervous disorders. The first technique he tried was hypnosis; but since he had little success with it, he dropped it and continued to search for a better way to help his patients. He felt that he had found one when he became acquainted with Dr. Joseph Breuer's "talking cure," through which patients were able to get rid of their symptoms by talking about their experiences and problems. Freud expanded and developed this technique into what we now know as **psychoanalysis,** which we'll discuss in greater detail in Chapter 15.

As Freud listened to his patients—mostly middle-aged, upper-middle-class Viennese women—while they talked about their concerns and recited many of their experiences, he began to see significant threads emerging: the lifelong influence of experiences in early childhood, the existence and importance of infantile sexuality, the significance of the content of dreams, the way so much of our lives is ruled by deeply rooted elements of which we are not consciously aware. On the basis of these and other observations, he formulated his theories, sometimes illustrating his points by writing up individual case histories.

STRUCTURE OF PERSONALITY   According to Freud, the *id,* the *ego,* and the *superego* are three different parts of the personality, each of which serves a different function and develops at a different time (Freud, 1923/1950). These three components, of course, are not physically present in the brain; rather, they are forces that Freud assumed to exist, from his observations of people's behaviors and expressed thoughts and feelings.

Id   The **id** (Latin for *it*) is present at birth. It consists of such basic needs as hunger and thirst and the need for sex. Freud called these needs the *life instincts* and believed them to be fueled by a form of energy he called the **libido.** The life instinct is called **eros,** after the Greek god of love. The id also contains a *death instinct* (called **thanatos**), responsible for aggressiveness and destruction. The id cries out for satisfaction *right away.* It operates on the **pleasure principle,** which demands immediate gratification no matter what. Hungry babies cry to be fed; they do not care if their mother is sound asleep or their father is looking after another child; to infants, their own need is paramount, and they will stop their demands only when it is met.

To Freud, these life and death instincts are the bases for *all* human behavior throughout life. They are drives that motivate behavior. Each instinct consists of a bodily *need* (with hunger, for instance, the need is food) and a psychological *wish* (a desire for food). The need gives birth to the wish, and the wish leads to behavior.

People do not always gratify their instincts directly; sometimes they use substitute objects—a process known as *displacement*. When displacement produces something that is socially valuable, it is called *sublimation*. (Displacement and sublimation are discussed further below.)

Ego   The **ego** (Latin for *I*), the aspect of personality generally known as "common sense," develops soon after birth, when infants realize that the things they want will not come automatically and that they will have to figure out a way to get them. It operates on the **reality principle,** by which people work out plans and then take some kind of action—test their plans in some way—to see whether they are on the right track. This process is known as *reality testing*. Infants ruled by the id lie screaming in the crib until they are fed; but hungry toddlers, under the guidance of the ego, make their way to the cookie jar. The id (irrational and unconscious) feels and unthinkingly expresses emotion; the ego (rational and largely conscious) *thinks* and acts upon its analysis of the situation. The ego tries to find a way to gratify the id, while still considering reality.

Superego   The **superego** (Latin for *over the I*), the last part of the personality to develop, appears in early childhood. It operates on what we might be tempted to call the "perfection principle." It represents the values that parents, and then other representatives of society, communicate to the child as ideals. The superego lets children internalize the concepts of right and wrong, so that they can control their own behavior according to whether they themselves consider a given action right or wrong. The superego consists of the **ego-ideal** (the "shoulds," for which we have received approval, to which we aspire, and of which we feel proud) and of the **conscience** (the "should-nots," for which we have been punished and now punish ourselves through guilt).

The superego is the moral taskmaster of the soul, the agent that tries to prevent the id from acting upon its impulses, especially the sexual and aggressive ones. It aims to divert the ego from its realistic approach toward a moralistic one. The superego is nonrational like the id, and controlling like the ego; yet it is in opposition to both of them. It is the original killjoy. The ego *postpones* instinctual gratification: the superego tries to block it completely. If it succeeds too well, it produces a rigid, inhibited personality; when it fails, it creates an antisocial personality.

DEFENSE MECHANISMS OF THE EGO   According to Freud, then, the personality consists of three components: id, ego, and superego. The id and the superego are fundamentally opposed in their aims. The id aims for immediate gratification, while the superego aims to conform to societal ideals. The role of the ego is to mediate between the id and the superego.

People become anxious when they worry that their instincts will get out of control, and the ego develops defense mechanisms to deal with this anxiety. **Defense mechanisms** distort reality to make it easier to deal with. Furthermore, they are unconscious, so that the person is not even aware that any distortion has taken place and is completely convinced that his or her viewpoint is the only correct one. We all engage in these common defenses at some times; they don't represent a disorder unless they take a severe form.

Displacement   As was noted above, people do not always gratify instincts directly; they may use substitute objects. Use of a substitute is known as **displacement.** This is

Ego   *According to Freudian theory, the aspects of personality generally known as common sense; operates on the reality principle to mediate between the id and the superego.*
Reality principle   *In Freudian theory, the operating principle for the ego, through which the ego attempts to find acceptable ways to gratify the id.*

Superego   *According to Freudian theory, the aspect of personality which represents the values that parents and other agents of society communicate to the child. The superego results from resolution of the Oedipus or Electra complex.*
Ego-ideal   *In Freudian theory, an aspect of the superego that represents the "shoulds," for which we have received approval, to which we aspire, and of which we feel proud.*
Conscience   *According to Freudian theory, an aspect of the superego that represents the "should-nots," for which we have been punished and now punish ourselves through guilt.*

Defense mechanisms   *According to Freudian theory, an unconscious way to combat anxiety through the distortion of reality.*

Displacement   *Freudian defense mechanism in which a person gratifies an urge indirectly, by substituting a safer or more available object, person, or activity.*

(Rosenwald Collection, National Gallery of Art, Washington)

Sublimation, a Freudian defense mechanism, can be seen in the sharply satirical drawings of Honoré Daumier, who used the pen rather than the sword to attack elements in society that aroused his indignation. Here he caricatures corrupt jurists, one of his favorite targets.

Sublimation Freudian defense mechanism characterized by rechanneling uncomfortable feelings (like sexual anxiety) into acceptable activities (like schoolwork).

Repression Freudian defense mechanism characterized by the unconscious blocking from consciousness of anxiety-producing urges or experiences.

Regression Freudian defense mechanism characterized by returning to behaviors of an earlier time in one's life.

Projection Freudian defense mechanism characterized by attributing one's own unacceptable thoughts and motives to another.

the process that is taking place when you check your impulse to yell at your boss, and then go home and yell at the first member of your family who is unlucky enough to cross your path.

Sublimation Displacement can have positive as well as negative effects. When it produces an achievement that is socially valued, it is called **sublimation.** Thus, a baby may suck on a pacifier when the breast is not available; a child who is discouraged from masturbating may play with blocks; and Leonardo da Vinci may have painted madonnas when what he really wanted was to feel close to his mother, from whom he had been separated as a child.

Repression In an anxiety-producing situation, a person may block certain urges or experiences from consciousness. This is called **repression.** People may be unable to remember a painful experience, may be unable to see an object or person in plain sight, may be unaware of feelings that at one time they expressed freely, or may be physically disabled without any organic reason (as in the case of a man who is sexually impotent with his wife because he considers the sexual impulse aggressive and is afraid of hurting her).

Regression In anxiety-producing situations, people often **regress.** That is, they return to the behavior of an earlier time in life, to try to recapture remembered security. A little boy, for instance, may react to the birth of a baby brother or sister by wetting his bed and sucking his thumb, behaviors he engaged in when *he* was the baby. Or, after the first marital quarrel, a newlywed may "go home to Mother." Once the crisis is past, the immature behavior will probably disappear, but if such behavior is a person's pattern, it is likely to reappear at the next sign of trouble.

Projection One way of dealing with unacceptable thoughts and motives is to **project** them, or attribute them to someone else. Thus, Jimmy may talk about how much his sister hates him instead of how much he hates her. Or a man may accuse his wife of adultery, not because she has given him any reason to doubt her fidelity, but because he himself is attracted to other women.

Reaction formation When people consider some of their own feelings unacceptable, they may replace these feelings with opposite feelings—a process known as **reaction formation.** A woman who hates her mother because she always felt that the mother favored her sister over her may loudly proclaim her love, complete with extravagant gifts and grand gestures. This kind of mechanism may have motivated a marketing analyst in Tampa, Florida, who led a drive against sex education books in public libraries because he claimed they would pervert the morals of children. While in the midst of this censorship attempt, the crusader was arrested for, and later pleaded no contest to, sexual misconduct involving an 8-year-old girl and a teenage boy ("Banning sequel," 1982). This man may well have replaced his unacceptable sexual urges toward children with what he saw as the opposite, the wish to maintain the innocence of children by not exposing them to books about sex.

How can we distinguish a reaction formation from a true feeling? Usually, a reaction formation involves compulsiveness and going to extremes. When "the lady doth protest too much," we are alerted to the possibility that things may not be what they seem.

Rationalization Another way of dealing with a difficult situation is to **rationalize,** that is, to justify our behavior by pretending that the difficulty doesn't exist. The fox

Reaction formation *Freudian defense mechanism characterized by replacing an anxiety-producing feeling with its opposite.*

Rationalization *Freudian defense mechanism characterized by justifying one's behavior in a difficult situation by pretending that the difficulty does not exist.*

(Drawing by Lorenz; © 1986 The New Yorker Magazine, Inc.)

"Mary Boone was not avoiding me. I was avoiding her."

This cartoonist uses another Freudian defense mechanism— rationalization—in depicting an artist's insistence that she, not the influential gallery owner she wants to impress, is doing the avoiding.

tells himself, "I don't want those grapes just out of reach, because they must be sour"; or, biting into a particularly sour lemon, "I'm clever to have chosen such a sweet fruit." The college we didn't get into wouldn't have been as much fun as the one where we are now, the job we didn't get would have been a dead end, the lover we lost would have kept us from meeting the far superior person we are now involved with.

People rationalize for another purpose, too—to make themselves feel better about doing something they basically feel they shouldn't be doing. When a department store makes a mistake in your favor, for example, do you pocket the money, telling yourself, "They overcharge, anyway, so this is really coming to me"? If so, you are rationalizing.

PSYCHOSEXUAL DEVELOPMENT According to Freud (1905/1949b), personality develops in a sequence of five stages, beginning in infancy. Four of these stages are named for parts of the body that are primary sources of gratification in each phase. These sensitive body parts are called the **erogenous zones.** A person whose needs are not met at any one stage or who is overindulged at that time may become fixated at the particular stage. **Fixation** is an arrest in development that results when the conflicts of a particular stage are not appropriately resolved. The sequence of the shifts of instinctual energy from one body zone to another is always the same; it is the level of a child's maturation that determines when these shifts will take place. Freud believed that a person's lifelong personality is largely determined during the first three of the stages that are listed in the following paragraphs. A major element of his theory is the concept of _infantile sexuality_—that the human sexual drive does not appear full-blown at puberty but has been present since birth, even though the sexual feelings of infants and young children are different in form from those of adolescents and adults.

Oral stage (birth to 12–18 months) The erogenous zone during the **oral stage** is the *mouth,* through which the baby gets pleasure from eating, sucking, and biting. Sucking, then, accomplishes something besides just getting nutrition into the body—it is a source of pleasure in itself. People fixated in the oral stage may, as adults, become so gullible that they will "swallow" anything, become dependent, say cruel things (that is, be orally sadistic), or take the same kind of pleasure from absorbing knowledge and acquiring possessions as they once did from ingesting food.

Anal stage (12–18 months to 3 years) During the second year, the child's instinctual energy shifts to another erogenous zone, the *anus,* as the child learns to control elimination; this is Freud's **anal stage.** Toddlers find the very act of withholding or expelling feces sensually gratifying. Toilet training is important. A child who is trained too strictly may become obsessively neat, cruel and destructive, or obstinate and stingy; a child who is praised extravagantly for producing bowel movements may be inspired to be productive in other realms as well.

Phallic stage (3 to 6 years) The **phallic stage,** which gets its name from *phallus,* a term for the penis, begins when the child feels pleasure in the *genital* region. At this point the child may discover masturbation.

Oedipus, a king in Greek literature, killed his father and married his mother, not realizing who either one was. Freud gave the name of this tragic figure to the **Oedipus complex**—the concept that every little boy falls in love with his mother during the phallic stage and has murderous thoughts toward his father. According to Freud, a boy lavishes love and affection on his mother and competes with his father for the mother's love and affection. Unconsciously the boy wants to take his father's place, but, recognizing his father's power, he is afraid of him. Since he has learned that little girls don't have a penis, he concludes that someone must have cut it off and fears that his father, angry at his attempted usurpation, will do the same to him. The resulting anxiety is the **castration complex.** Fearful, the boy represses his sexual

Erogenous zones *Sexually sensitive areas of the body.*

Fixation *According to Freudian theory, an arrest in development which results when the conflicts of a particular stage are not appropriately resolved.*

Infantile sexuality *Freud's concept of the human sexual drive as something that does not appear full-blown at puberty but is present from birth, even though the sexual feelings of infants and young children are different in form from those of adolescents and adults.*

Oral stage *According to Freudian theory, the psychosexual stage of infancy (birth to 12–18 months), characterized by gratification in the oral region; feeding is the major situation in which this gratification occurs.*

Anal stage *According to Freudian theory, the psychosexual stage of toddlerhood (12–18 to 36 months), in which the child receives pleasure through anal stimulation; toilet training is the major situation in which gratification occurs.*

Phallic stage *According to Freudian theory, the stage of psychosexual development of the preschool child (3 to 6 years), characterized by gratification in the genital area.*

Oedipus complex *Phenomenon described by Freud in which the male child in the phallic stage feels sexual attraction for his mother and rivalry toward his father.*

Castration complex *Phenomenon described by Freud in which the male child, seeing that girls do not have penises, becomes fearful of his own castration by an angry father.*

strivings toward his mother, stops trying to rival his father, and begins to identify with him.

Once Freud had identified the Oedipus complex, he had to conceptualize a mechanism for female sexual development. What he came up with was the **Electra complex;** many consider the reasoning behind it quite tortuous. A little girl becomes aware that she does not have a penis, thinks it is a very valuable thing to have, and feels incomplete because of her lack. She envies anyone who has a penis, and becomes especially attracted to her father because of his possession of this organ. Thus, she competes with her mother for her father's affections. At the same time, she does love her mother and doesn't want to lose her mother's love. Therefore she becomes anxious and represses her ambivalent feelings. Eventually she identifies with her mother, but she cannot resolve her **penis envy** until she grows up and gives birth to a son "who brings the longed-for penis with him" (Freud, 1905, quoted in Schaeffer, 1971, p. 19). (Apparently the woman who never has children or is blessed only with daughters is doomed to suffer penis envy all her life.) Freud maintained that little girls never *completely* overcome penis envy (so that females are left generally envious and suffering from low self-esteem), and that they do not resolve the phallic stage as well as little boys do.

At about the age of 5 or 6, children resolve the Oedipus complex or the Electra complex when they realize that the risks of competing with the same-sex parent are too great. They identify with the parent of the same sex and internalize parental standards to develop a superego. Identification with the same-sex parent helps to relieve the anxiety brought about by the Oedipus and Electra complexes. This process is known as *identification with the aggressor.* Freud felt, however, that identification with the same-sex parent is never total and that all people continue to possess some traits of the other sex. He also felt that boys develop a superego more readily than girls do. (For a discussion of identification, in both Freudian terms and other terms, see Chapter 9.)

Latency stage (6 years to puberty) The **latency stage** is a period of relative sexual quiet between the turbulent phallic and genital stages. Boys and girls in this stage tend to avoid the opposite sex, but they are not totally asexual during this time, since they masturbate, engage in sex play, ask sexual questions, and tell sex-oriented jokes.

Genital stage (from puberty on) The **genital stage,** which occurs because of the hormonal changes that accompany puberty, marks the entry into mature sexuality, when the person's major psychosexual task is to enter into heterosexual relationships with people outside the family.

We have barely touched on Freud's rich and complex theory, which he spelled out and elaborated upon in many volumes. We do discuss other aspects of his theoretical framework in other places in this book, for they permeate many topics in the study of psychology. For now, though, let's see how well Freud's theory has held up over the years.

EVALUATION OF FREUDIAN THEORY Probably the single most important contribution Freud made to the study of human personality was his emphasis on the **unconscious,** that vast network of stored, often repressed passions and ideas that direct our conscious thoughts and behavior. Freud likened the human mind to an iceberg, in which only the smallest part, the conscious (like the tip of the iceberg), is exposed, while the much larger part, the unconscious, is hidden beneath the surface.

Another vastly important contribution was Freud's emphasis (even though it sometimes appears to be an overemphasis) on the importance of early experience in later development.

The single most controversial element of his body of thought was his insistence

According to Freud, every little boy goes through a stage when he falls in love with his mother and sees his father as a rival. This is known as the Oedipus complex.

Electra complex *According to Freudian theory, the female counterpart of the Oedipus complex, in which the little girl in the phallic stage feels sexual attraction for her father and rivalry toward her mother.*

Penis envy *Freudian concept that the female envies the penis and wants one of her own.*

Latency stage *According to Freudian theory, a period of relative sexual calm during middle childhood (6 years to puberty) that occurs after the Oedipus or Electra complex is resolved.*

Genital stage *Freudian term for the psychosexual stage of mature adult sexuality, which begins during adolescence.*

Unconscious *Network of stored, often repressed, factors that affect conscious thoughts and behaviors.*

on the sexual drive as the primary motivating force for behavior throughout life, even from infancy. Several of his followers, including Jung and Adler (whose theories are discussed in this chapter), broke with him over this issue. According to contemporary critics, he overemphasized sex as the primary motivating force of behavior throughout life; but he is generally respected for bringing the concept of infantile sexuality out into the open.

In recent years, the focus of criticism has shifted to Freud's perception of women as inferior creatures, anatomically (because they don't have a penis), psychologically (because, not having a penis, they do not experience either the Oedipus conflict or castration anxiety), morally (because, not undergoing these two conflicts, they do not develop as strong a superego as boys do), and culturally (because, not having such a strong superego, they are not capable of sublimating baser desires into creative and productive work that will advance civilization). Freud maintained that "penis envy" prevented girls from developing as strong a superego as boys do; but in fact girls show more guilt (Bronfenbrenner, 1960), suggesting that they have a *stronger* superego. One of Freud's early followers, Karen Horney, broke with him over his view of women.

Other voices have criticized Freud for other reasons. Humanists take issue with his view of human beings as creatures at the mercy of base instincts that will cause trouble if they are not controlled. Because he based his theories on the lives of troubled people who had come to him for help, Freud did not appear to appreciate the strength of the healthy human psyche. Furthermore, it is questionable whether we can appropriately theorize about normal development on the basis of observations of people with emotional problems.

Because many of Freud's theories are vague and hard to define, it has been difficult to design research projects to confirm or refute them. Still, researchers have tried and tried. Thousands of attempts to test Freud's theories have been made over the years, with varied results (Fisher & Greenberg, 1977; Luborsky, Crits-Christoph, & Mellon, 1986; Winson, 1985). Research findings do show evidence for the importance of early experience and the existence of the unconscious. Oral and anal personality types, children's erotic feelings for the parent of the other sex and their hostility toward the same-sex parent, and male fears of castration as related to erotic arousal also receive some validation from scientific studies. Other research, however, indicates that identification occurs for reasons having at least as much to do with parental characteristics of warmth and nurturance as with "fear of the aggressor"; that women achieve sexual identification as easily as men; and that the libido, the idea of a sexual latency period in middle childhood, and the death instinct don't stand up scientifically. As far as psychoanalysis as a treatment is concerned, the jury is still out. On the basis of available research, it can be neither accepted nor rejected. It did, however, serve to popularize "talk therapy," which in a number of forms is widely used today, as we'll see in Chapter 15.

Some recent criticism has focused on the way Freud's own defense mechanisms seem to have entered into the formulation of his theories. For example, it is possible that Freud may have ignored blatant evidence of parental maltreatment and sexual seduction of children, while claiming that children were naturally aggressive, masochistic, and sexually seductive toward their parents (Masson, 1985; Tribich & Klein, 1981). One reason advanced for this selective blindness is the possibility that Freud may have suspected—and not wanted to acknowledge—the likelihood of his own father's having been sexually seductive; another might be Freud's inability to own up to sexual fantasies about his own daughters (Krüll, 1986; Tribich, 1982).

In general, Freud's followers differed from him in a number of ways. They did not place the same all-encompassing emphasis on sex and aggression as motivators of human behavior, and they were more concerned with the way social interaction affects development. Let's meet four of these neo-Freudians: Jung, Adler, Horney, and Erikson. We'll begin with Carl Jung.

Carl Jung, a Swiss physician who believed that personality has historical, or "racial," origins.

Analytic Psychology: Carl Jung   Carl Jung (1875–1961) was at one time considered by Freud to be his "heir to the throne." But Jung, a Swiss physician, split with Freud for both personal and intellectual reasons. Among their major theoretical differences were Jung's rejection of sexuality as the major determinant of behavior; his conviction that life is directed in large part by the positive and purposeful goals people set for themselves and not only by repressed factors; and his emphasis on growth and change throughout life, in contrast to Freud's belief that personality is unalterably set in childhood. Jung emphasized the process of developing an individual personality and the search for meaning in life.

The most controversial aspect of Jung's theory is his mystical belief in the historical (or racial) origins of personality. He believed that the roots of personality go far back before the birth of the individual, through past generations, to the dawn of humanity. From our distant ancestors we inherit common predispositions that mold the way we will look at and respond to life. Our personalities are thus collectively (in his term, "racially") determined. To learn more about the evolution of this collective personality, Jung steeped himself in the study of mythology, religion, and primitive beliefs and rituals, as well as in dreams and the manifestations of neuroses and psychoses.

Jung saw the mind as consisting of the ego (the conscious mind), the **personal unconscious** (repressed or forgotten material), and the **collective unconscious** (that part of the mind which is derived from ancestral memories). The collective unconscious is made up of **archetypes,** emotionally charged ideas that link universal concepts to individual experience. Archetypes can best be thought of as symbols or as common themes that are found through the generations and in all parts of the world.

According to Jung, we have many archetypes that we are born with and that influence our behavior. For example, the *archetype of the mother* results when the baby perceives the mother, not only according to the kind of woman she is and the experiences the baby has of her, but also according to the preformed concept of a mother that the baby is born with. An important archetype is the **persona** (the social mask one adopts). Then there are the **anima,** the repressed feminine side of a man's personality, and the **animus,** the repressed masculine side of a woman's personality. The anima and animus are examples of Jung's belief that personality consists of opposite tendencies. People openly express one tendency but retain its opposite in the unconscious. We also have archetypes for birth, death, God, the child, the wise old man, and others.

Much more widely accepted were Jung's constructs of the *introvert* (the person oriented toward his or her inner, subjective world) and the *extrovert* (the person oriented toward the outer, objective world). A person may often be described in one of these terms till middle age, when the other attitude emerges from the personal unconscious.

Jung considered the midlife transition important in other ways, too. This is the time of life, said Jung (1931/1953), when a person wants to throw off the persona, or mask, that has characterized the way he or she has been dealing with other people, and to express the feelings and emotions that have been repressed up until then. This helps to explain a commonly noted phenomenon: men tend to become more nurturant and emotionally expressive in middle age, as women become more assertive and career-oriented.

Like Freud's work, Jung's is hard to substantiate through research and experimentation. Although Jung has not had nearly the impact of his "master," his influence reaches farther than is generally recognized. It was Jung, for example, who expressed the optimistic viewpoint that the humanists later expanded on and who enunciated the concept of self-actualization through goal-directed behavior. Furthermore, artistic expression of Jung's theories can be seen in many contemporary films, plays, and novels, and perhaps in the general move toward mysticism that has characterized many aspects of contemporary society.

Personal unconscious   *According to Jungian theory, a component of the mind characterized by repressed or forgotten material.*

Collective unconscious   *According to Jungian theory, a component of the mind derived from ancestral memories.*

Archetypes   *According to Jungian theory, the symbols or common themes that are found through the generations and in all parts of the world.*

Persona   *Jungian archetype of the social mask one adopts.*

Anima   *Feminine archetype in man.*

Animus   *Masculine archetype in woman.*

(Umeda Art Boeki, Osaka)

This painting by Magritte, "The Ready-Made Bouquet," seems to illustrate Jung's concept that each of us carries within us an archetype of the other sex. Here we see the anima, *the feminine archetype, contained within a man.*

Alfred Adler, a Viennese physician who believed that early experiences are the most important determinant of personality. He coined the term "inferiority complex."

Inferiority complex *According to Adler, the basis for the drive to achieve, to complete oneself, and to overcome feelings of inadequacy.*

Superiority complex *According to Adler, overcompensation for feelings of inferiority.*

Individual Psychology: Alfred Adler   Alfred Adler (1870–1937), a Viennese physician like Freud, also broke with Freud, largely because of differences about sexuality and the role of the unconscious. Adler felt that people are primarily social, not sexual; that social motivations are more powerful than sexual ones; that the style of life a person chooses determines how he or she will satisfy sexual needs, rather than vice versa; and that it is more important to explore conscious, goal-directed behavior than unconscious motivation. Although he believed that social nature is inborn, he also maintained that the kinds of social experiences we have early in life—those with other people, especially parents and siblings—influence the way we will deal with relationships throughout life.

Adler coined the term **inferiority complex.** He felt that people try to compensate for their feelings of inferiority, sometimes by *overcompensating* and developing what he called a **superiority complex.** It's possible that his interest in dealing with feelings of inferiority and with the importance of early experiences was an outgrowth of his own sickly childhood. A major impetus in life, according to Adler, is the urge toward superiority, not over other people, but over one's own sense of inferiority, which stems initially from a child's feelings of inadequacy because of small size and lack of power. The inferiority complex drives us to achieve, to complete ourselves, to overcome early feelings of inferiority, and to become self-fulfilled.

As the founder of *individual psychology*, Adler emphasized the uniqueness of each person. In this belief, he was the precursor of the humanists, since he emphasized the concept of an individual style of life, or the way each person strives to overcome his or her inferiority feelings and develop a sense of self-worth.

Like Jung, Adler considered behavior to be goal-directed, instead of being motivated by unconscious factors. He believed in a *creative self*, a personal system that interprets experiences and seeks out those that will be fulfilling. Instead of emphasizing basic universal drives, Adler focused on the *uniqueness* of personality, which prods each of us in a different direction to find those satisfactions in life that will be personally fulfilling.

Adler was very influential through his analysis of the effect of birth order on personality; through his emphasis on the great influence of social, rather than sexual, factors; and through his stress on conscious, goal-directed behavior.

We all feel unwanted sometimes. According to Adler, the urge to overcome our sense of inferiority is the drive that leads to achievement.

Cultural Psychology: Karen Horney   Another disciple of Freud who was strongly influenced by him and then went off in new directions was Karen Horney (1885–1952). Horney was also a physician trained in psychoanalysis. She was convinced that Freud overestimated the importance of biological factors in determining personality while he neglected social and cultural ones. Particularly, she rejected Freud's concept of penis envy. Horney maintained that when a woman does wish to be a man, it is not an anatomical feature that she would like to possess but "all those qualities or privileges which in our culture are regarded as masculine, such as strength, courage, independence, success, sexual freedom, right to choose a partner" (Horney, 1939, p. 108).

Horney attributed anxieties (which she called *neuroses*, the term used by Freud) to a child's difficulty in dealing with a potentially hostile world full of such adverse factors as domination; indifference; erratic behavior; lack of respect; too much or too little warmth, admiration, or responsibility; and so forth (Horney, 1945). The anxious child, she theorized, deals with the world by "feeding" one or more of ten needs that she characterized as neurotic because she considered them irrational. These needs are the needs for affection and approval, for a partner who will take over one's life, for power, for prestige, for personal achievement, for personal admiration, for self-sufficiency and independence, and for perfection and unassailability; the need to exploit others; and the need to restrict one's life within narrow borders. She later grouped these needs into three basic ways of responding:

Karen Horney, a physician trained as a psychoanalyst, maintained that when a woman does wish to be a man, it is not his penis that she envies but all the masculine privileges endowed by her culture.

■ Moving *toward* people (becoming dependent upon them)

■ Moving *against* people (becoming hostile and rebellious)

■ Moving *away* from people (withdrawing into the self)

The major difference between healthy and neurotic people, Horney said, is that healthy people can integrate these three attitudes, sometimes giving in to others, sometimes fighting, and sometimes keeping to themselves, whereas the "neurotic" is inflexibly committed to one of these directions, regardless of whether or not it is appropriate in particular circumstances.

Psychosocial Theory: Erik H. Erikson   Erik Erikson (b.1902), a contemporary psychoanalytic theorist who was born in Germany but has spent most of his life in the United States, has carried on Freud's tradition of modifying original theories to keep up with changing times.

Erikson's major contribution to personality theory is his emphasis on the conflict between inborn instincts and societal demands. He maintains that the particular culture a person grows up in determines what these conflicts will be. This theory, which incorporates both the psyche and society, describes a progression of eight stages throughout life. In each stage the person is faced with a crisis, the resolution of which can have either a good or a bad outcome, depending on his or her ability to strike a healthy balance. For example, beginning in infancy, babies must develop the right ratio of *trust* (so that they can form intimate relationships) to *mistrust* (so that they can protect themselves in a sometimes hostile world). Many of Erikson's writings (1950, 1963, 1968) focused on childhood and adolescence, but he also built upon Jung and Adler's belief in adult development and extended his own life stages into old age. (For a detailed discussion of Erikson's theory, see the chapters on development in Part IV.)

Right: Erik H. Erikson, a psychoanalyst, emphasized the conflict between inborn instincts and societal demands, and the role of society in forming personality. He described a progression of eight stages of personality development, from infancy through old age.

Humanistic Approaches

Like psychoanalysis, ***humanistic psychology*** focuses on internal motivators of behavior, but it differs from classical analytic thinking in its optimistic confidence in our positive natures. Philosophically, humanists are in the same camp as the eighteenth-century philosopher Jean-Jacques Rousseau, who believed that people are "noble savages" who will become productive, fulfilled, happy, good human beings—unless unfavorable experiences interfere with their ability to express their finest natures. This contrasts sharply with the psychoanalysts' view of people as captives struggling to free themselves of dark and dangerous instinctual urges. While psychoanalytic theories maintain that our lives are determined by both inner and outer forces, humanistic approaches emphasize self-determination and free will.

Unlike the early psychoanalysts, whose background was medical, the humanists tend to come from disciplines such as education and psychology. Their viewpoint, which is a *phenomenological* one, stresses the importance of the subjective, unique experiences of each person and the potential all of us have for self-fulfillment through spontaneity, creativity, and personal growth.

Self-Actualization Theory: Abraham H. Maslow   Abraham Maslow (1908–1970) made his greatest contribution to humanistic psychology through his preoccupation with healthy people rather than sick ones. Focusing on joy, enthusiasm, love, and well-being, rather than on conflict, shame, hostility, and unhappiness, Maslow studied creative people who were functioning at a high level in society. From these studies he drew conclusions about healthy personality development.

Maslow's theory of human motivation rests on what he saw as a *hierarchy of needs*. Needs, according to the theory, are of two basic kinds; D needs (to correct *deficiencies*) and B needs (to achieve a higher level of *being*). Maslow felt that all human beings have to meet certain basic needs of survival first, before they can even think about needs on the next higher level. Not until they are not deficient with regard to any of their most basic needs can they strive to fulfill those higher-order needs that provide the most intense kinds of spiritual and psychic gratification.

Thus, people who are gasping for air or suffering from starvation have one overriding motivation—basic survival. When that is ensured, they can turn their attention to concerns of safety—freedom, say, from fear and pain. Feeling relatively safe, they then seek intimacy in their relationships with family, friends, and lovers. Once comfortably nurtured by affectionate ties with other people, they can then turn their attention to meeting their own basic need for self-respect. Not until we feel healthy, safe, loved, and competent can we seek the ***self-actualization*** that comes from pursuit of knowledge, appreciation of beauty, playfulness, self-sufficiency, insight into truth, or any of the other fifteen principal B values.

What kind of person does achieve self-actualization? Maslow (1950/1973) identified 38 persons who he thought had fully realized their potential. This select group included such historical giants as Albert Einstein, Ludwig van Beethoven, Abraham Lincoln, and Eleanor Roosevelt, along with more obscure people whom Maslow knew personally. After closely studying these people's lives, Maslow identified 16 characteristics that distinguished self-actualizers (presented in Table 13-2).

Although Maslow's theory has been inspirational to many people and has introduced a welcome focus on the healthy personality capable of scaling the heights of self-fulfillment, he has been criticized for a lack of scientific rigor, especially in the subjectivity of his criteria for self-actualization. This is not surprising, since he protested against overreliance on science and described the detached, highly objective, proof-oriented scientist as an example of a closed-minded person who resists anything resembling a peak experience.

Maslow's hierarchy of needs is also subject to some degree of criticism. Although it is clear that someone struggling to survive is rarely concerned with any of the higher-order needs, the order of priority for the other needs, once we get beyond survival, seems to vary for different people, and at different times for the same person. Most of us, for example, know people who are more concerned with achieving

Abraham Maslow, a humanistic psychologist, drew conclusions about healthy personality development from his studies of creative people who were functioning at a high level.

TABLE 13-2 CHARACTERISTICS OF SELF-ACTUALIZING PEOPLE

1 Realistic viewpoint toward life
2 Acceptance of themselves, other people, and the world around them
3 Spontaneity
4 Focus on solving problems rather than thinking about themselves
5 Need for privacy and a certain degree of detachment
6 Independence and an ability to function on their own
7 Unstereotyped appreciation of people, things, and ideas
8 History of peak experiences (profoundly spiritual experiences that may be mystical or religious in nature, and that often occur when a B value is actualized, at the point at which a person gains insight into some truth)
9 Identification with the human race
10 Deeply loving and intimate relationships with a few people
11 Democratic values
12 Ability to separate means from ends
13 Sense of humor that is lively and not cruel
14 Creativity
15 Lack of conformity
16 Demonstrated ability to rise above the environment, rather than merely adjust to it

Source: Adapted from Maslow, 1950/1973.

(Culver Pictures)

Eleanor Roosevelt, the wife of Franklin D. Roosevelt, was a notable example of Maslow's "self-actualized person." Originally a shy, awkward girl, she became politically active to help her husband—and then she became an international force in her own right as she campaigned for human rights.

success in a career (that is, with esteem needs) than with developing close personal relationships ("belongingness" and love needs). And most of us have experienced conflicts between work (or school) and relationships, and we may give one of these a higher priority on one occasion and reverse the priorities on another. The concept is useful, then, for thinking about human motivation; but as in most issues concerning human beings, we cannot describe an invariant sequence.

Person-Centered Theory: Carl Rogers   Carl Rogers (1902–1987), one of the most influential contemporary theorists, held a life-affirming view of human beings as powerful architects of themselves. Rogers formulated his theory of personality out of his background as a therapist to troubled people, but his view of the human psyche, unlike Freud's, is an optimistic picture of human strength. His view of personality centers on the concept of the self—the core of personality. He maintained that we all ask ourselves, "Who am I, really?" and that the way we answer this question and the degree to which we accept and value ourselves for the persons we are determines how we feel.

Rogers acknowledges an unconscious that guides much of our behavior; but, again unlike the psychoanalysts, he sees unconscious processes as *positive* motivators for behavior. Self-knowledge and self-regard come about, he says, through:

■ Our early experiences in which we gain mastery over the environment

■ The high regard of others shown by their expressions of affection, admiration, and acceptance (essential for us to have a positive view of ourself)

■ *Congruence* (agreement between the ideal self and the real self)

When the person we would *like* to be (ideal self) and the person we see ourself as (real self) are similar, we are congruent. The congruent person functions at the highest level. Such a person is open to experience and is not defensive and therefore views people and things accurately, gets along well with others, and has a high level of self-esteem. The goal of this healthy personality is growth toward self-actualization.

A person who has an *incongruent* view of the self becomes tense and anxious and may resort to defense mechanisms or even retreat into fantasy to preserve that view of the self. What causes an incongruent view? Sometimes it comes about because people are torn between what they think and what they believe other people think they should think or do. For example, suppose a woman with a strong sex drive

Congruence   According to Carl Rogers, a situation in which the person we would like to be (our ideal self) and the person we see ourself as (our real self) are similar.

The humanistic psychologist Carl Rogers's view of personality centers on the degree of congruence between the person you would like to be and the person you think you are.

Behaviorism *School of psychology that emphasizes the study of observable behaviors and events and the role of the environment in causing behavior.*

The behaviorist B. F. Skinner believes that you learn how to be the kind of person you are just as you learn everything else—by being rewarded or punished for various behaviors.

wants to think of herself as a good person. If she has been taught that sex is evil, she may repress her sexuality, even in marriage, so that she will not think of herself as a bad woman. When we are incongruent, we can change our behavior to conform to our picture of our ideal self, or change our goal to something more realistic. Rogers's person-centered therapy aims to bring about congruence through a nurturing, nondirective method (see Chapter 15).

Like Maslow, Rogers did much to promote a positive view of humankind. He saw the brighter face of our personality rather than the darker side stressed by the Freudians; and unlike the behaviorists, he saw us as controlling ourselves rather than being buffeted by outside forces. His person-centered approach to therapy has been influential.

Although Rogers tried to stimulate research on his theories, it has been difficult to design research projects to study them, since many of his terms and concepts are vague and hard to define operationally.

Environmental (or Learning) Approaches

Give me a dozen infants, well-formed, and my own specified world to bring them up in and I'll guarantee to take any one at random and train him to become any type of specialist I might select—doctor, lawyer, artist, merchant-chief, and, yes, even into beggar-man and thief, regardless of his talents, penchants, tendencies, abilities, vocations, and race of his ancestors. (Watson, 1924, p. 76)

These words were written by one of the major historical figures in **behaviorism,** the American psychologist John B. Watson (1878–1958). Watson, who was known as "the father of behaviorism," agreed with the *tabula rasa* (Latin for *blank slate*) view of personality. According to this point of view, the newborn infant is an empty slate. Environmental experience will imprint both personality and destiny upon the child. The theories fitting this philosophy are quite different from the other three kinds of approaches we talk about in this chapter, which all place great emphasis on various inborn traits or drives. Environmental approaches view human beings as almost infinitely pliant, or capable of being shaped "to order," not only in childhood, but throughout life. Watson believed, for example, that most emotions are learned. In the famous experiment with "little Albert" described in Chapter 5, he demonstrated how fear could be classically conditioned in a baby.

Environmental theories have their roots in Ivan Pavlov's work on classical conditioning and in Edward Thorndike's work on operant conditioning (described in Chapter 5), as well as in Watson's experiments. More recent work by environmentalists also emphasizes the way internal, cognitive factors (like our thoughts and feelings) affect our behavior, along with such external influences as rewards and punishments.

Radical Behaviorism: B. F. Skinner According to B. F. Skinner (b. 1904), whose research on the ways animals—and people—learn is also discussed in Chapter 5, we learn how to be the kind of people we are, just as we learn everything else. The entire concept that most people call personality, with its unconscious motivation, its moral underpinnings, and its emotional overlay, does not exist. Human behavior, Skinner says, can be divided into the different kinds of activity that we either do or don't do, depending on what we have been rewarded or punished for in the past and on what consequences we expect in the future. Rewards are much more powerful than punishments in shaping behavior.

Human behavior, then, is *lawful,* in the sense that it follows certain basic laws, or principles, of learning. It is merely a result of the chaining together of a number of stimulus-response sequences. No matter how unproductive a behavior might seem to be, it would not persist unless there was some "payoff" for the person doing it. Children may throw frequent temper tantrums, for example, because tantrums often bring results—either things the children want or the attention of their parents. They will continue to pitch tantrums as long as they get something from them.

This theory has been criticized for seeing people as empty shells and for oversimplifying the significance of learning principles, but it is optimistic in that it sees the possibility of change. An extreme view of the effect of change is demonstrated in *Walden Two,* a novel in which B. F. Skinner describes a utopian community that rewards desirable behaviors, thus bringing about a perfect society. At least one commune, in Virginia, tried to put Skinner's ideas into practice, but it later dropped its emphasis on behaviorist principles (Samuel, 1981). There are, however, many successful case histories of people who *have* seemed to change aspects of their behavior as a direct result of the application of learning principles, structured in behavior therapy programs (discussed in Chapter 15).

Social-Learning Theory: Albert Bandura   Human beings are not pigeons confined to a cage whose only stimuli are, say, different-colored bars. Our widely varied behavior takes place in extremely complex surroundings. How do we learn to do things in the first place, so that we can then be rewarded or punished for them? According to Albert Bandura (b. 1925) and other social-learning theorists (whose approach was presented in Chapter 5), we see other people perform various behaviors; we copy them; and then, when we are rewarded, we continue to do these things. If we don't get positive feedback, we eventually stop these behaviors. This point of view goes beyond basic learning principles to take into account the social context in which learning takes place.

The social-learning theorist Albert Bandura believes that we develop our personalities by observing and copying other people, and then continuing to perform the kinds of behaviors that are rewarded.

The process of observing and imitating others, called *modeling,* seems to play a part in the way children learn aggressive or altruistic behaviors. When children observe someone else acting aggressively—a real-life adult, an adult seen on film, or a cartoon character—they are more likely to act aggressively themselves than if they do not see any model at all or if they see a model acting in a kindly, gentle, helpful way. Furthermore, they're more likely to imitate behavior when they see the person responsible for it being rewarded than when they observe punishment or no consequence at all (Bandura, 1965, 1977; Bandura, Ross, & Ross, 1961, 1963; Bandura & Walters, 1963).

Although social learning theory, because of its strong emphasis on specific behaviors, does not give a good picture of the whole person, it has made a strong contribution to personality theory. A major plus is the therapy derived from it that is used to help people rid themselves of phobias and other situation-related anxieties. (More will be said about this in Chapter 15.)

Trait Approaches

The fourth broad category of personality theories we'll talk about—the trait theories—consists of several explanations for personality that resemble psychoanalytic and humanistic points of view in their focus on *internal* influences on personality, as opposed to the *external* factors emphasized by environmentalists. According to trait theories, personality is consistent from situation to situation not because of an emotional outlook colored by early experience, or because of ancestral memories, or because of universal needs. Rather, trait theories focus on specific attributes peculiar to the individual.

Some trait approaches are "type" theories that divide people into distinct categories and neatly classify them as one type or another. Other trait theories look at people not so much in terms of one type or another, but as blends of many different characteristics that people have to a greater or lesser extent. We will examine two trait theories that fit into the second category: those of Gordon W. Allport and Raymond B. Cattell.

Psychology of the Individual: Gordon W. Allport   Because he was concerned with the uniqueness of each individual, rather than with the personality of the "average" person, Gordon Allport (1897–1967) sought ways to identify specific traits that would account for each person's characteristic behavior.

Allport maintained that each of us has a personal disposition that consists of up to three kinds of traits: cardinal traits, central traits, and secondary traits (1937, 1961). A **cardinal trait** is one that is dominant and therefore colors virtually every aspect of a person's behavior and attributes. Few people have a cardinal trait, but one example might be found in the character played by Jack Lemmon in the film *Tribute*. The hero of this movie was *always* funny. He made jokes in every conceivable situation—when his marriage was breaking up, when his young son was trying to be intimate with him, when he was facing his own imminent death from cancer. For this man, humorousness was clearly a cardinal trait. Among historical figures, we think of the amorousness of Casanova and the plotting of Machiavelli. Few people have one overriding trait such as these, which characterizes their whole personality.

Central traits are the handful of characteristic tendencies that we would ordinarily use to describe a person ("fun to be with," "generous," "enjoys trying new things," "has an offbeat sense of humor and a quick temper"). According to Allport, we need to know only five to ten central traits to know a personality fairly well.

Then there are **secondary traits,** which we display from time to time but which are not strong enough to be regarded as integral parts of our personality, because they appear in only a relatively small range of situations.

To Allport, personality is the dynamic organization of a person's traits, which determines how he or she will act. Allport distinguished personality from *character*, which he considered an ethical concept, a judgment of a personality; and from **temperament,** which he defined as those biological aspects of functioning that show little change with development. (See the discussion of temperamental traits in the box "Your Temperament and Personality.")

Allport was not interested in looking at large groups of people and identifying general principles of behavior (the *nomothetic,* or *dimensional,* approach to studying personality), but in determining what makes one person "tick" (the *idiographic,* or *morphogenic,* approach). This very emphasis makes it difficult to study personality in terms of his theory, since every researcher would have to study every person separately.

Allport was more interested in what people are like than in how they got that way. He was as uninterested in delving into their past for repressed unconscious motivation as in looking at the culture to come up with environmental influences on personality. He wanted to *describe* personality rather than *explain* it. In his effort to do this, Allport and a colleague, H. S. Odbert (1936), analyzed about 18,000 terms found in a dictionary to determine which ones represented true personality traits, which ones represented temporary states, and which ones were judgmental. They finally came up with a total of 4541 personality traits (Allport & Odbert, 1936).

Allport's influence led to a heightened interest in studying individual cases rather than large groups of people, in relating people's behavior to their underlying personality traits, and in the development of personality tests.

Factor Theory: Raymond B. Cattell   Raymond Cattell (b. 1905) believes that personality traits develop in response to both psychological and environmental elements, and that although there are thousands of **surface traits** (clusters of traits readily seen by ordinary observers), these are less important than the crucial **source traits** (the underlying determinants of those clusters). The source traits interact to produce surface traits and account for people's behavior and enable us to predict future behavior.

Cattell's major contribution to the literature on personality has been his use of a statistical technique, **factor analysis,** to reduce the thousands of surface traits to just 16 source traits.

To come up with his basic list of source traits, Cattell (1965) rated several hundred adults on a large number of personality traits. He and his colleagues then

Cardinal trait   *According to Allport, a characteristic that is dominant and therefore colors virtually every aspect of a person's behavior and attributes.*

Central traits   *According to Allport, the few characteristic tendencies needed to describe an individual.*

Secondary traits   *According to Allport, characteristics that are displayed occasionally but are not strong enough to be regarded as integral parts of a personality.*

Temperament   *Characteristic style of approaching people and situations.*

Surface traits   *According to Cattell's theory, clusters of characteristics that are readily seen by ordinary observers.*

Source traits   *According to Cattell's theory, characteristics that are the underlying determinants of the total personality cluster.*

Factor analysis   *Statistical technique used by Cattell to determine the factors underlying scores on a larger group of measures.*

YOUR TEMPERAMENT AND PERSONALITY

What kind of baby were you? Did you smile and laugh almost all the time? Or were you a screamer, whose infant crying jags were followed in toddlerhood by temper tantrums? Do you, by and large, have the same kind of disposition now as an adult —predominantly either cheerful or glum? Such characteristic moods often show up right from birth, demonstrating distinct differences in temperament, a person's characteristic style of approaching people and situations.

After following hundreds of babies from birth through middle childhood in a large-scale project known as the New York Longitudinal Study (NYLS), researchers identified nine different aspects of temperament that appear inborn (Thomas, Chess, & Birch, 1968). Subsequent research suggests that these traits may remain fairly stable in adulthood (Burks & Rubenstein, 1979; Kagan, 1982; Thomas & Chess, 1977). These nine temperamental elements are activity level; regularity in biological functioning (sleeping, eating, eliminating); readiness to accept new people and situations; adaptability to change; intensity of responses; sensitivity to noise, light, and other sensory stimuli; mood (cheerfulness or unhappiness); distractibility; and persistence.

Although such differences in temperament are not, of course, the only determinants of behavior, they are important in many ways, right from birth. One of the major trends in recent research has been an exploration of the degree to which children affect the people around them. A child's temperament influences the way other people, especially parents, will act toward him or her. It is easier to be warm and loving to a baby who is usually cheerful and whose wants you can anticipate and meet relatively easily than it is to a baby who cries constantly, resists being cuddled, and often seems impossible to please. Parents who get along best with children who are difficult or slow to warm up are the ones who have learned to adapt their child-rearing patterns to their children's individual needs (Thomas & Chess, 1977). Some children, in fact, seem to change their behavioral styles over the years, apparently reacting to the kind of parental handling they get.

Temperamental differences are important in adulthood, too. Our temperamental styles tend to influence our choices of friends and spouses, other people's inclinations to be close to us, the way we get along with others, the way we spend our leisure time, and the way we earn our living (Burks & Rubenstein, 1979; Kagan, 1982). When a husband and wife do not get along, for example, the problem may lie in a lack of fit between temperaments; recognizing, accepting, and accommodating to their differences may enable a couple to forge a new, stronger relationship. Similarly, in furthering our own aims, we need to recognize when we are letting our temperaments direct our lives in unproductive ways, so that we can look at more appropriate ways to fulfill our basic temperamental styles (Burks & Rubenstein, 1979).

---

developed a questionnaire known as the **Sixteen Personality Factor Questionnaire (16PF)** (Cattell, Saunders, & Stice, 1950). Each of the source traits is bipolar, and test takers receive ratings on each one to show their personality profiles. Cattell feels that the three most important traits for describing personality are how outgoing or reserved a person is, how stable or emotional, and how intelligent. (See Figure 13-1, page 470, for three contrasting personality profiles based on Cattell's source traits.)

Critics charge that Cattell was arbitrary in extracting and naming his source factors and that the scales are not valid predictors of behavior; however, Cattell is constantly refining the techniques and the test is well regarded in some quarters.

Another issue, the **person-situation controversy,** revolves around the stability of traits over different situations, that is, whether behavior is influenced more by personality traits or by circumstances—a major source of debate among personality theorists (see the box "The Person-Situation Controversy" on page 471).

Depending on your own background and your own personality (your basic way of approaching life), you may feel more comfortable with the explanation of personality in one of these categories of theories than with those in the others. Still, each of the four approaches described makes its own important contribution to our understanding of personality. We have, for example, derived an understanding of the unconscious aspects of our behavior from the psychoanalytic theorists. We have a better awareness of individual components of personality as a result of the description and

Sixteen Personality Factor Questionnaire (16PF) Questionnaire developed by Cattell and his colleagues to measure personality profiles by rating test takers on 16 personality dimensions.

Person-situation controversy Conflict over whether behavior is consistent over time and situations or whether it changes to meet the demands of different situations.

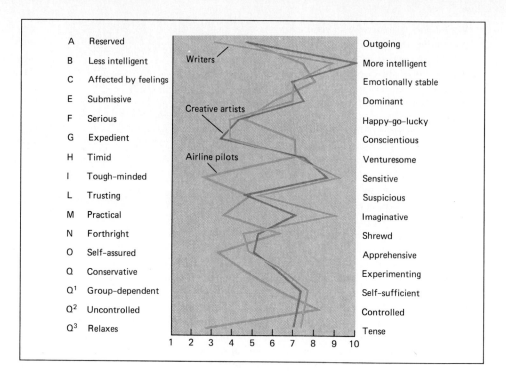

A	Reserved		Outgoing
B	Less intelligent		More intelligent
C	Affected by feelings		Emotionally stable
E	Submissive		Dominant
F	Serious		Happy-go-lucky
G	Expedient		Conscientious
H	Timid		Venturesome
I	Tough-minded		Sensitive
L	Trusting		Suspicious
M	Practical		Imaginative
N	Forthright		Shrewd
O	Self-assured		Apprehensive
Q	Conservative		Experimenting
Q^1	Group-dependent		Self-sufficient
Q^2	Uncontrolled		Controlled
Q^3	Relaxes		Tense

FIGURE 13-1 *16PF personality profiles developed by Cattell for three groups of subjects: airline pilots, creative artists, and writers. (Source: Adapted from Cattell, Eber, & Tatsuoka, 1970.)*

TABLE 13-3 SITUATIONAL ETHICS

Would you . . .	Percent who said "yes" or "probably"	Percent who said it is, or probably is, unethical	Percent who would, or probably would, be more likely to do it if sure they wouldn't get caught
Drive away after scratching a car without telling the owner?	44%	89%	52%
Cover for a friend's secret affair?	41%	66%	33%
Cheat on your spouse?	37%	68%	42%
Keep $10 extra change at a local supermarket?	26%	85%	33%
Knowingly buy a stolen color TV set?	22%	87%	31%
Try to keep your neighborhood segregated?	13%	81%	8%
Drive while drunk?	11%	90%	24%
Accept praise for another's work?	4%	96%	8%

Note: Responses indicate how 23,340 readers of *Psychology Today* answered a variety of questions about moral behavior. Respondents tended to be female (69 percent), young (67 percent in twenties or thirties), well educated (only 12 percent had no college experience), and relatively nonreligious (only 11 percent rated themselves as very religious).

Source: Hassett, 1981.

Think about two or three people you know well, and try to call to mind a few of their personality traits. Can you describe these people consistently, or do their behaviors vary from one situation to another? Do you have a friend who is almost always fun to be with but sinks into long spells of depression when her work isn't going well? Is a relative of yours talkative and vivacious when he's with the family, but shy with outsiders? Is a woman you know frugal when it comes to spending money on herself but a spendthrift when she buys presents for her family? The person-situation controversy revolves around questions like these. How much of people's behavior retains an internal consistency, and how much varies in response to the particular situations they find themselves in (or maneuver themselves into)?

Most people tend to think of personality as something that is fairly stable over time and in different situations. This commonsense belief is in agreement with the ideas of psychoanalysts and trait theorists who see behavior as consistent because of certain characteristics within a person. Environmentalists, on the other hand, maintain that situation-specific behavior is more typical.

It's sometimes hard to judge consistency, since we usually don't see people in a complete range of situations. If your friend never calls you or makes excuses not to see you when she's depressed, you'll have a limited view of her. Your point of view about your relative may vary, depending on whether you usually see him in the family or in a large crowd (Mischel & Peake, 1982).

More than 50 years ago, Hugh Hartshorne and Mark May (1928a, 1928b) set out to study honesty in children. They set up a variety of circumstances giving children opportunities to lie, cheat, and steal. Some would lie but not cheat, some would cheat but not steal, and some would steal in one setting but not in another. Many factors seemed to influence the children's behavior, including the likelihood of their being caught. These researchers concluded that it was impossible to characterize some children as honest and others as dis-

THE PERSON-SITUATION CONTROVERSY

honest, and that there was no way of predicting what any one child would do in any given situation. For years their study has been widely cited by those who believe that behaviors are largely determined by the situation and that basic personality traits do not exist.

A recent analysis of the findings in this study and of those in studies that measured extroversion (outgoingness), punctuality, friendliness, certain kinds of movement, and conscientiousness reached an opposite conclusion, however: that there *is* impressive evidence for the existence of broad personality traits (Epstein & O'Brien, 1985). According to this analysis, knowing these traits will give us enough information to predict a person's behavior averaged over a number of situations and occasions, even though we may not be able to say what he or she will do in any particular situation. Thus, we can expect a person with a basically outgoing personality to be this way most of the time, "but it would be foolish to wager that someone with a high score on extroversion will greet you with a slap on the back and play a practical joke on you when you meet him or her at 2:00 P.M. tomorrow" (Epstein & O'Brien, 1985, pp. 516–517).

In their analysis of the research on honesty in children, Epstein and O'Brien contend that Hartshorne and May insisted on an impossibly strict measure to support the concept of the unified trait of honesty, and that their findings were also corrupted by the inclusion of some tests of very low reliability. They concluded that some people *are* more honest than others, even though they may sometimes stray from the path. They reached similar conclusions for the traits measured in the other studies.

The Stanford University psychologist Walter Mischel (1968, 1973) at one time took an extreme environmentalist position, maintaining that people's behavior was determined more by whether they were likely to be rewarded or punished than by their internal traits, but he has modified this stance somewhat (1977). For one thing, he has come to accept the point made by Kenneth Bowers (1973) that people often create the situations they find themselves in. Competitive people turn cooperative sessions into competitive ones, aggressive children create chaos as soon as they join a group, and certain people typically surround themselves with particular types of other persons—such as the woman who always gets involved with a man who disappoints her or the employer who always hires incompetent workers. A man may justify his speeding, for example, by saying that his car rides so smoothly at high speeds that it's hard to keep it within the legal limit, or that the highway he takes is so full of other fast-moving cars that he would feel foolish going any slower; yet this man *chose* both his car and his route. What, then, makes him a speeder—some risk-taking, aggressive, rebellious, or impatient characteristic within himself, or the highly pressured situations he gets himself into?

A recent questionnaire answered by readers of the magazine *Psychology Today* showed that people do vary in the level of honesty they display in different situations (see Table 13-3, opposite). If you ask yourself and a few other people the questions in this questionnaire, you may get a more personal slant on the difference between basic personality traits and situational influences. If your conclusions are the same as those in the most recent literature, you'll find that behavior seems to arise from the interaction between a person's dominant personality characteristics and the particular dimensions of a specific situation. By and large, at the level of individual items, behavior is situationally specific and unstable, whereas it is much more general and stable when you average it over situations and occasions.

TABLE 13-4   MAJOR POINTS OF CONTROVERSY IN PERSONALITY THEORIES

1 Is sex behind everything? Or are other drives—for power, achievement, recognition, and social standing—equally important or at times more important?

2 Are people controlled by ''bad,'' primitive instincts that need to be repressed? Or are we ''good'' social creatures, the ''noble savages'' envisioned by the French philosopher Rousseau, unless harmful experiences interfere with our ability to express our nature?

3 Is our behavior directed by rational, conscious thought processes or by irrational, unconscious motivations?

4 Can we exert free will over our lives, or is our behavior directed by forces beyond our control, either internal or external?

5 Can the behaviorists' findings about the ways animals learn be applied to human beings to explain our personality development?

6 Can we inherit the beliefs of our ancestors? Or are we born with no ancestral memory?

7 Are we consistent in our behaviors? Or do we change according to the situation?

8 Can we develop a theory of normal personality development by studying troubled people?

Source: Hassett & Editors of *Psychology Today.*

measurement performed by trait theorists. We have a stronger sense of our own power to affect our lives as a result of the humanistic emphasis on positive, healthy aspects of personality. And the environmental approach helps us to appreciate the way situations can affect our behavior. As in many of the topics discussed in this book, no one point of view has all the answers. A blend of several approaches enhances our understanding of ourselves and others.

Major points of controversy among the personality theories are listed in Table 13-4 above.

TESTING PERSONALITY

While one Ph.D. candidate was thinking about a topic for her doctoral dissertation, a number of her friends were confiding in her about their extramarital sexual relationships. She did a computer search of the social science literature. Although she found a number of articles pointing out the neuroticism and immaturity of people who engage in extramarital sex, she was not able to locate any studies that had used standard personality measures or standard measures of marital adjustment to compare women having affairs and monogamous women. Since she felt that such studies would be useful to marriage counselors wanting to help couples dealing with extramarital affairs, she chose to do this kind of study for her dissertation. She administered standard tests to two groups of women, one monogamous and one having extramarital sex. She found that the personalities of the two groups of women did not differ, but that their marriages did (Oursler, 1980).

This, then, is one reason for developing personality tests—to come up with information that can help solve practical problems. Counselors use information from personality tests to advise people in choosing careers, in understanding their difficulties in getting along with others, and in making a wide range of decisions. The United States government has used personality tests to identify people who are too disturbed to serve in the armed forces. An increasingly popular use of personality tests is for screening job applicants, to determine their emotional and temperamental suitability for the work they are seeking.

The other major purpose of personality testing is for basic research. By measuring different aspects of personality, researchers look for similarities and differences among individuals and among groups, measure the effectiveness of various kinds of psychotherapy, look for personality changes that occur throughout the life span, and look for relationships between personality and various kinds of behaviors.

Although personality testing has been used since early in the twentieth century, many psychologists are skeptical about its value, especially in employment and government. Their skepticism stems from inconsistencies within the tests and difficulties in measuring their effectiveness. For one thing, authors of different tests define personality differently (when they define it at all), and there is no agreement about what personality tests measure. Then, the studies assessing the effectiveness of tests have, for the most part, been poorly designed (Hogan, Carpenter, Briggs, & Hansson, 1985). When personality tests are developed and used appropriately, however, they provide information that is helpful, for example, in predicting job performance, especially when it is used together with other criteria, like the results of aptitude tests (Hogan et al., 1985).

How do we decide whether a particular personality test is a "good" measure? The basic criteria of **reliability** and **validity,** which we discussed with regard to intelligence tests in Chapter 7, also apply to personality tests. A test is reliable if it yields approximately the same results on retests, and it is valid if it measures what it is supposed to be measuring. We'll keep these criteria in mind as we look at some of the most common tests used to measure personality.

Reliability *Consistency of a test in measuring the performance of an individual or group.*
Validity *Degree to which a test measures what it is supposed to measure.*

Types of Personality Tests

The type of personality test chosen in any particular situation usually reflects the tester's own theory of personality, the purpose for which the test is being given, and the testing situation. Let's look at the ways in which the most common objective and projective tests differ from one another.

Objective Tests   *Objective tests* call for short replies, are usually answered in writing rather than through conversation, and consist of a standardized list of questions. The interpretation of objective tests is less subjective than that of projective tests and requires less skill and training on the part of the examiner; still, it is not cut and dried. Objective tests are stronger than projective techniques in both validity and reliability.

Objective tests *Tests that typically require short written responses to a standardized list of questions.*

MINNESOTA MULTIPHASIC PERSONALITY INVENTORY (MMPI)   During the 1930s, J. C. McKinley and Starke R. Hathaway, both from the University of Minnesota Medical School, wanted to bring some standardization to psychiatric diagnosis. They collected more than 1000 potential test questions and then posed them to both mental patients and apparently healthy people; these were about thoughts, feelings, attitudes, previous life experiences, and physical and emotional symptoms. They kept 550 true-false statements that clearly differentiated between the patients and the nonpatients. Thus the **MMPI** was born. It has gone on to become the most widely used test of personality and mental health.

The MMPI is still used to look for evidence of emotional disturbance, but it is also widely used as a general measure of personality traits. This test has generated so much research that by 1976, there were some 3500 references on it in the literature (Anastasi, 1976). The test scores require considerable skill to interpret, since the *patterns* of answers are significant, rather than the answers to single questions. The answers are characterized in two ways—on four scales that check the overall validity of the answers, and on ten clinical scales that demonstrate specific traits. For sample items on some of these measures, see Table 13-5 (page 474).

The MMPI is currently being revised, to set new norms and to enhance its ability to predict patients' responses to different kinds of therapy. A major reason for updating the test is that people do not think the same today as they did when the original norms were established in the 1930s and 1940s. We have more flexible notions of men's and women's roles, we're more likely to question authority and established beliefs, and we're more sophisticated, so that what may have been questionable 40 or 50 years ago may be perfectly normal today. For example, a woman who said "true" to the statements "I like mechanics magazines" and "I would like to be a soldier" would have been assumed to be abnormally masculine under the old scoring system. This is no longer the case ("Widely used," 1986).

MMPI *Minnesota Multiphasic Personality Inventory; the most widely used test of personality and mental health.*

TABLE 13-5 SOME OF THE VALIDITY AND CLINICAL SCALES OF THE MMPI, AND PARAPHRASES OF SOME ITEMS FROM EACH KIND OF SCALE

Scale Name	Sample Item and Example of Response (These Items Are Usually Not Answered in These Ways by Normal People)	Characteristics of High Scores on This Scale
Validity scales		
Lie	Once in a while I poke fun at others' mistakes. (False)	Denial of common personal faults; defensiveness.
Cannot say	Many blanks or "cannot says"	Evasiveness or uncooperativeness.
Frequency	My nose often swells up so it is larger than normal size. (True)	Eccentricity or carelessness.
Clinical scales		
Hypochondriasis	I feel "butterflies" in my stomach several times a day or oftener. (True)	Overconcern about health; exaggeration of real or imagined physical ailments.
Depression	I have had several days in a row where I could not get over feeling "blue." (True)	Feelings of hopelessness and worthlessness.
Hysteria	I frequently notice trembling or shaking in various limbs of my body. (True)	Complaints of physical ailments when under stress; overenthusiasm suggestive of immaturity.
Paranoia	It is hard for me to think of anyone I could call an enemy. (False)	Defensiveness, suspiciousness, and jealousy.
Psychasthenia	I always wipe my feet two or three times before entering a building, even if there is no doormat. (True)	Obsessive-compulsiveness; excessive introspection that dwells on fears and self-doubts.

Source: Adapted from Samuel, 1981, p. 165.

Recently, an effort has been made to establish new norms by questioning a large sample of normal men and women from the midwest. The MMPI profiles in this contemporary sample showed higher levels of emotional disturbance than those in the original sample (Colligan, Osborne, Swenson, & Offord, 1984). Why should this be? One interpretation might be that people are under more psychological or physical stress today, but the answer probably lies in changed mores and perceptions. The answers given by healthy people today would have seemed aberrant in earlier times. It's clear, then, that new norms are needed.

Besides the first criticism of the MMPI—that the old norms need to be updated—the other major objection to the test is that it is often used outside the clinical setting for which it was developed. For example, 80 percent of police departments around the country use the MMPI to screen job applicants (R. Hogan, 1986), even though it is not effective in predicting police officers' job performance (Hogan et al., 1985). This demonstrates one common problem with tests—that the test itself may be fine, but the uses to which it is put are inappropriate.

CATTELL'S SIXTEEN PERSONALITY FACTOR QUESTIONNAIRE (16PF) Another objective test is the Sixteen Personality Factor Questionnaire (16PF) developed by Raymond Cattell, which was discussed earlier in this chapter. In this test, as we noted, the 16 source traits are bipolar, and test takers receive a rating on each trait; the result is a personality profile.

Projective Tests   Relatively unstructured tests that try to discover what and how a person is thinking, on both conscious and unconscious levels, are called *projective tests.* They present ambiguous material in either words or pictures and ask questions that call for open-ended answers. The way the test taker interprets the material and then formulates his or her answer provides important clues to personality. The material in a projective test has been described as "a sort of screen" on which the test taker "'projects' his characteristic thought processes, needs, anxieties, and conflicts" (Anastasi, 1976, p. 559). These tests are used more often for people in therapy, and less often for basic research or for nontherapeutic counseling, such as academic or vocational counseling. The Rorschach test and the Thematic Apperception Test (TAT) are the most frequently used projective tests.

RORSCHACH TEST   What do you see in the inkblot shown in Figure 13-2? This inkblot is similar to those used in the *Rorschach test,* which was developed in 1921 by the Swiss psychiatrist Hermann Rorschach. (The inkblot designs actually used in the test are never published anywhere else.) If you were really taking the Rorschach test, you would be shown some or all of ten standardized inkblot cards and asked to tell what you saw in each one. The examiner would keep a record of your answers, including any comments you might volunteer, any gestures you might make, and any emotional expressions you might show. You would then be questioned closely about your answers, to get you to clarify and elaborate upon them.

Your answers would then be analyzed and scored on several dimensions: *location* (what part of the blot did you talk about—the entire blot or part of it, and which parts?), *determinants* (did you talk about color, form, or movement in the blot?), *content* (what did you see—animal or human forms, or some other type of object?), and *popularity* (is your response similar to those of many other people, or is it novel?).

There are a number of questions about the reliability and validity of the Rorschach test. The number of responses a test taker makes is related to his or her age and level of intellect and education, which should not, of course, be influences upon a pure measure of personality (Anastasi, 1976). Then there are the effects of experience: you're more likely to see boots in the blots if you've just been hiking in the woods, whereas you're more apt to see an airplane if you live near an airport (Sundberg, 1977).

Projective tests   Personality tests that use relatively ambiguous material, the responses to which provide clues about the test taker's personality.

Rorschach test   Widely used projective personality test in which the test taker describes what he or she sees in a series of inkblots; answers are scored on several dimensions.

FIGURE 13-2   *This inkblot is similar to one used in the Rorschach test, a projective personality test. (Source: Rorschach, 1921.)*

FIGURE 13-3 *Sample item from Murray's Thematic Apperception Test (TAT). (Source: Murray, 1943.)*

Thematic Apperception Test (TAT)
Projective personality test in which the test taker makes up stories about ambiguous pictures; these stories are scored for themes.

The Rorschach test is widely used. Its most useful application may be as a direct measure of a person's cognitive style or ways of organizing perceptions, or as part of a structured interview in the hands of a skilled clinician (Goldfried, Stricker, & Weiner, 1971).

THEMATIC APPERCEPTION TEST (TAT)   Look at the picture in Figure 13-3, and make up a story describing what the people shown are thinking and doing, what went on beforehand, and what will happen next. If you were actually taking the **Thematic Apperception Test (TAT),** this might be one of a series of cards you would be shown. Your stories would be analyzed according to which of the people you identify with, what personality characteristics and basic needs you ascribe to them, what environmental pressures you see as significant, the overall plot line of the story, and the story's eventual outcome.

The TAT has been modified for several special purposes—for children, vocational counselees, and participants in attitude surveys. One picture of four adults of different ages was specially drawn for a study looking at the way middle-aged adults perceived their age and sex roles in the family (Neugarten & Gutmann, 1958). The differences between the ways 40- to 54-year-olds saw the people in the cards and the ways people from 55 to 70 years old saw them enabled the researchers to draw some conclusions about personality changes in the years from 40 to 70. For example, the younger group saw an older man in the picture as the authority figure, while the older group saw an older woman in that way. The researchers, Bernice L. Neugarten and David L. Gutmann, concluded that women, as they age, become more tolerant of their aggressive impulses, while men become more tolerant of their nurturant impulses.

Although considerable standardization has been done on the TAT and norms have been published for all aspects of the ways people respond to each card, research has shown that responses are influenced by subjects' fatigue, hunger, and emotional states (Anastasi, 1976). Again, the impact of such temporary conditions interferes with the interpretation of more enduring personality characteristics. In order to put the stories in proper perspective, the examiner needs to know something about the test taker's life outside the testing situation. Age, for example, would be significant in assessing the character a person identifies with. Other clues in the story might reflect events or circumstances of special significance to the test taker.

The Rorschach test and the TAT share with other projective tests, such as sentence-completion and word-association tests, certain problems in interpretation. Because answers are so open-ended, interpretation relies to a great extent on the examiner's subjective assessment. As a result, it is difficult to come up with good indexes of reliability among different scorers and between one test session and another. It is also difficult to assess validity.

On the positive side, these tests have several advantages. Because they are interesting, they often serve as a good way for an examiner or a therapist to establish rapport with a client. Since the "right" answer is less obvious than in objective tests, projective tests are harder to fake. And they seem to help therapists expand their knowledge of the client.

Interview Techniques   Talking to people is, of course, a time-honored way of finding out about them. When we ask them questions, we not only get the basic reply, but can get clarification or expansion of their answers. Furthermore, we can see how a person behaves as he or she is talking to us. Does Ms. A. seem comfortable and self-assured, answering our questions directly and easily, or does she avoid looking us in the eye, hesitate for a long time before answering, and change her answers frequently? What does Mr. B. look like? Does he seem to pay reasonable attention to his grooming? Is he dressed appropriately? Is he clean?

Interviews vary along a number of dimensions, one of which is the degree of standardization. There is the highly *structured* interview, in which the interviewer has drawn up a particular set of questions, which is given to every person interviewed. The *unstructured* interview, on the other hand, takes form as it progresses, differing in each case. With this procedure, the interviewer is not confined to a particular set of predetermined questions, but can follow interviewees along paths that they open up, to explore any issues that arise, including some the interviewer may never have thought of. Virtually all therapists use some form of interview to find out about their clients, as we shall see in our discussion of therapeutic procedures in Chapter 15.

Ethics of Personality Testing

"The Fourth Amendment was designed to protect our people from unreasonable search and seizure. Yet today our Government is engaged in a much more insidious form of search than going into someone's home or through personal papers. We are now searching their minds, trying to pry out the most hidden and intimate thoughts," said United States Congressman Cornelius E. Gallagher during the course of hearings on the use of personality tests by federal agencies (Gallagher, 1965). The committee conducting the hearings maintained that it was none of the government's business how people feel about their parents, what their sex life is like, or what their religious beliefs are. Questions on all these topics appear in many personality tests.

When we realize how much confidential information about people can be learned through projective and objective testing, we realize why this is such a sensitive area. Should these questions be asked at all in hiring, in academic admissions, and in other situations in everyday life? Or do they constitute an invasion of privacy? When they are asked, who should ask them? And how should the results be handled? These are all difficult questions.

One danger in personality tests is the possibility of their falling into the wrong hands, being administered and interpreted by unqualified people, and thereby subjecting test takers to biased treatment. Another is the possibility that the test *results* may fall into the wrong hands.

We also need to be aware of a different sort of ethical issue. Since different racial groups show different kinds of personality profiles on the MMPI, with blacks appearing to show more emotional disturbance than whites, we need to look closely at what the tests are really measuring. Since these tests were standardized and validated only with white populations, the differences in the scores of nonwhite test takers may have more to do with cultural differences than with emotional ones (Cross, Barclay, & Burger, 1978; Gynther, 1972). If so, nonwhite test takers might be unfairly denied entry into military service, employment, and other opportunities that depend on test results.

The entire issue of emotional health is, of course, extremely complex. How do we decide when a person crosses the line between health and illness? Who decides? How do we define various states and degrees of health or illness? And how can disturbed people best be helped? We will be grappling with these questions in Chapters 14, 15, and 16.

SUMMARY

1 Personality is the constellation of relatively consistent ways of dealing with people and situations that makes each person unique.
2 According to the psychoanalytic theory of Sigmund

Freud, people are governed by a constant conflict between their biological urges and the need to tame them. In Freud's view, there are three different parts to the personality: the id, the ego, and the superego. The id, which operates on the pleasure principle and contains the life and death instincts, wants immediate gratification of instinctual needs. The ego, which operates on the reality principle, tries to find acceptable ways to gratify the id. The superego, which consists of the ego-ideal (the "shoulds" of behavior) and the conscience (the "should nots" of behavior) represents parental and societal values.

3   According to Freud, people develop defense mechanisms to combat anxiety. These are largely unconscious and distort reality. Among them are displacement (indirect gratification of an urge), sublimation (rechanneling uncomfortable feelings into acceptable activities), repression (blocking anxiety-producing urges or activities from consciousness), regression (returning to the behaviors of an earlier time in one's life), projection (attributing one's unacceptable thoughts to another), reaction formation (replacement of an anxiety-producing feeling with its opposite), and rationalization (justifying one's own behavior).

4   Psychosexual development, in Freudian theory, is a series of shifts in the primary area of the body in which one receives sexual gratification. The body parts that act as primary sources of gratification are known as erogenous zones. According to Freud, there are five psychosexual stages. Failure to be appropriately gratified in a particular stage can result in fixation at that stage. This is reflected in a person's personality traits.

5   According to Freud, from birth to 12–18 months, the period of infancy, the child is in the oral stage, in which the erogenous zone is the area around the mouth. Feeding is particularly important in determining the successful (or unsuccessful) resolution of this stage. From 12–18 months to about 3 years, the period of toddlerhood, the child is in the anal stage; at this time, the erogenous zone is the anal region, and the nature of the toilet training experience is important. During the phallic stage (from 3 years to about 6 years), when the erogenous zone shifts to the genital region, young boys must resolve the Oedipus complex and young girls the Electra complex. In both of these situations the young child falls in love with the parent of the other sex and resents the same-sex parent. When the anxiety produced by this situation becomes too great, the young child represses the unacceptable feelings and identifies with the same-sex parent, internalizing parental standards and developing a superego. Then, between the ages of about 6 and 12, the child is in a calm period known as *latency*. From puberty on, the child is in the genital stage of mature sexuality.

6   Freud's theory is controversial. Probably his most important contribution is his emphasis on the role of the unconscious in motivating behavior. His emphasis on the sexual drive as the primary motivating force for behavior throughout life, even in infancy, is the most controversial aspect of his theory.

7   Carl Jung, who broke away from Freud because of Freud's emphasis on sexuality, believed in the historical ("racial") aspects of personality. Alfred Adler also broke away from Freud because of differences over the role of sexuality in motivating behavior. According to Adler, people struggle with the need to overcome inferiority. Karen Horney attributed anxieties (*neuroses*) to the child's difficulty in dealing with a potentially hostile world. Erik Erikson is concerned with the effects of cultural and societal factors on personality. He sees psychosocial development as a lifelong process that occurs in a series of eight stages. In each stage, the individual must resolve a particular crisis.

8   Humanistic theories emphasize the subjective, unique experiences of the individual and the potential each person has for self-fulfillment. Abraham Maslow believed that people are motivated by a hierarchy of needs. Once a person's basic needs are met, he or she can strive to fulfill the need for self-actualization. Carl Rogers believed that everyone needs to discover who his or her "real self" is, to become that person, and to find acceptance for the person he or she is. To function at the highest level, we need agreement (congruence) between the person we would like to be and the person we see ourself as actually being.

9   Environmental (or learning) approaches include B. F. Skinner's radical behaviorism and Albert Bandura's social-learning theory. According to Skinner, we learn behaviors on the basis of reward and punishment. Bandura believes that we learn by observing and imitating models. If we are rewarded for imitating behaviors, we are likely to repeat them.

10   Trait theories focus on internal influences on personality and are concerned with specific attributes peculiar to the individual. Gordon Allport believed that each person has a personal disposition made up of several types of traits. A cardinal trait, which few people have, is a dominant trait that colors virtually every aspect of a person's behaviors and attributes. Central traits are the handful of characteristic tendencies that could be used to describe an individual. Secondary traits are traits that are displayed occasionally but are not strong enough to be considered an integral part of a personality. Raymond B. Cattell defined surface traits as the cluster of traits readily seen by an observer, and source traits as a much smaller number of traits that are the underlying determinants of the surface traits.

11   The person-situation controversy revolves around the question whether personality is consistent and stable over times and situations or whether people's behavior is more situation-specific. Behavior seems to arise out of an interaction between people's dominant personality characteristics and the particular situation they find themselves in. People have a number of broad personality traits; if these are known, it is possible to predict behaviors averaged over a number of situations and occasions. However, knowing these traits may not enable us to predict a person's behavior in any particular situation.

12   Psychologists have devised different ways to assess personality. These include objective tests (such as the MMPI and the 16PF) and projective tests (such as the Rorschach

test and the TAT). In addition, interviews, which may be structured or unstructured, are often used.

13 A number of important ethical considerations surround personality testing. These include inappropriate use of tests and the danger that test results will fall into the wrong hands.

KEY TERMS

Anal stage (page 458)
Anima (461)
Animus (461)
Archetypes (461)
Behaviorism (466)
Cardinal trait (468)
Castration complex (458)
Central traits (468)
Collective unconscious (461)
Congruence (465)
Conscience (455)
Defense mechanism (455)
Displacement (455)
Ego (455)
Ego-ideal (455)
Electra complex (459)

Erogenous zones (458)
Eros (454)
Factor analysis (468)
Fixation (458)
Genital stage (459)
Humanistic psychology (464)
Id (454)
Infantile sexuality (458)
Inferiority complex (462)
Latency stage (459)
Libido (454)
MMPI (473)
Objective tests (473)
Oedipus complex (458)
Oral stage (458)
Penis envy (459)

Persona (461)
Personality (452)
Personal unconscious (461)
Person-situation controversy (469)
Phallic stage (458)
Pleasure principle (454)
Projection (456)
Projective tests (475)
Psychoanalysis (454)
Rationalization (457)
Reaction formation (457)
Reality principle (455)
Regression (456)
Reliability (473)
Repression (456)
Rorschach test (475)

Secondary traits (468)
Self-actualization (464)
Sixteen Personality Factor Questionnaire (16PF) (469)
Source traits (468)
Sublimation (456)
Superego (455)
Superiority complex (462)
Surface traits (468)
Temperament (468)
Thanatos (454)
Thematic Apperception Test (TAT) (476)
Unconscious (459)
Validity (473)

SUGGESTED READINGS

BANDURA, A. (1977). *Social learning theory*. Englewood Cliffs, NJ: Prentice-Hall. A brief statement of the principles of social learning, written by the leading spokesperson for this approach.

BURKS, J., & RUBENSTEIN, M. (1979). *Temperament styles in adult interaction: Applications in psychotherapy*. New York: Brunner/Mazel. A fascinating exploration by two psychotherapists of temperament styles in adult behavior and of ways in which therapy can build on these styles. Case histories illustrate six temperamental styles identified by the authors; these styles, in turn, are based on the nine dimensions of temperament identified by Thomas, Chess, and Birch.

FREUD, S. (1965). *The interpretation of dreams*. New York: Avon/Discus. An eloquent presentation of Freud's revolutionary and controversial analysis of the significance of dreams. (Original work published 1900)

MASSON, J. M. (1985). *The assault on truth*. New York: Penguin. A controversial book which proposes that Freud suppressed evidence that some of his patients may have been sexually mistreated as children.

ROGERS, C. R. (1980). *A way of being*. Boston: Houghton Mifflin. A collection of essays that describes Rogers's person-centered approach and provides insight into his personal experiences and attitudes.

SKINNER, B. F. (1982). *Beyond freedom and dignity*. New York: Bantam/Vintage. A controversial plan for a scientific program to alter people's behavior. This book is considered one of the most important in modern psychology.

THOMAS, A., CHESS, S., & BIRCH, H. G. (1968). *Temperament and behavior disorders in children*. New York: New York University Press. A report on the New York Longitudinal Study that emphasizes the different characteristics that show up from birth and the ways these characteristics interact with methods of child rearing.

WINSON, J. (1986). *Brain and psyche*. New York: Vintage. Winson's controversial attempt to reconcile psychoanalysis and neuroscience by looking for the neurological underpinnings of the mind.

C H A P T E R

14

ABNORMAL PSYCHOLOGY

PREVIEW QUESTIONS

- Why is it so difficult to diagnose mental disorders?

- What are the rationales underlying explanations of mental disorders as a breach of morality, an illness, faulty learning, ineffective adaptation, and warped development?

- What is the core of the controversy over the third edition of the *Diagnostic and Statistical Manual of Mental Disorders* of the American Psychiatric Association (DSM III)?

- What is the range of mental disorders?

- Why do people try to commit suicide, and how can concerned friends and family help avert suicides?

The middle-aged man known to students at the University of Wisconsin as "Snowball" was a familiar figure on State Street in Madison until his recent death. Dressed in shabby, dirty clothes, he carried his possessions—including his window-washing equipment—with him in an assortment of shopping bags and twine-wrapped boxes. As he went about his daily life, he carried on an unending, unintelligible conversation with himself. His background was a mystery—where he was from, how he had lost his home, why he didn't seem to have any family or friends. The only things most of us in the university community knew about his present life were that he earned a little money washing windows, that it was hard to stay close to him because of the strong odor of urine he exuded, and that his appearance and his behavior seemed to signal severe emotional disturbance.

"Snowball" is, unfortunately, typical of many who populate the streets of cities around the country. These lost souls—young and old, male and female, black and white—are members of an army of homeless people who live on the fringes of urban society. Most of these people are harmless to the public; their only offense is the obviousness of their desperate situation. The harm they do is to themselves. In winter, some freeze to death; in sleep, some are preyed upon by sadistic attackers; in their terrible poverty and isolation, some starve. Many are on the streets because they suffer from emotional disorders that prevent them from holding a job or living with other people in the community. They are a constant reminder that despite our society's great technological virtuosity, when it comes to helping the emotionally disturbed in our midst, we are often mired in the past.

When I see these people, sometimes mumbling to themselves, sometimes ranting to passersby, I often wonder what brought them to this pass. An occasional newspaper story describes early promise, loving relatives, a past with some successes—and then a plunge into the darkness of mental illness.

—From the notebooks of Diane Papalia

Abnormal psychology *Scientific study of the causes of emotional and behavioral disorders.*

Virtually all of us have a personal interest in **abnormal psychology,** the study of emotional disturbance and abnormal behavior. Who among us does not number among our family members, our friends and neighbors, or our co-workers someone who displays eccentricities, who suffers from depression that prevents work or study, whose everyday life is restricted by unrealistic fears, who drinks to such excess that work or family life suffers, who cannot hold a job, or who shows some other sign of what is generally considered abnormal behavior? Who among us has not at some time behaved in a way that seemed odd even to ourselves?

Yet not every passing mood, unusual action, or quirk of personality assumes great significance. What, then, constitutes abnormal behavior? How do we explain it—as breach of morality, illness, result of faulty learning, misguided adaptation, or warped development? What causes it? And what can be done about it? We will deal with the first three of these questions in this chapter and with the fourth in Chapter 15, which describes various types of therapies for psychological problems. (Related topics, such as substance abuse, mental retardation, Alzheimer's disease, and disorders related to eating, sleep, and sexuality, are all discussed elsewhere in this book.)

This chapter is devoted to the study of psychological disorders. However, there is often no sharp break between what is "normal" and what is "abnormal," and so we'll be as explicit as we can in our definitions. All the disorders we discuss affect large numbers of people, even though they may represent only small percentages of the population at large. Like a pebble thrown into a pond, the problems of one troubled person ripple out to affect families and friends, the community that must arrange for care, and all of us who as taxpayers are called upon to support needed services. We become intensely aware of the truth in John Donne's statement that "no man is an island, entire of itself; every man is a piece of the continent, a part of the main." Mental disorders affect us all.

APPROACHES TO ABNORMAL PSYCHOLOGY

What Is Abnormal?

Shortly after midnight on Friday, June 16, 1978, Sylvia Frumkin decided to take a bath. Miss Frumkin, a heavy, ungainly young woman who lived in a two-story yellow brick building in Queens Village, New York, walked from her bedroom on the second floor to the bathroom next door and filled the tub with warm water. A few days earlier, she had had her hair cut and shaped in a bowl style, which she found especially becoming, and her spirits were high. She washed her brown hair with shampoo and also with red mouthwash. Some years earlier, she had tinted her hair red and had liked the way it looked. She had given up wearing her hair red only because she had found coloring it every six weeks too much of a bother. She imagined that the red mouthwash would somehow be absorbed into her scalp and make her hair red permanently. Miss Frumkin felt so cheerful about her new haircut that she suddenly thought she was Lori Lemaris, the mermaid whom Clark Kent had met in college and had fallen in love with in the old "Superman" comics. She blew bubbles into the water. (S. Sheehan, 1982, p. 3)

It is immediately clear—not only to a psychiatrist but to any reasonably aware person—that the young woman here given the pseudonym "Sylvia Frumkin" is acting and thinking in a bizarre way, a way we would have no trouble at all designating abnormal.

What is it about this woman's thinking and behavior, however, that make them abnormal? Many normal, healthy people in our culture are heavy and ungainly, many wear their hair in unbecoming ways, many color their hair with ineffective products. Many daydream, fantasizing themselves as other persons.

Sylvia Frumkin is not like these other people. She has been diagnosed as suffering from a schizophrenic disorder (*schizophrenia* will be defined later in this chapter). For one thing, she cannot distinguish reality from fantasy. She does not just imagine herself as *like* "Lori Lemaris, the mermaid"; she is convinced that she *is* this fictional creature. For another thing, a person of Sylvia Frumkin's apparent basic intelligence and position in society would be expected to know that mouthwash is not a hair dye and cannot be absorbed into the scalp. It is not ignorance or naiveté that makes her think this way, but a disorder in the nature of her thinking.

This, then, is one element of some forms of psychological abnormality: *inability to recognize reality*. People who "hear voices," people who imagine that hordes of enemies are conspiring against them, and people who fear injury at the hands of invaders from outer space are all out of touch with the real world. Their lack of orientation to reality tends to make them act in strange ways, ways that may be destructive to themselves or others. (However, some patterns of thought and behavior are considered abnormal, even though they do not involve an inability to recognize reality.)

Another way in which Sylvia Frumkin's thought and behavior are abnormal is their *statistical rarity*. Most people do not think the way she does, and most people do not act the way she does. During the thirteenth century, people who thought that the earth was flat were mistaken, but they were not harboring an abnormal belief: most people believed that the earth was flat. Anyone thinking that now, however, would be in the distinct minority and would, therefore, be exhibiting an abnormal point of view, contrary to scientific facts that have been well established and widely taught in our society.

Being different from other people is not always considered abnormal, of course. Albert Einstein, for example, exhibited thought processes that were unique, and yet he was honored for his difference, not institutionalized, because his behavior was desirable. To be considered abnormal, a person's unusual thoughts or behavior must also be considered *undesirable*. The type of abnormal thought and behavior we discuss in this chapter is undesirable, and thus is considered abnormal even if it is not rare, as, for example, in the case of clinical depression, a fairly common disorder.

Abnormality has other faces, too. Sylvia Frumkin does not perform productive work, does not have an intimate sexual relationship, has no friends, has great difficulty getting along with her parents and her sister, has trouble getting from one place to another, and constantly loses her possessions. She is dysfunctional in all these basic areas of life. Furthermore, she is unhappy much of the time. Although normal people are not always happy, of course, they are not subject to the severe bouts of depression, rage, fearfulness, or confusion that are often hallmarks of an abnormal condition.

Since human beings are so variable, it is extremely difficult to come up with an all-encompassing definition of abnormality. The preceding points, however, cover the most important deviations from the model in our society of a normal, psychologically healthy person: a person who generally perceives reality fairly accurately, who behaves somewhat similarly to most other people in most situations, who does productive work either in the home or at a paid or volunteer job, who can handle the tasks of everyday living, and whose moods remain fairly constant and appropriate to circumstances.

Not all people who deviate from this profile, of course, are severely disturbed. Certainly, many people who show abnormal behaviors are not as dysfunctional as Sylvia is, nor do they exhibit all the symptoms she does. Some people may differ from the healthy model in just one respect. For example, someone may be unusually sad or fearful much of the time and yet still be able to hold a job, take care of a family, and in general get along day by day. Or a person may go through a temporary episode of strange behavior but then go back to leading a fairly normal life. Furthermore, the degree of impairment at any one time varies greatly: it may be so mild that a person is on the border between normality and abnormality, or so intense that institutionalization and intensive treatment are called for.

Way of Looking at Abnormal Behavior: Models

The woman dresses bizarrely, speaks incomprehensibly, behaves outlandishly, and frightens her neighbors, who recognize her strangeness. She must be possessed by evil spirits, they believe. To get rid of the evil spirits, she must be put to death. At another time and another place, such a woman would be seen to be suffering from an illness, which is best treated by one or more chemical substances. In still other circumstances, people would believe that this woman has learned to behave eccen-

The belief that mental illness was a result of sin and possession by the devil set the stage for thousands of witchcraft trials, such as the trial of George Jacobs in Salem, Massachusetts, in 1692, shown in this painting.

trically as a response to her environment, and therefore must be taught the "right" responses, so that she can adapt normally.

These are examples of *interpretations* of abnormal behavior as, respectively, a moral lapse, a medical condition, and learning wrong responses. The way we interpret, or explain, abnormality influences the way we treat it and has important implications for society at large, as well as for affected people. Therefore, it is important to understand the various *models*, or theories, that try to explain abnormal attitudes and behavior.

Moral Model   During the Middle Ages, psychological disorders were sometimes thought to stem from a sinful rejection of divine wisdom. The explanation of mental illness common at that time was that it resulted from sin and possession by the devil. This explanation is known as the ***moral model***. It seems that most of the unfortunates who were burned as witches were sane and confessed to such crimes as intercourse with the devil or participation in satanic cults only during torture (Davison & Neale, 1986). Still, the idea that abnormality was tied to sin and the devil may even have been held by some of these victims. Traces of the moral model remain today in the words of mental patients themselves, who often speak of their condition in moral terms, generally ascribing their problems to a lack of willpower or other personal inadequacies.

Moral model   *Explanation of mental illness, common during the Middle Ages, as a result of sin and possession by the devil.*

Medical Model   Another view of abnormality also existed in the Middle Ages—that it was the result of some underlying medical problem. During lunacy trials in Britain, odd behavior was typically attributed to physical illness or injury or to emotional shock (Neugebauer, 1979). This attitude, which is prevalent today, opens the way to helping the emotionally disturbed by absolving them of blame for their condition.

The medical origins of some abnormal behavior are seen clearly in conditions in which a physical illness or an event like a stroke or accident affects personality and judgment as well as physical functioning; in drug addiction; and in senile dementia, which presumes an organic deterioration of the brain. As we'll see later in this chapter, findings of unusual chemical balances in the blood systems of persons diagnosed with schizophrenic or depressive disorders seem to indicate that these conditions, too, have physical causes.

When we speak of abnormal psychology as "psychopathology" or "mental illness" as distinguished from "mental health," we are thinking in terms of the medical model. An acceptance of this explanation leads to our calling people who act strange "sick," turning their care over to physicians, placing them in hospitals or treating them as outpatients, and treating them with a wide variety of physical techniques (such as drugs, electroconvulsive—or "shock"—therapy, sleep, and vitamins). This explanation de-emphasizes both individual responsibility for behavior and social forces that may be contributing to a person's problem.

A major criticism of the *Diagnostic and Statistical Manual of Mental Disorders*, or DSM III (which was published in 1980 by the American Psychiatric Association and is discussed in detail later in this chapter), is that it relies on this **medical model** to explain virtually all deviance. Over half of the more than 230 disorders listed in DSM III are *not* attributable to organic causes, and looking at human behavior only in terms of illness limits our understanding and restricts our ability to help (Schacht & Nathan, 1977).

Psychoanalytic Model Lucy R., a young English governess, consulted Sigmund Freud because she had lost her sense of smell and yet was plagued by strong imaginary odors. She had also lost her appetite, her energy, and her ability to sleep normally. Freud diagnosed Lucy's problem as *hysteria*, a neurosis that resulted from repression of some idea or feeling and caused her to convert psychic energy into physical symptoms. During the course of treatment, Freud's initial diagnosis appeared to be confirmed by Lucy's admission that she was in love with her employer, a widower, but was embarrassed by her feelings and was trying to put them out of her mind. As she expressed her repressed sexual longings, she became able to live with them, and her sense of smell returned to normal (Freeman & Strean, 1981).

According to Freud's theories, abnormal behavior results from conflicts between the id and the superego, conflicts too great for the ego to handle. These conflicts can be aggravated by serious errors in child rearing committed by parents who either understimulate or overstimulate their children during the oral, anal, or phallic stage of early childhood. As a result of the child's own inborn needs and the parents' blunders, the child becomes fixated in one period or another and is unable to develop normally.

When the **psychoanalytic model** was developed at the beginning of the twentieth century, it represented a major advance in thinking. It did not place the responsibility for abnormal behavior on sin, lack of will, or disease. Rather, it assigned blame to a number of factors—family, friends, and physiology—and thus inspired scientists to look further for the causes of mental illness.

On the other hand, by limiting its emphasis to the experiences of early childhood, psychoanalysts give short shrift to the possibility that some traumatic event in adulthood could trigger psychopathology. Furthermore, although their stress on early parenting may provide a ready target for blame, this is not necessarily beneficial to the patient. "The advantage of a blame-free interpretation of behavior is that energy is not wasted on vendettas but can be spent on returning the mad person to normal" (Siegler & Osmond, 1974, p. 76). However, the psychoanalytic explanation of abnormal behavior did give rise to a way of treating it, described fully in Chapter 15.

Behavioral Model Psychologists who use the **behavioral model** do not draw upon unconscious id-superego conflict or physical illness to explain disorders. Instead, they believe that abnormal ways of thinking and acting are learned, largely through conditioning and modeling. Thus, a little girl may have learned to protect herself against an abusive father, but when in adulthood she either avoids all men or seeks out abusive ones, her behavior is no longer adaptive (helping her to adapt to her

Medical model *Explanation of mental disorders as a result of illness.*

Psychoanalytic model *Explanation of mental disorders as a result of conflict between the id, ego, and superego.*

Behavioral model *Explanation of mental disorders as abnormal ways of thinking and acting that are learned, largely through conditioning and modeling.*

TABLE 14-1 THREE MAJOR MODELS OF MENTAL ILLNESS

	Medical	Psychoanalytic	Behavioral
Emphasis	Brain	Mind	Behavior
Causes of illness	Biochemical imbalance, physical illness, or injury	Disturbed dynamics, childhood experiences	Learned habits
Methods of study	Neurosciences (neurochemistry, behavioral genetics)	Introspection (free association, dream analysis)	Controlled experiments (use of conditioning, animal research)
Types of illness	Moderate to severe (depression, mania, schizophrenia)	Mild ("neuroses," personality disorders)	Mild to severe (anxiety, phobias, personality disorders, addictions)
Methods of treatment	Medication	Psychotherapy	Behavior modification

Source: Adapted from Andreasen, 1984.

environment) but is instead maladaptive (interfering with her adjustment). At this point learning theorists design a treatment that involves teaching new, adaptive ways of behaving.

While traditional learning theorists have been concerned with maladaptive *behaviors*, cognitive theorists have emphasized the way that maladaptive *thoughts* influence behavior. This orientation, a result of the "cognitive revolution," suggests that how we think about events influences how we behave. A number of currently popular therapies emphasize changing these underlying thought patterns.

For a summary and comparison of the three most important models of abnormality, see Table 14-1.

Other Models   Since the subject of psychological disorder is so complex, so compelling, and so important for both individuals and society at large, it is not surprising that it should be explained in so many different ways. Besides the models already described, a number of other viewpoints have their adherents.

SOCIAL-CONSEQUENCE MODEL   Thomas S. Szasz (1974), a psychiatrist (and thus someone who is medically trained), vigorously attacks the notion of psychological disorders as illnesses. Szasz is the most prominent proponent of the **social-consequence model**, according to which such disorders are problems of living—problems that arise out of difficulties in coping with society. The difficulties are conflicts between a person's needs, opinions, aspirations, and values and those of other people or of society. They are not medical in origin but stem instead from ethical conflicts, legal definitions, and cultural standards. Their consequences are social rather than medical. Instead of assuming the role of patient, it is more appropriate for people to take responsibility for their own actions, to do something about them, and to suffer the appropriate consequences when they are harmful to others.

Szasz's criticisms sometimes seem to oversimplify complicated situations and do not provide explanations for all abnormal behavior, but they do raise issues that are all too often ignored or taken for granted.

FAMILY, OR SYSTEMS, MODEL   The **family, or systems, model** sees psychological difficulties as arising from an entire family setting rather than from one person. Only one family member may actually show abnormal behavior. But according to this

Social-consequence model
Explanation of mental disorders as problems of living rather than medical illnesses.

Family, or systems, model
Explanation of mental disorders as arising from an entire family setting, with its own patterns of functioning, rather than from one person.

model, the abnormality is not confined to that person but is a symptom of psychopathology within the family. Practitioners of family therapy look at the family as a system, with its own patterns of functioning. Communications in a family that includes a disturbed person are, in this theory, specially constructed to create one disturbed person (called the "identified patient") so that the other family members can continue to function "normally." When the identified patient is helped, the entire family may be thrown into turmoil, and its members may be forced to develop new patterns of relating to each other (Bateson, Jackson, Haley, & Weakland, 1956; Herr & Weakland, 1979).

Sociocultural model *Explanation of mental disorders that emphasizes the role of society in determining what is abnormal.*

SOCIOCULTURAL MODEL   The **sociocultural model** emphasizes the role of society in causing disturbed behavior. An extreme example of socially induced abnormality is found in a group of people who seem to flout every human instinct—a mother who roughly flings her baby to the ground and laughs when the child is hurt; a husband who does not take his sick wife to the hospital but lets her die and buries her secretly so that he can make money by selling her medicine; an adult who snatches food from the mouth of a starving old man and then remorselessly leaves him to die.

Who are these people, whose behavior shouts out its abnormality? They are typical members of the Ik tribe, who live in Africa in the mountains spanning the borders of Uganda, Sudan, and Kenya (Turnbull, 1972). Their alienation from one another and from almost everything we have come to call "human" or "normal" demonstrates what can happen to a society of people who live in a harsh environment where food is so scarce that survival depends on total selfishness. Even though the behavior of the Ik is abnormal by our standards, it is in accordance with the norms (standards of behavior) of their particular society. We see, then, how much of a role culture plays in determining what is normal—and what is abnormal.

The sociocultural model recognized that less severe pressures can also take their toll. Discrimination against women, blacks, the elderly, and homosexuals; poverty and its stresses; the strains of living in an overcrowded, high-pressure urban environment—all these factors are pointed to as causes of disturbed and disruptive behavior.

Humanistic model *Explanation of mental disorders as a result of failure to achieve self-actualization (self-fulfillment).*

HUMANISTIC MODEL   According to Carl Rogers (1970), Abraham Maslow (1954/1970), and other humanists, abnormal behavior represents a failure to achieve self-actualization (self-fulfillment). It is the result of lack of growth and fear of change, a culmination of poorly made choices in life. This explanation is the **humanistic model**. Like the behaviorists, the humanists pay little attention to what may have caused an abnormality, focusing instead on what can be done once it exists. Their perspective is optimistic, since it assumes that people's own choices have done much to cause their troubles and that they can now make new choices which will change their lives and resolve their psychological problems.

Of course, none of the models described here can serve as an umbrella explanation for all abnormality. In some instances, one basic approach may seem to provide the most reasonable explanation and the most promising implications for treatment, while in others a completely different perspective is more appropriate. The things we need to realize are how little we actually do know about the causes of abnormal behavior; how much one disturbed person differs from another not only in the disturbance itself but in every other aspect of life capable of influencing the cause, the course, and the treatment of disturbance; and how important it is to keep an open mind.

How Common Is Abnormality?

The kind of behavior we talk about in this chapter is distressingly common. In the largest and most thorough survey done to date, researchers associated with the Na-

Drug abuse is distressingly common in our society. Adults like these, who function well on the job and in other areas of life, engage in recreational use of dangerous mind-altering drugs such as marijuana and cocaine—and the most abused drug in the United States today, alcohol. Is their behavior normal? Questions like this illustrate the difficulty of classifying behavior as abnormal.

tional Institute of Mental Health (NIMH) interviewed about 10,000 Americans in Baltimore, St. Louis, and New Haven. About 1 to 5 adults (or about 29 million people, if the results are assumed to represent all Americans) were found to suffer from some kind of psychological disturbance in any 6-month period (Eaton et al., 1984; D. X. Freedman, 1984; Myers et al., 1984; NIMH, 1984; Regier et al., 1984; Shapiro et al., 1984). Only one-fifth of these people sought treatment for mental health problems (usually from general physicians), the percentage varying on the bases of sex and of the specific disorder. Women were twice as likely as men to receive treatment, and about half of people diagnosed as schizophrenics were treated, compared with only 18 percent of those who abused drugs or alcohol (Robins et al., 1984).

Anxiety has replaced depression as the leading mental health problem in this country; it is followed by substance abuse (alcohol and drugs—in a 4 to 1 ratio) and affective disorders (such as depression and bipolar disorder). The most disabling disorder, schizophrenia, afflicts 1 percent of the adult population (see Table 14-2). (The technical terms used here will be defined later in this chapter.)

TABLE 14-2   MAJOR MENTAL DISORDERS IN THE UNITED STATES

Disease	Number of People Affected within a 6-Month Period in the United States	Percentage of adults affected	Percent who are treated
Anxiety	13.1 million	8.3	23
Alcohol and drug abuse	10.0 million	6.4	18
Depression	9.4 million	6.0	32
Schizophrenia	1.5 million	1.0	53

Sources: Eaton et al., 1984; D. X. Freedman, 1984; Myers et al., 1984; NIMH, 1984; Regier et al., 1984; Shapiro et al., 1984.

Who is most likely to suffer from a mental disorder? People under 45 and people who are not college graduates have higher rates than older people and college graduates. Blacks and whites have about the same rates. Men and women also have comparable rates, but they differ in the prevalence of specific conditions. Women are more likely to suffer from depression or anxiety disorders (like phobias, panic disorders, and obsessive-compulsive disorder); men are more likely to experience substance abuse and antisocial personality (both of which tend to affect people under 45).

MEASURING AND DIAGNOSING ABNORMALITY

Problems and Issues

Researchers use various measures to determine how "normal" people are. Specially trained interviewers draw conclusions based on behavior and also ask subjects about the presence of various symptoms that are generally considered indicative of psychological difficulties (such as bouts of depression; certain physical ailments linked to mental state, like stomach ulcers and migraine headaches; and drinking, eating, and sleeping habits). Sometimes during the course of an interview and sometimes by administering questionnaires, investigators ask questions designed to elicit attitudes (such as, "Do you agree or disagree with this statement: 'I sometimes can't help wondering whether anything is worthwhile any more'?"). The researchers then develop indexes of mental health based on the subjects' answers in the various categories and on their own observation.

Diagnosis of emotional disturbance is extremely difficult and is a constant source of controversy among mental health professionals. In one well-known study, titled "On Being Sane in Insane Places" (1973), David Rosenhan had several colleagues join him in faking a symptom, with the purpose of being admitted to mental hospitals. After saying they had been hearing voices over the past 3 weeks that said "empty," "hollow," and "thud," the eight "fakers" were diagnosed as suffering from schizophrenia and admitted to hospitals (12 hospitals in 5 states were involved). After admission, the pseudo patients spoke no more about the voices and immediately began acting normally. Still, during the time they were in the hospital, anything they did—including taking notes—was considered to be a symptom of illness. Although none of the hospital employees ever seemed to suspect that these people might not be disturbed, some of the *real* patients voiced their suspicions that the "pseudos" were journalists or investigators. After 1 to 7 weeks of hospitalization, all the pseudo patients were discharged as "schizophrenics in remission" (temporarily symptom-free).

Rosenhan sees this study as evidence that psychiatrists cannot recognize mental health when they see it, since normal people were admitted to mental hospitals and then discharged, not as healthy but as only temporarily symptom-free. Spitzer (1976), however, who has severely criticized the design of the study, sees its findings as proof that diagnosis of mental illness is relatively accurate, since the staff psychiatrists had no reason to think the pseudo patients were lying when they described their symptoms and because they were kept in the hospitals for a much shorter period than is usually the case. Spitzer also maintains that discharging them as "in remission" was correct inasmuch as it was a precaution warranted by the apparent severity of their symptoms at the time they were admitted.

What this study illuminates more than anything else is the great difficulty in deciding who is normal and who is not. What are the major issues here? First, it is difficult even for highly educated professionals to determine whether someone is truly disturbed or is just pretending to be disturbed. Second, once people have been labeled abnormal, other people (in this case, hospital staffs) look at them in that way without stopping to question the diagnosis. Third, even though these "patients" were discharged more quickly than most real schizophrenics would have been and were recognized as being free of symptoms at discharge, they were still considered ill. Once having shown signs of abnormality, they were not considered to have recovered, even after they were seen to be behaving normally.

DSM III

In 1952, in an effort to make it easier to diagnose various mental disorders, the American Psychiatric Association drew up a guidebook called *Diagnostic and Statistical Manual of Mental Disorders* (DSM). DSM has been revised twice. Its third edition, **DSM III**, the last to be published so far, appeared in 1980 and, like the first two editions, has been controversial. The incomplete draft of the newest revision, DSM III-R, has already aroused strong opposition. Even highly qualified mental professionals disagree on the definitions of many disorders.

DSM III *Third edition of Diagnostic and Statistical Manual of Mental Disorders, a guidebook to diagnosis, published by the American Psychiatric Association.*

The goals of the framers of DSM seem clear enough—to help clinicians treat and manage patients, to make diagnostic categories as reliable as possible, to provide information useful to clinicians of various theoretical persuasions, to reflect up-to-date research data, to bring some consistency to the use of diagnostic terms, and to eliminate terms that are no longer useful.

Normality and abnormality are not all-or-nothing propositions, of course. Most of us recognize that many people have idiosyncrasies that might be considered abnormal and yet can still lead relatively normal lives, and even people who are so disturbed that they need to be institutionalized often have periods of acting quite normally. Therefore, the assumption of DSM III that having a mental disorder and not having a disorder are not totally different conditions, but are rather two ends of a continuum, seems unassailable.

Why, then, has this document aroused such a storm of controversy in psychological and psychiatric circles? The answer has to do in part with the basic difficulty in diagnosing psychological problems. We can often determine an abnormal physical condition by taking a temperature, measuring blood chemistry, seeing an obvious symptom like unusual bleeding. We can often determine that a crime has been committed by applying a clear standard: stolen property, for example, or the inflicting of bodily harm. But in assessing psychological abnormality, personal opinions, attitudes, cultural norms, and moral standards enter in to muddy up the situation.

For example, one of the controversial differences between DSM III and its predecessor, DSM II (1968), was that DSM III dropped homosexuality as a mental disorder, unless a homosexual was unhappy about his or her sexual orientation and *wanted* to become heterosexual—a condition referred to as *ego-dystonic homosexuality*. In the revision of DSM III that is now in progress, DSM III-R, it is proposed that ego-dystonic homosexuality be dropped. A disorder related to homosexuality will now be part of a category that includes several disorders in sexual functioning, such as marked feelings of inadequacy related to self-imposed standards of masculinity or femininity (such as size or shape of sex organs, or level of sexual performance), distress about having a pattern of repeated sexual conquests in which the person feels that he or she is "using" sex partners, and persistent distress or confusion about one's sexual orientation.

Another major controversy has revolved around accusations of sex bias. Critics charge that DSM III takes a male-dominated point of view and defines psychological health differently for men and women. Women who *over*conform to traditional female roles (such as passivity, dependency, and slenderness) are regarded as disturbed, but so are women who refuse to conform to such roles (showing aggressiveness, competitiveness, independence, and adventurousness) (Broverman et al., 1970; M Kaplan, 1983a, 1983b). According to these contradictory diagnoses, then, women could be labeled unhealthy either way. Defenders of DSM III maintain that if such charges were correct, women would be diagnosed as abnormal more often than men in all categories, which is not the case; on the contrary, some categories, especially several personality disorders, are more frequently diagnosed in men (Kass,

TABLE 14-3 MAJOR CATEGORIES OF DISORDERS

Category	Examples
Disorders usually first evident in childhood or adolescence	Mental retardation, Tourette's syndrome, hyperactivity, anorexia nervosa
Organic mental disorders	Alzheimer's disease (senile dementia)
Substance-use disorders	Abuse of or dependence on such drugs as alcohol, barbiturates, amphetamines, PCP, LSD
Schizophrenic disorders	Disorganized, catatonic, paranoid, undifferentiated, and residual schizophrenia, all of which involve thought disturbances or hallucinations or both
Paranoid disorders	Differing severities of paranoia, which involves the delusion that one is being persecuted
Psychotic disorders not classified elsewhere	Brief reactive psychosis (psychotic symptoms lasting from a few hours to two weeks in response to a trauma)
Affective disorders	Disorders of mood such as depression and mania
Anxiety disorders	Phobias, panic disorders, obsessive-compulsive disorder, post-traumatic stress disorder
Somatoform disorders	Hypochondriasis, conversion disorder, psychogenic pain disorder, in all of which the person exhibits physical symptoms for which no physiological basis can be found
Dissociative disorders	Multiple personality, amnesia, fugue, all of which involve a sudden, temporary alteration in consciousness, identity, or motor behavior
Psychosexual disorders	Masochism, sadism, inhibited orgasm, premature ejaculation, gender identity disorders
Factitious disorders	Physical or psychological symptoms that are under the control of the individual, as determined by some outside observer (like the production of severe psychological symptoms that make the patient seem psychotic)
Disorders of impulse not classified elsewhere	Kleptomania (compulsive stealing), pyromania (fire setting), pathological gambling
Adjustment disorders	Impaired functioning in response to some stressful life event (divorce, illness, natural disaster) or a developmental stage (leaving the parental home, becoming a parent), which may include a depressed or anxious mood or inhibition with work
Psychological factors affecting physical condition	Tension headaches, asthma, ulcerative colitis, acne
Personality disorders	Paranoid, narcissistic, antisocial, passive-aggressive, schizoid, borderline
Conditions not attributable to a mental disorder that are a focus of attention or treatment	Malingering, problems in school or on the job, marital problems, parent-child problems

Source: DSM III, 1980.

Spitzer, & Williams, 1983; Williams & Spitzer, 1983). Women do seek treatment more often than men, perhaps because they are referred more often for therapy, although the reason could also be that women are more conscious of health issues and are more willing to admit a need for help.

Sex bias has also been charged in connection with three new categories proposed for DSM III-R: periluteal phase dysphoric disorder, self-defeating personality disorder, and sadistic personality disorder (Fisher, 1986). Why are these categories considered sexist? Critics charge that the expression *periluteal phase dysphoric disorder* (originally *premenstrual dysphoric disorder*) suggests that women with menstrual problems are showing psychiatric symptoms rather than biological ones; that *self-defeating personality* blames the victim and might be wrongly applied to people who are trapped in abusive situations through no fault of their own; and that *sadistic personality disorder* could be used as a legal defense for rapists and abusers of women and children.

Still another argument concerns the elimination of the term *neuroses*, because of the shift in DSM III away from Freudian orientation, as well as its framers' conviction that there is no universally accepted definition of the term. Others criticize DSM III for its medical explanations of abnormal behavior. Many professionals reject the concept of considering *all* psychological disorders a form of "mental illness," and some reject the very concept of mental illness.

Despite all the objections to DSM III, however, it is still the most comprehensive guide we have and is the culmination to date of continuing efforts to define abnormal behavior as specifically as possible. The mental disorders classified therein are those that the American Psychiatric Association defines as a "clinically significant behavioral or psychological syndrome or pattern that occurs in an individual and that is typically associated with either a painful symptom (distress) or impairment in one or more important areas of functioning (disability)" (DSM III, p. 6). Implicit in this definition is the existence of a behavioral, psychological, or biological dysfunction, as distinct from a social dysfunction, that is, as distinct from a conflict between a person and society (like juvenile delinquency). If a disturbance is only social, the American Psychiatric Association considers it a social deviance rather than a mental disorder. Table 14-3 shows the major categories of disorders in DSM III.

DSM III organizes information along five different *axes*, or main organizational categories: three clusters summarizing ways to diagnose a specific disorder and two that provide additional information to be called upon to plan treatment and predict the outcome for a particular patient. The axes are organized as follows:

- *Axis I*: Clinical syndromes (such as organic mental disorders, affective disorders, and schizophrenic disorders). Conditions that are a focus of attention or treatment but are not attributable to a mental disorder (such as underachievement in school, isolated antisocial acts, and career uncertainty).

- *Axis II*: Personality disorders (in which specific personality traits interfere with social or occupational functioning or cause distress—such as dependent, paranoid, and schizotypal disorders) and specific developmental disorders (such as late speech or retarded arithmetical abilities).

- *Axis III*: Physical disorders and conditions.

- *Axis IV*: Severity of psychosocial stressors (ranging from mild, like the stress caused by a change in work hours, to extreme, like that caused by a death in the family).

- *Axis V*: Highest level of adaptive functioning in the past year (with regard to social life, job, and use of leisure time).

To see how psychiatrists use these axes in diagnosis, see Table 14-4 (page 494).

TABLE 14-4   DIAGNOSIS OF A PSYCHOLOGICAL DISTURBANCE USING DSM III

The director of psychological services at a major corporation has referred a long-term employee, a 62-year-old man who is slated for early retirement, to a psychiatrist because of the worker's depression, which has caused a high rate of absenteeism. The psychologist knows that this worker used to be absent often because of a drinking problem, but he thinks that the man is not drinking now and feels that there are other problems. The psychiatrist's diagnosis, based on the axes listed in DSM III looks like this, as presented in DSM III (1980, p. 30).

Axis I: Major depression, single episode, with melancholia; alcohol dependence, in remission

Axis II: Dependent personality disorder (provisional; rule out borderline personality disorder)

Axis III: Alcoholic cirrhosis of liver

Axis IV: Psychosocial stressors: anticipated retirement and change in residence with loss of contact with friends
Severity: Moderate

Axis V: Highest level of adaptive functioning past year: Good

---

The remainder of this chapter will focus on describing and discussing the most common disorders affecting people in our society.

TYPES OF ABNORMALITY

Anxiety Disorders

(Jeffrey Reed/Medichrome)

We all feel anxious sometimes, but not all anxiety becomes severe enough to be considered part of an anxiety disorder that interferes with one's life.

Psychoses *Mental disorders whose symptoms interfere with total functioning, involve a break from reality, and make it difficult for an affected person to get along without a major support like heavy medication or institutionalization.*

For months after a devastating automobile accident that left her two closest friends dead, Robin, age 17, had nightmares about the crash, although during her waking hours she could not remember it. She could not concentrate on her schoolwork, she felt detached from her family and classmates, and she was plagued by guilt feelings because she had survived while her friends had not.

Allan, a college sophomore, has to get up 2 hours earlier than his roommate, even though both have the same schedule of morning classes, because of the elaborate rituals he goes through every single morning. Among other things, Allan brushes his teeth exactly 150 times, takes both a bath and a shower, changes his bedsheets, and checks to be sure all his books are in alphabetical order.

Many people experience mild degrees of conditions like these. Everyone who has been through a trauma feels some aftershock, and who among us has not double-checked something we were positive we had already done just a few minutes before (like turning on an alarm clock or engaging the emergency brake of a car)? When feelings like these don't affect the way we function in day-to-day living over a period of time, we take them in our stride.

Robin and Allan cannot do this, because their functioning is severely impaired. They are suffering from conditions that Sigmund Freud called *neuroses,* to describe mental disorders arising from anxiety, disorders whose symptoms interfere with normal functioning but do not block it entirely. Conditions that used to be termed *neuroses* (until the publication of DSM III in 1980) include phobias, obsessions and compulsions, some depressions, and some amnesias. These conditions do not represent a break from reality, and although they interfere with normal functioning, they do not call for hospitalization.

Under the classification used by the American Psychiatric Association in DSM III, the term *neurosis* is no longer used. Disorders that used to be called *neuroses* are now classified as anxiety disorders, affective disorders, somatoform disorders, and dissociative disorders. Let us look at some of these before we go on to examine **psychoses**—severe conditions that affect total functioning, involve a break from reality, and make it virtually impossible for an affected person to get along in the world without a major support like heavy medication or institutionalization.

In anxiety disorders, either anxiety is the main symptom or it appears when people try to master other symptoms (confronting whatever they're phobic about or resisting a compulsion, for example). What do we mean by **anxiety?** It can be defined as a state of apprehension, fearful uncertainty, or dread caused by anticipated threat. It is often accompanied by such physical symptoms as shortness of breath, rapid heartbeat, sweating, and trembling. **Anxiety disorders**—phobic disorders, obsessive-compulsive disorders, panic disorders, generalized anxiety disorders, and post-traumatic stress disorders—are fairly common, affecting some 8.3 percent of adult Americans, or some 13 million people (DSM III, 1980). Panic, phobic, and obsessive-compulsive disorders affect more women than men and seem to run in families (Myers et al., 1984; Robins et al., 1984).

Forms of Anxiety Disorders PHOBIC DISORDERS Some 11 million Americans (7 percent of the adult population) suffer from some kind of **phobia,** an unrealistic fear that interferes with normal living (Robins et al., 1984). The most common, **simple phobia,** is a persistent, irrational fear of some particular aspect of the environment. People may be so afraid of animals that they won't visit a family with a pet; so afraid of thunder and lightning that they go down into the cellar, or to the foyer of an apartment house, during every thunderstorm, even in the middle of the night; so afraid of enclosed places that they won't ride in an elevator; or so afraid of heights that they won't go to a child's third-floor classroom on open school night.

The most severe phobia, and the one for which people most often seek treat-

Anxiety State of apprehension, fearful uncertainty, or dread caused by anticipated threat.

Anxiety disorders Psychological disturbances, affecting about 8.3 percent of the adult population of the United States, including phobic disorders, panic disorders, and generalized anxiety disorders.

Phobia Unrealistic fear that interferes with normal living.

Simple phobia Most common type of phobia, consisting of a persistent, irrational fear of some particular aspect of the environment.

(Drawing by B. Tobey; © 1975 The New Yorker Magazine, Inc.)

"*Not on your life! Come and get it.*"

Identification with the feelings and situations portrayed underlies much of the humor in cartoons. Anxiety disorders are common enough in our society to allow people to identify with the phobic fear of height shown by the woman here.

Agoraphobia   Most severe phobia, for which people most commonly seek treatment; manifested as inability to go out of the house, be in large unfamiliar places, drive, or travel by public conveyance.
Social phobia   Type of phobia in which a person is terrified of being in situations where he or she can be scrutinized by others.

ment, is **agoraphobia.** Agoraphobia generally takes the form of inability to go outdoors, to be in large unfamiliar places (like theaters and department stores), to drive a car, or to travel by bus or train. The condition affects women about four times oftener than men and is experienced by about 0.5 percent of the adult population (DSM III, 1980). Another type of phobia is **social phobia,** terror of situations in which one can be scrutinized by others.

OBSESSIVE-COMPULSIVE DISORDERS   Allan, the fanatically fastidious college student, is plagued by **obsessions** (persistent ideas, thoughts, images, or impulses that seem senseless even to him and yet invade his consciousness against his will) and by **compulsions** (repetitive, irrational behaviors that he feels obliged to carry out even though he can't see any point to them himself). Obsessive-compulsive disorders affect about 100,000 American adults (somewhat less than 0.1 percent of the population) (Robins et al., 1984).

The most common obsessions center on violence (for example, fear of killing one's child), contamination (fear of becoming infected by shaking hands or by eating from unclean utensils), and doubt (wondering over and over whether one has done something terrible, like hurting someone in a car accident). The most common compulsions drive someone to count (for example, steps, actions, or figures in wallpaper), to wash the hands, or to touch (every piece of furniture in a room or every garment in a closet). Obsessive-compulsive adults almost always realize how senseless these thoughts and actions are, and they usually try to resist them. Resistance, however, causes so much anxiety that it's easier for such people just to give in to the symptoms, even when doing so may disrupt their lives to the point that they cannot go to school or hold a job (Spitzer, Skodol, Gibbon, & Williams, 1983).

Obsessions   Persistent ideas, thoughts, images, or impulses that seem senseless even to the person who has them and invade consciousness against the person's will.
Compulsions   Repetitive, irrational behaviors that a person feels obligated to carry out even though he or she cannot see any point to them.

(Drawing by Woodman; © 1986 The New Yorker Magazine, Inc.)

"But that's what you said yesterday—'Just one more cord'!"

Many people will also identify with the obsessive-compulsive traits shown by the man in this cartoon.

So-called compulsive eating, sexual activity, gambling, and drinking are not true compulsions, because the activities themselves can be pleasurable and the only reason a person drawn to them would want to resist them would be because of their consequences. So-called obsessive preoccupations with problems on the job, in an unrequited love affair, or in some other area are not true obsessions, because no matter how much a person may brood about these things, the problems themselves are real and so the thoughts are meaningful, even if excessive.

POST-TRAUMATIC STRESS DISORDER   The kind of reaction Robin had to the car crash she had been in is considered a disorder only because of its degree of severity. Virtually everyone who experiences a traumatic event feels some aftereffects. Only when these effects are more severe and long-lasting than usual is the person considered to be suffering from ***post-traumatic stress disorder,*** a condition common among veterans of military combat and among survivors of rape, natural disasters, and such unnatural disasters as concentration camps and bombing attacks. Typical symptoms involve dreams about the event, sleep disturbance (sometimes caused by fear of such dreams), guilt, and overreaction to sights or sounds associated with the traumatic event. When symptoms appear within 6 months of the trauma and last no longer than 6 months, the prognosis is more favorable than it is when the symptoms emerge after a latency period of months or even years and last longer than 6 months.

Post-traumatic stress disorder
Anxiety disorder characterized by re-experiencing a traumatic event.

OTHER ANXIETY STATES   ***Panic disorders*** are characterized by recurrent attacks of fear of some nameless, formless doom. Sometimes these attacks occur unpredictably; at other times they develop a discernible pattern, coming up in connection with some particular activity (like driving a car or going into a dark room). The attacks are usually signaled by a rush of physical symptoms, such as dizziness, trouble in breathing, choking, chest pain, sweating, and faintness (see Figure 14-1).

Panic disorder   Anxiety disorder characterized by recurrent attacks of terror that include physical symptoms such as dizziness, breathing difficulties, and sweating.

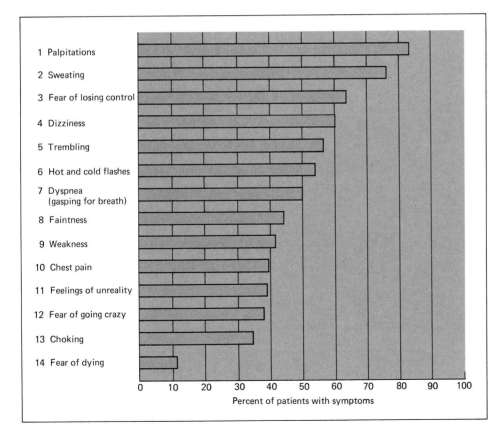

FIGURE 14-1 *Frequency of symptoms with panic attacks. More than 1 million Americans suffer symptoms like these in response to a variety of situations, which may include such everyday activities as going out to mail a letter. (Source: Adapted from Katerndahl, 1984.)*

The person may suddenly be seized by a fear of dying, going crazy, or doing something uncontrolled. Women are more likely than men to experience panic attacks. The attacks usually last for several minutes but occasionally persist for hours. Panic disorders affect 0.8 percent of the adult population, or 1.2 million Americans (Robins et al., 1984).

Generalized anxiety disorder is a more diffuse kind of anxiety, without the specific symptoms of the other anxiety disorders. Affected people usually cannot ascribe their discomfort to any particular situation or event. They just know that they feel anxious, and they may exhibit such physical symptoms as shakiness, "jitters," sweating, dry mouth, insomnia, distractibility, and a general state of uneasy anticipation. Such symptoms must go on for at least a month to warrant this diagnosis.

Causes of Anxiety Disorders   There are, of course, many explanations for the causes of anxiety and several models of anxiety, along the lines of models of abnormality in general. The earliest theories about the various anxiety disorders concentrated on psychological disturbances caused by early experiences (the psychoanalytic model). Later theories focused on learning, specifically the learning of bad habits (the behavioral model). The prevailing theory today attributes anxiety largely to physiological problems (the medical model). Since the medical model is the subject of the most research, let's look first at evidence for a biological basis of anxiety.

MEDICAL MODEL OF ANXIETY   The belief that anxiety may be due to a chemical imbalance in the brain owes much to recent research pointing to a physiological aspect of anxiety, although other factors also seem important. Biology is not the whole story.

In one set of studies, researchers used a PET scanner (described in Chapter 2) to get images of the brains of people suffering from panic disorder. They found a difference in blood flow between the right and left sides of the brain, apparently caused by an abnormality in the area of the brain that is believed to control emotions (Reiman et al., 1984). Evidence that panic disorders seem to run in families suggests that the condition is at least partly hereditary (Fishman & Sheehan, 1985).

Research on obsessive-compulsive disorders has found that some people are more vulnerable to them, possibly because of a biological predisposition—an inborn tendency, which may be activated by factors in the environment. It has also been found that neurological abnormalities, such as unusual EEG patterns and frontal lobe dysfunctions, may exist in susceptible people; and that these people seem to have abnormal levels of the neurotransmitters serotonin and norepinephrine. Furthermore, since identical twins are more **concordant** (similar) for obsessive-compulsive disorders than fraternal twins are, a hereditary basis for such a tendency may exist (Turner, Beidel, & Nathan, 1985).

PSYCHOANALYTIC MODEL OF ANXIETY   Psychoanalysts have traditionally thought that anxiety (which they term *neurosis*) develops through four stages:

1   Inner conflict between the drives of the id and the fears induced by the superego
2   Presence of sexual drives
3   Inability of the logical, rational influence of the ego to help a person work through a conflict
4   Burrowing underground of powerful drives, which then seek expression through anxiety or related behaviors

Not all psychoanalysts agree with this explanation. As we pointed out in Chapter 13, several of Freud's followers broke with him over the role he gave to sexual feelings. Alfred Adler (1929, 1930), for example, maintained that anxiety disorders ensue from feelings of inferiority, which have their roots in childhood, when children feel inadequate because of their small size and their relative inability to help

---

Generalized anxiety disorder
Mental disorder characterized by feelings of anxiety that cannot be ascribed to any particular event or situation.

Concordant   *Alike in a certain characteristic.*

themselves. And recent findings about biological factors in anxiety disorders are leading some contemporary analysts to broaden their views about people with these disorders and to combine medication with psychotherapy (A. M. Cooper, 1985).

BEHAVIORAL MODEL OF ANXIETY   Learning theorists hold that anxiety disorders arise initially from learning the wrong behaviors (for example, a child might learn such behaviors by observing a phobic parent). The disorders are then maintained when they are reinforced (for example, a girl who doesn't like to go to school might be rewarded for the stomachache she gets every morning by being allowed to stay home with her mother). Some learning theorists, such as Joseph Wolpe (1978), take a fairly mechanistic view, believing that thought obeys the same basic laws that govern motor behaviors and the autonomic processes of breathing and circulation. On the other hand, Bandura (1968, 1974) stresses the importance of the intervening influence of thought as essential in producing changes in human behavior.

In view of the great variety of anxiety disorders, it is likely that no single factor is at their root, but that they result from a combination of factors: an inborn tendency, caused by inherited neuroanatomical or biochemical abnormalities, is then triggered by stress.

The hero of the rock opera "Tommy" sees his mother's lover kill his father; the boy then becomes deaf, blind, and mute. A mental health practitioner would probably diagnose this as conversion hysteria, one of the somatoform disorders.

Somatoform Disorders

You didn't hear it, you didn't see it,
You won't say nothing to no one!
Never tell a soul
What you know is the truth.

After Tommy, as a 10-year-old, sees his mother's lover kill the boy's father, he is admonished by the preceding words. Going even further than his mother and eventual stepfather intend him to, Tommy dutifully becomes deaf, blind, and mute. The rest of the rock opera *Tommy* (as sung by the group The Who), in which the tragedy occurs, tells of the family's efforts to restore the boy's senses. The doctor who sees him reports,

The tests I gave him show no sense at all.
His eyes can see, his ears can hear,
His lips can speak,
But still he does not answer to my call.

Neither gypsy (the "acid queen") nor faith healer can help the boy, who eventually regains his abilities only after his mother, in a violent outburst, smashes a mirror in front of him.

What Are Somatoform Disorders?   *Tommy* is an extreme example of the **somatoform disorders.** These conditions, which derive their name from the Greek word *soma* (body), are characterized by a display of physical symptoms for which no physical basis can be found. Such symptoms, which are common in wartime, seem to arise from psychological needs. ***Conversion disorder***, Tommy's apparent affliction, can cause a person to become paralyzed, lose the sense of smell or pain, suffer seizures, or even experience false pregnancy.

Causes of Somatoform Disorders   DSM III offers two possible explanations for somatoform disorders. One explanation is that a person keeps an internal conflict or need out of awareness by losing the ability to perceive. (Tommy seems to fall into this category.) The second explanation is that a severe symptom might be a "secondary gain" received by avoiding an activity. Thus, an opera singer who really hates to perform in public loses his voice and *cannot* go on. Or a woman whose husband wants a divorce becomes paralyzed and holds on to him through her need.

Somatoform disorder *Mental disorder characterized by physical symptoms for which no physical basis can be found.*
Conversion disorder *Type of somatoform disorder in which a person may become paralyzed, lose the sense of smell or pain, suffer seizures, or experience false pregnancy.*

A recent study of 35 pairs of twins found that somatoform disorders seem to run in families (Torgersen, 1986). However, they do not seem to be caused by a hereditary predisposition as much as by similarities in childhood experiences. Identical twins did have a higher concordance rate (29 percent) than fraternal twins (10 percent), but they were also likely to have had more similar childhood experiences. Only two pairs of fraternal twins were concordant for somatoform disorder; these had been closer as children than almost all the other sets of fraternal twins.

Dissociative Disorders

A shy, timid 22-year-old, who was given the pseudonym "Sybil" by the writer who told her story (Schreiber, 1975), first consulted a psychiatrist because there were periods in her life when she seemed to "black out" totally, forgetting what she had done for long stretches of time. Soon after she began therapy, Sybil underwent a drastic personality change in the middle of a session, leading her psychiatrist to suspect that Sybil was a rare example of a dissociative disorder, multiple personality.

Forms of Dissociative Disorders   A *dissociative disorder* involves a sudden temporary alteration in consciousness, identity, or motor behavior. In *multiple personality,* as the term implies, a person has more than one distinct personality, and the alteration consists of each personality's coming to prominence at different times, totally submerging the other or others. The personalities are usually quite different (as in the most famous multiple personality in literature, Dr. Jekyll and Mr. Hyde), and each may be unaware of the other.

Sybil's case proved to be much more complicated than her psychiatrist first suspected; the course of therapy brought out a total of 16 separate personalities living at different times in Sybil's mind. These personalities were all very different from each other. They ranged in age from infancy to middle age; two were male; and they all had different talents, abilities, ways of speaking and moving, and images of themselves.

Sybil's first additional personality had been born when, as a 3-year-old, Sybil needed a route to escape (at least mentally) from the tortures inflicted upon her by her cruel and disturbed mother. From that time on, Sybil would create new personalities whenever she had to deal with an unbearable situation. Fortunately, Sybil's case had a happy ending. After more than 11 years of psychoanalysis, she was able to integrate all her personalities into one personality (the seventeenth), which was, at last, a whole person capable of dealing with life.

Multiple personality is, fortunately, quite rare, as are the other dissociative disorders, described below.

Amnesia is a general term for a variety of memory disorders, including psychogenic amnesia and psychogenic fugue. In *psychogenic amnesia,* a person may forget events that occurred during a certain period of time, often a few hours before or after a disturbing event, as Robin, the girl who had been in the automobile accident, forgot the events just before it. *Psychogenic* means *caused by psychological factors;* psychogenic amnesia usually begins after an extremely stressful event and ends suddenly, without coming back. In its more pervasive forms, it can cause people to forget who they are, forcing them to assume a new identity; or people may feel that their sense of their own reality is lost.

In *psychogenic fugue,* people may be so severely affected that they forget their identities and assume new ones. They may suddenly disappear from home or work, forgetting who they are; and the new identity such a person assumes may be very different from his or her former one—an entirely new personality. Fugues often follow traumatic experiences like marital quarrels or natural disasters and are associated with heavy drinking. They are usually brief and are followed by complete recovery without recurrence.

Dissociative disorder   Mental disturbance involving a sudden temporary alteration in consciousness, identity, or motor behavior.

Multiple personality   Dissociative disorder in which a person has two or more distinct personalities, each of which comes to prominence at different times.

Amnesia   General term for a variety of memory disorders.

Psychogenic amnesia   Dissociative disorder in which a person may forget events that occurred during a certain time period. It usually follows a traumatic event and may end suddenly.

Psychogenic fugue   Dissociative disorder in which a person may forget his or her identity and assume a new one.

In *depersonalization disorder,* people temporarily lose or change their sense of their own reality. They may seem to see themselves from a distance, outside the body; they may feel "mechanical" or like characters in a dream; and they may feel that parts of the body have changed in size. These sensations are often accompanied by a sense of lack of control over one's actions.

Depersonalization disorder
Dissociative disorder in which a person temporarily loses or changes the sense of his or her reality.

Causes of Dissociative Disorders   Severe sexual abuse or violent abuse in childhood, like the kind suffered by "Sybil," is common in the histories of adults suffering from dissociative disorders. The link between such abuse and a dissociative disorder is explained by learning theorists as an avoidance response that helps to protect the victim, by allowing him or her to "escape" into another personality. The psychoanalytic explanation, on the other hand, attributes such disorders to massive repression, in which one part of the mind splits off from another part to let the affected person erase unacceptable thoughts from consciousness. Such thoughts may be related to abuse or, more often, may go back to the sexual wishes of the Oedipal stage. Psychoanalytic theorists do not say, however, why ordinary repression is not enough for people who suffer from dissociative disorders—why they need to block out an entire part of the personality or acquire a new identity.

Both points of view are speculative; the causes of these disorders are basically unknown.

Affective Disorders: Depression and Mania

All of us have good moods and bad ones. Some of us are moodier than others, more prone to swings in the dominant emotional tone that colors our psychic lives. It's easy to understand moods that seem related to the events in our lives—the euphoria we float in when we fall in love, or the depression we sink into when we are fired from a job. Most people also accept the notion of "waking up on the wrong side of the bed" or "waking up with a song in my heart" and think little about ordinary shifts in mood. When these emotional states do not interfere with the way we lead our lives—or when such interference is confined to a brief period of time—most people can adapt quite well.

Sometimes, however, such moods are more severe. When they are either so good that a person seems to be flying—or so bad that his or her entire life looks bleak—and when they persist over time to such a severe degree that they interfere with day-to-day functioning, a person is said to be suffering from one of the **affective disorders,** or disorders of mood. These disorders affect more than 9 million American adults (6 percent of the adult population) (Robins et al., 1984).

Affective disorders   *Mental disturbances characterized by disorders of mood.*

John Custance was a person of just such severe moods. He wrote that he had fallen in love "with the whole Universe" (Custance, 1952). When he was in a state of great well-being, his senses were much keener than usual, allowing him to see, feel, and hear intensely. He had a sense of mystic communion with God and with all humankind. Sexual activity became a religious experience. He felt enormously powerful, as if all his wishes, even the most extravagant, were coming true; and as if all his ambitions, even the most unrealistic, would be realized.

On the surface, this sounds like a state we would all like to be in. At the time John Custance was experiencing all these euphoric feelings, however, he was in an acute manic episode, which drove him into wild and irrational behavior. He insisted on giving away large sums of money that he could ill afford to prostitutes who came up to him on the street. He made a shambles of a church whose representatives had denied his request for money to help a particular young woman. Because of episodes like this he landed in a psychiatric institution.

John Custance's illness had an even darker side—depression. From the heights of the grandiosity that characterized his manic periods, he would plunge into the depths of black moods in which he was overcome by an overpowering, nameless dread, a sense of his own wickedness and worthlessness, and a terrifying succession of hallucinations that drove him to try to take his own life on three different occasions.

Custance, whose accounts of his illness, written while he was in its throes, have made a major contribution to the psychiatric literature, was suffering from what is commonly known as *manic-depressive disorder.* It is categorized by DSM III as **bipolar disorder**, one of the major affective disorders.

Affective disorders range in severity from a relatively mild **mania** (the elated phase of bipolar disorder) or **depression** (the sad phase of bipolar disorder, or a condition that may occur independently) to an extreme state of either mania or depression. In bipolar disorder, the two extremes alternate; the disorder consists of one or more manic episodes, which generally alternate with depressive episodes. Depression without mania, or **unipolar disorder,** may be classified as a chronic minor affective disorder, a chronic depressive disorder, or a major depressive disorder that is either psychotic or not, depending on the severity and other characteristics of the condition. A depression or other disorder is considered a psychosis if the impairment is so severe that it interferes grossly with ordinary functioning.

Among a random sample of American adults, 1 in 20 can expect to experience a major depressive episode at some time in their lives, 1 in 30 will experience the fairly common chronic mild depression known as **dysthymic disorder** (or *dysthymia*), and about 1 in 100 will be affected by mania (Robins et al., 1984). For a profile of those at greatest risk for affective disorders, see Table 14-5.

In some ways, depression and mania are two faces of the same illness, with many characteristics in common. The course of either one may be chronic (continuing over a span of years) with periods of normal functioning between episodes. Or a person may experience only a single episode. Episodes may occur singly, spaced years apart—or several may occur one right after another, and then not appear again for a long time. Either kind of affective episode often follows chronic physical illness,

Bipolar disorder *Mental disorder characterized by one or more manic episodes which generally alternate with episodes of depression.*

Mania *Aspect of bipolar disorder characterized by extreme elation irrational behavior, and grandiose thinking.*

Depression *Psychological disturbance characterized by sadness and difficulties in eating, sleeping, and concentrating.*

Unipolar disorder *Depression without manic episodes.*

Dysthymic disorder *Chronic mild depression.*

TABLE 14-5   RISK FACTOR PROFILE FOR AFFECTIVE DISORDERS

	Depression (Unipolar Disorder)	Manic-Depression (Bipolar Disorder)
Sex	Twice as many women affected	Both sexes affected equally
Age	Under 40 at greatest risk	Under 40 at greatest risk
Average age of onset	Middle to late thirties	Late twenties
Socioeconomic status	Lower levels at greater risk	Higher levels at greater risk (especially well-educated persons and high achievers)
Race	No difference	No difference
Religion	No difference	More prevalent in certain groups (Jews from central and eastern Europe; Hutterites in midwestern United States)
Interpersonal relationships	Affects unmarried and unattached, especially separated and divorced women	No difference
Life events	More vulnerable after loss of important personal relationship	More vulnerable after loss of important personal relationship

Source: NIMH, 1984.

severe psychosocial stress, or alcohol dependency. More severe manic and depressive disorders may follow less severe ones. And both unipolar disorder and bipolar disorder tend to run in families, giving rise to the possibility that they may be at least partly inherited. This possibility does, indeed, seem to be confirmed from recent research, which we'll look at in a little while.

In other ways, depression and mania do differ from each other, so that it makes sense to discuss them separately. Let's look at each of them.

Depression Cal, a successful advertising executive, has suddenly lost all interest in life. Nothing seems to matter any more—not his job, or his family, or the tennis games he once enjoyed so much. Food no longer tastes good, and so Cal eats much less of it; he has lost 30 pounds over the course of a few weeks. He lies awake for hours and then falls asleep only to awaken abruptly after an hour or two, to lie awake again for hours before drifting off shortly before dawn.

Cal's difficulty in concentrating, his slower thinking, and his indecisiveness affect his work at the advertising agency, but even though his boss has asked him what is wrong and expressed genuine concern, Cal doesn't care about his poor work performance, the opinion of his colleagues, or the danger of losing his job. He is obsessed with thoughts of suicide; he is preoccupied with various methods he might use to end his life. Cal is in the midst of a *major depressive episode.*

Laurie, a college senior, feels that she is losing control of her life. She is overwhelmed with schoolwork and on academic probation for the first time. She has no friends, feels alienated from her family, and wants a boyfriend desperately but is afraid to talk to men. She hates the way she looks, feels as though she never has any fun, has no energy for or interest in activities that might be enjoyable, and feels worthless and frightened. Although this is the worst she has ever felt, she cannot remember a time since high school when she has been really happy. Laurie is considered to be suffering from dysthymia, which is often referred to as *depressive personality.*

Laurie's and Cal's symptoms are typical of their respective types of depression. They consist not only of the sad and despairing mood itself, but of other kinds of behavior as well. Depressed people often experience some kind of change—sleeping or eating much more or less than usual, suddenly having trouble concentrating, suffering loss of energy or interest in previously enjoyed activities, losing all desire for sex or seeking it out constantly. Sometimes these symptoms are present without sadness. In major depressions with psychotic features, additional symptoms are often present. Some severely depressed people hear voices, think that parts of their body are either missing or not functioning, suffer from disordered and confused thinking, or have delusions of persecution because they feel sinful, guilty, and deserving of punishment.

Major depressive episodes may begin at any age, even in infancy; but the symptoms of depression are somewhat different at different ages. Depressed children, for example, are likely to experience separation anxiety, to cling, to refuse to go to school, and to be afraid that their parents will die. Dysthymic depression usually begins early in adult life, although it may begin in childhood or adolescence, or in later adulthood, sometimes following a major depressive episode. It is hard to know how many old people are depressed, since symptoms of depression in the elderly are often misdiagnosed as organic brain syndrome.

Depression can take different forms. It can be unipolar or bipolar. It can range in severity from a fairly mild interference with one's normal state to an extreme psychotic condition that calls for institutionalization. The onset of a depressive episode is variable; depression sometimes develops over a period of days or weeks and at other times is a sudden reaction to severe stress.

Not every bout of unhappiness, of course, should be called *depression*. Normal reactions to life stresses and losses often include a period of sadness and grief. It is only when such a mood persists over a long time, interfering with ordinary functioning, that it is termed *depression*. The greatest danger in depression is suicide.

All people feel sad at some times. When unhappiness persists over a long time and interferes with ordinary functioning, it is considered depression. People of any age can suffer from this condition—which, fortunately, can often be helped by various kinds of treatment.

Mania (Bipolar Disorder)   Normally, Ellen, a suburban real estate broker, is fairly reserved. In her manic phases, however, she is euphoric, talkative, and exuberant. Someone meeting her for the first time when she is in these phases is likely to be fascinated by this flamboyant woman whose liveliness makes her the "life of the party." Only those who know her well realize how excessive her moods are at these times. When Ellen is in the middle of a manic episode, she goes off in all directions at once, making extensive plans to take part in all sorts of activities—political, occupational, sexual, and religious. She becomes very sociable. She thinks nothing of picking up the phone to call old friends in the middle of the night—since she seems to need practically no sleep at these times, it doesn't occur to her that her friends do need sleep. As her powers of judgment fail, she spends money recklessly, takes risks in the car and on the ski slopes, and flirts outrageously with her friends' husbands, often ending up in bed with them. Men are especially attracted to her at these times, as she becomes highly dramatic, turning into a lively companion, full of jokes, amusing stories, and advice on a wide range of topics that she really knows nothing about.

Manic episodes like this tend to come upon a person suddenly, escalate rapidly, and last from a period of a few days to a few months. People who experience them usually have their first before age 30. Most people who have a manic episode will eventually experience a major depressive episode.

Less research has been conducted into the causes of the manic side of affective disorders than into the depressive phase. From what has been done, however, it seems likely that some disturbance of brain chemistry underlies both these conditions.

Causes of Affective Disorders   In trying to locate the cause of mood disorders, researchers have looked at the body, the psyche, the mind, and the environment. What have they discovered?

GENETIC EXPLANATION   When the psychiatrist Larry Pardue, who had suffered from depression during his years as a college student and a physician in training, began to suspect that an unusually large number of his relatives were depressed, he searched his family tree. After he came up with a list of 19 close relatives who had shown signs of the condition, he published his findings, giving support to a theory that depression, or a tendency toward it, can be inherited (Pardue, 1975; Wingerson, 1982).

Other evidence for a hereditary basis for affective disorders comes from family studies. When identical twins (who have the same genetic inheritance) are more likely to be concordant for a trait—that is, when both are more likely to show it—than are fraternal twins (who are no more alike than any two siblings), there is a strong likelihood that the trait is at least partly hereditary. This is the case with affective disorders. Identical twins have a concordance rate of from 40 to 70 percent; the risk goes down to from zero to 15 percent for fraternal twins (NIMH, 1984). The rates are higher for bipolar disorder than for unipolar disorder, but the higher concordance rate for identical twins in both disorders suggests a strong genetic component to affective disorders. The fact that the concordance rate is less than 100 percent, however, suggests that people may inherit a predisposition for affective disorders, but that events or environmental factors probably play a role in triggering the expression of the disorder itself.

Further evidence for the heritability of affective disorders comes from a report that one or more genes associated with depression have been located at a specific point on chromosome number 6 (Weitkamp, Stancer, Persad, Flood, & Guttormsen, 1981). These genes are located near a cluster of genes that control a part of the body's immune system. Depression, then, may be related to a defect in the immune system of an affected person. In addition, very recent research has linked a dominant gene located on chromosome 11 with the development of bipolar disorder (Egeland et al., 1987).

BIOLOGICAL EXPLANATIONS Characteristics that may be inherited by some people who suffer from depression include abnormalities in the functioning of neurotransmitters, chemicals in the brain that either stimulate or inhibit other cells. At one time, scientists believed that depression and mania might be caused by having too many or too few neurotransmitters, but subsequent research suggests that this explanation was too simple. Instead, several other mechanisms have been implicated.

One line of research has found that patients with affective disorders have an abnormally high number of receptor sites for the neurotransmitter acetylcholine, making them abnormally sensitive to this substance (Nadi, Nurnberger, & Gershon, 1984). This finding may enable scientists to predict which people are at high risk for these conditions *before* any symptoms appear. Other studies suggest that a failure in the regulation of neurotransmitters may be the crucial mechanism causing these disorders (Siever & Davis, 1985).

Another link between mind and body lies in the association that depression has with various drugs and physical illnesses. Illnesses that cause depression include diabetes, syphilis, multiple sclerosis, and certain vitamin deficiencies. Illnesses that are associated with depression but for which no cause-and-effect relationship has been found include infectious diseases like mononucleosis and flu, endocrine disturbances, and asthma. Drugs that are associated with depression include female hormones (such as those found in birth control pills), some anticancer drugs, and corticosteroids (NIMH, 1984).

PSYCHOANALYTIC EXPLANATIONS Although "a unified, comprehensive, and precise psychoanalytic theory of depression has not fully emerged" (Isenberg & Schatzberg, 1978, p. 149), a number of different psychoanalytic explanations have been offered.

In the *libidinal* approach, taken by Freud and his followers, depression is explained as the result of lowered self-esteem that ensues from failure in adult love relationships. Such a failure, in turn, may be due to an oral fixation caused by problems in the mother-infant relationship.

Ego-psychological theory sees depression as the consequence of the realization that one is unable to live up to one's aspirations. Feeling like a failure, one becomes depressed.

According to *object-relations* theory (in which the word *object* is usually used with reference to a person), depression comes from a failure to reconcile good and bad feelings toward the mother. The resultant ambivalence causes guilt and tension and can then bring about depression later in life at the loss of some important object (which, as noted above, is usually a person but may also be a position in life, a job, physical health, or some other attribute). This approach sees depression as a reaction to loss. However, a review of the literature on the relationship between depression in adulthood and the loss of a parent in childhood found no evidence of cause and effect (Crook & Eliot, 1980).

COGNITIVE EXPLANATIONS Cognitive explanations attribute depression to the way people interpret their life experiences. These explanations include Beck's cognitive theory and Seligman's learned-helplessness theory.

Cognitive theory: Aaron Beck Beck noted that depressed people think poorly of themselves, criticize themselves, feel deprived, exaggerate their problems, and dwell on thoughts of killing themselves (Beck & Burns, 1978; Sacco & Beck, 1985). He and his colleagues believe that depressives suffer from a kind of basic thinking that distorts reality. These people magnify their failures, misinterpret innocuous statements about them as indicating that they are bad, react negatively to ordinary experiences, and are pessimistic about the future. Why do depressed people think this way? According to Beck, the reason is that they suffer from cognitive, as well as emotional, dysfunction.

Depressed people, for example, have trouble interpreting proverbs because they tend to think concretely rather than abstractly. They look at life in an all-or-nothing way, seeing things as either black or white. They misinterpret statements, focus on irrelevant details, make generalizations on the basis of a single incident, and evaluate experiences unrealistically, making either a mountain of an unimportant event or a molehill of an important one.

As depressed persons hold fast to their distortions in thinking, they become even more disturbed, and they develop a sense of purposelessness and hopelessness that makes them act in ways which make their depression worse. A depressed businessman, for example, stops seeing friends and colleagues, thinking, "What's the use? They'll be better off without me." By isolating himself, he loses the opportunity to get positive input that might raise his sense of self-esteem; by staying away from his business, he contributes to its decline; by expecting rejection and acting negatively, he alienates other people; and so his disordered thinking fuels itself, creating a self-fulfilling prophecy (Beck & Burns, 1978).

Depressed people also show other cognitive deficits (Seligman, 1975). When they are hospitalized, for example, their tested IQ drops and their ability to memorize definitions of new words deteriorates. This may be due to their belief that they cannot do these tasks; they do not try, and their belief becomes reality.

Beck regards stress as a major factor precipitating depression. Childhood stresses are especially important, since the kinds of stress that people undergo early in life often set the stages for the stressors that may set off depression later on. Thus, a person whose parents were divorced when he or she was a child may, as an adult, go into a clinical depression at the breakup of a love affair but may not be so severely affected by the loss of a job. Another person, one who had trouble living up to extremely high standards of achievement set by demanding parents, would be able to deal with the loss of a lover but would become depressed by a failure at work. Even people who are predisposed to depression, then, may escape it if the specific kinds of stressors they were sensitized to in their early years do not appear in adulthood (Sacco & Beck, 1985).

Even success can bring about depression, when people feel that they have not really created their own successes but have only "fallen into" them. What, for example, would make someone like Marilyn Monroe feel that life is not worth living? Her depression—or that of someone like her—might result from feeling that she receives attention, love, wealth, and other rewards not because of who she is or what she does, but only because of how she looks, a condition she had little or nothing to do with bringing about. (Cognitive theory does not provide the only possible explanation for Marilyn Monroe's psychological problems. It has been suggested that she may have been suffering from a disorder known as *borderline personality*—which is discussed later in this chapter, in the box on page 512.)

Learned-helplessness theory: Martin E. P. Seligman Disbelief in one's own effectiveness is the core of Seligman's learned-helplessness theory. This can be seen most clearly in reactive forms of depression, which usually follow events like the death of a loved one, rejection by a loved one, physical illness or injury, money troubles, flunking out of school, being fired from a job, growing old, or being faced with any problem that seems insoluble. It is the apparent insolubility of the problem, the belief that nothing the person can do will overcome the terrible blow that has brought such suffering, which leads to depression. People who feel that they have put forth their best efforts—and that those best efforts have not been good enough—become depressed, feeling that there is nothing more they can do.

Seligman (1975) formulated the learned-helplessness theory largely on the basis of animal studies, and he and others had trouble predicting depression in human beings according to it. Therefore, in the best scientific tradition, he has reformulated the model to take into account the fact that helplessness is more complicated in people than his original theory implied (Abramson, Seligman, & Teasdale, 1978;

TABLE 14-6 CAUSAL EXPLANATIONS FOR A BAD EVENT: "I FAILED MY MIDTERM EXAMINATION"

A. Internal explanation
  1. Stable explanation
    a. Global explanation: "I'm stupid."
    b. Specific explanation: "I'm stupid in this subject."
  2. Unstable explanation
    a. Global explanation: "I was feverish that day."
    b. Specific explanation: "I had trouble concentrating on that topic the other day."

B. External explanation
  1. Stable explanation
    a. Global explanation: "All evaluations are unfair."
    b. Specific explanation: "That teacher writes bad tests."
  2. Unstable explanation
    a. Global explanation: "It was Friday the thirteenth."
    b. Specific explanation: "My test booklet was missing a page."

Source: Peterson & Seligman, 1985, p. 923.

Peterson & Seligman, 1985). This reformulation rests on people's answer to the question *Why?* when they face uncontrollable events.

If, for example, you fail a midterm exam, do you attribute your failure to something about yourself (an *internal* cause) or something about the circumstance (an *external* cause)? Do you think that the cause will persist over time (be *stable*) or be fleeting (*unstable*)? Will this cause affect other aspects of your life (be *global*) or just this one event (*specific*)? For examples of the different kinds of causes, see Table 14-6.

Research has found that people are quite consistent in their explanatory styles. Those who are most likely to become depressed are the ones who tend to attribute unpleasant events to internal, global, and stable causes. In other words, they think that the fault lies in them, it affects everything they do, and it will always influence the events in their life: "I will always fail at whatever I do" (Peterson & Seligman, 1985, p. 927).

We'll talk about *therapy* for learned helplessness in Chapter 15. Here, though, we should note that *prevention* seems to lie in learning from an early age how to control important elements in one's life (Seligman, 1975).

SEASONAL EXPLANATIONS The ancient Greeks associated certain melancholy states with seasonal periods, and investigators over the centuries have looked at this link. Only in the twentieth century, however, has the phenomenon of seasonal variation in the incidence of affective episodes been studied systematically and have conclusions been reached that variations in light and temperature affect mood states and can trigger depressive episodes (Rosenthal, Sack, & Wehr, 1983). The syndrome recently identified as **seasonal affective disorder (SAD)** is treated with so-called *light therapy;* the syndrome and the treatment are discussed in Chapter 15.

Seasonal affective disorder (SAD)
Mental disorder in which seasonal variations in light and temperature trigger depressive episodes.

Suicide

Depression is a fatal illness for the 15 percent of victims who, overwhelmed by feelings of helplessness and hopelessness, decide that their only way out is to end their lives. Some 30 to 70 percent of all suicides in this country are believed to occur in people suffering from severe depression (NIMH, 1984). Although depression seems to carry the highest risk for suicidal behavior, many people suffering from schizophrenia, personality disorders, or no apparent mental illness at all kill themselves. Estimates of attempted and completed suicides vary enormously, largely because not all suicidal deaths are recognized as such and many attempts go unrecorded. By all counts, however, the numbers are high. Suicide is the tenth leading cause of death in the United States, the third for adolescents and young adults, and the second for whites between the ages of 15 and 34. By one estimate, almost 300,000 suicides took place between 1970 and 1980, averaging out to *one every 20 minutes* (*Morbidity & Mortality Weekly Report*, 1985).

Who Are the People Most Likely to Take Their Own Lives? Table 14-7 shows the major risk factors for suicide; but these bare facts come alive only when we consider the human lives involved:

■ An 18-year-old boy, despondent after a traffic accident that results in the wreck of his car, the revocation of his driving license, and the prospect of a trial, jumps off an icy bridge to his death. (In absolute numbers, most suicides occur among young white men. The gap between male and female suicides is widening.)

■ A 50-year-old man who has just been hospitalized for depression hangs himself because he believes the treatment will not help him. (Psychiatric inpatients are most vulnerable during the first week after admission—Copas & Robin, 1982).

■ A 16-year-old girl, constantly at odds with her parents because they disapprove of her boyfriend, breaks up with the boy and then shoots herself. (Girls and women attempt suicide about three times more often than boys and men do. But males are three times more "successful" in killing themselves, probably because they have generally used more lethal methods such as guns and ropes, while females have tended to take pills. This pattern is changing, as more females have turned to guns. Guns were the leading method for both sexes in 1980—MMWR, 1985).

TABLE 14-7 RISK FACTORS FOR SUICIDE

Characteristic	Highest Risk
Sex	Male (3 times as likely as females)
Race	White (2 times as likely as blacks)
Age	Highest rates: over age 45, especially in the fifties and sixties (but rates for younger people are increasing) Highest numbers: 15–34 years
Geographic location (U.S.)	The west (lowest rates in the northeast)
Season of year	Spring (March, April, May)
Family history	Other family members have attempted or carried out suicide
Personal history	Previous suicide attempts Previous psychiatric treatment Current or previous stressful life events
Health	Depression, schizophrenia, alcohol or drug abuse, physical illness
Personality	Dependency, helplessness, hopelessness, inability to accept help, difficulty forming close personal relationships, poor problem-solving ability (especially under stress)
Marital status	Divorced and widowed
Occupational status	Unemployed Medical doctors

Sources: Adapted from Boyer & Guthrie, 1985; *Harvard Medical School Health Letter*, 1986; *Morbidity and Mortality Weekly Report*, 1985.

What Makes People Resort to Suicide?   Many people become depressed—yet not all of them take the drastic step of suicide. Many people undergo severe life stresses— yet some of them are able to deal with them and continue living. What makes the difference?

BIOLOGICAL PREDISPOSITION   One line of research focuses on biochemical analysis. Such testing has found that people who have tried to commit suicide have lower levels of a substance known as 5-HIAA, a by-product of the neurotransmitter serotonin, in their spinal fluid, and that depressed patients who have made more frequent and more violent attempts have especially low levels of 5-HIAA. Other research suggests that high levels of cortisol, a compound found in the blood and the urine, are positively correlated with a higher risk of suicide (Boyer & Guthrie, 1985). Identifying such substances may help to predict which psychiatric patients are most likely to commit suicide.

INFLUENCE OF HEREDITY   Very few suicide risk factors occur among the Old Order Amish, a tightly knit community of people who live apart from society as most of us know it. They give each other a great deal of social support, encounter little stress in their everyday lives, rarely use or abuse drugs or alcohol, and consider suicide taboo. Thus it's easier among this group to isolate family patterns of suicide from the impact of other influences.

A recent study in an Amish community in Pennsylvania found a strong hereditary pattern for both affective disorders and suicide. Interviews with family members of the 26 persons who had committed suicide between 1880 and 1980 found that 24 of the 26 had had major affective disorders and that close relatives of the suicides also had a high rate of affective disorders. Furthermore, four multigenerational pedigrees (family trees) accounted for 73 percent of the suicides, even though they made up only 16 percent of the population in 1960 and 1980. This distribution suggests a strong role for inheritance, for major affective disorders and for suicide itself. Since not all those with affective disorders in these pedigrees tried to end their lives, however, it's clear that other factors, too, are at work. One of these factors may be the specific kinds of stress encountered, and another may lie in individual personality traits (Egeland & Sussex, 1985).

LIFE STRESSES   An argument with an important person in one's life, the end of a love affair or a marriage, a serious illness in oneself or a loved one, a court appearance for a criminal offense, the loss of a job, or the death of a spouse—all these factors are related to the risk of suicide (Boyer & Guthrie, 1985). And, as might be expected, different stressors assume different levels of importance at various stages in the life cycle.

Some professionals, for example, believe that teenage suicide rates have soared in recent years because adolescents today are under much more stress than their counterparts were in earlier days (Elkind, 1984). They are pressured to grow up more quickly, to assume more responsibility, to achieve at higher levels. Feeling unable to meet the demands placed on them, more adolescents may resort to suicide. Often, however, these young people do not really want to die. They want only to change their lives, and their suicide attempts are actually desperate pleas for attention and help.

Stresses that appear much later in life account for the high rate of suicide among the elderly, who have had to face many losses—of beloved friends and family members, of meaningful work, of physical health, and perhaps even of mental acuity. Older men may be at particular risk because they contrast their present role in life with the achievements of younger men and feel that they have outlived their usefulness.

At some time in your life someone you care for may be at the brink of committing suicide. Many people intent on killing themselves keep their plans secret, but signals of risk may appear well beforehand. By learning to recognize the warning signs of suicide and the kinds of actions that can prevent it, you might be able to save a life that is precious to you.

WARNING SIGNS OF SUICIDE
- Withdrawal from family or friends
- Talking about death, the hereafter, or suicide
- Giving away prized possessions
- Abuse of drugs, alcohol, or both
- Mood changes, such as anger, boredom, or apathy
- Unusual neglect of appearance
- Difficulty concentrating on work or school
- Staying away from work, school, or other usual activities
- Complaints of physical problems when nothing is actually organically wrong
- Changes in sleeping or eating habits—sleeping or eating much more or much less than usual

WHAT A CONCERNED PERSON CAN DO
- Talk to the person about his or her suicidal thoughts. Bringing up the subject will not put ideas into the mind of someone who has not al-

PSYCHOLOGY IN YOUR LIFE

HELPING TO PREVENT SUICIDE

ready thought of suicide, but it will bring feelings out into the open.
- Tell others in a position to do something—the person's parents or spouse or other family members, a close friend, a therapist, or a counselor. It's better to break a confidence than to let someone die.
- Do as much as possible to relieve the real-life pressures that seem intolerable, whether that means calling a rejecting boyfriend or girlfriend, lending money, or interceding with an employer.
- Show the person that there are other options besides death, even though none of them may be ideal. One therapist talked nonjudgmentally to a suicidal pregnant teenager, raising the possibility of a number of steps, including having an abortion, placing the baby for adoption, keeping the baby, telling her parents, telling the baby's father, and committing suicide.

She was able to rank the steps in order of preference, and suicide no longer headed the list. She and the therapist were now " 'haggling' about life'' (Shneidman, 1985). This therapist believes that it is important to remind the patient ''that life is often the choice among lousy alternatives. The key to well functioning is often to choose the least lousy alternative that is practicably attainable'' (p. 32).
- Consider the impact of choice of method. Suicide rates declined in England and Wales between 1960 and 1975, apparently because natural gas—which had been a popular method—was no longer in use. In the United States and in Australia, the number of suicides in which the method was barbiturates declined in proportion to the number of prescriptions written for barbiturates. Since the number of suicides involving guns has risen in recent years, gun control legislation would probably decrease such deaths. Many suicides are impulsive, and if a convenient means is not at hand, the depressed person may not go any further or may at least defer the action long enough to get help. Furthermore, a person who leans toward one method of suicide may be reluctant to use another (Eisenberg, 1980).

HEARING ABOUT OTHER SUICIDES   Two recent studies suggest that televised news reports of suicides and television dramas about suicide are related to an increase in suicides and suicide attempts among teenagers (Gould & Shaffer, 1986; Phillips & Carstensen, 1986). The authors of both these studies raise the possibility that an ''imitative effect'' causes some teenagers to attempt suicide. The correlations in these studies do not, however, necessarily indicate that there is a cause-and-effect relationship. Furthermore, even if reports about suicide do contribute to a rise in the suicide rate, their influence accounts for only a small part of the variation in the rate (Eisenberg, 1986).

Since suicide is often not so much a wish for death as a desire to avoid unbearable pain, either physical or emotional, friends and families of troubled people can often do a great deal to help those they love find support and courage to go on living; see the box ''Helping to Prevent Suicide.''

Personality Disorders

Charles Manson (the cult leader who was convicted of the brutal murders of seven Californians, including the actress Sharon Tate), as a boy, lied, stole, and played hooky from school repeatedly. As a young teenager, he began to engage in petty theft, for which he wound up in a succession of 18 state schools, reformatories, and other juvenile institutions. He graduated to car theft, the exploitation of naive young hippies, and murder. Because of his charismatic personality, he attracted many followers.

What Is a Personality Disorder?   Charles Manson is considered to have a personality disorder. In Chapter 13 we talked about *personality* as characteristic, consistent ways of seeing, thinking about, and relating to people and experiences in our lives. When these ways do not contribute to effective functioning, and when they are so rigid that even though they are maladaptive they continue to govern a person's life and to interfere with social or occupational functioning, we say that the person is suffering from a ***personality disorder.***

Personality disorders encompass a wide range of behaviors. They are more vaguely defined than some of the other disorders discussed in this chapter, but they still present distinctive profiles. Although these disorders vary considerably, they do have certain features in common. Most show up at a very early age and become more deeply ingrained over the years. Most people affected with them don't see anything wrong with the way they are functioning. They think it's the rest of the world that is out of step, that their own behavior is perfectly natural. It is easy to perpetuate this illusion, since the behavior of people with personality disorders does not interfere with everyday life to the same extent as behaviors associated with many other disturbances. When it does, these people usually do not recognize the degree to which they themselves are creating their own difficulties.

One personality disorder that has major implications for society in general is the disorder which is believed to have affected Charles Manson, *antisocial personality disorder;* it is described in the next section. Another, which was first identified in DSM III and is currently very controversial, is ***borderline personality disorder;*** it is described in the box "The Borderline Personality" (page 512) and Table 14-8.

The Antisocial Personality   Our prisons are full of them, and our hospitals and morgues are full of their victims. They frustrate law enforcement officers, social workers, the clergy, and their own parents, usually from a very early age. These people seem unreachable by most means. They commit acts that range from petty disobedience to unspeakable brutality, and then seem to feel no remorse. As children they don't respond to the ordinary rewards and punishments that motivate other youngsters. As adults they're resistant to most societal structures. They manipulate others, persistently violate other people's rights, have shallow emotions, need self-aggrandizement, cannot tolerate constraints, and have an underdeveloped conscience. Such people, often called *sociopaths* or *psychopaths*, are said to have the disorder **antisocial personality.**

Charles Manson is a typical sociopath, both in behavior and in personal history. He was the son of a teenage prostitute, he never knew his father, and he was abandoned by his stepfather when he was still a baby. At the age of 5, he lost his mother, too, since she was imprisoned for robbery. Such a pattern of growing up without both parents, being removed from home (as Manson was when he was sent to live with an aunt and uncle, and then again when he was sent to one juvenile institution after another), and living in poverty is common among sociopaths.

There is no clear correlation between antisocial personality and unstable family life, however, nor is there any known organic basis, such as specific brain damage. There is, however, a correlation with abnormal EEGs and with abnormal skin conductance of electricity, indicating a possible physiological element. This factor seems hereditary, as shown by adoption studies and by the higher concordance rates

(Eric Roth/Picture Cube)

Many people are in prison because they have antisocial personality disorder, a condition that makes them immune to the moral, familial, and societal restraints which govern the behavior of most of us. The disorder seems to run in families, spurred by both heredity and environment; it affects many more males than females.

Personality disorders *Mental disorders characterized by maladaptive behavior patterns that appear at an early age, become more ingrained over time, and are not viewed as abnormal by the person exhibiting them.*

Borderline personality *Personality disorder characterized by instability in several areas, including mood, self-image, and relationships.*

Antisocial personality *Personality disorder characterized by behaviors that violate the rights of others.*

It has been suggested that Marilyn Monroe, Adolf Hitler, Lawrence of Arabia, Zelda Fitzgerald, and Thomas Wolfe were all borderline personalities; and this disorder has been diagnosed in many lesser-known people (Sass, 1982). Although *borderline personality* had been recognized for years by psychoanalysts, it came to prominence only fairly recently and was not given "official status" as a psychiatric disorder until DSM III was published in 1980. Its prevalence is variously cited as between 3 and 15 percent of the population and 20 to 50 percent of psychiatric patients (*Harvard Medical School Mental Health Letter*, 1985b; Sass, 1982; Tanne, 1983).

The diagnosis is a difficult one, and the name is confusing. What are people with this syndrome on the borderline of? At one time they were thought to be teetering between neurosis and psychosis (particularly, between neurosis and schizophrenia). Today the "border" seems to be considered the person's identity. Borderline personalities are people who have trouble knowing who they are: more than anything else, they are unstable and unpredictable. Instability is the most crucial characteristic of the disorder; it can show up in interpersonal relations, mood, and self-image.

Other than instability, no single feature is always present; but the characteristics listed in Table 14-8 provide general criteria for diagnosis

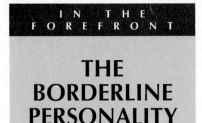

IN THE FOREFRONT

THE BORDERLINE PERSONALITY

(DSM III, 1980). People suffering from borderline personality are hard to be close to. They have intense, but usually short-lived, relationships with others. They drive others away because their moods are mercurial. They are loving one minute and full of anger the next; their emotional needs are immense; they become too dependent; and they habitually take advantage of other people's feelings for them. This disorder seems closely related to several other personality disorders (narcissistic, histrionic, and antisocial disorders) and to depression. Some of the typical self-destructive behaviors (like drinking, sexual promiscuity, or gambling) associated with borderline personality may be desperate attempts to shake off depression.

The cause of the disorder is hard to pin down, and more research is called for. Since the category includes so many different types of people, it is possible that the subtypes have different causes. There is some evidence for a genetic basis: traits

often seem to run in families, and borderline personality resembles some aspects of affective disorders and schizophrenia, in which heredity seems to play a key role. The environment may also be important; but the role of experience is not clear, either in early childhood or later in life. Some observers believe that disturbed and unstable family relationships early in life—which may include parental rejection, abuse, or separation—may prevent a child from forming a stable sense of self (Groves, 1981; *Harvard Medical School Mental Health Letter*, 1985b).

Treatment usually consists of psychotherapy, psychiatric drugs, or a combination of therapy and drugs. Short-term hospitalization is sometimes called for in extreme cases. The most effective treatment seems to be long-term individual psychotherapy, one or more times per week for several years. Such therapy usually focuses on help in coping with immediate problems, support at times of extreme disorganization and emotional instability, and attempts to help the patient understand and change self-defeating behavior. The condition tends to persist over a period of years; its victims continue to have problems with impulse control and with personal relationships. Many borderline patients, however, do become more stable and function better by their mid-thirties (*Harvard Medical School Mental Health Letter*, 1986).

(Wide World Photos)

Marilyn Monroe, the beautiful, talented movie actress who died of an overdose of sleeping pills at the age of 36, may have suffered from a borderline personality. The trauma of a childhood in which she didn't know her father and lived in a series of foster homes may have been a major factor in her difficulties in forming a stable sense of self, the key feature of this disorder.

TABLE 14-8 DIAGNOSTIC CRITERIA FOR BORDERLINE PERSONALITY DISORDER

1 *Impulsivity or unpredictability* in at least two areas that are potentially self-destructive, such as money, sex, gambling, drug or alcohol abuse, shoplifting, overeating, or physical self-damage.
2 Pattern of *unstable and intense relationships* with others, marked by changing attitudes that run the gamut from idealizing people to devaluing them, and by the manipulation and exploitation of other people.
3 *Inappropriate, intense, or poorly controlled anger,* marked by outbursts of temper.
4 *Identity disturbance,* shown in uncertainty about self-image, gender identity, long-term goals, values, and loyalties. (Typical statements are, "I feel like my sister when I am good" and "I don't know who I am.")
5 *Changeable moods,* with marked shifts into depression, irritability, or anxiety; these moods usually last from a few hours to a few days before giving way to normal ones.
6 *Intolerance of being alone,* leading to frantic efforts to avoid being alone and to depression when solitude is unavoidable.
7 *Physical self-damage* that can include attempts at suicide, self-mutilation, recurrent accidents, or physical fights with others.
8 Chronic feeling of *emptiness or boredom.*

Note: To be diagnosed as having borderline personality disorder, a person has to have at least five of these characteristics as a usual and habitual pattern (not limited to occasional episodes of illness). They either impair the person's everyday life to a significant extent or cause great unhappiness.

Source: Adapted from DSM III, pp. 322–333.

for identical than fraternal twins (*Harvard Medical School Mental Health Letter,* 1985a). Most sociopaths are male: about 3 percent of American men, but fewer than 1 percent of American women, are estimated to have antisocial personality disorder. The condition seems to run in families, affected by both genetic and environmental influences.

Schizophrenic Disorders

Earlier in this chapter we met "Sylvia Frumkin," whose life has been exhaustively detailed in a sensitive, compassionate book (S. Sheehan, 1982). In many ways, Sylvia is typical of people suffering from schizophrenic disorders, the most severe and disabling of all the psychological disturbances. Her bizarre and handicapping symptoms, the early onset of her disorder, the great difficulty she has had receiving effective treatment, and the devastating impact her condition has had on her own life and on that of her family are all typical. In other ways, however, no single patient can be considered typical, since no one feature is always present in this disorder. It seems, in fact, that a cluster of separate illnesses make up the syndrome known as ***schizophrenia.***

Traditionally schizophrenia has been broken down into four subtypes—disorganized, catatonic, paranoid, and undifferentiated (DSM III, 1980); see Table 14-9 (page 514). These categories have proved hard to use, however. It is often difficult to decide which subtype a person belongs in—and even when a diagnosis of a particular subtype is made, this system does not help therapists to decide how to treat the person (Davison & Neale, 1986). A more recent distinction is between positive and negative symptoms of schizophrenia, described in the next section, "Symptoms of Schizophrenia." This classification seems potentially more useful, since it has implications for prognosis and treatment.

Symptoms of Schizophrenia If we look at Sylvia's symptoms and check them against DSM III, we are struck by the many ways in which she corresponds to the definition. First of all, schizophrenia is clearly considered a psychosis, a psychological disorder characterized by a loss of contact with reality. How do schizophrenics show this split from the real world?

Schizophrenia Psychosis characterized by at least one of the following: delusions, hallucinations, or thought disturbances.

TABLE 14-9 TRADITIONAL SUBTYPES OF SCHIZOPHRENIA

Type	Distinguishing Characteristics
Disorganized	Person tends to be incoherent and act silly or incongruous or show no emotion at all. Not likely to suffer from major delusions, although minor delusions and hallucinations are common. Behaves oddly, showing grimaces and other strange mannerisms, complaining of imaginary ailments, and withdrawing socially. This subtype is the most disabling. It shows up early, cuts the patient off from normal life, and continues to get worse, with virtually no hope of recovery.
Catatonic	Person seems to be in a trance, often holding the body in a contorted, rigid posture, not speaking, not showing any signs of hearing or seeing what goes on around him or her. Sometimes these periods of stupor alternate with extremes of excitement. If not supervised, the catatonic may hurt self or others.
Paranoid	Person has delusions of grandeur or of being persecuted, or hallucinations with either of these themes. Likely to be full of anxiety and anger and to show these feelings by being argumentative or by actual violence. May worry about gender identity, afraid of being homosexual. With other people, either stilted and formal or extremely intense.
Undifferentiated	Person has prominent delusions, hallucinations, incoherence, or grossly disorganized behavior. Does not fit into any of the other categories.

Source: DSM III, 1980.

Some of the symptoms of schizophrenia are considered *positive symptoms,* since they are behaviors shown by schizophrenics and not other people. Another group of symptoms are referred to as *negative symptoms,* since they represent defects in normal abilities (Andreasen & Olsen, 1982). Patients whose symptoms come from both groups about equally are in the category *mixed schizophrenia.*

Schizophrenics whose symptoms are mostly positive differ in a number of important ways from those with mostly negative symptoms. One of the most important distinctions is in prognosis. People with positive symptoms have a better chance of improving, since negative symptoms are both more crippling and more resistant to treatment. People with negative symptoms are likely to have had a poorer overall adjustment before the onset of schizophrenia and to have a lower level of functioning afterward, as well as impaired cognitive functioning and a history of brain injury, neither of which is typically found in "positive" schizophrenics.

Among the positive symptoms of schizophrenia are *delusions,* in which people believe they are being persecuted, think that other people can hear their thoughts, or are convinced that their thoughts have been removed from their head; *disturbances of thought,* marked by incoherence or illogical thinking (they shift ideas quickly from one topic to another, completely unrelated one, without seeming to be aware of the disjointed quality of their thoughts); *hallucinations,* in which they hear voices, see apparitions, or feel sensations (like snakes crawling around inside their bodies); repeated instances of *bizarre or disorganized behavior* (like collecting and hoarding garbage); and *inappropriate emotional responses* (laughing when talking about a sad or frightening experience).

Negative symptoms include *vague, impoverished speech* (leaving out words or putting them together without any grammatical frame); *blunted or flat emotional responses* (showing very little emotion or none at all); *inability to experience pleasure or feel intimacy;* and *difficulty paying attention.*

Other features of schizophrenia are a disturbed sense of self, withdrawal from the real world into a private world of fantasy, inability to work toward a goal, and abnormalities of posture and motor movements (rigidity, jumping around, grimacing). No single feature is always present, but at some phase of the illness either delusions, hallucinations, or thought disturbances always appear (DSM III, 1980).

(Grunnitus/Monkmeyer Press)

People affected by the catatonic type of schizophrenia, like this woman, will sometimes stand rigidly in one bizarre posture for hours, resisting all efforts to move them.

Course of Schizophrenia Schizophrenic disorders usually begin during adolescence or early adulthood. Here, too, Sylvia Frumkin is typical: she went from being a bright, achieving child to being an adult who is unable to function even marginally.

Schizophrenia generally goes through a preliminary phase, called the *prodromal* phase, which marks a deterioration in functioning before the illness goes into its active phase. During the *active* phase, the psychotic symptoms appear. This phase is followed by a *residual* phase, during which some of the psychotic symptoms may persist while others go into remission and disappear, at least for the time being. The symptoms must last for at least 6 months to warrant a diagnosis of schizophrenic disorder.

A diagnosed schizophrenic who shows no signs at all of the illness is considered to be *in remission*. Most commonly, schizophrenics have increasingly severe attacks of symptoms and become more and more impaired with each episode. Those for whom the prognosis seems to be best are people who appeared quite healthy before they showed any symptoms, people whose illness seemed to have been precipitated by disturbing life events, people whose illness came on suddenly and in midlife as opposed to adolescence or early adulthood, and people whose relatives have suffered from depressive or manic disorders. Although complete recovery is occasionally reported—as by the author of the book *I Never Promised You a Rose Garden* (H. Green, 1964)—it is uncommon, especially if the condition has persisted more than 5 years (Manschreck, 1981).

Men and women are equally likely to become schizophrenic, but the illness shows up differently in the two sexes (Lewine, 1981). Its onset is earlier for men—usually before age 25—whereas for women it more often appears after age 25. Symptoms are different, too: men are more apt to show negative symptoms and women positive ones. These differences are attributed variously to hormonal influences, to females' earlier maturation (which may slow the development of schizophrenia), and to different kinds of psychosocial stress. Women, for example, are more apt to develop the illness at times of family conflict and childbirth, whereas in men it is associated with leaving the parental home, getting a job, and being in competitive situations.

Schizophrenia is more common among the poor than among the middle and upper classes: 6 percent of slum dwellers are likely to be diagnosed as having a schizophrenic disorder at least once, compared with 1 to 2 percent of the general population (Robins et al., 1984; U.S. Dept. of Health and Human Services, 1981b). This difference in the incidence of schizophrenia may point to the role of psychosocial stress in triggering the disorder.

Causes of Schizophrenic Disorders: Current Perspectives There are many theories about the cause of schizophrenia, but most of the available research seems to point to a combination of factors: an inherited biological predisposition, which is then triggered by environmental stress. Let us now look at the evidence for this point of view.

GENETIC FACTORS *Evidence for genetic transmission* Can parents pass schizophrenia on to their children? Is there a gene for schizophrenia that travels through generations as a hereditary condition like any other? A large body of evidence points to the likelihood of a genetic predisposition for schizophrenic disorders. This predisposition is probably carried by several different genes, each of which has a small additive effect, so that the more of these genes a person has, the greater the inherited predisposition for schizophrenia. It is also possible that different kinds of schizophrenia are affected by different genes (Faraone & Tsuang, 1985). Where does this evidence come from? The data are mostly from studies of adopted children, of twins, and of families. Let us consider each of these lines of research.

Adoption studies: The strongest evidence of an inherited predisposition for schizophrenia comes from studies of adopted children. First, children who are born to schizophrenic women and are then removed from their mothers at an early age and adopted by families that have no schizophrenic members are more likely to develop schizophrenia themselves than are adopted children whose biological mothers were not schizophrenic (Heston, 1966; Kety, Rosenthal, Wender, Schulsinger, & Jacobsen, 1975). On the other hand, children of normal biological mothers who are adopted into families in which an adoptive parent later becomes schizophrenic are no more likely to develop the disorder themselves than are children in the general population (Kety, Rosenthal, Wender, & Schulsinger, 1968). In other words, the association exists between schizophrenic adults and the parents who conceived them, not the ones who raised them, suggesting a hereditary component for schizophrenia.

Twin studies: Studies of identical and fraternal twins also support a genetic link. The identical twin of a schizophrenic (who has exactly the same genetic legacy) is four times more likely to develop the disorder than is the fraternal twin of a schizophrenic. The geneticist Irving I. Gottesman has said, "If you are a betting person, the existence of an identical twin to a schizophrenic is still the best single predictor of future schizophrenia" (1979, p. 57). In the rare cases when identical twins have been reared apart, they are just as likely to be concordant for schizophrenic disorders as those brought up together (Gottesman & Shields, 1966).

Family studies: Another way of investigating the heritability of a trait is to look at a person's family tree and to ask, "What are the risk rates that the relatives of this person will develop the disorder, as compared with the population at large?" When consanguinity (blood relationship) studies have been done, researchers have found that relatives of people with schizophrenic disorders are more likely to develop the disease themselves than are unrelated people, and the closer the blood relationship (the more genes shared), the higher the risk (Erlenmeyer-Kimling, Cornblatt, & Fleiss, 1979). In the general population, for example, the risk of developing schizophrenia is about 1 percent; the risk for a person with one schizophrenic parent is 11 to 12 percent; and the risk for a person with two schizophrenic parents is about 40 percent (Erlenmeyer-Kimling et al., 1979).

How hereditary, then, are schizophrenic disorders? In none of these lines of research—adoption studies, twin studies, or family studies—is the risk rate 100 percent. Not all children of schizophrenic parents go on to develop schizophrenia, nor do all identical twins of affected persons get the disease themselves. This imperfect correlation leads to the assumption that some people inherit a predisposition to this disorder that may never be expressed unless something occurs to bring it out. This "something" may be a stressful situation.

The predisposition to schizophrenia may show up in other ways. Relatives of schizophrenic patients sometimes show eccentricities that could be considered muted forms of schizophrenic symptoms—unsociability, coldness, hypersensitivity, fanaticism, or militancy. These relatives are often diagnosed as "neurotics" (Wender & Klein, 1981b).

It is also possible that a "schizoid trait" can actually be desirable in some contexts (Claridge, 1972). When carried by a highly intelligent person who has grown up in a secure, nurturing environment, such a trait may lead to unusual creativity. This trait may lead a person to use language in unusual ways, to make up words, to put them together in new combinations, and to make other novel and creative connections among ideas. In less favorable circumstances, the trait may lead someone into the madness of schizophrenia.

We still do not know how a hereditary tendency toward schizophrenia interacts with the environment to produce the illness. Gottesman (1979) suggests that heredity accounts for about 80 percent of the cause of schizophrenia, but that the 20 percent environmental factor is critical "in determining whether the person who is at high risk for genetic reasons does or does not break down" (p. 69). For example, a person with a very mild predisposition toward schizophrenia may function normally until late in life when major stresses may trigger a schizophrenic reaction. For example, the combination of death of a spouse and onset of deafness, both of which may bring about social isolation, might have this effect.

Furthermore, what one person experiences as highly stressful events, another may take in stride, not reacting strongly to them and, therefore, not experiencing ill effects. This may explain why two people with the same genetic predisposition (like identical twins) may not react identically to what appear to be the same environmental factors.

How genetic transmission may be manifested: Brain dysfunctions   Inherited vulnerability to schizophrenia may lie within the functioning of the brain. With the development of sophisticated techniques (such as the advanced x-ray techniques described in Chapter 2), researchers have identified a number of abnormalities that suggest that at least 20 to 35 percent of diagnosed schizophrenics have some sort of brain impairment (Seidman, 1983). This is a high enough proportion to suggest that physiological abnormalities may cause the syndrome in some people. Since brain abnormality is not found in the majority of schizophrenics, however, it is clear that this is not the only answer.

In one recent investigation by magnetic resonance imaging (MRI) comparing the brains of 38 schizophrenics and 49 normal subjects, differences showed up between the two groups. The schizophrenics had significantly smaller frontal lobes, as well as smaller skulls and cerebrums, possibly suggesting abnormal early development that retarded brain and skull growth. The patients with "negative" symptoms were more likely than those with "positive" symptoms to have smaller cerebrums and skulls, but no more likely to have smaller frontal lobes (Andreasen et al., 1986).

In other studies, patients with "negative" symptoms were found to have the most severe brain defects, which may explain the fact that their illness is usually more severe and resistant to treatment. Their brains are more likely to show enlargement of the ventricles (small, pouchlike cavities) and cerebral atrophy (deterioration of brain tissue), especially in the frontal lobe. Dysfunctions of the brain stem and cerebellum are also suspected (Seidman, 1983).

Findings of damage in the frontal lobe seem to support the role of the neurotransmitter *dopamine* in creating a chemical imbalance in the brain. Amphetamines, which can cause or worsen schizophrenic psychosis, release dopamine into the brain pathways. Neuroleptic drugs (like chlorpromazine, or Thorazine), on the other hand, which are widely used to reduce the agitation of schizophrenics, work by blocking receptors and preventing the transmission of dopamine. Thus, just by knowing how these drugs work, we may be able to conclude that too much dopamine in the brain may cause schizophrenic symptoms. We still cannot come to a definitive conclusion, however, because even though an impressive amount of research points to dopamine as a causative factor, researchers have not been able to find any consistent changes in metabolites or enzymes related to the group of neurotransmitters that includes dopamine. It is possible, then, that dopamine plays a secondary rather than a primary role in causing schizophrenia (Nathan & Harris, 1980). On the other hand, another link to dopamine is revealed in the finding of nearly twice the usual number of dopamine receptors in the brains of schizophrenics (Iversen, 1979). This may mean, then, that schizophrenics get double the effects from the same level of dopamine.

Patients with "positive" symptoms show abnormally high levels of arousal in reacting to various experiences, suggesting a possible failure to appropriately inhibit the arousal system in the brain stem. This may result from dysfunction in the limbic region, in the midbrain, and in the area of the upper brain stem. Defects in attention and defects in arousal have also been found in bipolar illness. People diagnosed with bipolar disorder show greater dysfunction of the right hemisphere of the brain, whereas those diagnosed as schizophrenic show greater dysfunction of the left hemisphere (Seidman, 1983).

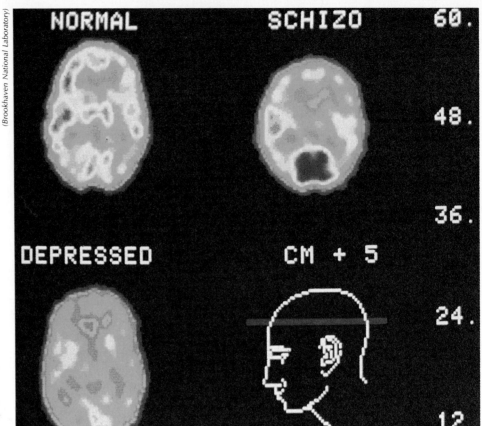

(Brookhaven National Laboratory)

This picture shows differences in the metabolism of the blood sugar glucose in the brains of a normal, a depressed, and a schizophrenic person, as shown by PET scanning. The red line on the profile of the head shows the brain area scanned. The color scale shows the units of glucose metabolized. The normal brain is shown at top left. The schizophrenic brain, top right, shows a decreased glucose metabolic rate in the frontal cortex region. The brain of the depressed subject, lower left, shows reduced rates all over the brain.

Another new technique has found physiological differences in brain activity in persons with schizophrenia and bipolar disorder. Through positron-emission tomography (PET), scientists can monitor chemical activity in the brain. Using this technique, they have seen differences in the metabolism of the sugar glucose (which provides more than 80 percent of the energy used by the brain) in psychotic patients. Those with schizophrenia show a lower level of glucose metabolism in the frontal cortex, and those with bipolar disorder show a higher level of activity in the right temporal region during their manic phases. PET scanning may thus aid in diagnosing a patient without clear-cut symptoms, and offer a clue to the origin of these psychoses as well.

Furthermore, there are other unexplained physical differences, such as the "peculiar-looking" capillaries (tiny blood vessels) found in the brains of some schizophrenics, especially in those of persons with chronic cases (Nichol & Heston, 1979). The fact that capillary peculiarities are also found in mentally retarded people, in old people with senile dementia, and in epileptics points to another possible avenue of research. We need to remind ourselves, however, that almost every line of research over the years has found some differences between normal people and at least some people with schizophrenia (Herbert, 1982). Since some of these differences—for instance, higher rates of tuberculosis—were later explained as results of the disease rather than causes (as outgrowths of poor care, for example), we need to be cautious about interpreting whatever new data we find.

One question that researchers constantly have to ask themselves has to do with the difference between correlation and causation. Suppose faulty enzymes or differences in enzyme levels are, indeed, found between schizophrenics and healthy people. Is it possible that the schizophrenic behavior has in some way changed the biochemical balance, rather than having been caused by it? Although this does not seem likely, it is possible, and it does have to be taken into account.

The difference in brain dysfunction among persons with schizophrenia—the kind, the extent, and whether it exists at all—indicates that there are different forms of the disorder, probably with different causes, and that psychosocial causes play a role in some patients.

ENVIRONMENTAL FACTORS   In contrast to explanations of schizophrenia which look for answers *inside* the affected person—such as the psychoanalytic explanation (which is not discussed here) and the genetic explanation—environmental approaches focus on the world he or she lives in.

"Family pathology"   Schizophrenia has been attributed to the stress of living in families that are disorganized and unhealthy because of conflicts between the parents or because of mental illness in one or both parents (Lidz & Fleck, 1960). It has also been thought that parents could cause their children to become disturbed by saying one thing verbally but sending contradictory messages with body language, facial expressions, or actions. Such mixed messages are called a *double bind,* because no matter how the receivers of them react, they can't win. A familiar example is the mother who complained that her son never acted affectionate but drew away from his kisses or hugs (Bateson, Jackson, Haley, & Weakland, 1956).

One problem with these explanations is that they don't explain why some people who grow up in chaotic families are able to lead satisfying, fulfilling, normal lives, nor do they explain why some people who grow up in homes that appear loving and orderly do go on to develop schizophrenia. In addition, we come back to the problem of causation versus correlation. It is eminently possible that parents become disturbed and that homes become disorganized *because* a family member has schizophrenia—in other words, that the causation goes in the other direction. Perhaps something in the child comes out at an early age to disturb the parent-child relationship. The parents' attempts to be affectionate may, for example, be rebuffed by an angry child. Then, later, the stresses of living with a symptomatic schizophrenic take their toll on the entire family.

Life stress as a trigger   Current thinking generally considers disorganized family life and other stressful situations to be contributory causes of schizophrenia in someone who is already genetically predisposed. Researchers who have studied the children of schizophrenic parents have found a number of risk factors that, *in combination with inherited susceptibility,* may trigger the illness. These factors include habitually confused and negative communication from parents (like the double bind); poor emotional bonding with the mother during the first 3 years of the child's life; separation from parents into an unstable home life; complications of childbirth; and cognitive, intellectual, motor-coordination, or social deficits in childhood (Watt, 1984). Other observers have identified as the triggering stress the financial and social strains of lower-class living in industrial countries, especially in times of political upheaval and high unemployment (Warner, 1986).

It is a truism in science that the more theories we have about something, the less we know about it. This is certainly true of schizophrenia. Our search for answers may be more productive if we broaden it to include many different causes, rather than try to isolate one single cause. With this point of view, maybe we can come up with some partial answers here and there and eventually fit them together to form one picture. Until then, research continues.

Obviously, theories about the causes of psychological disturbances influence the ways these disturbances will be treated, as we'll see in Chapter 15 when we discuss various kinds of therapy now in use.

SUMMARY

1 Abnormal psychology is the study of emotional disturbances and abnormal behavior. It is difficult to develop an all-encompassing definition of what is abnormal.

2 In our society, the psychologically healthy person is considered to be someone who perceives reality fairly accurately, who behaves somewhat similarly to most other people in most situations, who does productive work, who can handle the tasks of everyday living, and whose moods remain fairly even and appropriate to the situation. Of course, not all people who deviate from this profile are severely disturbed.

3 Throughout history, people have offered different explanations of the causes of abnormality and, therefore, different ideas of how to treat it. During the Middle Ages, mental disorders were thought to be the result of sin and possession by the devil; this position is called the moral model. The medical model considers mental disorders to be the result of illness. According to the psychoanalytic model, abnormal behavior is the result of conflict among the id, the ego, and the superego. The behavioral model maintains that abnormal ways of thinking and acting are learned, largely through the mechanisms of conditioning and modeling.

4 Additional viewpoints about the cause of mental disorders include the social-consequence model, which holds that many disorders that the medical model would view as illnesses are more appropriately considered problems of living that arise out of difficulties in coping with society. The sociocultural model focuses on the role of society in causing disturbed behavior. The humanistic model views abnormal behavior as a result of the failure to achieve self-actualization. None of the models can account for all types of mental disorders.

5 About 1 in 5 American adults (about 29 million people) suffer from some kind of psychological disturbance in any 6-month period. Only about one-fifth of these seek treatment, the percentage varying with sex and the specific disorder. Anxiety, substance abuse (of alcohol and drugs, in a 4 to 1 ratio), and affective disorders (such as depression and bipolar disorder) are the three most common mental health problems.

6 Diagnosis of mental disorders is difficult. The third edition of the *Diagnostic and Statistical Manual of Mental Disorders* (DSM III) is a controversial document published by the American Psychiatric Association in an effort to make diagnosis easier.

7 DSM III has eliminated the term *neurosis*. Disorders that used to be called neuroses are now classified as anxiety disorders, certain affective disorders, somatoform disorders, and dissociative disorders. People with these disorders have difficulty coping with some aspects of their lives but generally do not need hospitalization.

8 Anxiety is a state of apprehension, fearful uncertainty, or dread caused by some real or imagined threat. Anxiety disorders include phobic disorders, obsessive-compulsive disorders, post-traumatic stress disorder, panic disorders, and generalized anxiety disorders. Anxiety disorders affect some 8.3 percent of adult Americans.

9 A phobia is a persistent, intense, and unrealistic fear of an object or situation, such as snakes or open spaces. Obsessions are persistent unwanted ideas, thoughts, images, or impulses that cannot be eliminated rationally; compulsions are urges to repeat certain unwanted acts. Post-traumatic stress disorder may occur after a traumatic event such as military combat and may involve nightmares about the event and overreaction to stimuli that recall it. Panic disorders are attacks of terror that include such physical symptoms as dizziness, difficulties in breathing, and sweating. In generalized anxiety disorders, people feel anxiety without being able to ascribe their discomfort to any particular situation or event.

10 Medical, psychoanalytic, and behavioral explanations of anxiety disorders have been offered. The medical approach looks to biological explanations. According to the psychoanalytic approach, these conditions are the result of conflict between id, ego, and superego. Learning theorists hold that anxiety disorders arise from inappropriate learning.

11 Somatoform disorders, such as conversion disorders, are characterized by physical symptoms for which no physical basis can be found. They are thought to arise from psychological factors.

12 Dissociative disorders involve sudden temporary alterations in either consciousness, identity, or motor behavior. Examples include multiple personality, psychogenic amnesia, psychogenic fugue, and depersonalization disorder. Psychoanalytic theorists hold that these disorders are the result of repression. Learning theorists consider them to be avoidance responses.

13 Affective disorders—depression and mania—are disorders of mood. They affect about 6 percent of American adults and take a number of different forms and levels of severity. Although depressive episodes differ in intensity, depressed people in general have difficulty sleeping, eating, and concentrating. People suffering from depression with psychotic features may also experience delusions, hallucinations, and disordered and confused thinking. Researchers studying depression have offered genetic and physiological explanations, psychoanalytic explanations, and cognitive explanations. During a manic episode, people show extremely elated behavior. Bipolar disorder is the condition consisting of one or more manic episodes generally alternating with depressive episodes.

14 Fifteen percent of people with severe depression eventually take their own lives. Possible explanations for suicide include a biological predisposition (which may be inherited), particular life stresses, and hearing about other suicides.

15 Personality disorders are maladaptive behavior patterns that appear at an early age, become more ingrained over time, and are not viewed as abnormal by the person exhibiting them. Two personality disorders are antisocial

personality (characterized by behaviors which violate others' rights) and borderline personality (characterized by impulsive, unpredictable, manipulative behavior).

16 Schizophrenia is a disorder characterized by loss of contact with reality. DSM III describes four major subtypes of schizophrenic disorders: disorganized, catatonic, paranoid, and undifferentiated. Other classification systems describe "positive" and "negative" symptoms. Positive symptoms include delusions, disturbances of thought, hallucinations, bizarre and disorganized behavior, and inappropriate emotional responses. Negative symptoms include vague and impoverished speech, blunt or flat emotional response, inability to experience pleasure or feel intimacy, and difficulty paying attention. Although no single symptom is always present, delusions, hallucinations, or thought disturbances always appear at some phase of the illness. Schizophrenic disorders afflict about 1 percent of adult Americans.

17 Current perspectives on the cause of schizophrenic disorders consider genetic factors and environmental factors, such as double-bind situations and stress. There appears to be an inherited susceptibility for schizophrenia that is "triggered" in an unfavorable environment.

KEY TERMS

Abnormal psychology (page 482)
Affective disorders (501)
Agoraphobia (496)
Amnesia (500)
Antisocial personality (511)
Anxiety (495)
Anxiety disorders (495)
Behavioral model (486)
Bipolar disorder (502)
Borderline personality (511)
Compulsions (496)
Concordant (498)

Conversion disorder (499)
Depersonalization disorder (501)
Depression (502)
Dissociative disorder (500)
DSM III (491)
Dysthymic disorder (502)
Family, or systems, model (487)
Generalized anxiety disorder (498)
Humanistic model (488)
Mania (502)

Medical model (486)
Moral model (485)
Multiple personality (500)
Obsessions (496)
Panic disorders (497)
Personality disorder (511)
Phobia (495)
Post-traumatic stress disorder (497)
Psychoanalytic model (486)
Psychogenic amnesia (500)
Psychogenic fugue (500)
Psychoses (494)

Schizophrenia (513)
Seasonal affective disorder (SAD) (507)
Simple phobia (495)
Social-consequence model (487)
Social phobia (496)
Sociocultural model (488)
Somatoform disorder (499)
Unipolar disorder (502)

SUGGESTED READINGS

AMERICAN PSYCHIATRIC ASSOCIATION. (1980). *Diagnostic and statistical manual of mental disorders.* (3d ed.). Washington, DC: American Psychiatric Association. The most recent edition of the DSM. This controversial document (DSM III) contains criteria for diagnosing mental disorders.

CHERNIN, K. (1985). *The hungry self.* New York: Times Books. A probing analysis of women's often troubled relationship with food. After looking at the cultural significance and personal consequences of eating disorders, the author concludes that eating problems often conceal identity problems that stem from troubled mother-daughter relationships.

KLAGSBRUN, F. (1976). *Too young to die.* Boston: Houghton Mifflin. A straightforward, readable picture of the myths and realities of youthful suicide that explores motives, describes symptoms of depression, and suggests ways to help those thinking about ending their lives.

SEIDENBERG, R., & DECROW, K. (1983). *Women who marry houses.* New York: McGraw-Hill. A penetrating discussion of agoraphobia, the fear of leaving home, with an emphasis on the female case.

SHEEHAN, S. (1982). *Is there no place on earth for me?* Boston: Houghton Mifflin. An absorbing, true account of "Sylvia Frumkin," a paranoid schizophrenic who spent 17 years of her life in and out of mental institutions.

SPITZER, R. L., SKODOL, A. E., GIBBON, M., & WILLIAMS, J. B. W. (1983). New York: McGraw-Hill. A collection of 54 case histories that include information about diagnosis, treatment, and prognosis.

C H A P T E R

15

THERAPY

■ What are the differences among the three major forms of therapy—psychotherapy, medical therapy, and environmental therapy?

■ What are the differences among dynamic, behavioral, and humanistic psychotherapy?

■ How have the cognitive, interpersonal, and brief approaches influenced psychotherapy?

■ What impact has the shift of chronically mentally ill people from hospital to community care had on both patients and society?

■ Is therapy really effective?

■ Is one method superior to the others?

■ How important is the "fit" between client and therapist?

Dr. L. asks me to go into the personal "space" near my 15-year-old daughter (whom I'll call "Molly" here to preserve her privacy). I walk toward Molly, who is standing in the middle of the room, and I stand right in front of her, as close as I can without touching her. I don't put my arms around her the way I used to do so often and so easily when she was little. Dr. L. says, "You came very close to Molly—and then you backed off."

I feel silly about this exercise, and I feel angry with Dr. L. for what she has said. Probably both feelings stem from the fact that the exercise has touched a raw nerve. Over the past couple of years Molly and I have been having fierce, intense arguments. I have been tentative about going into her space—wondering whether I need to be invited, whether I am welcome.

Three of us—my husband and Molly and I—have come to see Dr. L., a clinical psychologist who specializes in family therapy, to help our family resolve the problems we all know exist but don't know how to solve. Molly and I argue constantly. She keeps doing things she knows her father and I don't approve of. He and she hardly talk at all. He talks to me and she talks to me and I talk to both of them. I don't like being in the middle. Our other two daughters feel that we're not paying enough attention to them— and they're probably right. And things don't seem to be getting any better.

Like many families that go into family therapy (which is one of the kinds of treatment for psychological problems that are described in this chapter), we were catapulted into the experience by a rebellious adolescent. In the process, all of us learned much about ourselves as individuals, about our relationships with each other and with my husband's parents and my own, and about some of the family myths that our children were trying to live up to.

Our ten sessions in family therapy helped our family to function better. It helped us express thoughts and feelings that we had kept hidden. It helped us see how much we love each other. It cleared away much of the emotional confusion that had settled like a dense fog on some family beliefs, obscuring their origins.

Today, some ten years later, Molly and I are again close and again hugging each other. When problems arise (as they do in all families), we try to remember some of the concepts that we learned in family therapy.

—From the notebooks of Sally Olds

Family therapy is only one kind of treatment offered for emotional troubles. In this chapter we look at many different kinds of treatment for psychological problems, some of which deal only with the mind (as in the "talking cure," psychoanalysis), some of which treat the body (through drugs, surgery, or electroconvulsive therapy), and some of which combine physical and psychological approaches (such as administering drugs along with sessions of psychotherapy).

Most people who seek treatment, or **therapy,** for some kind of psychological problem do so because they feel powerless to change actions, thoughts, or feelings that prevent them from achieving life goals and being happy (Morse & Watson, 1977). In this chapter we describe people who receive therapy (these people are usually called *clients* or *patients*), people who administer it (*therapists*), and the means therapists employ. We also describe and evaluate various kinds of therapy.

...y General term for a variety of ...atments for psychological problems.

WHO UNDERGOES THERAPY?

Some people who seek psychological counseling or treatment are basically healthy but are undergoing a severe crisis in their lives. Others have such disabling emotional problems that they cannot function in the community. These groups of people are the extremes; in between are a wide variety of people experiencing a wide range of psychological problems. Although about 1 adult American in every 5 is estimated to have a mental health problem in any 6-month period, a large percentage of those who need treatment do not receive it, according to a major survey undertaken by the National Institute of Mental Health that looked at adults in Baltimore, St. Louis, and New Haven, examining the prevalence of 15 disorders listed in DSM III (Myers et al., 1984; Regier et al., 1984; Shapiro et al., 1984). The kind of problems people have, as well as their sex, affects their chance of being treated. Thus, only 18 percent of people who abuse drugs or alcohol receive treatment, compared with 53 percent of people suffering from schizophrenia; and women are twice as likely as men to receive treatment (Shapiro et al., 1984).

Most of those who do receive help fall into one of the following categories. First, they may be *psychotics*—people with schizophrenic or depressive disorders, who are most likely to be receiving drugs, to be institutionalized, or both. Second, they may be people suffering from *anxiety disorders,* whose functioning is impaired and who are most likely to be receiving psychotherapy. Third, they may be people who are *psychologically shaken*—temporarily overwhelmed by stressful events or experiences such as illness, loss of a job, childbirth, divorce, the death of someone close, and the like. These people usually respond to a "first aid" kind of therapy. Fourth, they may be *unruly* people—acting-out children or teenagers, self-indulgent spouses, antisocial personalities, alcoholics, compulsive gamblers—who are usually brought to therapy by others. Fifth, they may be *discontented*—people who are seeking more joy, happiness, and contentment. This category accounts for the bulk of clients for "human potential" programs, which do not claim to cure any specific problem but promise life enhancement and self-fulfillment. Sixth, they may be *professional therapists* who are undergoing therapy themselves as part of their training (J. Frank, 1979).

WHO PROVIDES THERAPY?

Most of us receive help from many people for our psychological problems. We talk to friends, relatives, teachers, family doctors. We often feel better after sharing our concerns with these people, and we often get good advice from them. We would not, however, refer to them as "therapists." A **therapist** is someone who is specially trained to offer a definite kind of treatment. In some societies this definition could apply to witch doctors and practitioners of voodoo. In our society therapy is usually provided by one of the following:

Therapist *Professional specifically trained to offer a definite kind of treatment for psychological problems.*

■ *Clinical psychologists,* who hold a Ph.D. in psychology and generally have special clinical training. A clinical psychologist may also have a Psy.D. or a master's degree and work under the supervision of a doctoral-level psychologist.

(© Mieke Maas/Image Bank)

Troubled people often go first to the family doctor, who either provides help or refers them to a psychotherapist.

■ *Medical doctors,* the health professionals most often consulted by people with emotional problems. Medical doctors may prescribe medicine, may offer supportive counseling, may refer a patient to another professional—or may do all these things.

■ *Psychiatrists,* medical doctors with advanced training in psychiatry. A combination of psychiatric and medical training helps psychiatrists identify physical conditions that may be causing psychological problems and permits them to prescribe drugs.

■ *Social workers,* who have a master's degree, and often advanced training, in psychiatric theory and practice.

■ *Psychoanalysts,* who may be any of the foregoing who have advanced training in psychoanalysis (a technique based on Freudian theory) and have undergone analysis as part of their training.

■ *Psychiatric nurses,* who hold an R.N. degree and have advanced training in psychiatry.

■ *Counselors,* who may hold a doctoral or master's degree in education.

WHAT FORMS DOES THERAPY TAKE?

Therapy for psychological problems can take many forms. Problems are complex, and people are complex. What helps one person will not necessarily work with another; the solution for a problem that stems from a physiological cause will necessarily be different from one for a problem arising from a troubled family environment. Later in this chapter, suggestions are offered for choosing a type of therapy and the particular person to administer it.

Psychotherapy **Treatment that focuses on thoughts, feelings, and behaviors.**

The three major forms of therapy are psychotherapy, medical therapy, and environmental therapy (social treatment). **Psychotherapy** focuses on thoughts, feelings, and behaviors. Psychotherapists use procedures that aim to make a client's personality, behavior, or attitudes (or all three) more productive, more positive, and more life-enhancing. Psychotherapy may focus on helping clients understand the reasons underlying their problems, or it may ignore the reasons and concentrate only on changing undesirable behavior. It may explore a client's past history or focus almost entirely on the here and now. It may emphasize words or actions, thoughts or behavior.

The focus is different in each of the two other major forms of treatment for psychological problems. **Medical therapy** focuses on the body and uses such tools as drugs, surgery, or electric shock. The third approach, **environmental therapy,** is social. It changes people's environment in some way, perhaps by placing them in an institution or in a foster home, changing a work situation, or structuring their lives around new activities.

Psychotherapy

The nonmedical forms of treatment use words and behaviors as their tools, rather than prescription pads or scalpels. Psychotherapists do not make any physiological changes in their clients' bodies. They do not prescribe drugs, perform surgery, or intervene physically in any other way—unless they are offering drugs or surgery in addition to a basic course of psychotherapy. By the conclusion of a successful course of psychotherapy, the recipient should have learned something and should have gained greater control over his or her life.

The three major "schools" of psychotherapy are dynamic, humanistic, and behavior therapies.

Dynamic therapies emphasize the thoughts, feelings, and past life of the client and the need for insight into them in order to change personality; they have grown out of the psychoanalytic theory of Sigmund Freud (see Chapter 13). Although relatively few people today enter classical analysis, Freudian philosophy is still a basic element of most contemporary dynamic psychotherapy.

Humanistic therapies have their basic foundation in the view of personality espoused by Jung and Adler and then enunciated by Maslow and Rogers (also described in Chapter 13). They are much more diverse than dynamic therapies. They emphasize the unique qualities of each person's vision of the self and they try to change people's outlook and to help people become self-fulfilled through achieving their potential.

Behavior therapies are based on learning theories that grew out of the work of such researchers as Pavlov, Watson, Skinner, and Bandura (as described in Chapter 5). These therapies do not delve into the client's thoughts and motives, but focus instead on specific, observable actions. They concentrate on the behavior that the first two schools may regard only as *symptoms* of the deeper problem. Behavior therapists work primarily on changing behavior, using techniques developed from controlled research studies. Originally, behavior therapists did not acknowledge the role of thought in behavior, but this orientation has changed considerably. Today, many seek to change the way a client thinks, with the aim of changing the client's behavior. To do this, behavior therapists use a variety of cognitive techniques.

The three orientations have arisen from different sources, draw on different techniques, and emphasize different aspects of development. They are all constantly evolving and giving birth to new outgrowths and approaches, some of which will be described later in this chapter. We'll discuss such important trends as *brief* therapy and the *interpersonal* (group and family) approach.

In a recent survey of more than 400 counseling and clinical psychologists, about 11 percent identified their orientation as psychoanalytic, about 9 percent as person-centered (that is, humanist), about 7 percent as behavioral, and about 12 percent as cognitive-behavioral (see Table 15-1). Modern therapists tend to draw their methods from more than one school. About 41 percent of the psychologists surveyed called themselves *eclectic,* indicating that they integrate aspects of two or more schools into

Medical therapy *Treatment that focuses on the body and uses such tools as drugs, surgery, and electric shock.*

Environmental therapy *Treatment that focuses on changing a person's environment in some way; social treatment.*

Dynamic therapy *Psychotherapeutic approach that emphasizes the need for insight into thoughts, feelings, and past life as a way to bring about changes in personality.*

Humanistic therapy *Psychotherapeutic approach that aims to help clients grow by removing constraints upon their self-fulfillment.*

Behavior therapy *Psychotherapeutic approach that uses experimentally established learning principles to overcome maladaptive habits.*

TABLE 15-1 THEORETICAL ORIENTATIONS OF 415 RESPONDENTS

Orientation	Number	Percent
Psychoanalytic	45	10.84
Behavioral	28	6.75
Cognitive or rational-emotive	50	12.05
Person-centered	36	8.67
Gestalt	7	1.69
Family	11	2.65
Eclectic	171	41.20
Other	67	16.14
Total	415	99.99

Source: Adapted from D. Smith, 1982.

a treatment course for an individual client (D. Smith, 1982). This often works well, since, as Strupp (1973, 1975) has pointed out, all kinds of psychotherapy contain certain common ingredients. They all include a helping relationship similar to the parent-child relationship, as well as a power base from which the therapist can influence the patient; and they all depend for their success on the client's ability and willingness to learn. Let us look more closely at each approach.

Dynamic Therapies   What do we mean when we say that a therapy is "dynamic"? One of the meanings of *dynamic* is "characterized by or tending to produce continuous change" (*American Heritage Dictionary*, 1971). All therapy, of course, aims to bring about change—and is considered a dismal failure when it does not. Dynamic therapists, however, aim for a particularly far-reaching kind of change. They seek to restructure basic personality by changing the way a person looks at life and reacts to it. How do they bring about change? By helping people develop insight into, or awareness of, the vast and powerful psychological forces buried deep within their unconscious.

The first type of therapy incorporating this goal and this approach was the psychoanalytic treatment invented by Sigmund Freud. Many of the therapists who followed him incorporated most of his ideas about the reasons for the psychological difficulties people encounter, but they have introduced a number of changes into the process. Today, therefore, a great many people receive therapy incorporating Freudian thought but with modifications in philosophy or technique.

Psychoanalysis   *Therapeutic approach, originally developed by Freud, that aims to eliminate anxiety by giving the patient insight into unconscious conflicts which affect behavior and emotions.*

Free association   *Psychoanalytic technique in which the patient says whatever comes to mind, without censoring anything.*

PSYCHOANALYSIS   If you were to embark upon a treatment of classical **psychoanalysis,** you would enter an intense, long-lasting doctor-patient relationship. You would be seeing your doctor—the *analyst*—from three to five times per week, 45 or 50 minutes each time, for several years. You might lie down on a couch as the analyst sat behind you, to free both of you from the distractions that might interfere with your free flow of thoughts and with your therapist's total concentration on what you were saying. The analyst would say very little, while you, as the *analysand,* would be encouraged to say whatever came into your mind, without censoring anything. This process is known as **free association.** You would also be encouraged to talk about your dreams, the content of which is considered very important in uncovering hid-

(© Cesar Paredes 1985/The Stock Market)

This woman, undergoing classic psychoanalysis, is on the traditional analytic couch. She lets her thoughts flow freely and shares them with her therapist, not censoring anything. While this analyst's pipe and beard are reminiscent of Freud, they are not required for a successful course of therapy.

den thoughts. Your analyst would point out to you the symbolic nature of events and people in your dreams.

As you talked, you would give your analyst clues to the unconscious forces behind your anxiety. By asking questions, the analyst would stimulate you to think about these influences on your personality and to gain insight into them. Freud believed that many of the causes that underlie the basic conflict between id and superego are sexual in nature and that repressed sexuality is the cause of most emotional problems.

When patients do not speak freely—when they have trouble free-associating or remembering dreams or discussing a particular topic—they are considered to be *resisting therapy* because talking about certain events causes them too much anxiety. That, of course, is why they repressed these topics in the first place, and so all analysands are expected to resist to some degree. Becoming aware of your **resistance** helps you identify especially significant elements in your unconscious.

Another important feature of analysis is **transference.** You would often react to the therapist as if he or she were an important person in your life: the mother who neglected you, for example, or the lover who left you. An analyst will sometimes provoke a patient to bring about transference. As you recognized your emotions and re-enacted conflicts based in an earlier relationship (usually the parent-child relationship), you would get the opportunity to work through these strong feelings. **Countertransference** refers to a therapist's feelings for a patient, who can awaken elements from the therapist's own emotional history.

Very few people go through strictly classical psychoanalysis today. Even people who can afford to spend $50 to $150 for each private session of analysis, or who have access to a low-cost analytic institute, are often not able or willing to spend the time. Furthermore, not everyone can benefit from this type of help. The ideal analysand is bright, articulate, and not too sick. The people who do best in analysis are those who do best in most treatment programs, the clients for whom therapists use the nickname YAVIS (*y*oung, *a*ttractive, *v*erbal, *i*ntelligent, and *s*uccessful).

PSYCHOANALYTICALLY INSPIRED PSYCHOTHERAPY   Another reason so few people receive classical psychoanalysis is that most therapists have moved toward a short-term, goal-directed approach that is more directive and relies on less frequent therapy sessions. The basic tenets of Freudian analysis are still alive and well, but they are most often offered in modified forms. Usually, therapy sessions take place only once or twice a week, rather than three to five times per week. Therapist and patient generally sit in chairs facing each other. Contemporary therapists tend to be more directive than classical analysts, raising pertinent topics when they think it's appropriate, rather than waiting until the patient brings them up. (For an example of a session between a psychoanalytically inspired therapist and a client, see the section on psychoanalysis in the box "Some Typical Therapeutic Dialogues," page 530.)

Ego-analytic therapy is widely considered the most important modification of psychoanalysis. It goes beyond classical Freudian therapy. In order for the classical analytic therapist to help patients deal with their instinctual drives (the id), the ego must be essentially intact and healthy. Some people who have grown up in a disturbed environment, however, suffer from impaired ego development. The ego analysts (starting with Erikson, Horney, and Anna Freud) emphasize the importance of strengthening and building an impaired ego before therapist and patient can deal effectively with personality and behavioral conflicts. Thus, ego analysts draw on techniques and interpretations that are based on, but different from, those used by strict Freudians. Although ego analysts do encourage patients to look to the past to uncover the root causes of their present behavior, they put more emphasis on the present. In their belief in personal control, they encourage patients to take charge of their lives and to change them for the better (Blanck & Blanck, 1974; Davison & Neale, 1986; Kurshan, 1986).

Resistance *Psychoanalytic term for the inability of a patient to speak about certain anxiety-producing events.*

Transference *Psychoanalytic term for a patient's reaction to the therapist as if the therapist were an important person in the patient's life; this process allows the patient to work through conflicts from earlier relationships.*

Countertransference *Psychoanalytic term for a therapist's feelings for a patient, who can awaken elements from the therapist's own emotional history.*

Ego-analytic therapy *Modification of psychoanalysis that focuses on the ego rather than the id by emphasizing patients' ability to control their own lives.*

Although the following three dialogues represent only brief moments in a course of therapy, they can help to provide a glimpse of the kind of interaction that goes on between a therapist and a client in three different kinds of therapy: psychoanalytically inspired, person-centered (Rogerian), and rational-emotive (cognitive). They illustrate some of the purposes of therapy (to bring about various types of change), and they show the differences in tone and emphasis between therapists and types of therapy.

If you went to a therapist with one of these orientations, the dialogue given here would be representative of the sort of experience you might expect to have. But bear in mind that many therapists today are eclectic—they use ideas and techniques from various sources.

PSYCHOANALYSIS

The dialogue below marked the beginning of a psychoanalysis that was to change the reporter Lucy Freeman's life. As she wrote in her book *Fight against Fears* (1951), "There was no one moment of change. . . . Certain seconds stood out sharper than others when truth hit home with the impact of a body-blow" (p. 317). This sense of an accumulation of insights into one's emotional distress is typical of dynamic therapy, as the therapist helps

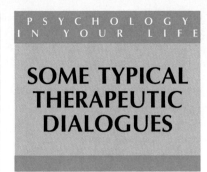
the client become aware of the significance of specific events in the past and how they have aroused fear, anger, guilt, or other emotions that live on long after the initial event is forgotten. A principal aim of psychoanalysis is to recall those events and identify their emotional ramifications, and, with the insight gained, to resolve the feelings.

"What are you thinking?" John [the therapist] asked softly.

I was worrying lest my shoes dirty the couch. It did not seem good manners to rest one's feet on furniture, even if that was accepted as high style for psychiatry.

"Nothing," I muttered. . . . "It doesn't seem right to talk about myself."

"Everyone should be interested in himself, first," John said. "The people who refuse to think about themselves realistically never understand themselves or anyone else."

He added, reflectively, "Perhaps you were never allowed to talk about

yourself and now you feel nobody cares what you say."

Nobody cares? How often I felt nobody cared. Everyone but I seemed to have someone who cared.

"Maybe you don't care about yourself," he said.

"What difference does that make?" I asked sharply. I had never worried whether I liked myself or not.

"If you do not like yourself, you cannot like anyone else," he said.

I was too surprised to answer. The first tears in years flowed to my eyes. (L. Freeman, 1951, pp. 35–37)

PERSON-CENTERED THERAPY

The following dialogue shows how a therapist helped a client to fully experience the feeling of being a dependent, pleading little boy, a feeling he had held back with great effort. At first, people are often afraid of "negative" emotions such as anger, fear, self-pity, sexual arousal, hostility, and laziness. However, Rogers feels that it is important for the client to allow these feelings to come forth and to let them find a balance with "positive" emotions, those that are loving, tender, courageous, and venturesome.

Client (C): There's kind of two pulling feelings about it. Or two "me's" somehow. One is the scared one that wants to hold on to things, and that one I guess I can feel pretty clearly right now. You know, I kinda need things to hold on to—and I feel kinda scared.

Humanistic Therapies As opposed to dynamic therapies, which aim to *rebuild* personalities, the humanistic therapies aim to *free* them. Humanistic therapists believe that potentially actualized personalities already exist even if they are buried under constricting attitudes; their role, as they see it, is to work with people to remove constraints upon self-fulfillment.

As we saw in Chapter 13, the humanists' explanations of personality are optimistic. They have faith in people's ability to live life to the fullest, even if that means changing long-held attitudes and behaviors. For humanistic therapists, the people who receive therapy are never "patients"—they are not invalids under the care of a doctor. Rather, they are always *clients,* partners in therapy. In fact, humanistic therapists respect the client as a sort of "senior partner," since it is the client, rather than the therapist, who is considered primarily responsible for the success of therapy. It is the client who has to want to change—and it is the client who is capable of the kind of improvement in living that will lead to self-fulfillment.

In keeping with the keenly individualistic flavor of humanism, this point of view has spawned many different therapeutic approaches. Each one emphasizes some-

Therapist (T): M-hm. That's something you can feel right this minute, and have been feeling and perhaps *are* feeling in regard to our relationship, too.

C: Won't you let me *have* this, because, you know, I kinda *need* it. I can be so lonely and scared without it.

T: M-hm, m-hm. Let me hang on to this because I'd be terribly scared if I didn't. Let me *hold* on to it. *(Pause)*

C: It's kinda the same thing—*Won't* you let me have my thesis or my Ph.D. so then. . . . 'Cause I kinda *need* that little world. I mean . . .

T: In both instances it's kind of a pleading thing too, isn't it? Let me *have* this because I need it *badly.* I'd be awfully frightened without it. *(Long pause.)*

C: I get a sense of . . . I can't somehow get much further. . . . It's this kind of *pleading* little boy, somehow, even . . . What's this gesture of begging? *(Putting his hands together as if in prayer)* Isn't it funny? 'Cause that . . .

T: You put your hands in sort of a supplication.

C: Ya, that's right! Won't you *do* this for me, kinda. . . . Oh, that's *terrible!* Who, me, *beg?* (C. R. Rogers, 1961, pp. 112–113)

RATIONAL-EMOTIVE THERAPY

The therapist in this dialogue tries to pin the client down quickly to a few basic irrational ideas, challenge the client to validate these ideas, show why they cannot work, explain how to replace them with more rational ones, and teach the client how to think more logically, avoiding self-defeating attitudes.

Therapist (reading from form client had filled out): Inability to control emotions; tremendous feelings of guilt, unworthiness, insecurity; constant depression; conflict between inner and outer self; overeating; drinking; diet pills. . . . All right, what would you want to start on first?

Client: I don't know. I'm petrified at the moment!

T: You're petrified—of what?

C: Of you!

T: No, surely not of me—perhaps of yourself!

C: *(Laughs nervously)*

T: Because of what I am going to do to you?

C: Right! You are threatening me, I guess.

T: But how? What am I doing? Obviously, I'm not going to take a knife and stab you. Now, in what way am I threatening you?

C: I guess I'm afraid, perhaps, of what I'm going to find out—about *me.*

T: Well, so let's suppose you find out something *dreadful* about you—that you're thinking foolishly, or something. Now why would that be awful?

C: Because I, I guess I'm the most important thing to me at the moment.

T: No, I don't think that's the answer. It's, I believe, the opposite! You're really the least important thing to you. You are prepared to beat yourself over the head if I tell you that you're acting foolishly. If you were not a self-blamer, then you wouldn't care what I said. It would be important to you—but you'd just go around correcting it. But if I tell you something really negative about you, you're going to beat yourself mercilessly. Aren't you?

C: Yes, I generally do.

T: All right. So perhaps that's what you're really afraid of. You're not afraid of me. You're afraid of your own self-criticism.

C: *(Sighs)* All right.

T: So why do you have to criticize yourself? Suppose I find you're the worst person I ever met? Let's just suppose that. All right, now why would you have to criticize yourself?

C: *(Pause)* I'd have to. I don't know any other behavior pattern, I guess, in this point of time. I always do. I guess I think I'm just a shit.

T: Yeah. But that, that isn't so. If you don't know how to ski or swim, you could learn. You can also learn not to condemn yourself, no matter what you do. (Ellis, 1979, pp. 206–207)

---

what different goals and uses somewhat different techniques. We will discuss two humanistic approaches—person-centered therapy and gestalt therapy.

PERSON-CENTERED APPROACH The **person-centered approach,** developed by Carl Rogers (1951) and formerly called *client-centered therapy,* views the client as a person in search of self. It is based on the conviction that we all have within ourselves vast resources for self-understanding and for changing our self-concepts, basic attitudes, and behavior, and that the therapist's role is to provide the climate for people to draw upon their own resources to reach complex, complete development (C. R. Rogers, 1980). Rogers was named most often as the most influential psychotherapist, living or dead, by the 400 practicing psychologists who answered the survey summarized earlier (in Table 15-1).

In Rogerian philosophy, the therapist is not an expert on whom the client can depend but an accepting, understanding friend who will be the client's companion during the search for self. The therapist has no preconceived goal, does not seek to diagnose the client's problems, and does not try to lead the client. On the contrary, the therapist looks to the client—to see the world as the client sees it and to under-

Person-centered approach
Humanistic psychotherapeutic approach, developed by Rogers, which provides a climate for clients to draw upon their own resources to fulfill themselves.

stand that world through the client's eyes. Progress toward the client's goal of **self-actualization,** or self-fulfillment, comes about through the relationship between client and therapist.

What conditions in this relationship create the climate for growth? The three basic elements are not limited to the relationship between therapists and client, but also apply to relationships between parent and child, teacher and student, and administrator and staff. They are acceptance, empathy, and congruence.

Acceptance Acceptance is unconditional positive regard. If a therapist accepts clients totally and unconditionally as they actually are at the moment—even if they are expressing "negative" feelings—they will gain the strength to change and grow. Being accepted by someone else helps clients develop a more caring attitude toward themselves.

Empathic understanding *Primary empathy* consists of a sensitive, active listening through which the therapist focuses on the client's world from the client's point of view. The therapist is thus able to understand the client's feelings (even those the client may not be consciously aware of), clarify them, and communicate this understanding to the client.

Advanced empathy offers clients a new way of looking at themselves and their world. The therapist takes the information given by the client and advances interpretations that may suggest more productive ways of behaving. These suggestions are offered very carefully and gently; the therapist wants to offer a new perspective, but does not want to pressure the client into seeing things the way the therapist does.

Congruence Congruence is genuineness or realness. People who are congruent do not try to appear different from what they are. They are themselves. They do not put up a front (of, say, professionalism or authoritarianism) or try to mask their emotions. They let the other person see what they are feeling and thinking. As clients understand and prize themselves, they will accept their experiences as real and become more genuine. They perceive themselves differently, getting to know their own feelings and attitudes and not those that have been imposed upon them by other people.

By the end of person-centered therapy, clients have come to recognize their own responsibility for their emotions, opinions, and actions and are able to experience the new self in action. How do therapists help clients reach this point? They clarify the clients' feelings and the topics under discussion, often by doing nothing more than using different words to restate what the clients have just said; ask nonspecific questions to encourage clients to bring up those topics that are most important to them; and, throughout, show acceptance of clients and what they are saying. (See the section on person-centered therapy in the box "Some Typical Therapeutic Dialogues.")

GESTALT THERAPY The term *gestalt* refers to the arrangement of the parts of something into a whole which is meaningful in a way that the individual parts are not. Gestalt psychology explains personality through this concept of the whole as greater than the sum of its parts. Gestalt psychologists believe that psychological problems often stem from a difficulty in integrating the various parts of the personality into a well-organized whole. Frederick S. (Fritz) Perls (1944) drew upon the gestalt viewpoint for a therapeutic approach that focuses on the patient's understanding the present rather than the past. **Gestalt therapy** helps clients make themselves aware of the whole self, mostly through direct appeals to the physical self and the emotional self rather than to the intellectual self.

This kind of therapy incorporates a high level of activity and direction on the part of the therapist, who is much more in charge than in person-centered therapy. The therapist actively seeks to make clients aware of contradictions in their actions,

Gestalt therapy *Humanistic psychotherapeutic approach, developed by Perls, which helps clients become more aware of the whole self.*

often by pointing out how clients' nonverbal behavior belies what they say. The therapist stresses the concept of each person's assuming responsibility for what he or she does, urging clients to speak in terms of "I did" rather than "it happened." Role-playing, games, and visual imagery are all important techniques in gestalt therapy that emphasize joining fragments of the self into a unified being.

Behavior Therapies   Behavior therapy is markedly different from either dynamic or humanistic psychotherapy. It did not evolve entirely from the treatment of troubled people, as the dynamic and humanistic therapies did; rather, it developed in part from laboratory research on the way humans and animals learn. It is rooted, therefore, in the psychology of learning, which, as we saw in Chapter 13, explains human personality through basic learning principles. If maladaptive behavior has been learned, it can be unlearned. Thus, we can define behavior therapy as the use of experimentally established principles of learning to overcome habits that are not adaptive for the person.

Behaviorists maintain that negative habits and attitudes are learned responses and that the best way to get rid of them is to learn new, positive responses. They do not concern themselves with unconscious conflicts that underlie behavior. Instead, they are concerned with the behavior itself. Therefore, the therapist's job is to help the client unlearn maladaptive behavior and learn some new behavior to replace it. Dynamic therapists believe that eliminating any specific behavior will merely take away one symptom, which the person will soon replace with another maladaptive behavior; behavior therapists disagree. They contend that the maladaptive behavior itself is usually the problem.

Since they believe that people learn abnormal behavior according to the same principles that govern the learning of normal behavior, behavior therapists regard the abnormal not as an indication of mental illness, but as the result of faulty learning. They refer to many of the conditions classified as mental disorders in DSM III (such as sexual deviance, conduct disorders, and phobias) as *behavior disorders* or *problems of living* (Rachman & Wilson, 1980).

Behaviorists delve into people's past experiences only as much as is necessary to find out how past events are maintaining undesirable behavior in the present. Their focus is on the present: What is the client doing now? What should the client be doing instead? They don't aim to reorganize the personality but confine their goal to eliminating the behavior that brought the client to therapy in the first place.

Behavior therapists' scientific principles and their ties to the laboratory can be seen in their methods. Their criteria for choosing a particular technique for a particular problem, their descriptions of their techniques, and their measurements of results are all as precise as possible.

There has been a relaxation, however, in the application of some of these standards. Behaviorists used to take a vehement "antimentalistic" approach that denied that thought, feelings, or social interaction had anything to do with controlling behavior, but present-day behaviorists, like dynamic or humanistic therapists, recognize that people can exercise self-control and self-direction to change the way they act. Not only in our environment are our behaviors shaped, but in our hearts and minds, as well.

For example, if a client came to therapy with a drinking problem, a contemporary behavior therapist might decide not to focus directly upon the problem behavior, the drinking. The therapist might consider it more productive to change the conditions that have created the client's need or desire to drink. If the therapist felt that the drinking was related to problems at work, he or she might help the client become more assertive with a boss or learn techniques of becoming more relaxed in the boss's presence. Or the therapist might use a cognitive approach to raise the client's level of self-esteem to reduce feelings of weakness and helplessness in relation to the boss.

All these techniques would still be considered behaviorist, because they are based on learning principles, are focused on the here and now, and are oriented toward changing current behavior. But "focusing on the relationship rather than on the drinking per se clearly reflects a more mentalistic and complex approach to problem drinking than strict learning principles would admit" (Morse & Watson, 1977, p. 274).

Behavior therapists have developed a number of different techniques. The use of any particular procedure will depend on the specific problem being treated, the personality of the individual client, and the orientation of the therapist. What are some of these methods?

SYSTEMATIC DESENSITIZATION   Were you afraid of the ocean as a small child? If so, your father may have taken you to the water's edge and stood with you, holding your hand, till you were comfortable watching the waves. Next, he might have encouraged you to dip a foot in the water between waves, lifting you up when a wave approached. Then he may have stayed with you, still holding tight, while a wave washed over your ankles. In this way you would have conquered your fear, bit by bit, till you were able to splash merrily. If so, you experienced a form of **systematic desensitization** that, as Wolpe (1982) points out, is commonly offered not only to children, but also to beginning mountain climbers, trapeze artists, and members of societies that require ceremonial ordeals.

Systematic desensitization is a popular approach that has been effective in dealing with various anxiety disorders, including phobias. It is based on classical conditioning, and it aims to help a client gradually replace undesirable responses with desirable ones. It works by inducing a relaxed (nonanxious) state and then exposing the client to a series of progressively stronger anxiety-producing stimuli, until he or she is desensitized to a stimulus as strong as those encountered in real life. The treatment is often offered in two phases: *in imagination,* in which the client mentally visualizes the anxiety-producing situations; and *in vivo,* in which the client confronts the anxiety-producing stimuli in real life. The first situation in either phase is a very weak anxiety producer, and clients do not go on to anything more threatening until they can respond without anxiety at each level.

Systematic desensitization *Behavior-therapy technique, based on classical conditioning, in which clients are gradually exposed to a hierarchy of anxiety-producing stimuli and taught to relax at each level until they have overcome their fear of the object or situation.*

(© Jacques M. Chenet/Woodfin Camp)

Dr. Carol Zimmerman helps a man overcome his fear of heights by supporting him through systematic desensitization. Since he is actually on a high roof, he has clearly made considerable progress already. His hands are tightly clutching the ledge, however, showing that he still has a way to go.

AVERSIVE THERAPY **Aversive therapy** combines an unpleasant situation with a behavior that a client wants to get rid of. It has been used to help problem drinkers, smokers, and sexual offenders, among others. People who have taken the drug Antabuse (disulfiram), for example, will become violently ill if they drink even the smallest amount of alcohol while the drug is in their system. Repeated experiences of drinking and feeling sick will often remove any desire to drink. Aversive therapy is useful only when clients continue to use it to change their behavior after they are no longer in the therapeutic situation (Bootzin, 1975).

Aversive techniques are often used in conjunction with positive approaches that help a client learn new behaviors. Thus, a person who drinks to overcome shyness at meeting new people may get training in social skills, or a child molester may take part in a program that associates sexual arousal with appropriate adult partners. The positive approaches are often used first, with aversive therapy reserved until the client has learned how to make acceptable responses and still wants to get rid of an unacceptable one.

MODELING THERAPY Imitation is not only the "sincerest form of flattery"; it is often the most effective way to learn a new behavior. We learn how to swim, dance, play tennis, and do all sorts of things by watching other people and then imitating what they do. We learn ways of getting along in the world by watching our parents and then behaving as they do. According to social-learning theorists, the people we copy, or *model* ourselves after, exert a major influence over us. If our models cope well with life, we are likely to learn and practice good coping mechanisms. If not, we copy their maladaptive ways. Behavior therapists maintain that we can learn adaptive behavior by seeing and copying well-adjusted people consciously provide models of desirable behavior.

Modeling therapy can take several forms. *Live modeling* consists of observing actual people. *Symbolic modeling* involves watching people on film. (Peter, the little boy in Chapter 5, was helped to overcome his fear of rabbits by watching other children playing with one.) To treat phobias, either one of these can be paired with *desensitization,* in which the client uses a relaxation technique along with seeing the models; and with *participation,* in which the client actually takes part in the anxiety-producing activity. Such combinations of therapies enable clients to overcome their phobias by seeing others demonstrating an absence of anxiety. Modeling therapy is also used to help aggressive children learn more appropriate behavior patterns.

POSITIVE REINFORCEMENT (OPERANT THERAPY) People learn to behave in certain ways when they are rewarded for doing so. On the basis of this principle, behavior therapists have treated many psychological problems with **operant therapy**, in which clients are rewarded for changing their behavior. The secret to a successful program of operant therapy lies partly in the value of a specific reward to a specific person. Such a program has to follow a sequence in which the therapist identifies the behavior to be changed, establishes what the client would consider a motivating reward, and then gives the reward when the client performs the target behavior.

Positive reinforcement can work with or without the client's awareness. In one case, a hospitalized woman who had virtually stopped eating was in danger of starving to death; she was rewarded, at first, by the therapist's speaking to her every time she lifted her fork to eat; later, she was rewarded only when she lifted the food toward her mouth, chewed, and swallowed (Bachrach, Erwin, & Mohr, 1965). When she did not eat anything, the therapist left her alone until the next meal. After a while, weight gain, rather than the act of eating by itself, brought additional rewards. As her weight began to rise (from a low of 47 pounds), her rewards broadened: she was given the company of another patient during mealtimes, was allowed to go for walks around the hospital grounds, and was shampooed. Upon her discharge from the hospital, therapists instructed her family in ways to reward her behavior, and 2 1/2 years after discharge she was maintaining an adequate weight.

Aversive therapy Behavior-therapy technique which combines an unpleasant situation with a behavior that a client wants to get rid of.

Modeling therapy Behavior-therapy technique in which the client learns new behaviors by observing and imitating models.

Operant therapy Behavior-therapy technique in which the therapist uses a system of rewards to change the client's behavior.

In one important operant technique, the "token economy" program, the client is very much aware of reinforcement. In such a program, clients receive tokens (often plastic poker chips) every time they exhibit the target behavior. They accumulate their tokens and use them to "purchase" goods or privileges.

Contemporary behavior therapists encourage clients to feel responsible for their successes (for the woman who had stopped eating, the weight gain constituted the success). This positive attitude helps to maintain the benefits after the course of therapy has ended. We can see that this is a cognitive approach, since thought processes are important in maintaining a behavior.

COGNITIVE-BEHAVIORAL THERAPIES **Cognitive-behavioral therapies** stress the identification of distortions in thinking, show clients how such distortions contribute to their distress, and help them substitute more accurate appraisals and interpretations of reality. Cognitive therapists do not try to interpret unconscious factors. They use some behavioral techniques and also stress inner experience. Below, we discuss two important cognitive behavioral therapies—Albert Ellis's rational-emotive therapy and Aaron T. Beck's cognitive therapy.

Rational-emotive therapy: Albert Ellis **Rational-emotive therapy** (RET) operates on a belief that thought and emotion are closely intertwined and a conviction that psychological problems are caused by faulty thought. This approach focuses on helping people solve their emotional troubles by examining their thinking, finding the flaws in it, and making it more logical and realistic.

RET takes an alphabet-soup approach to personality. As explained by Ellis (1974, 1958), therapy usually starts at C, the client's upsetting emotional *consequence* (the feeling of depression, anxiety, or worthlessness that has brought the client into therapy). The client usually attributes C to A, the *activating experience* (such as being rejected by a lover). It is up to the therapist to make the client see that there had to be some kind of intervening factor, B, the client's *belief system*, to get from A to C.

The therapist might point out to a client—let's call him "Joe," and let's say he has been rejected by Mary—that people get rejected all the time and that they don't all feel as depressed as Joe does. Some people get angry, some are inspired to write a song, and some just shrug their shoulders and find someone else. Therefore it's obvious that A didn't *cause* C. What did? Joe's own irrational beliefs: his beliefs that Mary's rejecting him means that he's worthless, that something is terribly wrong with him, that he'll never find anyone else he'll love as much, and that he deserves to be punished for failing to get Mary to accept him.

The therapist then moves on to D—to *dispute* with Joe his irrational beliefs, making Joe ask himself such questions as "Where is the evidence that no desirable woman will probably ever accept me?" and "By what law do I deserve to be punished for being so inept?" Joe can then rephrase his belief system to include such thoughts as "It is not awful, but merely very inconvenient and disadvantageous for Mary to reject me," "Although my life may be less enjoyable now and therefore worth less, I am never a worthless person," and "It is highly likely that some day I'll find another desirable woman."

Joe can now move on to E—new and better-functioning *effects*. Such effects include his ability to stop indulging in irrational thought the next time he goes through a similar activating experience, whether it's being jilted by a woman, fired from a job, or refused for an apartment. (For an example of a session between a rational-emotive therapist and a client, see the section on rational-emotive therapy in the box "Some Typical Therapeutic Dialogues.")

Cognitive therapy: Aaron T. Beck As we pointed out in Chapter 14, Beck and his colleagues see depression as a result of people's unrealistically negative views of themselves, the future, and the world (Sacco & Beck, 1985). These therapists build on their conviction that people's behavior stems from the way they think. They base their treatment on their belief that people can focus on and communicate their negative thoughts, that they can change the way they think, that changing the way they think will change the way they feel and act.

Cognitive therapists challenge and contradict their clients' thoughts, and they also try to demonstrate through action how illogical they are. For example, a therapist will direct a woman who is afraid to speak to men to go out of her way to do so. Only by actually seeing that what she fears most does not come true will such a woman recognize the lack of logic in her thinking and see how it has warped her life.

This active approach characterizes a variety of short-term treatment programs, which generally consist of fifteen to twenty-five 50-minute sessions. Beck and his colleagues use a variety of cognitive and behavioral techniques, primarily with nonpsychotic patients who suffer from unipolar depression (Beck & Burns, 1978; Sacco & Beck, 1985). During the course of therapy they help patients learn to identify "automatic" thoughts (the thoughts that pop into people's heads unbidden), to connect these thoughts with their depression, to see when these thoughts are unreasonably negative, to substitute more reasonable thoughts, and to change the assumptions that interfere with healthy functioning.

In one case, a patient spent most of his time in bed and protested that he was "too weak" to walk. The therapist asked him how far he thought he could walk. When the man said, "Just a few feet," the therapist suggested they experiment to see whether the man might be able to walk farther than he had thought. This proved to be so, and after getting the patient to walk around the ward and get a soda as a reward, the therapist got his own reward by seeing the patient playing Ping-Pong the next day.

Group and Family Approaches GROUP THERAPY Like our closest animal relatives, the great apes, people are social creatures. We live in groups, we function in groups, and we malfunction in groups. A vast number of the people who seek therapy do so precisely because of their difficulties in getting along with others. It's not surprising, then, that some of the early psychotherapists quickly began to treat people in groups. **Group therapy** is a treatment approach in which two or more clients are seen together, rather than individually. Sigmund Freud and his immediate follower, Carl Jung, believed strongly in the personal basis of psychopathology and did not explore group therapy. But another early analyst, Alfred Adler, believed just as strongly in the role of social factors in causing emotional problems and in the use of social situations to cure them; therefore, he did use the group format, in child-guidance centers and with alcoholics (Bloch, 1979).

Group therapy Therapeutic technique in which two or more clients are seen together rather than individually.

(Joan Menschenfreund/Stock Market)

In group therapy, people learn from hearing about other people's problems and from hearing other people's reactions to their own troubles. Some problems are especially suitable for airing in a group situation, as the members learn from and help each other.

Today, practitioners from all the major schools of psychotherapy, as well as from the newer offshoots, do much of their work with groups of clients, as well as with individuals. Groups may be composed of people who have similar problems (such as drug abusers, overeaters, child beaters, or sex offenders), or they may consist of a mix of people with different problems.

What do people get from group therapy that they can't get from one-on-one treatment? They learn that they are not alone—that other people's problems are just as bad as their own, or worse. They get feedback about themselves from the other group members, as well as from the therapist. In the group they play out the problems in relating to other people that may have brought them into therapy in the first place. They learn from each other, by seeing how other people work out their problems and by listening to advice and suggestions. They feel better about their own worth as they see that they can help others. They feel free to express their feelings in a safe environment.

What kinds of people do best in group therapy? In a discussion of long-term dynamic psychotherapy groups composed of people looking for help with a variety of different problems—and ultimately, for a basic personality change—Bloch (1979), not surprisingly, predicts success for the same clients who do best in other kinds of therapy: those who are motivated, relatively sophisticated in exploring and talking about their emotions, and convinced of the value of this kind of therapy. Poor candidates for group therapy include those who will get little from it (such as people with severe symptoms of schizophrenia, who are too out of touch with reality to participate productively) and those who interfere with other people's ability to benefit (such as severe depressives, whose unreachability frustrates and dispirits other group members).

Some problems that can be effectively tackled in a group are poor self-concept, inability to express or control emotions, anxiety, depression, ineffective coping with stress, and difficulties in getting along with or being intimate with other people (Bloch, 1979). Other problems that respond very well to highly structured groups focused on specific behavioral manifestations are drinking and eating too much, mistreating children, and compulsive gambling.

Most groups are composed of between five and eight members—enough people for the group experience to be effective and not so many that any individual will be lost. They usually meet once a week at a set time for 1 1/2 to 2 hours. Some are *closed*: that is, membership is restricted to those who joined at the beginning. Others are *open*: people are permitted to leave at different points and can be replaced with new people.

Family therapy Form of group therapy that changes maladaptive behaviors by changing family roles and communication patterns.

FAMILY THERAPY **Family therapy** is similar to group therapy in its focus on interaction among people, but it differs in several important ways. First, "The group does not have a history. It has no past and no future. The family has both" (Foley, 1979, p. 464). Second, the family therapist's role is as a model or teacher; the group therapist, by contrast, is more of a facilitator (Yalom, 1975). Third, and perhaps most important, the goal of family therapy is to strengthen the family group itself, along with its individual members, whereas the goal of a therapy group is to self-destruct when its individual members have resolved their conflicts.

The basic premise of family therapy is that the *presenting problem*, the symptom that sends someone into therapy—a husband's drinking, a wife's depression, a runaway child—is never the basic problem. Instead, family therapists see these surface problems as signals that something is seriously wrong with the entire family (Napier, 1978). It is the family *system* that is not operating properly. This may be because of poor communication that prevents family members from knowing each other's feelings. It may be because a family believes in a "myth" that has been handed down from generation to generation ("Our family is unlucky" or "We are a family that likes to fight"). It may arise from a misguided conviction that all members of a family have to think alike. Or it may be due to other reasons, like alliances between some family members that exclude others (such as between one parent and one child) or inhibitions on the expression of feelings (Bentovim, 1979). Often a problem in the parents' marriage—which they think they are concealing from the children—surfaces in one child's rebelliousness (the child subconsciously reasons, "If I focus their attention on my troubles, they'll have to stay together to handle me").

In this kind of therapy, the entire family is the patient. By helping people to understand how their family works, counselors can often help them see what each one is doing to perpetuate disruptive patterns and how they can change these patterns. Family therapists, who may come from any of the major schools of therapy, work in a number of different ways. They may see the entire family every time, or alternate with separate sessions for one or more members. They may see a family for 1 hour a week, for one 2-hour session every two to four weeks, or on some other schedule. They may be able to resolve a problem in four or five sessions—or they may stay with a family for a year or more. These variations depend on the therapist's orientation, the family's inclinations, and the severity and kind of problem.

COUPLES THERAPY "What did you see in each other that made you want to spend your lives together?" a psychotherapist asks two troubled clients. A smile comes to both clients' faces as the man says, "Her sense of humor," and the woman says, "I could see kindness in him." In an effort to recapture their former happiness—which has turned into a polite, joyless distance—this long-married pair have consulted a therapist who specializes in helping couples. Such therapists work with both the married and the unmarried, with both heterosexual and homosexual couples, with couples who have been together a long time and with those in the early stages of a relationship. **Couples therapy** aims to improve the relationship between two people, frequently by helping them communicate better.

Although the techniques used vary, depending on the particular people and problems involved and the therapist's orientation, the focus is usually on issues between the two people. The partners usually see the therapist together, although some therapists alternate between seeing the couple and seeing each partner separately. The therapist assumes that conflict is normal within every relationship and that it is how two people deal with everyday issues (like child rearing, money, time, sex, in-laws, changing gender roles, and so forth) which establishes the quality of their relationship. Some couples, like the one in the example above, deal with conflicts by ignoring them—until they realize that although they seem like a "perfect pair," they have erected barriers between them.

The overriding need for most couples is to learn how to communicate with each other. Very often, one partner feels that the other person should *know* how he or she feels without needing to put feelings and opinions into words. At other times, attitudes come out only in anger. The goal of therapy is to help each partner learn how to communicate real needs and feelings in ways that the other person can hear, and then to help the couple learn how to negotiate differences and resolve conflicts (Guerney, 1977). One behavioral strategy is called *caring days*: first, one partner does kindnesses for the other; on a subsequent day, the other partner goes out of his or her way in return (Stuart, 1976, cited in Davison & Neale, 1986). This approach breaks the cycle of distance and suspicion, shows the partners that, by giving, they are able to affect each other in a positive way, and motivates them to keep up this kind of expression of their regard for each other.

Sometimes the conflict or distance between two people is so great that separation seems to be the best option for the well-being of both. "Divorce therapists" help people about to separate or those who have just gone through a separation to deal with problems related to loss of the partner—loss in self-esteem and the need to structure a new way of life. This kind of counseling is so new that little research has been done on its effectiveness, but it will probably generate studies soon (Davison & Neale, 1986).

Couples therapy Therapeutic technique that helps two people improve their relationship by focusing on interpersonal issues and communication problems.

(Freda Leinwand/Monkmeyer Press)

The greatest problem bringing couples to therapy is difficulty in communicating. Therapists help partners gain the courage to share their thoughts and feelings with each other, and they offer specific suggestions for improving communication skills.

Brief Therapies   The actor, writer, and film director Woody Allen has often spoken of his psychoanalysis, which has gone on for some 25 years. In something of an understatement, Allen has said, "You don't learn anything in a dramatic rush" (Gittelson, 1979). Classical Freudian analysis is the longest-lasting psychotherapy generally offered today; it is fairly common for analysis to last 5 years or longer.

It's surprising, therefore, to realize that Freud started out offering analysis as a **brief therapy**, lasting from a few months to a year. In fact, he required only a single 4-hour session to cure the composer Gustav Mahler's impotence with his wife. In this session Freud pointed out to Mahler that he was identifying his wife with his mother, saying, "I take it that your mother was called Marie. How comes it that you married someone with another name, Alma, since your mother evidently played a dominating part in your life?" Mahler, impressed, told Freud that his wife's full name was Alma Maria, but that he always called her "Marie" (Goleman, 1981, p. 62). Thus the composer quickly arrived at an insight into his problem, and was cured.

A contemporary therapist has also reported a high success rate with single sessions (lasting only 2 hours), during which he identifies one major problem and offers at least one suggestion for beginning to solve it. Although he does not claim that this kind of therapy will solve serious emotional problems, he sees it as an "impasse service," which helps overcome emotional "roadblocks" (Bloom, cited in Goleman, 1981).

For the most part, however, conventional therapy is open-ended, so that a client has no idea how long it will last. This often poses problems, since therapy is expensive, time is precious, and there are not enough therapists for all those who need help. As a result, over the past 20 years, a number of time-limited therapeutic approaches have developed, most of them lasting no more than 15 or 20 sessions (Goleman, 1981).

How do therapies operate within such strict limitations? They work mainly by focusing on one, or just a few, troubling symptoms, rather than making an effort to reorganize a whole personality. Brief therapies come from all the schools we have discussed and have much in common. They tend to be supportive, emphasizing the client's strengths and offering a "safe," accepting atmosphere. The therapists are usually active, not hesitating to give practical advice and not insisting that all insight develop from the client. They often use aids like hypnosis, various conditioning techniques, and drugs (prescribed by themselves if they are physicians or by doctors with whom they work closely).

The best candidates for brief therapy are intelligent people troubled by an easily identified, sharply focused problem who are strongly motivated to change. The worst are impulsive, self-centered, self-destructive, masochistic, negativistic, rigid, and very dependent people (Goleman, 1981). As was true of group therapy, the people who do best with brief therapy are the ones who do best with any therapy.

These, then, are the major kinds of psychotherapy. (For a summary and comparison of the three major psychotherapeutic schools, see Table 15-2.) As we indicated, psychological problems are often treated in other ways, too—medically or socially. We'll now describe medical and environmental therapy; then, we'll evaluate the comparative effectiveness of the various forms of treatment.

Medical Therapy

We're all familiar with the bodily sensations tied to our emotional states—the butterflies zooming around in our stomach before an important exam or the tension headache that appears when we are worried. Emotional states can also contribute to illness; the link is discussed in detail in Chapter 16. In this section we discuss various physiological methods (like drugs, surgery, and electric shock) that are often used to treat psychological disorders. These therapies are frequently used along with some type of psychotherapy.

TABLE 15-2 SUMMARY OF THE THREE MAJOR PSYCHOTHERAPEUTIC SCHOOLS

	Dynamic	Humanistic	Behaviorist
Roots of school	Psychoanalytic theory.	Humanism.	Learning theory.
Historical development	Treatment of troubled individuals.	Treatment of troubled individuals.	Laboratory research in learning.
Theory about causes of abnormal behavior	Unconscious forces, especially sexual urges.	Inhibition of natural growth and motivation; distortion of self-perception.	Faulty learning.
Attitude toward recipient of therapy	"Patient" (sick person), to be healed by doctor or expert.	"Client," equal partner with therapist.	"Student," to be taught by therapist.
Aim of therapy	Reorganize patient's total personality.	Help client move toward self-actualization.	Teach client new adaptive habits and attitudes to replace old maladaptive ones.
Approach	Patient may lie on couch and free-associate. Therapist does not raise issues but does interpret meaning of patient's information.	Client and therapist face each other as both raise issues.	Therapist devises specific program to focus on target behaviors. Some cognitive approaches try to eliminate distortions in thinking.
Important time frame	Past.	Present and future.	Present and future.
Length of therapy	Three to five 45-minute sessions per week for several years.	Variable, but time-limited.	Variable; time-limited.

People have long believed there are times when the body can make the mind sick. This belief has given rise to a range of therapies that aim to cure mental illness by treating the body. The earliest form of such treatment was surgery. Much later, electroconvulsive therapy (sometimes known as *electric shock therapy*) began to be used. Another kind of physical treatment for emotional distress—the administration of medicinal drugs—has become so common that it has amounted to a revolution in the care of the psychologically disturbed. We'll look briefly at surgery and electroconvulsive therapy and then look more intensively at the ways different kinds of drugs are used to treat different kinds of mental illness.

Psychosurgery   If you wander through the halls of a museum of natural history, you might see an exhibit of ancient human skulls into which holes have been drilled with a sharp instrument. Archeologists have determined that such holes were caused by the mental health experts of the day, who practiced *trepanning*, a procedure that used a circular saw to cut out a portion of bone from the skull. The assumption is that this was done to treat mental illness or to relieve intractable pain. Thus we see that *psychosurgery*, the destruction of apparently normal brain tissue in order to alleviate severe psychiatric disorders, has a very long history.

We don't have any accounts in the medical literature of psychosurgery, however, until 1891, and it was not widely adopted until the 1930s (Valenstein, 1986). At that time a procedure known as *prefrontal lobotomy* was often performed; it involves cutting the nerve pathways in the two frontal lobes of the brain. Prefrontal lobotomies were done by the thousands during the 1940s and early 1950s for schizophrenic behavior disorders, obsessions, and severe pain. Lobotomies seemed to provide at least temporary relief of symptoms in 30 to 60 percent of patients, letting

Psychosurgery Destruction of apparently normal brain tissue to treat severe psychiatric disorders.

some leave institutions and come home to live. However, this irreversible operation had a darker side. The patients' personalities often changed radically, leaving them apathetic shells of their former selves; some 5 percent developed convulsions; and more than 6 percent died (Barahal, 1958; Rosen, 1982).

The popularity of psychosurgery in those years was due partly to a lack of effective alternative treatments, partly to the belief that disturbances of the brain caused mental illness, and partly to the eagerness of several prominent neurosurgeons to practice their new specialty. Psychosurgery continued even after it became obvious that it did not always work, and that in some cases the cure was worse than the disease. Its use did not decline dramatically until the 1950s, with the advent of psychoactive drugs.

About 35,000 operations were performed between 1936 and 1978, but the number performed each year was declining toward the end of this period: in 1971, for example, only 300 were performed—and those by only six neurosurgeons (Valenstein, 1986). Today, lobotomies are no longer performed; what little psychosurgery is carried out today takes the form of restricted operations on relatively small areas. Only a small number of patients, for whom drugs provide no relief, receive even this restricted psychosurgery. The recent operations have fewer drastic side effects, but it is unlikely that this radical treatment will ever be widely used again.

Electroconvulsive Therapy   The application of electric current through the brain to produce a convulsion, or seizure, is known as *electroconvulsive therapy (ECT)*. This treatment has been in use since the late 1930s, and in 1980 it was administered to more than 33,000 hospitalized psychiatric patients (NIH, 1985a). The typical ECT patient is a middle-aged, middle- to upper-income white woman suffering from severe depression who has found drug therapy ineffective (Sackheim, 1985). The patient receives from six to twelve treatments, usually three per week.

A treatment consists of the following procedure. The patient is first given a sedative and a muscle relaxant and is strapped to a padded bed. The person administering the treatment attaches electrodes (devices that conduct electricity) to one or both sides of the patient's head, and briefly passes a strong electric current through the brain. The patient usually becomes unconscious, goes rigid for a few seconds, has strong convulsions for a couple of minutes, and stays unconscious for about half an hour.

Upon awakening, the patient is apt to be groggy and confused for a period lasting from several minutes to several hours, remembering neither the shock nor anything that happened just before it. Memory loss for events up to 6 months before ECT and difficulty in learning new material may persist for up to 2 months afterward. The degree of memory deficit depends on the number of treatments received, on the placement of the electrodes, and on other factors (NIH, 1985a).

Electroconvulsive therapy is often effective in alleviating the despair of severely depressed and suicidal patients, but not for patients who are suffering from milder or reactive depression. It is as effective as lithium in treating patients with bipolar disorder (mania), and it seems to help patients with "positive" symptoms of schizophrenia.

Why does ECT work? One theory is that depression is caused by an imbalance of chemicals in the brain, and that the seizures affect these chemicals. A recent investigation (Costain, Cowen, Gelder, & Grahame-Smith, 1982) supported this theory: it found that depressed patients given electroconvulsive therapy showed brain changes ordinarily associated with the increased transmission of the brain chemical dopamine. Another possibility is that because the shock brings about temporary memory loss, it breaks the patient's pattern of disturbing thoughts.

In any case, this form of therapy, too, has generally given way to drug treatment. ECT is usually resorted to only when drug therapy would not be effective, as, for example, with elderly people who could not tolerate the side effects of drugs. The

Electroconvulsive therapy (ECT)
Application of an electric current through the brain to produce a convulsion; often effective in treating severe depression.

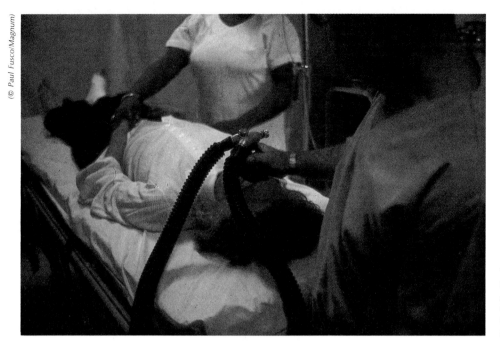

The controversial therapy involving the administration of electric shock is used less often these days than it used to be. It helps alleviate severe depression in some people who do not respond to antidepressant drugs.

treatment is quite controversial. Its opponents charge that it is medical abuse forced on people who are psychologically unable to make an informed decision, who will suffer memory loss, and who may also suffer psychological damage. Its advocates maintain that its safety has been demonstrated by controlled studies and that it often helps patients for whom no other treatment will work.

Drug Treatments   When Freud wrote about a vast and powerful unconscious that held the roots of our personality development and about the striking results he achieved by taking neurotic patients deep into their repressed memories, he started a revolution. Now, another far-reaching change has affected the way we look at and care for millions of people. Freud's was the revolution of the unconscious. Today, we are witnessing a revolution of the biochemical.

The revolutionaries today are professionals who explain psychological disturbance in terms of the balance of chemicals in the pathways of our brains, and who treat it by administering drugs that travel through those pathways. Their influence has even spread to general practitioners, who now dispense **psychoactive** (mind-altering) drugs to millions of patients every year.

Psychoactive   *Mind-altering.*

Besides lifting the spirits of ordinary people at times of illness or other stress, this biochemical revolution has helped to empty and close institutions that used to house the mentally ill. It has enabled people who were once a menace to themselves and to those around them to live freely in the community, hold jobs, and be among normal people, even though it has not cured their illnesses or magically made them normal. It has relieved the guilt of many parents, explaining their children's disturbances as the result of inborn chemical imbalances rather than emotionally scarring life experiences.

Because so many psychological disorders respond so well to psychoactive drugs, many researchers have become convinced that these disorders have biochemical causes. In some cases the successful drug treatment of a condition has inspired research that has indeed shown a biological basis for the disorder; in other cases, the jury is still out.

What role do drugs play in the treatment of psychological disturbance? What can they do and not do? When are they indicated? In the following paragraphs, we'll consider these questions.

WHAT DISORDERS CAN BE HELPED BY DRUGS? The medications developed so far have been used most effectively with people suffering from the following conditions.

Schizophrenia In the late 1940s, physicians found that a certain antihistamine had a calming effect on patients undergoing surgery. Before long, scientists had developed a chemical relative of this drug that they administered to agitated schizophrenic patients. They then discovered that this new drug, chlorpromazine (its trade name is Thorazine), not only calmed these patients but also eliminated a number of the specific symptoms of their condition. Many patients who took it stopped hearing voices and hallucinating and were no longer oppressed by paranoid delusions. This drug and its chemical relatives in the phenothiazine family (which also includes trifluoperazine, marketed as Stelazine) have become known as *antipsychotic* drugs, as *neuroleptics* (because they produce neurological side effects), and as *major tranquilizers*. They are not addictive, and they do not induce sleep.

Some of these drugs work dramatically for patients with "positive" schizophrenic symptoms like delusions and hallucinations, controlling their most disabling symptoms and enabling them to live outside an institution, in the community. They do not, however, seem to help patients with "negative" symptoms like a withdrawn, apathetic state (Andreasen & Olsen, 1982). Even when the drugs do work, they do not cure the condition: when people with schizophrenic disorders stop taking their medicine, their symptoms come back within a few weeks. Furthermore, even when they are on the medication, many patients still need extensive social support and cannot lead a normal life (Wender & Klein, 1981b). The difference between the medicated and nonmedicated states for most such persons is the difference between being able to walk alone on a public street, aware of the people and events in everyday life, and sitting on the floor of a bare hospital room, staring unseeingly at blank walls.

Antipsychotics are widely used today—too widely, according to critics, who maintain that they are used primarily to make patients easy to manage. These critics point also to the drugs' troubling side effects, which include blurred vision, trembling, constipation, and dryness of the mouth. The most worrisome side effect is **tardive dyskinesia**, a disorder that produces involuntary facial twitches and body contortions and affects a sizable number of those who have taken these drugs for a period of years. Some 40 to 50 percent of patients in state mental hospitals suffer from this disabling side effect (Kolata, 1979).

When patients are taken off the drugs, the side effects may or may not disappear—and the handicapping symptoms of schizophrenia reappear. These facts have caused a great deal of controversy in psychiatric and legal circles. Today, many hospitalized mental patients are going to the courts to insist on their right to refuse antipsychotic drugs, and many psychiatrists and hospital directors maintain that psychotic patients are unable to make sound decisions about their treatment (Appelbaum, 1982).

Depression (unipolar disorder) The use of chlorpromazine inspired the development of an entire class of antidepressive drugs, the tricyclics. They had been synthesized before the turn of the century but were not used until the late 1950s, when chemists noted their chemical resemblance to chlorpromazine. Initial trials with them were successful in raising people's spirits, and they have been widely prescribed to treat clinical depression and certain other psychological disorders (NIH, 1984b). The most common of the tricyclic compounds are amitriptyline hydrochloride (Elavil), imipramine hydrochloride (Tofranil), doxepin hydrochloride (Sinequan), protriptyline hydrochloride (Vivactil), and nortriptyline hydrochloride (Aventyl). Lithium (described in the next section) has also proved effective as a long-term preventive treatment for recurrent depression (NIH, 1984b).

Another group of antidepressants in common use today is made up of monoamine oxidase (MAO) inhibitors (like isocarboxazid, or Marplan; phenelzine sulfate,

Tardive dyskinesia *Side effect of antipsychotic drugs that produces involuntary facial twitches and body contortions.*

or Nardil; and tranylcypromine sulfate, or Parnate), also developed in the 1950s, when a new drug for tuberculosis "caused some elderly TB patients to dance in the corridors of their sanitariums" (Clark, 1979, p. 100).

There are limitations on the use of antidepressants. Although they are very effective in treating the kind of despair that seems to well up from nowhere, helping some 70 percent of people with endogenous depression (Wender & Klein, 1981a), they do little, if anything, for the person depressed over an upsetting life event like death of a family member or the loss of a job. Furthermore, even when they work well, they don't take effect for a week or longer. If a person is so desperately low in spirits that he or she is suicidal, it is dangerous to rely only on the antidepressants; immediate electroconvulsive therapy may have to be given until the medicine has a chance to work.

Like all drugs, antidepressants have side effects. Tricyclics produce relatively minor ones like constipation, dryness of the mouth, and dizziness, but MAO inhibitors can lead to dangerously high blood pressure if the patient eats certain foods, such as chocolate or cheese, which contain a certain amino acid.

A group of "second-generation" antidepressants are now being tested for patients who cannot be helped by the drugs in current use (Noll, Davis, & DeLeon-Jones, 1985). Amoxapine (Ascendin) seems to hold promise in the treatment of depressed persons with such psychotic symptoms as hallucinations and delusions who have not found relief from other treatment. Structurally, amoxapine is different from tricyclics and MAO inhibitors and like antipsychotic drugs. Its side effects are like those of the antipsychotics—tardive dyskinesia, as well as impotence and inhibited or painful ejaculation in men, and inability to reach orgasm in women (Noll et al., 1985).

Another form of treatment is, in a sense, analogous to drug therapy, although it uses light instead of drugs. **Light therapy** is now being used with patients diagnosed as having **seasonal affective disorder (SAD)**. See the box "Light Therapy for Seasonal Affective Disorder" (page 546).

Light therapy Treatment for seasonal affective disorder in which the depressed person is exposed to special fluorescent lights for several hours before dawn and after dusk.

Seasonal affective disorder (SAD) Psychological disturbance in which seasonal variations in light and temperature trigger depressive episodes.

Bipolar disorder ("manic-depression") About the same time these other drugs were making their appearance in the late 1940s and early 1950s, the drug lithium (actually, the chemical lithium carbonate) was found to control the extravagant excesses of manic states. Although it is a treatment rather than a cure, it often eliminates the manic symptoms entirely, and has therefore been used increasingly since about the early 1970s (NIH, 1984b). Although lithium is not habit-forming, it does have side effects. It can affect the thyroid gland and the kidneys and can cause mild hand tremors and weight gain, as well as other slight effects. In excessive doses it can be poisonous, and since there is a fine line between therapeutic and toxic levels, anyone on lithium should have regular blood tests, as well as regular thyroid and kidney examinations.

Another problem with lithium is in getting patients to take it. Since many manics don't like to give up the euphoria of their high states, some psychiatrists adjust the dosage of lithium to temper the mania without getting rid of it completely.

Anxiety disorder In 1975, the antianxiety drug *diazepam* (Valium) was the most popular drug in America; 61.3 million prescriptions were written for it (Boffey, 1981). Since then, largely as the result of extensive publicity about its abuse and the danger of its being habit-forming, Valium has become less popular. In 1980, about 33.6 million prescriptions were written for it.

Valium—like its chemical cousins meprobamate (Miltown) and chlordiazepoxide (Librium)—is one of a class of drugs formally termed *benzodiazepines* and informally (and somewhat misleadingly) referred to as "minor tranquilizers," to differentiate them from the phenothiazines, or "major tranquilizers." Although they are both called *tranquilizers*, these two classes of drugs are very different. Unlike the phenothiazines, the benzodiazepines do not alleviate psychotic symptoms and can be

In the spring and summer, Sheila,[*] 32, is a lively, cheerful bundle of energy. At her job, on Wall Street, she is an achiever; she does volunteer work at a local girls' club, jogs every morning, and still feels like partying at night. By the end of October, though, she is a different person. She falls into bed exhausted at 8 P.M. and sleeps through her alarm the next morning. Not only does she give up running, volunteering, and partying, but it is all she can do to keep her job. Aside from her perpetual lateness, she has trouble concentrating, has little motivation, and finds it almost impossible to initiate a new project. At work and in her personal life, she is irritable and suspicious of other people. Although she has no trouble forming close relationships with men in the warm months, she cannot sustain an emotional tie over the winter.

All winter, Sheila's roommate tries unsuccessfully to cheer her up. She has nicknamed Sheila "Lights," because of Sheila's habit of turning on all the lights in the apartment. Adding to Sheila's depression is her tendency to eat more and gain weight every winter. Her only relief from this gloomy state comes during the 2-week vacation she takes every January on some sunny Caribbean is-

*"Sheila" is a composite of several typical cases.

LIGHT THERAPY FOR SEASONAL AFFECTIVE DISORDER

land. Once there, the "summertime" Sheila reappears briefly, not to show up again until mid-March.

Sheila suffers from what has recently been defined as seasonal affective disorder (SAD), a psychological disturbance in which seasonal variations in light and temperature trigger depressive episodes.

Seasonal variations in mood have been recognized since ancient times. Researchers have sought to tie them to holidays (like Christmas), climate, and biological rhythms, with no success. The most recent—and promising—theory is based on intensity and duration of light. Since the early 1980s, a group of psychiatrists affiliated with the National Institute of Mental Health have been studying and treating people suffering from recurrent winter depressions (N. E.

Rosenthal, 1985; Rosenthal, Sack, & Wehr, 1983; Rosenthal et al., 1984; Wehr et al., 1986). Sheila is typical of these patients—they feel sad every winter, have little energy, sleep more than usual but never feel rested, withdraw from family and friends, eat either more or less, and have trouble concentrating and doing their work.

Rosenthal and his colleagues had (at the time of this writing) treated about fifty such "winter depressives," using light therapy. For 5 to 6 hours each day, the patient sits in front of special fluorescent lights that include all the colors in natural daylight, from red to ultraviolet. Patients are not to stare directly at the lights; they read, sew, or do some other activity, and only glance regularly at the lights. Most patients experience some improvement within a week (Wehr et al., 1986). It's possible that the light exerts an effect on neurotransmitters or endocrine functioning.

This therapy is certainly promising—and for most people, more accessible than a tropical holiday—but Rosenthal (1985) emphasizes that his findings are only preliminary. Studies need to be replicated with more subjects and different kinds of light, and more extensive visual tests need to be done (even though no eye problems have showed up in the patients treated so far).

(NIMH)

Dr. Norman Rosenthal, shown here with a patient, has treated people for seasonal affective disorder, using light therapy. Before treatment, such people have experienced depressive episodes triggered by seasonal variations in light and temperature.

addictive. The most common side effects of the benzodiazepines are drowsiness and unsteadiness (from large doses), and a tendency to exaggerate the effect of alcohol when taken along with it. The benzodiazepines are effective in treating *general* anxiety—which a person feels in almost any kind of situation. For panic disorders or *specific* anxiety—anxiety that shows up only in certain circumstances, like taking a test or riding in an airplane—the benzodiazepines do not seem to be effective.

Panic disorders are often treated successfully with antidepressants such as imipramine (a tricyclic antidepressant) and phenelzine (an MAO inhibitor) (D. V. Sheehan, 1982). Antidepressants and tranquilizers are sometimes prescribed together for specific goals. High rates of success have been reported in treating phobic patients with a combination of tricyclics and minor tranquilizers (Wender & Klein, 1981b).

HOW DO DRUGS WORK? As we learned in Chapter 2, billions of nerve cells interconnect in the human brain. At the synapses where they form junctions, the nerve cells release the chemicals called neurotransmitters, which travel to other nerve cells and activate impulses that affect thought, mood, and movement. Once a neurotransmitter has activated a cell and a new impulse is initiated, the chemical is reabsorbed into the nerve cell that sent it out. According to the theory of chemical imbalance, problems arise when too much or too little of a particular neurotransmitter is released and when the receptors absorb it too quickly or too slowly. In other words, an excess or a deficiency of any neurotransmitter will cause deviations from the normal.

The neurotransmitter dopamine is the chemical that seems implicated in schizophrenia. Dopamine activates cells in parts of the brain that process thoughts and feelings, and when there is too much of it, it causes psychotic disorders of thought and mood. Antipsychotic drugs counter this effect by blocking the dopamine receptors so that the brain cells cannot absorb it.

Depression appears to be caused by a deficiency of other neurotransmitters, either norepinephrine or serotonin. Antidepressant drugs attack this problem in two ways. Tricyclics increase levels of one chemical or the other, and MAO inhibitors block an enzyme that breaks down norepinephrine, allowing it to remain longer in the brain.

Lithium seems to act similarly to the antipsychotic drugs in reducing the sensitivity of dopamine receptors, while at the same time raising levels of serotonin, as the antidepressants do.

HOW WELL DO DRUGS WORK? Psychoactive drugs have taken millions of people from a state of being half alive, and miserable, to a richer life in the society of normal people. Still, these medications are not a cure-all for psychological distress. First of all, they don't always work. Even the ones with the highest rates of success for a particular disorder are not effective with everyone suffering from the condition. And even when drugs *are* able to eliminate symptoms, the side effects they leave in their wake sometimes seem as bad as the original condition or worse, and so their use has to be discontinued. For people who cannot be helped by drugs, we need alternate forms of treatment—and we need continued research to find new ways to help. (Later in this chapter, we will compare drug therapy with the other therapies.)

Environmental Therapy

Sometimes the best course of treatment requires changing a person's environment. This may involve the most extreme kind of change—placement in a psychiatric hospital. Or it may involve a less radical alternative—such as residence in a hostel, a small group home, or a foster home. It may involve sending a person to a day-care center—a sheltered environment that offers therapy as well as constructive activities. Such alternative care may offer training in everyday living activities like personal grooming, using public transportation, budgeting, shopping, cooking, and doing laundry. It may also offer vocational training or work in a sheltered workshop.

Institutionalization Institutionalization of the mentally disturbed has a long history, stretching back to the seventeenth and eighteenth centuries. Its goal was humanitarian—to provide refuge, or "asylum," for the mentally ill. It also protected society: by locking up the disturbed (especially those prone to violence), the normal were safeguarded. Eventually, in the nineteenth century, mental health professionals began to offer specialized treatment to the inmates of sanitariums. By and large, however, attempts to cure institutionalized people proved disappointing. People so disturbed that they needed to be hospitalized were rarely able to benefit from treatment, and many people remained in mental hospitals from early adulthood until their deaths, as disturbed as the day they had entered. Fewer than 5 percent of those who were in an institution for more than 2 years ever left it (Paul, 1969).

Yet no one knew what else to do with the severely disturbed. More and more hospitals were built, and more and more patients were consigned to them. During the 1950s, more than 500,000 Americans were in the wards of mental hospitals, their number increasing by nearly 10,000 per year (Clark, 1979). Hospitals were crammed with four times the number of patients they had originally been built to house, and in many cases were nothing more than foul, dangerous storehouses for people who seemed barely human.

Deinstitutionalization Movement, begun in the 1950s, to shift the chronically mentally ill from hospital to community care.

Deinstitutionalization Since the 1950s, a movement known as ***deinstitutionalization*** has resulted in the shifting of chronically mentally ill people from hospital to community care. Millions of patients have left mental hospitals and gone home to live in their own communities and to receive treatment as outpatients. (See Figure 15-1.) This movement stemmed from four major factors. First, there was the advent of antipsychotic and antidepressant drugs. Second, there was a new philosophy of mental health: the idea that most mentally ill patients could get better treatment in their home communities than in hospitals. Third, there were legal pressures against involuntary hospitalization except for people thought likely to harm themselves or others. Fourth, there were financial pressures on state governments, and home care was considered cheaper than hospitalization (H. R. Lamb, 1984).

What happened in Ypsilanti, Michigan, is typical. The regional psychiatric hospital there had been built in 1931. It was designed to house 900 patients, but by the 1950s, it was straining to care for 3400 who were packed within its walls. In 1979, there were again only 980 patients (Clark, 1979). The patients who remained could now receive more individual, humane attention in more pleasant surroundings.

But what has happened to patients who have left such hospitals? Those who receive adequate alternative help in the community are often better off, and no worse off, than they would be in a hospital. In a review of ten studies comparing institutional and noninstitutional care of patients with serious mental illness, Kiesler (1982) concludes that patients who receive care outside an institution do better on the job or at school, maintain better long-term relationships, have better psychiatric evaluations, and in general do better on other measures of independent living. Furthermore, hospitalized patients are more likely to return to mental hospitals after discharge than noninstitutionalized patients are to ever be admitted at all. Hospitalization becomes self-perpetuating.

But many patients do not receive good care outside the hospital, partly because services are not available and partly because they are so ill that they cannot make the best choices for themselves or follow a consistent treatment program. The few excellent community-based programs that do exist can treat only a very small minority of the patients who need them. Most released patients get little or no follow-up care or supervision and are left on their own. Very many live a revolving-door existence, going into and out of institutions until they would echo the plaint that became the title of a book about a schizophrenic woman, *Is There No Place on Earth for Me?* (S. Sheehan, 1982).

The destiny of the typical psychotic patient released from an institution is a life

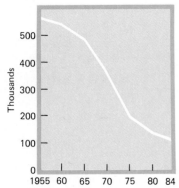

FIGURE 15-1 *Average daily population in state and county mental hospitals, 1955–1980 (1984 estimated). Treating disturbed people in the community has not proved to offer the kind of care that society had hoped for. (Source: NIMH in Morganthau, 1984).*

(Ilse Friesem/Monkmeyer Press)

The United States has not been able to keep its promise to provide the mentally ill with treatment and rehabilitation within the community. Instead, deinstitutionalization has added many former mental patients to the great number of homeless people who fend for themselves on the streets.

on the fringes of society. After struggling to get along either in a family thrown into turmoil by the disturbed person's presence or in a lonely furnished room, the patient shows up far too often at a hospital emergency room, to be readmitted once more to a psychiatric facility. About half of all released inpatients return to an institution within a year of discharge (Bassuk & Gerson, 1978). Many of those who remain in the community end up sleeping in alleys and doorways, starving or freezing, prey to criminal assaults. People suffering from chronic, disabling mental illness are thought to account for some 25 to 50 percent of the 250,000 to 3 million homeless people in the United States (H. R. Lamb, 1984); see Figure 15-2. There is evidence, too, that some of the mentally ill who would formerly have been treated in mental hospitals are now turning up in jails (Teplin, 1983).

The promise of "community mental health," so widely heralded in the 1960s—the provision of treatment and rehabilitation within community settings—has been a tragic failure. The American Psychiatric Association has blamed this failure on fed-

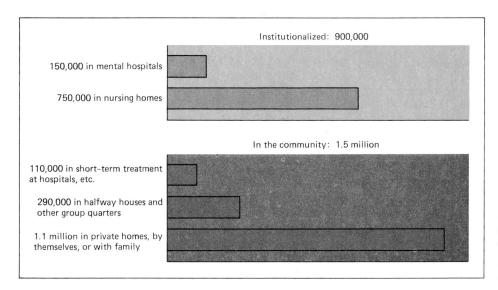

FIGURE 15-2 *The mentally ill among us. Psychologically disturbed people account for a large proportion of the homeless in the United States; estimates vary from 25 to 50 percent. (Source: NIMH in Morganthau, 1984.)*

Institutionalized: 900,000

150,000 in mental hospitals

750,000 in nursing homes

In the community: 1.5 million

110,000 in short-term treatment at hospitals, etc.

290,000 in halfway houses and other group quarters

1.1 million in private homes, by themselves, or with family

Fewer disturbed people are being cared for these days in mental hospitals, as the result of a number of societal changes, most specifically the advent of a wide array of psychoactive drugs. Still, while the total number of institutionalized patients is lower, more people are admitted and readmitted—though for shorter stays.

eral, state, and local governments that do not provide enough money for basic medical and social services; "patients' rights" lawyers who get their clients out but do not get care for them; and mental health professionals who do not deal with the most severely ill patients and do not realize the extent of the problem (H. R. Lamb, 1984).

Although the number of patients in mental hospitals at any one time is two-thirds lower than it was 20 years ago, more people are admitted and readmitted, but for shorter stays. Mental hospitals in the United States receive about 1,800,000 admissions each year, and 70 percent of all national funds spent on mental health go to hospital care (Kiesler, 1982). One reason for this is that Medicaid has become the largest single program in the country for funding mental health and Medicaid pays primarily for institutional care rather than alternative types of care.

Society needs to allocate some resources to find out what kind of care is best for which kinds of patients—and then to provide it. The American Psychiatric Association has called for revamping of the mental health system. One important change would increase funding to provide basic care and services for the homeless mentally ill and would ensure coordination of these services by having each patient cared for by a single health worker (H. R. Lamb, 1984).

EVALUATING THE VARIOUS THERAPIES

We have discussed a large number of therapies available to treat psychological problems. To come to any conclusion about their effectiveness, we have to ask some critical questions. The rest of this chapter will address the following:

1 Is therapy better than no therapy?
2 Is any one therapy "best"?
3 Is a particular therapy best for a particular problem?
4 Is a combination of therapies better than a single therapy?
5 Is there a common denominator for all therapies?

Is Therapy Better Than No Therapy?

"Everyone has won and all must have prizes," the dodo announced as he judged the race in *Alice in Wonderland*. Luborsky, Singer, and Luborsky (1975) cited this "dodo bird verdict" to illustrate their belief "that all the psychotherapies produce some benefits for some patients" (p. 995). This belief is supported by a number of studies which have found that a large percentage of troubled people benefit by *any* kind of psychotherapy.

The consensus of contemporary researchers is far different from early reports on the efficacy of psychotherapy, which now seem overly skeptical and negative. The most influential of the earlier critics of therapy was Hans J. Eysenck (1952, 1965, 1969), who argued that about two-thirds of all "neurotics" improved over a 2-year period whether they received therapy or not, that any effects of psychotherapy were small or nonexistent, and that "current psychotherapeutic procedures [had] not lived up to the hopes which greeted their emergence fifty years ago" (1965, p. 136). The only therapy Eysenck credited with positive results was behavior therapy.

Since Eysenck came to this conclusion, however, there have been more comparison studies, and they have been better designed. Luborsky and his colleagues (1975) point out that 80 percent of studies evaluating the benefits of psychotherapy have found mainly positive results even for minimal treatment, and that about two-thirds of the comparisons of psychotherapy with control groups of untreated people show significant differences.

Most of these studies deal only with short-term treatment, lasting from 2 to 12 months, and most rely on the therapist's judgment of the client's improvement. Since therapists like to feel that their efforts help people, they are apt to be biased in the direction of seeing improvement. But studies that have used more objective standards—such as the ratings of independent clinical judges or hospital discharge and readmission rates—find results similar to those based on therapists' judgments. Our answer to question 1, then, is *yes*: in general, therapy is better than no therapy.

Is Any One Therapy "Best"?

The fiercest contemporary controversies orbit around psychotherapy versus drug therapy and around dynamic therapies versus behavior therapies. Let's look at the evidence on these issues.

Psychotherapy versus Drug Therapy   Should patients use their mouths to talk or to take drugs? The controversy between pro-drug and anti-drug forces compares therapists to bartenders (Klerman, 1978). Should the psychiatrist mix a therapeutic "cocktail"—say, family therapy with a tranquilizer or group therapy with a neuroleptic—or be a "prohibitionist" and avoid drugs altogether, or be a dispenser of drugs alone, for those who "like their drinks straight"? To answer these questions, it helps to review the evidence for the effectiveness of talking and drug therapies.

EVIDENCE ON PSYCHOTHERAPY   A number of researchers have sought to determine the effectiveness of psychotherapy. One analysis of data from 375 studies assessed people who received psychotherapy, compared with people who received no treatment (they had applied for it but were kept on waiting lists) and with people who received a different kind of treatment. The conclusion was that "the average client receiving therapy was better off than 75 percent of the untreated controls" (Smith & Glass, 1977, p. 754). A follow-up analysis that had more rigorous standards for control groups supported these findings (Landman & Dawes, 1982).

How much psychotherapy does it take to help people? One research team analyzed 114 studies, mostly involving clients suffering from anxiety or mild depressive disorders and therapists who were psychodynamic in nature; no treatment was behavioral or drug-based. After 8 sessions, about 50 percent of the clients showed measurable improvement; after 26 sessions, about 75 percent showed improvement; after 1 year of weekly sessions, about 85 percent showed improvement. No single treatment was 100 percent effective in alleviating any disorder (Howard, Kopta, Krause, & Orlinsky, 1986). These findings emphasize the benefits to be gained from time-limited, "brief" therapy. They suggest that 26 sessions are a good time frame for treatment when resources are limited, and that 52 weekly sessions will give the maximum benefit.

EVIDENCE ON DRUG THERAPY   The controversy over drugs has to do largely with the anxiety disorders. The value of drugs in treating such severe emotional difficulties as schizophrenia, major depression, and mania is generally accepted.

People who are *anti-drug* say that drug therapy makes patients too dependent on their doctors, that it increases their beliefs in magical treatment, and that it does not encourage them to struggle to gain insight into their personality problems. Social critics maintain that giving drugs to disturbed people implies that their problems are biomedical and thus labels these people as "sick," when, in fact, their problems may have arisen out of a discriminatory social climate. Other critics question the effectiveness of drugs, maintaining that improvements credited to drugs might in fact be due to placebo effects. A ***placebo*** is a treatment that seems the same as an experimental treatment but actually has no physiological effect—such as a pill that substitutes sugar or something else for an active ingredient. Any effect such a "sugar pill" has on a person is assumed to be psychological. Placebos are often given to the control subjects in experiments, so that any difference between an experimental and a control group will clearly be the result of the difference in the content of the medication and will not be affected by the fact that one group is getting medication and the other is not.

Placebo Treatment that seems the same as an experimental treatment but has no physiological effects.

People who feel that there is a place for drug therapy also raise questions. As we said earlier, even those drugs with the highest success rates for a particular disorder are not effective with everyone suffering from that condition. Moreover, even when drugs do work, their side effects may be so severe that their use has to be discontinued.

Since large-scale drug therapy is relatively recent, there is still a great deal of controversy about proper doses, and we do not know much about long-term effects. We still have to develop criteria for releasing hospitalized patients into the community, so that we will not have large numbers of people floundering about without a caring structure simply because drugs have helped them get rid of their obvious symptoms. We have to ask ourselves how many people are getting drugs to alleviate the ordinary anxieties of everyday life, when they would be better advised to develop psychological reserves of strength to deal with adversity. We have to ask whether doctors prescribe pills simply because that is the fastest, easiest thing to do, even if some other treatment might be more effective.

People who are strongly *pro-drug* believe that medication is all a patient needs and that psychotherapy on top of drugs may interfere with the drug regimen. They compare psychoactive drugs with those used in general medicine, like insulin for diabetes, and say that nothing else is necessary. Many "biological psychiatrists" feel that psychotherapy will arouse patients and make them more tense by stirring up painful inner conflicts, thus undoing the valuable effects of the drugs.

Some people whose conditions seem to have a biochemical basis respond dramatically to drug treatment. If they have not been severely handicapped emotionally by the consequences of their conditions, they can often walk away from their therapist's office clutching a prescription and requiring nothing more than a periodic checkup to be sure that things are still going well.

For most people, however, drugs are most profitably used in conjunction with some kind of psychotherapy. No matter how effective the drugs are in getting rid of troubling symptoms, people still need to develop some insight into their lives, or need to learn behaviors that are more appropriate than those they were practicing before therapy. The drugs may be a catalyst enabling a person to participate actively in and derive benefit from psychotherapy, and the psychotherapy may be able to take different focus because the drugs control the most troubling symptoms. (We will look at the way drugs and therapy are combined in our answer to question 4—"Is a combination of therapies better than a single therapy?")

Psychoanalytically Oriented Therapy versus Behavior Therapy Neither psychoanalytical nor behavioral therapy has been shown to be of significant value in treating psychoses (either schizophrenia or severe depression); but both are commonly used in the treatment of a wide range of other disorders. In most studies comparing the two for the typical person who comes to therapy with a variety of anxiety symptoms, very little difference emerges.

One explanation for this may lie in findings from interviews with therapists from different schools. Behavior therapists, who emphasize the importance of persuading clients to practice new behaviors, often work with them for "a year of corrective emotional experience," which can be "what the Freudians refer to as transference" (R. Russell, 1981, p. 20). And eclectic therapists, who emphasize the importance of helping a client achieve insight, give specific behavioral suggestions. In sum, these interviews confirm the conclusion in Gurman and Razin (1977) that "the differences among therapists are more evident in how they think than how they or their patients behave" (R. Russell, 1981, p. 17).

The bulk of well-designed comparative studies show little advantage in behavioral methods over nonbehavioral ones in treating affective and anxiety disorders, even though studies using mathematically sophisticated meta-analysis statistical techniques suggest that behavior therapy has a slight advantage over dynamic and humanistic therapies (Stiles, Shapiro, & Elliott, 1986). This advantage might arise because most of the comparative research is carried out by adherents of cognitive-behavioral theory. (Researchers' theoretical viewpoints are often correlated with their findings, perhaps because of the way they design their evaluative studies or because of the particular criteria they use.)

More confirmation of these findings has come from studies focusing on cognitive therapy. Treatment is better than no treatment. But cognitive-behavioral therapy is no better than other behavior-therapy techniques: it is no more effective than desensitization, and a combination of these two therapies is no better than either one used alone (Berman, Miller, & Massman, 1985; Miller & Berman, 1983).

Our answer, then, to question 2—"Is any one therapy best?"—is that while therapy is generally more effective than no therapy, in most cases there is no clearly demonstrated superiority of one type of therapy over another.

Is a Particular Therapy Best for a Particular Problem?

The first report of the Commission on Psychiatric Therapies of the American Psychiatric Association stated that drug therapy is essential in the treatment of schizophrenia and that psychoanalytically oriented therapies "contribute little additional benefit to pharmacotherapy," though there is some value to various forms of behavior therapy and psychosocial rehabilitation (Pines, 1982). In major depressions, however, the commission recommends psychotherapy in addition to drugs. Drugs are also indicated in the treatment of other illnesses that appear to have a physiological basis, such as Tourette's syndrome (a neurological disorder characterized by muscular and vocal tics), some forms of childhood hyperactivity, and some kinds of panic attacks.

One recent study found that people with schizophrenic disorders get more benefit from a combination of family therapy and neuroleptic drugs than from individual supportive therapy in conjunction with drugs (Falloon et al., 1982). Therapists educated patients and their families about the nature, course, and treatment of schizophrenia; helped family members to identify tensions; and taught them how to improve their problem-solving skills. After 9 months, only one of the patients in the family therapy group had relapsed, compared with eight who had been treated individually. Moreover, the family-treated patients had spent less than 1 day in the hospital, on the average, compared with more than 8 days for those in the other group.

Is any one therapy best for depression? In a recent major study, the National Institute of Mental Health compared four groups of 239 moderately to severely depressed patients. One group received 16 weeks of cognitive-behavioral therapy, one received 16 weeks of interpersonal psychotherapy, one received the antidepressant drug imipramine, and the fourth group received a placebo and weekly supportive visits from an experienced psychiatrist (NIMH, 1986).

All the groups showed improvement, even those getting the placebo, but the most severely depressed patients in the "placebo condition" got little benefit, and the greatest improvement showed up among patients in the three groups receiving active treatment. After the 16 weeks of treatment, there were no differences among these three groups, although the drug did work faster than the two forms of psychotherapy, showing an advantage by the eighth to the twelfth week of treatment. Predicting which patient would do well in a specific treatment seemed to depend on different characteristics for each of the four approaches. Researchers are now analyzing these differences, which include the severity of depression; whether the depression is endogenous or in reaction to a life event; the patient's marital status; the patient's expectation of improvement; and various social, cognitive, and occupational factors. Other research will focus on following up the patients to see whether the improvements last, analyzing the importance of the individual therapist's skill, and identifying the mechanisms of change.

Our answer to question 3, however, is that for most psychological disorders, the match between therapist and client may be much more important than the particular theory the therapist espouses. (For more on this, see the discussion of question 5—"Is there a common denominator for all therapies?")

Is a Combination of Therapies Better Than a Single Therapy?

"In practice, most psychiatrists and even many nonmedical psychotherapists are active bartenders, mixing various 'cocktails' of drugs and psychotherapy" (Klerman, 1978, p. 221). The combination of these two kinds of therapy often operates as a "two-stage rocket" in the treatment of depression (p. 222). The first stage, the drug, attacks the prominent symptoms—anxiety, insomnia, tension, and so forth—getting the depressed person out of the "symptomatic orbit." The psychotherapy that constitutes the second stage helps the client become more competent in everyday life, adjust socially, gain insight into his or her situation. Drugs seem to make such a person more accessible to psychotherapy, and the combination seems superior to either treatment alone.

Luborsky and his associates (1975) also found advantages with combined treatments. When they compared drugs plus psychotherapy for a variety of psychological disorders with either drugs alone or psychotherapy alone, and when they compared medical care alone for psychosomatic illness with medical care plus psychotherapy, the combination won out almost all the time. They concluded, "A combination of treatments may represent more than an additive effect of two treatments—a 'getting more for one's money'" (p. 1004). We seem to have a synergistic effect here. That is, the combination of two different treatments provides a therapy that is much more effective than just adding the benefits of one to those of the other. The combined force of the treatments has an energy all its own.

Our answer to question 4, then, would be *yes*—a combination of therapies does seem to be more effective than one therapy used alone.

Is There a Common Denominator for All Therapies?

What do all psychotherapies have in common? They all offer some kind of systematized explanation for a client's problems, with a set of principles the client can use to guide future behavior, and they all offer a helping relationship with a professionally trained person. When they work, they improve clients' self-esteem and sense of personal competence and give clients confidence that they can make it in the world. "The chief problem of all patients who come to psychotherapy is demoralization, and the effectiveness of all psychotherapeutic schools lies in their ability to restore patients' morale" (J. Frank, 1974, p. 271).

Therapeutic alliance Emotional bond and involvement between therapist and client.

In determining the success of treatment, the **therapeutic alliance** (an emotional bond and involvement between therapist and client) is more important than what kind of therapy is used. "You have to get along. It could be Sigmund Freud himself, but if he rubs you the wrong way, you should go to another therapist" (Cummings, quoted in Sobel, 1980, p. 104). All good therapists recognize the importance of the right fit between therapist and client.

Clients need to feel comfortable with the therapist's personality, orientation, and general approach. The most successful clients of both psychotherapists and behavior therapists report finding their therapists warm, genuine, and empathic. Sloane and his colleagues (1975) found that clients whose therapists like them, are comfortable with them, and find them interesting make better progress. Stiles and his associates (1986), however, did not find a link between therapeutic outcome and therapists' warmth, understanding, and attempts to provide new perspectives for clients. They emphasize the client's contribution as the most important predictor of a successful outcome—how involved the client is in the therapy and how willing he or she is to reveal personal information and feelings. Luborsky and Auerbach (1985) emphasize the relationship itself as more important than either therapist or client

Faced with the bewildering array of therapies and therapists, how can people choose the best kind of therapy for their problems and the best person to administer it? There are no hard-and-fast answers, but the following dialogue may be helpful.

Q: How do I know if I need therapy?
A: Let's answer that question with other questions. Are you often unhappy? Do you have problems making and keeping close relationships? Do you have trouble doing schoolwork or holding a job? Do irrational fears get in the way of your everyday life? Has there been a big change in your habits—sleeping too much or not enough, overeating or losing your appetite, losing interest in activities and people you used to enjoy? Do you think about suicide? Do you generally feel out of control of your life? If you have problems like these, it's time to speak to a therapist.

Q: How do I start?
A: With a thorough physical examination, since some emotional problems are related to physical health. Your family doctor may be able to recommend a therapist. Someone you know who has had a good therapeutic experience can give you a name. You could go to your college's counseling and psychological service. Check the yellow pages to find a family service agency or a mental health center. Or you could contact the closest school of medicine or major teaching hospital that has an outpatient psychiatric clinic. Such clinics often offer psychological testing, diagnostic screening by psychia-

CHOOSING THERAPY AND A THERAPIST

trists, and the ongoing services of psychologists and social workers.

If you go first to an interdisciplinary team, you'll find out whether your problems are physically caused, you'll have access to professionals qualified to prescribe medication, and you'll reap the benefits of several heads.

Q: How can I tell whether a particular therapist is right for me?
A: Only through a personal meeting can you tell if a therapist is right for you. Besides checking out a therapist's basic professional qualifications, to be sure he or she has the appropriate credentials, you'll know whether you feel comfortable with his or her personality, values and belief systems, and psychological orientation. Does he or she seem like a warm, intelligent person who would be able and interested in helping you? Is he or she willing to talk about the techniques to be used? Does he or she make sense to you?

If you get a good feeling from the first therapist you see, there's no need to shop around. If you feel at all un-

comfortable, however, it's worthwhile setting up one-shot consultations with one or two others before you make up your mind. The therapist's attitude toward your interest in talking to another therapist may be the first barometer of his or her suitability. If you are not in need of emergency care, be prepared to spend at least as much time shopping for a therapist as you would for a new car. Your decision may have lifelong ramifications, and it pays to invest time and money to make it as wisely as possible.

Q: How much will I have to spend?
A: As of this writing, cost of therapy varies from no fee to $150 or more for a 45-minute session. Therapists in private practice charge more than those affiliated with centers or large institutions, and psychiatrists usually charge more than psychologists, who in turn charge more than social workers. Many therapists charge on a sliding scale, based on what the client can afford, and many health insurance plans cover the costs.

Q: What should I do if I start with a therapist and then decide that he or she is not helping me?
A: First, ask yourself whether you're displeased because your therapy is raising difficult, painful issues that you don't want to deal with. Then express your dissatisfaction to your therapist and deal with it in your sessions. Finally, if you are convinced that your therapy is either ineffective or harmful, find another therapist (not one referred by your current therapist!).

alone. The fit between the two people seems better when they're similar in such characteristics as age, occupation, marital status, and religious activity, and in the values they hold.

Like anyone else, therapists continue to learn as they practice, and this learning pays off for their clients. By and large, experienced therapists from any school achieve better results with clients than novices do, probably because they take the initiative more and are more realistic, more patient, more interested in the client's history, more willing to wait for information, more prone to interpret material, more variable in the way they behave during interviews, and more effectively expressive (Gurman & Razin, 1977; R. Russell, 1981).

Since the fit between therapist and client is so important to the success of therapy, how are people seeking therapy to choose the right therapist? Luborsky (1979) has suggested that clients try several therapists and select one on the basis of their feelings. He also proposed that, to make this process easier, therapists should supply film clips or videotapes of themselves doing therapy. And Hogan (1979) recommends that therapists become aware of their own limitations, techniques, and values and that they share this awareness publicly, to make the selection of a therapist less like a blind date. (For suggestions on finding a therapist, see the box "Choosing Therapy and a Therapist.")

Our answer to question 5, then, is that all therapies do have a "common denominator": the therapeutic alliance.

Therapy has made an enormous difference in the lives of many people. It has opened their eyes to the possibilities around them. It has enabled them to be more loving, more productive, more content with themselves. It has allowed them to live in the company of their fellows in society rather than being forced into the isolation of institutionalization. It has often, quite simply, wrought miracles. In other instances, therapy has been a grave disappointment to those who sought and participated in it. The more we understand about what it can and cannot do, the better we will be able to benefit from its great capacity to help.

SUMMARY

1 One in every five adult Americans is estimated to have a mental health problem in any 6-month period. Whether a person receives therapy depends on the particular problem (53 percent of schizophrenics get therapy, for example, compared with only 18 percent of alcohol or drug abusers) and the sex of the person (women are twice as likely as men to go for therapy).

2 Recipients of therapy fall into several categories: psychotics, people suffering from anxiety disorders, the psychologically shaken, the unruly, the discontent, and professional therapists.

3 A therapist is someone who is specially trained to offer a definite kind of treatment. In our society, a therapist is generally a clinical psychologist, medical doctor (perhaps with advanced training in psychiatry), social worker, psychoanalyst, psychiatric nurse, or counselor.

4 The three major forms of therapy are psychotherapy, medical therapy, and environmental therapy (social treatment).

5 Psychotherapy is nonmedical treatment. There are three major "schools" of psychotherapy: dynamic, humanistic, and behavioral. Important current trends include brief therapy and group and family approaches. Many psychotherapists use elements from two or more approaches in their therapy, calling themselves "eclectic."

6 The goal of dynamic therapy is to restructure personality by changing the way a person looks at and reacts to life. In this approach the patient is helped to develop insight into the vast and powerful forces in his or her unconscious. Psychoanalysis is a type of dynamic therapy, developed by Sigmund Freud, which uses techniques such as free association and dream analysis to determine repressed instinctual drives and defenses in the unconscious that influence behavior. During psychoanalysis, the patient gains insight into these forces.

7 Because classical psychoanalysis is so time-consuming and costly, many psychoanalytically oriented therapists have moved toward psychoanalytically inspired psychotherapy, which is more directive, less frequent, briefer, and goal-directed.

8 An important modification of psychoanalysis is ego-analytic therapy, which emphasizes a person's ability to control his or her own life.

9 The goal of humanistic therapies is to free personalities in order to help clients grow. In Carl Rogers's person-centered approach, the therapist views the client as an individual in search of self. The goal of therapy is self-actualization (self-fulfillment). Therapists provide clients with acceptance ("unconditional positive regard") and empathic understanding so that clients come to accept their experiences as real and thus get to know their true feelings and attitudes rather than those imposed by others.

10 The goal of gestalt therapy, a type of humanistic therapy developed by Fritz Perls, is to make the client aware of the whole self. Gestalt psychotherapists believe that psychological problems often stem from a difficulty in not being able to integrate the various parts of the personality into a well-organized whole. Gestalt therapists actively seek to make clients aware of contradictions in their actions. They use a variety of techniques including role-playing games, and visual imagery.

11 Behavior therapy uses experimentally established principles of learning to overcome habits that are not adaptive for the individual. The client is seen as someone who has learned inappropriate behaviors, and the aim of therapy is to eliminate the undesirable behaviors and replace them with appropriate ones. Behavior therapists use a wide variety of techniques based on learning principles; these techniques include systematic desensitization, aversion

therapy, modeling, and positive reinforcement (operant therapy).

12 Cognitive-behavioral therapies, such as Ellis's rational-emotive therapy and Beck's cognitive therapy, use behavioral techniques but stress the identification of distortions in thinking, show clients how such distortions contribute to their distress, and help them substitute more accurate appraisals and interpretations of reality.

13 Today, therapists from all the major schools sometimes do their work with groups rather than single individuals. In family therapy the entire family is the patient. The goal of family therapy is to strengthen the family group. By helping people understand how their family works, therapists can often help them see what each family member is doing to perpetuate disruptive patterns and how they can change these patterns. Couples therapy focuses on interpersonal issues between two people, often emphasizing communication problems.

14 Brief therapies are time-limited approaches, generally lasting for no more than 15 or 20 sessions.

15 Medical therapies include psychosurgery, electroconvulsive therapy, and drug treatment. Psychosurgical techniques, which involve the destruction of apparently normal brain tissue to alleviate severe psychiatric disorders, were once quite common but are rarely used today. Electroconvulsive therapy involves the application of electric current through the brain and is often effective with severely depressed, suicidal patients. Drug therapy is now extremely common. Schizophrenia, depression, bipolar disorder, and anxiety disorders often respond successfully to drugs. The biochemical revolution has helped numerous sufferers of mental disorders to live in the community. However, drug therapy is not always successful and frequently entails unwanted side effects.

16 Seasonal affective disorder (SAD) is a seasonal variation in mood; the sufferer generally becomes depressed in the wintertime. "Light therapy" appears to be an effective treatment.

17 Environmental (or social) therapy involves changing the individual's environment. Deinstitutionalization is the shift of chronically mentally ill people from hospitals to community care, such as placement in a hostel, small group home, or foster home. Since many patients do not receive good care outside the hospital and often become homeless, the community mental health movement is widely regarded as a failure.

18 Although some early research questioned the value of psychotherapy, more recent research indicates that it is effective for many people. No one type of psychotherapy is considered to be the most effective overall, although particular types of therapies seem to be especially well suited for particular problems. In many cases, however, the "therapeutic alliance," or match between the patient and the therapist, seems to be more important than the particular therapy used. Drug therapy is especially effective in treating disorders such as schizophrenia, depression, and mania; however, drugs are not equally effective for all patients. For most, drugs are most profitably used along with psychotherapy.

KEY TERMS

Aversive therapy (page 535)
Behavior therapy (527)
Brief therapy (540)
Cognitive-behavioral therapies (536)
Countertransference (529)
Couples therapy (539)
Deinstitutionalization (548)
Dynamic therapy (527)
Ego-analytic therapy (529)
Electroconvulsive therapy (542)

Environmental therapy (527)
Family therapy (538)
Free association (528)
Gestalt therapy (532)
Group therapy (537)
Humanistic therapy (527)
Light therapy (545)
Medical therapy (527)
Modeling therapy (535)
Operant therapy (535)
Person-centered approach (531)

Placebo effect (551)
Psychoactive (543)
Psychoanalysis (528)
Psychosurgery (541)
Psychotherapy (526)
Rational-emotive therapy (536)
Resistance (529)
Seasonal affective disorder (SAD) (545)
Self-actualization (532)

Systematic desensitization (534)
Tardive dyskinesia (544)
Therapeutic alliance (554)
Therapist (525)
Therapy (525)
Transference (529)

SUGGESTED READINGS

GOLEMAN, D., & SPEETH, K. R. (Eds.). (1982). *The essential psychotherapies.* New York: New American Library. A collection of essays by such important psychotherapists as Freud, Adler, Jung, Ellis, Beck, Wolpe, and Rogers. The editors introduce each section with a brief biography of the therapist.

NAPIER, A., & WHITAKER, C. A. (1978). *The family crucible.* New York: Harper & Row. A moving account of the process of family therapy, focusing on the problem of the "identified" patient.

VALENSTEIN, E. S. (1986). *Great and desperate cures: The rise and decline of psychosurgery and other radical treatments for mental illness.* New York: Basic Books. An absorbing cautionary tale—scholarly yet fascinating.

WOLPE, J. (1982). *The practice of behavior therapy.* New York: Pergamon. A thorough discussion of behavior therapy. It contains information on cognitive approaches, assertiveness training, and treatment of inhibited sexual response, as well as other techniques. Includes many case histories.

CHAPTER

16

HEALTH PSYCHOLOGY

PREVIEW QUESTIONS

■ How does the interpretation of a potentially stressful event influence the ability to cope with it?

■ How do psychological factors influence decisions about eating, exercising, smoking, and drinking?

■ How do these activities affect psychological and physical health?

■ What can be done to prevent illness, or to recover from illness?

■ How do emotional states influence the functioning of the immune system?

The first time I saw my baby daughter, she was 2 months old. She looked up at me with her dark eyes and I felt true bliss. Then when she held my hand all the way home from the airport, it was heavenly. The social worker from the adoption agency had warned me that I might not feel anything, or that I might feel let down the first time I saw her. Instead I felt the thrill of welcoming this wonderful little girl into my life.

I knew from my studies and my observations that the birth or adoption of a first baby is a major transition in parents' lives. I knew that parenthood is an adventure that can be thrilling, frightening, fulfilling, challenging, enriching, exhausting—and in some ways like a ride on a roller coaster. But as much as you might know academically, there's a whole new dimension when your own life is affected. My husband Jonathan and I were eager to set off on this adventure and to raise our child the best way we knew how, even though we realized that parenthood would bring all sorts of stress.

For us, the stress began long before our baby's birth, as we came to the decision to adopt a child. Since we wanted an infant rather than an older child, and since it is difficult to find infants to adopt in the United States, we decided to look for a baby from another country. Because we knew other couples who had adopted babies from South America, we went to an agency that arranged such adoptions, and set the wheels in motion to adopt a child from Chile.

By starting those wheels in motion, we also set ourselves off—on a journey through several emotional ups and downs. Jon and I got to know ourselves and each other more deeply as we answered questions about the most intimate details of our personalities, our personal histories, and our feelings about our own parents, each other, and the meaning of parenthood—and as we demonstrated to strangers that we had the qualities needed to adopt a child.

We had already filled out some of those probing forms, and we were a little nervous, when we went to the adoption agency for our first interview. When the social worker asked us why we had asked for a girl, I tried to think of an answer that would put me in a good light. My husband jumped in with, "So she can have a daughter she can take shopping in Bloomingdale's!" and I had to laugh. In naming one of my favorite activities and one of my favorite New York department stores, he put his finger on one of the things I was looking forward to doing with my little girl. Fortunately, the social worker laughed too, the ice was broken, and some of our anxiety was dispelled.

That was only the beginning, though. There were more interviews. There were the references needed from five "community leaders" who would vouch for us as prospective parents. There was the endless stream of papers we had to fill out and have translated into Spanish. Even after we had the thrill of hearing that we had been approved, there was the uncertainty of not knowing how long a wait we would have (it could be anywhere from 6 months to 2 years). And then we heard the exciting news, only a few months later, that a healthy little girl had been born, and that within about 2 months she would be ours. We had her name all picked out—Anna Victoria.

Despite the emotional support we received from our friends and family, the frustration of waiting during those last months became almost unbearable. At this point all we could do was shop! We outfitted Anna's room; we filled her closets with clothing in

*every size she'd need for her first 2 years; we bought carloads of equipment "essential"
for the contemporary baby.*

*We dealt with the stress of these months by talking to people who had been through
the process, and by continuing to remind ourselves that hitches and snags and delays
were to be expected and that we would just "go with the flow" until we had Anna at
home. This attitude stood us in good stead when our papers seemed to take forever to be
processed, when we couldn't make telephone contact with our Chilean lawyer and
pediatrician, and when the flight down to pick up our baby was postponed because of
fog in Santiago. But now, at last she was here.*

—From the notebooks of Diane Papalia

Conceiving or adopting a baby is just one of many basically happy events that
involve some stress. For most of us, virtually every day in our lives contains
stress—some of which we welcome, some of which we weep at, and most of
which most of us handle quite well. Coping with stress in positive ways (as through
the use of humor, through calling on personal and social resources, through a positive interpretation of stressful events—and through shopping!) can make the difference between being energized by stress and being weakened by it.

In this chapter we talk about health psychology, a new specialty that is concerned particularly with the management of stress but also with a number of other
subjects that demonstrate the close tie between mind and body. Among these subjects are the steps that we can take to keep ourselves and our children healthy, to
prevent illness, and to recover from illness. We look at the most important psychological, social, and biological influences on our well-being and see the important
implications that findings in this field have for our own lives.

WHAT IS HEALTH PSYCHOLOGY?

Why does one student have a perfect attendance record, while another loses a day or
two of every month because of illness? Why are some young people still beginning to
smoke, at a time when study after study has shown that cigarette smoking is the
single most important cause of preventable illness and death? Do most people consistently do the kinds of things that will help keep them healthy? These are just a few
of the questions that absorb practitioners of a new subfield, health psychology. What
is this specialty?

To answer this question, we first have to ask, "What is health?" According to the
World Health Organization, health is "a state of complete physical, mental, and
social well-being and is not merely the absence of disease and infirmity" (Danish,
1983). Although we rarely if ever achieve this ideal condition, its definition serves as
a concise statement of a goal. The exciting premise of the new discipline of health
psychology is an observation made by an ancient Greek philosopher, Democritus,
that people "pray to their gods for health; they do not realize that they have control
over it themselves" (Stone, 1979, p. 4).

Today, more than at any time in recorded history, we have an impressive degree
of control over our own health. In the past, until as recently as the beginning of the
twentieth century, the major causes of death were acute conditions (conditions that
come on quickly and end quickly) such as tuberculosis, pneumonia, and other infectious diseases. Today's leading causes of death are chronic illnesses (conditions
which linger for a long time) like heart disease and cancer, and injuries from highway accidents. To a considerable extent, these causes of death are affected by our
own lifestyles and decisions. We can structure our lives and our societies in ways
that will go far to keep us healthy.

Health psychology *Scientific study of the psychological factors that promote health, cause illness, and affect recovery from illness.*

Health psychologists *Psychologists who focus on the role of psychology in helping people to adopt health-promoting lifestyles, to prevent and recover from illness, to deal with stress, and to use and expand health-care systems.*

Researchers in the field of **health psychology** use the findings of the last 100 years of scientific study of behavior and behavior modification in an effort to discover the psychological factors that promote health, influence illness, and affect recovery from illness. **Health psychologists** are psychologists who conduct research and use the findings of research to help people develop healthful lifestyles, to manage stress and other aspects of their lives, to prevent illness, to speed recovery from illness, and to make the best use of the health care system in recovering from acute illness and in adjusting to chronic disease. This is one of the newest subfields in the science of psychology; and it offers many opportunities for research and for applying the results of research to improve the lives of present and future generations. No field is more relevant to our day-to-day lives.

As we examine the kinds of issues that engage health psychologists, we want to keep several themes in mind. The following threads run through much of the discussion in this chapter.

Biopsychosocial model *Model according to which biological, psychological, and social factors interact to affect health and illness.*

Biomedical model *Model according to which illness is purely a result of biological factors, and psychological and social influences are ignored.*

■ *In discussing health and illness, we cannot separate the mind from the body.* Health psychology subscribes to a **biopsychosocial model** of health. According to this model, biological, psychological, and social factors interact to affect health and illness. This model is in sharp contrast to the traditional **biomedical model**, which considers illness to be purely the result of physiological factors, largely ignoring psychological and social influences. When we use the biopsychosocial model for diagnosis and treatment, we need to consider the interaction of factors from all three spheres of a person's life.

■ *Social and psychological factors can influence health in a number of different ways.* Some mental states cause changes in tissue function. Thus, stress may affect the release of hormones or neurotransmitters. Some voluntary behaviors, such as smoking or drinking, have direct effects on body organs. And some attitudes prevent people from seeking medical care or following treatment recommendations, interfering with recovery from illness (Krantz, Grunberg, & Baum, 1985).

■ *To promote and maintain good health, we need to have a sense of control over our bodies and our lives.* People who believe that they can control their own lives may be more apt to adopt healthful lifestyles. Furthermore, considerable research has shown that people tend to consider most stressful those events and situations which they feel they can neither predict nor control.

■ *Each of us can play an active role, rather than a reactive one, in becoming healthy and staying healthy.* Instead of assuming little responsibility for our health, and taking action only when illness strikes, we can do a great deal to stay healthy, to fend off illness, and to extend our years of vigorous life. We'll be discussing some of the most important and best-researched preventive measures in this chapter.

STRESS

Even before that first mysterious moment when something in your mother's body received a signal that you were ready to leave the security of her womb, your existence was not free of stress. A fetus may be assaulted by a barrage of environmental insults—drugs, nicotine, maternal disease, x-rays, environmental pollutants. Then there is the trauma of birth, quickly followed by discomforts (such as hunger), by events that arouse fear (a crash of thunder) or anxiety (encountering a strange person), by frustrations (not being able to make our wishes known), by difficulties (learning a new skill), by pain (a stomach cramp), and by innumerable other reminders that no environment is all serenity and bliss. Moreover, even basically positive or good events can have stressful aspects. Stress is not characteristic only of painful experiences. It is also present in the leap of excitement as a baby welcomes the mother's return at the end of the working day, in the bursts of giggling that follow a child's being tossed up in the air in exuberant play, in the heady excitement of a toddler's first shaky steps toward a wider world. Through coping—adapting to stress in positive ways—we develop in many ways.

What Is Stress?

What exactly is stress? Different researchers define it differently. Some focus on particular events or stimuli that cause stress; others focus on physiological and psychological reactions to such events. In this book we use the term *stressors* for events that are capable of causing stress, even though they do not always do so. We use the term *stress* for the physiological and psychological reactions to stressors.

Stressor *Event capable of producing stress although not necessarily doing so.*

Stress *Physiological and psychological reactions to stressors.*

A great deal of stress is expected as part of the normal life cycle. Such stressors as assuming a new job, getting married, having a baby, and being widowed, for example, are not unexpected in the lives of most people. These are *normative* stressors—as opposed to *nonnormative* stressors, which involve some totally unanticipated event, like being caught in an earthquake or a bank robbery. Hans Selye, M.D., a major figure in the history of stress research until his death in 1982, believed that some stress is essential for life. He maintained that "complete freedom from stress is death" (1980, p. 128).

Reacting to Stress

Physiological and Cognitive Aspects of Stress A PHYSIOLOGICAL PERSPECTIVE One major area of research is the body's physiological response to stressors. That response can take the form of hormonal changes.

Selye (1982) defined stress as "the nonspecific (that is, common) result of any demand upon the body." This reaction is called *nonspecific* because, according to Selye, it is always much the same, regardless of the source or type of stressors. In other words, the same response is brought about by dissimilar situations—a concept that is quite controversial. A *specific* response, on the other hand, is distinctive; it varies according to the kind of demand a particular stressor makes on a particular person.

Let's consider some examples. Sweating is a specific response to heat; shivering is a specific response to cold; tired leg muscles are a specific response to bicycling up a steep hill. Heat, cold, and muscular exertion, as well as a host of other stimuli—such as joy, sorrow, drugs, and hormones—require the body to *do* something to bring itself back to a normal state. In other words, the body must adapt or adjust. The overall process of adaptation is *nonspecific* in the sense that it overrides specific individual responses (such as sweating) to specific individual demands for adjustment (such as heat). The work the body must do to adapt to a stressor is independent of the specific response. Thus, an increased output of energy is its nonspecific response to a stressful event.

This may seem clearer if we think of the body as like a house powered by electricity. When the house is too cold, we turn on the furnace. When it is too hot, we turn on the air conditioner. When it is too dark, we turn on a light. Each kind of equipment performs a different function—that is, each makes a *specific* response. But each one also draws on the house's overall supply of electricity. The increase in total electric power generated is the house's *nonspecific* response to the separate demands upon its ability to adapt.

Selye did his pioneering research with rats. He found that injecting rats with nonlethal doses of poison; subjecting them to cold, heat, infection, trauma, or hemorrhage; and pulling their tails led to a predictable group of physiological symptoms (Selye, 1982). Selye called these reactions the **general adaptation syndrome (GAS)** (1936), and he concluded that people under stress react similarly.

General adaptation syndrome (GAS) *Three-phase reaction to stress, described by Selye, consisting of alarm, resistance, and exhaustion.*

The GAS has three phases, or stages: alarm, resistance, and exhaustion.

1   *Alarm reaction*: Upon becoming aware of a stressor, a person or an animal goes into *shock* and *countershock*. In the shock condition, body temperature and blood pressure drop, heartbeat quickens, and muscles go slack. Then, in the countershock condition, the body makes an active physiological attempt to deal with the situation. The adrenal cortex enlarges and increases its output of adrenaline and other secretions, to give the body more energy; blood pressure and body temperature rise; pulse rate speeds up; the blood in the muscles circulates faster and coagulates more quickly.

2   *Stage of resistance*: With prolonged exposure to a stressor, a person or an animal puts up increased resistance to this stressor and less resistance to other stressors. As the organism tries to adapt or to escape, the adrenal cortex enlarges more, the thymus gland and spleen shrink, and stomach ulcers may develop. If the resistance is successful, the body returns to its normal condition. If it is not, the body collapses.

3   *Stage of exhaustion*: When a stressful event is severe enough and prolonged enough, exhaustion sets in, and many symptoms from the alarm reaction reappear. The body's ability to adapt and its supply of energy are limited. Sleep and rest may be able to restore the body to its previous levels of functioning, but this extreme effort by the body has taken its toll. At this point, the body is more vulnerable to disease. (For a diagram of the three stages of the GAS, see Figure 16-1, below.)

Selye made a major contribution to stress research by emphasizing the physiological effects of stress on the body. Today, however, it looks as if the stress response is more specific than Selye believed. Different stressors do seem to bring about different hormonal responses (J. W. Mason, 1968, 1975). Another problem is that Selye's model, which was developed using rats, does not take into account the individual nature of human beings' responses (Mikhail, 1981). What one person will find highly stressful may roll off the back of another. Jim, who is shy, may go into a tailspin at the thought of a blind date; his roommate Joe may be energized by a blind date but paralyzed by a physics exam that Jim doesn't give a second thought to. An event that overwhelms a person on one occasion (such as getting a parking ticket) will seem to be only a minor irritation on another. The way we perceive an event and the resources we have for coping with it seem to be factors that determine whether it will be stressful. This, essentially, is the cognitive perspective (Lazarus, 1980)—which we'll look at next.

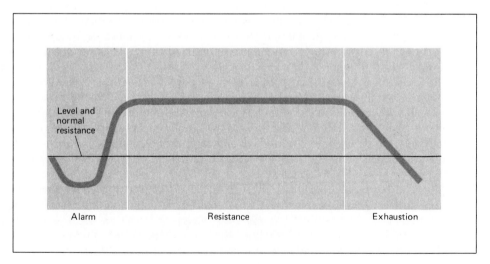

FIGURE 16-1 *General adaptation syndrome (GAS). According to Selye, the body reacts to stress in three major stages: alarm, resistance, and exhaustion. The alarm stage is the body's initial reaction, characterized initially by diminished resistance and then by mobilization of defenses. If the stressor continues, the stage of resistance occurs: the alarm reaction is replaced by above-normal resistance. If the stressor continues for too long, the body can no longer maintain its resistance and the stage of exhaustion is reached: the symptoms of the alarm reaction reappear and death may occur.*

For many people, speaking in front of a group is one of the most stressful experiences imaginable. Others find that it causes only mild nervousness, and still others enjoy being the center of attention. People are highly variable in the way they respond to potentially stressful events. According to the cognitive view, the way we perceive an event and our resources for coping with it determine whether it will be stressful for us.

A COGNITIVE PERSPECTIVE The cognitive view of stress is that stress is in the mind of the beholder. For example, suppose that you have just failed a course. The effect this experience will have on your life depends on whether you need the credit to graduate or to be admitted to graduate school, or whether—say—you want to drop out of college and have been waiting for a good excuse. Another example might be the death of a father of four adult children. The effects of this death may range from extremely slight, for a son who has never been close to his father and is now living far away, to extremely traumatic, for an unmarried daughter who has been keeping house for him.

The cognitive theory of stress, then, is that it is not just what happens which creates stress, but our reaction to what happens. The way we *feel* depends to a great extent on the way we *think* about the events in our lives. In this view, stress is a result of interaction between a particular person and a particular event (Holroyd & Lazarus, 1982; Lazarus, 1980). In most situations, stress depends on the way a person interprets the stressor, and that interpretation is based on previous experience with similar circumstances and on the person's present ability to cope.

The way we construe our relationship with the environment is a function of cognition, or thought. Thoughts influence the way we feel. At the same time, our emotions affect the way we perceive the world. Thus, emotion (feeling) follows cognition (thought), and vice versa. The key, according to Lazarus, is the transactions that take place between people and the environment. The way we feel, think, and act is a product of the way we interact as individuals with events. All our experiences—good and bad—are filtered through our unique personalities, our personal histories, and our viewpoints on life. By and large, we determine which of these experiences will be uplifting and which will be degrading. We do this in the way we act to shape our own lives and in the way we react to the shapes our lives assume.

Let's look at two free-lance graphic designers who have fallen behind a deadline. Charles interprets this as proof of his inadequacy, his slowness, and his inability to schedule time and assignments. Di, on the other hand, is buoyed up by the situation. She interprets it as showing that she simply has more work than she can handle, and that this in turn is evidence of her talent, competence, and popularity with art directors. Charles is paralyzed into inactivity, and Di is energized—by virtu-

Primary appraisal *A person's evaluation of implications that an event has for his or her well-being.*

Secondary appraisal *A person's evaluation of his or her ability to cope with a particular event.*

ally the same situation. These two people have appraised the same basic circumstances quite differently, with the result that these circumstances have a very different meaning for each of them.

The two critical factors in interpretation of a situation are **primary appraisal,** or evaluation of its implications for one's own well-being; and **secondary appraisal,** or evaluation of one's ability to cope with it (Lazarus & Folkman, 1984).

In primary appraisal, we determine what is at stake in a particular situation. We may see it as irrelevant when it does not seem to affect us one way or another; as benign or positive when it can preserve or enhance our well-being; and as stressful when it has already hurt us, when it threatens to hurt us, or when it is challenging. The main purpose of primary appraisal, then, is to discover the meaning of an event. In secondary appraisal, we consider the ways we might cope with the event and how effective these options might be.

In the case of the two free-lance artists, Di and Charles might have made very similar primary appraisals. Their work and how they do it are, clearly, important for their careers, their self-esteem, and their lives. But they have made very different secondary appraisals. Charles is not confident that he can cope with the situation effectively, while Di is entirely confident that she can.

Stress and Development   "It is only by inviting things to go wrong, inviting them to go in unexpected and inappropriate directions, that we will find out where it is that they indeed intend to go." These words by the poet William Dickey (1981) sum up a major reason why so many people continue to take risks—to court stress—throughout their lives. Although the negative aspects of stress can be grave, the positive aspects can be uplifting. A good argument can be made that most of our development throughout life arises from the stressful situations we encounter or create, not from the rafts of tranquility we drift upon from time to time.

Many men and women reach peaks of satisfaction by seeking change and by successfully navigating the unpredictable elements of life. When we reach out to try some new activity we're not at all sure we can master, we feel the familiar signs of stress. When we apply to a college we're not confident will accept us, when we take on a new job we don't have the experience to handle easily, when we make an overture to a man or woman whose interest in us we doubt, we are actively—if not consciously—choosing a stress-inducing situation. If we didn't overreach ourselves to some degree, however, we would never advance beyond our present levels of achievement and satisfaction. We would stop growing. The key to achieving success seems to lie in the ability to cope with the kind of stress we actively seek out and the kind thrust upon us by fate. Most of us do cope well most of the time. By analyzing the strategies used by people who cope effectively, we can improve our ability to grow from stress instead of being overwhelmed by it. We'll talk about these strategies later.

There's no way we can escape stress throughout life. Even if we could, we would lose more than we would gain. As researchers continue to point out, we all *need* some degree of stress in our lives. What we have to do is find the level that's right for us, and then develop ways of coping that will enhance our lives, not constrict them.

Just as we need different amounts of food, sleep, and companionship, we also need different amounts of stress. For instance, Martina does her best work when she is carrying an 18-hour course load, playing on the hockey team, acting in the campus theater group, and serving as a dorm adviser. The busier she is, the more she seems to accomplish. Her roommate, Tracy, on the other hand, needs large blocks of free time for quiet contemplation. She limits her course load to 14 hours, fills her free time with activities (like playing solos on her flute) that do not involve making commitments to other people, and enjoys "hanging out" with friends in an unstructured way. Martina would become unbearably restless under Tracy's schedule, and Tracy would bend under the weight of Martina's.

Although people do show individual differences in the way they react to stressors, most people are likely to find some kinds of experiences more stressful than others. An event is most likely to produce stress if it is *negative* rather than positive (losing a job is more stressful than being hired for a new one); *unpredictable* rather than predictable (being told not to report for work the next day is more stressful than having been forewarned that your company might go out of business); *uncontrollable* rather than controllable (being jilted by a lover is more stressful than doing the jilting yourself); and *ambiguous* rather than clear (an uncertain diagnosis is more stressful than a specific one). Now let's look at some of the research that backs up these statements. Since most of the data are correlational, we cannot come to definitive conclusions about causation, but we can draw some fairly strong inferences.

Stress and Life Events   MAJOR LIFE EVENTS   How much of an impact do the events that occur in our lives—both the good ones and the bad ones—have on our health? A considerable body of literature has grown up around this topic. Research suggests that when several "life events" occur within a rather short time, people have to make so many adaptations that their bodily resistance may be lowered. While stress does not seem to *cause* illness, it may make a person more vulnerable to illness.

The psychiatrist Thomas H. Holmes and his colleagues looked at the life events that some 5000 hospital patients reported as having preceded their illnesses and then developed a rating scale to assess the impact of what they called *life-change units* (LCUs). Holmes and Rahe (1967) found strong evidence that the more changes take place in a person's life, the greater is the likelihood of illness within the next year or two. They found relationships between life changes and the occurrence or onset of heart attack, accidents, tuberculosis, leukemia, multiple sclerosis, diabetes, psychiatric disorders, and all sorts of minor medical complaints.

Surprisingly, some of the stressful events patients reported seemed very positive—such as marriage, a new baby, a new home, a promotion at work, and an outstanding personal achievement. Even happy events, apparently, require adjustments to the changes they bring about (as we saw with Diane Papalia's adoption of Anna): these changes induce stress, and some people seem to react to stress by getting sick. The researchers did not emphasize the meaning events held for people; rather, they focused on how much the subjects had to adapt their response behaviors to these events.

After asking a sample population of 394 adults to assess a number of events according to the amount of adjustment each one required, Holmes and his colleagues (Holmes & Masuda, 1974; Holmes & Rahe, 1967) assigned numerical values to various events and developed the **Social Readjustment Rating Scale (SRRS)** (see Table 16-1). With this scale, a respondent checks off the number of events experienced during a particular time period. The sum of LCUs is the person's score. Holmes and Masuda (1974) found that about half the people who scored between 150 and 300 LCUs in a single year, and about 70 percent of those with 300 LCUs, became ill. This work represents a breakthrough in measuring stress. Its important contribution is its demonstration of an association between the number of life events that require adaptation and the development of illness.

Some of its conclusions are questionable, however (Lazarus, 1981; Lefcourt, Miller, Ware, & Sherk, 1981; D. V. Perkins, 1982; Rabkin & Struening, 1976). First, the correlation between life events and illness is quite modest. Then, the scale does not take individual differences into consideration. Two people might come up with the same number of LCUs, from the same kinds of events; yet one may stay healthy while the other gets sick. Why is this so? The answer seems to be that the events hold different meanings for each person. People are so complex that we cannot analyze their lives only in terms of numbers. Simply adding up LCUs does not tell us the context in which changes took place, how important a person felt they were, and how well (or poorly) he or she dealt with them. Moreover, subsequent research

(©Paul Sequeira/Rapho-Photo Researchers)

People commonly find major life changes stressful, even those that are typically considered positive in nature, such as moving into a new home.

Social Readjustment Rating Scale (SRRS) Tool to assess major life events undergone by person; large changes in life events are associated with illness.

TABLE 16-1 LIFE EVENTS AND WEIGHTED VALUES

Life Event	Value	Life Event	Value
Death of spouse	100	Son or daughter leaving home	29
Divorce	73	Trouble with in-laws	29
Marital separation	65	Outstanding personal	
Jail term	63	achievement	28
Death of close family		Wife beginning or stopping	
member	63	work	26
Personal injury or illness	53	Beginning or ending school	26
Marriage	50	Revision of habits	24
Fired at work	47	Trouble with boss	23
Marital reconciliation	45	Change in work hours	20
Retirement	45	Change in residence	20
Change in health of family	44	Change in schools	20
Pregnancy	40	Change in recreation	19
Sex difficulties	39	Change in social activity	18
Gain of new family member	39	Change in sleeping habits	16
Change in financial state	38	Change in number of family	
Death of close friend	37	get-togethers	15
Change of work	36	Change in eating habits	15
Change in number of		Vacation	13
arguments with spouse	35	Minor violations of law	11
Foreclosure of mortgage	30		
Change of responsibility			
at work	29		

Source: Adapted from Holmes & Rahe, 1967, p. 213.

suggests that various characteristics of an event influence its impact on health. As indicated before, negative, unpredictable, uncontrollable, or ambiguous events are more stressful than positive, predictable, controllable, or clear events. Finally, the original work did not address the fact that a great deal of stress results from *lack* of change—from boredom, loneliness, inability to advance at work, stable but unrewarding personal relationships, and lack of meaning or commitment in life. The worst drawback of the scale may be its implication that people are passive creatures who react rather than act, who are victims of their environment rather than agents who can effect change themselves.

To sum up, this research has earned an important place in the psychological literature by underscoring the relationship between stress and illness, but we still need to look further for answers to the question: Why do some people become sick from stress, while others are energized by it?

MINOR LIFE EVENTS: HASSLES AND UPLIFTS   In his poem "Shoelace," Charles Bukowski (1980) expresses lyrically what several psychologists have established through research:

> It's not the large things that
>   send a man to the madhouse . . .
> No, it's the continuing series
>   of small tragedies that send
>   a man to the madhouse . . .
> Not the death of his love
>   but a shoelace that
>   snaps with no time left . . .

Richard C. Lazarus and his colleagues (DeLongis, Coyne, Dakof, Folkman, & Lazarus, 1982; Kanner, Coyne, Schaefer, & Lazarus, 1981) developed measures of everyday *hassles* (their term for irritations) and *uplifts* (satisfactions); see Table 16-2. They found that hassles (mundane events like losing a wallet, getting stuck in traffic, and fighting with a teenage child at home or a boss or subordinate at work) are much better predictors of physical and psychological health than major life events. Some research suggests that such simple uplifts as playing with a child or listening to music may be able to reverse the potentially harmful effects of stressors (Cohen & Hoberman, 1983). Looking at everyday happenings as well as at major life events may deepen our understanding of the relationship between stress and health.

In many cases, effects of major life events are actually outgrowths of the daily hassles they create. It may not be the large, dramatic events in our lives that are most important, but what happens day in and day out. A widow's grief at losing the man she loved may be compounded by her need to learn how to balance a checkbook, how to handle household repairs, and how to manage on a smaller income. A man's distress over his divorce may have as much to do with his problems in getting the stains out of his shirts as in getting his wife out of his mind. Suppose a man has just learned that his brother, who lives far away, has died. Although the man may grieve, his brother's death hardly affects his life from day to day. If the man's business partner were to die, however, not only would he miss the partner personally, but he would also have to cope with many business problems caused by the partner's death. Lazarus (1981) predicts that illness would be likelier upon the death of the partner than the death of the brother.

We cannot conclude, however, that hassles cause stress. As we pointed out earlier, the fact that two variables show a correlation (a mathematical relationship, as explained in Chapter 1 and in the Appendix) does not necessarily mean that one of them causes the other. It is possible, for example, that people in poorer physical and mental health take hassles more seriously and are more gravely affected by them than healthier people are. It is also possible that poor health itself causes some of the hassles—for example, by making a person forgetful, clumsy, or argumentative.

Even more important, perhaps, are questions about what the "hassles scale" actually measures. Critics charge that many of the hassles listed (for example, being lonely, not having enough energy, or being afraid of rejection) actually resemble psychological symptoms. If the hassles are themselves symptoms, it is no wonder that they correlate well with other symptoms. Another methodological problem is the way the questions are posed, which may bias people's answers toward an overemphasis of the importance of hassles (Dohrenwend & Shrout, 1985).

CONTROL AND PREDICTABILITY OF LIFE EVENTS   Why should hassles and major life events be related to stress? One answer has to do with control. Most of us tend to feel as if we *should* be able to control our everyday lives. We *should* pick the route that's free of traffic, we *should* safeguard our belongings so that we won't be robbed, we *should* get along with other people, we *should* be able to make ordinary business decisions. When these "shoulds" don't operate, we feel at fault. We also feel helpless. Another answer has to do with a characteristic common to many major and minor life events: their unpredictability. A large body of literature indicates that uncontrollable and unpredictable events are more stressful than events we can control and predict.

Stressors such as noise, crowding, electric shock, arbitrary discrimination, dealings with bureaucracy, and demands for increased performance can affect the way we perform various tasks, and they affect us most negatively when we can neither control them nor predict their occurrence (Cohen, 1980). In one study, laboratory subjects did proofreading tasks while their ears were regularly assaulted by blasts of noise. Subjects who were told that they could stop the noise by pushing a button performed better on the task than subjects who could not do anything about the noise—even though the subjects who could push the button did not in fact push it (Glass & Singer, 1972). In another study, subjects did a proofreading task in crowded

TABLE 16-2 "HASSLES" AND "UPLIFTS"

Typical Hassles

1 Too many responsibilities
2 Concerns about physical appearance
3 Being lonely
4 Not enough personal energy
5 Concerns about getting ahead
6 Not enough time for entertainment and recreation
7 Job dissatisfactions
8 Concerns about the meaning of life
9 Fear of rejection
10 Too many things to do

Typical Uplifts

1 Relating well with your spouse or lover
2 Having enough time to do what you want
3 Being visited, phoned, or sent a letter
4 Having enough money for entertainment and recreation
5 Being with children
6 Free time
7 Music
8 Getting unexpected money
9 Spending time with family
10 Sex

Source: Adapted from Kanner, Coyne, Schaefer, & Lazarus, 1981.

and uncrowded rooms. The subjects in a crowded room who were told that they could walk out and work in a larger room did not actually do so, but they did perform better on the task than the subjects who did not have the option of moving (Sherrod, 1974).

One way people seek to establish control over their lives is to search for meaning in an experience ("Why did this happen? How does it affect my life now?"). The search may lead them to attribute it to something that they did. Blaming themselves can be a positive approach, because if they have caused an event, then they can prevent it from happening again or from having a devastating effect on their lives. This sequence of thought showed up in a study of 78 women with breast cancer and their families (Taylor, 1983). Ninety-five percent of the women offered some explanation for the occurrence of the cancer, and many of the causes suggested were factors under their control (like diet, stress, or the effect of certain carcinogens). Two-thirds believed that they could exercise at least some control over the course or recurrence of the cancer by changing their behavior or their way of thinking, a belief that helped them cope with their illness.

Other studies have found that uncontrollable, unpredictable stress interferes with people's humanitarian tendencies. Laboratory subjects who have been exposed to stress that they can neither predict nor do anything about are less sensitive to other people. They are less likely to help a "stranger" (actually, a confederate in the experiment) look for a lost contact lens, more likely to administer an electric shock to another "subject" (again, of course, a confederate), and less likely to recognize individual differences among people. (The way people behave toward each other is discussed in Chapters 17 and 18, which deal with social psychology.)

Why does uncontrollable, unpredictable stress have such wide-ranging effects? One explanation is learned helplessness—a theory first proposed by Seligman (1975) and introduced in Chapter 5, "Learning". A person who feels that nothing he or she can do will change some aspect of the environment, or make it predictable, loses the will to try to change other aspects of the environment. If we feel that nothing we do matters, the end result is a shrug of the shoulders—"Why try?" This attitude will show up on both the cognitive and the emotional level. It may lead to depression (as explained in Chapter 14, "Abnormal Psychology") and, in severe cases, even to death.

There is some research support for the learned-helplessness theory: people living under various conditions over which they have no control often do show signs of helplessness (S. Cohen, 1980). Such people include college students who live in crowded dorms, poor people who live in densely populated housing projects, and children who go to grade schools located in the noisy air corridors of busy airports.

Such findings have important implications for society. For example, it is useful to know that people are better able to deal with inevitable personal setbacks, and will be more helpful and sensitive to one another, when it is possible to control and predict events. But can this knowledge help us in the many situations where we cannot exert control or predict what is about to happen? In a sense, it can: simply knowing that we're apt to experience a higher level of stress is itself a type of predictability, and expecting a difficult time sometimes helps people to cope with it when it comes.

Coping with Stress

People who take on the physically and psychologically demanding job of air traffic controller generally have the kind of personality that flourishes in stressful situations. They must work on schedules that alternate long periods of boredom with short bursts of hectic activity, and they know that as they guide airplanes into and out of airports, they hold the lives of hundreds of people in their hands. Most people in this occupation handle stress well, probably because people who choose this work do so precisely because they find its demands challenging and feel they can handle the pressure.

These air traffic controllers hold highly stressful jobs, as they bear the responsibility for human lives. While people who choose this work generally handle stress well, the demands of the job led to a long, painful strike in the early 1980s, when workers demanded a shorter work week. The ensuing unemployment led to even more stress for workers and their families.

Yet even air traffic controllers have their tolerance levels: the union representing them cited the psychological strains inherent in the job as the major basis for its request for a shorter work week. When the request was denied, in August 1981, 13,000 union members went on strike. Ironically, the strike itself posed new stresses, and these energized some workers while demoralizing others. Most of the striking controllers expected to be back at their jobs within a month, but the strike was declared illegal and the controllers were fired. At the end of the year, the former controllers were no longer measuring the strike in terms of days out or salaries lost. They talked about it, instead, in terms of the changes in their lives (Barron, 1981).

Some of these workers suffered greatly. They were worried about money; they felt inadequate because their wives were now supporting their families (most air traffic controllers are men); they had marital problems; and they were generally anxious and upset.

After the initial shock, however, some of the displaced workers plucked victory from what to others was a crushing defeat. One 32-year-old, for example, went back to college, attained a 3.3 grade-point average in pre-law political science courses, and was seriously considering becoming a lawyer. This man was obviously coping positively with a stressful situation in a way that promised ultimate reward.

What exactly *is* coping? It is not the avoidance or elimination of stress, because a life with no stress would be a boring life. We all need some stress and the chance to deal with it. Dealing successfully with stress involves turning it from a problem into a challenge that presents an opportunity for growth.

A process-oriented definition of **coping** sees it as a constantly changing effort to manage demands that tax personal resources (Lazarus & Folkman, 1984). We cope in one of two major ways—either through problem-focused coping, in which we try to solve the problem; or through emotion-focused coping, in which we try to manage our emotional response to the problem. In problem-focused coping, we may change the environment or our own actions or attitudes (possibly confronting a person we see as responsible for the problem, or getting more information about a situation). In emotion-focused coping, we may use defense mechanisms like denial, intellectualization, projection, and so forth (described in Chapter 13); we may take drugs, legal or illegal; we may change consciousness through techniques like meditation (for a discussion of the way drugs and meditation affect us, see Chapter 4); or

Coping *Constantly changing effort to manage the demands that tax personal resources.*

we may force ourselves to think positive thoughts. We're more likely to use the first approach in situations we think we *can* change, and to use the second when we think we can*not* do anything about a threatening situation (Lazarus & Folkman, 1984).

For example, a striking air traffic controller can change his work environment by taking a different kind of job, or he might immerse himself in union-related activities to improve the working conditions of the present job. If he feels that he can't change the job, he might work on changing his own attitude—by seeking tension-releasing activities outside of work or by reminding himself that the gratifications of his job are partly due to its challenges and his ability to use his skills.

Effective copers tend to use both kinds of techniques—those that help them solve the problem at hand and those that help them feel better—in positive ways. Less effective copers may solve the immediate problem but at a high cost in terms of emotional and physical well-being, or may escape through drugs or meditation into a state that makes them feel better but does not do anything to change the source of their stress. Most of the time we use a combination of many acts and thoughts to cope with a specific situation. The particular ones adopted depend on the nature of both the stressor and the person under stress.

Why do some people handle stressful situations better than others? Why does one person build a new life after becoming permanently handicapped through illness or injury, or mourn a dead spouse but go on to form a close relationship with someone else, or rebound after losing a job under publicly embarrassing circumstances, to emerge apparently stronger from the ordeal—while another sinks into apathy, depression, or even suicide? The way we cope is influenced by our internal and external resources, our beliefs, our problem-solving and personal skills, our social support, and competing demands (Lazarus & Folkman, 1984). Some factors, of course, are obvious: for example, having enough money to pay your bills and enough time to do your work will reduce stress. It is also easier to deal with one stressor at a time than to deal with "stress overload": the more stressors we have at any one time, the harder it is for us to handle them. We'll look now at the influence of personality and social support, and at some techniques for reducing stress.

Personality   Our personality affects the way we handle stress. Later in this chapter we'll look at differences in the ways "type A" and "type B" personalities respond to stress, and we'll examine some possible relationships between personality and illnesses such as heart disease and cancer.

By observing people who handle stress well, researchers have identified an important personality style: ***hardiness.*** Kobasa and her colleagues have identified three characteristics of hardiness—commitment, challenge, and control (Kobasa, 1982a, 1982b; Kobasa, Maddi, & Kahn, 1982).

Commitment allows us to believe in the truth, importance, and interest of what we are and what we're doing, and thus to feel an overall sense of purpose in life. *Challenge* is based on the belief that change, rather than stability, is the normal condition of life. When we hold this attitude we can look at a stressful life event as an opportunity for personal growth, rather than as a threat. We're likely to be open and flexible, and we may even seek out new and interesting experiences, in the full and open knowledge that when we do so, we invite a certain measure of stress into our lives. The most important of these dimensions seems to be *control,* the belief that we are responsible for our own lives, that in some way we bring about stressful events, and that therefore we can do something about them (see Chapter 11 for a discussion of locus of control).

Although the concept of hardiness seems to hold promise for identifying personality characteristics that help people cope with stress, some researchers following up this theory have found that the "three C's" do not form a single construct. As was noted above, control appears to be the most important element. Thus, the theory may need some bolstering (Taylor, 1986).

Hardiness   *Personality style characterized by commitment, challenge, and control.*

Social Support   People who have family members and good friends to call upon usually cope with stress better than those who do not: they fall ill less often and recover from illness more quickly (Cohen & Wills, 1985; Weingarten, 1985). What do important people in our lives provide? They may give us tangible assistance by lending us money, driving us to a doctor's office, or baby-sitting; they may give us information about solving a problem; or they may support us emotionally by reassuring us and letting us know they care (Taylor, 1986).

In one study of men and women who had experienced a high degree of stress during the previous year, those who seemed healthiest (both physically and emotionally) had more easygoing personalities and were more apt to cope with a problem by doing something about it than by keeping their feelings to themselves or taking them out on the people around them. Some gender differences emerged. Self-confidence seemed more important in helping men deal with stress; and in times of stress women were more likely than men to turn to family members. Both these differences seem to reflect traditional sex roles: men are expected to be strong and self-sufficient, while women are allowed to admit vulnerability and seek help (Holahan & Moos, 1985).

Specific Coping Techniques   Myths and stereotypes about coping abound in our culture. A man whose wife has left him goes into a bar and downs one drink after another as he tells his troubles to the bartender. A nervous father-to-be paces back and forth, lighting up one cigarette after another. A fat person eats; a thin person stops eating; a depressed person goes to bed.

Fortunately, there are better ways to cope with stress. Some of them come to us naturally; others, we can learn. Training programs have been developed that help tense people learn how to relax, insecure people become more assertive and thus more self-confident, and uncertain people discover their own resources for coping (Holahan & Moos, 1985). Such programs help people replace harmful methods of coping (like those noted above) with positive methods. Meditation (discussed in Chapter 4) and biofeedback (discussed in Chapter 5) are two other ways to deal with stress.

"COMMONSENSE" TECHNIQUES   The reports of a number of new parents illustrate some common ways in which people cope with stress. When 109 pairs of new parents were asked about their coping strategies and were questioned on several measures of well-being at three successive time periods—midway during the pregnancy, about 6 weeks after the baby's birth, and from 6 to 8 months after birth—those couples who were found to be coping best reported specific helpful activities and attitudes (Miller & Sollie, 1980). These included:

- *Adaptability*: Ability to accept the unpredictability of day-to-day life with a baby, to learn patience, and to be flexible.

- *Communication*: Ability of husband and wife to share their feelings with each other.

- *Seeing parenthood as a shared responsibility*: Ability to break away from stereotyped household roles and to negotiate new ones.

- *Pursuing adult interests*: Continuing to participate in activities that were of interest before the birth of the baby.

- *Spending some time away from the baby.*

- *Looking to the future*: Talking about career goals, planning to implement them, and recognizing that parenting responsibilities ease as children mature.

- *Using friends, relatives, and neighbors as resources*: Getting information, advice, and help with child care from others.

**TABLE 16-3 SOME COPING STATEMENTS USED BY STUDENTS IN
A STRESS-INOCULATION PROGRAM**

Situation	Statements
Preparing for a stressor	What is it I have to do? I can develop a plan to deal with it. Just think about what I can do about it. That's better than getting anxious. No negative self-statements; just think rationally. Don't worry. Worry won't help anything. Maybe what I think is anxiety is eagerness to confront it.
Confronting and handling a stressor	Just "psych" myself up. I can meet this challenge. One step at a time. I can handle the situation. Don't think about fear, just about what I have to do. Stay relevant. This anxiety is what the doctor said I would feel. It's a reminder to use my coping exercises. This tenseness can be an ally, a cue to cope. Relax; I'm in control. Take a slow deep breath. Ah, good.
Coping with the feeling of being overwhelmed	When fear comes, just pause. Keep focus on the present; what is it I have to do? Let me label my fear from 0 to 10 and watch it change. I was supposed to expect my fear to rise. Don't try to eliminate fear totally; just keep it manageable. I can convince myself to do it. I can reason my fear away. It will be over shortly. It's not the worst thing that can happen. Just think about something else. Do something that will prevent me from thinking about fear. Just describe what is around me. That way I won't think about worrying.
Reinforcing successes	It worked; I was able to do it. Wait until I tell my therapist about this. It wasn't as bad as I expected. I made more out of the fear than it was worth. My damn ideas, that's the problem. When I control them, I control my fear. It's getting better each time I use the procedure. I'm really pleased with the progress I'm making. I did it!

Source: Adapted from Meichenbaum, 1975, pp. 250–251.

STRESS-INOCULATION TRAINING   Brian, a first-year college student, always breaks out in a cold sweat before taking an examination, is so tense and nervous that he forgets all the material he thought he had down pat, and (not surprisingly) gets a low grade on the test. Since Brian wants to do well at the university, he knows he will have to do *something* to overcome his debilitating test anxiety.

One thing Brian might do is seek out a program of **stress-inoculation training**. Such a program educates people about their reactions to stressors through active give-and-take between leader and participants, lets them rehearse ways to cope with specific stressors, and then has them practice coping skills on a variety of mild to severe stressors. This kind of program combines two important psychological approaches: cognitive therapy, which makes people aware of their feelings, and of what they themselves are doing and saying to themselves to bring about those feelings; and behavior modification, which shows them how to change their negative behaviors (Novaco, 1977). In one program directed at test anxiety, for example, students are encouraged to learn new, helpful statements that they can say to themselves to replace the anxiety-producing statements they have been making. Some examples of the new statements are given in Table 16-3.

Stress-inoculation training
Behavioral technique, designed to prevent stress, which combines cognitive therapy and behavior modification.

Living with Stress

Do people who know how to handle stress live longer? According to a study of 1200 persons over the age of 100, the answer seems to be *yes*. These centenarians' answers to questions about social, psychological, and biological factors indicated that they had a positive outlook on life and had rooted out negative attitudes and emotions (Segerberg, 1982). They seemed to exemplify the successful application of Selye's theory, which emphasizes the development of a "lofty long-range purpose" to live by (1974, p. 106). With such a purpose, people can make commitments, can express themselves fully, and can achieve a sense of security. "To accomplish this," says Selye (p. 110), "you must first find your optimal stress level, and then use your adaptation energy at a rate and in a direction adjusted to your innate qualifications and preferences."

In some ways, life is like theater. Every good play is built around a basic conflict which illuminates character, draws on the characters' reserves of strength, and—because the outcome is uncertain—maintains suspense. So it is with life. Stress is not necessarily a villain in our lives, and at times it may well be a hero. The role it plays depends largely on the way that we, the actors, read our lines and stage our actions. By responding creatively and effectively, we can often write our own happy endings.

WELLNESS AND HEALTH PRACTICES

How can we talk about health as a positive state, not just the absence of illness? It is helpful to use a new term—*wellness*. This term describes an ideal state of enriched health and enhanced life (Danish, 1983). According to this concept, even people who are disabled or who suffer from some health impairment can be considered *well* if they make an active effort to live their lives as fully as possible within the limitations of their condition.

Wellness Ideal state of enriched health and enhanced life.

Most people want to feel good. In one nationwide poll, 81 percent of Americans rated good health as second in importance only to a good family life (Rubenstein, 1982). And certain practices, such as those listed in Table 16-4, seem to be directly related to health; a survey of 7000 people, age 20 to 70, found that those who followed all seven of these habits were healthiest, followed by those who followed six, then by those who followed five, and so on (Belloc & Breslow, 1972). Yet many people who recognize the value of these and other behaviors do not practice them in everyday life. A recent survey found that people 18 to 29 years old practice the fewest health habits of any age group (Prevention Research Center, 1986).

How would you classify yourself in terms of seeking wellness? One team of researchers informally (and with tongue slightly in cheek) categorized people as "risk takers," "sensible people" who abstain from smoking and drinking, "health nuts," and "hypochondriacs" (Leventhal, Prohaska, & Hirschman, 1985). It's interesting, however—and frustrating to professionals interested in promoting wellness—to find that even within these categories people tend to be inconsistent. That is, correlations between different kinds of behaviors are fairly weak, within any category. You may watch your weight and drink moderately, but smoke heavily. Your cousin may jog daily and abstain from smoking and drinking, but be indiscriminate in choosing sexual partners. Your aunt may fail to use her seat belt when she drives to the annual gynecological checkup she wouldn't miss.

These inconsistencies show how hard it is to motivate people to follow certain health practices. The challenge for health psychologists is to identify the mechanisms that control such behaviors and then to encourage people to develop helpful behaviors and eliminate harmful ones (Leventhal, Prohaska, & Hirschman, 1985). Let's take a look at some of these mechanisms.

TABLE 16-4 SEVEN HEALTH HABITS

1 Eating breakfast
2 Eating regular meals and not snacking
3 Eating moderately to maintain normal weight
4 Not smoking
5 Drinking alcohol moderately or not at all
6 Exercising moderately
7 Sleeping regularly 7 to 8 hours a night

Source: Belloc & Breslow, 1972.

(Mark Olds)

Exercise provides a host of benefits, and you don't have to run a marathon to get them. Lower levels of exercise done regularly are even better, as this 2-mile-a-day jogger has learned.

Influences on Health Practices

Social Factors   If your parents and friends smoke, you're more likely to smoke yourself. If your culture considers a suntanned body beautiful, you're more likely to spend time in the sun than if it admires an ivory-pale complexion. If your parents taught you to brush your teeth when you were very young, you're likely to do it all your life without even thinking about it. In these behaviors and in other health practices, you are influenced by your culture, your socioeconomic level, your immediate family, and your friends.

Sociological Factors   If you are poor or poorly educated, or if you live in an area with poor health care facilities, you may not be able to guard your health well. You may not be able to afford a nutritious diet, you may not know what foods are nutritious, you may not obtain the immunizations that are available, and you may not be able to treat medical, dental, and psychological problems when they first arise—thereby allowing them to become severe.

Environmental Factors   One important presence in the environment is the legal structure. What role, for example, can official agencies play in promoting health? For years the federal government has issued statements warning of the health dangers of cigarette smoking—while at the same time providing financial subsidies to tobacco growers. There is a basic contradiction here.

Governmental regulations can play a major part in many aspects of wellness. If your state enacts and enforces laws requiring the use of seat belts for adults and safety restraints for children in cars, you're more apt to use them. Laws that mandate childproof caps on medicine containers, fireproof materials for children's pajamas, and helmets for motorcyclists encourage the use of these safety measures. Laws that prohibit smoking in public places protect people from their own smoke and from the smoke of others. Laws can do just so much, however, as this country learned during Prohibition. People who are determined to do something often violate the law.

Other environmental factors also affect health. One important source of stress for many people is the workplace. Among the on-the-job stresses reported in a survey of 915 female office workers are low pay, lack of promotions, monotonous work, too much work, problems with supervisors, and production quotas (Working Women Education Fund, 1981).

Emotional Factors   If you are undergoing emotional stress, you may be more likely to drive carelessly, overeat or undereat, or drink or smoke more than usual. Your emotions can affect your health in other ways, too. Emotional stress can affect the body's immune system, rendering you more susceptible to diseases that would not affect you so severely if you were in a more positive frame of mind.

Cognitive Factors   Your beliefs exert a great deal of control over your health. If you think that you could contract tuberculosis without being aware of it, you'll be more likely to get a chest x-ray than if you think you would get an early warning sign (Hochbaum, 1958). If you believe that something that you did caused your high blood pressure, you're more apt to take medicine and change your habits in an effort to cure it (Steele, Gutmann, Leventhal, & Easterling, 1983).

Physical Factors   If you cough when you smoke, feel nauseated when you drink, or feel uncomfortably full when you overeat, you'll be less likely to repeat these behaviors. Some people who exercise feel euphoric during and immediately after a workout (a "runner's high"), which is a strong factor in getting them to repeat the activity.

How Health Habits Can Affect Wellness

The way you eat, the amount of sleep you get, the extent of your physical activity, your use or nonuse of drugs, and all the other health-related things you do on a day-in, day-out basis are an essential part of your lifestyle. Your own experience tells you that certain habits can make you feel better immediately. (It feels better, for example, to wake up in the morning without a hangover than with one; it feels better to have the wind to run for a bus without having to stop for breath; it feels good to zip up your jeans without feeling that you're going to burst.)

Furthermore, research shows the importance of certain habits for long-term health. This is one area of our lives over which we can exert considerable control. The United States Centers for Disease Control (1980, in Taylor, 1986), for example, estimate that in this country, factors over which we have some control are associated with 50 percent of the deaths from the ten leading causes of death. We have the power to prevent much illness. The following sections, on a few specific aspects of health that have been the subject of substantial research, show how we can exercise such power.

Diet   What we eat determines (to a certain degree) how we look, how we feel about our looks, how we feel physically, and how likely we are to suffer from various diseases. Diseases like diabetes and gout are more common among people who eat a rich diet, and there is a link between diet and some other diseases, including cancer and heart ailments. We'll look closely at some aspects of diet and health.

DIET AND HEART DISEASE   Evidence has been mounting in recent years that high levels in the bloodstream of a fatty substance called **cholesterol** increase the risk of heart disease. Cholesterol forms fat deposits in blood vessels throughout the body, narrowing those vessels so severely that the blood supply to the heart can be cut off—which will lead to a heart attack. The link between cholesterol and heart disease has been definitively established by recent research, including a 7-year study of 3806 middle-aged men with high cholesterol levels. All the men followed low-cholesterol diets, and some received a drug to lower cholesterol. This study found

Cholesterol *Fatty substance whose level in the blood is related to dietary intake of fats. High levels are associated with increased incidence of heart disease.*

that lowering cholesterol levels can reduce the risk of heart disease and death (Lipid Research Clinics Program, 1984a, 1984b).

The most important determinant of cholesterol levels seems to be the kind and amount of food we eat. The current recommended diet emphasizes fish and poultry rather than red meat; low-fat or skim milk, low-fat yogurt, and cottage cheese rather than hard cheeses; margarine and oil rather than butter; a lowered intake of fats and oils in general; and reduced consumption of egg yolks—no more than two to four per week (American Heart Association, 1984). One particular kind of oil, fish oil obtained from eating certain kinds of fatty fish, seems to be associated with a *lower* risk of coronary disease (Knapp, Reilly, Alessandrini, & FitzGerald, 1986).

DIET AND CANCER Extensive research, worldwide, strongly suggests that there is a link between diet and the risks of certain kinds of cancer. Japanese-American women in the United States, for example, have higher rates of breast cancer than women in Japan, while people in Japan have higher rates of cancer of the stomach and esophagus than Americans do. Breast cancer seems to be related to the high-fat diet typical in the United States; stomach and esophageal cancers seem to be associated with the pickled, smoked, and salted fish that make up much of the diet of the Japanese (Gorbach, Zimmerman, & Woods, 1984).

DIET AND WEIGHT Maintaining appropriate body weight makes us feel good, both physically and psychologically. Body weight depends on calories: those taken in through food and those expended through exercise. Overweight in most cases is simply a case of eating more than the body needs.

Different people seem to have different caloric needs, and these predispositions seem to have a strong genetic component. A recent study compared 540 Danish adults who had been adopted with both their biological parents and their adoptive parents. The researchers classified parents and offspring as "thin," "median-weight," "overweight," or "obese," according to a "body-mass index" based on weight divided by height. A strong correlation showed up between the body mass index of the adoptees and their biological parents; but there was virtually no relationship between adoptive parents and children. The highest correlation appeared between mothers and their biological daughters (Stunkard et al., 1986).

Other research suggests that family environment does play a part in obesity, since positive correlations have been found between adoptive parents and children, fraternal twins, and even pet owners and their pets (Garn, 1966). However, it is often possible for children of overweight parents to control their weight by making changes in their lifestyle: eating less and exercising more.

EATING DISORDERS *Obesity* People who are 10 percent heavier than the "ideal" weight for their height and body build are considered *overweight*. The term *obese* is reserved for people who are at least 20 percent over the ideal weight. Current estimates indicate that fewer than one-fourth to fewer than one-half of American adults (from 21 to 46 percent) are within the weight range recommended for their sex, height, and body build, depending upon what normal range is considered acceptable (Prevention Research Center, 1986).

Obesity can lead to such health problems as high blood pressure, heart disease, certain cancers, allergies, and sinus attacks (NIH, 1985b). Obesity can also become a severe psychological problem, since it so drastically violates our society's standards of beauty. The National Institutes of Health (1985b) urge that the obese receive the same kind of medical attention given to people with other life-threatening disorders. Lower levels of overweight can also impair health, especially if there are other risk factors, like diabetes or hypertension. Physical risks include such conditions as high blood pressure, heart disease, and certain cancers.

Obesity is a difficult condition to treat. Although overweight people can lose weight on a variety of different diets, most of them regain the weight they have lost—and more. The most effective programs begin with reducing the amount of

Obesity Eating disorder characterized by being at least 20 percent over ideal weight; associated with a variety of medical problems.

LOSING WEIGHT BY APPLYING PSYCHOLOGICAL PRINCIPLES

- *Eat in only one place at regular times*: This will help you cut down on snacking, by limiting the number of places and times that have associations with eating and thus suggest, "It's time to eat."
- *Eat slowly*: This helps you get the most pleasure from the smallest amount of food, helps you fool yourself into thinking you're eating more than you actually are, and gives your body time to give you feedback on when you've had enough.
- *Don't do anything else while you're eating, such as reading or watching television*: This helps you make eating the "main event," so that you can concentrate on your food and be more responsive to your body's internal cues. It also keeps you from establishing habits ("If I'm at the movies, it's time to eat popcorn").
- *Reduce the availability of fattening foods*: If you can't resist chocolate-chip cookies, peanuts, or other high-calorie foods, don't bring them home. Throw out or freeze leftovers immediately, so that you won't be tempted to eat them. If you buy nuts, buy them with their shells on, so that you'll have to expend more effort to eat them; you'll probably eat less.
- *Allow for some variety in your diet—but not too much*: If you deprive yourself of all the foods you love, you'll binge when you get the chance. It's better, therefore, to incorporate a small serving of cake or ice cream or some other high-calorie treat into your menu instead of avoiding it completely. However, since people (and animals) eat more food when faced with a large variety, limit your meals to a few basic dishes instead of a wide choice.
- *Avoid fatty and rich-tasting foods, even when they're "dietetic"*: Foods that look, smell, and taste sweet, rich, or fatty—even when they're not—seem to stimulate the appetite.
- *Eat in the company of other people who are moderate eaters themselves*: You'll be inclined to eat more moderately when other people are witnesses to what you eat. Also, you'll be able to guide your intake by theirs.
- *Use small serving plates and glasses*: Food heaped on a small plate looks like more than the same amount on a large plate. Take advantage of this visual illusion to fool yourself into eating less.
- *Incorporate exercise into your daily schedule*: Aside from direct expenditure of energy in the activity itself, exercise increases perceived energy level, builds muscle mass (which uses more calories than fat does), and seems to reduce appetite. Programs that combine dieting, changes in behavior, and exercise result in more weight loss than any one of these methods alone. The most effective exercise schedules include sessions of at least 20 minutes each, three times a week, of activities that are strenuous enough to expend 300 calories per session or to raise the heart rate to 60 to 70 percent of its maximum (Thompson, Jarvie, Lahey, & Cureton, 1982). This generally means swimming, running, bicycling, dancing, or some other kind of aerobic activity (activity requiring high consumption of oxygen for a sustained period of time), rather than a more static exercise like weight lifting or sit-ups.

food eaten, and then use behavior modification techniques and increased exercise to keep the weight off. (A modified fast at the beginning often leads to quick weight loss, which motivates people to stay in a program long enough to learn healthier eating patterns.) However, even these programs have had only moderate levels of success. (For suggestions on losing weight that you can implement yourself, see the box "Losing Weight by Applying Psychological Principles.")

Anorexia nervosa **Anorexia nervosa** is an eating disorder which takes the form of a prolonged refusal to eat. The result is severe loss of weight, to the point where the person is 15 percent below normal body weight. Although the disorder affects people of both sexes and of varying ages (it can begin as early as 9 years of age, during the thirties, or even later), the typical patient is female and somewhere between puberty and the early twenties. She is usually bright, well-behaved, and appealing, and from an apparently stable, well-educated, well-off family. She is preoccupied with food—with cooking it, talking about it, and urging others to eat—but she either doesn't eat herself, or gorges herself and then purges by vomiting or using laxatives. She has a distorted sense of body image and sees herself as beautiful when she is at her most pathetically and grotesquely skeletal.

Anorexia nervosa *Eating disorder characterized by prolonged refusal to eat, leading to extreme weight loss (at least 15 percent under normal weight).*

Once the starvation begins, other symptoms appear. Menstruation usually stops, thick soft hair may grow over the body, and intense overactivity may occur. The usual course of anorexia involves a single episode with complete recovery, but between 15 and 21 percent of anorectic patients starve themselves to death (DSM III, 1980).

We don't know what causes anorexia. It may be a physical disorder caused by a disturbance in the hypothalamus, a hormonal imbalance, or a deficiency of a crucial neurotransmitter; or it may be a psychological disturbance related to depression, fear of growing up, or family malfunctioning. Most researchers link it to the emphasis in our society on slenderness as an ideal of beauty, which can put extreme pressures on a vulnerable person (Barker, 1979; Gold et al., 1986; Gwirtsman & Germer, 1981; Herzog, 1982). So far, research evidence has not conclusively borne out any of the hypotheses, and further study is needed.

Treatment of anorexia often involves hospitalization and drugs to encourage eating and inhibit vomiting, along with behavior therapy—eating is rewarded by privileges such as getting out of bed and leaving the room. Such immediate measures are usually combined with psychotherapy, which almost always involves the patient's family. The aim of therapy is to make patients more aware of their own feelings and needs, and to help them act in a self-directed, competent way (Bruch, 1978).

Bulimia Eating disorder characterized by episodes of "binge" eating (ingestion of huge quantities of food), followed by purging (vomiting or use of laxatives).

Bulimia Forty to 50 percent of women with anorexia nervosa will at some time develop **bulimia** (Johnson & Larson, 1982). This disorder, which is also most common in teenage and young adult women, is characterized by episodes of "binge" eating—ingestion of huge quantities of food (between 1000 and 5000 calories might be consumed in a single episode)—followed by vomiting or use of laxatives to purge the body (Johnson Stuckey, Lewis, & Schwartz, 1982). Bulimics are often depressed and commonly suffer such physical complications as hair loss, extensive tooth decay, and gastric irritation. Most women with bulimia are of normal weight. It is difficult to get precise figures on the incidence of bulimia, and estimates range widely—from 1 to 5 percent of the general population (Nagelberg, Hale, & Ware, 1983) and from 5 to 67 percent of college women (Hart & Ollendick, 1985; Polivy & Herman, 1985).

Once a binge begins, bulimics cannot stop eating; afterwards, they feel guilty, depressed, and panicky. In one study, bulimic women were asked to describe the factors that led to their binges. Heading the list was difficulty in handling emotions (Johnson et al., 1982). The emotions which these bulimics found it difficult to deal with were most likely to be sadness, loneliness, and irritability; and they experienced more fluctuations in mood than a sample of normal women (Johnson & Larson, 1982). Researchers have suggested that bulimics binge in order to regulate tension and moderate their mood swings, that they become addicted to food as others become addicted to alcohol or drugs, and that they purge themselves to avoid becoming fat.

The second item on the list of precipitating factors was restrictive dieting (Johnson et al., 1982). One team of researchers maintains that dieting may cause bingeing because dieters are so conscious of what they eat that they manage their food intake by cognitive means (knowing what they "should" or "should not" eat) rather than physiological means (feeling hungry or full) (Polivy & Herman, 1985). When for some reason they stray from their diet (eating foods that are not allowed, or eating more than is allowed), they lose all sense of control and overeat even more. These researchers conclude their review of the link between dieting and bingeing with the thought that "perhaps dieting is the disorder that we should be attempting to cure" (Polivy & Herman, 1985, p. 200). Recent studies do, however, indicate that antidepressant drugs are sometimes effective in treating bulimia (Pope, Hudson, & Jonas, 1983).

(c)1980 Tom McCarth/The Image Bank)

Sports that can be done from childhood throughout adulthood—such as running, swimming, bicycling, and walking—provide a good basis for the kind of moderate exercise that can be fun as well as healthful.

Exercise Whenever you hear a claim about a pill or a potion that is supposed to cure practically anything from warts or impotence to cancer, you can be fairly sure that it's fraudulent. There is one remedy, however, that has been scientifically shown to produce a wide range of health benefits. It can help to ward off heart disease, colds, and influenza; maintain healthy and attractive weight goals; make sex more exciting; make food taste better and digest more efficiently; build up energy; and put one in a happier state of mind. This seemingly magical panacea is physical exercise.

For some years Americans have heeded the call to get moving, but there are signs that the exercise boom has peaked, and that fewer people are engaging regularly in strenuous activity today than a few years ago (Prevention Research Center, 1986). In 1961 less than 1 out of 4 people engaged in regular physical activity; by the 1980s, between half and three-fourths of the population were doing so (Serfass & Gerberich, 1984). These people in running shoes, warm-up suits, and leotards are reaping the health benefits noted above, plus a few others, such as protection against ***osteoporosis***—a thinning of the bones that may occur in later life—and the possibility of improved cognitive functioning (McCann & Holmes, 1984; Notelovitz & Ware, 1983; Paffenbarger, Hyde, Wing, & Hsieh, 1984; Serfass & Gerberich, 1984; Thomas, Lee, Franks, & Paffenbarger, 1982; Tomporowski & Ellis, 1986).

Because we sometimes hear of a sudden heart attack during exercise, some people wonder whether the risks are worth the benefits. A recent study helps to put such fears at rest. When men who jogged, played singles tennis, chopped wood, or did other strenuous exercise for 2½ hours per week were compared with men who exercised for less than 20 minutes a week, the inactive men were three times more likely to die suddenly than the active ones. Among the active men, those who did suffer cardiac arrest were more likely to do so when they were exercising vigorously than when they were resting, accounting for the public perception of the dangers of strenuous exercise. Overall, however, this study and others strongly suggest that the benefits of exercise outweigh its risks (Siscovick, Weiss, Fletcher, & Lasky, 1984).

Health psychologists have found that people are more likely to adopt exercise as a lifelong habit if they're aware of its benefits, if they choose the right exercise for their own body build and lifestyle, if they take the time to warm up and cool down,

Osteoporosis *Thinning of the bones that may occur in later life, especially among women.*

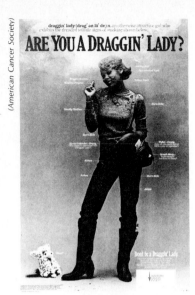

ARE YOU A DRAGGIN' LADY?

Efforts are being made to discourage young women in particular from smoking. Proportionately fewer men smoke these days, but the percentage of female smokers has remained about the same, causing women's rates of lung cancer and other smoking-related illnesses to come close to those of men.

and if they set goals and monitor their progress (Serfass & Gerberich, 1984). Children should be encouraged to make exercise part of their daily lives—especially activities they can continue doing as adults, such as running, swimming, bicycling, and walking. This is especially important, since recent studies have found that American children are at an appallingly low level of fitness, which observers attribute to cutbacks in school physical education programs and to increased time spent watching television ("Presidential council on fitness," 1986).

Use of Tobacco   If you wanted to do just one thing for your health, you would stay far away from tobacco. Cigarette smoking is the single most important cause of preventable illness and death in this country. It is the major cause of death from cancer of the lung, esophagus, larynx, and mouth; it contributes to death from cancer of the pancreas, kidney, and bladder; and it also contributes to heart disease and makes stomach ulcers worse (Fielding, 1985a; U.S. Public Health Service, 1982). Previous differences in rates of cigarette smoking between men and women may well account for much of the 7-year difference in life expectancy between the sexes (Miller & Gerstein, 1983). Furthermore, smoking during pregnancy affects the unborn baby: it increases the chances of producing a small baby or one who is dead at birth or dies soon afterward (U.S. Dept. of Health and Human Services, 1980a). And a body of evidence shows that "passive smoking" (breathing in smoke emitted by other people) can affect the health of nonsmokers (Bonham & Wilson, 1981).

In recent years, more people, including a growing number of teenage boys, have been using chewing tobacco or snuff (finely ground tobacco that is either sniffed or held in the mouth). These forms of tobacco also pose health dangers, including increased risk of cancer of the mouth, esophagus, larynx, and pancreas; gum disease; high blood pressure; and nicotine dependence (Connolly et al., 1986; NIH, 1986).

Even though fewer people are smoking today, many young people still start; most smokers first light up at about the age of 12 (Matarazzo, 1982). In 1984, 18.7 percent of American high school seniors smoked daily, compared with 29 percent in 1977; and 35 percent of adult men and 30 percent of adult women smoked, compared with 52 and 34 percent, respectively, in the 1960s (Johnston, O'Malley, & Bachman, 1985; USDHHS, 1985a). The percentage of male smokers dropped by one-third, while the percentage of female smokers has remained about the same; since the highest proportion of women smokers are in their early twenties, the number of female smokers is likely to increase. Yes, women have "come a long way" toward catching up with men in lung cancer incidence and mortality rates; women's rates are rising by about 6 percent per year (Horm & Kessler, 1986).

Because of its far-reaching effects on health, the use of tobacco presents several challenges for health psychologists—how to keep young people from starting to smoke, how to discourage young women in particular, and how to help smokers quit. Cigarette smoking *is* on the decline in this country, and most people who have stopped smoking have quit on their own, rather than in connection with the many counseling, behavior modification, and hypnosis programs or other programs set up to help smokers quit (Fielding, 1985b). The people who join these programs may be those who are unable to stop smoking on their own. The programs' fairly low rates of success may be due, then, to the fact that their enrollees constitute a "hard-core" group who find it hardest to stop.

Use of Alcohol   Alcohol is the leading problem drug in the United States. Ten million Americans can't handle it and are either "problem drinkers" or full-fledged alcoholics. When does alcohol become a problem? Drinking is a problem when it interferes with a person's ability to function on the job or in personal relationships, and when a person cannot control the desire for or use of alcohol. (For some warning signs of problem drinking, see the box "Do You Have a Drinking Problem?") People dependent on alcohol experience a variety of withdrawal symptoms when they stop

The key to a successful solution for a drinking problem is a willingness to admit to being an alcoholic. The following questions are recommended as a means of "self-testing" for a drinking problem.

EARLY SYMPTOMS
(FIRST STAGE OF ALCOHOLISM)

Yes   No

____ ____ Are you beginning to lie or feel guilty about drinking?

____ ____ Do you gulp your drinks?

____ ____ Do you try to have a few extra drinks before joining others in drinking?

____ ____ Must you drink at certain times—for example, before lunch or a special event, after a disappointment or quarrel?

____ ____ Do you drink because you feel tired, depressed, or worried?

____ ____ Are you annoyed when family or friends talk about your drinking?

____ ____ Are you beginning to have memory blackouts and occasional passouts?

DO YOU HAVE A DRINKING PROBLEM?

MIDDLE SYMPTOMS
(EXTENSION OF EARLY SYMPTOMS)

____ ____ Are you making more promises and telling more lies about your drinking?

____ ____ Are there more times when you need a drink?

____ ____ When sober, do you regret what you have said or done while drinking?

____ ____ Are you drinking more often alone, avoiding family or close friends?

____ ____ Do you have weekend drinking bouts and Monday hangovers?

____ ____ Have you been going "on the wagon" to control your drinking?

____ ____ Are memory blackouts and passouts becoming more frequent?

LATE SYMPTOMS
(ADVANCED STAGE OF ALCOHOLISM)

____ ____ Do you drink to live and live to drink?

____ ____ Are you obviously drunk on important occasions—for example, a special dinner or meeting?

____ ____ Do your drinking bouts last for several days at a time?

____ ____ Do you sometimes get the "shakes" in the morning and think it helps to take a "quick one"?

____ ____ Do blackouts and passouts now happen very often?

____ ____ Have you lost concern for your family and others around you?

Source: Ayerst Laboratories.

drinking. Drinkers can die from a large amount of alcohol taken at one time—or from liver or heart disease brought on by drinking over a period of years. Drivers who drink are two to four times as likely to suffer serious or fatal injuries in accidents as nondrinking drivers (Waller et al., 1986).

The mixture of alcohol and other drugs, especially tranquilizers, anticoagulants, barbiturates, and other sedatives, can cause depression, coma, or even death. Drinking during pregnancy—especially heavy drinking and binge drinking—can produce the **fetal alcohol syndrome,** which includes retarded growth, low intelligence, and poor motor development in the baby (Jones, Smith, Ulleland, & Streissguth, 1973). Because alcohol impairs judgment, reaction time, and motor ability, one of its most lethal effects is the high number of traffic accidents caused by drivers who have been drinking.

With all these dangers, why would anyone ever drink? The answer is, at least partly, that most people can handle alcohol in moderation and that for many people it enhances the enjoyment of life. Moreover, wine is a part of the rituals of many religions; small amounts of brandy are often recommended by doctors as a pain-

Fetal alcohol syndrome Mental, motor, and growth retardation in a child, caused by the mother's abuse of alcohol during pregnancy.

killer; and the relaxing qualities of alcohol contribute to social celebrations. Since alcohol is such a pervasive presence in modern society, people need to examine themselves to determine whether they are among those who either cannot drink at all or need to exercise special care. At the same time, societal institutions need to keep developing ways of helping those people who already have drinking problems to regain normal functioning.

Controversy has recently arisen over the claim that alcoholics who are taught "controlled drinking" techniques (ways to drink in moderation) do better than alcoholics who follow the conventional therapy—total abstinence from alcohol (Sobell & Sobell, 1975; Sobell, Sobell, & Ward, 1980). Critics of this claim say that patients who have been taught controlled drinking are often sick and rehospitalized within a year, and that over a 10-year period four such patients died of alcohol-related causes (Pendery, Maltzman, & West, 1982). However, a Canadian review panel supported "controlled drinking," the United States Department of Health and Human Services (1981a) considers it a realistic treatment for some problem drinkers, and in 1984 a United States federal panel agreed with the Canadian conclusions that researchers who advocate controlled drinking had *not* falsified their results (Marlatt, 1983). Still, this controversy will undoubtedly persist for some time.

Other Practices   Many other behaviors affect our health, including the drugs we do or don't take (a number of psychoactive drugs are discussed in Chapter 4), the amount of sleep we get (also discussed in Chapter 4), the extent and kinds of personal relationships we become involved in (discussed in Chapter 18), our sexual activity (discussed in Chapter 12), and the way we drive (use of seat belts is discussed in Chapter 5). Some behaviors that are directly related to our ability to prevent heart disease or cancer will be discussed later in this chapter.

Intervention: Promoting Good Health Practices

It's one thing to know the kinds of behaviors that contribute to good health. It's quite another to put them into effect. Ideally, good health habits should be established early in life, because ingrained behaviors are hard to change later on. It's hard to give up activities that we enjoy, like smoking, eating too much or eating foods that aren't good for us, and drinking. It's also hard to adopt new behaviors, such as exercising, eating sensibly, and performing monthly breast self-examinations. Health psychologists focus much of their effort on encouraging people to adopt behaviors that enhance health and to reduce those that carry health risks. A wide variety of programs have these aims; the degree of their success depends on the specific program and on the behavior in question. Long-term moderate successes, for example, have been noted in some programs (especially Alcoholics Anonymous and some of the programs modeled on it to attack other kinds of problems).

Interestingly, many of us seem to help ourselves better than formal programs can help us. Long-term success rates for people who stopped smoking and lost weight on their own have been reported at 68 percent, whereas most intervention programs have long-term success rates of between 10 and 45 percent (Leventhal & Cleary, 1980, Schachter, 1982). It is possible that people who can change on their own do not turn to formal programs, and so the programs treat those who have the most trouble. It is also possible that success rates in any single program are not high but the cumulative effect of several programs eventually bears fruit. Still, as the authors of one review of the literature state, "It is simply better to do something than nothing" (Leventhal & Cleary, 1980, p. 374). Many health psychologists urge the government, private industry, and community agencies to devote more efforts to preventing the development of problems (Nathan, 1983). Let's take a look at some of the most commonly used approaches for both preventing and changing behaviors that are dangerous to health.

Public Health Programs Community-based programs, which often rely on mass communication, have been instituted to educate schoolchildren about smoking, to encourage entire communities to change their eating habits, to get people to wear seat belts, to discourage driving after drinking, and to bring about other changes in behavior. The philosophy behind these programs is to repeat a message often enough, and also compellingly enough, that people will change their attitudes and eventually modify their behaviors. These community programs have had varying rates of success.

Some educational programs use fear as a motivator, showing horrible examples of what can happen if the desired behavior is not adopted. For example, antismoking campaigns have sometimes included vivid scenes of lung surgery. Such threatening messages do bring about temporary changes in attitudes, but the new attitudes rarely last long enough to change behavior. Furthermore, fear sometimes has unwanted results—it may, for instance, discourage people from getting x-rays. There seems to be a critical balance here: too little fear does not lead people to take action, and too much fear prevents them from thinking about the problem. The most effective approach seems to combine a message with a moderate level of fear and a concrete plan of action for a desired behavior. Smokers who saw a graphic picture of lung disease and then received specific instructions on controlling the urge to smoke and regulating environmental signals to smoke did smoke less at a 3-month follow-up (Leventhal, 1974). Of course, for smokers, 3 months is a short time, and many resume the habit. As smokers often say, "It's easy to stop smoking—I've done it plenty of times."

Can the mass media be used to change behaviors? Advertisers certainly believe that the media can be used in this way—and so do many health experts. One community-based study, the Stanford Heart Disease Prevention Program, involved a sample divided into four groups. For two of the groups, radio and television spots and programs, billboards, bus posters, and direct mail provided information on risk factors for heart disease, with the aim of encouraging people to reduce or stop smoking, to lose weight, to exercise, and to reduce their intake of sugar, salt, saturated fat, and cholesterol. In the third group, besides the media messages, certain people at high risk also received face-to-face instruction in behavioral techniques. The fourth group served as the control, receiving neither messages nor instruction. During three annual follow-ups, some changes had taken place in both "mass media" groups, but greater and longer-lasting changes had occurred in the third group, which had received personal instruction (Meyer, Nash, McAlister, Maccoby, & Farquhar, 1980); see Figure 16-2.

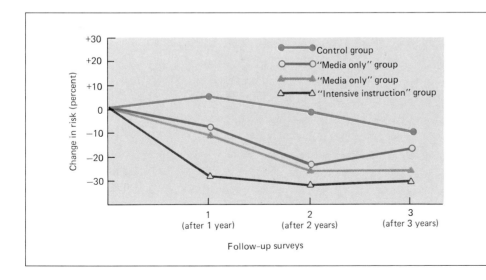

FIGURE 16-2 *Lowering the risk of cardiovascular disease. The risk of heart disease went down most for people in the Stanford Heart Disease Prevention Program who received face-to-face instruction and mass media messages about risk factors (△). But media messages alone do have an impact: people in the two samples that were exposed to them (○ and ▲) showed more reduction in "risk behaviors" than people in a control sample that received no instruction at all (●). (Source: Meyer et al., 1980.)*

Even though the mass media alone may not have brought about much measurable change in behavior, media programs can be important, because they provide an initial "push" for change. Before people can change their behavior, they need to be motivated, and motivation may come from information they see in a magazine or on a television screen. But an actual change in behavior may not occur for some time and therefore may not be linked directly to the media messages.

Changing Social Norms A norm is a standard of behavior. As societal standards change, many people change their ways. For example, let's consider smoking. Field rations for soldiers in the United States Army traditionally included cigarettes, and smoking was long considered an emblem of virility. In July 1986, however, the Army enacted new regulations. It prohibited smoking in Army facilities around the world, except in specially designated areas (Cushman, 1986). Many soldiers were unaffected by the new rule, since they had already given up the habit in accordance with today's image of masculinity, which emphasizes physical fitness. And exercise and smoking are incompatible. Meanwhile, the growing ranks of nonsmokers have become more militant, demanding smoke-free areas on planes, in restaurants, and in other public places. A number of smokers give up the habit because they feel uncomfortable around their nonsmoking friends (Fielding, 1985b). As more government agencies, employers, and proprietors of public places limit smoking, it will become even less of a norm. Even now, when we look at old movies on television, we may be startled to see how much more prevalent smoking was in films made 30 and 40 years ago than it is in movies being made today.

Another example is tanning. One standard of beauty that has contributed to a health hazard in the twentieth century is the bronzed, suntanned look, which has sent people flocking to beaches to get the dark complexion that looks so healthy but actually represents a serious risk of skin cancer. Perhaps the time has come to revive an older ideal, which was maintained by staying out of the sun as much as possible: the pale, ivory-skinned beauty of the nineteenth century.

As social norms change, the popular advertising image of a tanned man enjoying a cigarette will come to look as dated as a dandy in a powdered wig!

The artist Frederick Frieseke showed a young woman (left) using a parasol to protect her complexion from the sun, to conform to nineteenth-century standards of beauty. Our growing knowledge of the danger of too much sunlight may change social norms, and tan-seeking sunbathers like those shown at the right may forsake sunny beaches for more sheltered spots, even though they're not likely to go back to the restrictive clothing and restricted activities of an earlier time.

(Butler Institute of American Art)

(©Ian Berry/Magnum)

School Programs   Classroom-based teaching about a variety of health habits is a staple in many communities. It has been effective in passing on information about smoking and sometimes in encouraging antismoking attitudes. Unfortunately, it usually doesn't have much effect in preventing smoking (Leventhal & Cleary, 1980). This may be because it generally doesn't deal with the reasons young people usually start to smoke—because they want to feel and look grown-up or glamorous, or want to be accepted by their friends. Also, young people usually don't look ahead to the long-term consequences of smoking, which seem very remote.

Some newer programs for children and adolescents that do take these motivations into account have been more effective. Students in these programs have lower rates of smoking—15 to 20 percent lower than students in control groups (Fielding, 1985b). These programs rely on students about the same age as the target students, or a little older, to get across the message that smoking is not common among their peers and doesn't confer maturity or sexiness; to develop arguments against smoking and give students practice in using them; and to talk about ways in which the media promote smoking and about the immediate physical consequences of smoking.

Programs that aim to prevent alcohol abuse and alcohol-related traffic accidents among adolescents have had mixed results—some positive attitude changes, but little behavior change (Nathan, 1983). One notable exception was a program for seventh- to tenth-graders that touched many bases, including myths about alcohol, reasons for drinking, and the effects of alcohol on the family, driving, sports, fitness, and sexuality (Goodstadt, Sheppard, & Chan, 1982).

Individual Approaches   The range of approaches for helping people change their behavior includes psychotherapy, hypnosis, behavior modification, biofeedback, and medical treatment with drugs. Hospitalization is sometimes indicated, involving surgery for extreme cases of obesity, nutritional supplementation for anorexics, and *detoxification* (treatment to restore bodily functioning) for alcoholics and drug addicts. Different approaches help different people; no one kind of treatment has proved effective for all people in any one category.

Detoxification   *Treatment to restore physiological functioning that has been seriously affected by abuse of alcohol or other drugs.*

Self-Help Groups   The model for self-help groups, in which a number of people who share a common problem get together to help each other and—in the process—help themselves, has been Alcoholics Anonymous. This respected organization provides the emotional support of fellow alcoholics in helping people recognize why their drinking is a problem and in helping them to give it up (Zimberg, 1982). Support groups have helped people deal with a wide variety of behaviors, including overeating, smoking, gambling, and abusing their children. They often succeed where other, more formal programs do not.

ILLNESS

We've already mentioned some of the ways in which lifestyle can influence illness. In this section we examine two serious health problems and ways we may be able to protect ourselves against them.

Two Major Health Problems

Heart Disease   The leading cause of death in the United States today is heart disease; it accounts for almost half of all deaths every year. Furthermore, many people have to limit their activities considerably because of heart-related disability. Although heart disease is especially common among men and the elderly, it also affects women and people of all ages.

Coronary heart disease (CHD)
Narrowing and blockage of the coronary arteries that may lead to a heart attack.

Type A behavior pattern
Aggressive, impatient behavior possibly associated with coronary disease.

Type B behavior pattern *Relaxed, easygoing, unhurried behavior.*

What happens to the heart afflicted with **coronary heart disease (CHD)?** The coronary arteries are the vessels that bring blood to the heart; when these vessels narrow, the oxygen and nourishment that the heart needs cannot get through. Mild interference with the flow of these vital supplies may cause pain; a major blockage causes a heart attack. A number of behavior-related risk factors seem to be associated with CHD, including smoking, overweight, high intake of cholesterol, and a sedentary lifestyle. Another highly studied risk factor is the **type A behavior pattern.**

People with "type A" personalities tend to be impatient, competitive, aggressive, and hostile, acting as if they are in a race against time and are constantly faced by challenges. **"Type B"** personalities are more relaxed, easygoing, and unhurried. The significance for health of these two personality types is that type A people (mostly men) are more likely to suffer heart attacks in their thirties or forties, while type B people almost never have heart attacks before the age of 70 (Friedman & Rosenman, 1974). Type A women are more vulnerable to heart disease if they work at a paying job than if they are homemakers. Thus, with the steady influx of women into the labor force, the implications for the health of American women are grave.

Not all studies show the same close relationship between type A behavior and risk of heart attacks (Case, Heller, Case, Moss, & The Multicenter Post-Infarction Research Group, 1985). However, one line of research has implicated one aspect of type A behavior—*hostility*, stemming from *cynicism,* lack of trust in the basic goodness of other people and a belief that others are usually mean, selfish, and undependable (Barefoot, Dahlstrom, & Williams, 1983; Williams, Barefoot, & Shekelle, 1984). The constant vigilance required of someone who doesn't trust others may have physiological results, such as the secretion of hormones like *testosterone,* which is a factor in the clogging of arteries. Type A people also secrete much more of the hormone *noradrenaline* than type B people; this is a substance that may create the blood clots which cause heart attacks (Rosenman, 1983). Secretion of noradrenaline may be increased because type A people perceive their environment as stressful and challenging, and thus react physiologically, even to the mildest events, almost as if they are fighting for their lives.

Another possibility is that type A behavior is the result, rather than the cause, of certain physiological characteristics. For example, type A patients who were anesthetized for coronary bypass surgery were found to have greater increases in blood pressure than type B patients. This suggests that stressful events may produce more physiological arousal in type A people, who then cope with stress through type A behavior (Kahn, Kornfeld, Frank, Heller, & Hoar, 1980; Krantz & Durel, 1983).

It isn't easy for type A people to modify their behavior, since in our society this kind of behavior is associated not only with competitiveness, impatience, and a potential for hostility but also with occupational prestige, high income, and rapid career advancement (C. L. Cooper, 1981; Rosenman & Chesney, 1982). Type A behavior can be changed, however, by psychotherapy, relaxation and deep breathing, and self-monitoring.

In one recent study, 118 healthy Army officers who exhibited type A behavior were randomly assigned to one of two groups. Those in the treatment group received 9 months of counseling, which helped them reappraise some of their beliefs, construct new and more realistic goals, recognize the things that made them angry, learn how to avoid or change potentially stressful situations, and in general to practice new habits of thinking, feeling, and acting. The others served as a control group. Of the officers in the treatment group, 42 percent showed a marked reduction of type A behavior, compared with only about 9 percent of the controls (see Figure 16-3). The officers whose type A behavior decreased sharply showed a reduction in serum cholesterol levels, even though the eating habits of both groups were quite similar (Gill et al., 1985). Although we don't know whether these changes will last, the researchers who conducted this study maintain that it shows that type A behavior can be changed even in ambitious, leadership-oriented, middle-aged men—prime candidates for heart attacks.

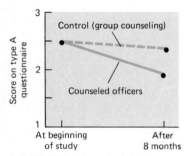

FIGURE 16-3 *A marked decrease occurred in the intensity of type A behaviors as reported by military officers who received counseling on ways to reduce them. The difference between the counseled men and women and a control group who did not receive counseling also showed up in reports by the officers' spouses and in videotaped observations. (Source: Adapted from Gill et al., 1985.)*

Cancer *Cancer,* the second-largest killer in the United States, is not a single disease. The term *cancer* refers to more than 100 different diseases caused by abnormal cell growth and proliferation. Certain risk factors are associated with certain kinds of cancers. Smokers, for example, are more likely to contract lung cancer than nonsmokers, and people who spend a lot of time in the sun are at higher risk of skin cancer than people who do not (Gorbach, Zimmerman, & Woods, 1984; Kopf, Rigel, & Friedman, 1986).

Cancer Group of diseases characterized by abnormal cell growth and proliferation.

One controversial line of research in *psychoneuroimmunology* has associated emotional states with the chance of contracting and recovering from cancer. Some studies have linked stress to the probability of developing cancer and have suggested that stress may reduce the effectiveness of the immune system (see the box "The Mind and the Immune System, page 590). Other work has shown an association between survival among cancer patients and certain personality traits. For example, in one long-term study, researchers examined 2020 middle-aged men during the late 1950s. In follow-up studies over the next 17 years, it turned out that men who had been depressed when they were first seen were twice as likely to have died from cancer as the other men, even when smoking, drinking, family history of cancer, and occupational status were the same (Shekelle et al., 1981). Another study found that polite, unaggressive, acquiescent people who get cancer seem to die sooner than patients who are combative and angry at their illness and their doctors (Derogatis, Abeloff, & Melisaratos, 1979).

Psychoneuroimmunology Scientific study of the way emotional states can influence the body's immune functioning.

However, other studies have not borne out these findings. In one study of 359 cancer patients, no correlation appeared between the course of the disease and a number of psychosocial factors (Cassileth, Lusk, Miller, Brown, & Miller, 1985). Warning that the scientific literature contains very few sound studies of a relationship between mental state and disease, Angell (1985) cautions against blaming the victim. We need to recognize that health and illness depend on multiple factors—psychological, social, and physical. We can exert some control over these factors, but our control does have limits. Although it's important to do as much as we can to prevent illness and to recover if we do become ill, it's just as important to remember that people who succumb to cancer, heart disease, or other ailments are not necessarily to blame for their illnesses. When we don't know the cause of a disease, it's often easier to ascribe it to a psychological factor than to admit our ignorance about it.

Health Care and the Patient-Practitioner Relationship

We can do a great deal on our own to influence whether we stay well, as we've seen. But even with the best of care and the most positive attitudes, we sometimes need the services of health care professionals, such as doctors, nurses, physicians' assistants, and midwives. Even when we're healthy, we move into the health care system for assistance with childbearing, for preventive measures like regular medical and dental checkups, and for instructions on procedures for checking our own health, like monthly breast examinations for women. Then, of course, despite our best efforts we sometimes suffer illness or injury. The way we deal with the system, in obtaining preventive care, in recovering from acute illness, or in adjusting to chronic conditions, has important implications for our lives.

Encounters with providers of health care are often fraught with anxiety. We're worried about our health, we may not like a practitioner's personality or have confidence in his or her ability, we may be embarrassed at the level of personal information we have to reveal, and we tend to feel out of control of our lives (Mentzer & Snyder, 1982; Stone, 1979). Some of this anxiety can be alleviated. A practitioner's warmth and friendliness and ability to communicate can help patients adjust to the health care setting (Mentzer & Snyder, 1982).

Furthermore, patients can do a great deal for themselves. At one time, "good" patients put themselves into their doctors' care and unquestioningly accepted their

When first-year dental students were going through stressful periods in the academic year, their saliva contained smaller amounts of IgA, a substance that protects against various infections, than it did at other times (Jemmott et al., 1983). Medical students showed lower immune responses during the week before final exams than they did during the first week after return from summer vacation (Kiecolt-Glaser, Speicher, Holliday, & Glaser, in press). Psychiatry residents taking oral exams had lower responses on two measures of the body's ability to fight invading organisms than matched residents who were not taking exams (Dorian, Keystone, Garfinkel, & Brown, 1982).

Similar changes in immune functioning have been noted in astronauts right after splashdown (Kimzey, Johnson, Ritzman, & Mengel, 1976) and in men whose wives had recently died of breast cancer (Schleifer, Keller, McKegney, & Stein, 1979). The new science of psychoneuroimmunology is the study of the way emotional states are related to the body's immune functioning. The immune system is the body's surveillance system. Its function is to recognize and destroy disease-causing microorganisms, and thereby prevent infections, allergies, and cancer. According to the biopsychosocial model of health, it is not an isolated

THE MIND AND THE IMMUNE SYSTEM

system, but is integrated with other body processes and is sensitive to changes in central-nervous-system (CNS) and hormonal functioning. Since changes in the CNS and the endocrine system occur in response to stress, we can see a link between stress and various diseases, ranging from the common cold to cancer. (See Figure 16-4.)

An important question for scientists in this field is this: Since many people are exposed to stress—sometimes even to the same kind of stress—why do some stay healthy while others fall ill? Some clues have started to emerge, providing a partial answer. One explanation is that different people see stress differently. Some people may see a project to be completed as a challenge that makes use of their ability, while others see it as a task that saps their strength. Immune functioning also seems to be

related to what kinds of experiences we've had in the past (an accumulation of stressors weakens the immune response) and what we expect for the future (ability to predict stress is helpful)—and to whether or not we have supportive friends and relatives who help us deal with stress (Maier & Laudenslager, 1985).

An important element is a sense of control over a situation. Dramatic experimental evidence for this has come from work with animals. Rats that received painful electric shocks which they could not shut off were found to have fewer lymphocytes (disease-fighting cells) in their bodies, but rats that could turn a wheel that would shut off the shocks, both for themselves and for the other rats, remained normal. Both groups of rats received the same numbers of shocks, suggesting that it wasn't the stress of the shocks that mattered, but the element of control (Laudenslager et al., 1983).

We have noted the importance of predictability and control in our ability to deal with stressful situations. The absence of these characteristics is associated with physical illness, as well as with diminished psychological and social functioning. Once again, we see the close relationship among many facets of our lives.

FIGURE 16-4 *The immune system is linked to other body processes. Changes in the central nervous system and the endocrine system can lower the immune response, making the body more vulnerable to various diseases.*

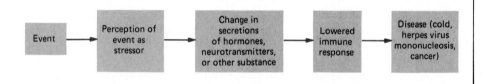

diagnosis and recommendations for treatment. Today, however, consumers of health care are more likely to be better informed and more assertive about seeking care. We tend to look upon our relationship with our doctors and other health care practitioners as partnerships. We are more apt to express our needs and our opinions, we feel free to consult other doctors for second (or third) opinions, and we pursue the kind of health care that we feel is best for us.

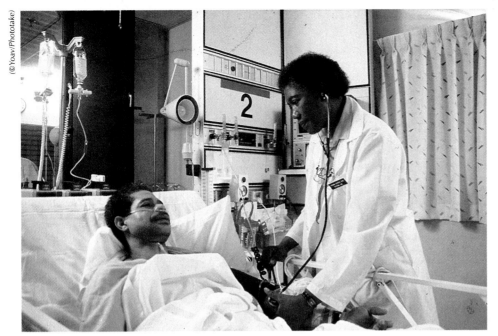

An illness that leads to hospitalization is stressful in itself, and that stress is aggravated by being in an unfamiliar place and being subjected to frightening procedures administered by strangers. All this adds to patients' sense that they are losing control over their lives. Sensitive providers of health care make special efforts to respect patients' dignity and reduce their feeling of helplessness.

This new attitude is good for our health. People who are overly concerned with being "good" patients may fail to ask crucial questions or volunteer important information, for fear of taking up a doctor's time. Furthermore, doctors' respect for patients results in patients' receiving information about the medical procedures they undergo and about the diagnoses and prognoses of their conditions. Most people want to know such information, even when a diagnosis is unfavorable, rather than being uncertain (Mentzer & Snyder, 1982). Even when people can't change the outcome, knowing what to expect gives them the feeling that they have a measure of control over their lives, an important element in coping with stress. Furthermore, people who understand why a certain course of treatment is recommended are more likely to follow through with it.

One of the most stressful health-related situations is hospitalization. In the typical institutional setting, patients' sense of control over their lives is almost nonexistent as they stay in unfamiliar settings, are required to wear hospital-approved garments, are considered fair game for onslaughts of medical students and residents taking innumerable histories, are unable to move around and get things for themselves. These and other common practices add to the patients' sense of helplessness, feelings of depression, and sense of being unable to cope. Fortunately, some forward-thinking hospital administrators are investigating ways to give patients back some sense of control over their lives, even when they are in institutions.

Sometimes such measures can be very simple ones. For example, in an experiment described in Chapter 1, researchers asked a group of nursing home residents to choose and care for a plant and also told these residents that they themselves were responsible for seeing that they got good care, for making decisions about how they spent their own time, and for changing things they did not like. Meanwhile, they gave a second group of residents a plant and told them that the nurses would water and care for it, and that the nurses were responsible for caring for residents and making them happy. On follow-up, the people in the first group were found to be happier, more active, and more alert, and they lived longer than the people in the second group. Apparently, something as simple as encouraging people to take charge of their own lives can enhance both the quality and the length of life (Rodin & Langer, 1977).

SUMMARY

1   Health psychology is the scientific study of the psychological factors that promote health, cause illness, and affect recovery from illness. Health psychologists subscribe to a biopsychosocial model, or a model that an interaction of biological, psychological, and social factors affects health and illness.

2   Different researchers define stress differently. We consider stress to consist of physiological and psychological reactions to stressors. Stressors are events capable of producing stress although not always doing so.

3   Selye considered stress to be the body's nonspecific response to any demand. He described a three-stage reaction to stress consisting of alarm, resistance, and exhaustion, known as the general adaptation syndrome (GAS). Selye performed his basic research using rats; its applicability to people has been questioned.

4   Lazarus sees stress as a result of a transaction between people and the environment. Whether or not a particular event is viewed as stressful depends on a person's interpretation of it. In reacting to a situation, people use two types of appraisal. In primary appraisal, a person evaluates the implications of an event for his or her well-being. In secondary appraisal, a person evaluates his or her ability to cope with the event.

5   An event is most likely to be perceived as stressful when it is negative, unpredictable, uncontrollable, or ambiguous or several of these.

6   Holmes and his colleagues found a relationship between the number of life changes (measured in life-change units, or LCUs) and vulnerability to illness. Although this work has been criticized on methodological grounds, it is widely considered to represent a breakthrough in measuring stress.

7   Lazarus and his colleagues found that "hassles" (irritating things that happen to people from day to day) were better predictors of physical and psychological health than were the major life events examined by Holmes and his associates. Lazarus's work has been criticized on methodological and conceptual grounds.

8   Stressors such as noise, crowding, electric shock, arbitrary discrimination, dealings with bureaucracy, and demands for increased performance can affect the way people perform various tasks. They affect people most negatively when they can be neither predicted nor controlled.

9   Coping is a constantly changing effort to manage the demands that tax personal resources. Problem-focused coping aims to solve the problems causing the stress, whereas emotion-focused coping aims to manage emotional responses to the problem. Effective copers tend to use both types of coping strategies.

10 A number of factors influence whether people handle stress effectively. These include personality, social support, and specific coping techniques. In this regard, hardiness has been identified as an important personality style.

11 Wellness is an ideal state of enriched health and enhanced life.

12 The practice of health behaviors is influenced by social, sociological, environmental, emotional, cognitive, and physical factors.

13 A number of health habits are related to disease. Specific aspects of diet are related to the development of heart disease and cancer. Obesity (being at least 20 percent above desirable weight) has been associated with a wide range of physical and psychological problems. Anorexia nervosa is a prolonged and severe refusal to eat characterized by extreme weight loss, leading to a body weight at least 15 percent under normal. Bulimia is an eating disorder characterized by episodes of bingeing and purging.

14 Exercise has been linked to a variety of health benefits. The benefits of exercise outweigh the slight risk of cardiac arrest during strenuous activity.

15 Tobacco and alcohol use have been associated with far-reaching health problems. Tobacco use is the single most important cause of preventable illness and death in the United States. Alcohol is the leading problem drug in the United States.

16 A variety of formal and informal intervention programs have been developed to foster good health and the practice of health-promoting behaviors. These include community-based public health programs, school programs, individual treatment, and self-help groups. These programs have met with varying degrees of success. In addition, changing social norms have affected health behaviors.

17 The leading cause of death in the United States is heart disease. A number of behavior-related risk factors, including the type A behavior pattern, have been associated with heart disease. People displaying type A behavior are impatient, competitive, aggressive, and hostile compared with the more relaxed type B personalities. It appears to be possible to modify type A behavior.

18 Cancer is the second leading cause of death in the United States. Different types of cancer have been related to different risk factors, including tobacco use (associated with lung cancer and other types of cancer) and overexposure to the sun (associated with skin cancers). One controversial line of research has examined the relationship between emotional states and the probability of contracting cancer and of recovering from cancer. These studies have yielded inconsistent results.

19 Psychoneuroimmunology is the scientific study of the way emotional states can influence the body's immune functioning. Changes in the central nervous system and endocrine system that occur in response to stress may decrease the effectiveness of the immune system and provide the link between stress and various diseases.

20 Use of the health care system can be anxiety-producing. The practitioner's warmth, friendliness, and ability to communicate can help patients adjust. Consumers of health care can also promote positive encounters with the health care system by being assertive about seeking care, by expressing needs and opinions, and by asking questions.

KEY TERMS

Anorexia nervosa (page 579)
Biomedical model (562)
Biopsychosocial model (562)
Bulimia (580)
Cancer (589)
Cholesterol (577)
Coping (571)
Coronary heart disease (CHD) (588)

Detoxification (587)
Fetal alcohol syndrome (583)
General adaptation syndrome (GAS) (563)
Hardiness (572)
Health psychologists (562)
Health psychology (562)
Obesity (578)

Osteoporosis (581)
Primary appraisal (566)
Psychoneuroimmunology (589)
Secondary appraisal (566)
Social Readjustment Rating Scale (SRRS) (567)
Stress (563)

Stress-inoculation training (574)
Stressor (563)
Type A behavior pattern (588)
Type B behavior pattern (588)
Wellness (575)

SUGGESTED READINGS

FIGLEY, C. R., & McCUBBIN, H. I. (Eds.). (1983). *Stress and the family: Vol. II. Coping with catastrophe.* New York: Brunner/Mazel. A collection of articles by leading researchers about coping with such catastrophic events as unemployment, rape, captivity, and chronic illness.

GOLDBERGER, L., & BREZNITZ, S. (Eds.). (1982). *Handbook of stress: Theoretical and clinical aspects.* New York: Free Press. A series of articles on physiological and psychological aspects of stress, as well as treatment and support strategies.

HANSON, P. G. (1986). *The joy of stress.* Kansas City: Andrews, McMeel & Parker. An easy-to-read book for the layperson, based on the scientific literature on stress, on how to make stress work for you rather than against you. The book contains many interesting exercises.

LEVY, S. M. (1985). *Behavior and cancer.* San Francisco: Jossey-Bass. A comprehensive discussion of the influences of lifestyle and of psychological and behavioral factors on the development and growth of human cancers.

McCUBBIN, H. I., & FIGLEY, C. R. (Eds.). (1983). *Stress and the family: Vol. I. Coping with normative transitions.* New York: Brunner/Mazel. The companion volume to Figley and McCubbin, discussed above. Chapters focus on the impact of family transitions such as marriage, parenthood, divorce, and dual-career situations.

PELLETIER, K. R. (1984). *Healthy people in unhealthy places: Stress and fitness at work.* New York: Delacorte/Seymour Lawrence. This readable book focuses on ways that individual workers and corporations can make the workplace more healthy. There is an appendix describing health promotion resources throughout the United States.

U. S. DEPARTMENT OF HEALTH AND HUMAN SERVICES. (1983). *The health consequences of smoking: Cardiovascular disease. A report of the Surgeon General.* A comprehensive review of the relationship between smoking and cardiovascular disease. It concludes that cigarette smoking should be considered the most important risk factor for coronary heart disease in the United States.

P A R T

VII

SOCIAL PSYCHOLOGY

We human beings are social creatures. From the moment of birth, we begin to be affected by those around us—our parents, our baby-sitters, our brothers and sisters, even other crying babies we don't know. This close tie with other human beings persists throughout life as we influence others and are, in turn, influenced by them. The specific ways in which this influence is demonstrated are often affected by the situation in which we find ourselves. In the next two chapters we'll look at such influences both in groups and in intimate relationships.

■ In *Chapter 17,* "Social Influence," we look mostly at the group. We see how the influence of a group of strangers can make us doubt the evidence of our own senses, how someone we think of as an authority can influence us to harm a person who has done us no injury, and how easy it is to slip into socially accepted kinds of behavior even if they're not our usual way of acting. We also look at the "up" side, the factors that encourage us to reach out to help others. And finally, we look at the way we form our attitudes and how those attitudes can change—a phenomenon that is particularly relevant for modern society as we strive to overcome discrimination based on prejudices against certain ethnic and racial groups.

■ In *Chapter 18,* "Interpersonal Attraction and Relationships," we focus on initial attraction, on friendship, and on love. We see what research tells us about why we like or love one person and not another—about the effect of external factors (such as where people happen to live) and of inner characteristics (such as personal warmth). We take a somewhat scientific look at that most unscientific emotion, love, and see how it affects our close relationships with others, both in and outside of marriage.

C H A P T E R

17

SOCIAL INFLUENCE

■ How does a group influence the behavior of individuals in it? What factors affect its influence?

■ What happened in an experiment in which students were randomly assigned to the role of "prisoner" or "guard"?

■ How can group opinion make people doubt the evidence of their own eyes?

■ How can "groupthink"—uncritical acceptance of an unwise course of action in order to maintain unanimity within a group—lead to disaster?

■ What makes ordinary people obey an authority figure who orders them to inflict pain on another person who has done them no harm?

■ What factors influence the decision to help a person in distress?

■ How are attitudes in general—and prejudices in particular—formed, and how can they be changed?

One Saturday evening some years ago, my husband Mark and I were walking along Rush Street in Chicago. The street was thronged with people headed for restaurants, nightclubs, jazz spots, and other attractions for those who, like us, were in a celebratory mood, looking for a "night on the town." As we were making our way through the crowd, we suddenly saw two husky men move to either side of two young women who were walking together a few yards in front of us. Each of the men grabbed one of the women and wrestled her to the ground. The women struggled and cried out. The men grimly went ahead, pinning the women down. Was this a "gangland" attack, reminiscent of Chicago in the Prohibition era? Or was it a robbery by a couple of hoodlums who were so arrogant that they dared to assault people in public view, confident that no one would intervene?

But one person did intervene. Mark broke away from me and confronted one of the men, asking loudly and angrily (to alert other would-be helpers in the vicinity), "What's going on here?" Continuing to pin down one woman with a well-muscled arm, one of the men used his free hand to pull out his wallet and flip it open to show his credentials. "We're cops. We're arresting these women for prostitution." By this time a crowd had gathered, as a slightly red-faced Mark walked over to me, and as I applauded "my hero," who had shown courage—both physical bravery and the courage to stick his neck out in a difficult, ambiguous situation.

—From the notebooks of Sally Olds

Social psychology *Scientific study of how people feel about, think about, are affected by, and act toward other people.*

Whan led Mark to intervene in this situation; and what prevented all the other people on the street, who had witnessed the same scene, from doing anything about it? This is one of the questions explored by researchers in **social psychology,** the scientific study of social influence. This branch of psychology has to do with how we feel about, think about, are affected by, and act toward other people. Much of psychology studies the individual alone—what individuals perceive, think, remember, and feel—and only incidentally relates these processes to the influence of other people. Social psychology, however, emphasizes the fact that human beings are social creatures from birth till death and that it is impossible to understand them without understanding how we act and react to others. Those others do not even have to be physically present: we learn social behavior and then make it part of our repertoire even when we are alone. For example, when you're alone at home, you probably still wear clothes and eat with a knife and fork.

Social psychology really came into its own only after World War II, possibly in response to the terrible questions raised by the Nazi holocaust, and especially to the mystery at the heart of this horrifying era: How could the citizens of a nation known for its cultural and intellectual values have carried out a crusade that resulted in the deaths of more than 12 million Jews, Gypsies, political dissidents, and other "undesirables"? How could so many ordinary persons who loved their families and behaved decently toward their neighbors have participated in or averted their eyes from millions of ghastly deaths (Steiner, 1979)?

To answer questions about people's behavior toward others, social psychologists use a wide variety of research approaches and techniques. They conduct experiments in the laboratory and in the field, sometimes in public places such as subways, elevators, and restaurants. Some studies call for a certain amount of deception (and thus raise ethical issues, as discussed in Chapter 1); other research is straightforward. Although much research in social psychology explores socially relevant topics—helping, obedience, conformity, and so on—considerable attention is also devoted to more basic topics like the ways attitudes are formed and changed. One body of research focuses on differences between the ways people behave when they are alone and how they act when they are with others.

In our two chapters on social psychology, we discuss both new and classic research into various aspects of social influence. We see the effect of the social situation on conformity and obedience—remembering, however, that personality interacts with situational factors to determine what a person will do at any time. In this chapter, we focus on the way people function in groups. We look at one important kind of social behavior—altruism, or helping others. We then see how attitudes are formed, how they can be changed, and how they relate to behaviors; and we look in detail at one specific kind of attitude—prejudice. In Chapter 18, we'll talk about the nature and influence of intimate relationships.

PEOPLE IN GROUPS

According to psychologists, if you are interacting with one or more other people, you are in a group. *Interaction* implies that the members of a group are aware of one another and take one another into account, and that their relationship has some continuity, involving either the past or an anticipated future (McGrath & Kravitz, 1982). In other words, the people milling about you on a crowded city street would not constitute a group of which you are a member, unless some event were to happen that would make you stop and pay attention to one another. On Rush Street, for example, the passersby who stopped to watch became part of a group.

We belong to many different groups throughout our lives, from the basic one—the family—to children's clubs, school classes, and a variety of associations based on the common interests of their members. The groups that are most meaningful—like families and friendship circles—have a long history and the expectation of a long-term future. Other groups—like the members of a psychology class or the guests at a party—last for only a short time and have no expected future; but these are still groups, because their members are interacting and interdependent at some time.

Norms and Roles: Defining Our Place in the Group

In the movie *Best Friends,* Goldie Hawn and Burt Reynolds play a couple who marry after having lived together for 3 years. When they meet each other's parents for the first time, both mothers—the man's and the woman's—impress on the woman her new responsibilities: pouring her husband's coffee and waiting on him at the table. She tells them that he not only knows how to do all of that himself but actually does it—only to be told that now that they're married, this is her job as a wife. She is now supposed to behave according to the way her mother and mother-in-law have interpreted the role of wife.

(Bettmann Archive)

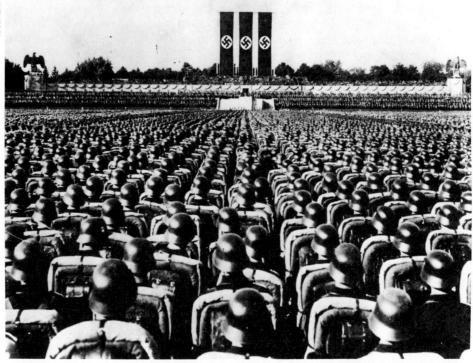

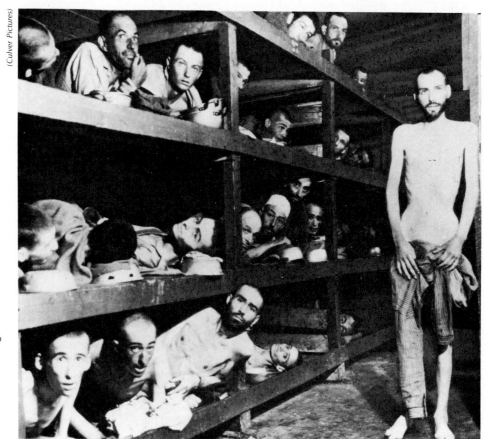
(Culver Pictures)

The tragedy of the Holocaust inspired a flood of research in social psychology. What could have motivated so many people (like the Nazi soldiers shown in the photo on the top at a rally in Nuremberg, who may have been decent, ordinary people) to carry out a crusade of horror that resulted in the cruel and inhuman death of more than 12 million other decent, ordinary people (such as the people in a concentration camp in the photo on the bottom)?

What Are Roles?   A *role* is a set of behavioral expectations for a specific social position. A role in turn is made up of a set of **norms,** which are society's definitions of the way we should behave—in other words, rules of behavior for people in various roles. Thus, norms in the United States dictate that men wear clothing that covers their pelvic area; a role—such as the role of a professional—might dictate that a man wear a suit, shirt, and tie. Norms govern virtually every aspect of our behavior in society, although they vary depending on which particular society we live in. (Thus, Italian men commonly walk arm in arm, but American men ordinarily do not.) For instance, we have norms for the roles of parent, worker, and spouse. (A worker is expected to be loyal, conscientious, and hardworking, for example.)

A *social role,* such as spouse, parent, or worker, is a particular social position that has acquired a substantial number of norms. But not every kind of behavior assumes the status of a social role. Thus, when a person travels by plane, there are a few behavioral expectations in the situation (buy a ticket, use a seat belt, etc.); but these would not warrant considering "airline passenger" a social role.

Norms can both enhance and restrict behavior. They oil the functioning of groups of people; and once you learn the norms in your culture, you know how to behave in many different situations. On the other hand, they can stifle independence, since most people's natural tendency seems to be to follow norms, even when these are not the most effective or humane way to act. In this chapter, we will see some instances in which people obey orders because of previously learned norms, and others in which they conform to group decisions when they might think and act quite differently if they were alone. We will also see that different people act differently in similar situations, showing the power of individual personality traits.

How Much of Our Behavior Is Determined by Norms and Roles?   In an ingenious experiment, Philip G. Zimbardo and his colleagues at Stanford University established how powerful an influence a situation and society's definition of roles within that situation have on behavior (Zimbardo, Haney, Banks, & Jaffe, 1977). They recruited 21 emotionally stable, physically healthy, mature, law-abiding college students to take part in a study on prison life. They randomly assigned 11 to act as prison guards for a 2-week period and assigned the other 10 to play the part of prisoners.

The "prisoners" were picked up in a surprise arrest, handcuffed, fingerprinted, "deloused," given uniforms with ID numbers and stocking caps, and put in 6- by 9-foot windowless cells in the basement of a temporarily unused college building. The "guards" were issued khaki uniforms, reflector sunglasses (to prevent eye contact with prisoners), billy clubs, whistles, handcuffs, and keys. Rules were established that simulated the restrictiveness and depersonalization of prison life: prisoners had to obtain permission to write a letter, smoke a cigarette, or go to the toilet; and silence was enforced at many times during the day.

The researchers wanted to find out how these normal, healthy volunteers would react, and whether their responses would give clues about the violence that characterizes real prison life. They found out so much that they had to release four prisoners within the first few days—and then end the entire experiment early, after only 6 days and nights.

The experiment had worked too well. These two groups of volunteers, at first indistinguishable in personality and health, developed traits related to their roles as prisoners and guards. The four prisoners who were released early suffered from depression and anxiety, and one of them had a psychosomatic rash over his entire body. One prisoner went on a hunger strike; some became "model" prisoners, obeying every command, no matter how arbitrary; others withdrew into themselves.

The guards all became authoritarian and abusive, though to varying degrees. Some were "good guys" who did little favors for the prisoners and were reluctant to punish them, and some were "tough but fair," just doing their job as they saw it. More than one-third of them, however, acted hostile, arbitrary, and cruel and used

Role   Set of behavioral expectations (or norms) for a specific social position.

Norms   Society's definitions of how we "should" behave.

Social role   Social position that has acquired a substantial number of norms.

(© Van Bucher/Photo Researchers)

Different societies have different social norms. It is common for French men, like these, to greet each other with a kiss; but such demonstrations of affection are rare in the United States, even among men who are close friends or relatives.

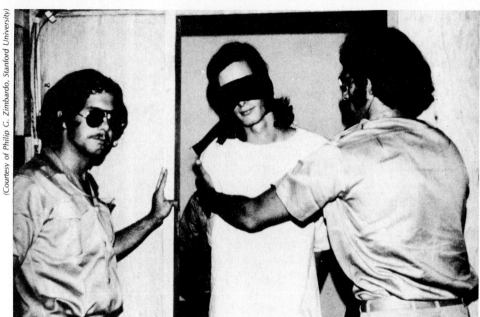
(Courtesy of Philip G. Zimbardo, Stanford University)

In their "prison" experiments, Philip Zimbardo and his colleagues were surprised to learn how quickly and thoroughly people pick up "appropriate" norms for the roles they play. Normal college students assigned to be prisoners, like the one shown blindfolded in this picture, tended to become passive and helpless, while students designated as guards tended to become authoritarian and abusive.

their new power to degrade and humiliate the prisoners. Typically, the guards would give commands and orders to the prisoners and threaten and insult them. The prisoners tended to become passive, increasingly doing and saying less and less that would call attention to themselves—behaving in general like classic cases of learned helplessness.

The researchers were surprised by the "relative ease with which sadistic behavior could be elicited from normal, non-sadistic people, and the extent of the emotional disturbance which emerged in young men selected precisely on the basis of their emotional stability" (p. 213). The kind of behavior that showed up during the 6 days of the experiment seemed a direct product of the environment. Therefore, Zimbardo and colleagues concluded, "to change behavior we must discover the institutional supports which maintain the existing undesirable behavior and then design programs to alter these environments" (p. 214).

Prisons need not be built of concrete and steel; they can exist in our minds. Many of us play out our roles as oppressors or victims in a "prison of the mind" constructed by prejudice. This study helps us see how quickly people can pick up the "appropriate" norms for the roles they play.

Conformity and Groupthink: Why We Go Along with the Group

Conformity   Before you read any further, look carefully at the boxes in Figure 17-1. One of the lines in the square on the right is the same length as the single line in the square on the left. Which one?

You probably had no trouble choosing the matching line. This makes the findings from some experiments on conformity all the more startling.

Conformity Change in opinion, behavior, or both in response to real or imagined pressure from others.

WHAT IS CONFORMITY?   **Conformity** is a change in opinion, behavior, or both in response to real or imagined pressure from others.

In Solomon Asch's pioneering studies (1955, 1956), a group of male college students were told that they were participating in experiments on perception. Each subject sat at a table with a group of seven confederates—people who were posing as subjects but who were actually working with the experimenter. All the "subjects" were then shown cards like the ones in Figure 17-1 and given the problem described above. The confederates were called upon to answer before the real subject was. All the participants gave their answers aloud in front of the entire group.

On some trials the confederates answered correctly, but on others every confederate gave the wrong answer—contradicting what the real subject could see perfectly well. In the trials where the confederates gave the wrong answer, about 1 out of 3 of the real subjects conformed; that is, they went along with the majority, changing their own opinion in response to the pressure they felt from the others in the group. Overall, about 3 out of 4 subjects gave the incorrect, conforming answer at least once. The majority of subjects did trust their own judgment most of the time, but a disturbingly large number of wrong answers were given.

WHAT AFFECTS CONFORMITY? *Differences among people* Significant differences showed up among the subjects. Those who remained independent differed from each other: some seemed confident in their own judgment, some acted withdrawn, and some appeared tense and doubtful but determined to do as well as they could. The conforming subjects included some who were not aware that they had been influenced by the majority and some who still felt that they were right but did not want to seem different from the others. The largest subgroup of the conformers, however, came to doubt the evidence of their own senses.

Both the independent and the conforming subjects agonized. One independent student was puzzled and hesitant when he gave his (right) answers. At one point he grinned in embarrassment and whispered explosively to his neighbor, ''I always disagree—darn it!'' When he finally learned the true nature of the experiment, he was relieved and exultant, saying, ''I do not deny that at times I had the feeling: to heck with it, I'll go along with the rest.'' Another subject, who had gone along with the majority in 11 out of 12 trials, seemed nervous and confused during the interview after the experiment and freely described his own pathetic loss of confidence in the face of overwhelming disagreement, saying things like, ''If I'd been first I probably would have responded differently'' and ''If they had been doubtful I probably would have changed, but they answered with such confidence.'' Midway through the experiment, this subject had begun to suspect its true nature; at an earlier point, he had assumed that the others were seeing an optical illusion. But even these suppositions did not give him confidence in himself (Asch, 1951, pp. 177–178).

Differences in situations Changing various experimental conditions resulted in a number of interesting findings (Asch, 1956). If just one other person in the group

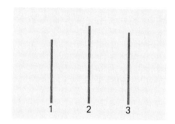

FIGURE 17-1 *Asch's line-drawing task. Subjects were shown these cards and asked to choose the line in the picture on the bottom that was the same length as the line in the picture on the top. (Source: Asch, 1955.)*

(Drawing by Vietor; © 1978 The New Yorker Magazine, Inc.)

''Wait a minute, you guys—I've decided to make it unanimous after all.''

Pressure to conform to the opinions held by other members of a group often makes people disregard their own critical judgment, sometimes to the point where they even ignore the evidence of their senses.

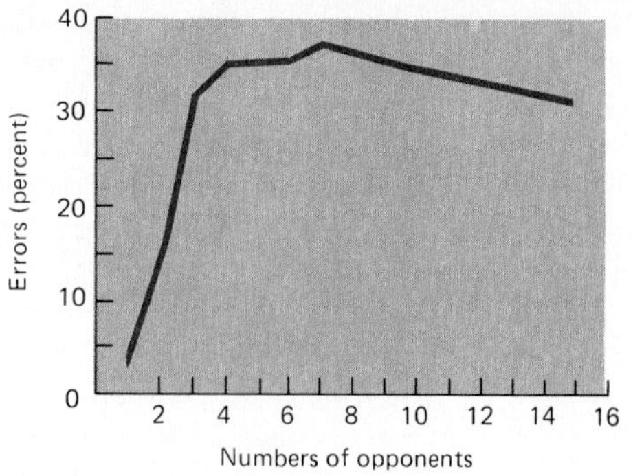

FIGURE 17-2 *The size of the opposition had an effect on conformity. When a subject had just 1 opponent, the subject erred 3.6 percent of the time. With 2 opponents, the error rate rose to 13.6 percent. With 3 to 15 opponents, the error rate jumped to from 31.2 percent to 37 percent. (Source: Asch, 1955, p. 35.)*

agreed with the subject, the subject was much more likely to hold fast to his position. If, however, the person who originally agreed with the subject later switched to the majority position, the subject was apt to switch, too.

The size of the opposition was important, too. In a series of trials, subjects were confronted with from 1 to 15 persons who held a unanimous (and wrong) position. The reactions of the subjects showed that the size of the unanimous majority did not have to be very large to induce conformity. When a subject was confronted with only one person and that person held a differing opinion, the subject was not likely to change his response. When confronted with two people taking different positions, the subject was more likely to conform. Being confronted with three unanimous dissenters, however, resulted in the maximum level of conformity—the same level as with a very large unanimous group (see Figure 17-2).

CONFORMITY VERSUS INDEPENDENCE   Despite the surprisingly high level of conformity that led so many people to mistrust the evidence before their eyes, *most of* the answers from subjects in Asch's experiments were, in fact, correct, even in the face of unanimously wrong answers offered by peers. For a discussion of the factors that may encourage independent expression, see the box "What Makes People Willing to Go Against the Crowd?"

Conformity is not always bad. If no one's behavior conformed to group norms, we would seldom if ever know what to expect, and we would be faced constantly with thousands of decisions about everyday activities. We would not be able to count on other drivers' stopping at a red light, on other passengers' making way for us to get off a crowded bus, on other moviegoers' taking their turn in the line at the box office. Much of the time, conforming behavior is simply convenient, both for ourselves and for others. The important thing is to know when conformity is appropriate and when it conflicts with norms and values that should have priority. This is often difficult, even for people in high places.

Groupthink   "How could we have been so stupid?" John F. Kennedy asked this question in 1961, after he and his close advisers had seen their decision to invade the Bay of Pigs in Cuba turn into a military and political fiasco. The answer proposed by Irving L. Janis (1971, 1982) was **groupthink:** uncritical acceptance of an unwise course of action by members of a closely knit group, in order to preserve unanimity. Groupthink, then, is a distinct kind of conformity.

Although it is often said that "two heads are better than one," the perils of groupthink cast some doubt on this idea. It is true that when two or more people turn their joint attention to a problem, they often come up with more possibilities than any one of them would think of alone, and that this can result in a better solution. But when the members of a group become too concerned about preserving unanimity,

Groupthink *Uncritical acceptance of an unwise course of action by members of a close-knit group in order to preserve unanimity.*

All of us sometimes find ourselves in situations where we hold opinions that are different from those held by most of the people around us. We are often torn between expressing our true opinions and feeling true to ourselves, on the one hand, and covering up the way we feel, on the other.

To find out why some people are willing to speak up against majority opinion, Santee and Maslach (1982) presented their subjects (120 male and female college students) with several hypothetical problems in human relationships that reflected the kinds of problems real people are likely to encounter.

For example:

> Geraldine and Lennie are college students who have been living together in an apartment near the campus. Lennie's allowance buys the food and they are sharing the rent. Geraldine has told her parents she is rooming with another girl, and now her parents are coming to visit their daughter. They have never seen her apartment. Geraldine has asked Lennie to move out for the time that her parents are in town. Should he? (1) Yes. His moving out will save a lot of

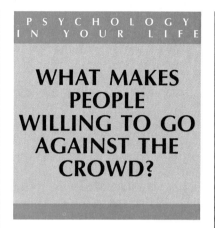

WHAT MAKES PEOPLE WILLING TO GO AGAINST THE CROWD?

trouble with her parents. (2) No. It would be hypocritical for them to pretend, so Geraldine should tell her parents before they come. (3) Yes, but Geraldine should pay for Lennie's new accommodations and food. What do *you* think is the best solution for this problem? (p. 694)

Undergraduates who had previously read the stories served as judges, rating solutions as good or poor. (In this case they considered the first two good and the third one poor.) Participants were divided into two groups: a "peer opinion" condition (the experimental group) and a control group. Those in the experimental group could hear three other people (confederates) agree unanimously on a solution or disagree about two "good" solutions; those in the control group heard no other opinions. Students in the experimental group chose the majority solution 63 percent of the time (70 percent when peer opinion was unanimous); those who did not know what other students said (the controls) chose it only 51 percent of the time.

Even more interesting than this expected difference in conformity was a relationship between independent answers and self-concept. Before the experiment, all subjects had taken tests to measure their self-esteem, willingness to call attention to themselves, shyness, social anxiety, and self-consciousness. Those who had high self-esteem and were willing to be conspicuous in public were more likely to dissent from unanimous peer opinions than those who were shy, anxious, and self-conscious in public.

they lose the ability to think critically. When the members of a group put loyalty to the group above all else, groupthink takes over. Individuals do not deliberately suppress thoughts that would expose the folly of current or proposed plans. But they become so involved in wanting the group to continue being a "good group" that they unwittingly push to the back of their minds any nagging thoughts that would "spoil the cozy, 'we-feeling' atmosphere" (Janis, 1971, p. 218).

Groupthink makes people become overoptimistic, rationalize decisions instead of seriously reconsidering them, fail to consider ethical or moral consequences, hold on to stereotyped views of opponents that cloud judgment, put pressure on anyone who casts doubt on the group's policy, censor their own critical thinking, believe falsely that everyone else fully agrees with a policy, and try to protect the group from evidence that its policies are unsound (Janis, 1971).

President Kennedy learned a painful lesson from the Bay of Pigs in 1961 and was able to prevent groupthink in his handling of the Cuban missile crisis in 1962. He used some of the techniques later recommended by Janis, which include:

1 Alerting group members to the dangers of groupthink
2 Having the leader remain impartial
3 Instructing everyone to express any objections and doubts
4 Assigning one or more group members to play the role of devil's advocate by taking an opposing viewpoint
5 Occasionally subdividing the group into small groups that meet separately
6 Paying attention to all warning signals from a possible rival
7 Calling a "second-chance" meeting to re-evaluate the preliminary decision

8 Inviting outside experts to come in and challenge the group's views
9 Encouraging group members to sound out group thought with trusted associates
10 Having several independent groups work on the same question at the same time

Obedience: Why We Comply with Demands of Authority Figures

Milgram's Studies Suppose that you have answered a newspaper ad for subjects to take part in an experiment on memory and learning, directed by a professor at a prestigious university. You go to the psychology lab, where you meet an experimenter wearing a laboratory coat, and another subject—a pleasant-looking man in his fifties. You are told that the experiment has to do with the effects of punishment on learning and that you have been chosen to be the "teacher." You see the other subject—the "learner"—being strapped into a chair in an adjacent room and attached to an electrode, and you hear the experimenter tell him that whenever he makes a mistake in learning a list of word pairs, he will receive an electric shock. The shocks will be painful, but they will not cause any permanent tissue damage.

Back in the main lab, you are seated in front of a shock generator which has 30 switches ranging from 15 to 450 volts and labeled from SLIGHT SHOCK to DANGER—SEVERE SHOCK. The experimenter tells you to give the test to the learner and to give him a shock whenever he makes a mistake or fails to answer. You are to start at the lowest level of shock and keep increasing the jolt with each error.

How far do you think you would go in following these instructions? Would you stop when the learner began to show some discomfort—if he grunted, say, at 75 volts? Would you stop at 120 volts if he complained? Would you stop at 150 volts if he demanded to be released? Or would you keep giving shocks until you reached 285 volts and the learner was screaming in agony? Suppose that at any of these points, you turned to the experimenter for guidance and he told you to continue. Would you then go all the way to the maximum—450 volts—even if you heard no more sounds from the next room?

A sample of college students, psychiatrists, and middle-class adults were presented with this same description. If you have reacted to it the way they did, you feel a sense of revulsion and are sure that you—and virtually all normal people, except for a lunatic fringe of perhaps 1 to 2 percent—would refuse to obey the experimenter at an early point (Milgram, 1974). Yet when such an experiment was actually performed (with the cooperation of a confederate, an actor who only pretended to be receiving shocks), the results were very different.

In 1963, Stanley Milgram conducted this experiment, which was not about learning and memory but about **obedience,** compliance with the demands of an authority figure. Milgram wanted to determine the extent to which ordinary people would obey an authority figure who ordered them to hurt another person. Milgram and the rest of the psychological community were startled by the results. Of the 40 men from a wide range of occupations who were the subjects, 25 (or 62.5 percent) obeyed commands fully and continued to give shocks to the highest voltage possible. Only 15 broke off in response to the "learner's" protests. Milgram (1974) pressed on with more experiments, introducing variations, until almost 1000 adults had taken part. The results were basically the same. A distressingly high proportion of subjects, even though many of them disapproved of the "teaching tactics" of the experiment and were troubled by their own role in it, obeyed orders and administered what they thought were painful shocks to an innocent person.

Even those who disobeyed often showed great agitation, as we can see from this transcript of a defiant subject:

> The man is banging. He wants to get out. . . . I'm sorry. If the man wants to get out I'd just as soon stop. . . . I don't want to administer any more [extremely excited]. . . . I will gladly refund the check, but I will not harm this man. . . . I'm sorry, I will not give him any more if

Obedience *Compliance with the demands of an authority figure.*

he obviously wants to get out. There is no money in the world that will make me hurt another individual. (Milgram, 1965, p. 67)

The frightening conclusion from Milgram's studies is the realization that many ordinary, decent people are, in some circumstances, ready to obey an authority who orders them to inflict pain on another person. If this is true, it helps to explain many atrocities throughout history and forces us to examine the elements in society that exalt the value of obedience over individual thought.

Still, some people always seem to find the strength to fight against officialdom—even in a reign of terror like Nazi Germany. In these experiments, too, some of the subjects were able to resist authority. What makes people able to resist? When Milgram's studies were analyzed according to characteristics of the situation—how many people were present, whether the experimenter was in or out of the room, and so forth—it turned out that both aspects of the situation and personality traits of the individual people in it affected behavior.

For example, subjects who were in the same room as the victim were much more likely to defy orders (60 percent did), and subjects who actually had to place the victim's hand on the shock plate were even more likely to resist (70 percent defied orders); see Figure 17-3. As the subject's level of involvement with the learner increased (from neither seeing nor hearing him, at first, to hearing, seeing, and then touching him), the subject was less inclined to inflict injury. This link between remoteness from a stranger and greater willingness to do harm may have implications for modern warfare, in which it is possible to kill millions of unseen people simply by pushing a button.

A major difference in personal characteristics between obedient and defiant subjects was that the defiant subjects saw themselves as principally responsible for the suffering of the learner, while the obedient ones felt less responsible than the experimenter. Furthermore, the obedient subjects attributed twice as much responsibility for the learner's suffering to the learner himself, offering arguments like, "After all, he volunteered for the experiment, and he didn't learn very well in it" (Milgram, 1974).

Some of Milgram's subjects were horrified by the commands they received and flatly refused to administer the shocks. Apparently, some aspects of these people's personalities led them to transcend the situation. Yet it is difficult to predict the way someone will behave either from knowing his or her personality or from knowing the situation he or she is in. It is important to remember that what we do depends on the interaction between *who* we are and *where* we are. Even though prediction is difficult or impossible, it is still important to look for the roots of behavior, especially of

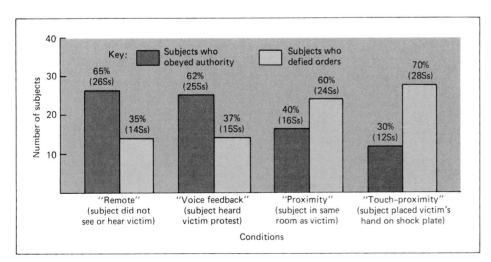

FIGURE 17-3 *Level of obedience in relation to experimental conditions. In Milgram's experiments, the more closely a subject was involved with a victim, the less likely the subject was to obey an order to inflict apparently painful electric shocks. The highest level of obedience occurred among subjects who neither saw nor heard the people who were supposedly receiving the shocks, and the lowest level of compliance occurred among subjects who had to touch the supposed victims. (Source: Adapted from Milgram, 1974.)*

behavior involving aggression and altruism, which have a strong impact on the way we function individually and as a society.

Critiques of Milgram's Studies Milgram's work has been assailed on two major grounds. First, critics maintain that the experiment itself was immoral. It deceived people and faced them with a disturbing truth about themselves, causing them extreme stress for which they were not prepared and which may have caused long-term psychological harm (Baumrind, 1964). Milgram (1974) has denied that his procedures caused lasting harm and has pointed to the fact that more than 8 out of 10 subjects said afterward that they were glad to have taken part, 4 out of 5 felt that more experiments like this should be carried out, and 3 out of 4 said that they had learned something of personal importance. One 39-year-old social worker said, one year after his participation, "What appalled me was that I could possess this capacity for obedience and compliance to a central idea, i.e., the value of a memory experiment, even after it became clear that continued adherence to this value was at the expense of violation of another value, i.e., don't hurt someone else who is helpless and not hurting you. I hope I can deal more effectively with any future conflicts of values I encounter" (Milgram, 1974, p. 54).

Second, critics also hold that the findings have little relevance to the real world. The subjects trusted Yale University (where the experiment took place) not to do anything cruel or immoral; as voluntary subjects, they may have been particularly prone to obey a scientific researcher; they were repeatedly prodded to continue if they showed any doubt; the lab situation was so different from what a person would encounter in, say, wartime that it is impossible to generalize from one to the other (Baumrind, 1964; Orne & Holland, 1968). Milgram (1974) countered these arguments by setting up a similar experiment away from the university, and found that obedience was not significantly different there. He also asked hard questions, such as these:

> Is not the criticism based as much on the unanticipated findings as on the method? The findings were that some subjects performed in what appeared to be a shockingly immoral way. If, instead, every one of the subjects had broken off at "slight shock," or at the first sign of the learner's discomfort, the results would have been pleasant, and reassuring, and who would protest? (Milgram, 1974, p. 194)

Whatever we may conclude about the criticism of these experiments, they show to what lengths ordinary people will go in the name of obedience, force us to question our own commitment to values that transcend submission to authority, and raise questions about the ability of society to produce citizens who can tell whether obedience serves just or unjust causes.

ALTRUISM

Both helping and hurting other people are part of the long history of the human race. What makes us behave one way or the other? Are the tendencies toward these behaviors built into us, or are they drummed into us? What makes them surface when they do? In Chapter 11, "Motivation and Emotion," we discussed some of the reasons for aggressive behavior. Now let's take a look at the underpinnings of **altruism,** which is behavior performed for the benefit of someone other than the person doing it, with no anticipation of reward.

People help each other in many ways—by giving money, by giving blood, by giving time. Most of this help is offered to family and friends, but a great deal is extended to strangers we will never meet. Most of us perform a wide variety of helping actions that entail some cost, self-sacrifice, or risk on our part. We take part

Altruism *Behavior carried out to benefit another, without anticipation of rewards from external sources.*

in civil rights marches, participate in boycotts, put off our own goals to further other people's well-being. Virtually everyone either gives or gets some kind of help almost every day, and yet the great bulk of helping behavior goes unnoticed.

Over the past generation, psychologists have been delving into the reasons underlying altruistic behavior. Let's consider *when* and *why* we help others, and how altruism can be encouraged.

When Do We Help Others?

One way to examine altruistic behavior is in terms of a very specific kind of help— the kind given to a stranger in an emergency. Let's look at some examples.

The crowd on a subway platform in New York City was aghast as a 75-year-old blind man stumbled and fell between the cars of a train that was about to pull out of the station. One man in the crowd—Reginald Andrews, a 29-year-old unemployed father on his way home after having filed still another job application—leaped onto the tracks, yelled out a plea to stop the train, and pulled the blind man to safety into a narrow crawl space under the edge of the platform. "I wasn't thinking about the danger, just that, hey, somebody needs help," Andrews said later, when he was asked why he had put his own life in danger to help a complete stranger (McFadden, 1982).

How different Mr. Andrews's action was from that of 38 people who unwittingly spurred a long line of research studies designed to determine what makes some people take action to help a stranger, while others do nothing! Those thirty-eight were also New Yorkers—residents of an apartment complex who watched from their windows in the middle of the night while a brutal attacker stabbed a young woman named Kitty Genovese to death. Despite her piercing screams, and despite the fact that it was obvious what was happening—the killer came back for three separate attacks—not one of these neighbors came to her aid, and no one even picked up the phone to call the police until she was already dead (A. M. Rosenthal, 1964). Why? Were these people unfeeling monsters, indifferent to her plight?

Factors Affecting Altruism   The answers that have emerged from dozens of experiments are complex, but they do shed some light on why one person will risk his or her life while another will not help at all. Virtually all these studies have ruled out apathy as an answer. When people see that another person is in trouble, they are hardly ever indifferent. Even when they do not take any helpful action, they are often agitated and tense, concerned about the other person's health or safety, and torn about their own role. A number of factors help to explain why people do or do not stretch out a helping hand.

RECOGNITION THAT AN EMERGENCY EXISTS   Before you take action, you must first notice that an event is taking place and then interpret it as an emergency (Latané & Darley, 1968). When a situation is clearly a serious emergency, like the blind man's fall under the subway train, impulsive, immediate rescue attempts like Reginald Andrews's are more likely to occur (Piliavin, Dovidio, Gaertner, & Clark, 1981; Shotland & Heinold, 1985).

If a situation is ambiguous, you'll look around at the people near you to see how they're interpreting it. If you interpret an event as an emergency but no one else seems to be doing anything, you may decide that you were overreacting and then do nothing. This was brought out in a study in which smoke filled a room. When people were alone, they reported it; when they were with other people who did nothing, they ignored it, probably assuming that if there were a danger, somebody else would have done something (Latané & Darley, 1968). (How similar is this situation to those in Asch's conformity studies, in which people doubt their own judgment when the majority adopts a different point of view?)

NUMBER OF PEOPLE ON THE SCENE   Faulty interpretation was clearly not responsible for the failure to help Kitty Genovese. Ironically, the sheer number of witnesses to her ordeal was probably the major reason why no one helped her. Study after study has shown that people who are alone are more likely to help someone in trouble (Latané & Nida, 1981; Shotland & Heinold, 1985). When other potential rescuers are around, barriers go up.

The first barrier is the influence of other people in interpreting an event. If this is a crisis, why isn't someone else doing something about it?

The second barrier is the ability of the observer to diffuse responsibility. The observer may think, "Let George do it" or, "Why should I go out on a limb when there are all these other people around who can help?" Or the observer may assume, "If this really is important, surely someone else has already done something about it, and I don't need to."

A third barrier is the fear of looking foolish: "Suppose what looks like a crisis really isn't. Everyone will have seen me jump in with both feet—and then I'll look silly."

CHARACTERISTICS OF THE VICTIM   A man who collapses in a moving subway car is more likely to get help if he is carrying a cane than if he smells of liquor and is carrying a bottle wrapped in a brown paper bag (Piliavin, Rodin, & Piliavin, 1969). It is easy to understand why people would rather help a disabled person than a drunk. But some other characteristics of the victim are more difficult to explain. For example, a man with a cane who collapses in a subway train is *less* likely to get help if he is bleeding from the mouth (a sign of serious injury) than if he is not (Piliavin & Piliavin, 1972). A man is less likely to be helped if he has a large red birthmark on his face than if he is unmarked (Piliavin, Piliavin, & Rodin, 1975). These findings suggest that fear or disgust can cause inaction.

CHARACTERISTICS OF THE BYSTANDER   A bystander's personality, outlook on life, and current circumstances all affect whether he or she will help. People in a hurry, for example, do not stop to help as often as people who are unpressured. In one study, divinity students practiced a speech in one building and then set out to record it in another building. Some students were told that they were late for their taping appointments, some that they were on time, and some that they were early. On the way, each student passed a man lying in a doorway, his eyes closed and his head down, who coughed as the student went by. More than half the students who were early or on time stopped to help, but only 1 in 10 of those who thought they were late did. What was the topic of the students' speeches? It was the parable of the good Samaritan (Darley & Batson, 1973).

In another study, 32 people who had intervened during crimes in progress were found to possess distinctive personal characteristics (Huston & Geis, cited in Shotland, 1985). They were more likely to have been victimized themselves in the past, and this may have made them especially sympathetic to the victims. They were also self-assured and confident that they could handle the situation. Many had received special training in police work, first aid, or lifesaving, which might have accounted for their confidence.

In recent years, public health educators have offered training to the general public in such lifesaving techniques as cardiopulmonary resuscitation (CPR), a first aid technique for victims of heart attack and near-drowning; mouth-to-mouth resuscitation; and the Heimlich maneuver (to dislodge food that is choking someone). How effective is such training? According to a recent study of persons trained in a technique to stop bleeding from an artery, knowing what to do can save lives (Shotland & Heinold, 1985). In this study, training did not increase the *rate* of helping, but it did improve the *effectiveness* of help. Specifically, untrained witnesses who tried to help someone who appeared injured and bleeding heavily tended to try to find someone else to give direct assistance, while those who knew what to do did it themselves. Minutes were saved, and if a real emergency had existed, lives would have been saved, too. It seems, then, that training in crisis behavior could help people act in other emergencies, too.

Predicting Altruistic Behavior   When we see another person in serious trouble, we react on two levels: feeling and thinking. We become emotionally aroused, a response that may have been bred into us to preserve our species. Even day-old infants cry when they hear another baby cry (Sagi & Hoffman, 1976; Simner, 1971). The fact that such a response occurs so early in life suggests that it may be inborn, rather than learned. What we do learn is how to decide what to do. In a crisis, we ask ourselves what we stand to gain or lose by acting or by not acting. Will you feel too guilty if you do nothing? Will you be taking foolish risks by stepping in?

   Jane A. Piliavin and her colleagues at the University of Wisconsin have provided a *cost-benefit analysis* of when people will help. They hold that in deciding whether to help, we calculate the costs and benefits to us and try to minimize the costs and maximize the benefits. We are most likely to help when the reward for helping seems greater than the cost of helping. According to this analysis, you will help if you are so emotionally aroused that you respond impulsively, not even thinking of the costs to yourself; if your personal costs are low (you have time, and you are not risking your life); or if the situation holds out benefits to you (you find the victim attractive, you want to do something interesting, or you want to see yourself in the role of hero) (Piliavin, Dovidio, Gaertner, & Clark, 1981). Often, people feel distressed when they do not help someone in need but they still do not help, because the costs to themselves are too high.

Cost-benefit analysis   Explanation of altruistic behavior which maintains that people help others when the reward is greater than the cost.

Why Do We Help Others?

What makes people go out of their way to help others, in a variety of situations, often putting themselves at a disadvantage? A number of explanations have been offered; let's consider several of them.

We Inherit a Tendency toward Altruism   Since some children show altruism from a very early age and others do not, it is possible that some people are born with more generous, sharing natures. Altruism may be in their genes. Although altruism can, of course, hurt the person who engages in it, it *is* beneficial to the species at large. The existence of prosocial behavior in the animal kingdom suggests some hereditary, biologically adaptive reason for it.

   Sociobiologists, scientists who study the biological basis of social behavior in various animals (including the human species), point to many altruistic activities among animals. Chimpanzees adopt orphaned chimps, small birds such as robins and thrushes whistle to warn their fellows of the approach of a hawk (even though this may draw attention to themselves), and some honeybees commit suicide while defending their nests against intruders (Wilson, 1978). Many sociobiologists have concluded that there is some kind of genetic programming which makes us act altruistically. Most social psychologists, however, concentrate more on the learning and environmental factors that contribute to this kind of behavior.

Sociobiologists   Scientists who study the biological basis of social behavior in various animals.

We Learn to Be Altruistic   A great deal of research over the past few decades has indicated that people *learn* to be sensitive to other people and to help them. Altruistic children tend to have parents who help others, who expect their children to help others, and who let their children know in no uncertain terms how they should behave (Mussen & Eisenberg-Berg, 1977; Yarrow, 1978). In other words, among the norms such children learn are helping behaviors.

Donating blood is a very special kind of altruistic behavior. First, it requires that our bodies part with a substance essential for life itself. Then there are other costs. For many people the very idea arouses the fear of pain and of needles; the donation may interfere with everyday life because of prohibitions against smoking, drinking, or exercising—or because of possible faintness or dizziness—for a while afterward; and it requires an outlay of time and effort (Piliavin, Evans, & Callero, 1984).

It is in society's interest, however, to encourage people to donate blood. Today, the demand for blood is increasing, for both medical and social reasons. Health authorities emphasize the need to convert from a paid to a voluntary blood supply: such diseases as type B hepatitis and AIDS can be transmitted through infected blood, and the risk of infection has been higher with blood obtained commercially than with blood given by volunteers. To get ample supplies of blood, it is more efficient to en-

IN THE FOREFRONT

WHY PEOPLE BECOME REGULAR, COMMITTED BLOOD DONORS

courage previous donors to come back than it is to continually recruit new donors (Miller & Weikel, 1974).

Researchers are seeking, then, to find out why some people give blood over and over again in a "community responsibility" blood collection system. In such a system, donors do not get paid, nor do they or their families receive any reciprocal or insurance benefits if they should need blood

themselves. Donors would appear to have nothing to gain from giving blood, and they do incur costs like those listed above. Yet some people become habitual blood donors. Why?

Piliavin and her colleagues have studied the process by which people become regular, committed blood donors, and have identified the following basic categories of motivation for giving blood (Piliavin, Evans, & Callero, 1984):

■ *External social motives.* Most first-time donors fall into this category. They are likely to have been pressured to give blood by a friend, by coworkers, or by others aiming for a good showing in a community blood drive. Externally motivated people are more likely to come in with someone else and to respond to rewards like ice cream or a tee shirt. They want to avoid sanctions or criticisms.

■ *Community or social group responsibility.* Donors feel that giv-

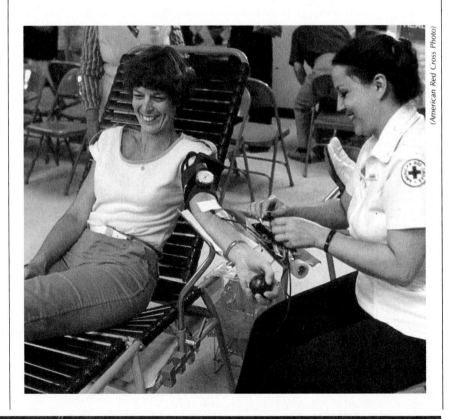

(American Red Cross Photo)

Donating blood has been compared to a risky sport like skydiving. At first, people are nervous and afraid when they are donating blood or skydiving; but the more often they do either activity, the more positive they feel about it, until they become "addicted" to the experience.

ing blood is something a good citizen should do, and they want to live up to societal standards of responsibility.

- *Personal moral obligation.* Donors see themselves as moral if they give blood, and as less moral if they do not. They want to live up to their own standards of morality.

- *Addiction to the experience.* Some donors are attracted to the act of donating blood for its own sake; they want to master the fear involved in doing it. For these donors, the initial negative state is replaced with a positive one. Giving blood has been compared to parachute-jumping: at first, participants feel fearful and anxious; but the more often they jump (or give blood), the more positive they feel about what they are doing—whether it's the exhilaration and sense of competence felt by the parachutist or the "warm glow" of having helped someone in need felt by the blood donor (Piliavin,

Callero, & Evans, 1982). Thus, by repeatedly doing something they were initially anxious about, they transform the experience into a positive one, even an addicting one.

Becoming a regular, committed blood donor, according to Piliavin et al. (1984), is a process involving several interrelated steps. First, donors need to feel that their "costs" will be unimportant. They become convinced as they find, for example, that the experience is not painful, as they have feared; that they do not have to wait a long time; and that there are no physical aftereffects. Second, they need to develop motives for donation that are internal—motives that are tied to their feelings about themselves rather than to external, social pressures. Third, they have to plan to donate again. Finally, they have to develop a *habit* of donation. In the earlier stages of regular blood donation, social pressures

dominate; later, internal motivations become increasingly important. During their first two experiences as donors, people think about why they are giving blood; but by the third or fourth donation they begin to define themselves as regular donors. Those who become committed are more likely to have come in alone the first time, to have waited a short time, to have suffered no physical aftereffects, and to have experienced positive feelings afterward.

Although Piliavin and her colleagues believe that blood donation is so distinctive an experience that their findings cannot be generalized to other altruistic acts, it does seem that the combination of minimal cost (little time lost and little physical discomfort) and maximum benefit (feeling good afterward) is the overriding element in determining a person's commitment to this kind of prosocial behavior. A similar kind of cost-benefit ratio may well apply to other forms of altruism.

(© Ellis Herwig/Stock, Boston)

Helping others makes volunteers, like these men dishing out food to the poor, feel better about themselves. Unhappy people often lift their own spirits by helping others who are less fortunate, and happiness often spurs people to take charitable actions toward others.

Being Altruistic Makes Us Feel Good   People like to feel virtuous. Since many of us have been raised to think that charitable behavior is praiseworthy, we have a good opinion of ourselves when we help someone else, and this is in itself rewarding. Helping behavior may also be closely allied to two kinds of emotional states—happiness and sadness.

When we're sad, helping others makes us feel better by making us feel as if we are better people (Baumann, Cialdini, & Kenrick, 1981). This would seem to bear out the traditional advice to unhappy people—that they will feel better if they do not brood about their own problems but instead do something nice for someone else.

We also seem to be more apt to help others when we're feeling happy, a conclusion reached by Baumann and his colleagues (1981) and confirmed by Rosenhan, Salovey, and Hargis (1981). In the latter study, students who imagined that they were being rewarded for hard work with a vacation in Hawaii were more likely to help a friend than those who imagined that their best friend was to be given the trip. When we feel fortunate, competent, and successful, our good feelings about ourselves often spur us to carry out good actions toward others.

In addition to these general factors, there may be more specific motivations for altruistic behavior. Some of the considerations that motivate people to donate blood, for example, are described in the box "Why People Become Regular, Committed Blood Donors" (pages 612–613).

How Can We Encourage Altruism?

To survive in a perilous world populated by predatory animals and hostile tribes, early humans had to develop certain patterns of behavior. One such behavior pattern, we can assume, would have been characterized by helping only those in their own small group and reacting with suspicion and aggression toward other groups. Today, however, these attitudes are no longer adaptive (Hamburg, 1983). In a world in which strangers are often dependent on each other for the necessities of life, we need to develop other ways of relating to those around us.

How, then, can we encourage altruism? One answer seems to lie in teaching children to solve their problems without resorting to violence, in discouraging them from aggressiveness early in life and rewarding them for alternative behaviors, and in teaching appropriate values—helping rather than hurting, caring about other people rather than indifference, cooperation rather than competition, and equality between the sexes rather than male dominance and machismo. We could, for example, expose boys "to the same training that girls have traditionally received in our society, and [encourage them] to develop similar kinds of socially positive, tender, cooperative, nurturant, and sensitive qualities, which are antithetical to aggressive behavior" (Eron, 1980, p. 244).

Another approach is biological, having to do with brain chemistry. Recognizing that human beings do inhibit their aggression in many situations, some researchers are trying to discover what brain chemicals are involved in the inhibitory process and whether similar substances can be developed to help people master antisocial aggression (Redmond, 1983).

Still another approach emphasizes the importance of positive solutions for individual, family, community, and societal problems. Some states have even passed laws that require people to help each other, as discussed in the box (opposite page) "Should We Legislate Helping Behavior?" Encouraging people to assume responsibility for their fellow human beings is not easy, but in the nuclear age especially, it is essential.

As the research summarized in the preceding pages indicates, a number of factors operate to prevent bystanders from helping strangers who fall ill, become injured, or are victimized by criminals. To try to get bystanders involved in offering help more often, a few states have passed "good Samaritan" laws—according to which people who witness serious crimes can be sued, fined, or even jailed for *not* acting. Such laws have been analyzed by a psychologist who has conducted extensive research on bystanders' responses (Shotland, 1985). Let's look at their possible benefits and the difficulties they present.

BENEFITS OF "GOOD SAMARITAN" LAWS

■ *Fixing responsibility.* Many people fail to act in emergencies, especially when there are other witnesses, because they do not feel that it is up to them to act. A good Samaritan law would hold bystanders responsible for doing nothing, regardless of what others did.

■ *Altering the cost-benefit ratio.* People often do not act because they believe that they run a greater risk of suffering a penalty (danger or inconvenience) by acting than by doing nothing. A good Samaritan law would impose a penalty for *not* acting.

DIFFICULTIES WITH "GOOD SAMARITAN" LAWS

■ *Witnesses may not be willing to admit that they saw a crime for fear of being prosecuted.* This would

dry up a rich source of information for police investigators.

■ *Enforcement is difficult.* It is difficult to separate errors of judgment from deliberate avoidance of civic duty. Very often only the witness knows his or her reason for delayed action or inaction. A person seeing a couple engaging in sexual intercourse, for example, may not realize that a rape is occurring; he or she may look away out of embarrassment or respect for privacy—and then be accused of ignoring a crime. Or a person may call for help too late—but who is to say what a "reasonable" time for reporting is?

It is possible that difficulties like these might be overcome by the way such laws are written. It also may be possible, however, that altruism cannot be legislated but must, instead, be instilled into people from a very early age, so that it becomes part of their outlook on life.

ATTITUDES

Components of Attitudes

You have an attitude toward practically everything and everyone in the world you have ever spent any time thinking about, and you have undoubtedly expressed opinions about many subjects. Your opinion is your attitude, put into words. An **attitude** is a learned, relatively permanent way of responding to someone or something in a favorable or unfavorable way. It consists of three elements: what you think (the cognitive component), how you feel (the emotional component), and how you tend to act out your thoughts and emotions (the behavioral component). For example, you probably have an attitude about extramarital sex. Cognitively, you may think it's harmful to a marriage; emotionally, you may feel jealous at the idea that your spouse might have sex with anyone else; and behaviorally, you may remain monogamous.

One problem with studying attitudes is that the three elements often contradict each other. For example, three separate national public opinion polls spanning the years from 1970 to 1977 showed that 75 to 87 percent of people in North America disapprove of married people's having sex with people they are not married to (National Opinion Research Center, 1977). Other surveys found that during the same period about half of all men and from one-fourth to one-half of all women were saying that they *had* had extramarital sex (Hunt, 1974). It seems, then, that the cognitive component of some people's attitudes about extramarital sex differs from the behavioral component.

Attitude Learned, relatively permanent way of responding to someone or something, which has cognitive, emotional, and behavioral components.

Much research about attitudes has focused on the interrelationships among the different elements—how a change in one affects the others—and how we form and modify our opinions and our actions. Knowing that there are three different components suggests that attitudes can be measured by using different scales for thoughts, feelings, and action. This method of measurement has important implications for efforts to *change* attitudes. If we try to change only the cognitive element—for example, to convince someone of the rationale behind civil rights laws without taking into account the charged emotions in race relations—we won't get very far.

Measurement of Attitudes

Usually, social scientists measure attitudes just as market researchers or ordinary people would—by asking people about their beliefs through interviews or questionnaires. Let's take a look at two of the most popular paper-and-pencil attitude scales, the Likert scale and the semantic differential.

The ***Likert scale*** (Likert, 1932) lists several statements and asks the subject to respond on a continuum from "strongly agree" to "strongly disagree." A statement, or series of statements, is presented, such as: "The drinking age in my state should be raised to 21." The subject is then asked to indicate the extent to which he or she agrees or disagrees. Likert used a 5-point spread, from "strongly agree" to "agree," "undecided," "disagree," and "strongly disagree." The subject gives the appropriate number or letter, and each response is given a point value. A person's attitude score is the sum of all his or her ratings. (See the discussion in Chapter 18 of Rubin's "liking" and "love" scales for an example of a Likert-type scale.)

The ***semantic differential*** (Osgood, Suci, & Tennenbaum, 1957) focuses on the meaning of a word or concept for a particular person. To determine this, the tester asks the subject to rate concepts (such as *father, nuclear power, Democrats,* or *black people*) on a series of bipolar (opposite) dimensions arranged on a 7-point scale. Each concept is usually rated on 15 or more bipolar scales, which reflect three major factors: evaluation of the concept itself (as in the scale "fair-unfair"); evaluation of its power (as in "strong-weak"); and evaluation of its activity level (as in "fast-slow"). When a subject rates a series of different concepts on the same dimensions, we can see similarities or differences in his or her attitudes toward different concepts. (See Figure 17-4.)

The concepts to be rated can be specially selected to fit a particular issue. Thus, if we want to see whether you feel differently toward different ethnic groups, we could ask you to rate Italians, Germans, Poles, and Scots on the same bipolar dimensions, and we could then assess similarities and differences in ratings. Similarly, we could compare your attitudes toward your mother and your father, toward different

Likert scale Measure of attitudes in which a subject responds to a series of statements on a continuum from "strongly agree" to "strongly disagree."

Semantic differential Measure of attitudes in which a concept is rated on a series of dimensions.

FIGURE 17-4 *Semantic differential. The respondent checks the appropriate segment of each scale—here, as it applies to the concept "father." Respondents can be asked to rate a variety of concepts, so that the different ratings can be compared. Generally, at least 15 scales are presented for each concept.*

```
                              FATHER
        Good     ____:____:____:____:____:____:____   Bad

        Clean    ____:____:____:____:____:____:____   Dirty

        Cruel    ____:____:____:____:____:____:____   Kind

        Slow     ____:____:____:____:____:____:____   Fast

        Valuable ____:____:____:____:____:____:____   Worthless

        Tense    ____:____:____:____:____:____:____   Relaxed

        Strong   ____:____:____:____:____:____:____   Weak

        Large    ____:____:____:____:____:____:____   Small
```

occupations, toward abstract ideas (like peace and war), and toward different brand names. The semantic differential has been applied to research on vocational choices and on consumers' reactions to different products; and it has also been used in clinical diagnosis (Anastasi, 1976).

Relying on self-reports poses problems, however. For one thing, the way a question is asked often affects the answer given. In a recent poll, 39 percent of Americans said that government spending for public welfare should be cut, while only 7 percent thought that "aid to the needy" should be cut (Marty, 1982). For another thing, people are not always honest with *themselves* about their true attitudes, let alone with researchers. It is usually best to use several different methods to measure attitudes.

Formation of Attitudes

How did you develop your attitudes toward people of other ethnic groups, toward the desirability of communism or democracy, or toward the importance—or unimportance—of a liberal arts education? Somehow, somewhere, you learned it. As with every other issue in psychology, different theories have been advanced to explain the formation of attitudes.

Learning Theories   When the American flag is carried past you or when you hear the familiar strains of "The Star-Spangled Banner," your tendency to stand and salute indicates learning. From early childhood, you associated these actions with the flag and the national anthem, you imitated what you saw your parents and teachers do, you were made to feel like a good citizen, and you associated these symbols of your country with positive qualities.

According to learning theory, we learn attitudes the same way we learn everything else. As we learn new information, we learn the feelings, the thoughts, and the actions associated with it. Experts in public relations, advertising, and sales put this principle into effect every time they couple information about a product with a pleasant association—a satisfying meal or a picture that conjures up happy thoughts. Learning theories see people as reactors rather than initiators, as primarily passive beings whose learning "depends on the number and strength of the positive and negative elements previously learned" (Freedman, Sears, & Carlsmith, 1981).

Cognitive-Consistency Theories   Suppose that you are a television network executive who supports peace-oriented organizations and who believes strongly in the need for people to get along with each other. The government publishes a major report indicating that certain programs carried by your network foster aggressive attitudes that could lead to crime, or even war. These programs are the highest-rated, most profitable ones on the network; if you were to suggest dropping them, you are sure you would be fired the next day.

What are you to do about these conflicts? You might try to make one attitude (your desire to keep your good job) consistent with your other attitude (your belief in furthering goodwill among people). One way is to question the report by pointing out problems in the design of the study or maintaining that the findings do not justify the conclusions drawn. Another way is to make minor—and probably meaningless—program changes that won't jeopardize your job. Either way, you can continue to think of yourself as a person concerned with the common good—and you can keep your job. This kind of behavior is an example of cognitive dissonance, discussed below.

Cognitive-consistency theories hold that a perceived incompatibility between a person's thoughts and actions (cognitive inconsistency) can cause discomfort, and that people try to reduce their discomfort by changing one or the other—either their thinking or their actions—to make the two consistent with each other. The most important of these theories is Festinger's cognitive-dissonance theory.

Cognitive-consistency theories *Theories which maintain that incompatibility between thoughts and actions can cause discomfort, which people then try to reduce.*

(Bettmann Archive)

Aesop's fox could not reach the grapes and decided he didn't want them, because they were sour anyway. According to cognitive-dissonance theory, the fox would have felt even more strongly about the sour grapes if they had been within reach but he had not wanted to make the effort to get them.

We all know Aesop's tale about the fox who could not reach the grapes and decided he didn't want them, because they were probably sour. Then there's the story of the fruit-loving monkey who couldn't get anything besides lemons and decided that they were the sweetest lemons he had ever tasted. According to cognitive-dissonance theory, which was proposed by Leon Festinger (1962), these opinions would have been even stronger if the fox and the monkey had had a choice—if the grapes had been within reach but the fox did not want to make the effort to get them, or if the monkey had chosen the lemons instead of some other fruit. The natural tendency to enhance the value of whatever we have chosen and to play down the choice we have not made is part of the basis for this influential theory.

Cognitive dissonance is a state of psychological discomfort that occurs when there is a basic incompatibility between our thoughts and our actions, or between two or more sets of ideas, attitudes, or opinions that we hold. To reduce the discomfort, we change something. The main focus of this theory is on explaining what people do to bring about consistency, or harmony.

Dissonance is inevitable whenever we make a choice. Since few choices are perfect, whatever we choose has some negative aspects, and whatever we do not choose has some positive aspects. If we think about these aspects we will experience an uncomfortable level of dissonance. We will wonder whether we have made the right choice—whether some other college would have given us a better education, whether some other car would have held up longer, whether some other spouse would have been more satisfying to live with. We try to reduce dissonance by telling ourselves that the alternative we have chosen is really more desirable and the one we have not chosen is less desirable.

Situations that can produce cognitive dissonance are those in which we do something contrary to our deeply held ideas about what is right or proper, those in which we hold a belief that appears to defy the rules of logic, those in which something happens that contradicts our past experience, and those in which we do something that doesn't fit our idea of who we are and what we stand for (Festinger, 1957).

Cognitive dissonance *State of psychological discomfort that occurs when there is a basic incompatibility between thoughts and actions, or between two or more sets of ideas, attitudes, or opinions that a person holds.*

A classic experiment demonstrating this effect was conducted by Festinger and Carlsmith (1959). They asked college students to work at a boring, tiring job for an hour. For 30 minutes, the students put spools on and took them off a tray, using one hand; and for the other 30 minutes they turned square pegs one quarter-turn at a time, using one hand. Then the experimenters gave the subjects a challenging task: to tell the next subjects about the job with the spools and pegs and to make it sound like fun. All the students were paid for telling the lie, but half received only $1 and the other half $20. The first subjects were then interviewed to find out what they really thought of the experiment. Those who had received the large payment were more likely to say that the job was dull; those who got only $1 were more likely to give a favorable opinion of their dreary hour (see Table 17-1).

Why was this so? It seems that the subjects who earned $20 could easily tell themselves that they had lied because they had been paid a lot of money to do so. The subjects who were paid only $1 could not come up with any good reason for lying; to get rid of their uncomfortably dissonant feeling, they simply changed their minds and decided that the job had not been so dull after all. They changed their attitudes to account for their behavior.

The practical lesson we can take from this is that if we want to change someone's attitude and future behavior, we'll do better to give modest rewards instead of large ones. If, for example, you want to encourage people to diet to lose weight, give them $2 for every pound they lose—not $50. Then they will be more motivated to continue to eat less; they will not be able to tell themselves that they are dieting only for the money.

Like all influential theories, cognitive dissonance has stirred up a great deal of analysis—and its share of heated controversy. It can also be modified in several ways.

We can't ignore the fact that we're all different from one another. You may be able to tolerate dissonance better than I can—you may shrug it off without feeling that you need to reduce it—or you may deal with it in a different way. Instead of downgrading the grapes as sour, the fox could have boosted his self-esteem by upgrading something else in the situation—perhaps the value of the exercise he got while trying to reach them. Furthermore, what is dissonant for me may be consonant for you.

Besides, sometimes information that arouses dissonance is useful. If we could not tolerate some dissonance, we would often distort reality, and we could never admit our mistakes. Admitting mistakes does create dissonance, but it is the only way we can profit from them and learn to do better in the future. If I tell myself that the car I bought is the best one on the market—even though I am dissatisfied with its performance in many ways—I may be able to maintain a consonant view of myself as an intelligent purchaser, but I will not be able to change to a vehicle that will meet my needs better and I'll be trapped with an inferior product.

TABLE 17-1 A BORING TASK, A LIE, AND COGNITIVE DISSONANCE

Question on Interview	Average Rating on Interview Questions		
	Control group (n = 20)	$1 (n = 20)	$20 (n = 20)
How enjoyable tasks were (rated from −5 to +5)	−0.45	+1.35	−0.05
Willingness to participate in similar study (rated from −5 to +5)	−0.62	+1.20	−0.25

Note: Subjects who had been paid either $1 or $20 for saying that their tasks were enjoyable, as well as control subjects who were not asked to lie, were interviewed following the study. Those in the $1 condition were more likely to give favorable opinions about the boring tasks than those in the other two conditions. n = number of subjects.

Source: Festinger & Carlsmith, 1959.

Self-Perception Theory   In the musical *Fiddler on the Roof,* Tevye the dairyman asks his wife, "Golde, do you love me?" After some evasiveness, she sings, "Do I love him? For 25 years I've lived with him, fought with him, starved with him. Twenty-five years my bed is his. If that's not love, what is?" Tevye asks, "Then you love me?" and Golde replies, "I suppose I do."

This exchange melodiously illustrates Daryl Bem's **self-perception theory** (1967, 1970). Bem disagrees with Festinger's cognitive-dissonance theory, the theory that an internal process first arouses dissonance and then reduces it. Bem says people form their attitudes much more simply. They infer their own attitudes in the same way that they infer the attitudes of other people—by observing behavior. Golde realizes that she has stuck with Tevye through many difficult years; she assumes, then, that she must love him. If you find yourself dressing with special care for what you had thought was going to be a casual evening, you realize, "This party and these people must mean more to me than I had thought." To figure out what our own attitudes are, we rely on the same external cues that we turn to when we try to decide what others think and feel.

Self-perception theory would explain the behavior of the subjects in Festinger and Carlsmith's study by suggesting that those students who lied about the boring task for only $1 might think, "I would not lie for so little money. Therefore, I must not have been lying; the task must have been interesting enough."

How do these two interpretations differ? Festinger emphasizes cognitive dissonance as an uncomfortable state that motivates people to reduce the discomfort. Bem, on the other hand, is concerned not with psychological discomfort but simply with the way people infer their attitudes in ambiguous situations by looking at their own behavior. To learn how we think, he says, we look at what we do.

Bem's theory has many practical applications. For one thing, it has implications about the value of participating in picketing, protest demonstrations, and other issue-oriented actions. If attitudes follow behavior, the more a person does on behalf of a particular cause—preserving the environment, for example, or strengthening a union—the more strongly he or she will believe in that cause.

Changing Attitudes: Persuasive Communication

How are we persuaded to change our attitudes? Everywhere you go, someone is trying to talk you into doing or believing something. Newspaper ads and radio and television commercials urge you to buy products and vote for candidates. Religious leaders exhort you to act in a way befitting the dictates of their congregations. Special-interest groups urge you to fight for the right to bear arms or for gun control; to keep the constitutional right to abortion or to overturn it; to support the Equal Rights Amendment or to defeat it. Teachers, friends, and relatives try to convince you of the wisdom and morality of some courses of action and the folly or evil of others.

What makes some of these persuasive communications more effective than others? The basic factors to consider are the source of a communication, its nature, and the characteristics of the audience. The following discussion is indebted to Elliot Aronson's (1984) clear analysis of these elements.

Where Does the Message Come From?   We are most likely to be influenced by people who are experts on the topic they're talking about, who have shown themselves to be trustworthy, who are arguing a point of view from which they personally have nothing to gain, who are not trying to win us over, and who are similar to us. For example, black junior high school students were more likely to have cleaner teeth after hearing a taped message on proper dental care from a black dentist than after hearing one from a white dentist (Dembroski, Lasater, & Ramirez, 1978).

Two points about the source of a message must be noted, however. First, there is a "sleeper effect": although a highly credible source has more impact immediately after delivering a message, this dissipates after 4 weeks—probably because most people forget where they first heard a message (Kelman & Hovland, 1953).

Second, in trivial matters, the factors described above become unimportant if we like the person who delivers a message, identify with him or her, and find him or her attractive. For example, a woman's beauty has a strong impact on an audience's opinion, even on topics irrelevant to her looks (Mills & Aronson, 1965). No wonder attractive young women look out on us from so many billboards, magazine ads, and television screens!

How Is the Message Stated?   Messages can appeal to our reason or to our emotions; they can be one-sided or can present both sides of a question; and they can differ in other ways. What makes one approach better in some situations but not in others? Sometimes the answer has to do with the nature of the topic being discussed; sometimes it has to do with the intelligence or self-esteem of the audience; sometimes it has to do with which message we heard first or last.

Appeals to emotions usually seem more effective than appeals to logic. Many persuasive campaigns, for example, are based on fear: What will happen to the world if you don't vote for this candidate? What will happen to you if you drink and drive? What will happen to your family if you don't buy life insurance? In general, a message that induces moderate fear is most likely to change your attitude. If a message frightens you too much, you'll "tune out" to get rid of the discomfort; and if it doesn't frighten you enough, it won't get your attention. The higher your opinion of yourself, the more likely you are to respond to a fear-arousing message—possibly because you have confidence in your ability to respond to the threat; because you're not afraid of fear itself but are motivated by it; or because the more you think of yourself, the better you want to take care of yourself (Leventhal, 1970).

The most effective health campaigns, such as those against smoking and heart disease, combine a moderately frightening message with specific instructions for change (see Chapter 16). Without specific guidelines for change, attitudes may change, but behavior does not (Leventhal & Cleary, 1980; Maccoby, Farquhar, Wood, & Alexander, 1977; Meyer, Nash, McAlister, Maccoby, & Farquhar, 1980).

Two-sided messages—messages that include both sides of an argument but attempt to refute one viewpoint—are more effective with intelligent audiences who are at least aware of the opposing views, and with audiences that are already leaning in the opposite direction. If someone is already leaning toward your position, don't confuse him or her by presenting arguments for the other side; but if you feel you're on hostile territory, you'd do better to present the arguments your audience is already in agreement with and to show why these arguments are wrong (Hovland, Lumsdain, & Sheffield, 1949).

Who Is Listening to the Message?   What characteristics of an audience make it most receptive to a message? Poor self-esteem is one, since people who do not think much of themselves are more easily influenced. A relaxed, well-fed state is another. One reason political candidates rely on informal get-togethers in private homes when seeking support is that people who have had something to eat and drink are more receptive (Dabbs & Janis, 1965; Janis, Kaye, & Kirschner, 1965). Another, of course, is that people are likely to be influenced when friends or neighbors whom they like and respect offer their homes to help a candidate.

Furthermore, listeners need to feel in charge of their own opinions. If you forewarn them, "I'm going to try to persuade you of the value of my point of view," they will put their guard up and be less persuasible (Freedman & Sears, 1965). Experimenters who use such phrases as "you have no choice but to believe this" are more likely to alienate listeners than to persuade them (Worchel & Brehm, 1970). You may have found, in your own experience, that when parents try hard to change their adolescent and grown children's attitudes, the children often feel that their freedom is being threatened and dig their heels in even more strongly. In this way, strenuous parental opposition can have a "Romeo and Juliet" effect, driving a young person into the arms of the sweetheart, the political involvement, or the way of life the parents are most against (Driscoll, Davis, & Lipetz, 1972).

(Advertising Council)

Campaigns against combining drinking and driving often use fear as a motivator, drawing on research that demonstrates its effectiveness— especially when it is moderate and when suggestions are given for alternative courses of action.

Finally, an involved audience is more likely to change its attitude. Handing out blank stationery and asking members of an audience to write to their congressional representatives then and there is likely to do two things—produce more mail than there would have been if you had asked them to write when they got home, and solidify their own attitudes on the topic.

The importance of personal involvement was brought out by one study in which 14 young women who smoked were asked to play the role of a person with lung cancer (Janis & Mann, 1965). They saw x-rays, talked with their "doctor," pretended to await surgery, and so forth. There were also 12 controls—smokers who heard tapes of role-playing sessions but did not take part themselves. The role-players became more antismoking in their attitudes than did the controls—more convinced that smoking is unhealthy and leads to lung cancer, and more interested in giving up smoking. Eighteen months later, both groups were smoking less, but the role-players were smoking less than the controls (Mann & Janis, 1968).

Attitudes and Behavior

The relationship between attitudes and behavior is not always clear. A popular tale in the business community points up the difficulty of using the attitudes that people *say* they hold to predict what they will actually *do*. Some years ago, the story goes, a major automobile manufacturer sponsored a survey to ask consumers what they wanted in a car. The overwhelming majority said they wanted a simple car, with a minimum of fancy styling and a maximum of safety. The manufacturer produced a car like this, and it was a financial disaster: hardly anyone bought it. And so the manufacturer sponsored another poll. This time, researchers asked consumers, "What does your neighbor like in a car?" "Oh, him," people would say. "He likes something with a lot of chrome on it, that makes a quick getaway, that's capable of high speeds on the highway." The manufacturer made *this* car, and it made a fortune.

Similarly, a recent poll on racial attitudes found that both black and white respondents are more likely to say that their neighbors dislike people of another race than that they themselves dislike such people (Meislin, 1987). The split between attitudes and behavior has been demonstrated in psychological research as well. Studies have found, for example, that people's general attitude toward religion doesn't tell us whether they'll go to church next Sunday. That depends also on whether it is raining, whether they wake up with a hangover, whether they like the preacher, and whether there is something else they want to do. However, their religious attitudes do predict their overall religious conduct over time (Fishbein & Ajzen, 1974; Kahle & Berman, 1979).

There are, however, some instances when knowing what people think can predict their later actions (Kahle, 1983; Kahle & Berman, 1979). Prediction tends to be fairly accurate under the following conditions:

1 *When other influences on our behavior are minimized*—our concern about what others will think, for example.
2 *When the measured attitude corresponds closely to the situation being considered.* It is easier to predict a man's behavior toward a specific female coworker if we know how he feels about her than if we know only how he feels about the Equal Rights Amendment (Steiner, 1979).
3 *When we are conscious of our attitudes as we act,* either because we are reminded to focus on them (as by being asked to think about them or by looking in a mirror); because we acquired them in especially powerful ways, such as personal experience; or because we are "inner-directed" people who believe in judging each situation according to our principles rather than adjusting our principles and behavior to fit the situation (Snyder, 1982; Snyder, Campbell, & Preston, 1982).

One review of several dozen studies on attitudes and behaviors concluded that knowing what people *say* their attitudes are allows us to predict with less than 10 percent accuracy what they will actually *do* (Wicker, 1969). Why should this be? One major reason is that we often don't know what our attitudes about a specific topic are until we are forced to take action. (As one newspaper columnist said during a strike when the paper was not being printed, "How do I know what I think if I don't write about it?") According to Bem's theory of self-perception, we often don't know what we think until we see how we act. For instance, a woman in college may *think* that she is opposed to cheating and that this is an important principle; but if she is in a situation where she thinks that cheating on an exam will make a difference between passing or failing a crucial course, and if she thinks she won't get caught, she may well look over her neighbor's shoulder (Wicker, 1969).

Furthermore, in some cases changing our behavior seems to change our attitudes. Schoolchildren who teach a moral code to other children, or enforce such a code, end up following it better themselves (Parke, 1974); people induced to testify to something they're not really sure of end up believing it (Klaas, 1978); and soldiers who act brutally toward an enemy population end up hating and denigrating them.

The crucial issue in the relationship between attitudes and behavior is that both what we *do* and what we *say we believe* are subject to other influences. We have certain standards about the kind of person we want to be, and the attitudes we express often conform to those standards, even though we do not always act the way we think we should. Also, we have a certain picture of ourselves that we want to present to the rest of the world, and we often say what we think other people want to hear—and end up believing it ourselves.

Prejudice

A black couple, both professionals, answer an ad for an apartment, only to be told, "Sorry, it's already rented," although a white couple who come afterward are shown the apartment. A woman seeking an entry-level job is asked by the personnel director, "Can you type?" and is offered a secretarial job, while a man with the same education and experience is sent to the sales department. A 75-year-old man in excellent command of his faculties is not consulted about whether or not he should have surgery; instead, his physician discusses his condition with his middle-aged daughter. Prejudice exists against people of virtually every racial and ethnic group and against the elderly, women, the handicapped, the poor, and people whose lifestyles are unpopular.

What Is Prejudice? *Prejudice* is a negative attitude held toward people solely because of their membership in some group and without knowledge of them as individuals. *Stereotypes* are oversimplified beliefs about the characteristics of members of a group, with no allowance for individual differences. Whether stereotypes are positive or negative, they short-circuit logical thought and reasonable judgment, and they rob the individual of the right to be judged for himself or herself. Prejudice is an attitude, encompassing both thoughts and feelings; *discrimination* is behavior aimed at a person one is prejudiced against.

Prejudice Negative attitude toward people held solely because of their membership in a particular group.

Stereotypes Preconceived, oversimplified beliefs about the characteristics of members of a group.

Discrimination Behavior aimed at a person against whom one is prejudiced.

How Do We Become Prejudiced? There are a number of theories of prejudice. One theory holds that prejudice develops as a natural by-product of competition over scarce resources; a second considers it an attitude that we learn in the same way we learn other attitudes; a third sees it as a manifestation of a certain kind of personality; and a fourth focuses on the way we use stereotypes in our thinking.

PREJUDICE AND COMPETITION According to one theory, prejudice is an outgrowth of competition. We compete—and we become prejudiced against our competitors. People of one ethnic or racial group often become violently prejudiced against the members of any other group vying for the same jobs. Prejudice has shown up, for example, in the American southwest, between Americans and Mexicans; in California, between whites and Chinese; in a small industrial town surrounded by farmland, between native Americans and German immigrants; and in large cities around the country, between blacks and whites (Aronson, 1980).

PREJUDICE AND LEARNING   A second theory holds that we learn to be prejudiced. When children hear the adults around them expressing prejudiced attitudes and see them showing prejudiced behavior, they acquire prejudice the same way they acquire any other societal norm. As we saw earlier, most people—children included—like to conform to societal norms and like to be accepted by others. If the most important people in a child's world are prejudiced against certain groups, the child will be, too. Furthermore, it's hard even for a child of relatively unprejudiced parents to avoid the barrage of stereotypes that come from picture books, television programs, and magazine ads.

Over the past several decades, however, prejudice has become unfashionable, and more people have been expressing unprejudiced attitudes. In 1942, people were much more likely than they were in 1980 to disapprove openly of blacks and whites' sitting together on buses, going to school together, or living in the same neighborhoods (Hyman & Sheatsley, 1956; Myers, 1983; National Opinion Research Center, 1980). This does not mean that prejudice itself has decreased as dramatically as public awareness of it has. It still exists in less obvious forms. One issue that has brought this out is school busing. Since whites do not oppose busing students from one primarily white school to another but do oppose busing between largely white and largely minority-group schools (McConahay, Hardee, & Batts, 1981), it seems clear that prejudice against minority groups exists.

PREJUDICE AND PERSONALITY   According to a third theory, there is such a thing as a "prejudice-prone personality." In an effort to determine whether certain people were more likely to develop prejudices, researchers devised the F scale (here, the F stands for *fascism*) to define what they called an **authoritarian personality** (Adorno, Frenkel-Brunswik, Levinson, & Sanford, 1950). Table 17-2 lists some of the items from this scale. The authoritarian personality emerged as one that tends to think in stereotypes, is emotionally cold, identifies with power, and is intolerant of weakness

Authoritarian personality Rigid, conventional, prejudice-prone person who thinks in stereotypes, is emotionally cold, identifies with power, and is intolerant of weakness.

TABLE 17-2   ITEMS FROM THE F SCALE

The United States is getting so far from the true American way of life that force may be necessary to restore it.

Familiarity breeds contempt.

He is, indeed, contemptible who does not feel an undying love, gratitude, and respect for his parents.

Reports of atrocities in Europe have been greatly exaggerated for propaganda purposes.

Homosexuality is a particularly rotten form of delinquency and ought to be severely punished.

It is essential for learning or effective work that our teachers or bosses outline in detail what is to be done and exactly how to go about it.

There are some activities so flagrantly un-American that, when responsible officials won't take the proper steps, the wide-awake citizen should take the law into his own hands.

Every person should have a deep faith in some supernatural force higher than himself to which he gives total allegiance and whose decisions he does not question.

Obedience and respect for authority are the most important virtues children should learn.

Nowadays when so many different kinds of people move around so much and mix together so freely, a person has to be especially careful to protect himself against infection and disease.

No sane, normal, decent person could ever think of hurting a close friend or relative.

Source: Adapted from Adorno et al., 1950.

---

in himself or herself as well as in others. Such a person is rigid and conventional, believes in the value of punishment, and willingly submits to higher authority without much questioning.

Adorno and his colleagues traced the traits characterizing the authoritarian personality back to patterns of child rearing, finding that the parents of people showing these traits tend to discipline their children harshly, withdrawing love and making their children feel insecure. The children feel dependent on, afraid of, and hostile toward their parents. Unable to express their anger toward their parents directly, they carry their negative feelings with them to adulthood, emerging as angry, fearful people who take out their aggression against groups they see as weaker than themselves.

Although these findings do give us insight into prejudiced people, they do not provide a clear explanation of prejudice. For one thing, although there is a correlation between child-rearing patterns, personality characteristics, and authoritarian thinking, we don't know what is cause and what is effect. For another, parents who raise their children in this authoritarian way tend to be prejudiced themselves, and so their children may develop prejudices through identification and imitation, not necessarily through personality development.

Another personality factor associated with prejudice is low self-esteem. People who do not feel good about themselves are, apparently, more prejudiced. Their negative attitudes about themselves may incline them toward negative feelings about others, possibly in an effort to feel better about themselves by feeling superior to other people.

PREJUDICE AND STEREOTYPES A fourth theory explains prejudice not in terms of social factors or personality but rather in terms of cognitive functioning—as an aspect of information processing. This theory suggests that stereotypes help people simplify their thinking. In a complex social environment that bombards us with all sorts of information, it is hard to understand and predict other people's behavior. Stereotypes become a handy (if sometimes dangerous) tool for drawing conclusions about people, especially those we don't know personally.

How does this work? We can see the process in the results of some recent experiments (Bodenhausen & Wyer, 1985). In one of these studies, subjects were asked to make parole recommendations for people convicted of different crimes and identified as "Carlos Ramirez" (Hispanic), "Ashley Chamberlaine" (upper-middle-class white Anglo-Saxon Protestant), or "John T." (no information about ethnicity). The person was said to have committed one of two crimes: either embezzling company funds by forging signatures, or brutally attacking a man in a bar after an argument. The subjects were given background information about the person (age and marital status, for example), information about his criminal record and the crime itself, and information about life circumstances that might have motivated the crime (such as "in need of cash to support his pregnant wife" for the embezzlement and "is experiencing great frustration in his personal life" for the assault).

When "John T." was supposed to be the criminal, no stereotype was evoked and subjects were much more likely to recommend parole if they felt that the criminal's life circumstances were strong motivating factors for the crime. But when the crime fit people's stereotypes ("Ramirez" having committed the assault or "Chamberlaine" having embezzled the money), the subjects were more punitive and less likely to recommend parole, even when there were mitigating circumstances. It seems, then, that when a stereotype is available, people use it, make a judgment based on it, and do not look for other explanations. They then use this judgment to confirm their stereotyped thinking.

How Can We Reduce Prejudice? Looking at possible explanations for prejudice gives us clues about how to reduce it. We can encourage cooperation instead of competition. We can teach open-mindedness instead of prejudice. We can encour-

Research suggests that children can be raised to be open-minded. When they are raised with respect and love, they like themselves better and are more likely to like others—even those who are different from them. Furthermore, children who are encouraged to cooperate with people of different races or religions end up liking themselves and others better than those who are taught to "look out for number one."

age people to examine and judge others rationally instead of mindlessly absorbing stereotypes. We can raise our children to feel good about themselves and to accept responsibility for their own lives instead of taking their problems out on others.

ENCOURAGING COOPERATION   To test the belief that prejudice will arise if one group can achieve its ends only at the expense of another, and that cooperating to achieve shared goals can overcome prejudice, Muzafer Sherif (1966) and his colleagues conducted the classic "Robbers Cave" experiment. They assigned healthy, bright, well-adjusted 11- and 12-year-old boys to one of two groups—the Eagles and the Rattlers—at a summer camp. First they set up various projects involving cooperation within each group, such as building a diving board, building a rope bridge, and cooking out in the woods.

Once each group had a strong, cohesive feeling, the next stage of the experiment pitted the Eagles and the Rattlers against each other in touch football, tug-of-war, and other games that awarded prizes to the winning team. The boys in each team became hostile to the other team, scuffling, calling names, and burning the other team's banner. The researchers then escalated the conflicts, setting up situations designed to favor one group over the other. The less-favored group reacted—not against the camp directors who were setting the rules, but against the boys in the preferred group.

Once the desired level of hostility had been achieved, the researchers dropped the competitive activities and brought the two groups together as much as possible. By this time, however, so much ill will had grown up between the two groups that it hung between them and even increased, even when the boys were all eating together or just sitting around watching movies.

The "Robbers Cave" experiment ended on a promising note. The researchers put the Eagles and Rattlers in situations where they had to cooperate to obtain a goal that was beneficial for both groups. When they *had* to get together to repair the water-supply system and to rescue a disabled camp truck, they did. In the process, the hostility between the groups evaporated. Eagles made friends with Rattlers, and both groups began to work and play together on their own.

In another effort to reduce prejudice through cooperation, Aronson and his colleagues developed an approach called the *jigsaw technique*. In classrooms with children of different ethnic and racial backgrounds, teachers assigned different parts of a single project to different children, and the children learned that they could do their own assignments only if they consulted, taught, and listened to each other. The children soon learned that when they encouraged other children they drew benefits for themselves, and they ended up liking school better, liking each other better, and liking themselves better (Aronson & Bridgeman, 1979; Aronson, Stephan, Sikes, Blaney, & Shapp, 1978; Geffner, 1978).

PREVENTING THE LEARNING OF PREJUDICE   To teach open-mindedness instead of prejudice, we can change the kinds of messages that people receive from society. We can examine the mass media for evidence of prejudice against various groups, and if it is found we can demand that the media show all groups from new, positive viewpoints.

Another learning approach is to change the rules of society to uphold the rights of all people, as the Supreme Court did in 1954 when it outlawed segregation in schools, and as legislatures and the courts have done in many more recent laws and decisions that have upheld the rights of racial and other minorities, of women, and of the elderly. The importance of rules in teaching open-mindedness is borne out by the powerful influence that changed behavior has on attitudes. Enforcing equal access to housing, for example, requires people to live together on an equal footing; we have known for years that white people who live in housing projects with black tenants develop more favorable attitudes toward black people than white residents of segregated housing projects do (Deutsch & Collins, 1951). The evidence supports Bem's self-perception theory. The white person may think, "If I live close to black people and we get along as neighbors, then I must like them." More recently, a 15-year study of black students who had gone to mainly white suburban schools found that they were more likely than those who had gone to mostly black city schools to live and work in racially mixed communities and to have white friends; black students who had gone to segregated urban schools tended to be less receptive and more hostile toward white people ("Study of black students," 1985).

TEACHING "MINDFUL" DISCRIMINATION   People who are prejudiced draw conclusions about others that are based on information (like skin color, religion, ethnic background, sex, or age) that is not relevant to the issue under consideration (such as intelligence, competence, or likability). Prejudice is thus a kind of mindless, automatic thinking. One group of researchers reasoned that if children could learn to make distinctions among people based on information that *was* relevant, they would be less likely to exhibit, and to act upon, prejudiced thinking. They would, in other words, be what these researchers described as "mindful."

That is, in fact, what happened after a specially designed program that trained sixth-graders to be more mindful (Langer, Bashner, & Chanowitz, 1985). In the first step in the program, the students were introduced to the idea that most problems do not have a single right answer but have several possible solutions, and thus they were encouraged to think inventively. Then they were asked questions involving different physical disabilities, to make them think whether specific handicaps were drawbacks or benefits in different kinds of situations. For example, they were shown a picture of a boy in a wheelchair and a boy with no apparent disability, and they were asked which one they would want to have as their partner for a variety of different activities, including checkers, soccer, and a wheelchair race. The students who had been trained in mindfulness were more likely than a control group of untrained sixth-graders to choose the boy in the wheelchair for the wheelchair race, less likely to choose him for soccer, and less likely either to prefer or avoid him for neutral activities like checkers. The trained students seemed to make more appropriate distinctions and to see people as individuals who were able or disabled, not globally, but only with respect to specific tasks.

RAISING INDEPENDENT, FAIR-MINDED CHILDREN The implications for child rearing of the findings of Adorno and his colleagues (1950) on the authoritarian personality indicate that we can do a great deal to help our children become unprejudiced by raising them with respect and love, in ways that will help them think well of themselves.

In many of the issues we have talked about in this chapter, self-esteem has turned out to be the key to living well in groups. People who think highly of themselves are less apt to become slavish conformists, blind obeyers, cruel aggressors, and prejudiced discriminators. People who like themselves are more likely to like others—and less likely to feel the need for someone else to look down on.

SUMMARY

1 Social psychology, the scientific study of social influence, focuses on how people think about, feel about, are affected by, and act toward other people. Social psychologists are concerned with the influence of the group on behavior. A group consists of two or more people who are interacting and interdependent at some time.

2 A role is a set of behavioral expectations for a particular social position. A role is made up of a group of norms, which are society's definitions of how people "should" behave. A particular position assumes the status of a social role when it accumulates a substantial number of norms. Norms can enhance behavior by letting people know how to behave in social situations; but they can also restrict behavior by stifling independence.

3 Zimbardo's study of the prison experience demonstrated how rapidly presumably normal people assume "appropriate" norms for the roles they play. It shows the powerful influence of the situation on behavior.

4 Conformity is a change in opinion, behavior, or both in response to real or imagined pressure from others. Asch's classic study of conformity showed that individuals often conform to group opinion even when the group opinion is clearly wrong. Since not all people in Asch's experiments did conform, however, we see that characteristics of the situation and the person affect behavior.

5 *Groupthink* refers to an uncritical acceptance by members of a close-knit group of an unwise course of action in order to preserve unanimity. It is a type of conformity.

6 Milgram's experiments on obedience to authority show that in some circumstances people will obey orders to inflict harm on another. A number of personal and situational factors influence a person's decision to obey. Participants were more likely to disobey if they were in the same room with the "victim" or actually had to place the "victim's" hand on a shock plate. They were most likely to obey when they were in the same room as the experimenter. Participants who felt principally responsible for the victim's suffering were least likely to obey.

7 Altruism is behavior carried out to benefit another, without anticipation of rewards from external sources. A number of factors influence whether helping occurs. These include the recognition that an emergency exists, the number of observers present, and characteristics of the victim and the bystander. According to Piliavin and her

colleagues, people use cost-benefit analysis in deciding whether to help; they try to minimize their costs and maximize their rewards.

8 Theoretical explanations of why people help others include the possibilities that they inherit the tendency, that they learn to be altruistic, and that helping makes them feel good. Studies of regular blood donors indicate that external motivating factors such as social pressures predominate in the early stages of regular blood donation but that internal motivation becomes more important later.

9 An attitude is a learned, relatively permanent way of responding to someone or something in a favorable or unfavorable way. Attitudes have three components: the cognitive (thoughts), the emotional (feelings), and the behavioral (actions). These three components may contradict each other.

10 Attitudes are often measured using questionnaires and interviews. The Likert scale and the semantic differential are important measurement instruments.

11 Social psychologists have shown considerable interest in attitude formation and attitude change. According to learning theory, people learn attitudes through conditioning. Cognitive-consistency theories hold that a perceived inconsistency between a person's thoughts and actions (that is, cognitive inconsistency) can cause discomfort, which must be reduced. According to Festinger's cognitive-dissonance theory, when there is a basic inconsistency between a person's thoughts and actions, or between two or more sets of ideas, attitudes, or opinions that a person holds, a state of psychological discomfort results. People are then motivated to reduce this discomfort. Bem's self-perception theory holds that people infer their attitudes from their behaviors.

12 A number of factors determine the effectiveness of persuasive communication in changing attitudes. These include the source of the message, how the message is stated, and characteristics of the audience. It is often difficult to predict a person's behaviors by knowing his or her attitudes.

13 Prejudice is a negative attitude held toward people solely on the basis of their membership in a particular group rather than on the basis of knowledge of them as individuals. Stereotypes are preconceived, oversimplified beliefs about the characteristics of members of a group. Discrim-

ination is behavior aimed at a person one is prejudiced against.

14 Theories of prejudice include the following: that it is a natural by-product of competition over scarce resources, that it is a learned attitude, that it is the manifestation of a certain type of personality (the authoritarian personality),

and that it is a result of using stereotypes to process information.

15 Ways to reduce discrimination include encouraging co-operation to achieve shared goals, teaching open-mindedness, teaching "mindful" discrimination, and raising independent, fair-minded children.

KEY TERMS

Altruism (page 608)
Attitude (615)
Authoritarian personality (624)
Cognitive-consistency theories (617)

Cognitive dissonance (618)
Conformity (602)
Cost-benefit analysis (611)
Discrimination (623)
Groupthink (604)
Likert scale (616)

Norms (601)
Obedience (606)
Prejudice (623)
Role (601)
Self-perception theory (620)

Semantic differential (616)
Social psychology (598)
Social role (601)
Sociobiologists (611)
Stereotypes (623)

SUGGESTED READINGS

ARONSON, E. (1984). *The social animal*. New York: Freeman. An award-winning introduction to many topics in social psychology, including conformity, prejudice, and attraction. Written in an enjoyable style.

JANIS, I. L. (1982). *Groupthink*. Boston: Houghton Mifflin. This is Janis's most recent discussion of "groupthink"; it contains an analysis of the Watergate cover-up.

MILGRAM, S. (1974). *Obedience to authority*. New York: Harper Colophon. Milgram's account of his famous experiments on obedience to authority. The book includes numerous transcripts of individuals' reactions in the experimental situation.

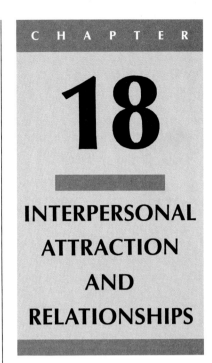

CHAPTER

18

INTERPERSONAL ATTRACTION AND RELATIONSHIPS

PREVIEW QUESTIONS

■ How do people explain the behavior of others—as due more to their personalities or their circumstances?

■ Do people explain their own behavior the same way?

■ How important are proximity, physical attractiveness, similarity, and other personal characteristics in creating impressions of other people?

■ What makes people enter, and stay in, relationships?

■ What do people look for in their friends?

■ What is love?

■ How does one choose a person to marry?

■ How does marriage affect people?

■ Why are some people lonely, and how can loneliness be overcome?

I first met Sue in 1971, when she was an undergraduate student in a class I was teaching in child development. I took to her friendly, outgoing personality right away. Then, when she became a graduate student in my department, we found that we had a great deal in common. As we got to know each other better, we grew to enjoy each other's company more and more. Sue's warm and caring nature showed itself in her ability to say something in virtually any social situation that would put people at their ease. This characteristic made me feel good when I was alone with Sue, and it also made it enjoyable to be with her in other people's company.

Sue and I enjoyed talking about our shared academic interests, clarifying our ideas as we discussed them together. Then we began to spend more and more nonacademic time with each other, often getting together for intimate talks about what was going on emotionally with both of us. Soon we found ourselves sharing some of the most important moments in our lives. Sue stood up with me at my wedding, and she drove me to the airport for my first meeting with the baby girl my husband and I would adopt as our own. I was with her when her father had open heart surgery; I was with her when she learned that she was pregnant with her first child; and I was with her just after the birth.

A few years ago, I moved 2000 miles away from Sue, so that our only contact for 2 years was an occasional letter or telephone call. But when we got together again, we felt as if we had seen each other only the day before—we were still close and comfortable. At this point, I'm sure that Sue and I will be friends for life, that even when we're geographically far away from each other, we won't have any emotional distance between us. I feel richer for having her in my life.

—From the notebooks of Diane Papalia

People are basically social animals who need other people. In many of the chapters in this book, we have seen how we affect other people and how they affect us. For example, as we saw in Chapter 16, social and emotional support from other people is often crucial in helping us through stressful situations. Throughout life, we influence and are influenced by our parents, our peers, our siblings, our teachers, our neighbors, our coworkers. The presence of friends and special "significant others" in people's lives can often predict their level of happiness (Lowenthal & Haven, 1968).

In this chapter, we look at specific types of ties with other adults—friendship, love, and marriage. In recent years, a considerable amount of research in social psychology has tried to unravel the mystery of how these relationships begin, develop, and either continue or dissolve. Our discussion emphasizes two aspects of these relationships—what attracts us to other people and what happens when attraction blossoms into close friendship or love.

STUDYING ATTRACTION AND RELATIONSHIPS

Before going on, stop to think about your three closest friends. If you are in a loving relationship, think about your partner, too. Why have you chosen these particular people for these special places in your life? What is it about them, of all the people you know? With an apology to Elizabeth Barrett Browning, let's ask ourselves, "Why do I like (or love) thee? Let me count the ways. . . . " Can you say why you were first attracted to each of these people—and why you became close to them?

Research

Findings from research in social psychology may be of some help in answering both these questions. Researchers have analyzed ***interpersonal attraction,*** the formation of an attitude that reflects a tendency to evaluate another person in a positive way. The research on attraction has focused on first impressions and how they are influenced by such factors as proximity (physical closeness in living quarters or daily activities), similarity, physical appearance, and personal characteristics such as warmth and competence. Psychologists have found, and emphasize, that there are no attributes that absolutely predict attraction. It is how you interpret another person's characteristics that determines whether or not you will be attracted. In other words, attraction depends on the interaction between your own traits, the other person's traits, and the situation in which you get to know each other.

In recent years, more research has focused on ***close relationships.*** In a close relationship, two people influence each other to a considerable degree, are dependent on each other in a variety of ways, are capable of arousing strong emotion in each other, and usually engage in various types of activities together over a long period of time. Researchers have studied how such relationships begin and become stronger, and why and how they sometimes end.

A number of theories describe the progression of relationships from superficial levels to deeper ones (Altman & Taylor, 1973; Backman, 1981; Levinger, 1974). As relationships deepen, the partners become more willing to disclose intimate facts and feelings and become more committed to each other. Although the initial research focused on the early stages of relationships (which are fairly easy to study), more recent research has shifted the focus to later stages, including maintaining the relationship and breaking up.

Some studies of attraction have taken place in naturalistic settings like housing developments (Festinger, Schachter, & Back, 1950) and dormitories (Newcomb, 1961), but much of the research has focused on ingenious laboratory-based studies. The subjects have been mostly white, middle-class college students. Since researchers interested in isolating a particular aspect of attraction have often set up situations that are more or less artificial, it is sometimes difficult to generalize their results to real-life situations. This problem exists, of course, for all lab-based experimental research. Recently, social scientists have been merging naturalistic and laboratory approaches to make their results more valid. They have been using analytic procedures borrowed from the laboratory, along with survey procedures applied to the context of everyday life (Backman, 1981).

Measuring Attraction

Psychologists measure interpersonal attraction in two principal ways—by listening to what people say and by looking at what they do.

Interpersonal attraction *Tendency to evaluate another person in a positive way.*

Close relationship *Association in which people influence each other, are dependent on each other, are capable of arousing strong emotion in each other, and usually engage in various types of activities together over a long period of time.*

TABLE 18-1 INTERPERSONAL JUDGMENT SCALE: MEASURE OF ATTRACTION

Personal Feelings (Check One)

_____ I feel that I would probably like this person very much.
_____ I feel that I would probably like this person.
_____ I feel that I would probably like this person to a slight degree.
_____ I feel that I would probably neither particularly like nor particularly dislike this person.
_____ I feel that I would probably dislike this person to a slight degree.
_____ I feel that I would probably dislike this person.
_____ I feel that I would probably dislike this person very much.

Working Together on an Experiment (Check One)

_____ I believe that I would very much dislike working with this person in an experiment.
_____ I believe that I would dislike working with this person in an experiment.
_____ I believe that I would dislike working with this person in an experiment to a slight degree.
_____ I believe that I would neither particularly dislike nor particularly enjoy working with this person in an experiment.
_____ I believe that I would enjoy working with this person in an experiment to a slight degree.
_____ I believe that I would enjoy working with this person in an experiment.
_____ I believe that I would very much enjoy working with this person in an experiment.

Source: Byrne, 1971.

Asking People How They Feel A researcher might ask you to describe characteristics that particular people have and feelings that you have toward these people. Approaches like this are called _self-report measures_. They are used in two basic ways: either to rate specific persons in your life or to rate a stranger with whom you have interacted in the context of an experiment.

The most widely used self-report measure of attraction is the Interpersonal Judgment Scale, which was developed by Donn Byrne (1971). On this scale you would rate someone on six different dimensions: (1) intelligence, (2) knowledge of current events, (3) morality, (4) adjustment, (5) your own feelings of liking or disliking, and (6) how much you would want to work with him or her. The two dimensions of this scale that are used to measure attraction are "liking" and "want to work with"; these are shown in Table 18-1. On other scales—those designed to measure romantic attraction—you would indicate how much you would like to date the other person, how much you would like that person as a spouse, and how sexually and physically attractive he or she seems.

Another set of self-report measures consist of the "liking" and "love" scales developed by Zick Rubin (1970). These are Likert-type scales (see Chapter 17)—scales that list a number of statements or attitudes and ask the subject to respond on a continuum from "strongly agree" to "strongly disagree." (For excerpts, see Table 18-2.)

Responses to these scales indicate that liking and loving are very different emotions. Love is not just a higher degree of liking; it is another feeling altogether. How do we know this? We can draw this conclusion because the "liking" and "love" scores are only moderately correlated. That is, if you like someone, there is not much basis for thinking that you will also love that person. High scores on Rubin's dimensions of affection and respect go along with liking; but love is associated with high scores on attachment, caring, and intimacy.

Looking at What People Do Another way to measure attraction is by observing what people actually do, rather than how they say they feel. Using so-called _unobtrusive measures,_ psychologists look at people. They note how much time a couple

TABLE 18-2 EXAMPLES FROM LIKING AND LOVE SCALES

From the Liking Scale

Affection

_____ is one of the most likeable people I know.

Respect

I have great confidence in _____ 's good judgment.

From the Love Scale

Attachment

It would be hard for me to get along without _____ .

Caring

If _____ were feeling badly, my first duty would be to cheer him (her) up.

Intimacy

I feel that I can confide in _____ about virtually anything.

All Statements Would Be Answered by Checking the Appropriate Spot on the Following Continuum

1	2	3	4	5	6	7	8	9

Not at all true;   Definitely true;
disagree completely.   agree completely.

Source: Z. Rubin, 1970

spend gazing into each other's eyes, how close they stand and whether they lean toward or away from each other, how much they touch, how willing they are to do favors for each other, whether their body postures are in _synchrony_ (that is, whether they assume the same posture at the same time), whether they attempt to see each other again, and so fourth (Byrne & Griffitt, 1973; Perper, 1985; Z. Rubin, 1970).

All these behaviors are barometers of attraction. For example, people whose scores on the "love" scale indicate that they love each other a great deal spend more time gazing into each other's eyes than couples who love each other less; this suggests that both measures are valid (Z. Rubin, 1970). By and large, however, very few studies have tried to find a relationship between self-report scales and behavioral measures of attraction (Triandis, 1977).

FORMING RELATIONSHIPS

How Do We Make Decisions about Other People?

Perceiving Others   Whether we like or dislike someone depends very much on the way we perceive his or her attributes and motivations. How do we arrive at our perceptions? Suppose you are standing in line waiting for a bus and you suddenly feel yourself being violently jostled. You will probably turn around to see who is pushing you—and you will probably try to come up with some explanation for what is happening.

If you see that a man wearing dark glasses and carrying a white-tipped cane has bumped into you, you'll assume that the man is blind, and you may then offer to help him get where he wants to go. If you see that the person who pushed you is a man wearing ragged clothes and reeking of alcohol, you'll assume he's drunk and may either ignore him or tell him to go away. If the jostler is a swaggering teenager who looks at you defiantly and curses you with a racial epithet, you may take a swing at him, call a police officer, walk away, or try to melt into the crowd. In each of these cases, the initial behavior is the same, but because of other cues, you attribute different reasons to the initial behavior—and you react very differently, depending on these attributions.

You form inferences about people on the basis of what they do, what they are like, and in what context their behavior is taking place. In your perception of them, you do not react passively. Even if you do nothing, your mental processes are active. You search your memory of your own experience to categorize clues about their behavior, and you interpret these clues in your own frame of reference to give a meaning to that behavior. A blind man, you'll conclude, can't help himself; a drunk one doesn't care; and a tough teen is acting out his aggressive feelings.

These examples are fairly clear-cut, but in most situations it is harder to decide why a person acts in a certain way. Yet we are continually examining the behavior of other people, trying to figure out their intentions and their emotional states, and trying to decide *why* they do what they do. The attributions we provide for other people's behavior are very important, because they determine how we will feel and act toward those other people.

Attribution Theory DISPOSITIONAL AND SITUATIONAL EXPLANATIONS OF BEHAVIOR According to **attribution theory**, we explain people's behavior either dispositionally or situationally. A *dispositional* explanation has to do with *internal* causes—such as personality traits or a person's own efforts. A *situational* explanation, on the other hand, has to do with *external* causes—such as a particular set of circumstances, or someone else's actions, or luck (Heider, 1958).

Attribution theory is intended to explain the way we make judgments about other people. If we believe, for example, that someone has shoved us for no good reason, then we're likely to be very angry. If we can come up with an explanation that seems logical (in other words, one that would explain why we ourselves might do the same thing in such a situation), we will understand the behavior and not be angry. Attribution theory has been an important theoretical framework for social psychological research in the recent years.

When we are trying to answer the question, "Why did that person behave that way?" we rely on three types of information: *distinctiveness, consensus*, and *consistency* (Kelley, 1967). A behavior is distinctive if it is associated with a particular stimulus. Consensus exists when a particular behavior is similar to the way most people act in a given situation. Finally, a behavior is consistent if it will recur in similar circumstances.

Suppose you are told about "Sharon," who laughs uproariously at a particular comedian. Sharon hardly ever laughs at comedians, but whenever she hears this one, she does laugh at him. Almost everyone else who hears this particular comedian laughs at him, too. A group of college students were asked whether they thought Sharon's laughter was caused by an internal quality (a tendency to laugh at comedians) or an external circumstance (the effect of this particular entertainer). Sixty-one percent attributed her laughter to the situation (the effect of the comedian); only 12 percent attributed it to something about Sharon herself (McArthur, 1972). Sharon's response was associated distinctively with this stimulus (the comedian), it is similar to those of other people (there is a consensus), and it is consistent over time. In other words, something about the situation has elicited it.

On the other hand, the students felt differently about "Paul." Paul, they were told, is enthralled by a certain painting, has almost always been enraptured by the same painting (even though practically no one else who sees this painting is), and is thrilled by almost any other painting. Some 85 percent of the students felt that Paul's fascination arose from Paul himself; almost none of them attributed it to the painting. Paul's reaction was consistent, but it was not distinctive and there was no consensus; this indicates that the source of his delight was internal. Paul's behavior is more appropriately attributed to something within himself (like his enthusiastic personality) rather than to something in the situation (such as the merit of a painting).

Attribution theory *Theory about how people make judgments about causes of behavior.*

"So! If it's good, it's Mister Coffee. If it's bad, it's me."

According to the concept of the fundamental attribution error, if this husband were enjoying coffee he made himself, he would be likely to reverse the attributions he makes for his wife's brew. Thus, he would underestimate the importance of situational influences (the coffee maker) and overestimate personality factors (his own superior ability to brew coffee).

THE FUNDAMENTAL ATTRIBUTION ERROR   When a psychologist heard that one of her graduate students was dropping out of the Ph.D. program, at first she blamed his decision on his laziness or his inability to cope with the program's intellectual demands. After some reflection, she realized that she had succumbed to the "fundamental attribution error." She had failed to consider the situational factors that played an important part in the student's decision to leave the program. His father, who lived 1000 miles away, had been quite ill, and the student wanted to be close to him and help his mother make decisions about his care. Furthermore, a government loan that the student had counted on to get him through the semester had not come through.

The **fundamental attribution error** is a common tendency to underestimate the importance of situational influences and to overestimate dispositional influences—that is, personality—in explaining behavior (Ross, 1977). We are more apt to make this error when we account for other people's behaviors than when we explain our own.

Research has supported the existence of this error. In one experiment, students were presented with essays favoring a particular point of view. Even when the subjects knew that the writers of the essays had been *told* to take this point of view, they tended to assume that the writers really believed what they were saying (Jones & Harris, 1967). In another study, students talked with a woman who acted either friendly or distant (Napolitan & Goethals, 1979). Even when students were told that the experimenters had instructed the woman to act the way she did, they judged her on her behavior. If she acted warm, they considered her a warm person; if she acted unfriendly, they assumed that she was that way in general.

In explaining our own behavior, we are more likely to acknowledge the importance of the situation—especially when we talk about our failures. We protect our egos by attributing our failures to the situation ("I couldn't fix the car because it's a junk heap") and our successes to ourselves ("I must be a good mechanic if I got rid of that rattle"). This was dramatically illustrated by a survey of candidates in 33

Fundamental attribution error
Tendency to underestimate the importance of situational influences and to overestimate that of dispositional influences (personality factors) in explaining behavior, especially the behavior of others.

political races. When asked why they thought they had won or lost, 75 percent of the winners attributed their victories to their own characteristics, emphasizing factors within their control, such as hard work, smart strategy, or service to constituents; while the losers overwhelmingly (90 percent) blamed the results on outside factors beyond their control, such as party makeup of the district, national and state trends, or lack of money (Kingdon, 1967).

This way of thinking, however, seems to be affected by cultural standards, as studies of shyness have indicated. In Japan, where 60 percent of people consider themselves shy, children are expected to assume the full burdens of their failures but to credit their success to their parents, their grandparents, their teachers, or Buddha. In Israel, which has a low rate of shyness, people are encouraged to accept full credit for their successes and to blame their failures on such external factors as inadequate teaching or prejudice. The Japanese style seems to discourage people from taking risks and to foster shyness, while the Israeli style encourages risk-taking, since the person has little to lose (Zimbardo & Radl, 1982).

What causes the fundamental attribution error? Why do we tend to make assumptions about the personalities of other people without considering how situations influence their behavior? For one thing, we *know* the influential factors in our own situation, but we may not know them for other people. We can easily point to various influences on our own behavior, but it is easier to assume that other people do things because that's the kind of people they are.

Let's go back to the example of being pushed. Suppose that you see that the jostler is a belligerent teenager. If you were to learn that someone who looked very much like you had just moments before pushed him and had called out an ethnic slur while doing it, the boy's action would make more sense, and you would not automatically assume that he was showing pure, unmotivated aggression.

What does the fundamental attribution error imply about intimate relationships? Any marriage counselor can recount tales of disputes in which partners explain their own behavior by referring to mitigating circumstances while they accuse their spouses of acting out of selfishness, inconsiderateness, thoughtlessness, repressed hostility, and other unfavorable personality traits. Also, we each bring our own experience and way of thinking to bear on an incident, and we attribute thoughts and feelings to others that may never have entered their minds.

"Such a bias sows the seeds for interpersonal misunderstandings. . . . It is very likely that we assign to another's personality what we should be viewing as a complex interaction between person and situation" (E. Jones, 1977, p. 321). We don't make enough allowance for the roles people assume, for external pressures they are subjected to, and for differences in their experiences and ours. Therefore, whenever other people do something we don't like or can't understand, the temptation arises to attribute their behavior to their personality. Once we have assigned a personality to them, we create self-fulfilling prophecies by giving off subtle cues that induce people to act the way we expect them to.

What Attracts Us to Other People?

For many years, research on attraction focused on the study of first impressions among white, middle-class college students in laboratory and field experiments. Even with these limitations, however, it uncovered a number of principles that explain what attracts us to other people. Paramount among these principles is that attraction results from the interaction between another person's characteristics and our appraisal of those characteristics. Diane Papalia's attraction to her friend Sue (described at the beginning of this chapter) occurred because Diane values warmth, friendliness, a caring nature, and other characteristics that Sue has. A person who

The more we see of other people, the more likely we are to become friendly with them. According to some research, next-door neighbors are more likely to be friends than are people who live farther apart.

wants a friend to possess athletic ability or a tendency to rebel against authority would most likely be attracted to someone else.

Before we can appraise another person's traits, we have to meet that person. First, then, we'll discuss the importance of proximity in friendship. Next we'll consider some personal characteristics that seem to influence attraction; and finally we'll consider how similarity affects attraction.

Proximity: "The Nearness of You" If you are a college student in the United States and I am a Sherpa animal herder living in a remote Himalayan village, it is highly unlikely that we will ever meet, let alone form a relationship. That seems fairly obvious. It is also unsurprising that there is a strong correlation between how close we live to someone and how friendly we become with that person. What *is* surprising is the strength of that correlation. You can test it yourself by making your own "friendship map." Plot out your neighbors in your dorm, in your apartment building, or on your street. In all likelihood, you will find that the closer you live to someone, the friendlier you are with that person, even if your proximity originally came about by chance.

RESEARCH ON PROXIMITY   The powerful impact of proximity was first brought out in a classic study of friendship patterns among married students living in a housing development called Westgate West (Festinger, Schachter, & Back, 1950). The complex consisted of 17 two-story buildings, with five apartments per floor. Residents had no choice over which apartment they lived in: when a unit became vacant, the next person on the waiting lists was assigned to it.

Again, it is not surprising that Westgate residents became friendlier with those in the same building than with those in other buildings. The surprising thing was the *extent* of this association. The two major elements influencing friendships were how many doors away one person lived from another, and in what direction a house faced. Next-door neighbors were most likely to be friends. After that, people living two doors away from each other were more likely to be friends than people separated by even a relatively short hall. People on the same floor were more friendly than people living on different floors.

The people who had the most friends were the ones whose apartments were near the mailboxes and near stairway entries and exits (where there was a lot of coming and going); those with the fewest friends lived in houses that faced outward toward the street. The people in these end houses, which had been assigned to them purely by chance, had fewer than half as many friends as people whose houses faced inward on the courtyard.

If you want to be popular, then, it makes sense to go where people are—get a room, an apartment, or a desk in a well-trafficked area, and go out of your way to see people often.

WHY IS THERE A RELATIONSHIP BETWEEN PROXIMITY AND ATTRACTION? The correlation between proximity and attraction is not just a matter of availability and convenience. After all, people living two doors away from each other are almost as "available" as next-door neighbors. Something else must be at work. It is possible that the more we see of someone, the more familiar that person becomes; and that we become comfortable with familiar people because we can predict the behavior of people we know well. If I know how you will react, I can tailor my own actions to do things that will please you and avoid doing things that will make you angry.

Another possibility is that if I know I will be seeing a lot of you, I will be more highly motivated to see your good points and to do whatever I can to keep our interactions pleasant. This conclusion is suggested by a study which found that people who expected to spend time with another person had more positive feelings toward that person than they had toward another person whom they did not expect to see again (Darley & Berscheid, 1967).

Then there is the "mere exposure" effect (Zajonc, 1968, 1970), which suggests that we like something or someone better after having been exposed to it, him, or her repeatedly. We often seem to prefer familiar musical works, paintings, and other works of art, and the same principle may hold for people.

Of course, proximity and familiarity don't always make us like someone. Even though proximity is related more often to attraction than to hostility, the great majority of violent assaults in this country are among relatives, neighbors, and others who know each other well (Steinmetz & Straus, 1974). Furthermore, if we dislike people the first time we meet them, being close to them is apt to increase our dislike (Schiffenbauer & Schiavo, 1976).

Let's look now at some additional factors that draw us to others.

Physical Appearance: "The Way You Look Tonight" Americans spend millions of dollars every year on clothing, makeup, hair care, and other services and products intended to make us look better. Research suggests that such expenditures may not be so extravagant, after all. A number of studies show that physically attractive people are more sought after, more highly regarded, and generally treated better. This begins in early childhood, when attractive nursery school children are more likely to be chosen as friends and less likely to be blamed by teachers for misbehavior (Dion & Berscheid, 1974). It continues during the school years, when good-looking children are more popular (Kleck, Richardson, & Ronald, 1974; Lerner & Lerner, 1977); and it persists in adulthood, when better-looking people are sought out more and treated better, and are thought to have better prospects for good sex lives, good marriages, and happiness (Ecker & Weinstein, 1983; Dion, Berscheid, & Walster, 1972; Snyder, Tanke, & Berscheid, 1977; Walster, Aronson, Abrahams, & Rottman, 1966).

In studying attractiveness, researchers generally ask an independent panel of judges to rate photographs of people on their attractiveness, assuming that a person can be considered attractive if enough judges agree that he or she is attractive. Then they set up experiments using subjects who were not involved in these ratings—and who do not even know that the effects of attractiveness are being studied—and correlate the results with the initial ratings.

One of the earliest studies on attraction sought to confirm the idea that we are drawn to people who are at about our own level of "social desirability"—a concept that included physical attractiveness. In 1966, Elaine Walster and her colleagues sponsored a "computer-match" dance for first-year students at the University of Minnesota. The researchers obtained scores on personality and aptitude tests for the 752 students who had bought tickets, had these students fill out questionnaires about themselves, and had them rated on attractiveness by four sophomores. Then they assigned them randomly to dates.

The students evaluated their dates at intermission (2½ hours into the dance), and then again 4 to 6 months later. The conclusions did not confirm the researchers' initial hypothesis that people of similar attractiveness will seek each other out. Nor did similar levels of personality and intelligence seem to attract people to each other. To the contrary, the single most important factor in how much the dates liked each other was how physically attractive they found each other. For both men and women, the more attractive their dates were, the more they wanted to date each other again and tried to do so (Walster et al., 1966). The often noted similarity in attractiveness between husbands and wives (McKillip & Riedel, 1983) must, therefore, have other causes. Maybe people drift toward their own level by trial and error. Studies indicate that people choose others of high social desirability when they expect those others to like them, but when they are afraid there is a strong chance of being rejected, they lower their sights to their own level of desirability or lower (Berscheid, 1983).

Of course, it is hard to find out about someone's inner self on a crowded, noisy dance floor; appearance may be the most readily available information. It is also possible that the first-year students in this study were responding to something else about their dates that is correlated with good looks. That something may be the kind of personality an attractive person develops as a result of the self-confidence generated by a lifetime of favorable treatment.

The fact that we respond according to the way we are treated was brought out in another study. Male college students were shown either a photo of a beautiful woman or one of an unattractive woman and were told they would be having a 10-minute "get-acquainted" phone conversation with her. The men imagined the beautiful woman to be friendly and socially skilled, with a good sense of humor, while the unattractive woman was seen as lacking these qualities. Observers who listened in on the phone conversations—which actually took place with women other than those in the photos—found that the men acted according to their preconceived notions. The ones who thought they were talking to a beauty were friendlier, funnier, sexier, and more interesting. The significant finding with regard to the way our looks affect our personalities is that the women picked up these cues. The women thought to be attractive *acted* friendlier, more animated, and more self-confident; the ones thought unattractive were more standoffish and withdrawn (Snyder et al., 1977). This study shows one effect that appearance, reflected through others' eyes, has on personality.

There may be several reasons why looks matter. First, it is a pleasure to look at someone beautiful. Also, since we assume that beautiful people have more desirable characteristics, we may believe that when we get a pretty package, we are getting more inside the package, too. Another element is status by association. If most people attribute positive traits to attractive people, and if attractive people are more popular and thus have the ability to choose their friends and lovers more freely, then whoever they choose must be special, too. Therefore we enhance our own status by associating with beautiful people. Still another possibility is that beautiful people, because they have been treated favorably over the years, may be more secure, more giving, more competent, and more satisfying to be with. Since the effects of looks on attraction go beyond first impressions (Huston & Levinger, 1978), there probably are many reasons for their power in bringing—and keeping—people together.

Other Personal Characteristics: "That Certain Something"   There are, of course, many other personal characteristics that attract us to people. These characteristics do not exist in a vacuum, but are filtered through our perceptions. It is not the trait itself that attracts us, but the way we perceive it. We may think that people have a good sense of humor if they laugh at our jokes—and if we meet them in situations that encourage laughter and high spirits. Proximity and physical attractiveness are important when we begin a relationship. Other factors—such as warmth and competence—assume special importance as we decide whether to keep it up.

WARMTH   To many people, warmth embodies consideration of other people, informality, sociability, humanity, generosity, a sense of humor, and good nature. These are the specific traits that a group of students attributed to a guest lecturer when they had been told ahead of time that he was a warm person (Kelley, 1950). Some students in the same class, listening to the same lecturer, had been told he was a "rather cold" person. *All* the students were told that he was industrious, critical, practical, and determined. Not only did the students who expected the lecturer to be cold evaluate him less favorably after his 20-minute class, but they also participated less in the discussion than those who had expected a warm person.

This classic experiment demonstrates the importance not only of personality characteristics themselves, but also of the way our interpretation and expectations of other people's personalities affect the degree to which we'll like and feel comfortable with them, the way we'll act toward them, and, consequently, the way they are likely to feel and act toward us. People often act the way we expect them to when they perceive the cues that we give.

COMPETENCE   People admire competence in others; no evidence indicates that many people are attracted to those of mediocre abilities or talents. But too much competence apparently makes other people feel insecure (Aronson, 1980). We like competent people much better when they make the kind of mistakes that let us see them as less perfect and more human. This is known as the *pratfall effect*. When competent people fall flat on their face as a result of their own errors, we tend to see them as more fallible, more human, and more likeable.

In one set of experiments, researchers played four tape recordings to subjects. The tapes consisted of interviews with either a man of mediocre ability or one so highly competent that he was almost perfect (he was an honor student, a yearbook editor, and a member of the track team, and he was able to answer 92 percent of a series of difficult questions asked during the interview). One tape of each person (actually the same actor playing both parts) was without incident, while the other portrayed the interviewee clumsily spilling coffee all over his new suit. The subjects rated the superior person who spilled the coffee as the most attractive of the four, the superior person who did not spill the coffee next, the mediocre person third, and the mediocre person who spilled coffee last (Aronson, Willerman, & Floyd, 1966).

Similarity: "We Think Alike"   The thrill of getting to know another person often comes from discovering that you both love the same books, hate the same politician, have similar goals in life, and do the same things in your leisure time. A great deal of research underscores the power of attitudinal similarity in bringing people together.

Assume that you are a subject in a "phantom other" experiment (Byrne, 1961, 1971). After you have answered an opinion questionnaire, you are presented with another person's answers to the same questions, and you are asked how you feel about this person. In fact, no such person exists. A researcher has carefully filled out the second questionnaire to make it more or less similar to your own answers: it may show anything from no agreement to total agreement. The closer the phantom's answers are to your own, the more likely you are to like that person (Byrne, Clore, & Worchel, 1966; Byrne & Griffitt, 1973; Byrne, London, & Reeves, 1968).

Does the same principle hold in real life? Apparently it does. One study of the importance of similarity differs from most others in the extended nature of the contact among the subjects and in the fact that none of the subjects was told how much the others were like him or different from him (Griffitt & Veitch, 1974). Thirteen men who had not known each other lived together for 10 days in a fallout shelter, after having first given the experimenter their attitudes on 44 issues. At the end of the first, the fifth, and the ninth days of confinement, each man was asked to list the three people in the group he would *most* like to remain in the shelter and the three he would *least* like to stay. There was a clear-cut correlation. People wanted to keep the ones most like them and wanted to get rid of the ones least like them.

Other studies have found additional common grounds, besides attitudes, for close relationships. Both friends and spouses tend to be similar in race, age, socioeconomic status, religion, education, intelligence, values, and leisure activities (Murstein, 1982; Werner & Parmelee, 1979). Similarities in personality are also a basis of attraction (Byrne, 1969). Complementarity theory holds that opposite personalities attract—that, for example, a shy person is drawn to an outgoing one and a talker to a listener. This seems sensible but does not show up in actual studies, even though some friends, lovers, and spouses do seem to become more complementary as their relationships develop (Berscheid & Walster, 1978; Fishbein & Thelen, 1981; Nias, 1979).

One limit on the effect of similarity brings to mind Groucho Marx's famous avowal, "I wouldn't join any club that would have me for a member!" People who have a low opinion of themselves are not attracted to others who remind them of themselves. Leonard (1975) tested 64 college students on a measure of self-esteem; got information on their education, work history, and vital statistics; and asked their opinions about 14 controversial topics. He then asked his subjects to rate several confederates, some of whom gave information that made them seem similar to the subject and some of whom seemed quite different. Only the subjects with high self-esteem were attracted to people who were like them; the reverse obtained for those who thought little of themselves.

Why are we attracted to people like ourselves? For one thing, they are reinforcing: they validate our own experience. If you think the same way I do, I think that I must be right myself. Since most of us like to be right, this is a significant reward. Also, since we think that our opinions are correct, we admire the judgment and thinking of those who share them. Also, we often assume that those who think like us will be favorably inclined toward us, and that in turn makes us favorably inclined toward them (Huston & Levinger, 1978).

We tend to be attracted to people who share our interests, values, and goals—and to people who like the same kinds of leisure activities.

Why Do We Enter and Stay in Relationships?

Over the course of a lifetime, we become attracted to many people, but we become intimate with relatively few of them. The hallmark of a close relationship—one based on either friendship or love—is interdependence. This usually incorporates an intimacy that comes about from **self-disclosure**, that is, sharing personal information, opinions, and feelings; considerable influence over each other's feelings, attitudes, and behavior; a high level of interaction; and the potential for strong emotion. How does such interdependence develop?

One model of the way a relationship develops, showing the interdependence between two people, can be seen in Figure 18-1. First, at stage 1, "zero contact," two people—P (for person) and O (for other)—are completely unaware of each other and have no relationship at all. At stage 2, "awareness," one or both know about the other, either through having noticed the other or having heard about the other from a third party; but no direct contact has taken place between them. This stage can be important in leading one or both people to make efforts to get to know the other

Self-disclosure Sharing of personal information, opinions, and feelings with another person.

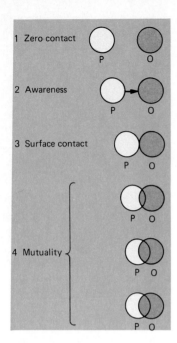

FIGURE 18-1 *Development of a relationship. Here, two people—P (person) and O (other)—go from complete unawareness of each other, through successively closer stages of awareness and contact, until they reach a point of mutual dependence. A relationship may stop moving on at any point in this progression. (Source: Adapted from Levinger & Snoek, 1972.)*

Exchange theory *Theory that people consider rewards and costs, as well as alternatives, in determining whether to enter a new relationship or stay in an existing one.*

Comparison level *Minimum benefit a person requires from a relationship.*

Comparison level for alternatives *Attractiveness of other possible ties, or of no relationship, compared with an existing relationship.*

person. Stage 3 is "surface contact," when the two begin to interact on a superficial level, possibly by exchanging small talk. Their interactions are brief, their contact may be defined by social roles (such as doctor and patient), and their impact on each other is limited. The relationship really takes hold when stage 4, "mutuality," is reached. Interdependence, or mutual dependence, may occur at levels ranging from very low to very high. The closer the people become, the more dependent each becomes on the other. They have a steadily increasing influence on each other's opinions, feelings, and behavior (Levinger & Snoek, 1972).

A relationship may stop moving on at any point in this progression. Only those people who reach the last stage, the stage of considerable interdependence (shown in Figure 18-1 by a large overlap), form close bonds, with a potential capacity for great joy and happiness—and for deep anger and sorrow.

Virtually all theories that attempt to explain why relationships progress to deeper levels draw to some degree on concepts of rewards and punishments. Rewards might include the fun we have doing things with certain people, the pleasure we get from looking at them, the satisfaction and self-validation of working toward common goals, the help they give us, or the boost in self-esteem that comes from feeling liked by them or admired by others because of them.

Sometimes people don't even have to do anything themselves to represent social rewards—they just have to be near us when we're feeling good for some other reason (Lott & Lott, 1974). Children like their teammates better when they win than they do when they lose; and children who receive approval from their teachers like their classmates better than children whose teachers ignore or criticize them (Lott & Lott, 1968). Adults like a stranger better when they meet him or her in a comfortable environment than when they have met in a hot, crowded room (Griffitt, 1970; Griffitt & Veitch, 1971). "It is through the relaxing evening before the fire, the excitement of a discussion, or the fun of a great party that the person who was always there will be liked even though he or she was not directly responsible for any of these pleasures" (Lott & Lott, 1974, p. 172). This carryover effect provides a rationale for marriage counselors' common advice that couples should make special efforts to plan good times together, so that they can each bask in the glow of shared pleasures.

Exchange Theory: We Calculate the Value of a Relationship *Exchange theory* is the most important contemporary theory of social relationships and the one most widely accepted by researchers in the field (even though they acknowledge that it may not tell the "whole story"). It maintains that we consider the rewards and the costs in everything we do, including our relationships, even though we're not always consciously aware that we're doing so (Homans, 1961; Thibaut & Kelley, 1958). The rewards in a relationship may include love, status, services, goods, information, and money (Foa & Foa, 1974). The costs can be either unpleasant aspects of the relationship, or simply the fact that we have to give up something else, like another relationship or the freedom and solitude of being uncommitted.

When we hear someone say something like, "I'm not getting enough from this relationship anymore," we recognize the common tendency to calculate the rewards and costs in a relationship and to deduct costs from rewards. If the reward is more than the cost, the relationship is profitable; if the reward is less than the cost, the relationship is unprofitable. Whether or not we enter and stay in a relationship, however, depends on more than simply calculating its rewards and costs. We also make various comparisons that may determine the fate of the relationship.

The **comparison level** in a relationship is the minimum benefit a person expects from it; this determines his or her satisfaction. If you get more than the minimum, you will be satisfied, but if you get less, you will be dissatisfied (Thibaut & Kelly, 1959). The **comparison level for alternatives** is the attractiveness of other possible ties, or of no relationship at all, compared with the existing relationship. Commitment—a moral obligation to remain with someone or dependence upon the other person—is rarely so nearly total that a person never thinks, "Could I get more from an attachment to someone else? Or would I be better off even if I were alone? Do the problems in this relationship outweigh its benefits for me?" This is analysis in terms of a comparison level for alternatives. Even if you are dissatisfied with an existing relationship, if you do not think you would be better off with someone else or alone, you will stay in it. But if you think you would be better off with an alternative, you will leave it.

Suppose you are in a less-than-perfect marriage. You may think about the alternatives and ask yourself such questions as: "What will my financial situation be like if I leave my spouse?" "How will I feel about myself if I leave?" "What will leaving do to my ties to children, in-laws, and friends?" "Could I attract someone else I would be happy with? If not, would I be more unhappy by myself than I am now?" If the probable outcome of leaving doesn't look any worse than the unhappiness you're now suffering, you'll probably leave. If it seems worse, you'll stay.

Exchange theory rubs many people—including many psychologists—the wrong way. "It seems to make of human behavior a rather selfish, egocentric endeavor [with a motif of] 'What can you do for me?'" writes Bernard Murstein (1971, p. 17), objecting to the theory's businesslike assessment of a person's emotional ledger. And yet, the theory *is* flexible enough to explain the behavior of an extremely generous, nurturant, giving person who considers the opportunity to take care of someone a reward. In such a person's system of exchange, a relationship that someone else might consider a loss would be extremely profitable.

Equity Theory: We Give and We Get   Most of us are most comfortable in relationships in which we feel we are getting about what we deserve. We're uncomfortable both when we feel we are being shortchanged and when we feel we are shortchanging someone else, and in such situations we try to restore a fair balance. This is the basic premise of **equity theory,** an offshoot of exchange theory. The focus of equity theory is on fairness in a relationship and on the discomfort that results when people are in relationships that feel unfair to them. It holds that people feel most comfortable in relationships in which there is an equitable (fair) distribution of rewards and costs and that they will strive to restore this state to relationships that they perceive as unbalanced (Hatfield, Traupmann, Sprecher, Utne, & Hay, 1984). This theory has long been applied to relationships in business and to casual social relationships. Elaine Walster and her colleagues cite considerable evidence to apply it to relationships between friends, between lovers or spouses, and between parents and children (Walster, Walster, & Berscheid, 1978).

Equity theory   Theory that people are most comfortable in relationships in which there is a fair distribution of rewards and costs and that they will try to restore equity (balance) in relationships perceived as unbalanced.

We can restore equity in two basic ways. We restore *actual equity* by changing what we are giving or what we are getting. A wife who feels exploited may stop cooking dinner, have an extramarital affair, or withhold some of her earnings, putting them into a separate bank account. Or she may decide to restore *psychological equity* by convincing herself that the inequitable relationship is, in fact, fair. She can minimize her inputs ("I'm not as good-looking, smart, or well educated as he is"), exaggerate her outcomes ("Even if I'm unappreciated, I get a chance to meet a lot of interesting people through him"), exaggerate her husband's inputs ("He earns so much money that he can give our family a good life"), or minimize her husband's outcomes ("He has to put up with a lot on his job that I don't have to on mine").

In casual relationships, the concept of equity is taken for granted. We do a neighbor a favor and expect that when we need one in return, we will get help. After we go to a party, we feel we should invite the host to our own home, or reciprocate in some other way. If a classmate pays for coffee one day, we reach for the check next time. It's harder to calculate equity in intimate relationships, because they are multifaceted and involve more interactions. Still, even if we don't measure or expect repayment for every service rendered, we expect a certain fairness in the relationship—in the services we give and receive and in the "value" of the other person.

When researchers analyzed 2000 questionnaires on mating and dating, they found that the respondents who were happiest in their relationships thought that their partners were about as desirable as they were, and that respondents who thought that their partners were much more or much less desirable were not as satisfied (Berscheid, Walster, & Bohrnstedt, 1973). Furthermore, relationships in which partners thought that they were fairly treated tended, on follow-up 3½ months later, to be more stable than those in which people thought that they were getting either too much or too little (Walster & Walster, 1978).

When partners in an intimate relationship are not equally matched on one trait, they often balance that by an inequality in the other direction on some other characteristic. For example, in Berscheid, Walster, and Bohrnstedt's study (1973), people who considered their partners more attractive than themselves tended to be richer, more loving, and more kind and considerate than those whose partners were at the same level of attractiveness or lower. Thus, we tend to keep our relationships in balance, often without being consciously aware of doing so.

These theories apply to many kinds of relationships, but we'll look closely now only at intimate relationships: friendship, love, and (since lovers often go on to become spouses) marriage and divorce.

INTIMATE RELATIONSHIPS

Friendship

Most of us want and need good friends. We want friends because they extend, or even replace, family support. We crave people we can trust absolutely. We yearn for someone we can call in the middle of the night when we're in trouble. Some friendships endure longer than marriages, provide a great measure of emotional and practical support, and in immeasurable ways contribute to the quality of life. During times of stress and in old age, people who have someone to confide in have a distinct psychological advantage over those who do not (Lowenthal & Haven, 1968). But it is not easy to achieve and sustain close friendships; there are even fewer guidelines for attracting and keeping friends than there are for attracting and keeping lovers.

Most of us have several different kinds of friends, to meet different needs (La Gaipa, 1977). We have social acquaintances (with whom we play tennis or study for an exam), good friends (whom we call up to go to a movie), close friends (whom we count on for help and support in times of need), and best friends (in whom we confide our deepest secrets). Friendships seem to develop first out of proximity, then out of similar background characteristics (such as age, sex, and race), then out of role relationships (with coworkers, fellow students, or fellow bowlers, for example), and then out of similarities in values and attitudes (Huston & Levinger, 1978).

In recent years, researchers have shown more interest in studying friendship, in seeing what happens during a relationship and what makes some friendships endure. One recent study is interesting in the way it seems to confirm theories discussed earlier in this chapter, at least for the short duration of the study. Eighty-four first-year college men and women filled out four questionnaires at 3-week intervals about same-sex friends they had just met and thought they might become good friends with. When the study ended 3 months later, researchers analyzed the differences between the pairs who had become good friends and those who had not, and found differences in both attitudes and behaviors (Hays, 1985).

There seemed to be a crucial time for building the friendships. Those pairs who were friends at the end of 3 months had experienced a flurry of shared activities and increasing affection and self-disclosure during a relationship-building period between 3 and 6 weeks after meeting. Those who did not become friends had had less and less to do with each other right from the start. The friendships followed the pattern described by Levinger and Snoek (1972) and shown earlier in Figure 18-1, as friends grew in openness, comfort, and mutual concern and shared more activities and personal information with each other. The importance of this 3- to 6-week

Having someone to confide in and someone to be a companion are two reasons for friendship. After an initial attraction, a friendship often follows a pattern starting with shared activities and increasing in affection and self-disclosure. Friends often live near each other, have similar characteristics (such as age, sex, and race), and share role relationships (such as being fellow students).

period may be, in social exchange terms, an exploratory period during which people sample the potential reward of a particular relationship before making a commitment to it (Hays, 1985).

Having confidants and having companions were cited most often as benefits of close friendships, and emotional distress and expenditure of time were cited most often as costs. Costs grew, too, as the friendships developed, but as long as the benefits outweighed the costs, people seemed willing to put up with the bad to get the good. Some dissatisfactions are probably inevitable in any relationship. In fact, one study of the social networks of 120 elderly widows found that the very people who provide the most social support—friends and relatives—are also responsible for a great deal of stress (Rook, 1986). Thus, the key to improving satisfaction may well be, as Hays suggests, to concentrate on improving the benefits rather than on eliminating the costs. This may apply to lovers and spouses, as well as to friends.

Recognition of the importance of a network of caring people has spurred a great deal of research on helping people who suffer from **loneliness,** as discussed in the box "Loneliness" (pages 648–649).

Loneliness Unpleasant and distressing feeling that results from deficiencies in social relationships.

Love

Everyone is an expert on love. Common knowledge and personal experience, for example, tell us that:

■ Women usually fall in love before men do and then keep on carrying the torch after a man has called it quits.

■ We don't fall in love with and marry people we know very well, but instead become crazy about fascinating strangers we meet away from our normal life and work.

■ Women need to be hard to get if they want to get a man.

These may be things we all "know"—but psychological research conducted over the past 20 years has proved them all wrong (Walster & Walster, 1978).

As an element in people's lives that is responsible for a major share of either

Who among us has never known some lonely times? Having no one to play with after the family moves to a new town, sitting home alone on New Year's Eve after a lovers' quarrel, sitting by yourself in a dorm room as you hear peals of laughter down the hall, being ignored by coworkers on a new job, and losing a loved one through separation or death are all common and painful situations. For most of us, such times are transitory, and we find emotional supports to help us shake off our sad and lonely feelings. For some people, however, loneliness is an unshakable part of daily life.

Loneliness is not a new problem. The Old Testament tells us that God said after creating Adam, "It is not good that the man should be alone: I will make him a help mate." The scientific study of the phenomenon is new, however, with serious research and theoretical work dating principally from the 1970s. Researchers are still seeking to learn the causes of loneliness, to formulate theories for understanding it, and to develop strategies to help lonely people.

WHAT IS LONELINESS?

Loneliness is not the same as aloneness. Some people are miserably lonely when surrounded by people, and others are content in solitude. Loneliness is a subjective experience

LONELINESS

that is defined in many different ways by lonely people and by social scientists. Virtually all the definitions agree that loneliness is unpleasant and distressing and that it results from deficiencies in a person's social relationships (Peplau & Perlman, 1982).

What causes such deficiencies? We can look at loneliness in three basic ways, focusing on emotional, cognitive, and social aspects. The emotional explanation states that people need both emotional intimacy with one special person and social support from a circle of caring people, and that when these are not present in someone's life, that person will feel lonely (Weiss, 1982). The cognitive view stresses the lonely person's interpretation of his or her life, especially with regard to expectations and desires. If a person wants and expects to have a certain level of social involvement and does not get it, that person will be lonely. The discrepancy between desire and reality causes the loneliness (Peplau & Perlman, 1979). The social view

looks to the institutions in society and to people's external circumstances. When these circumstances make it hard for people to make and keep friends, they will feel isolated and lonely (Rook, 1984).

The feeling of loneliness is bad enough in itself. What may be even worse is, the way it contributes to a host of physical and psychological problems, including depression, alcohol abuse, adolescent delinquency, aggressiveness, various forms of physical and mental illness, suicide, and higher mortality rates (Rook, 1984).

WHO ARE THE LONELY?

Those who are especially plagued by loneliness account for 11 to 26 percent of the American public (Peplau, Russell, & Heim, 1979). Their numbers are greatest among adolescents, young single adults, people who have been recently divorced, the unemployed, people with low incomes, and people who are housebound and handicapped (Peplau & Perlman, 1982; Rook, 1984).

Some people are lonely because of physical isolation (such as handicapped people who cannot leave their homes), but most are imprisoned by personal characteristics that interfere with forming relationships. Lonely people usually have poor social skills. They have trouble starting

happiness or unhappiness, love is at last coming in for its fair share of research and theorizing from social psychologists, who have finally joined poets, novelists, and songwriters in trying to unravel its mysteries. From interviews, laboratory experiments, and other tools of research, we are learning facts about love which may have a host of practical applications.

We have learned, for example, that the beliefs listed above are myths. Men fall in love more quickly than women and cling more tenaciously to a dying affair; we do date, fall in love with, and marry the boy or girl next door or down the street startlingly often; and men are most attracted to women who are easy for them to get but difficult for other men to get (Peplau & Gordon, 1985; Walster & Walster, 1978).

Most of us are lucky enough to love many different people in the course of our lives. How does this elusive feeling differ from person to person and relationship to relationship? Is the love between parent and child different, for example, from that between siblings, or between lovers caught in the heady excitement of a new romance, or between two people celebrating their fiftieth anniversary together? Social scientists have tried to answer these questions in a number of ways; we'll look at two of these approaches.

conversations, making phone calls, introducing themselves to others, taking part in groups, having a good time at parties, asserting themselves, taking social risks, offering and receiving confidences, responding to other people's overtures, and trusting others. They tend to have low self-esteem, to be self-conscious in social situations, and to blame themselves for their social failures (Rook, 1984). Some of these traits may cause these people's loneliness; others may result from it.

HOW CAN THE LONELY BE HELPED?

Because loneliness stems from many causes, alleviating it can take many different forms. Since the study of this common distress is so new, we are still in the process of developing different approaches and testing to see which ones are most effective. The approaches that appear most promising fall into one of the three basic categories. They either aim to help lonely people establish the kind of social ties they yearn for, try to prevent loneliness from evolving into even more serious problems like depression or suicide, or try to prevent loneliness from occurring in the first place.

Following are some of the specific steps that have been taken in all three approaches to help people climb out of the morass of loneliness.

Helping lonely people to establish personal ties:

■ Group training programs in social skills that use modeling, role-playing, feedback systems, and homework to help people learn how to start a conversation, talk on the phone, give and receive compliments, and make effective and appropriate overtures for physical intimacy.

■ Modifying dysfunctional beliefs through cognitive therapy programs, to enable people to see when they are engaging in self-destructive patterns of thinking (such as becoming obsessed by the fear that other people will laugh at them if they risk taking a social initiative).

■ Developing trust in other people through supportive therapy.

■ Helping people to learn about groups and locations in their communities where they might take part in interesting activities and meet other people, such as shopping malls, parks, special-interest organizations, and volunteer programs.

■ Encouraging cooperative projects in classrooms, housing projects, senior citizens' centers, and nursing homes to make it more rewarding for people to spend time with others.

Helping people cope with loneliness:

■ Transition programs for people who have just suffered an emotional loss, which offer both information and social support. Such programs have been run, with varying degrees of success, for recent widows, for the newly separated and divorced, and for the children of divorced parents.

■ Programs that help people to use solitary time in satisfying ways. This may involve encouraging them to find pleasurable daytime hobbies that they can pursue by themselves and helping them to find ways of being content on their own.

Preventing loneliness:

■ Identifying high-risk groups (such as those who have recently experienced a loss) and targeting special programs to them.

■ Providing transportation (such as jitneys, minibuses, and volunteer drivers) so that people can visit family and friends.

■ Establishing community centers where people can go for various activities (like after-school centers where children can do homework, day care centers for the elderly and disabled to help them and their caretakers, and gathering places for adolescents and single adults).

Passionate Love and Companionate Love   One distinction that has been made is between "passionate love" and "companionate love." *Passionate love* is "a wildly emotional state, a confusion of feelings: tenderness and sexuality, elation and pain, anxiety and relief, altruism and jealousy" (Walster & Walster, 1978, p. 2). It rarely lasts more than from 6 to 30 months, even though it may surface from time to time in a basically companionate relationship. *Companionate love,* sometimes called *conjugal love,* is like a loving friendship between a man and a woman that includes affection, deep attachment, trust, respect, appreciation, loyalty, and close knowledge of each other (Driscoll, Davis, & Lipetz, 1972). Even though it may be intense enough to make a person sacrifice in time of need—sometimes to the point of giving his or her life—it is a sensible emotion that follows Byrne's "law of attraction" (1971), which attributes attraction to reinforcement.

Triangular Theory of Love   An intriguing concept that goes beyond these two descriptions is the **triangular theory of love,** proposed by Robert J. Sternberg (1985c; Sternberg & Barnes, 1985; Sternberg & Grajek, 1984). According to this view, love has three faces—intimacy, passion, and commitment. *Intimacy* is the emotional

Triangular theory of love Theory, proposed by Robert Sternberg, that love has three components: intimacy (the emotional component), passion (the motivational component), and commitment (the cognitive component).

friendship
moves fall de

This French couple seem to be enjoying what one team of researchers call "passionate love." If they don't kill themselves falling out of windows and stay together more than 2 years, they will probably (according to the same researchers) develop "companionate love," a loving friendship that includes affection, deep attachment, trust, respect, appreciation, loyalty, and close knowledge of each other.

component. This involves self-disclosure, which leads to a sense of connection, warmth, and trust. _Passion_ is the motivational component. This is based on inner drives that involve a high degree of physiological arousal, which becomes translated into physical attraction and sexual desire. Finally, commitment is the cognitive component, the decision to love and to stay with the person one loves. The presence of one, two, or all three of these components produces a particular kind of love, and the match in the kinds of love felt by the two partners in a relationship determines the success of that relationship. Sternberg attributes problems in love relationships to mismatches of the components and to changes in the proportion of each component over time. The eight types of love relationships that result from different combinations of these three components are shown in Table 18-3 (opposite).

When we talk about love and friendship and intimate relationships, we are talking about the kinds of attachments that often lead to marriage, with all its joys and complexities. Social psychologists have studied some aspects of marriage, including how we choose our mates and how marriage affects us in various ways. In recent years, with the increase in the divorce rate in the United States, research on the dissolution of relationships, both before and after marriage, has increased as well.

Marriage and Divorce

Marriage and issues having to do with it affect all our lives. Nine out of 10 Americans marry at some time, and those who do not will be affected by the marriages of their friends and relatives. Now, for the first time in history, a married couple is as likely to be parted by divorce as by death (Weitzman, 1986). Thus, divorce, too, affects most of us either directly or indirectly. Let's see what social psychologists have to say about these topics.

How We Choose Someone to Marry   What would you want in a husband or wife? Probably you would want someone you love, someone who loves you, someone who will be your best friend, and someone with whom you can have a fulfilling sexual relationship. Today, in the United States, these attributes have largely replaced the bases for marriage that have been important throughout history—and that

TABLE 18-3 PATTERNS OF LOVING

Type	Description
Nonlove	All three components of love are absent. This describes most of our personal relationships, which are simply casual interactions.
Liking	Intimacy is the only component present. This is what we feel in true friendship and in many loving relationships. There is closeness, understanding, emotional support, affection, bondedness, and warmth. Neither passion nor commitment is present.
Infatuation	Passion is the only component present. This is "love at first sight," a strong physical attraction and sexual arousal, without intimacy or commitment. This can flare up suddenly and die just as fast—or, given certain circumstances, can sometimes last for a long time.
Empty love	Commitment is the only component present. This is often found in long-term relationships that have lost both intimacy and passion, or in arranged marriages.
Romantic love	Intimacy and passion are both present. Romantic lovers are drawn to each other physically and bonded emotionally. They are not, however, committed to each other.
Companionate love	Intimacy and commitment are both present. This is a long-term, committed friendship, which often occurs in marriages in which the physical attraction has died down but in which the partners feel close to each other and have made the decision to stay together.
Fatuous love	Passion and commitment are present, without intimacy. This is the kind of love that leads to a whirlwind courtship, in which a couple make a commitment on the basis of passion without allowing themselves the time to develop intimacy. This kind of love usually does not last, despite the initial intent to commit.
Consummate love	All three components are present in this "complete" love, which many of us strive for, especially in romantic relationships. It is easier to reach it than to hold onto it. Either partner may change what he or she wants from the relationship. If the other partner changes, too, the relationship may endure in a different form. If the other partner does not change, the relationship may dissolve.

Source: R.J. Sternberg, 1985c.

are still essential in many other societies around the world—such as consideration of finances or lineage by the nuptial couple's parents, and similarity in social background between bride and groom.

Similarity is still important, although not as much as it was in times past. Most of us continue to pick spouses of the same race and religion, and of similar age, intelligence, education, and socioeconomic status; although, with increasing rates of interracial and interreligious marriages, the number of exceptions to the "rule" of similarity is growing (Murstein, 1982).

Contemporary researchers tend to look at similarity as a screening device that "limit[s] the pool of marital eligibles rather than pushing the individual to marry anyone who has a similar cultural-social heritage" (Murstein, 1982, p. 652). Most of us do not have a vast smorgasbord of potential marriage partners to select from; we tend to be exposed to those similar to ourselves, and we choose from them. Thus similarity works as a screen devised by fate and circumstance. The theories of interpersonal attraction give insight into our ultimate choice among those who get through the screen.

How Marriage Affects Us   Although scientific research on marriage lags behind the interest most people have in the topic, we do know a little about how this almost universal state affects us. For one thing, it seems to keep us healthy. Married people are physically and mentally healthier than single, separated, divorced, or widowed people (Bloom, Asher, & White, 1978). Another interpretation, of course, is that healthier people are more likely to marry or to stay married. Probably, both explanations contribute to the positive correlation between health and marital status.

Over the past half century, there has been considerable change in the way husbands and wives think about their marriages and act in them. A major shift has been in gender roles, as men and women have widened their thinking—and their actions—to perform duties once considered to be the province of one sex or the other. This has led to another major change, in **power,** an issue that is explored in the box "Power in Marriage."

Power *Ability of one person to influence another person's behavior, thoughts, or feelings.*

Breaking Up BREAKING UP BEFORE MARRIAGE "The best divorce is the one you get before you get married" seems to be as relevant today as it ever was. The end of an intimate relationship is always painful, but research bears out common experience that the end of a premarital affair is less traumatic than a divorce (Hill, Rubin, & Peplau, 1976; Rubin, Peplau, & Hill, 1981).

In a study of 103 breakups among dating college students, part of a larger study of dating couples, a number of factors characterized affairs that ended. The young men and women who ended their relationships were more different from each other on such measures as age, educational aspirations, intelligence, and physical attractiveness than were the ones who stayed together. Furthermore, the couples who split were more likely to be unequally involved in the relationship; one was much more in love than the other. On Rubin's "love" and "liking" scales (1970), the partners' love was a better predictor of their staying together than was their liking for each other. Whether the couples had had sexual intercourse or had lived together were, on the other hand, totally unrelated to whether they stayed together.

Couples often used external factors to help them separate, as shown by the fact that breakups peaked at turning points of the school year (May–June, September, and December–January). The splits coincided with changes in living arrangements or schedules or times when questions arose regarding future plans ("Should we spend our vacation together?" "Should we get an apartment together?" "Should I accept a job out of town?").

The decision to divorce is rarely arrived at lightly, since the breakup of a marriage is one of life's most stressful events. It almost always involves great emotional pain, and major social and financial disruptions. The year after a divorce (which is usually more than 2 years after the initial separation) is usually an emotional low point for divorcing parents and their children.

The desire to break up is seldom felt equally by both partners. One person usually initiates the breakup—and that person is apt to feel freer, happier, guiltier, and less depressed and lonely than the other partner. The noninitiator has to deal with his or her feelings of rejection, as well as the end of a relationship that he or she wanted to continue (Hill et al., 1976). Contrary to popular myth, women are more likely to end a relationship than men are—even when they are the more involved partner. Furthermore, they cope better with rejection when the man ends the affair than men cope when the woman is the initiator. They may be more sensitive to their partner's feelings, better able to tell when he does not return their own depth of emotion, and thus more prepared either to accept or precipitate the break. Furthermore, women seem more in control of their feelings, possibly because of early socialization that emphasizes their power in the emotional domain—often at the expense of power in other aspects of life (Rubin et al., 1981).

BREAKING UP AFTER MARRIAGE On Holmes and Rahe's Social Readjustment Rating Scale of life stresses (1967), divorce is second only to the death of a spouse. Aside from the emotional turmoil that precedes, accompanies, and follows it, it requires a change of residence for at least one partner, a changed financial situation for both, generally a series of legal skirmishes, and often the necessity of working out disagreements about the care of children. It is no wonder that the year after the divorce (which is usually more than 2 years after the initial separation) is usually an emotional low point for both the divorcing parents and their children (Hetherington, Cox, & Cox, 1975).

Although most people don't go into marriage planning to make it a power play, it is not long before some issue comes up about which the couple disagrees. You want to eat Chinese food; your partner wants pizza. Or you want to go to one movie; your partner wants to see another. As the marriage progresses, more and more issues come up—where you'll live; how you'll spend your money; how or whether you'll worship; what your career goals are; how you'll allocate household chores; whether you'll have children, and if so, how many and when and who will take care of them. The way you resolve issues like these reflects the balance of power in your relationship. If you have more power than your spouse, you'll need to decide how you'll use it. If you have about equal power, you'll need to work out strategies for negotiation.

Power, in its social sense, refers to one person's ability to influence another person's behavior, thoughts, or feelings—in other words, to get the other person to do something, or to think or feel a certain way. Usually, the person in a relationship who has more resources has more power. Historically, husbands have had more power in marriage than wives. By law, they controlled the family property and made important decisions. By custom, they earned more money, they were better educated, and they had more prestigious jobs (Sears, Freedman, & Peplau, 1985). Today, however, marriages in which the husband is the undisputed head

POWER IN MARRIAGE

of the household are less common (Huston, 1983).

Who, then, does hold the power? This question is hard to answer. As women have obtained better jobs and earned more income, they have achieved more power in the household (Scanzoni & Scanzoni, 1976). In addition, physical attractiveness and social desirability are resources that can be held by either spouse. Power can also go to the partner who is less committed to the relationship. If one person—either husband or wife—cares more about staying married than the other does, the one who is more committed will have less power. That is, he or she will do more to accommodate the other partner (Waller, 1951).

Finally, though, in close relationships different people measure power in different ways; what one person sees as equal, another may consider very unbalanced. Some people say that their relationship is egalitarian because they share in day-to-day decisions; others say it is skewed because one partner is more influential in major decisions. The greatest number of people say that

their relationship is equal, a large minority say that it is male-dominant, and a small percentage term it female-dominant (Scanzoni & Scanzoni, 1976).

One review of the literature on power and marital satisfaction reports that the unhappiest marriages are those in which wives are dominant (Gray-Little & Burks, 1983). This may reflect the fact that the wife-dominant pattern is not socially sanctioned. If a man does not assume the amount of leadership that a woman has expected and wants, she may assume it herself, but she may be disappointed in her husband and unsure about her own role. The husband in such a marriage may withdraw even more, and the more he pulls back, the more his wife may try to force his involvement, thus leading to almost constant conflict. Husband-dominant marriages may be happier, possibly because they do fulfill cultural expectations.

The happiest marriages are egalitarian unions in which husbands and wives have equal power and make decisions jointly. This pattern is rapidly becoming the cultural ideal in the United States, and the one that more people aspire to (Peplau, 1979). As this pattern becomes more and more common, the male-dominant pattern may violate people's expectations and prove to be less satisfying. We see, then, that marriage responds to changes in society, as well as to the personalities of the people involved.

Despite the high rate of divorce today, the decision to separate is rarely made lightly. It is, however, made considerably more often than it used to be. Some changing societal trends that have reduced the barriers to divorce include the fact that women are less financially dependent on their husbands today; that both sexes face fewer legal obstacles, less religious opposition, and less of a social stigma; and that current wisdom decrees that it is not always best to stay together "for the good of the children." But, as Berscheid and Campbell point out, "Changes in societal conditions do not terminate relationships; people do" (1981, p. 210). These changed conditions, however, do affect the comparison level for the person considering divorce. The alternatives to marriage are not so costly as they used to be, and so divorce is a viable option for more people.

In marital breakups as in dating breakups, it is often the woman who decides to sever the tie, often after months or years of contemplation (Kelly, 1982). Again, the partner who makes the decision to divorce is usually in better emotional shape than the other partner, largely because of the sense of control over his or her own life and the absence of the need to deal with rejection. Other factors that affect the way a person will react emotionally include the presence or absence of a network of supportive friends and family, the effect of the situation on the children, the presence or absence of a lover who can serve as a "transitional person," and the degree of financial strain. Although divorce is often a positive step that results in healthier psychological functioning, "the substantial minority of men and women who [are] overwhelmed and disorganized beyond their recuperative powers . . . remind us that divorce is not a panacea for all. Indeed there is evidence that divorce results in clear psychological gain for just one spouse to the marriage more often than both are benefited" (Kelly, 1982, p. 749).

Interpersonal relationships are the source of our greatest joys and our deepest pain. Although psychology is intrinsically the study of the individual, we have seen throughout this book how the individual affects and is affected by other people. The more we care about someone, and the more we invest of ourselves in relationships, the more deeply we are affected by our ties with others. The burgeoning interest among researchers in exploring the ways people get along with each other offers hope for the well-being of the individual psyche—as well as for a society made up of many kinds of individuals.

SUMMARY

1 Interpersonal attraction is the tendency to evaluate another person in a positive way. It is an attitude. Attraction to another depends on interactions between one's own traits, the other's person's traits, and the situation in which the two get to know each other.

2 Social psychologists study interpersonal attraction by using naturalistic observation, self-report measures, and laboratory and field experiments.

3 *Person perception* refers to the ways we form impressions or perceptions of others. People try to give meaning to their own behaviors or the behavior of others by attributing causes to their behavior. According to attribution theory, we tend to explain people's behaviors either dispositionally (as being based on some internal factor, like a basic personality trait) or situationally (as being the result of an external cause, such as a particular circumstance). According to Kelly, three factors are important in attributing meaning to someone's behavior: distinctiveness, consensus, and consistency of the behavior.

4 Fundamental attribution error is the tendency to overestimate the importance of dispositional factors (like personality traits) and to underestimate the importance of situational influences (like a particular circumstance) in accounting for behavior. This error is particularly likely to operate when people explain the behavior of others. When people explain their own behavior, however, they tend to attribute it to situational factors. People are particularly likely to attribute their failures to the situation and their successes to themselves.

5 Studies have demonstrated that a person's initial attraction to another person is related to a number of factors. The proximity between two people affects their likelihood of becoming friends. A study by Festinger and his colleagues showed that next-door neighbors in a student housing development were most likely to become friends. From childhood on, physical attractiveness is an important element in how people view others. Attractive people are thought to possess a wide array of desirable traits. Other personal characteristics, such as warmth and competence, influence interpersonal attraction. In addition, people, particularly those with high self-esteem, are attracted to others who hold similar opinions. People also tend to like those who like them.

6 Close relationships incorporate self-disclosure, which occurs as relationships progress to deeper levels of intimacy. There are a number of theories about why people stay in relationships. The most important contemporary theory is exchange theory, the theory that people consider the rewards and costs in a relationship as well as their alternatives in deciding whether to get into a relationship and whether to stay in it. Equity theory, an offshoot of exchange theory, maintains that people are most comfortable in relationships in which there is a fair distribution of rewards and costs and that they will try to restore equity in relationships they perceive as unbalanced.

7 People maintain a number of different types of friendships, from social acquaintance to best friend. Friendships seem to develop first out of proximity, then out of similar background characteristics, role relationships, and similarities in values and attitudes. Recent research has focused on factors related to the development of friendships.

8 Loneliness is an unpleasant and distressing feeling that results from deficiencies in a person's social relationships.

Emotional, cognitive, and social explanations of these deficiencies have been offered. Most lonely people have difficulty forming relationships. Approaches to helping them focus on assisting them in establishing desired social ties, on preventing loneliness from evolving into even more serious problems such as depression and suicide, and on trying to prevent loneliness from occurring in the first place.

9 Sternberg's triangular theory of love holds that love has three components: intimacy (the emotional component), passion (the motivational component), and commitment (the cognitive component). Sternberg describes eight types of love relationships that result from different combinations of the three components.

10 There appears to be a relationship between marital status and physical and psychological health. Power is one person's ability to influence another's behavior, thoughts, or feelings. Historically, husbands have had more power in marriages than wives; but egalitarian marriages, in which both partners have equal power, are rapidly becoming the cultural ideal in the United States.

11 A number of factors influence breaking up, whether this occurs before or after marriage. Changing societal trends have reduced a number of barriers to divorce.

KEY TERMS

Attribution theory (page 636)
Close relationships (633)
Comparison level (644)
Comparison level for alternatives (644)
Equity theory (645)
Exchange theory (644)

Fundamental attribution error (637)
Interpersonal attraction (633)
Loneliness (647)
Power (652)
Self-disclosure (643)
Triangular theory of love (649)

SUGGESTED READINGS

BERSCHEID, E., & WALSTER, E. (1978). *Interpersonal attraction* (2nd ed.). Reading, MA: Addison-Wesley. A well-written and scholarly discussion about theories and measurement of interpersonal attraction, by two leading researchers.

KELLEY, H. H., et al. (1983). *Close relationships*. San Francisco: Freeman. Nine social psychologists discuss the impact of intimate relationships on human well-being. Information on therapy is included.

KLAGSBRUN, F. (1985). *Married people: Staying together in the age of divorce*. New York: Bantam. A well-researched and sensitively written book that draws upon published research, interviews with happily married couples, and the author's exploration of her own long-term marriage to examine such topics as the transition from passionate to companionate love, competition between spouses, the influence of family (including children) and friends on a couple's relationship, and sexuality.

POGREBIN, L. C. (1986). *Among friends: Who we like, why we like them, and what we do with them*. New York: McGraw-Hill. An absorbing analysis, for lay readers, of friendship in contemporary society. It illustrates findings from social science research with anecdotes gleaned from over 150 interviews and the author's own life. Interesting sections on differences between men's and women's friendships and on the changing patterns of friendships from infancy through old age.

WALSTER, E., & WALSTER, G. W. (1978). *A new look at love*. Reading, MA: Addison-Wesley. A delightful discussion of passionate and companionate love, with material on the dynamics of sexual attraction, how we choose a marriage partner, and the pain of passionate love. The book is liberally illustrated with cartoons and with quizzes for the reader to answer.

APPENDIX

STATISTICS

■ **BRANCHES OF STATISTICS**

■ **DESCRIPTIVE STATISTICS**

Central Tendency
Variability
Normal Distributions
Skewed Distributions
Correlation

■ **INFERENTIAL STATISTICS**

Sampling Methods
Testing Research Hypotheses

Would you describe yourself as above average in intelligence? Do you study less or more than other students? Is your sense of humor superior or inferior to other people's? Are you enduring an unusually stressful year? Are you likely to earn over $100,000 a year within the next decade?

The answers to all of these questions require **statistics,** a discipline that includes a variety of methods for collecting, organizing, analyzing and making inferences from numerical data. Statistics is a branch of mathematics that is used by psychologists as well as other social scientists to sort facts and draw conclusions. Psychology cannot use the precise measurements of pure sciences such as physics and chemistry. Height and weight can be measured accurately and precisely, but the measurement of memory, intelligence, humor, motivation and other broad personal attributes can only be estimated. Psychologists must rely heavily on statistics in developing tests of these attributes and in interpreting the results of research studies.

Although most mathematical calculations used in psychology are easily handled by computers, it is important to know how to interpret the computer output accurately. Therefore, the emphasis in this appendix will be on interpretation of statistics rather than on calculation.

BRANCHES OF STATISTICS

There are two branches of statistics: descriptive and inferential. **Descriptive statistics** provide a way to summarize data gathered from research. For example, you could determine the grade-point averages and study schedules of students in your psychology class and use descriptive statistics to summarize your findings. Instructors often use descriptive statistics to explain how students scored on examinations. **Inferential statistics** use data from a sample to generalize and predict results in a larger population. You would need inferential statistics to predict the intelligence and study schedules of future psychology classes composed of students similar to those in your own class. Both descriptive statistics and inferential statistics are needed in psychological research.

DESCRIPTIVE STATISTICS

Suppose that a researcher surveys a psychology class with 25 students and asks each student to record the total number of hours he or she has studied psychology during a specified week. The researcher collects the information and records the data as shown in Table A-1. How can the researcher organize these data to make your interpretation easier?

One way to organize the raw data in Table A-1 is to make a tally, or frequency distribution. A **frequency distribution** lists each score or observation, statistically known as X (in our example the number of hours of psychology study), and indicates how frequently each score or observation X occurs (see Table A-2).

Another possibility is to create a visual outline of the data, a graph. One commonly used graph is the **histogram,** or bar graph. The *horizontal axis,* or *abscissa,* shows the score of each person—in our example, the number of hours of psychology study. The *vertical axis,* or *ordinate,* represents the frequency of each score—in our example, the number of students who studied a set number of hours. Figure A-1 shows a histogram that is clearly more meaningful than Table A-1.

Often it is useful to compare the graphs of two or more sets of data. But constructing one histogram on top of another would be confusing. A better way to handle this comparison is to construct another type of graph from the histogram. By connecting the midpoints of the tops of the bars of the histogram, you can construct a

TABLE A-1 RAW DATA	
Student	Score X Hours of Psychology Study during Specified Week
John A.	6
Mike A.	3
Jane B.	4
Kara C.	9
Joann D.	10
Henry E.	20
Marshall G.	9
Jim I.	11
Tom J.	8
Bill J.	6
Tess L.	5
Dana M.	4
Leslie N.	6
Jack O.	0
Nancy O.	7
Ann P.	10
Sue Q.	6
Janice R.	7
Kenn S.	5
Louis S.	5
Willy T.	8
Lois T.	4
Carol V.	6
Tom W.	9
Bob Y.	7

TABLE A-2 FREQUENCY DISTRIBUTION	
Hours of Psychology Study X	Frequency
0	1
1	0
2	0
3	1
4	3
5	3
6	5
7	3
8	2
9	3
10	2
11	1
12	0
13	0
14	0
15	0
16	0
17	0
18	0
19	0
20	1

frequency polygon, as shown in Figure A-2 (page 660). A polygon is a closed figure with many angles. The frequency at both ends of the distribution is zero, closing the figure and making a polygon. Frequency polygons (unlike histograms) *can* be constructed on top of each other for easy comparison of the two distributions. Figure A-3 (page 660) uses frequency polygons to compare the amount of time 20 students spent studying psychology in 1 week with the number of hours they spent watching television during the same week.

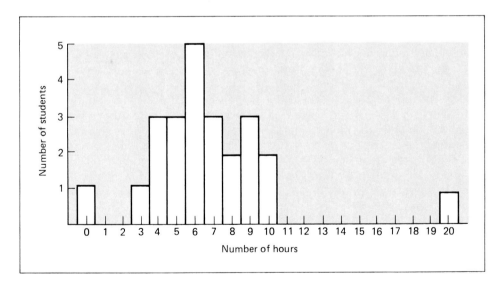

FIGURE A-1 *Histogram.*

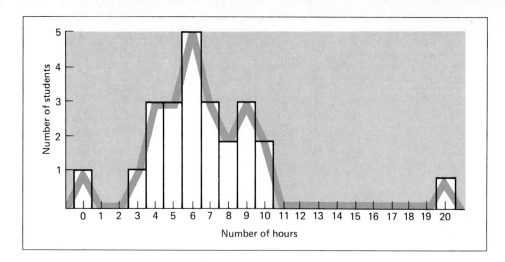

FIGURE A-2 *Frequency polygon.*

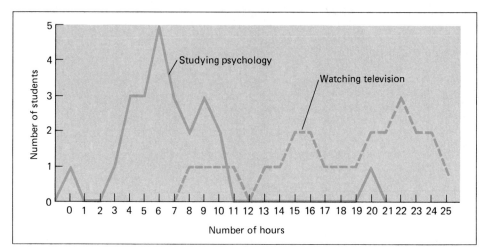

FIGURE A-3 *Comparison of frequency polygons. This comparison demonstrates that students spend more time watching television than studying psychology.*

Central Tendency

The purpose of descriptive statistics is to organize, summarize, and simplify data. Frequency distributions and graphs provide organization but can be cumbersome and confusing. It is helpful to know the **central tendency,** or the most typical and representative score in a distribution. The three most common measures of central tendency are the mode, median, and mean.

Central tendency   *Most typical or most representative score in a distribution.*

Mode   The ***mode*** (M_o) of a distribution is the score that occurs most frequently. In our example in Table A-3, 6 hours was the most common score. Although it is often easiest to compute, the mode is the least-used measure of central tendency. There are several reasons for this. In some distributions, particularly in small groups, scores occur only once and there is no mode. In larger groups, there is frequently more than one mode. Also, the mode is more subject to fluctuation in sampling than either the median or mean. Generally, the mode is useful when only one or two scores occur extremely frequently.

Mode   *Score that occurs most frequently in a distribution.*

Median   Just as a median strip divides a freeway in half, the ***median*** (*M*) divides a distribution in half, so that one-half the scores are above it and one-half are below it. The median, or midpoint, is easiest to compute if there is an odd number of observations, as in the example in Table A-3. To calculate the median, observations or scores must be arranged in order, from highest to lowest. If there is an odd number of

Median   *Midpoint of a distribution of scores, with the same numbers of scores above and below.*

TABLE A-3   CALCULATION OF MEAN, MEDIAN, AND MODE

Mean $(\overline{X}) = \dfrac{\Sigma X \text{ (sum of scores)}}{n \text{ (total number)}}$	Median (M) = midpoint	Mode (M_o) = most frequent score
X (score)	X (in order)	X (in order)
0	0	0
3	3	3
4	4	4
9	4	4
10	4	4
20	5 12	5
9	5 below	5
11	5	5
8	6	6
6	6	6
5	6	6 Mode
4	6	6
6	6 Median	6
0	7	7
7	7	7
10	7	7
6	8	8
7	8 12	8
5	9 above	9
5	9	9
8	9	9
4	10	10
6	10	10
9	11	11
7	20	20
$n = 25$ $\Sigma X = 175$	$M = 6$	$M_o = 6$

$$\overline{X} = \frac{175}{25} = 7$$

scores, there will be only one middle score to represent the median. However, when there is an even number of scores, there will be two middle scores; the median will then be found by averaging these two scores. For example, in the distribution:

$$1, 2, 3, 4, 5, 6$$

the median is computed by averaging 3 and 4, and would thus be 3.5. The median is not affected by extreme scores. If the person who studied psychology for 20 hours during the week instead had studied for 120 hours, the median would be unaffected.

Mean   The *mean,* the arithmetic average of all scores, is the most frequently used measure of central tendency. The mean, often symbolized as $\overline{X}$, is calculated by adding all scores (X's) and dividing by the total number of scores, as shown in Table A-3. The Greek letter Σ (capital sigma) is used by statisticians to indicate summation, or adding all scores. You are undoubtedly familiar with the mean from computing your college grade-point average. The mean is the most useful measure of central tendency, since it is an exact arithmetic measure, and it is commonly used in inferential statistics. However, it can be affected by extreme scores. In our example, if the student who studied psychology for 20 hours had instead studied for 120 hours, the mean would increase from 7 hours to 11 hours. Thus the score of only one student would have a profound effect on the mean for the entire group.

Mean   *Arithmetic average (often called simply "average"), arrived at by adding up all scores in a distribution and then dividing the total by the number of individual scores.*

Variability

After computing a measure of central tendency, a logical question is: How representative is this score? In other words, do the other scores spread out widely, or do they cluster around the mean and median? Consider the following sets of IQ scores:

	IQ scores		
Set 1	99	100	101
Set 2	40	100	160

Variability *Spread of scores in a distribution.*

Range *Simplest measure of variability; the difference between the largest and smallest scores in a sample.*

Although both sets share the same central tendency, there is an obvious difference in the spread of the scores, or **variability.**

Range The simplest measure of variability is the **range,** the difference between the largest and smallest scores. The range for the distribution in Table A-2 would be $20 - 0 = 20$ hours. Although it is easy to compute, the range reflects only the difference between the highest and lowest values and does not include any other scores. One extremely high or low score could have a strong impact. Indeed, everyone could have the same score except two people, and the range would reflect only the values of the two extremes.

Variance Another way to determine the variability of scores in a distribution is to compute the deviation of each score from the mean, as shown in Table A-4, column 2. The deviation is computed by subtracting the value of the mean from each score. In the example in Table A-4, the mean value of 7 was subtracted. Values below the mean have negative signs; values above the mean have positive signs. The total shown at the bottom of column 2 is zero. As a matter of fact, the sum of the deviations from the mean in any distribution will always equal zero (this is not very helpful in estimating variability).

Deviation computations have important uses. Statisticians have found that an interesting and widely used number can be derived by first squaring each deviation from the mean as in column 3 of Table A-4. The average of the squared deviations is then computed by totaling the figures in column 3 and dividing by the total number of cases, 25. This average of all the squared deviations from the mean score is called the **variance** and is symbolized by σ^2. In our example:

Variance *Measure of variability determined by computing the deviation of each score from the mean; the average of all the squared deviations from the mean score.*

$$\Sigma (x - \overline{X})^2 = 326; \; n = 25; \; \text{and} \; \sigma^2 = \frac{\Sigma(x - \overline{X})^2}{n} = 13.04$$

Standard Deviation The preferred and most widely used measure of variability is the standard deviation. The **standard deviation,** symbolized by σ, is simply the square root of the variance.

Standard deviation *Square root of the variance; the preferred and most widely used measure of variability.*

$$\text{Standard deviation} = \sqrt{\text{variance}}$$
$$\sigma = \sqrt{\sigma^2}$$

In our example in Table A-4, the standard deviation is $\sqrt{13.04} = 3.6$. Like the variance, the standard deviation takes every score into account, rather than just the two extreme scores used in computing the range. The most important advantage of the standard deviation over the variance is that the standard deviation is expressed in terms of the original unit of measurement (in our example, number of hours), whereas the variance is expressed in squared units of measurement. Larger values of standard deviations indicate that scores are widely scattered from the mean. Smaller values denote that most observations or scores are close to the mean. For example, suppose that a researcher studied the level of job satisfaction of individuals in the accounting and public relations departments of a company. In both departments the

TABLE A-4 COMPUTATION OF THE VARIANCE AND STANDARD DEVIATION

Column 1: Observation	Column 2: Deviation from mean ($\bar{X}$) $(x - \bar{X})$	Column 3: Squared deviation $(x - \bar{X})^2$
0	−7	49
3	−4	16
4	−3	9
4	−3	9
4	−3	9
5	−2	4
5	−2	4
5	−2	4
6	−1	1
6	−1	1
6	−1	1
6	−1	1
6	−1	1
7	0	0
7	0	0
7	0	0
8	1	1
8	1	1
9	2	4
9	2	4
9	2	4
10	3	9
10	3	9
11	4	16
20	13	169
$\Sigma = 175$	$\Sigma = 0$	$\Sigma = 326$
$\bar{X} = 7$		

Variance (average deviation squared):

$$\sigma^2 = \frac{\Sigma(x - \bar{X})^2}{n} = \frac{326}{25} = 13.04$$

Standard deviation:

$$\sigma = \sqrt{\sigma^2} = \sqrt{13.04} = 3.6$$

average score was 70 percent satisfaction. However, the standard deviation in the accounting department was 1 while the standard deviation in the public relations department was 10. The researcher can conclude that there is considerably more variation in job satisfaction in the public relations department than in the accounting department. The standard deviation can be used for considerable additional statistical interpretation.

Normal Distributions

Fortunately, mathematicians and statisticians have more concrete descriptions of "normality" than psychologists do. The **normal distribution,** or normal curve, was suggested by a mathematician named Quetelet who noted that many measurements fall into an orderly pattern. For example, if you were to observe the heights of a crowd of women at an airport, you would probably note that most are average height, some are slightly taller or shorter, and very few women are extremely short or extremely tall. If you were to continue with thousands of observations and plot the exact height values on a graph, your frequency polygon would probably resemble the smooth curve shown in Figure A-4 (page 664).

The normal distribution is a symmetrical bell-shaped curve; the left half is the mirror reflection of the right half. In a normal distribution, the mean, median, and mode all fall in the same location, the exact center of the curve. Most of the scores

Normal distribution Distribution of scores in the orderly pattern of a symmetrical bell-shaped curve on which the mean, median, and mode are all equal.

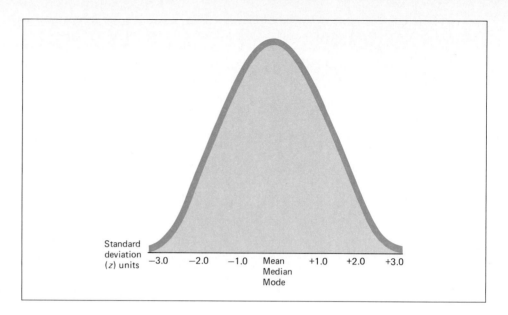

Standard deviation
(z) units −3.0   −2.0   −1.0   Mean   +1.0   +2.0   +3.0
                            Median
                            Mode

FIGURE A-4 *Normal distribution.*

are grouped around these measures of central tendency. Nearly all the scores in a normal distribution will appear within three standard deviation units on either side of the mean.

Consider the distribution of intelligence test scores. IQ tests have been developed to reflect a normal distribution of intelligence in the whole population. The mean IQ has been set at 100, and most intelligence tests have a standard deviation of 15 points. Since nearly all scores in a normal distribution are within ±3 standard deviation units, you can safely conclude that most people have IQs between 55 and 145.

Standard score Number of standard deviations a score is from the mean; z score.

The score of any individual on an IQ test can be translated into a **standard score,** or z score, by stating how many standard deviations the score is from the mean. The mean of the distribution has a z score equal to zero since it has zero or no deviation from itself. Scores above the mean are positive z scores; scores below the mean are negative z scores. A z score of +2 on an intelligence test would be 2 standard deviations above the mean: that is, 30 points above 100, or 130. Similarly, a z score of −1 on an IQ test would be 1 standard deviation below the mean, or 100 − 15 = 85. The standard score is always computed by subtracting the mean from the score and dividing by the standard deviation.

$$z = \frac{x - \overline{X}}{\sigma}$$

If you know the mean and standard deviation, you can determine a given individual's z score on any test. The z scores permit comparisons of scores on tests that have different means and standard deviations. Suppose you wanted to compare your score on a standardized test of perceptual speed with your IQ score of 120; that is, you want to find your *relative* standing on the two tests. Since the mean of the IQ test is 100 and the standard deviation is 15, you would compute your z score as follows:

$$z = \frac{120 - 100}{15} = \frac{20}{15} = \frac{4}{3} = 1.33$$

Your z score on the IQ test is 1.33. Now assume that your score on the test of perceptual speed was 85, the mean score on the test was 73, and the standard deviation was 12.

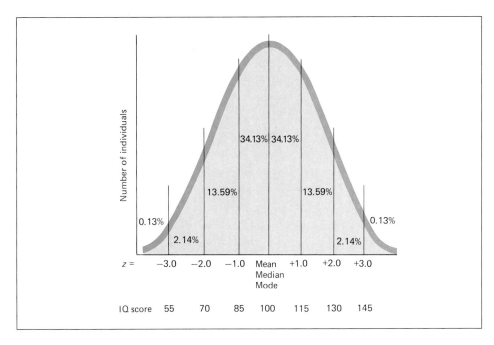

FIGURE A-5 *Percentages in a normal curve. In a normal distribution, more than two-thirds of the people will have IQs between 85 and 115. Only a fraction of 1 percent will have IQs below 55 or above 145.*

Your *z* score on the test of perceptual speed would then be computed:

$$z = \frac{85 - 73}{12} = \frac{12}{12} = 1.0$$

Thus, your score on the IQ test was higher than your score on the test of perceptual speed. Psychologists often compare individual scores on different tests. For example, a psychologist might want to know whether the person has more ability in language or math. By comparing relative *z* scores, psychologists can answer many types of queries about test results; *z* scores allow comparison of scores on tests of different lengths with different means and standard deviations.

As shown on Figure A-5, in a normal curve, more than two-thirds of the scores are within 1 standard deviation of the mean. Less than 5 percent of the scores are more than 2 standard deviations away from the mean, and a mere fraction of a percent are more than 3 standard deviations away (Figure A-6). If your IQ is 130, only slightly more than 2 percent of the population has scored above you.

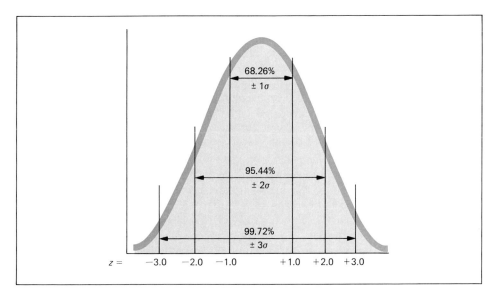

FIGURE A-6 *Total percentages in a normal curve. In any normal distribution, 68.26 percent of the scores will be within 1 standard deviation of the mean, 95.44 percent will be within 2 standard deviations, and 99.72 percent will be within 3 standard deviations.*

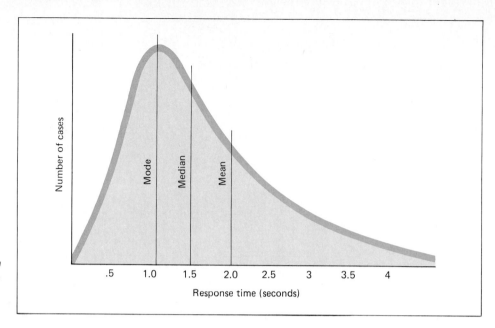

Skewed Distributions

Skewed distribution   Asymmetrical distribution of scores in which the mean, median and mode fall in different places.

Not all distributions of large populations are normal. Often the mean, median, and mode fall at different places and the distribution is said to be **skewed** (not symmetric). For example, response time often forms a skewed distribution. When people are instructed to press a buzzer in response to a flashing light, most will respond very rapidly; only a few will lag behind (see Figure A-7). Since skewed distributions do not possess the same attributes as normal distributions, assumptions about the percentage distribution of standard scores are inappropriate. Thus it is more difficult to compare individual scores among skewed distributions.

Correlation

Correlation   Measure of the relationship (association) between variables.

The focus thus far has been on describing distributions with only one variable. **Correlation** is the study of the relationship between measurements of two variables. The purpose of correlations is to determine whether two sets of measurements have any association with each other.

Scatterplot   Visual representation of the relationship between two variables.

Assume, for example, that you want to determine whether there is a relationship between high school grade-point average (GPA) and college GPA. To determine the relationship between these two variables, you might begin with a visual representation, a **scatterplot.** Figure A-8 presents a list of GPAs and a scatterplot. Each student is represented by 1 point on the scatterplot, with high school GPA indicated by distance along the vertical axis and college GPA indicated by distance along the horizontal axis. By glancing at the scatterplot, you can see that students with high GPAs in high school tend to have high GPAs in college (Ted, Tom, and Marcia). Similarly, those with low high school GPAs tend to have low GPAs in college (Bob and Susan). In other words, as high school GPA increases, college GPA tends to increase. There is then a *positive correlation* between the two variables because as one variable increases, the other also tends to increase.

When as the values of one variable increase, values on the other tend to decrease, correlation is said to be *negative,* or *inverse.* For example, as students spend more time watching television, they are likely to spend less time studying. As shown in Figure A-9, on a scatterplot points of positive correlation tend to slope upward, while the points of negative correlation slope downward. When there is no correlation or relationship between two variables, points appear randomly and without a specific direction.

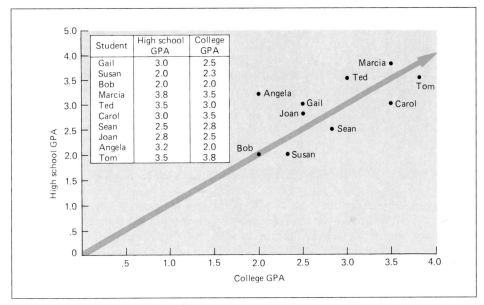

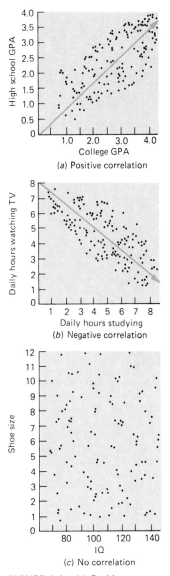

Student	High school GPA	College GPA
Gail	3.0	2.5
Susan	2.0	2.3
Bob	2.0	2.0
Marcia	3.8	3.5
Ted	3.5	3.0
Carol	3.0	3.5
Sean	2.5	2.8
Joan	2.8	2.5
Angela	3.2	2.0
Tom	3.5	3.8

FIGURE A-8 *Constructing a scatterplot.*

(a) Positive correlation

(b) Negative correlation

(c) No correlation

FIGURE A-9 *(a)* Positive correlation. *(b)* Negative correlation. *(c)* No correlation.

To determine the strength or extent of a relationship between two variables, you need to compute a correlation coefficient. A ***correlation coefficient (r)*** is a numerical value that indicates the strength and direction of the relationship between two variables. When there is no relationship between two variables, $r = 0$. Values of r range from -1.0 (perfect negative correlation) to $+1.0$ (perfect positive correlation). In perfect correlations, all values appear in an exact straight line on a scatterplot, as shown in Figure A-10.

However, most psychological variables have less than perfect correlation. The correlation coefficient is expressed as a decimal; the larger the numerical value of the decimal, the stronger the relationship. Usually r values of $\pm.80$ are considered very high. Note that strong correlations may be either positive or negative. The sign of a correlation coefficient merely indicates the direction of the relationship.

The actual computation of r is quite complex and will not be included in this appendix. Most statistics software packages for microcomputers include the Pearson product moment coefficient of correlation, which will compute the value of r for any two variables.

Correlation coefficient *Decimal value that indicates the strength and direction of a relationship, ranging from $+1.0$ (perfect positive correlation) to -1.0 (perfect negative correlation).*

FIGURE A-10 *(a)* Perfect positive correlation: $r = +1.0$. *(b)* Perfect negative correlation: $r = -1.0$.

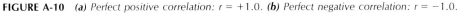

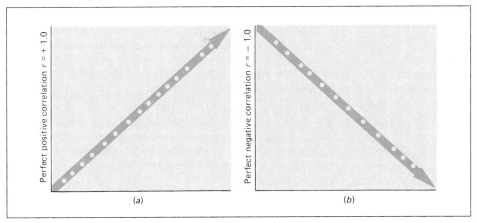

Statisticians and psychologists stress that correlation does not imply causation. For example, suppose that you found a perfect positive correlation between the number of librarians in several communities and the amount of alcohol consumed in those communities. Are the librarians alcoholics? Does reading books cause people to drink? Do alcoholics read more than others? Probably both of these variables are affected by another factor, the population of the community. The purpose of correlation is to determine the extent and direction of relationships rather than to identify causes.

INFERENTIAL STATISTICS

Often it would be either too expensive, too time-consuming, or totally impossible to measure an entire population. Inferential statistics allow researchers to predict and generalize from descriptive data they have collected and computed on just a small sample from the population. Whether standardizing an IQ test, assessing the popularity of a new product, or attempting to predict that an experiment can be replicated with the same results, psychologists must work with samples and rely on inferential statistics.

Sampling Methods

Several methods have been used to draw a sample from an entire population. You are undoubtedly familiar with the "man in the street" technique. A reporter stands at a specific location and asks a sample of three or four passersby for their opinions. This sampling technique is frequently seen on the evening news, but it has two serious defects. First, the sample size is usually extremely small, consisting of only a few people. Second, the sample is usually biased, being limited to a specific location rather than representing many geographic areas. For example, attitudes toward physical fitness may be quite different if the interviewer stands at a cocktail lounge as opposed to a health center. The "man in the street" technique is considered haphazard and is not an accepted sampling method for serious research.

A good sample should be representative of an entire population. As mentioned in Chapter 1, one appropriate sampling technique is the **random sample.** For a sample to be truly random, every member of the population must have the same chance of being selected for the sample. If you want to use a random sample of 200 students from a college population of 2000, it is acceptable to select every tenth name from a roster of college students. It would not be appropriate to select only first-year students or only students whose last names begin with A and B.

A sample becomes even more representative of an entire population when it is stratified. In a **stratified random sample,** the sample must represent in proportion the various relevant elements of the population. For example, suppose you were requested to select a stratified sample for a nationwide survey on the study habits of college students. If 54 percent of the population of all college students is male, then 54 percent of your sample should be male. You would also want to have proportionate representation on other relevant variables such as the student's major, year of study, grade average, and commitment to a career; and the size and geographic location of the college. As you can imagine, the choice of categories or strata to be represented is critical to the accuracy of a stratified random sample. Even in the most rigorous stratified sampling, there is always some degree of uncertainty. However, as the size of the sample increases, the level of uncertainty decreases.

Perhaps the most famous blunder in sampling occurred when Thomas Dewey was declared president of the United States by the media in a close election. When all the votes were counted, Harry Truman had a clear victory. Current political pollsters have developed more sophisticated techniques and prediction errors are now less likely.

Random sample *Sample in which each member of a population has an equal chance to be chosen for study.*

Stratified random sample *Sample that represents in proportion the various relevant elements of a population.*

Testing Research Hypotheses

Since psychological experiments cannot be performed on entire populations, sampling and inferential statistics are critical for testing hypotheses and doing research. All psychological experiments must begin with a ***null hypothesis,*** a statement that an independent variable will not affect a dependent variable. The null hypothesis describes conditions as they currently are believed to exist. For example, a null hypothesis might state that consuming vitamin pills will not affect scores on an intelligence test, or that increased ventilation will not affect tolerance of pain, or that attending ballets will not affect skiing skill. Until experimental evidence proves otherwise, we have no reason to believe that vitamin pills, ventilation, and ballet will cause these other specific changes in behavior.

> ***Null hypothesis*** *Statement that an independent variable will not affect a dependent variable.*

The null hypothesis is a statement that the researcher attempts to disprove or reject and usually takes the following form:

If . . . there is a change in the independent variable, *then* . . . this will not affect the dependent variable.

Suppose, for example, that psychologists wanted to determine whether financial motivation would affect scores on a final examination in psychology. They intend to offer students $10 for scores over 80 percent. The null hypothesis would then be stated:

If students are offered a reward of $10 for grades over 80 percent on a final exam, *then* this will not affect their scores on the final exam.

The psychologists would then attempt to disprove the null hypothesis with some degree of certainty.

As mentioned in Chapter 1, the psychologists would need to assign students to two groups: an ***experimental group*** that is offered the $10 reward and a ***control group*** that is not offered any reward. Students must be randomly assigned to the two groups; stratification would enhance the equality of the two groups.

> ***Experimental group*** *Subjects who receive the treatment of interest in an experiment.*
>
> ***Control group*** *Subjects who do not receive the treatment of interest in an experiment, who are then compared with the experimental group.*

In addition to the random assignment of subjects, the experimenters would need to control many other variables that might intervene. They must be certain that both groups use the same text, hear the same lectures, participate equally in controlled discussions, and meet at approximately the same time of day. Conditions on the day of the final exam must be identical for both groups. The only difference in the treatment of the two groups should be the independent variable, the offer of a $10 reward.

Suppose now that the results of the final exam have come in. The experimental group has an average score of 79, and the control group has an average score of 75. Is this difference meaningful or significant? Could this difference have occurred by chance? Would this difference hold for another group of students? To answer these questions, the experimenters must compare the means *and* standard deviations of the two groups. Consider the differences in the experimental and control groups illustrated in Figure A-11 (page 670). Clearly, the results with the smaller standard deviations show more noticeable differences.

How can we be sure that the difference in the two groups did not occur just by chance? It would clearly be unusual to find two groups with identical scores. Can we say that the difference here is really significant? For results to be statistically significant, we must be certain that the obtained difference was not just due to chance variations. In psychological experiments, we can reject the null hypothesis if the odds are 5 percent or less that the difference could occur by chance. Or, to state it another way, we can reject the null hypothesis if a difference of that size would not occur by chance 95 times out of 100.

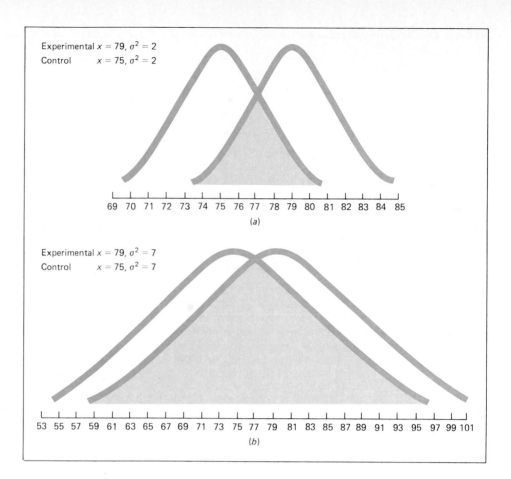

Experimental $x = 79$, $\sigma^2 = 2$
Control $x = 75$, $\sigma^2 = 2$

69 70 71 72 73 74 75 76 77 78 79 80 81 82 83 84 85
(a)

Experimental $x = 79$, $\sigma^2 = 7$
Control $x = 75$, $\sigma^2 = 7$

53 55 57 59 61 63 65 67 69 71 73 75 77 79 81 83 85 87 89 91 93 95 97 99 101
(b)

FIGURE A-11 *Comparison of experimental and control groups. Differences in means alone are not necessarily significant. In **a** and **b**, the mean difference is the same. However, **a**, which has less variability (a smaller value of σ), shows less overlap.*

t test Statistical test used to determine the significance of differences between two groups.

t Test Researchers use a **t test** to determine the significance of differences between experimental and control groups. The t test is a ratio of the means and standard deviations of the two groups. In Chapter 1 (Table 1-3, page 27), a hypothetical experiment was designed to determine whether computer-assisted instruction would affect scores on a final exam in introductory psychology. Students in the experimental group would receive computer-assisted training in addition to traditional instruction; students in the control group would receive only traditional instruction. At the end of the experiment, a t test would be used to compare the means and standard deviations of the scores of the two groups on the final examination. If there is a large difference in means and small variability, t will have increased value and be significant. If there is a small difference in means and large variability, t will have less value and will not be significant.

Analysis of variance Statistical test used to determine the significance of differences when there are more than two groups.

Analysis of Variance Suppose that some other researchers conduct a more complex experiment on motivation and scores on psychology tests. These experimenters study the effects of offering a $10 reward, a $25 reward, or a chance to win a microcomputer. In this case, the researchers would need four groups: three different "reward" groups and a control group. The t test is useful only for two groups, however. Therefore, a more complex procedure, an *F test* or **analysis of variance**, is required. The F test is named after an English statistician, R. A. Fisher, and uses ratios similar to the t test. As with the t test, an analysis of variance yields statements of significant differences among the groups. Since most experiments reported in journals employ more than two groups, analysis of variance is among the most common statistics used by psychologists.

SUMMARY

1 There are two branches of statistics. Descriptive statistics summarize data, and inferential statistics make generalizations and predictions from data.

2 Descriptive statistics can be summarized in table form on a frequency distribution or graphed on histograms and frequency polygons.

3 Central tendency is the most typical or representative score in a distribution. The three measures of central tendency are mode, median, and mean.

4 The mode is the score that occurs most frequently in a distribution.

5 The median is the midpoint or the score that ranks in the center of a distribution.

6 The mean of a distribution is the arithmetic average and is affected by extreme scores.

7 Variability is the spread or fluctuations within a distribution. The range is the simplest measure of variability and is computed by subtracting the lowest score from the highest score. The standard deviation is the best measure of variability, since it takes every score into account and can be used for additional statistical interpretation.

8 A normal distribution is a symmetrical bell-shaped curve where the mean, median, and mode are equal. Almost all scores fall within ± 3 standard deviation units of a normal curve.

9 Standard deviation units are called *z scores,* or *standard scores.* The *z* scores are used to compare scores on tests that have different means and standard deviations.

10 In a normal distribution, more than two-thirds of the scores are within ± 1 standard deviation of the mean.

11 When the mean, median, and mode fall in different places in a distribution, the distribution is skewed rather than normal.

12 Correlation is the study of the relationship between two variables and can be represented graphically in a scatterplot. A correlation coefficient is a decimal value that indicates the strength and direction of the relationship. Correlation coefficient values vary from $+1.0$ (perfect positive correlation) to -1.0 (perfect negative correlation). Values close to zero indicate there is no relationship between the variables.

13 Although correlation can indicate the strength of relationships, it does not imply causation.

14 The two main techniques used in inferential statistics are sampling and hypothesis testing.

15 A good sample should be representative of an entire population. In a random sample, every member of the population should have an opportunity to be chosen. In a stratified sample, relevant elements in the populations are represented in appropriate proportions.

16 Psychological experiments begin with a null hypothesis, a statement of conditions as they currently exist. The purpose of the experiment is to reject or disprove the null hypothesis.

17 When differences occur between the experimental and control groups, researchers must use a statistical test to be certain that the difference is significant and did not occur just by chance. If there are two groups in the experiment (one experimental group and one control group), a *t* test is used to measure the significance of the difference. If more than two groups are involved in the experiment, an *F* ratio test, or analysis of variance, must be used.

KEY TERMS

Analysis of variance (page 670)
Central tendency (660)
Control group (669)
Correlation (666)
Correlation coefficient (667)
Descriptive statistics (658)
Experimental group (669)
Frequency distribution (658)
Histogram (658)
Inferential statistics (658)
Mean (661)
Median (660)
Mode (660)
Normal distribution (663)
Null hypothesis (669)
Random sample (668)
Range (662)
Scatterplot (666)
Skewed distribution (666)
Standard deviation (662)
Standard score (664)
Statistics (658)
Stratified random sample (668)
t test (670)
Variability (662)
Variance (662)

SUGGESTED READINGS

HUCK, S. W., CORMIER, W. H., & BOUNDS, W. G., JR. (1974). *Reading statistics and research.* New York: Harper & Row. Focuses on the interpretation of statistics as used in research studies.

HUCK, S. W., & SANDLER, H. M. (1979). *Rival hypotheses: Alternative interpretations of data based conclusions.* New York: Harper & Row. Cleverly presents a number of well-known hypotheses of general interest and suggests alternative conclusions from possible data.

KIMBLE, G. (1978). *How to use (and misuse) statistics.* Englewood Cliffs, NJ: Prentice-Hall. Helps you to recognize how statistics can be used to intentionally distort data.

YOUNG, R. K., & VELDMAN, D. J. (1981). *Statistics for the behavioral sciences* (4th ed.). New York: Holt, Rinehart & Winston. Provides more extensive coverage of the topics in this appendix along with specific applications of inferential statistics in the behavioral sciences.

GLOSSARY

abnormal psychology Scientific study of the causes of emotional and behavioral disorders. (17, 482)

absolute threshold Lowest intensity at which a stimulus can be perceived. (77)

accommodation Process by which the lens changes shape to focus images at different distances onto the retina. (81)

acetylcholine Neurotransmitter that has been implicated in Alzheimer's disease. (50)

action potential (AP) "Firing" of a neuron, or the sending of a nerve impulse down its axon, from one end of the neuron to the other. (45)

activity theory Theory of aging which holds that in order to age successfully a person must remain as active as possible. (370)

acupuncture Ancient Chinese technique in which thin needles are inserted into the body at a number of carefully charted locations in order to block pain. (96)

adaptation Decrease in the response of the sensory system to continued stimulation. (78)

affective disorders Mental disturbances characterized by disorders of mood. (501)

aggression Any behavior intended

to hurt or destroy someone or something. (392)

agoraphobia Most severe phobia, for which people most commonly seek treatment; manifested as inability to go out of the house, be in large unfamiliar places, drive, or travel by public conveyance. (496)

alcohol Central-nervous-system depressant that causes blood pressure to drop and heart rate to increase. (149)

algorithm Problem-solving strategy in which every possible answer is exhausted until the correct solution (if one exists) is arrived at. (287)

alleles Alternative forms of a gene. When alleles are identical, a person is homozygous for a trait; when alleles are dissimilar, the person is heterozygous. (308)

altered state of consciousness (ASC) Any qualitative change in consciousness from the normal waking state. (119)

altruism Behavior carried out to benefit another, without anticipation of rewards from external sources. (608)

Alzheimer's disease Irreversible dementia characterized by memory loss, confusion, and other intellectual and personality deterioration. (47, 366)

amnesia General term for a variety of memory disorders that arise from different causes and affect memory

in different ways. (215, 500)

amphetamines Specific class of drugs that stimulate the central nervous system. (145)

anal stage According to Freudian theory, the psychosexual stage of toddlerhood (12–18 to 36 months), in which the child receives pleasure through anal stimulation; toilet training is the major situation in which gratification occurs. (458)

analysis of variance Statistical test used to determine the significance of differences when there are more than two groups. (670)

analytic introspection Technique developed by Wundt that uses self-observation to analyze the mind or break it down into its component elements. (10)

androgens Male sex hormones. (424)

androgynous Personality type integrating both typically "masculine" and typically "feminine" characteristics. (427)

anima Feminine archetype in man. (461)

animus Masculine archetype in woman. (461)

anorexia nervosa Eating disorder characterized by prolonged refusal to eat, leading to extreme weight loss (at least 15 percent under normal weight). (579)

anterograde amnesia Memory loss

that is characterized by the inability to create new permanent memories. (219)

antisocial personality Personality disorder characterized by behaviors that violate the rights of others. (511)

anxiety State of apprehension, fearful uncertainty, or dread caused by anticipated threat. (495)

anxiety disorders Psychological disturbances, affecting about 8.3 percent of the adult population of the United States, including phobic disorders, panic disorders, and generalized anxiety disorders. (495)

aphasia Language disturbance that often occurs following damage to the left hemisphere due to stroke or injury. (65)

applied research Research that addresses immediate ''practical'' problems. (23)

applied social psychologists Social psychologists particularly concerned with solving practical problems related to people in groups. (19)

archetypes According to Jungian theory, the symbols or common themes that are found through the generations and in all parts of the world. (461)

arousal Physiological state which we experience as an ability to process information, to react to an emergency, and to experience a wide range of emotions. (400)

artificial intelligence (AI) Branch of research that programs computers to solve problems by making them ''think'' the way human beings do. (289)

ascending reticular activation system Part of the reticular formation responsible for the waking process. (56)

associational rehearsal Process of encoding information in memory by making connections between new material and material already there. (200)

association cortex Area of the brain that receives input from many sensory and motor systems but does not have specific sensory or motor functions; it is free for such activities as language, thought, and memory. (59)

associative learning Kind of learning in which an association is formed between two events. Two types of associative learning are classical conditioning and operant conditioning. (160)

asymmetry of the brain Concept that there are differences in size, organization, and function between structures of the left hemisphere and right hemisphere of the brain. (63)

attachment Active, affectionate, reciprocal relationship specifically between two people; their interaction reinforces and strengthens the attachment, or bond. Often refers to infant's relationship with parents. (327)

attention State of focused mental activity. (103)

attitude Learned, relatively permanent way of responding to someone or something, which has cognitive, emotional, and behavioral components. (615)

attribution theory Theory about how people make judgments about the causes of behavior. (636)

auditory meatus Ear canal. (91)

authoritarian personality Rigid, conventional, prejudice-prone person who thinks in stereotypes, is emotionally cold, identifies with power, and is intolerant of weakness. (624)

autonomic arousal Heightened activity of a number of physiological responses such as heart rate and respiration. The increased action is controlled by the autonomic nervous system. (401)

autonomic nervous system Part of the peripheral nervous system that controls involuntary functions; consists of the parasympathetic and sympathetic divisions. (53)

autonomy versus shame According to Erikson, the second crisis of psychosocial development. Between 12–18 months and 3 years, the child develops a balance of autonomy (independence, self-determination) and shame. (323)

autosomal dominant inheritance Pattern of inheritance in which a specific gene is dominant; if it is inherited, it manifests itself in the person. (308)

autosomal recessive inheritance Pattern of inheritance in which a trait appears only if a person inherits two genes for it, one from each parent. If the person inherits only one gene for the trait, it will not appear in the person but may be passed on to his or her children. (308)

aversive stimulus Stimulus that the subject does not like; a type of punishment. (177)

aversive therapy Behavior-therapy technique which combines an unpleasant situation with a behavior that a client wants to get rid of. (535)

axon Tail-like fiber extension of a neuron, which carries nerve impulses to other neurons. (44)

axon hillock Swelling near the connection between an axon and the cell body. (45)

axon terminal Far end of the axon. (45)

basal ganglia Collection of cell bodies near the thalamus; the structures it comprises seem to be important in controlling movement. (58)

basic research ''Pure'' research that focuses on looking for answers which increase the total fund of human knowledge. (23)

basic trust versus basic mistrust According to Erikson, the first crisis of psychosocial development. From birth to 12–18 months, an infant develops a sense of whether or not the world can be trusted; the feeding situation and the quality of the mother-infant interaction are important determinants of the outcome of this stage. (323)

basilar membrane Tissue inside the cochlea that moves at the same rate as the vibrations of the sound wave. (91)

behavioral model Explanation of mental disorders as abnormal ways of thinking and acting that are learned, largely through conditioning and modeling. (486)

behaviorism School of psychology that emphasizes the study of observable behaviors and events and the role of the environment in causing behavior. (14, 466)

behavior therapy Psychotherapeutic approach that uses experimentally established learning principles to overcome maladaptive habits. (527)

binocular cues Cues in depth perception that depend on both eyes. (107)

binocular disparity Cue in depth perception that is based on each eye's having a different view of the world. (107)

biofeedback Technique that gives people information about their internal processes (like blood pressure and heart rate) so that they can learn to exert control over those processes. (183)

biological motion Patterns of movement of living organisms. (112)

biomedical model Model according to which illness is purely a result of biological factors, and psychological and social influences are ignored. (562)

biopsychosocial model Model according to which biological, psychological, and social factors interact to affect health and illness. (562)

bipolar disorder Mental disorder characterized by one or more manic episodes which generally alternate with episodes of depression. (502)

borderline personality Personality disorder characterized by instability in several areas, including mood, self-image, and relationships. (511)

bottom-up processing Explanation of pattern recognition that emphasizes the contribution of the stimulus. (102)

brain stem Part of the brain that contains the medulla, pons, and midbrain; is responsible for many basic functions. (56)

brief therapy Time-limited psychotherapy, generally lasting for no more than 15 to 20 sessions, which tends to focus on one or two symptoms or problems. (540)

bulimia Eating disorder characterized by episodes of "binge" eating (ingestion of huge quantities of food), which are followed by purging (vomiting or use of laxatives). (580)

caffeine Stimulant that raises heart and breathing rates and blood pressure. (144)

cancer Group of diseases characterized by abnormal cell growth and proliferation. (589)

cardinal trait According to Allport, a characteristic that is dominant and therefore colors virtually every aspect of a person's behavior and attributes. (468)

case history; case study Research method in which intensive information is collected about one individual or very few individuals. (24)

castration complex Phenomenon described by Freud in which the male child, seeing that girls do not have penises, becomes fearful of his own castration by an angry father. (458)

central nervous system (CNS) Brain and spinal cord. (51)

central tendency Most typical or representative score in a distribution. (660)

central traits According to Allport, the few characteristic tendencies needed to describe an individual. (468)

cephalocaudal principle Principle that development proceeds in a head-to-toe direction; upper parts of the body develop before lower parts. (315)

cerebellum Part of the brain connected to the back of the brain stem, involved primarily in the coordination of motor activity. (56)

cerebral cortex Gray matter that surrounds most of the brain, involved in most higher-level functions, such as thinking, remembering, and problem solving. (58)

cerebrum Most highly developed part of the brain; it is multifunctional and contains the hypothalamus, thalamus, basal ganglia, limbic system, and cortex; the forebrain. (57)

chimeric stimuli Stimuli that are not encountered in everyday life. (67)

cholesterol Fatty substance whose level in the blood is related to dietary intake of fats. High levels are associated with increased incidence of heart disease. (577)

chromosomes Tiny rod-shaped particles that carry genes, the transmitters of inheritance. In the normal person, there are 46 chromosomes in each cell. (308, 419)

chunking Technique for expanding the capacity of short-term memory by grouping items together in the mind. (196)

circadian rhythms Biological patterns in body functions that occur every 25 hours. (126)

classical (Pavlovian) conditioning Kind of learning in which a previously neutral stimulus (conditioned stimulus) acquires the power to elicit a response (conditioned response) after repeated pairing with an unconditioned stimulus that ordinarily elicits a particular response (unconditioned response). (160)

climacteric Medical term for menopause and the changes that occur at this time in a woman's life. (355)

clinical psychologists Psychologists who diagnose and treat emotional and behavioral disorders. (17)

close relationship Association in which people influence each other, are dependent on each other, are capable of arousing strong emotion in each other, and usually engage in various types of activities together over a long period of time. (633)

clustering Technique for organizing material to be remembered into categories. (201)

cocaine Stimulant made from the leaves of the South American shrub *Erythroxylon coca*. (145)

cochlea Coiled, fluid-filled structure; the inner ear. (91)

cognitive-behavioral theory of hypnosis View that attaining the hypnotic state depends on the subject's readiness to "think with" and imagine themes suggested by the hypnotist rather than on any trance-induction technique. (141)

cognitive-behavioral therapies Therapeutic techniques that identify distortions in thinking, show clients how such distortions contribute to their distress, and help them substitute more accurate appraisals and interpretations of reality. (536)

cognitive-consistency theories Theories which maintain that incompatibility between thoughts and actions can cause discomfort, which people then try to reduce. (617)

cognitive development Changes in thought processes, which affect learning, language abilities, and memory. (302)

cognitive dissonance State of psychological discomfort that occurs when there is a basic incompatibility between thoughts and actions, or between two or more sets of ideas, attitudes, or opinions that a person holds. (618)

cognitive learning View of learning that considers underlying thought processes involved in learning. (160)

cognitive maps Term developed by Tolman to describe the process of constructing a mental map of the environment by using the information gained by senses and kinetic clues about direction and distance. (18)

cognitive psychology Psychological school concerned with the way the mind processes information. (15, 269)

collective unconscious According to Jungian theory, a component of the mind derived from ancestral memories. (461)

comparison level Minimum benefit a person requires from a relationship. (644)

comparison level for alternatives Attractiveness of other possible ties, or of no relationship, compared with an existing relationship. (644)

compulsions Repetitive, irrational behaviors that a person feels obligated to carry out even though he or she cannot see any point to them. (496)

concordant Alike in a certain characteristic. (498)

conditioned response (CR) Response that comes to be elicited by a conditioned stimulus which has been repeatedly paired with an unconditioned stimulus. (162)

conditioned stimulus (CS) Initially neutral stimulus which, after re-peated pairings with an unconditioned stimulus, comes to elicit a conditioned response. (162)

conductive deafness Hearing loss, caused by a ruptured eardrum or a defect in the bones of the middle ear, where sound waves are prevented from reaching the cochlea. (94)

cones Receptors on the retina responsible for seeing color and small details. (81)

conformity Change in opinion, behavior, or both in response to real or imagined pressure from others. (602)

congruence According to Carl Rogers, a situation in which the person we would *like* to be (our ideal self) and the person we see ourself as (our real self) are similar. (465)

conscience According to Freudian theory, an aspect of the superego that represents "should-nots," for which we have been punished and now punish ourselves through guilt. (455)

consciousness Our awareness of ourselves and the world around us. (119)

conservation Piaget's term for the awareness that two stimuli that are equal (in length, weight, or amount, for example) remain equal despite perceptual alteration, so long as nothing has been added to or taken away from either stimulus. (319)

consolidation Shift of a fragile memory trace to a permanent change in physical structure; this shift represents the two phases of memory, short-term and long-term. (216)

content validity Degree to which a test covers a representative sample of the material under consideration. (239)

continuous reinforcement Pattern of reinforcement by which the organism is reinforced every time that it emits the desired response. (170)

control group Subjects who are not exposed to the independent variable; their performance is compared with that of the experimental group. (26, 669)

conversion disorder Type of somatoform disorder in which a person may become paralyzed, lose the sense of smell or pain, suffer seizures, or experience false pregnancy. (499)

coping Constantly changing effort to manage the demands that tax personal resources. (571)

cornea Transparent protective tissue at the front of the eye. (80)

coronary heart disease (CHD) Narrowing and blockage of the coronary arteries that may lead to a heart attack. (588)

corpus callosum Massive bundle of axons that enables the two hemispheres of the brain to communicate with each other. (63)

correlation Measure of the relationship (association) between variables. (23, 666)

correlation coefficient Decimal value that indicates the strength and direction of a relationship, ranging from +1.0 (perfect positive correlation) to −1.0 (perfect negative correlation). (24, 667)

cost-benefit analysis Explanation for altruistic behavior which maintains that people help others when the reward is greater than the cost. (611)

counseling psychologists Psychologists who administer and interpret psychological tests, interview and observe clients, and help resolve clients' problems. (17)

countertransference Psychoanalytic term for a therapist's feelings for a patient, who can awaken elements from the therapist's own emotional history. (529)

couples therapy Therapeutic technique that helps two people improve their relationship by focusing on interpersonal issues and communication problems. (539)

creativity Ability to see things in a new and unusual light and to come up with unusual solutions to problems. (290)

criterion-related validity Measure of the relationship between test performance and some independent outcome (criterion). (239)

critical period (1) Specific time during development when an animal or person needs to have appropriate experiences to bring about normal adult functioning. (2) Specific "sensitive time" during development when an event has its greatest impact. (112, 277)

cross-sectional method Data-collection technique in which subjects of different ages are measured on one occasion, providing information about age differences in behavior. (303)

cross-sequential method Data-collection technique which combines longitudinal and cross-sectional strategies. (303)

crystallized intelligence Ability to use information that has been learned; this kind of intelligence is influenced by culture and education. Compare with *fluid intelligence.* (233, 356)

cue-dependent forgetting Inability to remember information because appropriate retrieval cues are lacking. (214)

data Information collected through research. (20)

decibels (dB) Measurement of the loudness or intensity (amplitude) of sound waves. (90)

declarative memory Knowledge about facts. (199)

deductive reasoning Logical process in which the conclusion is certain if the information given is true. (289)

defense mechanisms According to Freudian theory, an unconscious way to combat anxiety through the distortion of reality. (See *displacement, sublimation, repression, regression, projection, reaction formation,* and *rationalization.*) (455)

deinstitutionalization Movement, begun in the 1950s, to shift the chronically mentally ill from hospital to community care. (548)

dementia Mental deterioration caused by organic brain disease; characteristic of about 10 percent of people over 65 years of age. (366)

dendrites Narrow, branching extensions of a neuron's cell body that receive incoming signals from other neurons. (44)

dependent variable Factor which

may or may not change as a result of the experimental manipulation of an independent variable. (26)

depersonalization disorder Dissociative disorder in which a person temporarily loses or changes the sense of his or her reality. (501)

depression Psychological disturbance characterized by sadness and difficulties in eating, sleeping, and concentrating. (502)

depth perception Ability to judge how far away an object is. (106)

description Information about what is actually occurring. (5)

descriptive statistics Statistical methods used to summarize data. (658)

detoxification Treatment to restore physiological functioning that has been seriously affected by abuse of alcohol or other drugs. (587)

developmental psychologists Psychologists who describe, explain, predict, and modify changes in behavior throughout the life span. (19, 302)

dichotic listening (shadowing technique) Technique in which one message is presented to one ear and another to the other ear. (104)

difference threshold Smallest difference in intensity between two stimuli that can be detected (also known as *jnd,* or *just noticeable difference*). (78)

discrimination (1) Learning to respond differently to two similar (but not identical) stimuli. (2) Behavior aimed at a person against whom one is prejudiced. (162, 623)

disengagement theory Theory of aging which holds that successful aging is characterized by mutual withdrawal between society and the elderly person. (370)

displacement Freudian defense mechanism in which a person gratifies an urge indirectly, by substituting a safer or more available object, person, or activity. (455)

dissociative disorder Mental disturbance involving a sudden temporary alteration in consciousness, identity, or motor behavior. (500)

divided attention Concentration on more than one activity at the same

time, often with a reduction in performance. (103)

double-blind technique Procedure in which neither subject nor experimenter knows who is in the experimental group and who is in the control group. (29)

Down's syndrome Chromosomal disorder caused by an extra chromosome 21 (or sometimes by the attachment of chromosome 21 to another chromosome), resulting in mental retardation and often heart defects and other physical abnormalities; the most common chromosomal disorder. (262)

drive Force inside an organism that motivates behavior. (385)

drug Chemical substance that produces physical, emotional, or behavioral changes in the user. (143)

drug abuse Nonmedicinal use of a drug that results in physical, mental, emotional, or social impairment. (143)

DSM III Third edition of *Diagnostic and Statistical Manual of Mental Disorders,* a guidebook to diagnosis, published by the American Psychiatric Association. (491)

dynamic therapy Psychotherapeutic approach that emphasizes the need for insight into thoughts, feelings, and past life as a way to bring about changes in personality. (527)

dyspareunia Painful intercourse, most common in women. (442)

dysthymic disorder Chronic mild depression. (502)

echoic memory Auditory sensory memory. (195)

ecological theory Theory that the relationships between different objects in a scene give us information about their sizes. (104)

educational psychologists Psychologists who do research on the learning process. (18)

ego According to Freudian theory, the aspect of personality generally known as common sense; operates on the reality principle to mediate between the id and the superego. (455)

ego-analytic therapy Modification of psychoanalysis that focuses on the ego rather than the id by em-

phasizing patients' ability to control their own lives. (529)

ego-ideal In Freudian theory, an aspect of the superego that represents the "shoulds," for which we have received approval, to which we aspire, and of which we feel proud. (455)

ego integrity versus despair According to Erikson, the eighth and last crisis of psychosocial development. The elderly person achieves a sense of acceptance of his or her life allowing the acceptance of death; the developmental alternative is despair, characterized by failure to accept one's life and, thus, one's ultimate end. (368)

egocentrism Inability to consider another's point of view; a characteristic of preoperational thought. (319)

Electra complex According to Freudian theory, the female counterpart of the Oedipus complex, in which the little girl in the phallic stage feels sexual attraction for her father and rivalry toward her mother. (459)

electroconvulsive therapy (ECT) Application of an electric current through the brain to produce a convulsion; often effective in treating severe depression. (542)

electroencephalograph Instrument that measures brain-wave activity. (122)

electromyograph Instrument that measures muscle movement. (123)

electrooculograph Instrument that measures eye movements. (123)

embryonic stage Second stage of pregnancy (2 to 8–12 weeks), characterized by rapid growth and development of major body systems and organs. (310)

emotion General term for a person's subjective reaction to the environment. Emotions involve neural and hormonal responses. When activated, emotions elicit an adaptive reaction that the individual experiences as pleasant or unpleasant. (383)

empty nest Transitional phase of parenting following children's leaving the parental home. (363)

encoding Process of getting information ready for storage in the memory system by classifying it in some way. (193)

endocrine system Network of glands that secrete hormones into the bloodstream. (68)

endorphins Opiatelike substances released by the brain which prevent pain signals from reaching the brain. (95)

engineering psychologists Psychologists concerned with designing, evaluating, and adapting machines to meet human needs. (20)

engram Memory trace. (209)

enkephalin Endorphin that is a powerful painkiller. (95)

environmental therapy Treatment that focuses on changing a person's environment in some way; social treatment. (527)

episodic memory Type of declarative memory that involves memory about our own experiences; also called *autobiographical memory*. (199)

equity theory Theory that people are most comfortable in relationships in which there is a fair distribution of rewards and costs and that they will try to restore equity (balance) in relationships perceived as unbalanced. (645)

erogenous zones Sexually sensitive areas of the body. (430, 458)

eros In Freudian theory, life instincts. (454)

erotica Materials designed to arouse sexual desire. (443)

estrogen Female sex hormone. (433)

ethologist Scientist who studies behavior in its natural environment. (384)

exchange theory Theory that people consider rewards and costs, as well as alternatives, in determining whether to enter a new relationship or stay in an existing relationship. (644)

experimental group Group of subjects exposed to the independent variable, the treatment of interest in an experiment. (26, 669)

experimental psychologists Psychologists who study basic psychological processes in animals and humans. (18)

experimenter bias Influence on experimental results caused by the experimenter's expectations. (29)

explanation Information about why events occur. (5)

extinction Gradual weakening of and failure to perform a learned (conditioned) response. (162)

factor analysis Statistical technique used by Cattell to determine the factors underlying scores on a larger group of measures. (468)

familial retardation Retardation for which no physical cause can be found; it is generally less severe than organic retardation and probably involves an interaction between genetic and environmental factors. (263)

family, or systems, model Explanation of mental disorders as arising from an entire family setting, with its own patterns of functioning, rather than from one person. (487)

family resemblance Degree to which members of a category share features in common. (283)

family therapy Form of group therapy that changes maladaptive behaviors by changing family roles and communication patterns. (538)

fetal alcohol syndrome Mental, motor, and growth retardation in a child caused by the mother's abuse of alcohol during pregnancy. (312, 583)

fetal stage Final stage of pregnancy (8–12 weeks to birth), characterized by rapid growth and continued development. (311)

fixation According to Freudian theory, an arrest in development which results when the conflicts of a particular stage are not appropriately resolved. (458)

fixed-interval schedule Pattern of reinforcement under which the organism is regularly rewarded according to a fixed time period. (171)

fixed-ratio schedule Pattern of reinforcement in which the organism is reinforced after making a specified number of responses. (171)

flashbulb memory Vivid recollections of what one was doing when one heard about a significant event. (206)

fluid intelligence Ability to solve novel problems; this kind of intelligence is influenced by neurological development. Compare with *crystallized intelligence*. (233, 356)

formal operations According to Piaget, the final stage of cognitive development, characterized by the ability to think abstractly. (345)

fovea Region of the retina specialized for detail vision. (83)

free association Psychoanalytic technique in which the patient says whatever comes to mind, without censoring anything. (528)

frequency distribution List of observations and how frequently each occurs. (658)

frequency theory Theory that the frequency by which the basilar membrane is stimulated determines what pitch is heard. (92)

functional fixedness Overreliance on traditional ways of solving problems, which inhibits novel solutions. (286)

functionalism School of psychology, represented by James and Dewey, concerned with what the mind does rather than its elements or structure. (12)

fundamental attribution error Tendency to underestimate the importance of situational influences and to overestimate the importance of dispositional influences (personality factors) in explaining behavior, especially the behavior of others. (637)

ganglion cells Cells in the eyes that carry all visual information to the brain. (81)

gender identity Awareness, developed in early childhood, that one is male or female. (419)

gender identity disorder Psychosexual disorder in which a person feels uncomfortable with his or her sex and behaves in ways that are generally associated with the other sex. (429)

gender identity disorder of childhood Disorder in which a young child develops a profound disturbance of the normal sense of maleness or femaleness. (429)

gender roles Behaviors, attitudes, and interests that a culture says are appropriate for males and females. (419)

gender stereotypes Generalizations

about masculine and feminine attitudes and behavior. (419)

general adaptation syndrome (GAS) Three-phase reaction to stress, described by Selye, consisting of alarm, resistance, and exhaustion. (563)

generalized anxiety disorder Mental disorder characterized by feelings of anxiety that cannot be ascribed to any particular event or situation. (498)

generativity versus stagnation According to Erikson, the seventh crisis of psychosocial development, characterizing midlife. The mature adult is concerned with establishing and guiding the next generation or else feels stagnation (personal impoverishment). (358)

genes Transmitters of inheritance, carried on the chromosomes. (308, 419)

genital stage Freudian term for the psychosexual stage of mature adult sexuality, which begins during adolescence. (459)

genotype Genetic composition of a person; the genotype may differ from the phenotype because of the possession of recessive genes. (308)

germinal stage First stage of pregnancy (fertilization to 2 weeks), characterized by rapid cell division and increasing complexity of the organism. (310)

gestalt laws Principles, described by gestalt psychologists, that govern the ways by which the perceptual system organizes sensory information. (100)

gestalt psychology School of psychology that emphasizes the pattern formed by the elements in the mind rather than the individual elements themselves. These elements form a whole that is greater than the sum of its parts. (12, 100)

gestalt therapy Humanistic psychotherapeutic approach, developed by Perls, which helps clients become more aware of the whole self. (532)

glial cells Cells that support and protect neurons. (44)

grammar Rules of sound, meaning, and syntax in a language. (270)

group therapy Therapeutic tech-

nique in which two or more clients are seen together rather than individually. (537)

groupthink Uncritical acceptance of an unwise course of action by members of a close-knit group in order to preserve unanimity. (604)

habituation Simple type of learning in which an organism stops responding to something that it has grown used to. (160, 248, 314)

hallucinogens Psychedelic drugs, such as LSD and PCP, that alter perception, thoughts, and emotions and produce hallucinations. (147)

hardiness Personality style characterized by commitment, challenge, and control. (572)

health psychologists Psychologists who focus on the role of psychology in helping people to use psychological research to adopt health-promoting lifestyles, to prevent and recover from illness, to deal with stress, and to use and expand health care systems. (19, 562)

health psychology Scientific study of psychological factors that promote health, influence illness, and affect recovery from illness. (562)

hemispheric lateralization Condition in which two structures of the brain, one in the left hemisphere and one in the right, look alike yet perform separate functions. (63)

heritability Proportion of variance in a trait that is due to genes; it applies to differences within a group rather than between groups. (254)

heroin Addictive narcotic. (150)

heterosexuals People who are sexually attracted to persons of the other sex. (440)

heterozygous Possessing two dissimilar alleles for a trait. (308)

heuristic Problem-solving strategy consisting of a rule of thumb for finding a solution. It may lead to a solution more quickly than an algorithm can; but it will not necessarily lead to a solution at all. (287)

hippocampus Brain structure important in memory. (216)

histogram Bar graph. (658)

holophrases First spoken words; they express a complete thought in a single word. (272)

homeostasis Equilibrium (balance) of vital functions maintained by coordinated adjustments of the autonomic nervous system. (55)

homosexuals People who are sexually attracted to persons of the same sex. (440)

homozygous Possessing two identical alleles for a trait. (308)

hormones Chemicals that can influence the rate or the direction of activity in distant target organs by speeding up or inhibiting the growth of cells in those organs. (68)

humanistic model Explanation of mental disorders as a result of failure to achieve self-actualization (self-fulfillment). (488)

humanistic psychology Optimistic view of personality that emphasizes healthy human behavior and the ability to exert considerable control over one's life; considered the "third force" in psychology. (15, 464)

humanistic therapy Psychotherapeutic approach that aims to help clients grow by removing constraints upon their self-fulfillment. (527)

hypnosis Procedure which produces a state of heightened suggestibility or susceptibility to outside influence. (96, 139)

hypothalamus Small organ in the brain that plays a vital role in mediating between the brain and the endocrine system. (57)

hypothesis Prediction about the results of research. (20)

iconic memory Visual sensory memory. (195)

id According to Freudian theory, the aspect of personality that is present at birth; the id operates on the pleasure principle and is characterized by the desire for immediate gratification. (454)

identification Process by which a person acquires certain characteristics, beliefs, attitudes, values, and behaviors of another person or group; one of the most important personality developments of early childhood. (335)

identity versus role confusion According to Erikson, the fifth crisis of psychosocial development, in which an adolescent must determine his or her own sense of self or suffer from identity confusion. (347)

ill-defined concept Concept for which the features and rules that connect members of a category are not obvious. (282)

illusions False perceptions. (111)

imaginary audience "Observer" who exists only in the mind of an adolescent who is as concerned with the adolescent's thoughts and behaviors as the adolescent is. (345)

incentives External, learned goals that motivate behavior. (387)

incus Tiny bone in the ear; the "anvil." (91)

independent variable Factor which is manipulated by the experimenter. (26)

inductive reasoning Logical process in which the conclusion drawn is probably correct. (289)

industrial and organizational psychologists Psychologists concerned with working people and the workplace. (20)

industry versus inferiority According to Erikson, the fourth crisis of psychosocial development, which occurs during middle childhood. Children must learn the skills of their culture or feel inferior. (324)

infantile sexuality Freud's concept that the human sexual drive does not appear full-blown at puberty but is present from birth, even though the sexual feelings of infants and young children are different in form from those of adolescents and adults. (458)

inferential statistics Statistical methods which use data from a sample to generalize and predict results in a larger population. (658)

inferiority complex According to Adler, the basis for the drive to achieve, to complete oneself, and to overcome feelings of inadequacy. (462)

inhibited female orgasm Situation in which a woman can become sexually aroused but is unable to reach orgasm. (442)

inhibited male orgasm In the male, inability to ejaculate. (442)

inhibited sexual desire (ISD) Persistent lack of sexual interest that is of concern to a person. (441)

inhibited sexual excitement A man's partial or complete failure to attain or keep an erection, or a woman's partial or complete failure to attain or keep vaginal lubrication and swelling. (442)

initiative versus guilt According to Erikson, the third crisis of psychosocial development, which characterizes children from about 3 to 6 years. Children develop initiative when they try out new things and are not overwhelmed by failure. (324)

insight Sudden, creative solution to a problem. (285)

insomnia Difficulty getting to sleep, staying asleep, or both. (135)

instincts Inborn, species-specific, relatively complex patterns of behavior which are biologically determined and which are usually important for species survival. (159, 384)

intelligence Constantly active interaction between inherited ability and environmental experience, which results in an individual's being able to acquire, remember, and use knowledge; to understand both concrete and abstract concepts; to understand relationships among objects, events, and ideas; and to apply and use all the above in a purposeful way to solve problems in everyday life. (229)

intelligence quotient (IQ) Mathematical score computed by dividing a person's mental age (MA) by his or her chronological age (CA) and then multiplying by 100: IQ = (MA/CA) × 100. (237)

interneurons Intermediary neurons that send messages from one kind of neuron to another. (43)

interpersonal attraction Tendency to evaluate another person in a positive way. (633)

interstimulus interval Time interval between presentation of the neutral stimulus and the unconditioned stimulus. (162)

interval schedule of reinforcement Partial-reinforcement schedule that requires a certain amount of time to pass between the presentations of reinforcement. (171)

intimacy versus isolation According to Erikson, the sixth crisis of psychosocial development, in which the young adult seeks to find a balance between making commitments to others and maintaining his or her own individuality. (358)

iris Pigmented set of muscles surrounding the pupil. (80)

jnd Difference threshold (just noticeable difference). (78)

language Means of communicating through spoken sounds that express specific meanings and are arranged according to rules. (270)

language acquisition device (LAD) Inborn ability to analyze language to extract grammatical rules. (275)

latency stage According to Freudian theory, a period of relative sexual calm during middle childhood (6 years to puberty) that occurs after the Oedipus or Electra complex is resolved. (459)

latent learning Learning that occurs but is not displayed until the organism is motivated to display it. (180)

law of effect Thorndike's principle that when an animal's actions are accompanied or closely followed by a satisfying experience, the animal will connect the two and will be likely to perform the same actions in a similar situation. (168)

law of exercise Thorndike's principle that the connection between a stimulus and a response is strengthened by repetition. (168)

learned helplessness Conviction that one's actions make no difference, which occurs when an organism learns that it cannot control important events in the environment. (186)

learning Relatively permanent change in behavior, which reflects knowledge, understanding, or skill achieved through experience (which may include study, instruction, observation, or practice). (159)

learning theorists Theorists who believe that the environment is most influential in learning language. (274)

lens Disk-shaped elastic structure in the eye that focuses light into a clear image. (81)

levels-of-processing model of memory Memory model of Craik and Lockhart, which holds that the ability to remember is dependent on how deeply we process information. (202)

libido In Freudian theory, sexual energy. (454)

life structure According to Levinson, the basic pattern of a person's life, consisting of both internal and external aspects. (359)

light therapy Treatment for seasonal affective disorder in which the depressed person is exposed to special fluorescent lights for several hours before dawn and after dusk. (545)

Likert scale Measure of attitudes in which a subject responds to a series of statements on a continuum from "strongly agree" to "strongly disagree." (616)

limbic system Part of cerebrum that mediates emotional responses and is involved in memory; it includes the septal area, the hippocampus, the amygdala, and parts of the thalamus. (58)

linguistic-relativity hypothesis Whorf's view that language affects perception and thought; also known as the *Whorfian hypothesis.* (278)

linguistics Study of language. (270)

locus of control Concept that explains events according to whether they result from efforts under one's control (internal) or from outside factors over which one has no control (external). (387)

loneliness Unpleasant and distressing feeling that results from deficiencies in social relationships. (647)

longitudinal method Data-collection technique in which the same people are measured more than once to see behavioral changes over time. (303)

long-term memory (LTM) Type of memory that seems to have unlimited capacity and may store information permanently. (194)

LSD (d-lysergic acid diethylamide) Synthesized drug with psychoactive properties. (148)

malleus Tiny bone in the ear; the "hammer." (91)

mania Aspect of bipolar disorder characterized by extreme elation, irrational behavior, and grandiose thinking. (502)

mantra Specific word or thought used repetitiously by someone practicing transcendental meditation. (138)

marijuana Derivative of the plant *Cannabis sativa,* which contains the mind-altering component delta-9-tetrahydrocannabinol, or THC. (147)

maturation Unfolding of biologically determined patterns of behavior, programmed by the genes. (159, 316)

mean Often called the "average," this is an arithmetic average, arrived at by adding up all the scores in a distribution and dividing that total by the number of individual scores. It is the most frequently used measure of central tendency. (Compare with the other two measures of central tendency, the *median* and the *mode.*) (661)

mean length of utterance (MLU) Average length of utterances, in morphemes. (272)

median Midpoint of a distribution of scores, with the same numbers of scores above and below. (660)

medical model Explanation of mental disorders that holds that they are the result of illness. (486)

medical therapy Treatment that focuses on the body and uses such tools as drugs, surgery, and electric shock. (527)

meditation Altered state of consciousness induced by a refocusing of attention. (138)

menarche First menstruation. (344)

menopause Cessation of menstruation, which typically occurs at about age 50. (355)

mental age Assessment of intellectual ability, determined by administering an intelligence test and matching the test taker's score with the average age of those who have scored similarly during the standardization of the test. (237)

methadone Addictive narcotic, sometimes used to treat heroin addiction. (150)

MMPI Minnesota Multiphasic Personality Inventory; the most widely used test of personality and mental health. (473)

mnemonic Device to aid memory. (224)

mode Score that occurs most frequently in a distribution. (660)

modeling Type of learning that involves observing and imitating other persons' behaviors. (182)

modeling therapy Behavior-therapy technique in which the client learns new behaviors by observing and imitating models. (535)

modification Change in, or control of, aspects of the environment in order to change behavior in a way that will benefit both the individual and society. (6)

monocular cues Cues about the distance of an object that can be seen with just one eye. (107)

moral model Explanation of mental illness, common during the Middle Ages, as a result of sin and possession by the devil. (485)

morpheme Smallest meaningful element of speech. (270)

morphine Opium derivative used to relieve pain and induce sleep. (150)

motherese Specialized kind of conversation that is addressed to young children and is important for language acquisition. (275)

motivation General term for the force responsible for arousal, direction, and persistence of behavior. (383)

motor (efferent) neurons Nerves that transmit information from the brain to the muscles and glands of the body. (43)

multifactorial inheritance Pattern of inheritance in which a trait is expressed either by a combination of several genes or through the interaction of genes with environmental factors. (308)

multiple-intelligence theory Gardner's theory that intelligence consists of seven independent "intelligences" which involve the ability to solve problems or create prod-

ucts valued within one or more cultural settings. (234)

multiple personality Dissociative disorder in which a person has two or more distinct personalities, each of which comes to prominence at different times. (500)

myelin Fatty tissue that covers some axons, allowing impulses to travel faster. (44)

myelinization Process that forms myelin on axons. (45)

nAch "Need to achieve." According to Murray, this need is characterized by a desire or tendency "to overcome obstacles, to exercise power, and to strive to do something difficult as well and as quickly as possible." (397)

narcolepsy Disorder characterized by an uncontrollable urge to sleep. (135)

narcotics Central-nervous-system depressants used to relieve pain and induce sleep. (150)

nativists Theorists who believe that there is an inborn capacity for learning language. (274)

nature-nurture debate Controversy over the relative influence of inherited traits (nature) and experience (nurture) on development. (304)

negative reinforcer Unpleasant stimulus which, when removed from a situation, increases the probability of the occurrence of a response. (169)

neodissociation theory of hypnosis View that a hypnotized person is functioning on more than one level of awareness. (140)

neonatal period First 28 days of life. (313)

nerves Bundles of axons. (51)

nervous system Network of cells, whose function is to detect stimuli, guide motor responses, and provide the framework for mental processes; it consists of the brain, the brain stem, the spinal cord, the cranial and peripheral nerves, and the ganglia. (40)

neurons Nerve cells that send and receive information to and from other parts of the body. (43)

neurotransmitter Chemical involved in transmitting messages between neurons. (47)

neutral stimulus Stimulus that does not automatically elicit a reflex response. (162)

nicotine Stimulant found in tobacco. (144)

nightmares Frightening dreams most likely to appear in childhood; they occur during REM sleep. (137)

night terrors Sleep disorder consisting of panic attacks which typically occur within an hour of falling asleep, during stage 4 sleep. (137)

nonnormative life events Biological and environmental influences on development that, while not happening to most people, may have a major impact on those who do experience them. (304)

normal distribution Distribution of scores in the orderly pattern of a symmetrical bell-shaped curve on which the mean, median, and mode are all equal. (663)

normative age-graded influences Biological and environmental influences on development that are highly similar for all people in a given age group. (304)

normative history-graded influences Biological and environmental influences on development common to people of a particular generation. (304)

norms (1) Society's definitions of how we "should" behave. (2) Standards of test performance. (239, 601)

NREM (non-rapid-eye-movement) sleep Four sleep stages, each with distinct EEG patterns, not typically associated with dreaming. (123)

null hypothesis Statement that an independent variable will not affect a dependent variable. (669)

obedience Compliance with the demands of an authority figure. (606)

obesity Eating disorder characterized by being at least 20 percent over ideal weight; associated with a variety of medical problems. (578)

objective tests Tests that typically require short written responses to a standardized list of questions. (473)

object permanence Realization that an object or person continues to exist even when no longer seen; according to Piaget, the most important cognitive acquisition of infancy. (236, 318)

obscenity Legal term for materials that are offensive to community standards, appeal to prurient interests (lust), and lack serious scientific, educational, literary, political, or artistic value. (443)

observational learning Learning based on the imitation of models. (181)

obsessions Persistent ideas, thoughts, images, or impulses that seem senseless even to the person who has them and invade consciousness against the person's will. (496)

Oedipus complex Phenomenon described by Freud in which the male child in the phallic stage feels sexual attraction for his mother and rivalry toward his father. (458)

olfactory mucosa Mucous membrane that contains the smell receptors. (97)

operant Response that an organism makes to bring about an effect. (168)

operant (instrumental) conditioning Type of learning in which the consequences of a behavior (that is, whether it is reinforced or punished) determine whether or not the behavior will be repeated. (160)

operant therapy Behavior-therapy technique in which the therapist uses a system of rewards to change the client's behavior. (535)

opium Narcotic used to relieve pain and induce sleep. (150)

opponent-process theory (1) Theory, proposed by Solomon, that an initial state will be opposed by an opposite reaction in the central nervous system which will reduce the intensity of the first state and produce its opposite. Thus, an initially negative state will be followed by a positive state, and vice versa. (2) Theory of color vision which proposes that opposite processes occur in three systems: blue-yellow, red-green, and achromatic; explains the phenomenon of afterimages. (88, 386)

optic disk Part of the eye with no photoreceptors; when an image is projected on this disk, it hits a blind spot. (81)

oral stage According to Freudian theory, the psychosexual stage of infancy (birth to 12–18 months), characterized by gratification in the oral region; feeding is the major situation in which this gratification occurs. (458)

organic amnesia Memory disorder that can be attributed to physiological illness or injury. (219)

organic retardation Generally severe mental retardation with a physical cause. (262)

osteoporosis Thinning of the bones that may occur in later life, especially among women. (581)

panic disorder Anxiety disorder characterized by recurrent attacks of terror that include physical symptoms such as dizziness, breathing difficulties, and sweating. (497)

papillae Taste buds on the tongue. (98)

parallel forms Alternative versions of a test which are so similar that they should yield similar scores; a way to measure reliability. (239)

paraphilia Sexual arousal only in response to unusually bizarre imagery, objects, or acts. (443)

partial reinforcement Pattern of reinforcement in which the desired response is rewarded only part of the time; also called *intermittent reinforcement*. (170)

PCP (phencyclidine hydrochloride) Stimulant, depressant, and pain killer. (148)

penis envy Freudian concept that the female envies the penis and wants one of her own. (459)

perception The way the brain interprets sensations to make them meaningful. (77)

perceptual constancy Awareness that objects and events in the environment remain the same even though they may appear different because of varying environmental conditions. (104)

peripheral nervous system Network of sensory and motor nerves that control muscles and glands. (51)

person-centered approach Humanistic psychotherapeutic approach developed by Rogers, which provides a climate for clients to draw upon their own resources to fulfill themselves. (531)

person-situation controversy Conflict over whether behavior is consistent over time and situations or whether it changes to meet the demands of different situations. (469)

persona Jungian archetype of the social mask one adopts. (461)

personal fable Conviction, typical in adolescence, that a person is special, unique, and not subject to the rules that govern the rest of the world. (345)

personal unconscious According to Jungian theory, a component of the mind characterized by repressed or forgotten material. (461)

personality Constellation of relatively consistent ways of dealing with people and situations that makes each person unique. (452)

personality disorders Mental disorders characterized by maladaptive behavior patterns that appear at an early age, become more ingrained over time, and are not viewed as abnormal by the person exhibiting them. (511)

personality psychologists Psychologists who study and assess individual differences in personality. (17)

phallic stage According to Freudian theory, the stage of psychosexual development of the preschool child (3 to 6 years), characterized by gratification in the genital area. (458)

phenotype Observable characteristics of a person. (308)

phi phenomenon Perceptual phenomenon used in a classic demonstration in perception that gave rise to the gestalt movement, in which stationary lights alternately flashed on and off are perceived as being in motion. (13)

phobia Unrealistic fear that interferes with normal living. (495)

phoneme Minimal sound unit of spoken language. (270)

phonemic restoration effect Phenomenon in which a listener reports hearing a speech sound that has been omitted from a passage. (103)

phrenology Pseudoscientific approach which contends that psychological attributes correspond to swellings and hollows in the skull, reflecting the development of particular areas of the brain. (40)

physical development Changes in the body such as changes in height, weight, brain development, and motor skills. (302)

physiological dependence Continued need for a drug in order to avoid the physical symptoms of withdrawal and to continue to function. (143)

physiological psychologists Psychologists who study the relationship between physiological processes and behavior. (18)

Piagetian approach Theory of intellectual development that describes qualitative changes in thinking which are typical of children of particular ages. (235)

pinna Outer ear. (91)

pituitary Endocrine gland called the body's "master gland" because it controls the activity of all the other glands. (69)

placebo Treatment that seems to be the same as the experimental treatment but has no physiological effects. (29, 96, 551)

place theory Theory that the ability to hear a sound of a certain pitch depends on the particular spot on the basilar membrane which is stimulated. (92)

pleasure principle In Freudian theory, the operating principle for the id, which attempts to gratify needs immediately. (454)

polygraph test Lie-detector test. (412)

population All the members of a group being studied. (22)

pornography Sexually oriented materials that a given individual or group of people consider morally or aesthetically objectionable. (443)

positive reinforcer Stimulus which when added to a situation increases the probability of the occurrence of a response. (169)

post-traumatic stress disorder Anxiety disorder characterized by re-experiencing a traumatic event. (497)

power Ability of one person to influence another person's behavior, thoughts, or feelings. (652)

prediction Forecast of future events on the basis of past events. (5)

prejudice Negative attitude held toward people solely because of their membership in a particular group. (623)

premature ejaculation Situation in which a man's ejaculation regularly occurs before he wants it to. (442)

premenstrual syndrome Psychological and physical state experienced just before and during the early phases of a menstrual period, characterized by physical discomfort and by psychological tension. (393)

presbycusis Hearing loss for high-frequency sounds. (93)

primacy effect Tendency to remember the items presented first in a series. (205)

primary appraisal Person's evaluation of the implications that an event has for his or her well-being. (566)

primary cortex Part of the cortex that receives direct input from various senses of the body and sends direct output to the motor system. (61)

primary mental abilities Thurstone's theory of intelligence, which identified seven relatively distinct factors. (232)

primary reinforcers Objects or events that are biologically important, such as food and sex, and whose appearance increases the probability of the occurrence of a response. (169)

primary sex characteristics Characteristics directly related to the sex organs and involved in reproduction. (435)

proactive interference (PI) Situation in which information learned earlier inhibits the ability to remember new information. (214)

procedural memory Memory for information about how to do various activities. (199)

progesterone Female sex hormone. (433)

projection Freudian defense mechanism characterized by attributing one's own unacceptable thoughts and motives to another. (456)

projective tests Personality tests that use relatively ambiguous material, the responses to which provide clues about the test taker's personality. (475)

protein synthesis Body's building of protein molecules from amino acids. (217)

proximodistal principle Principle that development proceeds in a near-to-far direction; parts of the body near the center develop before the extremities. (315)

psychoactive Mind-altering; term describing a drug that changes perception, mood, or thought processes. (143, 543)

psychoanalysis Therapeutic approach, originally developed by Freud, that aims to eliminate anxiety by giving the patient insight into unconscious conflicts which affect behavior and emotions. (13, 454, 528)

psychoanalytic model Explanation of mental disorders as a result of conflict between the id, ego, and superego. (486)

psychogenic amnesia Dissociative disorder in which a person may forget events that occurred during a certain time period; it usually follows a traumatic event and may end suddenly. (221, 500)

psychogenic fugue Dissociative disorder in which a person may forget his or her identity and assume a new one. (500)

psychological dependence Drug dependence in which users believe they must have the drug to feel good or normal. (144)

psychology Scientific study of behavior and of mental processes. (5)

psychometric approach Orientation to the study of individual differences in intelligence that emphasizes measurement using tests derived from factor-analytical statistical techniques. (231)

psychometric psychologists Psychologists who develop psychological tests and methods to score and interpret them. (19)

psychoneuroimmunology Scientific study of the way emotional states can influence the body's immune functioning. (589)

psychophysics Study of the relationship between physical aspects of stimuli and psychological perceptions of them. (77)

psychoses Mental disorders whose symptoms interfere with total functioning, involve a break from reality, and make it difficult for an affected person to get along without a major support like heavy medication or institutionalization. (494)

psychosexual dysfunction Recurrent and persistent disturbance in the sexual response cycle that is not caused by a physical condition or by medications. (441)

psychosocial development Changes in the emotional and social aspects of personality. (302)

psychosurgery Destruction of apparently normal brain tissue to treat severe psychiatric disorders. (41, 541)

psychotherapy Treatment that focuses on thoughts, feelings, and behaviors. (526)

puberty Physiological point at which a person is sexually mature and able to reproduce. (343, 435)

pubescence Time of the life span just before puberty, characterized by rapid physiological growth, maturation of reproductive functioning, and development of primary and secondary sex characteristics. (343, 435)

punishment Event that when administered following a response decreases the probability of the recurrence of that response. (177)

pupil Small hole in the center of the iris which allows light to enter the eye. (80)

random sample A sample in which each member of the population has an equal chance to be chosen for study. (23, 668)

range Simplest measure of variability; the difference between the largest and smallest scores in a sample. (662)

rational-emotive therapy Type of cognitive therapy, developed by Ellis, which emphasizes irrational thought processes as the root of emotional problems. (536)

rationalization Freudian defense mechanism characterized by justifying one's behavior in a difficult situation by pretending that the difficulty does not exist. (457)

ratio schedule of reinforcement Partial reinforcement schedule that requires a certain number of responses to be emitted for reinforcement to be given. (171)

reaction formation Freudian defense mechanism characterized by replacing an anxiety-producing feeling by its opposite. (457)

reaction range Range of variability in a trait due to the interaction of heredity and environment. (305)

reality principle In Freudian theory, the operating principle for the ego, through which the ego attempts to find acceptable ways to gratify the id. (455)

recall Measure of retention in which the subject has to reproduce from memory previously learned material. (203)

recency effect Tendency to remember the items presented last in a series. (205)

receptive field Specific areas of the retina to which given ganglion cells respond. (84)

receptor sites Specialized molecules on receiving neurons that bind with a neurotransmitter. (47)

recognition Measure in which the subject is confronted with material that has been previously learned, and is asked to identify it. (203)

reflex Inborn, unlearned involuntary reaction to stimulation. (52, 159, 315)

regression Freudian defense mechanism characterized by returning to the behaviors of an earlier time in one's life. (456)

reinforcement Event (or consequence) following a behavior which increases the probability that the behavior will occur again. (168)

reliability Consistency of a test in measuring the performance of an individual or a group. (239, 473)

REM rebound The body's making up for lost REM sleep. (127)

REM (rapid-eye-movement) sleep Sleep associated with dreaming; also called active or paradoxical sleep. (123)

replicate To repeat an experiment using the same methods and procedures to see whether the same results are obtained. (29)

repression Freudian defense mechanism characterized by the unconscious blocking from consciousness of anxiety-producing urges or experiences. (456)

research Systematic and objective collection of data. (20)

resilient children Children who bounce back from unfortunate circumstances; invulnerable children. (331)

resistance Psychoanalytic term for the inability of a patient to speak about certain anxiety-producing events. (529)

resting membrane potential (RMP) Difference in ions across the neuron membrane. (44)

reticular activation system (RAS) System of nerve pathways and connections within the brain stem. (401)

reticular formation Network of nerves located in the brain stem; it controls waking up and going to sleep. (56)

retina Tissue lining the back of the eye and containing the light-sensitive rods and cones; it is the most important part of the eye. (81)

retrieval Process of getting at information in memory. (193)

retroactive interference (RI) Situation in which information learned later inhibits the ability to remember previously learned information. (214)

retrograde amnesia Memory loss that is characterized by the inability to recall information learned before the onset of the amnesia. (219)

rods Receptors on the retina that are sensitive to black and white but not to color. (81)

role Set of behavioral expectations (or norms) for a specific social position. (601)

Rorschach test Widely used projective personality test in which the test taker describes what he or she sees in a series of inkblots; answers are scored on several dimensions. (475)

rote rehearsal Deliberate repetition of information to keep it in memory. (196)

samples Subgroups of a target population. (22)

scatterplot Visual representation of the relationship between two variables. (666)

schedules of reinforcement Patterns by which reinforcement is administered. (170)

schizophrenia Psychosis characterized by at least one of the following: delusions, hallucinations, or thought disturbances. (513)

school psychologists Psychologists who work directly with schoolchildren and their parents and teachers to deal with school-related problems. (18)

scientific method Systematic, objective, and organized way to get information, involving observation, description, and experimental investigation. (5)

sclera White outer part of the eyeball that contains receptors for pressure, temperature, and pain. (80)

seasonal affective disorder (SAD) Mental disorder in which seasonal variations in light and temperature trigger depressive episodes. (507, 545)

secondary appraisal Person's evaluation of his or her ability to cope with a particular event. (566)

secondary reinforcers Stimuli that become reinforcing after becoming associated with primary reinforcers. (169)

secondary sex characteristics Body changes occurring during adolescence that do not involve reproductive organs, such as breast development, growth, body and facial hair, and voice changes. (435)

secondary traits According to Allport, characteristics that are displayed occasionally but are not strong enough to be regarded as integral parts of a personality. (468)

sedatives and tranquilizers Central-nervous-system depressants that are calming and sleep-inducing. (149)

selective attention Concentration on some stimuli while others are ignored. (103)

self-actualization Self-fulfillment. (386, 464, 532)

self-disclosure Sharing of personal information, opinions, and feelings with another person. (643)

self-perception theory Bem's theory that people look at their own behavior and then form their attitudes by observing what they do. (620)

semantic differential Measure of attitudes in which a concept is rated on a series of dimensions. (616)

semantic memory Type of declarative memory that involves meaning independent of one's own experiences. (199)

semantics Study of meaning in a language. (270)

senescence Period of the life span that ushers in old age and is accompanied by decrements in bodily functioning; varies across age and people. (364)

sensation Stimulation of the sensory organs and the transmission of information about this stimulation through the nervous system. (77)

sensorineural hearing loss Hearing loss due to damage to the hair cells of the cochlea or to damage to the auditory nerve. (93)

sensory memory (SM) Type of memory that involves material which comes through the senses. This material disappears very rapidly unless it is transferred into short-term memory. (194)

sensory (afferent) neurons Nerves that transmit information from the body to the brain. (43)

serial-position curve Curve of remembering which demonstrates that in free recall there is a tendency to remember items learned first and last in a series and to forget those in the middle. (205)

set point Mechanism that maintains an individual's usual weight. (389)

sex differences Physical differences between males and females. (419)

sex-linked inheritance Pattern of inheritance in which genes for certain characteristics (often undesirable) are carried on an X chromosome. The genes are transmitted by the female and are generally expressed in the male. (308)

sex therapy Treatment designed to remove specific obstacles to sexual functioning. (443)

sexual burnout Boredom with the same sexual routine, marked by a sense of physical depletion and emotional emptiness and a negative sexual self-concept. (442)

shadowing technique (dichotic listening) Technique in which one message is presented to one ear and another to the other ear. (104)

shaping Reinforcement of responses that come progressively closer to the desired behavior until the desired behavior is reached. (174)

short-term memory (STM) Working memory, with a limited capacity; items remain in short-term memory for up to 20 seconds unless held there by rehearsal. (194)

signal detection theory Approach to psychophysics that emphasizes both the sensitivity of the senses and the motivations of observers. (77)

simple phobia Most common type of phobia, consisting of a persistent, irrational fear of some particular aspect of the environment. (495)

single-blind technique Technique in which subjects do not know if they are in the experimental group or the control group. (29)

Sixteen Personality Factor Questionnaire (16PF) Questionnaire developed by Cattell and his colleagues to measure personality profiles by rating test takers on 16 personality dimensions. (469)

skewed distribution Asymmetrical distribution of scores in which the mean, median and mode fall in different places. (666)

sleep apnea Sleep disorder characterized by periods of interrupted breathing. (136)

social-consequence model Explanation of mental disorders as problems of living rather than medical illnesses. (487)

social-learning theory Theory, proposed by Bandura, that behaviors are learned by observing and imitating models and are maintained through reinforcement. (181, 274)

social phobia Type of phobia in which a person is terrified of being in situations where he or she can be scrutinized by others. (496)

social psychology Scientific study of how we feel about, think about, are affected by, and act toward other people. (19, 598)

Social Readjustment Rating Scale (SRRS) Tool to assess the major life events undergone by a person; large changes in life events are associated with illness. (567)

social role Social position that has acquired a substantial number of norms. (601)

sociobiologists Scientists who study the biological basis of social behavior in various animals. (611)

sociocultural model Explanation of mental disorders that emphasizes the role of society in determining what is abnormal. (488)

somatic nervous system Part of the peripheral nervous system that controls reflex and voluntary actions. (53)

somatoform disorder Mental disorder characterized by physical symptoms for which no physical basis can be found. (499)

source traits According to Cattell's theory, characteristics that are the underlying determinants of the total personality cluster. (468)

spinal cord Long, stemlike structure that consists of nerve cell bodies and axons. (51)

split-half reliability Degree of similarity in scores on half of the items in a test compared with the other half. (239)

spontaneous recovery Reappearance of an extinguished response with no additional conditioning trials. (162)

standard deviation Measure of variability of scores; the square root of the average squared deviation around the mean. (238, 662)

standard score Number of standard deviations a score is from the mean; z score. (664)

standardization In test construction, development of procedures for giving and scoring a test; test items are administered to a large group of subjects representative of the population for whom the test is intended in order to determine the distribution of test scores. (238)

standardized Using the same measurement instruments and testing procedures for all participants. (25)

stapes Tiny bone in the ear; the "stirrup." (91)

statistics Branch of mathematics that uses a variety of methods for collecting, organizing, analyzing, and making inferences from numerical data. (658)

stereopsis Basis for 3D movies and slide viewers, which project a slightly different image to each eye and thus create the illusion of depth. (107)

stereotypes Preconceived, oversimplified beliefs about the characteristics of members of a group. (623)

stimulants Drugs that stimulate the central nervous system, producing increased energy, wakefulness, and elevated mood. (144)

stimulus Form of energy which can elicit a response. (77)

stimulus generalization Tendency to respond in the same way to a stimulus that is similar (but not identical) to the one used in the conditioning trials. (162)

storage Process of keeping material in memory. (193)

storage-and-transfer model of memory Multistore model of memory proposed by Atkinson and Shiffrin which holds that there are three types of memory: sensory, short-term, and long-term. (194)

stranger anxiety Normal wariness of strangers that usually begins at about 8 to 12 months of age. (332)

stratified sample Sample that shows a proportional representation of various important characteristics found in the larger population. (Also known as a **stratified random sample**.) (23, 668)

stress Physiological and psychological reactions to stressors. (563)

stress-inoculation training Behavioral technique, designed to prevent stress, which combines cognitive therapy and behavior modification. (574)

stressor Event capable of producing stress although not necessarily doing so. (563)

stroke Severe accident in the brain, occurring when a blood vessel in the brain suddenly bursts or is blocked, thus preventing oxygen from reaching parts of the brain and causing damage to a specific area. (65)

structuralism School of psychology, developed by Wundt and Titchener, that emphasized the study of elements of the mind. (11)

structure of intellect Model of intelligence proposed by Guilford, according to which intelligence is the result of the interaction of operations (the way we think), contents (what we think about), and products (the result of the application of a certain content, or our thinking a certain way about a certain issue). (232)

subjects Participants in research. (21)

sublimation Freudian defense mechanism characterized by rechanneling uncomfortable feelings (like sexual anxiety) into acceptable activities (like schoolwork). (456)

superego According to Freudian theory, the aspect of personality which represents the values that parents and other agents of society communicate to the child. The superego results from the resolution of the Oedipus or Electra complex. (455)

superiority complex According to Adler, overcompensation for feelings of inferiority. (462)

superstitious behavior Behavior that has been strengthened or weakened because it was accidentally reinforced or punished. (172)

surface traits According to Cattell's theory, clusters of characteristics that are readily seen by ordinary observers. (468)

synapse Junction between the axon of one neuron and the dendrites or cell body of a second, where neurons communicate with each other. (47)

synaptic cleft Tiny physical gap between the membrane of one neuron and that of another. (47)

synaptic vesicles Specialized organs

on the axon terminal of the sending neuron which squirt neurotransmitters into synapses. (47)

syntax Body of rules for structuring a language. (270)

systematic desensitization Behavior-therapy technique, based on classical conditioning, in which clients are gradually exposed to a hierarchy of anxiety-producing stimuli and taught to relax at each level until they have overcome their fear of the object or situation. (534)

tardive dyskinesia Side-effect of antipsychotic drugs that produces involuntary facial twitches and body contortions. (544)

telegraphic speech Speech that is characterized by many utterances and that sounds like words in a telegram. (273)

temperament Characteristic style of approaching people and situations. (468)

testosterone Primary male hormone produced by the testes. (433)

test-retest reliability Degree of similarity in scores when a test is given to the same person or group more than once. (239)

thalamus Part of the cerebrum that acts as a relay center for the senses to the cortex; it receives sensory information, which it sends to sensory areas of the cortex, and it sends motor information to the cortex. (58)

thanatology Study of death and dying. (372)

thanatos In Freudian theory, death instincts. (454)

Thematic Apperception Test (TAT) Projective personality test in which the test taker makes up stories about ambiguous pictures; these stories are scored for themes. (397, 476)

theory Explanation of the cause of behavior; theories organize data and provide directions for research. (20)

theory of misapplied constancy Theory that inappropriate interpretation of cues in an illusion is the result of having learned cues for maintaining size constancy. (111)

therapeutic alliance Emotional bond and involvement between therapist and client. (554)

therapist Individual specifically trained to offer a definite kind of treatment for psychological problems. (525)

therapy General term for a variety of treatments for psychological problems. (525)

threshold In an action potential, the value of membrane potential when the NA+ pores are completely open. (45)

tinnitus Continuous ringing or hissing sound in the ears. (93)

tip-of-the-tongue (TOT) problem Retrieval problem in which an item cannot be remembered although there is some knowledge of it. (202)

top-down processing Explanation of pattern recognition that emphasizes the observer's expectations and knowledge. (102)

transcendental meditation (TM) The best-known meditative technique in the west, developed by Maharishi Mahesh Yogi. (138)

transference Psychoanalytic term for a patient's reaction to the therapist as if the therapist were an important person in the patient's life; this process allows the patient to work through conflicts from earlier relationships. (529)

transsexual Person who has felt for at least 2 years that he or she is "trapped" in the body of the wrong sex, wants to live as a member of the other sex, and may want to be rid of his or her genitals. (429)

treatment Experimental manipulation. (28)

trial-and-error learning Learning by trying out a number of responses until the correct response is made. (168)

triangular theory of love Theory, proposed by Robert Sternberg, that love has three components: intimacy (the emotional component), passion (the motivational component), and commitment (the cognitive component). (649)

triarchic theory of intelligence Sternberg's theory describing three types of intelligence: componential (analytical ability), experiential (insight and creativity), and contextual (practical knowledge). (235)

trichromatic theory Theory that the visual system contains three color mechanisms (for red, green, and blue), and that combinations of the responses of these three mechanisms produce all sensations of color. (86)

t test Statistical test used to determine the significance of differences between two groups. (670)

two-factor theory Spearman's theory that intelligence consists of two kinds of factors: the g factor (general intelligence), an inherited intellectual capacity, which influences all-around performance; and several s factors (specific abilities), which account for the differences between scores on different tasks. (231)

tympanic membrane Eardrum; a tissue that vibrates as sound waves enter the ear. (91)

type A behavior pattern Aggressive, impatient behavior possibly associated with coronary disease. (588)

type B behavior pattern Relaxed, easygoing, unhurried behavior. (588)

typicality Degree to which a particular item is a good example of a concept. (283)

unconditioned response (UCR) The automatic response to an unconditioned stimulus. (162)

unconditioned stimulus (UCS) Stimulus that automatically elicits an unconditioned response, without the organism's having to learn (be conditioned) to respond. (162)

unconscious Network of stored, often repressed, factors that affect conscious thoughts and behaviors. (459)

unconscious inference theory Theory that perceptual constancies are a result of what is known from experience. (104)

unipolar disorder Depression without manic episodes. (502)

vaginismus Involuntary spasms of the vaginal muscles. (442)

validity Degree to which a test measures what it is supposed to measure. (239, 473)

variability Spread of scores in a distribution. (662)

variable-interval schedule Pattern of reinforcement by which the time period that must pass before a response is reinforced varies around some average. (171)

variable-ratio schedule Pattern of reinforcement in which the organism is reinforced after making a variable number of responses around some average number. (171)

variables Properties that vary, or can be varied for the purpose of an experiment, among members of a group. (23)

variance Measure of variability determined by computing the deviation of each score from the mean; the average of all the squared deviations from the mean score. (662)

violence Destructive action against people or property. (392)

visual capture Phenomenon by which visual information is more influential than information from the other senses. (79)

visual cortex Part of the cerebral cortex that is concerned with vision. (84)

Weber's law Law of psychophysics which states that more intense stimuli require larger changes before those changes can be perceived, whereas less intense stimuli require smaller changes. (78)

well-defined concept Concept specified by a set of unambiguous features, connected by a rule. (282)

wellness Ideal state of enriched health and enhanced life. (575)

word-superiority effect Principle in pattern recognition based on the observation that a letter can be identified more quickly if it is part of a word than if it stands alone. (103)

Yerkes-Dodson law Principle, according to Yerkes and Dodson, that optimal level of arousal varies depending on what you are doing; if you are doing something very easy, you will do best at a high arousal level; if you are doing something more complicated or more difficult, you will do best if your arousal level is somewhat lower. (402)

zygote One-cell organism resulting from the union of sperm and ovum. (306)

BIBLIOGRAPHY

Abramson, L. Y., Seligman, M. E. P., & Teasdale, J. D. (1978). Learned helplessness in humans: Critique and reformulation. *Journal of Abnormal Psychology, 87*(1), 49–74.

Abramson, P. R., & Hayashi, N. (1984). Pornography in Japan: Cross-cultural and theoretical considerations. In N. M. Malamuth & E. Donnerstein (Eds.), *Pornography and sexual aggression.* Orlando, FL: Academic.

Abroms, K. I., & Bennett, J. W. (1981). Parental contributions to trisomy 21: Review of recent cytological and statistical findings. In P. Mittler (Ed.), *Frontiers of knowledge in mental retardation: Vol. 2. Biomedical aspects* (pp. 149–157). Baltimore: University Park Press.

Action for Children's Television. (undated). *Treat TV with T.L.C.* One-page flyer. Newtonville, MA: Author.

Adams, C. G., & Turner, B. F. (1985). Reported change in sexuality from young adulthood to old age. *Journal of Sex Research, 21*(2), 126–141.

Adams, D. B., Gold, A. R., & Burt, A. D. (1978). Rise in female-initiated sexual activity at ovulation and its suppression by oral contraceptives. *New England Journal of Medicine, 299,* 1145–1150.

Adams, E. H., & Durell, J. (1984). Cocaine: A growing public health problem. In J. Grabowski (Ed.), *Cocaine: Pharmacology, effects, and treatment of abuse.* (NIDA Research Monograph 50, DHHS Publication No. ADM 84-1326). Washington, DC: U.S. Government Printing Office.

Adelson, J. (1979). Adolescence and the generation gap. *Psychology Today, 12*(9), 33–37.

Ader, R., & Cohen, N. (1982). Behaviorally conditioned immunosuppression and murine systemic lupus erythematosus. *Science, 215,* 1534–1536.

Adler, A. (1928). *Understanding human nature.* London: Allen & Unwin.

Adler, A. (1929). *Problems of neuroses.* London: Kegan Paul.

Adler, A. (1930). Individual psychology. In C. Murchison (Ed.), *Psychologies of 1930.* Worcester, MA: Clark University Press.

Adler, A. (1936). On the interpretation of dreams. *International Journal of Individual Psychology, 1,* 3–16.

Adorno, T., Frenkel-Brunswik, E., Levinson, D., & Sanford, R. N. (1950). *The authoritarian personality.* New York: Harper & Row.

Ainsworth, M. D. S. (1969). Object relations, dependency, and attachment: A theoretical review of the infant-mother relationship. *Child Development, 40,* 969–1025.

Ainsworth, M. D. S. (1979). Infant-mother attachment. *American Psychologist, 34*(10), 932–937.

Ainsworth, M. D. S., & Bell, S. (1977). Infant crying and maternal responsiveness: A rejoinder to Gerwitz and Boyd. *Child Development, 48,* 1208–1216.

Ainsworth, M. D. S., Blehar, M. C., Waters, E., & Wall, S. (1978). *Patterns of attachment: A psychological study of the strange situation.* Hillsdale, NJ: Erlbaum.

Allport, G. W. (1937). *Personality: A psychosocial interpretation.* New York: Holt.

Allport, G. W. (1961). *Patterns and growth in personality.* New York: Holt, Rinehart & Winston.

Allport, G. W., & Odbert, H. S. (1936). Trait-names: A psycho-lexicon study. *Psychological Monographs, 47* (Whole No. 211).

Allport, G. W., & Postman, L. J. (1958). The basic psychology of rumor. In E. E. Maccoby, T. M. Newcomb, & E. L. Hartley (Eds.), *Readings in social psychology* (3d ed.). New York: Holt.

Altman, I., & Taylor, D. (1973). *Social penetration: The development of interpersonal relations.* New York: Holt, Rinehart & Winston.

Amabile, T. M. (1983). *The social psychology of creativity.* New York: Springer-Verlag.

American Civil Liberties Union (ACLU). (1985, Fall). Polygraph tests are degrading, don't work—and should be banned. *Civil Liberties.*

American Heart Association. (1984). *Eating for a healthy heart: Dietary treatment of hyperlipidemia.* Dallas: Author.

American heritage dictionary of the English language. (1971). W. Morris (Ed.). Boston: Houghton Mifflin.

American Medical Association. (1985). Scientific status of refreshing recollection by the use of hypnosis (Report of Council on Scientific Affairs). *Journal of the American Medical Association, 253*(13), 1918–1923.

American Psychological Association (APA). (1986, February 1). APA resolution says reliability of polygraph test "unsatisfactory." News release.

American Psychological Association (APA). (undated). *Behavioral research with animals.* Washington, DC: Author.

Amoore, J. E., Johnston, J. W., & Rubin, M. (1964). The stereochemical theory of odor. *Scientific American, 210*(2), 42–49.

Anastasi, A. (1976). *Psychological testing* (4th ed.). New York: Macmillan.

Anastasi, A., & Schaefer, C. E. (1971). Note on concepts of creativity and intelligence. *Journal of Creative Behavior, 3,* 113–116.

Anders, T., Caraskadon, M., & Dement, W. (1980). Sleep and sleepiness in children and adolescents. In I. Litt (Ed.), *Adolescent Medicine. Pediatric Clinics of North America, 27*(1), 29–44.

Anderson, A. M. (1982, May 20). The great Japanese IQ increase. *Nature,* pp. 180–181.

Anderson, J. R. (1980). *Cognitive psychology and its implications.* San Francisco: Freeman.

Andreasen, N. C. (1984). *The broken brain: The biological revolution in psychiatry.* New York: Harper & Row.

Andreasen, N. C., Nasrallah, H. A., Dunn, V., Olson, S. C., Grove, W. M., Ehrhardt, J. C., Coffman, J. A., & Crossett, J. H. W. (1986). Structural abnormalities in the frontal system in schizophrenia. *Archives of General Psychiatry, 43,* 136–144.

Andreasen, N. C., & Olsen, S. (1982). Negative versus positive schizophrenia. *Archives of General Psychiatry, 39,* 789–794.

Angell, M. (1985). Disease as a reflection of the psyche. *New England Journal of Medicine, 312*(24), 1570–1572.

Anthony, E. J., & Koupernik, C. (Eds.). (1974). *The child in his family: Children at psychiatric risk* (Vol. 3). New York: Wiley.

Appel, L., Cooper, R., McCarrell, B., Sims-Knight, J., Yussen, S., & Flavell, J. (1972). Development of the distinction between perceiving and memorizing. *Child Development, 43,* 1365–1381.

Applebaum, P. S. (1982, March 21). Can mental patients say no to drugs? *The New York Times Magazine,* pp. 46, 51–57.

Arend, R., Gove, F., & Sroufe, L. A. (1979). Continuity of individual adaptation from infancy to kindergarten: A predictive study of ego-resiliency and curiosity in preschoolers. *Child Development, 50,* 950–959.

Aronson, E. (1980). *The social animal* (3d ed.). San Francisco: Freeman.

Aronson, E., & Bridgeman, D. (1979). Jigsaw groups and the desegregated classroom: In pursuit of common goals. *Personality and Social Psychology Bulletin, 5,* 438–446.

Aronson, E., Stephan, C., Sikes, J., Blaney, N., & Snapp, M. (1978). *The jigsaw classroom.* Beverly Hills, CA: Sage.

Aronson, E., Willerman, B., & Floyd, J. (1966). The effect of a pratfall on increasing interpersonal attractiveness. *Psychonomic Science, 4,* 227–228.

Asch, S. E. (1951). Effects of group pressure upon the modification and distortion of judgements. In H. Guetzkow (Ed.), *Groups, leadership and men: Research in human relations.* Pittsburgh: Carnegie Press.

Asch, S. E. (1955). Opinions and social pressure. *Scientific American, 193*(5), 31–35.

Asch, S. E. (1956). Studies of independence and conformity: A minority of one against a unanimous majority. *Psychological Monographs, 9* (Whole No. 416).

Aschoff, J., & Wever, R. (1982). Spontanperiodik des menschen bei ausschluss aller zeitgeber. In M. C. Moore-Ede, F. M. Sulzman, & C. A. Fuller, *The clocks that time us.* Cambridge, MA: Harvard University Press. (Reprinted from *Naturwissenschaften,* 1962, *49,* 337–342)

Aserinsky, E., & Kleitman, N. (1953). Regularly occurring periods of eye motility and concomitant phenomena during sleep. *Science, 118,* 273.

Ash, P., Vennart, J., & Carter, C. (1977, April). The incidence of hereditary disease in man. *Lancet,* 849–851.

Atkinson, J. W. (1957). Motivational determinant of risk-taking behavior. *Psychological Review, 64,* 359–372.

Atkinson, R. C., & Shiffrin, R. M. (1968). Human memory: A proposed system and its control processes. In K. W. Spence & J. T. Spence (Eds.), *The psychology of learning and motivation: Advances in research and theory* (Vol. 2). New York: Academic.

Atkinson, R. C., & Shiffrin, R. M. (1971). The control of short-term memory. *Scientific American, 225,* 82–90.

Bachrach, A. J., Erwin, W. J., & Mohr, J. P. (1965). The control of eating behavior in an anorexic by operant conditioning techniques. In L. Ullman & L. Krasner (Eds.), *Case studies in behavior modification.* New York: Holt, Rinehart & Winston.

Backman, C. W. (1981). Attraction in interpersonal relationships. In M. Rosenberg & R. H. Turner (Eds.), *Social psychology.* New York: Basic Books.

Baird, J. C. (1982). The moon illusion: II. A reference theory. *Journal of Experimental Psychology: General, 111,* 304–315.

Balkwell, C. (1981). Transition to widowhood: A review of the literature. *Family Relations, 30,* 117–127.

Ballinger, C. B. (1981). The menopause and its syndromes. In J. G. Howells (Ed.), *Modern perspectives in the psychiatry of middle age* (pp. 279–303). New York: Brunner/Mazel.

Baltes, P. B., & Kliegl, R. (1986). On the dynamics between growth and decline in the aging of intelligence and memory. In K. Poeck, H. J. Freund, & H. Ganshirt (Eds.), *Neurology* (pp. 1–17). Heidelberg, Germany: Springer-Verlag.

Baltes, P. B., Reese, H. W., & Lipsitt, L. (1980). Life-span developmental psychology. *Annual Review of Psychology, 31,* 65–110.

Bandura, A. (1964). The stormy decade: Fact or fiction? *Psychology in the School, 1,* 224–231.

Bandura, A. (1965). Vicarious processes: A case of no-trial learning. In L. Berkowitz (Ed.), *Advances in experimental social psychology* (Vol. 2). New York: Academic.

Bandura, A. (1968). A social learning interpretation of psychological dysfunctions. In P. London & D. Rosenhan (Eds.), *Foundations of abnormal psychology.* New York: Holt.

Bandura, A. (1974). Behavior theory and the models of man. *American Psychologist, 19,* 859–869.

Bandura, A. (1977). *Social learning theory.* Englewood Cliffs, NJ: Prentice-Hall.

Bandura, A., & Huston, A. (1961). Identification as a process of incidental learning. *Journal of Abnormal and Social Psychology, 63*(12), 311–318.

Bandura, A., Ross, D., & Ross, S. (1961). Transmission of aggression through imitation of aggressive models. *Journal of Abnormal and Social Psychology, 63,* 575–582.

Bandura, A., & Walters, R. H. (1963). *Social learning and personality development.* New York: Holt.

Banks, M. S., Aslin, R. N., & Letson, R. D. (1975). Sensitive period for the development of human binocular vision. *Science, 190,* 675–677.

Banning sequel. (1982, January). *American Society of Journalists and Authors Newsletter,* p. 10.

Barahal, H. S. (1958). 1,000 prefrontal lobotomies—A five to ten-year follow-up study. *Psychiatric Quarterly, 32,* 653–658.

Barash, D. P. (1977). *Sociobiology and behavior.* New York: Elsevier.

Barber, T. X. (1970). *LSD, marihuana, yoga, and hypnosis.* Chicago: Aldine.

Barber, T. X., & Wilson, S. C. (1977). Hypnosis, suggestions, and altered states of consciousness: Experimental evaluation of the new cognitive behavioral theory and the traditional trance-state theory of hypnosis. In W. E. Edmonston, Jr. (Ed.), *Conceptual and investigative approaches to hypnosis and hypnotic phenomena.* New York: New York Academy of Sciences.

Bard, P. (1938). Studies in the cortical representation of somatic sensibility. *Harvey Lectures, 33,* 143–169.

Barefoot, J. C., Dahlstrom, W. G., & Williams, R. B. (1983). Hostility, CHD incidence, and total mortality: A 25-year follow-up study of 255 physicians. *Psychosomatic Medicine, 45*(1), 59–63.

Barfield, R. E., & Morgan, J. N. (1974). *Early retirement: The decision and the experience and a second look.* Ann Arbor, MI: Institute for Social Research.

Barfield, R. E., & Morgan, J. N. (1978). Trends in satisfaction with retirement. *Gerontologist, 18*(1), 19–23.

Barker, P. (1979). *Basic child psychiatry* (3d ed). Baltimore: University Park Press.

Barnes, A., Colton, T., Gunderson, J., Noller, K., Tilley, B., Strama, T., Townsend, D., Hatab, P., & O'Brien, P. (1980). Fertility and outcome of pregnancy in women exposed in utero to diethylstilbestrol, *New England Journal of Medicine, 302*(11), 609–613.

Barnett, R. (1985, March 2). We've come a long way—but where are we and what are the rewards? Presentation at conference, Women in Transition, New York University's School of Continuing Education, Center for Career and Life Planning, New York.

Baron, R. A. (1977). *Human aggression.* New York: Plenum.

Barron, J. (1981, December 5). Ex-controllers facing hardships. *The New York Times,* p. 27.

Bartoshuk, L. M. (1974). Taste illusions: Some demonstrations. *Annals of the New York Academy of Sciences, 237,* 279–285.

Baruch, G., Barnett, R., & Rivers, C. (1983). *Lifeprints.* New York: McGraw-Hill.

Bassuk, E. L., & Gerson, S. (1978). Deinstitutionalization and mental health services. *Scientific American, 238*(2), 46–53.

Bateson, G., Jackson, D. D., Haley, J., & Weakland, J. (1956). Double-bind hypothesis of schizophrenia. *Behavioral Science, 1,* 251–264.

Baumann, D. J., Cialdini, R. B., & Kenrick, D. T. (1981). Altruism as hedonism: Helping and self-gratification as equivalent responses. *Journal of Personality and Social Psychology, 40*(6), 1039–1046.

Baumrind, D. (1964). Some thoughts on ethics of research: After reading Milgram's "Behavioral study of obedience." *American Psychologist, 19,* 421–423.

Baumrind, D. (1967). Child care practices anteceding three patterns of preschool behavior. *Genetic Psychology Monograph, 75,* 43–88.

Baumrind, D. (1970). Socialization and instrumental competence in young children. *Young Children, 26*(2).

Baumrind, D. (1985). Research using intentional deception: Ethical issues revisited. *American Psychologist, 40,* 165–174.

Baumrind, D., & Black, A. E. (1967). Socialization practices associated with dimensions of competence in preschool boys and girls. *Child Development, 38*(2), 291–327.

Bayer, A. E. (1967). Birth order and attainment of the doctorate: A test of an economic hypothesis. *American Journal of Sociology, 72,* 540–550.

Beard, R. J. (1975). The menopause. *British Journal of Hospital Medicine, 12,* 631–637.

Beck, A. T., & Burns, D. (1978). Cognitive therapy for depressed suicidal outpatients. In J. O. Cole, A. F. Schatzberg, & S. H. Frazier (Eds.), *Depression: Biology, psychodynamics, and treatment.* New York: Plenum.

Becker, B. J. (1983). *Item characteristics and sex differences on the SAT-M for mathematically able youths.* Paper presented at the annual meeting of the American Educational Research Association, Montreal.

Bell, A. P., & Weinberg, M. S. (1978). *Homosexualities: A study of diversity among men and women.* New York: Simon & Schuster.

Bell, A. P., Weinberg, M. S., & Hammersmith, S. K. (1981). *Sexual preference: Its development in men and women.* Bloomington: Indiana University Press.

Bell, S., & Ainsworth, M. D. S. (1972). Infant crying and maternal responsiveness. *Child Development, 43,* 1171–1190.

Belloc, N. B., & Breslow, L. (1972). Relationship of physical health status and health practices. *Preventive Medicine, 1*(3), 409–421.

Belmont, L., & Morolla, A. F. (1973). Birth order, family size, and intelligence. *Science, 182,* 1096–1101.

Belsky, J. (1980). A family analysis of parental influence on infant exploratory competence. In F. A. Pederson (Ed.), *The father-infant relationship: Observational studies in a family setting.* New York: Praeger.

Bem, D. J. (1967). Self-perception: An alternative interpretation of cognitive dissonance phenomena. *Psychological Review, 74*(3), 183–200.

Bem, D. J. (1970). *Beliefs, attitudes and human affairs.* Belmont, CA: Brooks/Cole.

Bem, S. L. (1974). The measurement of psychological androgyny. *Journal of Consulting and Clinical Psychology, 42*(2), 155–162.

Bem, S. L. (1976). Probing the promise of androgyny. In A. G. Kaplan & J. P. Bean (Eds.), *Beyond sex-role stereotypes: Readings toward a psychology of androgyny.* Boston: Little, Brown.

Benbow, C. P., & Stanley, J. C. (1980). Sex differences in mathematical ability: Fact or artifact? *Science, 210,* 1262–1264.

Benbow, C. P., & Stanley, J. C. (1983). Sex differences in mathematical ability: More facts. *Science, 222,* 1029–1031.

Benderly, B. L. (1981). Flashbulb memory. *Psychology Today, 15*(6), 71–74.

Bennett, W., & Gurin, J. (1982). *The dieter's dilemma: Eating less and weighing more.* New York: Basic Books.

Benson, H. (1975). *The relaxation response.* New York: Morrow.

Benson, H. (1983). *The relaxation response in the management of stress.* Paper presented at a seminar, Coping with Corporate Stress: Avoiding a Cardiovascular Crisis, New York.

Bentovim, A. (1979). Family therapy when the child is the referred patient. In S. Bloch (Ed.), *An introduction to the psychotherapies.* Oxford: Oxford University Press.

Berger, R. M. (1982). *Gay and gray: The older homosexual male.* Urbana: University of Illinois Press.

Berkowitz, L. (Ed.). (1979). *Advances in experimental social psychology* (Vol. 12). New York: Academic.

Berkowitz, L. (1983). Aversively stimulated aggression: Some parallels and differences in research with animals and humans. *American Psychologist, 38*(11), 1135–1144.

Berlyne, D. E. (1971). *Aesthetics and psychobiology.* New York: Appleton-Century-Crofts.

Berman, J. S., Miller, C., & Massman, P. J. (1985). Cognitive therapy versus systematic desensitization: Is one treatment superior? *Psychological Bulletin, 97*(3), 451–561.

Berscheid, E. S. (1983, March 25). Personal communication.

Berscheid, E. S., & Campbell, B. (1981). The changing longevity of heterosexual close relationships. In M. J. Lerner & S. C. Lerner (Eds.), *The justice motive in social behavior.* New York: Plenum.

Berscheid, E. S., & Walster, E. (1978). *Interpersonal attraction* (2d ed.). Reading, MA: Addison-Wesley.

Berscheid, E. S., Walster, E., & Bohrnstedt, G. (1973). The happy American body, a survey report. *Psychology Today, 7*(6), 119–131.

Biller, H. B. (1981). The father and sex role development. In M. E. Lamb (Ed.), *The role of the father in child development.* New York: Wiley-Interscience.

Birns, B. (1976). The emergence and socialization of sex differences in the earliest years. *Merrill-Palmer Quarterly, 22,* 229–254.

Blackburn, J. A., & Papalia, D. E. (1986, November). *Modification of figural relations performance: A comparison of two training approaches.* Paper presented at the annual meeting of The Gerontological Society of America, Chicago.

Blackburn, J. A., Papalia, D. E., & Foye, B. (1986, August). *Fluid ability training: A comparison of treatment procedures.* Paper presented at the annual meeting of the American Psychological Association, Washington, DC.

Blanck, G., & Blanck, R. (1974). *Ego psychology: Theory and practice.* New York: Columbia University Press.

Bloch, S. (1979). Group psychotherapy. In S. Bloch (Ed.), *An introduction to the psychotherapies.* Oxford: Oxford University Press.

Block, J. H. (1978). Another look at sex differentiation in the socialization behaviors of mothers and fathers. In F. Wenmark & J. Sherman (Eds.), *Psychology of women: Future direction of research.* New York: Psychological Dimensions.

Block, J. (1981). Some enduring and consequential structures of personality. In A. I. Rabin, J. Aronoff, A. M. Barclay, & R. A. Zucker (Eds.), *Further explorations in personality.* New York: Wiley-Interscience.

Blodgett, H. C. (1929). The effect of the introduction of reward upon the maze performance of rats. *University of California Publication of Psychology, 4*(8), 120.

Bloom, B. (1985). *Developing talent in young people.* New York: Ballantine.

Bloom, B. L., Asher, S. J., & White, S. W. (1978). Marital disruption as a stressor: A review and analysis. *Psychological Bulletins, 85,* 867–894.

Bluebond-Langner, M. (1972). Meanings of death to children. In H. Feifel (Ed.), *New meanings of death* (pp. 47–66). New York: McGraw-Hill.

Blumstein, P., & Schwartz, P. (1983). *American couples: Money, work, sex.* New York: Morrow.

Bodenhausen, G. V., & Wyer, R. S. (1985). Effects of stereotypes on decision making and information-processing strategies. *Journal of Personality and Social Psychology, 48*(2), 267–282.

Boffey, P. M. (1981, October 13). Worldwide use of Valium draws new scrutiny. *The New York Times,* pp. C1–C2.

Bolles, R. C., & Fanselow, M. S. (1982). Endorphins and behavior. *Annual review of psychology. 33,* 87–102.

Bolton, R. (1973). Aggression and hypoglycemia among the Qolla: A study in psychobiological anthropology. *Ethnology, 12,* 227–257.

Bonham, G. S., & Wilson, R. W. (1981). Children's health in families with cigarette smokers. *American Journal of Public Health, 7,* 290–293.

Bonnet, M. H. (1985). Effect of sleep disruption on sleep, performance, and mood. *Sleep, 8,* 11–19.

Bootzin, M. (1975). *Behavior modification and therapy: An introduction.* Cambridge, MA: Winthrop.

Botwinick, J., West, R., & Storandt, M. (1978). Predicting death from behavioral test performance. *Journal of Gerontology, 33*(5), 755–762.

Bouchard, T. J. (1981). The study of mental ability using twin and adoption designs. In *Twin research 3: Intelligence, personality and development.* New York: Liss.

Bouchard, T. J., Heston, L., Eckert, E., Keyes, M., & Resnick, S. (1981). The Minnesota study of twins reared apart. Project description and sample results in the developmental domain. In *Twin research 3: Intelligence, personality and development.* New York: Liss.

Bouchard, T. J., & McGue, M. (1981). Familial studies of intelligence: A review. *Science, 212*(29), 1055–1058.

Bourne, L. E. (1967). Learning and utilization of conceptual rules. In B. Kleinmuntz (Ed.), *Concepts and the structure of memory.* New York: Wiley.

Bourne, L. E. (1970). Knowing and using concepts. *Psychological Review, 77,* 546–556.

Bourne, L. E., Dominowski, R. L., & Loftus, E. F. (1979). *Cognitive processes.* Englewood Cliffs, NJ: Prentice-Hall.

Bousfield, W. A. (1953). The occurrence of clustering in the recall of randomly arranged associates. *Journal of General Psychology, 49,* 229–240.

Bower, G. H. (1973, October). How to . . . uh . . . remember. *Psychology Today,* pp. 63–70.

Bowers, K. (1973). Situationism in psychology: An analysis and a critique. *Psychological Review, 80*(5), 307–336.

Boyer, J. L., & Guthrie, L. (1985). Assessment and treatment of the suicidal patient. In E. E. Beckham & W. R. Leber, *Handbook of depression.* Homewood, IL: Dorsey.

Brady, J. V. (1967). Emotion and sensitivity of psychoendocrine systems. In D. C. Glass (Ed.), *Neurophysiology and emotion.* New York: Rockefeller University Press.

Brady, J. V. (1975). Towards a behavioral biology of emotion. In L. Levi (Ed.), *Emotions: Their parameters and measurement.* New York: Raven.

Brandt, J. (1983). Personal communication.

Bratler, T. E., & Forrest, G. G. (Eds.). (1985). *Alcoholism and substance abuse: Strategies for clinical intervention.* New York: Free Press.

Brecher, E. M. (1971). *The sex researchers.* New York: New American Library.

Brecher, E., & Editors of Consumer Reports Books. (1984). *Love, sex, and aging: A consumers union report.* Boston: Little, Brown.

Breland, K., & Breland, M. (1951). A field of applied animal psychology. *American Psychologist, 6,* 202–204.

Brim, O. G., Jr., & Kagan, J. (Eds.). (1980). *Constancy and change in human development.* New York: Wiley-Interscience.

Brinkley, J. (1986, March 28). U.S. blames new form of heroin for outbreak of overdose deaths. *The New York Times,* pp. A1, B6.

Brodbeck, A. J., & Irwin, O. C. (1946). The speech behavior of infants without families. *Child Development, 17,* 145–156.

Brody, E. B., & Brody, N. (1976). *Intelligence.* New York: Academic.

Brody, J. E. (1982, November 16). Noise poses a growing threat, affecting hearing and behavior. *The New York Times,* pp. C1, C5.

Brody, L. R., Zelazo, P. R., & Chaika, H. (1984). Habituation-dishabituation to speech in the neonate. *Developmental Psychology, 20,* 114–119.

Bromley, D. B. (1974). *The psychology of human aging* (2d ed.). Middlesex, England: Penguin.

Bronfenbrenner, U. (1960). Freudian theories of identification and their derivatives. *Child Development, 31,* 15–40.

Brouilette, R. T., Fernbach, S. K., & Hunt,

C. E. (1982). Obstructive sleep apnea in infants and children. *Journal of Pediatrics, 100*(1), 31–40.

Broverman, J. K., Broverman, D. M., & Clarkson, F. E. (1970). Sexual stereotypes and clinical judgments of mental health. *Journal of Consulting and Clinical Psychology, 34,* 1–7.

Brown, P., & Elliot, R. (1965). Control of aggression in a nursery school class. *Journal of Experimental Child Psychology, 2,* 103–107.

Brown, P. K., & Wald, G. (1964). Visual pigments in single rods and cones in the human retina. *Science, 144,* 45–52.

Brown, R. (1973a). Development of the first language in the human species. *American Psychologist, 28*(2), 97–106.

Brown, R. (1973b). *A first language: The early stages.* Cambridge, MA: Harvard University Press.

Brown, R., Cazden, C. B., & Bellugi, U. (1969). The child's grammar from I to III. In J. P. Hill (Ed.), *Minnesota symposia on child psychology* (Vol. 2). Minneapolis: University of Minnesota Press.

Brown, R., & Kulik, J. (1977). Flashbulb memories. *Cognition, 5,* 73–99.

Brown, R., & Lenneberg, E. H. (1954). A study in language and cognition. *Journal of Abnormal Social Psychology, 49,* 454–462.

Brown, R., & McNeill, D. (1966). The "tip of the tongue" phenomenon. *Journal of Verbal Learning and Verbal Behavior, 5,* 325–337.

Bruch, H. (1978). *The golden cage: The enigma of anorexia nervosa.* Cambridge, MA: Harvard University Press.

Bukowski, C. (Speaker). (1980). "The shoelace," on *Bukowski reads his poetry.* [Recording]. Santa Monica, CA: Takoma Records.

Burke, B. S., Beal, V. A., Kirkwood, S. B., & Stuart, H. C. (1943). Nutrition studies during pregnancy. *American Journal of Obstetrics and Gynecology, 46,* 38–52.

Burks, J., & Rubenstein, M. (1979). *Temperament styles in adult interaction: Applications in psychotherapy.* New York: Brunner/Mazel.

Bush, T. L., Cowan, L. D., Barrett Connor, E., Criqui, M. H., Karon, J. M., Wallace, R. B., Lyroler, H. A., & Rifkind, B. M. (1983). Estrogen use and all cause mortality: Preliminary results from the Lipid Research Clinics program follow-up study. *Journal of the American Medical Association, 249*(7), 903–906.

Butler, R. (1975). *Why survive? Being old in America.* New York: Harper & Row.

Butler, R. (1961). Re-awakening interests.

Nursing Homes: Journal of American Nursing Home Association, 10, 8–19.

Butterfield, E., & Siperstein, G. (1972). Influence of contingent auditory stimulation upon non-nutritional suckle. In J. Bosma (Ed.), *Oral sensation and perception: The mouth of the infant.* Springfield, IL: Thomas.

Butters, N., & Cermak, L. S. (1980). *Alcoholic Korsakoff's syndrome.* New York: Academic.

Byrne, D. (1961). Interpersonal attraction and attitude similarity. *Journal of Abnormal and Social Psychology, 62,* 713–715.

Byrne, D. (1969). Attitudes and attraction. In L. Berkowitz (Ed.), *Advances in experimental social psychology* (pp. 35–85). New York: Academic.

Byrne, D. (1971). *The attraction paradigm.* New York: Academic.

Byrne, D., Clore, G. L., & Worchel, P. (1966). The effect of economic similarity—dissimilarity on interpersonal attraction. *Journal of Personality and Social Psychology, 4,* 220–224.

Byrne, D., & Griffitt, W. (1973). Interpersonal attraction. *Annual Review of Psychology, 24,* 317–336.

Byrne, D., London, O., & Reeves, K. (1968). The effects of physical attractiveness, sex, and attitude similarity on interpersonal attraction. *Journal of Personality, 36,* 259–271.

Cain, W. S. (1981, July). Educating your nose. *Psychology Today,* pp. 49–56.

Calderone, M. S. (1983, May–July). Fetal erection and its message to us. *SIECUS Report,* pp. 9–10.

Campos, J. J., Langer, A., & Krowitz, A. (1970). Cardiac responses on the visual cliff in prelocomotor human infants. *Science, 170,* 196–197.

Cannon, W. B. (1927). The James-Lange theory of emotions: A critical examination and an alternative theory. *American Journal of Psychology, 39,* 106–124.

Carew, T. J., Hawkins, R. D., & Kandel, E. R. (1983). Differential classical conditioning of a defensive withdrawal reflex in *Aplysia californica. Science, 219,* 397–400.

Carlson, N. R. (1986). *Physiology of behavior* (3d ed.). Boston: Allyn & Bacon.

Carr, D. B., Bullen, B. A., Skrinar, G. S., Arnold, M. A., Rosenblatt, M., Beitins, I. Z., Martin, J. B., & McArthur, J. W. (1981). Physical conditioning facilitates the exercise-induced secretion of beta-endorphin and beta-lipotropin in women. *New England Journal of Medicine, 305,* 560–563.

Carrera, M. A. (1986, April 11). *Future directions in teen pregnancy prevention.* Talk presented to the annual meeting of the Society for the Scientific Study of Sex, Eastern Region.

Cartwright, R. D. (1978). *A primer on sleep and dreaming.* Reading, MA: Addison-Wesley.

Caruba, A. (1986, May 22). Personal communication.

Case, R. B., Heller, S. S., Case, N. B., Moss, A. J., & The Multicenter Post-Infarction Research Group. (1985). Type A behavior and survival after acute myocardial infarction. *New England Journal of Medicine, 312*(12), 737–741.

Cassileth, B. R., Lusk, E. J., Miller, D. S., Brown, L. L., & Miller, C. (1985). Psychosocial correlates of survival in advanced malignant disease. *New England Journal of Medicine, 312*(24), 1551–1555.

Castillo, M., & Butterworth, G. (1981). Neonatal localization of a sound in visual space. *Perception, 10,* 331–338.

Cattell, J. M. (1885–1886). The inertia of the eye and the brain. *Brain, 8,* 295–312.

Cattell, R. B. (1965). *The scientific analysis of personality.* Baltimore: Penguin.

Cattell, R. B., Eber, H. W., & Tatsuoka, M. M. (1970). *Handbook for the 16PF questionnaire.* Champaign, IL: Institute for Personality and Ability Testing.

Cattell, R. B., Saunders, D. R., & Stice, G. F. (1950). *The 16 Personality Factor Questionnaire.* Champaign, IL: Institute for Personality and Ability Testing.

Chase, M. H. (1981). The dreamer's paralysis. *Psychology Today, 15,*(11) 108.

Chasnoff, I. J., Burns, W. J., Schnoll, S. H., & Burns, K. A. (1985). Cocaine use in pregnancy. *Lancet, 313*(11), 666–669.

Cherniak, N. S. (1981). Respiratory disrythmias during sleep. *New England Journal of Medicine, 305*(6), 325–330.

Chess, S. (1983). Mothers are always the problem—or are they? Old wine in new bottles. *Pediatrics, 71*(6), 974–976.

Chilman, C. S. (1980). *Adolescent sexuality in a changing American society: Social and psychological perspectives* (NIH Publication No. 80-1426). Bethesda, Md.: U.S. Department of Health, Education, and Welfare, Public Health Service, National Institutes of Health.

Chilman, C. S. (1982). Adolescent childbearing in the United States: Apparent causes and consequences. In T. M. Field, A. Huston, H. C. Quay, L. Troll, & G. E. Finley (Eds.), *Review of human development.* New York: Wiley.

Chomsky, C. (1969). *The acquisition of syntax in children from five to ten.* Cambridge, MA: Massachusetts Institute of Technology Press.

Chomsky, N. (1965). *Aspects of the theory of syntax.* Cambridge, MA: Massachusetts Institute of Technology (MIT) Press.

Chomsky, N. (1968). *Language and mind.* New York: Harcourt, Brace, & World.

Cicirelli, V. G. (1980, December). Adult children's views on providing services for elderly parents. Report to the NRTA-AAARP Andrus Foundation.

Cicirelli, V. G. (1982). Sibling influence throughout the lifespan. In M. E. Lamb & B. Sutton-Smith (Eds.), *Sibling relationships: Their nature and significance across the lifespan.* Hillsdale, NJ: Erlbaum.

Claridge, G. (1972). The schizophrenias as nervous types. *Journal of Psychiatry, 121,* 1–17.

Clark, M. (1979, November 12). Drugs and psychiatry: A new era. *Newsweek,* pp. 98–104.

Clarke-Stewart, A. (1977). *Child care in the family: A review of research and some propositions for policy.* New York: Academic.

Clatworthy, N. M. (1980, May 1). *Morals and the ever changing college student.* Paper presented at the North Central Sociological Meeting, Dayton, OH.

Clausen, J. (1986, August 30). *Early adult choices and the life course.* Paper presented at the 81st annual meeting of the American Sociological Association, New York.

Clayton, V., & Overton, W. (1973). *The role of formal operational thought in the aging process.* Paper presented at the annual meeting of the Gerontological Society, Miami.

Clendinen, D. (1985, November 3). Race and blind justice behind mixup in court. *The New York Times,* p. 26.

Coe, W. C., & Ryken, K. (1979). Hypnosis and risks to human subjects. *American Psychologist, 34*(3), 673–681.

Cohen, D. B. (1974). Toward a theory of dream recall. *Psychological Bulletin, 81,* 138–154.

Cohen, D. B., & Wolfe, G. (1973). Dream recall and repression: Evidence for an alternative hypothesis. *Journal of Consulting and Clinical Psychology, 41,* 349–355.

Cohen, S. (1980). Aftereffects of stress on human performance and social behavior: A review of research and theory. *Psychological Bulletin, 88*(1), 82–108.

Cohen, S., & Hoberman, H. M. (1983). Positive events and social supports as buffers of life change stress. *Journal of Applied Social Psychology, 13,* 99–125.

Cohen, S., & Wills, T. A. (1985). Stress, social support, and the buffering hypothesis. *Psychological Bulletin, 98*(2), 310–357.

Cole, S. (1980). Send our children to work? *Psychology Today, 14*(2), 44.

Colegrove, F. W. (1982). The day they heard about Lincoln. In U. Neisser (Ed.), *Memory observed.* San Francisco: Freeman. (Reprinted from *American Journal of Psychology,* 1899, *10,* 228–255)

Coleman, J. (1980). Friendship and the peer group in adolescence. In J. Adelson (Ed.), *Handbook of adolescent development.* New York: Wiley.

Colen, B. D. (1982, March 7). Should the police use hypnosis? *This World, San Francisco Chronicle Magazine,* p. 22.

Coles, R., & Stokes, G. (1985). *Sex and the American teenager.* New York: Harper & Row.

Colligan, R. C., Osborne, D., Swenson, W. M., & Offord, K. P. (1984). The aging MMPI: Development of contemporary norms. *Mayo Clinic Proceedings, 59,* 377–390.

Condon, W., & Sander, L. (1974). Synchrony demonstrated between movements of the neonate and adult speech. *Child Development, 45,* 456–462.

Connolly, G. N., Winn, D. M., Hecht, S. S., Henningfield, J. E., Walker, B., & Hoffmann, D. (1986). The reemergence of smokeless tobacco. *New England Journal of Medicine, 314,*(16) 1020–1027.

Coons, S., & Guilleminault, C. (1982). Development of sleep-wake patterns and non-rapid eye movement sleep stages during the first six months of life in normal infants. *Pediatrica, 69*(6), 793–798.

Cooper, A. M. (1985). Will neurobiology influence psychoanalysis? *American Journal of Psychiatry, 142,* 1395–1402.

Cooper, C. L. (1981). *The stress check.* Englewood Cliffs, NJ: Prentice-Hall.

Copas, J. B., & Robin, A. (1982). Suicide in psychiatric inpatients. *British Journal of Psychiatry, 141,* 503–511.

Corby, J. C., Roth, W. I., Zarcone, V. P., & Kopell, B. S. (1978). Psychophysiological correlates of the practice of tantric yoga meditation. *Archives of General Psychiatry, 35,* 571–577.

Corkin, S. (1984). Lasting consequences of bilateral medial temporal lobectomy: Clinical course and experimental findings in H.M. *Seminars in Neurology, 4,* 249–259.

Cornsweet, T. N. (1970). *Visual perception.* New York: Academic.

Cory, T. L., Ormiston, D. W., Simmel, E., & Dainoff, M. (1975). Predicting the frequency of dream recall. *Journal of Abnormal Psychology, 84,* 261–266.

Costain, D. W., Cowen, P. J., Gelder, M. G., & Grahame-Smith, D. G. (1982). Electroconvulsive therapy and the brain: Evidence for increased dopamine-mediated responses. *Lancet, 2*(8295), 400–404.

Coyle, J. T., Price, D. L., & DeLong, M. R. (1983). Alzheimer's disease: A disorder of cortical cholinergic innervation. *Science, 219,* 1184–1190.

Craik, F. I. M., & Lockhart, R. S. (1972). Levels of processing: A framework for memory research. *Journal of Verbal Learning and Verbal Behavior, 11,* 671–684.

Craik, F. I. M., & Tulving, E. (1975). Depth of processing and the retention of words in episodic memory. *Journal of Experimental Psychology (General) 104,* 268–294.

Crawford, H. (1982). Cognitive processing during hypnosis: Much unfinished business. *Research Communications in Psychology, Psychiatry and Behavior, 7*(2), 169–178.

Crick, F. (1982, February). Do dendritic spines twitch? *Trends in Neuroscience,* pp. 44–46.

Crick, F., & Mitchison, G. (1983). The function of dream sleep. *Nature, 304,* 111–114.

Crook, T., & Eliot, E. (1980). Parental death during childhood and adult depression: A critical review of the literature. *Psychological Bulletin, 87*(2), 252–259.

Crook, T. H., & Miller, N. E. (1985). The challenge of Alzheimer's disease. *American Psychologist, 40*(11), 1245–1250.

Cross, D. T., Barclay, A., & Burger, G. K. (1978). Differential effects of ethnic membership, sex, and occupation on the California Personality Inventory. *Journal of Personality Assessment, 42,* 597–603.

Crosson, B. (1984). Role of the dominant thalamus in language: A review. *Psychological Bulletin, 96*(3), 491–517.

Curtiss, S. (1977). *Genie.* New York: Academic.

Cushman, J. H., Jr. (1986, July 8). Soldiers bid a farewell to smoking. *The New York Times,* p. A12.

Custance, J. (1952). *Wisdom, madness, & folly.* New York: Farrar, Straus, & Cudahy.

Cutting, J. E., & Proffitt, D. R. (1981). Gait

perception as an example of how we may perceive events. In R. Walk & H. L. Pick (Eds.), *Intersensory perception and sensory integration* (pp. 249–273). New York: Plenum.

Cytrynbaum, S., Bluum, L., Patrick, R., Stein, J., Wadner, D., & Wilk, C. (1980). Midlife development: A personality and social systems perspective. In L. Poon (Ed.), *Aging in the 1980s.* Washington, DC: American Psychological Association.

Dabbs, J. M., & Janis, I. L. (1965). Why does eating while reading facilitate opinion change? An experimental inquiry. *Journal of Experimental Social Psychology, 1,* 133–144.

Dalton, K. (1977). *The premenstrual syndrome and progesterone therapy.* London: Heinman.

Daniels, D., & Plomin, R. (1985). Origins of individual differences in infant shyness. *Developmental Psychology, 21,* 118–121.

Danish, S. J. (1983). Musings about personal competence: The contributions of sport, health, and fitness. *American Journal of Community Psychology, 11*(3), 221–240.

Darden, D. K., & Marks, A. (1985a, April). *Boredom and the analysis of role requirements.* Paper presented to Southern Sociological Society, Charlotte, NC.

Darden, D. K., & Marks, A. (1985b, August). *The meaning of boredom.* Paper presented to the Society for the Study of Symbolic Interaction, Washington, DC.

Darley, J., & Batson, C. D. (1973). From Jerusalem to Jericho: A study of situational and dispositional variables in helping behavior. *Journal of Personality and Social Psychology, 27,* 100–108.

Darley, J., & Berscheid, E. (1967). Increased liking as a result of the anticipation of personal contact. *Human Relations, 20* 29–40.

Davis, H. D., & Squire, L. R. (1984). Protein synthesis and memory: A review. *Psychological Bulletin, 96,* 518–559.

Davison, G. C., & Neale, J. M. (1986). *Abnormal psychology* (4th ed.). New York: Wiley.

Deaux, K. (1985). Sex and gender. *Annual Review of Psychology, 36,* 49–81.

DeCasper, A., & Fifer, W. (1980). Newborns prefer their mothers' voices. *Science, 208,* 1174–1176.

DeFries, J. C., & Plomin, R. (1978). Behavioral genetics. *Annual Review of Psychology, 29,* 473–515.

DeLongis, A., Coyne, J. C., Dakof, G., Folkman, S., & Lazarus, R. S. (1982). Relationship of daily hassles, uplifts, and major life events to health status. *Health Psychology, 1*(2), 119–136.

Dembroski, T. M., Lasater, T. M., & Ramirez, A. (1978). Communicator similarity, fear arousing communications, and compliance with health care recommendations. *Journal of Applied Social Psychology, 8,* 254–269.

Dement, W. (1960). The effect of dream deprivation. *Science, 131,* 1705–1707.

Dement, W., & Baird, W. P. (1977). *Narcolepsy: Care and treatment.* Stanford, CA: American Narcolepsy Association.

Denney, N. W. (1982). Aging and cognitive changes. In B. B. Wolman (Ed.), *Handbook of developmental psychology.* Englewood Cliffs, NJ: Prentice-Hall.

Denney, N. W., & Palmer, A. M. (1981). Adult age differences on traditional and practical problem-solving measures. *Journal of Gerontology, 36*(3), 323–328.

Dennis, W. (1960). Causes of retardation among institutional children: Iran. *Journal of Genetic Psychology, 96,* 47–59.

Deregowski, J. B. (1972). Pictorial perception and culture. *Scientific American, 227,* 83.

Deregowski, J. B. (1980). *Illusions, patterns and pictures: A cross-cultural perspective.* London: Academic.

Derogatis, L. R., Abeloff, M. D., & Melisaratos, N. Psychological coping mechanisms and survival time in metastatic breast cancer. *Journal of the American Medical Association, 242,* 1504–1508.

Deutsch, M., & Collins, M. E. (1951). *Interracial housing: A psychological evaluation of a social experiment.* Minneapolis: University of Minnesota Press.

DeVingues, R., & DeValois, K. (1975). Neural coding of color. In E. C. Carterette & M. P. Friedman (Eds.), *Handbook of perception* (Vol. 5). New York: Academic.

Diagnostic and statistical manual of mental disorders (DSM I). (1952). Washington, DC: American Psychiatric Association.

Diagnostic and statistical manual of mental disorders (DSM II). (1968). Washington, DC: American Psychiatric Association.

Diagnostic and statistical manual of mental disorders (DSM III). (1980). Washington, DC: American Psychiatric Association.

Dickey, W. (1981). I have had my vision. *The Key Reporter, 67*(1), 1–11.

Dickson, W. P. (1979). Referential communication performance from age 4 to 8: Effects of referent type, context, and target position. *Developmental Psychology, 15*(4), 470–471.

Dion, K. K., & Berscheid, E. (1974). Physical attractiveness and peer perception among children. *Sociometry, 37,* 1–12.

Dion, K. K., Berscheid, E., & Walster, E. (1972). What is beautiful is good. *Journal of Personality and Social Psychology, 24,* 285–290.

Dixon, R. A., & Baltes, P. B. (1986). Toward life-span research on the function and pragmatics of intelligence. In R. J. Sternberg & R. K. Wagner (Eds.), *Practical intelligence: Nature and origins of competence in the everyday world.* New York: Cambridge University Press.

Dodd, D. M., Kinsman, R., Klipp, R., & Bourne, L. E., Jr. (1971). Effects of logic pretraining on conceptual rule learning. *Journal of Experimental Psychology, 88,* 119–122.

Doering, C. H., Kraemer, H. C., Brodie, H. K. H., & Hamburg, D. A. (1975). A cycle of plasma testosterone in the human male. *Journal of Clinical Endocrinology and Metabolism, 40,* 492–500.

Dohrenwend, B. P., & Shrout, P. E. (1985). "Hassles" in the conceptualization and measurement of life stress variables. *American Psychologist, 40,* 780–785.

Dominick, J. R., & Greenberg, B. S. (1971). Attitudes towards violence: The interaction of television exposure, family attitudes, and social class. In G. A. Comstock & E. A. Rubinstein (Eds.), *Television and social behavior, Vol. 3: Television and adolescent aggressiveness.* Washington, DC: U.S. Government Printing Office.

Donnerstein, E. (1984). Pornography: Its effect on violence against women. In N. M. Malamuth & E. Donnerstein (Eds.), *Pornography and sexual aggression.* Orlando, FL: Academic.

Dorian, B. J., Keystone, E., Garfinkel, P. E., & Brown, G. M. (1982). Aberrations in lymphocyte subpopulations and functions during psychological stress. *Clinical and Experimental Immunology, 50,* 132–38.

Drachman, D. A., & Arbit, J. (1966). Memory and the hippocampal complex. *Archives of Neurology, 15,* 52–61.

Dreyer, P. H. (1982). Sexuality during adolescence. In B. B. Wolman (Ed.), *Handbook of developmental psychology.* Englewood Cliffs, NJ: Prentice-Hall.

Driscoll, R., Davis, K. E., & Lipetz, M. E. (1972). Parental interference and romantic love: The Romeo and Juliet effect. *Journal of Personality and Social Psychology, 24,*(1), 1–10.

Dryfoos, J. (1985). What the United States can learn about prevention of teenage pregnancy from other developed countries. *SIECUS Report, XIV,* 1–7.

Duncan, C. P. (1949). The retroactive effect of electroshock on learning. *Journal of Comparative and Physiological Psychology, 42,* 32–44.

Dunker, K. (1945). On problem-solving. *Psychological Monographs, 58*(5, Whole No. 270).

Dunn, J. (1985). *Sisters and brothers.* Cambridge, MA: Harvard University Press.

Durden-Smith, J., & DeSimone, D. (1982, April). The sex signals. *Playboy,* pp. 144–146, 226–242.

Dusek, D., & Girdano, D. A. (1980). *Drugs: A factual account.* Reading, MA: Addison-Wesley.

Dutton, D. G., & Aron, A. P. (1974). Some evidence for heightened sexual attraction under conditions of high anxiety. *Journal of Personality and Social Psychology, 30,* 510–517.

Dywan, J., & Bowers, K. (1983). The use of hypnosis to enhance recall. *Science, 222,* 184–185.

Eagly, A. (1983). Gender and social influence: A social psychological analysis. *American Psychologist, 38,* 971–981.

Eagly, A., & Carli, L. L. (1981). Sex of researcher and sex-typed communications as determinants of sex difference in influenceability: A meta-analysis of social influence studies. *Psychological Bulletin, 90*(1), 1–20.

Eagly, A., & Steffen, V. J. (1986). Gender and aggressive behavior: A meta-analytic review of the social psychological literature. *Psychological Bulletin, 100*(3), 309–330.·

Earle, J. R., & Perricone, P. J. (1986). Premarital sexuality: A ten year study of attitudes and behavior on a small university campus. *Journal of Sex Research, 22,* 304–310.

Eaton, W. W., Holzer, C. E., Von Korff, M., Anthony, J. C., Helzer, J. E., George, L., Burnam, M. A., Boyd, J. H., Kessler, L. G., & Locke, B. Z. (1984). The design of the epidemiologic catchment area surveys. *Archives of General Psychiatry, 41,* 942–948.

Ebbinghaus, H. (1913). *Memory: A contribution to experimental psychology* (H. A. Roger & C. E. Bussenius, Trans.). New York: Teachers College. (Original work published 1885)

Ecker, N., & Weinstein, S., (1983, April

16). *The relationship between attributions of sexual competency, physical appearance and narcissism.* Paper presented at conference of Society for Scientific Study of Sex, Eastern Region, Philadelphia.

Eckerman, C. O., & Stein, M. R. (1982). The toddler's emerging interactive skills. In K. H. Rubin & H. S. Ross (Eds.), *Peer relationships and social skills in childhood.* New York: Springer-Verlag.

Eckert, E. D., Heston, L. L., & Bouchard, T. J. (1981). MZ twins reared apart: Preliminary findings of psychiatric disturbances and traits. In *Twin research 3: Intelligence, personality and development.* New York: Liss.

Educational Testing Service. (1981). *Preliminary scholastic aptitude test.* Princeton, NJ: Author.

Edwards, C. P. (1977). The comparative study of the development of moral judgment and reasoning. In R. Monroe, R. Monroe, & B. B. Whiting (Eds.), *Handbook of cross-cultural human development.* New York: Garland.

Egeland, J. A., Gerhard, D. S., Pauls, D. L., Sussex, J. N., Kidd, K. K., Allen, C. R., Hostetter, A. M., & Housman, D. E. (1987). Bipolar affective disorders linked to DNA markers on chromosome 11. *Nature, 325*(26), 783–787.

Egeland, J. A., & Sussex, J. N. (1985). Suicide and family loading for affective disorders. *Journal of the American Medical Association, 254,* 915–918.

Ehrenreich, B., Hess, E., & Jacobs, G. (1986). *Re-making love.* Garden City, NY: Anchor Press/Doubleday.

Ehrhardt, A. A., & Money, J. (1967). Progestin induced hermaphroditism: I.Q. and psychosocial identity. *Journal of Sexual Research, 3,* 83–100.

Eibl-Eibesfeldt, I. (1972). *Love and hate.* (G. Strachan, Trans.). New York: Holt. (Original work published 1971)

Eiger, M. S., & Olds, S. W. (1987). *The complete book of breastfeeding.* New York: Workman.

Eimas, P., Siqueland, E., Jusczyk, P., & Vigorito, J. (1971). Speech perception in infants. *Science, 171,* 303–306.

Einstein, A. (1949). Autobiography. In P. Schilpp, *Albert Einstein: Philosopher–scientist.* Evanston, IL: Library of Living Philosophers.

Eisenberg, L. (1980). Adolescent suicide: On taking arms against a sea of troubles. *Pediatrics, 66,* 315–320.

Eisenberg, L. (1986). Does bad news about suicide beget bad news? *New England Journal of Medicine, 315*(11), 705–707.

Eisenberg, N., & Lennon, R. (1983). Sex differences in empathy and related capacities. *Psychological Bulletin, 94,* 100–131.

Eisenson, J., Auer, J. J., & Irwin, J. V. (1963). *The psychology of communication.* New York: Appleton-Century-Crofts.

Ekman, P., & Friesen, W. V. (1971). Constants across cultures in the face and emotion. *Journal of Personality and Social Psychology, 17,* 124–129.

Ekman, P., Friesen, W. V., & Ancoli, S. (1980). Facial signs of emotional experience. *Journal of Personality and Social Psychology, 39*(6), 1125–1134.

Ekman, P., Levenson, R. W., & Friesen, W. V. (1983). Autonomic nervous system activity distinguishes among emotions. *Science, 221,* 1208–1210.

Ekman, P., & Oster, H. (1982). Review of research, 1970–1980. In P. Ekman (Ed.), *Emotion in the human face* (2d ed.) (pp. 147–173). New York: Cambridge University Press.

Elkind, D. (1981). *The hurried child.* Reading, MA: Addison-Wesley.

Elkind, D. (1984). *All grown up and no place to go.* Reading, MA: Addison-Wesley.

Elliott, F. A. (1982). Neurological findings in adult minimal brain dysfunction and the dyscontrol syndrome. *Journal of Nervous and Mental Disease, 170*(11), 680–687.

Elliott, J. M. (1964). Measuring creative abilities in public relations and advertising work. In C. W. Taylor (Ed.), *Widening horizons in creativity.* New York: Wiley.

Ellis, A. (1958). Rational psychotherapy. *Journal of General Psychology, 59,* 35–49.

Ellis, A. (1974). *Humanistic psychotherapy.* New York: McGraw-Hill.

Ellis, A. (1979). Rational-emotive therapy. In R. J. Corsini, *Current psychotherapies* (2d ed.). Itasca, IL: Peacock.

Elton, D., Stanley, G., & Burrows, G. (1983). *Psychological control of pain.* Sydney: Grune & Stratton.

Engen, T. (1982). *The perception of odors.* New York: Academic.

Epstein, R., Kirshnit, C. E., Lanza, R. P., & Rubin, L. C. (1984). Insight in the pigeon: Antecedents and determinants of an intelligent performance. *Nature, 308,* 61–62.

Epstein, S., & O'Brien, E. J. (1985). The person-situation debate in historical and current perspective. *Psychological Bulletin, 98*(3), 513–537.

Erikson, E. H. (1950). *Childhood and society.* New York: Norton.

Erikson, E. H. (1963). *Childhood and society* (rev. ed.). New York: Norton.

Erikson, E. H. (Ed.). (1965). *The challenge of youth*. New York: Anchor.

Erikson, E. H. (1968). *Identity: Youth and crisis*. New York: Norton.

Erlenmeyer-Kimling, L., Cornblatt, B., & Fleiss, J. (1979). High-risk research in schizophrenia. *Psychiatric Annals, 9*(1), 79–102.

Eron, L. D. (1980). Prescription for reduction of aggression. *American Psychologist, 35*(3), 244–252.

Eron, L. D. (1982). Parent-child interaction, television violence, and aggression in children. *American Psychologist, 37*(2), 197–211.

Esquirol, J. E. D. (1838). *Des maladies mentales considerées sous les rapports medical, hygienique, et medico-legal* (Vols. 1–2). Paris: Bailliere.

Evans, E. F. (1982). Basic physics and psychophysics of sound. In H. B. Barlow & J. D. Mollon (Eds.), *The senses* (pp. 239–250). Cambridge: Cambridge University Press.

Eysenck, H. J. (1952). The effects of psychotherapy. *Journal of Consulting Psychiatry, 16*, 319–324.

Eysenck, H. J. (1965). The effects of psychotherapy. *International Journal of Psychiatry, 1*, 97–142.

Eysenck, H. J. (1967). *The biological basis of personality*. Springfield, IL: Thomas.

Eysenck, H. J. (1969). *The effects of psychotherapy*. New York: Science House.

Eysenck, H. J. (1976). *Sex and personality*. London: Open Books.

Eysenck, H. J., & Kamin, L. (1981). *The intelligence controversy*. New York: Wiley.

Fagan, J. F. (1982). Infant memory. In T. M. Field, A. Huston, H. Quay, L. Troll, & G. Finley (Eds.), *Review of human development*. New York: Wiley-Interscience.

Fagan, J. F., & McGrath, S. K. (1981). Infant recognition memory and later intelligence. *Intelligence, 5*, 121–130.

Falloon, I. R., Boyd, J. R., McGill, C. W., Razini, J., Moss, H. B., & Gilderman, A. M. (1982). Family management in the prevention of exacerbations of schizophrenia. *New England Journal of Medicine. 306*(24), 1437–1440.

Fancher, R. E. (1979). *The pioneers of psychology*. New York: Norton.

Fancher, R. E. (1985). *The intelligence men: Makers of the IQ controversy*. New York: Norton.

Fantz, R. L. (1956). A method for studying early visual development. *Perceptual and Motor Skills, 6*, 13–15.

Fantz, R. L. (1963). Pattern vision in newborn infants. *Science, 140*, 296–297.

Fantz, R. L. (1964). Visual experience in infants: Decreased attention to familiar patterns relative to novel ones. *Science, 146*, 668–670.

Fantz, R. L. (1965). Visual perception from birth as shown by pattern selectivity. In H. E. Whipple (Ed.), New issues in infant development, *Annals of the New York Academy of Science, 118*, 793–814.

Fantz, R. L., Fagan, J., & Miranda, S. B. (1975). Early visual selectivity. In L. Cohen & P. Salapatek (Eds.), *Infant perception: From sensation to cognition: Basic visual processes* (Vol. 1, pp. 249–341). New York: Academic.

Fantz, R. L., & Nevis, S. (1967). Pattern preferences and perceptual-cognitive development in early infancy. *Merrill-Palmer Quarterly, 13*, 77–106.

Faraone, S. V., & Tsuang, M. T. (1985). Quantitative models of the genetic transmission of schizophrenia. *Psychological Bulletin, 98*(1), 41–66.

Farber, S. (1981). Telltale behavior of twins. *Psychology Today, 15*(1), 60.

Farley, F. (1986a). The big T in personality. *Psychology Today, 20*(5), 44–52.

Farley, F. (1986b, April 12). Personal communication.

Federal Bureau of Investigation (FBI). (1983). *FBI law enforcement bulletin*. Washington, DC: Author.

Fenton, G. W. (1975, August). Clinical disorders of sleep. *British Journal of Hospital Medicine*, 120–144.

Feron, J. (1982, February 5). Hypnosis is on trial at Stouffer hearing. *The New York Times*, pp. B1–B2.

Feshback, S., & Weiner, B. (1982). *Personality*. Lexington, MA: Heath.

Festinger, L. (1957). *A theory of cognitive dissonance*. Stanford, CA: Stanford University Press.

Festinger, L. (1962, January). Cognitive dissonance. *Scientific American*, pp. 93–102.

Festinger, L., & Carlsmith, J. M. (1959). Cognitive consequences of forced compliance. *Journal of Abnormal and Social Psychology, 58*, 203–210.

Festinger, L., Schachter, S., & Back, K. (1950). *Social pressures in informal groups: A study of human factors in housing*. New York: Harper & Brothers.

Fielding, J. E. (1985a). Smoking: Health effects and control (First of two parts). *New England Journal of Medicine, 313*(8), 491–498.

Fielding, J. E. (1985b). Smoking: Health effects and control (Second of two parts). *New England Journal of Medicine, 313*(9), 555–562.

Fields, H. L., & Basbaum, A. I. (1978). Brainstem control of spinal pain-transmission neurons. *Annual Review of Physiology, 40*, 217–248.

Fillion, T. J., & Blass, E. M. (1986). Infantile experience with suckling odors determines adult sexual behavior in male rats. *Science, 231*, 729–731.

Filsinger, E. E., & Fabes, R. A. (1985). Odor communication, pheromones, and human families. *Journal of Marriage and the Family, 47*(2), 349–359.

Fishbein, D., & Thelen, M. H. (1981). Psychological factors in mate selection and marital satisfaction: A review. *Catalog of Selected Documents in Psychology, 11*, 84.

Fishbein, M., & Ajzen, I. (1974). Attitudes toward objects as predictive of single and multiple behavioral criteria. *Psychological Review, 81*, 59–74.

Fisher, K. (1986, February). DSM-III-R. *APA Monitor*, pp. 18–24.

Fisher, S., & Greenberg, R. P. (1977). *Scientific credibility of Freud's theories and therapy*. New York: Basic Books.

Fishman, S. M., & Sheehan, D. V. (1985). Anxiety and panic: Their cause and treatment. *Psychology Today, 19*(4), 26–32.

Fiske, E. B. (1981, March 17). Youth outwits merit exam, raising 240,000 scores. *The New York Times*, pp. A1, C4.

Flavell, J. H., Beach, D., & Chinsky, J. (1966). Spontaneous verbal rehearsal in a memory task as a function of age. *Child Development, 37*, 283–299.

Flynn, J. R. (1984). The mean IQ of Americans: Massive gains 1932 to 1978. *Psychological Bulletin, 95*(1), 29–51.

Foa, U. G., & Foa, E. B. (1974). *Societal structures of the mind*. Springfield, IL: Thomas.

Foley, V. D. (1979). Family therapy. In R. J. Corsini, *Current psychotherapies* (2d ed.) (pp. 460–499). Itasca, IL: Peacock.

Forman, G., & Siegel, I. (1979). *Cognitive development: A life-span view*. Belmont, CA: Wadsworth.

Foulkes, W. D. (1964). Theories of dream and recent studies of sleep formation consciousness. *Psychological Bulletin, 62*, 236–247.

Fouts, R. S. (1974). Language: Origin, definitions, and chimpanzees. *Journal of Human Evolution, 3*, 475–482.

Fox, J. R. (1983, January 18). *Inhibition, aggression, and kinship*. Paper presented at seminar, Recent Studies Concerning Dominance, Aggression, and Violence, Rockefeller University, New York.

Fox, N. A., & Davidson, R. J. (Eds.). (1984). *The psychobiology of affective development*. Hillsdale, NJ: Erlbaum.

Fox, R., & McDaniel, C. (1982). The perception of biological motion by human infants. *Science, 218*, 486–487.

Frances, S. J. (1979). Sex differences in nonverbal behavior. *Sex Roles, 5*, 519–535.

Francke, L. (1983, April 17). A growing number of programs to prevent child abuse. *The New York Times*, p. A1.

Frank, J. (1974). Psychotherapy: The restoration of morale. *American Journal of Psychiatry, 131*(31), 271–274.

Frank, J. (1979). What is psychotherapy? In S. Bloch (Ed.), *An introduction to the psychotherapies*. New York: Oxford University Press.

Frank, M. (1973). An analysis of hamster afferent taste nerve response function. *Journal of General Physiology, 61*, 588–618.

Freedman, D. X. (1984). Psychiatric epidemiology counts. *Archives of General Psychiatry, 41*, 931–933.

Freedman, J. L. (1984). Effect of television violence on aggressiveness. *Psychological Bulletin, 96*(2), 227–246.

Freedman, J. L., & Sears, D. O. (1965). Warning distraction, and resistance to influence. *Journal of Personality and Social Psychology, 1*, 262–266.

Freedman, J. L., Sears, D. O., & Carlsmith, J. M. (1981). *Social psychology* (4th ed.). Englewood Cliffs, NJ: Prentice-Hall.

Freeman, D. (1983). *Margaret Mead and Samoa*. Cambridge, MA: Harvard University Press.

Freeman, L. (1951). *Fight against fears*. New York: Crown.

Freeman, L., & Strean, H. S. (1981). *Freud and women*. New York: Ungar.

Freeman-Longo, R. E., & Wall, R. V. (1986, March). Changing a lifetime of sexual crime. *Psychology Today*, pp. 58–64.

Frequent bear forages to obtain favorite tidbits. (1983, June 22). *The New York Times*, p. 16.

Freud, S. (1949a). Instincts and their vicissitudes. In J. Riviere (Trans.), *Collected papers of Sigmund Freud* (Vol. 4, pp. 60–83). London: Hogarth. (Original work published 1915)

Freud, S. (1949b). Three essays on the theory of sexuality. In J. Strachey (Ed. and Trans.), *The standard edition of the complete psychological works of Sigmund Freud* (Vol. 7). London: Hogarth. (Original work published 1905)

Freud, S. (1950). The ego and the id. In J. Strachey (Ed. and Trans.), *The standard edition of the complete psychological works of Sigmund Freud*. London: Hogarth. (Original work published 1923)

Freud, S. (1955). *The interpretation of dreams*. New York: Basic Books. (Original work published 1900)

Freud, S. (1963). *Dora: An analysis of a case of hysteria*. New York: Collier. (Original work published 1905)

Fried, P. A., Watkinson, B., & Willan, A. (1984). Marijuana use during pregnancy and decreased length of gestation. *American Journal of Obstetrics and Gynecology, 150*, 23–27.

Friedman, M., & Rosenman, R. H. (1974). *Type A behavior and your heart*. New York: Knopf.

Friedman, J., Globus, G., Huntley, A., Mullaney, D., Naitoh, P., & Johnson, L. (1977). Performance and mood during and after gradual sleep reduction. *Psychophysiology, 14*, 245–250.

Frodi, A. (1976). Experiential and physiological processes mediating sex differences in behavioral aggression. *Göteborg Psychological Reports, 6*(16), 18.

Fromkin, V., Krashen, S., Curtiss, S., Rigler, D., & Rigler, M. (1974). The development of language in Genie: Acquisition beyond the "critical period." *Brain and Language, 1*, 81–107.

Frueh, T., & McGhee, P. (1975). Traditional sex role development and amount of time spent watching television. *Developmental Psychology, 11*(1), 109.

Gallagher, C. E. (1965). Opening remarks. Testimony before the House Special Subcommittee on Invasion of Privacy. *American Psychologist, 20*, 955–988.

Gallup, G. G., & Suarez, S. D. (1985). Alternatives to the use of animals in psychological research. *American Psychologist, 50*(10), 1104–1111.

Galton, F. (1883). *Inquiries into human faculty and development*. London: Macmillan.

Galton, F. (1979). *Hereditary genius: An inquiry into laws and consequences*. New York: St. Martin's. (Original work published 1869)

Garcia, J. (1981). The logic and limits of mental aptitude testing. *American Psychologist, 36*(10), 1172–1180.

Garcia, J., & Koelling, R. A. (1966). Relation of cue to consequence in avoidance learning. *Psychometric Science, 4*, 123–214.

Gardner, B. T., & Gardner, R. A. (1969). Teaching sign language to a chimpanzee. *Science, 162*, 664–672.

Gardner, H. (1979, March 29). Exploring the mystery of creativity. *The New York Times*, pp. C1, C17.

Gardner, H. (1985). *Frames of mind*. New York: Basic Books.

Garmezy, N. (1983). Stressors of childhood. In N. Garmezy & M. Rutter (Eds.), *Stress, coping and development in children*. New York: McGraw-Hill.

Garn, S. M. (1966). Growth and development. In E. Ginzberg (Ed.), *The nation's children* (pp. 24–42). New York: Columbia University Press.

Gazzaniga, M., & LeDoux, J. E. (1978). *The integrated mind*. New York: Plenum.

Gebhard, P. H., Gagnon, J. H., Pomeroy, W. B., & Christenson, C. V. (1965). *Sex offenders: An analysis of types*. New York: Harper & Row.

Geffner, R. (1978). *The effects of interdependent learning on self-esteem, interethnic relations, and intra-ethnic attitudes of elementary school children: A field experiment*. Unpublished doctoral dissertation, University of California, Santa Cruz.

Geller, E. S. (1984). A delayed reward strategy for large-scale motivation of safety belt use: A test of long-term impact. *Accident Analysis and Prevention, 16*(5/6), 457–463.

Geller, E. S. (1985). Seat belt psychology. *Psychology Today, 19*(5), 12–13.

Geller, E. S., Bruff, C. D., & Nimmer, J. G. (1985). *The "flash for life": Community-based prompting for safety belt promotion*. Unpublished manuscript.

Geller, E. S., & Hahn, H. A. (1984). Promoting safety belt use at industrial sites: An effective program for blue collar employees. *Professional Psychology: Research and Practice, 15*(4), 553–564.

Geller, E. S., Paterson, L., & Talbott, E. (1982). A behavioral analysis of incentive prompts for motivating seat belt use. *Journal of Applied Behavior Analysis, 15*, 403–415.

Gescheider, G. A. (1985). *Psychophysics: Method, theory, and application*. Hillsdale, NJ: Erlbaum.

Geschwind, N. (1979). Specializations of the human brain. *Scientific American, 241*(3), 180–199.

Geschwind, N., & Galaburda, A. M. (1985). Cerebral lateralization. Biological mechanisms, associations and pathology: I. A hypothesis and a program for research. *Archives of Neurology, 42*, 428–459.

Gesell, A. (1929). Maturation and infant behavior patterns. *Psychological Review, 36*, 307–319.

Getzels, J. W., & Jackson, P. W. (1963). The highly intelligent and the highly creative adolescent: A summary of some research findings. In C. W. Taylor & F. Baron (Eds.), *Scientific creativity: Its recognition and development.* New York: Wiley.

Gewirtz, H. B., & Gewirtz, J. L. (1968). Caretaking settings, background events, and behavior differences in four Israeli childrearing environments: Some preliminary trends. In B. M. Foss (Eds.), *Determinants of infant behavior* (Vol. 4). London: Methuen.

Gibson, J. J. (1979). *The ecological approach to visual perception.* Boston, MA: Houghton Mifflin.

Gil, D. G. (1971). Violence against children. *Journal of Marriage and the Family, 33*(4), 637–48.

Gill, J. J., Price, V. A., Friedman, M., Thoresen, C. E., Powell, L. H., Ulmer, D., Brown, B., & Drews, F. R. (1985). Reduction in type A behavior in healthy middle-aged American military officers. *American Heart Journal, 110*(3), 503–514.

Gilligan, C. (1982). *In a different voice: Psychological theory and women's development.* Cambridge, MA: Harvard University Press.

Ginzberg, E., et al. (1951). *Occupational choice: An approach to a general theory.* New York: Columbia University Press.

Gittleson, N. (1979, April 22). Maturing of Woody Allen. *The New York Times Magazine,* p. 104.

Gladue, B. A., Green, R., & Hellman, R. E. (1984). Neuroendocrine response to estrogen and sexual orientation. *Science, 225,* 1496–1499.

Glanzer, M., & Cunitz, A. R. (1966). Two storage mechanisms in free recall. *Journal of Verbal Learning and Verbal Behavior, 5,* 351–360.

Glass, A. L., Holyoak, K. J., & Santa, J. L. (1979). *Cognition.* San Francisco: Freeman.

Glass, D., Neulinger, J., & Brim, O. (1974). Birth order, verbal intelligence and educational aspirations. *Child Development, 45*(3), 807–811.

Glass, D., & Singer, J. E. (1972). *Urban stress: Experiments on noise and social stressors.* New York: Academic.

Gleason, J. B. (1967). Do children imitate? *Proceedings of the International Conference on Oral Education of the Deaf* (Vol. 2), pp. 1441–1448.

Goertzel, V., & Goertzel, M. G. (1962). *Cradles of eminence.* Boston: Little, Brown.

Gold, P. W., Gwirtsman, H., Avgerinos, P. C., Nieman, L. K., Gallucci, W. T., Kaye, W., Jimerson, D., Ebert, M., Ritt-

master, R., Loriaux, L., & Chrousos, G. P. (1986). Abnormal hypothalamic-pituitary-adrenal function in anorexia nervosa. *New England Journal of Medicine, 314,* 1335–1342.

Golden, N. L., Sokol, R. J., Kuhnert, B. R., & Bottoms, S. (1982). Maternal alcohol use and infant development. *Pediatrics, 70,* 931–934.

Goldfried, M. R., Stricker, G., & Weiner, I. R. (1971). *Rorschach handbook of clinical and research applications.* Englewood Cliffs, NJ: Prentice-Hall.

Goldgabern, D., Lerman, M. I., McBride, D. W., Saffiotti, U., & Gajdusek, D. C. (1987). Characterization and chromosomal location of a cDNA encoding brain amyloid of Alzheimer's disease. *Science, 235,* 877–880.

Goldman, R., Jaffa, M., & Schachter, S. (1968). Yom Kippur, Air France, dormitory food and eating behavior of obese and normal persons. *Journal of Personality and Social Psychology, 10,* 117–123.

Goldsmith, M. F. (1985). Possible herpes virus role in abortion studied. *Journal of the American Medical Association, 251,* 3067–3070.

Goleman, D. (1980). 1528 little geniuses and how they grew. *Psychology Today, 13*(9), 28–53.

Goleman, D. (1981). Deadlines for change. *Psychology Today, 15*(8), 60–69.

Goleman, D. (1984a, February 21). The aging mind proves capable of lifelong growth. *The New York Times,* pp. C1, C5.

Goleman, D. (1984b, November 6). Studies of children as witnesses find surprising accuracy. *The New York Times,* pp. C1, C4.

Goleman, D. (1986, March 4). Concentration is likened to euphoric states of mind. *The New York Times,* pp. C1, C3.

Goodenough, D. (1967). Some recent studies of dream recall. In H. Witkin & H. Lewis (Eds.), *Experimental studies of dreaming.* New York: Random House.

Goodner, C. J., & Russell, J. A. (1965). Pancreas. In T. C. Ruch & H. D. Patton (Eds.), *Physiology and biophysics.* Philadelphia: Saunders.

Goodstadt, M. S., Sheppard, M. A., & Chan, G. C. (1982). An evaluation of two school-based alcohol education programs. *Journal of Studies on Alcohol, 43,* 352–369.

Gorbach, S. L., Zimmerman, D. R., Woods, M. (1984). *The doctors' anti-breast-cancer diet.* New York: Simon & Schuster.

Gordon, E., & Terrell, M. (1981). The changed social context of testing. *American Psychologist, 36*(10), 1167–1171.

Gottesman, I. I. (1962). Differential inheritance of the psychoneuroses. *Eugenics Quarterly, 9,* 223–227.

Gottesman, I. I. (1979). Schizophrenia and genetics: Toward understanding uncertainty. *Psychiatric Annals, 9*(1), 54–78.

Gottesman, I. I., & Shields, J. (1966). Schizophrenia in twins: 16 years consecutive admission to a psychiatric clinic. *British Journal of Psychiatry, 112,* 809–818.

Gould, M. S., & Shaffer, D. (1986). The impact of suicide in television movies. *New England Journal of Medicine, 315,* 690–694.

Gould, S. J. (1981). *The mismeasure of man.* New York: Norton.

Gray-Little, B., & Burks, N. (1983). Power and satisfaction in marriage: A review and critique. *Psychological Bulletin, 93*(3), 513–538.

Green, H. (1964). *I never promised you a rose garden.* New York: Holt.

Green, R. (1976). One hundred ten feminine and masculine boys: Behavioral contrasts and demographic similarities. *Archives of Sexual Behavior, 5,* 425–446.

Greenberg, M., & Morris, N. (1974). Engrossment: The newborn's impact upon the father. *American Journal of Orthopsychiatry, 44*(4), 520–531.

Greenberg, S. B., & Peck, L. (1974). Personal communication.

Greenberger, E., & Steinberg, L. (1986) *When teenagers work: The psychological and social costs of adolescent employment.* New York: Basic Books.

Greenblat, C. S. (1983). The salience of sexuality in the early years of marriage. *Journal of Marriage and the Family, 45,* 289–299.

Greenwell, J., & Dengerink, H. A. (1973). The role of perceived versus actual attack in human physical aggression. *Journal of Personality and Social Psychology, 26*(1), 66–71.

Gregory, R. L. (1973). *Eye and brain* (2d ed.). New York: World University Library.

Grief, E. B., & Ulman, K. J. (1982). The psychological impact of menarche on early adolescent females: A review of the literature. *Child Development, 53,* 1413–1430.

Griffitt, W. B. (1970). Environmental effects on interpersonal affective behavior: Ambient effective temperature and attraction. *Journal of Personality and Social Psychology, 15,* 240–244.

Griffitt, W. B., & Veitch, R. (1971). Hot and crowded: Influence of population density and temperature on interpersonal affective behavior. *Journal of Personality and Social Psychology, 17,* 92–98.

Griffitt, W., & Veitch, R. (1974). Preacquaintance attitude similarity and attraction revisited: Ten days in a fallout shelter. *Sociometry, 37,* 163–173.

Grinspoon, L., & Bakalar, J. B. (1979). *Psychedelic drugs reconsidered.* New York: Basic Books.

Grossman, H. J. (1983). Classification in mental retardation. Washington, DC: American Association on Mental Deficiency.

Grotevant, H., & Durrett, M. (1980). Occupational knowledge and career development in adolescence. *Journal of Vocational Behavior, 17,* 171–182.

Group for the Advancement of Psychiatry. (1973). *The joys and sorrows of parenthood.* New York: Scribner's.

Groves, J. E. (1981). Borderline personality disorder. *New England Journal of Medicine, 305*(5), 259–262.

Gruneberg, M. M., Morris, P. E., & Sykes, R. N. (Eds.). (1978). *Practical aspects of memory.* London: Academic.

Guerney, B. G., Jr. (1977). *Relationship enhancement.* San Francisco: Jossey-Bass.

Guilford, J. P. (1959). Three faces of intellect. *American Psychologist, 14,* 469–479.

Guilford, J. P. (1967). *The nature of human intelligence.* New York: McGraw-Hill.

Guilford, J. P. (1977). *Way beyond the I.Q.* Buffalo, NY: Creative Education Foundation and Bearly Limited.

Guilford, J. P. (1982). Cognitive psychology's ambiguities: Some suggested remedies. *Psychological Review, 89*(1), 48–59.

Guilleminault, E., Eldridge, F., & Simmons, B. (1976). Sleep apnea in eight children. *Pediatrics, 58,* 23–30.

Gummerman, K., & Gray, C. R. (1971). Recall of visually presented material: An unwonted case and a bibliography for eidetic imagery. *Psychonomic Monograph Supplements, 4*(10).

Gurman, A. S., & Razin, M. (1977). *Effective psychotherapy: A handbook of research.* New York: Pergamon.

Alan Guttmacher Institute. (1981). *Teenage pregnancy: The problem that hasn't gone away.* New York: Author.

Gwirtsman, H. E., & Gerner, R. H. (1981). Neurochemical abnormalities in anorexia nervosa: Similarities to affective disorders. *Biological Psychiatry, 16,* 991–995.

Gynther, M. D. (1972). White norms and black MMPIs: A prescription for discrimination? *Psychological Bulletin, 5,* 386–403.

Haan, N., & Day, D. (1974). A longitudinal study of change and sameness in personality development: Adolescence to later adulthood. *International Journal of Aging and Human Development, 5*(1), 11–39.

Haas, A., & Sherman, M. (1982). Conversational topic as a function of role and gender. *Psychological Reports, 51*(2), 453–454.

Hall, C. S. (1966). *The meaning of dreams.* New York: McGraw-Hill.

Hall, C. S., Domhoff, G. W., Blick, K. A., & Weesner, K. E. (1982). The dreams of college men and women in 1950 and 1980: A comparison of dream contents and sex differences. *Sleep, 5,* 188–194.

Hall, E. (1983), A conversation with Erik Erikson. *Psychology Today, 17*(6), 22–30.

Hall, E. (1984). Sandra Scarr: What's a parent to do? *Psychology Today, 18*(5), 59–63.

Hall, G. S. (1916). *Adolescence.* New York: Appleton.

Hamburg, D. (1983, January 19). *The evolutionary background of human behavior.* Lecture given at the American Museum of National History, New York.

Hamilton, S., & Crouter, A. (1980). Work and growth: A review of research on the impact of work experience on adolescent development. *Journal of Youth and Adolescence, 9*(4), 323–338.

Hammond, C. B., Jelovsek, F. R., Lee, K. L., Creasman, W. T., & Parker, R. T. (1979). Effects of long-term estrogen replacement therapy. II. Neoplasia. *American Journal of Obstetrics and Gynecology, 133,* 537–547.

Harkins, E. (1978). Effects of empty nest transition on self-report of psychological and physical well-being. *Journal of Marriage and the Family, 40*(3), 549–556.

Harlow, H. (1958). The nature of love. *American Psychologist, 13,* 673–685.

Harlow, H. (1962). The heterosexual affection system in monkeys. *American Psychologist, 17,* 1–9.

Harlow, H. F., & Harlow, M. K. (1962). The effect of rearing conditions on behavior. *Bulletin of the Menninger Clinic, 26,* 213–224.

Harlow, H. F., & Harlow, M. K. (1969). Effects of various mother-infant relationships on rhesus monkey behaviors. In B. M. Foss (Ed.), *Determinants of infant behavior* (Vol. 4). London: Methuen.

Harlow, H. F., & Zimmerman, R. R. (1959). Affectional responses in the infant monkey. *Science, 130,* 421–432.

Harrell, R. F., Woodyard, E., & Gates, A. (1955). *The effect of mothers' diets on the intelligence of the offspring.* New York: Bureau of Publications, Teacher's College.

Harris, B. (1979). Whatever happened to little Albert? *American Psychologist, 34*(2), 151–160.

Hart, K. J., & Ollendick, T. H. (1985). Prevalence of bulimia in working and university women. *American Journal of Psychiatry, 142*(7), 851–854.

Hartman, M. (1976). A descriptive study of the language of men and women born in Maine around 1900 as it reflects the Lakoff hypothesis in "Language and woman's place." In B. L. DuBois & I. Crouch (Eds.), *The sociology of the languages of American women* (pp. 81–90). San Antonio, TX: Trinity University Press.

Hartmann, E. (1981). The strangest sleep disorder. *Psychology Today, 15,* 14–18.

Hartmann, E., Baekeland, F., & Zwilling, G. R. (1972). Psychological differences between long and short sleepers. *Archives of General Psychiatry, 26,* 463–468.

Hartmann, E., & Brewer, V. (1976). When is more or less sleep required? A study of variable sleepers. *Comprehensive Psychiatry, 17*(2), 275–284.

Hartshorne, H., & May, M. A. (1928a). *Studies in the nature of character: Vol. 1. Studies in deceit.* New York: Macmillan.

Hartshorne, H., & May, M. A. (1928b). *Studies in the nature of character: Vol. 2. Studies in self-control.* New York: Macmillan.

Harvard Medical School Mental Health Letter, (1985a, July). The antisocial personality, Part I. *2*(1), 1–4.

Harvard Medical School Mental Health Letter (1985b, December). Borderline personality disorder, Part I. *2*(6), 1–3.

Harvard Medical School Mental Health Letter. (1986, February). Suicide, Part I. *2*(8), 1–4.

Hashim, S. A., & Van Itallie, T. B. (1965). Studies in normal and obese subjects with a monitored food dispensary device. *Annals of the New York Academy of Science, 131,* 654–661.

Hasset, J., and the Editors of *Psychology Today.* (1981, November). Is it right? An inquiry into everyday ethics. *Psychology Today*, pp. 49–56.

Hatfield, E., Traupmann, J., Sprecher, S., Utne, M., & Hay, J. (1984). Equity and intimate relations: Recent research. In W. Ickes (Ed.), *Compatible and incompatible relationships*. New York: Springer-Verlag.

Hay, D. F., Pedersen, J., & Nash, A. (1982). Dyadic interaction in the first year of life. In K. H. Rubin & H. S. Ross (Eds.), *Peer relationships and social skills in childhood*. New York: Springer-Verlag.

Hayden, A., & Haring, N. (1976). Early intervention for high risk infants and young children. Programs for Down's syndrome children. In T. D. Tjossem (Ed.), *Intervention strategies for high risk infants and young children*. Baltimore: University Park Press.

Hayes, C. (1951). *The ape in our house*. New York: Harper & Row.

Hayflick, L. (1974). The strategy of senescence. *Gerontologist, 14*(1), 37–45.

Hays, R. B. (1985), A longitudinal study of friendship development. *Journal of Personality and Social Psychology, 48*(4), 909–924.

Hearnshaw, L. S. (1979). *Cyril Burt: Psychologist*. Ithaca, NY: Cornell University Press.

Hearst, E. (1979). One hundred years: Themes and perspectives. In E. Hearst (Ed.), *The first century of experimental psychology*. Hillsdale, NJ: Erlbaum.

Hebb, D. O. (1949). *The organization of behavior*. New York: Wiley.

Hebb, D. O. (1955). Drive and the C.N.S. (conceptual nervous system). *Psychological Review, 62*(4), 243–254.

Hebb, D. O. (1978). On watching myself get old. *Psychology Today, 12*(6), 15–23.

Hecht, S., Shlaer, S., & Pirenne, M. H. (1941). Energy at the threshold of vision. *Science, 93*(2425), 585–587.

Heckler, M. M. (1985). The fight against Alzheimer's disease. *American Psychologist, 40*(11), 1240–1244.

Heide, F. J., & Borkovec, T. D. (1983). Relaxation-induced anxiety enhancement due to relaxation training. *Journal of Clinical and Consulting Psychology, 51*(2), 171–182.

Heide, F. J., & Borkovec, T. D. (1984). Relaxation-induced anxiety: Mechanisms and theoretical implications. *Behavioral Research and Therapy, 22*(1), 1–12.

Heider, E. R., & Olivier, D. C. (1972). The structure of the color space in naming and memory in two languages. *Cognitive Psychology, 3*, 337–354.

Heider, F. (1958). *The psychology of interpersonal relations*. New York: Wiley.

Heiman, J. R., LoPiccolo, L., & LoPiccolo, J. (1980). The treatment of sexual dysfunction. In A. Gurman & D. Kniskern (Eds.), *Handbook of family therapy*. New York: Brunner/Mazel.

Helmreich, R. (1968). Birth order effects. *Naval Research Reviews, 21*.

Henker, F. O. (1981). Male climacteric. In J. G. Howells (Ed.), *Modern perspectives in the psychiatry of middle age*. New York: Brunner/Mazel.

Herbert, W. (1982). Schizophrenia: From adolescent insanity to dopamine disease. *Science News, 121*(11), 173–175.

Herbst, A. L., Ulfelder, H., & Poskanzer, D. (1971). Adenocarcinoma of the vagina. *New England Journal of Medicine, 284*(16), 878–881.

Hering, E. (1920). *Grundzuge der Lehr vs. Lichtsinn*. Berlin: Springer-Verlag.

Heron, W. (1961). Cognitive and physiological effects of perceptual isolation. In P. Solomon, P. E. Kubzansky, P. H. Leiderman, J. H. Mendelson, R. Trumbull, & D. Wexler (Eds.), *Sensory deprivation*. Cambridge, MA: Harvard University Press.

Herr, J., & Weakland, J. (1979). Communication within family systems: Growing older within and with the double-bind. In P. K. Regan (Ed.), *Aging parents*. Los Angeles: University of Southern California Press.

Herzog, D. B. (1982). Bulimia in the adolescent. *American Journal of Diseases of Children, 136*, 985–989.

Heston, L. L. (1966). Psychiatric disorders in foster-home-reared children of schizophrenic mothers. *British Journal of Psychiatry, 112*, 819–825.

Heston, L. L., & White, J. A. (1983). *Dementia*. New York: Freeman.

Hetherington, E. M. (1965). A developmental study of the effects of sex of the dominant parent on sex role preference, identification and imitation in children. *Journal of Personality and Social Psychology, 2*, 188–194.

Hetherington, M., Cox, M., & Cox, R. (1975). *Beyond father absence: Conceptualizing effects of divorce*. Paper presented at the biennial meeting of the Society for Research in Child Development, Denver.

Hilgard, E. R. (1977). The problem of divided consciousness: A neodissociation interpretation. In W. E. Edmonston, Jr. (Ed.), *Conceptual and investigative approaches to hypnosis and hypnotic phenomena*. New York: New York Academy of Sciences.

Hilgard, J. R. (1970). *Personality and hypnosis: A study of imaginative involvement*. Chicago: University of Chicago Press.

Hilgard, J. R. (1979). *Personality and hypnosis* (2d ed.). Chicago: University of Chicago Press.

Hill, C. T., Rubin, Z., & Peplau, L. A. (1976). Breakups before marriage: The end of 103 affairs. *Journal of Social Issues, 32*(1), 147–168.

Hingson, R., Alpert, J. J., Day, N., Dooling, E., Kayne, H., Morelock, S., Oppenheimer, E., & Zuckerman, B. (1982). Effects of maternal drinking and marijuana use on fetal growth and development. *Pediatrics, 70*(4), 539–546.

Hirsch, H. V., & Spinelli, D. N. (1970). Visual experience modifies distribution of horizontally and vertically oriented receptive fields in cats. *Science, 168*, 869–871.

Hobson, J. A., & McCarley, R. W. (1977). The brain as a dream state generator: An activation-synthesis hypothesis of the dream process. *The American Journal of Psychiatry, 134*(12), 1335–1348.

Hochbaum, G. (1958). *Public participation in medical screening programs: A sociopsychological study* (Public Health Service Publication No. 572). Washington, DC: U.S. Government Printing Office.

Hoffman, H. J., & Solomon, R. L. (1974). An opponent-process theory of motivation III: Some affective dynamics in imprinting. *Learning and Motivation, 5*, 149–164.

Hoffman, M. (1977). Sex differences in empathy and related behaviors. *Psychological Bulletin, 84*, 712–722.

Hogan, D. B. (1979). *The regulation of psychotherapists: A study in the philosophy and practice of professional regulation* (Vol. 1). Cambridge, MA: Ballinger.

Hogan, R. (1986). Personal communication.

Hogan, R., Carpenter, B. N., Briggs, S. R., & Hansson, R. D. (1985). Personality assessment in industry: A historical and conceptual overview. In J. Bernardin & D. Bownas (Eds.), *Personality assessment in organizations*. New York: Praeger.

Holahan, C. J., & Moos, R. H. (1985). Life stress and health: Personality, coping, and family support in stress resistance, *Journal of Personality and Social Psychology, 49*(3), 739-747.

Holmes, D. S. (1984). Meditation and somatic arousal reduction. *American Psychologist, 39*(1), 1–10.

Holmes, T. H., & Masuda, M. (1974). Life

change and illness susceptibility.. In B. S. Dohrenwend & B. P. Dohrenwend (Eds.), *Stressful life events: Their nature and effects*. New York: Wiley.

Holmes, T. H., & Rahe, R. H. (1967). The social readjustment rating scale. *Journal of Psychosomatic Research, 11*, 213–218.

Holroyd, K. A., & Lazarus, R. S. (1982). Stress, coping, and somatic adaptation. In L. Goldberger & S. Breznitz (Eds.), *Handbook of stress*. New York: Free Press.

Holton, G. (1972). On trying to understand scientific genius. *American Scholar, 41*, 95–110.

Homans, G. C. (1961). *Social behavior: Its elementary forms*. New York: Harcourt Brace Jovanovich.

Hooker, E. (1957). The adjustment of the male overt homosexual. *Journal of Projective Techniques, 21*, 18–31.

Hoova, R., Gray, L. A., & Fraumeni, J. F., Jr. (1977, September 10). Stilboestrol (Diethystilbestrol) and the risk of ovarian cancer. *Lancet*, pp. 553–534.

Horel, J. A. (1978). Neuroanatomy of amnesia. Critique of the hippocampal memory hypothesis. *Brain, 101*, 403–445.

Horm, J. W., & Kessler, L. G. (1986, February 22). Falling rates of lung cancer in men in the United States. *Lancet*, pp. 425–426.

Horn, J. (1978). Human ability systems. In P. B. Baltes (Ed.), *Life-span development and behavior* (Vol. 1). New York: Academic.

Horn, J. (1983). The Texas adoption project: Adopted children and their intellectual resemblance to biological and adoptive parents. *Child Development, 54*, 268–275.

Horn, J., & Donaldson, G. (1980). Cognitive development II: Adulthood development of human abilities. In O. G. Brim & J. Kagan (Eds.), *Constancy and change in human development*. Cambridge, MA: Harvard University Press.

Horney, K. (1939). *New ways in psychoanalysis*. New York: Norton.

Horney, K. (1945). *Our inner conflicts*. New York: Norton.

Houts, M. (1981). The accuracy/fallibility of eyewitness reporting. *Trauma, 23*, 1–6.

Hovland, C. I., Lumsdaine, A. A., & Sheffield, F. D. (1949). *Experiments on mass communication. Studies in social psychology in World War II* (Vol. 3). Princeton, NJ: Princeton University Press.

Howard, K. I., Kopta, S. M., Krause, M. S., & Orlinsky, D. E. (1986). The dose-effect relationship in psychother-

apy. *American Psychologist, 41*(2), 159–164.

Hoyenga, K. B., & Hoyenga, K. T. (1979). *The question of sex differences*. Boston: Little, Brown.

Hubel, D. H. (1963). The visual cortex of the brain. *Scientific American, 209*(30), 54–62.

Hubel, D. H. (1979). The brain. *Scientific American, 241*(3), 44–53.

Hubel, D. H. (1982). Explorations of the primary visual cortex, 1955–1978. *Nature, 299*, 515–524.

Hubel, D. H., & Wiesel, T. N. (1959). Receptive fields of single neurons in the cat's striate cortex. *Journal of Physiology, 148*, 574–591.

Hubel, D. H., & Wiesel, T. N. (1979). Brain mechanisms and vision. *Scientific American, 24*(3), 150–162.

Huesmann, L. R., Eron, L. D., Klein, R., Brice, P., & Fischer, P. (1983). Mitigating the imitation of aggressive behaviors by changing children's attitudes about media violence. *Journal of Personality and Social Psychology, 44*(5), 899–910.

Hull, C. L. (1943). *Principles of behavior*. New York: Appleton-Century-Crofts.

Hulse, S. H., Egeth, H., & Deese, J. (1980). *The psychology of learning* (5th ed.). New York: McGraw-Hill.

Hunt, E., & Love, T. (1982). The second mnemonist. In U. Neisser (Ed.), *Memory observed*. San Francisco: Freeman. (Original work was paper presented to the American Psychological Association in Honolulu, September, 1972)

Hunt, M. M. (1974). *Sexual behavior in the 1970's*. New York: Dell.

Hunt, M. M. (1982). *The universe within: A new science explores the human mind*. New York: Simon & Schuster.

Hunziker, U. A., & Barr, R. G. (1986). Increased carrying reduces infant crying: A randomized controlled trial. *Pediatrics, 77*(5), 641–648.

Hurvich, L. M. (1981). *Color vision*. Sunderland, MA: Sinauer Associates.

Hurvich, L. M., & Jameson, D. (1957). An opponent-process theory of color vision. *Psychological Review, 64*, 384–404.

Huston, T. L. (1983). Power. In H. H. Kelley, E. Berscheid, A. Christensen, J. H. Harvey, T. L. Huston, G. Levinger, E. McClintock, L. A. Peplau, & D. R. Peterson, *Close relationships*. New York: Freeman.

Huston, T. L., & Levinger, G. (1978). Interpersonal attraction and relationships. *Annual Review of Psychology, 29*, 115–156.

Hyde, J. S. (1981). How large are cogni-

tive gender differences? *American Psychologist, 36*(8), 892–901.

Hyde, J. S. (1984). How large are gender differences in aggression? A developmental meta-analysis. *Developmental Psychology, 20*, 722–736.

Hyde, J. S. (1986). *Understanding human sexuality* (3d ed.), New York: McGraw-Hill.

Hyman, B. T., Van Hoesen, G. W., Damasio, A. R., & Barnes, C. L. (1984). Alzheimer's disease: Cell-specific pathology isolates hippocampal formation. *Science, 225*, 1168–1170.

Hyman, H. H., & Sheatsley, P. B. (1956). Attitudes toward desegregation. *Scientific American, 195*(6), 35–39.

Hypnotized man remembers too much. (1978). *American Bar Association Journal, 64*, 187.

Inouye, E. (1965). Similar and dissimilar manifestations of obsessive compulsive neuroses in monozygotic twins. *American Journal of Psychology, 121*, 1171–1175.

Irwin, P. (1985). Greater brain response of left-handers to drugs. *Neuropsychologica, 23*, 61–67.

Isenberg, P., & Schatzberg, A. F. (1978). Psychonanalytic contribution to a theory of depression. In J. O. Cole, A. F. Schatzberg, & S. H. Frazier. (Eds.), *Depression: Biology, psychodynamics, and treatment*. New York: Plenum.

Iverson, L. L. (1979). The chemistry of the brain. *Scientific American, 242*(3), 134-147.

Izard, C. E. (1971). *The face of emotions*. New York: Appleton-Century-Crofts.

Izard, C. E. (1977). *Human emotions*. New York: Plenum.

Izard, C. E. (1979). Emotions as motivations: An evolutionary-developmental perspective. In R. A. Dienstbier (Ed.), *1978 Nebraska Symposium on Motivation* (pp. 163–200). Lincoln: University of Nebraska Press.

Izard, C. E., Huebner, R. R., Resser, D., McGinnes, G. C., & Dougherty, L. M. (1980). The young infant's ability to produce discrete emotional expressions. *Developmental Psychology, 16*(2), 132–140.

Jacobsen, H. (1977). Current concepts in nutrition: Diet in pregnancy. *New England Journal of Medicine, 297*(19), 1051–1053.

Jacobsen, J. L., & Wille, D. E. (1986). Influence of attachment patterns on developmental changes in peer interaction from the toddler to the preschool period. *Child Development, 57*, 338–347.

James, W. (1884). What is an emotion? *Mind, 9,* 188–205.

Janis, I. L. (1971). Groupthink. *Psychology Today, 5,* 43.

Janis, I. L. (1982). Counteracting the adverse effects of concurrence-seeking in policy planning groups: Theory and research perspectives. In I. H. Brandstatter, J. H. Davis, & G. Stocker-Kreichgauer (Eds.), *Group decision making.* New York: Academic.

Janis, I. L., Kaye, D., & Kirschner, P. (1965). Facilitating effects of eating while reading on responsiveness to persuasive communication. *Journal of Personality and Social Psychology, 1,* 181–186.

Janis, I. L., & Mann, L. (1965). Effectiveness of emotional role-playing in modifying smoking habits and attitudes. *Journal of Experimental Research in Personality, 1,* 84–90.

Jarvik, K. F., Kallman, F., & Klaber, N. M. (1957). Changing intellectual functions in senescent twins. *Acta Genetic Statistica Medica, 7,* 421–430.

Jasper, H. H. (1958). The ten twenty electrode system of the International Federation. *Electroencephalography and Clinical Neurophysiology, 10,* 371–375.

Jay, T. B. (1980). Sex roles and dirty word usage: A review of the literature and a reply to Haas. *Psychological Bulletin, 88,* 614–621.

Jemmott, J. B., III, Borysenko, J. Z., Borysenko, M., McClelland, D. C., Chapman, R., Meyer, D., & Benson, H. (1983). Academic stress, power motivation, and decrease in salivary secretory immunoglobulin A secretion rate. *Lancet, 1,* 1400–1402.

Jensen, A. R. (1969). How much can we boost IQ and scholastic achievement? *Harvard Educational Review, 39,* 1–123.

Johansson, G. (1973). Visual perception of biological motion and a model for its analysis. *Perception & Psychophysics, 14,* 201–211.

Johansson, G. (1975). Visual motion perception. *Scientific American, 232,* 76–88.

Johnson, C., & Larson, R. (1982). Bulimia: An analysis of moods and behavior. *Psychosomatic Medicine, 44,* 341–351.

Johnson, C. L., Stuckey, M. K., Lewis, L. D., & Schwartz, D. M. (1982). Bulimia: A descriptive survey of 316 cases. *International Journal of Eating Disorders, 2,* 3–16.

Johnson, R. N. (1972). *Aggression in man and animals.* Philadelphia: Saunders.

Johnston, L. D., O'Malley, P. M., & Bachman, J. G. (1985). *Use of licit and illicit drugs by America's high school students, 1975–1984* (DDHS Publication No. ADM 85-1394). Rockville, MD: National Institute on Drug Abuse.

Johnston, L. D., O'Malley, P. M., & Bachman, J. G. (1986). *Drug use among American high school students, college students, and other young adults: National trends.* Rockville, MD: National Institute on Drug Abuse.

Jones, E. (1977). How do people perceive the causes of behavior? In I. Janis (Ed.), *Current trends in psychology.* Los Altos, CA: Kaufmann.

Jones, E., & Harris, V. A. (1967). The attribution of attitudes. *Journal of Experimental Social Psychology, 3,* 2–24.

Jones, H. E. (1930). The retention of conditioned emotional reactions in infancy. *Journal of Genetic Psychology, 37,* 485–497.

Jones, K. L., Smith, D. W., Ulleland, C., & Streissguth, A. P. (1973). Patterns of malformation in offspring of chronic alcoholic mothers. *Lancet, 1(7815),* 1267–1271.

Jones, M. C. (1924). A laboratory study of fear: The case of Peter. *Pedagogical Seminary, 31,* 308–315.

Jones, M. C. (1957). The late careers of boys who were early- or late-maturing. *Child Development, 28,* 115–128.

Jones, M. C., & Mussen, P. H. (1958). Self-conceptions, motivations, and interpersonal attitudes of early- and late-maturing girls. *Child Development, 29,* 491–501.

Jost, H., & Sontag, L. (1944). The genetic factor in autonomic nervous system function. *Psychosomatic Medicine, 6,* 308–310.

Jung, C. G. (1933). *Modern man in search of a soul.* New York: Harcourt, Brace & World.

Jung, C. G. (1953). The stages of life. In H. Read, M. Fordham, & G. Adler (Eds.), *Collected works* (Vol. 2). Princeton: Princeton University Press. (Original work published 1931)

Just, M. A., & Carpenter, P. A. (1980). A theory of readings: From eye fixations to comprehension. *Psychological Review, 87,* 329–354.

Kacerguis, M., & Adams, G. (1980). Erikson stage resolution: The relationship between identity and intimacy. *Journal of Youth and Adolescence, 9(2),* 117–126.

Kagan, J. (1958). The concept of identification. *Psychological Review, 65(5),* 296–305.

Kagan, J. (1971). *Personality development.* New York: Harcourt Brace Jovanovich.

Kagan, J. (1979). Overview: Perspective on human infancy. In J. Osofsky (Ed.), *Handbook of infant development.* New York: Wiley.

Kagan, J. (1982). Canalization of early psychological development. *Pediatrics, 70(3),* 474–483.

Kahle, L. R. (1983). *Attitudes, attributes, and adaptation.* London: Pergamon.

Kahle, L. R., & Berman, J. (1979). Attitudes cause behaviors: A cross-lagged panel analysis. *Journal of Personality and Social Psychology, 37,* 315–321.

Kahn, J. P., Kornfeld, D. S., Frank, K. A., Heller, S. S., & Hoar, P. F. (1980). Type A behavior and blood pressure during coronary artery bypass surgery. *Psychosomatic Medicine, 42,* 407–414.

Kalat, J. W. (1984). *Biological psychology* (3d ed.). Belmont, CA: Wadsworth.

Kamin, L. J. (1974). *The science and politics of IQ.* Potomac, MD: Erlbaum.

Kandel, E. R. (1976). *The cellular basis of behavior.* San Francisco: Freeman.

Kandel, E. R. (1979). Small systems of neurons. *Scientific American, 241(14),* 66–76.

Kanellakos, D. P. (1978). Transcendental consciousness: Expanded awareness as a means of preventing and eliminating the effects of stress. In C. D. Spielberger & I. G. Sarason (Eds.), *Stress and anxiety* (Vol. 5). New York: Wiley.

Kanner, A. D., Coyne, J. C., Schaefer, C., & Lazarus, R. S. (1981). Comparison of two modes of stress measurement: Daily hassles and uplifts versus major life events. *Journal of Behavioral Medicine, 4(1),* 1–39.

Kaplan, H. S. (1979). *Disorders of sexual desire.* New York: Simon & Schuster.

Kaplan, M. (1983a). The issue of sex bias in DSM-III. *American Psychologist, 38,* 802–803.

Kaplan, M. (1983b). A woman's view of the DSM-III. *American Psychologist, 38,* 786–792.

Kass, F., Spitzer, R. L., & Williams, J. B. W. (1983). An empirical study of the issue of sex bias in the diagnostic criteria of DSM-III Axis II personality disorders. *American Psychologist, 38,* 799–801.

Katerndahl, D. A. (1984). Panic attacks: Psychologic response or medical illness? *Postgraduate Medicine, 75(8),* 262.

Keesey, R. E., & Powley, T. L. (1975). Hypothalamic regulation of body weight. *American Scientist, 63,* 558–565.

Kelley, H. H. (1950). The warm-cold variable in first impressions of persons. *Journal of Personality, 18,* 431–439.

Kelley, H. H. (1967). Attribution theory in social psychology. *Nebraska Symposium on Motivation, 15,* 192–238.

Kellogg, W. N., & Kellogg, L. A. (1933). *The ape and the child.* New York: McGraw-Hill.

Kelly, J. B. (1982). Divorce: The adult perspective. In B. Wolman (Ed.), *Handbook of developmental psychology.* Englewood Cliffs, NJ: Prentice-Hall.

Kelman, H. C., & Hovland, C. (1953). "Reinstatement" of the communicator in delayed measurement of opinion change. *Journal of Abnormal and Social Psychology, 48,* 326–335.

Kermis, M., Monge, R., & Dusek, J. (1975). *Human sexuality in the hierarchy of adolescent interests.* Paper presented at the Annual Meeting of the Society for Research in Child Development, Denver.

Kety, S. S., Rosenthal, D., Wender, P. H., & Schulsinger, F. (1968). The types and prevalence of mental illness in the biological and adoptive families of adopted schizophrenics. In D. Rosenthal & S. S. Kety (Eds.), *Transmission of schizophrenia.* London: Pergamon.

Kety, S. S., Rosenthal, D., Wender, P. H., Schulsinger, F., & Jacobsen, B. (1975). Mental illness in the biological and adoptive families of adopted individuals who have become schizophrenic: A preliminary report based on psychiatric interviews. In R. R. Fieve, D. Rosenthal, & D. Brill (Eds.), *Genetic research in psychiatry.* Baltimore: Johns Hopkins University Press.

Kiecolt-Glaser, J. K., Speicher, C. E., Holliday, J. E., & Glaser, R. (in press). Stress and the transformation of lymphocytes by Epstein-Barr virus. *Journal of Behavioral Medicine.*

Kiesler, C. A. (1982). Mental hospitals and alternative care: Noninstitutionalization as potential public policy for mental patients. *American Psychologist, 37*(4), 349–360.

Kiester, E., Jr. (1986). Spare parts for damaged brains. *Science 86, 7*(2), 33–41.

Kihlstrom, J. F., & Evans, F. J. (1979). *Functional disorders of memory.* Hillsdale, NJ: Erlbaum.

Kihlstrom, J. F., & Harakiewicz, J. M. (1982). The earliest recollection: A new survey. *Journal of Personality, 50*(2), 134–148.

Kimmel, D. C. (1974). *Adulthood and aging.* New York: Wiley.

Kimura, D. (1985, November). Male brain, female brain: The hidden difference. *Psychology Today,* pp. 51–58.

Kimura, D., & Harshman, R. A. (1984). Sex differences in brain organization for verbal and nonverbal functions. *Programs for Brain Research, 61,* 423–441.

Kimzey, S. L., Johnson, P. C., Ritzman, S. E., & Mengel, C. E. (1976, April). Hematology and immunology studies: The second manned Skylab mission. *Aviation, Space, and Environmental Medicine, 47*(4), 383–390.

Kingdon, J. W. (1967). Politicians belief about voters. *The American Science Review, 61,* 137–145.

Kinsey, A. C., Pomeroy, W., & Martin, C. E. (1948). *Sexual behavior in the human male.* Philadelphia: Saunders.

Kinsey, A. C., Pomeroy, W., Martin, C. E., & Gebhard, P. H. (1953). *Sexual behavior in the human female.* Philadelphia: Saunders.

Klaas, E. T. (1978). Psychological effects of immoral actions: The experimental evidence. *Psychological Bulletin, 85,* 756–771.

Klatzky, R. L. (1980). *Human memory* (2d ed.). San Francisco: Freeman.

Klaus, M. H., & Kennell, J. H. (1982). *Parent-infant bonding.* St. Louis: Mosby.

Kleck, R. E., Richardson, S. A., & Ronald, L. (1974). Physical appearance cues and interpersonal attraction in children. *Child Development, 45,* 359–372.

Kleinginna, P. R., Jr., & Kleinginna, A. M. (1981). A categorized list of emotion definitions, with suggestions for a consensual definition. *Motivation and Emotion, 5,* 345–379.

Kleitman, N. (1960). Patterns of dreaming. *Scientific American, 203,* 81–88.

Klerman, G. (1978). Combining drugs and psychotherapy in the treatment of depression. In J. O. Cole, A. F. Schatzberg, & S. H. Frazier (Eds.), *Depression: Biology, psychodynamics, and treatment.* New York: Plenum.

Knapp, H. R., Reilly, I. A. G., Alessandrini, P., & FitzGerald, G. A. (1986). In vivo indexes of platelet and vascular function during fish-oil administration in patients with atherosclerosis. *New England Journal of Medicine, 314,* 937–942.

Kobasa, S. C. (1982a). Commitment and coping in stress resistance among lawyers. *Journal of Personality and Social Psychology, 42*(4), 707–717.

Kobasa, S. C. (1982b). The hardy personality: Toward a social psychology of stress and health. In G. Sanders & J. Suls (Eds.), *Social psychology of health and illness.* Hillsdale, NJ: Erlbaum.

Kobasa, S. C., Maddi, S. R., & Kahn, S. (1982). Hardiness and health: A prospective study. *Journal of Personality and Social Psychology, 42*(1), 168–177.

Koff, E., Rierdan, J., & Sheingold, K. (1980, April). *Memories of menarche: Age and preparedness as determinants of subjective experience.* Paper presented at the annual meeting of the Eastern Psychological Association, Hartford.

Kohlberg, L. (1964). The development of moral character and moral ideology. In M. Hoffman & L. Hoffman (Eds.), *Review of child development research* (Vol. 1). New York: Russell Sage Foundation.

Kohlberg, L. (1966). A cognitive-developmental analysis of children's sex-role concepts and attitudes. In E. E. Maccoby (Ed.), *The development of sex differences.* Stanford, CA: Stanford University Press.

Kohlberg, L. (1976). Moral stages and moralization. In T. Lickona (Ed.), *Moral development and behavior.* New York: Holt, Rinehart & Winston.

Kohlberg, L. (1968). The child as a moral philosopher. *Psychology Today, 2*(4), 25–30.

Kohlberg, L. (1969). Stage and sequence: The cognitive developmental approach to socialization. In D. A. Goslin (Ed.), *Handbook of socialization theory and research.* Chicago: Rand McNally.

Kohlberg, L., & Gilligan, C. (1971, Fall). The adolescent as a philosopher: The discovery of the self in a postconventional world. *Daedalus,* 1051–1086.

Kohler, W. (1927). *The mentality of apes.* New York: Harcourt, Brace & World.

Kolata, G. (1979). Mental disorders: A new approach to treatment? *Science, 203*(5), 36–38.

Kolata, G. (1981). Clues to the cause of senile dementia. *Science, 211*(6), 1032–1033.

Kolata, G. (1986, January). Weight reduction may start in our cells, not psyches. *Smithsonian,* pp. 91–97.

Kokmen, E. (1984). Dementia-Alzheimer type. *Mayo Clinic Proceedings, 59,* 35–42.

Kolb, B., & Whishaw, I. (1980). *Fundamentals of neuropsychology.* San Francisco: Freeman.

Komisar, L. (1987). *Corazon Aquino.* New York: Braziller.

Kopf, A. W., Rigel, D., & Friedman, R. (1986). The incredible increasing incidence of malignant melanoma in the United States. *Skin Cancer Foundation Journal, 4,* 21,93.

Koulack, D. (1970). Repression and forgetting of dreams. In M. Bertini (Ed.), *Psicofisiologia del sonno e del sogno: Proceedings of an International Symposium,* Rome, 1967. Milan: Editrice vita e pensier.

Koulack, D., & Goodenough, D. (1976). Dream recall and dream recall failure: An arousal-retrieval model. *Psychological Bulletin, 83,* 975–984.

Krantz, D. S., & Durel, L. A. (1983). Psychobiological substrates of the Type A behavior pattern. *Health Psychology, 2,* 393–412.

Krantz, D. S., Grunberg, N. E., & Baum, A. (1985). Health psychology. *Annual Review of Pschology, 36,* 349–383.

Kreutzer, M., & Charlesworth, W. R. (1973). *Infant recognition of emotions.* Paper presented at the biennial meeting of the Society for Research in Child Development, Philadelphia.

Kreuz, L. E., & Rose, R. M. (1972). Assessment of aggressive behavior and plasma testosterone in a young criminal population. *Psychosomatic Medicine, 34,* 312–332.

Krueger, J. M., Pappenheimer, J. R., & Karnovsky, M. L. (1982). The composition of sleep-promoting factor isolated from humans. *The Journal of Biological Chemistry, 257*(4), 1664–1669.

Krüll, M. (1986) *Freud and his father.* (A. J. Pomerans, Trans.) New York: Norton.

Kübler-Ross, E. (1969). *On death and dying.* New York: Macmillan.

Kupfersmid, J., & Wonderly, D. (1980). Moral maturity and behavior: Failure to find a link. *Journal of Youth and Adolescence, 9*(3), 249–261.

Kurshan, M. (1986, October 10). Personal communication.

Kutchinsky, B. (in press). *Obscenity and pornography: Behavioral Aspects.*

LaBarge, E. (1981, November). Counseling patients with senile dementia of the Alzheimer type and their families. *Personnel and Guidance Journal,* pp. 139–142.

LaFerla, J. J., Anderson, O. L., & Schalch, D. S. (1978). Psychoendocrine responses to sexual arousal in human males. *Psychosomatic Medicine, 40,* 166–172.

La Gaipa, J. J. (1977). Testing a multidimensional approach to friendship. In S. W. Duck (Ed.), *Theory and practice in interpersonal attraction* (pp. 249–270). London: Academic.

Lakoff, R. (1973). Language and women's place. *Language in Society, 1*(2), 45–80.

Lamb, H. R. (1984). *Homeless mentally ill.* Washington, DC: American Psychiatric Association.

Lamb, M. E. (1979). Paternal influences and the father's role: A personal perspective. *American Psychologist, 34*(10), 938–943.

Lamb, M. E. (1981). The development of father-infant relationships. In M. E. Lamb (Ed.), *The role of the father in child development* (2d ed.). New York: Wiley-Interscience.

Lamb, M. E. (1982). Sibling relationships across the lifespan: An overview and introduction. In M. E. Lamb & B. Sutton-Smith, *Sibling relationships.* Hillsdale, NJ: Erlbaum.

Landman, J. T., & Dawes, R. M. (1982). Psychotherapy outcome: Smith and Glass' conclusions stand up under scrutiny. *American Psychologist, 37*(5), 504–516.

Lange, C. (1922). *The emotions.* Baltimore: Williams & Wilkins. (Original work published 1885)

Langer, E. J., Bashner, R. S., & Chanowitz, B. (1985). Decreasing prejudice by increasing discrimination. *Journal of Personality and Social Psychology, 49*(1), 113–120.

Langer, E. J., Beck, P., Janoff-Bulman, R., & Timko, C. (1984). An exploration of relationships among mindfulness, longevity, and senility. *Academic Psychology Bulletin, 6*(2), 211–226.

Langer, E. J., Chanowitz, B., & Blank, A. (1985). Mindlessness-mindfulness in perspective: A reply to Valerie Folkes. *Journal of Personality & Social Psychology, 48*(3), 605–607.

Langer, E. J., & Rodin, J. (1976). The effects of choice and enhanced personal responsibility in an institutional setting. *Journal of Personality and Social Psychology, 34*(2), 191–198.

Lashley, K. (1950). In search of the engram. *Symposia of the Society of Experimental Biology, 4,* 454–482.

Lassen, N. A., Ingvar, D. H., & Skinhoj, E. (1978, October). Brain function and blood flow. *Scientific American,* pp. 62–71.

Latané, B., & Darley, J. M. (1968). Group inhibition of bystander intervention in emergencies. *Journal of Personality and Social Psychology, 10*(3), 215–221.

Latané, B., & Nida, S. (1981). Ten years of research on group size and helping. *Psychological Bulletin, 89*(2), 308–324.

Laudenslager, M. L., Ryan, S. M., Drugan, R. C., Hyson, R. L., & Maier, S. F. (1983). Coping and immunosuppression: Inescapable but not escapable shock suppresses lymphocyte proliferation. *Science, 221,* 568–570.

Lazarus, L. W., Stafford, B., Cooper, K., Cohler, B., & Dysken, M. (1981). A pilot study of an Alzheimer's patients' and relatives' discussion group. *Gerontologist, 21*(4), 353–357.

Lazarus, R. S. (1980). The stress and coping paradigm. In L. Bond & J. Rosen (Eds.), *Competence and coping during adulthood* (pp. 28–74). Hanover, NH: University Press of New England.

Lazarus, R. S. (1981). Little hassles can be hazardous to health. *Psychology Today, 15*(7), 58–62.

Lazarus, R. S. (1982). Thoughts on the relations between emotion and cognition. *American Psychologist, 37*(9), 1019–1024.

Lazarus, R. S. (1984). On the primacy of cognition. *American Psychologist, 39*(2), 124–129.

Lazarus, R. S., & Folkman, S. (1984a). Coping and adaptation. In W. C. Gentry (Ed.), *Handbook of behavioral medicine.* New York: Guilford.

Lazarus, R. S., & Folkman, S. (1984b). *Stress, appraisal, and coping.* New York: Springer-Verlag.

Ledger, M. (1983, April). To watch a thief. *Pennsylvania Gazette,* pp. 32–38.

Lefcourt, H., Miller, R., Ware, E., & Sherk, D. (1981). Locus of control as a modifier of the relationship between stressors and moods. *Journal of Personality and Social Psychology, 41*(2), 357–369.

Leibowitz, H. W. (1971). Sensory, learned, and cognitive mechanisms of size perception. *Annals of the New York Academy of Sciences, 188,* 47–62.

Lemon, B., Bengston, V., & Peterson, J. (1972). An exploration of the activity theory of aging: Activity types and life satisfaction among in-movers to a retirement community. *Journal of Gerontology, 27*(4), 511–523.

Lenneberg, E. H. (1967). *Biological functions of language.* New York: Wiley.

Lenneberg, E. H. (1969). On explaining language. *Science, 164*(3880), 635–643.

Lennie, P. (1980). Parallel visual pathways: A review. *Vision Research, 20,* 561–594.

Lennon, M. C. (1982). The psychological consequences of menopause: The importance of timing of a life stage event. *Journal of Health and Social Behavior, 23,* 353–366.

Leonard, R. L. (1975). Self-concept and attraction for similar and dissimilar others. *Journal of Personality and Social Psychology, 31,* 926–929.

Lerner, R., & Lerner, J. (1977). Effects of age, sex and physical attractiveness on child-peer relations, academic performance, and elementary school adjustment. *Developmental Psychology, 13*(6), 585–590.

Leshner, A. I. (1978). *An introduction to behavioral endocrinology.* New York: Oxford University Press.

Lester, B. (1975). Cardiac habituation of the orienting response to an auditory signal in infants of varying nutritional status. *Developmental Psychology, 11*(4), 432–442.

Lester, R., & Van Thiel, D. H. (1977). Gonadal function in chronic alcoholic men. *Advances in Experimental Medicine and Biology, 85A,* 339–414.

Leventhal, H. (1970). Findings and theory in the study of fear communications. In L. Berkowitz & E. Walster (Eds.), *Advances in experimental social psychology.* New York: Academic.

Leventhal, H. (1974). Attitudes: Their nature, growth and change. In C. Nemeth (Ed.), *Social psychology: Classic and contemporary integrations.* Chicago: Rand McNally.

Leventhal, H., & Cleary, P. D. (1980). The smoking problem: A review of the research and theory in behavioral risk modification. *Psychological Bulletin, 88*(2), 370–405.

Leventhal, H., Prohaska, T. R., & Hirschman, R. S. (1985). Preventive health behavior across the lifespan. In J. C. Rosen & J. Solomon (Eds.), *Prevention in health psychology.* Hanover, NH: University Press of New England.

Levin, J., & Arluke, A. (1985). An exploratory analysis of sex differences in gossip. *Sex Roles, 12,* 281–285.

Levine, M. W., & Shefner, J. M. (1981). *Fundamentals of sensation and perception.* Reading, MA: Addison-Wesley.

Levinger, G. (1974). A three-level approach to attraction: Toward an understanding of pair relatedness. In T. L. Huston (Ed.), *Foundation of interpersonal attraction.* New York: Academic.

Levinger, G., & Snoek, J. G. (1972). *Attraction in relationship: A new look at interpersonal attraction.* Morristown, NJ: General Learning Press.

Levinson, D. (1986). A conception of adult development. *American Psychologist, 41*(1), 3–13.

Levinson, D., Darrow, C., Klein, E., Levinson, M., & McKee, B. (1978). *The seasons of a man's life.* New York: Ballantine.

Levy, G. (1985). Right brain, left brain: Fact and fiction. *Psychology Today, 19*(5), 38–44.

Levy, J., Trevarthen, C., & Sperry, R. (1972). Perception of bilateral chimeric figures following hemispheric disconnection. *Brain, 95,* 61–78.

Lewine, R. R. J. (1981). Sex differences in schizophrenia: Timing of subtypes. *Psychological Bulletin, 90*(3), 432–444.

Lewis, C., & Lewis, M. (1977). The potential impact of sexual equality on health. *New England Journal of Medicine, 297*(11), 863–869.

Lidz, T., & Fleck, S. (1960). Schizophrenia, human integration, and the role of the family. In D. D. Jackson (Ed.), *The etiology of schizophrenia.* New York: Basic Books.

Lieberman, M., & Coplan, A. (1970). Distance from death as a variable in the study of aging. *Developmental Psychology, 2*(1), 71–84.

Likert, R. (1932). A technique for the measurement of attitudes. *Archives of Psychology, 40.*

Limber, J. (1977). Language in child and chimp? *American Psychologist, 32,* 280–295.

Lincoln, R. (1986). Smoking and reproduction. *Family Planning Perspectives, 18*(2), 79–84.

Linn, M. C., & Petersen, A. C. (1985). *Emergence and characterization of gender differences in spatial ability: A meta-analysis.* Unpublished manuscript, University of California, Berkeley.

Lipid Research Clinics Program. (1984a). The lipid research clinic coronary primary prevention trial results: I. Reduction in incidence of coronary heart disease. *Journal of the American Medical Association, 251,* 351–364.

Lipid Research Clinics Program. (1984b). The lipid research clinic coronary primary prevention trial results: II. The relationship of reduction in incidence of coronary heart disease to cholesterol lowering. *Journal of the American Medical Association, 251,* 365–374.

Lipsitt, L. (1982). Infant learning. In T. M. Field, A. Huston, H. Quay, L. Troll, & G. Finley (Eds.), *Review of human development.* New York: Wiley-Interscience.

Livson, F. (1976). *Sex differences in personality development in the middle adult years: A longitudinal study.* Paper presented at the annual meeting of the Gerontological Society, Louisville, KY.

Lloyd-Still, J., Hurwitz, I., Wolff, P. H., & Schwachman, H. (1974). Intellectual development after severe malnutrition in infancy. *Pediatrics, 54,* 306.

Locke, J. (1959). *An essay concerning human understanding* (Vol. 1). New York: Dover. (Original work published 1690)

Loftus, E. F. (1979). *Eyewitness testimony.* Cambridge, MA: Harvard University Press.

Loftus, E. F. (1980). *Memory.* Reading, MA: Addison-Wesley.

Loftus, E. F. (1983). Silence is not golden. *American Psychologist, 38*(5), 564–572.

Loftus, E. F., & Loftus, G. R. (1980). On the permanence of stored information in the human brain. *American Psychologist, 35*(5), 409–420.

Loftus, E. F., Miller, D. G., & Burns, H. J. (1978). Semantic integration of verbal information into a visual memory. *Journal of Experimental Psychology, 4,* 19–31.

Loftus, E. F., & Palmer, J. C. (1982). Reconstruction of automobile destruction: An example of interaction between language and memory. In U. Neisser (Ed.), *Memory observed.* San Francisco: Freeman. (Reprinted from *Journal of Verbal Learning and Verbal Behavior,* 1974, *13,* 585–589)

Long, P. (1986). Medical mesmerism. *Psychology Today, 20*(1), 28–29.

Longino, C. F., & Kart, C. S. (1982). Explicating activity theory: A formal replication. *Journal of Gerontology, 37*(6), 713–721.

Looft, W. R. (1971). *Toward a history of life-span developmental psychology.* Unpublished manuscript, University of Wisconsin, Madison.

Lopata, H. (1973). Living through widowhood. *Psychology Today, 7*(2), 87–98.

Lopata, H. (1977, September–October). Widows and widowers. *The Humanist,* 25–28.

Lopata, H. (1979). *Women as widows.* New York: Elsevier.

Lorayne, H. (1975). *Remembering people.* New York: Stein & Day.

Lorenz, K. (1966). *On aggression.* London: Methuen.

Lott, A. J., & Lott, B. E. (1968). A learning theory approach to interpersonal attitudes. In A. G. Greenwald & T. M. Ostrom (Eds.), *Psychological foundations of attitudes.* New York: Academic.

Lott, A. J., & Lott, B. E. (1974). The role of reward in the formation of positive interpersonal attitudes. In T. L. Huston (Ed.), *Foundations of interpersonal attraction.* New York: Academic.

Lowenthal, M., & Haven, C. (1968). Interaction and adaptation: Intimacy as a critical variable. In B. Neugarten (Ed.), *Middle age and aging.* Chicago: University of Chicago Press.

Lubar, J. (1985, April). *Biofeedback—A*

modern approach for health mainte-nance. Paper presented at the meeting of The Biofeedback Society of America, New Orleans.

Luborsky, L. (Speaker). (1979). *Predicting outcomes of psychotherapy* (Tape recording). New York: BMA Audio Cassettes.

Luborsky, L., & Auerbach, A. H. (1985). The therapeutic relationship in psychodynamic psychotherapy: The research evidence and its meaning for practice. In R. E. Haks & A. J. Frances (Eds.). *Psychiatry update: American Psychiatric Association annual review* (Vol. 4). Washington, DC: American Psychiatric Association.

Luborsky, L., Crits-Christoph, P., & Mellon, J. (1986). Advent of objective measures of the transference concept. *Journal of Consulting and Clinical Psychology, 54*(1), 39–47.

Luborsky, L., Singer, B., & Luborsky, L. (1975). Comparative studies of psychotherapies. *Archives of General Psychiatry, 32*, 995–1008.

Ludwig, A. M. (1969). Altered states of consciousness. In C. Tart (Ed.), *Altered states of consciousness.* New York: Wiley. (Reprinted from *Archives of General Psychiatry,* 1966, *15,* 225–234)

Luria, A. R. (1968). *The mind of a mnemonist* (L. Solotaroff, Trans.). New York: Basic Books.

Lynn, D. (1974). *The father: His role in child development.* Monterey, CA: Brooks/Cole.

Lynn, R. (1966). *Attention, arousal and the orientation reaction.* Oxford, England: Pergamon.

Lynn, R. (1982). IQ in Japan and the United States shows a growing disparity. *Nature, 297,* 222–223.

Lyons, R. D. (1983, October 4). Decrease in casual sex. *The New York Times,* p. C3.

Maccoby, E. E. (1980). *Social development.* New York: Harcourt Brace Jovanovich.

Maccoby, N., Farquhar, J. W., Wood, P. D., & Alexander, J. (1977). Reducing the risk of cardiovascular disease: Effects of a community-based campaign on knowledge and behavior. *Journal of Community Health, 3,* 100–114.

Maccoby, E. E., & Jacklin, C. N. (1974). *The psychology of sex differences.* Stanford, CA: Stanford University Press.

MacFarlane, A. (1975). Olfaction in the development of social preferences in the human neonate. In Ciba Foundation Symposium 33, *The Human Neonate in*

Parent-Infant Interaction. Amsterdam: Associated Scientific Publishers.

MacFarlane, A. (1978). What a baby knows. *Human Nature, 1*(2), 74–81.

MacLeod-Morgan, C. (1982). EEG lateralization in hypnosis: A preliminary report. *Australian Journal of Clinical and Experimental Hypnosis, 10,* 99–102.

Maier, S. F., & Laudenslager, M. (1985). Stress and health: Exploring the links. *Psychology Today, 19*(8), 44–49.

Makepeace, J. M. (1981). Courtship violence among college students. *Journal of Family Relations, 30*(1), 97–102.

Malamuth, N. M. (1981). Rape proclivity in males. *Journal of Social Issues, 37*(4), 138–157.

Malamuth, N. M. (1984). Aggression against women: Cultural and individual causes. In N. M. Malamuth & E. Donnerstein (Eds.), *Pornography and sexual aggression.* Orlando, FL: Academic.

Malamuth, N. M., & Check, J. V. P. (1984). Debriefing effectiveness following exposure to pornographic rape depictions. *Journal of Sex Research, 21*(1), 1–13.

Malamuth, N. M., & Donnerstein, E. (Eds.). (1984). *Pornography and sexual aggression.* Orlando, FL: Academic.

Mamay, P. D., & Simpson, P. L. (1981). Three female roles in television commercials. *Sex Roles, 7*(12), 1223–1232.

Mann, L., & Janis, I. L. (1968). A follow-up study on the long-term effects of emotional role-playing. *Journal of Personality and Social Psychology, 8,* 339–342.

Manschreck, T. C. (1981). Schizophrenic disorders. *New England Journal of Medicine, 305*(27), 1628–1632.

March of Dimes. (1983). *Genetic counseling.* White Plains, NY: Author.

Marcia, J. E. (1966). Development and validation of ego identity status. *Journal of Personality and Social Psychology, 3,* 551–558.

Margules, M. R., Moisset, B., Lewis, M. J., Shibuya, H., & Pert, C. (1978). Beta-endorphin is associated with overeating in genetically obese mice (ob/ob) and rats (fa/fa). *Science, 202,* 988–991.

Marion, R. W., Wiznia, A. A., Hutcheon, G., & Rubinstein, A. (1986). Human T-cell lymphotropic virus Type III (HTLV-III) embryopathy. *American Journal of Diseases of Children, 140*(7), 638–640.

Marks, W. B., Dobelle, W. H., & MacNichol, E. F. (1964). Visual pigments of single primate cones. *Science, 143,* 1181–1183.

Marlatt, G. A. (1983). The controlled-

drinking controversy. *American Psychologist, 38*(10), 1097–1110.

Marshall, S. P. (1984). Sex differences in children's mathematic achievement: Solving computations and story problems. *Journal of Educational Psychology, 76,* 194–204.

Marty, M. E. (1982, April 15). Watch your language. *Context.*

Maslow, A. H. (1970). *Motivation and personality.* New York: Harper & Row. (Original work published 1954)

Maslow, A. H. (1973). Self-actualizing people: A study of psychological health. In R. J. Lowry (Ed.), *Dominance, self-esteem, self actualization: Germinal papers of A. H. Maslow.* Monterey, CA: Brooks/Cole. (Original work published 1950)

Mason, J. W. (1968). Organization of psychoendocrine mechanisms. *Psychosomatic Medicine, 30,* 565–608.

Mason, J. W. (1975). A historical view of the stress field. *Journal of Human Stress, 1,* 6–12, 22–37.

Mason, R. M. (1985). Artificial intelligence: Promise, myth, and reality. *Library Journal, 110*(7), 56–57.

Masson, J. M. (1985). *The assault on truth.* NY: Penguin.

Masters, W. H. (1983, December 9). Personal communication.

Masters, W. H. (1986). Sex and aging—expectations and reality. *Hospital Practice, 21*(8), 175–198.

Masters, W. H., & Johnson, V. E. (1966). *Human sexual response.* Boston: Little, Brown.

Masters, W. H., & Johnson, V. E. (1970). *Human sexual inadequacy.* Boston: Little, Brown.

Masters, W. H., & Johnson, V. E. (1979). *Homosexuality in perspective.* Boston: Little, Brown.

Masters, W. H., & Johnson, V. E. (1981). Sex and the aging process. *Journal of the American Geriatric Society, 29,* 385–390.

Masters, W. H., Johnson, V. E., & Kolodny, R. C. (1985). *Sex and human loving.* Boston: Little, Brown.

Matarazzo, J. D. (1982). Behavioral health's challenge to academic, scientific, and professional psychology. *American Psychologist, 37*(1), 1–14.

Matas, L., Arend, R., & Sroufe, L. A. (1978). Continuity of adaptation in the second year: The relationship between quality of attachment and later competence. *Child Development, 49,* 547–556.

Matlin, M. M. (1983). *Perception.* Boston: Allyn & Bacon.

Matlin, M. M. (1987). *The psychology of*

women. New York: Holt, Rinehart & Winston.

Matlin, M. M. (1988). Sensation and perception (2d ed.). Boston: Allyn & Bacon.

Mayer, D. J., Price, D. D., & Rafii, A. (1977). Antagonism of acupuncture analgesia in man by the narcotic antagonist naloxone. Brain Research, 121, 369–372.

McArthur, L. A. (1972). The how and what of why: Some determinants and consequences of causal attribution. Journal of Personality and Social Psychology, 22, 171–193.

McBurney, D. H., & Collings, V. B. (1984). Introduction to sensation/perception (2d ed.). Englewood Cliffs, NJ: Prentice-Hall.

McBurney, D. H., & Gent, J. F. (1979). On the nature of taste qualities. Psychological Bulletin, 86, 151–167.

McCann, I. L., & Holmes, D. S. (1984). Influence of aerobic exercise on depression. Journal of Personality and Social Psychology, 46(5), 1142–1147.

McClelland, D. C. (1965). Achievement and entrepreneurship: A longitudinal study. Journal of Personality and Social Psychology, 1(4), 389–392.

McClelland, D. C. (1973). Testing for competence rather than for "intelligence." American Psychologist, 28(1), 1–14.

McClelland, D. C. (1985). Human motivation. Glenview, IL: Scott, Foresman.

McClelland, D. C., Atkinson, J. W., Clark, R. A., & Lowell, E. L. (1953). The achievement motive. New York: Appleton-Century-Crofts.

McClelland, D. C., & Winter, D. G. (1969). Motivating economic achievement. New York: Free Press.

McConahay, J. B., Hardee, B. B., & Batts, V. (1981). Has racism declined in America? It depends upon who is asking and what is asked. Journal of Conflict Resolution, 25(4), 563–579.

McCormack, T. (1985). Making sense of research on pornography. In V. Burstyn (Ed.), Women against censorship (pp. 183–205). Toronto: Douglas & McIntyre.

McCormick, D. A., & Thompson, R. F. (1984). Cerebellum: Essential involvement in the classically conditioned eyelid response. Science, 223, 296–299.

McFadden, R. D. (1982, December 22). Passenger saves blind man's life on IND tracks. The New York Times, p. B1.

McGrath, J. E., & Kravitz, D. A. (1982). Group research. Annual Review of Psychology, 33, 195–230.

McKillip, J., & Riedel, S. L. (1983). External validity of matching of physical attractiveness for same and opposite sex couples. Journal of Applied Social Psychology, 13, 323–337.

McKinley, D. (1964). Social class and family life. New York: Free Press.

McKinnon, D. W. (1968). Selecting students with creative potential. In P. Heist (Ed.), The creative college student: An unmet challenge. San Francisco: Jossey-Bass.

Mead, M. (1928). Coming of age in Samoa. New York: Morrow.

Mead, M. (1935). Sex and temperament in three primitive societies. New York: Morrow.

Meichenbaum, D. A. (1975). Self-instructional approach to stress management: A proposal for stress innoculation training. In C. D. Spielberger & I. G. Sarason (Eds.), Stress and anxiety (Vol. 1). Washington, DC: Hemisphere.

Meislin, R. J. (1987, January 8). Racial divisions seen in poll on Howard Beach attack. The New York Times, p. B2.

Mentzer, S. J., & Snyder, M. L. (1982). The doctor and the patient: A psychological perspective. In G. S. Sanders & J. Suls (Eds.), Social psychology of health and illness. Hillsdale, NJ: Erlbaum.

Metzger, B. E., Ravnikar, V., Vileisis, R. A., & Freinkel, N. (1982, March 13). "Accelerated starvation" and the skipped breakfast in late normal pregnancy. Lancet, pp. 588–592.

Meyer, A. J., Nash, J. D., McAlister, A. L., Maccoby, N., & Farquhar, J. W. (1980). Skills training in a cardiovascular health education campaign. Journal of Consulting and Clinical Psychology, 48(2), 129–142.

Mikhail, A. (1981). Stress: A psychophysiological conception. Journal of Human Stress, 7, 9–15.

Milavsky, J. R., Stipp, H. H., Kessler, R. C., & Rubens, W. S. (1982). Television and aggression: A panel study. New York: Academic.

Milgram, S. (1965). Some conditions of obedience and disobedience to authority. Human Relations, 18, 67–76.

Milgram, S. (1974). Obedience to authority. New York: Harper & Row.

Miller, B. C., & Myers-Walls, J. A. (1983). Parenthood: Stresses and coping strategies. In H. I. McCubbin & C. R. Figley (Eds.), Stress and the family, Vol. 1: Coping with normative transitions. New York: Brunner/Mazel.

Miller, B. C., & Sollie, D. L. (1980). Normal stress during the transition to parenthood. Family Relations, 29, 459–465.

Miller, C., & Swift, K. (1976). Words and women. Garden City, NY: Doubleday.

Miller, E., Cradock-Watson, J. E., & Pollock, T. M. (1982, October 9). Consequences of confirmed maternal rubella at successive stages of pregnancy. Lancet, pp. 781–784.

Miller, G. A. (1956). The magical number seven, plus or minus two: Some limits on our capacity to process information. Psychological Review, 63, 81–97.

Miller, G. H., & Gerstein, D. R. (1983). The life expectancy of nonsmoking men and women. Public Health Reports, 98(4), 343–349.

Miller, N. E. (1969). Learning of visceral and glandular responses. Science, 163, 434–445.

Miller, N. E. (1985a). Rx: Biofeedback. Psychology Today, 19(2), 54–59.

Miller, N. E. (1985b, April). Some professional and scientific problems and opportunities for biofeedback. Presidential address to the meeting of the Biofeedback Society of America, New Orleans.

Miller, N. E. (1985c). The value of behavioral research on animals. American Psychologist, 40(4), 423–440.

Miller, R. C., & Berman, J. S. (1983). The efficacy of cognitive behavioral therapies: A quantitative review of the research evidence. Psychological Bulletin, 94(1), 39–53.

Miller, T., & Weikel, M. K. (1974). Blood donor eligibility, recruitment, and retention. In American Red Cross, Selected readings in donor motivation and recruitment, 2, 53–62.

Mills, J., & Aronson, E. (1965). Opinion change as a function of communicator's attractiveness and desire to influence. Journal of Personality and Social Psychology, 1, 173–177.

Mills, J. L., Graubard, B. I., Harley, E. E., Rhoads, G. G., & Berendes, H. U. (1984). Maternal alcohol consumption and birth weight. Journal of the American Medical Association, 252, 1875–1879.

Milner, B. (1966). Amnesia following operation on the temporal lobes. In C. Witty & O. Zangwill (Eds.), Amnesia. London: Butterworth.

Milner, B. (1970). Memory and the medial temporal regions of the brain. In K. H. Pribram & D. E. Broadbent (Eds.), Biology of memory. New York: Academic.

Mischel, W. (1973). Toward a cognitive social learning reconceptualization of personality. Psychological Review, 80, 252–283.

Mischel, W. (1968). Personality and assessment. New York: Wiley.

Mischel, W. (1977). On the future of personality measurement. *American Psychologist, 32,* 246–254.

Mischel, W., & Peake, P. K. (1982). Beyond déjà vu in the search for cross-situational consistency. *Psychological Review, 89,* 730–755.

Mishkin, M. (1982). A memory system in the monkey. *Philosophical Transactions of the Royal Society of London, 298,* 85–95.

Mitchell, D. E., Freeman, R. D., Millodot, M., & Haegerstrom, C. (1973). Meridional amblyopia: Evidence for modification of the human visual system. *Vision Research, 13,* 535–558.

Molfese, D., Molfese, V., & Carrell, P. (1982). Early language development. In B. Wolman (Ed.), *Handbook of developmental psychology.* Englewood Cliffs, NJ: Prentice-Hall.

Money, J., & Erhardt, A. A. (1972). *Man and woman, boy and girl.* Baltimore: Johns Hopkins University Press.

Montemayor, P. (1983). Parents and adolescents in conflict: All families some of the time and some families most of the time. *Journal of Early Adolescence, 3*(1–2), 83–103.

Moore-Ede, M. C., Sulzman, F. M., & Fuller, C. A. (1982). *The clocks that time us.* Cambridge, MA: Harvard University Press.

Morbidity and Mortality Weekly Report (MMWR). (1985, June 21). Suicide—U.S., 1970–1980. Atlanta: Center for Disease Control.

Morgan, A. H. (1973). The heritability of hypnotic susceptibility in twins. *Journal of Abnormal and Social Psychology, 82,* 55–61.

Morgan, P. (1984). The big whiff. *Pennsylvania Gazette, 83*(3), 37–40.

Morganthau, T. (1986, January 6). Abandoned. *Newsweek,* pp. 14–19.

Morris, C. D., Bransford, J. D., & Franks, J. J. (1977). Levels of processing versus transfer appropriate processing. *Journal of Verbal Learning and Verbal Behavior, 16,* 519–533.

Morris, D. (1969). *The naked ape.* New York: Dell.

Morris, D. (1977). *Manwatching.* New York: Abrams.

Morse, S. J., & Watson, R. J. (Eds.). (1977). *Psychotherapies: A comparative casebook.* New York: Holt, Rinehart & Winston.

Mosher, D. L. (1965). Interaction of fear and guilt in inhibiting unacceptable behavior. *Journal of Consulting Psychology, 29,* 161–167.

Mosher, D. L., & Abramson, P. R. (1977). Subjective sexual arousal to films of masturbation. *Journal of Consulting and Clinical Psychology, 45,* 796–807.

Moss, H. A. (1967). Sex, age, and state as determinants of mother-infant interaction. *Merrill-Palmer Quarterly, 13,* 19–36.

Moss, R. J. (1986, September). Prejudicial esteem. *Psychology Today,* p. 20.

Mowrer, O. H. (1960). *Learning theory and the symbolic processes.* New York: Wiley.

Moyer, K. E. (1976). *The psychobiology of aggression.* New York: Harper & Row.

Mullaney, D. J., Johnson, L. C., Naitoh, P., Friedmann, J. K., & Globus, G. G. (1977). Sleep during and after gradual sleep reduction. *Psychophysiology, 14,* 237–244.

Murphy, D. P. (1929). The outcome of 625 pregnancies in women subjected to pelvic roentgen irradiation. *American Journal of Obstetrics and Gynecology, 18,* 179–187.

Murray, H. A. (1938). *Explorations in personality.* New York: Oxford University Press.

Murray, H. A. (1943). *Thematic apperception test.* Cambridge, MA: Harvard University Press.

Murstein, B. I. (1971). Critique of models of dyadic attraction. In B. I. Murstein (Ed.), *Theories of attraction and relationships.* New York: Springer-Verlag.

Murstein, B. I. (1982). Marital choice. In B. B. Wolman (Ed.), *Handbook of developmental psychology.* Englewood Cliffs, NJ: Prentice-Hall.

Mussen, P. H., & Eisenberg-Berg, N. (1977). *Roots of caring, sharing, and helping: The development of prosocial behavior in children.* San Francisco: Freeman.

Mussen, P. H., & Jones, M. C. (1957). Self-conceptions, motivations, and interpersonal attitudes of late- and early-maturing boys. *Child Development, 28,* 243–256.

Mussen, P. H., & Rutherford, E. (1963). Parent-child relations and parental personality in relation to young children's sex role preferences. *Child Development, 34,* 589–607.

Myers, D. G. (1983). *Social psychology.* New York: McGraw-Hill.

Myers, J. K., Weissman, M. M., Tischler, G. L., Holzer, C. E., Leaf, P. J., Orvaschel, H., Anthony, J. C., Boyd, J. H., Burke, J. D., Kramer, M., & Stoltzman, R. (1984). Six-month prevalence of psychiatric disorders in three communities. *Archives of General Psychiatry, 41*(10), 959–967.

Myers, N., & Perlmutter, M. (1978). Memory in the years from 2 to 5. In P Ornstein (Ed.), *Memory development in children.* Hillsdale, NJ: Erlbaum.

Myers-Walls, J. A. (1984). Balancing multiple role responsibilities during the transition to parenthood. *Family Relations, 33,* 267–271.

Nadi, N. S., Nurnberger, J. I., & Gershon, E. S. (1984). Muscarinic cholinergic receptors on skin fibroblasts in familial affective disorder. *New England Journal of Medicine, 311,* 255–230.

Naeye, R. L., & Peters, E. C. (1984). Mental development of children whose mothers smoked during pregnancy. *Obstetrics and Gynecology, 64*(5), 601–607.

Nagelman, D. B., Hale, S. L., & Ware, S. L. (1983). *Prevalence of eating disorders in college women.* Paper presented at the American Psychological Association, Anaheim.

Nagy, M. (1948). The child's theories concerning death. *Journal of Genetic Psychology, 73,* 3–27.

Napier, A. (1978). *The family crucible.* New York: Harper & Row.

Napolitan, D. A., & Goethals, G. R. (1979). The attribution of friendliness. *Journal of Experimental Social Psychology, 15,* 105–113.

Nass, G. D., Libby, R. W., & Fisher, M. P. (1984). *Sexual choices: An introduction to human sexuality* (2d ed.). Monterey, CA: Brooks-Cole.

Nathan, P. E. (1983). Failures in prevention. *American Psychologist, 38*(4), 459–467.

Nathan, P. E., & Harris, S. L. (1980). *Psychopathology and society* (2d ed.). New York: McGraw-Hill.

Nathanson, C. A., & Lorenz, G. (1982). Women and health: The social dimension of biomedical data. In J. Z. Giele (Ed.), *Women in the middle years.* New York: Wiley-Interscience.

National Academy of Sciences. (1982). *Ability tests: Consequences and controversies.* Washington, DC: National Academy Press.

National Center for Health Statistics. (1986). *Maternal weight gain and the outcome of pregnancy, United States, 1980.* Vital Statistics (Series 21, No. 44. DHHS Pub. No. 86-1922). Washington, DC: U.S. Government Printing Office.

National Institutes of Health (NIH). (1984a). *Drugs and insomnia.* NIH Consensus Development Statement, 4(10). Washington, DC: U.S. Government Printing Office.

National Institutes of Health (NIH).

(1984b). *Mood disorders: Pharmacologic prevention of recurrences.* NIH Consensus Development Statement, 5(4). Washington, DC: U.S. Government Printing Office.

National Institutes of Health (NIH). (1985a). *Electroconvulsive therapy.* NIH Consensus Development Statement, 5(1). Washington, DC: U.S. Government Printing Office.

National Institutes of Health (NIH). (1985b). *Health implications of obesity.* NIH Consensus Development Conference Statement, 5(9). Washington, DC: U.S. Government Printing Office.

National Institutes of Health (NIH). (1986). *Health implications of smokeless tobacco use.* NIH Consensus Development Conference Statement, 6(1). Washington, DC: U.S. Government Printing Office.

National Institute of Mental Health (NIMH). (1984). *Depression: What we know.* (DHHS Pub. No. ADM 85-1318). Washington, DC: U.S. Government Printing Office.

National Institute of Mental Health (NIMH). (1986, May). *NIMH treatment of depression collaborative research program.* Summary of presentations at the annual meeting of the American Psychiatric Association.

National Institute on Aging. (1980). *Senility: myth or madness.* Washington, DC: U.S. Government Printing Office.

National Institute on Drug Abuse (NIDA). (1985). *Treatment of cocaine abuse.* Washington, DC: U.S. Government Printing Office.

National Opinion Research Center. (1977). *General social surveys code book for 1972–1977.* Chicago: University of Chicago Press.

National Opinion Research Center. (1980). *General social surveys, 1972–1980.* Storrs, CT: Roper Public Opinion Research Center, University of Connecticut.

Neisser, U. (1982). Memory: What are the important questions? In U. Neisser (Ed.), *Memory observed.* San Francisco: Freeman.

Nelson, K. (1973). Structure and strategy in learning to talk. *Monographs of the Society for Research in Child Development, 38*(Nos. 1–2).

Nelson, K. (1979). The role of language in infant development. In M. Bornstein & W. Kessen (Eds.), *Psychological development from infancy.* Hillsdale, NJ: Erlbaum.

Nelson, K. (1981). Individual differences in language development: Implications for development and language. *Developmental Psychology, 17*(2), 170–187.

Nelson, T. O. (1977). Repetition and depth of processing. *Journal of Verbal Learning and Verbal Behavior, 16,* 151–172.

Neugarten, B. (1968). Adult personality: Toward a psychology of the life cycle. In B. Neugarten (Ed.), *Middle age and aging.* Chicago: University of Chicago Press.

Neugarten, B. (1975, January 18). The rise of the young-old. *The New York Times,* p. 29.

Neugarten, B., & Gutmann, D. L. (1958). Age-sex roles and personality in middle age: A thematic apperception study. *Psychological Monograph, 72*(17, Whole No. 470).

Neugarten, B., & Hagestad, G. (1976). Age and the life course. In H. Binstock & E. Shanas (Eds.), *Handbook of aging and the social sciences.* New York: Van Nostrand Reinhold.

Neugarten, B., Havighurst, R., & Tobin, S. (1968). Personality and patterns of aging. In B. Neugarten (Ed.), *Middle age and aging.* Chicago: University of Chicago Press.

Neugarten, B., Moore, J. W., & Lowe, J. C. (1965). Age norms, age constraints, and adult socialization. *American Journal of Sociology, 70,* 710–717.

Neugebauer, R. (1979). Medieval and early modern theories of mental illness. *Archives of General Psychiatry, 36,* 477–484.

Newcomb, T. M. (1961). *The acquaintance process.* New York: Holt, Rinehart & Winston.

Newman, H. H., Freeman, F. H., & Holzinger, K. J. (1937). *Twins: A study of heredity and environment.* Chicago: University of Chicago Press.

Newton, N., & Modahl, C. (1978). Pregnancy: The closest human relationship. *Human Nature, 1*(3), 40–49.

Nias, D. K. (1979). Marital choice: Matching or complementation? In M. Cook & G. Wilson (Eds.), *Love and attraction.* Oxford, England: Pergamon.

Nichol, S., & Heston, L. (1979). The future of genetic research in schizophrenia. *Psychiatric Annals, 9*(1), 32–53.

Nickerson, R. S., & Adams, M. J. (1979). Long-term memory for a common object. *Cognitive Psychology, 11,* 287–307.

Nieberg, P., Marks, J. S., McLaren, N. M., & Remington, P. L. (1985). The fetal tobacco syndrome. *Journal of the American Medical Association, 253,* 2998–2999.

Nisan, M., & Kohlberg, L. (1982). Universality and variation in moral judgment: A longitudinal and cross-sectional study in Turkey. *Child Development, 53,* 865–876.

Nisbett, R. E. (1968). Taste, deprivation and weight determinants of eating behavior. *Journal of Personality and Social Psychology, 10,* 107–116.

Noll, K. M., Davis, J. M., & DeLeon-Jones, F. (1985). Medication and somatic therapies in the treatment of depression. In E. E. Beckham & W. R. Leber (Eds.), *Handbook of depression.* Homewood, IL: Dorsey.

Notelovitz, M., & Ware, M. (1983). *Stand tall: The informed woman's guide to preventing osteoporosis.* Gainesville, FL: Triad.

Novaco, R. W. (1977). A stress inoculation approach to anger management in the training of law enforcement officers. *American Journal of Community Psychology, 5,* 327–346.

O'Barr, W. M., & Atkins, B. K. (1980). "Women's language" or "powerless language"? In S. McConnell-Ginet, R. Borker, & N. Furman (Eds.), *Women and language in literature and society* (pp. 93–110). New York: Praeger.

O'Brien, C. P., Stunkard, A. J., & Ternes, J. W. (1982). Absence of naloxone sensitivity in obese humans. *Psychosomatic Medicine, 44,* 215–218.

O'Connor, D. (1982, May 13). Personal communication.

O'Connor, M. J., Cohen, S., & Parmelee, A. H. (1984). Infant auditory discrimination in preterm and full-term infants as a predictor of 5-year intelligence. *Developmental Psychology, 20,* 159–165.

O'Connor, R. D. (1972). Relative efficacy of modeling, shaping, and the combined procedures for notification of social withdrawal. *Journal of Abnormal Psychology, 79*(3), 327–334.

Oelsner, L. (1979, March 8). More couples adopting victims of genetic defects. *The New York Times,* pp. A1, B14.

Offer, D., & Offer, J. B. (1979). Normal adolescent males: The high school and college years. *Journal of the American College Health Association, 22,* 209–215.

Olds, S. W. (1985). *The eternal garden: Seasons of our sexuality.* New York: Times Books.

Olton, D. S. (1979). Mazes, maps and memory. *American Psychologist, 34,* 583–596.

Orne, M. T. (1977). The construct of hypnosis: Implications of the definition for research and practice. In W. E. Edmonston, Jr. (Ed.), *Conceptual and investigative approaches to hypnosis and hypnotic phenomena.* New York: New York Academy of Sciences.

Orne, M. T., & Holland, C. C. (1968). On the ecological validity of laboratory deceptions. *International Journal of Psychiatry, 6*(4), 282–293.

Orr, W. C., Martin, R. J., & Patterson, C. D. (1972, May). When to suspect sleep apnea—the Pickwickian syndrome. *Resident and Staff Physician,* pp. 101–104.

Osgood, C. E., Suci, G. J., & Tennenbaum, P. H. (1957). *The measurement of meaning.* Urbana: University of Illinois Press.

Oskamp, S., & Mindick, B. (1981). Personality and attitudinal barriers to contraception. In D. Byrne & W. A. Fisher (Eds.), *Adolescents, sex, and contraception.* New York: McGraw-Hill.

Oskamp, S., Mindick, B., Berger, D., & Motta, E. A. (1978). Longitudinal study of success versus failure in contraceptive planning. *Journal of Population, 1,* 69–83.

Ostrove, N. (1978). Expectations for success on effort-determined tasks as a function of incentive and performance feedback. *Journal of Personality and Social Psychology, 36,* 909–916.

Oswald, P. F., & Peltzman, P. (1974). The cry of the human infant. *Scientific American, 230*(3), 84–90.

Oursler, J. D. (1980). *The role of extramarital involvement in personal adjustment, marital adjustment and counseling of middle class women.* Unpublished doctoral dissertation, St. John's University, New York.

Paddock, J. (1975). Studies on antiviolent and "normal" communities. *Aggressive Behavior, 1*(3), 217–233.

Paffenbarger, R. S., Hyde, R. T., Wing, A. L., & Hsieh, C. (1986). Physical activity, all-cause mortality, and longevity of college alumni. *New England Journal of Medicine, 314,* 605–613.

Pagano, R. R., Rose, R. M., Stivers, R. M., & Warrenburg, S. (1976). Sleep during transcendental meditation. *Science, 191,* 308–309.

Paivio, A. (1975) Perceptual comparisons through the mind's eye. *Memory and Cognition, 3*(6), 635–647.

Palmer, S. E. (1975). Visual perception and world knowledge: Notes on a model of sensory cognitive interaction. In D. A. Norman, D. E. Rumelhart, & The LNR Research Group, *Explorations in cognition.* New York: Freeman.

Paloma, M. M. (1972) Role conflict and the married professional woman. In C. Safilious-Rothschild (Ed.), *Toward a sociology of women.* Lexington, MA: Xerox.

Papalia, D. E. (1972). The status of several conservation abilities across the life span. *Human Development, 15,* 229–243.

Papalia, D. E., & Bielby, D. D. (1974). Cognitive functioning in middle and old age adults: A review of research based on Piaget's theory. *Human Development, 17,* 424–443.

Papalia, D. E., Blackburn, J. A., & Foye, B. (1986). *Report of cognitive training project.* Unpublished manuscript.

Papalia, D. E., Blackburn, J. A., Foye, B., & Serlin, R. (1986). Modifiability of figural relations performance: A comparison of two training approaches. Unpublished manuscript.

Papalia, D. E., & Olds, S. W. (1982). *A child's world* (3d ed.). New York: McGraw-Hill.

Pardue, L. (1975). Familial unipolar depressive illness: A pedigree study. *American Journal of Psychiatry, 132*(9), 970–972.

Parke, R. D. (1974). Rules, roles, and resistance to deviation: Recent advances in punishment, discipline, and self-control. In A. Dick (Ed.), *Symposia of child psychology* (Vol. 8). Minneapolis: University of Minnesota Press.

Parke, R. D. (1977). Some effects of punishment on children's behavior—revisited. In E. M. Hetherington & R. D. Parke (Eds.), *Contemporary readings in child psychology.* New York: McGraw-Hill.

Parke, R. D. (1978, October 31). *Babies have fathers, too.* Paper presented at seminar, Advances in Child Development Research, sponsored by American Psychological Association and Society for Research in Child Development, New York Academy of Sciences, New York.

Parkes, C. M., Benjamin, B., & Fitzgerald, R. (1969). Broken heart: A statistical study of increased mortality among widowers. *British Medical Journal, 4,* 740–743.

Parkes, J. D. (1977, May 7). The sleepy patient. *Lancet,* pp. 990–993.

Parmalee, A. H., Wenner, W. H., & Schulz, H. R. (1964). Infant sleep patterns: From birth to 16 weeks of age. *Journal of Pediatrics, 65,* 576.

Patterson, G. R., Chamberlain, P., & Reid, J. B. (1982). A comparative evaluation of a parent-training program. *Behavior Therapy, 13*(5), 638–650.

Paul, G. L. (1969). Chronic mental patients: Current status—future directions. *Psychological Bulletin, 71,* 81–94.

Pavlov, I. P. (1927). *Conditioned reflexes.* London: Oxford University Press.

Pedersen, D. M., & Wheeler, J. (1983). The Müller-Lyer illusion among Navajos. *Journal of Social Psychology, 121,* 3–6.

Pedrick-Cornell, C., & Gelles, R. J.

(1982). Elder abuse: The status of current knowledge. *Family Relations, 31,* 457–465.

Peel, E. A. (1967). *The psychological basis of education* (2d ed.). Edinburgh: Oliver & Boyd.

Pendery, M. L., Maltzman, I. M., & West, L. J. (1982). Controlled drinking by alcoholics? New findings and a reevaluation of a major affirmative study. *Science, 217,* 169–175.

Penfield, W., & Roberts, L. (1959). *Speech and brain mechanisms.* Princeton, NJ: Princeton University Press.

Peplau, L. A. (1979). Power in dating relationships. In J. Freeman (Ed.), *Women: A feminist perspective* (2d ed.). Palo Alto, CA: Mayfield.

Peplau, L. A., & Gordon, S. L. (1985). Women and men in love: Gender differences in close heterosexual relationships. In V. E. O'Leary, R. K. Unger, & B. S. Wallston (Eds.), *Women, gender, and social psychology.* Hillsdale, NJ: Erlbaum.

Peplau, L. A., & Perlman, D. (1979). Blueprint for a social psychological theory of loneliness. In M. Cook & G. Wilson (Eds.), *Love and attraction.* Oxford, England: Pergamon.

Peplau, L. A., & Perlman, D. (1982). *Loneliness: A sourcebook of current theory, research and therapy.* New York: Wiley-Interscience.

Peplau, L. A., Russell, D., & Heim, M. (1979). The experience of loneliness. In I. H. Frieze, D. Bar-Tal, & J. S. Carroll (Eds.), *New approaches to social problems: Applications of attribution theory.* San Francisco: Jossey-Bass.

Perkins, D. N. (1981). *The mind's best work.* Cambridge, MA: Harvard University Press.

Perkins, D. V. (1982). The assessment of stress using life event scales. In L. Goldberger & S. Breznitz (Eds.), *Handbook of stress.* New York: Free Press.

Perls, F. S. (1944). *Ego, hunger and aggression: A revision of Freud's theory and method.* Atlanta: Knox.

Perper, T. (1985). *Sex signals.* Philadelphia: Institute for Scientific Information.

Persky, H., Lief, H. I., Strauss, D., Miller, W. R., & O'Brien, C.P. (1978). Plasma testosterone level and sexual behavior of couples. *Archives of Sexual Behavior, 7*(3), 157–173.

Peterson, C., & Seligman, M. E. P. (1985). The learned helplessness model of depression: Current status of theory and research. In E. E. Beckham & W. R. Leber, *Handbook of depression.* Homewood, IL: Dorsey.

Peterson, L. R., & Peterson, M. J. (1959). Short-term retention of individual verbal items. *Journal of Experimental Psychology, 58,* 193–198.

Petersen, R. C. (1984). Marijuana overview. In M. D. Glantz (Ed.), *Correlates and consequences of marijuana use* (DHHS Pubiication No. ADM 84–1276). Washington, DC: U.S. Government Printing Office.

Petri, E. (1934). Untersuchungen zur erbedingtheit der menarche. *Z. Morph. Anth., 33,* 43–48.

Petri, H. L. (1986). *Motivation: Theory and research.* Belmont, CA: Wadsworth.

Phillips, D. P., & Carstensen, L. L. (1986). Clustering of teenage suicides after television news stories about suicide. *New England Journal of Medicine, 315,* 685–689.

Piaget, J. (1932). *The moral judgment of the child.* New York: Harcourt, Brace & World.

Piaget, J. (1952). *The origins of intelligence in children.* New York: International Universities Press.

Piaget, J. (1972). Intellectual evolution from adolescence to adulthood. *Human Development, 15,* 1–12.

Pihl, R. O., Zeichner, A., Niaura, R., Hagy, F., & Zacchia, C. (1981). Attribution and alcohol-mediated aggression. *Journal of Abnormal Psychology, 90,* 468–475.

Piliavin, J. A., Callero, P. L., & Evans, D. E. (1982). Addiction to altruism? Opponent-process theory and habitual blood donation. *Journal of Personality and Social Psychology, 43*(6), 1200–1213.

Piliavin, J. A., Dovidio, J. F., Gaertner, S. L., & Clark, R. D. (1981). *Emergency intervention.* New York: Academic.

Piliavin, J. A., Evans, D. E., & Callero, P. (1984). Learning to "give to unnamed strangers." In E. Straub, D. Bar-Tel, J. Karylowski, & J. Reykowski (Eds.), *Development and maintenance of prosocial behavior.* New York: Plenum.

Piliavin, J. A., & Piliavin, I. M. (1972). Effects of blood on reactions to a victim. *Journal of Personality and Social Psychology, 23*(3), 353–361.

Piliavin, J. A., Rodin, J., & Piliavin, J. A. (1969). Good samaritanism: An underground phenomenon? *Journal of Personality and Social Psychology, 13,* 289–299.

Piliavin, I. M., Piliavin, J. A., & Rodin, J. (1975). Costs, diffusions, and the stigmatized victim. *Journal of Personality and Social Psychology, 32*(3), 429–438.

Pines, M. (1979, January). Superkids. *Psychology Today,* pp. 53–63.

Pines, M. (1981). The civilizing of Genie. *Psychology Today, 15*(9), 28–34.

Pines, M. (1982, May 4). Movement grows to create guidelines for mental therapy. *The New York Times,* p. C1.

Pirenne, M. H. (1948). *Vision and the eye.* London: Chapman & Hall.

Plutchik, R. (1962). *The emotions: Facts, theories, and a new model.* New York: Random House.

Plutchik, R. (1980). *Emotion: A psychoevolutionary synthesis.* New York: Harper & Row.

Plutchik, R. (1983). Emotions in early development: A psychoevolutionary approach. In R. Plutchik & H. Kellerman (Eds.), *Emotion: Theory, research and experience. Vol 2: Emotions in early development* (pp. 221–257). New York: Academic.

Pokorny, J., & Smith, V. C. (1986). Colorimetry and color discrimination. In K. R. Boff, L. Kaufman, & J. P. Thomas (Eds.), *Handbook of perception and human performance* (Vol. 1). New York: Wiley.

Polivy, J., & Herman, C. (1985). Dieting and bingeing: A causal analysis. *American Psychologist, 40,* 193–201.

Pomeranz, B., & Chiu, D. (1976). Naloxone blockade of acupuncture analgesia: Endorphin implicated. *Life Sciences, 19*(11), 1757–1762.

Pope, H. G., Hudson, J. I., & Jonas, J. M. (1983). Antidepressant treatment of bulimia: Preliminary experience and practical recommendations. *Journal of Clinical Psychopharmacology, 3*(5), 274–281.

Porter, R. H., & Moore, J. D. (1981). Human kin recognition by olfactory cues. *Physiology and Behavior, 27,* 493–495.

Premack, A. J., & Premack, D. (1972). Teaching language to an ape. *Scientific American, 277,* 92–99.

Prentice, A. M., Whitehead, R. G., Watkinson, M., Lamb, W. H., & Cole, T. J. (1983, March 5). Prenatal dietary supplementation of African women and birthweight. *Lancet,* pp. 489–492.

Presidential council on fitness. (1986, March 26). *The New York Times,* p. A27.

Press, A. (1982, April 16). Judge to jury: Overruled. *Newsweek,* p. 59.

Prevention Research Center. (1986). *Prevention index '86: A report card on the nation's health.* Emmaus, PA: Rodale.

Prial, F. J. (1983, January 22). Cable TV is said to top networks in movie violence. *The New York Times,* p. 46.

Purtilo, D., & Sullivan, J. (1979). Immunological bases for superior survival in females. *American Journal of Diseases of Children, 133,* 1251–1253.

Rabkin, J. G., & Struening, E. L. (1976). Life events, stress, and illness. *Science, 194,* 1013–1020.

Rachman, S. J., & Wilson, G. T. (1980). *The effects of psychological therapy* (2d ed.). Oxford, England: Pergamon.

Raleigh, M. J., McGuire, M. T., Brammer, G. L., & Yuwiler, A. (1984). Social and environmental influences on blood serotonin concentrations in monkeys. *Archives of General Psychiatry, 41*(4), 405–410.

Raven, J. C. (1983). *Raven Progressive Matrices Test.* San Antonio, TX: Psychological Corporation.

Raynor, J. O., & Entin, E. E. (1982). *Motivation, career striving, and aging.* Washington, DC: Hemisphere.

Read, M. S., Habicht, J.-P. Lechtig, A., & Klein, R. E. (1973, May 21–25). *Maternal malnutrition, birth weight, and child development.* Paper presented before the International Symposium on Nutrition, Growth and Development, Valencia, Spain.

Rechtschaffen, A., Gilliland, M. A., Bergmann, B. M., & Winter, J. B. (1983). Physiological correlates of prolonged sleep deprivation in rats. *Science, 221,* 182–184.

Rechtschaffen, A., & Kales, A. (1968). *A manual of standardized terminology, techniques, and scoring system for sleep stages of human subjects.* Washington, DC: U.S. Government Printing Office.

Redmond, D. E. (1983, January 18). *Brain chemistry and human aggression.* Paper presented in a seminar, Recent Studies Concerning Dominance, Aggression, and Violence, sponsored by the Harry Frank Guggenheim Foundation, Rockefeller University, New York.

Reed, C. F. (1984). Terrestrial passage theory of the moon illusion. *Journal of Experimental Psychology: General, 113,* 489–500.

Regier, D. A., Myers, J. K., Kramer, M., Robins, L. N., Blazer, D. G., Hough, R. L., Eaton, W. W., & Locke, B. Z. (1984). The NIMH epidemiologic catchment area program. *Archives of General Psychiatry, 41*(10), 934–941.

Reichard, S., Levson, F., & Peterson, P. (1962). *Aging and personality: A study of 87 older men.* New York: Wiley.

Reicher, G. M. (1969). Perceptual recognition as a function of meaningfulness of stimulus material. *Journal of Experimental Psychology, 81,* 275–280.

Reid, J. R., Patterson, G. R., & Loeber, R. (1982). The abused child: Victim, instigator, or innocent bystander? In D. J. Berstein (Ed.), *Response structure and organization.* Lincoln: University of Nebraska Press.

Reiman, E. M., Raichle, M. E., Butler, F. K., Herscovitch, P., & Robins, E. (1984). A focal brain abnormality in panic disorder, a severe form of anxiety. *Nature, 310,* 683–685.

Reisenzein, R. (1983). The Schachter theory of emotion: Two decades later. *Psychological Bulletin, 94*(2), 239–264.

Reiss, I. L. (1980). *Family systems in America* (3d ed.). New York: Holt, Rinehart & Winston.

Reiss, I. L. (1986). *Journey into sexuality: An exploratory voyage.* Englewood Cliffs, N.J.: Prentice-Hall.

Relman, A. S. (1982). Marijuana and health. *New England Journal of Medicine, 306*(10) 603–604.

Rice, B. (1979). Brave new world of intelligence testing. *Psychology Today, 13*(4), 27–41.

Richards, W. (1970). Stereopsis and stereoblindness. *Experimental Brain Research, 10,* 380–388.

Richardson, D. W., & Short, R. V. (1978). Time of onset of sperm production in boys. *Journal of Biosocial Science,* Suppl. 5, 15–25.

Richter, C. P. (1957). On the phenomenon of sudden death in animals and man. *Psychosomatic Medicine, 19,* 191–198.

Riegel, K. F., & Riegel, R. M. (1972). Development, drop, and death. *Developmental Psychology, 6*(2), 306–319.

Rimmer, R. H. (1984). *The X-rated video guide.* New York: Arlington.

Rips, L. P., Shoben, E. J., & Smith, E. E. (1973). Semantic distance and the verification of semantic relations. *Journal of Verbal Learning and Verbal Behavior, 12,* 1–20.

Ritvo, E. R., Freeman, B. J., Mason-Brothers, A., Mo, A., & Ritvo, A. M. (1985). Concordance for the syndrome of autism in 40 pairs of afflicted twins. *American Journal of Psychiatry, 142,* 74–77.

Rivlin, R., & Gravelle, K. (1984). *Deciphering the senses.* New York: Simon & Schuster.

Robbins, L. C. (1963). The accuracy of parental recall of aspects of child development and of childrearing practices. *Journal of Abnormal and Social Psychology, 66,* 261–270.

Roberts, A. H. (1985). Biofeedback: Treatment, training, and clinical roles. *American Psychologist, 40*(8), 938–941.

Roberts, W. W., & Kiess, H. O. (1964). Motivational properties of hypothalamic aggression in cats. *Journal of Comparative and Physiological Psychology, 58*(2), 187–193.

Robins, L. N., Helzer, J. E., Weissman, M. M., Orvaschel, H., Gruenberg, E., Burke, J. D., & Regier, D. A. (1984). Lifetime prevalence of specific psychiatric disorders in three sites. *Archives of General Psychiatry, 41,* 949–958.

Robson, K. S., & Moss, H. A. (1970). Patterns and determinants of maternal attachment. *Journal of Pediatrics, 77*(6), 976–985.

Rock, I. (1983). *The logic of perception.* Cambridge, MA: Massachusetts Institute of Technology Press.

Rodin, J. (1981). Current status of the internal-external hypothesis for obesity. *American Psychologist, 36,* 361–372.

Rodin, J. (1983). *Obesity: An update.* Invited address, American Psychological Association, Anaheim, CA.

Rodin, J., & Langer, E. (1977). Long-term effects of a control-relevant intervention with the institutionalized aged. *Journal of Personality and Social Psychology, 35,* 897–902.

Roffwarg, H. P., Herman, J. H., Bowe-Anders, C., & Tauber, E. S. (1976). The effects of sustained alterations of waking visual input on dream content. In A. M. Arkin, J. S. Antrobus, & S. J. Ellman (Eds.), *The mind in sleep: Psychology and psychophysiology.* Hillsdale, NJ: Erlbaum.

Rogers, C. R. (1951). *Client-centered therapy.* Boston: Houghton Mifflin.

Rogers, C. R. (1961). *On becoming a person.* Boston: Houghton Mifflin.

Rogers, C. R. (1970). *Carl Rogers on encounter groups.* New York: Harper & Row.

Rogers, C. R. (1980). *A way of being.* Boston: Houghton Mifflin.

Rogers, M. F. (1985). AIDS in children: A review of the clinical, epidemiological and public health aspects. *Pediatric Infectious Disease, 4*(3), 230–236.

Rolls, E. T., Rolls, B. J., Kelly, P. H., Shaw, S. G., Wood, R. J., & Dale, R. (1974). The relative attenuation of self-stimulation, eating and drinking produced by dopamine-receptor blockade. *Psychopharmacologia, 38,* 219–230.

Rook, K. S. (1984). Promoting social bonding. *American Psychologist, 39*(12), 1389–1407.

Rook, K. S. (1986). Reciprocity of social exchange and social satisfaction among older women. *Journal of Personality and Social Psychology, 52*(1), 145–154.

Rorschach, H. (1921). *Psychodiagnostics.* Bern: Huber.

Rosch, E. H. (1975). Cognitive representations of semantic categories. *Journal of Experimental Psychology: General, 104,* 192–233.

Rosch, E. H., & Mervis, C. B. (1975). Family resemblances: Studies in the internal structure of categories. *Cognitive Psychology, 7,* 573–605.

Rosch, E. H., Mervis, C. B., Gray, W. D., Johnson, D. M., & Boyes-Braem, P. (1976). Basic objects in natural categories. *Cognitive Psychology, 8,* 382–439.

Rose, F. (1986). The quest for thinking machines. *Science Digest, 94,*(5), 36–42.

Rosen, H. (1982). Lobotomy. In *Encyclopedia Americana* (Vol. 17, p. 635). Danbury, CT: Grolier.

Rosenhan, D. L. (1973). On being sane in insane places. *Science, 179,* 250–258.

Rosenhan, D. L., Salovey, P., & Hargis, K. (1981). The joys of helping. Focus of attention mediates the impact of positive affect on altruism. *Journal of Personality and Social Psychology, 40*(5), 899–905.

Rosenman, R. H. (1983, June 14). *Type A behavior in corporate executives and its implications for cardiovascular disease.* Paper presented at a seminar, Coping with Corporate Stress: Avoiding a Cardiovascular Crisis, New York.

Rosenman, R. H., & Chesney, M. A. (1982). Stress, type A behavior, and coronary disease. In L. Goldberger & S. Breznitz (Eds.), *Handbook of stress.* New York: Free Press.

Rosenthal, A. M. (1964). *Thirty-eight witnesses.* New York: McGraw-Hill.

Rosenthal, N. E. (1985). Antidepressant effects of light in seasonal affective disorder. *American Journal of Psychiatry, 142*(2), 163–170.

Rosenthal, N. E., Sack, D. A., Gillin, C., Lewy, A. J., Goodwin, F. K., Davenport, Y., Mueller, P. S., Newsome, D. A., & Wehr, T. A. (1984). Seasonal affective disorder: A description of the syndrome and some preliminary findings with light therapy. *Archives of General Psychiatry, 41*(1), 72–80.

Rosenthal, N. E., Sack, D., & Wehr, T. A. (1983). Seasonal variation in affective disorders. In T. A. Wehr & F. K. Goodwin (Eds.), *Circadian rhythms in psychiatry.* Pacific Grove, CA: Boxwood.

Rosenzweig, M. R. (1984). Experience, memory and the brain. *American Psychologist, 39,* 365–376.

Rosenzweig, M. R., & Leiman, A. L. (1982). *Physiological psychology.* Lexington, MA: Heath.

Ross, L. (1977). The intuitive psychologist and his shortcomings: Distortions in the attribution process. In L. Berkowitz (Ed.), *Advances in experimental social psychology.* New York: Academic.

Rotter, J. B. (1966). Generalized expectancies for internal versus external control of reinforcement. *Psychological Monographs, 80,* 1–28.

Rotter, J. B. (1975). Some problems and misconceptions related to the construct of internal verus external control of reinforcement. *Journal of Consulting and Clinical Psychology, 43,* 36–67.

Rovee-Collier, C., & Lipsitt, L. (1982). Learning, adaptation, and memory in the newborn. In P. Stratton (Ed.), *Psychobiology of the human newborn.* New York: Wiley.

Rubenstein, C. (1982, July). Psychology's fruit flies. *Psychology Today,* pp. 83–84.

Rubenstein, C. (1982). Wellness is all: A report on *Psychology Today's* survey of beliefs about health. *Psychology Today, 16,* 62–72.

Rubin, D. C. (Ed.). (1986). *Autobiographical memory.* New York: Cambridge University Press.

Rubin, D. C., & Kozin, M. (1984). Vivid memories. *Cognition, 16*(1), 81–95.

Rubin, D. H., Krasilnikoff, P. A., Leventhal, J. M., Weile, B., & Berget, A. (1986). Effect of passive smoking on birth-weight. *Lancet, II*(8504), 415–417.

Rubin, L. B. (1979). *Women of a certain age.* New York: Harper & Row.

Rubin, L. B. (1983). *Intimate strangers: Men and women together.* New York: Harper & Row.

Rubin, Z. (1970). Measurement of romantic love. *Journal of Personality and Social Psychology, 16*(2), 265–273.

Rubin, Z., Peplau, L. A., & Hill, C. T. (1981). Loving and leaving: Sex differences in romantic attachments. *Sex Roles, 7*(8), 821–835.

Rugh, R., & Schettles, L. B. (1971). *From conception to birth: The drama of life's beginning.* New York: Harper & Row.

Rumbaugh, D. M., & Gill, T. V. (1973). Reading and sentence completion by a chimpanzee. *Science, 182,* 731–733.

Runck, B. (1980) *Biofeedback-issues in treatment assessment.* Rockville, MD: National Institute of Mental Health.

Runeson, S., & Frykholm, G. (1983). Kinematic specifications of dynamics as an informational basis for person-and-action perception: Expectation, gender recognition, and deceptive intention. *Journal of Experimental Psychology: General, 112,* 585–615.

Russell, M. (1976). Human olfactory communication. *Nature, 260,* 520–522.

Russell, R. (1981, March 5). *Report on effective psychotherapy: Legislative testimony.* Presented at a public hearing,

The Regulation of Mental Health Practitioners, conducted at the City University of New York by Assemblyman Mark Alan Siegel of the New York State Assembly Committee on Higher Education.

Rutter, M. (1983). Stress, coping, and development: Some issues and some questions. In N. Garmezy & M. Rutter (Eds.), *Stress, coping and development in children.* New York: McGraw-Hill.

Rutter, M. (1984). Resilient children. *Psychology Today, 18,* 57–65.

Sabin, L. (1972, February). Why I threw out my TV set. *Today's Health,* pp. 70–71.

Sacco, W. P., & Beck, A. T. (1985). Cognitive therapy of depression. In E. E. Beckham & W. R. Leber (Eds.), *Handbook of depression.* Homewood, IL: Dorsey.

Sachs, J., Bard, B., & Johnson, M. L. (1981). Language learning with restricted input: Case studies of two hearing children of deaf parents. *Applied Psycholinguistics, 2,* 33–54.

Sackheim, H. A. (1985, June). The case for ECT. *Psychology Today,* pp. 36–40.

Sagi, A., & Hoffman, M. (1976). Empathetic distress in newborns. *Developmental Psychology, 12*(2), 175–176.

Sahakian, W. S. (1976). *Learning systems, models, and theories.* Chicago: Rand McNally.

Sajdel-Sulkowska, E. M., & Marotta, C. A. (1984). Alzheimer's disease brain: Alterations in RNA levels and ribonuclease-inhibitor complex. *Science, 225,* 947–949.

Salans, L. B., Knittle, J. L., & Hirsch, J. (1968). The role of adipose cell size and adipose tissue insulin sensitivity in the carbohydrate intolerance of human obesity. *Journal of Clinical Investigation, 47,* 153–165.

Samuel, W. (1981). *Personality: Searching for the sources of human behavior.* New York: McGraw-Hill.

Sanders, R. (1986, April). Eye to eye. *UCSF Magazine,* pp. 3–15.

Santee, R. T., & Maslach, C. (1982). To agree or not to agree: Personal dissent amid social pressure to conform. *Journal of Personality and Social Psychology, 42*(4), 690–700.

Sass, L. (1982, August 22). The borderline personality. *The New York Times Magazine,* pp. 12–15, 66–67.

Savage-Rumbaugh, E. S., Sevcik, R. A., Rumbaugh, D. M., & Rubert, E. (1985). The capacity of animals to acquire language: Do species differences have anything to say to us? *Philosophical*

Transactions, Royal Society of London, B308, 177–185.

Saxe, L., Dougherty, D., & Cross, T. (1985). The validity of polygraph testing: Scientific analysis and public controversy. *American Psychologist, 40*(3), 355–366.

Scanzoni, L., & Scanzoni, J. (1976). *Men, women, and change: A sociology of marriage and family.* New York: McGraw-Hill.

Scarr, S., & Weinberg, R. A. (1983). The Minnesota adoption study: Genetic differences and malleability. *Child Development, 54,* 260–267.

Schacht, T., & Nathan, P. E. (1977). But is it good for psychologists? Appraisal and status of DSM III. *American Psychologist, 32,* 1017–1025.

Schacter, D. L. (1983). Amnesia observed: Remembering and forgetting in a natural environment. *Journal of Abnormal Psychology, 92*(2), 236–242.

Schachter, S. (1971). *Emotion, obesity, and crime.* New York: Academic.

Schachter, S. (1982). Don't sell habit breakers short. *Psychology Today, 16*(8), 27–34.

Schachter, S., & Gross, L. P. (1968). Manipulated time and eating behavior. *Journal of Personality and Social Psychology, 10,* 98–106.

Schachter, S., & Singer, J. (1962). Cognitive, social, and physiological determinants of emotional state. *Psychological Review, 69,* 379–399.

Schaeffer, D. L. (1971). *Sex differences in personality.* Belmont, CA: Brooks/Cole.

Schaie, K. W., & Gribbin, K. (1975). Adult development and aging. *Annual Review of Psychology, 26,* 65–96.

Schank, R. C., & Hunter, L. (1985). The quest to understand thinking. *Byte, 10*(4), 143–155.

Scharf, B., & Buus, S. (1986). Audition I. In K. R. Boff, L. Kaufman, & J. P. Thomas (Eds.), *Handbook of perception and human performance* (Vol. 1). New York: Wiley.

Schiamberg, L. B., & Chun, C.-H. (1986, May 26). *The influence of family on educational and occupational achievement.* Paper presented at the annual meeting of The American Association for the Advancement of Science, Philadephia.

Schiffenbauer, A., & Schiavo, R. S. (1976). Physical distance and attraction: An intensification effect. *Journal of Experimental Psychology, 12,* 274–282.

Schildkraut, J. J., & Kety, S. S. (1967). Biogenic amines and emotions. *Science, 156,* 21–30.

Schleifer, S. J., Keller, S. E., McKegney, F. P., & Stein, M. (1979, March). *The influence of stress and other psychosocial factors on human immunity.* Paper presented at the annual meeting of the Psychosomatic Society, Dallas.

Schmeck, H. M., Jr. (1976, June 10). Trend in growth of children lags. *The New York Times,* p. 13.

Schreiber, F. R. (1975). *Sybil.* Chicago: Regenery.

Schultz, D. P. (1969). The human subject in psychological research. *Psychological Bulletin, 72,* 214–228.

Schultz, D. P. (1981). *A history of modern psychology.* New York: Academic.

Schulz, R. (1978). *The psychology of death, dying, and bereavement.* Reading, MA: Addison-Wesley.

Scovern, A. W., & Killman, P. R. (1980). Status of electroconvulsive therapy: Review of the outcome literature. *Psychological Bulletin, 87,* 260–303.

Sears, D. O., Freedman, J. L., & Peplau, L. A. (1985). *Social psychology* (5th ed.). Englewood Cliffs, NJ: Prentice-Hall.

Sears, P. (1977). *Life satisfaction of Terman's gifted women: 1927–72: Comparison with the gifted and with normative samples.* Paper presented at 5th Annual Conference, School of Education, University of Wisconsin, Madison.

Sears, P., & Barbee, A. (1978). Career and life satisfaction among Terman's gifted women. In *The gifted and the creative: A fifty-year perspective.* Baltimore: Johns Hopkins University Press.

Sears, R. R. (1977). Sources of life satisfaction of the Terman gifted men. *American Psychologist, 32,* 119–128.

Sears, R. R., Maccoby, E. E., & Levin, H. (1957). *Patterns of child rearing.* New York: Harper & Row.

Segal, J., & Yahraes, H. (1978). *A child's journey.* New York: McGraw-Hill.

Segerberg, O. (1982). *Living to be 100.* New York: Scribner's.

Seidman, L. J. (1983). Schizophrenia and brain dysfunction: An integration of recent neurodiagnostic findings. *Psychological Bulletin, 94*(2), 195–238.

Seligman, M. (1975). *Helplessness: On depression, development and death.* San Francisco: Freeman.

Selman, R. L., & Selman, A. P. (1979). Children's ideas about friendship: A new theory. *Psychology Today, 13*(4), 71–80, 114.

Selye, H. (1936). A syndrome produced by diverse nocuous agents. *Nature, 138,* 32.

Selye, H. (1974). *Stress without distress.* Philadelphia: Lippincott.

Selye, H. (1980). The stress concept today. In I. L. Kutash, L. B. Schlesinger, & Associates (Eds.), *Handbook of stress and anxiety.* San Francisco: Jossey-Bass.

Selye, H. (1982). History and present status of the stress concept. In L. Goldberger & S. Breznitz (Eds.), *Handbook of stress: Theoretical and clinical aspects.* New York: Macmillan.

Séquin, O. E. (1907). *Idiocy: Its treatment by the physiological method.* New York: Bureau of Publications, Teachers College, Columbia University. (Original work published 1866)

Serfass, R. C. & Gerberich, S. G. (1984). Exercise for optimal health: Strategies and motivational considerations. *Preventive Medicine, 13,* 79–99.

Shapiro, C. M., Bortz, R., Mitchell, D., Bartel, P., & Jooste, P. (1981). Slow-wave sleep: A recovery period after exercise. *Science, 214,* 1253–1254.

Shapiro, S., Skinner, E. A., Kessler, L. G., Von Korff, M., German, P. S., Tischler, G. L., Leaf, P. J., Benham, L., Cottler, L., & Regier, D. A. (1984). Utilization of health and mental health services. *Archives of General Psychiatry, 41*(10), 971–978.

Shatz, M., & Gelman, R. (1973). The development of communication skills: Modifications in the speech of young children as a function of listener. *Monographs of the Society for Research in Child Development, 38*(5, Serial No. 152).

Shaywitz, S., Cohen, D., & Shaywitz, B. (1980). Behavior and learning difficulties in children of normal intelligence born to alcoholic mothers. *Journal of Pediatrics, 96*(6), 978–982.

Sheehan, D. V. (1982). Current concepts in psychiatry: Panic attacks and phobias. *New England Journal of Medicine, 307*(3), 156–158.

Sheehan, S. (1982). *Is there no place on earth for me?* Boston: Houghton Mifflin.

Sheehy, G. (1976). *Passages.* New York: Dutton.

Shekelle, R. B., Raynor, W. J., Ostfeld, A. M., Garron, D. C., Beliauskas, L. A., Lin, S. C., Malizia, C., & Paul, O. (1981). Psychological depression and 17-year risk of death from cancer. *Psychosomatic Medicine, 43*(2), 117–125.

Sheperd-Look, D. L. (1982). Sex differentiation and the development of sex roles. In B. B. Wolman (Ed.), *Handbook of developmental psychology.* Englewood Cliffs, NJ: Prentice-Hall.

Sherif, M. (1966). *In common predicament: Social psychology of inter-group conflict and cooperation.* Boston: Houghton Mifflin.

Sherman, L. W., & Berk, R. A. (1984, April). The Minneapolis domestic violence experiment. *Police Foundation Reports,* pp. 1–8.

Sherrod, D. R. (1974). Crowding, perceived control, and behavioral aftereffects. *Journal of Applied Social Psychology, 4,* 171–186.

Shields, J. (1962). *Monozygotic twins brought up apart and brought up together.* London: Oxford University Press.

Shiffrin, R. M., & Atkinson, R. C. (1969). Storage and retrieval processes in long-term memory. *Psychological Review, 76,* 179–193.

Shipp, E. R. (1985, November 4). Teenagers taking risks: When pregnancy is the result. *The New York Times,* p. A16.

Shneidman, E. S. (1984). *Death: Current perspectives.* Palo Alto, CA: Mayfield.

Shorter, M. A., & McDarby, D. (1979). *Chemical survival: A primer for western man* (2d ed.). Phoenix, AZ: Do It Now Foundation.

Shotland, R. L. (1985). When bystanders just stand by. *Psychology Today, 19*(6), 50–55.

Shotland, R. L., & Heinold, W. T. (1985). Bystander response to arterial bleeding: Helping skills, the decision-making process, and differentiating the helping response. *Journal of Personality and Social Psychology, 49*(2), 347–356.

Shotland, R. L., & Straw, M. K. (1976). Bystander response to an assault: When a man attacks a woman. *Journal of Personality and Social Psychology, 34,* 990–999.

Siegel, S., Sherman, J. E., & Mitchell, D. (1980). Extinction of morphine analgesic tolerance. *Learning and Motivation, 11,* 289–301.

Siegler, M., & Osmond, H. (1974). *Models of madness, models of medicine.* New York: Harper & Row.

Siever, L. J., & Davis, K. L. (1985). Overview: Toward a dysregulation hypothesis of depression. *American Journal of Psychiatry, 142*(9), 1017–1031.

Simner, M. L. (1971). Newborn's response to the cry of another infant. *Developmental Psychology, 5*(1), 136–150.

Singer, J. L., & Singer, D. G. (1983). Psychologists look at television: Cognitive, developmental, personality, and social policy implications. *American Psychologist, 38*(7), 826–34.

Siscovick, D. S., Weiss, N. S., Fletcher, R. H., & Lasky, T. (1984). The incidence of primary cardiac arrest during vigorous exercise. *New England Journal of Medicine, 311*(14), 874–877.

Sitaram, N., Weingartner, H., & Gillin, J. C. (1978). Human serial learning: Enhancement with arecoline and impairment with scopolamine. *Science, 201,* 274–276.

Skeels, H. M. (1966). Adult status of children with contrasting early life experiences. *Monographs of the Society for Research in Child Development, 31*(Whole No. 3), 1–65.

Skeels, H. M., & Dye, H. B. (1939). A study of the effects of differential stimulation on mentally retarded children. *Program of the American Association of Mental Deficiency, 44,* 114–136.

Skinner, B. F. (1938). *The behavior of organisms.* New York: Appleton-Century-Crofts.

Skinner, B. F. (1951). How to teach animals. *Scientific American, 185,* 26–29.

Skinner, B. F. (1953). *Science and human behavior.* New York: Macmillan.

Skinner, B. F. (1957). *Verbal behavior.* Englewood Cliffs, NJ: Prentice-Hall.

Skinner, B. F. (1961). Teaching machines. *Scientific American, 205,* 90–102.

Skinner, B. F. (1982, August 23). *Intellectual self-management in old age.* Paper presented at the annual meeting of the American Psychological Association, Washington, DC.

Slag, M. F., Morley, J. E., Elson, M. K., Trence, O. L., Nelson, C. J., Nelson, A. E., Kinlow, W. B., Beyer, H. S., Nuttall, F. Q., & Shafer, R. B. (1983). Impotence in medical clinic outpatients. *Journal of American Medical Association, 249*(13), 1736–1740.

Sloane, R. B., Staples, F. R., Cristol, A. H., Yorkston, N. J., & Whipple, K. (1975). *Psychotherapy.* Cambridge, MA: Harvard University Press.

Slobin, D. I. (1971). Universals of grammatical development in children. In W. Levelt & G. B. Flores d'Arcais (Eds.), *Advances in psycholinguistic research.* Amsterdam: New Holland.

Smith, D. (1982). Trends in counseling and psychotherapy. *American Psychologist, 37*(3), 802–809.

Smith, D. W., & Wilson, A. A. (1973). *The child with Down's syndrome (mongolism).* Philadelphia: Saunders.

Smith, M. C. (1983). Hypnotic enhancement of witnesses: Does it work? *Psychological Bulletin, 94*(3), 387–407.

Smith, M. L., & Glass, G. V. (1977). Meta-analysis of psychotherapy outcome studies. *American Psychologist, 32,* 752–760.

Snodgrass, S. E. (1985). Women's intuition: The effect of subordinate role on interpersonal sensitivity. *Journal of Personality and Social Psychology, 49,* 146–155.

Snow, C. E. (1972). Mothers' speech to children learning language. *Child Development, 43,* 549–565.

Snow, C. E. (1977). Mothers' speech research: From input to interaction. In C. D. Snow & C. A. Ferguson (Eds.), *Talking to children: Language input and acquisition.* Cambridge: Cambridge University Press.

Snow, C. E., Arlman-Rupp, A., Hassing, Y., Jobse, J., Joosten, J., & Verster, J. (1976). Mothers' speech in three social classes. *Journal of Psycholinguistic Research, 5,* 1–20.

Snow, M. E., Jacklin, C. N., & Maccoby, E. E. (1983). Sex-of-child differences in father-child interaction at one year of age. *Child Development, 54,* 227–232.

Snyder, M. (1982). When believing means doing: Creating links between attitudes and behavior. In M. Zanna, E. Higgins, & C. Herman (Eds.), *Consistency in social behavior: The Ontario symposium* (Vol. 2). Hillsdale, NJ: Erlbaum.

Snyder, M., Campbell, B., & Preston, E. (1982). Testing hypotheses about human nature: Assessing the accuracy of social stereotypes. *Social Cognition, 1*(3), 256–272.

Snyder, M., Tanke, E. D., & Berscheid, E. (1977). Social perception and interpersonal behavior: On the self-fulfilling nature of social stereotypes. *Journal of Personality and Social Psychology, 35,* 691–712.

Snyder, S. H., & Reivich, M. (1966). Regional location of lysergic acid diethylamide in monkey brain. *Nature, 209,* 1093.

Sobel, D. (1980, October 26). Freud's fragmented legacy. *The New York Times Magazine,* p. 28.

Sobell, L., Sobell, M., & Ward, E. (1980). *Evaluating alcohol and drug abuse treatment effectiveness.* New York: Pergamon.

Sobell, M., & Sobell, L. (1975). The need for realism, relevance, and operational assumptions in the study of substance dependence. In H. D. Cappell & A. E. LeBlanc (Eds.), *Biological and behavioral approaches to drug dependence.* Toronto: Alcoholism and Drug Addiction Research Foundation of Canada.

Solman, R. T., May, J. G., & Schwartz, B. D. (1981). The word superiority effect: A study using parts of letters. *Journal of Experimental Psychology: Human Perception and Performance, 7,* 552–559.

Solomon, R. L. (1980). The opponent-process theory of acquired motivation: The costs of pleasure and the benefits of pain. *American Psychologist, 35,* 691–712.

Solomon, R. L., & Corbit, J. D. (1974). An opponent-process theory of motivation I. Temporal dynamics of affect. *Psychological Review, 81,* 119–145.

Sontag, S. (1972, September 23). The double standard of aging. *Saturday Review,* pp. 29–38.

Soutek, A. J., & Wyatt, R. J. (1981). The chemistry of crankiness. *Psychology Today, 15*(10), 120.

Spearman, C. (1904). General intelligence objectively determined and measured. *American Journal of Psychology, 15,* 201–293.

Sperling, G. (1960). The information available in brief visual presentations. *Psychological Monographs, 74*(Whole No. 498).

Sperry, R. (1982). Some effects of disconnecting the cerebral hemispheres. *Science, 217,* 1223–1226.

Spiegel, D. (1984). Hypnosis. *Harvard Medical School Mental Health Letter, 1*(4), 3–5.

Spiess, W. F. S. (1977). *The psychophysiology of premature ejaculation.* Unpublished doctoral dissertation. State University of New York at Stony Brook.

Spitzer, R. L. (1976). More on pseudo science in science and the case for psychiatric diagnosis: A critique of D. L. Rosenhan's "On being sane in insane places" and "The contextual nature of psychiatric diagnosis." *Archives of General Psychiatry, 33,* 459–470.

Spitzer, R. L., Skodol, A. E., Gibbon, M., & Williams, J. B. W. (1983). *Psychopathology: A case book.* New York: McGraw-Hill.

Sports people. (1982, August 11). *The New York Times,* p. B8.

Squire, L. R., & Slater, P. C. (1978). Anterograde and retrograde memory impairment in chronic amnesia. *Neuropsychologia, 16,* 313–322.

Sroufe, L. A., Fox, N. E., & Pancake, V. R. (1983). Attachment and dependency in a developmental perspective. *Child Development, 54,* 1615–1627.

Sroufe, L. A., & Wunsch, J. (1972). The development of laughter in the first year of life. *Child Development, 43,* 1326–1344.

Stapp, J., Tucker, A. M., & VandenBos, G. R. (1985). Census of psychological personnel: 1983. *American Psychologist, 40*(12), 1317–1351.

Stark, R., & McEvoy, J. (1970). Middle-class violence. *Psychology Today, 4,* 52–65.

Starr, B. D., & Weiner, M. B. (1981). *The Starr-Weiner report on sex and sexuality in the mature years.* New York: Stein & Day.

Steele, D. J., Gutmann, M., Leventhal, H., & Easterling, D. (1983). *Symptoms and attributions as determinants of health behavior.* Unpublished manuscript, University of Wisconsin-Madison.

Steinberg, L. D. (1981). Transformations in family relations at puberty. *Developmental Psychology, 17*(6), 833–840.

Steiner, I. D. (1979). Social psychology. In E. Hearst (Ed.), *The first century of experimental psychology.* Hillsdale, NJ: Erlbaum.

Steinmetz, S. K., & Straus, M. A. (Eds.). (1974). *Violence in the family.* New York: Dodd, Mead.

Stenchever, M. A., Williamson, R. A., Leonard, J., Karp, L. E., Ley, B., Shy, K., & Smith, D. (1981). Possible relationship between in utero diethylstilbestrol exposure and male fertility. *American Journal of Obstetrics and Gynecology, 140,* 186–193.

Sternberg, R. J. (1979). Stalking the IQ quark. *Psychology Today, 13*(4), 27–41.

Sternberg, R. J. (1985a). *Beyond IQ.* Cambridge: Cambridge University Press.

Sternberg, R. J. (1985b). Human intelligence: The model is the message. *Science, 230*(4730), 1111–1118.

Sternberg, R. J. (1985c, August). *A triangular theory of love.* Paper presented at the annual meeting of the American Psychological Association, Los Angeles.

Sternberg, R. J., & Barnes, M. L. (1985). Real and ideal other in romantic relationships: Is four a crowd? *Journal of Personality and Social Psychology, 49*(6), 1586–1608.

Sternberg, R. J., Conway, B. E., Ketron, J. L., & Bernstein, M. (1981). People's conceptions of intelligence. *Journal of Personality and Social Psychology, 41*(1), 37–55.

Sternberg, R. J., & Davidson, J. (1982). The mind of the puzzler. *Psychology Today, 16*(6), 37–44.

Sternberg, R. J., & Grajek, S. (1984). The nature of love. *Journal of Personality and Social Psychology, 47*(2), 312–329.

Sternberg, S. (1966). High-speed scanning in human memory. *Science, 153,* 652–654.

Sternberg, S. (1967). Two operations in character-recognition: Some evidence from reaction-time measurements. *Perception and Psychophysics, 2,* 45–53.

Sternberg, S. (1969). The discovery of processing stages. *Acta Psychologica, 30,* 276–315.

Sternglanz, S., & Serbin, L. (1974). Sex role stereotyping in children's television programs. *Developmental Psychology, 10,* 710–715.

Stiles, W. B., Shapiro, D. A., & Elliott, R. (1986). Are all psychotherapies equivalent? *American Psychologist, 41*(2), 165–180.

Stjernfeldt, M., Berglund, K., Lindsten, J., & Ludvigsson, J. (1986). Maternal smoking during pregnancy and risk of childhood cancer. *Lancet, I*(8494), 1350–1352.

Stone, G. C. (1979). Health and the health system: A historical overview and conceptual framework. In G. C. Stone, F. Cohen, & N. E. Adler (Eds.), *Health psychology.* San Francisco: Jossey-Bass.

Strasser, S. (1984, January 23). A town on the edge of fear. *Newsweek,* p. 27.

Streib, G. F., & Schneider, C. J. (1971). *Retirement in American society: Impact and process.* Ithaca, NY: Cornell University Press.

Stroop, J. R. (1935). Studies of interference in serial verbal reactions. *Journal of Experimental Psychology, 18,* 643–662.

Strupp, H. (1973). On the basic ingredients of psychotherapy. *Journal of Consulting and Clinical Psychology, 41,* 1–8.

Strupp, H. (1975). Psychoanalysis, "focal" psychotherapy, and the nature of the therapeutic inference. *Archives of General Psychiatry, 32,* 127–135.

Study of black students by Center for Social Organization of Schools and Rand Corporation. (1985, September 17). *The New York Times,* p. C1.

Stump, A. (1975, October 4–10). "That's him—the guy who hit me!" *TV Guide* pp. 32–35.

Stunkard, A. J., Foch, T. T., & Hrubec, Z. (1986). A twin study of human obesity. *Journal of the American Medical Association, 256,* 51–54.

Stunkard, A. J., Sorensen, T., Hanis, C., Teasdale, T. W., Chakraborty, R., Schull, W. J., & Schulsinger, F. (1986). An adoption study of human obesity. *New England Journal of Medicine, 314,* 193–198.

Suedfeld, P. (1975). The benefits of boredom: Sensory deprivation reconsidered. *American Scientist, 63,* 60–69.

Sullivan-Bolyai, J., Hull, H. F., Wilson, C., & Corey, L. (1983). Neonatal herpes simplex virus infection in King County, Washington. *Journal of the American Medical Association, 250*(22), 3059–3062.

Summers, W. K., Majovski, L. V., Marsh, G. M., Tachiki, K., & Kling, A. (1986). Oral tetrahydroaminoacridine in long-term treatment of senile dementia, Alzheimer type. *New England Journal of Medicine, 315*(20), 1241–1245.

Sundberg, N. D. (1977). *Assessment of persons.* Englewood Cliffs, NJ: Prentice-Hall.

Suomi, S., & Harlow, H. (1972). Social rehabilitation of isolate-reared monkeys. *Developmental Psychology, 6*(3), 487–496.

Suomi, S., & Harlow, H. (1978). Early experience and social development in Rhesus monkeys. In M. Lamb (Ed.), *Social and personality development.* New York: Holt, Rinehart & Winston.

Sutton-Smith, B. (1982). Birth order and sibling status effects. In M. E. Lamb & B. Sutton-Smith (Eds.), *Sibling relationships: Their nature and significance across the life-span.* Hillsdale, NJ: Erlbaum.

Swacker, M. (1975). The sex of the speaker as a sociolinguistic variable. In B. Thorne & N. Henley (Eds.), *Language and sex: Difference and dominance* (pp. 76–83). Rowley, MA: Newbury House.

Szasz, T. (1974). *The myth of mental illness* (rev. ed.). New York: Harper & Row.

Talland, G. A. (1969). *The pathology of memory.* New York: Academic.

Tanfer, K., & Horn, M. C. (1985). Contraceptive use, pregnancy and fertility patterns among single American women in their 20's. *Family Planning Perspectives, 17*(1), 10–19.

Tanne, J. H. (1983). The "borderline" personality. *Medical World News, 24*(8), 50–67.

Tanner, J. M. (1973). Growing up. *Scientific American, 229*(16), 34–43.

Targ, D. B. (1979). Toward a reassessment of women's experience at middle-age. *Family Coordinator, 28*(3), 377–382.

Tart, C. (Ed.). (1969). *Altered states of consciousness.* New York: Wiley.

Taukermannova, M. (1973). Smiling in infants. *Child Development, 44,* 701–704.

Taylor, C. W., Smith, W. R., & Ghiselin, B. (1963). The creative and other contributions of one sample of research scientists. In C. W. Taylor & F. Barron (Eds.), *Scientific creativity: Its recognition and development.* New York: Wiley.

Taylor, S. E. (1983, November). Adjustment to threatening events: A theory of cognitive adaptation. *American Psychologist*, pp. 1161–1173.

Taylor, S. E. (1986). *Health psychology*. New York: Random House.

Templeton, R. D., & Quigley, J. P. (1930). The action of insulin on the motility of the gastrointestinal tract. *American Journal of Physiology, 91,* 467–474.

Teplin, L. A. (1983). The criminalization of the mentally ill: Speculation in search of data. *Psychological Bulletin, 94*(1), 54–67.

Terman, L. M. (1921). In symposium: Intelligence and its measurement. *Journal of Educational Psychology, 12,* 127–133.

Terman, L. M., & Oden, M. H. (1959). *Genetic studies of genius, V. The gifted group at mid-life.* Stanford, CA: Stanford University Press.

Terrace, H. S. (1979). How Nim Chimsky changed my mind. *Psychology Today, 13*(6), 65–76.

Terrace, H. S. (1985). In the beginning was the "name." *American Psychologist, 40*(9), 1011–1028.

Terrace, H. S., Petitto, L. A., Sanders, R. J., & Bever, T. G. (1979). Can an ape create a sentence? *Science, 206*(4421), 891–206.

Teuber, H.-L., Milner, B., & Vaughan, H. G., Jr. (1968). Persistent retrograde amnesia after stab wound of the basal brain. *Neuropsychologia, 6,* 267–282.

Thibaut, J. W., & Kelley, H. H. (1959). *The social psychology of groups.* New York: Wiley.

Thomas, A., & Chess, S. (1977). *Temperament and development.* New York: Brunner/Mazel.

Thomas, A., Chess, S., & Birch, H. G. (1968). *Temperament and behavior disorders in children.* New York: New York University Press.

Thomas, G. S., Lee, P. R., Franks, P., & Paffenbarger, R. S. (1982). *Exercise and health: The evidence and the implications.* Cambridge, MA: Oelgeschlager, Gunn, & Hain.

Thompson, A. P. (1983). Extramarital sex: A review of the research literature. *Journal of Sex Research, 19*(1), 1–22.

Thompson, J. K., Jarvie, G. J., Lahey, B. B., & Cureton, K. J. (1982). Exercise and obesity: Etiology, physiology, and intervention. *Psychological Bulletin, 91,* 55–79.

Thompson, R. A., & Lamb, M. E. (1983). Security attachment and stranger sociability in infants. *Developmental Psychology, 19*(2), 184–191.

Thompson, R. A., Lamb, M. E., & Estes, D. (1982). Stability of infant-mother at-tachment and its relationship to changing life circumstances in an unselected middle-class sample. *Child Development, 53,* 144–148.

Thorndike, E. L. (1911). *Animal intelligence.* New York: Macmillan.

Thurstone, L. L. (1938). *Primary mental abilities.* Chicago: University of Chicago Press.

Tolman, E. C. (1932). *Purposive behavior in animals and men.* New York: Century.

Tolman, E. C. (1948). Cognitive maps in rats and men. *Psychological Review, 55,* 189–208.

Tomlinson-Keasey, C. (1972). Formal operations in females from eleven to fifty-six years of age. *Developmental Psychology, 6*(2), 364.

Tomporowski, P. D., & Ellis, N. R. (1986). Effects of exercise on cognitive processes: A review. *Psychological Bulletin, 99*(3), 338–346.

Torgersen, S. (1986). Genetics of somatoform disorders. *Archives of General Psychiatry, 43,* 502–505.

Triandis, H. C. (1977). *Interpersonal behavior.* Monterey, CA: Brooks/Cole.

Tribich, D. (1982, January 14). Personal communication.

Tribich, D., & Klein, M. (1981). On Freud's blindness. *Colloquium, 4,* 52–59.

Troll, L. (1985). *Early and middle adulthood.* Monterey, CA: Brooks/Cole.

Trotter, R. J. (1983, August). Baby face. *Psychology Today,* pp. 14–20.

Tryon, R. C. (1940). Genetic differences in maze learning in rats. *Yearbook of the National Society for Studies in Education, 39,* 111–119.

Tulving, E. (1962). Subjective organization in free recall of "unrelated" words. *Psychological Review, 69,* 344–354.

Tulving, E. (1972). Episodic and semantic memory. In E. Tulving & W. Donaldson (Eds.), *Organization and memory.* New York: Academic.

Tulving, E. (1977). Cue-dependent forgetting. In I. Janis (Ed.), *Current trends in psychology.* Los Altos, CA: Kaufmann. (Reprinted from *American Scientist,* January–February 1974)

Turnbull, C. (1972). *The mountain people.* New York: Simon & Schuster.

Turner, S. M., Beidel, D. C., & Nathan, R. S. (1985). Biological factors in obsessive–compulsive disorder. *Psychological Bulletin, 97*(3), 430–450.

Unger, R. K. (1985). Epilogue: Toward a synthesis of women, gender, and social psychology. In V. E. O'Leary, R. K. Unger, & B. S. Wallston (Eds.), *Women, gender, and social psychology* (pp. 349–358). Hillsdale, NJ: Erlbaum.

U.S. Attorney General's Task Force on Family Violence. (1984).

U.S. Bureau of Census. (1983). *America in transition: An aging society* (Current Population Reports, Series P-23, No. 128). Washington, DC: U.S. Government Printing Office.

U.S. Department of Health and Human Services (USDHHS). (1980a). *Let's talk about drug abuse.* Rockville, MD: National Institute on Drug Abuse.

U.S. Department of Health and Human Services (USDHHS). (1980b). *Project sleep: The national program on insomnia and sleep disorders.* Rockville, MD: U.S. Public Health Service.

United States Department of Health and Human Services (USDHHS). (1981a). *Fourth Special Report to the U.S. Congress on Alcohol and Health* (DHHS Publication No. ADM 82-1080). Washington, DC: U.S. Government Printing Office.

U.S. Department of Health and Human Services (USDHHS). (1981b). *ADAMHA data book* (rev. ed.) (DHHS Publication No. ADM 81-662). Washington, DC: U.S. Government Printing Office.

U.S. Department of Health and Human Services (USDHHS). (1981c). *Q & A: Alzheimer's Disease.* Chicago: Alzheimer's Disease and Related Disorders Association. (Original work published by National Institutes of Health, NIH Publication No. 80-1646.)

U.S. Department of Health and Human Services (USDHHS). (1983). *Biofeedback* (Publication No. ADM 83-1273). Washington, DC: U.S. Government Printing Office.

U.S. Department of Health and Human Services (USDHHS). (1985a). *Health: United States* (DHHS Publication No. PHS 86-1232). Washington, DC: U.S. Government Printing Office.

U.S. Department of Health and Human Services (USDHHS). (1985b). *Q & A: Alzheimer's disease* (NIH Publication No. 85-1646). Washington, DC: U.S. Government Printing Office.

U.S. Department of Health, Education, and Welfare. (1971). *The institutional guide to DHEW policy on protection of human subjects.* Washington, DC: Author.

U.S. Department of Justice. (1986). *Attorney General's Commission on Pornography, Final Report,* Vols. 1–2. (Classification No. J1.2:P 82(v. 1–2). Washington, DC: U.S. Government Printing Office.

U.S. Public Health Service. (1982). *The health consequences of smoking: Cancer.* Rockville, MD: Author.

U.S. Senate Special Committee on Aging. (1986). *Aging America: Trends and projections* (1985–86 ed.). Washington, DC: U.S. Department of Health and Human Services.

Valenstein, E. S. (1986). *Great and desperate cures: The rise and decline of psychosurgery and other radical treatments for mental illness.* New York: Basic Books.

Valentine, C. W. (1930). The innate bases of fear. *Journal of Genetic Psychology, 37,* 485–497.

Vandell, D., Wilson, K., & Buchanan, N. (1980). Peer interaction in the first year of life: An examination of its structure, content, and sensitivity to toys. *Child Development, 51,* 481–488.

Vandenberg, S. G. (1967). Hereditary factors in normal personality traits (as measured by inventories). In J. Wortes (Ed.), *Recent advances in biological psychiatry* (Vol. 9, pp. 65–104). New York: Plenum.

Van Harreveld, A., & Fifkova, C. (1975). Swelling of dendritic spines in the fascia dentata after stimulation of the perforant fibers as a mechanism of post-tetanic potentiation. *Experimental Neurology, 49,* 736–749.

Vaughan, D., & Asbury, T. (1977). *General ophthalmology* (8th ed.). Los Altos, CA: Lange.

Vaughan, V., McKay, R. J., & Behrman, R. (1979). *Nelson textbook of pediatrics* (11th ed.). Philadelphia: Saunders.

Verbrugge, L. (1979). Marital status and health. *Journal of Marriage and the Family, 41,* 467–285.

Veroff, J., Douvan, E., & Kulka, R. (1981). *The inner American.* New York: Basic Books.

Victor, M., Adams, R. D., & Collins, G. H. (1971). *The Wernicke-Korsakoff syndrome.* Philadelphia: Davis.

Visual cues compensate for blindness in one eye. (1983, September 13). *The New York Times,* p. C2.

von Noorden, G. (1981). New clinical aspects of stimulus deprivation amblyopia. *American Journal of Ophthalmology, 92,* 416–421.

Wadden, T. A., & Anderton, C. H. (1982). The clinical use of hypnosis. *Psychological Bulletin, 91*(2), 215–243.

Waid, W. M., & Orne, M. T. (1982, July–August). The physiological detection of deception. *American Scientist, 70,* 402–409.

Waldrop, M. M. (1985). The machinations of thought. *Science 85, 6*(2), 38–45.

Walk, R. D., & Gibson, E. (1961). A comparative and analytical study of visual depth perception. *Psychology Monographs, 75*(15), 170.

Walker, L. J. (1984). Sex differences in the development of moral reasoning: A critical review. *Child Development, 55,* 677–691.

Wall, P. D. (1978). The gate control theory of pain mechanisms: A re-examination and re-statement. *Brain, 101,* 1–18.

Wallace, R. K., & Benson, H. (1972). The physiology of meditation. *Scientific American, 226,* 85–90.

Waller, P. F., Stewart, R., Hansen, A. R., Stutts, J. C., Popkin, C. L., & Rodgman, E. A. (1986). The potentiating effects of alcohol on driver injury. *Journal of the American Medical Association, 256,* 1461–1466.

Waller, W. (1951). *The family* (rev. ed. by Reuben Hill). New York: Dryden.

Wallerstein, J. S. (1983). Children of divorce: The psychological tasks of the child. *American Journal of Orthopsychiatry, 53,* 230–243.

Wallerstein, J. S., & Kelly, J. B. (1980). *Surviving the break-up: How children actually cope with divorce.* New York: Basic Books.

Walster, E., Aronson, V., Abrahams, D., & Rottmann, L. (1966). Importance of physical attractiveness in dating behavior. *Journal of Personality and Social Psychology, 4*(5), 508–516.

Walster, E., & Walster, G. W. (1978). *A new look at love.* Reading, MA: Addison-Wesley.

Walster, E., Walster, G. W., & Berscheid, E. (1978). *Equity theory and research.* Boston: Allyn & Bacon.

Warm, J. S., & Dember, W. N. (1986). Awake at the switch. *Psychology Today, 20*(4), 46–53.

Warner, R. (1986). Hard times and schizophrenia. *Psychology Today, 20*(6), 50–52.

Warren, R. M. (1984). Perceptual restoration of obliterated sounds. *Psychological Bulletin, 96,* 371–383.

Warren, R. M., & Warren, R. P. (1970). Auditory illusions and confusions. *Scientific American, 223,* 30–36.

Warrington, E. K., & Weiskrantz, L. (1970). Amnesic syndrome: Consolidation or retrieval? *Nature, 228,* 628–630.

Waters, E., Wippman, J., & Sroufe, L. A. (1979). Attachment, positive affect, and competence in the peer group: Two studies in construct validation. *Child Development, 50*(3), 821–829.

Watson, J. B., & Rayner, R. (1920). Conditioned emotional reactions. *Journal of Experimental Psychology, 3*(1), 1–14.

Watson, J. S. (1924). *Behaviorism.* New York: People's Institute.

Watson, J. S. (1967). Memory and "contingency analysis" in infant learning. *Merrill-Palmer Quarterly of Behavior and Development, 13,* 55–76.

Watt, N. F. (Ed.). (1984). *Children at risk for schizophrenia: A longitudinal perspective.* New York: Cambridge University Press.

Webb, W. B. (1971). Sleep behavior as a biorhythm. In P. Coloquohon (Ed.), *Biological rhythms and human performance* (pp. 149–177). New York: Academic.

Webb, W. B. (1975). *Sleep: The gentle tyrant.* Englewood Cliffs, NJ: Prentice-Hall.

Webb, W. B. (1979). Are short and long sleepers different? *Psychological Reports, 44,* 259–264.

Webb, W. B. (1984). [EEG tracings of stages of wakefulness and sleep]. Unpublished raw data.

Webb, W. B., & Bonnet, M. H. (1979). Sleep and dreams. In M. E. Meyer (Ed.), *Foundations of contemporary psychology.* New York: Oxford University Press.

Webb, W. B., & Cartwright, R. D. (1978). Sleep and dreams. *Annual Review of Psychology, 29,* 223–252.

Webb, W. B., & Friel, J. (1971). Sleep stage and personality characteristics of "natural" long and short sleepers. *Science, 171,* 587–588.

Wechsler, D. (1939). *The measurement of adult intelligence.* Baltimore: Williams & Wilkins.

Wechsler, D. (1944). *The measurement of adult intelligence* (3d ed.). Baltimore: Williams & Wilkins.

Wechsler, D. (1955). *Wechsler adult intelligence scale manual.* New York: Psychological Corporation.

Wechsler, D. (1958). *The measurement and appraisal of adult intelligence.* Baltimore: Williams & Wilkins.

Wechsler, D. (1974). *Manual: Wechsler intelligence scale for children* (rev. ed.). New York: Psychological Corporation.

Wechsler, D. (1981). *Wechsler adult intelligence scales revised* (WAIS-R). New York: Psychological Corporation.

Wehr, T. A., Jacobsen, F. M., Sack, D. A., Arendt, J., Tamarkin, L., & Rosenthal, N. E. (1986). Phototherapy of seasonal affective disorder. *Archives of General Psychiatry, 43,* 870–875.

Weinberg, J. (1982). *Sexuality: Human needs and nursing practice.* Philadelphia: Saunders.

Weiner, B. (1972). *Theories of motivation: From mechanism to cognition.* Chicago: Markham.

Weiner, B. (1974). An attributional interpretation of expectancy–valve theory. In B. Weiner (Ed.), *Cognitive views of human motivation.* New York: Academic.

Weiner, B. (1985). An attributional theory of achievement motivation and emotion. *Psychological Review, 92*(4), 548–573.

Weingarten, H. R. (1985). Marital status and well-being: A national study comparing first-married, currently divorced, and remarried adults. *Journal of Marriage and the Family, 47*(3), 653–662.

Weinstein, S. (1968). Intensive and extensive aspects of tactile sensitivity as a function of body part, sex, and laterality. In D. R. Kenshalo (Ed.), *The skin senses.* Springfield, IL: Thomas.

Weiss, R. S. (1982). Issues in the study of loneliness. In L. A. Peplau & D. Perlman (Eds.), *Loneliness: A sourcebook of current theory, research, and therapy.* New York: Wiley-Interscience.

Weitkamp, L. R., Stancer, H. C., Persad, E., Flood, C., & Guttormsen, S. (1981). Depressive disorders and HLA: A gene on chromosome 6 that can affect behavior. *New England Journal of Medicine, 305,* 1301–1306.

Weitzman, L. (1986). *The divorce revolution.* New York: Free Press.

Weitzman, L. J., Eifler, D., Hokada, E., & Rosa, C. (1972). Sex role socialization in picture books for pre-school children. *American Journal of Sociology, 77,* 1125–1150.

Wender, P. H., & Klein, D. F. (1981a). *Mind, mood, and medicine.* New York: Farrar, Straus, & Giroux.

Wender, P. H., & Klein, D. F. (1981b). The promise of biological psychiatry. *Psychology Today, 15*(2), 25–41.

Werner, C., & Parmelee, P. (1979). Similarity of activity preferences among friends: Those who play together stay together. *Social Psychology Quarterly, 42,* 62–66.

Wever, E. G. (Ed.). (1960). *Experiments in hearing.* New York: McGraw-Hill.

Whisnant, L., & Zegans, L. (1975). A study of attitudes toward menarche in white middle class American adolescent girls. *American Journal of Psychiatry, 132*(8), 809–814.

Whitbourne, S. K. (1985). *The aging body.* New York: Springer-Verlag. [Adapted from C. P. Lebo & R. C. Reddell (1972). The presbycusis component in occupational hearing loss. *Laryngoscope, 82,* 1402–1403]

White, B. L. (1971, October 21–22). *Fundamental early environmental influences on the development of competence.* Paper presented at Third Western Symposium on Learning: Cognitive Learning, Western Washington State College, Bellingham, WA.

Whorf, B. L. (1956). *Language, thought, and reality.* Cambridge, MA: Massachusetts Institute of Technology Press.

Wickelgren, W. (1977). *Learning and memory.* Englewood Cliffs, NJ: Prentice-Hall.

Wicker, A. W. (1969). Attitude versus actions: The relationship of verbal and overt behavioral responses to attitude objects. *Journal of Social Issues, 25,* 41–78.

Widely used mental test undergoing treatment. (1986, August 19). *The New York Times,* p. C1.

Wilbur, R. (1986). A drug to fight cocaine. *Science 86, 7*(2), 42–46.

Will, J. A., Self, P. A., & Datan, N. (1976). Maternal behavior and perceived sex of infant. *American Journal of Orthopsychiatry, 46*(1), 135–139.

Williams, D. R., & Williams, H. (1969). Auto-maintenance in the pigeon: Sustained pecking despite contingent nonreinforcement. *Journal of the Experimental Analysis of Behavior, 12,* 511–520.

Williams, H. L., Holloway, F. A., & Griffiths, W. J. (1973). Physiological psychology: Sleep. *Annual Review of Psychology, 24,* 279–316.

Williams, J. B. W., & Spitzer, R. L. (1983). The issue of sex bias in DSM-III. *American Psychologist, 38,* 793–798.

Williams, R. B., Barefoot, J. C., & Shekelle, R. B. (1984). The health consequences of hostility. In M. A. Chesney, S. E. Goldston, & R. H. Rosenman (Eds.), *Anger: Hostility and behavior medicine.* Washington, DC: Hemisphere.

Willis, S. L., Blieszner, R., & Baltes, P. B. (1981). Intellectual training research in aging: Modification of performance on the fluid ability of figural relations. *Journal of Educational Psychology, 73,* 41–50.

Wilson, E. O. (1978). *On human nature.* Cambridge, MA: Harvard University Press.

Wilson, E. O. (1980, December). The ethical implication of human sociobiology. *Hastings Center Report,* pp. 27–29.

Wilson, R. S. (1983). The Louisville twin study: Developmental synchronies in behavior. *Child Development, 54,* 298–316.

Wingerson, L. (1982). Training the mind to heal. *Discover, 3*(5), 80–85.

Winick, M., Brasel, J., & Rosso, P. (1969). Head circumference and cellular growth of the brain in normal and marasmic children. *Journal of Pediatrics, 74,* 774–778.

Winson, J. (1985). *Brain and psyche.* New York: Anchor.

Winterbottom, M. R. (1958). The relation of need for achievement to learning experiences in independence mastery. In J. W. Atkinson (Ed.), *Motives in fantasy, action and society* (pp. 453–478). Princeton, NJ: Van Nostrand.

Witelson, S. F. (1985). The brain connection: The corpus callosum is longer in left-handers. *Science, 229,* 665–668.

Wittgenstein, J. (1953). *Philosophical investigations.* New York: Macmillan.

Wolff, P. H. (1969). The natural history of crying and other vocalizations in early infancy. In B. Foss (Ed.), *Determinants of infant behavior* (Vol. 4). London: Methuen.

Wolozin, B. L., Pruchnicki, A., Dickson, D. W., & Davies, P. (1986). A neuronal antigen in the brains of Alzheimer patients. *Science, 232,* 648–650.

Wolpe, J. (1978). Cognition and causation in human behavior and its therapy. *American Psychologist, 33*(5), 437–446.

Wolpe, J. (1982). Behavior therapy versus psychoanalysis. *American Psychologist, 36*(2), 159–164.

Woodworth, R. S., & Schlosberg, H. (1954). *Experimental psychology.* New York: Holt.

Worchel, S., & Brehm, J. (1970). Effect of threats to attitudinal freedom as a function of agreement with the communicator. *Journal of Personality and Social Psychology, 14,* 18–22.

Working Women Education Fund. (1981). *Health hazards for office workers.* Cleveland: Author.

Wright, J. T., Waterson, E. J., Barrison, I. G., Toplis, P. J., Lewis, I. G., Gordon, M. G., MacRae, K. D., Morris, N. F., & Murray-Lyon, I. M. (1983, March 26). Alcohol consumption, pregnancy, and low birthweight. *Lancet,* pp. 663–665.

Yalom, I. (1975). *The theory and practice of group psychotherapy* (2d ed.). New York: Basic Books.

Yarrow, L. J., Rubenstein, J. L., & Pedersen, F. A. (1971). *Dimensions of early stimulation: Differential effects of infant development.* Paper presented at the biennial meeting of the Society for Research in Child Development.

Yarrow, M. R. (1978, October 31). *Altruism in children.* Paper presented at program, Advances in Child Development Research, New York Academy of Sciences.

Zajonc, R. B. (1968). Attitudinal effects of mere exposure. *Journal of Personality and Social Psychology, 9* (Monograph Supplement No. 2, Pt. 2).

Zajonc, R. B. (1970, February). Brainwash: Familiarity breeds comfort. *Psychology Today,* pp. 32–35, 60–62.

Zajonc, R. B. (1976). Family configuration and intelligence. *Science, 197*(4236), 227–236.

Zajonc, R. B. (1980). Feeling and thinking: Preferences need no inferences. *American Psychologist, 35*(2), 151–175.

Zajonc, R. B. (1984). On the primacy of affect. *American Psychologist, 39*(2), 117–123.

Zajonc, R. B., & Bargh, J. (1980). Birth order, family size and decline in SAT scores. *American Psychologist, 35,* 662–668.

Zaslow, F. (1987). Personal communication.

Zeigler, H. P. (1973). Trigeminal deafferentation and feeding in the pigeon: Sensorimotor and motivational effects. *Science, 182,* 1155–1158.

Zeigler, H. P. (1975, August). The sensual feel of food. *Psychology Today,* pp. 62–66.

Zelazo, P., & Kearsley, R. (1981, February). *Cognitive assessment and intervention in developmentally delayed infants.* Final report to the Bureau of Education for the Handicapped, Grant No. G007603979.

Zelnik, M., Kantner, J. F., & Ford, K. (1981). *Sex and pregnancy in adolescence.* Beverly Hills, CA: Sage.

Zelnik, M., Kim, Y. J., & Kantner, J. F. (1979). Probabilities of intercourse and conception among U.S. teenage women, 1971 and 1976. *Family Planning Perspectives, 11*(3), 177–183.

Zelnik, M., & Shah, F. K. (1983). First intercourse among young Americans. *Family Planning Perspectives, 15*(2), 64–72.

Zigler, E., & Seitz, V. (1982). Social policy and intelligence. In R. J. Sternberg (Ed.), *Handbook of human intelligence.* Cambridge: Cambridge University Press.

Zilbergeld, B., & Evans, M. (1980, August). The inadequacy of Masters and

Johnson. *Psychology Today,* pp. 28–30.

Zimbardo, P., Andersen, S., & Kabat, L. (1981). Induced hearing deficit generates experimental paranoia. *Science, 212*(26), 1529–1531.

Zimbardo, P., Haney, C., Banks, W. C., & Jaffe, D. (1977). The psychology of imprisonment: Privation, power and pathology. In J. C. Brigham & L. S. Wrightsman (Eds.), *Contemporary issues in social psychology.* Belmont, CA: Wadsworth.

Zimbardo, P., & Radl, S. L. (1982). *The shy child.* New York: Doubleday.

Zimberg, S. (1982). Psychotherapy in the treatment of alcoholism. In E. M. Pattison & E. Kaufman (Eds.), *Encyclopedic handbook of alcoholism.* New York: Gardner.

Zimmerman, W. (1970). Sleep mentation and auditory awakening thresholds. *Psychophysiology, 6,* 540–549.

Zuckerman, M. (1979). *Sensation-seeking: Beyond the optimal level of arousal.* Hillsdale, NJ: Erlbaum.

Zuckerman, M., Buchsbaum, M. S., & Murphy, D. L. (1980). Sensation-seeking and its biological correlates. *Psychological Bulletin, 88,* 187–214.

ACKNOWLEDGEMENTS

PART-OPENING PHOTOGRAPHS

Part I: Oskar Schlemmer, *Four Figures and a Cube,* copyright Familie Schlemmer, Stuttgart.

Part II: Charles Demuth, *Acrobats,* 1919; Collection, Museum of Modern Art, New York, gift of Abby Aldrich Rockefeller.

Part III: Roger de la Fresnaye, *The Conquest of the Air,* 1913; Collection, Museum of Modern Art, New York, Mrs. Simon Guggenheim Fund.

Part IV: Helen Lundeberg, *Double Portrait of the Artist in Time,* 1935; National Museum of American Art, Smithsonian Institution, Museum Purchase.

Part V: Ernest Stock, *Marathon Dancers;* © Three Lions.

Part VI: Pablo Picasso, *The Red Armchair,* 1931; Art Institute of Chicago, gift of Mr. and Mrs. Daniel Saidenberg, 1957.72.

Part VII: August Macke, *Lady with Green Jacket;* © Three Lions.

CHAPTER 1

Chapter-opening photograph: © Gordon R. Gainer/Stock Market.

Figure 1-1: Stroop, J. R. (1935). Studies of interference in serial verbal reactions. *Journal of Experimental Psychology, 18,* 643–662. Copyright 1935 by the American Psychological Association. Reprinted by permission.

Figures 1-2 and 1-3: Stapp, J., Tucker, A. M., & VandenBos, G. R. (1985). Census of psychological personnel: 1983. *American Psychologist, 40*(12), 1317–1351. Copyright © 1985 by the American Psychological Association. Reprinted by permission of the publisher and author.

CHAPTER 2

Chapter-opening photograph: © 1979 Tom Myers/Photo Researchers.

Figure 2-12: Rosenzweig, M. R., & Leiman, A. L. (1982). *Physiological psychology.* Reprinted by permission of D. C. Heath, Publishers.

Figure 2-13: Hunt, M. M. (1982). *The universe within: A new science explores the human mind.* Copyright © 1982 by Morton Hunt. Reprinted by permission of Simon & Schuster, Inc.

Figure 2-14: Kalat, J. W. (1984). *Biological psychology,* 2d edition. © 1984, 1981 by Wadsworth, Inc. Adapted by permission.

Figure 2-15: Lassen, N. A., Ingevar, D. H., & Skinhoj, E. (1978). Brain function and blood flow. *Scientific American, 239,* 62–71. Reprinted by permission of the publisher and authors.

Figure 2-16: Drawing by Carol Donner, in Geschwind, N. (1979). Specializations of the human brain. *Scientific American, 241*(3), 180–199. Copyright © 1979 by Scientific American, Inc. All rights reserved.

Figure 2-20: Courtesy of Roger Sperry.

Figure 2-22: Rosenzweig, M. R., & Leiman, A. L. (1982). *Physiological psychology.* Adapted by permission of D. C. Heath, Publishers.

Table 2-1: Carlson, N. R. (1986). *Physiology of behavior,* 3d edition. Adapted by permission of Allyn & Bacon, Publishers.

CHAPTER 3

Chapter-opening photograph: © 1984 Xenophon A. Beake/Stock Market.

Figure 3-1: Hecht, S., Schlaer, S., & Pirenne, M. H. (1941). Energy at the threshold of vision. *Science, 93*(2425), 585–587. Copyright 1941 by The Science Press. Reprinted by permission.

Figure 3-4b: Mitchell, D. E., Freeman, R. D., Millodot, M., & Haegerstrom, C. (1973). Meridional amblyopia: Evidence for modification of the human visual system. *Vision Research, 13,* 535–558. Reprinted by permission of Pergamon Press and the authors.

Figure 3-5: Drawing by John Langley Howard, in Hubel, D. H. (1963). The visual cortex of the brain. *Scientific American, 209*(30). Copyright © 1963 by Scientific American, Inc. Reprinted by permission.

Figure 3-7: Cornsweet, T. N. (1970). *Visual perception.* Copyright © 1970 by Harcourt Brace Jovanovich, Inc. Reprinted by permission of the publisher.

Figure 3-13: Dvorine Color Vision Test. Copyright © 1944, 1953, 1958 by Israel Dvorine. Published by The Psychological Corporation. Reproduced by permission. All rights reserved.

Figure 3-15: Levine, M. W., & Shefner, J. (1981). *Fundamentals of sensation and perception.* Addison-Wesley, publisher. Reprinted by permission of the author.

Figure 3-16: Matlin, M. W. (1983). *Perception.* Reprinted by permission of Allyn & Bacon, publisher.

Figure 3-19: Whitbourne, S. K. (1985). *The aging body.* Adapted from Lebo, C. P., & Reddell, R. C. (1972). The presbycusis component in occupational hearing loss. *Laryngoscope, 82,* 1402–1403. Copyright 1972 by Laryngoscope Company. Reprinted by permission of Laryngoscope Company and Springer-Verlag.

Figure 3-20: Weinstein, S. (1968). Intensive and extensive aspects of tactile sensitivity as a function of body part, sex and laterality. In Kenshalo, D. R. (Ed.), *The skin senses.* Reprinted by permission of Charles C Thomas, Publisher, Springfield, IL.

Figure 3-21: Amoore, J. E., Johnston, J. W., & Rubin, M. (1964). The stereochemical theory of odor. *Scientific American, 210*(2), 42–49. Copyright © 1964 by Scientific American, Inc. All rights reserved. Adapted by permission.

Figures 3-28 and 3-29: Palmer, S. E. (1975). Visual perception and world knowledge: Notes on a model of sensory-cognitive interaction. In Norman, D. A., Rumelhart, D. E., & LNR Research Group, *Explorations in cognition.* Copyright © 1975 by W. H. Freeman & Co. Reprinted by permission.

Figure 3-38: *Street Scene for the Theater,* after Bernardo Prevardi and Donato Bramante; Museum of Art, Carnegie Institute, Director's Discretionary Fund, 1974.

Figure 3-39: *Violin and Bow,* by J. D. Chalfont; Metropolitan Museum of Art, George A. Hearn, 1966.

Figure 3-44: Deregowski, J. B. (1972). Pictorial perception and culture. *Scientific American 83*(227) Copyright © 1972 by Scientific American, Inc. All rights reserved.

Table 3-2: Hurvitch, L. M. (1981). *Color vision.* © 1981 Sinauer Associates. Reprinted by permission.

CHAPTER 4

Chapter-opening photograph: © Bill Binzen/Photo Researchers.

Quotations from Webb, W. B. (1975). *Sleep: The gentle tyrant.* Prentice-Hall. Reprinted by permission of the author.

Figure 4-1: Reproduced by permission of Wilse B. Webb.

CHAPTER 5

Chapter-opening photograph: © Jean-Marc Barey/Vandystadt-Photo Researchers.

Quotations from Skinner, B. F. (1953). *Science and human behavior.* Copyright © 1953 renewed 1981 by B. F. Skinner. Reprinted by permission of Macmillan Publishing Company.

Quotation from Tolman, E. C. (1948). Cognitive maps in rats and men. *Psychological Review, 55,* 189–208. Copyright 1948 by the American Psychological Association. Reprinted by permission of the publisher and author.

Figure 5-4: Hulse, S. H., Egeth, H., & Deese, J. (1980). *The psychology of learning* (5th ed.). © McGraw-Hill

Book Company. Reprinted by permission.

Figure 5-6: Skinner, B. F. (1961). *Teaching machines.* Copyright © 1961 by Scientific American, Inc. Adapted by permission. All rights reserved.

Figure 5-7: Blodgett, H. C. (1929). The effect of the introduction of reward upon the maze performance of rats. *University of California Publication of Psychology, 4*(8), 120. Adapted by permission of University of California Press.

Table 5-1: Geller, E. S. (1984). A delayed reward strategy for large-scale motivation of safety belt use: A test of long-term impact. *Accident Analysis and Prevention, 16*(5/6), 457–463. Copyright © 1984, Pergamon Press, Ltd. Adapted by permission.

CHAPTER 6

Chapter-opening photograph: © Bill Binzen/Photo Researchers.

Quotations from Glass, A. L., Holyoak, K. J., & Santa, J. L. (1979). *Cognition.* Reprinted by permission of W. H. Freeman.

Quotation from *American Bar Association Journal* (1978). Hypnotized man remembers too much, *64,* 187. Reprinted by permission.

Figures 6-2 and 6-3: Sperling, G. (1960). The information available in brief visual presentations. *Psychological Monographs, 74,* 1–29. Copyright 1960 by the American Psychological Association. Reprinted by permission of the publisher and author.

Figure 6-5: Tulving, E. (1962). Subjective organization in free recall of "unrelated" words. *Psychological Review, 69,* 344–354. Copyright 1962 by the American Psychological Association. Reprinted by permission of the publisher and author.

Figure 6-6: Loftus, E. F. (1980). *Memory,* p. 25. © 1980, Addison-Wesley Publishing Company, Inc., Reading, MA. Reprinted by permission.

Figure 6-7: Allport, G. W., & Postman, L. J. (1958). The basic psychology of rumor. In Maccoby, E. E., Newcomb, T. M., & Hartley, E. L. (Eds.), *Readings in social psychology* (3d ed.).

Figures 6-9, 6-10, 6-11: Nickerson, R. S., & Adams, M. J. (1979). Long-term memory for a common object. *Cognitive Psychology, 11,* 287–307. Reprinted by permission of the publisher and author.

Table 6-1: Craik, F. I. M., & Tulving, E. (1975). Depth of processing and the retention of words in episodic memory.

Journal of Experimental Psychology (General), 104, 268–294. Copyright 1975 by the American Psychological Association. Reprinted by permission of the publisher and author.

Table 6-2: Hulse, S. H., Egeth, H., & Deese, J. (1980). *The psychology of learning* (5th ed.). © 1980 McGraw-Hill Book Company. Reprinted by permission.

CHAPTER 7

Chapter-opening photograph: © 1985 Lawrence Migdale/Photo Researchers.

Quotation from Anastasi, A. (1976). *Psychological testing* (4th ed.). Copyright © 1982 by Anne Anastasi. Reprinted by permission of Macmillan Publishing Company.

Figure 7-1: Guilford, J. P. (1977). *Way beyond the I.Q.* © 1977 Creative Education Foundation and Bearly Ltd., Buffalo, NY. Reprinted by permission.

Figure 7-2: Raven Progressive Matrices Test. © 1938, 1947, 1962, 1976, 1983 by J. C. Raven. All rights reserved.

Figure 7-3: Horn, J., & Donaldson, G. (1980). Cognition development II: Adulthood development of human abilities. In Brim, O. C., & Kagan, J. (Eds.), *Constancy and change in human development.* Reprinted by permission of Harvard University Press.

Figure 7-5: PSAT question reprinted by permission of Educational Testing Service, copyright owner. Solution copyright © 1981 by The New York Times Company. Reprinted by permission from the *New York Times,* March 17, 1981, p. C4.

Tables 7-3 and 7-4: Wechsler, D. (1981). Wechsler adult intelligence scale—revised (WAIS-R) and Intelligence Classifications on WAIS-R. © 1981 by The Psychological Corporation. All rights reserved.

CHAPTER 8

Chapter-opening photograph: © Enrico Ferorelli/DOT.

Quotations and Table 8-1: Lenneberg, E. (1969). On explaining language. *Science, 164*(3880), 635–643. Copyright 1969 by The American Association for the Advancement of Science. Reprinted by permission.

CHAPTER 9

Chapter-opening photograph: © Erika Stone/Peter Arnold.

Figure 9-2: Papalia, D. E., & Olds, S. W. (1982). *A child's world* (3d ed.). © 1982 McGraw-Hill Book Company. Reprinted by permission.

Figures 9-3a, 9-3b, and 9-4: March of Dimes (1983). Public health information booklet, *Genetic counseling*. Reprinted by permission.

Figure 9-5: Reproduced by permission of Everett Davidson.

Figure 9-6: Denver Developmental Screening Test. © 1969, William J. Frankenburg, M. D., and Josiah B. Dodds, Ph.D., University of Colorado Medical Center. Adapted by permission.

Figures 9-7a and 9-7b: Hunziker, U. A., & Barr, R. G. (1986). Increased carrying reduces infant crying: A randomized controlled trial. *Pediatrics, 77*(5), 641–648. © 1986. Reproduced by permission.

Table 9-5: Trotter, R. J. (1983). Baby face. *Psychology Today, 17*(8), 14–20. Copyright © 1983 American Psychological Association. Adapted by permission.

CHAPTER 10

Chapter-opening photograph: Jeffrey W. Myers/Stock, Boston.

Quotation from Peel, E. A. (1967). *The psychological basis of education* (2d ed.). Oliver & Boyd. Reprinted by permission of the author.

Quotation from Kohlberg, L. (1969). The cognitive-development approach. In Goslin, D. A. (Ed.), *Handbook of socialization theory and research*. Houghton Mifflin Company. Reprinted by permission of David A. Goslin.

Quotation from Streib, G. F., & Schneider, C. J. (1971). *Retirement in American society: Impact and process*. Cornell University Press. © G. F. Streib. Reprinted by permission.

Table 10-3: Lickona, T. (Ed.). (1976). *Moral development and behavior*. Holt, Rinehart & Winston. Reprinted by permission of Thomas Lickona, Ph.D.

CHAPTER 11

Chapter-opening photograph: Alan Carey/Image Works.

Figure 11-1: From *Love and hate* by Irenaus Eibl-Eibesfeldt, translated by Geoffrey Strachen. Copyright © 1971, 1972 by Methuen and Co. Ltd. and Holt, Rinehart & Winston, Inc.; reprinted by permission of Henry Holt and Co.

Figure 11-2: Maslow, A. (1954). *Motivation and personality* (3d ed.). Revised by Robert Frager et al. Copyright 1954, 1987 by Harper & Row, Publishers, Inc. Copyright © 1970 by Abraham H. Maslow. Reprinted by permission of Harper & Row, Publishers, Inc.

Figure 11-4: Schachter, S. (1971). *Emotion, obesity, and crime*. Reprinted by permission of Academic Press.

Figure 11-5: Weiner, B. (1974). An attributional interpretation of expectancy-value theory. In Weiner, B. (Ed.), *Cognitive views of human motivation*. Adapted by permission of Academic Press and the author.

Figure 11-6: Berlyne, D. E. (1970). Novelty, complexity, and hedonic value. *Perception and Psychophysics, 8*, 284. © 1970 Psychonomic Society. Reprinted by permission.

Figure 11-8: Plutchik, R. (1980). A language for the emotions. *Psychology Today* (2). Copyright © 1980 American Psychological Association. Reprinted by permission.

Figure 11-12: Waid, W. M., & Orne, M. T. (1977). The physiological detection of deception. *American Scientist, 70*, 404. Reprinted by permission of Scientific Research Society.

CHAPTER 12

Chapter-opening photograph: Paula M. Lerner 1986/Picture Cube.

Quotation from Reiss, I. L. (1980). *Family systems in America* (3d ed.). Holt, Rinehart, & Winston.

Figure 12-3: Alan Guttmacher Institute (1981). *Teenage pregnancy: The problem that hasn't gone away*. Reprinted by permission.

Figure 12-4: Hyde, J. W. (1986). *Understanding human sexuality*, (3d ed.). Reprinted by permission of McGraw-Hill Book Company.

CHAPTER 13

Chapter-opening photograph: © Costa Manos/Magnum.

Quotation from Anastasi, A. (1982). *Psychological testing* (5th ed.). Copyright © 1982 by Anne Anastasi. Reprinted by permission of Macmillan Publishing Company.

Figure 13-1: Cattell, R. B., et al. (1970). *Handbook for the 16PF*. Copyright © 1970 by the Institute for Personality and Ability Testing, Inc. All rights reserved. Reproduced by permission.

Figure 13-2: Hans Huber Publishers.

Figure 13-3: Reprinted by permission of the publishers from Henry A. Murray, *Thematic Apperception Test*, Cambridge, MA, Harvard University Press. Copyright 1943 by the President and Fellows of Harvard College. © 1971 by Henry A. Murray.

Table 13-4: Hassett, J., Editors of *Psychology Today*. (1981). Is it right? An inquiry into everyday ethics. *Psychology Today, 15*, 49–56. Reprinted by permission of James Hassett.

Table 13-5: Samuel, W. (1981). *Personality: Searching for the sources of human behavior*. Adapted by permission of McGraw-Hill Book Company.

CHAPTER 14

Chapter-opening photograph: M. De-Camp/Image Bank.

Quotation from Sheehan, S. (1982). *Is there no place on earth for me?* Copyright © 1982 by Susan Sheehan. Reprinted by permission of Houghton Mifflin Company. This material originally appeared in slightly different form in *The New Yorker*, Spring 1982.

Quotation from Townshend, P. (1969). "You Didn't Hear It" and "Go to the Mirror Boy." *Tommy*. Copyright © 1969 by Fabulous Music Ltd. All rights in the United States, its territories and possessions, Canada, Mexico and the Philippines controlled by Towser Tunes, Inc. Reprinted by permission of Towser Tunes, Inc. All rights reserved. International copyright secured.

Quotations from *Harvard Medical School Mental Health Letter* (1985). Borderline personality disorder, part I, *2*(6), 1–3. Reprinted by permission.

Figure 14-1: Katerndahl, D. A. (1984). Panic attacks: Psychological response or medical illness? *Postgraduate Medicine, 75*(8, June), 262. Adapted by permission of McGraw-Hill Book Company.

Table 14-1: Andreasen, N. C. (1984). *The broken brain: The biological revolution in psychiatry*. Copyright © 1984 by Nancy C. Andreasen. Adapted by permission of Harper & Row, Publishers, Inc.

Table 14-6: Peterson, C., & Seligman, M. E. P. (1985). The learned helplessness model of depression: Current status of theory and research. In Beckham, E. E., & Leber, W. R. (Eds.), *Handbook of depression*. Reprinted by permission of The Dorsey Press.

Table 14-7: Boyer, J. L., & Guthrie, L. (1985). Assessment and treatment of the suicidal patient. *Ibid.*, and *Harvard Medical School Mental Health Letter* (1986). Suicide, part I, *2* (8, February), 1–4. Adapted by permission.

CHAPTER 15

Chapter-opening photograph: Russ Kinne/Photo Researchers.

Quotations from Ellis, A. (1984). Rational-emotive therapy. In Corsini, R. J., et al., *Current psychotherapies* (3d ed.), 206–207. Reprinted by permission of F. E. Peacock, Publishers, Itasca, IL.

Definition of *dynamic* from *The American*

Heritage Dictionary of the English Language. © 1971 by Houghton Mifflin Company. Reprinted by permission.

Quotation from Freeman, L. (1951). *Fight against fears.* Crown Publishers, Inc. Reprinted by permission of Lucy Freeman.

Quotation from Rogers, C. R. (1961). *On becoming a person.* Reprinted by permission of Houghton Mifflin Company.

Table 15-1: Smith, D. (1982). Trends in counseling and psychotherapy. *American Psychologist, 37*(3), 802–809. Copyright 1982 by the American Psychological Association. Adapted by permission of the author.

CHAPTER 16

Chapter-opening photograph: Alan Berner, from *A Day in the Life of America.*

Quotation from Bukowski, C. (1972). "The Shoelace." *Mockingbird Wish Me Luck.* © 1972 by Charles Bukowski. Reprinted by permission of Black Sparrow Press.

Box 16-2: "Do You Have a Drinking Problem?" (n.d.). Reprinted by permission of Ayerst Laboratories, Division of American Home Products Corporation.

Figure 16-1: Selye, H. (1980). The stress concept today. In Kutash, I. L., Schlesinger, L. B., et al. (Eds.), *Handbook of stress and anxiety.* Reprinted by permission of Jossey-Bass.

Figure 16-2: Meyer, A. J., Nash, A. L., Maccoby, N., & Farquhar, J. W. (1980). Skills training in a cardiovascular health education campaign. *Journal of Consulting and Clinical Psychology, 48*(2), 129–142. Copyright 1980 by the American Psychological Association. Reprinted by permission of the author.

Figure 16-3: Gill, J. J., et al. (1985). Reduction in type A behavior in healthy, middle-aged American military officers. *American Heart Journal, 110*(3), 503–514. Reprinted by permission of C. V. Mosby Company.

Table 16-1: Holmes, T. H., & Rahe, R. H. (1967). The social readjustment rating scale. *Journal of Psychosomatic Research, 11* (August), 213. © 1967 Pergamon Press, Ltd. Reprinted by permission.

Table 16-2: Kanner, A. D., Coyne, J. C., Schaefer, C., & Lazarus, R. S. (1981).

Comparison of two modes of stress measurement: Daily hassles and uplifts versus major life events. *Journal of Behavioral Medicine, 4*(1), 1–39. Reprinted by permission of Plenum Press and the authors.

Table 16-4: Belloc, N. B., & Breslow, L. (1972). Relationship of physical health status and health practices. *Preventive Medicine, 1*(3), 409–421. Reprinted by permission of Academic Press.

CHAPTER 17

Chapter-opening photograph: James Holland/Stock, Boston.

Photograph from Milgrim's experiment: Copyright 1965 by Stanley Milgrim; from the film *Obedience,* distributed by Pennsylvania State University, PCR.

Quotations from Zimbardo, P., Haney, C., Banks, W. C., & Jaffe, D. (1977). The psychology of imprisonment: Privation, power and pathology. In Brigham, J. C., & Wrightman, L. S., (Eds.), *Contemporary issues in social psychology.* Reprinted by permission of Wadsworth Publishing Company.

Quotation from Santee, R. T. & Maslach, C. (1982). To agree or not to agree: Personal dissent amid social pressure to conform. *Journal of Personality and Social Psychology, 42*(4), 690–700. Reprinted by permission of the American Psychological Association.

Quotation from Asch, S. E. (1951). Effects of group pressure upon the modification and distortion of judgements. In Guetzkow, H. (Ed.), *Groups, leadership and men: Research in human relations.* Carnegie Press.

Quotation from Milgram, S. (1965). Some conditions of obedience and disobedience to authority. *Human Relations, 18,* 67–76. Copyright owned by Estate of Stanley Milgram. Reprinted by permission.

Quotations from Milgram, S. (1974). *Obedience to authority: An experimental view.* Copyright © 1974 by Stanley Milgram. Reprinted by permission of Harper & Row, Publishers, Inc.

Quote from Bock, J. & Harnick, S. (1964). "Do You Love Me?" *Fiddler on the Roof.* © Copyright 1964 by Alley Music Corp./Trio Music Co., Inc. All rights administered by Hudson Bay Music Inc.

Used by permission. All rights reserved.

Figures 17-1 and 17-2: Asch, S. E. (1955). Opinions and social pressure. *Scientific American, 193*(5), 31–35. Copyright © 1955 by Scientific American, Inc. All rights reserved.

Figure 17-3: Milgram, S. (1974). *Obedience to authority: An experimental view.* Copyright © 1974 by Stanley Milgram. Reprinted by permission of Harper & Row, Publisher, Inc.

Figure 17-4: Anastasi, A. (1982). *Psychological testing* (5th ed.). Copyright © 1982 by Anne Anastasi. Reprinted by permission of Macmillan Publishing Company.

Table 17-1: Festinger, L., & Carlsmith, J. M. (1959). Cognitive consequences of forced compliance. *Journal of Abnormal Psychology, 58,* 207. Copyright 1959 by the American Psychological Association. Reprinted by permission of the author.

Table 17-2: Adorno, T., Frenkel-Brunswik, E., Levinson, J., Sanford, R. N., et al. (1950). *The authoritarian personality.* Copyright 1950 by the American Jewish Committee. Reprinted by permission of Harper & Row, Publishers, Inc.

CHAPTER 18

Chapter-opening photograph: Janeart 1985/Image Bank.

Quotation from Kelly, J. B. (1982). Divorce: The adult perspective. In Wolman, B. (Ed.), *Handbook of developmental psychology.* Copyright © 1982. Reprinted by permission of Prentice-Hall, Inc., Englewood Cliffs, NJ.

Figure 18-1: Levinger, G., & Snoek, J. D. (1972). *Attraction in relationship: A new look at interpersonal attraction.* General Learning Press. Reprinted by permission of the authors.

Table 18-1: Byrne, D. (1971). *The attraction paradigm.* Reprinted by permission of Academic Press and the author.

Table 18-2: Rubin, Z. (1970). Measurements of romantic love. *Journal of Personality and Social Psychology, 16*(2), 265–273. Copyright © 1970 by the American Psychological Association. Reprinted by permission of the publisher and author.

INDEXES

NAME INDEX

Abeloff, M. D., 589, B 7
Abrahams, D., 640, 641, B 31
Abramson, L. Y., 506, B 1
Abramson, P. R., 433, 434, 445, B 1, B 21
Abroms, K. I., 262, B 1
Adams, C. G., 440, B 1
Adams, D. B., 433, B 1
Adams, E. H., 146, B 1
Adams, G., 350, B 15
Adams, M. J., 212, B 22
Adams, R. D., 220, B 31
Adelson, J., 351, B 1
Adler, Alfred, 14, 134, 258, 335, 460, 462, 498, 527, 537, B 1
Adorno, T., 624, 625, 628, B 1
Ainsworth, Mary D. Salter, 325, 328–330, B 1, B 3
Ajzen, I., 622, B 9
Alessandrini, P., 578, B 16
Alexander, J., 621, B 19
Allen, C. R., 504, B 8
Allport, Gordon W., 207, 467–468, B 1
Alpert, J. J., 313, B 13
Altman, I., 633, B 1
Alzheimer's Disease and Related Disorders Association, 48, 49
Amabile, T. M., 291, 294, 295, B 1
American Bar Association Journal, 211, B 14
American Civil Liberties Union (ACLU), 413, B 1
American Heart Association, 578, B 1
American Heritage Dictionary of the English Language, 528, B 1
American Medical Association, 142, 211, B 1
American Psychiatric Association, 440, 486, 493, 494, 549–550, 553
(See also *Diagnostic and Statistical Manual of Mental Disorders*)

American Psychological Association (APA), 9, 22, 30, 119, 142, 166, 243, 413, B 1
American Society of Clinical Hypnosis, 142
American Society of Journalists and Authors Newsletter, 457, B 2
Amoore, J. E., 98, B 1
Anastasi, A., 241, 243, 249, 250, 291, 473, 475, 476, 617, B 1, B 2
Ancoli, S., 410, B 8
Anders, T., 136, 137, B 2
Andersen, S., 30, 365, B 33
Anderson, A. M., 256, B 2
Anderson, J. R., 289, B 2
Anderson, O. L., 433, B 17
Anderton, C. H., 142, B 31
Andreasen, N. C., 487, 514, 517, 544, B 2
Andrews, Reginald, 609
Angell, M., 589, B 2
Anthony, E. J., 333, B 2
Anthony, J. C., 489, 495, 525, B 8, B 21
Appel, L., 322, B 2
Applebaum, P. S., 544, B 2
Aquino, Corazon, 357
Arbit, J., 220, B 7
Arend, R., 329, B 2, B 19
Arendt, J., 546, B 31
Aristotle, 8
Arlman-Rupp, A., B 28
Arluke, A., 422, B 18
Arnold, M. A., 95, B 5
Aron, A. P., 409, B 8
Aronson, E., 620, 621, 624, 627, 642, B 2, B 20
Aronson, V., 640, 641, B 31
Asbury, T., 83, B 31
Asch, Solomon E., 601–603, 609, B 2
Aschoff, J., 126, B 2
Aserinsky, E., 123, B 2

Ash, P., 311, B 2
Asher, S. J., 652, B 4
Aslin, R. N., 82, 113, B 2
Atkins, B. K., 422, B 22
Atkinson, J. W., 397, B 2, B 20
Atkinson, R. C., 193, 194, 209, B 2, B 27
Auer, J. J., 271, B 8
Auerbach, A. H., 554, B 19
Averinos, P. C., 580, B 11

Bachman, J. G., 145–147, 582, B 15
Bachrach, A. J., 535, B 2
Back, K., 633, 639, B 9
Backman, C. W., 633, B 2
Bacon, Francis, 118
Baekeland, F., 130, B 12
Baird, J. C., 111, B 2
Baird, W. P., 135, B 7
Bakalar, J. B., 148, B 12
Balkwell, C., 373, 374, B 2
Ballinger, C. B., 355, B 2
Baltes, P. B., 356, 369, B 2, B 7, B 32
Bandura, Alfred, 28, 181–183, 274, 336, 351, 467, 499, 525, B 2
Banks, M. S., 82, 113, B 2
Banks, W. C., 601–602, B 33
Barahal, H. S., 542, B 2
Barbee, A., 259, B 27
Barber, T. X., 141, B 2
Barclay, A., 477, B 6
Bard, B., 276, B 26
Bard, P., 407–408, B 3
Barefoot, J. C., 588, B 3, B 32
Barfield, R. E., 371, B 3
Bargh, J., 258, B 33
Barker, P., 580, B 3
Barnes, A., 312, B 3
Barnes, C. L., 49, 367, B 14
Barnes, M. L., 649, B 29
Barnett, R., 362, 363, B 3

Gaertner, S. L., 609, 611, B 24
Gagnon, J. H., 445, B 10
Gainsbauer, A., 411
Gajdusek, D. C., 49, B 11
Galaburda, A. M., 64, B 10
Gall, Franz, 40
Gallagher, C. E., 477, B 10
Gallucci, W. T., 580, B 11
Gallup, G. G., 22, B 10
Galton, F., 236, 253, B 10
Garcia, J., 176, 250, B 10
Gardner, B. T., 279, B 10
Gardner, H., 231, 234–235, 245, 251, 260, B 10
Garfinkel, P. E., 590, B 7
Garmezy, N., 332, 333, B 10
Garn, S. M., 578, B 10
Garron, D. C., 589, B 27
Gazzaniga, M., 64, B 10
Gebhard, P. H., 430, 439, 445, B 10, B 16
Geffner, R., 627, B 10
Gelder, M. G., 542, B 6
Geller, E. S., 173, B 10
Gelles, R. J., 398, 399, B 23
Gelman, R., 319, B 27
Genovese, Kitty, 609, 610
Gent, J. F., 98, B 20
George, L., 489, B 8
Gerberich, S. G., 581, 582, B 27
Gerhard, D. S., 504, B 8
German, P. S., 489, 525, B 27
Gerner, R. H., 580, B 12
Gershon. E. S., 505, B 21
Gerson, S., 549, B 3
Gerstein, D. R., 149, 582, B 20
Gescheider, G. A., 77, B 10
Geschwind, N., 64, 65, B 10
Gesell, A., 4, 316, B 10
Getzels, J. W., 291, B 10
Gewirtz, H. B., 325, B 11
Gewirtz, J. L., 325, B 11
Ghiselin, B., 291, B 29
Gibbon, M., 496, B 28
Gibson, E., 109, B 31
Gibson, J. J., 104, B 11
Gil, D. G., 399, B 11
Gilderman, A. M., 553, B 9
Gill, J. J., 588, B 11
Gill, T. V., 279, B 26
Gilligan, Carol, 324, 345, 347, 349, 423, B 11, B 16
Gilliland, M. A., 128, B 24
Gillin, C., 546, B 25
Gillin, J. C., 49, B 28
Ginzberg, E., 352, B 11
Girdano, D. A., 144, 148, 151, B 8
Gittleson, N., 540, B 11
Gladue, B. A., 71, 441, B 11
Glanzer, M., 205, B 11
Glaser, R., 590, B 16
Glass, A., 207, B 11
Glass, D., 258, 569, B 11
Glass, G. V., 551, B 28

Gleason, J. B., 275, B 11
Globus, G. G., 129, B 10, B 21
Goddard, A., 250, 254
Goertzel, M. G., 291, B 11
Goertzel, V., 291, B 11
Goethals, G. R., 637, B 21
Gold, A. R., 433, B 1
Gold, P. W., 580, B 11
Golden, N. L., 312, B 11
Goldfried, M. R., 476, B 11
Goldgabern, D., 49, B 11
Goldman, R., 391, B 11
Goldsmith, M. F., 311, B 11
Goleman, D., 122, 233, 259, 368, 540, B 11
Goodenough, D., 133, B 11, B 17
Goodner, C. J., 388, B 11
Goodstadt, M. S., 587, B 11
Goodwin, F. K., 546, B 25
Gorbach, S. L., 578, 589, B 11
Gordon, E., 250, B 11
Gordon, M. G., 312, B 32
Gordon, S. L., 648, B 23
Gottesman, I. I., 307, 516, B 11
Gould, M. S., 510, B 11
Gould, Stephen Jay, 249, 253, 254, B 11
Gove, F., 329, B 2
Grahame-Smith, D. G., 542, B 6
Grajek, S., 649, B 29
Graubard, B. I., 313, B 20
Gravelle, K., 95, B 25
Gray, C. R., 221, B 12
Gray, L. A., 355, B 14
Gray, W. D., 284, B 25
Gray-Little, B., 653, B 11
Green, H., 515, B 11
Green, R., 71, 429, 441, B 11
Greenberg, B. S., 396, B 7
Greenberg, M., 333, B 11
Greenberg, R. P., 460, B 9
Greenberg, S. B., 428, B 11
Greenberger, E., 352, 353, B 11
Greenblat, C. S., 438, B 11
Greene, "Mean" Joe, 107
Greenwell, J., B 11
Gregory, R. L., 105, B 11
Gribbin, K., 247, B 26
Grief, E. B., 344, B 11
Griffiths, W. J., 123, 126, B 32
Griffitt, W. B., 635, 643, 644, B 5, B 11, B 12
Grinspoon, L., 148, B 12
Gross, L. P., 391, B 26
Grossman, H. J., 261, B 12
Grotevant, H., 352, B 12
Group for the Advancement of Psychiatry, 362, B 12
Grove, W. M., 517, B 2
Groves, J. E., 512, B 12
Gruenberg, E., 489, 495, 496, 498, 501, 502, 515, B 25
Grunberg, N. E., 562, B 17
Gruneberg, M. M., 223, B 12
Guerney, B. G., Jr., 539, B 12

Guilford, J. P., 229, 232, 290, 291, B 12
Guilleminault, C., 130, B 6
Guilleminault, E., 136, B 12
Gummerman, K., 221, B 12
Gunderson, J., 312, B 3
Gurin, J., 389, B 3
Gurman, A. S., 552, 555, B 12
Guthrie, L., 508, 509, B 4
Gutmann, D. L., 476, B 22
Gutmann, M., 577, B 29
Guttmacher Institute (Alan Guttmacher), 436, B 12
Guttormsen, S., 504, B 32
Gwirtsman, H. E., 580, B 11, B 12
Gynther, M. D., 477, B 12

Haan, N., 357, B 12
Haas, A., 423, B 12
Habicht, J.-P., 311, B 24
Haegerstrom, C., 81, 82, 113, B 21
Hagestad, G., 354, B 22
Hagy, F., 393, B 24
Hahn, H. A., 173, B 10
Hale, S. L., 580, B 21
Haley, J., 488, 519, B 3
Hall, C. S., 133, 134, B 12
Hall, E., 358, 359, 369, 422, 423, B 12
Hall, G. Stanley, 9, 351, B 12
Hamburg, D., 614, B 12
Hamburg, D. A., 356, B 7
Hamilton, S., 352, B 12
Hammersmith, S. K., 440, 441, B 3
Hammond, C. B., 355, B 12
Haney, C., 601–602, B 33
Hanis, C., 389, 578, B 29
Hansen, A. R., 583, B 31
Hansson, R. D., 473, 474, B 13
Harakiewicz, J. M., 302, B 16
Hardee, B. B., 624, B 20
Hargis, K., 614, B 25
Haring, N., 263, B 13
Harkins, E., 363, B 12
Harley, E. E., 313, B 20
Harlow, H. F., 330, 331, 433, B 12, B 29
Harlow, M. K., 330, 331, 433, B 12
Harrell, R. F., 257, B 12
Harris, B., 166, B 12
Harris, John E., 223
Harris, S. L., 517, B 21
Harris, V. A., 637, B 15
Harrison, Tom, 410
Harshman, R. A., B 16
Hart, K. J., 580, B 12
Hartman, M., 422, B 12
Hartmann, E., 130, 131, 137, B 12
Hartshorne, H., 471, B 12
Harvard Medical School Mental Health Letter, 508, 512, 513, B 12
Harvard University Project, 260
Hashim, S. A., 390, B 12
Hasset, J., 470, 472, B 12
Hassing, Y., B 28
Hatab, P., 312, B 3

Kaplan, H. S., 441, B 15
Kaplan, M., 491, B 15
Karnovsky, M. L., 127, B 17
Karon, J. M., 355, B 5
Karp, L. E., 312, B 29
Kart, C. S., 370, B 18
Kass, F., 491, 493, B 15
Katerndahl, D. A., 497, B 15
Kaye, D., 621, B 15
Kaye, W., 580, B 11
Kayne, H., 313, B 13
Kearsley, R., 247–248, B 33
Keesey, R. E., 389, B 15
Keller, Helen, 269
Keller, S. E., 590, B 27
Kelley, H. H., 636, 642, 644, B 16, B 30
Kellogg, L. A., 280, B 16
Kellogg, W. N., 280, B 16
Kelly, J. B., 332, 653–654, B 16, B 31
Kelly, P. H., 49, B 25
Kelman, H. C., 620, B 16
Kennedy, John F., 206, 604
Kennell, J. H., 331, B 16
Kenrick, D. T., 614, B 3
Kermis, M., 353, B 16
Kessler, L. G., 489, 525, 582, B 8, B 14, B 27
Kessler, R. C., 396, B 20
Ketron, J. L., 230, 231, B 29
Kety, S. S., 412, 516, B 16, B 26
Keyes, M., 254, B 4
Keystone, E., 590, B 7
Kidd, K. K., 504, B 8
Kiecolt-Glaser, J. K., 590, B 16
Kiesler, C. A., 548, 550, B 16
Kiesler, E., Jr., 67, B 16
Kiess, H. O., 392, B 25
Kihlstrom, J. F., 221, 302, B 16
Killman, P. R., 216, B 27
Kim, Y. J., 435, B 33
Kimmel, D. C., 355, B 16
Kimura, D., 64, B 16
Kimzey, S. L., 590, B 16
King, Martin Luther, Jr., 206
Kingdon, J. W., 638, B 16
Kinlow, W. B., 433, B 28
Kinsey, A. C., 430, 439, B 16
Kinsman, R., 282, B 7
Kirkwood, S. B., 311, B 5
Kirschner, P., 621, B 15
Kirshnit, C. E., 285, B 8
Klaas, E. T., 623, B 16
Klaber, N. M., 307, B 15
Klatzky, R. L., 197, B 16
Klaus, M. H., 331, B 16
Kleck, R. E., 640, B 16
Klein, D. F., 516, 544, 545, 547, B 32
Klein, E., 359, 361, B 18
Klein, M., 460, B 30
Klein, R., 396, B 14
Klein, R. E., 311, B 24
Kleinginna, A. M., 384, B 16
Kleinginna, P. R., Jr., 384, B 16
Kleitman, N., 123, 132, 133, B 2, B 16

Klerman, G., 554, B 16
Kliegl, R., 356, 369, B 2
Kling, A., 48, B 29
Klipp, R., 282, B 7
Knapp, H. R., 578, B 16
Knittle, J. L., 390, B 26
Kobasa, S. C., 572, B 16
Koelling, R. A., 176, B 10
Koff, E., 344, B 16
Koffka, Kurt, 12
Kohlberg, Lawrence, 344, 345, 347–348, 423, 428, B 16, B 22
Kohler, W., 12, 285, B 16
Kokmen, E., 49, B 16
Kolata, G., 49, 390, 544, B 16
Kolb, B., 50, 63, B 16
Kolodny, R. C., 442, 443, B 19
Komisar, L., 358, B 16
Kopell, B. S., 138, B 6
Kopf, A. W., 589, B 16
Kopta, S. M., 551, B 14
Kornfeld, D. S., 588, B 15
Koulack, D., 133, B 17
Koupernik, C., 333, B 2
Kozin, M., 206, B 26
Kraemer, H. C., 356, B 7
Kramer, M., 489, 495, 525, B 21, B 24
Krantz, D. S., 562, 588, B 17
Krashen, S., 277, B 10
Krasilnikoff, P. A., 312, B 26
Krause, M. S., 551, B 14
Kravitz, D. A., 599, B 20
Kreutzer, M., 325, B 17
Kreuz, L. E., 393, B 17
Krowitz, A., 109, B 5
Krueger, J. M., 127, B 17
Krüll, M., 460, B 17
Kübler-Ross, Elisabeth, 372, B 17
Kuhnert, B. R., 312, B 11
Kulik, J., 206, B 5
Kulka, R., 362, 363, 400, B 31
Kupfersmid, J., 347, B 17
Kurshan, M., 529, B 17
Kutchinsky, B., 445, B 17

LaBarge, E., 49, B 17
LaFerla, J. J., 433, B 17
La Gaipa, J. J., 646, B 17
Lahey, B. B., 390, 579, B 30
Lakoff, R., 422, B 17
Lamb, H. R., 548–550, B 17
Lamb, M. E., 329, 331, 333–335, B 17, B 30
Lamb, W. H., 311, B 24
Landman, J. T., 551, B 17
Lange, C., 406–407, 410, B 17
Langer, A., 109, B 5
Langer, E. J., 29, 122, 591, 627, B 17, B 25
Lanza, R. P., 285, B 8
Larson, R., 580, B 15
LaRussa, Tony, 172
Lasater, T. M., 620, B 7

Laskley, K., 218, B 17
Lasky, T., 581, B 27
Lassen, N. A., 61, B 17
Latané, B., 609, 610, B 17
Laudenslager, M. L., 590, B 17, B 19
Lazarus, L. W., 49, B 17
Lazarus, Richard S., 411, 564–569, 571, 572, B 7, B 14, B 15, B 17
Leaf, P. J., 489, 495, 525, B 21, B 27
Lechtig, A., 311, B 24
Ledger, M., 394, B 17
LeDoux, J. E., 64, B 10
Lee, K. L., 355, B 12
Lee, P. R., 581, B 30
Lefcourt, H., 567, B 17
Leibowitz, H. W., 111, B 17
Leiman, A. L., 54, 59, 70, B 25
Lemmon, Jack, 468
Lemon, B., 370, B 17
Lenneberg, Eric H., 271, 272, 275, 277–279, B 5, B 17
Lennie, P., 84, B 17
Lennon, M. C., 355, B 17
Lennon, R., 422, B 8
Leonard, J., 312, B 29
Leonard, R. L., 643, B 17
Leonardo da Vinci, 456
Lerman, M. I., 49, B 11
Lerner, J., 640, B 18
Lerner, R., 640, B 18
Leshner, A. I., 69, B 18
Lester, B., 257, B 18
Lester, R., 312, B 18
Letson, R. D., 82, 113, B 2
Levenson, R. W., 410, B 8
Leventhal, H., 575, 577, 584, 585, 587, 621, B 18, B 29
Leventhal, J. M., 312, B 26
Levin, H., 259, 394, B 27
Levin, J., 422, B 18
Levine, M. W., 91, B 18
Levinger, G., 633, 644, B 18
Levinger, T. L., 642, 643, 646, B 14
Levinson, D., 359–361, B 18
Levinson, D., 624, 625, 628, B 1
Levinson, M., 359, 361, B 18
Levson, F., 370, B 24
Levy, G., 63, B 18
Levy, J., 66, 67, B 18
Lewine, R. R. J., 515, B 18
Lewis, C., 420, B 18
Lewis, I. G., 312, B 32
Lewis, L. D., 580, B 15
Lewis, M., 420, B 18
Lewis, M. J., 390, B 19
Lewy, A. J., 546, B 25
Ley, B., 312, B 29
Libby, R. W., 439, B 21
Lidz, T., 519, B 18
Lieberman, M., 370, B 18
Lief, H. I., 433, B 23
Likert, R., 616, B 18
Limber, J., 280, B 18
Lin, S. C., 589, B 27

Lincoln, Abraham, 206, 464
Lincoln, R., 312, B 18
Lindsten, J., 312, B 29
Linn, M. C., 420, B 18
Lipetz, M. E., 621, 649, B 7
Lipid Research Clinics Program, 578, B 18
Lipsitt, L., 320, 321, B 18, B 26
Livson, F., 357, B 18
Lloyd-Still, J., 257, B 18
Locke, B. Z., 489, 525, B 8, B 24
Locke, J., 8, 118, B 18
Lockhart, R. S., 193, 202, B 6
Loeber, R., 327, 398, 399, B 24
Loftus, E. F., 200, 205, 208–210, 215, 286, B 4, B 18
Loftus, G. R., 210, 215, B 18
London, O., 643, B 5
Long, P., 142, B 18
Longino, C. F., 370, B 18
Looft, W. R., 346, B 18
Lopata, H., 374, B 18
LoPiccolo, J., 445, 446, B 13
LoPiccolo, L., 445, 446, B 13
Lorayne, H., 223, B 18
Lorenz, G., 354–355, B 21
Lorenz, K., 392, B 18
Loriaux, L., 580, B 11
Lott, A. J., 644, B 18
Lott, B. E., 644, B 18
Love, T., 221, B 14
Lowe, J. C., 354, B 22
Lowell, E. L., 397, B 20
Lowenthal, M., 632, 646, B 18
Lubar, J., 184, B 18
Luborsky, L., 460, 550, 554, 556, B 19
Ludvigsson, J., 312, B 29
Ludwig, A. M., 119–121, B 19
Lumsdaine, A. A., 621, B 14
Luria, A. R., 221, B 19
Lusk, E. J., 589, B 5
Lynn, D., 333, B 19
Lynn, R., 256, 403, B 19
Lyons, R. D., 438, B 19
Lyroler, H. A., 355, B 5

Maccoby, E. E., 259, 334, 393, 394, 420, 421, 425, 428, B 19, B 27, B 28
Maccoby, N., 585, 621, B 19, B 20
MacFarlane, A., 97, 313, 314, B 19
Machiavelli, Niccolò, 468
MacLeod-Morgan, C., 139, B 19
MacNichol, E. F., 86, B 19
MacRae, K. D., 312, B 32
Maddi, S. R., 572, B 16
Maharishi Mahesh Yogi, 138
Mahler, Gustav, 540
Maier, S. F., 590, B 17, B 19
Majovski, L. V., 48, B 29
Makepeace, J. M., 398, B 19
Malamuth, N. M., 444, 445, B 19
Malizia, C., 589, B 27
Maltzman, I. M., 584, B 23
Mamay, P. D., 426, B 19

Mann, L., 622, B 15, B 19
Manschreck, T. C., 515, B 19
March of Dimes, 309, 310, B 19
Marcia, J. E., 350, B 19
Margules, M. R., 390, B 19
Marion, R. W., 312, B 19
Marks, A., 404, 405, B 7
Marks, J. S., 312, B 22
Marks, W. B., 86, B 19
Marlatt, G. A., 584, B 19
Marotta, C. A., 49, B 26
Marsh, G. M., 48, B 29
Marshall, S. P., 420, B 19
Martin, C. E., 430, 439, B 16
Martin, J. B., 95, B 5
Martin, R. J., 137, B 23
Marty, M. E., 617, B 19
Marx, Groucho, 643
Maslach, C., 605, B 26
Maslow, Abraham H., 15, 386–388, 464–466, 488, 527, B 19
Mason, J. W., 564, B 19
Mason, R. M., 292, B 19
Mason-Brothers, A., 307, B 25
Massman, P. J., 553, B 3
Masson, J. M., 460, B 19
Masters, William H., 430, 438, 440–446, B 19
Masuda, M., 567, B 13
Matarazzo, J. D., 582, B 19
Matas, L., 329, B 19
Matlin, M. M., 79, 85, 91, 92, 96, 104, 111, 421–423, B 19, B 20
May, J. G., 103, B 28
May, M. A., 471, B 12
Mayer, D. J., 96, B 20
McAlister, A. L., 585, 621, B 20
McArthur, J. W., 95, B 5
McArthur, L. A., 636, B 20
McBride, D. W., 49, B 11
McBurney, D. H., 98, 99, B 20
McCann, I. L., 581, B 20
McCarley, R. W., 132, 135, B 13
McCarrell, B., 322, B 2
McClelland, D. C., 250–251, 261, 397–400, 590, B 15, B 20
McConahay, J. B., 624, B 20
McCormack, T., 445, B 20
McCormick, D. A., 57, 218, B 20
McDaniel, C., 112, B 10
McDarby, D., 150, B 27
McDougall, William, 384
McEvoy, J., 399, B 28
McFadden, R. D., 609, B 20
McGhee, P., 426, B 10
McGill, C. W., 553, B 9
McGinnes, G. C., 324, 410, B 14
McGrath, J. E., 599, B 20
McGrath, S. K., 322, B 9
McGue, M., 307, B 4
McGuire, M. T., 412, B 24
McKay, R. J., 313, B 31
McKee, B., 359, 361, B 18
McKegney, F. P., 590, B 27

McKillip, J., 641, B 20
McKinley, D., 399, B 20
McKinley, J. C., 473
McKinnon, D. W., 291, B 20
McLaren, N. M., 312, B 22
McNeill, D., 202, B 5
Mead, Margaret, 351, 426, B 20
Meichenbaum, D. A., 574, B 20
Meislin, R. J., 622, B 20
Melisaratos, N., 589, B 7
Mellon, J., 460, B 19
Mengel, C. E., 590, B 16
Mentzer, S. J., 589, 591, B 20
Mercer, Jane, 248–249
Mervis, C. B., 283, 284, B 25
Metzger, B. E., 311, B 20
Meyer, A. J., 585, 621, B 20
Meyer, D., 590, B 15
Mikhail, A., 564, B 20
Milavsky, J. R., 396, B 20
Milgram, S., 606–608, B 20
Miller, B. C., 363, 573, B 20
Miller, C., 422, B 20
Miller, C., 553, B 3
Miller, C., 589, B 5
Miller, D. G., 210, 215, B 18
Miller, D. S., 589, B 5
Miller, E., 311, B 20
Miller, G. A., 196, B 20
Miller, G. H., 149, 582, B 20
Miller, N. E., 22, 184, 185, B 20
Miller, N. E., 367, B 6
Miller, R., 567, B 17
Miller, R. C., 553, B 20
Miller, T., 612, B 20
Miller, W. R., 433, B 23
Millodot, M., 81, 82, 113, B 21
Mills, J., 621, B 20
Mills, J. L., 313, B 20
Milner, B., 220, B 20, B 30
Mindick, B., 436, B 23
Miranda, S. B., 314, B 9
Mischel, W., 471, B 20, B 21
Mishkin, M., 220, B 21
Mitchell, D., 127, B 27
Mitchell, D., 386, B 27
Mitchell, D. E., 81, 82, 113, B 21
Mitchison, G., 132, B 6
Mo, A., 307, B 25
Modahl, C., 312, B 22
Mohr, J. P., 535, B 2
Moisset, B., 390, B 19
Molfese, D., 271, 276, B 21
Molfese, V., 271, 276, B 21
Money, J., 424, 429, B 8, B 21
Monge, R., 353, B 16
Monroe, Marilyn, 506, 512
Montemayor, P., 351, B 21
Moore, J. D., 97, B 24
Moore, J. W., 354, B 22
Moore-Ede, M. C., 126, 127, B 21
Moos, R. H., 573, B 13
Morbidity and Mortality Weekly Reports, 508, B 21

Morelock, S., 313, B 13
Morgan, A. H., 140, B 21
Morgan, J. N., 371, B 3
Morgan, P., 96, B 21
Morganthau, T., 548, 549, B 21
Morley, J. E., 433, B 28
Morolla, A. F., 258, B 3
Morris, C. D., 203, B 21
Morris, D., 433, B 21
Morris, N., 333, B 11
Morris, N. F., 312, B 32
Morris, P. E., 223, B 12
Morse, S. J., 525, B 21
Mosher, D. L., 433, 434, B 21
Moss, A. J., 588, B 5
Moss, H. A., 330, 425, B 21, B 25
Moss, H. B., 553, B 9
Motta, E. A., 436, B 23
Mowrer, O. H., 274, B 21
Moyer, K. E., 392, B 21
Mueller, P. S., 546, B 25
Mullaney, D. J., 129, B 10, B 21
Multicenter Post-Infarction Research Group, The, 588, B 5
Murphy, D. L., 402, B 33
Murphy, D. P., 311, B 21
Murray, H. A., 397, 476, B 21
Murray-Lyon, I. M., 312, B 32
Murstein, B. I., 643, 645, 651, B 21
Mussen, P. H., 344, 428, 611, B 15, B 21
Myers, D. G., 393, 624, B 21
Myers, J. K., 489, 495, 525, B 21, B 24
Myers, N., 322, B 21
Myers-Walls, J. A., 363, B 20, B 21

Nadi, N. S., 505, B 21
Naeye, R. L., 312, B 21
Nagelman, D. B., 580, B 21
Nagy, M., 372, B 21
Naitoh, P., 129, B 10, B 21
Napier, A., 538, B 21
Napolitan, D. A., 637, B 21
Nash, A., 336, B 13
Nash, J. D., 585, 621, B 20
Nasrallah, H. A., 517, B 2
Nass, G. D., 439, B 21
Nathan, P. E., 486, 517, 584, 587, B 21, B 26
Nathan, R. S., 498, B 30
Nathanson, C. A., 354–355, B 21
National Academy of Science, 246, B 21
National Center for Health Statistics, 311, B 21
National Institute of Mental Health (NIMH), 395, 489, 502, 504, 505, 507, 548, 549, 553, B 22
National Institute on Aging, 368, B 22
National Institute on Drug Abuse (NIDA), 150, B 22
National Institutes of Health (NIH), 135–137, 542, 545, 578, 582, B 21, B 22
National Opinion Research Center, 615, 624, B 22

Neale, J. M., 429, 485, 513, 529, 539, B 7
Neisser, U., 224, B 22
Nelson, A. E., 433, B 28
Nelson, C. J., 433, B 28
Nelson, K., 272, 274, B 22
Nelson, T. O., 303, B 22
Neugarten, Bernice, 354, 363, 370, 427, 476, B 22
Neugebauer, R., 485, B 22
Neulinger, J., 258, B 11
Nevis, S., 314, B 9
Newcomb, T. M., 633, B 22
Newman, H. H., 307, B 22
Newsome, D. A., 546, B 25
Newton, Isaac, 290, 291
Newton, N., 312, B 22
New York Longitudinal Study (NYLS), 469
New York Times, The, 106, 172, 286, 473, 582, 627, B 10, B 24, B 28, B 29, B 31, B 32
Nias, D. K., 643, B 22
Niaura, R., 393, B 24
Nichol, S., 518, B 22
Nickerson, R. S., 212, B 22
Nida, S., 610, B 17
Nieberg, P., 312, B 22
Nieman, L. K., 580, B 11
Nimmer, J. G., 173, B 10
Nisan, M., 347, B 22
Nisbett, R. E., 390, B 22
Noll, K. M., 545, B 22
Noller, K., 312, B 3
Notelovitz, M., 581, B 22
Novaco, R. W., 574, B 22
Nurnberger, J. I., 505, B 21
Nuttall, F. Q., 433, B 28

O'Barr, W. M., 422, B 22
O'Brien, C. P., 390, 433, B 22, B 23
O'Brien, E. J., 471, B 8
O'Brien, P., 312, B 3
O'Connor, D., 434, B 22
O'Connor, M. J., 314, B 22
O'Connor, R. D., 182, B 22
Odbert, H. S., 468, B 1
Oden, M. H., 259, B 30
Oelsner, L., 262, B 22
Offer, D., 351, B 22
Offer, J. B., 351, B 22
Offord, K. P., 474, B 6
Olds, S. W., 39, 70, 76, 158, 163, 193, 307, 342, 382, 385, 418, 435, 438, 524, 598, B 8, B 22, B 23
Olivier, D. C., 279, B 13
Ollendick, T. H., 580, B 12
Olsen, S., 514, 544, B 2
Olson, S. C., 517, B 2
Olton, D. S., 220, B 22
O'Malley, P. M., 145–147, 582, B 15
Oppenheimer, E., 313, B 13
Orlinsky, D. E., 551, B 14
Ormiston, D. W., 132, B 6

Orne, M. T., 140, 413, 608, B 22, B 31
Orr, C. W., 137, B 23
Orvaschel, H., 489, 495, 496, 498, 501, 502, 515, 525, B 21, B 25
Osborne, D., 474, B 6
Osgood, C. E., 616, B 23
Oskamp, S., 436, B 23
Osmond, H., 486, B 27
Oster, H., 410, B 8
Ostfeld, A. M., 589, B 27
Ostrove, N., 400, B 23
Oswald, P. F., 325, B 23
Ousler, J. D., 472, B 23
Overton, W., 345, B 6

Paddock, J., 394, B 23
Paffenbarger, R. S., 581, B 23, B 30
Pagano, R. R., 138, B 23
Paivio, A., 202, B 23
Palmer, A. M., 356, B 7
Palmer, J. C., 210, B 18
Palmer, S. E., 102, B 23
Paloma, M. M., 363, B 23
Pancake, V. R., 329, B 28
Papalia, D. E., 4, 118, 131, 133, 134, 228, 268, 302, 307, 320, 345, 369, 452, 482, 561, 567, 632, 638, B 4, B 23
Pappenheimer, J. R., 127, B 17
Pardue, L., 504, B 23
Parke, R. D., 177, 334, 623, B 23
Parker, R. T., 355, B 12
Parkes, C. M., 374, B 23
Parkes, J. D., 137, B 23
Parmalee, A. H., 130, 314, B 22, B 23
Parmalee, P., 643, B 32
Paterson, L., 173, B 10
Patrick, R., 358, 427, B 7
Patterson, C. D., 137, B 23
Patterson, G. R., 327, 398, 399, B 23, B 24
Paul, G. L., 548, B 23
Paul, O., 589, B 27
Pauls, D. L., 504, B 8
Pavlov, Ivan P., 161–164, 168, 169, 179, 285, 466, 527, B 23
Peake, P. K., 471, B 21
Peck, L., 428, B 11
Pedersen, D. M., 111, B 23
Pedersen, F. A., 425, B 32
Pedersen, J., 336, B 13
Pedrick-Cornell, C., 398, 399, B 23
Peel, E. A., 345, B 23
Peltzman, P., 325, B 23
Pendery, M. L., 584, B 23
Penfield, W., 41, B 23
Peplau, L. A., 648, 652, 653, B 13, B 23, B 26, B 27
Perkins, D. N., 291, B 23
Perkins, D. V., 567, B 23
Perlman, D., 648, B 23
Perlmutter, M., 322, B 21
Perls, F. S., 532, B 23

SUBJECT INDEX

Ganglion cells, 81, G 7
Gender, 419–429
    sex and gender differences, 419–427
    (See also Sexuality)
Gender differences, 419–427
    (See also Sex differences)
Gender identity, 419, G 7
    disorders of, 429, G 7
    theories of, 428
Gender identity disorder, 429, G 7
Gender identity disorder of childhood,
    429, G 7
Gender roles, 419, G 7
Gender signals, 433
Gender stereotypes, 419, 427, G 7
General adaptation syndrome (GAS), 563,
    G 7
Generalization of learning, 176
Generalized anxiety disorder, 498, G 7
Generativity versus stagnation, 358–359,
    G 7
Genes, 308, 419, G 7
Genetic defects, 308
    predicting, 311–313
Genetics:
    and affective disorders, 504
    and schizophrenia, 515
    trait transmission, 306–309
    (See also Heredity)
"Genie," case study of, 277–278
Genital stage, 459, G 7
Genotype, 308, G 7
German measles, 311
Germinal stage, 310, G 7
Gestalt laws, 100–102, G 7
Gestalt psychology, 12, 100, G 7
    on problem solving, 285–286
Gestalt therapy, 532–533, G 7
Gifted, intellectually, 258–261
Glaucoma, 83
Glial cells, 44, G 7
Goal-oriented behavior, 181
"Good Samaritan" laws, 615
Grammar, 270, G 7
Ground, figure and, 102
Group intelligence tests, 243–244
Group therapy, 537–538, G 7
Groups:
    control and experimental, 26, 669,
        G 4, G 6
    people in, 599–608
    self-help, 587
Groupthink, 604–606, G 7
Gustation, 98–100

Habituation, 160, 248, 314, G 7
Hallucinogens, 147–149, G 7
Handedness, 64
Handicapped, intelligence of, 247
Hardiness, 572, G 7
Hassles, 568–569
Health:
    in adulthood, 354–355

Health (Cont.):
    and aging, 364–367
    biopsychological versus biomedical
        model of, 562
Health practices:
    influences on, 576–577
    and patient-practitioner relationship,
        589–591
    promoting good, 584–587
    wellness and, 575–587
Health psychologists, 19, 562, G 7
Health psychology, 19, 559–593
    definition of, 562, G 7
    illness, 587–591
    stress, 562–575
    wellness and health practices, 575–587
Hearing, 90–94
    loss of, 93–94
Heart disease, 587–588
    coronary (CHD), 588, G 4
    diet and, 577–578
Helping behavior, 608–615
Hemispheric lateralization, 63–67, G 7
Hemophilia, 308
Heredity:
    and affective disorders, 504
    and aggression, 392
    and altruism, 611
    and development, 304–309
    and intelligence, 253–255
    and schizophrenia, 515–519
    and suicidal tendencies, 509
Heritability, 254, G 7
Heroin, 150, G 7
Herpes, 311–312
Heterosexuals, 71, 440–441, G 7
Heterozygous, 308, G 7
Heuristic, 287, G 7
"Hidden observer," 140
Hierarchy of needs, 386, 464
Hippocampus, 58, 216, G 7
Histogram, 658, G 7
Holophrases, 272, G 8
Homeostasis, 55, G 8
Homosexuals, 440–441, G 8
    biological basis for homosexuality, 71
    and DSM III, 491
Homozygous, 308, G 8
Hormones, 68, G 8
    and gender differences, 424
    and sexual arousal, 432–433
Humanistic model of abnormality, 488
Humanistic psychology, 15, 464, G 8
    on personality, 453, 464–466
Humanistic therapy, 530–533, 541
    definition of, 527, G 8
Hunger, 388–391
Hypnosis, 139–142
    definition of, 139, G 8
    and memory, 210–211
    for pain, 96
    practical applications of, 142
    susceptibility to, 140
    theories of, 140–141

Hypoglycemia, 393
Hypothalamus, 57, 68, 389, G 8
Hypotheses, 20, 669–670, G 8
Hysteria, 486

Iconic memory, 195, G 8
Id, 454, G 8
Identification, 335–336, G 8
Identity versus role confusion, 347, G 8
Idiographic approach, 468
Ill-defined concept, 282–284, G 8
Illness, 587–591, G 8
Illusions, 109–111, G 8
Imaginary audience, 345, G 8
Immune system, mind and the, 590
Incentives, 387, G 8
Incus, 91, G 8
Independence, conformity versus, 604
Independent variable, 26, G 8
Individual psychology, 462
Inductive reasoning, 289, G 8
Industrial and organizational psycholo-
    gists, 20, G 8
Industry versus inferiority, 324, G 8
Infancy:
    cognitive development in, 317–318
    memory in, 321–322
    physical development in, 313–317
    psychosocial development in, 322–324
    (See also Children)
Infantile sexuality, 458, G 8
Inferential statistics, 658, 668–670, G 8
Inferiority complex, 462, G 8
Information-processing theory:
    on intelligence, 247–248
    on problem solving, 286
Informed consent, 30
Inheritance, genetic (see Genetics; Hered-
    ity)
Inhibited female orgasm, 442, G 8
Inhibited male orgasm, 442, G 8
Inhibited sexual desire (ISD), 441, G 8
Inhibited sexual excitement, 441, G 8
Inhibition of neurons, 48
Initiative versus guilt, 324, G 8
Insight, 285, G 8
    and intelligence, 289
    and problem solving, 288–289
Insomnia, 135–136, G 8
Instinctive drift, 176
Instincts, 159, 384, G 8
Institutionalization, 548
Instrumental conditioning (see Operant
    conditioning)
Insulin, 388–389
Intellectually gifted, 258–261
Intelligence, 227–265
    artificial, 289, 292, G 2
    and creativity, 291
    definition of, 229, G 8
    extremes of, 258–263
    fluid versus crystallized, 233–234
    influences on, 253–258

Intelligence (Cont.):
  and insight, 289
  people's conception of, 230
  testing of, 236–253
  theories of, 229–236
Intelligence quotient (IQ), 237, G 8
Interaction, group, 599–608
Interference and forgetting, 211, 214
Internal cues, 390–391
Interneurons, 43, G 8
Interpersonal attraction, 631–655
  definition of, 633, G 8
  studying, 633–634
Interpersonal Judgment Scale, 634
Interpersonal relationships (see Relationships, interpersonal)
Interstimulus interval, 162, G 8
Interval schedule of reinforcement, 171, G 8
Interviews, 25–26
  in personality testing, 476–477
Intimacy versus isolation, 358, G 8
Intimate relationships, 646–654
Introspection (see Analytic introspection)
Introverts, 434
Involuntary functions, 53
Invulnerables (see Resilient children)
Iris, 80, G 9

James-Lange theory of emotion, 406, 407, 410
Jigsaw technique, 626–627
jnd (just noticeable difference), 78, G 9

K complex, 125
Kidneys, 68
Korsakoff's syndrome, 58, 220

L-dopa, 50
Laboratory experiment, 28
Lamaze delivery, 96
Language, 267–297
  of animals, 279–281
  children's learning of, 271–274
  critical period in learning, 277–278
  definition of, 270, G 9
  gender differences in, 420, 422–423
  learning a, 271–278
  and left hemisphere, 65–66
  linguistic-relativity hypothesis, 278–279
  studying, 269–271
  theories about, 274–277
Language acquisition device (LAD), 275, G 9
Lanugo, 313
Late adulthood (see Elderly)
Latency stage, 435, 459, G 9
Latent learning, 180, G 9
Lateral hypothalamus, 389
Laughing, 325

Law of effect, 168, G 9
Law of exercise, 168, G 9
Learned helplessness, 185–187, G 9
  and affective disorders, 506–507
Learning, 157–189
  aggression, 394–396
  altruism, 611
  associative, 160–179, G 2
  biofeedback and, 183–185
  biological influences on, 174–176
  cognitive perspectives on, 179–183
  definition of, 159, G 9
  in infancy, 320–321
  language, 271–278
  latent, 180
  observational, 181–183, G 11
  practical insights into, 183–187
  and prejudice, 624–627
  and sexual arousal, 433–434
Learning theorists, 274, G 9
Learning theory:
  on attitudes, 617
  on personality, 453, 466–467
  on problem solving, 285
Left-handedness, 64
Lens, 81, G 9
Lesion of brain, surgically induced, 41
Let-down response, 70
Levels-of-processing model of memory, 202–203, G 9
Libidinal theory of depression, 505
Libido, 454, G 9
Lie detector tests, 412, 413
Life-change units (LCUs), 567
Life events:
  control and predictability of, 569–570
  stress and, 567–570
Life expectancy, 367
Life stress (see Stress)
Life structure, 359–360, G 9
Light, adaptation to, 84–85
Light therapy, 507, 545, 546, G 9
Light waves, 79, 85
Likert scale, 616, 634, G 9
Limbic system, 58, G 9
Linguistic-relativity hypothesis, 278–279
Linguistic speech, 271–274
Linguistics, 270, G 9
  controversies in, 277–281
Lithium, 547
Little Albert experiment, 165–166
Live modeling, 535
Lobes of brain, 59–60
Lobotomy, 541–542
Localization of function, 41
Locus of control, 387, G 9
Loneliness, 647–649, G 9
Long life, stress and, 575
Long-term memory (LTM), 194, 199–202, G 9
Longitudinal method, 303, G 9
Love, 647–650
  triangular theory of, 649–650, G 16
Love scale, 634

LSD (d-lysergic acid diethylamide), 148, G 9
Luteinizing hormone experiment, 71

Machismo, 395
Magnetic resonance imaging (MRI), 43
Major depressive disorder, 503
Males, gender characteristics of, 419–427
Malleus, 91, G 9
Mania, 502, 504, G 9
Manic-depressive (bipolar) disorder, 502, 504, G 3
  drug therapy for, 545
Mantra, 138, G 9
Maps, cognitive, 180–181, G 4
Marijuana, 147–148, G 9
Marriage, 650–654
  power in, 653
  sex and, 437–440
Maternal influences on prenatal development, 311–313
Maturation, 159, 316, 317, G 9
  (See also Physical development)
Mean, 661, G 9
Mean length of utterance (MLU), 272, G 9
Median, 660, G 9
Medical doctors as therapists, 526
Medical model, 486, G 9
  of abnormality, 485–486
  of anxiety, 498
Medical therapy, 540–547
  definition of, 527, G 9
Meditation, 137–139, G 9
Medulla, 56
Memory, 191–225
  biological basis of, 215–218
  in childhood, 322
  as cognitive process, 193–215
  contents of, 204–208
  declarative, 199, G 5
  disorders of, 218–221
  episodic, 199, G 6
  exceptional, 221, 224
  and forgetting, 208–215
  iconic, 195, G 8
  improving, 222–223
  in infancy, 321–322
  legal implications of research, 210
  levels-of-processing model of, 202–203, G 9
  long-term, 194, 199–202, G 9
  permanence of, 215
  procedural, 199, G 12
  semantic, 199, G 14
  sensory, 194–195, G 14
  short-term, 194–198, G 14
  storage-and-transfer model of, 194, G 15
  testing, 204
Memory trace, 218
  decay of, 209–211
Menarche, 344, G 9
Menopause, 355, G 9

Mental age, 237, G 9
Mental development (see Cognitive development)
Mental health facilities, 548
Mental retardation, 261–263
Methadone, 150, G 10
Method-of-loci system, 221–222
Midbrain, 56
Middle adulthood (see Adulthood)
Midlife crisis, 356
Minnesota Multiphasic Personality Inventory (MMPI), 473–474, G 10
Misapplied constancy, theory of, 111
Mnemonics, 221, 224, G 10
Mode, 660, G 10
Modeling, 182, G 10
    identification and, 335–336
    live, 535
    symbolic, 535
Modeling therapy, 535, G 10
Modification, 6, G 10
Monoamine oxidase (MAO) inhibitors, 544–545
Monocular cues, 107, G 10
"Moon illusion," 111
Moral development, 345–347
Moral model, 485, G 10
Morpheme, 270, G 10
Morphine, 150, G 10
Mother-child attachment, 328–332
Motherese, 275–277, G 10
Motivation, 383–405, G 10
    achievement, 396–400
    aggression, 392–396
    arousal, curiosity, and boredom, 400–405
    determinants of, 383–384
    hunger and eating, 388–391
    theories of, 384–388
    (See also Emotion)
Motor cortex (see Cerebral cortex)
Motor development, early, 315–316
Motor (efferent) neurons, 43, G 10
Mourning, 372–374
MRI (magnetic resonance imaging), 43
Mueller-Lyer illusion, 109
Multifactorial inheritance, 308, G 10
Multiple-intelligences assessment, 251–253
Multiple-intelligences theory, 234, G 10
Multiple personality, 500, G 10
Muscles, 53–54
MYCIN (program), 292
Myelin, 44, G 10
Myelinization, 45, G 10
Myopia, 81, 82
Myotonia, 430

nAch, 397–400, G 10
Naloxone, 96
Narcolepsy, 135, G 10
Narcotics, 150–151, G 10
Narrative-chaining memory aid, 222

Nativists, 274, 275, G 10
Naturalistic observations, 26
Nature-nurture debate, 304, G 10
    and gender differences, 424
Nearsightedness, 81, 82
Needs, hierarchy of, 386, 464
Negative evaluation and aggression, 394
Negative reinforcer, 169, G 10
Neodissociation theory of hypnosis, 140, G 10
Neo-Freudians, 460–463
Neonatal period, 313, G 10
Nerves, 51, G 10
Nervous system, 40–67, G 10
    components of, 51–67
    study of, 40–43
    working of, 43–50
Neural-endocrine interactions, 70–71
Neuroleptics, 544
Neuromodulator, 95
Neurons, 43, G 10
Neuroscientists, 40
    (See also Physiological psychologists)
Neuroses, 493, 494
Neurotransmitters, 47–50, G 10
Neutral stimulus, 162, G 10
Nicotine, 144–145, G 10
    (See also Smoking)
Night blindness, 83
Night terrors, 137, G 10
Nightmares, 137, G 10
Nodes in the myelin, 45
Nomothetic approach, 468
Noninvasive techniques, 41–43
Nonnormative life events, 304, G 10
Non-rapid-eye-movement (NREM) sleep, 123, 125, G 10
Norepinephrine, 393, 412
Normal distributions, 663–665, G 10
Normative age-graded influences, 304, G 10
Normative history-graded influences, 304, G 10
Norms, 239, 599–602, G 10
    social, and health practices, 586
NREM (non-rapid-eye-movement) sleep, 123, 125, G 10
Nuclear magnetic resonance, 43
Nucleus, 44
Null hypothesis, 669, G 10
Nutrition:
    and intelligence, 257
    (See also Diet)

Obedience, 606–608, G 10
Obesity, 389–390, 578–579, G 10
Object permanence, 236, 318, G 10
Object-relations theory of depression, 505
Objective tests, 473–474, G 10
Obscenity, 443, 444, G 11
Observational learning, 181–183, G 11
Obsessions, 496, G 11

Obsessive-compulsive disorders, 496–497
Occipital lobe, 59, 60
Oedipus complex, 458, G 11
Old age (see Elderly)
Olfaction, 96–98
Olfactory mucosa, 97, G 11
Operant, 168, G 11
Operant (instrumental) conditioning, 160, 167–179, 321, G 11
    and seat belt use, 173
Operant therapy, 535–536, G 11
Opinions (see Attitudes)
Opium, 150, G 11
Opponent-process theory, 87–89, 385–386, G 11
Optic disk, 81, G 11
Oral stage, 458, G 11
Organic amnesia, 219–220, G 11
Organic retardation, 262, G 11
Organization for meaningful association, 222
Organizational psychology (see Industrial and organizational psychologists)
Orgasm, 431–432
Orienting response, 257
Osteoporosis, 58, G 11
Ovaries, 68
Overeating, 388–391, 578–579

Pain, 95–96
Pancreas, 68
Panic disorder, 497–498, 547, G 11
Papillae, 98, G 11
Parallel forms, 239, G 11
Paraphilia, 443, G 11
Parasympathetic nervous system, 54
Parenthood, 328, 362–363
Parents, gender differences and, 425
Parietal lobe, 59, 60
Partial reinforcement, 170, G 11
Participation in therapy, 535
Passionate love, 649
Patient-practitioner relationship, 589–591
Pavlovian conditioning (see Classical conditioning)
Pavor nocturnus, 137
PCP (phencyclidine hydrochloride), 148–149, G 11
Peer relationships in childhood, 336–337
Peg-word memory aid, 222
Penis envy, 459, G 11
Penny-drawing experiment, 212–213
People in groups, 599–608
Perception:
    of biological motion, 112
    definition of, 77, G 11
    depth, 106–108, G 5
    and experience, 111–113
    gestalt laws of, 100–102, G 7
    and memory, 209–211
    and sensation, 75–115

Racial discrimination, intelligence testing and, 245–246
Racial stereotypes, 623
Radical behaviorism, 466–467
Random sample, 23, 668, G 13
Range, 662, G 13
Rapid-eye-movement (REM) sleep, 123, 125, 127, G 13
RAS (reticular activation system), 401, 404, G 13
Ratio schedule of reinforcement, 171, G 13
Rational-emotive therapy (RET), 531, 536–537, G 13
Rationalization, 457–458, G 13
Reaction formation, 457, G 13
Reaction range, 305, G 13
Reality principle, 455, G 13
Recall, 203, 204, G 13
Recency effect, 205, G 13
Receptive field, 84, G 13
Receptor sites, 47, G 13
Recessive trait (see Genetics; Heredity)
Recognition, 203, 204, G 13
Recovery, spontaneous, 162, 176, G 15
Reflex, 52, 159, 315–316, G 13
    unconditioned, 162, G 16
Refractory period, 432
Regression, 456, G 13
Rehearsal, 196, 200, 211, 222
    associational, 200, G 2
    rote, 196, G 14
Reinforcement, 168–169, G 13
    positive (operant therapy), 535–536, G 11
    schedules of, 170–172, G 14
Relationships, interpersonal:
    close, 633
    entering and staying in, 643–646
    forming, 635–646
    intimate, 646–654
    studying, 633–634
Relearning, 204
Reliability, 239, G 13
    split-half, 239, G 15
    of test, 473
    test-retest, 239, G 16
REM rebound, 127, G 13
REM (rapid-eye-movement) sleep, 123, 125, 127, G 13
Replicate, 29, G 13
Repression, 209, 456, G 13
Research, psychological, 20–31
    basic and applied, 23
    definition of, 20, G 13
    ethics in, 22, 29–31
    methods in, 23–29
    subjects of, 20–23
Resilient children, 331–333, G 13
Resistance, 529, G 13
    to stress, 564
Resolution, sexual, 431
Response, 162
Response-oriented behavior, 181

Resting membrane potential (RMP), 44, G 13
Retardation, 261–263
Reticular activation system (RAS), 401, 404, G 13
Reticular formation, 56, G 13
Retina, 81, G 13
Retinal ganglion cells, 84
Retirement, 370–371
Retrieval, 193, 214–215, 221, G 13
Retroactive interference (RI), 214, G 13
Retrograde amnesia, 219, G 13
Review boards for psychological research, 23
Right-handedness, 64
RMP (resting membrane potential), 44, G 13
"Robbers Cave" experiment, 626–627
Rods, 81, G 13
Role theory, 371
Roles, 599–602, G 13
    social, 601, G 15
Rorschach test, 476–477, G 14
Rote rehearsal, 196, G 14
Rubella, 311

Sadistic personality disorder, 493
Samples, 22, G 14
Sampling, 22–23
Saturation of light, 86
Scatterplot, 666, G 14
Schachter-Singer theory of emotion, 408–409
Schedules of reinforcement, 170–172, G 14
Schizophrenia, 513–519, G 14
    causes of, 515–519
    drug therapy for, 544
    subtypes of, 514
    symptoms of, 513–514
School health programs, 587
School psychologists, 18, G 14
School psychology, 18
Scientific method, 5, G 14
Sclera, 80, G 14
Seasonal affective disorder (SAD), 507, 545, 546, G 14
Seat belt use, operant conditioning and, 173
Secondary appraisal, 566, G 14
Secondary reinforcers, 169, G 14
Secondary sex characteristics, 435, G 14
Secondary traits, 468, G 14
Sedatives, 149–150, G 14
    (See also Tranquilizers)
Selective attention, 103, G 14
Self-actualization, 386, 464–465, 532, G 14
Self-actualization theory, 464–465
Self-concept, 531–532
Self-defeating personality, 493
Self-disclosure, 643, G 14
Self-help groups, 587

Self-perception theory, 620, G 14
Self-regulation, 183
Self-reinforcement, 183
Self-report measure, 634
Semantic differential, 616, G 14
Semantic memory, 199, G 14
Semantics, 270, G 14
Senescence, 364, G 14
    (See also Elderly)
Senility (see Dementia)
Sensation, 77, G 14
    and perception, 75–115
Sensation-seeking, 402
Senses, physiology of, 79–100
    (See also specific senses)
Sensitization, 217
Sensorimotor stage, 317–318
Sensorineural hearing loss, 93, G 14
Sensory deprivation, 403–404
Sensory functioning in elderly, 364–365
Sensory memory (SM), 194–195, G 14
Sensory neurons, 43, G 14
Sensory thresholds, 77–78
Septal area, 58
Serial-position curve, 204–206, G 14
Serial recall, 204
Serotonin, 217, 412
Set point, 389, G 14
Sex chromosome, 308
Sex differences, 419–427, G 14
    in handedness, 64
    and intelligence, 258
Sex flush, 431
Sex-linked inheritance, 308, G 14
Sex therapy, 443–446, G 14
Sexual arousal, 432–434
Sexual burnout, 442, G 14
Sexual development, 343–344
Sexual orientation, 440–441
Sexual response cycle, 431–432
Sexual violence, pornography and, 444
Sexuality, 430–446
    in adolescence, 353, 435–436
    in adulthood, 436–440
    in childhood, 435
    in elderly, 440
    life-span perspective on, 434–440
    orientation in, 440–441
    physiology of, 430–434
    psychosexual problems, 441–446
    (See also Gender)
Shadowing technique (dichotic listening), 104, G 5, G 14
Shape constancy, 106
Shaping, 174, G 14
    of animals, 175
Shock reaction, 564
Short-term memory (STM), 194–198, G 14
Sibling attachment, 334–335
Signal-detection theory, 77, G 14
Similarity:
    and attraction, 642–643
    rule of, 100, 101